DAVID LEAN

The 1985 portrait by Cornel Lucas

DAVID
LEAN

A biography by

KEVIN BROWNLOW

RESEARCH ASSOCIATE CY YOUNG

RICHARD COHEN BOOKS • LONDON

ALSO BY KEVIN BROWNLOW

The Parade's Gone By…
How It Happened Here
The War, the West and the Wilderness
Hollywood: The Pioneers
Napoleon: Abel Gance's Classic Film
Behind the Mask of Innocence

BRITISH LIBRARY CATALOGUING IN PUBLICATION DATA:
A CATALOGUE RECORD FOR THIS BOOK IS AVAILABLE FROM THE BRITISH LIBRARY

ISBN 1 86066 042 8

FIRST PUBLISHED IN GREAT BRITAIN 1996 BY
RICHARD COHEN BOOKS
7 MANCHESTER SQUARE
LONDON W1M 5RE

DESIGNED BY RIDGEWAY ASSOCIATES

PRINTED IN GREAT BRITAIN BY
BUTLER & TANNER LTD, LONDON AND FROME

*"I hope the money men don't find out
that I'd pay them to let me do this."*

DAVID LEAN

DAVID LEAN *A Biography*

CONTENTS

PART ONE
A CHILD OF LIGHT

PART TWO
THE POET OF THE FAR HORIZON

INTRODUCTION

THIS book began as an attempt by David Lean to write his autobiography. An American publisher, Robert Stewart, had been trying to persuade David to write his memoirs since interviewing him on the set of DOCTOR ZHIVAGO in 1965. Stewart had been so impressed by David's comments on film-making that he begged him to put them on paper. But David was no writer and he turned down Stewart's requests until the end of his life, when illness confronted him with days of inactivity. A friend gave him the thought - why not find someone to interview you about your life and turn that into your autobiography? Which is where I came in.

The silent cinema had a profound influence on David and he knew of my 1968 book on the silent era, *The Parade's Gone By...*, and liked its extensive use of interviews. It also helped that we already knew each other. In 1984, my partner David Gill and I were asked by Thames Television to make a series on the British cinema. The company hoped for a series as lavish as our thirteen-part tribute to the silent cinema, *Hollywood* (1980), on a fraction of the budget and in a quarter of the time. David Gill suggested a way out of our dilemma by asking the leading British directors to make the documentaries themselves. Alan Parker, Lindsay Anderson and Sir Richard Attenborough accepted the challenge. The next director we approached was Sir David Lean.

I could never imagine him making a documentary - although in researching this book I discovered that he had made more than one - and my mental image was of a colossal crew laying a hundred yards of track for the opening shot. But both David Gill and I wanted very much to meet him, and here was a splendid opportunity.

David was living at the Berkeley Hotel with his wife, Sandy. He was 77, an age at which many men are fading away in old people's homes, yet he swept into the room with the ease and energy of a thirty-year-old. He looked magnificent: tall and exceptionally handsome, he wore a blue suit with a dazzling white shirt - buttoned at the neck, no tie - and looking as if he would be equally at home in a toga. He had an extraordinary face, the ears were large enough for a Buddha, but it was the powerful nose, the determined, sometimes grim set of the mouth and the strong chin that reminded one of a Roman bust. He could have been a highly successful leading man. In fact, he was impeccably cast as The Great British Film Director.

His voice was that of a man accustomed to command, yet it could be remarkably intimate and confiding. His vocabulary was limited; he therefore provided shades of meaning by the way he emphasised his words. He was a first-rate story-teller who could conjure up pictures with beautifully modulated emphasis. "A huge hall" means what it says. But when you heard David Lean say "a huu-uuge hall" you had no doubt that its scale exceeded Xanadu's. He had, in his youth, narrated for the newsreels and would have made an exceptional broadcaster.

To the casual visitor, which is what David Gill and I were that day, he was a profoundly charming man. He encouraged you to talk and he was a good listener. But you quickly found out that small talk was not his *forte* and you were wasting an opportunity if you indulged in it. We spent two or three hours in his suite, mesmerised by what he had to say and surprised at how indiscreet he was, and just before we left we were introduced to his wife, Sandy. She was tall, blonde, young and charming, and one's impression of David was that he led an enchanted life.

To our astonishment, David agreed to make the film for our TV series. He saw an opportunity of explaining how he felt the British film industry had gone wrong. It was a heady moment for us, thinking we would enable a remarkable film to be made. A few weeks later, David invited us back to the Berkeley and told us that he had decided not to proceed with the documentary but to embark on a feature about Stanley and Livingstone instead. He showed us some of his research and reminisced about his early days. I asked him if there were any directors he had worked with in the Thirties who had been unjustly neglected. "Have you heard of Bernard Vorhaus?" he asked.

We hadn't. When we got back to the office our researcher, Jo Wright, opened the London telephone directory and found a Bernard Vorhaus living in St John's Wood. We rang the number and a secretary said Mr Vorhaus was too busy to come to the phone but would call back. And so he did. He turned out to be an American, in his late seventies, out of the industry since the McCarthy era, when he had been blacklisted. It took some time for his film-making memory to return - and his memories of David Lean, who had cut his very first feature.

As it happened, the National Film Archive was at that moment printing up some of Vorhaus's 'quota quickies,' including a couple edited by David. They impressed the NFA's David Meeker so much that he organised a retrospective. Thus, as a direct result of David's reminiscence, Bernard Vorhaus returned to the United States to be honoured by a tribute at the Museum of Modern Art.

When David heard that Vorhaus was alive, he said he would get in touch, but it was typical of him that he didn't; he was hopelessly anti-social. And when David was dying, and it was too late, he expressed his regret that he had not made the effort.

WHEN I first met David, in 1985, he was releasing A PASSAGE TO INDIA, his first film since RYAN'S DAUGHTER in 1970 which was dismissed by critics with such disparagement that he went into a kind of purdah. But A PASSAGE TO INDIA was welcomed with critical praise and a new career had opened up for him. He was, once again, "bankable" - or so he thought. But in the midst of that triumph he suffered a personal disaster: his wife, Sandy, left him. Another woman came into his life, another Sandra - Sandra Cooke, an art dealer, as dark as Sandy was fair, with a talent for interior design. She eventually became David's sixth wife.

The project on Stanley and Livingstone never progressed as far as a script. David worked for a while on a film of J.G. Ballard's novel, *Empire of the Sun*, but he pulled out of that as well. When so many projects were being offered to him, it was no surprise that he turned aside from ours.

Nevertheless, he was very co-operative when Richard Attenborough wanted to interview him for his own British cinema film. I couldn't resist going over with the crew to David's new house at Sun Wharf, Narrow Street, in Docklands. It was largely unfurnished and workmen were making last-minute adjustments. I thought that the spacious interior resembled the villa of a Roman Consul.

David was very friendly and Attenborough treated him with deference - after all, David had given him his first film role in IN WHICH WE SERVE more than forty years before. The interview was so effective that Attenborough talked of making a whole series of interviews. David had that effect of enthusing you, making you believe you could do things you had never thought about before.

Through Maggie Unsworth - another veteran of IN WHICH WE SERVE - I was kept in touch with David, as if there were a role waiting for me which had yet to be disclosed. In March 1988, David celebrated his 80th birthday and Sandra organised a party at Narrow Street which was packed with old colleagues. I was introduced to an American journalist named Stephen Silverman who told me he was writing a book about David's career. To my surprise, I felt a twinge of remorse; even though the idea of writing a biography had not crossed my mind, I felt as though my territory had been invaded. When I asked David about Silverman's book he said "It's just about the films." Although it was a comparatively short book, triggered by the restoration and re-release of LAWRENCE OF ARABIA, Silverman did a remarkable job of winkling out of David facts about his family background and many other insights he had probably not expected to reveal. Silverman wrote the text, which was superbly illustrated, and brought the book out inside two years.

So I was surprised when I was contacted by Robert Stewart and told that David was planning his autobiography and that he had requested my help. I was puzzled at the thought of David participating in one of those "as told to" books. It was as if he had decided to produce a film instead of directing it. When I met Stewart I explained I was far too busy on a television series to become involved.

When he suggested that I just do the interviews, I relented. The prospect of listening to David Lean recalling his career was an enticing one and would enable me to find out more about the silent films he worked on.

WE arranged to start work in January 1990 at Sun Wharf. As I picked my way over the rubble and surveyed the acres of historic docklands under the most massive redevelopment since Victorian times, I wondered why David had chosen to live there. For when he moved in, few other people lived around him (I later realised this was one of the attractions). The old residents had been re-housed and the anticipated invasion by "yuppies" had not yet occurred.

I began to understand David's move when I watched his films. One of the first productions on which he served as "assistant in direction" - but virtually directed it himself - was MAJOR BARBARA which was largely set in Limehouse, in just the part of the river on which he now lived. Both GREAT EXPECTATIONS and OLIVER TWIST had scenes on the Thames, the latter ending with the death of Bill Sikes on the roof of a warehouse not unlike the original Sun Wharf. And David's Tangye forbears had launched the *Great Eastern* at the Isle of Dogs which David could see from his windows.

David's new home lay on a curve in the river. An intensely visual man, and a true romantic, he found the river exhilarating. During our sessions he would break off to point out a passing ship or a fleeting change of light. I realised that one could spend an entire day staring out of the window. (When working, his desk was placed with its back to the window.)

On that first encounter, David was dressed in his usual impeccable style, in a white polo-neck jersey, dark grey trousers and white socks. What was unusual was that he wore no shoes; there was something wrong with his legs. He didn't know exactly what was wrong but I noticed a change in him. He had an unaccustomed glow in his cheeks. He told me he had fired his doctor. "I got a bill for £7000. The doctor said, 'I would prefer cash.' "

His new doctor, Peter Wheeler, who became a close friend, instead of taking him off Cortisone put him back on it and he got better. "Three and a half months wasted," said David.

David's condition was more serious than I realised, for he needed a wheelchair. A Filipino, Fred, looked after him and he had a personal assistant called Sarah Foster, a cheerful, sturdy girl who had worked for the Queen Mother.

David was unstinting during our interview sessions. Not that he always answered my questions; sometimes a simple question would be followed by "the David Lean stare". I had been warned about this. His eyes would shift focus from me to the river and he would fall silent. To all intents and purposes he had departed the room. One had to be patient and wonder, Was he bored? Was he thinking of something else? Was he offended? Was he waiting for another question? If not, would I shatter his concentration by asking it? I decided to remain silent myself, which usually proved the right course, although occasionally he had been waiting for the next question! Eventually, I developed a technique of taking notes. After one exceptionally long silence, he suddenly stared at me and demanded to know what I was writing...

It turned out that we were at cross-purposes. David thought I was anxious to do a biography whilst I thought he was set on doing his autobiography. Clearly, Robert Stewart had Spiegeled us both and here we were, working together on a joint project, neither of us knowing what form it would eventually take. Sadly, it was David's death that decided the matter.

One morning David said, "Now, about the book. We ought to talk about conditions." My heart sank. I knew that film directors were often experts in legal matters. With a sinking feeling, I pulled out my notebook and headed a page "Conditions". David explained that his lawyer's name was Tony Reeves. I wrote this down.

"Now," he said, "I believe that a book should contain plenty of illustrations. Don't you agree?"

As the author of half-a-dozen film books, all of which were packed with pictures, I agreed wholeheartedly.

"Really good pictures," he said.

"Absolutely," I said. There was a long pause.

"That's all. Just bloody good pictures."

It was at that moment that I fell for David Lean.

IN 1986, David decided that his next film would be NOSTROMO, based on Joseph Conrad's novel. Steven Spielberg agreed to produce it, although when the two men disagreed about the script, Spielberg stood down and Serge Silberman took over. Because of David's recurrent bad health, the project was subject to constant delays.

Upon Sandra Cooke fell the burden of David's illness and the pressures building up on NOSTROMO. Having furnished and decorated Sun Wharf, Sandra decorated a fifteenth-century olive mill in the South of France which David had acquired. David loved the place, and also the fact that it was close to the Victorine Studios in Nice where his hero, Rex Ingram, had made pictures in the Twenties. NOSTROMO would be based there.

From my point of view, a visit to Sun Wharf was one thing, a flight to Nice and a long weekend was quite another. I was working flat out on a documentary series about D.W. Griffith, so it was not possible to get away as often as I would have liked. But when I did reach the Moulin du Jardinier, it was hard to leave.

The house was on a hill overlooking an epic sweep of Provence with the

Alpes Maritimes as a backdrop. The first Sunday morning the church bells tolled, the sun lit up the villages, magpies chattered and there was the delicious smell of coffee in the air. Yet from David, growling frustration! As far as I could see, David didn't *do* anything. He sat all day, fed by his devoted "family", and grumbled. "Yet he doesn't want to leave," I wrote in my notebook. "I cannot see how he can pull himself out of this to the point where he has the energy to direct." (I discovered later that he *had* been working non-stop all summer.)

While the thermometer soared and Sandra and Sarah sunbathed by the swimming pool, David and I tucked ourselves into a shady corner and he reminisced about his life and work. I think he imagined that my visits would be an enjoyable diversion, a way to occupy himself so he could pretend to himself that he was working. However, my churning up the past unsettled him far more than he expected.

But the Moulin du Jardinier was much more conducive to reminiscence than Sun Wharf. Since we were uninterrupted except for arrivals of coffee, David could launch into far longer streams of consciousness than was possible in London, where the telephone rang constantly and where visitors appeared at all too frequent intervals. He was short-tempered when his concentration was broken and astonishingly rude to the perpetrator. I had heard that Cortisone affects people in this way, but I suspect David always had a short fuse. While admitting that he could be as choleric as a gout-ridden colonel, I grew extremely fond of him.

Sandra was an exotic-looking creature. She sounded very English though she looked vaguely Oriental. She was born in Northumberland and had a Russian background. She wore her black hair in a fringe, with black around her eyes like a silent film star. She was slim and I judged her to be in her late twenties. I was surprised to discover that she was born in 1939. She always seemed to be organising something - which unsettled David who undoubtedly felt *he* should be organising something, preferably NOSTROMO.

"Does your wife talk all the time on the telephone?" he asked me one day (he hadn't yet married Sandra). "She never stops. Deirdre's coming round tomorrow - she'll still talk for half an hour. It makes me mad, jealous of the telephone. She'll talk to it and not to me. I think I need a private phone so I can talk to her."

Our conversations ranged widely and I realised that, in many ways, I had been preparing all my life for this book. As I listened to David, I heard him mention name after name which set off a flood of memories of my own, for I had met them, worked with them or interviewed them years before. Like David, I have had the opportunity to work at almost every job connected with making films. This is not only ideal training for a film historian, it has enabled me to realise why David had some of the attitudes he had. Because so many of his films were made on massive budgets, and because the films that I directed, with

Andrew Mollo, were made on shoestrings, many people have assumed I must feel antipathy to David's work. Quite the opposite is true. On a small film, expectations are as low as the budget. On a multi-million-dollar epic, the whole world is watching and the survival of a studio can depend on the outcome. What David achieved with that burden on his shoulders is astonishing.

I was startled at what we had in common. We admired the same films, the same directors - I only wish I had worked with him on a film rather than a book, for I would happily have been one of his "dedicated maniacs". He didn't ask after your family, slap you on the back or shower you with presents. He was, as he once admitted, a very emotional man "but being English I take a lot of care to cover it up."

When he recommended a book I made sure I read it, for I gathered that he read seldom and his enthusiasm was therefore all the more significant. He said that one of his favourite books was *The Summing Up* by Somerset Maugham, whom he had met in 1948. "At the end of dinner I sat down near him and we had quite a long conversation, and he said, 'I'm leaving at ten. I am told that my name is up in lights again in Piccadilly Circus and I'm going to drive round to have a look.' To think he once had four plays on at the same time in the West End and he wanted to go and see his name up in lights again.

"I don't know what it is about Maugham. He appeals to me enormously. I find him tremendously sad, and I suppose it's a kind of alone-ness which in some way matches something within myself."

Anyone interested in David Lean should read *The Summing Up*, for the philosophy of the two men is remarkably similar. Maugham's life has parallels with David's, too, although he was a child of the upper middle-class. The incident which devastated his childhood was the death of his mother when he was eight, which meant that he was farmed out to relations, a vicar and his wife. The vicar forbade him to go to the theatre, so when he discovered it he was entranced. Maugham was unable to follow his brother to university. As a professional writer, he claimed to be indifferent to criticism; in fact, he was as sensitive to it as David Lean. He was always impeccably dressed and was extremely generous - in private. He had a passion for Capri, as did David, and was as overwhelmed by the South Pacific as Gauguin, or Fletcher Christian.

As one reads *The Summing Up*, observation after observation seems relevant to David: "I have been attached, deeply attached, to a few people; but I have been interested in men in general not for their own sakes, but for the sake of my work... I had an instinctive shrinking from my fellow men that has made it difficult for me to enter into any familiarity with them. I have loved individuals; I have never much cared for men in the mass... I have known a number of actors very well... but I have never been able to look upon them as human beings... However brilliant a scene may be, if it is not essential to his play the dramatist must cut it... Those who possess an aesthetic sense of unusual delicacy diverge sexually from the norm to an extreme and often pathological degree."

David has been described, accurately, as a perfectionist, but during all the years he strove to achieve that impossible aim he must have been comforted by Maugham's remark: "Perfection is a trifle dull. It is not the least of life's ironies that this, which we all aim at, is better not quite achieved."

WHEN David died, in April 1991, the book was not complete. People asked me, "How much did you get out of him?" I usually say that I think he told me everything he wanted to tell me. That is very different from telling me everything he could have told me. He had, for instance, refused to discuss his aborted project about the mutiny on the Bounty because he knew it would dredge up miseries he was trying to forget; he also found it difficult to talk about his marriages and love affairs. He refused point-blank to discuss Ann Todd.

But all that work, all that information, could hardly be abandoned. Since David had liked my approach with *The Parade's Gone By...* - which was essentially an oral history - I thought the least I could do was to adopt a similar approach with his biography. Whenever I see names listed in the acknowledgements of biographies - particularly those dealing with films - I am disappointed that while the facts may be there, the voices are not. So I have made sure that at least in this book, those who knew and worked with David are given close-ups and not merely long-shots.

With Robert Stewart's agreement, and with the help of David's lawyer, Tony Reeves, and his widow, Lady Lean, I carried on with the project, incorporating David's memories with those of others. This research, which David himself would probably not have sanctioned, was to lead me down some fascinating paths - to his collaborators, fellow film-makers, friends, family, wives and girlfriends.

David had given me the impression that, by comparison with his brother, Edward, he was virtually illiterate, and that there was not the slightest chance of his writing his own book. This impression was reinforced by a well-known failure to write letters (I received one, typed by a secretary, but John Mills, a friend for fifty years, told me he had received none). I contacted his collaborators and asked for letters; no one had any. Pamela Mann produced a description of a trip to the Far East which he had duplicated for his friends and family and for a long time that appeared to be the extent of David Lean's literary output.

One day, Adrian Turner, who was writing a book on LAWRENCE OF ARABIA, interviewed Barbara Beale, with whom David had a seven-year relationship. Barbara informed Turner that she had deposited a great many letters from David at the University of Reading. When I read those, I realised that when David wrote a letter it could be as epic as one of his films. He typed them himself, very slowly, with two fingers, and it often took him days. His spelling might be endearingly shaky but he wrote in a direct and often pictorial way that would have been ideal for an autobiography.

There is something entirely fitting that Barbara Beale should have deposited David's letters at Reading, for the town features strongly in David's life. It was here, at Reading Station, in a scene reminiscent of BRIEF ENCOUNTER, that T.E. Lawrence left the refreshment room without his first draft of *Seven Pillars of Wisdom*. It was never seen again. David would go to school at Reading and it is in the Reading area that David's son, Peter, now lives. And nearby lives Isabel, Peter's mother and David's first wife.

If David failed at anything, it was at being a father. To Peter's regret, his father had walked out on him when he was little more than a baby and had had little to do with him since. Peter is level-headed about it and understands his father's attitude better than I do; but one can tell how profound is the sense of loss. However, Peter lightens up at any mention of films.

On one of my visits, Peter led me down the long path of the spectacular garden created by his wife, June. It was spring and the profusion of flowers would have won David's admiration. At the end of the garden was a small shed, housing lawnmower, rakes and flowerpots. In the middle of this organised chaos, Peter pointed to a curious object, a Pathé-Baby projector of 1923, wreathed in cobwebs like a relic from Miss Havisham's. This was the first projector David ever owned. With it, he showed his first shaky home movies that led to feelings of fury and frustration, for the brief bursts of movement were so unsatisfactory and so amateurish. This was the machine that by its very inadequacy led him to do so much better.

Back in the house, a modest suburban villa similar to the one in Croydon where David was born, Peter showed me a desk owned by David's uncle Edmund. In the drawers were other treasures: the first splicer David owned, the one with which he made his first attempts at the craft which he would so quickly master. There was a bottle of 1928 film cement, its top jammed solid. Most poignant of all, perhaps, a tiny still of Charlie Chaplin in THE GOLD RUSH in a passe-partout frame, presumably made by David, which came from his bedroom at Park Lane, Croydon. From the same period was an exercise book with the call signs of early radio stations scribbled down as David located them on his cat's whisker wireless.

These mementos, so meaningless to a casual observer, are all that survives from a childhood full of unhappiness, but one which gave way to the most scintillating career an English film-maker has enjoyed.

Every biographer, particularly those dealing with figures from the cinema, feels himself pursued by the Four Horsemen of the Apocrypha. I have tried to avoid those stories which sound too perfect to be authentic, and wherever possible I have had facts corroborated. The book is as accurate as I can make it, but for the benefit of future biographers I have provided source notes with references to the transcripts of my interviews.

I know this will not be the last biography of David Lean - I hope it won't - but I suspect it will be the most affectionate. I cannot judge whether I have done justice to his life. He has certainly enriched mine.

Kevin Brownlow,
London 1993-5

DAVID LEAN *A Biography*

ACKNOWLEDGEMENTS

I HAVE received so much help in compiling this book that I hardly know where to start in recording my thanks. The list that follows is absurdly long, but everyone on it contributed something crucial.

Robert Stewart, formerly of Charles Scribner's Sons, came to me with the idea, which I strongly resisted, but somehow he made it happen. I am very grateful to him, for it has been an extraordinary experience. His company was subsequently taken over, and I am indebted to Richard Cohen for his rescue in the last reel. Also to Patricia Chetwyn, Robyn Karney, Mary Sandys and Christine Shuttleworth for all their hard work. Maggie Unsworth had a great deal to do with involving me, whilst her son, Tim Unsworth, handed over all the research he did for the *South Bank Show*'s tribute to David Lean. Kay Walsh, David's second wife, was unstintingly generous with her time and her memories, even though she was at work on her own book. Norman Spencer, like the ideal production man that he is, showed me diaries, documents and even verbatim reports of meetings. Gerald McKnight gave me his research for a David Lean biography he had planned in 1983. Adrian Turner not only provided vital leads, he gave me access to his manuscript for his monograph on LAWRENCE OF ARABIA. Peter Lean, David's son, was a source of constant surprises, and I owe a great deal, too, to his mother Isabel. Bob Morris, author with Lawrence Raskin of another monograph on LAWRENCE, produced a bound volume of my manuscript which helped get it published. Ron Paquet, who maintains a David Lean archive in Canada, kept me regularly fuelled with rare material. Stephen Silverman, who wrote the most recent book on David, sent me the uncut manuscript. Barbara Beale put me up at her house in Almeria and allowed me to interview her for several days, also providing from her collection some of the best stills in the book. Since she has also donated her collection of letters and documents to the University of Reading, I owe her an especial debt. Linda Wood not only typed the entire manuscript - more than half a million words in its original form - but served as its first (unofficial) editor, as well as historical adviser. She has herself written the only study of the work of the first director David worked for, Maurice Elvey. Cy Young spent months doing research while I was hard at work on a documentary series on D.W. Griffith.

I must acknowledge the assistance of the British Film Institute and the National Film Archive, upon which all film historians are dependent. But I must record my sadness that the BFI decided to close their lending library. This has cost me a fortune. Other libraries have little in the way of film books, so I faced either the prospect of queueing up for the BFI reading room - and since I had a full-time job this wasn't possible - or buying the books I needed to consult. There is precious little money in film history and for the sake of future projects, a proper lending library, like the one operated for so long by the BFI, must be restarted in London.

It should be put on record that only one person refused to be interviewed: Peter O'Toole. He is writing his own memoirs, so nothing will be lost. Teddy Darvas was the first person I interviewed, and he encouraged me so much with his enthusiasm for David, with fascinating reminiscences, backed up with scripts, documents and videos, that I expected everyone else would prove an anti-climax. But David Lean left such a legacy of enthusiasm and admiration that I was given an astonishing degree of help and I wish there was a better way of showing my gratitude than a mere listing of names. To describe the contribution of each person, however, would double the length of this book: The Academy of Motion Picture Arts and Sciences, Sir Anthony Havelock-Allan, John Allinson, Eric Ambler, the late Lindsay Anderson, Nigel Andrews, George Andrews, Malcolm Arnold, the late Dame Peggy Ashcroft, Kate Ashe, Don Ashton, Richard Bates, BECTU Oral History Project, Mary Benson, Keith Best, Dick Best, Maurice Blundell, the late Robert Bolt, Osmond Borrodaile, Michael Bott (Reading University), the late Pierre Boulle, Dallas Bower, John Box, Lord Brabourne, Melvyn Bragg, Patrick Cadell, John Calley, Christopher Calthrop, Vera Campbell, John Chapman, the late Group Captain Lord Cheshire, Julie Christie, Arthur C. Clarke, the late George Clark, Michael Clarke, John and Catrine Clay, Anne Coates, Sid Cole, Tim Collins, Diana Cooke, Maurice Cooke, George Correface, Eric Cross, Group Captain John Cunningham, Betty Curtis, Patricia Danes, James D'Arc, John Howard Davies, Ernest Day, Clive Donner, the late Douglas Dunlop, Paul Dunstan, Christine Edzard, Bernard Eisenschitz, Sarah Ellis, Eileen Erskine, Bill Everett, Allen Eyles, Faraway Productions, Gerry Fisher, Geraldine Fitzgerald, Kate Fleming, Geoffrey Foot, Sarah Foster, Roy Fowler, Eddie Fowlie, Julian Fox, Pamela Francis, Stuart Freeborn, Harold French, Joyce Gallie, Clive Gardner, Michael Gee, John B. Gent, David Gill, the late Sidney Gilliat, Richard Goodwin, Marius Goring, Lavinia Graecen, Guy and Jo Green, Paul Gregory, Vanda Greville, Val Guest, Sir Alec Guinness, Shama Habibullah, the late Gordon Hales, Christopher Hampton, Peter Handford, Robert A. Harris, John Hawkesworth, Peggy Hennessey, David Henry, Katharine Hepburn, John Heyman, the late James Hill, Dame Wendy Hiller, Valerie Hobson, Richard Hogben, Frank Holland, Kees T'Hooft, Sir Anthony Hopkins, Attai Hossain, Richard Hough, Philip Hudsmith, Alan Hume, John Huntley, Peggy Hyde-Chambers, Christopher Jones, John Justin, Pauline Kael, Phil

Kellogg, Willie Kemplen, Deborah Kerr, Brigid Kinally, Brigitte Kueppers, Fred Lane, Tony Lawson, David Lean Investment Trust, Doreen Lean, June Lean, Lucy Lean, Lady Sandra Lean, Lady Sandy Lean, Leighton Park School, Richard Lester, Gloria Loomis, Dr Rachael Low, Kevin Macdonald, Tom Manning, Joe Marks, Dick May, Gerald McKee, Donald Mead, David Meeker, Sarah Miles, Harry Miller, Sir John Mills, John Mitchell, Andrew Mollo, Micheal de Mordha, Sheridan Morley, the late Robert Morley, Laura Morris, Oswald Morris, Inger-Grethe Mortensen, Irving Moskovitch, Patrick Moules, Eunice Mountjoy, Ronald Neame, Peter Newbrook, Julie Nightingale, Sir Anthony Nutting, Robert O'Brien, Jim Painten, Steven Pallos, James Pople, the late Dennis Potter, Gerald Pratley, Sir David Puttnam, Anthony Quinn, Santha Rama Rau, Tony Reeves, Jeffrey Richards, Jocelyn Rickards, David Robinson, Nicolas Roeg, Norman Roper, Win Ryder, George Rylands, Alison Samuel, Michael Santoro, Feroze Sarosh, Prunella Scales, Richard Schickel, Paul Scofield, the late Judy Scott-Fox, Jim Sheehan, David Shipman, Tony Sloman, Society of Friends Library, Martin Sopocy, Maud Spector, Julian Spiro, Anthony Squire, Patrick Stanbury, George Stevens Jr, Roy Stevens, Cathy Surowiec, Diccon Swan, Hilary and Dr Sheila Tangye, Peter Tanner, Peter Taylor, Jacqueline Thiédot, Ralph Thomas, the late Sid Thawley, the late Ann Todd, André de Toth, Wayne Tourell, David Tree, Turner Entertainment Co., Rita Tushingham, University of California Los Angeles, University of Reading, Pedro Vidal, Peter Viertel, Bernard Vorhaus, Stephen Walters, Nicholas Wapshott, Charles Ware, Dr Peter Wheeler, L.P. Williams, F.L. Woolley, Harry Wynder, Joan Young, Freddie Young, Fred Zentner, Fred Zinnemann.

With special thanks for the support of the Estate of Sir David Lean

The caricature of David Lean is by Gary (Gary Smith) of *The Sunday Times*

This book was edited by Adrian Turner

PART ONE

A CHILD OF LIGHT

"Miss Clayton has told me a terrible thing about you. She's afraid you will never be able to read or write."

DAVID LEAN'S MOTHER TO DAVID, AGED SEVEN

CHAPTER ONE

A FAMILY OF FRIENDS

"It is said that famous men are usually the product of an unhappy childhood."
Winston Churchill[1]

"WHO'S David Lean?" said the man on the telephone.

I had tracked down David Lean's birthplace, 38 Blenheim Crescent in South Croydon, and discovered it empty and derelict. I had slipped a note through the letter-box asking any future occupier to get in touch as I would value the chance of seeing inside. To arouse interest, I mentioned that David Lean had been born here in 1908.

A year passed, and when a developer called me I had forgotten all about the note. "Tell you the truth," he said, "the name David Lean doesn't mean much to me or my colleague."

"The great film director," I said, holding back my amazement. "LAWRENCE OF ARABIA, DOCTOR ZHIVAGO...."

"Oh, yes, I've heard of them. It's the name David Lean that we knew nothing about."

All the more reason to write this book, I thought. The developer invited me down to see the house, before it was altered out of all recognition.

"David Lean," he mused. "That ought to add five hundred pounds to the place. If you want to put a plaque up we'd be only too pleased."

No. 38 was a yellow brick house when it was built in 1908, the year when the Leans moved in, calling it Fairview. The house was substantial, with three storeys. As we approached it through the overgrown garden, I noticed the creepers had encircled the front door as though Miss Havisham lived there. The door had to be pushed violently; on the floor were scores of letters, a museum of junk mail. It was a miracle mine had been found. An old newspaper headline was visible beneath them: "Should Empty Homes be used for the Homeless?"

We picked our way to the kitchen, partly destroyed by fire. The flames had burned their way through later alterations and revealed the original Edwardian tiles. The electricity had long ago been switched off, and the developer pointed the way with a heavy-duty torch. It lit up the soot-blackened wall, and in the silence I became aware of a curious chafing sound, very soft, very eerie. The torch beam moved slowly up the wall and revealed at the top a spectacular butterfly, slowly moving its wings. The smoke-blackened kitchen had become a habitat for butterflies - quite uncanny, since David was passionate about butterflies as a small boy.

Upstairs, I could see the brambles had reached waist height in the small back garden, and then I saw the reason why the Leans probably bought the house - beyond the garden was a field. In those days there was no fence, and it must have seemed as if the garden stretched to infinity. The fact that the field has survived in the middle of residential Croydon is amazing enough; in those days it probably formed part of a farm, and the rural atmosphere, with trams clanking in the distance, must have been very appealing.

The bedrooms were exceptionally large for homes in the area, I was assured, and equally unusual was the room in which David was born, facing the street, which had a nanny's room attached. On the floor above were generous servants' quarters. Even in this fire-damaged state, the house was on offer for £77,000. In reasonable condition, it would have fetched £120,000. And its price in 1908? £60.

And yet when David went back to see it, after living abroad as a tax exile for years, he had been shocked.

"My parents must have been very poor," he told me, "because it was a miserable little place. A small street in South Croydon - awfully simple and plain."

No. 38 was by no stretch of the imagination "miserable" unless, like David Lean, you had spent a large proportion of your life in luxury. Nor could his father be described as poor.

Francis William le Blount Lean was a chartered accountant. In the Intermediate Examination of the Institute of Chartered Accountants in June 1898 he had passed first in all England. Even in his finals, in June 1900, he had received a prize for being placed fifth.[2] Although accountants, even prize-winning ones, were limited to salaries of two or three pounds a week when they were starting out, he was in 1908 a much-respected partner in the firm of Viney, Price and Goodyear. And he had been married for four years.

That Frank Lean was not ashamed of Fairview is suggested by a symbol of family pride, a visitors' book, bound in red morocco. In it were the signatures of distinguished headmasters - from Leighton Park, Sidcot and the Flounders Institute - friends and relatives of Francis Lean. But the most distinguished name of all appeared against the date of Wednesday, 25 March 1908. The name was written in bold letters in red ink: DAVID LEAN. There were no further entries.[3]

Frank Lean also announced the arrival of his son in more conventional fashion in *The Times*:

"LEAN on 25th inst. at 38 Blenheim-crescent, South Croydon, the wife of FRANCIS WILLIAM LE BLOUNT LEAN (née Tangye) of a son named David."

There was an announcement, too, in *The Friend*.[4]

The newspaper Frank Lean normally bought to read on the train was the *Daily Mail*, and on an inside page of that day's edition he might have glanced at a Special Law Report headed "Oliver Twist Recalled".

Two Poor Law relieving officers in the Chatham and Rochester districts of the Medway Union sued an alderman for libel. The alderman had tried to get a deserted young wife with her sick baby into the workhouse, and the two officers had behaved in such a way as to frighten the life out of her. The alderman was surprised to discover that the counsel for the plaintiffs was none other than (Henry) Charles

David Lean, aged 9 months, and his mother, Helena Annie Lean.

Dickens, KC, a son of the novelist. Did he not mean to imply, asked Mr Dickens, that what had happened was as bad as the events in *Oliver Twist*?

As if that was not coincidence enough, the paper was full of events which would resonate through David Lean's life and work.

A proposal for a Channel tunnel was rejected because it would provide an ideal route for a military invasion. No one was in any doubt which army the paper had in mind. Kaiser Wilhelm II might be a grandson of Queen Victoria, but he was regarded as greedy and treacherous. Ever since the Germans had defeated the French in the Franco-Prussian War in 1871, the English had half-expected the echo of jackboots in Whitehall. The very day of David's birth, the Kaiser was paying an official visit to the King of Italy at Venice in the hope, no doubt, of forging closer military links. The paper reported a speech by Prince von Bülow, the Imperial German Chancellor, about the relative strengths of the British and German navies. He had no wish to create alarm: "We wish to live in peace and quiet with England," he declared. But the speech did nothing to allay the suspicions of those who felt a war with Germany was inevitable.

Had he not been a Quaker, Frank would have been ideal officer material; one can picture him in command at Jutland. Thickset, handsome and dogmatic, he was part of a family so accomplished they were hard to measure up to.

"I was always a little bit in fear of the Leans," said David, who would himself one day inspire the same emotion. "They were very austere, very dry, very headmasterly."

Grandfather Lean, handsome, tall and bearded, was principal from 1870-1899 of a famous Quaker teachers' training college called the Flounders Institute in Yorkshire. William Scarnell Lean had assisted William Booth, who later founded the Salvation Army, in his evangelistic work in London (a fact which David would recall when working on the film of MAJOR BARBARA). In 1864, he married Marianna Bevan and had ten children.

He was an eloquent man; they said he had the "golden tongue" among Quaker preachers and he passed this gift to his son. He was also artistic and although the most puritanical among the Quakers did not approve, he painted watercolours of the Lake District and wrote poetry.

William Lean was seventy-five when David was born and although he had visited Frank and Helena shortly before the happy event, he died that same year without having seen his grandson.

His eldest boy, Bevan, in 1902 became the headmaster of the Quaker School, Sidcot, near Cheddar Gorge, in Somerset, a post he held for twenty-eight years until his retirement in 1930.

"I remember the wife of one of my cutters talking to me not long ago," said David, "and she said, 'You're not Bevan Lean's nephew?'

"I said, 'Yes, he was my uncle.'

"She couldn't get over it. I mean, to hell with my being a film director!"

Even more famous in Quaker circles was Frederick Andrews. William Scarnell Lean's sister, Anna Maria, married this extraordinary man in 1877, when he first took up his appointment as headmaster of the Quaker school at Ackworth, near Pontefract, in Yorkshire. Andrews, who had been a pupil at the school, remained headmaster from 1877 to 1920.

Well over six feet tall, Frederick Andrews was a much-loved figure. Unlike many educationalists of the time, he was fond of children and treated them in a direct, friendly way, which endeared him to them for the rest of their lives.

Despite his religion, Andrews tolerated the theatre, which he enjoyed "moderately", but responded with much more excitement when the cinema came into his life. One of his favourite films was Douglas Fairbanks's THE THREE MUSKETEERS which he saw shortly before his death.

There is no record of David meeting Frederick Andrews, but it seems impossible they would not have met since he lived until 1922, when David was fourteen.

Both sides of David's family came from Cornwall, but it was his mother's side which fascinated David. Helena Annie Tangye was known as "the beauty of the Tangyes".

"My mother's family I loved," said David. "They were good-looking people, very artistic with a lot of gift in them. The Tangyes were artists, inventors and engineers. There were the two brothers - James and Joseph - who launched the

Richard Tangye and the Great Eastern.

Great Eastern down on the Isle of Dogs. The *Great Eastern* was Brunel's ship, the first cable-laying ship to cross the Atlantic. Brunel couldn't launch it and it became a national joke. The Tangye brothers went there and said, 'Let us try.' They used their hydraulic jacks and down she went. They always said, 'We launched the *Great Eastern* and the *Great Eastern* launched us.'"[5]

David's talents perhaps owed more to this remarkable family than to the Quaker educationalists. The Tangyes were Quakers too, but they had the spark of romance. Their very origins might have been immortalised in a Sabatini novel. In 1404, Tannegui du Chatel attacked the coast of England in revenge for the killing of his brother at Dartmouth the year before. He spent two months here and the records refer to the existence of John Taynggy later in the century.

The family genius, however, did not flower until after the Industrial Revolution. Born in 1833, Joseph Tangye was a farmer and a coal merchant at Illogan, a mining community near Redruth, in Cornwall, and his wife Ann ran the village shop. Ann was a redoubtable figure; during a cholera epidemic, she stayed when everyone else had fled, keeping the village shop open. She had three girls and six boys (although one died young). It was these boys, James, Joseph, Edward, Richard and George, who were to start the famous Tangye engineering company.

As soon as they were old enough, the boys were put to work in the smithy of Ann's father, Edward Bullock. This suggests the old evil of child labour; in fact, the boys loved the place. Edward Bullock was fond of them and treated them with imagination and tact. He made them all think they were indispensable. Even if there was nothing for one of the brothers to do, he would put him in charge of the "Grunt". As the hammer fell, he would call out, "Now, Dick, grunt!"

The oldest boy James's earliest memories were of his grandfather among the great pumping engines of the Wheal Torgus Tin Mine. James was later involved in the construction of the Clifton suspension bridge. He became a prominent engineer, developing an idea of his grandfather's for a safety fuse for blasting powder. In 1855, he joined his brother Joseph in Birmingham and two years later, the celebrated family business began.

"They started a huge engineering firm in Birmingham," said David. "When I was young, you couldn't go on any railway station without seeing Tangye Gas Engines, Tangye Pumps, Tangye this and Tangye that."

Edward Tangye was obliged to work on his father's farm, but he, too, was more interested in engineering. He became a locomotive driver on the West Cornwall Railway and when this work came to an end, instead of returning to the farm, he set out to emigrate to the United States. His ship, in the hands of a drunken crew, was wrecked off the English coast with the loss of two hundred lives. Edward was rescued and, still determined to emigrate, he eventually settled in the wilds of Wisconsin. Once his brothers' business was thriving, they invited Edward back to England to join them, and he did so. He married his cousin, Ann Cowlin, and they had twelve children, one being David Lean's mother, Helena Annie.

"I remember a ship's lifebelt," said David, "hanging in the house that my grandmother lived in at Knowle - the Manor House - where they had a lovely conservatory with white grapes and black grapes, which I thought was the most glamorous thing I'd ever seen in my life."[6]

The grandmother, who lived to a ripe old age, is remembered by the family as being a woman remarkable for her coldness.

Richard Tangye, the fourth son, had a chip on his shoulder. He was educated at Sidcot, and became a junior teacher there at the tender age of fifteen. Only four-feet-ten, his life was made a misery by the other boys. Ambitious, clever and apparently utterly selfish, he had an excellent grasp of financial matters. Each brother had gifts that complemented the others, and Richard was able to bring what the others lacked - a sense of salesmanship.

The fifth brother, George, also a pupil at Sidcot (its thousandth), followed his brothers into the Birmingham firm. He was a generous, genial man who helped to support Sidcot in his later years, and who lived until 1920, when David was twelve, providing the ideal link for the boy to his family's history.

A family row broke up the partnership in 1872 when Richard quarrelled with his brothers. Yet he was the one to receive a knighthood - although he received it for his work in municipal affairs and for his philanthropy. Part of this philanthropy was devoted to the arts - an unusual interest for a Quaker. Richard and George felt that a great industrial community like Birmingham should have an art gallery and a school of art, and in 1880 they put up the money for both.[7]

As Edward used to say, "David, we've certainly come up from the mines."

With this extraordinary background, it is hardly surprising that David should have so prized his Tangye origins. One of his earliest feuds with his brother Edward - born three years later - was waged over the fact that he had been christened Edward Tangye Lean, after Helena's father.

David was jealous of Edward anyway, though he felt that, as the older boy, the Tangye name was his by right of seniority. David was one of the few people to call his brother Edward; everyone else called him Tangye.

Ironically, when David fell for the actress, Ann Todd, her name was Ann Tangye. She was married to Nigel Tangye, a first cousin. He was precisely the romantic and flamboyant type that David most admired - a pilot and a writer. Fortunately, once the drama was over, Nigel Tangye bore him no malice.[8]

As for his mother, David felt that she had inherited little of the Tangye talent. "Women in those days were kept under lock and key," he said. "She'd do embroidery, but she had no artistic flair. Of her sisters, Aunt Florence - called Florrie, of course - was very good-looking and painted extremely well."

Another sister, Evelyn, left the Quakers, to the dismay of both families, and joined the Church of England.

"Florrie and Evvy never broached the subject of religion because it would have meant a head-on confrontation. I think she must have been a flirt in her way. She was always fond of the clergymen, which made things worse for Florence."

David's uncles were somewhat more imposing characters. "Everyone went in fear and trembling of these brothers. My mother told me, 'We were always expected to stand up when any of the boys entered the room.' This applied to the younger brothers, too. The eldest brother was called Claude. He ended up as a rather important gentleman, Medical Officer for Health for Wiltshire.

"Then there was Walter. He was theatened by TB - tuberculosis was a forbidden subject - and was sent to British Columbia in Canada. I remember him coming back one Christmas and telling us about life in the wilds. He had nearly come to grief because he went to pick some berries on a bush and was startled by the arms of a bear coming round the other side. I thought this was terrifically glamorous, as indeed it was.

"Then there were two farmers. Reginald and my favourite, Clarence, whom I adored. His wife, Winnie, warm as toast, came from the Eveson family in the Midlands. They were successful coal merchants and they must have been rich. Winnie never got any money from them, as far as I could make out, because she and Clarence were always broke."

During the writing of this book, I was contacted by Dr Sheila Tangye and her sister Hilary, daughters of Reginald, who thought they might be able to shed some light on the family. I visited them at their home in Barnes, and learned about the dark side of the Tangye family.

"The Tangyes have the most appalling tempers," said Hilary. "We can lay people flat if we want to, we can annihilate people. Dad said that no one could live with Aunt Helena. She had such an awful temper, it's no wonder Frank couldn't live with her. He tried to come back and couldn't bear it."

Their father was the youngest but one of the twelve. David's mother was his eldest sister.

"The family of twelve," said Sheila, "was divided into the first few, who were educated in a very liberal and expensive way, and the rest. Reginald went to Blundell's [at Tiverton, in Devon] until he was fifteen, when he was taken away and given no further education. All Dad remembered of his childhood was 'Good morning Ma, Good morning Pa, Good evening Ma, Good evening Pa.' No love, no affection, nothing. He became a farmer - it was the only thing he knew how to do."

Reginald went to British Columbia with brothers Lance and Walter. When Lance fell ill, he brought him home. The First World War broke out and he was unable to go back. He married Imogen in 1916, and David and Edward used to spend the summer holidays with the family in the mid-twenties.

Reginald fell ill with cancer and died in 1933. "The awful thing was," said Sheila, "that as Dad was dying, Aunt Helena used to visit in her car. She would go up the back stairs and Dad would hear her going from room to room, looking in drawers, but never going to see him." [9]

Around 1910, the Leans moved from Croydon to a village called Merstham, between Redhill and Reigate. David's brother, Edward, was born here on 23 February 1911.

"We had a very pleasant house called the Fryennes," David remembered. "I went back only a few years ago. It had a beautiful lawn and it was positioned opposite the church."

It was a church the Leans never visited; they attended the Dorking and Horsham Meeting House. Frank's brother, Edmund Wylde Lean, who besides being a Quaker was also a chartered accountant, would bring his two children,

Isabel and Barbara, down from Ealing.

David may have regarded himself as an extrovert, but he was also very shy and was silent and awkward when meeting people. His cousin, Isabel, was even more painfully shy. Their first encounter was, to put it mildly, cool and distant. The parents were disappointed. Since the children met so few others of their own age, they hoped that a friendship might be established. Two decades later, Isabel would become David's first wife.

David Lean, 1910.

Saturday, 1 August 1914 was the start of the Bank Holiday weekend and the Leans had gone to the seaside resort of Sheringham in Norfolk. It was unusually hot. David was six years old and Edward was three. The newspapers were full of the talk of war, but the British hoped to stay out of it, assuming an assassination in Sarajevo in the remote Balkan state of Bosnia concerned only the Central Powers and Russia. They were more alarmed by the prospect of civil war in Ireland, between those who wanted Home Rule and those, like Carson, who were arming against it.

When the Germans invaded neutral Belgium, the British government sent an ultimatum demanding the removal of troops by midnight, 4 August 1914. Half an hour before the deadline, King George V held a council sanctioning war against Germany. Next day, the Territorials were mobilised. David was woken at his holiday guest house by an unusual sound.

"I remember a motorbike riding along the front at dead of night, the driver shouting 'Volunteers out!' I remember it vividly because everyone thought there was going to be an invasion immediately."

The Leans returned to Merstham and before long the family had two soldiers billeted on them. The smell of their uniforms was a faint memory for David of his childhood.

The war caused David's parents considerable anxiety. Since no Quaker would take up arms - war being contrary to the will of God - Frank would eventually register as a conscientious objector, like his brothers. But the war seemed such a clear-cut issue - a great nation going to the rescue of a helpless small one - that it caused Frank to re-examine his Quaker principles.

The Quakers had been founded in the seventeenth century as an extreme sect of the Puritan movement. Their founder, George Fox, driven to despair by what he saw as the hypocrisy of so-called Christians, claimed that Christ would speak to anyone; you did not need a magnificent edifice or an authorised parson to permit you to speak to God.

While this appealed to many as a simple truth, it struck the authorities as blasphemy, especially when the Quakers refused to pay church taxes of the time, known as "Tithes". Quakers were persecuted under Cromwell and Charles II, five hundred dying in English prisons.[10] They were first called Quakers in 1650 by Justice Bennett of Derby when George Fox, accused of blasphemy, "bid them to tremble at the work of God."[11]

Quakers believed that by meeting together in a simple building and sitting in "an energetic and expectant silence", God might make use of any worshipper as a minister. They believed in frugal living and absolute honesty in everyday affairs. This, combined with their self-discipline, gave them a reputation which enormously enhanced their business dealings. They stood also for the abolition of slavery, the institution of women's rights, temperance, the abolition of capital punishment, penal reform and the care of the mentally ill.

Originally they were known as "Children of Light", a description which would have appealed to David. Where he would eventually part company with the Quakers was over their puritanism. While they recognised that instrumental music was unlikely to arouse anything but pleasant and sociable sentiments, they felt that the time it took to learn to play an instrument should be put to more valuable uses; the desire for excellence, they felt, put one in spiritual danger. David, who never learned to play an instrument, was nonetheless drawn to music, not to mention the desire for excellence.

The Quakers rejected the other arts, too. The theatre, for instance, could harm the personality.

"The art of acting is based on impersonation," wrote John Punshon. "Friends were unhappy with this, for it could not be sincere to express a grief or happiness one did not feel and one only had to look at the lives of actors and actresses to see the sort of damage such insincerity could do." There was a subtle form of Quaker humour, wrote Punshon, "but the belly laugh is not one of their gifts."[12]

The effect on David was contradictory; while he rejected all the outdated Quaker restrictions, he was nonetheless thoroughly indoctrinated. He never regarded actors with anything less than suspicion and he buried himself in his "frivolous amusements" as though in a religious order.

"I'm not a Quaker now, though I have kept a lot of my Quaker upbringing," said David. "Moral overtones, really. Never tell a lie. Never cheat. And be highly suspicious of great show. I find it very difficult when I go into a place like St Peter's in Rome and see people swinging incense and gold about. I feel it is too ostentatious. Quite wrongly. I don't know why one shouldn't be too ostentatious. But that's from way back in Quaker meeting houses, you know. I think it's a very good religion, very good. I like the simplicity of it. I think it's quite good to go to a meeting, which I don't, and sit for an hour in silence every week, and just think a bit with other people. I don't know what I am now. I don't think, as Mrs Moore says, that it's a godless universe. But I wouldn't know what God is. I cannot believe it's all accidental. We're still trying to find out, like plumbers trying to mend Swiss watches, what makes us tick, aren't we? I just don't know. Nobody knows."[13]

In November 1914, a "Declaration on the War" was distributed by the Society of Friends: "All war is utterly incompatible with the plain precepts of our Divine Lord and Lawgiver."

The proper service of a Quaker in wartime was to save life. Young Quakers, who were not expected to enlist, could become ambulance drivers in the Friends' Ambulance Unit. When it became clear that the war was going to continue, even Quakers had second thoughts. One correspondent to *The Friend*, Bernard Ellis, argued that it was the first duty of all "to overcome the criminal, bind and punish him" and to meet force with force.[14] A couple of Quakers remonstrated with Ellis and he returned to the fray in November 1915, amid rumours of conscription. Quakers, he said, should take service in the Army and Navy "to preserve the freedom of the country in which Quaker ideals may flourish during the ensuing peace."[15]

One of those who responded to this letter was Frank Lean.

"The young man Friend finds himself at the present time in a position of no little difficulty," he wrote. "Anxious to show himself no coward, the appeal to the man in the trenches comes with great force, but once again it is shown that man's foes are to be found among his own household!"[16]

It was a terrible time for Quakers. They were given no clear lead. Even so eminent a Quaker as Frederick Andrews, headmaster of Ackworth, refused to condemn those of his former pupils who joined the armed services.

In 1916, Herbert Asquith's government presented the bill inaugurating conscription. That same month, at a Quaker meeting, many Friends refused to compromise by undertaking "alternate service" (hospital or farm work) because they felt that even hospital or farm work would indirectly support the prosecution of the war. During the passage of the bill, which became law in February, a minute was passed at the Kingston Monthly Meeting (of which Croydon was a part) stating that "many of our members were not prepared to place body and soul at the disposal of the military authorities."

"My father was highly respected," said David. "My mother, too. They were obviously sincere people who believed what they said. They were not doing it because they were cowards. Some Quakers, after all, went to the front in the Ambulance Unit and brought in the wounded from the battlefield under fire."

The conscription bill contained a conscience clause, and from March 1916, War Office Tribunals interviewed what became known as "Conscientious Objectors". Most of these tribunals were travesties of justice. Some Friends were refused exemption and forced into the army, to be transported to the front, where, if they refused to obey orders, they could be shot as deserters.[17] At his tribunal, however, Frank Lean was exempted on medical grounds.

"A few years earlier," said David, "he had a mastoid operation and a lump of his ear was taken out. For the rest of his life, his ear looked very strange. You could see a bigger hole there than there should have been and that excluded him from military service."

Because the Leans were Quakers, the Church of England village school would not admit David and in July 1915, the family decided to return to Croydon.

Francis William le Blount Lean.

Frank bought Warham Mount, a large Victorian house with a splendid garden at 3 Warham Road (since demolished). There had been a Zeppelin raid on Croydon in February, when bombs had killed nine and wounded fifteen, and while such events were hushed up, and dealt with anonymously by the papers as "visits", it was common knowledge in the district. Frank may have acquired his house as a direct result since many people fled London for the country.

David was sent to a kindergarten called Miss Clayton's at 60 Park Lane, East Croydon. Here it became apparent that brilliant families do not always produce brilliant children. By the standards of the time, with their ruthless emphasis on the three Rs, David was dim. By comparison with his brother, who was still only four, he was alarmingly backward.

"I remember my mother coming back one afternoon from a visit to Miss Clayton. She said, 'Dave, Miss Clayton has told me a terrible thing about you. She's afraid you will never be able to read or write.' And she burst into tears."

Imagine the tests that must have preceded this revelation. Imagine the frustrated astonishment as Miss Clayton vainly tried to persuade David to write something more than his name, to spell "cat" or "dog". Imagine the growing sense of shock that perhaps she had given a place in her school to a child who was mentally deficient. Had she been told at that moment that the dunderhead before her would become the most accomplished Englishman in his field, garlanded with honours - including a knighthood - she might have retired at once.

As it was, the appalling news filled the Leans with more dread than the war itself. The kindest theory was that perhaps the boy had some brain disease. The suspicion that he was mentally deficient they refused to acknowledge. This was perhaps a good thing, but it had its destructive side, for Frank Lean decided that the boy was being sluggish on purpose and began to bully him. As for David, he often sat glumly and silently - David Lean's silences would later become legendary in the film industry.

"I forget the real miseries," said David. "I just block them out, so my childhood is a series of blanks."

David's problem as a child was one of worthlessness. There was nothing he did that provoked admiration. His father, whom he looked up to, regarded him as a dullard, albeit with hidden reserves. His mother may have thought more of him but he did not value her opinion. She had a pedantic regard for the niceties of behaviour. She felt ill one evening and retired to bed and David asked, "Has Mum got a stomach-ache?" Helena was shocked and said, "Dave, you don't say 'stomach' to a lady."[18]

She was the only one to call him "Dave" and to the end of his life he loathed being called "Dave". He associated it, presumably, with being treated like a backward child. He was convinced he had a handicap and he retreated more and more into his private world of fantasy.

An English child in the First World War was not subject to the fears of a child in the front-line villages of France, shelled, occupied, evacuated, shelled again. And not even this Quaker child was made to feel that the war was wrong. For that would be unpatriotic.

"War wasn't awful in those days at all. It was glorious," recalled David. "There was no suggestion that people were getting horribly wounded. The *Illustrated London News* used to produce these dramatic pictures of scenes from the front and they were stirring, thrilling. But it was generally acknowledged that you never asked anybody a question about the war if they'd been at the front. It was taboo.

"We were out on the lawn at Warham Mount. It was a Sunday, a beautiful summer's day with a clear blue sky. My father said, 'Listen!' We all stopped talking and the only way to describe it is to say that the air was moving slightly. My father said, 'Those are the guns in France.' The whole place was trembling. Very strange and rather frightening."

On the night of 23 September 1916, the Leans were woken by a sound that chilled them all. It was as though a railway engine with rusty wheels was churning its way through the sky.

"My brother and myself went into my parents' bedroom with its big brass bedstead and my father took us to the window and we saw this silver Zeppelin, lit up by searchlights, with the bursts of the anti-aircraft shells exploding around it."

At half past twelve, the L31 was over Purley and as David and his family watched, the Croydon searchlight picked it up again. Two flares from the Zeppelin drowned it. Ten high explosive bombs and twenty-two incendiaries were dropped on Streatham. The L31 then disappeared from view.

"When we came back to the bed," said David, "I saw my mother sprawled across it. She had fainted."

Such dramatic incidents, though, were rare. David was far more aware of the long summer holidays, when life in Croydon barely seemed to move, when he felt almost paralysed by boredom. And as his brother became more articulate, David felt increasingly outclassed and isolated.

"I think I was my mother's favourite, and my brother was certainly my father's favourite, no doubt about that. I think my mother was sorry for me because I was absolutely eclipsed by this young brother of mine."

Edward was emerging as a very bright, very amusing child but quieter than David, who was regarded as an extrovert. They hardly played together at all; the fact that Edward was three years younger was constantly held up as a measure of David's backwardness.

David did not enjoy the pursuits he was expected to enjoy. Reading was an effort and he avoided it as much as he could. He had no interest in the visits to The Friends' Meeting House. Boys of low academic ability were forgiven if they shone at sport, but David wasn't much good at this either, and games requiring mental ability, like chess, completely defeated him. He would spend longer and longer gazing into space, actually deep in thought but to his father, merely confirming his worst suspicions.

David was developing an inner eye, which perceived different things to his contemporaries. It was as though he was an observer from another time. Taking no notice of cricket, which obsessed his friends, he was fascinated by such mundane matters as methods of transportation.

"Horses and trams were an important part of my childhood; the clop-clop-clop of horses' hooves on cobbles and the noise of tram bells and the tram wheels on the tracks. The trams have disappeared along with the horses. I can remember people going round and collecting the horse manure. I can see the cart wheels, bright silver from friction, the metal lining in place of a tyre, gleaming, highly polished silver, like a railway line. Buses were a rarity in my part of the world. It was nearly all trams and the exciting flash and crackle as the arm travelled along the wire - I used that in DOCTOR ZHIVAGO."

Towards the end of the war, David left Miss Clayton's - no doubt to her relief - and joined his prep school. He became one of the sixty-five day boys at The Limes, on the summit of Melville Avenue. The school was known as a preparatory school because, like others of its kind, it prepared boys for public school and the Royal Navy. It was unusually well equipped for the period - when some prep schools had more in common with Dotheboys Hall of *Nicholas Nickleby* - with a science laboratory, a carpentry shop, a gym and extensive playing fields.

The playing fields were lined with poplars and hanging from their branches by silken threads David found puss-moth caterpillars. He became fascinated with butterflies and from this flourished a deep love for natural history. At the end of his life, goaded by nostalgia, he asked his personal assistant to find some examples of these butterflies. By then, the puss-moth butterfly had become an endangered species.

"He told me that he used to watch butterflies all the time," recalled Sandra Lean, David's widow. "He would never catch butterflies, however. If a bee entered the house, or a wasp, he would not kill it. He would catch it in a glass and release it out of the window. And the same applied to butterflies. He was fascinated with butterflies and their colours."

One of the few books with David's name in it which survives from his childhood is *The Look About You Nature Book* by T.W. Hoare. Judging from its battered state, it was much loved. The fifty-six colour plates were obviously pored over, and the book must have accompanied David on country expeditions. Its cover has almost fallen off.

During the latter part of the morning of 11 November 1918, the boys at The Limes heard a curious series of sounds from Croydon - first the air-raid warning, then the church bells, which had been silent for so long, pealing into the autumn air. The matron, Miss Murray, marched in to the dining hall and told the masters that the Armistice had been signed. None of the boys understood the significance of the word - least of all David - and the masters had to explain it. The boys rushed out to the playground and cheered themselves hoarse. Despite their yelling they could still hear the crowds cheering and the racket from Croydon as maroons were fired and bugles sounded the All Clear. The boys at The Limes would be of military age well in time for the next war.

CHAPTER TWO

THE BREAK

FRANCIS Lean was a pillar of the establishment in the City, where he worked, and in Croydon where he lived. He was particularly valued for his contributions to his religion.

"He used to speak at the Croydon Meeting House,[1] much to my embarrassment," said David. "In a Quaker meeting there are no set sermons, anybody can stand up and speak whenever they like. My father used to speak quite a lot and everybody used to come up to my mother afterwards and say, 'Oh, we did enjoy your husband this morning.'"

Francis William le Blount Lean lies like a dark shadow over David's life. I tried on several occasions to persuade him to give me a word picture of the man, and each time he managed to avoid doing so. When he was obliged to describe some aspect of his father, it was delivered in dour tones. He gave the impression that had he cast a film of his life, his father would have been played by Charles Laughton, a combination of Captain Bligh and Mr Barrett, of Wimpole Street fame.

And yet Kay Walsh, David's second wife, recalled him with admiration.

"He was extraordinary, because he was an absolute smasher. If you think David and Edward were handsome, my God, this man! He was a beauty. I would have gone missing for him any day."[2]

Norman Spencer, David's production manager, met Frank in later years.

"He was an all-round man, not at all narrow-minded. David's mother had a curiously narrow mind, I felt. I always regarded David's father as a very nice, dignified, square kind of man, a charming Henley gentleman."[3]

Born in Birmingham in 1879, Frank Lean was accustomed to success. He was the author of a work imposingly entitled *Companies Act 1907. A Classified Abridgement of the Principal Provisions Affecting Directors, Secretaries and Auditors.* He had a first-class business mind, and it was a pity that none of it was inherited by his son.

"He had the sort of brain that analysed everything, docketed everything, and put everything into neat categories in his mind," said a member of the family. "David didn't fit in anywhere."[4]

In the light of his career, perhaps it was positively helpful that Frank and Helena refused to allow David to go to the cinema. Had he been allowed to go on a regular basis, it is possible that the shattering impact that the moving picture made on him would have been dissipated.

"My father wasn't allowed to go to the theatre when he was a boy because it was a place of sin. Gradually, the stage became legitimate and he used to take us all off to the theatre and that was fine. But the cinema..! My parents regarded it as a place of wickedness."[5]

David told Stephen Silverman that his parents were pretty advanced, as a lot of Quakers in those days were, but that they regarded cinemas as "absolute dens of vice." They objected to the wildly emotional portrayals of people like Pola Negri and Nazimova. Since the Leans did not visit the cinema anyway, this seems questionable. It was, as Lean acknowledged, much more a question of class.

"I suppose the real reason was that the cinema was the entertainment of the common people and there were very common people performing in it."[6]

For much the same reason he was denied children's comics. "My brother and I used to read *The Rainbow* in the six-foot forest of artichokes in the kitchen garden. I loved the flow of brightly coloured illustrations telling their stories in pictures. Because of this, I was fascinated by the outside of those forbidden cinemas with their display of stills from their current attraction. Sword fights, ships, deserts and glamorous men and women."[7]

David's brown studies gradually veered more towards fantasy and magic. If his parents denied him the cinema, his father would sometimes take him to see a magician called Captain Maskelyne and his show.

"They were wonderful illusionists. You'd see a blank stage and a lake would appear, and then a swan swimming on the lake. I don't know how the hell it was done. They also did sawing people in half, which I suppose is looked upon as commonplace now. But it was absolute magic to me."[8]

Another illusion showed a motor-cycle and rider circling around the stage, then entering a wooden crate which was hoisted in the air. A ray was aimed at the crate which disintegrated, leaving no trace of motor-cycle or rider...

"I always see myself as Captain Clive Maskelyne, in tails, saying, 'Now ladies and gentlemen, watch carefully. Yes, it's a door. Yes, it's opening. Someone is coming in...' It's as if I were telling a story, in very simple terms, and I would think to quite a low-brow audience."[9]

Fortunately, David was able to visit the cinema by proxy, thanks to the charwoman at Warham Mount, a lady of Irish origin called Mrs Egerton.

"She loved the cinema. She knew I wasn't allowed to go, so she described the cinema to me. I couldn't understand it. I remember saying, 'But what happens when they talk?'

"'Well,' she said, 'they open their mouths and then writing comes up on the screen - what they're saying.'

"'Writing comes...what do you mean? It can't look any good.'

"'It does. It looks as if they're talking.'

"I learned about the movies from Mrs Egerton. She was a stout woman with a jolly, sweet face. She was very respectably dressed in the kind of Cockney way that people like her dressed in those days. She had a tremendous sense of humour and was very warm. She really loved me. It was the first love, I think, that I ever experienced."

Mrs Egerton was married to a horse-cab driver who wore a bowler hat and moustache.

"I can still see him with a whip, sitting on the top of his cab. And it seemed rather incongruous, because loving her as I did, I found it rather hard to accept him."

It was entirely fitting that Mrs Egerton should have adored Charlie Chaplin, though she could hardly have known that he had borrowed his walk from a South London horse-cab driver.

"We had a huge kitchen in the basement of Warham Mount," said David. "She imitated Chaplin very well and she would sit me on a kitchen chair and I remember her walking round and round our great kitchen table with her toes turned out, then breaking into a run and skidding round the corners on one leg. I used to roll around with laughter. When I finally saw him, she was absolutely bang on.

"Mrs Egerton represented the public of those days and my mother couldn't possibly have understood what Mrs Egerton appreciated in Charlie Chaplin. When my mother expressed her distaste of Charlie Chaplin, something happened to her mouth. It was because he was a common, vulgar little man. He would pick up a child, and you could tell that the child had peed on his lap. Now that appalled her. She regarded it as a considerable lapse of taste.

"I learned later from my mother, who was somewhat put out by it, that Mrs Egerton came to her one day and asked if she would contemplate Mrs Egerton adopting me. I could hardly believe it and I still don't understand it to this day.

"I really loved Mrs Egerton, but I never dreamed of running away with her and never considered myself unloved. But she was my first 'other woman.' She was gay, she laughed a lot and she had a large dose of that lovely cockney vulgarity. By comparison, my mother and father seemed to belong to a museum - ruffles, stiff collars, ties and politeness. Mrs Egerton had sex."[10]

Since 1920, David's school, The Limes, had been under the headmastership of Major Harold Atkinson.[11]

"The very mention of his name brings back his smell," said David. "Brilliantine in his hair, Turkish cigarettes - he seemed terribly sophisticated. Nothing about The Limes excited me. I was not good at anything, but it was all reasonably pleasant."[12]

A former pupil of The Limes who remembered the schoolboy David was

Maurice Cooke of Purley.

"I tell you one thing that has always puzzled me," he said. "David was two years older than me - I was born in 1910 - and yet we were always in the same class. We moved up together. He can't have been very bright, can he?"

And that, of course, was the problem. It was to the Major's credit that he and his staff managed it with such tact that David was only vaguely aware of it.

"I don't know if he noticed, or if anyone else noticed. I doubt it. He was never depressed or anything. Major Atkinson was a very fine teacher, very fair and was particularly strong with boys who weren't good at something - football, for instance. He was a great encourager."[13]

David had a toy engine to play with at home, but it was only when Frank and Helena took the boys to Cornwall on holiday that his love affair with steam engines began. (He later haunted railway stations to watch the trains.)

"Paddington was the magic place," said David. "That's where the great holiday started. My father always took me down to see the engine of the Cornish Riviera Express that was to pull us down to Cornwall. I loved these steam engines and that's probably why I put them in my films.

"You left for Cornwall about ten-thirty in the morning and you got down there about five. First stop Exeter. It was Dawlish where the train suddenly came out beside the sea. That was very exciting. We stayed at the Carbis Bay Hotel. There were tremendously long beaches with hardly anybody on them. Yet I remember my mother walking miles down the beach, away from my father, my brother and myself, and only then did she get into her bathing costume. She went into the sea as far as her middle and that was all, and we didn't go anywhere near her because she was undressed, as it were. The prudery was extraordinary. I think I'm still a bit of a prude now because of all that."[14]

Towards the end of David's days at The Limes, he began to notice, whenever he came home, that the atmosphere at Warham Mount was becoming more and more strained. Helena was depressed, and when Frank came home in the evening, he was tense and silent.

Rumours passed like an electric current around the Lean and Tangye families. Of those relatives who were told - or who sensed - what was happening, only one did anything for David.

"I don't know if they saw things going on that I didn't see; I rather suspect they did. But for my eleventh birthday, Uncle Clement gave me a Kodak Box Brownie camera. It seems nothing now, but in those days it was the most enormous compliment. To be given a camera under normal circumstances, you'd have to be at least seventeen. It was the first time somebody gave me something which made me feel special.

"Everybody said, 'He'll never be able to use it' but actually I became very good and mad keen for taking pictures."

The Box Brownie had been introduced in 1900 at five shillings. Fifty thousand were sold within the year. It was a simple affair, the equivalent of today's "point-and-shoot" cameras, except that it used roll film with only eight exposures. It had a good lens, and David learned about photography by printing his own films.

"When you took photographs in those days, you printed them on daylight printing paper. You put the negative into a frame, you held the frame up to the sunlight and as the sun penetrated, it got darker and darker and when it reached what you thought was the correct density, you took it out and put it in hypo. It was a sort of secret of mine. I felt, 'I can do this', and so I just loved cameras. I still do.

"I was not the kind of child who rushed to their parents and said, 'Look at this!' because I didn't think my opinion was of any account. I always had this brother who was way ahead of me. I might show an unusually good photograph to my mother, but that was one of the awful things. Nothing I did really impressed anybody. Nevertheless, that Box Brownie really started me off."[15]

In 1921 there was a dismal change of existence for David. The family moved from Warham Mount to Park Lane in East Croydon, near Miss Clayton's and the Quaker meeting house. The curious thing about the move was that it was in no sense an improvement. Whereas Warham Mount had four storeys and a beautiful garden, the new

A view of Park Lane, Croydon, from an Edwardian postcard.

house - 97 Park Lane - had a much smaller garden and was a semi-detached house of three storeys.

"We can't have had a drop in our standard of living. It must have been that father was preparing to leave us when we moved to that miserable little house at Park Lane. He must have been preparing for the break."

Frank Lean had met a handsome, red-haired war widow. So deep was the injury caused by this liaison that I have been asked not to identify the woman. I shall call her Margaret Merton. Born in 1888, she came from a prosperous middle-class family. Her father was that unusual figure in the Edwardian era - a militant atheist.

Margaret was a pianist of ability, who gave public concerts in Croydon. There are two versions of how she met David's father. One is that Frank attended a charity concert at which she played. The other is that they met at a charity dance in George Street, Croydon. Since Frank loved music but could not dance a step, this seems less likely. In any case, Frank was immediately attracted to her and became friendly with her small son, Stephen, aged six.

At first the friendship was platonic. Margaret was even invited to Warham Mount for tea. Stephen remembered her coming home and saying, "It was extraordinary. They didn't have a carpet on the stairs, they had lino!"

Perhaps because they sensed their marriage was doomed, and they did not want its disintegration to be observed by their Quaker Friends, Frank and Helena decided to make a clean break. In March 1921, a letter of resignation arrived at the Kingston Monthly Meeting (which in those days included Croydon). Theodora Clark and Percy Harris were asked to visit the Leans in order to compile a report.

The report survives. I expected to read an honest appraisal of their marital state - Quakers being famous for their honesty - and possibly stern admonition from the two Friends. Instead, the report, dated 11 May 1921, merely quoted how the Leans (one can safely assume Frank did all the talking) had fallen out of sympathy with Quaker ideas.

"1. They find our meetings for worship very frequently lacking in interest. They consider that the advantages of our freedom are outweighed by the necessity of having, from time to time, to listen to unedifying addresses. They feel, too, that the music and especially perhaps the opening hymn, in the Congregational Church Service, is distinctly helpful in inducing a spiritual uplift and sense of unity in the congregation. They find the absence of music in our meetings a definite loss.

"2. They are not in sympathy with the pacifist position and consider that the Society stresses this matter far too much. In their opinion, Friends fail to realize that the freedom and security of life and property which they now enjoy are due largely to the baulking of the German attempt to invade this country by the entry of England into the war.

"3. In their judgment, the Society of Friends concerns itself too much with political matters and is too prone to offer advice to the Government on various questions that arise from time to time."

The visitors expressed their regrets, hoped that the resignation would not sever friendships, and assured them of a welcome should they ever decide to return to the Society.

"We enquired as to David and Edward and it appears likely that they will attend the children's class at Purley Congregational Church, but the parents did not desire that their names should be removed from our register unless and until the boys themselves, on reaching maturity, should express a wish for this to be done.

"In conclusion we made it clear to our Friends that we all wished them Godspeed in their new surroundings and assured them that they had the cordial sympathy and understanding of their Friends in Park Lane."[16]

The resignation was accepted.

The breakup of the marriage was an agonisingly slow process, with Frank slipping away whenever he could to see Margaret, who had taken a flat overlooking Kew Green. She and Frank felt compelled to come together, but they resisted it as long as they could.

Divorce in those days was worse than bereavement. Married couples would often endure any torment rather than inflict this fate upon themselves. The stigma sometimes led to suicide. It was not uncommon for the husband to take a mistress and for life to continue, in all outward respects, as before. This is what happened in this case - for a while.

David never knew why his father left. In later years, however, Edward's wife, Doreen, became a confidante of Helena who said that she felt it had been her fault that the marriage had failed.

"I had had a miscarriage after Edward was born, and I refused to let my husband anywhere near me."

Coolness developed into hostility, and the tension between his parents quickly became all too apparent to David.

"My most vivid memory is of hearing loud voices at 97 Park Lane, and going upstairs and finding my father in my mother's bedroom, he in his braces, my mother in tears, and my father turning to me as I came in and saying, 'David, I can't stand it any longer. I'm going.'"[17]

When Frank made the final break, he and Margaret left the district and went to live in Hove.

"Brighton we always called it. If Brighton came up in any conversation it was a terrible thing because that was where they were."[18]

David and Edward suffered a double displacement; not only had they lost their father, but he had moved into another family, with a substitute son.

Stephen, when he first met Frank, was instructed to call him "Uncle", which became "Uncle Bluncle", eventually shortened to "Buncs". Because of the delicate nature of the relationship, everybody else found this a convenient way of referring to him.

Buncs evidently felt guilty for the rest of his life.

"David's mother," said Stephen, "retreated into her Cornish Tangye background and absolutely refused any question of a divorce. The family was very much split - not so much on her side as on Buncs' side. They were Quakers, too, and Buncs I know had terrible struggles with his conscience. Two or three of his brothers and sisters came out on his side. The others cut off from him."

Surprisingly, Stephen recalled being taken several times to the Meeting House at Park Lane, but once Frank resigned he seemed to abandon all his hold on religion. He even took Margaret and Stephen to the cinema every week!

The final split occurred in 1923, when David was fifteen. "When my father left," he said, "I became the mainstay for my poor mother, who collapsed under the strain of the breakup of her marriage. She was desperately unhappy. She used to spend her time crying and to this day I cannot abide tears. If my wife starts to cry, I say, 'Stop crying!' in a brutal way, because it reminds me of my mother. I spent my life with tears.

"It was looked upon as a terrible thing to happen, for Quakers particularly. My father must have had tremendous courage to do it, for he was regarded as a thoroughly wicked, immoral man.

"People who did that sort of thing in those days were riddled by guilt. They feel that they're wicked people. That's the thing about Anna Karenina, isn't it? One of the points surely was that she really agreed with the people who condemned her. I went to immense efforts to avoid questions about my parents because I was so dreadfully ashamed that they weren't together."[19]

Frank Lean kept in touch with his boys - there was no question of his having abandoned them. And yet they felt abandoned. They were both devastated by his departure. For David, the future became enshrouded by gloom and he couldn't wait for the holidays to be over so he could get back to boarding school. His mother used her tears as a way of keeping David at home.

He retreated more and more into his private world.

CHAPTER THREE

THE LAWS OF LIP

1921 may have been wretched in many ways, but it also proved a year of destiny for David Lean.

One summer afternoon he had slipped in to the Scala Cinema, North End, Croydon with a friend from The Limes. Since they were only thirteen, they could get a decent seat for sixpence. The Scala advertised "Luxurious seats with arms in every part of the house". There were 882 of these seats and the auditorium was decorated with hunting scenes by a French artist. The atmosphere was heightened when the Scala orchestra took their places and their conductor, Señor Luna, strode to the podium.

The curtains parted and David was suddenly aware of a powerful beam of amber coloured light, stabbing through the cigarette smoke. The screen was bathed in this same amber colour and the orchestra burst into a dramatic theme, and David saw the main title of his first film: THE HOUND OF THE BASKERVILLES. Following the credits came lengthy introductory titles. As David struggled through them, he realised that he would have to improve his standard of reading.

THE HOUND OF THE BASKERVILLES was directed by Maurice Elvey. In those days, British films were produced on minuscule budgets, and this one went no closer to Dartmoor than Surrey. But that was hardly something David would have noticed. He was delighted by the huge photographs which moved, and thrilled by the silhouettes of the hound - its body alive with magical phosphorescence. With the music changing to reflect the mood of each scene, the shots of armed prison warders on horseback pursuing a wanted man across the moor and the fights in moonlight - the powerful beam of light changing the colour on the screen to blue - were almost unbearably exciting.

Seen today, the production is a workmanlike telling of Conan Doyle's famous story, with Eille Norwood as a handsome, but rather self-conscious, Sherlock Holmes. It contains occasional crudities of production which would have affronted the David Lean of later years. But for a boy who had never before seen a moving picture, it was unforgettable.

The source of this miracle appeared to be the rectangular shaft of arc light from the projector.

"I would look at that light as a pious boy might react to a shaft of sunlight in a cathedral. I still find it a slightly mystical experience. Something to do with forbidden and secret things. Something very much to do with magic and something connected with a far, far distant me who once told stories in caves and drew pictures on their walls.[1]

"Mrs Egerton was the one who fired my enthusiasm. I don't think I'd thought too much about the cinema before Mrs Egerton. And she was so mad about it she enthused me with it. And as with anybody who loves something very much, they conjure up visions. And the visions she conjured up didn't leave me with any great surprise when I actually sat in the cinema and saw a film for the first time. It worked just like Mrs Egerton said it did.

"My mother was a confidante of mine and she knew I went to the cinema, but she never told my father."[2]

David regarded the cinema primarily as a means of escape - "getting out of the suburbs of London and into a really magic house."[3] At the Scala, the Orpheum or the Palladium, he saw things he thought he would never see.

"I had suddenly discovered life though the movies. Intercut that with Croydon and you have an idea of how exciting it was."

David objected to the suburbs because of their dreariness: "Same

North End, Croydon, showing the Scala cinema on right.

houses, same trains, same suits and umbrellas." Thanks to his gifts of concentration, he was able to transfer the films he saw from the screen into his head, so that while he walked around his "dreadful town" he was actually living in a movie. He would sometimes emerge from the cinema and wonder why no one was staring at him, because he had become the star of the film he had just seen.

Legend has it that all silent films were accompanied by a tinkling piano. And, to begin with, they often were. But as the cinema became more sophisticated, so did the musical accompaniment and even small towns boasted cinemas with orchestras. Other cinemas installed organs and only the humblest places depended upon the piano.

"I was fascinated by these pictures on a screen and by the orchestra playing. People today don't know what silent movies were like. They were a very powerful medium, the silent picture combined with an orchestra. Its impact was something quite different from a talkie. Just marvellous really."[4]

David was still curious about the magical beam of light. In the interval, he used to look back at the projection port and wonder what went on there. In the silent days, films were generally tinted and toned - amber for day, blue for night, red for fire. These colours suffused the projector beam and David used to regard that beam, as it changed colour, as the symbol of his new passion.

"You have no idea how the movies were despised by the middle classes in England," said David. "They were cheap entertainment for the poor. I remember begging my mother one Saturday evening not to look after me but to go and see a Douglas Fairbanks film, THE MARK OF ZORRO. I still remember a shot where Fairbanks knocks a sword out of his rival's hand and it sticks into the ceiling and in the close-up it quivers. My mother didn't go. She wouldn't have liked it anyhow. If it had been the theatre, she might have reacted differently."[5]

The local paper, the *Croydon Times*, expressed the attitude of many of the older generation to this new form of entertainment.

"The movie appeals to the appetites and fancies of pre-historic man," pontificated A. D'Arcy Chapman. "Indulgence of the appetite it feeds, and of the faculties it particularly engages, weakens that very tender plant - zest for things that ameliorate. Now, of all things that ameliorate, the mastery of knowledge and its daughter wisdom are of the first importance. The key to knowledge is the mastery of the printed page. The movie turns millions away from the effort to attain that mastery... the average movie meets its observers at the most primitive part of their natures... the movie-seeing habit provokes no celebration."[6]

David did eventually persuade his mother to go with him to the cinema. "One of my favourite films ever," said David, "was WHITE SHADOWS OF THE SOUTH SEAS. I'd seen it already four times and I took my mother for the fifth. It was at the Regal, Marble Arch. When we came out, I said, 'Well, what did you think?' And she said, 'Oh son, I just can't look at those black people.'"[7]

David did not disappoint his parents in the examination required for public schools, the Common Entrance. He did just as badly as they had feared, and for a while it looked as if he would fail to gain entry into any public school. There were fearful places known as "Crammers" which specialised in forcing boys through the Common Entrance exam.

But Helena was still a Quaker even if Frank was not, and she was determined that the boy should go to a Quaker school.[8]

Realising he would never get David into one of the top schools like Charterhouse or Cheltenham College, Frank contacted Charles Evans, the head-master of Leighton Park, a Quaker School at Reading, where his predecessor, John Ridges, had been a friend of the Lean family. Evans was the son of a former head of Sidcot and Ackworth, and was thus familiar with the Lean family himself.

Evans wrote to Major Atkinson at The Limes asking for an appraisal of the boy. Atkinson's reply, which rests in the archive of Leighton Park School, would have cheered the hearts of David's parents had they been permitted to read it:

"The boy has been with me for some time and I have found him to be keen, honest and extremely hardworking. However, two terms ago I was of the opinion that he never would be suitable for public school life owing to the fact that he did not appear to make any progress in his work, and therefore I advised his father to give him an outdoor life. Since then he has made very rapid progress and appears to have turned the corner (I say this in spite of the marks obtained). He is by no means at his best during examinations, but I can honestly say I shall be very sorry when he leaves me as I have found he is liked by every master and boy in the school. Finally, I can only add that it is my firm opinion that he will be a credit to any school."[9]

Charles Evans wrote this letter of acceptance to Frank Lean:

"Mr Atkinson tells me that he thinks David appears to have turned the corner in his progress; he evidently has hopes that the boy will now make a start in his intellectual work. I am quite prepared to carry in the school a certain number of boys dull at books who bring other qualities to the community. My view is that those closely connected with Friends have first claim in such cases. In the circumstances, I propose that David should sit again for the Common Entrance Examination in March. I will find a place for him in May if he shows then that he has made fair progress between the two examinations.

"P.S. Is David fond of games and good at them?"[10]

Alas, no record survives of David's second try at the Common Entrance, but it must have satisfied Mr Evans since he accepted him for the spring term of 1922. However, on the Leighton Park entry form, against the question, "Has he shown aptitude for any particular study?" was written the emphatic answer, "No." The entry form noted that David's favourite leisure pursuits were "Natural History, Birds, Moths, Caterpillars, etc. Carpentry."

There was no mention of photography or the cinema.

David joined Leighton Park a year later than his fellow pupils, but the staff were able to smooth over the fact. Like most schools, there was an initiation ceremony and, in the case of Leighton Park, new boys were made to eat soap.

The school was progressive; Quakerism was implicit rather than explicit and less than half the boys in David's day were Friends. Compared to the major public schools, which have been described so often in such grim detail, Leighton Park was astonishingly tolerant. There was no corporal punishment, no fagging, no cadet corps. The importance of hobbies as a factor in education was accepted and great emphasis was placed on self-discipline. (It didn't always work, as the school history readily admits.) The fact that religion was not forced upon the boys was welcomed by David. Leighton Park was an unconventional school producing unconventional people who did not fit into predetermined moulds.

David could not get over his good fortune in being sent to this exceptional school. It was the first real freedom he had known.

"It was a very good school. They were very broadminded; they had only about forty percent Quakers. We had a Negro boy there and we had a Chinese boy, and you wouldn't expect this of Quakers."

Academically, he still regarded himself as a dud. "Hopeless at mathematics. Still am. I have to count on my fingers if I wish to add. Latin? Hopeless. They asked me to give it up."[11]

A class mate, F.L. Woolley, had a different memory. "I don't remember David being academically hopeless. I thought he was quite bright. Take English, for instance. It was clear that he had a brain, but he didn't devote it in the way the school wanted it devoted."[12]

Despite its progressive and relaxed approach, Leighton Park had its rules and rituals. Boys attended Reading Meeting on Sunday morning in dark suits, with stiff collars, gloves and bowler hats - straw hats in summer. The outfit was known as "Sunday Penitentials". The ritual involved asking another boy for a "Sunday", which was like signing up partners at a dance, although the card listed not foxtrots but all the Sundays of the coming term. David had to find boys willing to accompany him to Morning Meeting in Church Street. It was a way of making friends, and David, who was growing into a handsome youth, with his aristocratic nose, and brown hair rippling back from a broad forehead, had no difficulty.

"My best friend was a chap called Chivers, of the Chivers Marmalade family, although my closest friendship was with a very glamorous fellow called Patrick Goodbody, an Irishman who came from the Argentine. Frightfully good looking and sort of dashing."

David remembered Hugh Foot (later Lord Caradon) who also suffered from sibling rivalry and persuaded his parents not to send him to the same public school as his brother, Dingle Foot, whom he regarded as much brighter than he was. Michael Foot, the future Labour Party leader, joined the school just as David was leaving.

"The sons of Quaker industrialists like Cadbury and Rowntree sent their boys there. I remember a boy from the Reckitt family - Reckitt's Blue - who died of meningitis in the middle of a holiday."

David became friendly with a boy named C.E.F. Plutte. He was German, and his father was the English representative for one of the big German cable companies. Plutte's sister became David's first love.

"We were far too young. It was ridiculous. There was no sort of affair - it was all as pure as the driven snow."[13]

With his passion for natural history, David appealed to Charles Evans, the headmaster. An elderly, dignified man, he was surprisingly gentle for a schoolmaster - too much so, according to some former pupils.

One of David's contemporaries, Leslie Newbigin (eventually Bishop of the Church of South India), knowing Evans to be a keen naturalist, concealed a gramophone in the bushes and played a record of a nightingale singing when the bird was out of season. Evans was completely hoodwinked, and in his excitement summoned a meeting of the entire school to tell them of the extraordinary event.

Maurice Blundell and his friend, Jim Renton, kept two owls and a goat at the school farm.

"On parents' visiting days the pets were exhibited," said Blundell, "our goat being tethered to a stake with a card giving particulars of age nailed to the top of the stake. I remember seeing some of the visitors in fits of laughter. David had put sweetener on the card to induce the goat to eat it and the visitors were taking photographs."

David in those days was seldom without his camera, and when he saw the boys doing something interesting he would ask them to hold their position and he would photograph them.

"If there was a lark," said Maurice Blundell, "David would be part of it. I remember Anthony Heal, a boy from the London furniture shop family, bringing his bike on to the drive and doing stunts - violent turns, skidding, etc. David was directing him, telling him what he wanted for his photographs, before a master came up and stopped them for making a mess of the drive."[14]

David was a popular boy, always surrounded by a group of friends. The fact that he did not shine in the classroom or on the sports field - he excelled only at the high jump - undoubtedly helped his popularity, for he made no boy feel competitive towards him. And since all he really cared about was photography, films and natural history, he felt competitive towards nobody.

"From the age of fourteen until I was nineteen, I spent all my money on film. I used to take pictures all round the school, or on holiday. Then I spent nearly all my spare time in the darkroom - and the last of my money on enlarging paper. BB Bromide paper, I still remember the name."[15]

The school magazine, *The Leightonian*, recreated a typical Saturday afternoon in June, when David was in his last term:

"After lunch at school he gets straight on his bicycle and goes down to buy some enlargement paper in Broad Street. He bicycles up again, through the heat, to his study for his camera, and then goes to some forbidden territory of Reckitt House, which was a glorious wilderness and then out of bounds. He takes various photographs which we can be sure were anything but slapdash, comes straight back to the darkroom, develops his negatives, fixes and washes them and has them drying before tea. Then on with the enlargements as quickly as possible afterwards, using the special magic solution from Broad Street."[16]

Leighton Park was ahead of other schools in its attitude to the cinema. In David's time, the cinema - at least in its "educational" form - featured in school activities surprisingly frequently. There was even a lecture on the subject, although most lectures were of the old-fashioned lantern variety. David was enthusiastic about these too.

"We had a beautiful lantern, which gave an excellent picture on the screen. On Saturday evenings, M. So-and-so would arrive and give us a lecture on, say, his travels in Switzerland. Some were very well put together."[17]

David's class was taken to the 1924 Empire Exhibition at Wembley - an event he recreated in THIS HAPPY BREED. Not for a decade had London had such an attraction, with its coloured lights, artificial waterways and sideshows. At the Palace of Engineering was a foretaste of television with moving pictures clearly visible (via back projection) on a fourteen-inch screen. And a small cinema presented De Forest Phonofilms - short moving pictures that talked, three years before THE JAZZ SINGER.

In 1925, the Cadbury family gave Leighton Park its own 35mm film projector. The Headmaster, not being familiar with these things, borrowed a film, produced by the League of Nations Union, about the settlement of the Aaland Island dispute. Nearly three hundred people came to see it, many of them boys from other Reading schools. The Headmaster imagined it was full-length, like other films he had seen, but it proved to be a single reel, and at a mere fifteen minutes, the show proved something of an anti-climax.

On another occasion, David and his schoolfellows were overjoyed to find that a trip to the Vaudeville Cinema, Reading, had been substituted for afternoon school. This was to see another documentary, an altogether more remarkable one - Robert Flaherty's NANOOK OF THE NORTH, a study of the Eskimo. David never forgot the experience and he became an avid follower of the drama-documentaries created by Flaherty, Schoedsack and Cooper, and Van Dyke.

Apart from NANOOK, documentaries of this period were invariably dull, lacking the very qualities they needed to make them educational. Later in life, David revealed a prejudice against them which may have dated back to his schooldays, when the gulf between the factual and fictional films was far wider than it is now.

For fictional films, he could take his pick from the cinemas in Reading. "There were special holidays," said David, "when the boys were allowed to see a movie. But I used to sneak to the cinema on Wednesdays and Saturdays. When the lights came up you were terrified that you'd find one of the masters sitting three or four seats away from you."[18]

According to the school history, discipline was "only fair. The attitude to work was generally poor. There was a general loosening of control and an easy-going, tolerant attitude that was in keeping with the time."[19]

This might surprise the present generation, which assumes its grandparents to have been fanatical disciplinarians. But after the war there was a revolution in the attitude of young people which was even more disruptive than the upheaval in the sixties. The older generation was blamed for the war, Victorian values were scoffed at and faith in authority was shattered. Bewildered and insecure, the older generation often thought it prudent to accommodate the rebels rather than to try to suppress their rebellion.

A serious problem occurred in the summer term of 1925 over prep - work which had to be done after class ready for the next day's lesson. An attempt to allow the boys to do this when and where they wanted failed, and so a "segregation room" was set up in which malefactors could be confined. The rule was that boys should spend a whole month in the segregation room and masters could put their entire class in if they felt it necessary. The school magazine referred to the place as a "compression room or sardine tin... it had been a seething mass of incorrigible humanity" throughout the term.

To outsiders, all appeared calm. A young master who had just joined the school was impressed by the apparent diligence of the boys, and had just put such a comment in the Duty Book when there was an explosion of noise and the door to the segregation room burst open. The whole school poured past him. Gangs of boys began racing round the grounds, hunting for the prefect, who had sensibly vanished. The master had visions of the Russian Revolution, but the boys were rounded up and prep was resumed.

"Later," said the master, "a group of boys came to apologise to me and to explain that nothing personal was meant. It was just a riot to let off steam."

When he told other members of the staff, they said they rather expected something of the kind to happen. The incident was allowed to pass.[20]

David never mentioned these exploits, but there can be little doubt he took part in some of them. An associate of a later period, Norman Spencer, considered that David was always a bit of a delinquent.

"Even when famous and knighted, he still believed himself to be the original delinquent of his youth. He was always against the run of society. He wouldn't recognise the term, but he was an anarchist - a nihilist."[21]

The only thing David dreaded at Leighton Park, apart from mathematics, was the arrival of letters from his mother. The final split between his parents had occurred in 1923, but in 1925-26, Frank attempted to return.

"He went back," said Stephen "for the last turn of his conscience. My mama and I came home to find a letter on the table. But it lasted only about two months and he couldn't stand it and came back again. He then cut off from Helena altogether. After that she was always referred to as 'Madam'."

Helena poured out her misery to her son in letter after letter, making David feel more and more responsible.

In the holidays, Frank Lean did his best to atone for the disaster he had brought upon his family by taking his sons on elaborate trips to the Continent. Frank had the cheerful contempt for foreigners of so many of his generation.

"Now we're going on a boat," he would tell David and Edward. "When we get to Calais, hold your noses."[22]

"In those days," said David, "young people didn't travel much. It was too expensive and it was considered not quite on in some strange way. But my father was very good about taking us abroad - he used to take my brother and I on what in those days were quite exotic trips. I remember travelling on the Rhinegold Express to Basle. I thought the only people who could run a railway were the English. I was absolutely

David and Edward on the Continent, taken by their father.

astounded to find these huge picture windows, comfortable seats and beautiful food served at the tables."[23]

On a trip to Paris, Frank took the boys to the Folies Bergère. "This really horrified me - girls with bare breasts. God, what a prude I was! I suppose in some crude way he thought, 'This is the way they're going to be taught about Life.' Oh dear, oh dear."

David was more impressed by the paintings in the Louvre. He bought large reproductions which, framed with passe-partout, he displayed in his study.

Edward had arrived at Leighton Park in 1924. He was placed in Townson House, while David was in School House. Edward was much more serious about education than David. His schoolfellows regarded him as more withdrawn. He was also a voracious reader, in contrast to his brother who claimed to have been brought up on Jules Verne and R.M. Ballantyne, but whose favourite reading, apart from film magazines, was *The Boys' Own Paper*.

"There was a chap who wrote in *The Boys' Own Paper* I was dotty about called Major Charles Gilson. I used to follow his serials. I think they had a huge effect on my film-making in a curious way, because he had a story-telling gift that I thought was wonderful. I loved being taken by the hand and led along the story path. He started all that in me, which I still love today."[24]

The only writing David attempted was a diary which he began at fourteen and abandoned when he discovered that Edward was reading it. "I've forgotten how I found out - it mortified me, because I put my deepest secrets into it."[25]

David never kept another diary.

Edward's presence at the school was a constant goad. David airily referred to him as "The Intellectual" but Edward also took up photography about this time and quickly became proficient, on occasion keeping his brother out of the darkroom.

The staff were perceptive enough to realise that David needed some recognition of his seniority. The year after Edward arrived, they made David a House Prefect.

It was at Leighton Park that David encountered one of the greatest influences on his life.

"His name was Scott Goddard. He was a dapper man. He wore glasses, a rather neat moustache and carefully combed hair. He always dressed well and he must have been in his forties. He came from Rye in Sussex.

"He used to take Musical Appreciation and other subjects. I owe him an enormous amount. He was very tough with me. He used to say, 'David, you've just got to pull yourself together. There's more in you than you think. You've got to read this!' or 'You've got to listen to this!' Some of the best things in me come from him. He introduced me to Botticelli's Primavera, to Dutch

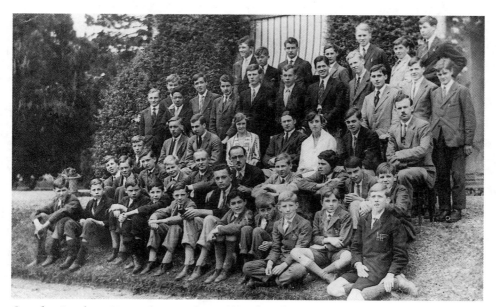

David at Leighton House; he is in the middle of the front row. Behind him, his hand on David's shoulder, is Scott Goddard.

seventeenth-century painting and, in particular, Vermeer.

"Scott Goddard used to go up to London once a week and he used to come into the dormitory - I used to pretend to be asleep - and he'd always leave under my pillow a postcard from the National Gallery or the Tate.

"He had a beautiful study, lined with books, with a splendid HMV gramophone with a mahogany horn which he used in Musical Appreciation. It was on this gramophone that I heard those horns of Richard Strauss for the first time. I loved looking around his study; it was filled with beautiful things.

"I liked him very much but he was homosexual and he was in love with me. The first time he made an approach to me, the fear gave me such strength that I laid him on the floor of his own study, held him down and said, 'I'm not going to let you up until you swear to me that you'll never do that again.' And there, on the floor of his study, he swore that to me. And he never did."

David met him again in the thirties. He was very seedy and down at heel.

"He said he would leave school when I left school, and I never believed him. He did. He had wanted to come and live with my mother and myself, the idea being to get closer to me. Obviously that had terrified me.

"I said, 'How are you, Scott?'

"He said, 'Better. The horrors of sex are beginning to leave me and I'm happier these days.'"

David took him to Oddenino's restaurant and Edward, who had also been his pupil, set him up as music critic on the *News Chronicle*.

"I don't think I'd be half the chap I am today but for Scott Goddard."[26]

The school had encountered some unusual boys - like the one who arrived on the first day of term, took one look at the place and went straight home - but the staff had never had to deal with anyone quite like David Lean. His reports indicate how much they liked him, however much they were required to disapprove. When he first arrived, his report noted "an interest which should help him in all departments of school life." He was "cheerful, even when he grouses." He had the power of mental association, "but he lacks the will to work at distasteful subjects."

His report for December 1923 was marked "Trouble at home" and Scott Goddard had added, "extremely perspicacious." Whenever there was something requiring organisation and staging, rather than academic achievement, David was in his element.

"He is greatly to be congratulated on his help," said the report of July 1923. "Full of ideas - both in a Form Social and a House Social. In his work, he repays personal attention - often finds it difficult to progress without it."

A year later, David's work showed "encouraging improvement" and they described him as "executive and masterful, almost to domineering!... He has been of a very great help to his Form and his Form Master." And in 1925, when he was seventeen, he was making good as a House Prefect, a position he deserved, and was described as "a boy of courage and we admire him for it."

David in his study, Leighton Park.

But where did his career lie? The moment he showed flair for one particular subject, and the masters attempted to encourage him, the enthusiasm popped like a soap bubble and they found him hurtling off after some other bright light. The school magazine, in a profile written years later, decided that the common factor of all his interests was "wild-eyed excitement". One can sense that this profile, written anonymously in 1956, was the work of a friend who had loved David, but whose affection was returned only briefly:

"He could always be dazzled by magic - the magic of an apparatus, situation or a person - and as long as the magic held he was given over to it so completely that there was nothing else in the world. (This was, of course, seductive in the extreme as long as one was being magical, but no less wounding when the magic ran out.) Various important types of magic were the Mediterranean, S.W. Brown, jazz, Richard Strauss, Vermeer, Lindbergh's transatlantic flight, cameras and enlargers, Charlie Chaplin, wireless sets and butterflies, Sonning, typewriters, Rudolph Valentino, Merit Halves, the possibility of life on Mars, Philip Newbigin, and the microscope.

"In a careerist sense, this hotch-potch of interests did not add up. It could not be said that because of his interest in the dysticus he was a zoologist, or an art critic or a painter because of the Tate or the Louvre, and if one simply took the sum of interests and multiplied their quality by ten, there would still be no place in the world for such a monster of dilettantism. But, of course, it was not these things in themselves which were important, except to some limited extent as mapping the outline of his potentialities; what was essential was the quality of vision he put into all of them. In this sense the situation was like a beam of light thrown on to a screen, so great was the concentration of his enthusiasm."[27]

Sex was rapidly becoming the chief obsession for David and his friends. David was now strikingly good-looking and he managed to attract the attentions of the opposite sex even in a boys-only school.

"The maids were called skivvies. One of the first kisses I ever had was with a maid at the top of School House at Leighton Park. I was in charge of changing the sun chart - a meteorological device into which you slide a card and it registers how many hours of sunshine you have had per day. I used to meet this maid, Alice, up there and I once kissed her. Terrific thrill. After that, we used to have pretty regular meetings, but it had to be very surreptitious and quick for fear of somebody coming up the stairs."[28]

Otherwise, sexual opportunities were limited.

"I remember a chap who was sent away on a tramp steamer to South America and I'll bet my bottom dollar it was because they suspected he masturbated. Masturbation sort of governed the youth of that time.

"I remember my father writing a letter to me on four pages of foolscap in which he said, 'Please be careful with this letter, because I shall be handing it on to Edward when the time comes.'

"His writing was hard for me to read. He kept referring to the laws of lip. And I thought, 'The Laws of Lip? What on earth can the Laws of Lip be?' It conjured all sorts of extraordinary pictures in my mind. Later, I realised he meant the laws of life.

"On the last day of term, when you left the school, the headmaster used to give what everybody knew as the Wine and Women Gas, when his wife left the table and a sort of informal atmosphere would be encouraged.

"I remember it started off with, 'Now you're going out into the world and you are going to meet girls. When you go on a seaside holiday and you want to bathe, never insist that the girls should bathe if they put up any sort of objection. You see…' And then he'd stammer for a bit and start talking about chickens and eggs. And he'd then explain that there was a period every month where girls had a perfectly natural thing, and he'd say, 'Now to come back to the egg. You have opened an egg sometimes, haven't you, and seen a spot of blood on it…' And this would lead to a discussion of the period. And I remember sitting at the table absolutely gaping, and walking across the playing fields afterwards with Pat Goodbody saying, 'What's he talking about? Blood?'

"Pat said, 'Oh yes, I've got a sister. Don't you know about that?'

"He then explained it all to me, because Pat was very sophisticated. And that's how I left school. I was as innocent as that at the age of eighteen."

David told me he had left Leighton Park when he was nineteen, and his reports speak of his staying on for an extra year. But the records show that he left in the Christmas Term of 1926, when he was eighteen. One reason his parents might have wanted him to stay was that neither they nor he had the slightest idea what he was going to do with his life.

This little still from Chaplin's THE GOLD RUSH hung on David's bedroom wall at Park Lane, Croydon.

"The aunts and everybody used to say what a dear boy David was," said Dr Sheila Tangye. "He had infinite charm but absolutely no brains and you didn't know what to put him at."[29]

As David was expected to become a farmer, he had spent the long summer holidays of 1925 and 1926 staying with Uncle Reggie and Aunt Imogen on their farm with his cousins Sheila and Hilary.

His favourite relations, however, were his Uncle Clarence and Aunt Winnie. Now he was sent to their farm at Clevelode, Worcestershire, for a training course, in the hope that the life might appeal to him. It was to be a very short apprenticeship.

"Winnie said one day that her brother's wife was coming down to lunch. Her name was Cissie. A field drain had to be cleared out and I was down there with mud up to my knees, digging, when I became conscious against the sky of a woman looking at me.

"She said, 'I'm Cissie.'

"It was the first time in my life that I'd had a woman look at me and I knew she felt that I was attractive. I climbed out of the mud and shook hands with her. She had slightly red hair. I was still at school. I must have been seventeen or eighteen. She was older than me, about twenty-five."

She might have looked youthful, but she must actually have been around forty. In 1907, she had married an income tax official, but an affair with a wealthy coal merchant, Noel Eveson, broke up the marriage and she was now Mrs Eveson, the kind of woman they referred to in the twenties as a divorcee. But David knew nothing of all this.

"We went back in her car and had lunch at the house. During lunch she said to me, 'You don't know anything of this district. Let me show you the countryside.'

"And we went to Bredon Hill and for the first time in my life I was conscious of this tremendous sexual appeal between us. I remember we lay in the grass and I put my hand on hers and she responded and put her hand on mine. And we kissed. And before we knew it we were making love. The first time I'd ever made love to a woman. I told her so and she wouldn't believe me.

"And there started an affair between us. We used to meet in London, and Clarence and Winnie guessed there was something going on and were shocked. I mean, her brother's wife. Not very funny. I was starting off in grand shape.

"She told me that her husband was wildly unfaithful to her. I remember her telling me, 'Yesterday I found a huge envelope full of French letters [condoms]. I took a needle and punctured every one of them.'

"She was jolly nice, and we had a rip-roaring love affair. I don't think any young man could have asked for better. We used to stay at the Berners Hotel. Bold as brass, ordered a double bedroom."[30]

David was unusual for his generation in that he felt that sex should be central to life, and not a furtive pastime, carried on outside the normal course of activity.

"My great friendship with Clarence and Winnie was severely marred by this affair. Years later, I was on a boat going out to India when I received a cable telling me that my Aunt Winnie had died and had left me all she had. It was nothing, some shares which amounted to a few thousand quid. But I'd no idea she was so fond of me. And Clarence had died before her. I got into awful trouble with both of them, but the story of her leaving me all she had sort of cancels it out. I was terribly touched."[31]

CHAPTER FOUR

CITY LIGHTS

AFTER Leighton Park, David returned to the drabness of home life in Croydon. His mother took no part in his hobbies, gave no encouragement to his enthusiasms. When he came home, bursting with excitement from the cinema, she sat silently in her chair. She was an attractive woman and was undoubtedly fond of David, but from all accounts she had little personality, certainly not enough to raise the spirits of an adolescent who described himself as extrovert, but was far more often the opposite. Yet she was extremely possessive and, now that she had lost Frank, she clung to David with a desperation he found disturbing. He spoke of the "tyranny of the tears."

"David had an awful time in Croydon," said his first wife, Isabel. "His mother didn't know how to cope with him. She was completely lost."

David immersed himself in photography and somehow found the money to buy a Pathe-Baby 9.5mm camera, ostensibly for the benefit of his brother. But when he realised he would be dependent on processing at the Pathescope factory he was exasperated; any delay in getting a print was more than he could bear. The best you could hope for from Pathescope was forty-eight hours for processing by direct reversal. Pathescope placed great emphasis on home processing and made an outfit for doing it yourself. David invested in his own developer and thereafter purchased only negative cassettes, or "chargers".

"I remember taking my mother to the Derby and filming it and coming home and developing it myself," said David. "I didn't know enough to make a print. I dried the negative by hanging it around the sitting room and then I projected it in negative form. I think my mother thought I'd gone mad.

"With the projector, I just showed films to myself. Occasionally I would drag my mother in. I turned the sitting room into a cinema, but it was all so amateur. I had so little money and it just wasn't good enough."[1]

The professional presentations provided by the big theatres with live orchestras in London were irresistible. David used to take the train from East Croydon to Victoria and the tube to the West End and see the latest releases - invariably American.

"I had enormous love for the American films. They influenced me tremendously."[2]

In 1926, at his favourite cinema, the Tivoli in the Strand, home of the new Metro-Goldwyn-Mayer productions, he saw King Vidor's THE BIG PARADE, an epic of the war presented with full orchestra and sound effects. David would never forget its impact and a scene in DOCTOR ZHIVAGO was based on the farewell scene from the Vidor picture, with its wild troop movements preventing the frantic girl from reaching her lover.

Herbert Brenon's Foreign Legion adventure BEAU GESTE, made in 1926 with Ronald Colman, gave David his first sight of the desert and made a considerable impact on him. A reissue of the 1920 melodrama, WAY DOWN EAST - with its astonishing climax depicting Lillian Gish floating on an ice-floe towards a massive waterfall - made David aware of D.W Griffith, whose career he had virtually missed. (He later saw Griffith's INTOLERANCE at the Film Society and decided it was the greatest film he had ever seen.)

If Vidor and Griffith impressed him, he was overwhelmed by the talent of Rex Ingram. "He was my idol. He was absolutely staggering. Wonderful."

David saw Ingram's 1921 film THE FOUR HORSEMEN OF THE APOCALYPSE about a year after its release, in Reading. This saga of a family, part French, part German, which moves to Europe in time to be divided by the Great War became his favourite silent film.

A lifetime later, in the seventies, David was in Los Angeles with his production designer, John Box, when THE FOUR HORSEMEN was screened during the Los

THE FOUR HORSEMEN OF THE APOCALYPSE, directed by Rex Ingram. David's favourite silent film.

Angeles Film Festival, with a fine print from MGM and a forty-piece orchestra.

"You've never seen it, have you?" said David to John Box. "You've got to see it."

"He was doing the brother thing to me," said Box. "He was teaching me about the cinema. What was strange was that during the performance he was watching me to see if I was liking it. And, of course, I loved it; I remember being quite transported.

"It was one of his three great movies. You can see its effect in some of his films. He told me, 'It must have taken Rex Ingram out of his little shell into the big world, and it took me out of my little shell and showed me the big world.' Rex Ingram gave him new horizons."[3]

David was delighted by John Box's reaction; he had thought his own response conditioned purely by nostalgia.

"It was an extraordinary and touching experience," he wrote, "to re-live, exactly as it was, a highlight out of one's past. To meet again one's boyhood idols exactly as they were - their faces perhaps a little younger with the passing years - or to find oneself impressed in exactly the same way by a powerful image.

"The recall was so strong that for a second or two I could actually smell the Central Cinema in Reading. I had sneaked in just as the lights were dimming. That was a magic moment. The glow of light from the orchestra pit, the dim outline of the conductor - his baton poised, waiting. I can almost see myself as if in a Close Shot. Fourteen years old, a stiff collar and tie, tense with anticipation. Then a Medium Shot from my point of view. A sudden sweep of velvet curtains revealing the white screen which throws the conductor into silhouette as his arms descend and the orchestra crashes out."[4]

David also admired Ingram's 1926 production, MARE NOSTRUM.

"I saw it at the Tivoli. That was the first time I realised without a doubt that there was somebody behind the camera, guiding everything, directing everything and choosing the angles. Here was somebody saying, 'Look at it from here', and making it more dramatic by the choice of angles."[5] In later years, whenever he saw a book on film history, David looked up the name Rex Ingram.

"He was tremendously good looking," said David, "better looking than most of the stars he worked with. He was married to a wonderful looking woman named Alice Terry. Nowadays, if you look up Ingram's record, you see him described as 'a great pictorialist'. You know, they accuse me of being pictorial. It probably has to do with Rex Ingram. Anyway, I'm really grateful for it."[6]

When the show was over, the orchestra had played the National Anthem and the crowds had poured into the West End streets, David would emerge in a daze. He was in no hurry to get back to Croydon. He used to take the tube to Victoria Station and linger in the refreshment room, sipping coffee, indulging in his recently acquired habit of chain-smoking and waiting for the last train home, hoping his mother was already asleep in bed.

"Doesn't it sound terrible? I used to let myself in and creep through the front door and I'd hear my mother's voice upstairs saying, 'Is that you, Dave?' I hated being called Dave and that used to drive me mad."

"There was a kind of enormous innocence about David," said his fifth wife, Sandy. "He was very naive, probably very undeveloped emotionally for many years, maybe all his life. But I think his relationship with his mother was a very simple one. It was about being the dutiful older son and doing what a dutiful older son ought to do, even though he hated to. I don't think there was much complication there; he had the Quaker sense of duty. He wasn't a tearaway in the way his brother was."[7]

If the atmosphere was tense when David lived alone with his mother, things became positively bizarre when Edward came home in the holidays.

"We used to have lunch on the oak table in the dining room. I suppose the furniture was left over from the bigger house. As soon as the meal was anywhere near finished, my brother would get up from the table - and this was an accepted thing - he would stamp out of the room, up the stairs and you'd hear his bedroom door slam and the key turning in the lock. You never saw him again until evening. I never dared go into that bedroom.

"We objected to his behaviour, but it didn't make any difference. I spent all my time with my mother. I hardly saw my brother at all. We hardly spoke to each other. That went on for years."

David took refuge in a secret activity: radio.

"I had a crystal set. It was about the best quality you could get in those days but you couldn't get any distance. Then I built valve sets. I was good at building valve radios. You had a little more distortion, but you could hear *much* further. I mean, you could get Paris and that was a huge kick. I used to lie in my bedroom with my earphones on. I suppose it shut off at midnight, but that seemed terribly late to me, you know, and really wicked listening."[8]

Next to the cinema and radio, David's principal source of magic and excitement was Croydon Airport which was a mere bicycle ride away. Established as part of the Air Defence of London in 1915, it gradually became the principal Civil Customs Aerodrome of Great Britain.

David knew the place from 1919, the start of civil aviation in Britain, when the Plough Lane aerodrome was a grass runway and a cluster of temporary sheds. Even then it was grandly known as the Air Port of London. (Heathrow and Gatwick were still meadowland.) The runway actually crossed Plough Lane, and there was a level-crossing for planes.

Many famous aviators launched or completed their epic flights from here - Charles Kingford Smith, Alan Cobham (a particular favourite of David), Jim

Mollison, Amy Johnson. Vast crowds gathered to watch the planes take off and land.

David's fondest memory was from 1927 when he saw Charles Lindbergh arrive at Croydon.

"It was in the papers that he was flying the Atlantic, then he was seen over Ireland and he landed in Paris. We knew that he was coming to Croydon and the crowds were enormous. I can see him now, a tall, blond, slim figure as he climbed out of his tiny plane, The Spirit of St Louis."[9]

David liked going to the cinema, he liked watching the trains and the planes. He was nineteen years old, had had his first love affair, and lived with his mother. How was this lonely, unpromising boy to earn his living?

Scott Goddard had stirred an appreciation of classical music, but it was jazz that David listened to on his radio. He even had a daydream of becoming a jazz pianist. The only drawback was that he couldn't play a note. After the experience with Clarence and Winnie, the idea of farming appealed less than before. But he was nineteen years old. It was high time he had a job.

His father realised that he had to give the boy a helping hand. He invited him to join the firm, Viney, Price and Goodyear, in a junior capacity at 8 St Martin's-le-Grand, opposite the General Post Office in the City of London.

David wore the uniform of the City worker - black jacket, pin-striped trousers, a rolled umbrella and, most humiliating of all, because his big ears lent him such a comic aspect whenever he put anything on his head, a bowler hat. His father saw him wearing a pullover one day and ordered him never to repeat the offence.

At the office, he sat in what he called his "white cell". Although the girls in the office amused him, nothing could compensate for the deadliness of the routine. He was allergic to mathematics and came close to a nervous breakdown when he was expected to pass the accountancy exams in which his father had triumphed thirty years before.

"I used to to check and recheck figures that had been checked before and would be checked again. It was as boring as hell. I put this in KWAI, actually."[10]

In a fog of misery, David would buy the *Evening Standard* at Cannon Street station and sit in the corner of a third-class carriage on the journey home to further misery at 97 Park Lane. Once a week, the *Standard* carried a film review by Walter Mycroft, a critic who impressed David with his love of movies and his lack of malice. (Mycroft later became a producer at BIP Elstree, though David never met him.)

After enduring this for a few months, David went to see his father and asked what was going to happen to him if he stayed on.

"You're not very good," said his father. "I don't think you'll ever pass any of the accountancy exams."

And then he made a remark which shattered his son.

"Look, I'm sending Edward up to Oxford, but to be quite frank, you're not worth it."

David recalled agreeing with him. "By then I was absolutely convinced that I wasn't worth anything. But it had a terrible effect on me. It put the final nail in my coffin. I don't think my father had any idea he was being as cruel as he was.

"Both my parents were convinced that I was a lowbrow, an ordinary kind of chap who hadn't got any real taste. The fact was that I was a terribly lonely young man and I wrapped myself in a lot of dreams and eventually confided them to the camera. I wanted to talk to people, but I only let it out to the camera. It's a funny thing to say, but it's true. And the camera became my friend.

"I've always been convinced I was a second-rater. I have jokes with Robert Bolt about this. I always say to him, 'You're my brother again.' He fits the pattern completely: highly educated, he's read all the classics, which I haven't, and he is in all respects the literary gentleman.

"I have had fun in the movies, but it's been more through working with other people than producing what I thought was any good. And it's a damn shame, really, because until lately I've never had any fun out of my success as a movie-maker. I've never enjoyed it. I've always thought, 'This is some sort of fluke.'"[11]

One afternoon, Helena invited to tea Aunt Edith, the wife of Clement Tangye, who had given David his Box Brownie camera.

"She said, 'How is David enjoying the office?'

"My mother said, 'Well, I don't think he likes it very much.'

"My aunt said, 'You know, I see no accountancy magazines in the house at all, there are nothing but film magazines. Why doesn't he go in for films?'

"Now, it sounds absolutely dotty, but until Aunt Edith said this to my mother, it had never entered my head that I could go into films. They were a sort of glamorous secret that I knew existed, but they were far too

David and his father, presumably taken by Edward.

glamorous for me. They were my great escape from East Croydon, and because I hadn't been allowed to go to the cinema for so long, they had acquired an even greater aura of glamour. I knew there were a few film studios, but never did I think I could belong to them, because I felt such a very second-rate person."[12]

David gave the matter considerable thought and, two weeks later, he put the improbable notion to his father.

"Dad, do you know anybody in films?"

"Why do you ask?"

"I would love to have something to do with films."

"This is mad. What can you hope to do?"

"I don't know. I just know I love them and it would be a tremendous thing for me if I could work on a film."

Frank thought that his son might just have well been thinking of running away and joining a circus.

"Look, David," he said, "It's a precarious way of earning a living. Forgive me for saying so, but if you could be as successful as somebody like Basil Dean [a famous stage director whom Frank possibly knew since he also came from Croydon] I could understand it. You can't possibly reach that kind of standard, you haven't got it in you."

David persisted and his father finally admitted that he knew the Gaumont accountants. Gaumont had studios at Lime Grove, in Shepherd's Bush, and in Islington, where the Gainsborough films were made. David was initially sent there, to meet an executive called Harold Boxall, whom he would encounter again during the Second World War. Boxall offered a probationary period of two weeks without pay. If he survived that, he would receive ten shillings a week.

David agreed with enthusiasm and was sent to Lime Grove where he met V. Gareth Gundrey, a writer, producer and occasionally director. A war veteran, Gundrey had an artificial leg. "He was the boss of the studio," said David. "Very important. He was a strange man, heavy-set, tall, the kind of rough-looking man you would never connect with the movies. Very nice, bright and highly intelligent."[13]

Gundrey asked what David was aiming at. "Was it perhaps something to do with the writing of scenarios?"

David replied, "I want to be doing the work of a director and to be present at the actual shooting."

This was what David thought the man would want to hear. He had no idea what job he wanted to do. All he wanted was to get inside the studios.

Gundrey asked an employee to give David a conducted tour. The first building in the country designed specifically for film work, the Gaumont studios were expanding, and construction work was under way next door. The original studio was a two-storey building opposite the swimming baths. On the lower floor were the scene dock, the prop department and laboratory and upstairs was the glass studio, infested with sparrows' nests.

"It was like a giant greenhouse, because they used the daylight coming through the glass to augment the studio lights."

The idea had been to use daylight as the sole source of light. But, as one veteran remembered, it seldom worked. "If it was a foggy day - and it often was - the studio became a pea-souper. On a cloudy day the cameraman would turn on a few lamps to provide sufficient exposure, then the sun would come out, bathe the set in light and ruin the shot."[14]

The management installed roller blinds and tried other remedies. When David was shown through, men were engaged in painting the glass black - "so it resembled a patchwork quilt" - and a fog dispersal plant was being installed.

The arc lights were dangerous, according to David, "because they had no glass covering and one could get what was known as "Klieg eyes". The moisture in the eye would dry up and it seemed as if one would never see properly again."

David was intrigued to notice that Gaumont was run like a factory and, although the style was dying out, employees still wore white coats with coloured piping on their collars - red for the camera department, blue for electricians, mauve for a director.

David was escorted into the camera room where he saw a Bell and Howell camera. He asked what it had photographed.

"I was told the last picture it worked on was ROSES OF PICARDY. Now, ROSES OF PICARDY was directed by Maurice Elvey, and it had John Stuart in the lead, and Lilian Hall-Davis, whom I thought was just wonderful. I saw it at the New Gallery, Regent Street. It was a bloody good picture.

"I remember touching the camera and being thrilled to be able to put my hand on the very machine through which the original negative of ROSES OF PICARDY had been run. I always had that kind of feel about important things in the movies, and I copied it for BRIDGE ON THE RIVER KWAI. At the end of the film, before the bridge is blown up, Alec [Guinness] takes a walk and I asked him, as he walked, to put his hand on the rail of the bridge and pat it.

"It's still in the film. You can see him touching the bridge and that's to do with touching the Bell and Howell camera that photographed ROSES OF PICARDY."

David could hardly have started on a lower rung of the ladder - a runner-cum-teaboy, and an unpaid one at that. In some notes he prepared for a 1943 radio interview, David recalled those early days: "I was an easy target for the good-humoured leg-pulls of the studio personnel who kept me running for things which sounded important to me but never existed. It was, 'Go to the property department and get me a sky-hook... Go to the chemist and get me a four-foot chemical fade-out... Go to the camera department and get me a rubber-necked lens that sees round corners...'"

The first film David worked on was called QUINNEYS, which was directed by Maurice Elvey, the man who had made THE HOUND OF THE BASKERVILLES, the first film he had ever seen, as well as ROSES OF PICARDY.

Elvey's background was almost as extraordinary as Chaplin's. His real name was William Seward Folkard and, according to his biographer, Linda Wood, he was raised in poverty, received no education and began working for a living at the age of nine. He was short and stocky, with a fine-honed, sensitive face and the accent of an educated man. To round off the impression he wore pince-nez, owned a country house at Godstone, and some of the most attractive girls in the business were his mistresses. He had energy and enthusiasm and he was well known as the most prolific director in the country.[15]

"Many times a day," said David, "he would chuckle, remove his pince-nez, and say, 'Amazing thing!' The amazing thing might be anything from a costume which had been produced for his approval or the failure of one of the lights."[16]

The drawback to Elvey was that he would make whatever he was given and not show any interest in improving the script. He would shoot as written, and the result often showed the weakness of his material.

"People used to laugh at Maurice Elvey," said David, "but I don't know why, because he was very efficient and good in his way and did some excellent pictures."

Set in London's Soho Square, QUINNEYS featured John Longden, Alma Taylor, who was a big star at the time, and Cyril McLaglen, brother of Victor, who had gone to Hollywood. It was about a Yorkshire antiques dealer, Joe Quinney (Longden), who acquires some Chippendale chairs and makes a cool £200 profit from an American, only to learn that they are fakes.

"I remember going on a set and being terribly impressed," said David. "It seemed magic to me, drawing rooms and even shops, built in a studio. The shops were supposed to be out in the sunlight; they weren't in the sun at all, but were lit by a sun arc. There was an atmosphere which was wonderfully exciting to me. It still is. I suddenly thought, 'This is it.'

"The directors were nearly all eccentric characters. They shouted a lot and were fond of megaphones. Few of the actors had stage experience and the director kept up a running commentary as the scene was being played. 'What is he pulling out of his pocket, darling? My God! It's a gun. Look at the door, darling. There's another knock...'

"There was always a three-piece orchestra. Piano, violin and jack-of-all-instruments who could play drums, accordion or oboe. They could play anything for any mood and they were a real help to almost every actor. I often wish I could have had them later; nothing like music for removing self-consciousness.

"The star actress was generally asked if there was any tune she would like and I shall never hear 'In a Monastery Garden' without thinking of Estelle Brody. She was a big Gaumont star and if a scene had anything to do with love, despair, remorse or religion it was 'In a Monastery Garden'."[17]

David had arrived in the industry at a fortuitous moment, for it had at last broken out of a three-year depression.[18] Not that it had ever exactly flourished in Britain. British films were never especially popular, not even at home, where audiences queued up to see American films. As Hollywood had proved again and again, good films required high budgets, because quality demanded time, and time was always the most expensive commodity.

High-quality films depended on confident investment. In England, films were regarded with ill-disguised contempt by most investors, including the banks. Why bother to invest in the product? Invest in the buildings - the picture palaces, which were replacing the fleapits of the early days. The Americans would guarantee the flow of films. Obligingly, they did so.

The film business was the only industry which did not increase its output when it expanded its markets. A town like Reading needed four hundred pictures a year at most. The entire world needed only four hundred pictures a year - after all, there were only 364 days to see them in and English cinemas were closed on Sundays. The Americans were perfectly willing to produce all of them and they needed no help from the British - or the French, Germans or Russians. In fact, they produced closer to seven hundred, and were past masters at keeping foreign films out of the United States. Thus British pictures were produced against hopeless odds - pitiful budgets, exhibitor resistance and audience indifference.

But the year 1927 brought a ray of hope. A "quota" system had been established, which meant that British cinemas were required by law to show a certain percentage of British pictures within a calendar year.

"Before it reached the Statute Book," wrote Linda Wood, "it is possible to argue that Britain did not possess a film industry as such; films were made, but in a spasmodic and haphazard fashion."[19]

The Cinematograph Films Act, 1927, which became law in January 1928, had an immediate result. The studios took on extra people - like David Lean - and re-equipped, ready for what many were convinced would be a boom.

David was lucky to be at Gaumont. Some of the studios would use the Act as an excuse to make pictures at the lowest possible cost for the least demanding audience. It was no coincidence that these studios were often making films for American companies. The Americans regarded the Act as a tax, or a fine. The Act could also be undermined, or bypassed, by showing the films once, early in the morning, when the cleaners were still in the auditorium. Then regular American films could be screened for the rest of the day. Had David been employed at a studio making nothing but quota films, his enthusiasm might have been snuffed out.

Once his two-week probationary period was up, David graduated to a properly paid position as a number boy - at ten shillings a week. This was the lowest grade on the camera crew, and was the silent-era equivalent of a clapper boy. David was required to carry the equipment and hold up the slate board with the numbers on it at the front of every shot.

His father, who had half expected him back at the office, now presented him with a handsome volume called *Moving Pictures - How They Are Made and Worked*. On the flyleaf, in his impeccable handwriting, he wrote an inscription:

"David Lean

With best wishes for his future work from his father,

F. W. Le B Lean, 11th August 1927."

The book was packed with unusual photographs of American films in production and was full of valuable information.[20]

The coolness of the inscription was not due to any lack of affection, as one might assume. It was probably due to the fact that Frank expected David to use the book at the studio, and so he avoided the more intimate inscription of his Christmas present that year, Emil Ludwig's biography of Napoleon, on the flyleaf of which he wrote:

"David with much love from his dad. F. W. Le B Lean 1927"

Having come almost straight from public school, David was aware of class differences at Gaumont. In a country where class barriers had been relaxed only slightly since the Victorian era, factory employees belonged to the working class. It was unusual to have a "gent" on the shop floor. But David didn't sense any hostility. In fact, his mother complained after a few weeks that he was acquiring a Cockney accent. He explained that almost everyone spoke like that in the studio.

But the British class system denied most of the studio workers a sense of vocation. David found that the continental technicians at Gaumont, like the mercurial Italian, Baron Giovanni Ventimiglia, who had photographed Hitchcock's first major film, THE LODGER, regarded themselves as artists, whereas the British felt they were there "to do a job of work".

Few felt as passionately about films as he did. One talented young cameraman, who had worked his way up from the labs since the war, had left only a month before he arrived; they might well have had something in common. His name was F.A. (Freddie) Young and he was at the time waiting to hear from producer-director M.A. Wetherell about a production no one seemed to want to finance on Lawrence of Arabia.

Luckily, the other camera assistant at Gaumont had an immense knowledge of cinema. He had left school at sixteen and was a year older than David. His name was Henry Hasslacher, whose father was a German émigré and whose mother was an upper-class Englishwoman. For some whimsical reason, he decided to change David's name.

"David Lean?" he said. "Most certainly not. From now on you are going to be Douglas."

"A famous American film star was called Douglas MacLean," said David. "I protested that I hated the name of Douglas, but there was nothing I could do about it. Because he started calling me Douglas, other people in my stratum called me Douglas. I used to meet people for years afterwards who would say 'Hello, Douglas.' I always used to think that people imagined I was faking it when I said my real name was David.

"Henry Hasslacher was tremendously highbrow and he wrote as a film critic under the name of Oswell Blakeston. He was homosexual and I used to dread going into the darkroom with him to unload the day's work. In between scrambles in the darkroom, I got to know quite a lot about Oswell Blakeston."[21]

Oswell Blakeston was an associate editor and frequent contributor to *Close Up*, an intellectual film magazine of the kind David grew to deplore. It was probably read by nobody else at Gaumont, but it figured strongly in David's life, whether he understood it or not. Some of its articles were in French, and some of those in English might as well have been, so abstruse was their language. But while much of the magazine was pretentious and absurd, some of it was vivid, intelligent and well-written. There were reports from locations of current films - for instance, an interview with G.W. Pabst while he was making PANDORA'S BOX with Louise Brooks. And it was beautifully produced, with striking stills.

It was through the pages of *Close Up* that David encountered vituperative criticism, a change from the kind of thing he was accustomed to in the *Daily Mail* and the *Evening Standard*. He had been deeply moved by F.W. Murnau's first Hollywood film, SUNRISE, but *Close Up* sneered at it for its "internationalism" and derided it for its pretension. David was dismayed, and he and Hasslacher had long discussions about the value of criticism of this sort.[22]

Through *Close Up*, David also heard about the Russian classics. The British censor had banned the films for fear that their revolutionary fervour might incite the British masses. They were screened for the intellectual élite at the Film Society in London but somehow David failed to see them. Through *Close Up* - and from Hasslacher himself - David also received his first glimmerings that the British film industry was not quite as splendid as he thought it was.

Close Up brought out a British Film number, as they had a Soviet Film number, not to celebrate the films this time so much as to weep over the lost opportunities.

"The truth is," wrote the magazine's editor, Kenneth Macpherson, "that the average attitude of England and the English to art is so wholly nonchalant and

clownish that it is quite useless to expect any art indigenously to flower there...
There are men and women of intellect, power and conviction who could build
the English cinema to a position of triumph to equal the Russians. Save them and
for God's sake get rid of the licentious rabble that destroys them."[23]

While some of the technicians were as good as any in Hollywood - and a few,
like Hitchcock, would add to their number - the general standard of film-making
in England was sloppy. According to Hasslacher, the kind of things that
occurred, even at so prestigious a studio as Gaumont, were beyond belief.

When a cameraman followed an actor through his viewfinder on an interior
set, he failed to notice until the rushes were screened that he had inadvertently
picked up the stage manager, sitting in his white coat, at the edge of the set.
Since the actor had finished his contract and was off to Germany, there was no
hope of reshooting the scene. So the cameraman took a ruler and scraped the
emulsion from the offending portion of the negative. Nobody complained; it was
regarded as another example of "modern photography".[24]

English directors were known to fall behind schedule so seriously that they
would simply cross out scenes in the script and put themselves ahead. When John
Ford tore out pages from a script for the same purpose, many years later, it so
astonished everyone it became one of Hollywood's most frequently quoted
stories. In England, it seems, it was routine.[25]

David was startled by these revelations, but he did not succumb to the
pervasive anti-British prejudice that affected so many of his more highbrow
colleagues. He was proud of being part of the British film industry, and
fortunately for him, he belonged to a studio that justified his faith in it. At ten
shillings a week, for a bit of fetch and carry, he was on his way.

CHAPTER FIVE

THE END OF THE RAINBOW

As the weeks passed, David was able to observe each stage of the production of QUINNEYS. When he made friends with the Gaumont projectionist, whose name was Matthews, he finally reached the end of the rainbow - that shaft of coloured light that so fascinated him whenever he went to the cinema.

"One day, he said to me, 'Look, Douglas, if you keep deadly quiet, and don't show yourself, you can come into the box and look through the porthole.' Now, the projection room in the studio was where the director, and a very privileged few, saw what had been shot the day before. I was tremendously grateful to Matthews for that, and I used to sneak in and see most of the rushes of the film that I was working on.

"One day, Matthews said to me, 'I'll give you a signal and you come into the box this afternoon around four o'clock and see a roll of cut stuff which Mr Elvey is running.'

"The lights went out, and my God, there were those scenes I had only glimpsed at rushes - a close-up, a long shot, it went to a close-up of Alma Taylor and a close-up of Cyril McLaglen and it looked as if they were talking to each other, interspersed with titles."

A few days earlier, David had seen two separate shots. One was of an explosion, the screen filling with smoke. The other was the same as the first, except that the set was badly damaged. Now he saw that the director had cut the two explosions together to resemble one continuous shot.[1]

"I was knocked backwards by the effect one could get by cutting from a long shot to a close-up, or a close-up of a woman intercut with a close-up of a man. It seemed so real, much better than it seemed in the studio when we did it.

"The director in those days always cut his own films. It was a rough and ready job because we had no Moviolas, so you could only see it in action in the projection theatre. In the cutting-room, you looked at the film through a magnifying glass against an illuminated ground glass screen. As the actor starts to sit in the chair in the long shot, you'd go to the last three or four pictures [frames] of his bottom taking his seat in the medium shot and it looked as smooth as anything, and it still does.

"I went to see Mr Elvey and asked if I could help him. 'My dear boy,' he said, 'I see no reason why you shouldn't.' And I came into the cutting-room at Gaumont, where he worked. I used to watch him run a piece of film from his nose to the full stretch of his arm, three feet - do it again - six feet. Once he'd cut a section of the long shot, I used to wind up the rest, mark it with its number and put it in a can, just as we do today. I was so interested that I became fairly efficient at keeping track of the film. I used to come every day and I proved quite useful to him."[2]

Gaumont employed girls as cutting-room assistants, but there were no unions then and, providing David was not needed elsewhere, the management had no objection to a camera assistant working in the cutting room. David was able to move from department to department, learning as he went, the finest apprenticeship any future director could have. People responded to his modesty and enthusiasm and found themselves helping him.

"I was an assistant to an assistant director called Dickie Beville. He had been in submarines during the war. I remember him meeting me one day in the underground passage at Gaumont.

"He said, 'Never let me see you like this again.'

"'What?'

"'You're sauntering aimlessly. You're going to meet all sorts of bosses here. You don't know them, but they'll know you and if they see you slouching along, head down, they won't think anything of you. Always carry a piece of paper and walk fast.'

"And so I carried a piece of paper and walked fast. I began to do all sorts of

SAILORS DON'T CARE. David watches from the wings, behind cameraman Baron Ventimiglia. Director W.P. Kellino stands holding script. Just behind him, Jack Harris, David's future editor. The two sailors are Alf Goddard and John Stuart.

quite important jobs. I was always willing to stay late and to finish something. I just loved it."

David worked on SAILORS DON'T CARE, directed by W.P. Kellino, the father of Roy Kellino, a veteran of music hall who had made comedies from the earliest days. David imitated his style of directing, complete with breathy, commercial-traveller accent: "'Now, my dear, I want you to take his hand with love in it...' He was very, very peculiar. He was a deplorable man, really. There are some people in show business that I cannot abide. They're not vulgar, yet they are and they put a sort of gentility over it all. He was like that.[3]

"The cameraman was Baron Ventimiglia. 'Venty' he was called. He was a very eccentric chap, very dark about the chin. In those days they used to make masks for every scene, masks with gauze in them. And I used to have to make these masks. I'd go out and buy the gauze and show it to the Baron and he'd peer through the samples and say 'That.' I'd cut the gauze and put it into a two-ply frame and hand the mask to Venty. He'd put it in the matte box of the camera and with a cigarette burn a hole in it. If people were seated at a table, for instance, the hole would leave the centre clear, but all round the edge would be fuzzy.

"I remember him sometimes tearing these masks with his teeth in a fury and I'd think, 'That's another half hour's work tonight.' The big thrill was being allowed to turn the handle of the camera on an actual scene. But this rare privilege was usually reserved for moments when the camera was perched on the edge of a cliff or on the top of a moving train. At which time the cameraman usually found it necessary to attend to business elsewhere."[4]

THE PHYSICIAN, *Wargrave Station, March 1928. David stands behind the German director, George Jacoby (centre). German Weinert arcs are being used, with American Bell and Howell cameras.*

Ventimiglia was one of the Continental technicians working in the British film industry. Before the war, Italy had produced the most sophisticated and epoch-making films and Italian technicians were highly prized; there were several at Gaumont. But since the war, Italian films had lost their pre-eminence and Germany was now looked to for innovation. Gaumont imported the German, George Jacoby, who had directed a remake of QUO VADIS? in Italy, and in England a film called THE FAKE. In 1928, David worked on Jacoby's THE PHYSICIAN as assistant cameraman. Maurice Elvey hovered over it as producer.

Whereas Elvey favoured the classical approach of editing and camera angles to emphasise dramatic points, with a restricted use of camera movement, Jacoby was fascinated by camera movement. He disliked what he called "tricks" - dramatic angles, fast cutting, superimposition - and looked forward to the day when he could achieve "perfect natural continuity" with a moving camera, following the actors through doorways and around furniture, eliminating the sudden jumps and mixes he found disturbing. He envisaged a mobile crane that could create "the single-take movie".

Jacoby's attitude might have appealed more to David had it not proved to him the wastefulness of the prowling camera - it took eighteen hours to view all the rushes. Gaumont, regarding him as a kind of Erich von Stroheim, exploited the fact as publicity for the film.

Jacoby's film featured a German actress named Lissi Arna. "A young man who worked with me as an assistant was dotty about Lissi Arna," said David. "When the film was finished, she took the boat to go back to Germany. Sure enough, he gathered up the courage, bought a huge bunch of red roses, went to the station, found her in her carriage and gave her the roses. She looked at the roses, looked at him, and said, 'Why didn't you tell me before?' And then the train pulled out."

In May 1928, David worked on Maurice Elvey's PALAIS DE DANSE, which was shot on location at the celebrated dance hall in Tottenham. This film survives at the National Film Archive and is proof of what good work was being done at Gaumont in the late twenties.

It is a fast-paced thriller in the American style, from an original screenplay by John Longden and his actress wife, Jean Jay, stylishly directed by Elvey and well shot by Percy Strong. The climax takes place on the glass dome above the crowded dance floor. The hero struggles with the villain - one of the most repellent characters in British films, played by an unrecognisable John Longden - and they crash through the glass, clinging to beams as the people below watch in horror.

The glass dome was reconstructed at Lime Grove and the scenes at the dance hall were all shot on location. David had to help organise fifteen hundred local people as extras for the climactic sequence, which was filmed with five cameras. To ensure the extras turned up, although they couldn't have been kept away with clubs, a fancy dress contest was organised, with the judges including the star of the film, Mabel Poulton.

"I remember working for another director," said David, "a charming man called Edwin Greenwood. He was educated, which was an exception in those days, very thin with glasses. I helped him on WHAT MONEY CAN BUY with Madeleine Carroll and John Longden. Before she became an actress, Madeleine Carroll had been a Birmingham schoolmistress, and Greenwood was mad about her. I remember him in the cutting-room looking at the film through a magnifying glass, picking up the scissors and saying, 'Darling, forgive me', as he put the scissors through the film. He was endearing."[5]

David also played a small part as a man who picks up Madeleine Carroll. But, alas, this film, like the majority of silent films, is lost.

It was on this film with Madeleine Carroll that David's career as a camera assistant nearly came to an abrupt end. He walked into the dark room, closed the door and turned on the white light instead of the red. A series of close-ups of Madeleine Carroll were ruined and David was fired on the spot.

"My next job was the most humiliating one I've ever had," said David. "It was offered to me out of compassion by the kind-hearted studio manager and was that of wardrobe mistress."

In the autumn of 1928, Maurice Elvey fulfilled a long-cherished ambition when he embarked on BALACLAVA, an epic about the Charge of the Light Brigade. Interiors were to be shot at Lime Grove, with exteriors at Aldershot, and some scenes were to be in colour. It was Gaumont's biggest film to date.

The other "wardrobe mistress" turned out to be Geoff Boothby, an assistant director and former military man, who later worked with Alexander Korda. David and Boothby had to drive down with the costumes to the location, dress the extras - there were hundreds of them - and recover the costumes after the day's shooting. Besides the British cavalrymen, there were a mass of "Russians" who had to be outfitted in the greatcoats and shakoes of the period.

David was not quite up to the task. A system of colour codes had been worked out to protect the extras from injury. The soldiers would wear uniforms of one colour and the dummies uniforms of another. David dressed a soldier in the wrong colour and the unfortunate man was stabbed in the rear by a lance. The last David saw of him he was running as hard as he could, considering his condition, away from the battlefield. It was not the last he heard of the matter, however, and he never worked in the wardrobe department again.[6]

No better action sequence can be seen in any British silent film than Elvey's splendidly shot charge. While not handled with the cinematic pyrotechnics of the Errol Flynn version of 1936, the Elvey sequence was so well staged that in the reckless travelling shots one might be racing alongside the 11th Hussars in a brilliant Crimean War newsreel. Only in the cutaways to the Russian gunners is the film let down - oddly enough by the poor standard of costuming.

David cannot take the blame for this, since he was only "wardrobe mistress", not costume designer. The Historical Adviser, Captain Oakes-Jones, was meticulous about the British details, but let the Russians take care of themselves. They have the quality of amateur dramatics and the film is less of an achievement as a result.

I first saw this charge on my 9.5mm home movie projector when I was a boy. A few years later, I found myself having tea with Maurice Elvey. He was then in his seventies and ekeing out his retirement by practising his fine calligraphic hand on the menus for Soho restaurants. Yet he seemed vigorous and had an excellent memory. I asked him how he shot the charge.

"I had six hundred cavalrymen waiting for my command," he said. "I was on a special platform with a public address system. A standby prop man, Arthur Charge, was setting the last of the detonators. I was worried about where he was placing them. I called, 'Oh, Charge...' Unfortunately, I had forgotten there was a microphone and the entire army galloped off..."[7]

This sounds like the six hundred horsemen of the apocrypha but, amazingly, the story is confirmed by Alan Lawson, who had taken over from David as Gaumont's number boy.

"The charge was staged with army co-operation at Long Valley, Aldershot," said Lawson. "There was a very stern sergeant-major in charge. Most of the cavalrymen were raw recruits. If they got thrown, the horses went straight back to barracks. The soldiers had to walk back."[8]

When BALACLAVA had finished its first run, Gaumont decided to reissue it with sound. An experimental sound recording had been made using the British Acoustic selenium cell system. It was recorded by A.W. Watkin, Britain's most famous sound recordist of later years.[9] But David was not involved in this.

His first experience with sound was on Elvey's elaborate fantasy of the future, HIGH TREASON, released in August 1929. A newly completed stage at Lime Grove was hastily sound-proofed while the film was being shot. It also used British Acoustic sound, apparently with much intelligence, though we shall never know as only the silent version has survived.

Influenced by Fritz Lang's METROPOLIS, it shows how the latest Hollywood and Continental techniques have been absorbed by Elvey, and Percy Strong, his resourceful cameraman. The technique is so polished, it makes HOUND OF THE BASKERVILLES resemble an Edison one-reeler of 1907.

Set in an England of 1950, HIGH TREASON is an anti-war parable with a tragic ending. A futuristic London curiously resembles the kind of city that Albert Speer planned for Hitler: grotesque government blocks looming above the Thames, with airships floating overhead and autogyros landing by the river. A

HIGH TREASON (1928). A film set in a war-torn future. David can just be seen beneath the white lamp on left.

border incident between Europe and the Atlantic States puts the country in a state of war, and when terrorists blow up the Channel Tunnel, war seems inevitable.

The film is remarkably prophetic in some ways, yet also naive, as science-fiction invariably is. But it is no sillier than Korda's much-vaunted THINGS TO COME whose star, Raymond Massey, has a small role in HIGH TREASON as a spokesman for peace.

David could remember nothing of consequence of this film apart from the sound system. However, he had kept a number of stills from it, and in one exterior he can be glimpsed, working as assistant director. It is likely that he worked on the editing, because this was a talking picture and in some auto-biographical notes he wrote, "Reprieve came along in the form of talkies... I made a dive for the cutting rooms."

There are several rather slow sequences which cry out for "Russian cutting", as it was known, that technique of fast cutting derived from Abel Gance and the early Americans, which the Russians had made their own.[10] Yet Elvey never adopted it and, more curious still, neither did David, not even in such an obvious place as the charge of the dragoons in DOCTOR ZHIVAGO. Such flamboyant editing went against his principles; both David and Elvey shared an unshakable belief that cutting at its best should never be noticed.

There was almost as much fuss made about the arrival of sound at Gaumont, David recalled, as when THE JAZZ SINGER first opened. Few people remembered all the European experiments - the optical sound system of Eugene Lauste before the war, Tri-Ergon in Germany and the De Forest Phonofilm shorts made at

Clapham. Not to mention British Acoustic which was the Danish Petersen-Poulsen system in patriotic disguise.

"They were doing a film of a music hall sketch called THE NIGHT PORTER with Donald Calthrop," said David. "It was directed by Sewell Collins. He was an American who came from the stage and was a well-educated man. He took quite a liking to me. I'd wheedled my way into his cutting room, keeping the cuts and handing him bits of films. Sewell Collins hadn't the foggiest idea how to synchronise sound and picture. There was only one person in the studio who could cut and synchronise sound and picture, and he was called John Seabourne who cut the Gaumont Sound News. Seabourne said to Collins, 'I can spare you an hour.'

"Thank God, Collins was completely unmechanical, and at the end of the hour he was as blank as he had been at the beginning. But I had picked up the idea of it and how it worked.

"Synchronisation was very crude. You had to hold the film together tightly in your hand, and move it laboriously, sprocket by sprocket, foot by foot, through your fingers, and make marks with a grease pencil every so often.

"The fact that I cut THE NIGHT PORTER with Sewell Collins gained me the position of being a kind of director's help in the cutting room, because lots of them found it very difficult. It *was* very difficult, too. But I managed to get the hang of it, and then, gradually, synchronisers came in which kept sound and picture level."[11]

David on an unidentified set at Gaumont, caught on five frames of film as he dashes out of the way before a take. Even as a camera assistant, the intensity and excitement of film-making is reflected in his face.

A crisis developed at Gaumont Sound News when John Seabourne was offered a much better job and departed.

"The job was not given to me," said David, "but to a dear chap called Roy Drew who made a fatal mistake. With newsreels you had neither the time nor the money to make prints of everything, so you worked direct from the negative. By the time you saw the first print, something like four hundred copies had been run off and you'd made four hundred mistakes. Roy Drew cut in a shot of the Graf Zeppelin upside down. It was an easy mistake to make, but all the copies had to be reprinted and he was fired."[12]

This suggests that Roy Drew was drummed out of Gaumont. Far from it; he stayed at Gaumont until 1959. But David was given his job at Gaumont Sound News and Drew became his assistant. Fortunately, the two men liked each other and worked well together. Drew's Zeppelin disaster was apparently quickly forgotten.

Despite his enthusiasm for all that was new, David was not entirely in favour of sound. He shared the opinion of Hasslacher/Blakeston and the *Close Up* crowd that silent films were reaching a peak of technical and artistic achievement that talking pictures could not match. Just as it was discovering more and more ways of speaking visually, of becoming an international language, the silent picture was made redundant.

By their very nature, talking pictures were obliged to give first place to dialogue. Since the techniques of recording sound were guarded by technicians as closely as the formula for a nuclear device, it was difficult for directors to override them. Sound men cared nothing for the art of the cinema; they wanted their dialogue and effects recorded to proper technical specifications. If actors had to pause in front of a flower vase, in which was hidden the microphone, then so be it. Cameras made a racket, so they had to be imprisoned in booths. Tracking dollies squeaked, so booths had to be immobile. Stage directors were brought in who were familiar with dialogue but not with cinema. For a while, a talking picture was liable also to be a tedious one.

"They moved into drawing rooms, as it were," said David. "Some of the films were interesting enough, but I lost a lot of my keenness for the cinema."

David also mourned the lost magnificence of the theatre orchestras in the first-run theatres, such as the Shepherd's Bush Pavilion, just round the corner from the Gaumont Studios, where Louis Levy - with whom David was later to work - conducted the orchestra. David was transfixed by the splendour of the huge cinema - which was less than four years old - and the music, which so impressed him he was convinced that the string section included thirty violins. In fact, the entire orchestra consisted of no more than twenty-two players together with an organist. While this could not compare to the big Broadway theatres, such as the Roxy with more than a hundred players, it was fairly large for England.

Remarkably quickly, Hollywood pictures shook themselves down and combined the best of the silent technique with the new technology. David was deeply impressed by Lewis Milestone's pacifist masterpiece of 1930, ALL QUIET ON THE WESTERN FRONT. Years later, whenever the question of a tracking shot was raised, this was the film he thought of.

"When that attacks starts and they [the French soldiers] start coming over the top, he tracks along the whole length of that trench. It's a fantastic effect. You could ask him why he does that, and I suppose he would answer that he thought it would raise the dramatic intensity rather than having a still camera showing men get up over the top and running."[13]

In the autumn of 1929, Oswell Blakeston's satire on pretentious French avant-garde cinema, entitled I DO LOVE TO BE BESIDE THE SEASIDE, was shown by the Avenue Pavilion.[14] When talkies came in, the Pavilion continued loyally to show silent films. The cinema called itself "The House of Silent Shadows". Owned by Gaumont, it was at 101 Shaftesbury Avenue and was managed by Leslie Ogilvie, an acquaintance of Blakeston. The Pavilion advertised in *Close Up* and the magazine regularly praised its lone efforts in showing continental films of the kind that had been given short shrift on their initial distribution, or that exhibitors wouldn't touch.

David and Blakeston saw a midnight showing at the Pavilion of Jacques Feyder's THERESE RAQUIN under its English title THOU SHALT NOT. Based on Zola's novel, it is now a lost film, one of the most eagerly sought-after of the entire silent era.

"It was one of those continental films which were quite new to me," said David. "They weren't the same sort of films that the Americans or the English were making, they were more intimate. And they were another step away from reality, because the people looked different, the ideas were different. When I went to THERESE RAQUIN I was enveloped in what I can only describe as a kind of darkness from the story, and that gave me a lot of help; it's stuck with me ever since."

David must have had distinctly mixed feelings when, in August 1930, the Avenue Pavilion was overtaken by progress and converted into the first Newsreel Theatre in the country as the Gaumont British Movietone News Theatre.

CHAPTER SIX

COMMITMENT

DAVID'S life had been so fulfilling and so hectic from the day he entered the film industry that a private life scarcely existed for him.

He had had his affair with Cissie and, perhaps, the occasional fling with a girl from the studio. His recollection was that contact with women was rare, although he remembered a girl called Kathy, or Kay, Meakin, of whom he was fond. But when he met his cousin Isabel again, he fell in love with her.

They had last met in 1922, when they were fourteen years old, on a family holiday in Swanage, in Dorset. Isabel and David had paired up, and went everywhere together.

"Edward was always about six yards behind us," said Isabel, "trying to find out what we were talking about."[1]

Isabel and her sister, Barbara, were attractive girls, but Barbara was scholastic, too clever, too much like Edward for David, who preferred Isabel, despite her shyness. She was reassuringly like himself.

"I hadn't got any brain for books and things," she said. "I was practical. I loved gardening. I was quiet and fairly serious."[2]

Like David, Isabel had a painful childhood. Her father had walked out when she was five.

"I remember mother saying, 'I think he is going,' and I said, 'I'll be your little boy.' We didn't hear anything from him for several years. Mother had to battle on alone. He sent money, but it must have been awfully little. We moved from Ealing to Maidenhead where mother's two sisters lived. I was fifteen when I was told my father was coming back. I remember him walking in, and his first remark was, 'You should have a father around the house.'

"And then he bought Fairmead in Knockholt, a very nice house with a large garden, right on top of the Downs. Daddy didn't make friends in the village so we led a rather lonely life up there."

When Isabel and Barbara were old enough, their father bought them a car, an Austin Seven.

"We roared up and down the country lanes. Once daddy saw us and said, 'One day that young woman is going to have an accident.' He didn't know it was me."

When David and Isabel met again, he started bombarding her with letters.

"He wrote that he was falling in love with me and wanted to see me. What did I think? I was very attracted to him. We led such a sheltered life that I hadn't known any boys at all."

Isabel, who had also worked as a trainee in a dress shop off Shaftesbury Avenue, was taking a domestic science course at the National Training School of Cookery in Wilton Road, Victoria.

"My father didn't know what to do with me as I wasn't bright at school. He found out from his lady friend (I imagine - how else would he know?) that there was this domestic science course. It went on for thirteen weeks: dressmaking, cooking, housekeeping. It was recognised training for housewifery. I have a certificate as a matter of fact. I got the highest marks in my term."[3]

Victoria was where David changed from the electric train to the tube for Goldhawk Road, the nearest station to Lime Grove. He delivered his letters by hand to the school and Isabel went home each evening to Knockholt, reading them on the train.

She did not write back - "I wasn't good at letter writing" - but she telephoned David and arranged to meet him at Knockholt. She had signed on for a woodwork course in the village, so her parents thought they knew where she was going when she set off in her Austin Seven in the evening. In fact, she drove to the station and met David.

After a few weeks of these covert visits, David suggested a trip to Paris and Isabel eagerly accepted. For a girl who lived such a cloistered existence, it was a prospect both romantic and immensely daring. She breathed not a word to her parents. David bought the tickets and on the train from Victoria to the Dover ferry, Isabel became aware of a man sitting opposite, looking at them. She was convinced he thought they were eloping.

They arrived in Paris in the evening. David was a fairly seasoned traveller, thanks to his father, but for Isabel, accustomed to rural Kent, the lights of the Champs-Elysées were simply astounding. They had no money, so they stayed in a cheap hotel. As Isabel put it, in the quaint motoring slang of the twenties, "We took that trip on the smell of an oily rag."

David was succinct in his memory of the romantic weekend.

"She was awfully nice," he said. "We fell in love and she became pregnant which was wicked."[4]

Isabel did not realise she was pregnant for a month or so, and even now she remembers how pleased David was when he first realised he was to become a father. Nothing of this was revealed to the family at first. The two young people, both twenty-two, simply announced their engagement. Frank Lean was brutally direct, as always: "You won't be able to have any family. You're first cousins," he wrote. Isabel's father, Edmund Lean, simply declared, "You cannot marry him."

When Isabel revealed the reason for the marriage Frank was sympathetic and said, "Right, get married. What a pity you didn't tell me before." Edmund became angry. Coincidentally, it appears, David discovered that Edmund was conducting an affair at a rendezvous familiar to him and wrote to Isabel in high moral dudgeon, referring to, "that father of yours."

"He is selfish to a degree... It is hard to keep myself from writing him a stinging letter telling him what I think of him and his underhand moral life. Much more tempting because he imagines himself undetected. As for meeting him at his office, I have thought it over and I am sure it would be foolhardy. Firstly, I can see no useful purpose being served. Secondly, I could no longer conceal my knowledge of the Berners Hotel and so on, which would, thirdly, lead to a very probable and bad display of temper from both of us.

"I just despise him. And one day I shall strip him of his happiness as he has tryed [sic] to do with us. I hate him from the bottom of my heart - he is a joke, trying to look genuine. My dear, we must endeavour to be patient, it only amounts to that, because they can't keep us apart for ever. I'll work as hard and as well as I can in trying to bring this damnable period down to a minimum... Don't be browbeaten by that swine, rather clear out than stand his hypocritical insults."[5]

When Edmund began to lock Isabel in her room, she decided she would follow this advice. In her Austin Seven, she drove to David's mother at Croydon. David was at home and Edward was away at Oxford.

David's mother was sympathetic; after all, her own father, Edward Tangye, had married his cousin. Isabel's father, by contrast, disowned her.

"My daughter will burn in hell," Edmund informed a startled Edward, when he encountered him in a London street.

Isabel stayed at Park Lane for several weeks. She and David used to clear aside the furniture in the living room and dance to gramophone records. It was decided that they would be married from Park Lane at the local church of St Matthew's. Frank Lean had to return from Hove and behave as though he and Helena had never been apart. So well did he play the role that Isabel was barely aware of the problem and had no idea they were coming together for the first time for several years. Unsurprisingly, Edmund Lean refused to attend.

"There was some chicanery about changing the date of the wedding so that the nine-month period was within the marriage, otherwise it would have been absolute wickedness," recalled David.

The wedding was held on 28 June 1930, with twenty or thirty relatives and friends in attendance. Afterwards, David and Isabel left for their honeymoon at Land's End, Cornwall. Isabel, who had been given a Box Brownie by her mother, took some impressive photographs of David. David's wedding present was a Pekinese pup called Fifi. Edward sent them a postcard from Oxford. He used to address the couple as "The Girls":

"I hope you are misbehaving yourselves and forgetting what the verger said about This and That... Dad says he thinks marriage will do that David girl good - it will give him an aim in life (really!) which implies the previous absence of religion."

He ended the note with a joke at their mother's expense.

"Aunt Florrie told a long story about how some friend of hers committed suicide in some river and the body was later washed up. Long pause. 'How dreadful,' says mum. 'Was she drowned?' Au revoir, mes enfants."

Mr and Mrs David Lean rented a two-room flat at 24 Royal Crescent, Holland Park. It consisted of an elegant sweep of early Victorian stucco houses which overlooked their own private gardens.

At first, married life was pleasant enough. David took Isabel to some of his haunts, such as Croydon Airport. She disliked the noise. They visited Brooklands for the motor-racing which Isabel found more exciting. They took long trips by bus and occasionally went to art galleries.

"But I don't remember that we went out a lot because we didn't have the money."

Edward had given them a wedding present of a large modern gramophone. It stood unusually high and needed no horn and they spent many evenings listening to music.

"David enjoyed music," said Isabel. "Old Scott Goddard had given him a taste for that and he knew which records he wanted, which operas and which symphonies."

He also played dance music and they danced together in their little room high above Holland Park.

Isabel did not particularly care for the cinema, which might have created an unspoken barrier between them. She never regarded it as anything more than a mild amusement and went only occasionally.

They made friends with a young medical student, Charles Clinton-Thomas, and his wife, who lived in the flat above, and sometimes friends from Leighton Park would drop by.

David's present to Isabel, Fifi the dog, turned out to be an embarrassment. It was oversexed and would fly hopefully at the legs of whoever came in. They had to give the animal away and the replacement was a more amenable Pekinese called Benjamin.

Although David regarded himself as being "miserably poor", his weekly salary of five pounds was well above the national average, which stood at three pounds.[6] Nevertheless, Isabel could barely make ends meet. "We nearly starved on it. Five pounds a week wasn't enough, even in those days. If David had a chop, then I couldn't afford one for myself. That's how we went on."

Frank sent his son an occasional five pounds to add to their income.

David and Peter, 1931.

On the evening of 1 October 1930, Isabel felt the first stabs of labour pains. She sat in a chair, gripping the arms, as the pain became more and more severe, while David rushed out to get a taxi. They drove to a nursing home in Ealing where a bed had been organised by his father's companion, Margaret Merton.

The baby was born in the early hours of 2 October, and the proud parents named him Peter David Tangye Lean. That night, David sat down and wrote "A Letter to My Son". He never finished it however - and his son never received what might have been a touching and poignant document.[7]

When mother and child returned after the customary two weeks in the nursing home, life in the little flat was turned upside down. Isabel found it hard to look after the baby and do all the housework. With David out six days a week, and often seven, returning tired after lengthy overtime, Isabel was to all intents and purposes a single mother. Men were not expected to do housework in those days and David was not a pioneer in this regard.

"He wasn't practical in that way," said Isabel, charitably. "He was artistic."

David had not wanted marriage, and he didn't care for children, so he was hardly the best of fathers. After a while, the very fact of coming home filled him with gloom.

"It was a hell of a climb up those stairs," he said. "And to live there with a baby that never stopped crying, and a dog, and having only enough money to scrape through,was wretched."[8]

Peter did not cry more than most babies but crying babies, David wrote, "drive me up the wall." Isabel, herself exhausted by sleepless nights, had little energy left for keeping the flat as immaculate as David expected. For David's perfectionism was not restricted to his work. When he came home to find nappies strung up to dry, he would grow exasperated. But his life did not look so bad to outside observers.

"Charles Clinton-Thomas used to say to David, 'You've got the best wife, the best baby and the best dog,'" said Isabel. "His wife was very fiery, so he thought the peace below was more what he would like."

Otherwise, Isabel was lonely. David's father endeared himself to her by his kindness. "He used to ask me out to lunch. I had no one to look after Peter, so I would put him into his cot asleep - he would sleep in the mornings - then fly to the underground, meet Buncs in the City, and he would give me a lovely lunch - then I would fly back again. Of course, Peter by then was in his cot crying. But Buncs was the only friendly relative I had. My sister was in Paris."[9]

One of the few friends who came to dinner at Royal Crescent was Roy Drew, David's assistant at Gaumont Sound News. Drew first met David on HIGH TREASON, and, like almost everyone else at Gaumont, knew him as "Douglas".

One of David's first jobs when he arrived at Gaumont had been to edit the footage of the annual University Boat Race, which was a national institution.

Cameras were stationed along the route, between Mortlake and Putney, and as soon as one camera had shot its section of the race, the film was rushed by car or motorcycle to the laboratory. There it would be given priority and as soon as it was developed, it was rushed to David and Drew's cutting-room.

Then there was a second race, between Gaumont and the other newsreel companies, as to who could get their film into the cinemas first. David claimed he had his film on a cinema screen at Shepherd's Bush within three hours of the end of the race.

A few days after the birth of Peter, David and his assistant, Drew, were involved in high drama.

"The Newsreel was issued twice weekly," wrote Roy Drew, "and we worked on the Monday release over the weekend - editing on Saturday night and printing on Sunday."[10]

On Sunday morning, 5 October 1930, Keith Ayling, the Gaumont Sound News Editor, telephoned David and Drew and informed them of a disaster. The airship R101 had crashed in France with the loss of most of its passengers and crew. They rushed in to try and cut something together, but they were outclassed by their rivals at British Movietone News.[11]

David was enthralled by aviation, and the race between the R100 and R101 had occupied a great deal of space in the press and in the newsreels. While the R100, designed by Barnes Wallis (later the inventor of the Dam Busters' bouncing bomb) was privately financed, the R101 was government financed. It had taken six years to build this colossus, which was bigger than a wartime

Zeppelin - seven hundred and seventy-seven feet long - and it had cost the country a million pounds, which it could ill afford. It was planned to build a fleet of these airships - which were as luxurious as any ocean liner, and which could fly to India in a quarter of the time it took to go by sea.

The Secretary of State for Air, Lord Thomson, wanted the airship to take him to India and back in time for an Imperial conference later that month. Tests and trials were cancelled, and the Air Ministry, embarrassed by the cost, forced the designers and builders to give the ship a clean bill of health. Sir Sefton Brancker, Director of Civil Aviation, was convinced the airship was not entirely airworthy. He was among those killed to prove how right he was. Strong winds buffeted the airship and probably ripped the gasbags in the nose, the ship tipped forward into a dive and crashed into the ground at Beauvais in northern France.

The first newsreel company to receive the news was Movietone. Paul Wyand was woken at five-thirty and reached Croydon Airport by seven. Here a charter plane took him through driving rain to Beauvais.

The Gaumont Sound News production manager did not hear the report until eight o'clock. He had dispatched a cameraman by ten, while Keith Ayling rounded up a scratch laboratory staff from executives and colleagues in various parts of London. Meanwhile, David and Drew assembled what they could from what they had.

They had the cameraman photograph the front page of the Sunday paper, with the grim headline and photographs of the victims. David then cut to the R101 at its mooring mast. Gaumont already had interviews with Lord Thomson, Sir Sefton Brancker and an airship expert, Major G.H. Scott, who also died in the wreckage. David cut these together, linked them with rough titles made on a typewriter, and ended the item with a shot of the R101 on its first trial in January, 1930.

This is the version that survives at the National Film Archive. It is a curiosity, for it begins in silence, and bursts into sound for the interviews. It desperately needs a commentary, although commentaries had not yet come into general use. The same thought clearly occurred to David. And both David and Roy Drew confirm that they gave it a commentary. This "mute" version might have been a rough preliminary to try and beat the other newsreels. It is impossible to be certain, because the newsreel companies consistently lied about their achievements.

Gaumont told the trade paper, *The Bioscope*, that they had chartered a plane from Heston aerodrome for their cameraman, who filmed the wreckage. Because he flew back at dusk, they provided him with flares to make the landing easier. The works manager, Mr Hitchcock, personally developed the negative; Keith Ayling and H.W. Bishop prepared the titles and helped turn out prints. Was it true? What is certain is that David wrote a commentary and read it himself. The records show there was a second, longer edition with commentary. But the implication is that no Gaumont cameraman flew out. Movietone allowed them to dupe their footage. Movietone had their newsreel on the screen at six-thirty on Sunday evening, Gaumont not until ten o'clock.

Isabel was in the nursing home when all this took place, and she remembered reading about the disaster in a newspaper. Yet she never knew about David's involvement until I told her about it, sixty-two years later.

Soon after this event, David and Roy were joined in their cutting-room by a young man called Ted (E.V.H.) Emmett.

"He had a great love for films and took a meagre job to break in to the film industry. The result was some interesting conversations on the films of the day between the three of us," said Roy Drew.

"I used to write commentaries and speak them," said David, "and Emmett was always badgering me for a job. I thought he was a bloody awful bore. One day, out of absolute desperation, I said, 'All right, have a go.' He took over, did a trial run for a week, and in amazement I said to myself, 'He's better than you are.' And I said, 'You've got the job.' He wrote the commentaries and spoke them and became famous for it."

Ted Emmett's rise-and-fall inflection still represents the voice of wartime Britain for many people of my generation, and it is fascinating to realise that he was given his start by David Lean.

Considering that David was dealing every day with events of world-shattering significance, it is strange that he never took any more than a professional newsreel man's interest in them.

The Gaumont Sound News, and the silent Gaumont Graphic, had reported on the Wall Street Crash and the subsequent Depression in the United States; they were less forthcoming when the Depression struck England. For the newsreels were essentially entertainment; as the modern tabloid papers report only sex and violence, for the sake of entertainment, so the newsreels presented world history in terms of parades, manoeuvres, beauty contests and sporting events, with the odd disaster thrown in. Any item which might have had political consequence was invariably ignored.

Entertainment industries generally thrive in a depression. Even when Germany was crippled by inflation, its film industry flourished, for the need for amusement is all the greater in a crisis. But the economic recession did cause problems for English films.

"One day, the bosses at Gaumont called us all in and we were addressed by Mr Gell. He was in charge of all sorts of things, including the newsreels, and he was as tough as blazes. He just said, 'Overtime is going to be stopped from next Monday.'

"I can see his face now, pinched-up rat face. He was an awful man and, of course, he timed it perfectly, because the film industry was in one of its terrible declines, and he knew we couldn't get other work. And he was quite right. We had to come crawling back and accept five pounds a week and no overtime - and we *had* to work overtime.

"People like Gell and Hagen [the head of Twickenham Studios] - and there were lots of them - treated us technicians abominably. And I must say I was all for the technicians. Puffin Asquith was one of the first members of the union, and I was one of the very early ones, too."[12]

Frank Lean's wedding present to David and Isabel was a two-week Mediterranean cruise. Isabel placed Peter in the care of Aunt Helena and in June 1931 they set out.

"I remember we saw Buncs before we went," said Isabel. "David managed to tell him that we hadn't even got money for our train fare to Southampton. So Buncs naturally forked out. Rather shocking.

"David was very much taken with Gibraltar and the long street with its tiny shops selling silk, shawls, fans and fancy umbrellas. He bought three pairs of soft, Japanese silk pyjamas and I wore them all to go through customs. But I

David and Isabel (r) on the cruise which Frank Lean gave them as a wedding present.

didn't get any - they were all for lady friends he'd met on the ship."[13]

From Gibraltar, the ship called at Naples and David and Isabel went to Pompeii. David spoke of Pompeii in one of our conversations, while saying nothing about this cruise.

"I was mad about Pompeii. It was my first experience of the ancient world."

I asked him how he was able to visit it.

"Can't remember," he replied, having blanked out the whole painful memory of Isabel.

I asked him if his father had taken him.

"Might have done. It was like wandering through an ancient field. I remember walking around it in tears. I found it tremendously moving."[14]

For David, Pompeii had a double significance. Not only was it part of the ancient world of his romantic imagination, it was a location in one of his favourite films, Rex Ingram's MARE NOSTRUM. He was startled to realise, when he saw the building that Alice Terry was shown visiting in the film, that it was in fact a Roman brothel.

According to David's second wife, Kay Walsh, he met a girl on this cruise called Jo Kirby. "When Isabel was on her bunk, he would go for a stroll on the deck with Jo. He told me this. He had little confessions when I would just say, 'Enough, enough, enough.'"[15]

Although the friendship was probably innocent enough on the cruise, it seems that David began seeing Jo Kirby after their return. David's first marriage was already under threat.

CHAPTER SEVEN

FLIGHT

By 1931, Edward had left Leighton Park and was at Oxford, where he became editor of the university magazine, *Isis*. A predecessor in this role was Peter Fleming, the husband of David's favourite actress, Celia Johnson.

While a student, Edward wrote two novels, one of which, *Storm in Oxford*, was subtitled "A Fantasy". It was certainly a fantasy as regards Edward's relationship with David, for it was the story of two brothers regarded as a curiosity at Oxford "because of their astonishing fondness for each other". (In fact, those who knew both men were convinced David loved Edward, despite David's jealousy of his intellect; he was certainly very proud of him.)

The main character, a flamboyant young man with the exotic name of Lorenzo, has been expelled from public school for taking responsibility for the actions of his younger brother, Ludovici. It is arguable that Edward, after a while, had begun to regard David as the younger brother. He often behaved like one.

There are many attempts to capture brotherly love - it is contrasted with homosexual infatuation - and perhaps it is significant that these are the least successful parts of the book. The set-pieces are as magnificently visual and energetic as the best of David's work - for example, the Charles the Second party is a drunken orgy in which the rowing hearties march on Ludovici's room and smash everything in it, beating him up savagely for good measure and hurling him into the river.

Edward was clever and talented, funny and charming. But he was also disturbed and had a difficult time at Oxford. Isabel always kept in touch with him and she used to try and get him out of scrapes with girls.

Edward Tangye Lean.

"He wrote asking me to send certain messages to these girls because they liked him and he didn't like them very much."[1]

David, meanwhile, was at his own university - Gaumont Sound News - and was enjoying it considerably more than Edward was enjoying Oxford. The work was creative and highly responsible; the newsreels were seen by millions around the world and speed and precision were essential. David was not naturally a fast worker. He liked to ponder something for a long time before coming to a decision. That was out of the question in newsreels, and perhaps it was good for his professional life that he sometimes had to act like an automaton. For he was gaining in confidence and in technical precision.

He was happy to help other young enthusiasts. Sid Cole, a future editor himself, and later a television producer, responsible for the *Robin Hood* series in the fifties, was a student at the London School of Economics in 1930. He was determined to get into the movies, and a fellow student, Kathy Meakin, a former girlfriend of David's, gave him an introduction.

"I went along to Shepherd's Bush and spent a night watching what went on at Gaumont News. David cut the material which had come in on negative - there was no time to print it. I remember going to a neighbouring cafe and when I came back they already had a print and the commentator was putting the narration on. David was very friendly and obliging and I just sat back and watched. I've always remembered David gratefully for being helpful in that way."[2]

Early in 1931, Keith Ayling, the News Editor, was tempted away from Gaumont to British Movietone News. He asked David to join him, and since the job paid more, and Movietone were the last word in newsreels - financed and equipped by Fox in America, although distributed in England by Gaumont-British - David had little hesitation in agreeing. He was sad to leave Gaumont, his alma mater, and Roy Drew, although he kept in touch and Roy visited him at Movietone, where David showed him the latest editing equipment shipped from the United States. David joined Sidney Wiggins, chief cutter, and Raymond Perrin, in April 1931.

There is a mystery here. Keith Ayling seems to have had a link with Paramount, at their studios in France, as well as the British and Dominions Studio at Elstree in Hertfordshire. For no sooner had David joined him, than he loaned him out to Herbert Wilcox's B&D to cut his first feature film, delaying his move to Movietone.

The film was called THESE CHARMING PEOPLE, adapted from the play, *Dear Father*, by Michael Arlen. The director was the famous Louis Mercanton, who had made QUEEN ELIZABETH with Sarah Bernhardt in 1912, and thus permitted Adolph Zukor, in the United States, to launch the era of the feature film. Mercanton, who was brought up in England, had specialised in "international" films in France. It was far from a "quota quickie" and David was thrilled to be entrusted with it.

David's hallmark as a newsreel editor was his ingenuity. Newsreel events were invariably shot with a single camera and lacked proper coverage. An ice hockey item, for instance, sent over from Canada, should have had the five cameras that Percy Strong used on PALAIS DE DANSE. Instead, it would be covered from a single position, with no cutaways, and it was David's job to convert a series of shots punctuated by camera flashes into a fast-moving and exciting sequence - straight on the negative, so that once he'd cut it he could not change his mind.

When he viewed the rushes of THESE CHARMING PEOPLE, he was overjoyed to see how much coverage he had to play with - long shots, close-ups, travelling shots. This meant he had to spend much longer than

THESE CHARMING PEOPLE: *David's future wife, Ann Todd, in her second film role, Nora Swinburne and Cyril Maude as Colonel Crawford. David made such a mess of the editing of this film that he was fired.*

he anticipated in the cutting room. He had hoped to go on the set and watch the film being made, but there was no time. The leading players included Cyril Maude, Godfrey Tearle and Nora Swinburne. In a smaller role was David's future wife, Ann Todd, though it would be seventeen years before they finally met each other.

David was nervous about his first feature assignment. Not wanting to spend his career cutting newsreels, he was anxious to prove how skilful he could be once he had the coverage he needed. He fairly danced through the footage, choreographing it as he had always wanted to choreograph his newsreels, and when he had finished the first reel he was understandably proud of his achievement.

Paramount had its European headquarters in Joinville, a suburb of Paris, and it was here that decisions were made affecting the British operation. It was here, too, that Alexander Korda was at work. Quite how the first reel of THESE CHARMING PEOPLE was seen by Korda remains a mystery. David said Korda was the producer, but Walter Morosco took the credit. I can only assume Louis Mercanton took it over to Paris to show it to his brother, Roger, who was editing Korda's picture, MARIUS.

Korda and the Mercanton brothers had probably never seen cutting like it in their lives. David had put everything he knew into this single reel of a society comedy. The following morning he was fired. Korda, far from being impressed by a future genius of the cinema, had been appalled.

"I had vastly overcut it," said David. "It jumped about all over the place. It was abominable."

David was not drummed out of the company. Like Roy Drew at Gaumont, he was merely reduced to the ranks. THESE CHARMING PEOPLE was handed over to an editor considered more competent, and David was demoted to assistant editor.

The company gave him what they, no doubt, considered a consolation prize: a screen test to see if he had any promise as an actor. Despite his outsize ears, he was more attractive than many leading men.

"I remember him telling me that they didn't think he would make an actor," said Isabel. "I think he was much too shy."

The test survives, or at least part of it, and the youthful face of David Lean has a resentful cast. He is asked to turn, and he squints crossly at the intensity of the lights. David may not have been a Quaker, but he still had a lot of the Quaker in him. I doubt he could ever have become an actor; his puritan streak would not have permitted it. A handful of actors may have won his admiration, but he retained a distaste for the breed throughout his life.[3]

By the time THESE CHARMING PEOPLE was released in July, David was cutting newsreels again at the Movietone News cutting-rooms in Newman Street. However, he claimed to have continued working on feature films as well.

"Every night I used to go to the cinema to watch American films and see how they were cut," he said. "I picked up the technique pretty quickly and I realised what a terrible hash I'd made of THESE CHARMING PEOPLE.

"The editor I was working with gradually realised that I was better than he was and let me cut the pictures he was working on. I had to be anonymous. He took the credit."

Just as it is hard to be sure which features David worked on without credit, it is equally hard to discover which newsreels he edited since the companies kept no records and several editors were employed. Fortunately, Peter Lean kept stills belonging to his father, frame enlargements franked "British Movietone News", which were blown up from items David had cut. These were probably the first he did for Movietone.

One newsreel opened with coverage of the 1931 tennis championships at Wimbledon and included an interview with a German player called Cillie Aussem. The final item in the same newsreel was entitled "BRITISH DESTROYERS LAY DEPTH CHARGES: Anti-submarine school at Portland operates against imaginary enemy craft in the Channel."

Superbly photographed shots of destroyers, moving at speed on a high summer's day, with dark, carefully filtered skies contrasting with the gleaming white of the bow waves, are intercut with sync sound material of the officers on the bridge - "Hard to starboard! Depth charge crew set up!"

The depth charges are fired in close shot and David cuts on action to long shot at exactly the right moment as they are hurled out to sea, and explode aft of the destroyer with a tower of white spray. The microphones of the time could not cope with the explosions, so the sound track is rather feeble, but visually it is first-rate, and perfect training for the man who would edit and co-direct a film called IN WHICH WE SERVE.

Because of the demands of the newsreels, visits to the cinema and possible moonlighting on features, David was rarely at home with Isabel and his young son. And on those rare occasions when he was home, he seemed discontented and withdrawn. Isabel grew deeply disheartened. The marriage was barely a year old and she imagined he was having wild flings with glamour girls at the studio. And since he never discussed his work with her, he merely fed her suspicions.

In the winter of 1931-32, David and Isabel moved from Holland Park to a slightly larger flat in Hampstead which afforded a beautiful view over the Vale of Health on Hampstead Heath. The address was Flat 2, 20 East Heath Road, just by Squire's Mount, where Gerald du Maurier, the famous actor, lived with his family, including - until her marriage in the summer of 1932 - the novelist Daphne du Maurier. Isabel often saw them walking on the Heath. When the pond in the Vale of Health froze solid, she parked Peter in his pram and taught herself to skate.

The flat may have been ideal in terms of its position, but it had minor drawbacks. In the flat above was an elderly retired clergyman and his wife.

"She used to scream at this poor man," said Isabel. "She was so loud, we could hear it distinctly. It was terrible."

This was another irritation for the highly-strung David when he returned exhausted from the cutting-room. But he was out most of the time and Isabel was left alone with Peter. She admitted that their life was "mediocre" and she was deeply upset by David's indifference as a father. For Peter was a beautiful child and she was justifiably proud of him.

However, David does seem to have been deeply attached to his wife and son, as a letter written by him at this time shows. Letters from David are rare enough at any time, but at this period they are unique. Isabel kept this one, which was undated but appears to be early 1932. It was written at home:

"Monday midnight. Here is a fine husband to return to. I've rung up Edward just now and Bettinson [Ralph Bettinson, a screenwriter at B&D] and myself are going down to see him tomorrow night by car as we mean to talk over train robbery stories with him, and if he had any good ideas I think he will be able to make a nice bit of money out of it. I have an idea it will end up with staying the night so I am taking my pyjamas with me. Anyhow, I will ring you up dear before we go, sometime in the late afternoon. Remember, dear, we have John Myers and Nina Batchelor coming on Wednesday. I think what we had last time was very good so what about some more salmon dear?

"The Vogelbird [their dog] has been a very good boy. His naughty papa gave him a good supper for his pains. Best not to tell you what, my dear. Haven't heard any more about work. But Lachman's secretary asked for my address this afternoon, whatever that may mean. He goes to Paris tomorrow anyhow.

"I have spent far too much money and have been extravagant - had a big meal at Stone's Chop House tonight and then went to the Bow Bells again.

"Well dear, I'm going to have a bath and take the dog out again. Be kind to him darling. He is rather dear and has been so good over the weekend. Give our dear little Peter a kiss from me and tell him I'll be back soon. God bless you and forgive me for rushing off. It isn't because I don't love you. I do - more than anyone. David."

Harry Lachman was an American who, in 1929, had made a film hailed as the first British all-talkie (there is a dispute about that) called UNDER THE GREENWOOD TREE. He had just finished shooting a Foreign Legion melodrama at B&D called INSULT.

Lachman wanted to do the editing in Paris, and David had evidently been recommended. Shortly after David wrote his letter to Isabel, he was told to report to the Paramount-Joinville studios outside Paris.

Although David felt confident enough about handling the material, this was the first time he had been abroad entirely on his own. He spoke no French and he was accustomed to his father making all the arrangements, even when he travelled with Isabel.

"I didn't enjoy it very much," said David, "and I didn't enjoy Paris. I was pretty unadventurous at this stage and slightly nervous about being abroad. I was married, I had a baby, it was all rather difficult."

What he failed to tell me, and what perhaps added to the difficulties, was the fact that Isabel followed him to Paris with Peter. David was startled, but the French film people were delighted to see the child and were so charmed by his looks that they wanted to put him in a film.

David suddenly became paternal, and protective. "Not on your life," he said, telling Isabel of the tricks film people played to get reactions from children in front of the camera.[4]

"INSULT had Sam Livesey, Roger Livesey's father in it. Also John Gielgud.

John Gielgud (right) starred in INSULT, *a drama set in North Africa and directed by Rex Ingram protégé Harry Lachman. With Sam Livesey and Elizabeth Allan.*

He was then a young man - and what a nice man he was. Harry Lachman had worked with Rex Ingram at the Victorine Studios in the South of France. He was a jolly good director and rather a good painter. He had a Chinese wife, I remember. But the picture wasn't terribly good." [5]

INSULT was released in July 1932. The following month, David walked out on his wife and son. He would feel guilty about it for the rest of his life and block out the memory of the event, as did Isabel, as much as she could, for if it was a difficult decision for him, it was traumatic for her. She still finds it hard to talk about.

"One day he told me he was going," she said. "I watched him pack. When he got up to go, Peter said, 'Bye, bye.' It made David laugh. But it didn't make him stay."

No one knows for certain where David went. Kay Walsh believes he moved in to a terraced house in Godfrey Street, Chelsea, with Jo Kirby, the girl he met on his honeymoon cruise. (They certainly lived together here, but it is difficult to determine when their liaison began.) Isabel found it impossible to comprehend what had happened.

"I used to stand at the window, waiting, hoping. For six months, I wept every night."

David sent so little money that Isabel couldn't support the baby and pay the rent, so eventually she gave up and went home to Knockholt to live with her parents. Her father had recovered from the shock of the marriage - he probably felt vindicated - and he was delighted to have his grandson in the house.

Frank Lean and Margaret took Peter and Isabel to Readymoney Cove, in Fowey, in Cornwall where they had a family reunion with Grandmother Tangye.

"Edward drove, I navigated and we went to stay in a fisherman's cottage. We had a marvellous fortnight there. Across the bay lived Daphne du Maurier.

"Buncs was so kind. He was like a father to Peter. Edward carried him about on his shoulders. I was a skeleton - I weighed six stone because I had so little money to live on. And, of course, I hadn't let anybody know. So it was a wonderful holiday."[6]

From David, Isabel heard nothing. Not even when Peter fell ill and had to be operated on; not even when she had a motor accident with Peter while driving Frank's Talbot.

"He did remember Peter's birthdays," said Isabel. "Of course, he was distracted. He found me terribly dull - look at all those interesting girls, all those people in the studio."

David blamed the failure of his marriage on the almost total ignorance in which young people of his generation were kept regarding sexual matters.

"It was a disaster," he said, "because we knew nothing - nothing. I think that ignorance was terrible. I don't think it does any good at all, now looking at it. I think how wonderful it is today when everybody seems to know everything. It doesn't do any harm, does it?

"We should never have got married. I mean, the impact of sex when it has been a complete mystery is the greatest force in the world, isn't it? It caused terrible misery in all sorts of families, and, of course, the Quaker families were stricter still."[7]

David's second wife, Kay Walsh, said: "He couldn't have any untidy bits hanging around, so he let Edward take over the emotional side of Isabel and Peter and everybody that he ought to have been worrying about."[8]

Isabel was perhaps the first to learn that when David Lean walked out of someone's life, he closed an iron door behind him.

Years later, discussing relationships, David advised a friend to be ruthless. "You see, you must cut. Anything that's finished is finished. You must just pretend people aren't there. Once you've made the decision, you've got to cut people out of your life."[9]

CHAPTER EIGHT

TOP FLIGHT

BERNARD Vorhaus was a young American who had worked as a writer at Paramount and MGM in Hollywood, but had never managed to become a director. In England, however, thanks to the quota system, he was about to have his chance.

Vorhaus knew the importance of a good editor. The man who usually cut "quota quickies" at Wembley Studios was, he felt, without talent. Vorhaus, wanting someone quick and with a strong sense of pace, had been struck by the standard of editing on Movietone newsreels - so much faster and more imaginative than their rivals.

He knew Keith Ayling and rang him up for advice. Ayling recommended David, said that he hated to lose him but would not stand in his way. Vorhaus and David liked each other on sight. Vorhaus was tall, good-looking and wore a beard, which was so unusual among young men in those days that street kids used to shout remarks about it. He had a soft New York accent and he was full of enthusiasm for films.

David admired the way he would pick up a miserable "quota quickie" with a rock-bottom budget and transform it into something worthwhile by pulling ideas out of the air. He liked the way that Vorhaus would forget about exterior establishing shots and spend the time with his actors. Then, while David started editing, he would go on holiday, taking a hand-held 35mm De Vry camera, and shoot his exteriors himself, with doubles, where necessary. This gave him the opportunity to wait for the right light, and to travel considerable distances, neither of which he could afford with the crew in tow. As soon as he got back, and his footage had been developed, David would insert the shots into the cutting-copy. Vorhaus would check it through and the picture was complete.

"He really worked on a shoestring," said David. "Highly inventive, with a real love for film and as clever as a wagonload of monkeys." [1]

Although Ayling had been loaning David out from Movietone to work on features, Vorhaus was under the impression he had a man new to feature film editing. Perhaps David did nothing to disillusion him.

"I wasn't uneasy about having a cutter who had never cut feature films before," said Vorhaus, "because I always decided myself exactly how I wanted the cutting to be. But that's not to detract for a moment from the brilliance and imagination of David's cutting."

Their first film together was SMONEY FOR SPEED, trade-shown in March 1933, and starring John Loder and Ida Lupino. She was thought to be fifteen, and this was only her second picture.

"Ida was a very intelligent woman," said Vorhaus. "She was not particularly literate but she had great dramatic imagination. She came from a traditional stage family (her father was Stanley Lupino) and they had a little stage in their house."

Vorhaus thought that there might have been a romance with Ida Lupino, and David admitted he fell "madly in love" with her. She eventually went to Hollywood and became one of the few women directors.

Director Bernard Vorhaus gave David Lean a break when he hired him to edit his MONEY FOR SPEED; Cyril McLaglen (left), Ida Lupino, John Loder.

It was at this period that David began to gain his reputation for being a lady-killer. His good looks, his charm and his boyish enthusiasm caused women to fall for him as soon as they met him. He was exceptional, even in an era when charm was commonplace.

Eric Cross, who photographed MONEY FOR SPEED, joked that at rushes, if David was there, no girl was safe once the lights had gone down. But as women quickly found out, they took second place to his first love. Vorhaus was particularly impressed with David's dedication.

"He worked right through the night in the cutting-room to stay on time so that he could be on the set in the daytime to watch how I was shooting, so it was quite clear to me that he was tremendously keen to make films."

When shooting was over, Vorhaus moved into the cutting-room to make sure that David was cutting it as he wanted. "After a bit, I thought this was not necessary at all. If I asked David to do a particular thing he did it absolutely perfectly.

"In our second film, GHOST CAMERA, for instance, there was one scene of a trial and reporters rush to the telephones. I wanted some fast cutting - you had a close-up of one journalist saying, 'M for mother' then a cut to the next - 'U for

Uncle' - and the next - 'R for Red' and at the end a close-up of the telephone operator's reaction, 'MURDER!' What I wanted done was bang, bang, bang and he wasn't afraid to cut very fast. Usually cutters at that time thought it couldn't be done. David did it superbly."

Vorhaus only managed to keep David on for the second picture, which was made at Twickenham, because they were so behind on another production that Jack Harris, their regular editor, was too busy. Once Harris was available, however, the association between Vorhaus and David came to an end.

Despite the fact that he had now cut several features, David gave me the impression that he returned to B&D as a first assistant, or assembly cutter, helping to cut quota quickies. An American, Merrill White, had taken over as head of the editing department.[2]

"I was working away by myself in the cutting-room at nine or ten at night when Merrill came up and said, 'Ah, David. I thought as much.'

"He was the overall boss and he put me up to fully-fledged editor again. He was a tall, tousle-haired man who had been cutter for Lubitsch in Hollywood. We used to take the 'quickies' - he'd take the first four reels and we'd work together until midnight, and then we'd go over to a feature film [an A film] and I'd take the first three reels and he'd take the next three reels and we'd spend two or three hours and go home at God knows what time in the morning. I became very good, I must say. And Merrill thought I was good.

"Merrill taught me that you can make any cut look smooth - whether it matches or not. And I can do that even now. I can take mismatches and I can make them look as if they match. He taught me more about cutting than anybody I knew. I looked on him as a sort of god."[3]

David was one of perhaps thirty editors trained by White. All of them stayed in the business for years.[4]

Among the thousand and one things Merrill White taught David was to adopt a nonchalant attitude to sound. While other editors were so daunted by the new equipment that some had nervous breakdowns, David refused to be intimidated.

"When sound came in," said David, "it slowed everything down. The soundtrack became a tyrant. Having to lace up and run track and picture together. Bloody cumbersome. You need a rhythm to edit well."

So he followed Merrill White's advice, learned the dialogue by heart and lip-read the actors, so he hardly needed the sound track.

"I could throw the film about with the old abandon."

This technique enabled him to do his cutting on a simple Moviola designed for picture only. But to make sure all was well, he had the assistant write the key words of dialogue on the clear spacing of the optical track. David also learned how to read sound tracks and could "see" the sound of an orchestra and point out where, say, the bassoons came in.

David learned that editing had a great deal in common with music, and he felt that to be successful it should be smooth, with an even tempo, and not jerky and strident.

"People always said, 'Oh, you're the one that cuts out the naughty bits, are you?' Everybody thinks that a cutter is somebody who cuts out stuff. That is not the case, of course. He does cut out stuff, but half the effects, when you sit in the movie theatre, are caused by the juxtaposition of pictures. And as a cutter, you select what the audience shall look at and when."[5]

David's expertise was becoming well known in the industry. He could have become arrogant and aloof, but he was a great encourager.

Over at Ealing Studios, a young assistant called Peggy Hennessey had been given the opportunity to cut a film by an American director called Al Parker. The problem was that she had to do a roughcut in two days. In a panic, she managed to put a roughcut together, and then rang David begging for help. He came over from Wembley late that evening and they looked at the film. At the end he said, 'You've nothing to worry about.' He was marvellous about encouraging young people. Al Parker was pleased with the cut, and I became a fully-fledged editor as a result."[6]

"After a while I became a sort of film doctor," said David. "If they had a film that was much too long, or a film they were in trouble with, I used to come in and re-cut it. In fact, if I get too old to direct a movie, I wouldn't mind going back to that. I love the feel of film. I love the smell of it. The smell has changed slightly. We used to make the joins with acetate, and the cutting-rooms would have this perfume around them. Now that's gone. Go and sniff nail-polish remover nowadays if you want to call to mind the old cutting-rooms.[7]

"I worked on a lot of bad pictures, and bad pictures are very good for one's ego, because the worse they are, the more chance you have of making them better. And I started to think, as numerous people who work with me think, that I could do better than they could - and that gave me a real urge to do something in the way of direction."[8]

It was an urge he resisted, partly because he was nervous about the idea, partly because he was offered nothing but quota quickies.

His growing fame as a film doctor meant that even though he might have worked all day on one picture, he might also have to drive to another studio and work all evening on another. One of these was THE SONG OF THE PLOUGH, directed by John Baxter in 1933. But David's dedication and his dash from studio to studio tended to puzzle people such as L.P. Williams, the art director for Herbert Wilcox at B&D, who later became art director on BRIEF ENCOUNTER.

"He was a funny chap, David. I worked within twenty-five yards of him at

B&D for years, and you never went out with him, he never asked you to parties or anything. He was just at the studio, then he'd get into his Invicta car and disappear. Where? I don't know. Nobody knew. I always understood David was at Cambridge. I found out later he certainly wasn't. But that was the impression one had."[9]

At Ealing, David (with Ian Thomson) cut TIGER BAY, a tropical melodrama starring Anna May Wong, a Chinese-American actress who had played with Douglas Fairbanks in THE THIEF OF BAGDAD ten years earlier. A cut above the basic "quota quickie", it was directed by an art director, John Wills. Apart from its superb cinematography, by American cameraman Robert G. Martin, with operator Alan Lawson from Gaumont, David regarded it as a routine assignment, one of those feebly financed films, all shot in the studio, in which the extras walk unnaturally slowly, as if afraid of running out of set.

Again at Ealing, David cut SECRET OF THE LOCH, directed by Elvey's old colleague, Milton Rosmer, who had made the sound reissue of BALACLAVA. The director of TIGER BAY, John Wills, reverted to his role of art director on this low-budget thriller about the Loch Ness monster, featuring the veteran stage actor Seymour Hicks, and the star of Von Stroheim's GREED, Gibson Gowland.

If SECRET OF THE LOCH was notable for anything, it was for David's meeting Vera Campbell. She had been trying to get a job at Ealing, but had only found one in the canteen - and she wasn't much good at that. She went to see the studio manager, Bill Lott, and David was standing in his office, complaining that he hadn't enough people in his cutting-room.

"What about her?" he asked, "I wouldn't mind having her. She could be some sort of help."

Vera was very young and, despite her glasses, very pretty. She was so thrilled to get into the cutting-room that she was not even shocked by the muddle she found.

"They didn't file their trims at all. All the sequences were wrapped up together in a great big roll. When you got it out of the tin, you had to go through every piece of film to find what you wanted. I had quite a good pictorial memory. I looked over David's shoulder, and I went to rushes and I'd memorised it all and he said, 'Oh, you're really quite bright.' I was frightfully pleased at this."[10]

Vera found David only too willing to explain and to demonstrate to his assistants the mysteries of editing.

"He'd say, 'Come on, we're going to see the roughcut.' Bang. Everyone would drop whatever they were doing and we'd all crowd into the little theatre. It was so exciting. He'd show his very first cut, too. He had none of the inhibitions of so many editors who go off with the cutting copy under their arm. It was a party. It was great fun. And he would say, 'What do you think of it?'

and he would listen to you. He was very good that way.

"But he didn't make friends easily. He joked and laughed a bit, but he seemed a bit shy. He did silly things and giggled a lot; it was as though he was embarrassed. He was not at ease with people like Thorold Dickinson, the supervisor at Ealing."

Vera noticed that David never wrote anything - not so much as a note. He dictated all his notes in the theatre, and she wrote them down.

"In the cutting-room, he wasn't a disciplinarian, but he was very demanding. You never knew when you were going home until David stood up and said, 'Let's call it a day.' Or he might say, 'Let's go up to town' and off we'd go and have a party somewhere.

"I thought David very clever and I admired him tremendously. I was fascinated also by the fact that he was so wicked. I remember at Ealing I took him some mail and he was working at the bench, winding away, underneath a window. He looked through it, took one letter and tore it in half and threw it out of the window. I said, 'Why did you do that?' He said, 'It was a dentist's bill - seven pounds. Well, he won't get that.'"[11]

The director of SECRET OF THE LOCH, Milton Rosmer, evidently tried to continue the work started by Scott Goddard. He introduced David to Chekhov and aroused his enthusiasm for Spain with travel books.

The cutting-room people found Rosmer's film "killingly funny", especially when an inoffensive lizard was enlarged via the Schüfftan process to the size of a prehistoric monster.

John Mitchell, who was a junior projectionist in the theatre adjoining David's cutting-room (and who, fifty years later, would be sound recordist on A PASSAGE TO INDIA), remembered that they used an iguana as the monster.

"In those days, back projection was pretty crude. The screen was always tearing. The iguana ended up as a very blown-up image. David was much in evidence on the floor. He wasn't just receiving the material in the cutting room but was making comments on the set."[12]

Alas, he had no hope of rescuing a film which had all the faults of the poverty-stricken British film of the time - poor back projection, feeble models, an inept script and bad acting; it was as though none of those responsible had been to the cinema since 1908.

From Ealing, David returned to B&D. Following the huge financial success of Alexander Korda's THE PRIVATE LIFE OF HENRY VIII, City money flowed freely into the British film industry for a couple of years, allowing ambitious producers, such as Korda and Herbert Wilcox, to concentrate on making high-quality (and high-budget) films.

As part of his assault on the international market, Wilcox produced NELL

GWYN with Anna Neagle. David worked with Merrill White on this - he insisted it was in a minor capacity - and he remembered the fuss caused in America over Neagle's cleavage and her lack of shame at being the King's mistress. An absurd moral ending was concocted showing her in the gutter. This did nothing for the box-office success of the film, and B&D's annual report for 1935 showed a deficit of over £25,000.

David also cut, with Merrill White, BREWSTER'S MILLIONS, another high-budget film. This Jack Buchanan vehicle was directed by Thornton Freeland, an American who had made FLYING DOWN TO RIO with Fred Astaire and Ginger Rogers. The casting director was an aristocratic young man called Anthony Havelock-Allan who eventually became David's producer.

David's first experience as a "film doctor" was probably Ealing's JAVA HEAD, a remake of an American silent. The film was directed by an American, J. Walter Ruben, whom the producer Basil Dean, with his usual tact, described as "an uncouth Hollywood type," and starred Anna May Wong, John Loder and Ralph Richardson. It was officially edited by Thorold Dickinson[13] but Rachael Low, in her history of the British film, says that it was rescued by the skills of Edward Carrick, art director, Dickinson, Carol Reed, an assistant to Basil Dean, who had just started directing himself, and David Lean.[14]

Watching the film today, one can sense that Ruben did not provide nearly enough coverage. There are transitions which would not be acceptable in a more polished production, and some sequences are held together with an inordinate number of wipes - often a sign of desperation. So, perhaps, David was relieved not to have his name on it.

It must have given David some satisfaction, however, to know that he was getting Basil Dean out of a spot. David's father had known Dean and had held him up as the supreme and shining example, but Dean, thought David, was a tinpot tyrant, only too willing to pick on the weak and defenceless.

Even though he was not working on very inspiring films, David was enjoying himself enormously. In 1934, he was thrilled when an inspiration of his youth - the great Douglas Fairbanks - came to work at B&D. David went up to the sound booth and looked down on Alexander Korda directing Fairbanks in THE PRIVATE LIFE OF DON JUAN.

"I got the biggest kick seeing Fairbanks run up a staircase - nobody could run up a staircase like Fairbanks. It was wonderful."[15]

In the mid-thirties a number of British producers, such as Korda, Wilcox, Dean and Michael Balcon, were trying to make films which would enhance the reputation of the British film industry. However, the "quota quickies" - supported by the American distributors in Britain in order to enhance the Hollywood films - were still made in huge numbers.

The front page of the *British Film Reporter*, a home-produced version of the *Hollywood Reporter*, warned in June 1934 of "SUICIDE VIA THE QUICKIE ROUTE. Stop this sausage-mill production. Each Pound-a-Footer is Blow to British Prestige." The report said, "Although designed ostensibly to assist the British film industry, the quota system is undermining the prestige of British films almost as fast as worthwhile productions are building it."

The reporter, Neville C. Thomson, had conducted his own survey at his local cinema, and reported a swelling chorus of protest.

"The present state of affairs is grossly unjust to the men and women engaged in production. It is lop-sided logic to argue that the quota film, bad as it may be, gives a lot of people work. That is penny wisdom and pound foolishness... We must get to work on the quickies before the quickies take us over the cliff."[16]

Some of the "quickies" bored David so much that he allowed his interest in women to affect his work.

As Julian Wintle, who assisted David on some of these quota films, told another assistant editor, Gordon Hales: "David would often be absent when he should have been cutting the picture. He would pick up a girl and start an affair. To finish the affair, he would send them passion fruit."

"Julian said that for a screening on Monday, David would come in on the previous Thursday or Friday and say, 'We'd better cut the picture.' He would work without stopping until the cut was screened. I read later that the difference between genius and other people is tremendous reserves of power."[17]

David appears to have regarded each love affair rather like a film: a burst of romance, a surfeit of attention, impeccable behaviour and charm, and the poor girl imagining her life hereafter will be pure Paramount Pictures. Then the passion fruit, the lid is placed on the affair and the can put on the shelf.

One of David's close friends was Dr Charles Clinton-Thomas, his former neighbour from Holland Park. He and his brother Tony, with their girlfriends - Charles now divorced from his fiery wife - often went out with David. Because of his Quaker upbringing, David was abstemious, although he chain-smoked. Charles remembered that David would wait until the two men were drunk, and then pounce on their girls.

"He always got away with it," said Mary Clinton-Thomas. "Women just loved him. And men loved him too. It takes a lot of charm and personality to overcome sexual jealousy, but David had both in abundance."[18] Charles and Tony went on holidays with David to the South of France, or skiing in the mountains. Such was David's evangelistic zeal for cinema that Charles abandoned medicine and followed David into the film industry. There he discovered that men like David Lean could be numbered on the finger of one thumb, and he quickly returned to medicine, becoming the surgeon he had always so much wanted to be.

During 1935, David worked on only one film worthy of the name. TURN OF THE TIDE was an honest attempt to make an authentically British film using land and sea as the French had so successfully used them, with ordinary working people mingling with actors who did not look like refugees from Mayfair. It was one of several attempts to create a school of documentary-drama under the influence of Robert Flaherty.

TURN OF THE TIDE was important because it was the first feature of a millionaire Methodist named J. Arthur Rank, a Yorkshire flour miller who had gone into films because he found sermons boring and wanted a more dynamic way for religion to reach young people.[19]

The film was based on a 1922 novel by Leo Walmsley called *Three Fevers*. David might have heard Walmsley when he lectured at the Public Hall, Croydon, on his war experiences in the Royal Flying Corps. Walmsley, who had taken part in a filming expedition to Africa, thought that Flaherty's films, such as MAN OF ARAN, were vastly overrated and he soon resigned from his position as technical adviser on TURN OF THE TIDE.

Walmsley was convinced it would be a ghastly flop and was startled to read glowing notices in the national papers. The critic of the *Sunday Chronicle* even regarded it superior to MAN OF ARAN.

David was probably called in as a "doctor" for he has no credit (nor has Ian Dalrymple who also worked on it). I learned of his association when he was very ill, and, while his memory was not impaired, his speech was and he could only manage a few words at a time. I wondered later if he had confused it with THE LAST ADVENTURERS, another drama of fishermen which he edited two years later. But no, he remembered the director - Norman Walker - he indicated his military moustache and said, "Very pleasant but not very talented."

To this day, film distribution is all too often a dishonest business; it is childishly simple to conceal profits, to exaggerate expenses and to ruin those who might otherwise prove competitors. But when applying their usual sharp practice to TURN OF THE TIDE, Wardour Street cheated the wrong man.

J. Arthur Rank might have remained on the sidelines, a mild-mannered producer of uplifting films, had it not been for this film. It was highly praised and many people wanted to see it. But the distributors kept it out of the main circuits. Consequently, Rank set up his own distribution company - General Film Distributors - and proceeded to buy the main circuits. It was not quite as simple as that, but as his biographer Alan Wood put it: "Within ten years or so, J. Arthur Rank was to be the biggest force in films in Britain, the owner of Pinewood and Denham Studios, of Gaumont and Odeon cinemas, with interests in every branch of the business and his film empire was valued at £50,000,000."

Why was Rank so keen on films? To John Wesley, the founder of Methodism, the theatre was "Satan's own ground", so old Joseph Rank refused to allow his children to visit the theatre, let alone the picture house. Like David, J. Arthur Rank came late to the cinema and it therefore held all the more fascination for him.

In January 1933, Adolf Hitler was appointed Chancellor of Germany. While this signalled the end of democracy in Germany, it also meant - to everyone's surprise - the end of the great era of German cinema. Hitler and his National Socialist party blamed the Jews for the war - and for every other ill - and resolved to suppress them. No one had the slightest idea how many Jews had contributed to the masterworks of the German silent era until they began to flee the country, turning up in the United States, France, Italy and Britain. Whilst the German cinema never recovered its prestige, the British was greatly enriched.

Among the refugees were Dr Paul Czinner and Elisabeth Bergner, who were assumed to be a married couple, but were actually only living together.[20]

An assistant asked Czinner what kind of doctor he was. "Sexual psychology," was the reply, though he is usually said to have been a doctor of philosophy. Born in Budapest in 1890, Czinner began as a playwright and turned to directing on the stage in Vienna. He became friends with Carl Mayer and worked with him on scripts. He created an enviable reputation for the films he made with Elisabeth Bergner. Czinner belongs to a school of European directors who specialised in *Kammerspiel* technique, where, in small-scale, intense stories, thoughts were conveyed by the actors through gesture and expression rather than words.

It was fortunate that Bergner was in such sympathy with him. Regarded as "the modern Duse", Bergner was akin to Garbo and Dietrich in the fanatical devotion she aroused among audiences, both male and female. She had the smooth, untroubled face of a child and combined heartbreaking innocence with a radiant sense of humour. She could switch from languid sophistication to impishness with the roll of an eye.

When Bergner arrived in England, she immediately took the leading role in Margaret Kennedy's play, *Escape Me Never*, continuing the saga of the Sanger family which had begun with an earlier play, *The Constant Nymph*. ESCAPE ME NEVER would be Czinner's third film in Britain.

Although Herbert Wilcox was technically in charge of the production, its real producer was The Hon Richard Norton, son and heir of Lord Grantley, who had secured the finance through United Artists, as he had done for Korda and THE PRIVATE LIFE OF HENRY VIII.

"He took a liking to me," said David. "He gave me some wonderful chances and he was the one who put me on to Czinner."

When Czinner agreed to use David as editor, Norton paid him an astonishing thirty pounds a week. The assistant director, Dallas Bower, was paid only twenty.

Griffith Jones as Caryl Sanger in ESCAPE ME NEVER: *David's first triumph.*

The company went on location to Cortina d'Ampezzo, in the Dolomites, and then on to Venice. Alas, David was not expected to go too. Nor did the cameraman, Georges Perinal, the great French cinematographer, who was working elsewhere and would only shoot the interiors. The company hired a German cameraman for the exteriors, the brilliant Sepp Allgeier.[21]

Through Allgeier's thrilling images, David would encounter the city of Venice for the first time in his cutting-room. He also became acquainted, through the lens of his Moviola, with an astonishingly lovely, dark-haired girl called Penelope Dudley Ward.

With the company on location, David set to work as soon as the rushes had been rubber-numbered and logged by his first assistant Patricia Danes, another veteran of silent pictures.

She regarded him as the nicest person she had ever known. "And a jolly good editor," she added. "They seemed terrible hours we did, but I loved working with him. It wasn't like work. David made it so interesting. He used to explain everything he did - not many of them did that."[22]

When the company returned, David told Czinner that he had finished the first cut of all the material. Czinner was far from pleased. "What? What first cut? We haven't viewed the rushes yet."

David patiently explained that in England it was the practice for the editor to make the first cut and he suggested they view it together in the projection room. Czinner refused.

"Take the cutting-copy," he ordered, "and put it back into the rushes and then I will take a look at it, not before."

After Czinner swept out, David and Patricia Danes went through the laborious process of breaking down the cutting copy and restoring the rushes.

David had not realised the importance Czinner placed on rushes. "He used the theatre as a glorified Moviola," said Philip Hudsmith, Czinner's colleague of later years, "so that he could analyse the dramatic content of a scene."[23]

When the editing was complete, David could not resist telling Czinner that the final cut of the location sequences closely resembled the original cut that he had made. Czinner looked at him a long time through his mild blue eyes and said, "Not quite, David."

When the company returned, David, in his customary way, spent his days on the set where he could observe the shooting and offer editorial advice to Czinner. Assistant director Dallas Bower found David an intriguing character. He had never known a man get into such entanglements with women - how he managed to do a day's work was beyond him.

"One of the things I found so extraordinary about him was that he had this appalling inferiority complex as far as his brother was concerned - he felt he had no intellectual ability at all.

"We used to see the rushes before Paul saw them and and make bets as to which takes he'd choose. Poor old Paul was obsessed by Elisabeth's eccentricities - he was concerned whether she was holding an apple at a certain angle while eating it, or whether her foot was turned in. I remember David saying, 'You know perfectly well the take he'll want me to use is the one where she turns both feet in, despite the fact that it isn't properly centred.'

"I remember we got frightfully fed up on one occasion when Paul, who was habitually late anyway, failed to turn up. David said, 'Let's go for a spin. I'm browned off.' He had an enormous Invicta car, with a bonnet from here to infinity. So I got into this thing. I've never been faster with anybody before or since. Literally, before you could say 'pop goes the weasel,' we found ourselves at Hatfield. Marvellous driver."[24]

Czinner's terrible time-keeping meant that David had to stay later than ever in the cutting-rooms. There was a rumour in the business that he held the industry record for a car journey from Elstree to Marble Arch where he lived in an apartment block called Mount Royal.

"I used to go to Lyon's Corner House at Marble Arch and have breakfast at about five and then went to bed for five or six hours. I got up at lunchtime and drove back to Elstree." David had low blood pressure and he hated getting up early.[25]

The unfortunate unit was called each day at the normal time - eight thirty - though the Czinners might arrive at midday. But Lean never lost his respect for the director.

"I'll tell you why," he said. "There are so many jerks about and Czinner was solid. He was highly intelligent. He seemed rather sinister, but he wasn't. He never did a terrible film. All right, his set-ups, the way he arranged his scenes - you could dismiss them as being obvious, but they were very well done and he had this gift, which very few people have as directors - Willy Wyler had it to a huge extent - of giving a kind of weight to a scene. I don't know how it's done. I know I can do it myself, but I'm buggered if I know how I do it. Some directors are not solid and there are some who have this solidity."

If Czinner had a fault, it lay in a somewhat Continental disregard for the eyeline rule. This is the foundation of film directing, which some of the finest directors, paradoxically, have taken no notice of at all. John Ford and Griffith both ignored it, and caused confusion among their audiences. The eyeline rule makes it easy for the audience to know who is talking to whom, which character is moving where. If you photograph someone talking off right, the person listening must be looking off left. If they also look off right, it will appear that the listener is looking at a third person the audience hasn't yet met. If an army shoots left, their enemy must shoot back right, otherwise, again, they will both appear to be shooting in the same direction at a phantom army which never appears.[26]

On the set, David could tactfully point out to Czinner when he had crossed this invisible line. Czinner's lack of interest in this kind of thing did not endear him to cameraman Georges Perinal.

"Peri was a terrific technician," said Dallas Bower, "but everything had to be planned to the nth degree. Paul never planned anything, so Perinal constantly had to be on his guard. He rather took the view that it was a good thing Paul had David Lean at his elbow."

ESCAPE ME NEVER was David's introduction to the use of music in sound films. Czinner was a trained musician - he is said to have written a violin concerto at the age of nine - and had been a friend of Richard Strauss. To compose the music for his new film, Czinner hired William Walton and paid him three hundred pounds, an astronomical sum. Walton's work on the film enabled him to help pay the mortgage on a house in South Eaton Place, but, as he put it, it nearly drove him to a lunatic asylum.[27]

ESCAPE ME NEVER opens with a burst of music and sunlight in Venice, a foretaste of SUMMERTIME. It is the nearest to a David Lean film that one can find among the whole group of films he edited. Its sets are cathedral-like when they have to be - no expense was spared and the finest designers were employed. The locations are unusually and stunningly shot. The playing is exceptional and full of emotion and the dialogue carefully thought out. And there are steam trains.

The film is full of resonances into David's own life. The story involves two brothers - Sebastian, obsessed with his work, and Caryl, obsessed with an exquisite girl, Fenella (Penelope Dudley Ward[28]). The first brother takes her easily from the second. There is a climactic fight when the brothers confront one another in front of Fenella, and Caryl shouts, "You get away with everything! You take everything! You're the genius! Oh God, I could kill you for this." And he proceeds to attempt to do so.

The central figure, however, is the enchanting Gemma Jones (Bergner), a madcap character who dismisses Fenella as "the Eiffel Tower in winter". She is struggling to bring up a baby on her own. She carts it around Venice and hauls it up the Dolomites and the audience takes little notice of it until towards the end. Now she has married Sebastian and life is hard for her and the baby falls ill...

Bergner's performance is among the finest in all cinema. If a film editor admires a performance after scrutinising it several hundred times, then it must have value.

"There was one scene," said David, "where she heard her baby has died which, just looking in that tiny Moviola lens, always made the

Elisabeth Bergner as Gemma Jones in ESCAPE *ME NEVER.*

hair go up at the back of my head. She was very talented. She did too much looking over teacups, but she was a damned good actress."[29]

Czinner does not entirely shake the film free of its theatrical origins, and David sometimes has to put up with long dialogue exchanges covered in one master shot. But elsewhere his editing is impeccable, even when Czinner's action lacks continuity. When Gemma sits down for a difficult encounter with Fenella, so beautifully is the cut executed that your eye is diverted from the fact that while in the long shot Fenella stands upright, in the closer shot she is leaning against the mantelpiece.

When Czinner provides David with only one cutaway sequence (a cutaway is a shot or sequence used to conceal a jump cut) during the ballet where he needs two, David does a daring thing. Gemma is shown wandering down the hospital steps after hearing about her baby, and slumps at the bottom. A policeman moves her on. David cuts back to the ballet, and then returns to exactly the same scene, this time played silent, like a memory.

ESCAPE ME NEVER was an immense success in England and covered its cost in one cinema in the West End alone. In America, thanks to the isolationism of its distribution system, its popularity was limited to New York.

It was this film that established David Lean as a top flight film editor.

"I'll always remember ESCAPE ME NEVER," said David, nostalgically. "I found out there was a scene by a tiny lake called Lake Messurina above Cortina. Whenever I'm in that part of the world, I drive up to Messurina and I know it is just from cutting that film."[30]

Although he never mentioned it, I discovered that David had gone to Venice and Lake Messurina as soon as the film was finished. He went with Jo Kirby. Among the correspondence sent to me for the book by David's lawyer, Tony Reeves, was a note from a "Joe Kirby" which contained a forwarding address. Jo Kirby proved to have died in 1979, but her son, John Clay, the writer, invited me to his London home.

Jo Kirby never mentioned David to her two sons, but she did reminisce about him to John Clay's wife, Catrine.

"She always said, 'He was the love of my life and I never got over it.' She didn't talk about his films. She didn't love David because he was someone important - he wasn't when she knew him - but because he was David. His influence on her was in photography and it was tremendous. They took photographs together, and at times you don't really know who took which. She went on all her life loving photography and taking very good pictures."[31]

John Clay said that somewhere in the attic were some home movies. When he finally produced them, I ran them on an editing table which could cope with shrunken film. I was astonished to see that they were a record of the 1935 cruise to Italy.

Jo Kirby came from a similar background to David. Her house in Cheshire - Hallswood in Neston - was similar in scale to Warham Mount. Her mother was Italian, and came from an artistic family, whereas her father was a chartered surveyor whose company had been involved in the construction of the Mersey Tunnel. She had thrived in this atmosphere, and one part of her relished her position in society - she could be snobbish on occasion - while the other part longed to get away from it. David was her ideal companion, for beneath his conventional public school exterior, there was a wild spirit.

He fulfilled her artistic desires by teaching her photography. Under his tutelage, she took photographs, which he later printed for her on toned paper, producing prints of exhibition standard. She had a remarkable eye.

Jo Kirby, at her wedding to Eric Clay.

"When they set up house together," recalled Catrine Clay, "her parents never knew. Officially she was living with a girlfriend. Only later did her parents discover what was going on and they were absolutely livid. They summoned her back but she managed to find an excuse to leave her parents and took the train to London. She hadn't told David she was coming. She had no idea where to find him.

"She said she was feeling desperate and she went out for a walk at night. She didn't know where she was, and she just walked round London. You have to understand that she was an extremely 'feet on the ground' type of person. So this is an extraordinary incident for that reason. She came up to Piccadilly Circus in a kind of trance and there he was and he came towards her. And he said he had been doing exactly the same thing."[32]

David left Jo Kirby later in 1935, or early the following year, because he had met a young actress, Lu-Anne Meredith. On the rebound from David, Jo Kirby met the man she would marry, Eric Clay.

Later, when she had already started going out with Eric Clay, she was travelling from London to Cheshire with him. She was supposed to have finished completely with David. She was on the train, and suddenly said she simply couldn't bear it any longer. She got off the train and caught the next train back to London.

This scene, so similar to one enacted by Celia Johnson in BRIEF ENCOUNTER a decade later, should, by all the laws of drama, have brought about a reconciliation. Alas, it did not.

"But she knew, in her hearts of hearts," recalled Catrine, "that it would never have worked. He was just too interested in other women and she had the feeling that he just never would be faithful. She was dead right about him, but I don't think being dead right makes much difference to how you feel. David Lean was the only man she ever talked to me about."[33]

When Jo Kirby returned to Cheshire, a final coincidence: her main suitor was a man called Philip Toosey, who would later distinguish himself in the Second World War by his conduct in a Japanese prisoner-of-war camp. He was upset by the performance of Alec Guinness in a film called THE BRIDGE ON THE RIVER KWAI which was said to have been based on him.[34]

CHAPTER NINE

LOVE CUTTING

DAVID thought he would one day become a director, though he was very cautious about predicting when this would be. In 1935, he was invited to join the John Stafford company at Elstree, with a vague promise that he would eventually be able to direct. Meanwhile he would simply continue as editor.

Among the films he cut for them was BALL AT THE SAVOY. David was intrigued by the Savoy background - he had nostalgic memories of the Savoy Hill radio station from the 2LO days - and by the fact that the suave Hollywood actor, Conrad Nagel, was the star. But even more intriguing than Nagel was a glamorous "Dorchester Girl" called Lu-Anne Meredith, playing the part of Mary.

Although managed by a British promoter, Felix Ferry, the Dorchester Girls were American. They danced at the famous Park Lane hotel in a troupe known as Les Girls. Most of London's most eligible bachelors were after them; one even had an affair with the Duke of Kent, which had to be hushed up, and another later married Marcus Sieff.

David fell for Lu-Anne on celluloid. She was not particularly gifted as an actress, but she was charming and very pretty.[1] David embarked on what he called "love cutting", working late, cutting around the awkward bits of her performance and going back and forth through all the out-takes, doing everything he could to improve the performance.

The female lead, Marta Labarr, happened to be the girlfriend of the director, Victor Hanbury. David and Hanbury had tremendous fights about the editing but Hanbury lacked the knowledge necessary to re-cut the picture, so Lu-Anne had her moment of glory on the silver screen, courtesy of David's editing.

When the film had its opening, David went up and introduced himself. Lu-Anne was used to men pretending to know her and she simply snubbed him. She had no idea who he was, while he felt he knew her intimately. He persevered and Lu-Anne was quickly charmed. They moved into a flat in a block called Cygnet House in the King's Road, Chelsea.

Lu-Anne dreamed of marriage, and David went so far as to speak to her mother over the transatlantic telephone. But he was not yet a free agent.

"It had been four years since David left me," said Isabel. "Edward came to Knockholt for the weekend and told me, 'David is not coming back. Please divorce him.' So I did. I went by myself to the Law Courts in the Strand. I hadn't anybody to go with me - father had been ill. I remember going up the stairs and standing in the box. I remember them asking me questions and I remember the judge nodding his head. Then it was all over."[2]

David did not defend the action. Isabel received a small sum from him for maintenance, but a few years later she received a letter from David's solicitor saying it would shortly be coming to an end.

I asked Isabel if, looking back on it, she was sorry she had married David Lean. "No," she said firmly. "I loved him." [3]

Why David went so far as to ask for a divorce, and then failed to go through with the marriage to Lu-Anne, is unknown. His relationship with her came to an abrupt end, David vanished and the iron door was slammed. Lu-Anne was devastated. She didn't want to go back to America, and the Dorchester period was over, so she married a man from one of the theatrical agencies who promised to take care of her.[4]

David had fallen for a Hungarian actress in BALL AT THE SAVOY called Esther Kiss. "He worshipped her, but wouldn't do anything about it because of her husband," said Kay Walsh. Esther Kiss was married to Steven Pallos, a member of the Korda organisation, whom David liked.

Now that he had reverted to his bachelor existence, David again rented a flat in the Mount Royal building at Marble Arch. It was new, and few of its flats were occupied, though those that were seemed to be inhabited by film industry people. But David's exalted salary of thirty pounds a week enabled him to indulge his passion for travel. He decided to go to Italy.

"On the way to Capri, starting off across the Bay of Naples, I sat on my sofa seat on this boat, which was open-decked, and I saw a chap sitting opposite me, quite a few years older than I was, and I thought, 'My God, that's Noël Coward.' He was reading. I never spoke to him, of course. I was fascinated. Obviously I never dreamed that I would ever work with him.

"You landed at the harbour at Capri, got a bus up the hill, and you walked into the piazza, a fascinating place where you met all kinds of people, strange, beautiful. And if you went down through the piazza to the other side of the island, there was Piccolo Marina, the little harbour, and above that was a place called the Pensione Weber, owned by two German sisters. I stayed there until my money ran out and then I'd come back to England to cut another film."[5]

Paul Czinner's next film was to be SAINT JOAN by George Bernard Shaw, a prestige production all the more remarkable because of Shaw's stubborn refusal - since a brief attempt in 1930 - to permit his plays to be filmed. Alexandre Benois, who had designed NAPOLEON for Abel Gance, had produced an impressive series of designs. David expected to be asked to edit it.

"Paul, in a fit of total madness," said Dallas Bower, "decided that he was concerned about the Catholic public and was worried Fox wouldn't put up the money if there was a Catholic boycott. Without telling anyone - without even telling Shaw - he submitted it formally to Father Martindale, who was the Papal representative in London. And one of the famous Shaw postcards arrived: 'Under no circumstances will you use my play.'"

Shaw wrote to James Bridie, whom Czinner had approached to write the screenplay, "I have now cried off the film and excommunicated Czinner with bell, book and candle."[6]

"Everyone was very put out," said Dallas Bower, "It transpired that in the middle of that week, Czinner and Bergner had dinner with J.M. Barrie. And in clouds of pipe smoke, he said, 'Why don't you make *As You Like It*? You did so very well with it in Germany.' And the following day, without knowing what Barrie had said, I remarked, 'By all accounts Elisabeth is a wonderful Rosalind. Why don't you....'

"Elisabeth said, 'That clinches it. That's what we're going to do.'"[7]

In the bar-cum-restaurant at Mount Royal, David met some of the other tenants, both English and American: Noah Beery, who had played Sergeant Lejaune in BEAU GESTE; mouth organist Larry Adler, who was evicted for having a girl in his room; Will Hay, the comedian; Marcus Sieff, the future millionaire owner of Marks and Spencer; and a young producer from Central Europe called Sam Spiegel, who made a play for David's French girlfriend, Monique Denys-Amiel.

"One of the people I met at Mount Royal was Robert Wyler, the younger brother of William Wyler," said David. "I became great friends with him. He directed a couple of films which were not successful, and he wrote a bit - not successfully - but he was a thoroughly nice man, and a bit nuts, I think.

"When I came back from Capri, Dr Czinner asked to see me. He said, 'We are going to do Shakespeare's *As You Like It* with Elisabeth and Laurence Olivier. We'd like you to cut it.'"

David said he'd think about it and went back to Robert Wyler. Wyler, who knew that David was an idiot as far as money and contracts were concerned, devised a plan. He pointed out that David was already earning a high salary and if the plan failed he would still be offered other pictures. Wyler's plan required David to have a hat - something he had not worn since his City bowler.

"Now," said Wyler. "you come into the office and you sit down and you put the hat on the desk opposite Czinner. He will say, 'We want you to cut AS YOU LIKE IT and we hope you'll be doing it for the same salary.' They may be very generous and offer you another five pounds. You say, 'I'm sorry, I can't accept that. If I'm going to work with you again I want a big rise. I want to be equal to the top American people. I want sixty pounds a week.'"

David was sure they would never agree to it.

Wyler said, "There will be tremendous exclamation about the sixty pounds, so let them say, 'Ridiculous, never heard of such a thing!' and gradually take your hat off the desk and put it in your lap and start to push your chair back. You say, 'I'm very sorry to hear this,' and you start walking towards the door. I guarantee they won't let you open it."

David did as Wyler suggested. "I asked for sixty pounds, picked up the hat, went for the door and they said, 'Wait a minute.' I laughed."

They asked for time to discuss the proposition. It was a vast sum for an editor. They pointed out that David was English, as if that fact placed a limit on his salary. David said that he was as good as the Americans.

"I went back the next day and they had thought it over and they agreed to the sixty pounds a week. It was double anything that the English were ever paid for cutting. So in no time, I was as rich as Croesus. It was a tremendous salary and it became a kind of joke that an English chap had done this. I was highly respected for it, at the same time. And that was all due to Bobby Wyler."[8]

As David, at the age of twenty-eight, became the highest paid editor in Britain, Isabel was visited by a bailiff. She and Peter had moved to Wembley and were finding it difficult to make ends meet.

David now had four assistants at his cutting-room at B&D: Vera Campbell, Gordon Pilkington, Nicky Bruce (the son of the Russian ballerina Tamara Karsavina), and a very junior assistant, Dick Best, whose sole job was to splice the reels on the foot-operated Bell and Howell joiner.

David used his assistants efficiently. He had his Moviola fitted on a low stand, and he sat in a wooden arm chair in the middle of the room. One assistant stood on his left and fed him the shots and the other stood on his right. To this assistant he handed the trims, which were hung on the trim bin.

"I have never seen this system before or since," said Dick Best. "All the editors I know like to be alone when they are 'creating.' I certainly did when I began editing, and I sat as far in the corner as I could - with an eye on the door awaiting the enemy! David had his back to the door, all of which proves that he was firmly in charge even then.

"We all knew he was earning sixty pounds a week, a phenomenal sum in those days. I believe Jack Harris at Twickenham was getting twenty-five. He was considered the finest editor when David started directing.

"David was treated almost like a guru by his assistants. I am sure, had there been only one chair in the bar at the Red Lion, David would have hunched in it, and we would have been sitting at his feet absorbing his psychology of life. He was very much into psychology then.

"At least two of us rushed to buy an identical sports jacket to the one he had found in Shaftesbury Avenue - pale blue with half-belt and 'blouse' type back. Very dashing!

"To me, David is the patron saint of cinema. More than anyone, he knew exactly what made a film tick."[9]

When AS YOU LIKE IT fell behind schedule, David suggested that Peggy Hennessey, who had cut three pictures since working with David on ESCAPE ME NEVER, was brought in to cut a couple of sequences.

The salary he was earning enabled him to sell his Invicta and buy a Lagonda sports car. He was so proud of it that he gave each of his assistants a ride up the A1 - one passenger at a time - at the then indictable speed of seventy miles per hour.

On AS YOU LIKE IT, David encountered a figure who would leave as deep an impression on him as he had left on the cinema itself. Carl Mayer had been responsible for the scripts of many of the classics of the cinema - THE CABINET OF DR CALIGARI, THE LAST LAUGH and SUNRISE. David, who admired all those films, particularly SUNRISE, regarded his meeting with Mayer as "one of the joys of my life".

"I got to know Carl Mayer very well," he said, "He was a dear man, he had grizzly white hair, very short, always a smile in his eyes and he used to come up and see me in the cutting-rooms.

"I remember showing Czinner and Mayer a reel I'd just cut and the lights went up and Carl said, 'My dear, you have cut too short the sving ins and the sving outs.'

"I said, 'What's a swing in and a swing out?' And he then explained it to me. He said, 'With a good actor, he takes the line and then gives his reply. A bad actor just replies. You don't see him absorb the line and then come in with his line.'

Laurence Olivier did not enjoy working on AS YOU LIKE IT with Elisabeth Bergner - nor did David. Photograph by Harry Saunders.

"And I remembered Merrill White saying to me, 'You can tell how good an actor is by the number of pictures you can use before he opens his mouth and after he shuts it.'

"And that's also true, and that's the swing in and the swing out. If someone gives a line to an actor and they reply, it's pat-ball, but a really great actor takes it and wallop - as it's left his racquet something is happening and in your mind's eye you are seeing it whiz across that net to be replied to by the other player."[10]

David's work on AS YOU LIKE IT added to his already glittering prestige. And yet, behind the confident façade there still was the inadequate "younger" brother struggling to overcome what he regarded as his own ignorance. Years later, after his involvement with Olivier's HENRY V, Dallas Bower approached David with the idea of filming MACBETH with Olivier.

"David gave me the most marvellous dinner at the White Tower and he said, 'Why you've asked me I can't think because I won't be able to handle it. Didn't you notice me fumbling an awful lot on AS YOU LIKE IT? The trouble with me is I've never understood what Shakespeare's lines were all about.'

"This extraordinary admission! I said, 'No, I didn't notice you fumbling because I had such a dreadful time myself, quite frankly.' I had to finish it. Bergner had appendicitis two-thirds of the way through. Czinner decided he had to be at her side, so there it was, and we were behind schedule. I had to do two sequences - the Phoebe sequence and all the pickups had to be done. I had two Hollywood cameramen, Hal Rosson and Lee Garmes, to cope with and I must say they were wonderful. David must have had the most awful battle with it. Of course, he cut it excellently. He was on the set very little."[11]

Laurence Olivier disliked Bergner and Czinner and did the film much against his will. David remembered him as a surly young man, whom Czinner cajoled from take to take with caviar sandwiches. Although he thought AS YOU LIKE IT a better film than HENRY V, he felt that Bergner, being Austrian, was miscast.

"During the production, Paul Czinner may have been late," said Vera Campbell, "but David was very naughty, too. He was having a romp with some girl and off he went in his car for the weekend. I got a telegram from him saying, 'STILL FIFTY MILES AWAY STALL THE DOCTOR'.

"Czinner turned up and said, 'Where's David?' I made up some fantastic story."

Vera would get in early and David might not arrive until after lunch. This meant that they would have to work late. Vera had to take digs at Borehamwood because on many occasions they worked too late for public transport. And no one was paid any overtime. Around ten in the evening, the technicians would gather at the canteen - a wooden shack with a tin roof and an open stove - and the sergeant would fry them sausages, bacon and eggs.

"David was much more relaxed by this time," said Vera Campbell. "We used to talk about our conscience towards our industry. How awful the waste was, and how we would reorganise the film industry. How disgraceful it was to have more than five takes of anything. (I took him to task about that when I met him after one of his big films!)

"I used to get very cross because, despite the late nights, I didn't want to do anything else except be in the cutting-rooms with the boys. It was lovely. But David would say, 'Well, Vera, you'd better get some sleep.' We'd have a little fight about it. I'd say, 'I don't see why it should be me when the boys aren't going.' I'd be chucked out and told to go home. And next morning I'd go around and say, 'What have you been doing? How far have you got?' I was terribly jealous of the work. I couldn't bear to miss anything.

"We were working on New Year's Eve. We all piled into the cars and drove to the Albert Hall and we bunked in with the floats for the Chelsea Arts Ball. As the doors opened, the floats went in and we'd all be hanging on like mad. We put on paper hats and made ourselves look jolly. We usually knew someone who had a box and some champagne and we used to scrounge our way round, dancing like crazy." [12]

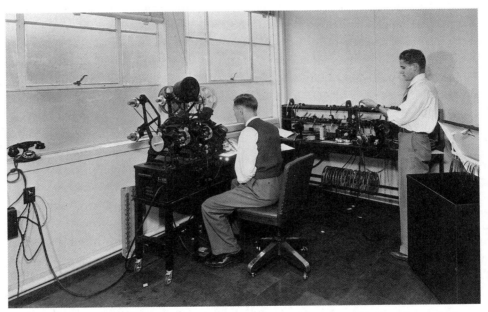

A typical cutting-room of the 1930s - the editor makes the cuts on the Moviola while the assistant makes the splices and files the trims.

CHAPTER TEN

DREAMING LIPS

KAY Walsh is now remembered as one of the leading film actresses of her generation, appearing in such notable films as IN WHICH WE SERVE, OLIVER TWIST, TUNES OF GLORY and THE RULING CLASS. In 1936, she was a chorus girl who had recently embarked on a few parts in film and in the theatre.

Kathleen Walsh was twenty-two years old. Her grandparents had come over from Ireland and settled in Pimlico, a decision for which she would always be grateful since it was close to Chelsea and fine houses.

As children, Kay and her sister, Peggy, lived with their grandmother, Betsy. "She was a darling, really, but a bit of a tippler. She would go to the Six Bells in the King's Road for her daily refreshment. There was a little cinema on the corner of Old Church Street and she would leave us there for an afternoon. It's rather classy now and cut up into four cinemas. Then it was a fleapit and smelled of dry wee-wee. There was a woman at the piano with the light shining on her, and another woman who pumped disinfectant into the air. I thought it had the scent of sweet lavender, and that the picture palace - my palace - was the most wonderful place in the world."

Kay was first taken to the cinema at the age of three, in 1917, and the experience gave her the finest possible education in cinema, even if the more conventional aspects of her education were overlooked.

"I had no education whatsoever," she insists, although, like so many self-educated people, she is very well-read, with a remarkable feeling for the language. In her early eighties, she looks many years younger, the upward-tilted eyes and the humorous mouth still recognisable from the films of her youth. If she speaks with that slightly intimidating Mayfair accent considered so necessary for stage and film work in the thirties, she has a sense of humour which had me in paroxysms of mirth. Despite the fact that she was hard at work on an autobiography herself, she answered all my questions with unstinting generosity, occasionally saying, "I'm not giving you that," and then telling me anyway.

On Friday 25 September 1936, Kay and her friend Betty had been to Leicester Square to see MY MAN GODFREY, starring Carole Lombard and William Powell. As they got home - a little house in Warwick Mews, near Little Venice in London, for which she paid eighteen shillings a week - the phone was ringing, and Kay rushed upstairs, thinking it was her fiancé calling from Switzerland. It wasn't; it was a woman called Beryl.

"I thought, 'Oh, my God. She knows I've been working and she's going to borrow money from me.'

"She said, 'Kay, will you help me? I've got three boys here and they're driving me crazy. Will you take them off my hands and give them a cup of coffee? They're really quite nice.'

"I was so relieved she wasn't going to borrow any money I said, 'Yes, of course, I will.'"

Ten minutes later, a taxi drove up with three young men - David Lean, Reggie Mills and Charles Clinton-Thomas. They knew that Kay was an actress and had just done a film with James Mason and Valerie Hobson.[1] She learned that David was a film editor and Reggie was his assistant, and they were cutting DREAMING LIPS with Elisabeth Bergner. Kay loved Bergner[2] and had cried all through ESCAPE ME NEVER, so they became immediate friends.

"We had coffee, beer and my wind-up gramophone. The room was blue with smoke - we were all chain smokers. They were very nice and when they left I opened the window to get rid of the smoke and went to bed thinking what a nice, sweet, cuddly bear Reggie Mills was."

Kay went to work in a "quota quickie" at Nettlefold Studios, Walton-on-Thames, and she stayed at the local pub. Betty, a chorus-girl who sometimes shared the Warwick Mews house, rang up to say that a mass of flowers had arrived with a card from David, thanking her for the delightful evening. When she returned there were two more phone messages from David. And when he rang again, he asked Kay to have tea with him and suggested they go and listen to gramophone records.

They met in a gramophone shop next door to Lyon's Corner House in Coventry Street, which was to become their "club" later on. They were jammed together in a booth no bigger than a phone box, listening to jazz records and chain smoking.

"Then he said to me - I must have been so stupid - 'Would you like to come back and hear these on my radiogram?' Because listening to them in a booth was not ideal. I said yes, that would be lovely."

By this time, David had moved out of Mount Royal and rented a room from Beryl at 2 Montagu Place. David had a front room on the second floor and Reggie Mills had a room at the back. Beryl ran it very well, with two North Country maids who served breakfast.

"David played the records," said Kay. "Stephane Grappelli, Django Reinhardt, Benny Goodman, Jack Teagarden, Harry James... The radiogram was wedged between the windows, the only piece of furniture that wasn't Beryl's. I sat on the chair, he sat on the radiogram, struck a graceful pose and showed me his magnificent profile.

"I looked at this beautiful piece of sculpture and thought, 'I've been jammed in a booth with this man and in my little mews house and I hadn't noticed what a stunning creature he is."

David told her that he had made a hash of his life, that he was divorced and had a little boy of five whose education he was worried about. Kay told him of a remarkable man called A.S. Neill, whose book, *Summerhill*, described his educational experiments at Dartington Hall and Bedales.

"We drank sherry and played some more records. We talked about films and books, books and films, and then he got off the gramophone and lit two cigarettes and put one in my mouth. I saw Paul Henreid and Bette Davis do it years later.[3] I thought it was thrilling and romantic. He told me I was the most unusual person he'd ever met - he'd been thinking about me ever since our first evening. He took the cigarette out of my mouth and kissed me. He locked the door against a possible invasion by Beryl, turned out the lights and made love to me.

"That evening, we went to the Café Royal, in Regent Street, and had dinner on the balcony from where we looked down at Bohemia. I went home that night to my little flat. I had been struck by lightning."

Kay broke off her engagement to her fiancé - Pownell Pellew, the ninth Viscount Exmouth - and threw herself into the vortex with David Lean.

"We worked all day and danced all night and slept through the weekend, waking late on Sunday to make love, to read the Sunday papers and to breakfast on eggs and bacon. And, of course, we went out to a film. We were asked everywhere - we were an attractive couple, we enjoyed life enormously. His tune

Kay Walsh photographed by David.

for me was, 'I've Got You Under My Skin' by Cole Porter and our restaurant was Oddenino's, just behind the Café Royal.[4]

"I only had one doubt about him. He did not read and he had no interest in my passion - the theatre. He liked the Corner House, he liked smoking, and he liked cutting and talking films.

"I dragged him to the theatre. The first play I made him see was *I Have Been Here Before* by J.B. Priestley and what David enjoyed most was Wilfrid Lawson giving a stunning performance. Next time I pushed him into a theatre was to see *On Your Toes* with Vera Zorina. He loved that because of 'Slaughter on Tenth Avenue.'

"But normally, if you went to the theatre with David, it had to have a screen, a projectionist and maybe a Wurlitzer coming up. We loved the Academy Cinema and Studio One in Oxford Street and the Rialto in Coventry Street and would watch one, sometimes two or three films a day."

David took her to run-throughs of DREAMING LIPS, which was almost complete. At one of these, he introduced her to Carl Mayer.

"I loved Carl," said Kay. "We used to meet him at the bar of Scott's, the fish restaurant in a side street by the London Pavilion. He always brought us a bunch of violets, a film magazine or a cutting from a newspaper. He was so *gemütlich*. David used to say, 'She's written a story - darling, tell Carl.' And suddenly I'm telling this great man these frightful stories which David thought were so wonderful."[5]

DREAMING LIPS - a story of musicians, in which the wife of an orchestra leader has an unhappy affair with a star soloist - was financed by Max Schach. An émigré from Czechoslovakia, Schach had had one success, ABDUL THE DAMNED, made for British International Pictures. On the strength of this, Schach advanced the Czinners £100,000 for two films. When the first, DREAMING LIPS, flopped, Max Schach vanished.

"There was despair in the cutting-rooms," said Kay Walsh. "David and I went up to Max Schach's office at the top of Regent Street - the furniture had gone and it was absolutely bare. Unopened mail littered the floor. And David, who had been earning sixty pounds a week, was flat broke. He had saved nothing - not one penny. Schach owed everyone money. David was owed several weeks."

It was not the best time to find another job. David's reputation as the highest paid cutter in England was suddenly a hindrance. For, after a boom, in 1936 the industry had entered its worst slump since 1924. There was widespread unemployment and acute distress. Of six hundred and forty companies registered between 1925 and 1936, only twenty remained by 1937.

By this time, Kay had met David's brother, Edward, who now worked on the liberal paper, the *News Chronicle*. Edward was editor of the leader page, ballet critic and book reviewer.

"Edward was terrifying to start with," said Kay. "He had startling looks. He looked a bit like David, but he hadn't got that sculpted look. Edward was depressed and envious of his brother's tremendous success with women. And David was envious of his brother's superior mind."

Edward was living at 56 Curzon Street, above the Mirabelle restaurant, and since he was going to Egypt for a month, he offered them his flat. "We moved into this luxurious flat with his wonderful library - all his D.H. Lawrence books that I grabbed and drank in - but we had no money. David's room with Beryl was two pounds a week and he hadn't got two pounds. I had some money because I'd been in this film with James Mason."

Edward's flat was a short walk from the Curzon, which was London's most luxurious and expensive cinema.[6] Opened in 1934, it was run by the Marquis de Casa Maury, a decorative artist who had been impressed by the elegant simplicity of some of the cinemas he'd seen in Paris. The Curzon was fitted with unusually comfortable seats and the three rows of club seats at the back provided unparalleled luxury.

"Oh, the love seats at the back!" said Kay. "We didn't have the money for those doubles. We often queued in the pouring rain - there was no cover, no protection - and we would see Raimu, Gabin, Jouvet. We adored those films.

"We would come out and just near 56 Curzon Street was a tiny Italian cafe. We would duck in there, soaking wet, and just have enough money for a couple of cups of coffee. All the most gorgeous prostitutes used to come in and I noticed their beautiful clothes and shoes.

"Back at No 56, we were intimidated by the porter, who knew that we weren't married and could see that we were a little dirty at the hem. We were always a little scared by him.

"When Edward came back there was nothing for it but for David to move in with me and that is where we spent the months when he was unemployed.

"Despite earning sixty pounds a week, he had no car and no overcoat. When he moved in, he arrived in a small van, and out came his radiogram, which had to be hauled in through the window as it wouldn't go up my narrow stairs. He had a 16mm camera, a projector, a small laundry box with some clothes, a pile of debts and that was that. No books, no pictures. It was over in minutes."

Warwick Mews was an idyllic spot in those days.[7] Like all mews, it was built as stables to house the carriages and horses for the wealthier houses nearby. It was reached through an impressive arch. In the first house lived a chimney sweep - still an essential occupation in the thirties, when most houses had coal fires. Then there was Mr French, the builder and decorator.

"It didn't matter if there was a lavatory seat outside my door when we came back at night. We left our door-key on the drainpipe. Trees hung over the wall of the garden beyond the wall. It was safe and peaceful."

Their local cinema was The Regal, Harrow Road, which cost them only ninepence. One night, coming back from the cinema, David stopped on the bridge across the Grand Union Canal. Just below, on a green verge, artists had built little studios. The gate was ajar...

"The setting was so beautiful," said Kay. "The canal, the painted boats, the little studio. I sat there looking at his magnificent head. He told me, 'I am not what you think I am.' He was honest and warned me that life with him would be very, very difficult, and that he had damaged so many women and didn't want to damage me.

"But one is so arrogant when in love - so sure that love will take care of absolutely everything. We walked back, stopping to kiss every minute as lovers do, and I thought, 'I will love him until the day I die.' And I very nearly did.[8]

"He never changed his address and I never badgered him. The denial game had started! Reggie Mills would bring his post over from Montagu Place and most of it was from the Inland Revenue. One was a colossal bill from Belgium, because he had crashed his car on his way back from a trip from Italy - he was certain he could get it shipped over, but now he couldn't even pay the bill to have it repaired. Reggie was a loyal go-between and never betrayed him in any way, but one or two little love letters slipped under my nose. Quite a catalogue. So that's when I heard about 'Love in a Haystack' - when he was staying with Clarence and Wynne - and that's when I heard about Jo Kirby. And Lu-Anne Meredith.

"Edward used to give us tickets for the ballet. The Opera House was not full and David and I would be in a box, thank God, because we looked all right from the waist up, but down below his trousers were frayed beyond repair. We hadn't got our bus fare home! He liked ballet well enough. I loved it. I was a trained dancer - Greek and mime were my forte."

Sometimes at Warwick Mews, David would pin a white tablecloth to the wall, set up his Bell & Howell projector and give Kay a film show.

"These were the films he had taken on his holidays and they were magnificent. Without doubt he would be a film director extraordinaire. There was always a gorgeous red-headed girl or a blonde in them and I'd say. 'Who's that beauty?' And he'd say, 'Oh, that's Charles Clinton-Thomas's fiancée' or something like that. Lies, of course. Whoppers."

Kay had no dreams of being an actress - she didn't think she would be good enough. She wanted to be a writer. One day in 1936, when David and Kay were strolling down the Edgware Road, he made a remark which revealed his dreams if not his ambitions. He greatly admired Fritz Lang's DR MABUSE films, written by his wife, Thea von Harbou.

"I will be Fritz Lang," he declared, "and you will be my Thea von Harbou."[9]

In December 1936, Kay opened at the Embassy Theatre, Swiss Cottage, in a play called *The Melody That Got Lost*, with Lady Tree, Esmond Knight, May Hallett and Victoria Hopper, the wife of Basil Dean. After Dean saw the play, Kay found herself offered a year's contract at Ealing Studios.

"I've never suffered so much in my life as I suffered at that studio," she said. "They were absolute monsters, and they all thought I was Basil Dean's girlfriend to start off with. They were all Freemasons; they would never give David a job because he had the wrong handshake. He went after a job once and came back and said, 'No hope.'"

Kay was assigned to a comedy with George Formby called KEEP FIT. It was a job many talented actresses had been tested for. But when she got the job, Kay was dismayed that David failed to show any particular interest

"I never remember him saying, 'Let me hold your script to see if you know your lines,' or 'What will you wear? What's the cameraman like?' People who are living together, whether married or not, must have some things in common. They must be interested in each other. 'Did you have a good day, dear? Would you like a gin and tonic?' But he never had that. My interest was in him."

When she returned, tired, from Ealing, she found that David was invariably out. Kay would wait up for him, anxious and upset, and would arrive at the studio next morning, exhausted. Despite his seeming indifference, Kay was anxious about David's morale; he was clearly becoming depressed.

"I had seen so much poverty and unemployment and so much violence as a child, I knew what it meant for a man to hang on to his sanity. Unemployment is a terrible thing; it diminishes. The inactivity was seriously affecting David. One day he came back from the Corner House and said, 'I just went past the Tourist Bureau. Oh, I would love to go on a cruise. It would do me so much good.'

"And I thought, 'Why not? I've got the money.' It cost me fifty pounds. I carried on working with Formby at Ealing. While David was away he sent me a telegram asking for five pounds. I cabled him the money. He always found money for film stock and when he came back he showed the film to me and Reggie. There was a girl carrying a huge teddy bear. I had a feeling afterwards that the girl and that teddy bear were somehow connected with my five pounds. I laughed when I was thinking about it - far removed from any rage or anything. From my point of view, it was unconditional love. But long afterwards I had the feeling that he had picked up a girl who was going on a cruise and he had said, 'I will join you.'

"There was a part of David nobody knows about, the Beckett side of him. When they talk about David looking into the distance, David's not thinking about the scene or the lens. He's looking into his guilty sub-conscious half the time. This, as I discovered later, was a disturbed, split man."

One night Kay and David had a tremendous row. She locked him out and watched him walk angrily away into the rain. But he came back.

"As a kind of coming-together gift to ourselves, we decided to go on a smashing holiday, a binge. I got four hundred pounds for this Formby film, but I had asked for it to be paid weekly - sixteen pounds a week - because I was so scared of all my responsibilities."

In 1937, another World War seemed inevitable. The Spanish Civil War was proof that Fascist Italy and Nazi Germany had no compunction about dropping bombs on civilians. Mussolini, the Italian dictator, was not an unpopular figure in England, but the combination of anti-Fascist propaganda and the slump caused tourism to Italy to fall away. Il Duce tried to offset this by encouraging people with what Kay called "Mussolini tickets", a cheap method of travel which included accommodation. Tickets were classified from A to D.

"It was so glamorous," said Kay. "We arrived in Paris at six on the Golden Arrow and the night train went out at eleven.[10] David wanted a cup of tea, and where do you think we went? W. H. Smith - they had a tea room on the first floor of their shop on the Place de la Madeleine. That's a bit of Croydon creeping through!"[11]

When they reached Italy, they started off with the A tickets, staying at the Excelsior in Naples. Then David introduced Kay to his enchanted island.

"We used to row around Capri in Sandalinas with glass bottoms. David would have a bath towel over his head, filming underwater life like Jacques Cousteau. And he took wonderful films of me, but not because he wanted to photograph *me*. I would climb mountains only to find later when I saw it that he wanted a little figure to break up a cloud, and I'd sweated up there for three hours.

"The biggest hotel in Capri was the Quisisana[12] - the elegant Duchess of Kent stayed there. Meals were served in the garden and there was a glass dance floor, and David looked absolutely stunning in a shirt and slacks. We were an attractive couple and we would hear this chatter-chatter from Noël Coward and Somerset Maugham. I don't know who the other people were, but they were in the Mountbatten class. We danced till three in the morning.

"As for Fascism, David had no time and no mind for politics. We never discussed politics. They were something that we left to Edward. Films were a substitute for real life. What you and I may know of real life would be a Moviola away, if you know what I mean. We hardly listened to the news, we were in such a whirl the whole time."[13]

From Capri they returned to Naples and then sailed to Venice, via Dubrovnik in Yugoslavia. David did not mention his visit to Venice; instead, he suggested that they went up to the mountains to see the other locations of ESCAPE ME NEVER - the Grossglockner glacier in the Dolomites and Cortina d'Ampezzo, It was here they reached the Es of the Mussolini tickets - a wooden hut with no running water.

"We were in Cortina for three or four days, and it rained incessantly. On our way to the Grossglockner, we went to the Post Office, and there, believe it or not, in white stockings, black shoes and a little dirndl was Elisabeth Bergner."

Bergner invited them to dinner at her hotel. "We were getting ready in the bathroom and there was a crash on the door of our little wooden hotel and it was old Czinner. 'Are you making love, my darlings? Are you both in the bath together?' He couldn't resist it.

"Anyway, we went to dinner with them. I was besotted by Bergner as an actress, and this was the first time I'd met her. I remember feeling that I was a very ordinary, very simple guest with a great actress and there was a little bit of a performance which I would rather have done without. David was completely at ease. I think he probably had a love affair with her on the Moviola and she was very pleased. She and Paul loved him.

"I had met Paul with David when they were finishing DREAMING LIPS. It was a showing of the final cut and Carl Mayer was there. At the end of the film, Bergner drowns herself. And Carl said to me, 'You see how clever your David is, Kay?' And he explained that it was David's idea to turn the last shot upside down so that 'THE END' could undulate with the water.

"They had an appointment with their architect at four in the morning and we all went climbing up the mountain. I could hear the sound of a brook where the land was plotted out for the house that was never built. When we came back to London, we had to take beer bottles back to the pub, the Warwick Castle, so we could put a shilling in the gas meter."

David's mother had moved from Croydon to Mayfield in Sussex in 1934. At weekends, David and Kay might go down to her house, Twelve Paths, where Kay would be puzzled by the strange way in which David addressed her - "Would mum like her chair by the window?" He was never able to use the Quaker style of "thee" and "thou" and this was his compromise.

Helena was still a handsome woman, but Kay found her embittered, full of suppressed anger at the loss of Frank, and at David's habit of bringing down his girlfriends. Kay learned that David, every time he found a new girl, presented her to his mother, his father and his brother. It was a sort of ritual for all of them. Kay wondered if it was done simply to antagonise Edward.

She was struck by Edward's powerful personality and his strange study, which was painted black with black curtains and a black carpet and, as she put it, "full of black moods". Edward belonged as much to that cottage as he did to his flat in Curzon Street.

"He would be up in the morning and whether we liked Sibelius or not, it came blasting through that thin little house. Or he would charge out like

Rochester with a wild look. But underneath it all, there was something touching and attractive and extremely artistic…"

David set up a darkroom at Warwick Mews, and Kay had acted as his model. She now found that Edward was a skilful photographer, too. During a walk in the woods they found a plover's nest.

"Edward took photographs of the eggs in the nest and then we went back to lunch. In half an hour he left the table, went back and took another photograph when there was a little crack in the shell and he did that every half-hour until the little beak appeared and the whole bird came through. David was a wonderful photographer but I think Edward was better."

Each time David and Kay left Mayfield to return to London, Helena, whose house was near the railway line, would wave her handkerchief at the window, just as she and David and Edward used to wave to their father when he went up to the City.

"It always upset David, this memory of the handkerchief waving and the train going out… And we were usually accompanied by a bag of Cornish pasties and two pounds which she gave us, together with something to eat for the rest of the week, because all we had was our train fare."

When Kay, as well as David, was out of work, she was imaginative in her suggestions as to how they should spend their days.

"I had the idea that we should have the best free entertainment in the world - and that was the Law Courts. The big question was: should we take a bus from Warwick Avenue to Fleet Street or should we walk? If we took a bus, it was sixpence. If we walked there and back, it might have meant three-and-six to have our shoes soled and heeled. This was serious and it had to be thought out.

"The Law Courts provided pure theatre. It was tremendous fun just sitting there, watching the judges, the barristers and the witnesses. You could always tell the liars. We saw the most astonishing characters.

'We would go across the road to something called the ABC - the Aerated Bread Co. We would have milk and a dash and a roll and butter, and that was our lunch. Milk and a dash did not mean brandy. The dash was a drop of that filthy stuff called Camp Coffee that came out of a bottle. That was our lunch - and then back for the matinee and my God, it was wonderful.

"I also got him doing something that I had loved as a very small child - I took him to the music hall at the Met., Edgware Road. I used to go to the Holborn Empire with my father and I saw all those wonderful stars. It was so far from films, so far from David's background in every way. But he took to it because he could see the fun of it, the skill of it - he could see the discipline and the star quality of these music hall people. He was really excited about it, as well he might be.

"David liked the urchin he could see in me. In a way, I was his link with Mrs Egerton."

CHAPTER ELEVEN

CLIMBING BACK

AT long last, David got another editing job - THE LAST ADVENTURERS - in which Kay Walsh was cast. Like THE TURN OF THE TIDE, it was intended to be an authentic British film, shot on location in the style of Flaherty. The producer, Henry Passmore, and the cameraman, Eric Cross, with whom David had worked on MONEY FOR SPEED, joined the crew of a North Sea trawler and sailed into the Arctic Circle, filming exteriors which were so impressive that Passmore was able to raise the money for the rest of the film.

"But hardly any of them were used," said Eric Cross. "They insisted on a love story and Henry was disgusted, of course. Roy Kellino took over as director in the studio. David came on the set occasionally and I remember asking him to do a bit of direction and he said, 'No, I'm not ready for it yet.'"[1]

Kay Walsh, who also thought David should have directed the film, was taken aback at the speed with which he cut the film. Suddenly, they were both out of work again. "It was his damn fault for being so quick, otherwise we would have had a few more weeks' salary."[2]

Although Kay had dutifully paid her employment stamps from the moment she first joined the theatre, David had never bothered, so he was not eligible for the dole. After a few weeks, Kay thought of selling her clothes to raise money for food.

"I went on a bus with my suitcase to a dress agency in the Edgware Road. The woman offered me only two pounds, so I had to put them into the suitcase again and got back on the bus."

In the autumn of 1937, Kay was offered work on another George Formby film, I SEE ICE. The cameraman was Ronald Neame, whose talents would not be fully revealed until he joined David Lean and Anthony Havelock-Allan as a founder member of Cineguild.

Delightful as the Formby films were, they did not need imaginative camera-work, they simply needed to be brightly illuminated. But that illumination could sometimes reveal too much - there were complaints from Basil Dean that Kay Walsh was looking tired.

"Somebody said, 'Of course she's tired, she's out with David Lean every night.' And that was the first I'd ever heard of David Lean," said Ronald Neame.[3]

But Kay only wished she *had* been out with David. His absences, after their romantic trip, which Kay had hoped would prove the start of a new life, were profoundly depressing.

"Ronnie had a terrible time," said Kay. "He needed something stronger than gauze over the lens - he needed linoleum. You could put a pencil under my eye and it wouldn't fall out for the bags. Dean [director], Kimmins and Ronnie would see the rushes and come back with long faces. I was terrified I'd get the sack."[4]

When the lack of work threatened to become a way of life, David decided to ask his father for financial help. Frank and Margaret had moved to London - to 23 Norfolk Road, St John's Wood - and David went to see him, leaving Kay outside.

"David came out of the house," said Kay. "Buncs had refused to lend him fifty pounds, but he was carrying a silver cigarette box and he stuffed fifty cigarettes into David's pocket. David gave them right back. And we were dying for a fag!

"I borrowed fifty pounds from someone else and the first thing I did with it was to buy him an overcoat and two suits. Edward said, 'Katy, you have a Keynesian flair.'"

Perhaps Frank had good reason for his refusal, for he had not been ungenerous in the past. Perhaps some vestige of his Quaker morality would not allow it. David had been earning the astonishing sum of sixty pounds a week for two years and had nothing to show for it. Perhaps Frank thought it disgraceful that Isabel and Peter had not benefited - and perhaps he felt that a harsh period with no money at all would be a salutary lesson.

By an extraordinary coincidence, when I visited the Tangye sisters I was shown a short story from *Isis*, written by Tangye Lean long after he had ceased to edit the paper. Published in the issue of 2 November 1938, the story was called "In Debt". It was about a young man, who worked in the film industry and was trying to borrow money from his father.

I sent a copy of the article to Kay Walsh. She confirmed that Edward had written an account of David's attempt to borrow money from Frank. Instead of calling him David, Edward calls him Jonathan, and he made him an actor rather than a technician:

"'We don't see much of each other, do we?' said his father. 'You come round here two or three times running, and we don't see each other again for months. Sherry?'" And he tilted the liquid abruptly into a glass.

"Jonathan took it, smiling oppressedly at his hand. 'No,' he said. 'I suppose that's true.' He thought bitterly: 'But whose fault is it? You're glad enough to see me when I'm working - boast about me when I'm in a part - but now I'm out you'd rather meet a corpse.'"

Jonathan explains that the slump has thrown about three-quarters of those who had been involved in film-making out of work. Jonathan says, "You have a way of making me feel it's my fault" and asks for a loan.

His father says, "I'm afraid it's out of the question. The slump's hit me too, you know. Only yesterday we had to dismiss four people from the accounts, and the directors have accepted a cut of eighteen percent. To be frank, I'd hoped round about now you'd be in a position to relieve me from some of these burdens - it would have more than compensated me for the cost of your education... You know, Jon, this is a hard thing to say now, but I'm afraid you inherit your mother's carelessness about money. A sort of blind spot... After all, you were earning forty pounds a week only a year ago. Couldn't you have saved out of that? You see, I can't help asking myself what would be the use of lending you money, whether it wouldn't be kinder to let reality impress some of its harsher side on you."

The father is somewhat ashamed of himself. Jonathan decides to go. Father holds out the cigarette box and scoops out a handful. Jonathan takes only one and the story ends on an anti-climax.

"When the door had closed and he was outside on the doorstep it seemed to him for a clear, swift moment that he had no friends, had never had, and the last chance of raising money was gone."[5]

David's former assistant, Vera Campbell, was now living in Chelsea. Upstairs was a man called Peter Witt, an impresario who had staged several musicals.

George Bernard Shaw with Gabriel Pascal.

Vera had been out of work for some time when Witt recommended that she went and saw a friend of his, Gabriel Pascal, who was about to make a film with George Bernard Shaw.

"Peter made an appointment and I went along to Pascal's office at Bruton Street, where he was having his breakfast, boiled eggs, talking to everyone. Very Hungarian."

Pascal was a stocky, fiery, utterly un-English character with a dazzling, gap-toothed smile. His ambition to persuade George Bernard Shaw to let him film his plays was regarded by everyone as ridiculous and futile.

"Pascal interviewed me for the job. Peter had told him I was an editor. I said, 'I don't really feel I could take on a whole film just yet - I could do the rough cut, but I couldn't carry the whole film through.' I recommended David.

"Pascal said, 'Oh, I've heard of him. He's no good.'

"I was so angry. I said, 'What do you mean, he's no good?' At the end of my outburst, he said, 'Right. I will see him.'

"I telephoned David and told him. But neither of us heard anything for some time, because Gabby hadn't clinched it with Shaw."

Pascal was born Gabor Lehol in 1894 in Transylvania. After military school in Hungary, he began his career as an actor, with a stock company in Hamburg. He claimed to have worked in Germany with Max Reinhardt (though in fact he had worked with the less distinguished Robert Reinert).

In Berlin, Pascal had a liaison with his landlady's young sister. He refused to marry her and was in Holland when his son, Peter, was born. He did not return as he was busy romancing the munitions millionaire, Sir Basil Zaharoff, in an attempt to make films using blocked currency in China.

Pascal arrived in England and set about persuading Shaw to give him the rights to make films from his plays. Although Shaw had been one of the very first people to have been photographed and recorded on the Movietone system, he was sceptical about the cinema and had hated a German film of *Pygmalion* which was made in 1935. But his sympathy for eccentrics encouraged him to meet Pascal, a man with hardly any film experience.

David was flat broke when he was finally summoned to meet Pascal. There is an industry legend that he walked all the way from London to Pinewood to get the job. In fact, he only had to walk to Bruton Street, which is near Berkeley Square. Pascal and David took to each other at once.

"I had never encountered anything like him in my life," said David. "He appeared to me like an exotic flower - the orchid department. He was short, stocky, with jet black hair with a little grey in it, swept straight back over a bald head. The funny thing was that Pascal and I were complete opposites, but I liked him very much and he liked me. It was an interesting sort of mix."

Pascal was aware that David had been out of work and there was no scheme devised by Robert Wyler to inflate his salary. David was lucky to get forty pounds a week.

Vera Campbell had all but given up when David telephoned her to say they would both be working on PYGMALION. David had quite forgotten it was Vera who had suggested him in the first place...

As David got to know Pascal, so he heard the astonishing story of how he secured PYGMALION.

"There are various versions of it," said David, "but this is the true one. Pascal came to England. He had no money and he went to a Hungarian agent and said, 'I want to make films in this country of the works of famous English writers. Who do you represent?'

"The man said, 'Well, I represent H. de Vere Stacpoole.' He wrote *The Blue Lagoon*. 'No, no, no,' said Gabby. 'Bigger please.'

"The man mentioned a few more names and Gabby said, 'No, no, no,' and he got up to Somerset Maugham, whom I'm sure he didn't represent, and Gabby said, 'Well, yes - but who else?'

"And the agent said, 'I'll tell you the most important man I represent, Bernard Shaw.'

"So Gabby said, 'Well, get him.' The agent didn't know Bernard Shaw, so he said, 'Well, he's a very difficult gentleman. This will be very confidential. I'm afraid I must ask you to leave the room, and I'll talk to him on the telephone.'

"Gabby left the room. The agent looked him up in the phone book and there he was: Shaw, G.B., Whitehall Court. He rang him up and the voice said, 'Yes, who is that?'

"The agent said, 'Well, you don't know me, but I have a gentleman here who wants to make films of your plays.'

"Shaw asked him a few questions and to his amazement said, 'Bring him along at four o'clock this afternoon.' The agent put down the phone, called in Gabby and said, 'We have an appointment.'

"Gabby said, 'I'd like to take you to lunch, but I have no money. Will you lend me a pound? So the agent gave Gabby a pound, they both went out to lunch and after lunch Gabby said, 'I'm going to have a haircut and shave,' and after that they went along to Whitehall Court. They were shown into the study and Shaw said, 'Now, what do you want to do?'

"Gabby said, 'I would like to make a film of your *Pygmalion*.'

"Shaw opened a drawer and handed him a mimeographed list of the regulations for Hollywood producers; you cannot alter one line of dialogue without permission, you cannot cast without permission, you cannot do this, you cannot do that. Gabby read it all through and said, 'Master, I accept.'

"To which Shaw said, 'Mr Pascal, how much money have you got?'

"And Gabby put his hand in his pocket and took out half a crown. 'This is all I have in the world, and it is change from the pound that this gentleman lent me this morning.'

"Shaw said, 'Mr Pascal, you're the first honest film producer I have ever met. I'm going to let you have *Pygmalion*.' As they went towards the door, Shaw shuffled the agent out first. Keeping Gabby behind, he drew out a pound note and gave it to him. 'Please, Mr Pascal,' he said, 'take my advice, never owe money to an agent.'"[6]

Shaw had entrusted to Pascal a gold-mine of literary properties. But Pascal - known as "the hobo producer" during his brief visit to Hollywood - was inept at setting up deals and after two years, negotiating with everyone who would see him, he still had nothing to show for it. Even his fellow Hungarian, Alexander

Korda, turned him down, possibly out of pique, since he had been after Shaw's plays himself.

The trouble was that no one in the film industry wanted unadulterated Shaw. But in the spring of 1937, Pascal met Nicholas Davenport who formed a syndicate and put up the first £10,000. J. Arthur Rank agreed to distribute the film, subject to guarantors being found if it went over budget.

The original script of PYGMALION, by Cecil Lewis and W.P. Lipscomb, was not regarded as entirely satisfactory, though it had the blessing of Shaw, and David was under the impression that Shaw himself had written it. Since Shaw had insisted that Pascal should have complete artistic and production control - which was another way of way of saying *he* had it - lengthy script conferences were held. David attended several of these.

The ending of the play was not cinematic, so the script-writing consortium came up with a sequence showing Eliza returning to Professor Higgins' study to find him listening to a recording he had made during her first visit. In her new, refined voice she enunciates the next lines. We see Higgins from the back, still in his hat. He has to say something ambiguous which would suggest that the two are going to live together - or get married.

"Unless my ego plays me false," said David, "I think the line, 'Eliza, where

The marbles scene in PYGMALION *between Professor Higgins (Leslie Howard) and Eliza Doolittle (Wendy Hiller) was enhanced by a Leslie Howard ad lib. When Eliza swallowed one, he remarked, 'Don't bother, there are plenty more - have another!'*

the devil are my slippers?' was my idea and I remember getting a great kick when I saw *My Fair Lady* and found they too had used it."[7]

David was much in awe of Shaw's dialogue and was startled when Leslie Howard made a suggestion for the "Flintstone" scene. The scene shows Professor Higgins teaching Eliza how to speak with the aid of such accessories as a candle and marbles. The idea for Eliza putting a marble in her mouth may have come from Professor Tilly, a speech training expert who acted as adviser; when she swallowed one accidentally, Leslie Howard remarked, "Don't bother, there are plenty more - have another!" This raised such a laugh on the set that it was sneaked into the final film.[8]

People felt that the picture had to include a scene of Eliza at the ball, which was not in the play. The director, Anthony Asquith, was delegated to go to Shaw and persuade him. He was invited to lunch and the two men discussed music. When Asquith finally broached the subject, Shaw dismissed it. Mrs Shaw came to Asquith's rescue and made Shaw listen to his outline. Asquith, trembling with nerves, began to read. Shaw was struck by one phrase - "Eliza comes up the stairs with the frozen calm of the sleepwalker." This appealed to Shaw and he kept repeating the phrase, and the result was that he agreed to write the scene. The ball scene was intended to last four minutes on the screen. Shaw's script was forty-five pages.

"I remember our gloom when the lengthy Shaw version arrived," said David. "I also remember hearing that the Hungarian, Karpathy, was a Shaw joke about Pascal himself. Pascal madly proud, of course."[9]

For the part of Eliza, Shaw had selected Wendy Hiller, whom he had encountered playing *Saint Joan* at the Malvern Festival in 1936. He declared she would be "the film sensation of the next five years."[10] But Shaw quarrelled with Pascal's choice of Leslie Howard for Professor Higgins and wanted Charles Laughton.

Leslie Howard, the most urbane of Englishmen, was actually the son of a Hungarian, although born in London. His real name was Leslie Howard Stainer. Pascal chose him not only as leading actor but initially as director. Howard asked for someone to help him, and Pascal hired Anthony Asquith, who had, like David, been going through a bad patch. He had been under contract to Max Schach and had not worked for two years. He was about to abandon the cinema and join the newly-formed BBC Television drama department.

Although Pascal persuaded Shaw to accept Leslie Howard, Shaw always believed him fatally miscast. "He thinks he's Romeo," he said, referring to the MGM production in which Howard co-starred with Norma Shearer. He felt the public would want him to marry Eliza, "which is just what I don't want."[11] Pascal withheld the ending until the last possible moment - and covered himself by shooting two others, just in case.

"Gabby was a considerable person," said David. "Everybody laughed at him - I laughed at him - but he was an enormous person in his way. And Shaw, obviously no fool, saw something of it.

"Gabby was absolutely bowled over by Shaw and he did everything right and everything wrong. I remember the time Shaw came down to launch the shooting of PYGMALION. A terrific upheaval went on and Gabby said, 'I've got to have the most beautiful armchair.' And so this armchair was produced and brought on to this set in preparation for Shaw, and I thought, 'Don't do this, it's not going to go down at all well.'

"Shaw finally came on the set just before lunch and sat down in the chair and then, to my horror, I saw Gabby go up to him and kiss him on his bald pate. I thought, 'This is going to be a disaster.' Not at all. He adored it."[12] Gabriel Pascal, wrote Michael Holroyd, was "stimulating, disruptive, unpredictable." Anthony Asquith, by contrast, was mild-mannered, insecure and shy, yet he was the true director of the film and its success was largely his responsibility. Shaw described him as "a sensitive and inventive youth (who) doesn't know the difference between the end of a play and the beginning,"[13] which one can attribute to Shaw's habit of giving Pascal all the praise and blaming everyone else for interfering.

When Anthony Asquith was a child, something about his nose made his mother, Margot, give him the nickname of "Puffin" and it stuck to him throughout his life. He was a remarkably gifted child, capable of speaking French and German fluently at the age of seven, and devoted to music. His father was the Liberal Prime Minister, so 10 Downing Street was his home, his playground and his school, for his delicate health required him to be taught by a governess until he was nine.

Asquith had become fascinated by the cinema when he was at Oxford, though it was virtually unprecedented for a man of his background to go into pictures, and at first the technicians did not know what to make of him. He was short, with a shock of reddish-golden curls, rather fey, with a curiously high-pitched voice: he would have been accepted in the theatre, but the cinema was rougher and tougher. Wally Patch, an actor on BOADICEA, recalled that it was the moment he was kicked in the groin by a horse, and picked himself up without a murmur, that he was accepted. And no one could resist either his charm or his enthusiasm.

Asquith, aware as any of his background, tried to reduce the class differences by dressing scruffily. He looked upon his fellow-workers as friends. But these fellow-workers were startled when this junior assistant suddenly leapfrogged over all of them with SHOOTING STARS, a melodrama about the film industry which he wrote and co-directed. This, with two of his other silent films, UNDERGROUND and COTTAGE ON DARTMOOR, became classics of British cinema.

While regretting the passing of his beloved silent film, he embraced sound with characteristic élan and directed TELL ENGLAND, a drama of the Gallipoli campaign which included a battle sequence of rapid cutting, à la Gance and the Russians. This combination of expertise and enthusiasm, rare in British cinema, endeared him to David.

"Puffin was a bloody good director," said David. "His trouble was that he had all sorts of wonderful ideas but he had such a tentative approach to carrying them out that many of them never came to any sort of fruition. He'd say, 'Oh, I'm afraid this is absolutely ridiculous.' He was so self-effacing, and he was a sweet, sweet man.

"I learned how difficult directing was from watching Asquith at work. I realised that when a difficulty came up, I could keep my mouth shut and say nothing. It is so easy to sit on the sidelines and you're jolly lucky if you don't have to open your mouth. Poor old Puffin had to open his mouth and come up with a solution.

"While Puffin was a good director, he could have been a first-rate director if he hadn't had this diffidence. He almost let his actors do too much on their own - an actor could get away with murder on one of Puffin's pictures because Puffin would feel he shouldn't push his ideas. But I learned a lot from him."[14]

Asquith shot PYGMALION in continuity, giving the actors a better chance to develop their characterisation. Bob Huke, who described his role as "second assistant clapperboy"[15] on the film, noticed that David was on the floor far more than an editor normally would be, and Asquith used to discuss it all with him.

"Puffin liked to block it all in, and we'd be booted off the stage and we'd go out and sit in the sun. Hazel Wilkinson, the continuity girl, took the notes. The blocking might take half a day, Puffin talking it over with David and [cameraman] Harry Stradling and [operator] Jack Hildyard. On the ballroom sequence, we were sitting in the sun all morning."[16]

David said that he directed a lot of the montage sequences with Wendy Hiller and Leslie Howard and that Asquith had said, "It's a damn shame. You should be up there as co-director."

But Vera Campbell remembered David doing more than simply the montage sequences.

"Puffin and David directed that film," she said. "Puffin was such a dear, and quite firm. He would never have any unpleasantness and he got on well with David. But David gradually pushed and pushed until Puffin was doing comparatively little and David was taking a lot of control as the cutter on the floor. He spent more time on the floor than anywhere else - that's why we worked so late.

"As for Leslie Howard, he would sit in on the evening sessions. Pinewood was very social in those days. But he would get bored easily. If he felt in the

Esme Percy's role as Count Karpathy (left) was written especially for the film by Shaw and based on Pascal. Leslie Howard is behind Scott Sunderland as Colonel Pickering and Wendy Hiller.

mood he would say, 'I suggest we do this,' but he didn't direct."[17]

David gave Asquith entire credit for directing the film. "Leslie would come in every so often with a word or two. From then on, Leslie got a taste for directing. He could move easily from being a star to being a co-director.[18] He was the most charming man I've ever met but he was always late. One was boiling with anger, and yet he did it continually.

"You'd say to yourself, 'I'll tell him what I think of him this time because he's really buggered up the whole afternoon.' And he'd come in and put his arms out and say, 'I am just dreadfully sorry' and come out with some long story of whom he met and how he was detained and within five minutes one had forgiven him everything.

"He preferred doing movies to the stage, which in those days was an extraordinary thing to hear. I remember him saying, 'Look, it will probably take me three runs to get this,' and he'd go at one of Shaw's long speeches with a real attack and speed and he was talking so fast that he was tripping over the words. About the third or fourth time he'd get it perfectly. Wonderful nerve and verve. In those days people just didn't talk as fast as that.

"He was so good at reactions that he made it very difficult for me as the cutter. You could have played practically the whole shot on his close-up, running the dialogue of the other people on him, he was so good at it. He knew all about stillness. He just looked at the other person.

"Sometimes I'd watch him on the set and I'd think, 'Well, you've gone too far. You're doing absolutely nothing.' See him on the screen, see that same shot in close-up - it's riveting, because he's concentrating and thinking. He was always more interesting than the person who was talking."[19]

"It was a great game to work for Pascal," said Anthony Asquith, "especially if you learned how to do it. One time David Lean and I were at the cutting stage and we showed a reel of it to Gabby who asked for some impossible cut, but by this time we knew him. We'd say, 'Right you are. In half an hour we'll show it to you.' Then we'd go and have a leisurely cup of coffee and show him the same reel again, not having touched a single frame of it; and this time it was, according to Gabby, *p-a-r-f-a-i-t.* But although there were times when he would ask you for something quite absurd, the next time it could be something absolutely splendid and constructive."[20]

On one occasion, Pascal accused David of altering a close-up. David insisted it was exactly as Pascal had seen it before, but Pascal, suspecting he had been hoodwinked once or twice, adopted his cavalry officer persona and David, who was exhausted, burst into tears.

Being a workaholic and addicted to stimulants like coffee and cigarettes, David was sometimes seized by sudden weeping fits. He would have to slip out of sight until the attack had passed.[21]

To write the music, William Walton was offered five hundred and fifty guineas, a considerable advance on the three hundred pounds he had earned for ESCAPE ME NEVER. But Walton declined Pascal's blandishments and it was Arthur Honegger (responsible for the scores for Abel Gance's LA ROUE and NAPOLEON) who accepted Pascal's offer.

Honegger conducted the London Symphony Orchestra at the music session, and asked Pascal for his opinion.

"Well, I think it is very good, but unfortunately my director does not like the way you have orchestrated the main theme," said Pascal.

Asquith had said nothing. Pascal said he would explain, as Asquith was too shy. Asquith cornered Pascal in the restaurant where he was lunching with the composer.

"Gabriel," said Asquith, "in future, if you wish me to support you in your lies, I would appreciate it if you gave me some warning."

"Do not insult me," said Pascal. "I challenge you to a duel. Choose your weapons - swords or pistols?"

"Well, for my part," said Asquith, "Swords *and* pistols."

"And that was the end of it," said David. "We all laughed about it afterwards. It was a sort of madness, but it had a kind of glorious sense about it in a way."

Two days before the premiere, there was a preview, after which Shaw's wife,

Charlotte, said, "This is the finest presentation of my husband's work."

According to Michael Holroyd, Pascal had been trembling with nerves, clutching Charlotte's hand and almost wringing these words from her. Pascal was especially nervous about the ending for which Asquith had shot three different versions. Pascal had selected the "romantic" one, expecting Shaw to be furious. But Shaw brushed it aside, saying it was of no consequence and at the same time blaming it on one of "twenty directors who seem to have turned up there and spent their time trying to sidetrack me and Mr Gabriel Pascal, who really does know chalk from cheese."[22]

Shaw, who came to no further shooting after the first day, was convinced that Pascal was the onlie begetter of his film, and that the multiplicity of interfering directors included Asquith, Leslie Howard and David Lean. After the preview, however, Shaw wrote to Pascal a triumphant note: "An all-British film, made by British methods, without interference by American script writers, no spurious dialogue, but every word by the author, a revolution in the presentation of drama in the film. In short, England über alles."

What he did not know was that some of his dialogue had been written by Kay Walsh.

"Puffin Asquith wouldn't believe, neither would Gabby Pascal, that I wrote some of the dialogue for David when he was cutting PYGMALION. I used to say to David, 'For God's sake, don't say that the girl you live with wrote this because you'd be disqualified immediately. Just present it as an idea.' He wasn't a thief like so many people in the industry. He very sensibly kept quiet and said, 'What about this?'"[23]

The lines were invariably accepted. Another line, written by Shaw for the original play, was Eliza's "Not bloody likely." Pascal and Asquith anticipated an objection from the film censor and had even taken out insurance to cover the cost of a re-take of the scene. To everyone's surprise, the line was allowed to remain in the film.

After all the hard work, Vera Campbell remembered everyone being seized by post-natal depression. "David came into the cutting-rooms one night and said, 'Gabby's very depressed, everyone's very depressed about the film's chances in the States. They say it's too highbrow.' I remember saying, 'Highbrow? It's a Cinderella story. It's not highbrow just because it's written by GBS."

Vera was right. The picture had been lavishly praised in England and the American critics followed suit. It won an Academy Award for Best Screenplay - GBS did not attend the ceremony - and Pascal was picked with the Pope and Hitler as one of the ten most famous men of 1938. Hitler asked to see the film as did Mussolini, and it won the Volpi Cup at the 1938 Venice Film Festival.

Asquith received many offers to work in Hollywood, but turned them down. He was a man of the British cinema, at home only in England.

Half a century later, the film is still a most accomplished piece of work. Seen in an original print, the cinematography has the lustrous sheen and the glass-smooth camera mobility one would expect of a top Hollywood cameraman like Harry Stradling. David's precise contribution will never be known. How many tactfully whispered suggestions were taken up by Asquith, how many performances were helped in the cutting-room, how many transitions lost their ragged edges under his gentle persuasion, can only be a matter of conjecture.

One can sense his skill in combining the best sections of two travelling shots by disguising the cut as the camera passes a Covent Garden pillar; one can enjoy the perfection of his cuts on action as one admires the flourishes of a brilliant dancer. Certainly he employs a great many dissolves, but that was the fashion of the time, not - as happened later - the last resort of a timid editor.

"My next film," Leslie Howard told *Film Weekly*, "will be the psychological study of a newspaper baron - a man with a chain of papers whose power is sufficiently great to change the policy of the Government and to alter the shape of Europe. The film will be handled as a comedy-drama - but it will also contain a serious sociological message, showing the folly of allowing power to accumulate in the

David, Ellen Drew and cameraman (and later director) Bernard Knowles on FRENCH WITHOUT TEARS.

hands of one person. Anthony Asquith will direct... the cutter will be David Lean, a young man of considerable intelligence who has lots of ingenious ideas on film-editing. We three shall be entirely responsible for the picture."[24]

Such a project would hardly have been popular among potential financiers, most of whom would have had strong connections with newspaper barons like Northcliffe, Rothermere or Beaverbrook. It was Orson Welles who had the courage, talent and determination to make CITIZEN KANE... in America three years later.

Nevertheless, Asquith and David stayed together for a somewhat less ambitious, but more commercial film - FRENCH WITHOUT TEARS, which was made at Shepperton.

Based on a play by Terence Rattigan - the comedy drew on Rattigan's own experiences at a French tuition school in Normandy - the stage cast included Rex Harrison, Kay Hammond, Roland Culver and Trevor Howard, but since they meant little to British cinema audiences, and even less to American ones, Paramount (who had bought it as a vehicle for Marlene Dietrich!) insisted on Ray Milland and Ellen Drew, and took only Roland Culver from the stage version.

David continued his role of director-in-waiting, attending the shooting, always ready with an answer to a problem, or a discreet suggestion in the director's ear, and editing the picture at night.

Paramount adopted the Hollywood system of sneak previewing the picture, a

David appears to be directing the director, Anthony Asquith, in this photograph by David Tree. Jack Hildyard, later to photograph BRIDGE ON THE RIVER KWAI, is at left.

practice which was virtually unknown in Britain. Members of the audience at the Astoria, Finsbury Park, were given cards and asked to fill them in with a simple comment indicating their reaction. The producer, Mario Zampi, Asquith and David attended the showing, and since the card that pleased the company most read, "Bloody good - Jim", and since that was David's favourite expression, one wonders whether the editor was trying to help things along.

As a member of the illustrious Asquith unit, David was interviewed by Oliver Baldwin (Viscount Corvedale). The interviewer noted that as a member of this unit he was perfectly happy, "but he still has one ambition and that is to direct. His preference would be either for quick-moving thrillers or films of the type Bob Flaherty specialises in. Until then he is content to edit."[25]

"I remember one lively and noisy dinner," said Kay Walsh, "at which Mario Zampi was extolling the glories of Mussolini. I loved Zampi, despite this. He was so noisy and untalented, but so keen and ambitious that he sizzled.

"David and I were living in digs in Shepperton and I recall Tolly [Anatole] de Grunwald bursting in the next day to tell us of Chamberlain's broadcast and saying, 'War's declared.'"[26]

Just as Paramount released FRENCH WITHOUT TEARS, the Government closed all the cinemas. Asquith, using his considerable influence, persuaded his mother to hold a meeting of Cabinet Ministers, MPs and representatives of the ACT union. The government decision was rescinded and the film was rewarded with large and enthusiastic audiences.

Mario Zampi followed this with a comedy, SPY FOR A DAY, which he produced and directed himself, keeping David close at hand and lining up a formidable array of writing talent. The North Country comic Duggie Wakefield, brother-in-law of Gracie Fields, played a farmhand who resembled a German spy and was thus the target of both sides. It was made in a panic in the first week of war, with threats that the government was about to close all forms of entertainment.

Zampi also announced plans to make four pictures in a £150,000 programme for 1940. The first was to be called BUSINESS AS USUAL, a ubiquitous sign in wartime Britain, and the theme was to deal with international unity, with emphasis on the Empire. The British government showed its gratitude to Zampi by rounding him up with Filippo Del Giudice and others regarded as enemy aliens and interning them under Regulation 18B.

Other film industry people fled to Hollywood - their less timorous colleagues coined the phrase, "Gone with the Wind Up". Much as David admired American films, there was never any question of his leaving England. Film industry workers aged thirty and above - David was thirty-one in 1939 - were classified as being in Reserved Occupations. Providing David had a job in films, he was unlikely to be called up.

Unfortunately, there was at first no obvious government commitment to a wartime role for films. Even though the Germans had proved the massive propaganda value of cinema, the British had seldom taken films seriously, and it was hard for them to do so at a time of national emergency. The decline in production caused many dismissals and laboratory workers were the first to go. Other industry employees decided to jump before they were pushed.

Kay discovered that David's concern for his son's education had not been that of an anxious father, more the ploy of a clever lover. "He didn't want to see Isabel or Peter. I thought there was something wrong. I thought how much better, certainly better for the boy and better for David, if they could meet. But every time I said, 'Take him to GULLIVER'S TRAVELS,'[27] he went out with some other woman. He didn't go out with Peter."

Kay and David moved from Warwick Mews when, against all advice, Kay bought a small Regency terrace house, 13 Ivor Place, off Baker Street, around the corner from the Rudolf Steiner Hall, which would soon play an important role in their lives. It cost £230 and had a twenty-year lease.

"My little house had shutters with hearts carved in the middle. Maggie and Ethel had the tobacco shop next door - they proved wonderful in air-raids when water and gas were cut off. The shop on the corner was a baker's and across the road was Dan, who was bald and wore a cap. They thought I was extraordinary when I moved in, this peroxided blonde. But when they saw I had to get up at six in the morning, Dan would wake me with a call - 'Kay, cup of tea on the doorstep.' They were all absolutely sweet."[28]

David spent comparatively little time at Ivor Place before he moved into the Pinewood Club at Pinewood Studios.

"He didn't try and make himself attractive to women," said Ronald Neame, "he just couldn't help it. And, of course, he was a Quaker, but he also liked girls very much and the two sides of his nature quarrelled with each other. The Quaker side would not let him indulge himself. The other side wanted to indulge and it's been a battle he's had all through his life."[29]

Kay made several attempts to leave David. "I got so fed up with the whole thing," she said. "I thought, 'I really must cut this out. It's awful. This can't be love.' Life was so full of pain as far as I was concerned. We had been a couple working together, then surviving in unemployment - and when we should have been sharing the spoils - rejection and indifference. Why do such men go charging around? He was so attractive to women and women were so attractive to him, but you don't keep on and on and on. What was he searching for? I always think he was searching for something inside himself.

"Now he had got work and money, he just didn't come back. There was no reason to stay at Pinewood. It was an easy journey from the studio to

Marylebone Station. But there were swimming pools, billiard tables and pretty girls."[30]

Pinewood still had the air of the grand estate it had once been. Heatherden Hall, a mansion set in a hundred acres, had belonged to a wealthy politician who had turned it into a showplace with ballroom, Turkish bath and swimming pool and sixteen acres of formal gardens. For David, who loved the country, it must have seemed a yet more glorious version of Leighton Park, devoid of all the drawbacks of enforced education.

Kay soon discovered that David was having an affair with Leslie Howard's girlfriend, a French woman called Violette Cunnington.

"They weren't all from the cutting room. They were hairdressers and make-up girls - but it was Violette this time."

"I know David was very wicked with women," said Vera Campbell, who was equally annoyed with Violette, since she was interested in Leslie Howard. "But I noticed that it was never someone outside the industry. It was either somebody on the crew - a continuity girl - or it was an actress, or somebody on the floor. It was partly being on location and the drama and romance of making films. But I'm pretty certain that very often the girls started it. People always think it was David. I'm not so sure. And the curious thing was that he never stayed with them."[31]

The Phoney War had ended. Kay Walsh was in Ivor Place when a bomb hit nearby Madame Tussaud's.

"My little house shook. I went out to the cinema. It was summer and the sun was shining and I accidentally left the light on in the basement and the air-raid wardens were bashing the door down when I came back and I was carted off to Bow Street and fined. When I got back, I found a large piece of shrapnel on my bed. That was the beginning of the real war.

"I was quite shattered - not about the war, but about David. I had been having a singing lesson. I came out and looked into this blazing blue sky and there was a Messerschmitt and a Spitfire fighting. They were like knitting needles. It was a ballet up there.

"That day he rang and said he was coming to town. When he arrived, he said, 'I want you to come down with me to the docks.' I was terrified, but I would go anywhere with him. We went down to the docks. I was shattered by the haggard faces of the women and kids walking along, and bedding on the bassinets, all going down to the tube stations to get away from the bombing. Their little homes looked as if a giant had squashed the lot.

"The later it got, the redder the sky became from the glow of the bombs. It was so bright you could read the paper. And David stopped there and I felt he was photographing it. I was a terrible coward, terrified of the war. He wasn't afraid that he was going to be hit, even when the sirens were wailing.

"That night the Luftwaffe came over again and gave us another bashing and they didn't need any light because the red light of the docks showed them everything they wanted. And I could feel this man was storing up this scene for the future.

"I suppose he was a born landscape artist, and his canvas happened to be celluloid. You cannot have anything fiercer than the reality of the Luftwaffe bombing the docks of London, and yet I can remember his detachment."[32]

"One dreaded the moonlit nights," said David. "The bombers got the moon in the Thames and followed its reflection up the river. First of all the air-raid siren would go off, then there was a pause of about three minutes and then you would hear the sound of feet running on the pavement, because people used to like getting together.

"Quite a collection of people used to gather at Ivor Place. I remember Vera Campbell, who had been my assistant and was now a cutter herself. She was married to a chap called John Pratt who was Boris Karloff's nephew. She used to sit on her haunches on the floor in the basement. You would hear the whistle of the bomb, and then the bang, and at every bang she took a little hop.

"I said to her one night, 'Vera, you've got to stop hopping.' I was frightened enough myself. You heard these sticks of bombs exploding and you knew they were coming in a line towards you.

"I never went to the air-raid shelters. Never wanted to. I regarded it as a sort of moral collapse, I suppose, which is rather stupid. 'Now, come on, pull yourself together, face it out, don't go down the rat-hole.'

"The remarkable thing was that Vera, from being this hopper, became pregnant and was soon as cool as a cucumber. Then she became maddening in a different way - she used to knit through the raids. It was most extraordinary, the effects of pregnancy on fear."[33]

The cinema became a valuable morale-booster and, whatever their drawbacks, David was proud of the British propaganda films of the early war years.

"Trust Alexander Korda to come out with THE LION HAS WINGS.[34] Micky Powell had a large share in doing it and it was about the air force. I remember going to see it at the Leicester Square Theatre and thinking it was a fairly poor film, but it had some exciting things in it. One felt we'd got an air force and it put some of the backbone into one. It sounds very corny talking like this now, but it did in those days. Nowadays people just don't know what it was like to hear Churchill on the radio when one was frightened. What a man. You could say anything you like about him, but as a leader, as a backbone for a nation, they don't come like that any more. We could have done with a figure like that in the movies..."[35]

CHAPTER TWELVE

MAJOR BARBARA

FOR a producer eager to do business with Zaharoff, the arms dealer, it was a trifle ironic that Pascal's second Shaw production should be MAJOR BARBARA. Shaw's 1905 play has as its hero an armaments manufacturer, Andrew Undershaft, whose daughter is a Major in the Salvation Army.

Pascal, who had produced PYGMALION, intended to direct as well this time - or, at least, to claim the credit for doing so. Shaw insisted that he would only be involved if Pascal was director. Harold French was hired as co-director.

Harold French had been an actor and had directed Terence Rattigan's West End triumph, *French Without Tears*. He had made his first film, a "quota quickie" for Anthony Havelock-Allan, in 1937.

"Pascal did not know where to put a camera," said David. "So what he did was to engage Harold French to supervise the speaking of the lines. And because I'd been the cutter on PYGMALION, and knew a bit about camera angles, he engaged me to tell him where to put the camera and what lenses to use. When the time came, I said, 'Gabby, what kind of credit are we going to get?'

"He said, 'You are going to be assistant director.'

"I said, 'No, I'm not.'

"We had a long argument and in the end he agreed to put us up there as 'Assistants to the director.' He said to me, 'Whoever gives the most help I of course will put first.'

"What I didn't know, but would have known now, was that he had already signed a contract with Harold French that he came first. But as far as the camera was concerned, I really directed that picture."[1]

"Harold French was not a film man," said Kay Walsh, "and David was furious because he said Gabby had split the directing. I could see it was Gabby's cunning. He didn't want to throw too strong a light on to David. But I remember the passion David felt."[2]

However, it must have been apparent to Pascal that brilliant as David was, he had had no experience with actors. And although Pascal claimed *he* had, he was equally incapable of directing performances to a West End standard. What could have been more obvious than to hire a top West End director? And at the start of production, Pascal formed a much closer relationship with French than he did with David.

"I knew how bloody important David was," said French, "but as far as Gabby was concerned, he was just the cutter. I liked Gabby. He was an awful old pirate, of course, wicked old beast, but he had taste. He didn't know anything about directing, so I had to direct the early part. He walked about and shouted and made noises and had enormous personality, but the person who really made the picture was David Lean. Absolutely no doubt about that."

In fairness to Pascal, he did not exploit David. He did not hire him as editor and then take advantage of his goodwill to use him as an unpaid director. He hired him for his knowledge of cutting and to act as directorial adviser. After all, Pascal had already hired an editor, Charles Frend.

Pascal was not the sort of producer who, having found the money, did nothing. He cared passionately about the film, and was able to convince Shaw that it was in his interests that the play be shortened and in some areas completely rewritten.

Script conferences were held in style at Claridge's Hotel. David invariably attended, together with French, screenwriter Anatole de Grunwald and Pascal himself. Some of the suggestions this group put forward, and which Pascal conveyed to Shaw, struck GBS sometimes as being "beyond the wildest dreams of Sam Goldwyn." Shaw continued to revise the dialogue, making cuts and transpositions as he accepted or rejected Pascal's advice.[3]

Pascal arranged for the film to be shot at Denham Studios. Alexander Korda's grand epoch was over, and the studios were now managed by Richard Norton on behalf of Korda's rival, J. Arthur Rank. Because of the war, the place was empty. Two stages had been taken over by the Government as food storage depots and one was assigned to Pascal. As soon as he finished, Denham was to be requisitioned by Lord Beaverbrook's Ministry of Aircraft Production.[4]

David moved from the Pinewood Club into digs at Denham. He, Phil Samuels, Stanley Haynes (who had been on FRENCH WITHOUT TEARS) and editor Charles Frend stayed in a house run by a Miss Styles.

"She loved men and hated women," said Kay Walsh. "She was a superb cook and they loved her and adored being bachelors manqué. They'd all got a troubled background with a woman somewhere - certainly David and Stanley had - and they rather liked the idea that Miss Styles hated women, so they could say, 'Love you to come to dinner, darling, but you do know Miss Styles loathes women!'"

The casting, like the screenplay, had to have Shaw's approval. Since he had not approved of Leslie Howard for PYGMALION, he was no doubt delighted to have him drop out of MAJOR BARBARA. An actor called Andrew Osborn replaced him in the role of Adolphus Cusins.

Pascal was lunching with studio head Richard Norton one day, discussing casting, when his eye fell upon an exquisite blonde at a nearby table. He walked over and asked, "Sweet virgin, are you an actress?" Her name was Deborah Kerr and she was a former dancer. She was summoned a week later to Pascal's office.

"The room was filled with awe-inspiring men, among them David Lean and Vincent Korda," wrote Deborah Kerr. "Pascal lounged in a chair and made me stand in the middle of the room. His first words were, 'Take off your shoes, you are too tall.' Obediently, I took them off, hoping that I hadn't got a hole in my stockings. Pascal then said, 'Now, sweet virgin, ACT!'"

She plunged into a scene from *Cradle Song* but Pascal interrupted, demanding that she recite the Lord's Prayer.

"I launched forth nervously, hoping I could remember it, when the phone rang. Pascal said into the phone, 'Not tonight, Sweet Princess, not tonight.'

"Turning to me, he said, 'You will be my Jenny Hill.'"[5]

David felt that he had not properly appreciated Deborah Kerr. She was only eighteen, and Pascal bullied her ruthlessly during the shooting. But she recalled David one day sitting on top of a high folding ladder, and leaning down to say, "Deborah, you are going to be a star, you do realise that?"

After the success of PYGMALION, there was little doubt that Wendy Hiller would play Major Barbara. However, she needed make-up tests, and Pascal asked David to direct them with cameraman Ronald Neame.

Wendy Hiller was not easy to photograph, and Neame improvised something he called a Wendy Light. David was delighted by his enthusiasm and inventiveness and the two became close friends.

The first cameraman on MAJOR BARBARA was the American, Harry Stradling, who had shot PYGMALION. But when war was declared, he resigned from the picture and returned home. He was replaced by the Canadian, Osmond Borrodaile, but on location at Dartington Hall, Devon, he ran into trouble with a series of rushes which were marred by mysterious negative scratches. Richard Norton rang up Freddie Young, who was already something of a veteran, and asked if he would go down to sort the situation out. Young agreed, so long as Borrodaile did not object, but when he arrived he learned that Borrodaile had walked off the picture.

Considering that Freddie Young's name would one day become inseparable from that of David Lean, the first meeting should have been at the very least a Stanley and Livingstone affair. Instead of which, according to David, they were not even polite to each other.

"Freddie came on the set and I had the viewfinder. I said, 'The camera here, with a fifty.' He took the viewfinder and said, 'Don't teach your grandmother to suck eggs.' He tried to take over.

"I said, 'We'd better go to the director.' I went to Gabby and told him this story and I said, 'You've just got to choose between us. You have Freddie as cameraman and don't have me. Do what you like.'"

Freddie Young recalls working for a week on MAJOR BARBARA and then being recalled to work on another picture. He recommended Ronald Neame, who travelled to Sheffield with David to shoot the second unit sequence in the steel factory. David was very impressed with his work and he had soon taken over as director of photography. But progress was slow - largely due to Pascal - and after two weeks, they were a week behind schedule.

"Gabby blamed the new cameraman - me," said Ronald Neame. "He said, 'He's a young man, very good but very slow.' Well I knew I wasn't slow because I'd photographed God knows how many 'quota quickies'. C.M. Woolf, who was financing the film, wanted to take me off because Gabby had said I was the reason for him being so behind schedule. The entire unit, headed by David Lean, got together, gave an ultimatum to Gabby and said, 'This is not fair. You cannot fire the cameraman for being slow because we know it isn't true.' They supported me up to the hilt. It was a wonderful piece of camaraderie and I stayed on the film."

Ronald Neame's father had been a famous photographer, Elwin Neame, who was killed in a car crash when Ronnie was only twelve. His mother was a film star, Ivy Close, who played the lead in Abel Gance's epic LA ROUE. After a spell as an office boy with an insurance company, his mother found him a job as a messenger boy at BIP. He was promoted to assistant for Claude Friese-Greene, son of the pioneer William Friese-Greene, a talented cameraman but an alcoholic. One day, Friese-Greene collapsed on the set, and the company, not wanting to spend money on a replacement, asked if Neame could take over. He was twenty-three and he finished DRAKE OF ENGLAND for director Arthur Woods. He became a director of photography on countless "quota quickies".

Not only was Pascal having problems with cameramen on MAJOR BARBARA, he also realised he had made a major casting error. The actor playing Adolphus Cusins, Andrew Osborn, was nowhere near strong enough. Shaw watched Pascal struggling with an actor - presumably Osborn - and scribbled a note to him: "You might as well try to teach differential calculus to an umbrella stand."[6]

Harold French, who was the man who had to cope with Osborn's inadequacies, strongly recommended Rex Harrison, who had played in the stage version of *French Without Tears*. Pascal made the change and was so relieved when he saw Harrison in action he declared he saw in the actor "the face of a tortured Christ." David drily remarked, "Tortured by too tight boots, of course."[7]

Rex Harrison, who was almost exactly the same age, was handsome and debonair, a master of light comedy. "After me," said Noël Coward, "you're the best light comedian in the world."[8] David's Quaker instincts were offended by Harrison's vanity. He stared at himself in the mirror with undisguised admiration, and while he wore a pair of horn-rimmed glasses in the role of Cusins, he wore a monocle off the set.

Harrison was no more enamoured of David and dubbed him "the whispering cutter," because, as Harrison later recounted, "It was part of his job to give guidance even on the set, but so that it should not be too obvious he insisted on whispering his advice into Gabby's ear - which of course made it far more obvious than if he had come on and shouted his head off."[9]

Robert Morley was cast as the arms tycoon, Undershaft. Although he was far too young, he had the expansive, gentle quality Shaw described.

"Gabby wanted Undershaft to smoke a cigar," said Ronald Neame. "Gabby was a great cigar smoker and he used to have these big Monte Cristos. But he also wanted Undershaft to love cigars. So we came to this scene and he wanted Robert Morley to take the cigar out of the humidor and lovingly clip it and, even more lovingly, light it while the dialogue was going on. What we call taking the weight off the line. But Gabby took against the way that Morley was handling the cigar. There was David by the camera and there was Gabby by the camera and there was Harold French in the background. We'd get into the scene and the cigar would come out and it would be clipped.

David with Gabriel Pascal on MAJOR BARBARA.

"'No, no, no,' would come from Gabby.

"And David would say, 'What's the matter, Gabby?'

"Gabby would say, 'Robert, when you take the cigar from the humidor, you look at it first and you enjoy the look of it and then after you have looked at it you then reach for the clipper.'

"We'd go again. 'No, no, no,' says Gabby. 'Robert does not handle... he is not with the cigar.'

"And this went on for an hour. In the end Robert was saying, 'But Gabby, dear Gabby, I don't know what you want. I'm trying to do everything you want me to do. But I can't understand...'

"And Gabby said, 'I can no longer speak with you.'

"From that day on until the end of the film, Gabby refused to talk to Robert Morley. Gabby would say to David, 'Tell to Mr Morley that I would like him to...' And David would say, 'Did you hear that Bob?' And Morley would say, 'I'm here, aren't I?' It was all quite ludicrous. And it all started because he couldn't light a cigar properly."[10]

David recalled the craziness of working with Pascal. "Gabby would say things to Harold French like, 'Tell Mr Morley to stop being a homosexual.' It seems absolutely mad when I tell you but that's how we went on and we accepted it. You know, if you are in madness for four hours of an eight-hour day, by the third hour, you look on it as normal. We didn't think of it as madness at the time. We thought it was pretty eccentric, but not as mad as it sounds now."

"The crew knew he was a phoney," said Harold French, "but we were the only picture on the floor, so they didn't want to lose their jobs and they weren't going to let him know. And he could be awfully nice..."

All this was an ideal baptism of fire for an editor who thought he was too nervous to direct. It was proof positive that he could do it a great deal better than some and Pascal's absurdities gave him enormous boosts of confidence.

Wendy Hiller missed the helpful direction of Anthony Asquith and had no respect for Pascal as a director. Their relationship became strained.

"I remember David being stern with me," she said. "He said I must not call Gabby a liar when other people were present."[11]

Harold French found David somewhat aloof, but he responded to his enthusiasm.

"David took me into the cutting-room. He'd worked all night - he was apt to work all night if he was keen on something, hours meant nothing to him. And what I saw astonished me. It was Shaw's dialogue, but the camera wasn't on Morley as Undershaft. David had cut it so brilliantly that he'd given the scene to somebody else. Undershaft hardly appeared at all. You heard his dialogue but the whole thing was switched around. I couldn't help admiring it but I said, 'David, I can't pass it, after all it's Undershaft's scene.' David, with a twinkle - as far as he could twinkle - said, 'No, I just wanted to show you what can happen.'

"He hadn't changed the dialogue, everything was there - it was just sheer brilliance in the editing. Oh, that man was extraordinary."

The set designer of MAJOR BARBARA was to have been Vincent Korda, assisted by John Bryan. But after doing some preliminary work, Korda departed and Bryan took over. He would have an indelible influence on David's films, as well as Ronald Neame's.

"John Bryan very quickly became the best designer I have ever met, or am ever likely to meet," said Neame. "He was the cameraman's dream boy, and the director's, too. When one proposed a set with him, he would move to a sixteen-

Throughout his career, David laid great importance on his sets. 1. John Bryan's design for Joe Gargery's forge in GREAT EXPECTATIONS. *2. The final set, built on St Mary's Marshes in the Thames Estuary.*

3. Memories of Mount Royal; Celia Johnson goes to keep her illicit appointment in BRIEF ENCOUNTER *- a set somewhat simpler than David had planned. 4. Wilfred Shingleton's authentic-looking set for* HOBSON'S CHOICE, *with Brenda de Banzie, Charles Laughton and John Mills. 5. David on the cobbled street of the village of Kirrary, built by Stephen Grimes for* RYAN'S DAUGHTER. *Photograph by Ken Danvers.*

6. *The massive Moscow street built by John Box and team in Madrid for* DOCTOR ZHIVAGO. *Troops leave for the front at the outbreak of war in 1914.*

7. *India may be full of bazaars, but you cannot film in them without crowds of onlookers, so David had John Box build one specially for A PASSAGE TO INDIA, in the grounds of a Maharajah's palace. Photograph by Frank Connor.*

The town of Aqaba was entirely built by John Box and team in Almeria, Spain for LAWRENCE OF ARABIA.
8. John Box and assistant art director Terry Marsh with model for the set and, in background, Box's
original design. 9. The final result - Aqaba, with the Turkish gun pointing out to sea - Lawrence
attacked from the land.

by-twelve drawing pad and with a few deft strokes in charcoal he would give you exactly what you had in mind. The moment John began his sketches the film came to life. It was a remarkable talent.

"His sets, when built, were always what one wanted. But he was a perfectionist and had no compunction about making changes if he felt they were needed, no matter what the cost and no matter how much aggravation he caused the long-suffering construction department."[12]

MAJOR BARBARA was made at the height of the Blitz. Denham Studios, northwest of London, was close to Northolt Aerodrome, which was heavily defended as a fighter airfield, and to Denham airfield which was used for training pilots. Because Korda had used Denham to make his air force propaganda picture, THE LION HAS WINGS, the Germans had threatened to "bomb Denham out of existence." But the Luftwaffe succeeded only in destroying the office block and a screening room.

Each time there was an air-raid warning, shooting stopped and everyone took cover in the underground shelters. The interruptions infuriated David - "Bloody air-raid," he'd say. Because the film was falling behind schedule, a scheme was devised to help them keep going. Ronald Neame described how spotters were put on the roof of the studio, protected behind sandbags.

"When the normal siren went it ruined the sound if we happened to be shooting but that was all. David would say, 'Cut' and we'd wait until the air-raid had stopped. But we did not go to the shelters because we had our own people

Deborah Kerr as Jenny Hill, Wendy Hiller as Major Barbara and Sybil Thorndike as The General in MAJOR BARBARA.

on the roof, and their instructions were the moment they sighted a German plane they should ring the firebell where we were shooting and we went straight to the shelter. For two or three weeks we continued shooting and the firebells never went off. We just cut when the sirens went off, waited thirty seconds and carried on.

"The Electrical Trades Union complained bitterly. They said, 'It's all very well for you lot on the ground, but we're up there in the gantry. By the time we get down to the bloody shelter the bomb may have dropped.' So the way we sorted that out was that every electrician had a rope, fastened to the spot rails. The plan was that if the bell went, they would come down by rope.

"We were in the middle of this scene with Rex and Wendy when for the first time this bell goes off. For a moment, everyone freezes, because it hadn't happened before, then everybody started running. The first to run were me, David and the camera crew; we all ran leaving the camera running.

"The next day on rushes there is this great set, there's Rex and Wendy in the foreground. Dialogue. The bell goes, everybody freezes. Rex looks round, Wendy looks round, then into the top of the picture drop all these ropes and down the ropes come all the electricians. Everybody is running, and running faster than all the rest when he realised what was happening was Rex Harrison. Wendy had not been told about the bell because she had not been on call the day it had all been arranged, so she didn't know what had happened. So she stood there looking around. It provided enormous hilarity in rushes the next day."[13]

Ronald Neame noticed that it was inevitable that David would have a new girl on every film he worked on.

"On MAJOR BARBARA it was Hazel Wilkinson, the script girl. She was one of many girls who cried on my shoulder."

According to Neame, she left the film when the relationship broke up. She telephoned him for advice and he drove to see her one night. On the way home, distracted by an air-raid, Neame crashed into another car, fortunately without causing any injury.

"And I thought, 'This is the last time I bloody well try and take care of David's problems with his ladies!'"[14]

David's affair with Hazel Wilkinson was almost the last straw for Kay Walsh.

"I was always leaving David, but even when I was packing and planning to murder him, I still loved him. It was terrible. I can't tell you what it was like being in love with David. It was a killer and how I survived it I really don't know.

"I went to do war work in the country. I stayed with a friend of mine and her husband and we were making sandwiches and coffee for soldiers - big war work, you can imagine - gumboots in the country, absolutely beautiful. It was at Abinger, in Surrey.

"He wrote me a letter - I wish I had it - that he was going to shoot himself if

I didn't come back to him. Can you imagine? What had happened was that Gabby got fed up with him. He had said, 'You are no good to me. Find your woman.'

'I suppose I must have left little stones and breadcrumbs all around, like *Babes in the Wood*, so he could come after me. What was so wonderful was that I was striding across the fields to do my war work and there was this haggard schoolboy standing there, dirty and wet. He had walked all night long from Denham, hitching lifts on army lorries. And you were suspect in those days if you were walking alone. But all that for me; I couldn't believe it. He's never done it for anybody else because he's never had to. He's only just had to ring up for the Rolls. So when I say I had the best years of his life, I do claim it with some credibility.

"He took me to the woods and we sat down. He said he was terribly sorry and would I marry him? Like J.M. Barrie's little scullery maid in *A Kiss for Cinderella,* I said 'No' to David, but I had all my fingers crossed and when he asked me again…"[15]

MAJOR BARBARA was now so far behind schedule that J. Arthur Rank came to Denham demanding an explanation. Harold French was shockingly honest. He said that Pascal could not make up his mind, he was shooting far too many takes and was interfering in everything. When he returned to his chair, David said, "That was fatal. You shouldn't have said that. That will be the end of you as far as Gabby is concerned."

And so it was. Pascal became positively chilly and at the end of the week he dispatched a letter terminating French's contract. French, who was deeply relieved, was lunching at the Savoy when he received an urgent telephone call - the actors would not go on the floor unless he returned.

"Luckily there were only two or three weeks to go and we got through those pretty quickly. Then Gabby said, 'If I give you two thousand pounds would you have your name taken off as co-director?' I said, 'Yes, of course,' because there were no other jobs, it was wartime and I didn't care. So he gave me two thousand pounds, which I was delighted with. And my name still appears on the titles."[16]

After French had departed, David recalled, "Gabriel Pascal got fed up and left me to it."

David directed all the scenes of Robert Newton and Donald Calthrop in the Salvation Army shelter on his own. Both actors were advanced alcoholics. When the alarm went and everyone raced to the shelters, Calthrop and Newton would stay behind, retrieve their bottles and settle down on the property furniture for a solid period of self-indulgence until the company re-emerged.

Robert Newton was dark and Celtic and David regarded him as an actor in the style of Wilfrid Lawson. He liked both men, but he was particularly fond of Newton, even though he represented the kind of man who would cause a proper Quaker to shudder - an exhibitionist and a dedicated drinker.

Calthrop, who had played memorable villains in films like Hitchcock's BLACKMAIL, was a small, gentle man with a great deal of wit and charm, but his manner changed alarmingly when he had too many whiskies. During the film, having been told that two of his sons had been killed (one in fact survived), he embarked on a drinking bout, and died of a heart attack, leaving a number of scenes still to be shot with a double. "Gabby was very dramatic about this," said Neame. "There was a two-minute silence on the set the day after Donald died."

The editor of MAJOR BARBARA, Charles Frend, had been film critic for *Isis* when it was edited by David's brother.

"He was a jolly good editor," said David, "keen and very sensitive. In those days at Denham, the cutting-rooms were over by the Old House, which was down by the river.

"Somebody said, 'You'd better come over to the

Robert Newton as Bill Walker and Rex Harrison as Adolphus Cusins.

cutting-rooms. Charlie's in a terrible state.' I went over and Charlie saw me and charged at the wall of the cutting-room and bashed his head against it - bang, bang, bang - and collapsed on the floor. It was a kind of nervous breakdown. You can all too easily find yourself in this state in the cutting-room, because editing is a highly complicated process."

Whether it was Lean or Pascal or a combination of the two who triggered the breakdown, Frend retired from the picture and David took over the editing, although he left Frend with his credit. When I asked David about these events, he blamed Pascal.

"Gabby could be an awful bully, and I suppose he sensed some vulnerable points in Charlie and tore into him."

Frend later became a distinguished director for Ealing and David remained on good terms with him, hiring him at the end of his life as second unit director on RYAN'S DAUGHTER.

Films in those days were printed on highly inflammable nitrate stock and

David was a smoker. Since smoking was forbidden in the cutting-rooms, he would switch off the Moviola and say, "Must have a fag," and step outside.

"The trim-bin would be full, but out they'd all go!" said Vera Campbell. "I didn't smoke. All the boys would follow him out and there I was, muttering away, doing all the work."

As the air-raids over London continued, some of Vera's friends were bombed out and she offered to help them find digs in Denham. This meant that she was absent from the cutting-room for some time. When she got back, David was livid.

"I burst into tears and I said, 'Well, there is a war on, you know, David.' He didn't care. The war didn't seem to affect him. It was just the film, the film, the film.

"And yet he wanted to know what was going on. He listened to the news, he even listened to Lord Haw-Haw. He was interested but not involved, whereas Charles Frend had maps on the cutting-room wall with flags all over them."[17]

During the editing of MAJOR BARBARA, Vera Campbell was married from the little house in Ivor Place. Despite the rationing, Kay offered to put on a party and other friends succeeded in obtaining a joint of meat. The groom, Dr John Pratt, managed to get some champagne.

"We had a real party at that little house," said Vera, "and David, who had begrudgingly given me a week off for my honeymoon, appeared quite late in the day. He didn't kiss me, wish me happiness or say 'Good show' to Johnny or anything. He said, 'Well, I hope somebody's going to be responsible for the blackout.' And that was all. It didn't mean anything - but it meant a lot to me."[18]

Having heard David talk about Vera Campbell, I think she meant more to him than she realised and perhaps he was genuinely sorry she was getting married. But Vera's wedding was not the only one to take place during the making of MAJOR BARBARA.

Kay Walsh and David Lean were married at Marylebone Town Hall on 23 November 1940, a week after the end of shooting. As they emerged on the street, an air-raid siren went off, but no one took any notice.

"Gabriel Pascal was our best man," said Kay. "He had said, 'Find your woman' after all. Edward sent me a telegram: KATY YOU ARE MARRYING THE WRONG BROTHER.

"We spent some of the honeymoon at Pascal's Mumford's Farm. When we got back, David went to live with Miss Styles again. He couldn't come out and face being married. It was such an insult. But it was convenient for David, and he was there with his old pals."[19]

Eventually David and Kay moved into a picturesque little place in Denham village called Melgan Cottage, where David could - in his free moments - practise gardening, something he grew to love.

The marriage, however, was doomed. As David wrote, years later, "Wives who are quicker-witted and more intelligent and are leaders of their family do not show their husbands to advantage."

Pascal had gone so far over schedule that, paradoxically, he saved the studio. Beaverbrook's Ministry of Aircraft Production, which was to have taken over the studio, had found somewhere else. The film took an almost unbelievable eighteen months to complete and had cost an estimated £250,000.

"When the film was finished, I was at Anglesea in Wales," said Wendy Hiller. "Gabby had been cutting and cutting and I made him keep several speeches which were absolutely obligatory. Gabby sent a print out which I saw at a cinema in Bangor. When I realised that those vital speeches were not in the film, I went to the Ladies and wept and never saw the rest of it."[20]

MAJOR BARBARA had its grand premiere on 20 March 1941 in Nassau, in the Bahamas, the islands to which the Duke of Windsor had been exiled and where Gabriel Pascal had dreams of creating a film production centre. Pascal attended the premiere with Katharine Hepburn, whom he was romancing with a view to starring her in a version of Shaw's *The Millionairess*.

The film, which opened in London in April 1941, failed to make a profit and Shaw lost £20,000 because he put his royalty payment from PYGMALION into it. But for David, it was an experience of crucial importance.

The production had endured the sacking of a co-director, the replacement of cameramen, an editor and a leading actor and the death of another actor. And all the while, the bombs were raining down on the studio. This editor who was convinced he was not yet ready to direct - this "frightened rabbit" as he described himself - was able to witness the behaviour of a producer-director who was almost entirely incompetent, committing waste on a monumental scale in the middle of a war.

The experience left a deep and abiding impression.

CHAPTER THIRTEEN

49TH PARALLEL

THE press regarded the filming of 49TH PARALLEL as an escapade by a bunch of young men trying to avoid military service.

To make this ambitious propaganda picture, Michael Powell proposed taking actors and technicians across the U-boat infested Atlantic to Canada. Powell and his partner Emeric Pressburger had already conducted a thorough tour of Canada and cleared their project with the authorities. Approval was obtained from Duff Cooper, the Treasury Minister, and the Government produced £60,000 from the Films Division of the MoI, a figure later matched by J. Arthur Rank.

Powell persuaded Leslie Howard, Raymond Massey (himself a Canadian) Laurence Olivier and Elisabeth Bergner to take part. Eric Portman was to portray the commander of a U-boat crew stranded in the wilds of Canada. It comes as a surprise to learn from Powell's autobiography that Portman disliked films and fought his director every step of the way.

Freddie Young was to be the lighting cameraman, though Osmond Borrodaile, who had returned to Canada after the MAJOR BARBARA débâcle, would shoot the title backgrounds. Betty Curtis was the brave young woman who agreed to be continuity girl. She and the art director, David Rawnsley, sailed with Powell from Liverpool to Halifax, Nova Scotia. On the voyage Syd Streeter, head of construction, worked out how to build a full-size mock-up of a U-boat.

There was a script, of course, but until Pressburger and his collaborator, Rodney Ackland, had finished it, Powell improvised along the way. When it arrived, it covered only the action up to the escape of the Nazis by seaplane. The unit set out for Hudson Bay, Powell informing them that they would be following in Flaherty's footsteps, for it was here that he had made NANOOK OF THE NORTH. They faced bitter cold, drenchings from icy spray, sea sickness and the engine failure of their boat among a group of icebergs.

"The blast of cold air as you pass near them seems nearly to take the skin off your nose," said Powell.

Michael Powell had worked with Rex Ingram, whose MARE NOSTRUM also involved a German submarine. Powell's film was exactly the sort of adventure David had longed to take part in ever since he saw NANOOK, CHANG and WHITE SHADOWS IN THE SOUTH SEAS. Unfortunately, Powell initially picked John Seabourne, David's predecessor at Gaumont Sound News, as editor and second unit director. David's moment had yet to come. The fact that he had to hear of their adventures second-hand must have filled him with the desire one day to make distant and dangerous location pictures himself.

When Powell arrived at Corner Brook, Newfoundland, to rendezvous with Rawnsley and the submarine, he learned that Elisabeth Bergner had flown the coop and joined Paul Czinner in Hollywood.[1] This was a disaster, for her part had still to be completed at the studio.

The home-made submarine behaved a trifle erratically when she made her maiden voyage. The actors stood uneasily on the conning tower which shuddered violently. Eric Portman, still suspicious of Powell, remembered how an actor, Raymond Lovell, had nearly drowned when Powell staged an aircraft crash on Lake Winnipeg.[2]

With Freddie Young at the camera, Powell was in a launch racing towards the submarine. Inside the submarine were the explosives to be used in the destruction of the vessel, something of which Portman was fortunately unaware.

"David Lean, who had access to all the guide-tracks and sound tracks when he was editing the film dines out on what happened next," wrote Powell. "Amid a crossfire of orders and recrimination, he imitates Eric's panic-stricken yell of 'You bastard, you'll kill us all for your damn movie!' echoing over the water. And then a little voice just beside the camera saying, 'Keep rolling.'"[3]

Powell returned with an enormous number of rolls of exteriors and began to shoot interiors at an equally prolific rate. Then John Seabourne collapsed with duodenal ulcers and had to be replaced. Powell had another pet editor, Hugh Stewart, but he had joined the armed forces and told Powell, "You couldn't do better than David Lean."[4]

"David Lean!" wrote Powell. "I was staggered. Somehow it had never occurred to me that I could command the services of a craftsman like David Lean. My rise had been meteoric, and nothing was too big for me to tackle, but I was at heart the same little eager beaver who had persuaded Joe Rock to let me make THE EDGE OF THE WORLD. A load dropped from my shoulders. I realised what it would mean for the film to have a cutter, an editor, like David Lean to review and pass sentence on those thousands of feet of film."[5]

David was called in by Harold Boxall - the man who had given him his first job - and asked if he would take over the film. David, who knew he was the best editor in the country, remembered Robert Wyler's advice and asked for nearly twice what he had been getting from Pascal - seventy-five pounds a week.

To his dismay, he saw a look of relief pass over Boxall's face. He realised he could now have asked for three times his Pascal salary and perhaps faced a little haggling.[6]

David began work by reading Emeric Pressburger's script, all two hundred and twenty-five pages of it.

"I settled down with it after dinner and then I couldn't stop. I was reading it at seven the next morning. It was fabulous. I remember sitting in Denham labs, in one of the theatres there, and seeing a rough cut which ran for over five hours.[7] I saw Micky - he was still shooting - and he met me with absolute ice, you can imagine, because he thought I was going to ruin his film.

"I got down to it and it took me about six weeks. I cut the first two hours and a bit down to one hour. And the awful day came when I thought, 'Well, I'd better ask Micky to see it.' He came over to the labs and we ran it. The lights came on - dead silence. I couldn't restrain myself any longer and I said, 'Mr Powell, what do you think?'

"He stood up, looked at me and said, 'Absolutely brilliant.' He walked straight out of the projection room and I had carte blanche for the rest of it."[8]

In a sense, Powell never forgave him, for he had had to be ruthless with the hard-won material. David and Powell became friends of a sort, but David was always a bit puzzled by him.

"He was a strange character. Even his book was strange. He was the most difficult character I've worked with because he was so uncommunicative. The thing I remember most about Micky was the way he'd say, 'Now, what do you think should be done with this?'

"You'd think a bit and very carefully tread your way through a suggestion you thought would be good and he'd look at you straight in the eyeball with those blue eyes and say, 'Why?' Devastating. Micky had a wonderful audacity and I just loved watching his films."[9]

Michael Powell wrote his account of the editing of 49TH PARALLEL:

"We had spent countless hours and dollars on night sequences in the Canadian Pacific marshalling yards showing escaping Nazis on the run. Out it all went, neck and crop. The back projection plates for Leslie Howard's scene in the canoe were shot from the wrong angle if they were to cut with the exterior scenes.

"'Were there any others?' David asked, squinting down at his Moviola, concentrating on the film and ignoring the trembling director. No? Then he would find some in the London Films library, something out of SANDERS OF THE RIVER, perhaps.

"Close-ups were needed of the U-boat crew ransacking the Hudson Bay Company store; had these been shot? No? Then David would shoot them, with Powell's permission. He liked the U-boat sequence, but it needed an introductory scene of a submarine surfacing. He thought he had seen just what was needed in some captured German film at the MoI.

"This became the shot of the German U-boat surfacing from the depths, accompanied by Ralph Vaughan Williams' powerful chords of music which lift the audience out of their seats.

"We would also need a shot of the cargo boat sinking, seen through a binocular matte, to match the close shot of the U-boat commander in the conning tower of submarine. The Denham tricks department would make the matte, and Denham labs the combined print. He hoped that I didn't mind that he had asked the tricks department to check for steadiness all the back projection plates we had made on exterior. They had reported that they were all very good, he added casually. I was relieved that something was good. I began to dread David zoning in on me with a list of questions in his hand.

"I had been saved by some good editors, but never on this scale. I felt as a general with an unprotected rear must feel when he learns that some insubordinate young commander has arrived with reinforcements. I turned my attention to our actors."[10]

No matter how tactfully all this was done, it could not but arouse hostility and resentment. David felt himself cast in the role of the hatchet man who was cutting away at a lot of fine footage. But there was no alternative, and not even Powell could deny that he was utterly committed to the film and was endeavouring to make it work. David thought about it night and day and came back to Kay at Melgan Cottage utterly exhausted.

Eric Portman and Raymond Massey in 49TH PARALLEL.

In those days at Denham, when a film had reached its final stage, the editor might ask some fellow editors to look at it and make comments.

"I remember David asking me, among others, to look at 49TH PARALLEL," said Sid Cole. "When we'd finished, David asked us if there was anything that worried any of us. I said, 'Yes, there's a big jump in the chronological continuity.' I told him it was in the Canadian sequence, and he had the expression as though he were running an internal Moviola. 'I know where you mean,' he said. 'That's where I took two reels out.'"[11]

49TH PARALLEL was a triumph. It even did well in the United States, which had, after all, been the target of the propaganda, although America had by now entered the war.[12]

David's attitude was that of a man who had devoted to the film weeks of back-breaking toil and wished he had had the good fortune to have made it himself.

"I don't think Micky did all that good a job of it," he said. "It was good - but not as good as it should have been."[13]

The film opened at the Odeon, Leicester Square and afterwards J. Arthur Rank and Oscar Deutsch presided over a banquet at Claridge's. Rank asked Powell what he was planning next and Powell promised to send him an outline for a film about the RAF which would become ONE OF OUR AIRCRAFT IS MISSING.[14]

Pressburger wrote an original screenplay about a bomber crew forced to abandon their aircraft and parachute into occupied Holland. It has echoes of their previous film though, in this one, the crew manages to find its way back to base to fight again.

Powell united with Pressburger under the combined name of The Archers to make this film, which they asked David to cut.

"It was quite an exciting film in its day," said David. "Very small. What isn't realised today is that the phrase was a regular thing on BBC news bulletins. Terrible. It was a great thing for me, coming so soon after 49TH PARALLEL."[15]

Continuity girl Betty Curtis, having survived the rigours of icy Canada as well as the U-boat infested Atlantic, was miserable on ONE OF OUR AIRCRAFT IS MISSING because she felt she wasn't doing her job properly. She typed up far more information than the editor needed, and so she worked much later than she should have done and got behind in everything. She was grateful to David, who taught her the right way to do it.

"He explained as he went along. 'What I shall want to know is this... watch out for that.' David was kindness personified. He was never impatient, always helpful. I don't remember him being anything but patient with everyone. But at the time, of course, he was not solely responsible for the film."[16]

On David's recommendation, Ronald Neame was hired as lighting cameraman. Ronnie Neame had become a close friend and would spend as much time as he could in the cutting-room, learning the craft of editing from the best teacher in the business, a skill which proved invaluable when he became a director. Neame's camera operator was Guy Green.[17]

Guy Green, who came from Somerset, was a tall, good-looking young man with a diffident manner and a strong sense of humour. Green admired David and was impressed at how often he would appear on the set, intent and watchful.

"It was unusual for an editor to come up to me and say, 'You know that tracking shot was a little bit unsteady. Don't do that any more.'"[18]

Guy Green had that burning enthusiasm for films which so appealed to David and before long he was invited to dinner with David and Kay at the Café Royal.

"I was very young and innocent in those days and they talked about things I had never heard about. Their language was quite... well, to my ears it was amazing."[19]

Through working with Anna Freud, Kay had discovered psychoanalysis and the language of Freud. Seldom heard outside the consulting room, it was becoming second nature to her. Before long it would become familiar to David too, when he became one of the first people in the film industry to subject himself to Freudian analysis.

The opening sequence of ONE OF OUR AIRCRAFT IS MISSING depicted the abandoned bomber hitting a power line and blowing up. "Nobody could edit such a long opening sequence as casually, and with such feeling, as David Lean," wrote Powell.[20]

The seed for what became Powell and Pressburger's most celebrated picture, THE LIFE AND DEATH OF COLONEL BLIMP, was sown in an exchange between the young pilot (Hugh Burden) and the middle-aged rear gunner (Godfrey Tearle), in which the older man says he was just like the young idealist when he was in his twenties, and he will be an old Blimp like him when he is in his fifties.

"David Lean persuaded me to drop the scene from the final cut," wrote Powell, "arguing, 'It's got nothing to do with the plot. It's the sort of idea you could make a whole film about.' So we did."[21]

Powell frequently asked David for advice. Gordon Hales, a trainee who was inspired by David's editing, was on the set when Powell asked, "David, look, I'm planning to do this scene and I want the group shot to follow it - track or cut?"

David would not always produce a snap answer. He would lapse into what some assumed to be a brown study, and others mistook for dumb insolence. He would stare into the distance and think. The "David Lean Silence" again.

After a pause of disturbing length, the light would return to his eye, a quick smile would reward the listener's patience and the answer would be delivered with clipped confidence, followed by a self-deprecating, "I think. Don't you?"

Powell regarded David as the best film editor since D.W Griffith.[22] By chance, the set of ONE OF OUR AIRCRAFT IS MISSING was regularly visited by a man who was about to make his first film as a director and was looking for someone with great technical skill to assist him. The man's name was Noël Coward.

CHAPTER FOURTEEN

IN WHICH WE SERVE

THE telephone rang in Melgan Cottage, Denham Village, and Kay Walsh answered it. The voice said, "This is Noël Coward. I wish to speak to David Lean."

"I resisted the temptation to say, 'This is Gertrude Lawrence,'" said Kay. "I thought it was Patrick Barr, an actor friend, playing silly pranks. But it really was Noël Coward.

"What happened was this. There was a restaurant called the Ivy opposite the Ambassadors, off St Martin's Lane. It was run by an Italian called Mario and I got all this later from him. He knew somebody called Filippo Del Giudice. Sitting there late one night were Noël Coward and Carol Reed, talking over their brandy and cigarettes. Noël said, 'I'm going to direct a film about my friend Dickie Mountbatten.' Carol asked how he was going to do it and then said - and David never gave Carol credit for this - 'You can't direct a film without David Lean.'"

Coward had set about the project with his characteristic thoroughness and listened to recommendations from a great many people. He had seen MAJOR BARBARA and had visited the set of ONE OF OUR AIRCRAFT IS MISSING. His first idea had been to contact Ronald Neame but David was suggested by Anthony Asquith, Anthony Havelock-Allan and Filippo Del Guidice. The only problem lay with David himself.

Michael Anderson, who lived next door to the Leans, remembered David was very nervous at the prospect.

"He said, 'Noël Coward wants me to do this and I can't. I just can't.' It was Kay who encouraged David to direct. 'Of course you can,' she said. 'You'll do it and you'll do it wonderfully.'"[1]

Over the years, David had been offered several films to direct, all of them "quota quickies". This was the route Michael Powell had taken and he had reached the top relatively fast. But David turned them down. Was he too proud or too nervous?

"If you make a quickie and it's a terrible script and you shoot it in three weeks, once it's showing in the cinema nobody says, 'That poor chap only had three weeks to shoot it in, he had a rotten script and couldn't afford any really good actors.' Nobody says that. They say, 'He's a lousy director.'

"And so I waited. And it was bad luck for me that two things came together." [2]

Michael Powell had promised to give him a film to direct, and Kay Walsh had kept jogging Powell's memory. Now he was offered one, a film about the London Symphony Orchestra in the Blitz, written by Emeric Pressburger and Patrick Kirwan.[3]

"I was terribly torn," said David, "but I was more attracted by the Noël Coward film and I had to break the news to Micky. It was a ghastly decision to make. Micky was furious with me. 'You're like a cheap tart walking down Bond Street. You see an expensive, glittering jewel in a window and you just can't resist it.'"

When Italy entered the war in 1940, producer Filippo Del Giudice was interned for four months on the Isle of Man under Regulation 18B. This did not diminish his enthusiasm for his adopted country and, anyway, he was quickly released because the file on him proved he was a firm opponent of Fascism; it was absurd to have arrested him in the first place.

"I liked Del very much," said David. "He was very smooth. He had a huge house and a very glamorous girlfriend, an actress called Greta Gynt. He used to call himself 'The Butler,' meaning 'I am your butler.' Noël Coward used to make odd cracks about the butler relationship, but he really was a producer. He produced the money, he ironed out all sorts of troubles."[4]

Anthony Havelock-Allan, a producer of "quota quickies", worked with Del Giudice. Tall, charming and humorous, Havelock-Allan was married to actress Valerie Hobson. When Del Giudice decided he wanted to make a Big Picture with a Big Name, he asked Havelock-Allan to contact Noël Coward.

Alas, Coward felt about the cinema as David felt about the theatre.

Noël Coward came from a similarly suburban background to David, although his family was lower middle class, rather than plain middle class, and he lived in genteel poverty in such suburbs as Teddington, where he was born in 1899. His mother ran a boarding house and his father, an alcoholic, was a salesman for an organ company.

He started as a child actor in 1910 and in 1917 he had a small role in D.W. Griffith's propaganda epic, HEARTS OF THE WORLD. By 1921, he had his first play in the West End and real success came with the notoriety of *The Vortex*. By the age of twenty-six, he had his first Rolls-Royce. Coward adopted the persona of the languid, upper-class Englishman so impeccably that he was not merely accepted but courted by the very society people he depicted.

Success was tremendously important to him, yet his life was anything but smooth. Failure had caused him nervous breakdowns, more than one of his plays was greeted by boos and once, outside the stage door, he was spat upon. He felt uneasy with cinema, sensing it would somehow diminish the theatre. However, his work had been filmed by England's best directors - including Hitchcock - and a Hollywood version of CAVALCADE had won the Best Picture Oscar. But the films were not popular with the mass audience.

In 1938, Coward was asked by his friend Lord Louis Mountbatten to conduct a survey for the Royal Naval Film Corporation to establish what kind of films sailors wanted to see. Unusually for a member of the aristocracy, Mountbatten was a fervent champion of the cinema.[5] It was when Mountbatten told Coward the story of the sinking of his ship, *HMS Kelly*, off Crete in May 1941, that he saw the potential for a film.

"Absolutely heart-breaking and so magnificent," wrote Coward. "The Royal Navy means a great deal to me and here, in this odyssey of one destroyer, was the very essence of it."[6]

Coward put his idea to Mountbatten, who was "wildly enthusiastic", and in July 1941 Coward had a meeting at the Savoy with Filippo Del Giudice, Anthony Havelock-Allan and Charles Thorpe of Columbia Pictures, who were considering financing the film.

On 28 July, Coward started on a rough outline with Mountbatten of what they called *White Ensign*. Meanwhile, Del Giudice tried to raise the money. Columbia had withdrawn, since they did not regard Coward as a star name. Del Giudice approached C.M. Woolf of General Film Distributors, but negotiations broke down on the same point. By this time, the estimated cost of the project was £180,000.

When the first draft of the script was ready there was a meeting at Coward's studio - a bomb-damaged building near Victoria. Coward was accompanied by Gladys Calthrop (a cousin by marriage of Donald Calthrop, she had designed all Coward's successes from *The Vortex* onwards), Joyce Carey, one of his favourite actresses, and Lorn Lorraine, his secretary. David was accompanied by Anthony Havelock-Allan and Ronald Neame.

"I was pretty scared," said David, "because Noël was *the* British sophisticate and I was always frightened that he would make some quip that would make everyone roar with laughter and that I would be the butt of it."[7]

Coward read them his script. He read for more than three hours. The faces of the film men must have been a study in mixed emotions. Here they were, at the birth of the most exciting event in their careers, and yet it was perfectly obvious to all of them that the scenario, a sort of maritime *Cavalcade*, which covered the story of the Navy from 1922 to the sinking of the Kelly in 1941, was unworkable.

"It was not written as a film script," said David, "but as a kind of narrative. However, one could see that there *could* be a film script."

Noël Coward asked what they thought, and in between drinks they tried to express their feelings.

"Well," said David, "it's absolutely wonderful, but as you've got it, it'll take six or eight hours on the screen."

"I can't believe it," said Coward.

"It does everything and goes everywhere," said David.

"I thought that was the whole point about film, you *can* do everything and you *can* go everywhere," said Coward, somewhat caustically.[8]

"You're quite right,' said Havelock-Allan, "but it is much too big and takes up too much time away from the real issue, which is what the Navy is doing in this war."

David gave an illustration by acting out one small scene - up the stairs, into the room, delivering the dialogue. In the end, Coward understood.

At this point, the memories of those involved diverge. Havelock-Allan and Neame remembered that Coward suggested they took the script away and work on it themselves, and that they began work that very evening. David remembered saying that Coward needed a method of selecting the best of the material he had written and he asked if he had seen Orson Welles's CITIZEN KANE, which had won David's highest admiration.

"He went to see it, and from KANE he got the idea of the flashbacks. Quick as a knife, he took the narrative, cut it up, introduced this Carley float, which was a sort of raft all these ships carried, and he used the men clinging to the Carley float to jump from one part of the story to another."[9]

Coward's diaries support the fact that he worked further on the script, because he was concentrating on the second draft, on 16 October 1941, when the police arrived and issued him with two summonses from the Finance Defence Department.[10] Nevertheless, he continued re-drafting it and another meeting was arranged, at which the script was handed over.

Kay Walsh remembered David bringing it home. She read it and was rather surprised by some of the things in it: "A fat lady, for instance, straight out of one of my Ealing comedies, was clinging to the Carley float among all the sailors. I suppose it was possible that a cargo ship had been sunk with passengers aboard, but she struck a very false note."

David was now very excited about the venture. Kay told him that he had to ask for co-director's credit. At first David baulked at the idea but Kay was adamant and a sort of scheme was devised between them.

"I told David to say to them, 'You have a first-class cameraman, a first class producer, I'm a first class cutter. You'll be surrounded by the cream of the industry. If you want to discuss anything with me, I'll be in the cutting room.' All these other people had had him at the Moviola, but also had him on the set when they were in trouble. And they really did take advantage of him.

"Now this looks as if I'm shooting Noël down. Not at all; I thought he was the most wonderful man. I was absolutely potty about him. I loved working with him and for him. But I was determined that David should have co-directing credit. David thought if you write, produce, direct and act and you do the music and if you've got six [title] cards with Noël Coward, who is going to look at the seventh?"[11]

At the next meeting with Coward, Gladys Calthrop turned to David and said, "I suppose you want to be assistant to the director?"

Recalling his experience with Pascal, David said, "I'm sorry, I don't see it like that. I'll be more than that if I come and join you."

"What do you mean?"

"I'm not prepared to do the work I'll have to do without co-directing credit."

"There was a general gasp," said David, "and I remember Gladys Calthrop sticking out her chin, which was considerable, and saying, 'But everyone has heard of Noël. Who has heard of David Lean?'

"I said, 'One day I hope they will. But I'm going to stick on that.'

"Noël said, 'No, I've got a better idea. We'll have it produced, directed, written and photographed by Noël Coward, David Lean and Ronald Neame.'"

David did not agree with that either. Noël Coward was irritated. He thought for a while and then he snapped, "I agree."

But he wanted Ronald Neame's credit as cameraman on the same title card, which was highly unusual and a mark of the respect in which he held him. (Welles had done this for his cameraman, Gregg Toland, on CITIZEN KANE.)

Anthony Havelock-Allan received credit as Associate Producer, with Coward as Producer, though the film was really produced by Havelock-Allan.

Noël Coward had envisaged playing Mountbatten just as he was, with a titled wife and a chauffeur-driven Rolls. But Mountbatten had insisted that his co-operation should remain a private matter and that the captain in the film should not be modelled on him.

Coward was persuaded to alter the character so he drove a Ford and behaved in a more democratic fashion. No one, apart from those involved, would ever know just how closely Mountbatten worked on the film, how Noël Coward quoted his speeches almost verbatim, how he even wore his old naval officer's cap. Although Coward's Captain D (the D signified command of a flotilla of destroyers) lacked the exuberance and humour of Mountbatten, he was otherwise a reasonable facsimile. Mountbatten's ship, the *Kelly*, was renamed *HMS Torrin*.

Mountbatten even helped with the casting of some of the minor characters. Bernard Miles was summoned to a London studio where a Home Guard film in which he appeared was projected for a group which included Mountbatten. As Miles left, Mountbatten looked at him and said, "You'll do."

"High praise, dear boy!" murmured Coward.[12]

"I spent four or five hours with Mountbatten at Denham," said David, "and he told me the whole business of the sinking of the *Kelly*. He was a fascinating, very good-looking man. He told me the story of the dive bombing and the planes coming in and the first hits. And then the ship started to keel over and he gave the order to abandon ship and I remember him saying, 'As we were going over I suddenly had the old-fashioned idea that the captain should be the last to leave the ship, and I grabbed the binnacle. Before I knew it I was underwater and my lungs were bursting. I was actually under the ship as it was turning over. I came up the other side and gasped and got my first breath of air and that saved me.'

"It was wonderfully exciting and he delivered it in a throwaway manner. Mountbatten had enormous personality. I can imagine that if he came to us now and there were six of us here with four hundred Russians or Chinese coming down the road, he would say, 'Now each of you take a rifle and let's advance on them.' You would have got killed instantly of course. But one would have done it.

"Even after all these years a sort of tingle of electricity goes through me when I think of that man coming into a room and starting to talk. And he gave us a lot of help behind the scenes."[13]

David and Ronald Neame then sweated over the shooting script - a technician's guide to the way the story is to be translated into the pictures - so that David knew precisely what was going to happen before he went on the floor.

"David didn't carry anything in his head," said assistant director Norman Spencer. "The script was the blueprint and you deviated on pain of death. A word, an idea, a gesture - anything altered worried David. He said to me, 'If I haven't got a shooting script I feel on unsafe ground.'"[14]

"I worked on the script with one of Mountbatten's chaps," said David, "an Able Seaman called Terry Lawlor who had been badly burned in the *Kelly* action. You've got to know what they're doing on the bridge when the planes appear, how the guns are trained on approaching fighters, who gives the order to fire and so on.

"Bloody hard work it was, too. And as I did that I turned what Noël had written into a shooting script. I got no credit for it, but I was interested in doing it because it was my notebook for shooting the film."[15]

Betty Curtis, hired as continuity girl, never forgot David's meticulous preparation. "The picture was there, on paper," she said. 'This kind of preparation,' David once said to me, 'was the essence of a good director.'[16]

Kay Walsh acted out all the parts for David. He would pose her in the rough position of the actor in the shot and then write down all the details as if he were shooting. "He couldn't draw but he did little thumbnail sketches - hieroglyphics, like a child," she said.

Gladys Calthrop, who was Noël Coward's designer, hardly had the experience to build a destroyer in the studio, so she designed only the domestic interiors. David Rawnsley and Syd Streeter, who had built the submarine for 49TH PARALLEL, built the aft third of a destroyer on Stage Five at Denham on hydraulic rockers. The set, which was two hundred feet long and fifty-six feet wide, was built almost entirely of wood, although mounted on steel rockers. It was claimed to be the biggest moving set ever constructed on either side of the Atlantic. The studio floor had to be reinforced to take the weight of approximately one hundred tons.

An actress called Celia Johnson, the last person to push herself for a part, approached Noël Coward at a party and asked to play the Captain's wife. The only film she had made so far was A LETTER FROM HOME, a short documentary made for the MoI by Carol Reed. She therefore had to undergo camera tests. Since she did not have a conventionally photogenic face, Neame found it hard to light her. They conversed about plays and books and then Noël Coward launched into "The Walrus and the Carpenter".

"We recited that poem at each other until we nearly burst," wrote Johnson, "and it looked quite crazy in the rushes. But Noël seemed to like it and I got the part."[17]

Celia Johnson was the same age as David and they came from similar backgrounds. Born in 1908 in Richmond, Surrey, she was the daughter of a doctor. She went to St Paul's Girls School, where the head of music was Gustav Holst. At RADA, the principal was not impressed by her, but Alice Cachet, a teacher from France, recognised her talent. Her previous favourite had been Charles Laughton.[18]

"I think David was partly smitten by my mother's talents," said Kate Fleming, her biographer, "and partly by the fact that she did what she was told, and no bother. She just got on with the job. She was the epitome of the no-nonsense school."[19]

For David, Celia Johnson became a paragon of the acting profession, rivalled in his mind only by Katharine Hepburn.

Havelock-Allan drew on his experiences of "quota quickies" to suggest actors like James Donald and Derek Elphinstone. Michael Wilding was a Coward suggestion. The cast also inevitably included a number of Coward's favourites - Joyce Carey, Everley Gregg - and it included actors who would work again for David Lean, such as Bernard Miles, Penelope Dudley Ward and John Mills. The role of Freda's baby went to Juliet Mills, who was Coward's god-daughter. And the role of Freda herself went to Kay Walsh. This was not Kay's idea. Having had enough of being the butt of George Formby's jokes, she had "retired".

But Kay had done a test for Leslie Howard's film, THE FIRST OF THE FEW, and had been rejected. Coward, who had borrowed several screen tests, was viewing

Kay's with David and asked for it to be played again.

"I'd like to test that girl," he said.

David asked what appealed to him about her.

"She's got a nice, mousy quality," said Coward.

David said, "Please don't. It's my wife. I'll never get anything to eat, and she'll take on the whole responsibility of the film over the sink..."

Coward tested her and made sure she got the part.[20]

When the *Kelly* hit a mine, a stoker panicked as he heard it knock against the bottom of the boiler room. He deserted his post and fled to the deck. Coward wrote this incident into the film and Lean had to find an actor with the right combination of youth and vulnerability. He contacted Al Parker.

"Al Parker was the director of THE BLACK PIRATE with Douglas Fairbanks, in two-strip Technicolor. He directed a few films in England and then became an agent. Because he had been a director, he knew what you were doing and I trusted him. I rang him up and said, 'Al, I'm in a mess. Do you know anybody who could play the part of...' and I gave him the description of the chap who loses his head and runs from his post. He said, 'I haven't anybody on the books who could do it, but I'll ring you tomorrow.'

"He rang me back and said, 'I've got him. He's hardly done anything, but I think he'll be excellent. His name is Richard Attenborough.'"[21]

Even though IN WHICH WE SERVE was a propaganda film for the war effort, and even though it had the support of Lord Mountbatten and many in high places, it could not find a distributor to put up a guarantee. Del Giudice, who raised a little backing from a Major Sassoon, had to start production on Two Cities money. Had he been able to substitute a proper film star for Noël Coward, he would have had no such difficulty. The irony was that largely as a result of this film, virtually the entire cast would become stars - John Mills, Richard Attenborough, Bernard Miles, Kay Walsh, Celia Johnson, Michael Wilding....

In November 1941, Coward presided over a meeting of the whole unit. "I let fly about general inefficiency," he said, "and dropped a few dark hints about what might happen if an important propaganda picture like mine should be held up by the mismanagement and indolence of the studios."[22]

He had undoubtedly been warned about Bert Batchelor, the communist shop steward at Denham, who regarded Coward as little short of a fascist. As it happened, Batchelor would cause no disruption on this film; all Coward's problems came from the very authorities who were supposed to help him.

In December 1941, Jack Beddington, director of the Films Division at the Ministry of Information, rang Coward to say that the MoI would not be associated with the film since it showed a ship being sunk. This, the MoI believed, was bad propaganda.

Coward wrote in his diary, "Absolutely appalled by this utterly infuriating impertinence. Will ask Dickie [Mountbatten] to take script direct to Winston Churchill. Certain that there is a campaign still going on against me. Time will show."[23]

Mountbatten reassured Coward that he would handle the whole affair, and asked for a copy of the script to take to the King and Queen. Coward's hero-worship of Mountbatten reached a new peak. Later, on 8 April 1942, the King and Queen, together with the two Princesses, were brought to the set by Mountbatten. The Royal party watched Noël Coward make his Dunkirk speech and they were shown half an hour of cut sequences. The visit was covered by newsreels and David was shown shaking hands with his important visitors.

The film was now called IN WHICH WE SERVE, taken from the morning prayer said aboard ships of the Royal Navy. "Everybody thought it was a very silly title," said Ronald Neame. "However, I do remember Tony Havelock-Allan's mother telling someone her son had worked on a film called In Which We Breed."[24]

The royal visit: King George VI, Queen Elizabeth, Lord and Lady Mountbatten, J. Arthur Rank, Princess Elizabeth, David Lean, Noël Coward.

Three weeks before the film went on the floor, Coward asked that every member of the unit - electricians, sound men, carpenters - be sent a copy of the script. This created an unusual degree of personal involvement. And each actor received a letter from Coward asking him to arrive at the studio word perfect.

Shooting began on 5 February 1942. "David, Ronnie and I were quivering with nerves," wrote Coward.[25]

They began with the scene of the Christmas party in which William Hartnell was to play the marine. The actors - Wally Patch, John Mills - arrived on the set. But no William Hartnell. The scene was rehearsed with Michael Anderson, assistant director, in his part.

"I rushed out to get Hartnell," said Norman Spencer. "He was still getting dressed. We dragged him down to the set with the wrong boots and half made-up. Coward called for complete silence on the set and he tongue-lashed Hartnell in a way I'd never thought possible and fired him on the spot. Quarter past nine. First day of shooting. A big film. Hartnell out."[26]

"I would like to make something crystal clear to all of you," said Coward. "I expect to find the same discipline in this studio as I enjoy in the theatre. I have never yet in my career known an actor to be late for the first day's rehearsal. I wouldn't stand for it there and I am not standing for it here."[27]

Michael Anderson - at David's insistence - played the part with a moustache.[28]

Five days later, Coward wrote in his diary: "Tuesday 10 February 1942. Yesterday's rushes excellent. Whole staff working well and efficiently."[29]

It was perfectly apparent to the crew who was boss. And it wasn't David Lean.

"I had seen six deck chairs on the set," said Kay Walsh, "one had Noël Coward on it, another Gladys Calthrop - and at the back was one chair with David Lean on it. I watched it for two days. When I got home I said, 'What on earth were you doing sitting alone at the back? Those six people were as near to the camera as you dare get without casting a shadow. Who is going to say Action? Who is going to say Cut? Get that chair up there with those nobs or don't come back here.'

"This story must have got to Noël Coward because from then on he referred to me as Madam Nob."[30]

The Carley float scenes, which were shot in the studio tank, took seven days to complete. Seven days in which Coward and his fellow actors, smeared from head to foot with synthetic fuel oil, had to float all day in filthy, smelly water. Havelock-Allan had the job of ensuring that the water was eighty degrees.

"We all used to lower ourselves, holding our nose, into the water," said Richard Attenborough, "because the smell of the oil and sawdust was simply dreadful. But never the Master. Noël came up the slope, stood on the edge and dived into the tank with the most terrible belly-flop. He hadn't much hair and he came out of the water with the oil and stuff pouring off his face and he said, 'There's dysentery in every ripple.'"[31]

Mountbatten said later, "It was much worse than the real thing when you chaps had finished."

Coward's hatred of the tank brought out the worst in him. According to Ronald Neame, Noël Coward had two personalities, one the producer-director-writer, the other the actor.

"And like all actors he was a fourteen-year-old. It got to the point where Noël was practically leading a revolution against us. It was then that we attempted to talk to him and pointed out very forcibly that he was part of the management as writer and co-director. We were trying to put good material up on the screen but he was the one that should have kept the actors together supporting us. He said, 'When I am acting, I am an actor and you are the enemy.'"

One reason why the tank scenes took so long to shoot was the machine-gunning of John Mills. "They couldn't find out how to do it safely," said Mills. "You can't use real ammunition because we haven't finished the picture yet. Props sent out for dozens and dozens of contraceptives and fitted them on a long pipe and exploded them beneath the water. Of course, it was absolutely wonderful. They made the right noises and they looked perfect. So I can claim to be the only actor shot in the arm with a French letter."[32]

David had to direct Noël Coward in all the scenes in which he was in front of the camera. Had Coward been a megalomaniac and humiliated him before the crew, David might well have crawled back to the cutting-room for a decade or so. But Coward knew talent when he saw it, and he also recognised a true professional. He accepted David's direction and that acceptance added to David's stature in the eyes of the crew.

"Noël directed all the actors," recalled John Mills, "and David did all the camera set-ups. Noël never interfered at all. So David shot the picture. He was fascinated by what David was up to. I think Noël was brilliant just to let him carry on and shoot it. I never remember Noël saying, 'Well, let's have a look at another set-up.' The set-ups were David's."[33]

Continuity girl Betty Curtis had found that her work was far too complicated, and she needed an assistant. A girl called Maggie Sibley came straight from secretarial college to be interviewed by Noël Coward. She was sixteen, tall and thin with a pageboy bob. Coward turned to Gladys Calthrop and said, "She looks like a mad Degas."

Maggie thought that was the end of it but Coward asked her if she could start on Monday. At first she was over-eager, running to fetch a cup of tea for Noël Coward and falling flat on her face over the cables. But she quickly became an invaluable member of the unit, and eventually, as the redoubtable Maggie Unsworth, the longest serving member of David's team. She was on his first film, his last film and many of those in between.

"Gradually," said Maggie Unsworth, "you could see Noël gaining confidence in David and leaving him alone. Obviously, if David had a problem he would talk to Noël, but on the whole he let him get on with it. David's confidence grew and grew. He had wonderful back-up from Ronnie, Tony, Norman Spencer and all the people who were behind him. Whatever he wanted to do they would do it, sharply, quickly, efficiently."[34]

"I had a lucky break," said David, "because Noël got terribly bored. Finally he said, 'I think you'd better shoot everything that I'm not in and I won't trouble to come down to the studio. You're perfectly capable of doing everything.'

"And that's just what I did. When Noël wasn't in the scene, I was the director on the set. I felt so young and inexperienced I always expected the doorman would stop me coming in. The crew accepted me because I did know what I was doing technically. That was the awful thing, you see. I had been a good editor, but all I had to rely on as a co-director was my knowledge of technique. I knew where to cut in the close-ups, how effective it would be going from this to that. But I had never directed actors before.

"I suppose I more or less copied Noël when he left me on my own. I had a very nice cast and I just found myself obeying my instincts and with a great heave of moral courage said what I thought to them. Most of the time they listened to me and were kind. And the better they were - people like Celia - the easier they were.

"Celia played the Captain's wife and in a scene at Christmas she gives a speech in the wardroom. Holding up her glass she says, 'Ladies and gentlemen, I give you my rival. It's extraordinary that anyone could be so proud and so fond of her most implacable enemy. God bless this ship and all who sail in her.' And tears were pouring down my face. Wonderful."[35]

The sequence of the return from Dunkirk was directed in its entirety by David Lean, and counts as his first complete sequence as sole director. He had as extras the 5th Battalion Coldstream Guards.

"I remember this as the hardest and most exciting work I've ever done in my life as an assistant director," said Norman Spencer. "I was absolutely worn out at the end of the day with exhaustion and excitement at the whole thing - it was marvellous."[36]

Many of the troops had taken part in the actual operation, and many of the sailors were wounded veterans, convalescing. Mountbatten had taken one look at the professional extras attempting to play sailors, shuddered and substituted them with the real thing. Also a number of the girls who were playing nurses were authentic VADs.

The two directors of IN WHICH WE SERVE: *David Lean and Noël Coward.*

"When I saw David direct that scene," said Kay Walsh, "I knew there was no going back."[37]

Camera operator Guy Green was sent away on a destroyer to the South Atlantic to shoot second unit material.

"I remember David giving me a brief before we started," said Green. 'He said, 'When you're out on this destroyer, if you're attacked by a Stuka, try and get a shot of the bomb leaving the aircraft and follow it until it explodes.'"[38]

"The German aircraft which attack the *Torrin* were not models," said David. "They were supplied by the RAF from something called the Enemy Flying Circus, based at Duxford. It consisted of a small group of captured enemy planes which was used for battle practice and manoeuvres. RAF fighters would circle around them at a distance because if any plane could see these German markings they would open fire."[39]

One of the pilots, flying a Heinkel 111, was James Hill, a member of the RAF Film Unit who later became a film director. "It was all painted up with swastikas," he said, "and although everybody was alerted for miles around one couldn't help feeling a little uneasy."[40]

"We built the masts of the ship at Duxford," said David. "They were mounted on swivels. The pilot in charge of the German planes was a former garage mechanic called Suzy [Flight-Lieutenant R.F. Forbes]. He was covered in medals,

DFC and bar, AFC... One day, after work at Duxford, I said, 'Suzy, why are you doing this job?'

"He said, 'Well, I'll tell you. I was sent on a sortie over the Channel and I had a fight with a German plane. I ran out of ammunition and I guessed the German had, too. So I did a manoeuvre which would force him to shoot, if he had any ammunition left. He didn't shoot. We both knew the game was up. He came close and flew wing-tip to wing-tip and he pulled back his cockpit cover and took off his helmet. I did the same. He was blond. We flew alongside for some time, then he saluted and pulled off for France and I saluted and turned for England.

"'Until that moment I thought a machine was a machine. Of course, in a way, I knew there was a pilot there. But I didn't reckon for the blond hair. That really shook me. I realised I could never fire at another German again, because there was a young man like me in there.

"'I went back to the aerodrome and asked to see the commanding officer and told him this story. I thought I was going to get into God knows what trouble. He said he wanted to think about it and then he said he was starting this Enemy Flying Circus and did I want to run it? I said I would indeed, sir, how kind.'"[41,42]

When the film was released, Ronald Neame received a letter from a young boy who wanted to know why these German aircraft dropped British bombs. "He was quite right," said Neame. "We never thought anyone would notice!"

Filippo Del Giudice had run out of money. The whole project had been based on credit. The only hope left was for David to do an assembly of the first couple of reels and to show it to Sam Smith, head of British Lion.

British Lion was not then the grand organisation it became when Korda took it over. Smith ran it as a kind of poverty row outfit at Beaconsfield.

"I had worked for Sam Smith," said Kay Walsh. "I remember standing in the passage outside the theatre with Celia who was chain-smoking. Eventually, Sam Smith came out. He said, 'Well, Noël Coward and the Royal Navy is good enough for me.' And we were back shooting the next day."[43]

On Sundays, David and Kay dug for victory in their allotment. "We had the most wonderful marrows and cauliflowers. David was a great gardener and a great naturalist too. I have never met anyone like him in this regard. For me, a Cockney sparrow, to spend a day in the country with him was unforgettable. He had been a great bird's-nester when he was a boy. He knew the sound of every bird, he knew the clouds, he knew the flowers. He was a country boy.

"He told me once about going to the Quaker meeting with Buncs. He was about fourteen. Buncs picked a wild rose on the way and the whole meeting had been devoted to the beauty of the rose."[44]

Before IN WHICH WE SERVE was finished, this film about a naval tragedy had a tragedy of its own.

"We were shooting a scene of an explosion on a gun turret," said Norman Spencer, "a damaged gun turret, all twisted and misshapen. The camera was on a rostrum twenty feet high. The shot was a very simple one really. They had sacks of lycopodium, the old flash powder. They had a lot of film cans lying around. They filled them with this yellow powder, with electrical contacts in each one. On the word of command, somebody touched the wires, there was an enormous whoof, a sheet of flame, clouds of smoke and as the smoke cleared you saw dead and twisted bodies. It was a jolly good way of doing explosions. You put the sound on afterwards.

"We shot it once, and were lining up the second take. There was a chief electrician called Jock Dymore, a sturdy, ebullient man. He called out, 'Come on, chaps, let's get it in before lunch.'"

"Jock went on deck with his two chums to refill these film tins," said Ronald Neame, "and he carried a flash powder bottle. He took the lid off and didn't realise that the film tin was white hot from the previous explosion and it went off and blew the three of them off the deck and burned them in a dreadful way."[45]

"We had to sit on that rostrum," said Maggie Unsworth, "which had no sides, no protection, watching this drama. It was terrible."

"We were all shocked," said Neame. "Even David was shattered to the point where he said, 'Let's pack up shooting for the day.'

"As we were doing so, Coward arrived and asked why we weren't shooting. When we explained, he said, 'You can't stop even for something like that.' He told us that the show must go on, and how important the film was. I think if he'd been there and seen what we'd seen, he would have realised how shocking it all was."

Norman Spencer accompanied Jock Dymore to Hillingdon Hospital. "In the ambulance he was in a hysterical state of shock. He said, 'Norman, now listen…' and he gave me a tip for a horse-race at Lingfield. I remember when he was wheeled in to the casualty department, the nurse opened the blanket, looked at the doctor and he shook his head. Jock died in about half an hour. He was burned away by this terrible flame. One of the electricians, Ronnie Wells, worked almost to this day with a burned face, as bad as that chap who was burned in the Falklands. The smell of burned flesh is something I shall never forget."[46]

David edited IN WHICH WE SERVE, despite what the credits say. His first assistant, Thelma Myers, was made up to editor to satisfy the union. However, he had originally hired Reginald Beck.

"I started IN WHICH WE SERVE," said Beck, "and David promised me he wouldn't come into the cutting-room. After three weeks of shooting, he stole in

Freda (Kay Walsh) and Shorty (John Mills) encounter hostility in a railway compartment in a scene from IN WHICH WE SERVE.

one evening when I wasn't there and took a sequence which I'd cut and re-cut it. That was enough for me."

This may have been essential - to check whether a sequence worked to avoid expensive retakes. But by breaking his word, David offended Beck, and they never worked together again. "I'd hate to work for him," was Beck's opinion.[47]

The opening of IN WHICH WE SERVE was a documentary treatment of the laying of the keel of the *Torrin*, shot not by David but by Anthony Havelock-Allan and Ronald Neame at the Hawthorne-Leslie Yard at Newcastle. (The opening and closing narration is spoken by an uncredited Leslie Howard who did it as a favour to Coward.)

"The newspaper floating in the dock was my idea," said Havelock-Allan. "I had been one of those who, from 1936, thought war inevitable. When, in January 1939, the *Daily Express* published the headline 'NO WAR THIS YEAR,' I was outraged by it. Everybody I knew was, in a sense, pro-war and ready to go - war was inevitable, it had to be fought. And I remembered this headline and I thought, 'What a good idea. Let that be in the bilge, with the bottles and muck being swept away as the keel of this ship takes the water to fight Hitler.'

"Beaverbrook [proprietor of the *Express*] was absolutely furious, and didn't speak to Noël for a very long time. There was no question we were rubbing his nose in the fact that even a few days before the war he was still trying to tell us there wasn't going to be one.

"Noël was very good. He never said it wasn't his idea, he never said, 'One of my little darlings did it.' They thought he had written it into the script."[48]

IN WHICH WE SERVE had its premiere on 27 September 1942 at the Gaumont, Haymarket. It was the first time a premiere had been held on a Sunday. The showing, in aid of the Royal Naval Benevolent Trust, was attended by the First Lord of the Admiralty, the King of Greece, the High Commissioner for Canada[49] and Lord and Lady Mountbatten.

"The premiere was stuffed full of naval personnel," said David. "You couldn't look round without seeing admirals and famous wartime figures sitting there. One or two giggled quite a lot. They knew Noël, and found the idea of his being a ship's commander amusing.

"There was so much smoke in the auditorium I had to go up to the projection box and tell them to change to the lighter print - I had one standing by. Cigar smoke was an absolute killer of any light you try to thrust through it. They put on the lighter print, but the smoke still had the effect of flattening the photography."[50]

"Towards the end there was a great deal of gratifying nose-blowing," wrote Coward, "and one stern-faced Admiral in the row behind me was unashamedly in tears."[51]

All the survivors of the *Kelly* agreed that the film was astonishingly accurate.

Richard Attenborough had heard splendid things about the picture, and the impact of his brief appearance in particular, and he invited his parents down from the north, bought himself a dinner jacket and attended the great event. He eagerly awaited the cast roller to see his name on the screen for the first time. But there was no Richard Attenborough. His name had been left off.

"I took it up with Tony Havelock-Allan and he said, 'Oh dear, I'm afraid there's nothing I can do. It's a mistake.' I couldn't get over it for a week. It was my big chance, my parents were there, no name on the screen."[52]

David's father, reading his *Daily Mail* in St John's Wood, would have seen a headline 'BEST FILM OF THE WAR'. Looking closer he would have noticed that Noël Coward wrote, produced, directed and acted in it. Nowhere would he have seen the name of David Lean.[53] Beaverbrook's *Daily Express* had to admire the picture, their critic, Ernest Betts, calling it, "Human, deeply moving... brutally faithful and exact."[54]

C.A. Lejeune, who had been given the privilege of a visit to the set, said, "Coward has given us one of the most heart-warming, heart-stirring films this country has ever produced, either at peace or at war."[55]

Her rival on *The Sunday Times*, Dilys Powell, declared it was the best film about the war yet made in Britain or America, and she drew attention to the Dunkirk scene: "This sequence, with the tired British Expeditionary Force sleeping on their feet, but collecting themselves at the word of command into the disciplined movements of the soldier and marching steadily away to the sound of drum and fife, is conceived with a fine sense of pictorial narrative."[56]

The News of the World said, "This is Hollywood beaten to its knees by Noël Coward and the young men he gathered around him to make a film which will surely triumph as entertainment wherever it is shown."[57]

The film created enormous goodwill for Britain in the United States. Noël Coward was given an Award for Service to Freedom which was accepted on his behalf by Lowell Thomas, president of the Overseas Press Club and the man who had brought the exploits of Lawrence of Arabia to the attention of the world through his book and lecture.

The New York Film Critics gave their 1942 Award to the film. And in the 1943 Academy Awards, Coward received a special certificate for his "Outstanding production achievement on IN WHICH WE SERVE."

The film, which no distributor wanted to risk, had cost £240,000, considerably more than most films produced in England in 1942. But it made £300,000 in the UK alone - it was the year's most popular film - and it grossed $180,000 in America. It became one of Winston Churchill's favourite films.

Whatever criticisms can be made against it half a century later - the fact that so much of it is staged in a studio, the stiff-upper-lip dialogue of the officers, and the stereotyped remarks of the lower deck - one needs a heart of stone to resist its emotional impact.

After the film's release David, Neame and Havelock-Allan went to see Noël Coward at the Mitre Hotel in Oxford. At the next table was a group of people who were discussing IN WHICH WE SERVE.

"It's utterly ludicrous," said one, "this man playing the captain of a destroyer."

"Our conversation dried up and we all listened intently," said Neame. "Eventually, Noël Coward had to leave, and as he went he stopped by the table, turned to face them and said, 'Personally, I thought I was VERY GOOD!'"[58]

CHAPTER FIFTEEN

THIS HAPPY BREED

NOËL Coward was so delighted with the success of IN WHICH WE SERVE that he suggested his "little darlings" should film his plays. In order to make these films, Anthony Havelock-Allan persuaded David and Ronald Neame that they should form a company. "I invented the name Cineguild Productions," said Havelock-Allan, "which made Noël laugh. He thought it was very funny. The reason I did it was because there was a famous group in America called The Theatre Guild."[1]

Cineguild would become one of the handful of British film companies that discerning audiences grew to respect, like The Archers and Individual Pictures. Although its output was relatively small, practically all its films became accepted as classics of the British cinema. At least one of them was so quickly forgotten that not even the men who made it could remember it. The reason for their amnesia was that it was not a feature film, but a documentary.

Much as he admired Flaherty, and the expedition pictures he had seen as a boy, David's private opinion was that ordinary documentaries were not proper films. He seemed unimpressed by the achievements of the Crown Film Unit and when I showed him LISTEN TO BRITAIN, Humphrey Jennings' masterpiece evoking the wartime atmosphere, he was merely polite about it. I sensed a resentment, even after half a century, about the documentary boys, who had apparently made it plain that their films were infinitely superior to most feature films made in England at the time.

"The documentary directors hated us feature people," said David. "They used to look on us as sort of tarts making an easy buck. They were quite wrong. So we had a kind of distant war going on, which was a pity, and so I was never mad about these documentary directors."[2]

Because he felt so ambivalent about documentaries, he never advertised the fact that he actually directed one.

While Cineguild's first production - THIS HAPPY BREED - was on the floor at Denham studios, the Ministry of Information decided to make a series of documentaries for showing in countries the Allies hoped soon to liberate. Cineguild, as a feature production company, was not the MoI's first choice, but it came into the picture after the supervisor of the series, Basil Dearden, was recalled to Ealing Studios.

The first assignment, LA BATAILLE POUR L'AXE, later called L'ECHEC D'UNE

STRATEGIE (FAILURE OF A STRATEGY) was given in 1944 to editor Peter Tanner. David was director, Arthur Calder-Marshall was producer and Sidney Bernstein executive producer.

"The picture was planned as a very matter-of-fact account of the war (on both sides) from the Fall of France to the build-up to D-Day," said Peter Tanner. "It was to be factual and would contain no propaganda. The decision was taken to make it on the lines of MARCH OF TIME."

Peter Tanner's cutting-room at Denham was next door to the Cineguild cutting-room where Jack Harris was editing THIS HAPPY BREED. David divided his time between the two.

Between April and May 1944, Peter Tanner and David viewed thousands of feet of British, American, German and Italian newsreels. The Axis newsreels, which came in regularly in excellent quality prints, were duped by an agent in Lisbon, who, it was said, also duped the British newsreels for the Germans.

David on camera crane, with Ronald Neame (r)
filming THIS HAPPY BREED.

"David was an eye-opener to me," wrote Peter Tanner. "Time and time again he would pick just the right shot to illustrate a point succinctly. I learned much about editing from David which certainly helped me in later years. David's chief complaint was that he was bound to the length of shots in the original newsreel, which were often much too short or failed to make the point he needed. He used to sit swearing and fuming and running the material at high speed through the silent head of the Moviola. He used to ask for a certain shot that he had seen originally at the Imperial War Museum or the MoI and get quite annoyed if I didn't recall it instantly. He would then tell me what shots were on either side of the one he wanted. Amazing.

"I knew that we *had* to have a married print ready by D-Day, so I knew roughly when that would be. I believe that the first print went in on D-Day Plus Three and was shown in the first recaptured French town with cinema intact.

"Because it was all newsreel material, it was hard to file. We worked Saturday mornings in those days, and one Saturday my assistant had to go to the dentist. David came in and asked for a shot. It wasn't where it should have been. It was a shot of a tank moving through explosions. He became more and more exasperated as we searched and failed to find it. Finally, he called the whole HAPPY BREED crew in - Jack Harris, Marjorie Saunders and Cecilia Walsh[3] - and they ransacked the cutting-room while David paced up and down outside, chain-smoking. His other crew were hoping to leave at noon and soon it was one o'clock. They still hadn't found it.

"'That's it,' said David. 'But have it there first thing Monday.' My assistant came in on Monday, and I described the shot and he went to a can full of clips and things and said, 'Is that it?' I had pulled that roll out a hundred times and unrolled it too - but not far enough. There was something else at the front. The tank shot followed. But it shows that David never forgot a shot and would refuse to continue until he had it.

"He did much of the editing himself. You couldn't keep him away from the Moviola. I was delighted to have him take over. I was very inexperienced and to work with David Lean was an absolute thrill."[4]

If the surviving twenty-minute film proves anything, it proves that David's talents did not lie with documentary. His newsreel training enabled him to put the shots together effectively, although it must be admitted that the next film in the series, FAILURE OF THE DICTATORS, which David had little to do with, is more excitingly edited - "I learned from the master," said Peter Tanner, "and put the lessons to good use." [5]

The film has a few credits but the one noticeable by its absence is that of the director. The end credits say simply, "Written and produced by Cineguild". David borrows montages from German newsreels and drops in the occasional shot from a feature film and only occasionally is there the individual Lean touch - a close-up of boots in snow to symbolise the slow defeat of the Italians in the mountains. The film has some well-chosen shots - including an amazing shot from one German aircraft of another as it flies past the Parthenon. But it cannot compare even with the routine work of Humphrey Jennings.

David's film, over-dependent on maps, is somewhat confused in the story it is trying to tell, and looks like the work of someone who knows little about the war. Perhaps the only way David could have got it right was if the Allies had delayed the invasion. As it was, the liberated countries saw what was, to all intents and purposes, a rough-cut - the only time David Lean was guilty of that.

Forty years later, when David Lean was at Pinewood, Peter Tanner reminded him of the documentaries.

"He looked at me quite blankly and said that he couldn't recall them at all. I started to go into detail and he said, 'What was my contribution?'

"I said, 'You were only the director!' At which he roared with laughter."

Both Anthony Havelock-Allan and Ronald Neame could not remember them either. Eventually Havelock-Allan, confronted by pages of research compiled by Cy Young, recalled a few details.

"I don't think they had any importance," he said. "I never heard the results, never heard how well we'd done them or how well they'd done in the countries in which they were shown."[6]

Noël Coward's generosity to his "little darlings" at Cineguild, which should have sent his spirits soaring, actually caused David some anxiety. He knew from the Shaw films the difficulty of transforming theatre into cinema. IN WHICH WE SERVE had no theatrical antecedents. And nor, frankly, had he.

"It's awfully hard doing a stage play, it really is," said David. "You've got to bring in so many ideas to make it a screenplay. A film demands an intimate look at the scene that one cannot do on the stage.

"I remember 'Binkie' Beaumont once asked me to direct a stage play. I said, 'Binkie, no. I don't know enough about it. I wouldn't know how to bring the audience's focus on to a certain part of the stage. I'd be lost. No, I'm going to stick to my movies.'

"And I did. I was going to say I'd rather like to be on the stage at Drury Lane and have a crack at it, but that would be a kind of self-flattering fantasy."[7]

David turned down another flattering offer - to co-direct HENRY V with Laurence Olivier. He confessed his lack of knowledge of Shakespeare, and said he didn't want to tag along behind Olivier and Shakespeare merely as a good technician.

"I'm glad I didn't," said David. "Larry did it himself and he did it very well."[8]

The Cineguild triumvirate chose THIS HAPPY BREED as their first production. After IN WHICH WE SERVE, they still wanted a propaganda element to whatever they made. THIS HAPPY BREED was propaganda for the stoicism, humour and resilience of the British people. It was a small-scale play, covering several decades in the life of an ordinary British family. How could Cineguild give it a modern touch, and make it an even more attractive proposition? The answer was Technicolor.

"When I first wanted to do the picture in colour," said David, "everybody thought it was really disgraceful. I had all the highbrows at Denham saying, 'Why on earth are you doing it in colour?' I said, 'Why not? It's new and it excites me.'"

Technicolor was not exactly new - the company released its first picture in 1917 - though relatively few British films had been made in colour. And David was always an enthusiast for the latest technology.

"In order to make Technicolor less glorious," said Ronald Neame, "we had to exaggerate the age and dirt on everything before it would show on the screen. The tide mark round the bath, for example, the stains on the wall and the paintwork - it all had to be too much to make it come out right."[9]

"It's very difficult to get filth to look anything in colour," said Anthony

Havelock-Allan. "Rotting fish usually looks like Titania's Coach."[10]

The President of the Technicolor corporation was Herbert T. Kalmus who insisted that every Technicolor production needed a "Colour Consultant". In charge of this was Kalmus's wife, Natalie.

"We had a rather nice lady called Joan Bridges on the film," said David. "She was called Colour Consultant, and she was one of Natalie Kalmus's assistants. We were contractually supposed to take very strict notice of what they said. It was balls because they didn't really know.

"You can do almost anything with colour. I doubt if I have ever altered a picture because of the colour. And yet these Colour Consultants used to say, 'That napkin over there has got to have a little more grey in it, please. Just a bit too bright.'

"It was like the old days in the black and white films, when everyone had to wear a blue shirt because the cameraman said he couldn't cope with white shirts. Now actors wear white shirts and the wisdom of the past is looked upon as a lot of nonsense.

"It was a sort of affectation, I suppose, and Technicolor were pretty vehement in their criticisms. HAPPY BREED was the first colour picture I'd ever done and I wanted to mute the colours. In the early days, Technicolor was looked upon as bright and vulgar. I used to say to people, 'Make your hand into a kind of tunnel, put it up to your eye and notice as it comes to your eye that the colours increase in density.' And they'd hold their hand up and say, 'My God!'

"And I'd say, 'That's what the screen is doing to colour. Look through a camera and you'll find it looks brighter than seeing it by eye.' So we withdrew the colour when it became too obtrusive - I'd look through the camera and see a picture postcard on the mantelpiece looking like a bright red blob - I'd take that out."[11]

Eileen Erskine remembered the dismay of the female members of the cast when they were provided with clothes of muted colours, such as beige and grey. She only fully realised how progressive Cineguild had been when she saw the restored version of the film at the National Film Theatre half a century later, and realised how "modern" the colour looked.

THIS HAPPY BREED had been written by Noël Coward in 1939 and rehearsals had been interrupted by the war. The film went into production during the Haymarket run of the play.

The subject was close to Coward's heart, for it followed an English lower middle-class family from the end of the first war to the beginning of the second. Coward was the product of just such a family - in just such a suburb - but he had distanced himself to such a degree that when he wrote their dialogue it failed to ring as true as his upper-class dialogue.

Keeping an eye on the light; an anxious David Lean on location in Clapham for THIS HAPPY
BREED. Technicolor needed an enormous amount of light and the unwieldy three-strip camera,
seen here, took a long time to move. Director of Photography, Ronald Neame (right), looks
more confident. Operator Ralph 'Bunny' Francke.

"Noël's lower orders are very specially Noël's lower orders," said Havelock-
Allan. "They don't bear an exact relation to the people that he's writing about.
They're absolutely splendid theatrical copies. There is something a little
condescending about the writing. The condescension is that he escaped from it
and really, how awful they were, seen from his more superior and, by adoption,
upper-class attitude."[12]

Noël Coward played the role of the head of the Clapham family on the stage.
David felt he was totally wrong for the film and Coward took the implied
criticism in good heart. David suggested Robert Newton, and Coward gave his
approval. But David had the feeling that Coward never fully forgave him for not
letting him play the part himself.

"Noël used to think nothing of his writing ability and nothing of his ability to
compose music," said David. "What he loved and yearned for above anything else
was praise as an actor. And quite honestly, I don't think he was a terribly good
actor unless he came out with a cigarette-holder and a dressing-gown.

"Robert Newton may not have been right, but he had a good stab at it. I had
a great weakness for Bobby Newton. He used to drink far too much. And when
he had a couple of drinks, he would speak the absolute truth, which could be
horrifying. I remember him talking to a friend of mine after lunch, when he'd

had a couple of drinks, and he leaned across the table and said, 'Now I'm going to tell you about you.' And he did, bang, on the dot, you know. Withering. He could be cruel, but what he said was undeniably true. I loved him."[13]

Both David and Noël Coward were besotted by Celia Johnson after her brilliant performance in IN WHICH WE SERVE. She had since worked on a picture called DEAR OCTOPUS, directed by Harold French from the Dodie Smith play, and had written, "Never again will I do a film unless I am absolutely *mad* about the part."[14] Noël Coward had to beseech her to do a test for THIS HAPPY BREED.

Because the test was in Technicolor she found it more irritating than normal, complaining that the make-up made her, "very pale so that one looks like a ghost, all wan and rather blue. I felt it needed only a touch of phosphorescence and I could haunt with any old ghoul. It takes ages, too."[15]

Celia Johnson was placed in a "torment of indecision". Her home life was complicated and she did not want to do the film. She wondered how she could contribute to the war effort by "knocking the world sideways as a Cockney mother of three." But Coward swept aside her objections and insisted that her "great gift" should come first. And so, with great reluctance, she accepted.

"Accents were not her strong point," wrote her daughter and biographer, Kate Fleming, "and she never felt very comfortable in the part."

Fortunately, she admired her fellow players, and her director. "I like David Lean more and more," she wrote. "He is not only extremely efficient but very nice and thinks I am good which is always endearing."[16]

But that didn't mean she liked the picture. She thought she was the one weak spot and neither looked right nor sounded right. "To me, I don't look like a real person and that is so important on the movies. Still, Noël saw the first stuff we had done and seemed pleased with it all."

David remembered that she could hardly bear the film. "Whenever we finished a scene," he said, "she would go to her script, tear out the page we had just done and screw it up and throw it on the floor. Celia was wrong really, although she's such a wonderful actress, she's nothing to do with Clapham, even acting at her best."

"Celia was the only actress who thought acting was of secondary importance to living," said Ronald Neame. "She was first and foremost a wife and she loved her little home and she found Bob Newton difficult to work with. We all did a bit. Bob had been told by Noël that he must not drink and that any time he was drunk on the set he would forfeit five hundred pounds of his salary. It was in his contract. His salary for the whole film was, I think, nine thousand pounds, and this was very serious for him, so he didn't drink at all during the first weeks of the film.

"We always said we would let Celia go early on Saturdays. In those days, we worked on Saturdays and the reason we let her go at midday was that there was a shortage of petrol and she hadn't got a car - she had to go by train to London and then down to Nettlebed. If she missed that train she had to wait for two hours for another.

"We were going to rehearse a scene round about midday for the following Monday morning. It was a very important scene, a scene where Kay Walsh, who played her daughter, comes back after having run away with the young man. It was a very emotional scene. I remember David saying, 'Celia, let's go though it once.' And Celia said, 'It's just too bad, you do this to me all the time. You promise I can go at twelve o'clock, and you know how important it is for me, and now here we are…'

"And David said, 'Oh, just once, Celia, just once through, that's all.'

"And so Celia looked at her watch and said, 'Five minutes.' I'll always remember this. She played that scene with Kay Walsh - it was about three and a half minutes long - and by the time they'd finished their rehearsal there wasn't anybody on that set without tears in their eyes - electricians, everybody - because it was the most beautifully played emotional scene. The only one who wasn't affected was Celia, who looked at her watch and said, 'Well now, can I go please?'"[17]

Noël Coward had left for a tour of South Africa and Asia. "It was pleasant," he wrote, "to be concerned with the picture but not trapped by it. I could never quite prevent a sinking of the heart every time I drove through the gates of Denham Studios - they recalled so many leaden and difficult days - but at least in these circumstances, with David and Ronnie doing all the actual work, I could say what I had to say and get out again before the atmosphere really defeated me."[18]

Stanley Holloway examining Cinex strips (tests of rushes) with David, Robert Newton and Ronald Neame on the set of THIS HAPPY BREED.

Now that David was directing an entire film without Coward's help, his colleagues watched carefully to see how he handled the actors.

"He was a marvellous director," said Eileen Erskine. "He gave you so little direction. He was amazingly modest where actors were concerned, yet he seemed to have enormous regard for them."[19]

That charitable view was not shared by his closest colleagues.

"David wasn't very fond of actors or actresses," said Ronald Neame. "He knew they were very important to him and therefore he did his best, in a condescending way, to accept them as people. He wasn't like Hitchcock, who said they should be treated as cattle. But he didn't really like them. He was at his best with actors who were completely secure - and Celia was one of the most secure ladies I've ever known. He was not good with actors who were insecure, who were nervous, or who needed their confidence built.

"I'll always remember on THIS HAPPY BREED that when he'd got a take he liked, he asked every one of us technicians what we felt. And I remember John Mills saying, 'Well, what about the fucking actors then? Aren't you going to ask us what we think about it?'" [20]

"The actors came second," said Norman Spencer. "He calls 'Cut' and whispers to his camera operator, 'Did you get the composition right?' He hadn't got that talent Carol Reed had of saying to an actor, 'Oh, that was marvellous,' talking to them first and then going to the technicians. David lacked guile there." [21]

There are directors, mostly American, who give no direction to their actors; as Cecil B. DeMille used to say, "I hired you to act, so act." But David was deeply concerned about performance and despite his lack of empathy with actors, he did his best to guide them. The fact that Noël Coward, a harsh judge of acting, left David alone to direct his favourite plays with his favourite players, was evidence enough of his ability.

While David was shooting a film peripheral to the war, his brother Edward was deeply involved in the war effort. He had been with British Intelligence in the Norwegian landings and the Germans let it be known that there was a price on his head. He was re-trained and devoted the rest of the war to his work at the BBC. He had recently published a book, *Voices in the Darkness*, about the BBC campaign against the "attack on truth" led by Goebbels.

David, on the other hand, displayed little concern for the war, and he was not alone in his attitude. Celia Johnson was amazed by the outlook of the people at Denham studios.

"This is really the most extraordinary place," she wrote. "No one appears to take the faintest interest in the war. Literally not the faintest, though now and again they are annoyed because they can't get five hundred horses without going to Ireland for them…" [22]

By the time THIS HAPPY BREED went into production, in 1943, the tide of war was turning in the Allies' favour. The worst days of the Blitz were long over, and much of London lay in ruins. The City had been pulverised and the South would soon face attack from the V1 rockets. Meanwhile, David wanted to open the film with an impressive wide-angle view of London as it looked in 1919.

The standard view from Waterloo Bridge was out of the question since the bridge itself was under reconstruction and the buildings around St Paul's Cathedral were almost all damaged or destroyed by bombs. But by hauling the Technicolor cameras to the top of a gasometer in Battersea they were able to achieve a magnificent panorama of London which, from the distance, appeared to be undamaged. Had it been seen by the Germans, they might well have questioned their own propaganda.

For one scene, shot in the studio, David needed additional light. He also needed an additional piece of script, since Coward had omitted it. The problem of this scene, where Vi (Eileen Erskine) breaks the news of the death of the brother, Reg, in a motor accident, was solved by Ronald Neame who suggested a very slow track across the room, gradually revealing more and more of the garden and keeping the audience in suspense.

"They think they're going to see something," said Neame, "and then when we get to the other side of the set, the parents come round the corner and back into the house and we know that they've received the news."

David thought this was an excellent idea. But in order to hold the entire room and the garden beyond in focus, the scene had to be shot using a small aperture. Technicolor stock was very slow, so a considerable increase in the lighting was required.

Bert Batchelor, the ETU shop steward, refused to co-operate. "We can't get you this amount of light. We haven't enough brutes here to light it," he said.

When David insisted, Batchelor reminded him there was a war on, merchant crews were dying in the Arctic Sea trying to bring us oil and David wanted extra power for what appeared to be a whim.

"David stood up to him," said Kay Walsh. "I was so proud of him. It was pretty frightening to be faced by Bert Batchelor and David was a little bit of a moral coward. But he stood his ground."

Extra lights were brought in from Nettlefold and Pinewood Studios and the scene was shot. David followed the action of the play once the tracking shot came to a halt. Frank (Newton) and Ethel (Johnson) walk back slowly in stunned silence. There is no sound except for the radio. In the play, you heard it softly, but David keeps it playing bright dance music throughout the scene, adding a poignant counterpoint. Neither Frank nor Ethel bother to turn it off since they are not aware of it. The camera retreats and the scenes fades out.

"A literal depiction of such a terrible moment," wrote critic Gerald Pratley, "could not possibly be more moving or believable than this little gem of content by implication." [23]

"In choosing the set-ups," said camera operator Guy Green, "it was very much a collaboration. David was the dominating influence but he would welcome suggestions. He was very good about that. He was very happy to discuss with me and Ronnie - we would discuss a great deal. On the set I found him very sympathetic. He was great with technicians, and a wonderful film-maker. I think he was born to be one. It was in his blood."[24]

David was also sympathetic to the plight of other film-makers, particularly those he admired. When Carol Reed ran into trouble with THE WAY AHEAD and was unable to find a cameraman, David suggested giving a break to Guy Green.

"This was terribly generous," said Green, "because finding reasonable personnel during the war wasn't easy and David had to find another operator."

The operator was enormously important to David, and fortunately he found another congenial man, Ralph "Bunny" Francke. That act of generosity was returned ten-fold: Guy Green proved to be a cameraman of genius and went on to photograph David's two Dickens films so brilliantly that the visual style still seems fresh and daring.

Robert Newton had kept his drinking firmly in check, apart from one lapse at a

David with Robert Newton (as Frank Gibbons) and Celia Johnson (Ethel Gibbons) on the set of the 1924 Wembley Exhibition - a memorable moment of David's youth.

party when he insulted Noël Coward. Newton was later arrested in Haymarket for being drunk and disorderly.

In the final scene Newton, playing Frank Gibbons, was about to leave Sycamore Road and was wheeling his grandchild in its pram. Coward had written a long speech for Gibbons, which was addressed to the baby:

"There's not much to worry about really, so long as you remember one or two things always. The first thing is that life isn't all jam for anybody, and you've got to have trouble of some kind or another, whoever you are. But if you don't let it get you down, however bad it is, you won't go far wrong... You belong to a race that's been bossy for years and the reason it's held on as long as it has is that nine times out of ten it's behaved decently and treated people right..."

When Kay Walsh read this speech she said, "The baby can't sit up and say 'Rubbish!' I drew David's attention to it. I said, 'It won't do. This is Chamberlain.'

"I never considered that David had a great brain, but he could see that it was worth examining. Edward came down to us for the weekend and David said, 'Ed, what do you think about this?' He said, 'Kay's absolutely right.'"

Anthony Havelock-Allan felt the speech struck a false note. But Ronald Neame's reaction was entirely different; he wanted the speech retained.

By this time, Coward had returned from his tour of the Far East and was playing Gibbons on stage at the Opera House, Manchester.

"It was a very un-Noël part," said Kay Walsh, "with the braces, and wheeling the pram around. Anyway, he really did mince us. He was very cruel. And we were so scared. But here was this man who had toured Australia, travelled to America, was worn out from a Far East tour and here come these people from Denham who haven't lost a night's sleep, questioning the very work he was appearing in so successfully.

"David and Tony were there, but Ronnie was missing. It turned out he wanted his son Christopher in the pram." [25]

David recalled a "terrible argument" and said that after a difficult half hour Coward agreed to cut some of the speech. "We cut out quite a bit," said David, "but still it was there on the screen and it would embarrass me still, I think." [26]

Curiously, David's memory was at fault here because, in the event, the entire speech was cut.

When THIS HAPPY BREED was completed, David nervously showed it to Coward at Denham studios.

"I remember coming to a scene that I was very unhappy about [the death scene] and I said as it was coming on, 'Look, Noël, tell me what's wrong with this.' And he said, 'My dear, I think if you had her standing and him sitting, it might have helped.'

"Bang on, you see. He was always dead right at that sort of thing, at being able to put his finger on something that was wrong in the choreography, or in the sort of staging."[27]

When the film was premiered, Noël Coward was in India and the event was presided over by his mother. Although the critics did not receive it with the lyrical acclaim of IN WHICH WE SERVE, they were nonetheless enthusiastic.

C.A. Lejeune noted that it lacked the emotional surge of the naval picture, but "the only people who will find it dull are those bores and prigs who find life itself dull." She reserved her most fervent praise for Celia Johnson: "Often she looks awful but by thunder! as an actress she's superb."[28]

This time, David received the praise due to the director, and such criticism as there was was reserved for Coward.

"Should not the observation be a trifle less benevolent, the defence of the ordinary man a trifle less condescending?" asked Dilys Powell.[29]

Noël Coward had told David, "You must know precisely what every character has for breakfast, even though you must never show them eating breakfast."[30]

Yet on THIS HAPPY BREED that is precisely what David did. Almost wilfully, he took every mundane event the cinema avoided - washing up, drying clothes, a great many meals - and worked the dialogue into them. For a British film to do this was unusual enough, but to show the kitchen sink, albeit in muted Technicolor, was revolutionary.

Realising this treatment could become claustrophobic, he opened the film out in the manner of the Hollywood version of Coward's CAVALCADE - the Victory Parade, the General Strike, even the arrival of talkies (for which David used scenes from the 1929 MGM musical, BROADWAY MELODY) followed by Coward's line for a member of the audience, "You know I don't understand a word they say."

In the rigid class structure of British society, the lower middle-class Gibbonses were a rung or two below the Leans, but David worked in many personal details from his own upbringing.

A confrontation between the father and the errant son Reg takes place in an upstairs bedroom similar, one suspects, to the one David occupied at Park Lane, its walls decorated with photographs of Douglas Fairbanks and Charlie Chaplin. Robert Newton is obsessed with his crystal set, and for the last moments of the life of King George V, David shows silhouettes of old-fashioned wireless aerials against the night sky.

With the pram scene removed, the film ends as it began, the camera left alone in the house after the Gibbonses move out. The camera retreats up the stairs, through the window, and we dissolve to the long shots of South London with Coward's new song "London Pride" triumphant on the track.

Mainly due to problems with Technicolor, the picture took far longer to make than anyone had anticipated. It consumed ten months and cost the then excessive amount of £220,609. But it proved to be Britain's top moneymaking film for 1944.

Anthony Havelock-Allan thought the Cineguild team should be seen in the right places, so David and Kay, with Ronnie and his wife, Beryl, came to London and stayed at the Savoy and Claridge's.

"Noël would take us to the theatre," said Kay Walsh. "We went to see *Blithe Spirit* when he'd taken over from Cecil Parker. He would take us to the Ivy. It was a wonderful time."

It was at the Savoy that Havelock-Allan was able to introduce David to his hero, William Wyler, the famous director. Wyler, who made the classic tear-jerking propaganda picture, MRS MINIVER, was in Britain making a colour documentary called MEMPHIS BELLE, which required him and cameraman William Clothier to fly missions over Germany with the bomber crews. He and David became friends.

"He said he was flak-happy," said Kay Walsh, "and that he was doing penance. He was so ashamed of the food he'd put in the shelter scene in MRS MINIVER. He was a darling man." [31]

David's brother, Edward, was living with a divorcee, Doreen Sharp, and they had a son, Anthony, born in 1940. Because of the war, they had done nothing about getting married. When they came to live with David and Kay at Denham, during the doodle-bug raids, David decided to straighten out their lives and arranged for them to be married at Slough register office.

"If it hadn't been for David," said Doreen Lean, "I don't think I'd ever have married Tangye. There is a story that after the wedding I was heard to say, 'Well, now at least you can divorce me!' Because once I was married he could leave me whenever he liked, in the way David Lean treated his wives." [32]

CHAPTER SIXTEEN

BLITHE SPIRIT

WHEN Noël Coward presented Cineguild with BLITHE SPIRIT it was an extremely valuable property. The play had opened in London in July 1941 and by the time Cineguild had completed THIS HAPPY BREED it was still running. It had played eighteen months on Broadway. The American studios were after it, and although Coward wanted £80,000 and a percentage, his trust in Cineguild mirrored Shaw's trust in Pascal.

But David was even less happy about BLITHE SPIRIT than he was about THIS HAPPY BREED. If there was a kind of film he disliked it was polite comedy. "He had a strong prejudice against upper-class frivolity," said Anthony Havelock-Allan. "He considered it lighted-headed, unserious and unimportant. Whereas MY MAN GODFREY and NOTHING SACRED were my favourite films of the period, David didn't enjoy them. BLITHE SPIRIT wasn't his world. Nor was it Ronnie's. As a result, it was not a very happy picture."[1]

As David recalled: "I said to Noël, 'I'm not ready to do this sort of stuff. I know nothing about comedy, especially high comedy. And with this you haven't any yardstick to compare it with. It's completely unreal. A ghost of a dead wife in the house, the present wife can't hear her, the husband can and he talks to her - I don't know how to handle it.'

"He said, 'Nonsense, my dear. Of course you can.'"

The play was close to Noël Coward's heart because it was the last he wrote with Gertrude Lawrence in mind. She had gone to America, she had married and thus, he felt, had gone from his life. He portrays her as a ghost.[2]

There was little that could be done with the script. The play was the apple of Coward's eye and he did not want it expanded or altered. All that could be done was to add a fresh line here and there to get the actors out of one shot and into another.

"What do you boys want?" Coward would ask at script conferences. "Sitting room to bedroom? Good. Got a pencil and a bit of paper? Here you are."[3]

The action in the play was limited to a single room. The film had a composite set of a complete house in which to expand the action. Coward had only one stipulation: "It must be the sort of house you'd want to live in." Gladys Calthrop was on hand to ensure that at least it matched her taste.

The set had to be built on an exceptionally large scale because of the ghost. She had to be specially lit, and passing behind other players would cause terrible problems. The unit considered the old-fashioned double exposure "corny" and wanted to find a distinctive special effect.

"We must have plenty of space to work," Lean told C.A. Lejeune, "because we have to keep the spots on Kay Hammond and nigger out the rest of the cast. Technically, this movie's murder."[4]

"We played twenty-six minutes of the film in one room," said Anthony Havelock-Allan. "David never thought of himself as a comedy director, never thought that he wanted to be. And he therefore didn't have a very happy relationship with Rex [Harrison] who did know about comedy and sensed right away that David wasn't very sure of himself.

"It had one more handicap which I didn't see at the time, but should have done. The play is about Charles Condomine, a middle-aged novelist who has long ago forgotten the days of his raunchy youth, who's now soberly married to a nice but rather dowdy woman. Not very exciting, but his work goes well, he's happy, he's made money. And out of the past comes his first wife, who was obviously a dish and with whom he had a great deal of fun. She reminds him of all that, and he gets the seven-year itch. Rex Harrison looked about twenty-six years old [he was thirty-six] and it never occurred to me at the time. It's not

The ghost of Elvira (Kay Hammond), bathed in green light in the Technicolor print, and her successor (Constance Cummings) in a scene from BLITHE SPIRIT.

funny if it's a young man; it's only funny if it's a middle-aged man. It was at its funniest on the stage when it was played by Cecil Parker.

"Kay Hammond was very, very good on the stage, but she had a slow delivery and did not photograph very well. She had a potato nose and heavy-lidded eyes and did not look like Veronica Lake.

"What should have given us the clue was the scene after the first visitation and Condomine is left on the sofa holding a cushion, a seraphic expression on his face. He's got his young wife back and they've just had a tremendous romp and they're lying there exhausted and blissfully happy on the sofa. And the second wife, who's been waiting for him upstairs, comes down and says, 'What are you doing? Have you gone mad?'

"And the electrician next to me turned to his mate and said, 'What the hell is he wasting his time with that bug-eyed one for when he's got that dish waiting for him upstairs?' In other words, the wife, Constance Cummings, looked more sexually attractive to him than Kay. That again was absolutely dead against the thing. We weren't able to convey the intense pleasure it provided in the theatre, so it wasn't a success, but I do think David did a marvellous job for a man who didn't like that kind of comedy." [5]

David imposed a closed set on the film, as he remembered Paul Czinner had done for Elisabeth Bergner. This was possibly due to his insecurity, but certainly due to the fact that a long section of the film had to be rehearsed like a play and any interruption could have been devastating.

Despite his precautions, David was so bitterly disappointed by the first two days' rushes that he went to see Michael Powell.

David confessed that he had completely misunderstood what Noël was driving at in the sequence he was shooting. Powell said he often misunderstood what Emeric was driving at until the preview.

"No, no, Micky, this is serious. We have been shooting for two days, and I realise that it's all wrong. What am I to do?"

"Scrap it. Go back and reshoot it. You are the boss."

David said that if he were to tell the others that he'd made a mistake and they had to retake two day's work, they'd never forgive him.

"Do it in the projection room, at the end of the rushes. They're going to wait to hear what you're going to say anyway.'

"He gave a hollow laugh. 'You don't know Ronnie and Tony. They would never respect me again.'

"'Oh yes they will. We are all fallible. They will respect you for realising what you were doing and they'll respect you for saying so. And then they'll respect you for having the cheek to say you're going to retake it. You've got a ten percent contingency in the budget that will take care of that.'

"He groaned and said he would try." [6]

I thought that David might have simply been depressed by the rushes. He had to view them in black and white and I imagined they might have looked flat. But Havelock-Allan said David's distress had nothing to do with film stock or photography. He was finding it extremely difficult to direct the actors - or at least Rex Harrison.

Harrison's apparently effortless acting would seem to have required no direction, but he was actually as insecure as David himself. "Despite a certain arrogance," said Ronald Neame, "he didn't know if he was funny or not and I don't think David did either."[7]

"I was rusty after all those years away from the set," wrote Harrison, "and to start with was all fingers and thumbs. David was ill at ease with comedy and his tension communicated itself to me. I remember one occasion when I had struggled through a scene in rehearsal and Lean turned to Ronald Neame and said, "I don't think that's very funny, do you?" Neame echoed, 'I don't think it's very funny, no.' They could hardly have thought of a better way to hamstring an actor."[8]

Rex Harrison, with his rich experience of innuendo, undoubtedly thought David and Neame were being sarcastic. David denied flatly to Stephen Silverman that it had ever happened, and Neame could not recall it, either. Anthony Havelock-Allan did.

"Rex did something in a scene that was meant to be amusing. And when David cut he said to Ronnie in a loud voice, 'Is that funny?' meaning, quite genuinely, 'Have we a funny scene?' And that was what upset Rex. Like all actors, he took it for a criticism. What David was saying was, 'This is something that was obviously designed to be funny, and has been perfectly well played, and I don't know if it's funny because it's not my kind of humour.'"[9]

Rex Harrison, Margaret Rutherford and Constance Cummings.

"Rex Harrison just took me apart," said David. "We got into a most unfortunate state. He was being much too nice, and the whole point about his part is that the ghost of his dead wife comes back and the living wife thinks he's gone mad.

"Rex was playing it very sweetly because he liked being liked. And that is a failing of a lot of actors; they want to be liked by the audience. Very often they are right. If the whole audience goes out of the cinema saying, 'Oh, wasn't he wonderful? I love him!', it's a great plus. You have to have great strength of character to have the audience leaving saying, 'What a shit!'

"I said, 'Look, you've got to snap at her, Rex.'

"He said, 'But audiences will think me so rude.'

"Actors don't like being thought rude, or some of them don't. He'd say, 'Oh shut up, old girl.' You can't get a real snap in it if the actor just refuses to do it. And I got into a terrible state with Rex.

"He'd say, 'All right, we'll do another take.' And it would be exactly the same, which is an old actor's trick with directors. And you had to have a lot of courage to say, 'No, it's exactly the same. Cut. Let's go again.' In the end we were looking at each other with completely blank faces, neither of us giving way. I didn't know what to say, but what I eventually said was, 'Look, Rex, I know you think I'm no good as a director - that I have to accept - but you are going to do as I tell you to get this film right. If you don't, you know that I'm a bloody good cutter and I'm going to leave you in shreds on the floor.'

"That helped a lot, but he never really forgave me. He gave an interview shortly before he died in which he said, 'When you're on a comedy, it's awfully hard working for a director who has no sense of humour.' Really funny and really devastating.[10]

"In private life he was very amusing and very nice. He was one of the vainest men I ever met, but jolly clever. Even in MY FAIR LADY, in which, God knows, he was very good, he was a sort of cheat. I'm sure Bernard Shaw would not have approved and I don't think Professor Higgins was meant to be charming. He was a tough character. But he gave it another kind of dimension. Audiences loved him because he was charming and funny as only Rex can be. Good as it is, it is not really Professor Higgins, and yet he won every award for it."[11]

Everyone who worked with David agreed on one thing: you did not expect to have fun. David regarded the making of films as a deadly serious business. He had caught the spirit of those pioneers who felt that what they were doing was of almost religious significance. "He thought about film," said Anthony Havelock-Allan, "as a Jesuit thinks about his vocation."

David was not a man to crack jokes. He was, however, a talented raconteur, who used his voice well and needed time for his stories to take effect. He preferred low comedy to high, situation comedy to wordplay. He made me laugh frequently, although one would never describe this essentially serious character as a funny man. But there was no doubt he appreciated comedy; was it not Mrs Egerton's imitations of Charlie Chaplin which first drew him to the cinema?

Constance Cummings was curious casting for an upper middle-class English wife, for she was American. She had come to England in the mid-thirties and married playwright-producer Benn Levy, but she was fondly remembered in America from films like MOVIE CRAZY in which she had been the foil for Harold Lloyd. As one of those brave souls who stayed in London during the Blitz, she had been accepted as a British actress, and she could adjust her accent to a degree. But she was still cast as an American in films like THIS ENGLAND and THE FOREMAN WENT TO FRANCE.

"Why did they cast me? I don't know," she said. "Noël must have had something to do with it. We were friends and Benn had been friends of both Noël and Gertie [Lawrence]. I had been in BUSMAN'S HONEYMOON in which I was supposed to be an English bluestocking married to Lord Peter Wimsey. Some people complained about that!

"David Lean was very nice. He was utterly engrossed in what he was doing and for that reason seemed - aloof is not the right word - preoccupied, not responding with jokes. Rather like Laurence Olivier when he was rehearsing or directing, he would get so preoccupied you'd find you would speak to him and he wouldn't hear you. David was like that. Ronnie, as a director, wasn't like that. He was just as serious, he took his work as seriously, but the minute he'd got the scene as he thought it should be he was ready to joke with anybody.

"Maybe what I thought was his being quiet was the fact that he wasn't at ease with this really silly, surface kind of comedy. There was a lot going on inside David Lean.

"The thing I longed for was much more funny stuff," she added, no doubt remembering her days with Harold Lloyd. "Ronnie Neame and I used to get into a corner and joke. We called ourselves the Corn King and Queen - we used to get these wild ideas of things you could do photographically with the ghost, which couldn't be done on the stage. Ronnie even suggested some of these things to David. But David had to photograph the play as it was, because Noël wasn't around. Before he left, Noël gave instructions, 'Don't play around with it!' which was a pity in a way, because it is pretty difficult to have a third of a film in one room.

"I don't know whose idea it was when Condomine had to drive Elvira into Hastings for lunch, and she says she wants to drive. She gets into the driving seat and they go by a policeman [actually an RAC patrolman] who suddenly looks at this car with nobody driving. This wasn't in the play - it couldn't be. I longed to have the film full of things like that."[12]

Margaret Rutherford, the epitome of the charmingly dotty middle-aged Englishwoman, had been one of the attractions of the stage production, and she gave the film much of its endearing quality. David was very fond of her.

"I always thought she must have been aware of how eccentric she was, but not at all. For one scene she had to eat a sandwich. She'd say something, take a bite and munch away in a very funny exaggerated way. I went up to her on rehearsal and said, 'Margaret, a little less with the sandwich, I think.'

"And she'd do it again and I'd say, 'Even less still.'

"We broke for lunch and went to the restaurant at Denham and I remember looking across and there was Margaret eating a sandwich in exactly the same way as she did on Take One.

"She was a dear, sweet woman. She was good in everything she did. And she would take on a kind of majesty, walking across a stage like a duchess."[13]

"Noël didn't want a transparent ghost," said Ronald Neame. "He wanted Elvira (Kay Hammond) to look exactly like the ghost in the play. Gray chiffon lit with a green light that followed her everywhere, even when she went behind people or furniture. This was one of the toughest assignments I ever had as a cameraman, but it was worth it."

To achieve the effect, Kay Hammond had to cover herself with a thick liquid make-up and a wig of greenish grey "hair". David decided to shoot Elvira only when seeing her from Condomine's point of view. Whenever the wife looks at

The shadow of Margaret Rutherford as Madame Arcati, Joyce Carey, Rex Harrison, Hugh Wakefield, Constance Cummings.

her she isn't there. So effective were these simple devices that the film won an Academy Award for special effects!

Noël Coward was abroad for most of the time Cineguild were making BLITHE SPIRIT, so whenever they were confronted by a lack of Noël Coward dialogue, they had to make it up themselves. Then came the nerve-racking moment when David had to show the roughcut to its author.

"The lights came up after the showing and I said, 'Well what do you think?'

"Noël said, 'You've just fucked up the best thing I ever wrote.'

"I said, 'I'm sorry. I did warn you I didn't know anything about high comedy.'

"I got back at him because years later [in 1957] I was in New York and he did it on television with himself as Condomine and Lauren Bacall playing Elvira and it was really appalling. Mine was a masterpiece compared to what he did. I met him after and I said, 'You've just fucked up the best thing you ever wrote.'"[14]

The reaction in the industry was one of disappointment. Film people felt David had fallen back on the old method of setting up a group shot and tracking in. Or, as Rex Harrison rather more brutally put it, "David set up a stage set and just photographed it. Four of us got up in line and then Margaret Rutherford would walk down the middle pulling faces."[15]

Kay Walsh felt that David should never have touched it. She admired IN WHICH WE SERVE. "And then to do THIS HAPPY BREED in rooms just twelve feet by twelve, to have been able to move the camera around and turn that into a movie was to me absolutely magnificent. But to assume that he could then go into Coward's wittiest comedy and direct Constance Cummings, Margaret Rutherford, Kay Hammond and Rex Harrison was really asking too much. I think he was wrong to accept it. He simply wasn't ready for it."[16]

The reviews were nonetheless welcoming.

"BLITHE SPIRIT is the wittiest, funniest creation of the English screen," declared William Whitebait, concluding that René Clair's THE GHOST GOES WEST and I MARRIED A WITCH were millstones by comparison with this satire on spiritualism.[17]

"After months when British films popped up here and there only to distress and embarrass, there suddenly blossoms at the Odeon today a British comedy that, I think, surpasses the most competent and effervescent nonsense we have got from Hollywood in many a long year," wrote Simon Harcourt-Smith in the *Daily Mail*.

He admitted that in the opening sequences he feared that here was mere photographed stagecraft. "But suddenly the whole scope of action broadens, we find ourselves in the presence of that rare object - a work of art which, however minor, has been correctly translated from one medium to another - and on the whole, I think, gained in the process....Here is a production that should do something to redress the balance of the eighty odd million dollars we pay out every year for the privilege of looking at American films." [18]

C.A. Lejeune did not consider it a very good film, and felt that it might have been better had Noël Coward been around to encourage David Lean and Ronald Neame to take greater liberties with his material. [19]

Dilys Powell was not enthusiastic either, but grudgingly admitted it was probably "as good a film as could be made if the play was to be preserved entire." [20]

The lack of enthusiasm from Lejeune and Powell, the two critics who meant something to him, and from whom he had received such glowing reviews, might not have depressed David so much had Noël Coward's reaction not been so crushing. But David seemed to lose heart. [21]

"I went to the Odeon in Kensington and saw it with him," said Kay Walsh. "And I said, 'I know how you feel, I know it hurts. But you know, next week, look at all those faces, they will be sitting here looking at something else. Put it on that level.'" [22]

But to have put it on that level would have demeaned the craft he loved so much. It would have acknowledged its ephemeral nature, would have implied there was something trivial about it. Once a film director believes that, he has either graduated as a fully-fledged cynic, or he leaves the business.

The film was a failure in America, too. According to Sheridan Morley, it was subjected to misleadingly sexy posters "and an orgy of tasteless publicity." [23] While tasteless publicity has seldom hurt a film in America, audiences were not amused. It was partly the timing. Even people who were fond of Coward, like John Gielgud, disliked the play, feeling that a comedy about death was hard to accept in time of war. This had not hurt the stage version, but it may have had something to do with the failure of the film.

David Lean remembered that it was a great success in just one country - India - only because it featured a ghost.

Financially, the film itself is a ghost. According to Anthony Havelock-Allan, it has still to make its money back.

CHAPTER SEVENTEEN

BRIEF ENCOUNTER

ONE aspect of industry practice which astonished and dismayed David was the power wielded by the distributor. As an editor, he was aware of their tyranny only from a distance. He knew, though, that producers or directors had to secure finance from one of the big distribution companies, and if one of their middlemen considered the story commercial he would enquire the names of the proposed cast. If the names were not "box-office", the proposition would be turned down. The producer or director would then have two alternatives: abandon the idea or miscast a star.

"Not wishing to starve," wrote David, in one of his rare articles, "he would probably choose the second course and the film would proceed. When the film was finished, the agonising day would arrive when the distributor would see the rough-cut. This was a nerve-racking experience, and I have sat in on many such sessions. When the lights went up at the end of the show, all eyes would turn to the man from Wardour Street. The distributor was virtually in charge of production, story, cast and final presentation." [1]

In David's opinion, the change in this wretched condition took place when Filippo Del Giudice of Two Cities Films set out to make IN WHICH WE SERVE with Noël Coward. Only Sam Smith, of the grandly named but little known British Lion Corporation, was willing to invest in a major work of entertainment and propaganda.

It proved a very sound investment. From that moment, Del Giudice embarked upon the policy of leaving the creative side of film-making to the film-makers and, with IN WHICH WE SERVE behind him, he successfully fought off all the old Wardour Street controls and the following films appeared: THE FIRST OF THE FEW, THIS HAPPY BREED, THE WAY AHEAD, BLITHE SPIRIT, THE WAY TO THE STARS and HENRY V.

Meanwhile, two other film-makers had similar ideas: Michael Powell and Emeric Pressburger. They approached J. Arthur Rank and asked for financial support and the freedom to make the films as they wanted to make them. Rank agreed and Independent Producers was formed. Powell and Pressburger, calling themselves The Archers, produced THE LIFE AND DEATH OF COLONEL BLIMP, I KNOW WHERE I'M GOING and A MATTER OF LIFE AND DEATH.

Frank Launder and Sidney Gilliat, who had been screenwriters for Hitchcock, formed Individual Pictures and produced THE RAKE'S PROGRESS, I SEE A

DARK STRANGER and GREEN FOR DANGER. Ian Dalrymple (Wessex Films) made THE WOMAN IN THE HALL and ESTHER WATERS. Cineguild made BRIEF ENCOUNTER.

Anthony Havelock-Allan took Cineguild away from Two Cities because he saw no reason why they should give a large percentage to the parent firm. When they joined Independent Producers, that percentage went to Cineguild, which was another advantage of working for J. Arthur Rank.

Rank admitted frankly that he knew nothing about the making of films; he allowed his directors to make them as they thought best. It is therefore ironic that Rank's name produces the kind of reaction among cineastes that Krupps' produced among pacifists. He is still regarded as a soulless tycoon, taking over cinemas from dedicated film lovers and forcing on the public stereotyped soap operas of British life.

A soulless tycoon did indeed take over the Rank Organisation when it ran into financial squalls, but in this earlier period, thanks to his policy of allowing the film-maker to get on with his job without interference, Rank helped to create a brief but remarkable period in British cinema. One of the most admired films of that period - and surely the most famous - was BRIEF ENCOUNTER.

"I wanted to do something else after BLITHE SPIRIT," recalled David. "Tony Havelock-Allan, Ronnie Neame and I were all very keen on a book called *The Gay*

Celia Johnson in the refreshment room set of BRIEF ENCOUNTER.

Galliard which was about Mary Queen of Scots. And I said to Noël, 'I'd rather like to try something like that.'

"Noël said, 'My dear, what do you know about costumes? You know nothing. You don't even know how people walk. Stick to the contemporary scene. Stick to what you know. Don't be foolish. Here, I tell you what, I've got this sketch, have a go at that. I'll write you a script very quickly.'

Celia Johnson with the grit in her eye, with Joyce Carey and Stanley Holloway.

"And about ten days later he had a full script of *Still Life*.[2] I read it and said, 'Noël, I don't think it's any good. This woman arrives at a railway station and gets some soot in her eye, meets this man and they arrange to meet next Thursday, and it goes on and in the end they part. It's got no surprises in it. It's not intriguing. You're not saying to the audience, 'Watch carefully. This is interesting.'

"And he said, 'Such as?'

"And under pressure I said, 'Well, such as... supposing we started with a fairly busy waiting-room. There are two people sitting at a table, talking, a man and a woman. Through the door comes another woman who sits down at the table. As she sits talking and talking, you realise there's something not quite right going on and a train comes into the station. 'That's your train,' says the woman. 'Yes,' says the man, 'I must go. Goodbye.'

"'He shakes hands with the other woman and then you go back and explain that this is the last time they see each other. They were never going to see each other again. And you play the first scene in the picture - it made no sense to you at all and you didn't hear half the dialogue - again, and that's the end of the film, with an added piece, perhaps, with the husband.'

"He said, 'Say no more,' and off he went, for about four days, and he came back with what was essentially BRIEF ENCOUNTER."

Anthony Havelock-Allan insisted that Noël Coward did not write any of the script. "The script was written by David, and myself and Ronnie. You realise that *Still Life* was a half-hour playlet which takes place entirely in the waiting room of a station. We had to invent scenes that were not there. And there were lots of places where there was no dialogue. We said, 'Could they go for a row in the lake? Could they go to the cinema?' Noël said, 'Only if they go to a bad film.'"

"I wasn't so close to BRIEF ENCOUNTER as I was to the others because I went to America," said Ronald Neame. "During the six weeks I was away, David and Tony Havelock-Allan worked on a first draft screenplay and then I came back and joined them. Because we did everything as a trio, we all took credit for the screenplay.

"We all knew pretty well the way Noël wrote, and so we would fill in scenes. We would put stand-in dialogue until we saw Noël and I remember on one occasion he said, 'Which of my little darlings wrote this brilliant Coward dialogue?'

"We would go to his studio and give him an outline of what the scene should convey. 'Get out your little pencils,' he would say. He would then pace up and down the room, pouring out the dialogue quicker than our pencils could put it down. He worked very quickly. It was always said that he wrote the play of *Blithe Spirit* in three days. And he said, 'I did put it down in three days but it had the whole of my life behind it, you know.'" [3]

"There was a terrific hunt for the title," said David. "I remember Noël saying, 'We've got to think of a good title for this.' It was obviously going to be a small film. 'A brief something - something short.' Noël, Gladys Calthrop and I had various guesses, all bad, and it was Gladys Calthrop who suggested BRIEF ENCOUNTER." [4]

The first choice for the role of the doctor, Alec Harvey, was Roger Livesey, who had starred in THE LIFE AND DEATH OF COLONEL BLIMP. But when David and Havelock-Allan were shown a rough-cut of Anthony Asquith's THE WAY TO THE STARS they were struck by an actor in the secondary part of Squadron-Leader Carter, the commanding officer, who gets killed early in the film. The actor was Trevor Howard.

"He had one shot on an aerodrome - and I'll never forget it," said David. "A plane came in over the field and did a victory roll. Trevor Howard looked up and said, 'Lineshoot.' [5] It was wonderful. Just on that one word, the way he said it and the way he looked, I said, 'That's him.'" [6]

Noël Coward was shown the scene in THE WAY TO THE STARS and said, "Don't let's look any further." [7]

Trevor Howard's agent sent him the script and before he had time to read it, Havelock-Allan telephoned to ask when it would be convenient for him to go to the tailor for fittings.

"I'm afraid I can't," said Howard. "I'm taking my wife to the cinema."

No one had told him he had got the part.

From the moment the idea took shape, Coward and the Cineguild triumvirate wanted Celia Johnson to play Laura Jesson. She still loathed making films, and hated the enforced separation from her family, yet she knew she would have to play the part when Noël Coward read it to her in October 1944.

"That is the trouble with being an actress," she wrote to her husband, Peter Fleming. "You do want to act even in such an unsatisfactory medium as films, and a good part sets one itching. And it is a good part. It's about a woman, married with two children, who meets by chance a man in a railway waiting-room and they fall in love. And it's All No Good… It will be pretty unadulterated Johnson and when I am not being sad or anguished or renouncing I am narrating about it. So if they don't have my beautiful face to look at, they will always have my mellifluous voice to listen to. Lucky people."[8]

Modern audiences are often puzzled by the fact that this famous war-time film shows no sign of the war - lights are blazing, trains run on time, chocolate is purchased without coupons. But *Still Life* was written in 1935, and the film is set in the late thirties. The reason David put up with that outlandish peaked hat which Celia Johnson wears in the film was to signal both the date and the fact that she was meant to be provincial.

"Now, of course, people say, 'Oh, that hat. It dates the film.' Well, it was meant to."[9]

David arranged with Isabel to send their son, Peter, to Bedales, the progressive public school, and to see him from time to time. More often than not, he had to cancel. In a rare letter to Peter, David wrote, "I have to leave for Lake Windermere early on Sunday morning and we shall be away for two weeks on a railway station called Carnforth. We start work every night at ten-thirty and finish at six in the morning, and then sleep all day. I am not looking forward to it very much as you can imagine."[10]

According to David, the reason they went to Carnforth, which is in Lancashire, was because it was a long way from the South Coast and there was plenty of time to douse the lights in the event of an air-raid. But by 1945, the Germans were being defeated on all fronts and they had precious little air force to cope with the invading Allies and could only launch the occasional nuisance raid on Britain.

The main danger came from the VI rocket bombs and the even more devastating V2s, which were indifferent to the black-out. Though they had no particular target, apart from Greater London, the Ministry of War overrated their sophistication. A mass evacuation had been ordered in July 1944, obliging the LMS railway to move its staff from London. Office blocks at the main London termini remained empty for the rest of the war.[11]

The BRIEF ENCOUNTER company were regarded as official evacuees. They had

On location: David Lean gazes warmly at Celia Johnson as she rehearses a scene with Trevor Howard.

originally been assigned a London station but Carnforth was safer, even though large quantities of munitions were routed through it. The assistance of a Railway Transportation Officer was vital to ensure that the movements of the film train did not conflict with priority traffic.[12]

"Carnforth was quite a big station," said David. "The Royal Scot used to go through every night at one-fifteen and I used to stand on the edge of the platform shaking with excitement holding Celia's arm as the thing roared through within six feet of us. Just wonderful."[13]

The winter of 1944-5 was bitterly cold. When they weren't needed, the actors huddled in the waiting room where the stationmaster maintained a roaring fire. To his intense surprise, David enjoyed making the picture. He found himself in tears at some of the emotional moments.

"You'd think there could be nothing more dreary than spending ten hours on a railway station platform every night," wrote Celia Johnson to her husband, "but we do the whole thing in the acme of luxury and sit drinking occasional brandies and rushing out now and again to see the expresses roaring through."

However, she had appalling nerves over the responsibility of carrying the film.

"I am scared stiff of the film and get first night indijaggers before every shot but perhaps I'll get over that. It is going to be most awfully difficult - you need to be a star of the silent screen because there's such a lot of stuff with commentary over it - it's terribly difficult to do."[14]

However, despite shivering with cold by the time the early morning fish train from Scotland pulled in - and doing a scene with the stink of herrings in the air - Johnson managed to get a kick out of the experience. Even when she returned to what she described as "the awful factory dreariness of Denham," she continued to enjoy herself. She liked David and the other members of the unit, such as cameraman Robert Krasker,[15] and the feeling of victory was in the air.

While Carnforth Station was used for establishing shots, most of the film was shot at Denham studios. Exteriors were filmed in nearby Beaconsfield and, for the boating scene, at Regent's Park in London.

The art director was L.P. Williams, who had worked for Herbert Wilcox when David was at B&D. He had been in command of an SOE camouflage unit in Italy, had contracted amoebic dysentery and been invalided home. He had dropped into Denham to see what was going on, and was promptly given the job of designing BRIEF ENCOUNTER. Williams made sure that Coward's regular designer, Gladys Calthrop, was kept well away from the production.

"I did a lot of sketches and showed them to David and he said, 'Just the job. But we must show them to Noël Coward.'

"When we showed Coward the sketches he said, 'They're no bloody good. That's not the idea at all. The whole point of the thing is that these are absolutely ordinary people... living somewhere like Golders Green.'

"Once he told me what he wanted, no trouble from then on. But when you read a script, you're rather liable to put the people into the circumstances you'd like... The settings were more upmarket than Coward wanted."[16]

Joyce Barbour had been cast in the role of Dolly Messiter - the chattering friend who bursts into the refreshment room at the crucial moment when Laura and Alec are on the edge of a decision. But Barbour had been ill and had difficulty remembering her lines. She also suffered from camera fright and David found it impossible to cope with her. However, Barbour had been Coward's choice.

"Once an actor becomes entrenched in a part," said David, "and they've done several weeks' work, you cannot change them. Although on BRIEF ENCOUNTER we did change an actress - the woman who keeps talking and talking. I took Noël aside and said, 'Noël, it's just not working.' He saw the material and said, 'God almighty, it's dreadful. You've got to change her.'

"We did, and played Everley Gregg in the part."[17]

Celia Johnson found it difficult playing opposite Trevor Howard, who was having to learn film acting virtually from scratch. He did not seem a very bright man, and David wondered whether he had been absurdly optimistic in hiring him. Yet he was to prove one of the finest and most professional of all British film actors, the male equivalent of Celia Johnson, in fact, and it is a tribute both to him and to David that BRIEF ENCOUNTER contains one of his most sensitive performances, and the one by which he was always known. But to reach that exalted plane was extremely difficult for all concerned.

Howard had particular difficulty with the scene in the refreshment room where he is supposed to catalogue diseases. It had to be apparent, despite the dialogue, that he and Laura were thinking of something very different. Howard took ages to get this right, and while David ordered take after take, Trevor improved but Celia, worn down by the weariness of repetition, lost her spontaneity.

David admired Trevor Howard. But he came into sharp contact with what he considered Howard's bull-headed refusal to understand what the part was all about.

"There's a scene in which he begs her to come back to a flat he's borrowed from a friend. She refuses, gets on to a train and sits down, and we hear the doors banging all the way up the train, hear various whistles, the engine gives a hoot and there's a jolt and then it starts to move. She jumps out on the platform and we dissolve to her walking up a stairway to a front door. She rings the bell and Trevor Howard opens the door. It's raining and they talk about the weather. He lights the fire and says, 'I expect the wood was damp.'

"We did a rehearsal of this and Trevor came over to me and said, "David, will you please explain this to me. It's a fucking awful scene.'

"I said, 'What's fucking awful about it?'

"He said, 'They know jolly well this chap's borrowed a flat, they know exactly why she's coming back to him, why doesn't he fuck her? All this talk about the wood being damp and that sort of stuff.'

"I said, 'Look, Trevor, have you ever been out with a girl, ever been on a dance floor with her, and you know that you're going to make love, whether it's her place or your place, but you know this is going to happen? And then when you get there and the door is shut and you're alone, everything's changed and there's a kind of embarrassment that you hadn't got when you were surrounded by people?'

"He looked at me and said, 'Oh, God, you are a funny chap.'

"I said, 'Funny chap or not, that's the way we're doing the scene, now come on.'

"And that's the way we did it, and he just thought I was mad. He was so insensitive he didn't know what we were doing half the time. He later became a wonderful actor, but oh dear, there were a lot of things that went straight over his head."

The scene at the flat is interrupted by the unfortunate arrival of the owner, Stephen, which causes Laura to run out in panic. To play Stephen, Valentine

Dyall had been cast for his Puritan countenance - David would have encountered any number of those in his own family circle.

"The Valentine Dyall character is not sympathetic at all," said David. "That flat is really a hostile place, uncosy, unwelcoming. It's all to do with guilt. If the flat had been different, it would have taken away a whole colour. I don't think the audience should have thought, 'Well, come on. Now you're alone.' They're not alone. Laura's husband is there as far as she's concerned. And guilt is all over the place.

"You know, men can be terribly hostile to other men who they think are a success with women. I think Dyall suddenly saw red because there had been a woman there, although he must have known what was going to happen. And remember the times, remember the times.... that scene contained the horror of discovery, the overlay of guilt, the lot. It *should* have ended in ugliness."[18]

Anthony Havelock-Allan had an argument with David over the set for the flat in which the scene took place - or rather the entrance to the flat. Laura ignores the lift and walks up the stairs to the first floor, emerging in a strikingly modern corridor. What was such a modern block doing in an ordinary market town like Milford Junction? It is uncannily similar to Mount Royal, Marble Arch, where David lived.

"Neither David nor I thought there was anything wrong with the design of it. But he wanted her to go up to the fourth or fifth floor. I said to him that it would be ridiculous if she walks up and doesn't use the lift - and it would be a great deal more expensive. After all, this was a little black and white picture which none of us thought would set the world on fire. And he agreed, reluctantly.

"Funnily enough, I think he did live on the fifth floor at Mount Royal. Because I lived there too - on the fourth. I still don't know whether he was right or not. But it was about the only battle I ever won."[19]

David's intention was to spin out the suspense; would she or would she not join the doctor at their illicit meeting place? "I always feel conscious when I'm making a movie that it's an eavesdrop. BRIEF ENCOUNTER is a kind of eavesdrop on those two people; they're two of the least likely people to have a secret love affair, highly respectable and dead honest, and you are fascinated by the way it works with them."[21]

The parallel between his father and the woman he ran away with - both "highly respectable and dead honest" - must have made the story more personal than even Noël Coward could have realised.

In his book on David's films, Gerald Pratley wrote: "The only weaknesses are the synthetic Cockneys in the synthetic station buffet played by Stanley Holloway and Joyce Carey, the comedy of the lower orders once more rendered in caricature."[21]

This view is shared by the majority of critics and David himself disliked the comedy relief, saying, "They embarrass me every time I see them."

But, as Anthony Havelock-Allan pointed out, Coward was a skilful theatre writer and he knew that the story would be intolerably sad without those scenes.

"The most risky thing I ever did was in BRIEF ENCOUNTER," wrote David. "In a couple of very intimate scenes we dimmed the lights out during the scene so that the two characters were the only things illuminated. As a station bell rang we jumped up the lights on the background. It gave the scene a great added intimacy and didn't look in the least tricky."[22]

But however much the director helps with unusual effects, nothing can substitute for a good performance.

"Film acting is, in fact, thinking," said David. "I take a lot of trouble explaining to the actors the atmosphere I am trying to secure, then I talk to them about the situation they are in and I try to suggest to them what they are thinking. Most of the time it works, and it has the added benefit of not removing the actor's pride.

"This is as effective in long shots as in big close-ups. If somebody is running away from having murdered someone, if they're thinking right, they run or walk correctly, because the thought dictates the walk.

"When Celia jumped on to the platform in that scene, she made for the exit which was at the end of a slope. I couldn't tell you exactly how she does it - it starts with a walk, she goes into a little bit of a run, slows down, a bit of a run. I printed the first take and I said to Celia, 'Just one moment. How on earth did you do that? I could tell everything you were thinking by the way you were walking.' And don't forget she had her back to camera all the time.

"She said, 'Well, I don't know... she would, wouldn't she?'

"And that was all, and it worked because she was thinking, 'I shouldn't be doing this, but it's terribly exciting.' And every thought transmitted itself to the legs."[23]

On 4 May 1945 the BBC announced the news of the German surrender in Northern France.

"At the studio excitement became intense at lunch-time by the report that all Technicolor cameras had gone to the Palace," wrote Celia Johnson, "and bets were laid and work haphazard on account of having to rush out to listen to the radio between every shot. A sign of tremendous upheaval was stressed by the unprecedented buying of a bottle of rather nasty white wine by Tony Havelock-Allan at lunch-time on our table."[24]

At last the news came through that Churchill would give the official announcement for the end of the war in Europe - VE Day - at three o'clock on 8 May 1945.

On VE day, David and Kay, together with Norman and Barbara Spencer, were invited to a party given by Frank Launder at 38 Park Place in Mayfair. It was the former home of Gertrude Lawrence.

"David particularly wanted to see the crowds," said Norman Spencer. "We joined the throngs and pushed through boisterous, dancing people outside Buckingham Palace and Parliament Square and had to force our way through the people on foot to get to the party."

"It was stuffed with film technicians and actors like Trevor Howard," said Kay Walsh, "and there were a great many drunks. It was not a day of rejoicing for me. I was very unhappy at that party. David was looking for his escape route again."[25]

That evening, however, David encountered William Walton in St James's Park and such being the euphoria of the day, Walton broke a vow to avoid drink and they celebrated and congratulated each other on having survived.[26]

A cloud of mystery hangs over the editing of BRIEF ENCOUNTER, for there are two credits on the film: "Film Editor Jack Harris" and "Associate Editor Marjorie Saunders". Why would David, who only needed one editor because of union regulations, suddenly need two?

"Jack Harris was David's editor," said Charles Saunders, Marjorie's husband, himself a film editor. "Marjorie was Jack's assistant. When BRIEF ENCOUNTER came up, Jack was in the United States. David told Marjorie, 'You cut it. If there's anything wrong, I'll let you know.'

"We lived near the studio and she worked very long hours. Sometimes, she would ring me up and say, 'Darling, I'm stuck.' So I'd go and help her out."[27]

When Jack Harris returned from his trip to Hollywood, he went over what was virtually a fine cut. He made several cuts of his own, and there was no questioning of abandoning his credit, which was why Marjorie Saunders has such an unusual credit herself.

When it came to the music, Noël Coward had asked for Rachmaninov's Second Piano Concerto which was his favourite piece of music, though he had not used it in the play.

"There was a big argument over the Rachmaninov," said John Huntley. "Muir Mathieson said that it was wrong to adapt classical music. He felt every film should have a specially composed score. David Lean had agreed. But Noël Coward said, 'No, no, no. She listens to Rachmaninov on the radio, she borrows her books from the Boots Library and she eats at the Kardomah.'

"Muir said, 'I will only do it if you show her switching on the radio and if you respect the original music.'

"Coward was happy to play fast and loose with the music, but if you listen to it you'll hear that it begins with the first eight piano chords and ends with the last part of the third movement of the concerto.

"As the last bars of Rachmaninov were played, everyone dissolved into tears in the audience and even Muir admitted that no specially composed score could have been quite so effective as that Rachmaninov."[28]

"A lesson in humility may be good for everybody," said David, "but I didn't need a lesson in humility in those days. I was a very frightened young man."[29]

After Noël Coward's succinct reaction to BLITHE SPIRIT, David was understandably nervous about his - and the public's - response to BRIEF ENCOUNTER.

"I was making GREAT EXPECTATIONS down at Rochester when the first print came through," said David. "I suggested we ask the local theatre if they would run a preview. Rochester was a pretty tough town in those days and at the first love scene one woman down in the front started to laugh. I'll never forget it. And the second love scene it got worse. And then the audience caught on and waited for her to laugh and they all joined in and it ended in an absolute shambles. They were rolling in the aisles - partly, I must admit, laughing at the woman, she had such a funny laugh. I remember going back to the hotel, and lying in bed almost in tears thinking, 'How can I get into the laboratory at Denham and burn the negative?' I was so ashamed of it."[30]

Rochester was a foolhardy place to preview such a middle-class film because it was right next to Chatham Dockyards, and the cinema was packed with sailors. Even IN WHICH WE SERVE might have had a rough ride.

However, when the film reached the audience for which it was intended, the critical praise was so resounding that Rank's publicity department feared a backlash from working-class audiences - as if working-class audiences read newspapers like *The Observer*. In the industrial north it was advertised as being good - "in spite of the wild praise of the London critics."

C.A. Lejeune, writing in *The Listener*, said she would choose it as a desert-island film, "because it seems to me to catch, in words and pictures, so many things that are penetratingly true. The whole colour, the spring, the almost magical feeling of the discovery that someone's in love with you; that someone feels it's exciting to be with you; that is something so tenuous that it's hardly ever been put on the screen."[31]

Thus began the career of a classic - one of the most famous and fondly remembered of all British films. Its story, characters, settings and music have been the subject of critical debate, of mockery, of adaptation and a remake.

On 29 September 1947, the BBC broadcast a radio version, with acknowledgement to Coward and Cineguild. Trevor Howard recreated his role for an American TV version of *Still Life* in 1954 in which he played opposite Ginger Rogers(!). It was remade, with Sophia Loren(!!) as the provincial housewife and Richard Burton as the doctor, in 1974.

BRIEF ENCOUNTER was parodied by the comedy team of Mike Nichols and Elaine May and its scenes of parting at the station were recreated in a television commercial (directed by Alan Parker) for frozen food. Someone even made a homosexual version of BRIEF ENCOUNTER called FLAMES OF PASSION, which was the title of the film that Laura and Alec see in the cinema.[32]

In 1980, Celia Johnson and Trevor Howard were reunited on television in *Staying On*, Paul Scott's coda to *The Raj Quartet*. Perhaps some day the two films will be shown as a double-bill because *Staying On* shows what might have happened to Laura and Alec had they run away after all.

"Curiously enough," said Anthony Havelock-Allan, "we thought the only place it would be received well would be in France, because there is a 1937 French film called L'ORAGE with Charles Boyer and Michèle Morgan which was not unlike

Trevor Howard and Celia Johnson hurry away from the dreadful FLAMES OF PASSION. (The title, an in-joke, referred to a silent Herbert Wilcox film.)

ours. It was directed by Marc Allegret and it was a story of a Paris business man who goes to the South of France on business and meets a girl there and starts a romance. It all ends tragically and he goes back to his wife.

"There was a showing for the important French Gaumont circuit. They said, 'Oh no, it is nothing. We don't want it at all.' The film went to Cannes where it won the Critics' Prize.[33] Gaumont was then persuaded to have another look, and still thinking it was no good, they played it. The French people who saw it loved it - they still said what the French would say, that they didn't believe they didn't go to bed. I mean, they couldn't have it that two people could be in love and didn't somehow find the opportunity to go to bed. Only the English, they said, could do that."

David felt that they had gone too far, from a commercial point of view. "We defied all the rules of box-office success," he wrote. "There were no big star names. There was an unhappy ending to the main love story. The film was played in unglamorous surroundings. And the three leading characters were approaching middle-age. A few years ago this would have been a recipe for box-office disaster, but this wasn't the case with BRIEF ENCOUNTER. The film did very well in this country in what are known as 'the better-class halls' and [it had] a similar success, but on a smaller scale, in New York."

The film started its New York run at an art house called The Little Carnegie with a satisfactory week's receipts. "But at the end of the fifth week came a big surprise," wrote David. "The takings for Saturday broke the box-office record for the house. That was the fifth Saturday, when, in the normal way, business would be expected to be dropping off. This state of affairs can only have come about by word-of-mouth recommendation from those who had seen the film."[34]

The picture ran for a solid eight months and David subsequently became the first director of a British film since Korda to be nominated for an Academy Award.[35] David, Neame and Havelock-Allan were also nominated for their screenplay.

BRIEF ENCOUNTER had turned David into something of a public figure: his photograph had appeared in newspapers and magazines and he was approached one day by a total stranger at a railway station.

"The man was rather a horsy type, and he was in an absolute fury. He said, 'I am told you are the gentleman who directed a film called BRIEF ENCOUNTER. I would like to express my disapproval of you. I am exercising the greatest restraint in not hitting you.'

"I said, 'I'm sorry about that. But what do you mean?'

"He said, 'You showed that lady - Celia Johnson I think is her name - considering being unfaithful to her husband. Do you realise, sir, that if Celia Johnson could contemplate being unfaithful to her husband, my wife could contemplate being unfaithful to me?'"[36]

Even though BRIEF ENCOUNTER was an example of "cinema", as opposed to a filmed play - its technique of flashbacks and sometimes flashbacks-within-flashbacks still seems audacious today - David was keen to break away from Noël Coward. He had planned to move away after what he considered the disaster of BLITHE SPIRIT. Ronald Neame had already left to prepare the new production for Cineguild, GREAT EXPECTATIONS.

The next Coward film, THE ASTONISHED HEART, was therefore directed by a new team - Terence Fisher and Anthony Darnborough and produced by Sydney Box for Gainsborough - although Celia Johnson was still the star. Coward later remarked of it, "Nearly good, but not quite."[37]

"When David left Noël," said Kay Walsh, "Noël was magnificent. He could have said, 'I've done all this for you and put you on the map...' He did no such thing. He understood that this was a man who didn't want to put the camera in the stalls. David more or less indicated that he was trapped and he was right. Noël set him free."[38]

CHAPTER EIGHTEEN

GREAT EXPECTATIONS

So closely is the name of David Lean associated with that of Charles Dickens that he has been called "a visual novelist" and considered the nearest equivalent to Dickens in films.[1]

It was a surprise, therefore, to learn that David was not an authority on Dickens. All he had read before he made GREAT EXPECTATIONS was *A Christmas Carol*. What he needed, apparently, was solid ground on which to leap from his secure niche with Noël Coward.

He chose Dickens; one might say that Dickens had already been chosen for him. In the winter of 1939, Kay Walsh shared a studio dressing-room with the eccentric actress Martita Hunt. When Hunt discovered that Kay lived at Ivor Place, she said, "You've got to see my play tonight, it's just round the corner at the Rudolf Steiner Hall."

When Kay told David, he said, "Not bloody likely." But at Kay's urging, they went in a group with Anatole de Grunwald and Carl Mayer.

"We sat on little gilt chairs and in five minutes the whole lot of us were spellbound," said Kay. "It was Alec Guinness's adaptation of *Great Expectations*, produced by George Devine. Alec Guinness sat on one side of the tiny stage and Merula, his wife, on the other and they narrated. Marius Goring played the grown-up Pip, Yvonne Mitchell played little Estella, Vera Poliakoff the grown-up, Alec played Herbert Pocket and Martita was Miss Havisham. It was absolutely wonderful. And at the end when the audiences left, I took David and the others up to the footlights and introduced them to Martita, who wore a stunning make-up."[2]

David Lean said that unless he had seen the Alec Guinness stage version he would never have done the film. "It exerted a tremendous influence."[3]

As early as IN WHICH WE SERVE, Kay had suggested Cineguild should next go back to the Victorian era - she felt that they had had enough of "tin helmets and Oerlikon guns." For David's birthday in 1940, she gave him the Nonsuch edition of Dickens.

"When David got hold of Dickens, you couldn't get a word out of him."

David thought *Great Expectations* was "absolutely wonderful" and felt it would make an exceptional film. But he had to be sure that Ronald Neame and Anthony Havelock-Allan shared his enthusiasm.

Neame had been to America at the request of J. Arthur Rank who was anxious to break into the American market, and who wanted up-to-date information on Hollywood production methods. Profoundly impressed by what he saw, Neame made up his mind to produce the kind of film he felt Americans would enjoy.

When David suggested a film of GREAT EXPECTATIONS, Neame put the idea to Rank who simply said, "Go away and make it. Don't spend more than you have to. Tell us when we can see it."[4]

In awe of Dickens, David wanted an expert on Dickens to write the script. Havelock-Allan suggested Clemence Dane.[5]

"What she wrote was so awful I cannot even begin to describe it," said David. "It had practically every incident in the book but done in shorthand so one never got to grips with any one scene. She took snippets of everything and didn't give anything real weight. If I had done it, she would have turned on me and written letters to *The Times* about the desecration of Dickens. It was hideously embarrassing.

"I said to Ronnie, 'Look, it's no bloody good,' and I thought the sky would fall on my head for saying such a thing about Clemence Dane, of all people. And he said, 'Well, what are you going to do?'"

David decided they should both have a crack at it themselves. In January

At The Blue Boar, Rochester, Joe Gargery (Bernard Miles) bids farewell to Pip (John Mills) in GREAT EXPECTATIONS.

1945, just before production started on BRIEF ENCOUNTER, the two men, with their wives, went down to the Ferry Boat Inn at Fowey in Cornwall. Working day and night, they wrote a continuity.

"The first thing I did," said David, "sounds pretty curious today, but I don't think it's a bad idea when you're faced with somebody like Dickens. As I read the book for the umpteenth time, I wrote down in a sort of headline form those scenes, or parts of scenes, which I thought would make a good movie, and I left out anything I thought dull. I was rather encouraged by the Clemence Dane approach because it removed my fears of trespassing on the great. I ended up with a rough continuity which was full of gaps - Pip on the marshes at the beginning, the graveyard, Magwitch the convict...

"Then we sat down and tried to link up the episodes and fill in the gaps. That's how it worked and it worked rather well. What we did, we did proud; if we had a Dickens scene, we gave it full value.

"Lots of people have come a cropper on this, and I think Ealing Studios came a cropper on NICHOLAS NICKLEBY. They had every scene in the book in snippet form in the film. It just does not work. You have to cut, and give it weight and do it proud. You have to savour Dickens, you have to enjoy him. You can't just skip through in shorthand. This is why George Cukor's DAVID COPPERFIELD is still a good picture."

When David became immersed in BRIEF ENCOUNTER, Neame worked on the script with Havelock-Allan and later with Cecil McGivern, who became head of drama at the BBC. Another writer given a screen credit for her contribution was Kay Walsh.

"None of us could think of an end," said Neame. "Dickens never found a good one, and we struggled and struggled and finally Kay said, 'Why don't you let me have a go?' And we said, 'Jolly good luck. Nobody else has been able to do it. What makes you think you can?' 'Well,' she said, 'I'd like to try.'"[6]

"I thought if Pip had a long white beard," said Kay, "and Estella had put on forty pounds and they met in a graveyard, Wardour Street wouldn't come through with the money and anyway, you couldn't finish the film like that. And so I got the idea of Miss Havisham and her influence on Estella, who'd just been jilted. It seems so obvious now that she would repeat the pattern of Miss Havisham. What was really good was Pip coming back and the voices - 'Don't loiter, boy!' and the gate creaking and the camera going up the stairs and you think you're going in to Miss Havisham and it's not her at all, it's Valerie [Hobson] as Estella.

"John Mills was absolutely thrilled with the ending because it gave him the chance to pull the curtains down, for the mice to run out, and for 'I have come back, Miss Havisham!' and 'Out into the sunlight!' and all that."

David, Neame and Havelock-Allan were so delighted with Kay's skill that just before they left on location they offered her the job of running the scenario department for Cineguild, but she turned it down.

I remember seeing GREAT EXPECTATIONS and thinking it looked like no other film I had ever seen. It was extremely stylised, and yet it had a savage realism missing from British literary adaptations. It was also a rare example of pure cinema, combining the best of silent German cinema with a power all of its own.

David never embarked on a film without giving an immense amount of thought to the way it should look. This was unusual in a business where some directors never so much as glanced through the viewfinder, leaving the visual style entirely to the lighting cameraman.

David had been impressed by Michael Curtiz's CASABLANCA, with Humphrey Bogart, Ingrid Bergman and Claude Rains, and he tried to analyse why it made such an impact. After talking it over with Ronald Neame, he realised that cinematographer Arthur Edeson had used long focus lenses, which provided a heightened sense of intimacy by keeping the faces sharp while softening everything around them.

When production designer John Bryan heard what David had in mind, he realised his sets might disappear into that softness and brought the ceilings sharply down so they would appear in the picture. Forced perspective had been a feature of German silent films, and KANE revived the practice, but in few films would it be used with such boldness. Once the sets were built in this way, the furniture had to be designed to fit.

David was so intrigued by this idea that he allowed it to take precedence over his CASABLANCA scheme. "John's sets are all planned to be shot from one angle," David told Norman Spencer, "it takes away my freedom, but they're so bloody good I don't mind."[7]

"It was the first time I worked with John Bryan," said David.[8] "He had more imagination than all of us. He took GREAT EXPECTATIONS and did a super Cruikshank on it. He was not frightened to exaggerate, to depart from reality. He enjoyed it and searched for opportunities.

"Right at the beginning, when Pip is running along a dyke, we had a clear blue sky.

"I said to John, 'I'm worried about this. It looks flat and horrible.'

"He said, 'Don't worry, I'll put in an artificial cloud.'

"And we used an artificial cloud, painted on glass and superimposed along the top of the screen, and it doesn't look artificial but if you look hard, you'll see that it is. It made the shot.

"The trees in the churchyard were carefully designed so that you could almost see a face in them. The churchyard was built in the studio and the church itself was about ten feet tall. The forced perspective looked perfectly natural, but unnatural too, and that was great. Nearly all the sets used the technique. He'd say, 'For God's sake don't get nearer than six feet of the backing,' but he had daring, and that was the great thing."[9]

"What we were trying to do," David said shortly after the film came out, "was to create that larger-than-life picture which is really most characteristic of Dickens' kind of writing. The scenes of the boy, Pip, lying terrified in his bedroom after a night of fear, creeping downstairs at dawn and then stealing the food for the convict out on the marshes was something Dickens wrote as if he were inside the boy himself. We tried to make the audience share Pip's fear.

"If we hadn't done this, we should have been faced with quite a different problem - making the audience accept what is really a pretty exaggerated piece of melodrama. They might easily have found the convicts and their fustian dialogue just funny instead of terrifying if we had not built up the fear in the audience at the same time as we did in the boy - first of all, of course, with the sheer physical shock when Pip suddenly collides with the convict in the churchyard at the beginning of the film and hears the horrifying threats in his throaty voice.

"From then on we made everything larger than life, as it is in a boy's imagination. We made the audience share Pip's own exaggerated experiences. Dickens describes the voices which Pip imagines accusing him of horrible crimes; they seem to come from the hare hung head downwards in the back of the larder cupboard and even from the munching cows in the misty fields. They are not, of

Headed by Norman Spencer, cast and crew of GREAT EXPECTATIONS step off the landing craft.

course, meant to come from them really; they are in Pip's imagination. Some
people got this wrong when they saw the film; the cows stare and chew, but they
do not actually speak!

"As far as the scenes with Pip are concerned we were not aiming at reality.
What we wanted to create all the time was the world as it seemed to Pip when
his imagination was distorted with fear. That, after all, was what Dickens himself
did." [10]

Dickens's brilliance at creating characters, was matched by Cineguild's choice of
actors.

"You have to go for outsize characters," said David. "Who has ever seen a
lawyer like Jaggers? We were lucky that Francis L. Sullivan was alive and a good
actor. He was wonderful. I've seen other versions of GREAT EXPECTATIONS but
they can't touch him. [11]

"Miss Havisham was played by Martita Hunt, thank God. That part could so
easily descend into a kind of farce. She was another outsize character.

"Freda Jackson in a small part - Joe Gargery's wife - was a sort of shrew. She
was not frightened to raise her voice. When you ask some actors to shout with
passion they usually say, 'You're making me overact.'"

There was little doubt that Alec Guinness would recreate his stage role as
Herbert Pocket. Guinness's career in films had begun and ended with a day's
crowd work in an Ealing film called EVENSONG, directed by Victor Saville, and it
had put him off film work for life.

"I picked up a pound for my day's work, dressed as a Tommy," said Guinness.
"We were herded like cattle and with such contempt; being a drama student I had
rather grander ideas about how one should be treated as a performer and I swore
I was never going to do another film." [12]

Shortly before he was to be demobbed from the Navy, Guinness received a
telegram from an agent.

"I don't know how she found me. It was very clever of her. She said David
Lean and Ronald Neame wanted me to do a screen test. I said I was still in
uniform. But I did the test in a little room in North London, still in uniform.
David was there with a cameraman. I was hugely charmed by him. He had a
wonderful, almost Boy Scout enthusiasm."

Finlay Currie, who had made such an impression in 49TH PARALLEL, was cast
as the convict, Magwitch. When John Mills was offered the part of Pip, David
gave him a warning.

"You know, Nob, I want you to do this, but it's a coat hanger for all the
wonderful garments that will be hung on you."

Valerie Hobson was cast as the adult Estella (and her mother, Molly) and
Jean Simmons, a protegée of Gabriel Pascal, played Estella when young.

David enjoyed making GREAT EXPECTATIONS more than any film he had worked on. The company was based at Rochester, the historic Medway town with close links to Dickens. They stayed at the Royal Victoria and Bull Hotel - immortalised as the Blue Boar in Dickens's novel.

"We stayed there six weeks," said production manager Norman Spencer, "and had the run of the place. It was a Dickensian coaching inn in the High Street, painted with gloomy brown paint and plagued by thousands of flies, especially in the kitchen."

A small island in the River Medway proved an ideal spot for a number of scenes. The only question was how to get the crew and equipment across. Norman Spencer solved the problem by borrowing a landing craft from the Navy.

"As we set sail from Rochester Harbour, at eight in the morning, the sun was shining and David said, 'Isn't this wonderful? What other profession would you be in?'

"The only way on to the island was to sail up, put the flap down, and we all walked off. And then this boat would put its front up, back off and come back for us like a taxi.

"Until then we were marooned on this island. It had an old, broken-down eighteenth-century fort and I remember Finlay Currie saying, 'Oh, we'll soon have this habitable. Come on, let's get some firewood and build a fire.' And we became a funny little gypsy film crew, working on this island."[13]

Dickens based Joe Gargery's house on the forge in the village of Chalk, which was still in existence, although in a heavily built-up area. A replica was erected on St Mary's Marshes on the Thames Estuary.

"We wanted mist," recalled Ronald Neame, "and we used smoke canisters, the kind that used to be thrown overboard from destroyers to camouflage ships, and we put these about a quarter of a mile away from the set with a prevailing wind bringing the mist towards us. But after we'd been shooting a few minutes we suddenly heard, coming from the distance, the sound of ships' sirens. Of course it was a busy Estuary and the Thames was covered with our fog. It hung around for ages."[14]

Imagine David's unit, hard at work on the marshes, coughing as the artificial mist floats slowly across them. David, concentrating on his film to the exclusion of all else, looks up and sees two young boys. One of them is his son. He could hardly have been more surprised if Peter had come running along the marshes, past the gibbet, like Pip.

"It was his idea," said Peter Lean. "We didn't press ourselves upon him. A friend and I were invited to go and stay with him during the school holidays.

"Someone was supposed to have met us at the local station, but no one met us so we had to take a taxi to where they were filming. They were in the middle of a shot. We both stood there and he suddenly looked round and looked over at us as if to say, 'What the bloody hell are you doing here?'

"Then it suddenly dawned on him who I was and his look changed to 'Oh, you *are* supposed to be here.' But I'd seen the first one."[15]

Peter responded to the atmosphere exactly like his father. He was fascinated by the paraphernalia of film-making and revelled in the look of it all.

"It was so flat, all you saw was this sparse grass. The light was glorious. The russet-coloured sails of the old barges used to pass like ships that were not really there. When they let off the smoke pots they came out of that mist and vanished back into it. I was given one of these cartridges, about the size of a cigar. I kept it for years."[16]

The light on the marshes, and the problems with matching shots, together with the moods of the Thames estuary - one day as calm as a millpond, the next a surging ocean - resulted in several re-shot scenes and the firing of David's cameraman, Robert Krasker. David remembered this situation with some embarrassment.

"You have to cast technicians as you cast actors," he said. "Bob Krasker had photographed BRIEF ENCOUNTER and I took him on GREAT EXPECTATIONS. But I was devastated by the first two or three lots of rushes because the photography hadn't got the guts I wanted for Dickens. It's no good having those outsize characters, convicts and crooks and God knows who, in polite lighting. It doesn't work. If you're going to do Dickens you have to have very strong photography, black shadows and brilliant highlights. Bob's rushes were flat and uninteresting."

David told him that what he was doing seemed little different to BRIEF ENCOUNTER and that it needed to be "much more daring, huge great black shadows, great big highlights - over the top."

Krasker was a brilliant cameraman, on that everyone agreed. Part of his trouble was the fact that he was shooting on the Medway in misty conditions which were bound to register low in contrast. But he had done exteriors in sunlight, and they, too, had disappointed David.

Ronald Neame, himself a former cameraman, also believed that Krasker was not on top of his form. Neame suggested that Krasker could resign because of 'ill health' and Guy Green would be hired to replace him. David said to Neame, "Well, can you arrange it?"

"It was one of the most awful things I've ever had to do in my life and as the producer I had to do it," said Neame. "I said, 'David and I feel we should make a change. I know it won't affect your career and we'll do it very quietly and discreetly.' But obviously, Bob was very upset. To be taken off a film is a terrible thing." [17]

"I felt very badly about the situation," said David. "Guy Green had been operator with me on several pictures and I thought he was exceptionally good.

He had done part of a film for Carol Reed [THE WAY AHEAD] and I took a huge gamble and said, 'Will you take over?' He did and won the Oscar for it.

"And then I saw THE THIRD MAN, which Bob Krasker photographed, and I thought, 'Oh my God, what a terrible mistake I made. What an injustice.' Carol got it out of him later, because it was wonderfully photographed, all the contrast and guts he didn't have on GREAT EXPECTATIONS."

Guy Green was working on a film directed by Stanley Haynes called CARNIVAL.

"David saw some of the rushes and said, 'That's what I want.' That's how I got involved," said Guy Green. "But Bob Krasker was a wonderful cameraman. I don't know what went wrong, maybe it was a personality thing."[18]

Guy Green exceeded everyone's hopes. He insists that his lighting was straightforward but he cannot satisfactorily explain how he achieved some of the most impressive black-and-white photography ever seen.

"It was a bit like painting, except that you start with a black piece of paper instead of white. What was exciting for me about black and white photography was making the actors come out of it - stereoscopically. I played the dark against the light all the time. Whenever the actors moved, the down side would always be silhouetted a bit. It got to be plastic somehow.

"There was a wonderful word called gamma, which meant the contrast factor of film. Many people used to put too much light on and it would always come out flat. I evolved the idea of using very little light and from very few directions. And I insisted they developed the negative to the proper gamma, so I got this rich black and white feeling. David was very complimentary about it. 'I love it,' he said, 'because you put light on the actors and you can see them properly.' It was true; in half the movies I see today I can't see the actor's faces and it drives me up the wall.

"The final result was partly John Bryan, partly David and partly old Charles Dickens."

Although Bob Huke, who remained as camera operator after Krasker left the picture, grew to admire Green's work, he said that much of the inspiration came from David.

"He talked to us about the photographic style. He said, for instance, when we shot the children, we would use 35mm lenses, and 24mm, which was the widest lens in those days. Even on close-ups we'd use the 35mm, so the set around them would seem so much bigger. But when we shot them when they're grown-ups, we'd use longer lenses, 50mm and 75mm. So it was exactly the same set, but it was a vast, cavernous, shadowy place when they were kids, and it was a dreary, dirty, run-down house when they were adults.

"David had this fantastic ability, when discussing scenes or when he was blocking them, to find something extra to put in there that wasn't in the script.

He wanted to add something, to improve it. Sometimes he'd become quite desperate when he couldn't find anything..." [19]

The scene concerning old Miss Havisham - whose life is frozen at the moment of rejection, and who lives in her wedding dress, still seated at the dust-enshrouded wedding table - was a triumph of inspired art direction and cinematography.

"It was strange about Miss Havisham," said David. "Martita Hunt built up a kind of unapproachable privacy. It was entirely her and John Bryan. And I feel I'm delving into things I shouldn't delve into... It sounds absurd, but because of this invasion of privacy she somehow created, she became very remote. I never spoke to her about it. And I've no idea what she was like. I never worked with her again." [20]

When John Mills, as the adult Pip, returns to Miss Havisham's house and tears the place apart, David said that his head was filled with images from CITIZEN KANE.

"When John Mills pulls the tablecloth, I'll tell you what I did. To make it look quicker, I tracked against it, the tablecloth moving under the camera. It gave the scene a sort of unreal touch. If you saw the film you would hardly know the camera was moving, you would just be aware that there was a strange pictorial hullabaloo going on."

A film unit on location is perfect material for melodrama, with all the underlying tensions and sexual attractions. The events of one particular evening could have been conjured up by Dorothy L. Sayers.

"David always had to have a girl on any film he worked on,' said Ronald Neame. "It was inevitable." [21]

"To amuse ourselves," said Norman Spencer, "somebody suggested we did some table turning. We'd all had a few drinks. We sat around the table - John Mills, Maggie Furse, David, Ronnie and myself - with our hands splayed out and fingertips touching. The table started to 'talk' as it always does, tipping over slightly and thumping back. One thump for yes, two for no. It's a game which becomes more serious as you go on.

"Somebody said, 'Let's see who's doing it' - one thump for A, two for B and so on. It kept spelling out 'LOVE ME' 'LOVE ME' and all of a sudden Maggie Furse tumbles to the floor in a dead faint. David said, 'Oh we've had enough for the day.' We resuscitated her by getting her on a sofa, fanning her and giving her water and then we all went to bed. I think that was the beginning." [22]

When the location was over, Spencer went back with David to Corballis, the house in Denham to which he and Kay had recently moved. Spencer's wife was staying there.

"I thought it was a little odd," said Spencer. "He kept saying, 'Well, you don't have to go yet, why don't you come in?'

"And I said, 'I must get back.' And he said to me later, 'I'd have given anything if you hadn't left,' because he knew he was going to have to tell Kay. And that was the beginning of the end of their marriage. He said to me afterwards, 'God, you were so bloody dense. I was doing everything to get you to stay because I couldn't go in and face her.'"[23]

"When Norman and Bar left," said Kay, "David was very strange. I was back in Mayfield with his mother and Edward in the strange black study and those black moods. You know, when a place is absolutely choking with atmosphere? These moody Leans. I thought it had all gone during the war, and the war had, as Edward said, taken care of it. But when peace broke out, his war came out. It was awkward. I think we went to the cinema.

"One night he said, 'We're doing night shooting on the lot. There'll be thousands of extras. I'm rather proud of it. Would you like to come?' And I went down - I always had a lovely reception from the crew. I always think people must have been watching because I felt like someone in a play when David took me and introduced me to Maggie Furse.

"David told me nothing for a week or two. One night he said he realised that as a creative person he had to live alone and that he was very sorry. Total denial of everything.

"When David leaves you, you are rubbed out. It was like an amputation. He came with nothing - if it hadn't have been for the radiogram - and he left with nothing.

"A few days later, George Pollock rang from the studios. 'Katy, when it's convenient to come down, David would like the three scripts and some clean socks.' We had had the scripts bound in red leather - rather flash. Someone came and collected them and that was that."

Kay was driven up to London. Some friends took her into a beautiful flat in Montpelier Square and Eric and Louise Ambler rented her their old flat in Cavaye Place.

"I was as miserable as sin. I was in a deep state of grief. If you'd given me Buckingham Palace, I'd still have been miserable." [24]

Maggie Furse, costume designer and assistant to Sophie Harris, had been married to Roger Furse, the stage designer who, with Maggie, had done the costumes for HENRY V. When Roger Furse found out about the affair he was furious and traced David and Maggie to a flat in Hertford Street, behind the Curzon, which Emeric Pressburger found for them.

"Roger Furse was ready to kill him," said Kay. "I wanted to knife him and shoot her but I couldn't kill him because I wanted him there to love him."

Eventually, David and Maggie Furse moved to the Athenaeum Court (now Hotel) in Piccadilly. The glamorous French actress Simone Signoret, who was separated from Yves Allegret, lived there, too. David was attracted to her and she would sometimes come to his apartment for chats. But she did not reciprocate his interest "and I never made a pass at her - I was so shy," said David.

Maggie Furse has been characterised as a graceful, sophisticated person, who looked as if she had stepped from the cover of *Vogue*.

"It's difficult for me to describe Maggie Furse," said Kay, "because I absolutely loathed her and planned to murder her. I used to call her Gypsy Petulengro because she wore those swathe turbans, and curtain-ring earrings and all the dingle-dangles. She was all the things I wasn't - I was corduroy trousers and gumboots.

"Her father was a distinguished caricaturist in *Punch*, Arthur Watts. Maggie eventually became a very good friend of mine. It was difficult not to like her. She was a very courteous, very good person to work with once you put aside your wrath. Didn't matter whether you were a star or an extra, she really knew how to take care of actors."[25]

David later invited Ronald Neame to dinner at the White Tower where they were joined by Margaret Furse. David told him, "You are sitting next to the lady who is going to be my wife."

They never married, however, and the affair lasted little longer than the film.

"I've never seen a man,' said Anthony Havelock-Allan, "who was in more of a subconscious dilemma between his sensuality and his strict sense of morality. I don't know if you've ever read a book of Colette's called *Chéri*. David was a Quaker Chéri."[26]

"We're opposites in almost everything," Ronald Neame told C.A. Lejeune when GREAT EXPECTATIONS was released. "We quarrel violently all the time, but we're the greatest possible friends. We balance each other, because he's up in the air all the time, while my feet are on the ground. David lives at a high pitch of intensity. He never relaxes. At the end of a picture, he and his unit are worn out. His mind is absolutely set along one line. His only really passionate interest in life is films, because it's the one thing he knows backwards.

"When he's making a film, he's blind and deaf to everything else in the world. He'll sit at lunch and never utter a word. He has no small talk at any time, and is terrifically difficult to get to know, until you have him interested in the one thing he loves - pictures - then he'll talk all right.

"His greatest danger - and he's well aware of it - is that he won't allow himself to show heart and warmth. He was brought up a strict Quaker, and there's always a battle royal going on between the true David and the other one. Provided he doesn't become too cold, he'll easily be one of the world's great directors."[27]

The relationship between Ronald Neame and David underwent a profound change on GREAT EXPECTATIONS.

Cineguild at work: l-r John Bryan, Anthony Havelock-Allan, Ronald Neame, David Lean.

"David doesn't like producers," said Neame. "He gets a very close relation-ship with his unit, with the cameraman, the sound man, with the script girl - particularly with the script girl - but anybody coming on to the set from outside is automatically, 'What's *he* want?' And the producer comes into that category. So although we were still tremendously good friends, I was now the person who said, 'David, do you think we can get off this set tonight?' Instead of the person who says, 'It doesn't matter if it takes another week.'"

David was working on a shot in the evening and it had to be finished by six-fifteen. When the electricians switched the lights out, David said he would do the shot the following morning. Neame pleaded with him to see the rushes and if they were all right move on to the next scene.

"David said to me, 'All right, we'll move on to the next set. But you'll never do that to me again, Ronnie, you'll never do that again.' And he meant it. And I realised that David was becoming big and reaching the point where he could call the tune as a director. I didn't enjoy being the one behind the desk instead of helping to make the film. I found producing a not very rewarding job."

Despite his lack of theatrical training, David was already becoming adept at getting good performances. But actors usually had mixed feelings about him.

Alec Guinness admired David's handling of the nervous, insecure actor he was then.

"He was very good. I was overawed. It was the first proper film job I'd done. He didn't tell one how to perform. He just knew when something was not quite catching. He didn't know how to put anything right, he just knew what wasn't right.

'I had a close-up in which I had to laugh out loud and this is always difficult. Difficult laughing in the theatre, but suddenly, I thought, 'On film you will see that this is manufactured and I am not remotely amused.'

"We tried it once or twice and David said, 'Let's forget about the whole thing for a moment. Let's just wait twenty minutes,' and so he sat by my side and I hadn't seen that he had made a little signal to the camera to start turning in the course of the conversation and then he said something which made me laugh and he said, 'Cut.' So he got his shot on a totally false premise... but thank God. I was so grateful. I don't think I would ever have achieved it otherwise."[28]

According to Anthony Havelock-Allan, his then wife, Valerie Hobson, had precisely the opposite experience.

"David would really have liked to have been all the actors, the writer and the director. He would have liked to have had the same relationship to a film as an author to a book. I hadn't suggested Valerie for the part of Estella, but he thought it was a good idea. And on paper it was a good idea. She was supposed to be cold and haughty, beauty at a distance. But David didn't realise that Valerie was absolutely paralysed with nerves."

"Of the sixty-nine films I've made," said Hobson, "this was easily the un-happiest. I did not enjoy working for David. I was a young actress then. I'd got quite a few films behind me - quite a few successful films. I don't mean I thought it would be a piece of cake, but I loved costume things and I thought it was going to be very much my cup of tea. But he was such a cold director. He gave me nothing at all as an actress. In fact, he had the reverse effect; whatever talents I may have had, he nullified. I simply couldn't do it, I couldn't take off at all.

"I feel rather bashful giving my opinion on undoubtedly one of the great directors. He obviously improved a great deal, I don't know. Yet David was pleased. He said, 'Exactly what's needed, someone without any heart or feeling at all. Splendid.' I thought I very nearly disappeared altogether. It may well have been me, because I think everyone else bounded through their parts. From Francis Sullivan on, everybody was rounded and perfect. So it may well have been that he engaged this actress to be a waxwork dummy of a person who'd had all the heart bred out of them.

"Let's face it, I don't think Estella is a good part. It's very thinly written and it's only as good as you can fill it out. And I wasn't allowed to fill it out even with what talents I might have had.

"What was undermining for me was that David would go on and on with the takes. Somebody at a party the other day said, 'I shall always remember you sitting there crocheting.' I think I had one line to do. David took forty-three takes, because no emotion was supposed to show on my face at all.

"I had to be absolutely relaxed, and cold and heartless. David would neither see nor care - he was going on until he got what he wanted and then, in fact, he'd use take three. So I didn't enjoy the film, although I feel rather mean talking about it that way. He remained privately a very great friend."[29]

At the end of the film, a shot of Valerie Hobson staring into a mirror took longer to shoot than had been planned, and since it was lunchtime, David let everyone go and they returned to it that afternoon and got it in two or three takes. No one noticed that a ubiquitous cartoon of wartime rationing - a Chad - was reflected in the mirror.

The film had been on the circuit for about three months, when a man in Newcastle wrote to ask what it meant. In panic, Cineguild rescued the cutting-copy from the vaults and ran it in the theatre and sure enough, there it was. It seemed that a carpenter or an electrician had idly drawn it on the wall during their lunch-break.

It couldn't be seen until one particular light was switched on, when its reflection was dimly revealed, just behind John Mills's shoulder, as he says "I've never ceased to love you when there seemed no hope in my love." Nobody else noticed and it is still in the film.

The editor of GREAT EXPECTATIONS was once again Jack Harris. However, when Kay Walsh visited him, he complained that he felt as though he was contributing nothing. "I'm getting a bit tired of cutting off the number boards," he said. Nevertheless, the collaboration between David and Harris resulted in a brilliantly edited production.

The most famous cut in the film occurs at the beginning, and is one of the most celebrated shocks in all of cinema. On a wintry day, Pip runs along the edge of the marshes, past an ominous gibbet, to visit his mother's grave. In the churchyard are trees whose branches creak like a swinging corpse and disturb the boy. He looks around nervously to satisfy himself that no one else is there. When he has put the flowers on the grave, he turns and runs straight into the powerful body of a man, an escaped convict who snarls, "Keep still, you little devil, or I'll cut yer throat."

This scene still makes audiences jump.

"I see the audience as a dull, sweet-sucking mass," wrote David in some notes for a lecture, "defying you to arouse their interest. The more lethargic they are, the more they will react to a kick in the stomach. I can't resist showing the first reel of GREAT EXPECTATIONS. It's a happy memory for any director to make that great grey mass react in any way, and they certainly reacted to this."

When I asked David about it, I was surprised that he spoke more of the dialogue than of the editing.

"When I was planning the encounter between Pip and Magwitch, I thought the way the convict talked was over-the-top but wonderful. I was determined to use it. I thought, 'This is very near the edge of laughter. The audience might easily laugh. If I can make the audience frightened, they won't laugh because I'll put them in the position of the boy.' So I worked the whole shot out and planned the two minutes before it to make the audience jump. I did three takes, and only the last one really worked; only in that was the timing right."

In Karel Reisz's book *The Technique of Film Editing*, published in 1953 under the auspices of the British Film Academy, whose committee included David and Jack Harris, there is a detailed description of the sequence, written by Harris:

"The whole of this passage was planned in cuts before it was shot, although the director did, of course, shoot a certain amount of cover. The most difficult thing to get over by photography was the sudden appearance of the convict. The effect was finally obtained by panning with the boy until he runs straight into the stationary convict.

"The difficulty in editing was to decide the exact frame to leave the panning shot and to cut to the boy screaming. The effect aimed at was to leave the shot on the screen sufficiently long to let the audience see that the boy had run into a man - and not a very nice man, at that - but not sufficiently long to get a good look and be able to decide that he was after all recognisably human. As a matter of interest, there are fourteen frames from the time the convict appears to the close-up of Pip. The sound of Pip's scream starts four frames before the cut, at just the precise moment that the apparition is taken away from the audience's sight."[30]

On Wednesday, 6 June 1946, with England in the grip of postwar austerity, with food and clothing still on the ration and with London's bomb damage all too apparent, David flew to New York. It was his first trip to America, and as such should have made an indelible impression on him. Yet he never mentioned it. He referred to Ronald Neame and Jack Harris going over, but gave me the impression he remained in England, hard at work.

The reason for the secrecy was the fact that David was accompanied by Maggie Furse. In his account of the flight, written for the Pinewood house magazine, he gives the impression he was alone, though Norman Spencer remembered Maggie later complaining that the American clothes she had bought were badly finished.

A year after the end of the war in Europe, transatlantic flying was so new and so risky - David refers to Laurence Olivier's "narrow escape" - that to ord-inary people it had irresistible glamour. David must have wanted an adventure:

"A Transatlantic flight," he wrote, "is a mixture of extreme excitement and extreme boredom. The excitement starts when you sit sipping a cup of tea at

Airways House, and a loudspeaker voice announces, 'American Air Lines Flight Twenty-two. Will passengers please come to the main entrance where the bus for Heathrow is waiting.'"

David wrote in great detail about the flight which stopped first at Shannon where the plane hit a flagpole, obliging them to spend the night in Ireland while a replacement plane was flown out.

"Then comes the boredom - ten hours of it," wrote David. "Ten hours of . sitting and looking at the ocean ten thousand feet below - not even a ship - for hour after hour. It is the longest day I've ever known as we're racing West towards the sun, which is now beginning to set. Queer to think it's midnight in London. The Air Hostess is pointing something out to the passengers in front, and there below is one of the most magnificent sights I have ever seen - an iceberg three or four times the size of the Cumberland Hotel... dazzling white and emerald green, brighter than any jewel...

"Boston at night is a fantastic sight after six years of black-out. Thousands and thousands of lights, as far as the eye can see, flashing signs in all colours, and great double-track roadways, with bridges at every crossing."

When the Skymaster finally landed at New York's La Guardia airport, and the cabin door was opened, a wave of heat signalled the ground temperature of ninety-five degrees.

"If you'd like to hear about New York, I'll write about that in the next issue."[31]

Alas, he didn't and all we have to go on is this extract from an American trade paper:

"Lean came to America to test for himself audience reaction in this country. There was none of the usual fanfare that surrounds the visit of a famous director - he slipped quietly into New York and hid away at one of the older New York hotels. Passing up the glamour spots he was soon riding the subway to Brooklyn and the Bronx, where in the ordinary movie houses, he found for himself what made Mr and Mrs America and their children laugh and cry... Armed with this experience, Lean went back to England with a new and enlarged sense of timing and audience reaction that should make his work even more acceptable to the one hundred and forty million potential movie goers in this country."

David spent five weeks in the United States. When he tried to return to England for the music session on GREAT EXPECTATIONS, he found that all flights were cancelled because of a crash in Pennsylvania. It was several days before he could get back.

Kine Weekly interviewed him a couple of hours after his plane landed. He explained that he had made no business calls and met no one of importance. He had discovered, however, that American audiences, with few exceptions, regarded British pictures rather as the British regarded French productions - purely as art films.[32]

Composer Walter Goehr had been recommended to David, though when he heard the music, he was bitterly disappointed. He decided the only alternative was to cut back Goehr's score - there was no time to redo everything - and make way for the work of another composer. Kenneth Paxman and G. Linley were also credited alongside Goehr.

Goehr was a pet hate of Muir Mathieson, the studio's resident composer and orchestrator. "Muir was very possessive," said his assistant, John Huntley, "and wanted to conduct everything himself. Goehr evidently agreed and then ratted on him and took the conducting - and the credit - out of his hands."[33]

"I was told to book the big theatre at Denham," said Win Ryder, whose first job as sound editor this was, "I couldn't get it. The London Philharmonic Orchestra had a block booking. So I asked the editor, Alan Jaggs, if I could use the theatre and he said, 'Yes, if you get out when we come in.'

"So we'd nearly finished when suddenly the film stopped and the lights came on. David stood up. 'What happened?' I began to explain but he brushed past me and there was the entire orchestra standing in the narrow corridor outside with Alan, and David really tore into him. The chap went puce."[34]

The next day, Alan Jaggs received a letter from David apologising for his behaviour; he had not understood the situation and of course Alan had been absolutely right. "It was a most generous gesture," said Geoff Foot, who was shown the letter by Jaggs, "and most unusual in the film business."[35]

The last chore on GREAT EXPECTATIONS was the submission to the British Board of Film Censors to obtain its certificate. This censor board had been set up in 1913, and it still had the same secretary, J. Brooke Wilkinson. Although unofficial, the Board was supported by the industry and by every licensing authority. Without a certificate, a film would not be shown by any self-respecting cinema.

To David's astonishment, the Board demanded cuts. David had an interview with the censor at his office.

"He gave me a long lecture. He thought that when this boy Pip came up to London and visited Herbert Pocket and lived in luxury, it was tempting thousands of young boys with no education to come to London and lead a good life. I was absolutely dumbstruck."

Taking advantage of the meeting, David interrogated the censor.

"I asked why I was forbidden to show platonic scenes between a screen husband and wife in a double bed together. He replied, 'You pretend they are husband and wife, but the audience knows very well they are not really married. On further reflection, you will realise you are asking me why you are forbidden to show an unmarried actor and actress in bed together.'

"He then proceeded to explain that he looked upon himself as a shield for the more sensitive members of the public and surprised me by asking, 'Do you know one of the most blessed inventions of all time? It is the invention of the paragraph. My wife is a great reader and I often see her skip a paragraph, or sometimes a whole page. Do you realise why she does this? She does it because she has come to an unsavoury passage, and the new paragraph or the new page gives her a guide as to where she can start reading again... Now, Mr Lean, you cannot give your audience such guidance. You have no paragraph. They have to sit and watch and even if they closed their eyes they hear the words. I am here to protect thousands of decent men and women like my wife. You're an artistic sort of chap - please don't take me amiss - but you see my point, don't you?'

"And it went on and on. He had one of the filthiest minds I've ever encountered. He was seeing God-knows-what in everything. Even he realised he had gone a bit far, I think, hence all this talk about his wife turning the pages. Anyway, I talked him out of making the cuts, so GREAT EXPECTATIONS was released intact."[36]

Well, almost intact. A shot of a judge placing the black cap on his head had to be removed. And as the graveyard scene and the death by fire of Miss Havisham were considered too frightening for small children, the film was given an 'A' certificate which meant that children could not be admitted without an adult.[37] Ronald Neame argued long and hard against the injustice of the rating.

It was impossible to find a paddle steamer of the right period, so the art department checked at Lloyds for all surviving paddle steamers and found the Empress, dating from the latter half of the 19th century. New masts were stepped-in with square rigging and dummy sails, the funnel was lengthened and the paddle-boxes enlarged until it looked exactly right.

"The first time I saw the film with an audience," said Lean, "I went to the press show and as the boy ran into the convict, the whole audience went back in a wave and I knew I was in business. It was lovely. It really worked.

"It doesn't work so well on television because the screen doesn't take up enough space in the room, and the convict is only a small part of what you're looking at. But show that on the big screen and people jump today."

The film had been alarmingly expensive to make - £392,568 - even more costly than the Technicolor films. But no one had any doubt that it was among the greatest British films ever made.

The reaction to the film could hardly have been more ecstatic. Noël Coward noted in his diary, "a really fine film." Carol Reed, then Britain's pre-eminent director, encountered David in a corridor and expressed his envy with a joke - "Why don't you fall under a bus?"

Monica Dickens, granddaughter of the great novelist (and daughter of Henry Charles Dickens, the barrister), said, "It is a wonderful picture. I enjoyed every moment of it. Grandfather would have loved it."[38]

In the *News Chronicle*, Richard Winnington wrote: "Dickens has never before been rendered effectively into cinema terms: now the acceptable adjustment between the realism of the camera and Dickens' robustious enlargement of character is here made... A turn of speed, attained by cutting that is ingenious enough to hide its brilliance, rebukes the lethargy into which most contemporary films have fallen. The film could only have been made in England, and a large amount of the visual pleasure is derived from the superlative photography of the Medway Saltings."[39]

The *Daily Express* critic, Stephen Watts, wrote: "There is only one way to succeed in making a film of a classic, and that is to make a film which is in itself a classic... Here is a picture which is British to the backbone, yet belongs proudly to the cinema of the world. For beauty, good taste and intelligence, for dramatic and emotional content and expert polish in every department, it is beyond nationality. In brief, a classic." Watts' review was headlined, "Britain makes her greatest film."[40]

Rank's distribution department had a policy of playing a film for four weeks at one of their West End theatres, and then, irrespective of how well it was doing, they would withdraw it and send it on general release.

"I drove my car down the Haymarket where it was playing," said David, "and there were queues around the block, yet it was coming off the next day."[41]

Two days later, Rank went down to Pinewood, and David complained.

"He said, 'Well, David, it's company policy. We do that so we can get it out into the country.' I said, 'You know, it has a lot to do with luck if a film catches on, and this film has all the earmarks of catching on in a bigger way than any other film I've done. You are taking a terrible risk because very soon you're going to hit a film that's not going to catch on and you can't treat the one that catches on so badly.'

"He said, 'David, I'm awfully sorry, but that's the company policy.'

"In my opinion, it was this policy that helped ruin Rank."[42]

In America, GREAT EXPECTATIONS was one of the few films selected for a prestige run, purely on merit, at the Radio City Music Hall, which seated over six thousand people. This was, in David's view, "an enormous compliment." He was nominated again for an Academy Award.

David was now established as England's second greatest director, after Carol Reed. His position was noted by a young ex-serviceman of twenty-three called Robert Bolt. He recalled a fellow student nodding towards a poster for GREAT EXPECTATIONS and saying he would like to be in the situation that fellow Lean was in. Bolt had never heard of him. He cared little for films; he was more interested in poetry.[43]

The film had an indelible effect on a future generation of film-makers - particularly those who would eventually work with David himself. John Box was stunned by it and regards it as one of the six best films he has ever seen.

Anne Coates was at school, wading through a set book, *Wuthering Heights*.

"On a school outing we were taken to see GREAT EXPECTATIONS. And suddenly the whole thing came alive to me. These extremely boring books which I was ploughing my way through were suddenly up there on the screen and I was carried away. I thought, 'What a marvellous thing to be able to do.' I don't know why, I just felt this would be something I would like to do with my life."[44]

Anne Coates would become the editor of LAWRENCE OF ARABIA. Robert Bolt would write it and John Box would become its production designer.

In all the euphoria over the film's success, David was invited in December 1946 to Paris to receive the Cannes award for BRIEF ENCOUNTER. He took Celia Johnson, and invited Kay, who accepted eagerly. Edward had persuaded David to start psychoanalysis against all his prejudices, and he had not abandoned it. Kay felt perhaps the marriage might, in the end, be rescued. The Paris trip was enjoyable - she liked Celia Johnson - and she was pleasantly surprised when the French journalists treated her seriously as a significant figure of British cinema.

But, Paris or no Paris, there was to be no second honeymoon with David.

CHAPTER NINETEEN

OLIVER TWIST

NOËL Coward gave David a piece of advice he often quoted and tried to follow: "My dear, never come out of the same hole twice."

After GREAT EXPECTATIONS he did his utmost to find a fresh subject, mainly because he thought he ought to; however, there was only one in his mind.

"All I could think of, because I had read it and thought it would make a jolly good movie, was *Oliver Twist*. I felt guilty because it seemed pretty feeble to do another Dickens immediately after GREAT EXPECTATIONS, but I said, 'Come on. It's not a serious crime.'"[1]

"I did all I could to discourage him," said Kay Walsh. "I said, 'You can't do two great chunks in a row like that.' But no, he was absolutely obsessed by it."[2]

"There was considerable disappointment," wrote Gerald Pratley, "on the part of many of his admirers that at a time when Italian neo-realist directors were shooting films about post-war problems, Lean should choose to remain in the past and make a second film from Dickens."[3]

It wasn't simply a matter of exchanging one famous name for another - Coward for Dickens. David, who was not a great reader, had discovered the irresistible emotional power of Dickens, together with his remarkable cinematic qualities. (Was it not Griffith himself who claimed to have taken cross-cutting from the novels of Dickens?) Even Dickens's dialogue, David said, was just perfect for the screen.

David worked on the script with Stanley Haynes, who had been production manager on MAJOR BARBARA - "assistant in production", as Pascal's quaint credits put it - and had also been associate producer on Carol Reed's THE WAY AHEAD.

David's new secretary, Mary Benson, noted that David and Stanley Haynes were reasonably compatible, though she felt Haynes was rather a sad man, with an unhappy marriage, two divorces and a series of love affairs behind him.[4]

"He came from a very poor background," said Kay Walsh. "He was very bright and won scholarships and went into a seminary for some years. He was going to be a priest. Then he went to Oxford where he did classics. He became something of an expert on Dickens. He went into the film industry and worked with Victor Saville, who thought so highly of him that when Stanley wanted a house, he bought him one. Stanley would pay him back, but Victor wanted to set up this Catholic boy. So he had a good start, but he also had instability.

"He had been a damned good production manager, but he wanted to be a director. Everybody thought they could be directors. There was a kind of honeymoon period with Del Giudice being the adorable spendthrift and they gave him a film, CARNIVAL. He went on the set and his crew could tell that he did not know what to do. He came to see us in Denham once or twice, but what can you say? That was a pretty bad experience for him, but he became good with scripts with David."[5]

David and Haynes took almost exactly a month to produce the script - a record for David and impressive by any standards. They celebrated their achievement on 12 April 1947 with a note to Mary Benson: "Sat 2 am. Pixie dear, we've done it! Hope you approve. Our end almost makes us cry but then we are very tired and slightly hysterical. My chum is all in. David."

And underneath was written: "My hour is done, my glass is run, I never more shall see the sun. Stanley."[6]

However good their ending, the two men had had enormous difficulty with the beginning because Dickens opens the novel in such an abstract way:

"... And in this workhouse was born on a day and date which I need not trouble myself to repeat, in as much as it can be of no possible consequence to the reader, in this stage of the business at all events, the item of mortality whose name is prefixed to the head of this chapter."

Hardly a cinematic opening.

"It was Easter [1947]," said Kay Walsh, "and David and Stanley said 'Come on, let's go down to Brighton.' Stanley had a load of kids by a load of ladies, and the lot of us went down. We finished up in something called the Grafton overlooking the front and they rigged up a table and a typewriter and David and Stanley went to work. Stanley looked like Sidney Carton with wet bandages around his head and David was like a very depressed Einstein trying to find the cure for madness as he searched for an opening."

After four days, OLIVER TWIST was still without an opening. In desperation, they held a competition at Pinewood, offering a reward to anybody who would come forward with an idea they could use. Nobody accepted the challenge. No one, except Kay Walsh, who would be cast as Nancy, the doomed girlfriend of Bill Sikes.

"Finally, I said to David, 'Look, I've got a couple of pages here I've written on an exercise book. Have a look at it.'

"It read something like this: 'There was a terrible storm raging and over the hill comes a girl in labour and the storm is buffeting her and she is being pitched about from pillar to post and she is in great pain. In the distance she sees a light and she goes struggling on against the storm and she looks up and sees a bell and as she pulls the bell and sinks down the camera goes up to a sign - WORKHOUSE - and a baby cries and Oliver Twist is born.'

"It was only a page of scribble, but David read it and said, 'Where did you get this from?'

"I said, 'From being three or four and sitting in the flea pit. I couldn't read so I don't remember any of the titles. I just remember this girl pulling her shawl around her, and she had those great big eyes with lots of black around them and a tiny mouth and she sank into a ditch and the whole thing was stamped on me forever. And I communicated it to David, who was very quick on anything that was pictorially vivid. He developed it into something absolutely magnificent."[7]

Norman Spencer admired the opening immensely.

"David used to regard the audience as a friendly enemy. He used to say, 'I'd love to make a film in which there's no dialogue for at least the first quarter of an hour. I want to see the chap in the audience with a cigarette - he can't bring himself to light it because he's so gripped.' He always tried to start his picture without dialogue and OLIVER TWIST is a marvellous example of that. It really works one hundred percent."[8]

When cameraman Guy Green and art director John Bryan set up the opening, they had special effects clouds scudding across the night sky over the desolate moor. Green thought they looked first-rate in the rushes, but David declared, "We're going to have to retake this. It's too romantic. I want more edginess and more storm."

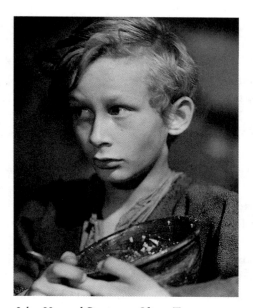

John Howard Davies as Oliver Twist

Oliver's mother, who staggers over the moor and then dies giving birth in the workhouse, was played by Josephine Stuart. As production manager, Norman Spencer had the task of finding a new-born baby.

He rang a Denham GP called Dr Phyllis Shipman and asked her if she knew of anybody who was about to give birth. "She said, 'You're in luck, because I'm pregnant.'

"Six weeks later the child was born. Taking a workhouse bed and a section of plaster wall, David and the crew went to her house, put Josephine Stuart into costume and into the bed in the drawing room and filmed the baby the day after she was born. Her father, Dr Eustace Shipman, played the doctor in the scene. Since the baby was a girl, she was named Olivia."[9]

The trade press had already announced the release of OLIVER TWIST in January 1947. It was not the Cineguild film, but a reissue of the low-budget 1933 version with Dickie Moore, directed by William Joyce Cowan and produced by Herbert Brenon. Distributor George Minter of Renown brought it back to take advantage of the Cineguild publicity.

Working at Renown was Keith Everson - now the celebrated film historian, William K. Everson.

"David Lean asked if he could come and see it. He was probably annoyed that Minter had taken advantage of the situation, but he didn't show it. He watched the film and afterwards told me how much he had enjoyed it and enquired about Herbert Brenon. He said he had always admired Brenon's work."[10]

Kay Walsh was still officially separated from David, but he and his work were always on her mind. She knew he was testing boys for the role of the Artful Dodger. Kay was appearing in Peter Ustinov's VICE VERSA, a school story involving many young actors. She rang David and told him she had found his Dodger - Anthony Newley.

"When we got to the casting of Charlotte, the servant of Sowerberry, the undertaker," said Norman Spencer, "David said, 'Let's get a really sexy little girl.' And Dennis Van Thal said, 'There's a sixteen-year-old who looks as though she's going to become a sex symbol.' It was Diana Dors and that was her very first film."

Robert Newton was the favourite for Bill Sikes - he had already played a similar role in MAJOR BARBARA and had enhanced his reputation in Carol Reed's ODD MAN OUT. But his reputation for drunken behaviour, however, had also spread to the insurance companies and there was a strong possibility that Rank would not employ him. Other actors were often reluctant to play with him. Newton seemed born for the part.

However, Robert Donat very much wanted the part, perhaps seeing an opportunity in playing the murderous Sikes to escape from the image of decency and gentleness which surrounded him.

Dickens described Fagin as "a very shrivelled old Jew, whose villainous-looking and repulsive face was obscured by a quantity of matted red hair."

The classic stage Fagin had been Herbert Beerbohm Tree.[11] It was clearly going to be the most difficult part to cast as well as the most difficult to play. The only actor who expressed any enthusiasm was, in David's eyes, the least likely to be able to do it.

Alec Guinness's entire screen career had thus far embraced one day as an extra and the part of Herbert Pocket. He was utterly charming and transparently lightweight. Or so David thought.

When he was at school, Alec Guinness and the boys used to stage shadow plays, using a sheet and a strong light.

"One of the scenes that I did, surely in shadow with something of a beard, was Fagin, demonstrating picking handkerchiefs and rags and things off a barrow and I could only do it if I could find some sort of funny voice to do it with. My chums at school were all rather impressed. Maybe that is why I wanted to play Fagin."

Guinness asked David Lean to lunch at the Savoy and said he wanted to play Fagin. David said, "You're out of your mind."

Guinness said, "What's wrong with British films as far as this actor is concerned is that you won't get away from your types. You won't find what is inside other people. I want to play Fagin and you won't hear of it."

David said, "No, that's nonsense."

Guinness said, "Do you think I can't look like Dickens drawings - like a Cruikshank? I'll just ask you for one thing. Give me a test."

"Of course I'll give you a test," said David.

"Don't come and look at the make-up, don't come and look at the clothes. Just let me appear on the set," said Guinness.

"Fair enough."

It was arranged that Guinness would make himself up in his dressing-room at the New Theatre (now the Albery) as if he were doing it for the theatre. David sent a make-up man to talk to Guinness to see what he was aiming at and together they would work towards the screen test which was to be held at Pinewood.

Norman Spencer remembered that David was convinced the test would be a waste of time and money. "He said, 'I can't see it. He's going to be covered in crepe hair and it'll look awful.'" Ronald Neame also thought Guinness would be too soft, too small.

When Alec Guinness walked on to the set as Fagin, David got the shock of his life.

"He came on looking not far removed from what he looks like in the film. Of course I was bowled over by it and he got the part without another word. He just had to walk on the set and we knew we were in business."[12]

"I did a test with Robert Donat," said Guinness, "who wanted to play Sikes, so we were both seeking after something. I got mine by the skin of my teeth and Robert didn't. He looked very good and he was a beautiful actor, but I don't think he'd got the vitality to cope."[13]

One of the unsung heroes of OLIVER TWIST, the make-up artist Stuart Freeborn, had a background that would have appealed to David. Born in 1914, he had left school at fourteen. His father wanted him go into insurance, to be something in the city. But Stuart longed for something artistic. Fascinated by the theatre and a very keen film-goer, he tried without success to become an extra. He did his own make-ups and even took his own photographs of himself in outrageous guises. He wrote to all the film studios and did his best to break into many of them.

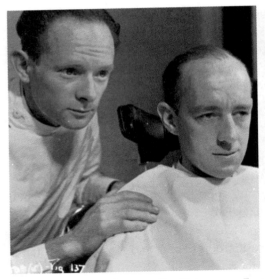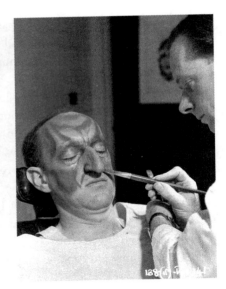

Stuart Freeborn making up Alec Guinness as Fagin.

This went on for years until he started an amateur cine society where his imaginative make-ups attracted publicity which led to an interview with Korda's company in 1936.

When he was hired for OLIVER TWIST - before Guinness asked David for the role - he realised that Fagin would be the most complicated job he had ever been faced with. Who on earth could play the role? He made a list of character actors and went over them with David.

David, who knew most of the names, was not enthusiastic about any of them. However, when Freeborn spoke to Alec Guinness and discussed the illustrations in Dickens by George Cruikshank, he began to see the young actor's extraordinary potential. It was then that the Pinewood test was organised

"I did some research," said Freeborn, "and got Cruikshank's drawings. The nose was typically cartoon, larger than life. I thought I could tone it down a bit, but then it wouldn't be the character everybody's used to looking at. Once you change the nose, it changed the whole thing and it doesn't look like Fagin at all."

David had suggested that Guinness should be made up twice - exactly like the Cruikshank drawings and then another version, toned down. Freeborn made a face-cast of Guinness, adding wrinkles and eye bags to age the youthful face. Guinness disliked ready-made beards, so his had to be made of loose hair, as were the eyebrows. The Cruikshank version contained the cartoon beaked nose. The toned down version had fewer wrinkles and a more normal nose.

"And he looked like Jesus Christ," said Freeborn. "It was extraordinary. David said, 'Forget that. It's not what we want at all.' So from there on it was the full nose."[14]

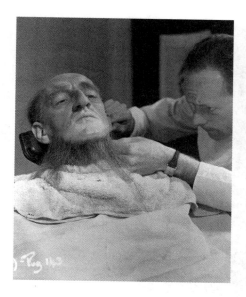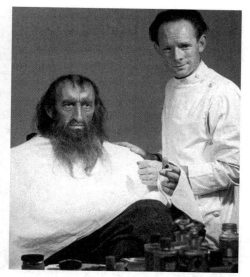

The Rank Organisation sent a copy of the script to the Production Code Administration in the United States to check for possible objections in America. The Code Administrator, Joseph I. Breen, passed the script, with eight minor changes. None of them concerned the character of Fagin. However, in a handwritten postscript, Breen said:

"We assume, of course, that you will bear in mind the advisability of omitting from the portrayal of Fagin any elements or inference that would be offensive to any specific racial group or religion. Otherwise, of course, your picture might meet with very definite audience resistance in this country."[15]

When Cineguild were informed of this, Freeborn asked, "What do we do? Do we go back to the Jesus Christ or what?"

David replied, "To hell with them. We're not going to change a thing."

For Guinness and Freeborn, it was a punishing regime. They arrived at Pinewood Studios at five-thirty and worked for three hours on the Fagin make-up. Then Freeborn had to have the other actors ready.

"Alec at that time wasn't really well known," said Freeborn. "He came in early every day and by the time anyone saw him he was fully made up. We'd been shooting for quite a few weeks when an assistant said, 'Hold everything, we might not get to you today, Alec.'

"Alec went down on the set and when he came back, he said, 'Do you know that nobody said good morning? Nobody even looked at me. And I suddenly realised they didn't know who I was. I'll be glad to get my make-up on so I've got friends again.'"[16]

The search for a boy to play Oliver received national coverage, and Cineguild

Bill Sikes (Robert Newton) forces Oliver (John Howard Davies) onto the roof of Fagin's hideout to escape the mob.

made a short film which was shown at the Rank cinemas. It attracted enormous interest, and even involved me.

My father brought home *The Leader* magazine every week, and one article asked, "Is there an Oliver Twist in modern Britain?"

My mother decided that the description by Dickens fitted me precisely. "A pale, thin child, somewhat diminutive in stature and decidedly small in circumference..."

The appeal was for boys between twelve and fourteen, but that was a blind for labour regulations. The boy they wanted had to be about nine. I was almost nine. I had acted in school plays. I was fascinated by films. I had even seen the 1933 OLIVER TWIST at school, and when the film was torn in the projector, and a ripped section fell to the floor, I picked it up and treasured it for months. And, as I learned from that film, even my name Brownlow was appropriate. What more could they want? I cannot be sure that my mother submitted my photograph, but she often spoke of putting me up for the part.

The publicity campaign resulted in fifteen hundred applications. All but eighty were weeded out, mine presumably among them, and an audition was held at the Victoria Palace. Under the supervision of Dennis Van Thal, the casting director, one boy after another was escorted backstage to play a scene

How David Lean put Dickens on the screen: 10. GREAT EXPECTATIONS: The shocking moment when Pip (Anthony Wager) is grabbed by the convict, Magwitch (Finlay Currie) in the lonely graveyard.

11. *In the bomb-shattered City of London on a Sunday morning, the Cineguild company film* GREAT EXPECTATIONS. *12. What the camera sees: Pip (John Mills) arrives in London.*

13. *(Overleaf) Pip (Anthony Wager) visiting Miss Havisham (Martita Hunt), "a living fossil", whose room is frozen at the moment of her interrupted wedding:* GREAT EXPECTATIONS.

14. *Alec Guinness, disguised only in a wig, as Herbert Pocket, with Pip (John Mills) in* GREAT EXPECTATIONS. 15. *Alec Guinness, in full disguise, brought humour and menace to Fagin; seen here with John Howard Davies as Oliver and Anthony Newley as the Artful Dodger in* OLIVER TWIST. 16. *(Overleaf) John Howard Davies as Oliver Twist in John Bryan's workhouse set.*

17. Filming the attempted escape of Bill Sikes (Robert Newton) with Oliver Twist (John Howard Davies).

with the actress Helen Burls. If any showed the slightest promise, they were rushed upstairs for a special audition with David and Ronald Neame.

At the end, David still wasn't satisfied. None of the boys matched the image in his mind of the ideal Oliver - they were the wrong size or the wrong weight, they couldn't act, or worst of all, "there was nothing in the eyes."

The final choice occurred by happy accident.

"My father was a film critic on the *Express* and features editor on the *Sketch*," said John Howard Davies. "I was allowed to listen to *Dick Barton, Special Agent* on the wireless. I was listening to this programme at my parents' flat off Finchley Road. My father's agent, Ted Lloyd, saw me in my dressing gown and said to my father, 'We've just been auditioning hundreds of boys for OLIVER TWIST and we're nowhere near finding the right one, but your son looks exactly the right type.'

"I can remember my father saying a couple of days later, 'Would you like to be in a film?' The only films I'd ever seen were cowboy films and I said 'Yes' immediately, and I was duly taken down to Pinewood to meet David Lean.

"He was extremely avuncular, very kind and gentle and I was dressed up in rags, much to my chagrin, because I thought I'd have a horse and a gun. A test was made, some photographs were taken and I got the part.

"It was as simple and as easy as that. The only thing that must have crossed their minds, as it certainly crossed mine, was that I had the wrong voice. But it didn't seem to worry them at all." [17]

Jack Davies was an old friend of David's. They had both worked at B&D - Davies as a writer - and at one point they were both keen on the same girl. Jack Davies also knew Ronald Neame, having lived in the same street in Golders Green.

"After David had interviewed and tested John," said Jack Davies's wife, Dorothy, "both he and the producer Ronald Neame had a problem. At that time it was against the law for children under the age of thirteen to work in film studios. John was only eight. But so determined was David to have John that they decided to risk being stopped by the educational authorities - they may have come to some arrangement with them in the end - and to ensure that as few people as possible should meet John, or know anything about him, until filming was completed. The press co-operated and all was well." [18]

On the set, John never heard a cross word.

"I think that must have been a deliberate policy, because when you are eight you can easily be upset by a display of bad temper. David was unfailingly nice, unfailingly courteous. He used various devices on me. When I felt inhibited about doing something, he would often shoot the rehearsal. He wasn't silly enough not to do the take. But I pretty soon cottoned on to this because my hearing was even better than his, with his large ears, and I could detect the sound of a Mitchell turning over. So I knew when he was taking and when he wasn't.

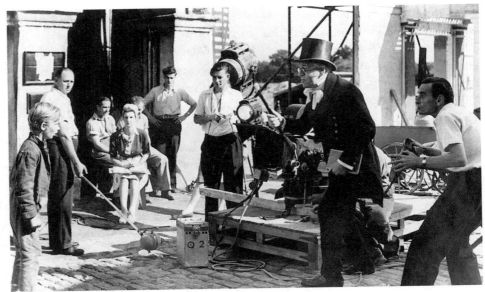

David directing John Howard Davies as Oliver Twist. Henry Stephenson in silk hat.

"There was one scene when Fagin is demonstrating the art of picking pockets and I was supposed to laugh. David and Alec Guinness put on a double act for me, falling about and hitting each other, putting their heads under each other's arms, pulling fingers out of their mouths, pretending they'd eaten them. It doesn't sound terribly funny now, but it was extremely funny then, and I was delighted by it. Alec was in his full Fagin make-up and David was in a suit. It was very incongruous."[19]

Directing children is an art of its own. Small boys tend to have a brief attention span, and John was no exception. He could be distracted by anything - a puff of smoke, a seagull swooping - and David's patient work would be wasted.

"I can remember David doing careful rehearsals, getting everything absolutely right," said Davies. "He did not do take after take. Sometimes he got it in one or two. When he was getting what he wanted, he was easily satisfied. But when he didn't he was very painstaking."

David felt that with children you should not direct, but rather suggest.

"I remember on one occasion when he had to faint in the courtroom. I spoke to him and described what he must be feeling - the room starting to go round and all the rest of it. Suddenly he dropped on the floor in front of me. His mother was very nice about that - a lot of women would have flown at me - but she saw that it was completely unintentional."

"He may have thought I fainted," said Davies, "but I didn't. I remember him saying, 'You've got to behave as though you'd suddenly become a rag doll. Just relax everything in your body. You've got to bear in mind the fact that you're not going to hurt yourself when you fall. Someone will be there to catch you.' Don't think there was actually, but he was marvellous."

"John was obsessed with wanting to see the set from the gantries," wrote Davies's mother, Dorothy. "I was terrified at the idea of climbing ladders and scaffolding to get him up there. David was anxious, too. Nevertheless, he took John by the hand and said, 'We're going up together.'

"A small tent had been erected for John on the set so that he could rest when there was no time to return to the dressing room. One day David came in and found me crying. I had just received news that my brother had died. David hugged and comforted me as if I were a child and consoled me until I had calmed down. Then he rearranged the shooting schedule so that I could go home. It was the sort of gesture that showed his compassion and understanding. I had already decided he was a great director. Now I thought of him as a friend."[20]

A distinguished visitor to the set: Mary Pickford.

During the shooting of OLIVER TWIST, several distinguished visitors came to the set including a small, middle-aged lady in an Edwardian-style hat who was allowed to peer through the viewfinder of the Mitchell. This was only fitting since she had bought the first Mitchell ever made for her own cameraman, Charles Rosher, in 1920. It was Mary Pickford, whose career was fading as David first went into films. He knew the debt that every film-maker owed her and her then husband, Douglas Fairbanks, for raising the standards of the industry.

Also during the production occurred the founding of the British Film Academy (now known as BAFTA), an organisation which, it was hoped, would parallel in reputation the Academy of Motion Picture Arts and Sciences in Los Angeles. Significantly, David was voted its first president.

"Because he never really dictated letters," said Mary Benson, "I wrote to everybody, all the directors, the top technicians, and the producers terribly dictatorial letters practically ordering them to join. I don't know how I managed to do that."[21]

At the official inaugural dinner of the Academy, held at Claridge's on 13 May 1947, Benson sat between Alexander Korda and Carol Reed, who discussed Charles Laughton and how Hollywood had spoiled him. Considering, however, that his work in America included such classics as THE HUNCHBACK OF NOTRE DAME and MUTINY ON THE BOUNTY, there must have been a lively discussion.

"David asked Korda what he does when he has an actor who can't act," wrote Benson in her diary. 'You go so far and then give up,' was the answer. Carol Reed discussed his marriage and said how difficult marriage is when you work in movies - 'there are so many gossips in films.' David would not have volunteered any details of his own marriage. He was still somewhat prudish and although fascinated by sex, he disapproved of salacious stories. Very few of his colleagues knew that he was being psychoanalysed.

"David went into analysis," said Kay Walsh, "because of his conflict with himself and maybe I came into it somewhere. I think he really did want to hang on to something normal, healthy and substantial - clock-winding and sharpening the knife for the Sunday joint. He was very aware that with this fire burning inside him something very destructive could happen. And he was always on the verge of it. It came out with his women and marriages - I imagine there was always a lot of anxiety there. People talk about his looking into the distance and I think he was thinking half the time, 'God almighty, what am I doing here?'

"He fitted analysis in between a day's work and meeting me and taking me out to dinner. I sometimes feel that anxiety can be such a weight that to be able to lie down for fifty minutes with total privacy and to be able to bring things up for which you might be in the Scrubs - the relief to be in good hands must have been enormous."

David's analyst was Dr Willi Hoffer, an Austrian-Jewish refugee from Vienna who had been an associate of Anna Freud. It was unusual for people to go into analysis in those days, and then as now it was an act of bravery, for the analyst forces his patient to face the worst things about himself, things he has always avoided.

Hoffer was the ideal analyst for David. A colleague spoke of

David told Kay Walsh that they would go on holiday together as soon as OLIVER TWIST *was complete - this photograph was taken just before he told her that he would not be joining her.*

his warmth and the "almost childlike emotional involvement" that were among his most endearing features. But when Hoffer began, the discipline was based on a formal, cold relationship which would not have appealed to David at all.

"The change," wrote Hoffer, "seems to me to be from an intellectual emotionally detached rapport between patient and therapist to one of intellectual intimacy based on a sublimated if not at times sublime, emotional closeness between the two partners, patient and therapist." [22]

Despite the fact that they were separated, David promised Kay they would go on holiday together. Halfway through OLIVER TWIST, the Rank management decided that sporadic holidays were both disruptive to the film and expensive. They considered the complete closure of the studio for two weeks - between 16-30 August - would be more sensible.

"We went out on the set after a day's shooting,' said Kay Walsh. "He said to me, 'I know you're going to understand but I'm not going to be able to go on holiday with you. I'm in a position in my analysis that I think I should just let you go on your own and I will go on my own.' That look of love and trust on my face! You would have to be deeply neurotic to love like that and Freud would have another word for it.

"He didn't like analysis. It's very hard work. The patient does the work and it's very painful facing up to who you really are. But eventually he ran and took flight. I think he was in flight all his life." [23]

David spent three years, five nights a week, in psychoanalysis and said at the time that it had made all the difference to his life. Later, though, David earnestly advised people against it. He said he suffered so much that he would never suggest inflicting it on anyone else, except as a last resort. When a family friend challenged him on the subject during the seventies, implying he had cut his analysis short, he flew into the worst rage that his niece, Sara, had ever seen.

To young people, David often appeared a distant, cold figure. Josephine Smith, a girl from the Rank publicity department, remembered him sitting silently on the set, deep in thought, with the entire crew waiting, waiting...

"I went back to the office and people asked me, 'Is he still sitting there?' And then Ronnie went down there to see what the problem was."

The problem was that David and Stanley Haynes had worked out a brilliant introduction for Bill Sikes, but could not get it on film. Cameraman Guy Green (who later married Josephine Smith) explained:

"David had devised a shot where Fagin was with the boys in his lair and a scuffle breaks out with the Artful Dodger. Fagin throws a pewter mug of beer - the operator whip panned as it hit the door - the door opened and Bob Newton appeared. And Bob had to say a line which he couldn't get right. So we kept having to play the beginning of the scene, pan across, hit the door, and Bob would

fluff it and we'd do it all over again. It went on for hours. It was a simple line -
'What yer goin' to do, Fagin?' - but he kept raising the inflection at the end and
ruining it."[24]

A more schedule-conscious director would have printed the best take for the
visuals and post-synchronised the line that Newton kept tripping over. But David
would never do anything by halves. The scene had to be perfect and he would go
on until it was. Looking at the shot in the film, one is so awe-struck that camera
operator Oswald Morris could follow the beer-mug as it flies through the air, in
impeccable focus, that one hardly takes in Bill Sikes's line.

Since the test with Robert Donat had disappointed everyone, David was able
to hire Newton, who was his first choice anyway.

"David had trouble with Bobby Newton," said Oswald Morris. "He was
inclined to ham it up and David was always battling with him to keep it down.
Bobby didn't think that was right and he kept hitting the bottle and David had his
work cut out coping with that. I must say he handled it very well. Once or
twice he would say, 'Bobby I think you'd better go home and have a rest.' He
never accused him of drinking."[25]

Considering David's puritanical attitude towards actors and alcohol, he
should have despised Newton. Yet he admired him and made far more
allowances for him than he later made for many a more conventional actor.

"In the later stages of the film," said David, "he used to get very muzzy. I
never knew whether he was drunk or not. He used to stand there in a kind of
dream. I used to go up to him and turn the camera over and I'd tap him on his
leg and say, 'Do you feel that?'

"'Yes, I'm beginning to feel that.'

"And I'd tap a bit harder and get ready. I'd tap him on the other leg and he'd
say, 'Yes, yes.' I'd say, 'Get ready, Bobby. Action!' And Bobby would go straight
into the scene and he would be magnificent."[26]

John Bryan's art direction was, if anything, more striking in this film than in
GREAT EXPECTATIONS, because the situations were even more dramatic. He used
forced perspective again, most memorably in the workhouse, with its bleak
expanse of brick, when Oliver asks for more.

"When you're faced with a cliché, you have to think very hard," said David.
"That scene has been reproduced so often. How do you photograph it? John
Bryan created the whole shot in forced perspective. You see the whole roof
behind him, the back of the man towering above the boy and it looks just
wonderful. Nobody would think that it's totally unreal."

"John Bryan made it bloody difficult, too," said cameraman Guy Green,
"although his sets were wonderful to photograph. He had Francis Sullivan as the
Beadle going along a tunnel, and it was impossible to light it. So I gave Sullivan a

lamp to carry with a light inside it which shone out in to the tunnel, and that was it.

"OLIVER TWIST was more difficult to photograph than GREAT EXPECTATIONS. That was a very photogenic picture. OLIVER was about grim, dirty interiors and I used a lot of diffused light, something which has become fashionable now with colour. I tried to get the effect of light coming through small dirty windows, and it had a kind of richness of its own. They do that now on television films - they bounce the light because they need very little of it. But I still like the harsh stuff now and again."[27]

Guy Green considered OLIVER TWIST probably his best work and during the shooting he learned that he and John Bryan had won Oscars for GREAT EXPECTATIONS. He went on the set and told David that he was the father of twins.

The film had received five nominations, including Best Director, and if ever a director deserved an Oscar it was David. It must have been with considerably mixed emotions that he heard the news. Later, he gave Guy Green his own award, a painting from the Leicester Galleries. No doubt John Bryan received one as well.

One of the most innovative scenes in OLIVER TWIST was the killing of Nancy (Kay Walsh) and its aftermath.

"I am not mad about violence on the screen," said David. "I know you have to have it every now and then but I'm absolutely sick of seeing gratuitous violence. I think violence is much more frightening if you leave it to the viewer to imagine.

"To do the death of Nancy as described - Bill Sikes hitting her on the head - would be disgusting. So I thought of the idea of the dog bolting for the door when Sikes picks up the cudgel. That's not in the book, but it worked a treat - the dog trying to get out, with the cries and bangs laid over it, and much more frightening than showing it because the audience fill in the gaps they haven't seen. They've seen nothing except that dog scrabbling at the door.

"How we came to do it was thanks to a fluke. One of the prop men brought out a stuffed cat and the bull terrier went absolutely mad. It barked and rushed at it and they had to tear the stuffed cat away from him. So when we were ready to film, we held the dog, turned the cameras over and pushed the stuffed cat's tail under the door. Then I said, "Action" and they let go of the dog and pulled the tail back and the dog rushes at the door and stayed there, barking and scrabbling. That was one of the best scenes in the picture.

"I was rather pleased with the rest of the sequence. I showed Sikes sitting there as the guilt began to creep over him. I showed her comb, her hairbrush, something on the floor, with the dog looking at it. You know, that's what movies are. Let the audience fill it in."[28]

Because they knew what caused them, the crew found the dog's reactions hysterically funny. In context, they give the scene a terrifying reality.

The dog, which the crew called Sikes, came from a dogs' home and had to be made up with cuts and scars to indicate that his owner maltreated him. "He was a Staffordshire bull terrier," said Norman Spencer. "He was a dear, sweet animal. I inherited him after the picture."

The climactic sequence, when the dog inadvertently leads the mob to Bill Sikes's hideout, was staged largely on the rooftops where Sikes forces the terrified Oliver to scramble over the tiles. A loose tile falls into the river far below with a splash. The roar of the mob suddenly ceases and a voice cries out, "There he is!"

"In real life," said Norman Spencer, "with a mob like that, a tile falling into the water wouldn't be heard. But it was another example of David's inbred sense of the dramatic." [29]

With Robert Newton invariably slightly drunk, accompanied by an eight-year-old, not even a safety net slung twenty feet below was sufficient protection. David had them secured with safety belts linked to wires - a device known as the Kirby's Flying Ballet harness.

"Once I had a Kirby," said John

Ossie Morris in pram, shooting a tracking shot with Eyemo camera; David, right, and focus-puller John Godar, left. It was while he was looking at this picture that David revealed the grim story behind Godar's conviction for murder.

Howard Davies, "I wanted to jump off and find out what it was like. I did get slightly worried about Robert Newton climbing that roof, because the structure did not seem to me to be terribly sound." [30]

At the end of the sequence, Oliver secures a rope on a chimney pot, and Sikes slips it round his shoulders. He begins the ascent when that loose tile falls, alerting a Peeler with a musket who opens fire. We see Sikes, hit in the back, falling out of frame, and the rope, loosely coiled around his neck, suddenly tightens in one of those close-ups which diverts our eyes from the horrifying violence but which make our imagination work harder. In a remarkably conceived shot, Sikes falls, the rope streams through shot and the focus-puller adjusts the lens so that when the rope suddenly goes taut we know only too well the reason why.

A terrible parallel to this, which occurred in real life, only came to light when I showed David a production still from OLIVER TWIST. He had been ill for some time, and as he stared at the photograph, many minutes ticked by in silence. Eventually he handed it back to me and said, pointing at one of the technicians, "That man was hanged."

I thought the illness had affected his mind, and said no more. But when I showed the picture to Ronald Neame, and pointed to the man, telling him what David had told me, he said, "I'm surprised. I would have thought it was this man here."

Gradually the story came out. John Howard Godar had been a clapper boy at Denham, working on such Korda films as THE FOUR FEATHERS. His mother, Madeleine, was in the wardrobe department and had worked on PYGMALION. Godar was now a focus-puller.

When his girlfriend fell for another man, Godar killed her with a knife (his violent behaviour had previously been restricted to his prewar days with the British Union of Fascists). He pleaded not guilty and a psychiatrist considered he was temporarily insane. Norman Spencer remembered him as an apparently placid, plump young man who wouldn't hurt a fly. The jury took only forty minutes to reach a unanimous verdict of guilty and Godar was hanged.

The murder occurred on the night of 6-7 June 1952 during the production of THE SOUND BARRIER.

"Extraordinary thing," said Peter Newbrook, whose assistant Godar was. "He was arrested, tried, convicted and hanged and we were still carrying on with the picture. It was very unnerving. It was a *crime passionel*; she goaded him and he was a very hot-tempered lad and that was it. They wouldn't have executed him in France."[31]

The editing of OLIVER TWIST was once again entrusted to Jack Harris. A new member of the cutting-room staff was Clive Donner, who became an editor and then a director, and who made his own version of the Dickens novel for television in 1983. As a second assistant he had the responsibility of synching up the rushes and was asked to have them ready for eight o'clock.

"David and Jack came in, I pushed the button and the rushes came on out of sync. I rushed upstairs and the projectionist and I re-synched them and we started again. At the end, as they were leaving, I said, 'I'm very sorry, David, dreadful mistake, I do apologise.' There was a cold silence. Then he said, 'Do it again, and your balls will drop off.'"[32]

To write the music, Muir Mathieson suggested David should engage an illustrious name for this very prestigious and very British film - William Walton, say, or Arthur Bliss. David eventually decided upon Sir Arnold Bax, Master of the King's Musick.

"Bax was great,' said John Huntley, "but was totally inexperienced at film and timing and all the rest of it. So in order to try and help, David wrote the most extensive notes on what he actually wanted the music to do."[33]

Huntley kept the notes and published some in his book on film music. Here is an example, for the scene when Fagin introduces his methods of picking pockets to Oliver.

"The boys have sat down to supper with Fagin, and after the Dodger has brought out his spoils for the day, Fagin raps the table with the toasting fork and says, 'To work.' I should like the music to accompany the whole scene of Fagin donning his hat, taking the walking stick and walking round like an old gentleman, and finally having his foot trodden on and his pockets picked, causing him to search frantically for his lost wallet and watch, which makes Oliver laugh so much. I think the music should start immediately after 'To work' and end on the dissolve to Oliver lying asleep. This is to me almost the most important piece of music so far, and I should like it to transform the scene into a comic ballet, with only one angry jar in it - the moment when Fagin gives the two boys who have failed to pick his pocket successfully a kick. This is important because, although I should like to emphasise the comedy in Fagin, I also want to retain his viciousness which is to develop more and more. In other words, Fagin as a character starts off in Oliver's eyes as an amusing old gentleman and gradually this guise falls away and we see him in all his villainy."[34]

When the film was in its rough-cut stage and had been shown to various people, there was one almost unanimous complaint. People were bewildered by Oliver's relationship with his benefactor, Mr Brownlow. Playing Mr Brownlow was Henry Stephenson whom David had always remembered as Sir Joseph Banks in MUTINY ON THE BOUNTY.

Because people felt the film was missing a scene to explain the relationship, David sought help from Eric Ambler who was at that moment scripting THE PASSIONATE FRIENDS which was to be directed by Ronald Neame.

"Those who had seen the cut film," said Ambler, "said 'What's Oliver gone there for? What's the connection between Oliver and Brownlow?' They were completely lost and asked me to fix it. David said, 'We want about thirty seconds to explain it.' So I wrote a little scene in the manner of Dickens. I used the Beadle, who could be retrieved for half a day, and Mr Brownlow discovering the child's birth certificate. That's all I did."[35]

When the film was over, the make-up artist, Stuart Freeborn, was not expecting any special thanks or praise.

"I thought, well, that's that. Nobody said thank you or anything, I've had a chance to do my job and I feel I did it all right."

But Freeborn was in for a delightful surprise. There was a preview at the local cinema in Uxbridge.

"The main curtains drew back and then David's voice came from behind the screen. He said, 'Before we see the film, I feel I would like to thank certain members of the unit. I would also like to thank Mrs Freeborn, because I know only too well what she's been going through for the last six months, having to get her husband off so early in the morning and all the problems he must have brought back with him in creating the character of Fagin.'

"So he had been aware of everything, despite the fact that he had been so distant at the time. The film went over very well. Everybody clapped and I felt, 'My God, it was all worth it.' It was a few months of agony but the best ones always are."[36]

David had invited Isabel and Peter to the preview at Uxbridge, which was held on Sunday 20 June 1948. It was the only time he had extended an invitation to his first wife and son - perhaps he thought they should see a film about the travails of an orphan boy...

David's father, perusing his *Daily Mail* in Norfolk Road, could not have failed to have noticed the paper's enthusiasm. David's direction was described as "inspired".

But other reviewers had reservations. The *News Chronicle* referred to it as "A thoroughly expert piece of movie entertainment... In any deeper aspect, the film profoundly disappoints... My impression is that Lean has become imprisoned by technique."

And Dilys Powell in the *Sunday Times* thought it suffered from the care with which it had been made: "There is no room in it for a mistake and none for the magnificent outbursts of rage, grief and passion which are the essence of Dickens... it is always admirable, often beautiful and sometimes a shade cold."

The most startling comment came from John Prebble in the *Sunday Express*: "Dear Mr Dickens... that gentle irony which enabled you to write so lovingly but so ignorantly of the lower classes has been ironed out. Your sarcastic reportage [has] gone and with it your mawkish sentiment and dishonest melodrama. In their place is a grim, harsh piece that reverberates the vertebrae... I do not think it matters whether this is good or bad Dickens. It does matter that it is a good film. The bad parts of it are yours."[37]

The film, which opened at the Odeon (formerly the Regal) Marble Arch, following a Royal premiere, was a huge commercial success. However, the full-blooded caricature of a Jew by Alec Guinness upset some Jews in England, as indeed had Dickens's novel one hundred and ten years earlier.

"The word 'Jew' is not mentioned in the film," said Alec Guinness. "I am married into a Jewish family anyway, and I said, 'It is not a Jew as far as I am concerned, just some curious Middle Eastern character in the East End.'"[38]

The Zionists, however, declared that Fagin was presented in the same way that Jews were vilified in the Nazi paper *Der Sturmer*. Their protests were overlooked, however, because the Zionists were anti-British, and in the struggle in Palestine, Zionist terrorists had killed British soldiers.[39]

When OLIVER TWIST went to America, it was expected to gather the same bouquets, and perhaps even the same Oscars, that GREAT EXPECTATIONS had enjoyed. To the dismay of everyone concerned, it was treated as something subversive. Guinness's portrayal was condemned as "the worst caricature of a Jew ever depicted in an English-speaking film."[40]

The New York film critics and the Board of Rabbis attacked the film's alleged anti-Semitism, and the release was postponed. The anti-Semitism charge may have been a handy stick with which to beat a British film. The Sons of Liberty (a New York Jewish organisation) had been picketing British films and their action caused exhibitors to withdraw several British releases, including three which were produced by Korda. Although he was Jewish, Korda decided to send no more films to America until the trouble was over.

Not all Jews objected to the film. Spokesmen for Jewish organisations in Britain denounced the boycott, claiming it was damaging Anglo-American relations and harmful to the new State of Israel itself. The American Council for Judaism opposed any ban, seeing a far greater danger in censorship. According to the Rank Organisation, OLIVER TWIST would have opened at Radio City Music

Alec Guinness as Fagin, John Howard Davies as Oliver Twist.

Hall; now its opening was postponed indefinitely.

"They picked upon the Fagin character and used it deliberately as a campaign," said Ronald Neame. "It was ridiculous, because we had these two villains: the intelligent, shrewd Fagin, with a great sense of humour, but a caricature up to a point, and we had Bill Sikes, a Gentile, who was far and away the worse villain. The attacks were ludicrous because we were certainly not anti-Semitic."[41]

Rank's American distributors, Eagle-Lion Classics, offered to test the film with a full sociological survey if the Anti-Defamation League would share the expense. But the League, an organisation opposed to racial and religious intolerance, would not co-operate. Nor would the National Community Relations Advisory Council, an association of Jewish agencies.

"Being brought up a Quaker," said David, "I was blissfully ignorant of anti-Semitism and when OLIVER TWIST went to the States and there was a row about Fagin, I couldn't believe it. I said, 'But this is just a Jewish villain. What's wrong with that?' in a naive way. It struck me as very peculiar."[42]

"When it came to be shown in Austria in the Cold War period," said Alec Guinness, "it was the only time the Russians and Americans were united about anything. All the Russians and all the American military walked out together leaving the rest of the audience there watching the film. So it was a political move."

In February 1949, a Jewish demonstration prevented the film being shown in Berlin. The demonstrators were mainly non-German displaced people, and it was reported that a large crowd of German spectators applauded when the German police finally drew their truncheons on the demonstrators, who were dismissed as Polish black marketeers. Two revolver shots were fired.

"On two successive nights," reported *Life* Magazine, "the Jews and police fought with clubs, rocks and firehoses around the Kurbel Theatre in Berlin's British sector.... Before riots ended, thirty-five Jews had been injured and three arrested. Seven policemen were hurt."[43]

There were fewer than a hundred demonstrators - outnumbered by the police - but they managed to fight their way into the cinema and the audience hastily left by the rear exits. The demonstration ceased only when a representative of the Jewish community announced that the film would not be shown.

"He was cheered by a group of Jews, who sang the Israeli national anthem."[44]

Since the film was not being shown in America, *Life* published a series of stills headed "Scenes from a Picture Americans Cannot See". It included all the arguments that David and Cineguild had advanced - that nowhere was Fagin called a Jew, that the non-Jewish Sikes was just as villainous.

"But between Dickens and director Lean, history had interposed the ghosts of six million murdered Jews and the spectre of genocide. It was hard to see why the producers had insisted on such complete fidelity and it was harder still to guess why the authorities had not only permitted the picture in Germany but refused to withdraw it immediately after the inevitable reaction came."[45]

Not until March 1950 did Eagle Lion submit the film to the Motion Picture Association for the Production Code Administration seal, without which it could not distribute the film in regular theatres. The seal was refused, the MPA citing a clause prohibiting films that "unfairly represent" a race or nationality. Eagle Lion appealed, and the seal was eventually issued, providing cuts were made. However, Eagle Lion still faced what amounted to a boycott; although one Texan circuit offered to show the film, they withdrew after pressure from New York exhibitors. Eventually, Eagle Lion were taken over by United Artists.

While United Artists were making up their mind what to do with the film, Columbia became interested in attempting to distribute it.

"Perhaps the anti-Semitic problem frightened the hierarchy of United Artists rather more than it did the old brigand Harry Cohn," said Norman Spencer. "He knew a good picture when he saw one and had a keen sense for a profit."[46]

Harry Cohn was head of Columbia, and David was asked by J. Arthur Rank to meet him at Claridge's. Cohn had been a vaudeville song plugger from the Lower East Side who had risen via slapstick comedies and poverty row dramas to the head of a much-respected production company. A shelf in his office was lined with the Oscars won for him by Frank Capra. Cohn behaved like a gangster, but Capra, and some of his other directors, found his honesty about films refreshing. He was, however, Jewish, and David assumed he was in for a tongue-lashing when he arrived at Cohn's suite.

"His first remark was, 'I kiss the feet of an artist,' which threw me. He said, 'I've just seen your picture. I don't know how you did it for money. I think it's just great.'

"He held his hand over one half of his face and said, 'This side of my face is artistic,' then he moved his hand, 'and this side's *commoishal*.' He thought the only trouble was, 'that accent and that schnozzle.'

"I said, 'Well, we can't do much about that.'

"He said, 'We can redub the accent and the schnozzle - we can make it turn up instead of turning down.'

"I was desperate. This was going to be horrible. I said, 'Look, Mr Cohn, it's now two or three years since we shot those scenes because of the hold-up over the anti-Jewish business. The boy [John Howard Davies] was this height, he's now this high, so we can't shoot anything with him in it.'

"He said, 'Oh, my God, I hadn't thought of that.'"[47]

Columbia did not release OLIVER TWIST, though Cohn would remember his meeting with David and would sow the seed for what would become David's greatest film, LAWRENCE OF ARABIA.

United Artists did eventually release OLIVER TWIST - on 30 July 1951 - with twelve minutes missing. Such scenes as Fagin counting jewels in a treasure box and his pickpocketing lessons were removed. Despite some good reviews, the film did poor business.

"I told them," said David, "they had turned it into an anti-Semitic picture. What they had done was to cut out everything that wasn't absolutely essential to the plot, so all the humour of Guinness's performance went. He was just a straight and unmitigated sod, Fagin. Madness. The Americans are only now beginning to see the film as it was supposed to be."[48]

Unsurprisingly, OLIVER TWIST was ignored by the Academy voters. GREAT EXPECTATIONS may have won Oscars for Guy Green and John Bryan but it had lost the award for Best Picture and Best Director to Elia Kazan's GENTLEMAN'S AGREEMENT, a film about anti-Semitism.

During the production, Guy Green recalled Robert Newton coming onto the set with his first costume which included a hat with a feather in it. David looked at him with dismay and said "This is terrible. Take him away and redress him."

David was addressing not some minor assistant, but Maggie Furse. It was a hint of the ending of their relationship, a parting which was confirmed when Norman Spencer met David in Shepherd's Bush one day.

"He was buying some flowers. I asked him who he was buying the flowers for. 'What do you mean?' he said. 'Me.' He was living in a little one-roomed flat in Athenaeum Court, Piccadilly. I thought it was terribly sad to be buying yourself flowers to put in your tiny bachelor apartment. But David was womanless for a time and he lived a sort of monkish, ascetic kind of life."[49]

And yet few directors were in such demand. Vivien Leigh wanted him. Alexander Korda wanted him. And, as we shall see, Ann Todd wanted him.

CHAPTER TWENTY

THE PASSIONATE FRIENDS

WHEN David finished OLIVER TWIST, he went on holiday with an exhilarating sense of freedom. He had repeated, perhaps even improved upon, the success of the earlier Dickens film, he had enhanced his reputation as England's greatest film director (with Carol Reed slightly ahead or slightly behind, according to one's loyalties) and it must have seemed, as far as it could in such an unpredictable business, that his judgment was infallible. Twenty years earlier, after all, he had been an utter washout, serving time in his father's office and staring at a lifetime of dreary routine.

By the time his holiday was over, he was enmeshed in company politics. He had become involved in the kind of situation he abhorred - being forced by circumstances to make a film he did not want to make. David's commitment to a film was so absolute that unless he was in love with the subject, he would far rather have nothing to do with it.[1]

Ronald Neame's directorial debut, TAKE MY LIFE, had given him sufficient confidence to repeat the experience and he asked author Eric Ambler to join him as writer and producer. Arthur Rank and John Davis were anxious to produce more films which appealed to women and asked them to consider making a love story.

"For better or worse," said Neame, "we chose THE PASSIONATE FRIENDS. We both felt we could bring the story up to date."

H.G. Wells's 1913 novel had already been made into a film in 1922 by the prolific Maurice Elvey. It was a difficult novel to film, being written in the form of a letter from a father to a son, about an affair with a woman who was not his mother. It was full of philosophical digressions, wild coincidences and a lengthy episode in the Boer War.

For Cineguild, THE PASSIONATE FRIENDS would become a title of some irony, for the project broke up one set of friendships and substituted it with others. David would always regret having anything to do with the film, although he was not entirely displeased with the result.

David made no secret of the fact that he thought Ronald Neame would not make a particularly good director. (He became one of the most successful in the business.) It was his theory that few former cameramen ever did. Yet here was Neame with a cast including Hollywood star Claude Rains, Marius Goring and Ann Todd, and a screenplay by the distinguished Eric Ambler. The Cineguild partners were highly competitive people, and they would not have been human if they were not occasionally envious of each other.

The competitive spirit had been heightened by the fact that Ambler, an author more famous in the United States than in Britain, had become a director of Cineguild. In 1944, with Peter Ustinov, he wrote THE WAY AHEAD for Carol Reed, a highly successful propaganda film, and since Cineguild lacked a professional writer, he was an undoubted asset.

In the winter of 1947, regarded as the worst of the century, Ambler produced THE OCTOBER MAN at Denham. It was a wretched experience; the central heating system at the studio was out of commission and the company had to make do with pitifully inadequate electric fires. Ambler said he accepted Neame's offer mainly because he thought Pinewood might be warmer.

His screenplay for THE PASSIONATE FRIENDS was well received and Rank quickly approved it. "In just a matter of weeks, the new wing of Cineguild was about to start production on a film of considerable importance," said Neame, "while Stanley and David had not yet found a subject. There was a danger that the tail might start wagging the dog."[2]

John Bryan joined the unit and began designing sets. While they were being built, Neame and Ambler went to the Villa d'Este on Lake Como to look for locations. There were strict currency restrictions at the time, and although Neame smuggled pound notes in his socks, they didn't have enough cash to visit the bar. They couldn't even afford a motor boat.

When I asked David to tell me about THE PASSIONATE FRIENDS, his reply was prefaced by a scowl like thunder and an immensely long David Lean Silence. Reluctantly, he told me what he remembered but asked me not to divulge Ronnie's name, as though the revelation could still affect his career or hurt his feelings. But since Neame told me his side of the story without requesting anonymity, I have censored nothing.

"It was a very unhappy situation, as you can imagine," said David. "It was one of the worst times I've had in my professional life. I should never have allowed myself to be put into that position. I wanted to help Ronnie, so I was torn in two directions. I saw the rushes and realised at once that it was no good. Then I took over. I stopped for two weeks, got the script and rewrote it with Stanley Haynes. We wrote like hell."[3]

David's account is incorrect, according to Neame, who says that David could not have seen the rushes since nothing had been shot. Neame says that Haynes called him about three weeks before shooting was due to start and requested a copy of the script, saying, "We're all in the same company, after all."

Neame sent him the screenplay and a few days later Stanley phoned again: "Ronnie, David and I want to have a very serious talk with you and Eric. It's about your script. We suggest the White Tower for dinner."

"The dinner was horrendous," said Neame. "I don't think any of us ate any-thing. David and Stanley felt our screenplay was a disaster and that to start production was madness. They begged us to accept the inevitable and postpone the start date until something could be done about it. Eric and I were completely shattered. By the end of the evening we had lost all confidence in ourselves. When someone as talented as David Lean says you've got a lousy script, you'd better believe it.

"I remember going home that night and thinking, 'Well, this is the end. I want to direct and I'm not going to be a director.'

"By the next evening, David and Stanley had made a plan. They would both come to our rescue. Eric would join them and work as a writer with them, while I, for the time being, would take over the pre-production producing chores. The three of them would make a new script, which they would deliver to me as it progressed. I would go to Arthur Rank and plead for a three-week extension of pre-production, a very costly request, because of artists' contracts, stage rental, etc. I would also talk to key members of the unit explaining the situation and, most difficult of all, tell Ann Todd the script that she had liked so much was to be scrapped and replaced by a new one, but that she should not be worried because the new script would be under the control of no less a person than David Lean.

"Up until this moment, my relationship with Ann had been excellent, but, as you can imagine, what was now happening was not very likely to encourage her confidence in me. Under the circumstances, she behaved very well.

"During the next few weeks, construction of the sets continued, and make-up and costume tests were made. The script pages came in very slowly and it soon became apparent that some of the sets already completed would not be needed and that other sets not anticipated in the budget would now have to be built."[4]

During this period, Neame and John Bryan went to Lake Annecy, in the hope that they could do better than the villa d'Este. Here they chose the final location for the lakeside terrace set.

For Eric Ambler, working on the script with David was traumatic. "David was learning to write for the screen. It was a very odd time. David didn't say it, but it was understood that what he wanted to get away from was BRIEF ENCOUNTER. Whereas that was what Ronnie had been aiming for - I suspect he wanted to make a better love story than David. What David really wanted to get away from was Noël Coward. He wanted to get away from the writing authority.

"Cineguild was there to service him. He wanted Ronnie to stay on as producer. He didn't want him going off, deserting the ship - his ship. So he had brought in Stanley Haynes. Stanley Haynes undoubtedly made a damn nuisance of himself, but he was trying to latch on to David so that he had a job.

"You have to consider that both David and Stanley were in psychoanalysis. During the discussions we had at the White Tower and at Stanley's flat, it was quite clear they were going to their analysts every day. David tried to work his analyst's observations into the film.

"He didn't want a writer to work with him, he wanted an amanuensis like Stanley. He wanted someone to interpret his thoughts. David had curious limitations. For instance, it was painful to watch him trying to write even a step outline for a script. He would stick out his tongue, frowning with intense concentration. He really had physical difficulty. But he had no difficulty in talking through the script. David reading would go like this - 'We have blah-blah-blah' - that was the dialogue. 'And then we come to a close-up, and gradually we move back from that...' It didn't matter what the story was, the visuals took precedence. He was really looking at it in a mental Moviola."[5]

"When we got back to England," said Ronald Neame, "a few more pages had come to the studio from David, Eric and Stanley, but the new starting date was rapidly approaching.

"I made the biggest mistake of my life. I actually started principal photography with less than fifty pages of the script, a script that bore no resemblance to the original. My hope was, by some miracle, to cope with the situation and save Rank from spending more money. I was a complete idiot. I was a lost soul and apart from the wonderful friendship of John Bryan and my wife, completely alone. There was no way I could have succeeded. At the end of the fourth day it is no exaggeration to say that I was near to suicide."

Ironically, it was Eric Ambler who called a halt. As producer, he was all too well aware of how little footage was being shot each day.

"Ann Todd started playing up," said Ambler. "She had the part of a 'Brief Encounter' with Trevor Howard and suddenly realised she'd got the wrong director. And it wasn't quite the right script either. And she just refused to play. I mean, it was quite disastrous. She would start arguing. She was determined that it wasn't going to work. Ronnie couldn't cope with her. Nobody could.

"I was the producer and there was nothing I could do. I said I was going to stop the picture. We couldn't go on spending money at that rate. We had commitments to Claude Rains and we had permission to pay him in dollars. You don't realise how difficult that was. That had to be a top level decision. He'd already been sitting there doing nothing for most of the time he'd been in the country.

"It then became necessary to decide how the picture was to be reorganised. I said that clearly Ronnie had to go as director. The obvious thing was for Ronnie to become producer. This was an acceptable public relations decision. I would be the writer. I resolved I would never again produce. And I knew I'd never make another picture with David."[6]

Ambler went to George Archibald, financial head of Independent Producers, who was understanding and helpful. It was agreed that David would take over, and at another meeting at the White Tower, Ambler was told he should discard his producer credit and Stanley Haynes would get a credit for adaptation.

"Ronnie lived in Fulmer at a big house called Mount Fidget," said Norman Spencer, associate producer on the picture. "He asked me to come over on the Saturday morning. He said, 'Look, I've decided I'm not a director. I can't go on with this picture. I'm going to produce and David's going to direct. It's going to be a bloody marvellous picture.'

"And then he told me to ask members of the crew to go to his house on Sunday morning and have coffee and he announced this so that everybody knew. Then he said that on Monday morning we were going to get the whole of the studio concerned with the film into the boardroom at Pinewood to announce his decision. It was an extremely brave thing to do."[7]

By the time that production resumed with David as director, Marius Goring - who had appeared in Neame's TAKE MY LIFE - had been replaced by Trevor Howard.

"David really disliked me," said Goring, "and didn't want me in the film. Of course, I didn't know this at the time. I found out later from Ronnie. I don't remember doing any scenes before David arrived."[8]

Once David reluctantly took over, he decided he would have to ride roughshod over the temperament of Ann Todd. "The trouble with you being in charge," he told Neame, "is that you put the red carpet down for her. You've got to be tough with her, you see."[9]

Ann Todd, who appeared in THESE CHARMING PEOPLE, from which David had been fired in 1931, had become perhaps Britain's one authentic star in the Hollywood mould, rivalled only by Margaret Lockwood. In 1945 she had played her most celebrated role in THE SEVENTH VEIL in which she starred as a pianist with psychological problems. British audiences gasped when her co-star, James Mason, smashes her hands as she plays the piano. She had recently been to Hollywood to appear in Alfred Hitchcock's THE PARADINE CASE in which she co-starred with Gregory Peck and Charles Laughton. Widely regarded as glacially beautiful, enigmatic and cool, the British fan magazines often referred to her as "the British Garbo".

"She was a little bit swollen-headed when she came on the set," said camera operator Ossie Morris. "You were told that she had just been working with Hitchcock and it was a great honour that she was now going to work with us."[10]

"We started again on minor sets at Pinewood," said Norman Spencer, "and then we did the big Albert Hall sequence. Ann Todd's work did not begin until the Albert Hall scene, which is why in her autobiography she has that recollection of David Lean swooping into her life on the camera crane. There was a crane,

David (far left) directs Ann Todd; Ossie Morris at camera, Guy Green with exposure meter:
THE PASSIONATE FRIENDS.

which was used to move into Ann and Claude Rains in their box, but at no point did we shoot in the real Albert Hall."

The Albert Hall scene was a recreation of the Chelsea Arts Ball, which David had once gate-crashed when he was an editor. Ann Todd recalled that the waiting was endless.

"If you were wearing costumes, you weren't allowed to take your dress off in case you were called, and then you had to get down there like lightning. Once, the call boy came up and said, 'Mr Lean's getting very angry that you are not coming down.'

"I said, 'I haven't been called.'

"So when I got down, I said, 'Mr Lean, I'm sorry. There was a muddle and I didn't get a call.'

"And he said, 'That's nothing to do with it. As an actress it's your obligation to come down.'

"I was very angry. I was in the dressing-room next to Claude. He came up to me and said, 'What's all the fuss about?' I told him. 'My God,' he said. 'You're a bigger person than that, surely? We're working in a factory. You get to the job at eight and you're paid for it. Don't make such a fuss.'

"I've never forgotten that. I've never been in a studio since, and been kept waiting, without thinking of him. After Claude, I wouldn't dare open my mouth."[11]

David, who had an aversion to the absurdities of star behaviour, sighed for the old days of Celia Johnson, whose only concern was to catch the train home to her family. He arranged for Ann Todd to be looked after and chauffeured by Maggie Furse. The result was that when Ann tried to discuss David with Maggie she would encounter a wall of loyalty which she could not penetrate.

"For an artist of his calibre," she thought, "it's odd that he doesn't have much of a feeling for people."[12]

"In the first week of filming," said Norman Spencer, "Trevor Howard tried to open the window of his dressing-room, broke the glass and cut an artery. He staggered into the corridor with blood spurting something like six feet. It was horrible. We sent for a doctor, and Dr Phyllis Shipman, Olivia's mother, came right away and stitched it up. We were shooting the scene in which Ann and Claude come out of the Albert Hall and meet Trevor.

"David, as usual, said, 'Well, can't we get a shot?' Trevor was a bit shaken, and they told David that he had this damn great bandage on his wrist. But we took the shot anyway by arranging Trevor's overcoat and a white scarf over his arm. I still think, watching the film, that he looks a bit pale."[13]

David was not thrown into the deep end with a new crew. He had his old Cineguild stalwarts supporting him, including John Bryan, who used a new method from Hollywood of moving sets on castors to speed up changes of set-up. He had Guy Green as lighting cameraman, proving his versatility with cinematography as different from OLIVER TWIST as silk from hessian. He was influenced by the gauzed, lustrous glamour lighting of Lee Garmes who had shot many of Marlene Dietrich's films for Sternberg, as well as Hitchcock's THE PARADINE CASE.

One unusual idea David re-introduced from the silent days, when set musicians were employed to provide the right mood for every scene. Obviously, he couldn't use music while shooting any more, but in between...

"David hated noise on the set," said Ossie Morris. "Even when people were lighting they had to be quiet, and he came up with the idea that maybe they'd be quieter if there was a pianist. He had a grand piano at the back of the set and a pianist played music quite softly. And everything else became softer. David had these very big ears and he could hear dialogue the other side of the stage."

One of the tunes constantly being played was, "People Will Say We're in Love."

"Operating for David," said Ossie Morris, "meant that he was over my shoulder on every set-up, watching every movement and saying, 'Now are you absolutely happy with that? Have you locked on the right frame? There was no movement when you panned at the end?' He really quizzed me, which did me the world of good and improved my standard of operating.

"David's great forte was that he saw everything in terms of cutting. He would often say, 'Now, Oz, I need literally thirty frames of this between so-and-so and so-and-so. Don't bother about the beginning, that's just a warm up. It's that little bit there, and don't bother about the end.'

"He didn't suffer fools gladly - he could tell very quickly if you were genuine or not, whether you knew what you were talking about. With David there was no second best. It was either right or wrong. I'm thrilled to have worked with him. I found him wonderfully dedicated, as did everyone who worked on that film."[14]

The film had some beneficial aspects, particularly the fact that it introduced David to Claude Rains, for whom he had enormous admiration. "I loved Claude. He was one of the very special people in my life."

Rains shared David's attitude towards his work. He believed in concentration to the same extent, too. In fact, he went even further than David, refusing all invitations to parties, devoting his time when not actually filming to studying the part. As a rule, he went to bed at eight in the evening and rose at four in the morning, putting in a quiet hour or two studying his lines before leaving for the studio.

Rains was among the most accomplished actors in Hollywood. His apparently effortless performances were achieved through mastery of his voice and mastery of timing. "He was very short," said David. "His heels were built up and he used to backcomb his hair; that added another inch. It wasn't straight vanity. He knew how to present himself. Presenting yourself is a large part of being a star actor.

"Claude always amused me because he carried timing to an almost absurd degree. You can almost put a Claude Rains scene to numbers: 'Yes,' pause of one, two, three, 'I'm not so sure.' Cross legs, two, three. 'What do you think?' And so on. It was that sort of technique, which is the basic technique of all acting, whatever anybody likes to say. You ain't got timing, you ain't got anything. It's tremendously important. I go in for it a lot myself.

"Claude told me that he started off as a call-boy at the Haymarket Theatre. He was a Cockney and one of the people he looked after was Sir Herbert Beerbohm Tree. Tree liked him and he was always there. Every evening when he came in, Tree would empty his pockets and put all his money on the dressing-table. Claude used to tidy it up afterwards while he was on the stage. One day he noticed several two-shilling silver coins. And Claude said, 'I don't know what came over me, but I found myself thinking one of these wouldn't be missed and I took it and put in my pocket. And this went on for several weeks. When there was a lot of change I took a silver coin and kept it.'

"One day Tree said to Claude, 'How much money have you got on you?'

"'I don't know sir.'

"'Well, could you see?'

"And Claude said, 'I put my hand in my pocket and took out all my change and there was the silver coin I'd just pocketed. Tree picked it up and examined it.'

"Tree said, 'Look at this closely, will you?' On it was scratched a 'T.' He said, 'I have suspected this for some time, and so I have been marking the coins. This is a terrible thing, a great disappointment to me. I want you to come along and see me on Sunday morning at my house.'

"And Claude, desperate, said, 'Of course.' He went to the house and Tree said, 'I've decided on your punishment. I think you might have a great future as an actor. The thing that's going to prevent it is that you don't speak properly. I've just written out a cheque. You're going to take that to Miss So-and-so and every weekend you're going to talk to her and she will teach you to speak English. That is your punishment.'

"And Claude went off and that woman taught him to use that wonderful voice that he had. And his first film part was in THE INVISIBLE MAN where only his voice was heard."

David encountered only one moment on THE PASSIONATE FRIENDS in which the great actor stumbled. "We rehearsed a scene in which Claude, as the husband, is alone with the wife and her lover. He suspects they are having an affair. He is very polite, however. 'How was the show?' 'Oh, fine,' they say. 'Good seats?' 'Very.' 'I'll get you a drink.'

"The first hint that you get that he knows is when he turns to Ann and says, 'Ice?' And Claude was saying it rather sweetly. I wanted the scene played very coldly. Claude had learned it on the boat coming over and he was word perfect. This was his interpretation. I was scared stiff - my first encounter with a Holly-wood star. Here I was telling this great actor what to do.

"I said, 'You're having them on toast. You've got them where you want them. It's a rather sadistic scene. You are, in a way, being very cruel. The wife gets it, the lover doesn't. It's got to be played in a quite different way.'

"He said, 'Oh my God, I've crossed the Atlantic to play it like this.'"

Claude Rains departed to reconsider the scene, and when he returned he did it impeccably.[15]

David Rawnsley, the art director of IN WHICH WE SERVE, had become head of Rank's Research Department. Inspired by the lack of studio space during the war, he had invented a device called Independent Frame. This was a producer's dream: it used back and front projection to ensure that no film-maker ever need set foot outside the studio again. Whatever location he needed, Independent Frame would faithfully reproduce it.

This was anathema to David (imagine LAWRENCE shot with Independent Frame!) who still had the ambition to do something along the lines of what Flaherty, and Schoedsack and Cooper, had done in the old days. He resolutely ignored Independent Frame (which was eventually revealed to be a complicated and expensive white elephant.) Although, like other film-makers of the time, he occasionally resorted to back projection, he didn't really approve of it. THE PASSIONATE FRIENDS included scenes in the Swiss Alps and David was determined to go there.

Left behind at Pinewood was eighteen-year-old Peter Lean. "They grandly gave me the title of Fourth Assistant Director," he said. "I was very, very green, having been brought up by my mother alone, and I was very young for my age. I worked with George Pollock in the office, reading through scripts with a stop-watch.

"I worked on the floor on THE PASSIONATE FRIENDS and loved every minute of it. I wasn't meant to be working on the same project as dad at all. I started with Ronald Neame. But all of a sudden there he was."

At Bedales, the progressive public school for which his father paid the fees, Peter had met the sons of Charles and Marjorie Saunders. Marjorie, who was Jack Harris's editing assistant on BRIEF ENCOUNTER, took Peter round the cutting-rooms at Denham.

"I thought this was a wonderful world," he said. "Terrific. All those Moviolas clattering away like mad. The smell of the film, it had a smell of its own, hadn't it? I kept some out-takes with Celia Johnson.

"I was not happy at school. I was pretty useless anyway. The highest marks I ever got were for art - and what good is art to anybody? I asked to leave Bedales a year before I should have. And I started at Pinewood at seventeen."

David may have paid for his education, but he materialised only on rare occasions.

"In a way, he wasn't like a father. He was like a nice sort of fairy godfather who came along at birthdays and at Christmas and took me out from time to time and gave me presents. I got an electric battery-operated power boat - I've still got it somewhere. It wasn't like that every Christmas or birthday, however, don't get me wrong." [16]

Peter, not being an essential member of the crew of THE PASSIONATE FRIENDS, was not taken on location, although David gave him his own trip to the mountains a year or so later.

"I chartered a BEA Viscount," said Norman Spencer, "and flew the whole crew to

There was no room in the boat for the director as well as the boatman, so David took over as boatman (in the final takes he wore a beret). Trevor Howard and Ann Todd are behind him. David took Ann for many romantic boat rides while they were on location.

Geneva." The company stayed at the Hotel de l'Abbaye, on the shores of the Lake. For most of them it was their first trip to a Europe at peace for ten years. Ann Todd, superstitious about her big success in THE SEVENTH VEIL, asked Spencer to ensure that her room was number seven. David changed the other numbers so they could be closer.

"We had terrible weather," said Spencer. "We had rain for days on end. It was sort of stair-rods rain; you couldn't shoot anything. We were well behind schedule. David was quite happy, because he'd started his relationship with Ann Todd. When you're on location there's always a holiday atmosphere - problems of husbands and wives and children are a long way away in England. Somehow the rain disappears.'

Finally, the sun came out and the company began shooting scenes on the lake. "David enjoyed piloting the Chris Craft motorboat. He'd take Ann and Trevor for rides, shooting across the lake at maximum speed, half out of the water. Ronnie was getting very worried back at home because first we had all this rain and now he sensed what was going on with David and Ann.

"Although David is normally a hard-working professional, on this occasion he'd get into the boat with Ann and they'd disappear for three-quarters of an hour and we'd all be waiting to shoot, tearing our hair. And then the boat would come racing back. He had only been taking her for a cruise. But it went a little to his head and even David was inclined to waste time.

"I remember Ronnie ringing me and saying, 'Norman, you're Associate Producer. Can't you do something to get them going?' It wasn't only the weather. David was taking more time than Ronnie thought he should. He felt somebody ought to crack the whip. Ronnie came from a school where you shot more minutes a day than David ever did. We shot well under a minute a day, whereas we should have been shooting two minutes a day.

"David would sometimes shoot just a few seconds. A shot of the motor-boat going round the corner. It's nothing, say ten seconds. Then a cloud comes up and you don't shoot again until the afternoon. Then you get a fifteen-second shot. That's the day's work: two shots, twenty-five seconds. Terrible. It looks awful from London, but you know the reasons when you're there." [17]

From Lake Annecy, the company moved to the Hotel des Alpes at Chamonix for the mountain scenes. It was here that the flirtation between David and Ann became serious.

"I adored Chamonix," said Ann, "because we were together. Of course everybody complained that he kept the camera on me because he loved me so much." [18]

On location at Chamonix, where the flirtation between David and Ann Todd became serious. Ann Todd and Trevor Howard right, Guy Green shading his eyes; David behind him.

A victim of this passionate friendship was Trevor Howard.

"Trevor was treated badly," said Norman Spencer. "He was ignored. It was Ann, Ann, Ann. Ann was the great thing, Ann was the lover. Trevor coped with it very well. He never complained. He just waited for the location to be over. When they got back to the studio he knew things would be different - it would not just be David, Ann and Trevor. Claude Rains and all the other actors would be there.

"When we left France, I was in the car with David and Ann and David started sobbing. He broke down. He had had such a wonderful emotional time that he couldn't bear to leave it. Suddenly, I suppose, he foresaw all the marriage problems waiting in England."[19]

The editor of the film was Geoffrey Foot, who had started his career at Ealing with Thorold Dickinson and had been assistant to Anthony Havelock-Allan in the Cineguild office before cutting Neame's TAKE MY LIFE and Marc Allegret's BLANCHE FURY.

"When David came back from location, I'd heard the rumours," said Foot. "I also knew they'd had terrible weather. I said to David, 'Rotten about the weather.' He said, 'It could have pissed with rain for another three weeks as far as I was concerned.'"

Working with the legendary David Lean, Britain's top editor, was nerve-racking for Geoffrey Foot.

"It was only my third picture solo, so I was very careful about cutting my first sequence. I showed it to him and he said, 'Yes. Jolly good.' He was charming. After that first sequence I think I got the feel for it fairly rapidly, and we were buddies after that. I grew very fond of him. He didn't cut anything himself - although I heard he did, he didn't with me. So it was something when you cut a sequence and he said, 'Good.'"

Since progress in the studio was as slow as it was on location - David was averaging forty-five seconds a day - Foot was able to do his editing very quickly and then, like David in the old days, he would go down to the set and watch the shooting.

"Quite often, on a difficult scene, he would clear the set of everyone but Guy Green, Ossie Morris and Maggie and just spend the morning rehearsing. After lunch, perhaps at four o'clock, he'd go for a take. Schedule? God knows. I don't think the schedule mattered."[20]

When THE PASSIONATE FRIENDS was finished, David thought it "very nearly very good. If you take me on and say, 'Where do you put it?' I'd say it's just on the edge somewhere. It could just go this way or just go that. And in fact it did. It was not a great success, but I'm quite proud of it. I think it's rather good. The trouble is you cannot have a real hit with a picture that doesn't go up at the end.

When I say go up, I don't mean that you're cheering. But you can be touched; it's got to have some kind of wave that reaches a certain height and I don't think it had that. It was rather cold."[21]

The critics generally agreed with him and drew comparisons with BRIEF ENCOUNTER. Thus despite its glamorous cast and locations, the film was not a huge commercial success. Perhaps its intricate method of telling the story through flashback - and sometimes flashbacks within flashbacks - made it confusing for general audiences. As the critic Milton Shulman wrote, "Mr Lean has a brief encounter with inflammation of the flashback."[22]

One of David's most ardent industry admirers, Gordon Hales, by now an editor himself, considered this film the crown of David's achievements.

"I was terribly impressed. I could go on for ages about the wonders of the film. There is a scene where his wife has gone out. Theatre tickets are left behind. Claude Rains looks. Cut to shot of tickets. Cut to Claude Rains from a different angle. He has a whisky. Does something else. Looks again and there is a different complementary angle of the tickets. It wasn't just a question of Lean running off an insert and cutting it in. That wonderful rescue from suicide in the tube station - when Rains takes his wife up the stairs and the total indifference of the underground attendant, whistling. I was just knocked out by the sheer impact of the film-making."

Following the completion of THE PASSIONATE FRIENDS, David was invited to take part in an illustrated lecture at the British Council theatre in Hanover Square for the British Film Academy. Jack Harris, Charles Frend and Stewart McAllister (Humphrey Jennings's editor) were also on the panel. Gordon Hales was in the audience.

"He said something unforgettable. He said, 'Partly as a result of OLIVER TWIST I became obsessed with the idea of showing thought on the screen. And I failed.'

"He had chosen the scene from THE PASSIONATE FRIENDS in which Claude Rains collects the key from hotel reception and walks about looking at the camera with furrowed brow. Lean said, 'Seeing it now, it's very heavy.' At the time, I didn't understand what was going on; but later on came a shot, slightly skewed, slightly out of focus, of the secretary looking and walking away, which to my mind recalled the thought process - 'Funny the way she walked off like that.' I didn't take him up on this, but when he said, 'I've abandoned trying to put thought on the screen,' I wish I'd said, 'Excuse me, Mr Lean, you've succeeded.'"[23]

When David decided to marry Ann Todd, he asked Kay Walsh to divorce him.

"I really didn't want to,' said Kay, "but I always promised that if there was really no chance of us getting together then yes. It was difficult for me to let him go with my obsession but I did promise that I would, and I knew it was a sane and proper thing to do. I didn't have to do it, but then I would have been like his mother, who just hung on to her man."[24]

Unusually for divorcing couples, David and Kay celebrated the event with dinner. But Nigel Tangye, who took the split very badly, sued Ann (Mrs Dorothy Ann Tangye) in a petition which alleged misconduct with David Lean at Aldwick, near Bognor, rather than the more romantic mountain location where it had actually occurred.[25]

Tangye was granted a decree nisi. Ann Todd described him to me as "a saint, he was very much in love with me," which accounts for the fact that he dropped his claim for £40,000 damages. He was given custody of their daughter, Ann Francesca.[26]

A few minutes later, in the same court, Kay Walsh (Mrs Kathleen Lean) of Cavaye Place, Fulham, was granted a decree nisi against her husband on the grounds of his adultery with Ann Todd.[27] David's brother and the entire Tangye family thought David's conduct disgraceful and they refused to speak to him.

David and Ann Todd were married on 21 May 1949 at a register office at Slough.[28] The obscure location was a successful attempt to foil the press. The papers carried the story as a mere paragraph: "David Lean called at Ann Todd's home in Selwood Place, Chelsea, early in the day and left by the back door."

Only a few friends, such as Stanley Haynes, knew about the ceremony. Neither Ann Todd nor her friend Diana Cooke remembered a wedding reception, but the press declared there was one, at Ilchester Place, and since they were camped outside the door, one can, on this rare occasion, believe them.

David had bought the house at 1 Ilchester Place, behind Kensington High Street near Holland Park, because it was grand. Michael Powell owned 2 Ilchester Place.

David had a good relationship with Ann Todd's son by her first marriage, David Malcolm.

"He was terrific," he said. "It was David Major and David Minor. He introduced me to the British Museum and used to take me there on Saturday mornings. He used to take me on the set and go through every aspect of production. He'd talk about sound - 'put the earphones on and listen to this' - and he'd sit me on the dolly and show me a tracking shot through the viewfinder.

"I asked him why, when you looked at a spoked wheel on the screen, it appeared to be going backwards. He spent hours on his Moviola in his study showing me why that happened.

"I said in real life people say 'Um' and 'Er' and hestitate a lot but that they didn't in his pictures. He replied, 'That's a serious question, it deserves a serious answer. In the cinema you are focused on that person and it would drive you nuts if they hesitated as much as they do in real life.'

"He did Dickens lectures from time to time, as a result of the films. He was regarded as an authority. He took me through Dickens, he made him interesting.

"He introduced me to slapstick and explained why Harold Lloyd could be as funny as Chaplin. We went once to see the Crazy Gang and arrived late and as we went to our seats in the third row of the stalls they all stopped and said, 'Would it be all right if we proceeded, or would you prefer us to go back to the beginning?' David waved his arm with an imperious gesture and said, 'Please, pray continue.' I was impressed by that.'

"He sat there, roaring with laughter at all the jokes about farts and bananas. He was still a small boy.

"When he turned his attention on you, you felt the heat. And when he didn't, you didn't."[29]

"Ann Todd organised the new house very efficiently," said Norman Spencer. "Her secretary, Mrs Ethel Tuke,[30] was installed in an upstairs office, paying bills, keeping accounts, diaries and so on. They employed a cook-housekeeper and Ann's old friend, Diana Cooke, known as 'Cookie,' took over the running and organising of all Ann's social affairs, personal appointments, wardrobe choosing and consequently a great deal of their joint social lives as well.

"Ann persuaded David that they should entertain more frequently - dinner parties, cocktail parties and the like for London theatrical and film personalities such as Alexander Korda, Terence Rattigan, Henry Sherek and many others."[31]

Ilchester Place had sliding doors, fitted with a tiny glass panel behind which David had projection equipment installed. Although David handled the 16mm equipment himself, a projectionist came from the studio to run the 35mm shows.

David tending his garden at Ilchester Place.

"David was provided with a plush study on the first floor where he and I met daily when we weren't shooting to discuss projects," said Spencer. "David was addicted to his Cona coffee machine, which was brought in by the housekeeper at eleven. And David became attached to Ann's green Rolls-Royce. Ann took taxis when he took the Rolls.

"The garden was small, but David organised it with flowers and one baby poplar tree planted on the lawn.

"I don't think David's life had ever been so organised, especially not in such an upper-middle class style. This was a new kind of life-style for David. It was Ann who insisted that now he was a famous film director he should live in a style befitting his status and move in the appropriate circles.

"A new element crept into Cineguild, because Ann understandably wanted pictures that gave her an opportunity to star. And David's biggest problem, all his life, was finding a subject to make into a film. He always felt, as he put it, constipated. We'd go into Hatchard's bookshop and he'd say, 'I bet that within six feet of us is the most marvellous film subject. But where?'"[32]

Among the stories that were considered was H.E Bates's 1944 novel, *Fair Stood the Wind for France*, for which David chose John Mills as the lead. Reading it now, one can see what appealed to David. A poignant love story set in a picturesque foreign location - the central region of France - it was a study of a sensitive, insecure man and how he deals with responsibility. Well written and full of suspense, the book was ideal for the kind of film the British industry was making at the time.

Yet David, with his loathing of anything to do with illness, had to face long passages describing, all too graphically, the hero's sufferings after a plane crash. That, and the superficial similarity to the plot of ONE OF OUR AIRCRAFT IS MISSING, may have been enough to deter him.

Also, there was no part for Ann Todd and she and David were seen more and more - by the industry as well as the press - as a glamorous team. Ann had a pet project of her own, a remarkable crime story which had formed the basis of a play in which she had starred. David reluctantly agreed to make the film.

CHAPTER TWENTY-ONE

MADELEINE

MADELEINE Smith became notorious in the 1850s when she was brought to trial on a charge of poisoning her lover. The facts have been argued over for more than a century - in novels, memoirs, essays, on radio, on television and in the theatre.[1] In 1950, Peter Hunt published *The Madeleine Smith Affair* in which he thanked Pinewood Films for the opportunity to examine "the abundant research material" gathered for the film.

Madeleine was the twenty-one-year-old daughter of a Glasgow architect. He owned a handsome house in Blythswood Square and was determined that she should make a suitable marriage from her own class. Unfortunately, while out walking with a chaperon, her eyes fell on a Frenchman, born in Jersey, called Emile L'Angelier. Good-looking, with a rakish moustache, he was not of her class: he was a clerk and earned a pitifully small salary. For this reason, Madeleine's father despised him and he was not permitted to call at the house. Madeleine began a furtive love affair, conducted almost entirely by letter. She wrote scores of passionate letters, almost all of which survive, while few of his remain.

Madeleine, who lived in fear of her father, was so enamoured of Emile that she referred to him as "my own darling husband" while only unofficially engaged. She kept the poor man shivering in the shadows, waiting for a note. Emile would not agree to running away with Madeleine; he wanted her, but he wanted her money as well.

To make their meetings less difficult, Madeleine moved her room into the basement. Emile's memorandum-book began to refer to the "pleasant hours" he spent with her. But he was an awkward character, a bit of a buffoon, and Madeleine met another man, William Minnoch, who appealed to her more. Emile's pride was hurt and he began to behave like a blackmailer.

Around this time, Madeleine purchased arsenic, ostensibly to dispose of rats. But there were no rats in Blythswood Square. She said it was for the family's country house. She continued to see Emile, and to provide him with cups of cocoa - often passed through the bars of the basement windows - after which he was invariably taken ill. Emile was frequently indisposed anyway, and was addicted to laudanum, and Madeleine's cocoa was not suspected. But when he died of arsenical poisoning, it appeared to be an open and shut case.

Madeleine Smith (Ann Todd) on trial in Scotland.

The jury returned a verdict peculiar to the courts of Scotland - Not Proven - meaning that whilst they could not clear her name, they were unwilling to see her hang. It was more a tribute to a brilliant defence than to Madeleine's innocence. The revelations in her love letters shocked the public more than the murder of the foreigner, who was dismissed as "a contemptible scoundrel" and generally thought to have got what he deserved. But after those love letters, the word "innocent" could never have been associated with Madeleine in the public's mind.

Madeleine lived to a ripe old age, and in 1926, a Hollywood film company approached her about an appearance in a film about her own case. When she refused, she was threatened with deportation as an undesirable alien from the United States, which she had made her home. She died in 1928 aged ninety-two.

In 1944, Ann Todd appeared in a theatrical version of the story called *The Rest Is Silence* by Harold Purcell. She carried the ivory-handled sunshade which Madeleine had held in court. Laurence Olivier considered filming the story, but the Rank Organisation bought the play, initially for Vivien Leigh, in a co-production with David O. Selznick. When this was abandoned, Ann Todd became the obvious choice.

"I had just married Ann Todd," said David, "and she begged me to direct it. It was a miserable film, one of the most difficult I've ever made. Something didn't fit. I don't know what."

Although the script was credited only to Stanley Haynes and Nicholas Phipps, working on it for months, according to his own account, was Eric Ambler. He then fell ill and withdrew. Nicholas Phipps, an actor who made a career out of being a sort of low-budget Noël Coward, and who was well-known in the industry as a script doctor, worked on the dialogue. Curiously enough, no use was made of the play which Rank had bought for Ann Todd. The script followed the facts closely enough for it to qualify as an original screenplay.

David, who had been involved on the script from the start, kept working on it at night while shooting during the day, which made the experience so unpleasant he was determined never to repeat it.

This, the last Cineguild production, was financed by Rank through an American distribution contract with Universal-International. Originally entitled THE TRIAL OF MADELEINE SMITH, and postponed from January to March, David started shooting in April 1949.

The unit went to Glasgow to shoot the opening exteriors, which included Madeleine's original house which still stood at 7 Blythswood Square.

"I attract spirits," said Ann Todd, "and in that house Madeleine Smith came and visited me. I get a certain reaction when I know. David went upstairs and I felt it very strongly. It was an extraordinary film. I felt most of the time we were making it that she was there. When I show it at home on cassette I still get a reaction."[2]

David may have married Ann Todd but, as Norman Spencer realised, there was little harmony between them.

"They didn't get on professionally. They had a lot of arguments. The same kind of arguments Ronnie had, David was now getting. Ann was very difficult. She was a very cerebral sort of actress and she wanted to work everything out. She is a curious woman. I like her very much, but she has a capacity to talk in that quick, nervous way, to ask you questions one after the other until she ties people up in knots. She used to tie David up in knots by saying, 'Wait a minute, what did you ask me? First of all you said you want this, now you say you want that...' We dropped more and more behind schedule and it became painful. MADELEINE was not a happy picture."[3]

Several French actors were considered for L'Angelier. David's secretary, Mary Benson, suggested Yves Montand, but he was not available. "We then went to Paris to meet Gérard Philipe," she said. "He was adorable, but he spoke hardly any English. We had tea with him, and he told us he was so busy he couldn't do it."

"He was a communist," said David. "In those days it was looked upon as very daring. He was a charming young man. He was absolutely unaffected. There was no business about being a film star. Very amusing, very light and oh, he was smashing." [4]

Eventually, an actor named Ivan Desny came to London, had dinner with David and Ann and got the part without a test. Little-known on either side of the Channel, he was twenty-six and had dubbed Trevor Howard's voice for the French version of BRIEF ENCOUNTER.

"I've heard several times that David Lean was difficult with actors," said Desny. "I did not think so. He made me feel at home on his set, talking to me as a grown-up, asking my advice. Being the director's choice helps tremendously.

"One morning we were all on the set, made-up, dressed and ready to shoot. After greeting us, David sent everybody to the canteen except Ann Todd and myself. He said, 'Somehow I don't feel it today.' He lit a cigarette and tried to work out whether Ann should be in the room already or whether I should be there first. After fifteen minutes, he said, 'Let's wrap it up.' He sent everybody home.

"Next morning, with steely precision, he said, 'Camera here... you do that... we cut to...' Practically two days' work was finished in six hours.

"He told me afterwards, 'If I had insisted on shooting yesterday, it would have been trash.' In a way he saved time, and a lot of footage. But who is the director today who could afford to dismiss the crew at ten in the morning because 'he does not feel it?'" [5]

David, who was still being psychoanalysed by Dr Hoffer, continued to introduce Freudian images into his films.

"He told me that he used some of these in MADELEINE," said Mary Benson. "L'Angelier drops his walking stick when he and Madeleine have a love scene on the floor. This was meant to indicate an orgasm." [6]

"There was one scene of me," said Ann Todd, "when I ran down the stairs David hurried up the camera just for that one shot [i.e. the shot was in slight slow-motion] and my Victorian skirt billowed out. The timing was extraordinary. He used to say that the little scenes in between the big scenes were sometimes more important than the big scenes themselves.

"The scene where I got into my wedding dress was not in the script. David had the brilliant idea of turning it into me being very happy and not giving a damn. I was now going to marry Minnoch and the audience gets a shock because I've changed so quickly. And at that moment you realise she's a bitch.

"David liked to have every detail right under his thumb. He was the first director I'd worked with in this country to have that sort of presence, to be the master on his set. There used to be moments when he'd get on the set and everything had left him. He'd go and sit very quietly, talking to nobody and we all had to sit quietly until the imagination came back."

For a scene on a beach, most economically minded directors would settle for the nearest stretch of sand with picturesque qualities, say Camber Sands in Sussex. But David wanted a photogenic and dramatic setting, and he and Ann loved Cornwall, so it was to Cornwall that he and the unit travelled for a scene in which Madeleine and Minnoch, played by Norman Wooland, take a ride together.

Ann Todd described in her autobiography how she couldn't sleep the night before because she had to face a horse which was to run away with her. The plan was to shoot a short dialogue scene with Wooland, then replace her with a double for the runaway scene.

Ann Todd as Madeleine Smith with Ivan Desny as L'Angelier.

"It was a lovely wild day, large waves and a wind; also a big crowd on the beach hoping to enjoy themselves. David was directing from the top of a fast camera car that could follow the horse along the sand."

When the camera assistant casually ran a tape measure across its nose, the horse took fright and reared up, pawing the air and neighing. Ann Todd screamed, her hat and veil fell off and David became "severe." They started again. David shouted "Action!" when suddenly a small plane appeared.

"It came straight at us and we all ducked. Flying very low, it skimmed along the beach. Assistant directors clung to the horse and me, seagulls screamed and the crowd, thinking the plane was part of the film, gazed fascinated and clapped. David lost his temper, clenched his fist and shouted at the plane as it prepared to attack again."

Only Ann Todd recognised the pilot as her ex-husband, Nigel Tangye. David never found out who it was, although he had the incident reported to the local flying club.

On the third attempt, the horse galloped away before the camera was ready, with Ann Todd clinging to its mane like "a sack of potatoes". It headed out to sea, but was brought up short when a wave struck it. Norman Wooland galloped after Ann and pulled her out. "I was really very, very frightened. David was furious with me and also with himself for losing a good shot because he couldn't keep the camera up with the horse."[7]

Eventually the double was used and the dialogue scene later restaged at Pinewood studios with Cornwall on the back-projection screen.

During production, the set was visited by the poet and novelist, L.A.G. Strong, and the cartoonist, David Low.[8]

They were collaborating on a book of Low cartoons to be accompanied by Strong's poems, which was published as *Low Company*. The cartoon, which is now in the National Portrait Gallery, was matched by this poem:

> *David Lean*
> *The calm, reflective brain, the brooding eye,*
> *The leap, the sombre peering through the lens,*
> *The taut intensity, the quick command,*
> *The sudden smile that warms the player's heart*
> *(Rehearsal was a strain): anxiety*
> *To please this difficult charmer melts away,*
> *The words are on the tongue, the muscles free.*
> *Silence. All are on their toes. His fingers snap*
> *for 'Action!' Yet another sharply seen*
> *And deeply suffered moment is secure*
> *For all to wonder at; and David Lean*
> *Sinks back fulfilled, exhausted. Then he's up*
> *Alert and glittering, to prepare the next*
> *Shot.*
> *Look at that posture, surely caught*
> *As one of his shots. Philosopher*
> *And artist, sensitive, dagger-hard*
> *To carve his picture; all compassion then*
> *For those who suffer with him; gay as a thrush*
> *When the work's over; nurse and task-master,*
> *Schemer and midwife, living on his nerves,*
> *(And other people's); long may David Lean*
> *Give blood transfusions to our British film*
> *And cure its long anaemia from his own*
> *Nervous intelligent tempestuous veins.*

It must have been strange for David to be working at Pinewood. Ronald Neame was directing THE GOLDEN SALAMANDER with Trevor Howard on one stage (with Oswald Morris as lighting cameraman) and Terence Fisher and Anthony Darnborough were directing THE ASTONISHED HEART with Celia Johnson and Noël Coward on another. In August, all Pinewood productions were paralysed by an electrician's strike.

The strike contributed to the unusually long schedule for MADELEINE, which took twenty-one weeks, compared to Neame's film which took only eleven weeks.

During the hiatus, David and Ann took a holiday in Rome, where Ann contacted her old friend, Ingrid Bergman, and David met Roberto Rossellini who was spearheading the movement which became known as Italian neo-realism.

"Rossellini represented the opposite of what David was doing," said Ivan Desny, "improvisation, disregard of classical rules... He met him at the time and was fascinated."

Desny felt that David had more in common with another Italian director, Luchino Visconti. "He was the only director to give me - in an entirely different range - the same sense of perfectionism. When David Lean was making a film he was making a Rolls-Royce. You can disagree with the shape or the colour, but you have to admit it is a Rolls. Perfection to the smallest detail."[9]

David Lean

Rossellini told David that as far as script-writing was concerned, the British planned ahead too much. "You prepare everything - the number of steps on a staircase, the number of windows in a room. You do the creative work months before going on the set, whereas your mind should be at its most creative when actually on the set, so as not to lose spontaneity of action when shooting; otherwise you look at the script and that reminds you of what you had worked out months ago, but your creative ability is then stale."[10]

However much he admired Rossellini, David could never have worked without a detailed script. But he liked Rossellini, then in the middle of an international scandal because of his relationship with Ingrid Bergman who had left Hollywood (and her husband) to be with him. To help them during this time of intense press speculation and condemnation, David and Ann invited Bergman to stay quietly with them at Ilchester Place when she needed to be in London.[11]

As with THE PASSIONATE FRIENDS, Geoffrey Foot was the editor of MADELEINE. "Now it's all together," I said, "Let's see it, just the two of us in the theatre. He sat

Leslie Banks as Madeleine's father, Ann Todd and Eugene Deckers. The deep focus style of photography owed a lot to CITIZEN KANE.

through it in silence and the lights went up and he said, 'Well, we've got a turkey, haven't we?'

"It ran about an hour-fifty then. He went back on the floor and did some extra shooting and then we organised a sneak preview."[12]

Assistant editor Clive Donner remembered the preview as the only real drama on the picture. It was held at the Gaumont Palace, Regents Park.[13] The advertised feature was a western and the place was packed. It was hardly the most receptive audience for a slow-moving, period melodrama. There were laughs in the wrong places, it was whistled and hooted at and Ann Todd left the theatre in tears.

"Back to the old drawing board that was, I can tell you," said Geoffrey Foot. "If anyone could rescue a picture it was David. But it was just not his cup of tea. We tried to recover it, but never got it."[14]

"We worked at it and worked at it," said Clive Donner. "What was wrong with that picture was that you could never get inside the character of Madeleine Smith. Because you must never know what she is thinking, there is nobody with whom you could identify. Nobody through whom you could tell the story. And so David never really got the drive of the film together.

"One day, David and Stanley Haynes announced they'd got a brilliant idea. 'We're going to have narration at the front.'

"I said, 'Oh, what a good idea. Just like HOUSE ON 92ND STREET.'

"David's mouth went down, the nostrils flared. 'Thank you very much,' he said. 'Days thinking that one up to be told that somebody else has already done it.'" 15

The harsh treatment of his film by the critics gave David something in common with Noël Coward, who had experienced such reactions in the theatre. David turned to him for advice. What did he think was wrong?

"I don't think," said Coward, "that you can make a film in which you, the writer-director, don't know in your own mind what was the outcome. In other words, did she do it or didn't she? And you've never said. You've left it open for the audience to choose and I think that is unsatisfactory as far as a dramatic picture or stage play is concerned."

The failure of his last two films shattered David. His magic carpet had been pulled from beneath him. His confidence was deeply shaken.

"MADELEINE was the worst film I ever made," said David, "and I don't think I put more sheer hard work into any picture. Beware of making any artistic creation for the wrong reasons! The negative forces create poltergeists. Nothing works, from script to cutting.

"I'll tell you a funny thing I've discovered over the years. If you have a scene which is really well-written, everything's easy. It's easy to photograph, it's easy to act and you shoot it very fast. If you have a scene where everything starts to go wrong, I always suspect the writing of the scene as having something to do with it.

"One of the essentials in the movies is for the audience to feel that they are in the hands of a good story-teller; they are being led, and what leads them is the intention of the scene. If it has the intention, you will nearly always win through. It somehow carries you on like a wave which breaks on the shore and carries you up that beach. All great things have an intention behind them. We didn't have a real intention on MADELEINE. Every scene was difficult; it was difficult to photograph, all the costumes were a pain in the neck and I think it was because of the script.

"It is rather a cold film. I was looking at it in the wrong way. I had no particular feelings for anybody in the picture and as far as movies are concerned that is pretty well fatal. I am not saying that one should sit back and say, 'This is going to excite the audience.' I've never done that. I sit back and say, 'Does it excite me?' Somehow it didn't and I think that's the answer." 16

In February 1950, Noël Coward lent David and Ann his home, Blue Harbour, Port Marie, in Jamaica. David made a remarkable colour home movie of this delayed honeymoon. It opened with shots of the chauffeur carrying out suitcases labelled KINGSTON JAMAICA and lashing them to the Rolls-Royce before driving down to the docks.

David and Ann chose to make the voyage on a Geest Line banana boat and hoped for an adventure. Not that the accommodation was anything but luxurious; the ship carried only a dozen passengers. During a violent storm, David filmed the waves pounding over the bow and flying high over the ship, a foretaste of RYAN'S DAUGHTER.[17]

There could have been no greater contrast to London in an austerity-ridden winter than the sun-drenched beaches of the West Indies, and David's camera does them full justice. He arranged for David Malcolm - Ann Todd's son from her first marriage - to fly out. He was only thirteen and as his plane had to make frequent refuelling stops, David sent morale-boosting telegrams to each airport - GETTING NEARER.

Once he arrived, he entrusted his camera to Ann and she filmed delightful shots of David Major and David Minor tumbling about in the surf. When they went on a boating trip, David took a glass-bottomed box, and leaning over the side, used it to film underwater shots.

The whole experience looks so idyllic in the home movie - similar to David's sojourn in the South Seas thirty years later - that I was surprised when Ann Todd dismissed it.

"The honeymoon wasn't any great success," she said. "It was a lovely place, but David wasn't an easy person to talk to. There are some people who shouldn't be married and David Lean was one of them."[18]

David had proposed to take twelve months off at the end of MADELEINE to prepare the script of THE GAY GALLIARD - about Mary Queen of Scots - for Ann. He had first considered it after BLITHE SPIRIT. The plan was for the script to be ready for Ann when she had completed two more pictures under her Rank contract. Neither of these were made.

David had barely started when John Davis of Rank began to scrutinise his work. Rank had lost about six million pounds in four and a half years and Davis's ruthlessness was the result.[19] In November 1949, redundancy notices had gone up at Pinewood and Rank announced they had no production plans after July 1950. Davis improved Rank's profit margin at the expense of the studio's most talented men.

"Independent Producers collapsed," said David. "The Rank Organisation pulled the money away from us. Micky Powell, Ian Dalrymple - all of us were left stranded. They got in Sydney Box and decided to make more entertainment pictures and I felt terribly lost."[20]

Rank's directors passed one by one to Korda. Carol Reed left after filming

ODD MAN OUT which may have been hailed as the best he had made, but it went over budget by a third. Other directors complained that after Rank had encouraged them to make films of the highest quality, they were suddenly penalised for their "extravagance".

Although David's last two pictures had cost - and lost - a lot of money, Rank and Davis did not want to lose him, or Cineguild. Rank's overtures, though, came to nothing when David's budgets on proposed new projects were too high. David left, with Ann Todd, to join Korda, and Cineguild, which had been under considerable strain for the past two years, was wound up.

David was just over forty. He had made some outstanding films but after two flops he faced an uncertain future.

Tangye Lean, by contrast, had been promoted to Comptroller of the BBC's European Services in 1949. (David used to tease his brother by saying he had sold out to the establishment by joining the BBC.)

As for his son, Peter had been doing his National Service. In August 1950, when he was nineteen he was demobbed. To celebrate the event, David took him to his tailor, Kilgore, French and Stanbury in Dover Street, and then to his barber, Vickery, in Cork Street.

"While we were at his tailor," said Peter, "he said, 'See that man over there? That's Jackie Coogan, the chap who was with Chaplin in THE KID.'"

David was appalled by the Cockney accent Peter had acquired in the RAF, just as his mother had been appalled by the accent he had briefly acquired at Gaumont. Peter was sent to Meriel St Clair, in Notting Hill Gate, to have elocution lessons. He recalls having to repeat, "How Now Brown Cow?" but not "The rain in Spain stays mainly in the plain."

As for employment, Peter was sent to seek advice from Frank Lean.

"My grandfather was still in his firm of chartered accountants," said Peter. "The son of one of his partners, Kit Price, ran a firm called Queen Anne's Hotel Supply Company, finding staff for the hotel business. I wasn't all that keen, but I was packed off to a hotel school in Switzerland, paid for by David. I always assumed he didn't want me around and this was the next best thing."[21]

However, Peter spent the first Christmas with his father for nearly twenty years. This was largely thanks to Ann Todd, who tried hard to make David see more of his son.[22]

"It was a private holiday for the four of us," said Peter. "Dad, Ann, me and Cookie. We flew from Northolt by Swissair the week before Christmas. We were supposed to have four or five days, but the weather was so good and we seemed to get on okay so he phoned my mother and asked if we could stay. We were there about ten days at the Hotel des Alpes.

"Ann Todd was always very charming to me. On that holiday, we used to walk arm in arm through the village. Great."[23]

Peter Lean on holiday at Chamonix,
photographed by his father.

In Peter's Motor Cycle Diary for 1950 appears this entry for Christmas Eve: "Soup, foie gras, lobster, Xmas pud, another pud, wine, coffee."

Back at Ilchester Place, Norman Spencer reported every morning to discuss possible ideas for the next David Lean film.

David had been enthralled by Grand Adventure ever since his father had taken him to see a lecture by Herbert Ponting, illustrated with the film he had shot of Captain Scott's expedition to the South Pole.

But a film of Scott's fateful expedition had already been made, starring John Mills. David and Spencer considered David Livingstone's journey into unknown Africa. David became fascinated by the struggle to conquer Everest, and for a while they struggled almost as hard to turn the story of Mallory and Irvine, who may have reached the summit in 1924, but were never seen again, into a film, even at one point bringing the Abominable Snowman into the equation.

"You see," said Spencer, "David could think of ideas like this, but he couldn't put the dramatics around it. You can't make a film about Everest unless somebody writes a good story for it."[24]

"The trouble with all these ideas," David told Stephen Watts in 1951, "they were all dated. They were all great stories of human courage, but the mystery had gone out of them. Aeroplanes had flown over Everest and the South Pole, Africa is no longer dark. By and large, man has explored this world of ours."[25]

What else in the world could he find to give him the theme for a film about man's exploration into the unknown?

CHAPTER TWENTY-TWO

THE SOUND BARRIER

"HE was a lion of a man," said David. "Grey hair, nearly white, the appearance of being tall - it was something to do with his presence. An enormous personality. He was highly intelligent and intensely professional. I like professionals. Professionals are people who will sacrifice good ideas for the whole. He was a great father figure. Fifteen minutes with him was worth two days with anyone else.[1]

"He could take any subject and talk on it for twenty minutes. You can't imagine how wonderfully exotic I found him, especially after my being around Quakers."[2]

Alexander Korda was the only film producer in Britain who operated like the moguls in Hollywood and cultivated the same sort of mystique. He combined the flamboyance of a David O. Selznick with the seriousness of an Irving Thalberg. Unfortunately, by the time David went to work for this pre-eminent figure, he was in his declining years.

Born Sandor Laszlo Kellner in 1893, Korda was a Hungarian Jew who began directing films in 1914. During the brief Communist regime in 1919, he was appointed by Bela Kun to the Directory of Arts. He was imprisoned in the subsequent Fascist terror and later fled with his wife, the actress Maria Corda, to Vienna where Korda became a prominent director. After an unhappy period in Hollywood, during which his marriage broke up, he went to Europe where he directed the first part of Marcel Pagnol's famous MARIUS trilogy. Just before moving to England, he had his first indirect encounter with David on THESE CHARMING PEOPLE.

He established London Films in 1932 and directed THE PRIVATE LIFE OF HENRY VIII the following year. This film, which made a star of Charles Laughton, was such a box-office triumph that Korda was able to provide jobs for many refugees from Hitler and to set about re-invigorating the British film industry. The film also financed Korda's love of the high-life.

Extravagance was Korda's dominant quality, and he lost his studios at Denham only a couple of years after they were opened. The beginning of the war found Korda in Hollywood - he was working for British intelligence as well as London Films - but he returned in 1943, and after a period heading MGM's British operation, he settled in magnificent headquarters at 144-6 Piccadilly.[3]

Once more he tried to re-invigorate the British cinema, and although his role was not as creative as it had been in the great days at Denham, his name appeared on some of the most distinguished films of the period, including THE FALLEN IDOL and THE THIRD MAN.

Korda was not entirely a benign influence on David. He revelled in luxury, spent huge sums on fine paintings, he married and divorced actresses (Maria Corda, Merle Oberon), he worked at a leisurely pace and, despite his brief fling with Communism, he was a self-confessed snob.

He was also elegant, erudite, amusing and highly intelligent. Unlike other producers, he knew the craft of making films from every aspect. He had such charm that he could spirit money from such unlikely sources as the Prudential Assurance Company, and he could cultivate friendships among the highest in the land, such as Churchill and Beaverbrook, the newspaper baron. In 1942, he was rewarded with the first knighthood given to a film personality, although it was almost certainly for his wartime intelligence work rather than for his films.

"He was rather vain," said David. "I remember him saying, 'I am the only person who had three writers working for me at the same time in the same office block - H.G. Wells, Lawrence of Arabia and Graham Greene.'

"It was in Alex's office at Piccadilly that I met Moura Budberg, whom I liked enormously. A fascinating woman, the lover of H. Bruce Lockhart, Maxim Gorky and H.G. Wells. He said, as she left the room once, 'I don't know why it is I always end up supporting my dead friends' ex-mistresses.'

"It was always fascinating if you spent an evening with him because you never knew who was going to drop in. He had a penthouse flat at Claridge's. I remember one evening being there and who should come in but Anthony Eden, who was Foreign Secretary. Alex knew all these people and he would go after titles for people. He once said to me, 'You are going to be in the Honours List. You are going to get a CBE, I know that, but for goodness sake don't get married and it'll happen some day.' Carol [Reed] had already been made a knight, you see. It took me twenty years."[4]

Korda's brothers were also important in David's life: Vincent, the painter, reluctantly dragged into an industry he disliked to work as an art director; Zoltan, still a bit of a firebrand, remaining left-wing long after Alex became a comfortable Tory, and making pictures about Africa and India. Zoltan Korda's THE FOUR FEATHERS, which was filmed in Egypt, was the nearest thing to LAWRENCE OF ARABIA the British had produced and was the best of Korda's series of adventure films which celebrated the glories of the British Empire.

Korda was tremendously proud of the fact that in his stable were the two greatest directors working in Britain: Carol Reed and David Lean. Although he was not the kind of producer who hovered on the set - he employed associate producers to do that - he wanted a direct line to these men. He did not want any self-styled "producer" in the way. He was dismayed when he learned that David had brought along his old associate from Cineguild, Stanley Haynes, expecting Korda to take him on as well. David had the difficult task of asking Haynes to give up his position as producer and stay on in a subordinate role.

"He said, 'All right, I'll leave you.' And he did. It was terribly sad because it was a kind of awful, private feud. I don't know what I should have done. I still feel guilty, but I think, in fact, that Alex was right about this production business - people do earn the title of producer too easily. Look at them today. Anyhow, Stanley left. He wouldn't work for me under those conditions.

"He tried to get a script ready of a Dickens story. He could not get the money for it and at the end of a four-or five-year saga of disasters he committed suicide. He wrote a suicide letter to my ex-wife, Kay Walsh. It was really terrible, and to this day she thinks that I was responsible. I wish he'd agreed to come with me because if he'd come on SOUND BARRIER - which was an enormous success - I think Alex would have taken him on board, because he would have contributed a lot. Bloody shame. I've only just got over that terrible incident, because I felt very, very badly about it." [5]

Norman Spencer would become David's associate producer.

THE SOUND BARRIER, David's first production for Korda, came about through his love of aeroplanes and his days spent watching them at Croydon aerodrome. The romance and the technology of air travel fascinated him.

Korda, who used to boast discreetly about having acquired David at a bargain price, thanks to his so-called "failures",[6] was not at first enthusiastic. He had burned his fingers in the thirties with an expensive flop called THE CONQUEST OF THE AIR and considered the subject of aviation was worth no more than a documentary.

David explained that he got the idea for THE SOUND BARRIER when he picked up the *Evening News* and read of the death of Geoffrey de Havilland, the son of the aircraft pioneer. His plane, which had fallen to pieces over the Thames estuary, was thought to be flying faster than sound. But Geoffrey de Havilland had been killed several years before, in September 1946. The accident that David read about occurred on 16 February 1950, and killed twenty-eight-year-old Squadron-Leader J.S.R Muller-Rowland, DSO, DFC. Newspapers drew a parallel between the two accidents, which probably led to the confusion in David's mind.[7] Muller-Rowland, too, was thought to have accidentally broken the sound barrier. There was a film here, to be sure, but was there a story?

To David's delight, Korda suggested that he undertake extensive research. "I spent months going to aircraft factories and talking to pilots," said David. "One of the chief difficulties, I think, was that all the flying people were worried that I was going to do a great big melodrama, that I'd overdo it; then after a short time they saw that I was serious about it, and they were a tremendous help. The more

I saw, the keener I became on the subject. This was all before we started to write it. Although we had a dramatic story we really had no story at all, we had a mass of background material." [8]

David had written a diary of his research and showed it to Korda who suggested that Terence Rattigan could write the script. "I think he would be wonderful at this," said Korda, "because he knows about aeroplanes, he's very inventive and he does not despise the cinema."

Korda called Rattigan on the spot. "Look," he said, "I'm sitting here with David Lean who's been going round aircraft factories and thinks there's a film to be made about planes flying faster than sound. He's got a whole lot of ideas in this diary. Would you be interested in putting it together into a script?"

Rattigan politely and firmly declined since he knew nothing about jets. It was only when David gave him his diary, which had several ideas for scenes scribbled in it, that he changed his mind. He saw that it could be a story primarily about human beings who were driven by an obsession with technology.

David and Rattigan agreed that this would not be an imitation of the great flying pictures of the past - WINGS, HELL'S ANGELS, DAWN PATROL - or any of the Second World War dramas which the British film industry was producing. THE SOUND BARRIER would be the story of the incredible achievements of civilian engineers and aviators in the few years since the war.

Terence Rattigan, who had already passed through David's life in 1939 when he was cutting FRENCH WITHOUT TEARS, was born in London in 1911. His parents both came from distinguished families of Irish lawyers. Frank, his father, was a diplomat, whose greatest friend had been Ronald Storrs, the foremost champion of T.E. Lawrence. Like David, Rattigan as a boy had sneaked out of the house to the bright lights, but he chose the theatre rather than the cinema.

With *French Without Tears* enjoying a long run in the West End, Rattigan indulged himself with a life of pleasure, Savile Row suits and a Rolls-Royce. Yet he was politically left wing; he even flirted with Communism. He took part in demonstrations with Michael Foot for Arms and Food for Spain and wrote an anti-Hitler play which was banned by the Lord Chamberlain.

During the war, Rattigan served in the RAF and put his experiences as an air gunner and wireless operator into a play, *Flare Path*, later reworked as the film THE WAY TO THE STARS, directed by Anthony Asquith. Rattigan detested writing film scripts as a rule, and had no respect - despite what Korda thought - for the cinema. But Rattigan was a man of considerable charm.

"I was terribly impressed by him," said David. "He was frightfully good-looking. He was well over six feet tall, with blue eyes, very well dressed. And he was practical and a very hard worker, like Noël.

"He took this diary of mine which had, let's say, twelve ideas in it for scenes. He wrote a script which contained ten of them, but much better than mine. We worked together and fiddled with it a bit. I loved working with him."

Rattigan felt that the death of two of Sir Geoffrey de Havilland's sons[9] would make a strong basis for the story. In the first draft, the main character, Ridgefield, was a self-made millionaire whose obsession is to create a plane which will break the sound barrier. This obsession leads to the death of his two sons whilst his daughter-in-law, Susan, asks whether technical progress is worth the sacrifice of men's lives.

When Rattigan delivered his first draft, there was a general sense of dismay. Apart from the fact that it was written in pencil, it was absurdly long, and theatrical without being especially dramatic. Rattigan, David and Norman Spencer had a meeting with Korda.

"He used to throw things at the ceiling over and over," said Norman Spencer, "and every now and again one or two of them stuck. Some of his ideas were terrible and some were wonderful. He said to Rattigan, 'Terry, you know what's wrong with this script? Change the son to a daughter.'

"And Rattigan said, 'My God, the whole thing works. Why didn't I think of that? I don't want a father and son. I want a father and daughter, then instead of the pilot being the son who's at war with his father...'

"So that slight melodramatic shape came out of it."[10]

This idea was undoubtedly a pragmatic one. Korda wanted Ann Todd to star in the film, if only because she and David as a team had something of the aura and

Ann Todd as Susan Garthwaite and Nigel Patrick as her test-pilot husband Tony examine the original newspaper which announced Geoffrey de Havilland's death.

publicity value of Vivien Leigh and Laurence Olivier. But even with that fundamental change to the narrative, the script remained depressingly theatrical. Norman Spencer took it upon himself to draft a critique to David:

"I want to explore those great spaces in the upper atmosphere more, with the pilot himself. I want to be excited not only by the plot situation in which he finds himself (is he going to be killed or not?) but by the atmosphere up there - the wonderment and fascination of a new element. It is a new world like the North Pole or the planet Mars is a new world. That is what the screen can show as well as human jealousies, childhood complexes and filial fear.

"And the test pilots. Not only *why* but what happens to them *when* they fly. *The intoxication of six hundred miles an hour at forty thousand feet.* For every ounce of neurotic dislike we take out we must put in an ounce of the romance of flight and we shall be getting somewhere."

Spencer's critique mirrored David's views and the two men had further discussions with Rattigan. When Rattigan produced the next draft, David had no hesitation in marking it, "Final Screenplay".

When Korda suggested Ralph Richardson for the part of Ridgeway, David was none too keen. "I said, 'Alex, he's so dull on the screen.' Everybody laughs now, but in those days he'd been in a series of films in which he played rather dreary, po-faced Englishmen."

David's observation to Korda was not exactly tactful because most of the films in which he felt Richardson was dull and po-faced had been produced by Korda - THINGS TO COME, THE MAN WHO COULD WORK MIRACLES, THE FOUR FEATHERS, THE LION HAS WINGS. But David was delighted by Richardson in THE SOUND BARRIER. "He gave a wonderful performance, the best he had given to that date."

Richardson played the role as a tough Northern businessman, just as it had been written by Rattigan.

"I liked him very much," said David. "He was very sweet, a true English eccentric who had no idea he was being eccentric. I had him again on ZHIVAGO and he had a day off. He said, 'I'm going fishing.' That night I came back to the hotel and there was a plate at my table with two beautiful trout and a note propped up in front saying, 'For my dear old trout.' That was typical of Ralphie.

"I wish I'd seen more of him on the stage, because he obviously excelled there. He was very original and daring. He's supposed to have been the greatest Cyrano, isn't he?[11]

"Rattigan wrote one of the pilots as the flying-by-the-seat-of-his-pants type, one of the new up-and-comers who started flying jets. This was played by John Justin, who was marvellous - very sensitive, a thinker.

"Nigel Patrick was a light comedian in the normal way. He wasn't very good in it because he had a kind of slickness about him which these chaps who know what real danger is haven't got.

"I remember we had a cockpit rigged up on the sound stage at Shepperton, and it had to be turned, twisted and buffeted. The test pilots I'd been working with - John Derry, from De Havilland, Mike Lithgow from Vickers and several others - had always wanted to come down and watch the film being shot.

"Nigel Patrick was up there on a rostrum in this cockpit pretending he was being buffeted by the sound barrier, and I felt really sorry for him. To have these men who really know, watching him in a cockpit with a camera on him, simulating what they do in reality... I was completely wrong. He wasn't embarrassed in the least, and I can never understand that. I can't to this day. I would have said, 'For God's sake don't bring them on.' It's worse than bringing Orson Welles on my set, because at least he directs and I direct. But this is a chap who can't fly a kite and he's pretending he's going through the sound barrier. Incredible."[12]

David and the chief technicians went down to recce the Vickers aerodrome in Hampshire, where most of the prototypes were kept and tested. After a test pilot made some low level passes, camera operator Peter Newbrook told David that it would be all but impossible to pan with a plane at that speed.

Cameraman Jack Hildyard solved the problem with what became known as the back-to-back camera - two Mitchell cameras pointing in opposite directions.

"The other operator, Denys Coop, and I tossed for who should take which position," said Peter Newbrook. "Denys won and took the first shot and I got the rotten one, the one that starts with the camera pointed vertically towards the sky to pick up the plane when it exited the frame from the first camera. The first part was not too difficult, as you could see the plane coming, but the second was a real by-the-seat-of-your-pants job.

"The other thing that David picked up on was that when the plane roared over, it seemed to cut a swathe through the long grass at the side of the runway and that was where the idea of the flattening grass and the delayed sound of the plane passing over came into his head - a lovely touch."

"We filmed the opening flying sequence," David told Gerald Pratley, "as a prologue to the credits for a very special reason, because round about the time we were doing the script, several people said that nobody would understand what the sound barrier was, so we thought we'd open the film on an incident that actually took place during the war. A pilot put his Spitfire into a dive, and he went faster and faster, and suddenly the machine started to shake, and he pulled on the stick to correct it, and the harder he pulled, the more the nose went down, until he finally throttled back and pulled out of the dive. Now the aeroplane had been shaking madly, and he didn't know quite what had happened. In fact, he had touched the edge, as it were, of the sound barrier, and we show this as the opening of the film, then follow it with the title 'Sound Barrier' so the

The back-to-back camera in action (left), filming the Vickers Supermarine swept-wing jet fighter, prototype 535, the "Swift", while a third operator covers it with a wild Arriflex.

first sequence describes what the film is about."[13]

David had a life-long dislike of second units. A second unit is a company working separately from the main unit, either for reasons of speed or because certain sequences are unusually difficult and require specialist knowledge. Such units usually require their own director. Although second units would create tensions on David's epics a decade later, he was pleased with the second-unit work on THE SOUND BARRIER.

"David wanted to shoot the aerial sequences," said Norman Spencer. "But Harold Boxall, who might be described as Korda's rottweiler, said, 'No, you can't. The picture will cost too much if you're going to finish the main shooting and then go up in the air. You must have a second unit."[14]

Fortunately, a remarkable aerial specialist called Anthony Squire was available. He could see at once what David meant when he said, "Look, I want to get the feel of the immensity of space. I'd like to see a wonderful cloudscape with just a little dot. Don't shoot close shots like everybody else so you can see the pilot. The dramatic part is the cloudscape."

Anthony Squire did not have the impression that David wanted to shoot the aerial material himself.

"Before THE SOUND BARRIER he was basically a studio man; he hadn't done much exterior work at all. Nothing would have been beyond him, but he would have been finding his feet much longer than me, because I was qualified, and accustomed to the air. I was a Sunderland Flying Boat ferry pilot during the war - Coastal Command, attacking submarines and serving as convoy escort."

Nevertheless, Anthony Squire was at pains to point out the respect David conveyed for him as a craftsman.

"At rushes one day I said to David, 'This is such a beautiful shot, the most beautiful we've done - I think it should come immediately before the Nigel Patrick character gets killed.'

"I saw the first showing of the picture and I said to David, 'I see you used that shot of the dive before Nigel Patrick was killed.' He said, in such a wonderful way, 'That's what you suggested, isn't it?' He had the reputation for being a tremendous big-head - he was in some ways, and perhaps more so later - but at this time it was just one technician talking to another."[15]

David, confined to the studios and the few exteriors required in the script, often envied Anthony Squire his aeronautical adventures. The second unit carried out a high-altitude flight, when Nigel Patrick flies Ann Todd to Cairo. They look down on Paris from a great height and he points out the Alps.

"These scenes were shot in a Mosquito with the famous test pilot John Derry[16] and we went up to thirty thousand feet," said Anthony Squire.

"Peter Newbrook lay in the nose and we all breathed through oxygen masks. After we'd done the shot of Paris and the Alps and we were on our way back across Northern France, Peter went very quiet and started murmuring nonsense. 'That's all right,' said John Derry, sitting there with his polka-dot bow tie which he tweaked occasionally, 'he's just run out of oxygen, I'll go down a bit and he'll wake up.'"

Making the planes appear at a convincing altitude was the problem on the rest of the aerial sequences.

"This is all supposed to be taking place where it's almost impossible to film, even nowadays, because it's so cold and the windows freeze over. Anyway, we had funny old planes, we were shooting out of open doorways and a cameraman friend of mine suggested we use infra-red film. It's cunning. You get that effect, with an ordinary sky, of a black, black sky and brilliant silvery-white clouds. And it solved our problems. It made it look like thirty thousand feet and it was probably shot at two thousand, just above whatever cloud there was. We couldn't get up beyond three or four thousand feet with our funny old crate, with us all standing in the doorway, and yet it looked out of this world."[17]

Weeks went by. Waiting for the sun to be in the right position took long enough, and the fickle English weather provided its own delays. Occasionally, the camera plane went out of action or the target plane would develop a fault.

The London Films hierarchy began to lose their nerve and talked of resorting to models. Norman Spencer passed this on to Anthony Squire.

"My heart fell. But I found out that David had no intention of stopping second-unit shooting or of doing model shots. He knew they could never match the stuff we were doing. 'Just go on shooting,' he said. It was wonderful to have a CO like that."

Nonetheless, David was the most exacting taskmaster. In the last flight sequence, where John Justin breaks the sound barrier, the second unit had the Swift pilot flying faster and faster, and reduced camera speeds made the plane move like forked lightning. But David, working in the cutting-room, said it was not fast enough.

"We've got to get one shot faster still, because this is breaking the sound barrier, which no one's seen and not many have heard, and it's really got to look fast."

"So, from a missile range at Aldershot or somewhere," said Anthony Squire, "he got some 16mm army film of a missile, and that's in the picture - one shot of a missile which is meant to be this aeroplane. But it's legitimate cheating."[18]

David had a new cameraman, Jack Hildyard, whom he had known since PYGMALION and who had been started in the business by Ronald Neame. Taking Hildyard's advice, David opted for travelling matte rather than back projection, because back projection was always obvious. Travelling matte meant that all the cockpit scenes had to be shot against a blue screen, the clouds being added optically in the laboratory. This was trickier than back projection because the background was blank until the lab had done its work.

In the studio, David had a Moviola on which he could view the second-unit footage and see exactly what was to appear behind the actor. Jack Hildyard also studied the backgrounds on the Moviola, so that if a cloud went over the sun, he could arrange for a shadow to pass over the cockpit as well. It was all incredibly expensive. But the superior quality justified the extra outlay, and THE SOUND BARRIER had the finest quality matte work anyone had ever seen.

"David said the cockpit shooting was the summit of his career as a technician," recalled Ann Todd.[19]

In the middle of the picture, Nigel Patrick suffered an attack of appendicitis and was rushed to hospital. David shot around him as much as possible and when there was nothing left to shoot the production was closed down. The big set of the living-room stood unused for three or four weeks, while both units were paid for by the insurance company. Even when Nigel Patrick returned, David had to wait until he had completely recovered before he dared risk the scene in which he had to carry Ann Todd over the threshold and into the living-room. To ease the action, David called upon the Kirby Flying Ballet harness he had used on the rooftops in OLIVER TWIST and suspended Ann from wires throughout the scene.

David then subjected Nigel Patrick to the sequence in which he breaks through the sound barrier, and his aircraft judders as though falling apart. This proved one of the most difficult effects to achieve. Art Director John Hawkesworth[20] eventually provided the solution with a mechanical hammer. It was hardly conducive to a restful convalescence, however, and Patrick was convinced he would have a relapse as the hammer pounded ear-splittingly off-camera, and the cockpit set thrashed as if mounted on a bucking bronco.

The marriage between David and Ann Todd was proving to be a disappointment for both of them. John Hawkesworth, who lived near them, said:

"Ann was determined to make him into a smart Kensington man. They had their big house in Kensington and had it furnished very well. They had their green Rolls-Royce and a chauffeur in a green uniform, and the chauffeur drove David to Shepperton every day. And then halfway through the film there wasn't any chauffeur any more. David was driving the green Rolls and gradually he was getting out of the trap that Ann had set for him."

"I think she thought that she would be leading lady in all his films from then on," said Anthony Havelock-Allan. "That's the impression he had, that she was proposing to use him as a stepping stone for her own career. And David didn't want to be a stepping stone for anybody's career except his own."

When tensions rose at Ilchester Place, David was able to find comfort in working on his garden. But on the studio floor, where tensions were high anyway, the two of them were face-to-face for hours on end, and there was no escape.

"They'd been doing a night scene," said Anthony Squire, "where Ann Todd comes to see the hole in the ground where Nigel Patrick has been killed. It took two nights to shoot, instead of one. I met David in the corridor and he said, 'Old boy, never put your wife in pictures.' She argued the toss for every single shot. I think she was a good actress, but she's a weakness in THE SOUND BARRIER.

"I remember in the hangar some stills man was asking for a shot of Ann and David said, 'Do we have to have all this Bert and Anna lark?' referring to Herbert Wilcox and Anna Neagle. He said it in front of everybody, so it was clear the marriage was going on the rocks."[21]

"The only row we had in front of people was on THE SOUND BARRIER," said Ann Todd. "I had to say to Nigel Patrick that I didn't want him to fly, that he had to think of me. It was a long speech, beautifully written by Rattigan.

"I felt that women, when they have something important to say, are inclined to get rather fierce. It's an animal thing. I felt she would be frightened and in her fear would bang him on the chest. At some terrible hour of the morning I played it the way I thought it ought to be played. And then I cried at the end and became very feminine.

"There was a terrible silence. 'Are you going to do it that way?' asked David.

"I said, 'Well, obviously I'm not. But I was going to, yes.' He said, 'Well, no man would stay in the audience. They'd just walk out.'

"It developed into a row. The camera crew became very embarrassed because he was so angry, and Nigel Patrick kept saying, 'It's all right, it's all right the way she's playing it.' Jack Hildyard said to David, 'You shouldn't say all that in front of the whole set.'

"David said, 'I don't want it played like that.'

"I said, 'You're the director. How do you want me to play it?' So he began this business of, 'Please, please don't go off and fly because you're being unkind to me.'

"I said, 'All right, I'll do it your way.' It was dreadful."

The film was shown in Paris, where it was dubbed into French. Ann and David saw this version, and discovered that Ann's French "double" had played the scene as she had wanted to play it - so far as the sound was concerned.

"Despite everything," said Ann, "David was a wonderful person to work for. There was always an excitement about him. I miss that nowadays."[22]

In the cutting-room, Geoffrey Foot was the editor, Peter Taylor the assembly editor and Valerie Leslie and Teddy Darvas the assistants.

"SOUND BARRIER was an amazing experience for me," said Teddy Darvas. "David was a wonderful teacher. When there was a problem on a sequence, everyone would stop for a cup of coffee and thrash it out, including me, the second assistant. My father had been at school with Alexander Korda in Budapest and we had come to England in 1938. When David realised I was not just a time-server, one of the many Hungarians Korda employed, he took me up and taught me.

"If you said something that was patently ridiculous, you wouldn't be ignored. David would patiently explain that it may be a good idea, but if you did that, something else was liable to happen. When I suggested he cut one of Ann Todd's biggest scenes with Nigel Patrick, instead of being funny, he carefully explained that I was absolutely right, the scene *was* too long, but if he cut it out it would damage the relationship when he dies later on. So I learned.

"On SOUND BARRIER there were a couple of really awful cuts. But David said he would rather have one bad cut than bore the audience for one minute."[23]

One of the most valuable lessons Darvas received was when David showed the film to Alexander Korda at his Piccadilly headquarters.

"David had a fantastic montage, a brilliant sequence when they build the plane which must have run about seven minutes. For some reason the end of the film was flat and when we ran the cut for Alex at the end of that sequence Alex just whispered to David, "Too dramatic."

*Ralph Richardson as Sir John Ridgefield, a character based on Sir Geoffrey de Havilland,
David Lean and director of photography Jack Hildyard.*

"The following day, David came in to the cutting-room and in ten minutes they cut it down to three or four shots and the rest of the film came to life. David always said that Alex saved THE SOUND BARRIER. He had this vision. He could see where David and Geoff could not."[24]

"There was a scene towards the end which I thought was one scene too many," said Geoffrey Foot. "Ann was coming through the empty house after her husband's been killed, carrying the baby. It was a real bit of American sentiment. I hated it. I always tried to get David to take it out. No, no, had to be in. I think it was partly because he was married to Ann. We did the fine cut and he said, 'Well, that's it. That's the cut.'

"I said, 'Apart from that scene.'

"He said, 'Not at that again are you?' He got all the film editors and their assistants into the theatre and ran the picture for them. 'That scene with Ann Todd,' said David, 'I want to keep it in, Geoff wants to take it out. What do you all think?'

"'Keep it in… Keep it in.'

"He turned to me and said, 'What do you think now?'

"I said, 'I still want it out.'

"He said, 'Right, you bugger. Take it out.'"[25]

The music for THE SOUND BARRIER was written by a young composer called Malcolm Arnold.

"When I was asked to do the film," said Arnold, "the film composers of Britain were amazed. John Hollingsworth said, 'I know David well, he'll ask you for a big tune, romantic feeling and all he wants is Rachmaninov, but it'll be Rachmaninov and Arnold. That's why he asked you.'

"That's the advice he gave me and that's what I did - just Rachmaninov with Arnold. But there is more than Rachmaninov in THE SOUND BARRIER. Where the Spitfire goes through the clouds, I made a rhapsody of it, which I recorded with the Royal Philharmonic in the Festival Hall. I asked David, 'Would you mind if I made it into a rhapsody?' and he said, 'No, it's publicity for the film.' I sent him a copy which I'm sure he used to play.

"I've used a tune for Ann Todd and Nigel Patrick many times, including the second movement of my Second Clarinet Concerto.

"I knew David had an ambition to be a jazz pianist, but he didn't play the piano, couldn't even read music. I said, 'In some of your spare and depressed moments, I'll come over to wherever you live and teach you to read music. I'll teach you the piano.' He never took up the offer."[26]

THE SOUND BARRIER was well received by virtually all the critics, "*including Lejeune and Powell*," wrote David. The premiere, held on 24 July 1952 at the Plaza, Piccadilly Circus, was a lavish occasion, attended by the Duchess of Gloucester, Frank Whittle, designer of the British jet engine, and Group Captain Douglas Bader, the crippled Battle of Britain pilot whose exploits were later filmed in REACH FOR THE SKY. Unusually for a film premiere, the event was covered by television cameras.

After the premiere, David and Ann arrived back at Ilchester Place to discover that David had forgotten his key. They decided to spend the night at the Savoy; the only problem was money. David had been impressed by Terence Rattigan's talk of his miraculous accountant, Mr Forsyth, to whom he entrusted all his financial problems. Mr Forsyth provided his spending money, and dealt with all the bills. David had decided to go to Mr Forsyth as well. Since Rattigan was permitted only the sum of two pounds and ten shillings a week, he could hardly be expected to pay for a double room at the Savoy. The management would not admit the famous pair until they had made a series of highly embarrassing and extremely late telephone calls.[27]

Korda engineered a tremendous publicity coup on 9 October 1952 when the Comet made its first record-breaking flight to Paris. Korda sponsored the forty-minute flight, which made aviation history, cutting the regular flying time in half. The plane carried Korda, David and Ann, Norman Spencer, three of Britain's top test pilots, and a group of journalists.

David and Ann Todd greeted by the crowds gathered to see the Comet on its maiden flight to Paris.

According to *Today's Cinema*, "the Paris traffic stopped in its tracks as the slim monster hurtled low above the Champs-Elysées and with a tight turn round the Eiffel Tower, repeated the process. For fifteen minutes, Parisians stopped and stared."[28]

"We taxied in at Orly," said Norman Spencer, "and the place was black with people watching this extraordinary aeroplane that made this funny noise and didn't have propellers."[29]

Thirty-five years before, Charles Lindbergh had landed at Orly with his primitive craft, The Spirit of St. Louis. David could never have expected to experience a similar thrill, but the *Today's Cinema* reporter described the scenes at Orly as the most remarkable he had ever seen. "Thousands of French men and women lined the airport barriers, whilst dozens of newsreel men and French radio commentators photographed and interviewed the stars of the party as they disembarked. Ann Todd and David Lean were literally besieged by the fans. Every newspaper in the capital carried front page stories of the Comet and the film. It was one of those occasions when it felt extra fine to be an Englishman."[30]

After the success of the Paris trip, Sir Miles Thomas, head of British Overseas Airways Corporation, gave David and Ann free tickets to travel on the Comet on her maiden voyage to South Africa. David took his cine-camera and recorded some beautiful footage when he went north, to Rhodesia, to see the Victoria Falls.

The visit to South Africa, arranged by a veteran distributor called Schlesinger, took on the glamour of a Royal Tour, judging by the *African Mirror* newsreels which David kept. Banners welcome Ann Todd and David Lean, huge crowds wave enthusiastically at the airports and along the roads, and the Royal South African Air Force band turns out at the cinema. At Johannesburg, Ann Todd's face dominates the front of a theatre, and next to it is a portrait of David. At one cinema, they are welcomed by the skirl of bagpipes and Ann is presented with an ostrich-feather cape.

David took one brief trip to Cape Town on his own. "It was a marvellous place, like the Grande Corniche in the South of France, although bigger and more exciting, with vast seascapes and cliffs.[31] I took a small plane run by a local airline to return to Johannesburg and as we took off I saw we were headed for the Drakensberg Mountains.

"After about thirty-five minutes, we felt as though the plane had been grabbed and shaken. We were plunged into darkness. They turned on the lights, and I saw the cabin door opening and the pilot emerging with blood streaming down his face, and going to the loo to wash himself. In a curious way I seem to attract people who are afraid of flying. On a turbulent flight to Bali, I had an old Indonesian, who was sitting next to me, put his arm round my neck and another chap kneeling in the aisle, and these two clung to me throughout the flight.

"This time it was a lady who came from a very rich South African family and she knelt on the floor and prayed and then put her arms around me and clung to me in terror. In those days, the flight took something like an hour and a half - it took us double that time. We had to slow down and dive and God knows what they were doing. We arrived at Johannesburg without further incident, but after that flight I found it took quite a lot of courage to get on a plane. I was just terrified of it, for about fifteen years."[32]

A month before David began flying on the Comet to Paris and Africa, he and his wife witnessed a terrible aviation disaster. The test pilot, John Derry, had become a close friend and used to visit them at Ilchester Place. Ann Todd felt there was a religious aura about him. "When he came into a room," she said, "everything lit up."

"I was very fond of John Derry," said David. "He was very, very quiet and interested in flying and in design where lots of these other pilots weren't."

On Saturday, 6 September 1952, at the Farnborough Air Show, David and Ann watched in horror while John Derry's plane disintegrated as it flew towards them.

"He was flying a new De Havilland machine straight down the runway," said David, "and it broke into pieces in front of everybody. It was an awful tragedy. A number of spectators were killed. Derry's wife was in the stands. So great was her shock, the poor dear, that she sat there as if nothing had happened. Another pilot had to come and take her away."[33]

David re-edited THE SOUND BARRIER for America - giving it a faster tempo - and he and Ann were sent over on the Comet[34] for the New York opening. The title had been changed to BREAKING THROUGH THE SOUND BARRIER, thus annoying David considerably. Korda's American distributor, Ilya Lopert, insisted that no one in America had heard of the sound barrier.

At the premiere was a US Air Force officer named Chuck Yeager, the first man to fly faster than sound. His feat, which had taken place on 14 October 1947, had been kept as classified information, which was presumably why the British thought they had been first.

"It was a good and very realistic action picture," wrote Yeager. "They used a Spitfire to break the barrier, which was amusing because that airplane wouldn't go faster than .75 Mach in a power dive. When the actor discovered that his stick froze at Mach 1, instead of pulling back, he pushed the stick forward and it somehow released. Any pilot who really tried that stunt would have drilled himself into the ground, but it worked as a dramatic moment in the picture, and I thoroughly enjoyed myself.

"When the lights came on, I realized that people seated around me thought they had watched a true story. I overheard one guy say to his wife, 'Where in hell was Uncle Sam?' I said to him, 'Hey, that was only a movie. We broke the barrier, not the damned British. And I'm the guy who did it.' I might have saved my breath. That movie was a hit, and many people who saw it believed it was a true story."[35]

THE SOUND BARRIER was voted as the Best Foreign Film by the National Board of Review in 1952 and the British Film Academy voted it the best film from any source. It was nominated as the Best Film of the year by the New York Film Critics and Ralph Richardson was voted Best Actor by the New York Critics and the British Film Academy. Rattigan's script was nominated for an Academy Award and London Films' sound department won an Oscar.[36]

Thirty-six years later, David Lean gave the first of the Directors' Guild lectures at the Museum of the Moving Image in London. THE SOUND BARRIER was the film chosen to precede David's talk. It had long been one of his favourite films, and he had mourned its disappearance, which he attributed to the fact that this story of early jet propulsion was already old-fashioned.

When the picture came to an end, David told his audience, "I'm feeling rather tearful at the moment because I like the picture. I thought it came off, and I found it very touching, partly because of the days it brought back to me in film-making. Tremendous excitement making that film.

"I've always been fascinated by adventure. I always think of the first man who went off in a boat and disappeared over the horizon, not knowing what he was going to find. I suppose I'm a romantic, but I find that frightfully exciting - the fact that we're still reaching out, trying to discover what we are, what the world is, what the universe is."

After THE SOUND BARRIER was finished, David began his long and difficult search for another subject. He was initially enthusiastic about an H.E. Bates novella called *The Cruise of the Breadwinner*. It was a tale of a battered old boat and its equally battered old skipper, on patrol off the South Coast during the war.

"I thought the old skipper an ideal part for Charles Laughton," said David. "I was astounded when he refused it. I could never get an explanation and years later I asked him why. 'My dear chap,' he said, 'If I played the skipper of a boat in war-time, the press would have given me hell. They'd have said, Charles Laughton, who spent the war in Hollywood, playing a war hero!'"

Then, with what he himself called his *"Boys' Own Paper* mentality", David came up with an idea for an underwater story about the Lost City of Atlantis. Jacques Cousteau came over from France for discussions, but he was more interested in talking about his own plans for making underwater documentaries than he was in David's idea.

David also thought that the next film after THE SOUND BARRIER should be a kind of sequel - a space story. He and Norman Spencer held discussions with Arthur C. Clarke, the future author of 2001: A SPACE ODYSSEY, who had written *The Exploration of Space* and was, in 1951, a well-known advocate of satellite communications technology. Eventually another writer was commissioned to prepare a treatment, but nothing came of it.

"I never met him again," said Arthur C. Clarke. "Funny thing was, we were both in Ceylon when he was making RIVER KWAI yet we never met. (Clarke's home is in Colombo.) My partner played a naval officer drinking in an exterior of the Mount Lavinia Hotel. I'm sorry we didn't meet."[37]

"We talked about Gandhi," said Norman Spencer, "and we discussed Lawrence of Arabia, which David had always wanted to do. It was talked of as an idea long before Spiegel came on the scene. David didn't know a lot about Lawrence, but he felt it was going to be marvellous action in the desert and cops and robbers stuff with the blowing up of the railways."[38]

But all this was far in the future. The next David Lean film would be neither space odyssey, nor underwater fantasy, nor desert epic. It would be a Northern comedy set in a bootmaker's shop in Victorian Salford.

CHAPTER TWENTY-THREE

HOBSON'S CHOICE

HAVING expunged his so-called "failures" with what the industry regarded as a triumph, David was assailed by fresh doubts. "THE SOUND BARRIER was such a terrific success," said Teddy Darvas, "he was terribly worried that anything he would do next would be slated by the critics."

While most film-makers maintained a healthy disrespect for critics, some to the point of ignoring reviews altogether, a few, like David, were devastated by bad notices. For him, they were the equivalent of a paternal lecture on how useless he was, with the added problem of knowing that his father would undoubtedly read them.

Yet no one could accuse David of taking on something safe and simple for his next project. Harold Brighouse's Northern comedy, *Hobson's Choice*, already had the status of a cherished national institution. Exceptionally for a British play, it had been premiered in America in 1915.[1]

The project came to David in a curious way. David's agent, Christopher Mann, also represented Wilfred Pickles, the famous radio personality whose programme *Have A Go* was listened to by most of Britain. Pickles told Mann that he wanted to make a film of *Hobson's Choice* and Mann turned not to David, who was hardly an obvious choice, but to the team of Frank Launder and Sidney Gilliat who had begun to specialise in comedy. Launder, indeed, had written the script for the 1931 version.[2]

The trouble was Launder and Gilliat were none too keen to cast Pickles. Mann - in a tricky position, for he also represented Launder and Gilliat - obliged them to consult Alexander Korda who shared their view. "What happened thereafter," said Gilliat, "was that Korda jumped the gun and bought the rights regardless. Neither of us knew until he told us. As soon as the news came out, Christopher Mann and Pickles accused us of betraying them. The whole situation was embarrassing and we decided to withdraw, at least temporarily, from the scene."[3]

Korda was taking a risk in offering the play to David for he was perceived as lacking a sense of humour despite his creditable work on BLITHE SPIRIT. Furthermore, Brighouse's play required an understanding of the distinctive Northern humour and David was in every fibre a Southerner. David saw the play at an Arts Theatre Club revival on 4 June 1952. An unusually good production, with David Bird as Hobson and Donald Pleasence as Willie Mossop, it gave David the courage to make the picture. The settings - late Victorian - were familiar to him from the Dickens films, as were the characters, who were broad caricatures. David may also have been encouraged to do the film since Ronald Neame had had a surprise hit in 1952 with Eric Ambler's adaptation of Arnold Bennett's THE CARD, starring Alec Guinness and set in the Potteries in the Midlands.

Korda had often heard David say he wanted to do a love story, and this *was* a love story, albeit a curious one. Hobson, who runs a boot shop in Salford, is the tyrannical father of three girls. The oldest, Maggie, has turned thirty and faces a dreary future as a spinster. Her sisters are prettier and flirtatious and have no shortage of suitors. Maggie determines to seize the first opportunity to escape - and that first opportunity is a poor one indeed: her father's timorous boot-hand, Willie Mossop. The only thing in this man's favour is his skill at crafting leather; otherwise, he falls flat on his face at every turn. Maggie sets about disentangling him from his girl, equipping him with his own shop and dragooning him into loving her. The marriage and the business prosper, while Hobson's business faces ruin. Without Maggie to look after him, he lurches around the streets, a hopeless alcoholic. Having pulled her husband up by his bootstraps, Maggie gives her father an ultimatum: she will return home on the condition that the two businesses are merged and that he takes no part in running it. Confronted by "Hobson's Choice", he has no alternative but to agree.

The play, about a strong-minded woman who refuses to be bullied by a man, was a distinctive product of the Suffragist era.

"I must admit I wasn't terribly enthusiastic," said Norman Spencer. "I thought, 'Well, a dear little Lancashire comedy.' Korda thought it was a good idea and Korda was quite far-seeing. We met Harold Brighouse. He was an old man who was a bit deaf and rather stunned by the whole thing. He said, 'I hope it'll be a nice film,' lost interest and went back up North again."

On 12 January 1953, six months after David saw the play, he and Norman Spencer moved into Korda's Piccadilly offices to start work on the script. At first they thought they might need a professional writer but after several meetings with "Wynyard Browne" - a *nom-de-théâtre* for a husband-and-wife team - they realised they could do the work themselves.

"There was the tight little play with everything there," said Spencer. "David got into the spirit of it all very quickly. I'd say 'Shall we go to lunch now?' and he'd say, 'Aye.'"

Roger Livesey, who had made such an impact in Powell and Pressburger's THE LIFE AND DEATH OF COLONEL BLIMP, was David's first suggestion for Hobson. But Spencer had another actor in mind, Charles Laughton. "I begged David to take him. I felt Livesey was overrated. Laughton was a Yorkshireman (Livesey came from South Wales) and he would be playing a Lancastrian, so you'd get regional accuracy, more or less, with international casting. And I thought it needed that size of character."[4]

David approached Korda with some doubt because Laughton had rejected THE CRUISE OF THE BREADWINNER and he hardly expected the actor to embrace this small-scale play.

Korda said, "David, I can tell you a lot about Charles Laughton. Charlie will do the most difficult scenes, like the eating scene in THE PRIVATE LIFE OF HENRY VIII, but give him something simple to do and he'll take three weeks and cause you endless trouble."[5]

Despite his memories of Laughton during the aborted production of I, CLAUDIUS, Korda contacted Laughton's agent, Paul Gregory. Korda played for flattery, claiming the part had been written especially for him. Laughton accepted the part and sent a telegram to David saying how honoured he was and how much he was looking forward to working with him. Teddy Darvas remembered that David was quite overcome that someone of Laughton's stature should have made such a gesture. Because of Laughton's existing commitments, a decision was made to postpone production until June 1953.

Charles Laughton ideally cast as Henry Hobson in HOBSON'S CHOICE.

"I adored Charlie," said David. "Someone asked Laurence Olivier if he had ever worked with a genius and he said, 'Yes, one: Charles Laughton.' Remember him as Bligh? I'm sure he was a cardboard cut-out in the script yet Charlie took it, threw it in the air, whirled it around, blew life into it and out came this extraordinary character. And that is a sort of genius, isn't it?"[6]

Born in 1888, in Scarborough, Laughton had become a major international star. He was famous for being "difficult" and for his obsession with his personal appearance, which led him to play sympathetic grotesques, such as Claudius and Quasimodo, or tyrants, like Bligh. Alfred Hitchcock, who made two pictures with him, once said: "It isn't possible to direct a Charles Laughton film, the best you can hope is to act as referee."[7] David decided to give him the minimum of direction.

"He was so full of inventiveness, and he was so entertaining to watch, that I just sat there, applauding him going through his part and giving various versions of it. I know directors got angry with him because they said he takes weeks to decide how to play a part. I remember he came to me after we'd been shooting for days and said, 'I've got it - feet on the ground and bubbles in the head.' And from then on, it took off. He went way over the top every now and then - my fault for not holding him back - but I just sat there, on a ninepenny seat in the stalls, just watching.

"Charlie was a fascinating man. We used to finish work at Shepperton and go to a pub to have a beer and chat about things. I found him immensely entertaining and interesting. Charlie knew it all in some strange way; he had a wonderful instinct. You would suggest something and he'd say, 'Yes, go on, go on,' and you'd find yourself following an oil slick.

"I didn't really believe it when he died and it came out that he was a homosexual. But I'm sure, looking back on it, that it's true. He had these wonderful soft sides to him, but he also had great strength."[8]

According to Teddy Darvas, David encouraged Laughton to be larger than life so that Maggie and Mossop would be more realistic by contrast. "David took advantage of Laughton's overacting," said Darvas, "but Laughton said in my hearing that he knew when the reviews came out he would be slated for going over the top. And it happened."[9]

Much to Laughton's delight, Robert Donat had been cast as Willie Mossop. Donat had played with Laughton in THE PRIVATE LIFE OF HENRY VIII .

"I like having rather mad shots at casting," said David, "and I thought Robert Donat could do it. I took him to dinner and he was full of doubts. I said, 'Bob, let's do a test and you'll see. If you think it's hopeless after doing the test, fair enough, but let's have a go.'"

Donat, a favourite of Korda's, was an actor of sensitivity and style, capable of high drama or elegant comedy, with the added advantage that he came from Manchester. He had become a major international star after winning an Oscar as the sad schoolmaster in GOODBYE MR CHIPS. In 1949 he had starred in the film of a Lancashire comedy, THE CURE FOR LOVE, which he also directed and produced.

Teddy Darvas was struck by how old Donat looked as he arrived on the set for his test. He was only forty-eight but suffered from chronic asthma. "I think this asthma was partly a hysterical thing," said Darvas, "but nonetheless it was a real illness. I saw this old man going down the trapdoor to his workplace and suddenly Willie Mossop appeared. It was absolute magic."[10,11]

The insurance company insisted that Donat pass a medical examination before they would accept the risk. According to Renée Ascherson, Donat's wife, this filled the actor with dread. "Robert's accountant told him that to make ends meet he had to do two films a year. During this time the insurance doctor was always at the back of his mind. He was terrified of the examination and the terror made it impossible for him not to have asthma."[12]

And this, sadly, is what happened. Donat's terror brought on a severe asthma attack and a few days before production was due to start the insurance company refused to pass him. Donat was devastated: "This failure may end my career," he wrote to a friend.[13]

"When we heard the news," said Paul Gregory, "Laughton's face was as long as the world. He said, 'Terrible news. My contract has been breached.' He said the only reason he wanted to do the part was to be able to play with Donat, whom he liked very much. He always had to have a crisis. He loved crises. So he refused to show up.

"David Lean called me and was very mild-mannered about the whole thing. I called Korda who said, 'You tell Charlie that if he wants me to go to the scandal sheets I will, unless he goes back to work.'

"This was a brutal reference to the fact that practising homosexuals were liable to be arrested in England. Laughton was made wretched by having to suppress this side of his nature. He was even baited about it by his wife Elsa Lanchester."

Because Laughton was, in Gregory's words, "frightened to death" by Korda, he went back to work. Fortunately, he loved David. "He thought he was wonderful," said Gregory, "But at the same time he was afraid of David. He feared anybody who he felt was really talented."[14]

David had rapidly to find another Willie Mossop. He offered the part to James Donald, who refused to do a test. Then he thought of John Mills and remembered a day when they were making GREAT EXPECTATIONS.

"We were out on the river in a rowing boat," said David, "doing the paddle-steamer scenes, and Johnny Mills was pretending to be seasick. He had us all in stitches. He's a very funny comedian and I thought, 'My God, Johnny could do it very well.'"

John Mills was again in a boat, a speed boat in the South of France, water-skiing with Rex Harrison, when he saw a man on the shore waving a piece of paper. It was a cable from David: "THIS IS AN SOS CAN YOU DROP EVERYTHING AND RETURN HOME IMMEDIATELY BOB DONAT ILL YOU CANT TURN DOWN WILLIE MOSSOP IN HOBSONS CHOICE CAN YOU"

"Of course, I'd seen the play many times," said Mills. "I took a plane home and went to see David. He told me they were stuck. David admitted he saw a big shambling man in the part rather than someone of my size and thought Bob Donat was better casting than I was. Did I think I could play it? I said, 'Absolutely.'"

An actor is trained to say "absolutely". Nevertheless, Mills was uncertain about the role. His fans regarded him as a hero - as the great explorer, SCOTT OF THE ANTARCTIC, or as the submarine commander in MORNING DEPARTURE - so David did his best to convince him that Mossop was a hero as well. "A boot boy ends up the owner of the most fashionable shoe shop in Manchester. That's the equivalent of a private rising to be a general."

As it turned out, his fans may have missed the gold braid, but they admired his versatility.

"John Mills's career was at a low ebb," said camera operator Peter Newbrook. "He had bought a secondhand Rolls-Royce convertible and I remember him saying, 'That's my last money. I don't know what's going to come up. But I'm going to enjoy myself.' He'd reached a point where he could no longer play young leading men. And he wasn't old enough to do the character parts he played later. Putting him in that picture opened up a whole new box of tricks for him."[15]

Mills later wrote that he would always be grateful to Willie Mossop. "I think I enjoyed him as much as any part I have played, and I needed him badly. I had not been in a really successful picture since MORNING DEPARTURE three years before."[16]

Prunella Scales had been cast as one of Hobson's daughters. "When I tested for the part of Vicky," she said, "David sat behind the camera and interviewed me in character. He was always extremely kind during the shoot and one day he said, 'Make sure your next film is in colour. It'll suit you better than black and white.'

"I'm afraid I didn't fulfil his hopes, having had a rather sketchy career in films, but I'm proud to have worked with him. I remember him being quiet and approachable with the ability to instil confidence despite my total lack of experience."[17]

The actress chosen to play Maggie, Brenda de Banzie, came from Manchester and had a difficult time. Laughton disapproved of her, saying "She doesn't understand the part in the least."

"David and Charlie took a kind of hate against her," said Norman Spencer. "I mean, they fell in love with each other in a kind of way. David thought Charlie was marvellous and poor Brenda was left out in the cold. It was the same pattern as Trevor Howard on PASSIONATE FRIENDS."[18]

David considered replacing her. Instead, he took her to a pub and lectured her on the art of screen acting.

"Brenda de Banzie was one of the tragedies of the British stage," said Teddy

Noël Coward advised David to set love scenes against wretched surroundings; Maggie (Brenda de Banzie) courts Willy Mossop (John Mills) against a polluted River Irwell.

Darvas. "She disappeared very quickly because there was a pool of character actresses in England, so why take Brenda de Banzie who will give you problems? Brenda was a nice woman but on the set she turned into a monster. She turned to David in front of the crew and said, 'The trouble with you, David, is that you direct for star quality.'"

Brenda de Banzie saw the first cut of the film and then had to do some additional shooting for which the sets were rebuilt.

"Brenda de Banzie was very sweet," said Teddy Darvas, "She was almost in tears when she realised what David had done for her and she thanked him generously. Then the extra shooting started and she was as bitchy as ever. The assistant director, Adrian Pryce-Jones, bought one of those printed cards and handed it to her. It said, 'Why be difficult when, with a little extra effort, you can be bloody impossible?' Even she had to laugh."

The art director on HOBSON'S CHOICE was Wilfred Shingleton, who had worked with John Bryan, and who created a much-admired set at Shepperton.[19] Cobbles for the streets were pre-cast and produced with indentations to ensure the deep puddles which would be crucial in Laughton's "moon walk" sequence.

A curious aspect of film-making of this period was that extras, or crowd artists, walked on tip-toe or on felt runners whenever dialogue was being recorded. David thought they looked like ballet dancers, quite ridiculous for a

Northern mill town where the working people wore clogs. David overruled the sound recordist and instructed the extras to walk normally. Since the sound was perfectly acceptable, this strange ritual died out.[20]

Many of the exteriors were shot on location in Salford, which still resembled the Manchester of the late nineteenth century. When David and Norman Spencer went up on a recce, people came out of their houses, wondering who the two strange men were.

"One woman asked us into her house," said Spencer. "She made us a cup of tea and said, 'Look, the wallpaper's peeling.' She thought we were from the council. A rumour had gone around that they were going to demolish these streets and build flats. She wanted to show us she needed another house."[21]

The company spent a week in Salford in September 1953. However, not all the settings were authentic: for the scene in which Maggie and Mossop leave the church, a set was built in Shepperton which was combined, seamlessly, with a travelling matte of distant Salford.

"David was always remembering what Noël Coward told him," said Teddy Darvas. "Play a love scene against a terrible slum. That's why he did the attempted kiss against the slum alley background."[22]

For the love scene by the canal, David chose the grimiest location he could find - the River Irwell in Peel Park, near the Royal Hospital. David told Brenda de Banzie and John Mills that they would have to wear gasmasks. He explained he would shoot over their shoulders, so the audience would see the canal, not their faces.

"The moment he said that," said Mills, "I accepted it straight away, whereas if another director had suggested it I might have said, 'Mmm, aren't you coming round the front?' I never felt that for a moment with David. I knew what he was going to do with it and felt it was going to be great.

"Anyway, we get there to shoot and the canal is now pristine, full of clear sparkling water. They'd heard a film company was coming to shoot and they dammed it and cleaned it up!"

The sun also shone, so burning tyres restored some of the characteristic Salford gloom. David instructed his property men to collect rubbish such as old cans and orange boxes and hurl them in the river. Lamp-posts were smeared with grime and the cinder path was splashed with black distemper. Just as all seemed ready, a cry was heard, "Mr Lean wants more scum!" An assistant ran into a shop and returned with dozens of packets of detergent powder which were poured into the river, making a bubbling foam of pollution. Salford was now back to what it was before the local council had applied its cosmetic skills.

The scene in HOBSON'S CHOICE which is invariably chosen for extracts on television is the brilliantly cinematic "moon walk" in which a hopelessly drunk Hobson lurches out of the Moonrakers pub and is transfixed by the sight of the moon reflected in a puddle. The huge set at Shepperton was vital for this sequence and the lights gleam on the cobblestones just as evocatively as they do in the Vienna of Carol Reed's THE THIRD MAN.

Clinging to a lamp-post, Hobson gazes at the moon, captive in a puddle, which is echoed by an eerie, "moon-mad" effect on the soundtrack. Hobson staggers towards the puddle and the moon disappears. He plumps his boot where the moon has been and as the ripples subside his own moon face is revealed in reflection. He pursues the moon from puddle to puddle until he thinks he finally has it captured. But it proves to be a reflection in a shop window. In this sequence, Laughton behaves much as Mrs Egerton must have acted when she was showing the young David the glorious antics of Charlie Chaplin.

The moon, originally intended to be an elaborate special effect, was nothing more than tracing paper on a hoop, lit by a brute (a high-intensity spotlight) and reflected in a puddle.

"When we came to Charles Laughton falling down the barrel chute into the cellar," said Norman Spencer, "it was my idea that it should be played almost in pantomime, with the sort of music you get in a music hall or circus when there's someone left on the high wire. This worried Laughton a lot. He said, 'Norman, that's great. But I want some help. I want to get an old music-hall comedian to show me how to go about it.'

"We got a chap called Billy Russell.[23] He was an old tumbler, a music-hall clown. We rigged up a hole in the studio floor with a slide and a rail and Laughton spent days working out how he was going to walk along the pavement and how he was going to fall down the hole. He didn't just fall in. He did all the business with the chain which was half invented by Billy and him."[24]

The arrival of Billy Russell caused one of the few ructions on an otherwise smooth-running production.

"David was furious because Russell cost something like two hundred guineas," said Teddy Darvas. "I went with Laughton to the Shepperton bar and he said, 'I know David is angry with me, but I will show you why I need Billy Russell.'

"Up against the bar he demonstrated when he staggered round the chains he ended up facing the wrong way. 'The reason I need Billy,' he said, 'is because of the old music-hall trick, the chassée, the quick movement of the legs so that Hobson faces the right way and can fall into the trap.'"[25]

Although a great fuss was made about the risk involved, the fall is a special effect. Hobson's wide-eyed horror is shown via a travelling matte; he descends slowly as if by parachute. David hated doing the process work, but it maintains the dreamlike atmosphere and put Laughton in no danger at all.

David Lean and Charles Laughton on the set at Shepperton.

When David first discussed the play with its author, Brighouse told him that one of the comic high spots would be Willie Mossop undressing on his wedding night. "I can assure you," said Brighouse, "it will bring the house down however long it runs."

In the film, Maggie goes to bed and the camera holds on Mossop as he takes off his jacket to reveal that he has no shirt, just a dicky and cuffs. He leans the dicky on the mantelpiece and places the cuffs neatly on either side. He is so shy he takes refuge under his nightgown merely to remove his trousers. Bang goes a door and he leaps to attention.

"Willie?" A call from the bedroom.

"Yes, Maggie, I'm ready." He takes a deep breath and the trumpet call of the battlefield is heard. He turns out the gaslight and marches into the bedroom to the swaggering sound of a military band.

"David shot it at length," said Teddy Darvas, "but the sequence was reduced with a dissolve. It is still bloody marvellous, but Brighouse was right; if it had been another minute longer it would have been funnier."[26]

"David slightly over-egged the pudding," said Norman Spencer. "On the stage it brings the house down because he's left alone in the room and he fiddles and faddles and suddenly Maggie marches in, gets hold of him by the ear and drags him into the bedroom. Curtain. I mean, that's good and funny. But when you make a film you think you can do it better and in the end he did it more elaborately but worse, because that original is marvellous."[27]

During the shooting of HOBSON'S CHOICE, on 21 July 1953, David went to Buckingham Palace. He had been awarded a CBE - Commander of the British Empire - an honour which had been accorded his brother, Edward, the year before.

"In order to keep things going," said Peter Newbrook, "Jack [Hildyard] and I had to keep a semblance of the picture going on the floor so we fooled around and did rehearsals. Of course, we shot nothing without him until he got back from his appointment with the Queen."[28]

When David's brother had received his CBE, Teddy Darvas suggested that David send him a congratulatory telegram. They were stilll not on speaking terms. In the hope of a rapprochement, David took Darvas' advice but he received no reply.

Now Darvas suggested that David write to Edward and say that if the Queen had forgiven him, perhaps his brother might. This broke the ice and the two men began a new, warmer relationship.

Malcolm Arnold had enjoyed working on THE SOUND BARRIER - it proved to be the film experience he relished most. He also had a marvellous time on HOBSON'S CHOICE. It was Arnold's Rabelaisian sense of humour that had decided Muir Mathieson to recommend him once again. He also worked extremely quickly. Arnold saw the fine cut on 14 November 1953 and was recording the music nine days later.

The territory was familiar to Arnold because he was the son of a shoe manufacturer. And David gave him his head, especially in the wedding-night scene. As Willie nervously prepares to enter the nuptial chamber, the music is of "expansive Straussian splendour," wrote Hugo Cole, "with an eloquent violin solo of a type that Arnold never allows himself to write in his concert music. The music changes to a brisk, semi-military march as Willie enters the bedroom."[29]

"David's advice was sound on everything except marriage," said Arnold. "Northerners adore the film and you know why? Because of the music. The shop opening, the Dance of the Puddles... David said, 'Try to get the flavour of Peel Park.'"

In the Dance of the Puddles there is a spine-tingling sound. "That was a musical saw," said Arnold, "played by a man who kept a cafe in Belgium, Jacques Loussier. They got him over at great expense and he was marvellous."[30]

Despite David's initial fears, the critics praised the film. Dilys Powell called it "a massively good-tempered success story."[31] William Whitebait in the *New Statesman* said "It is all very jolly. Personally, I could never have enough of Laughton when he lets go, as he does here." [32]

Philip Hope-Wallace, a theatre critic deputising for C.A. Lejeune, was less impressed by Laughton: "What is wanted (and David Bird in a recent stage revival hit it off perfectly) is a real foil for Maggie... Laughton offers something much clumsier and softer and less formidable, a great Fatty Arbuckle of a man, with a stummick, DTs and a musical drunk scene which would convulse you in the Chelsea Palace but is at odds with the comedy... What Mr Lean superbly furnishes is the high visual finish. This is Salford come alive... The after-rain gleam of the pavements, Peel Park on a Sunday, the ornaments in the parlour and the reflection of chimney stacks in the panes..."[33]

I saw the film early in 1954 when I was sixteen and already a passionate film enthusiast. I was accustomed to films that were either more dramatic or more amusing. This was neither high drama nor high comedy - it was mild without being bitter. Seeing it again for this book, I was struck by the quality of the photography and art direction and by Laughton's Hobson. He might have benefited from a touch of Mr Barrett or Captain Bligh, at least in the first half, so the confrontation with Mossop, during which he lashes him with his belt, could have carried more bite. He merely comes across as a lovable rogue and the lashing is an unpleasant and somewhat unconvincing surprise.

When I first saw HOBSON'S CHOICE, I already hated the artificiality of so many films with their painted backcloths, back projection and cameras that went through walls. Only on a second viewing did I notice the composite set of Hobson's shop - the camera moving from one room to another so unobtrusively that you are never aware of travelling through walls.

It is also now evident that David wanted to parody the famous opening of GREAT EXPECTATIONS. The film begins at night, in the rain, the camera craning back over the cobbled street to the sign of the boot, creaking in the wind. Inside, the camera examines the deserted shop, gliding over the elegant shoes and whipping to the clock as it strikes one. Branches bang against the skylight. Suddenly, the door flies open and a vast shadow casts the shop into darkness. We tilt up to Hobson, black against the street light, and he burps...

The film was well received in America and was entered for the 1954 Berlin Film Festival where it won the Golden Bear. The British Film Academy voted it the best British Film of the Year and David found himself the owner of an abstract bronze statuette by Henry Moore.

Since David had little appreciation of modern sculpture, the BFA's statuette gave him a jolt. He put it on his mantelpiece and over the months he grew to like it so much that when the time came to return it to the BFA he had a plaster cast made of it. He also bought a series of Henry Moore lithographs.

"At the end of SOUND BARRIER" said David, "Alex Korda knew I was unhappy with Ann. He never said a thing. But he called me into his office one day and said, 'David, I'd like you to think about doing a picture on the Taj Mahal.[34] You've got a very good eye, the best I've seen in anybody for a long time, and I think you could do that story.'

"I said, 'Look, Alex, this is absolutely mad. I've never been to India, I don't know anything about the Taj Mahal.'

"He said, 'My dear, you leave for India on Monday.' Once I realised it was inevitable, I said, 'Alex, I'd love to see Egypt on the way.'

"My brother and I were both mad about Pompeii. When he became a journalist - he was a leader writer for the *News Chronicle* - I remember him coming back from Egypt and saying, 'David, you've got to go to Egypt. Take Pompeii and throw it in the river. It'll knock your eyes out.'"

Korda agreed to David's request and plans were made for him to fly to Cairo, do some sightseeing, and then take a P&O ship from Suez to Bombay where he would be met by Vincent Korda.

"I arrived in Cairo in baking heat, the sun had set and I was tired out. I was staying at the Mena House which was out by the Pyramids. It was very old-fashioned and rather grand. I arrived in a state of exhaustion - the flight took all day - and all I wanted to do was go to bed.

"They got a man to show me to my room and I remember opening the doors to a very large double bedroom which had a musty smell. The man went over to the window and opened the shutters. I thought, 'What's that?'

"There were the Pyramids, illuminated by a full moon. My tiredness vanished instantly. I went downstairs to the concierge and said, 'How can I get near the Pyramids at this time of night?' He called a man over and this rather big, lumbering, attractive Egyptian, dressed entirely in white with a turban, came over. We walked off across the sand. In those days, there was nothing but a few tracks. Now the bloody fools have built an asphalt road and ruined it...

"As we approached the Pyramids, the guide said, 'There's going to be a dust storm.' I could see it coming. The sky went opaque and the effect, with the full moon, was startling, like a stage effect at Drury Lane. We found a place amongst some pieces of ancient stone and squatted as the dust came.

"There is something magical about being in a dust storm under a full moon. It comes in gusts, so you duck, then it softens and you can look up and you have this opaque sky again and the shape of the Pyramids.

"I've never lost the magic of that night. If I were a really rich man, knowing what I now know, I think I might spend every penny I have looking for ancient tombs."[35]

During the voyage to India, David received news that his Aunt Winnie had died and had left all her money to him. And it was during his stay in India that David met his future wife, Leila Devi - or Leila Matkar as she was then, being married to an Indian civil servant. David told her that she was the spirit of the Taj Mahal.

David had first met Leila when she was sitting in a gloomy room, suffering from a bout of depression. Enchanted by this soft, gentle, compliant woman - she was the antithesis of Ann Todd - David thought all she needed was to be taken out of the gloom and given love. [36]

"She must have been the embodiment of Indian womanhood, this lovely creature, so adored by people," said a mutual friend, the writer Attia Hosain. "She wasn't so beautiful if you looked at her feature by feature, it was the whole thing put together that was so impressive." [37]

David stayed in India for about a month. "I was knocked over by the first impact of the East," he wrote, several years later. "I suppose it was really the first time I realised the world was mine and that I needn't be fenced in. I came by boat from cold Europe, winter turning into spring at Suez and into summer in the Indian Ocean. [38]

"In one way, I felt completely at home in India; the snobbery, the class system, the hypocrisy and what is done and not done. I was slightly put out by that particular brand of mud wall stupidity and the extreme contrast of high intelligence. Then the sweetness, warmth and humour. Those nightmare pavements in Calcutta. The cows in Benares eating garlands off corpses as diesel engines rattle and rumble across the river. A Marabar 'Boum.'" [39]

In Agra, site of the Taj Mahal, David stayed at Laurie's Hotel. It was a hotel which would later play a decisive role in his life.

"This hotel was the first non-town hotel I'd been in. A lovely garden with huge flowering trees, parakeets and strange dark figures cutting the grass or bringing breakfast in the morning. The hotel was run by the Hotz Hotel Group. Originally Swiss people who had married English, with a touch, just a touch, of Indian en route. They also ran the Cecil Hotel in Old Delhi. The reigning Queen at the Cecil was a very amusing old girl called Mrs White."

Initially, the Cecil refused to accept David because he was a "film person". But once such an embarrassment was overcome, David became so closely attached to Mrs White that he called her "Mummy". She had run the hotel all her life and it was impeccably clean, with a garden of lawns, ancient trees and a profusion of bougainvillea. David used to sit in a white-pillared patio, drinking iced lime juice, as "Mummy" entertained him with stories of the Raj, an era which she missed desperately.

The purpose of David's trip to India - a film about the Taj Mahal - seemed forgotten. And, indeed, after David returned to England, Korda abandoned it. But that trip changed David's life: India, and other places far removed from

England, would have an extraordinary impact not only on his personality but also on his films. Ahead lay twenty years of living out of suitcases in hotels across the world. His only possessions would be his Rolls-Royce cars.

When David returned from India, he and Ann Todd invited Noël Coward to dinner. "David was talking about how well the women look after you in India," said Todd. "He was so insulting, not particularly to me, but it was aimed at me. I went upstairs, packed a suitcase and left the house. I went to the Berkeley and spent the night in a maid's room because the hotel was full. The next thing that happened was that David arrived at the Berkeley. He said, 'Just tell her to pack her case and come down quick.' He could be like that. He could be cruel. But that all went with being a genius. It was a veneer, something over what he really was.

"I don't think you can be married to a genius. David would go away into himself every now and then. David went dead on me, and he was never there."[40]

When I asked David about his marriage to Ann Todd, he refused to talk about it. Ann Todd said that she too had blocked out most of the incidents from her mind.

At the time, David was interviewed by Leonard Mosley of the *Daily Express*.

David said, "It wouldn't occur to me to ask Ann to give up a part in a play or film for my sake, even if it means separating herself from me. In fact, sometimes I insist on her playing in films or the theatre, knowing that it will keep us apart."

As he was talking, he was in Venice and Ann Todd was in Edinburgh, playing in the Old Vic production of *Macbeth*.

Mosley asked David if they missed each other.

"Need you ask?" said David, "And need you ask where I should like to have been on Monday night? It broke my heart not to be there."

Mosley wrote, "It was Lean who persuaded his wife to tackle Shakespeare… The Lean-Todd marriage is a success, but it is difficult to explain why. Both members of it are temperamental and emotional, both are moody and quick-tempered. Both are ambitious. But it succeeds, I think, because of a clever piece of feminine strategy.

"In this marriage, Ann manages the man in her life by always keeping him aware that he has the stronger personality of the two. She consults him about everything. She subtly infers [sic], in fact, that he is not only a great man at his own job, but is the power behind the scenes in her own triumphs too."[41]

When this article appeared, David had walked out on Ann Todd, his marriage was over. He would not see her again for more than thirty years.

CHAPTER TWENTY-FOUR

SUMMERTIME

SUMMERTIME, or SUMMER MADNESS as it was called in Britain, was David's favourite film, starring his favourite actress. It was made in Venice, one of his favourite places in the world. As he told a friend: "I've put more of myself in that film than in any other I've ever made."[1]

After the film was released, a Japanese fan magazine asked David what he wanted to achieve with the film. His answer survives in the form of notes. It is unusually candid, perhaps because he thought his comments would not be circulated on home territory.

"I have never yet made a picture," he wrote, "with any object in view other than to translate into moving pictures a story, a character, a love affair or a place which appeals to me and I would like to show to others. In a sense it's a child's desire, for like a child who finds a new toy, a strange animal or a brightly coloured flower, I want to show my discovery to others. I suppose that quality is what has made me become a film director.

"What appealed to me in the idea of SUMMERTIME? Loneliness. Why? Because I think that loneliness is in all of us, it is a more common emotion than love, but we speak less about it. We are ashamed of it. We think perhaps that it shows a deficiency in ourselves. That if we were more attractive, more entertaining and less ordinary we would not be lonely.

"The film is about a lonely woman who falls in love, and as I know no better remedy for the complaint I hope you will find it sympathetic."

David added that his film was entirely about Americans and Italians, and under normal circumstances he wouldn't feel himself knowledgeable enough to make films about foreigners - one reason he had never gone to Hollywood.

"But American tourists come to Europe in their thousands. Their voices are at this moment echoing round St Peter's in Rome, the Eiffel Tower in Paris and London's Piccadilly Circus. Their films have flooded all our cinemas. The American dollar has taken the place of gold, and beside my bed in Tokyo lies an American Bible. It really is too much, and in SUMMERTIME I couldn't resist having a good (and I hope affectionate) dig at them."

The most startling revelation among the notes was his declaration about writers: "The greatest mental and creative effort in any film is in the writing of the script. The writer not only creates the story but produces human beings out of his imagination, gives them words to speak and thoughts to think. He is the only truly creative person on a film. Without him, the actors would not have parts to play or words to speak, and the directors would be making documentary films, good enough in themselves, but without the force, the humanity and the appeal of a dramatic work of art."

David considered the director to be on a considerably lower plane.

"The director is an interpreter. His task is to translate the written word into pictures on a screen. I do not mean to minimise this process of translation. It is a highly complicated process of translation involving far too many people. It calls for the patience of a saint, the ruthlessness of a general and an unswerving determination to get what you want.

"It's spectacular. It's powerful. It's fascinating and it's very hard work. It's also conducive to egomania and what the French call *folie de grandeur*. The old-fashioned film director believed himself a kind of celluloid emperor, but this has now become a music-hall joke. Today we directors belong to a well-respected profession. At our head is Charlie Chaplin. He writes his own stories. He directs them. He acts in them and he even composes the music. He is the one truly creative artist the cinema has produced."[2]

SUMMERTIME was David's third film in colour. It was a co-production between Korda and British Lion in England and United Artists in America, who were the chief financiers. Korda's partner was Ilya Lopert, and Lopert's partner was Robert Dowling.[3] Their star was Katharine Hepburn.

"SUMMERTIME came about," said Norman Spencer, "because David couldn't find a subject. This became his perennial problem. It was one of the reasons for the great gaps in his schedule. He used to get into a creatively constipated state. A million possibilities flooded through his brain but he could not select the right one.

"Ilya Lopert said to Korda, 'There's a marvellous play in New York called *The Time of the Cuckoo* by Arthur Laurents.' Korda, doing his usual thing of coupling things together, said, 'David! Wonderful idea. Read it, tell me what you think.'

"One way of keeping in with the money men is to accept their ideas. David did not care for it as a play, but he liked the idea of a sex-starved, spinsterish schoolmistress from Akron, Ohio, going to Venice and being overtaken by the Latin approach to sex. That's what hit David."[4]

With David facing a lengthy sojourn abroad, it was necessary to find something to occupy Ann Todd. He did not relish the thought of her coming to Venice even on a visit.

"It was very important that we get something for Ann to do," said Katharine Hepburn, "which would interest her and flatter her, as David was wandering away. I was shrewd enough to know that if Ann was happy in her work, she was happy in her life, like most actors. (Isn't that a terrible thing to say?) I had great connections at the Old Vic with Michael Benthall and Bobby Helpmann.

"Ann Todd liked me. I was careful that she should like me. I flattered her a great deal. I could see what the situation was, so I think I behaved in a wildly tactful way from both their points of view." 5

Ann Todd was cast in the Old Vic production of *Macbeth*. Her Lady Macbeth would be one of her triumphs.

Arthur Laurents arrived in London on 22 November 1953 to discuss the script with David. Laurents, who had worked on Hitchcock's ROPE, agreed to write a screenplay, but when David began to read the result he was dismayed.

Laurents was sticking rigidly to his play - not surprisingly, since he had written it - and while he wanted to please David, he refused to alter his work out of all recognition. After several false starts, the collaboration ended.

David settled down to write the script with Norman Spencer. "We totally rewrote it," said Spencer. "The play was almost plotless, but we travelled far from the original, which was about this dumpy, middle-aged schoolmistress meeting this seedy, down-at-heel Italian. The play had starred Shirley Booth. Our script became so bloody glamorous it wasn't true."6

There were several other writers involved. Donald Ogden Stewart was brought in at the suggestion of Katharine Hepburn. A refugee from McCarthy who had moved to London, he was one of the wittiest and most urbane of script writers. However, one of his biggest successes - THE PHILADELPHIA STORY, which starred Hepburn and won him an Oscar - was the sort of polite comedy which David disliked. But since Stewart was such an agreeable fellow, David was optimistic. Pamela Mann, David's secretary, went to Stewart's home every day to work with him.

"It was disastrous," said Pamela Mann. "David was desperately disappointed. It was lacking in originality and ideas. And we were close to the shooting date."

The Hollywood writer S.N. Behrman was also brought in briefly. Then David had dinner with the novelist H.E. Bates who seemed far more suited to the task. Bates, though, was unable to start work at once. This made David realise that it was pointless sitting in London trying to write about Venice.

"David didn't have a car," said Pamela Mann. "Ann had the green Rolls. I had a little black Ford Anglia and I used to drive him everywhere. He never paid for the petrol or anything, despite the fact that I was only paid nine pounds a week.

"I remember driving him back from Donald Ogden Stewart's through Regent's Park and he said, 'We're going to do the script in Venice. And you're coming too.'

"I couldn't believe it. It was the first time I'd ever been away on location."7

First, however, David and Norman went ahead, on a recce. They left on 22 March 1954 and stayed at the Bauer Grunwald Hotel on the Grand Canal.

"David went around absorbing Venice," said Norman Spencer. "He sort of fell in love with it."

On 13 April they travelled to Rome to begin casting, using the Excelsior Hotel as their headquarters. Casting people brought in photographs and a great many actors were interviewed. One of them was Rossano Brazzi, an extremely good-looking man of thirty-seven. David, who disliked him on sight, had to admit he was perfect for the role.[8]

"We were slipping all the time towards the *jeune premier*," said Norman Spencer, "the idealised romantic leading man, and away from the Laurents play. Brazzi, by the way, had a wonderful wife [Lydia]. She was an exact replica of the Michelin man. She was enormous and in Venice would go around in the tiniest bikini, totally unselfconsciously. She was a wife-mother, as it were; she looked after him, gave him money to spend, told him what to do, acted almost like his agent."[9]

Returning to London, David and Norman had lunch with H.E. Bates who was now absorbed in the script. It was a kind of paid holiday for him, to work on somebody else's idea, writing for a different medium; it became even more of a holiday when he was invited to go out to Venice. Bates derived enormous pleasure from working with this insatiably curious, enthusiastic and charming film director and his genial associate producer, and they collaborated closely. Bates dedicated his book *The Sleepless Moon* to David.

Bates went out to Venice with David, Norman Spencer and Pamela Mann on 22 June 1954 travelling in luxury on the Orient Express.

"Every night," said Norman Spencer, "we'd go to the same restaurant and there'd be shrimps and lobster. It's a very claustrophobic city. Every two weeks, Venice repeats itself for the tourists; every two weeks there's the grand night ride on the Grand Canal in which there's a boat festooned with flowers and a tenor belting out 'O Sole Mio' through a tannoy and hundreds of gondolas with little grey and blue-haired ladies being punted along. It was all so artificial we got sick of it.

"I remember H.E. Bates saying when we sat down in the restaurant, 'Oh, not shrimps again. Just think if we were in England, we'd have roast leg of spring lamb, new potatoes, peas,' and we're all saying, 'Shut up, H.E., we can't bear it..'"[10]

"H.E. Bates was a wonderful writer," said David. "I knew him first through his short stories - some of the best English short stories ever written. And there are dozens of them. There was one short story when he describes the bubbles of water on a girl's back as she sits by a swimming pool. Terrifically sexy.

"I became very friendly with him and liked him enormously. A very charming, warm character. You can't compare him to someone like J.B.

Priestley, who was much gruffer, and had a bigger kind of personality. H.E. was very quiet and knew a lot about secrets.

"He and I wrote the script together. We rarely disagreed. On one occasion he bowed to me and perhaps I shouldn't have been so persuasive. He wanted the Rossano Brazzi character to be an Italian gigolo, who picked up American and English women in the tourist season. I remember he brings flowers for her at the end and runs along the platform. H.E. wanted the woman to reach out for the flowers but not to get them and for the train to disappear. The gigolo throws them on to the railway line and goes off down the platform thinking, 'Now who shall I pick up?'

"I thought it was too cynical, too hard. I'm not sure what I would have done today."[11]

It was not customary in the fifties for British pictures to be shot entirely on location. There were plenty of British studios, desperate for custom, where Venice could have been reproduced, with a little second-unit work for back-projection plates and establishing shots. Twenty years before, Dr Czinner had shot exteriors in Venice for ESCAPE ME NEVER and had filmed all the interiors in the studio. But David was determined to convey to an audience what he felt about Venice and that could only be achieved by shooting everything on location. David had been impressed by William Wyler's ROMAN HOLIDAY which had been filmed entirely in Rome.

Fortunately, Korda supported David. "I remember Alex Korda, before I left to start shooting, making a remark which was typical of Alex," said David. "He used to say very bright things every now and again. He said, 'Good luck, just remember that if I'd chosen some of the highly respected directors of the present moment, they would seek out all the side streets of Venice and never take a shot of the Grand Canal or the Piazza San Marco because that would be a cliché. They're not a cliché for nothing. For God's sake don't be shy of showing these famous places.'

"And of course I wasn't. It was bloody good advice, because you can easily end up in a dirty Venetian alley and think you're being arty. You're not."[12]

Pamela Mann remembered that David always talked about "eyefuls". "If you were going to a place like Venice, you showed all the "eyefuls". You didn't show the places nobody knows."[13]

And yet David loathed what he called "picture postcards" - the best view of a situation. He would always try to find an unusual way into a sequence, as he proved in the home movies of his first Venice trip, with Jo Kirby, where none of the shots are establishing shots of the Grand Canal, but are atmospheric close-ups of the play of light beneath a bridge, or long shots through sharply silhouetted pillars and mooring posts.

Only a small crew - including cameraman Jack Hildyard - went to Venice from

England; the majority of the crew were Italian. The cameras were rented from the Cinecittà studio in Rome.

The company used a little studio, which was in the hands of the receivers, called La Scalera - "a miniature Beaconsfield" as Norman Spencer described it - a stone's throw from a women's prison on the island of Giudecca.

David, Jack Hildyard and Peter Newbrook (operating Arriflex) above St Mark's Square, Venice.

"People asked where the Pensione Flora was," said Norman Spencer of the pretty place where Hepburn stays. "What Vincent Korda did was to rent an empty lot by the Grand Canal and he built a terrace so you got the real Grand Canal traffic going past. It was a marvellous idea. All the scenes in one direction were real and all the scenes in the other direction were in the studio." [14]

David fell in love with the Pensione set, and shot it from every conceivable angle until Ilya Lopert was desperate for him to leave it. Eventually, he did so. In the morning, as the unit travelled by barge to the next location, they saw men swarming over the set, knocking it down. No rushes had been seen, and to demolish a set before the lab had checked the rushes was a crime. David was terrified that the film may have been damaged.

The production manager, Ray Anzarut, had a fake telegram delivered to the cameraman - "ALL OK EXCEPT FOR FINAL SCENE MEN CAN BE SEEN WITH HAMMERS AT BOTTOM OF FRAME IS THIS ALL RIGHT" - and it was left on Lopert's desk.

"Half an hour later," said Peter Newbrook, "this speedboat comes along, its bow wave perpendicular, and there's Lopert, puce in the face, waving this telegram. David looked, realised it was a con and roared with laughter. He said, 'When I passed the set this morning it was certainly not funny. Pulling it down before we'd even seen the rushes! Don't ever do that again.'" [15]

The film industry has long been familiar with the front-office spy, the man delegated by the producer to report all that goes on. Lopert employed an assistant to do this job.

"He spied on me all the time," wrote David. "He timed rehearsals, the actual shooting of every set-up, and checked on my every movement. Lopert also had a wife who watched from her bedroom window overlooking the Grand Canal as we left for work in the morning. Every late departure was passed on to her husband."[16]

Casting locally proved surprisingly difficult. When they needed real American tourists as extras, no one responded to a notice put up in the American Express office; they had to be press-ganged from hotels. For the young boy who befriends Katharine Hepburn, an advertisement was taken in a Venice newspaper. No replies. David eventually persuaded a ten-year-old Neapolitan, Gaitano Audiero, to take the part. As for the maid at the Pensione Flora, it took two weeks of pleading with her boyfriend before she was able to start work.

Katharine Hepburn is one of the most celebrated of all film stars. She is wealthy, she has servants, she lives in two houses, one in New York and one in Connecticut. But she doesn't behave like a *grande dame*. She has a mischievous grin. She says outrageous things. She slops about in torn clothes. She appears to be more interested in you than you are in her, and thus she stimulates conversation. If the telephone rings in the midst of this conversation, she will snap down it and slam the receiver.

She will yell for some lunch for you both and will eat hers on a cushion on her lap, her legs stretched out on a chair. She is a comfortable person to be with, an amusing and invigorating companion. And besides, she has that attractive, brave-pioneer-woman's face and the voice to go with it.

I had visited her to talk about David Lean.

"We were good friends,' said Katharine Hepburn. "I don't know why he didn't fall for me."

"Maybe he did," I suggested.

"No, he didn't fall for me. You can always tell."

"He had a lot of trouble with his relationships," I said. "Why do you think that was?"

"Because he was interested in perfection, which is terribly important. And nothing seemed perfect to him. I think he was just hunting, hunting, hunting, his way through life."

"In private life as well as on the screen?"

"Oh, yes, yes, yes. Hopeless. He used to come here and sit. He and I had exactly the same feelings about what was important, and what wasn't important. So that's a very good basis for a friendship. Also most of the ladies fell madly in love with him. And I didn't at all. He was brilliant with film, he was brilliant in the medium. You couldn't get anyone who could touch him."[17]

Hepburn was forty-seven when she worked for David. He was a year younger.

"Kate was really one of the chaps, marvellous," Jack Hildyard told Julian Fox. "She knew exactly how she wanted to be lit, but she never questioned it after that."

"She got on very well with David," said Peter Newbrook, "They were great soul-mates because she was such a wonderful professional. She'd come in like an express train to Grand Central and she'd hit the mark. Not near it, but absolutely on it. You couldn't put a razor blade between the chalk mark and her feet." [18]

David said that she had taught him a professionalism he had seldom encountered among the English.

"Kate was wonderful. She had very definite views about people. A lot of people were scared of her. She was one of those electric personalities. I have never met anybody quite like Kate. You could put Charlie Laughton and Kate in a box - I don't suggest you do, God knows what would happen - but they were fascinating people, highly gifted, highly original.

"A lot of SUMMERTIME takes place in a pensione and Kate had a scene where she was walking across the terrace. She did a rehearsal and tripped over a loose tile. I thought, 'Oh, damn, what a nuisance. Let's do it once more.' She tripped again and I realised there was nothing wrong. I examined the spot and there was

no loose tile at all. She used the tripping to show her nervousness of the situation. She was adept at sliding things in like that, things you would never dream were invented." [19]

The most famous scene in SUMMERTIME is the one in which Hepburn, filming with her 16mm movie camera, steps back to obtain a wider angle and falls into the canal. Hepburn later blamed an eye infection on the polluted water.

Peter Newbrook dismisses the idea. "First of all, she only did it once. Michael Korda has written in his book that Katie had repeatedly done that scene, but it had to be done once only. [20]

"David and I selected the exact spot where she would fall in. This was adjacent to some steps, so it

The film's most famous image. Katharine Hepburn, as Jane, is trying to capture a shot on her cine-camera when she retreats slightly too far. Fortunately, the little boy, Mauro (Gaitano Audiero) has the presence of mind to grab the camera.

would be easier for her to be helped out. Having pinpointed the spot, the art department arranged with Council officials for the construction gang to lay in some very large tarpaulins so that when she fell in she would never fall in to any of the silt and filth that lay on the bottom of the canal.

"The fall was covered by two cameras. However, after the initial fall, she came out of the canal, was wrapped in towels and waited while the camera was repositioned for the various other shots in the sequence. She went back in the water several times, not by falling in but by walking down the steps.

"If anybody thinks that Katie took offence at going into the water I can tell you that nearly every night she would swim in the Grand Canal. We used to go back to our hotel in a private motorboat - she had Constance Collier, the actress, who was her coach and companion, with her for the whole trip. We had a lot of social evenings together. She used to wear a light safari thing and nothing underneath. She would stop the boat and tell the driver (in her strident but grammatically correct Italian) not to look and jumped off the stern of the boat, swam around for a while and then came back on board. This little pastime only took place after sunset, never in broad daylight. And she did it not once, but time after time, so that's all a myth about it being the company's fault for making her go in the water, to catch whatever she's alleged to have caught." [21]

As Hepburn said to Stephen Silverman when he confronted her with this fact: "I am a fool." [22]

"I'm not such a fan of Hepburn," said Norman Spencer. "She was a damn good performer, but a terrible nuisance on a film. First of all, she's yak-yak-yakking all the time and bossing everybody about. Even on the days when she wasn't called, she'd be on the set at half past seven in the morning saying, 'Now, how do you put the film in the camera?' David was an adoring mate of hers, and vice versa, but she really got in everybody's hair but David's.

"You see, once again David had a mate, and again a hate grew up and one of the hates on the film was poor Isa Miranda. David had seen her in that French picture *Au-delà des Grilles* in which she played a waitress with Jean Gabin." [23]

"When she arrived at the hotel," said David, "I went to meet her. I saw quite a different woman. I couldn't understand it. She didn't look like that woman I'd seen on the screen."

David had intended to dye her hair black, and he was particularly upset when the hairdresser explained that this was now out of the question since her head was full of stitches due to a recent face-lift.

"That was that," said David. "We were landed with a much-too-young matriarch of the Pensione." [24]

"David was furious," said Maggie Unsworth who, as Maggie Shipway, was continuity girl. "I think he was a bit angry with Ilya Lopert; he should have said when he was signing her, 'We like you as you are. Don't cut your hair, don't do this, don't do that.' Producers are supposed to do that kind of thing." [25]

When it came to shooting, Isa Miranda could not follow David's instructions. "I got absolutely desperate with her on a very simple scene. Finally I said, 'Look, Kate, can you have a go?' And she did."

"David did an unforgivable thing," said Norman Spencer. "It wasn't that Hepburn directed the scene, but he let her rehearse her, which I don't think is the right thing to do at all, because Isa Miranda was no fool. She knew she wasn't somehow clicking and the idea of Hepburn, this bossy woman who couldn't wait to tell people what to do, was a very bad angle." [26]

"I was nice to her," said Hepburn. "And David wasn't nice to her. He wanted to go in a certain direction and she paralysed him. I'm sure she must have nearly died. She just couldn't please him.

"I tried to be as tactful as I could with both of them so it didn't wind up in a terrible, terrible fight. To get what he wanted in the scene, I hit her so she'd burst into tears. I knew she couldn't burst into tears on her own. She didn't know I was going to do it, and it startled her, but she played the scene. I was very practical, I thought, and she was very grateful. And David was very grateful." [27]

"Shooting in Venice is very strange,' said Norman Spencer, 'because the water slows everything down. If you wanted to move to another location, we had to use great barges with lamps on them, barges with generators... everything was so slow."

It took an entire night to get one shot. As Rossano Brazzi and Katharine Hepburn are wandering along the canal and he buys her a gardenia, which she drops in the water, a boat floats past with young people singing and dancing.

"We took a long shot," said Spencer, "of the boat drifting under the bridge and that shot took one night. David was being exceptionally and annoyingly pedantic. He was peering through the viewfinder, saying to Jack Hildyard, 'What about a spot of red reflecting in the water there?' On and on. Everybody was hanging around and he was being far too self-indulgent. It was David Lean at his most maddening. The sort of thing that made people worry about the cost on a Lean picture. But he said, 'I want Venice to be the star of this picture,' which indeed it was." [28]

Other delays to the schedule could not be blamed on him. David wanted a spectacular shot of Piazza San Marco to be filmed at dusk, just as the hundreds of domed lamps go on. "I want the lights on," he said, "so you get that lovely effect of the sky, the people in the cafes and the sense of an evening starting." But the electricity people failed to put the lights on and another night was wasted. Gradually, the schedule slipped further and further behind.

"The night when Hepburn is taken out by Brazzi," said Norman Spencer, "we

Shooting on the terrace set built by Vincent Korda, David rehearses Katharine Hepburn, Darren McGavin and Mari Aldon. Jack Hildyard at camera.

used the Banda Municipale which plays twice a week in the Piazza San Marco. David wondered what they could play. They usually played Rossini, so I decided on 'The Thieving Magpie.' We did it at night when the crowds had gone and Venice was empty, right out in the Piazza San Marco with our extras and Katie Hepburn and Brazzi having dinner.

"David wanted to get a very good soundtrack and we went on recording this until about three in the morning and then David would say, 'Once more' and the bandsmen were getting so angry they were throwing their instruments down and saying, 'No, we want to go home.' He shot the band from the top of St Mark's Basilica, which meant we all had to wait an hour while we went up on the roof." [29]

"The trouble in a place like Venice," said David, "is the shopkeepers, because they see a chance of making money and say that their business is being stopped dead in its tracks. You are taking their customers away because the customers are watching us. They form a kind of blackmail ring and as soon as you bring out the camera and the actors they will make a terrible noise. They will hammer, clatter pans, shout, whistle. Anything to upset the shooting unless you agree on a price for their imagined loss of business. You just pay up. There's a price for doing anything."

When the company was shooting in the main square, the Piazza San Marco, they put up screens to obscure them from the inquisitive eyes and cameras of the tourists. Perhaps it was their success in camouflage that led David's son, Peter, who was on a camping holiday, to pass through the city without suspecting for a moment that his father had taken it over.

While they were shooting scenes on the steamer, Ilya Lopert - "an awful man in many ways," said Norman Spencer - marched up and demanded to know how they were going to make up the lost time. Lopert's solution was alarmingly simple. He ripped pages out of the script.

David, in a display of pique, went below with Maggie Shipway to type his letter of resignation. "But David," said Spencer, "would never resign and not shoot at all - so it came to nothing."

While they were aboard the steamer, David showed Spencer a novel he had been sent by a producer called Sam Spiegel. It was called *The Bridge on the River Kwai*.

During the production, Maggie Shipway fell ill. David sent her for a cure to Davos in Switzerland and paid all her medical expenses. Pamela Mann asked who was going to take over. David said she was. She protested that she knew nothing about continuity.

"It was quite frightening," said Pamela. "If you look at the scene of Katharine Hepburn signing in at the Pensione, you'll find that the pen goes from one hand to the other - the smoothness of the cut deceives the eye. I was mortified when Peter Taylor [the editor] told me about that. It never occurred to me to look.

"It was a real baptism of fire. But David was wonderful. You see, you never had to worry about cuts with David. He knew what made a good cut. Like a fool, I didn't capitalise on all that. Eventually I went back to being David's secretary."[30]

Towards the end of the autumn, the tourists had gone and Lopert wanted to stop shooting. They were thousands of dollars over budget. The unit were filming a scene with the camera on the train, and Katharine Hepburn is waving goodbye to Brazzi who is on the platform holding up a gardenia. A big Mitchell camera was mounted on the door of one carriage and Hepburn was in the carriage ahead.

"I was shooting her final close shot," said David, "as she sees the flower, nods, waves and sees him disappear from view. She somehow produced real tears and I was so delighted that I went along the corridor, put my arm around her and told her how pleased I was. Swallowing back the tears she said, 'You darned fool, you've given them the end of the picture.'

"She was right. The very next day Lopert started pressuring me over the cost of the picture. He said his wife would have to sell her jewellery. Within a week he left for Paris and a cable arrived the following morning telling the production manager that the sound camera was to be returned after exactly one more week's shooting - but I could have the Arriflex for a further week.

"I relayed this to Kate and she told me she would work for nothing until the film was finished to my satisfaction and that she would make arrangements that all her costumes would be handed over to her personally so we could shoot whatever scenes I chose. I finished the film with the Arriflex and I also finished it exactly on time.

"When I returned to the hotel that evening two policemen were waiting for me. Would I please come with them? On arrival at the police station, I was told that my work permit had expired and that I must leave Italy within forty-eight hours. I said, 'But I am going to have two weeks' holiday in Italy and have made arrangements to drive down to Sicily.' 'Sorry.' they said. After half an hour of pleading and argument their attitude began to soften. There were some whispered asides and finally the head man said, 'Please ask no more questions but take the train up to the frontier at Domodossola and catch the next train back. No-one will make any trouble.'

"They were obviously very embarrassed because the film was a good publicity boost for Venice and they, the police, had worked with me every day clearing the streets and canals and so forth.

"The following day it was all explained to me, unofficially. Lopert had heard via his spy system that Kate had made arrangements to keep all her clothes. He had put two and two together that we had a plan to continue shooting. He had given someone a big bribe in the police department to have me sent out of the country. Lopert was given one of the highest Italian decorations by the Italian Government for 'so lovingly presenting Venice on the screen.' He wore the little green button to the end of his days." [31]

"Lopert was wildly jealous of David to a degree that one can't imagine," said Katharine Hepburn. "He was a slightly crooked character, not trustworthy. And I don't think he even pretended to be trustworthy. I never knew about David, whether he was on to him, or wasn't on to him. I think David could usually control the situations he got into with his naiveté." [32]

By the end of October, 1954, everyone was back in London. Everyone but David.

David was reluctant to return to London, where the unresolved dilemma of Ann Todd faced him. He eventually came back in November, and moved into the Kensington Palace Hotel. He made no attempt to contact Ann. But one night, when Ann was safely out at the theatre, he and Jack Hildyard let themselves in to Ilchester Place and removed his belongings.

After a triumphant first night as Lady Macbeth, friends pressed into Ann

Todd's dressing room to shower her with congratulations. One of them asked where David was.

"I hedged and said he was still in Venice putting the finishing touches to his film with Katie Hepburn. He would soon be home, I told them.

"The next morning one of those same friends rang me up and told me, gently, the truth. 'Ann, you must know. David has been back a month.' And I found he had been living in an hotel, down the road from our London house. You can imagine how I felt.

"There had been a letter. It came one morning from Venice, out of the blue, a letter stating that he felt he wasn't cut out for marriage, he must live alone. All day long I lay like a ghost, shivering. My housekeeper couldn't understand. She wanted to send for the doctor, but he couldn't have helped me.

"What made the shock much worse was that we hadn't parted with angry words, a terrible scene. If we had, I think I could have borne it more easily. But in front of me I kept on seeing his smiling face as I had kissed him good-bye at the aerodrome to make his film. What had happened? WHY, WHY, WHY? I kept torturing myself.

"I thought if we could just have a talk, it would be all right, but I have not seen him from that day to this." [33]

A fine-cut of the picture was shown to Ilya Lopert and his partner Robert Dowling, and a row erupted because Dowling objected to a line of dialogue. Rossano Brazzi says to Katharine Hepburn: "You are like a hungry child who is given ravioli to eat. 'No,' you say, 'I want beefsteak.' My dear girl, you are hungry... eat the ravioli."

When Dowling insisted that the dialogue was removed, David insisted that it remained.

"Mr Lean," said Dowling, "I don't care what you say, this is my film. It belongs to me. If you keep it in for England, I shall cut it out for the United States and elsewhere."

"David was thunderstruck," said Norman Spencer. "He could not accept what he saw as the childish American naiveté of Dowling over what to David was an inoffensive line with subtle sexual meaning. The dialogue encapsulated the whole relationship between Hepburn and Brazzi, and in any case had always been in the script.

"David could hardly believe that Dowling would override him and had the power and intention to do so. David had never experienced such blunt producer power. David never quite realised that his films didn't belong to him." [34]

Nineteen fifty-five began with David moving into a service flat at Marsham

Court, Westminster. He confided to Norman Spencer that he had begun an affair with Leila Matkar.

"He said, 'It's such a relief to meet the Indian women who are so passive - and that's their strength. You see, cerebral women like Ann tie you up in knots, but the emotion isn't there.'

"When eventually I met Leila, she was a sort of Eastern Ann Todd. She never stopped talking. I never quite understood what David meant by all that."[35]

David renewed his other family relations, seeing his mother and father, and his brother, who was annoyed that yet another of David's marriages had collapsed. But at least David and Edward were on speaking terms.

His son was now working as assistant manager at the Lion Hotel in Guildford, where he had met a girl called June Thorpe whose father was district engineer for the Rank Organisation. Nobody knew about the relationship until the Wednesday before what was intended to be a quiet wedding, when Peter finally broke the news to Isabel. According to June, she nearly had a nervous breakdown. They later became extremely close.

"My mother phoned Dad up at Shepperton," said Peter, "and the next thing I knew he was flying down."

With memories of his own first wedding he subjected Peter to an interrogation.

"Do you have to?"

"No."

"Well, what are you doing it for?"

But when David realised that Peter had fully made up his mind, he bought champagne and provided a proper wedding dress, even though June had not intended to be married in that style. He announced that the honeymoon was all arranged and presented Peter with tickets for a trip to to Paris. He even produced Peter's passport.

The wedding took place at Guildford Register Office on Friday, 4 February 1955. Isabel was there, but she and David stayed aloof from each other. After the wedding and the reception, Peter and June went back to work before travelling to London in the early hours.

"We flew to Paris on the Air France 'Epicurean' Viscount," said Peter. "Dad saw us off. He gave us one hundred pounds' worth of francs and said, 'Don't dare come back with a penny of it.' That was quite something for me. I was earning four pounds a week at the time. He gave us a list of night clubs drawn up by Pamela Mann - and we managed five in four nights."[36]

"They were very excited, as well they might be," wrote Pamela Mann in her diary. "June in grey suit and little white feather hat, carrying a set of cream and blue matching luggage David had given them for their honeymoon present."[37]

Peter left his job as assistant manager at the Lion when he and June became managers of a small hotel in Streatham. When June became pregnant, she declared that she would not bring up a child in the hotel business. She felt the unsocial hours would be a strain. Since Peter had always been interested in cars, and especially the Lotus, he went to work for Colin Chapman, the founder of the company.

"He expected blood, sweat and tears all at the same time," said Peter. "And he was a very bad payer. I worked for him for twenty-two years and as one of the married men on the staff I was kept on during the winter when the others were laid off. When I wanted to leave he was staggered. 'What do you want to leave for? You've got a super job here at ten pounds a week!'"

Peter then became store manager at various garages, then back to storeman, from which he retired in 1995.

"On occasions, years later," said Peter, "I wished I'd never given up working in films. You meet so many really charming people. Some are right devils. But most are absolutely wonderful." [38]

The collapse of his marriage was not the only thing to deter David from staying in England. The disapproval of his relatives, the difficulty of bringing Leila to London and mounting financial problems all conspired to turn him into an exile.

His colleagues all assumed he was leaving as a tax exile. In a sense, this was correct. Yet David did not leave England to avoid surtax, but for another tax-related reason.

"I had an accountant who was also Terry Rattigan's accountant, a nice man called Forsyth. I was called along to the Income Tax Office, which was way out in the Great West Road direction. Their head man was called Mr Skinner. I said, 'You're very Dickensian.' He didn't know what I meant and I explained. And they said, 'Now, we've got to ask you several questions.' I couldn't answer any questions. I didn't know anything about finance whatever. In the end they shut this cardboard folio and said they were satisfied with my own company, Cineguild, but said they were going to challenge certain expenses of [Ann Todd's] company, Glendorgal, through which she had operated for some time before I met her.

"It transpired what they were claiming was £20,000. Mr Forsyth, who had nothing to do with her company, went into one of those freeze-frames so beloved of TV commercials.

"Outside in the corridor he explained that a husband is responsible for his wife's debts, that this amount of money would bankrupt me for the foreseeable future and that the only course he could see open to me was to become a tax exile, sell my interest in SUMMERTIME and leave the country. Korda gave me the £20,000 for the rights, my wife started divorce proceedings a little while later and laid claim to the house I had bought in Ilchester Place. I was almost completely broke." [39]

David was given a farewell party after dubbing SUMMERTIME. Teddy Darvas, Norman Spencer, Peter Taylor and Jacqueline Thiédot - who had been hired in Venice and had overcome all the problems of recording live sound in such a noisy location - toasted his departure.

"I'm all right," David told them. "I've bought an Aston Martin."

He left behind the Rolls-Royce, the house in Ilchester Place, the paintings, antiques, and even his home movies. He said farewell to Peter and June over a lunch in London. Thirty years would pass before they would see him again.

In Paris, David saw Jacqueline Thiédot, who had just returned herself. "He was full of strength and hope, like a college boy," she said. "He told me, 'Life begins at forty-eight.'"[40]

From Paris, David took the Orient Express, retracing the opening of SUMMERTIME as it crossed the causeway at Venice. He, too, had his 16mm camera with him.

"As I went over that causeway I could almost hear the dialogue of the picture being played in my head. I got terribly excited. I stayed at the same hotel - all the old faces were very pleased to see me - and wandered round all the places where we'd shot the film."[41]

One of David's rare letters from this period was written to camera operator Peter Newbrook:

"I can't resist writing to you a line now - I meant to do so a long time ago - but now I am jolted into activity by all these old familiar surroundings and especially the *sounds*.

"There are only two orchestras playing at once in the San Marco, but the sun is brilliant and that wonderful light is everywhere. I have been round to nearly all our old haunts as if on a revisit to a dream. But it's all very real, and now it seems as if the making of the film was a dream. Anyway, it wasn't, and the other night I saw the first colour print projected here in a little private theatre used by the Festival committee.

"The Venetians who saw it (no one we know) say it is the first time they have seen *their* Venice on the screen, and were most enthusiastic. I always thought that if people could at least say that our film gave a real picture of a city, I would be very happy. I have *such* a lot to thank you for - above all else, your never flaging [sic] enthusiasm and keeness [sic], and the knowledge I had that you were always ready to have a go at anything, no matter how tired you were - even if it meant trudging around the streets looking for locations at the end of a hard day.

"Anyway, it is all over and you have your reward by having those two really wonderful sunset shots in the picture. I think the best of their kind I have ever seen.

"Next time we have a crack at India. I am so excited and hope we will be together on that."[42]

Venice hosted the world premiere of SUMMERTIME on 29 May 1955. One hundred newspapermen were brought to Venice by Ilya Lopert from all over Europe and even from the United States. *Variety* estimated the cost of this at $36,000 and said that the City of Venice paid for most of it. Even though neither David nor Katharine Hepburn - who was with the Old Vic company in Australia - were present, Isa Miranda and Rossano Brazzi were in attendance, together with such stars as Gloria Swanson, Sylvana Pampanini and Joan Greenwood.

Six hundred people were ferried by gondola and jammed into the four hundred and fifty-two seat Palazzo Grassi. A girl who was voted 'Miss Summertime' either fell, or was pushed, into the Grand Canal, but since the photographic lights had been switched off, her effort was in vain.

"I first saw SUMMER MADNESS, a wonderful Venetian love story, under perfect conditions, i.e. in Venice," wrote the *Daily Herald* critic. "I went by gondola to see it presented in a seventeenth-century palace open to the velvet Venetian night. This week I wondered whether, seeing it in an ordinary cinema on an ordinary autumn day in London, I would still be enchanted. The magic remains."[43]

C.A. Lejeune thought it a combination of BRIEF ENCOUNTER and THREE COINS IN THE FOUNTAIN. "This dubiously moral heroine is brought to glowing life by Katharine Hepburn, whose wide awake face and probing fingers give the effect of receiving and storing up memories more delicately than I have seen the trick done since Garbo did it in the bedroom scene of QUEEN CHRISTINA."[44]

"Essentially," wrote Dilys Powell, "the film is a bit of autumn crocus-pocus. But it has two assets. It has Katharine Hepburn; and it has Venice.

"With love, with passion, Mr Lean and his director of photography Jack Hildyard have observed the great square of St Mark and the small canals with their face of exquisite corruption; the splendid panorama of the Grand Canal, the houses rising like cliffs over the narrow cracks of water, the gilded figures striking the hours. The eye is endlessly ravished.

"Yet without Katharine Hepburn we should, I fancy, have been left watching a novelette within a documentary. Miss Hepburn adds human distinction to the scene, and she adds it not only by the nervous vitality of her playing, but by her own physical beauty. Throughout the film she insists that she is old and faded, and all the time we look at a woman with an austerity of profile, an elongated, wiry elegance of body which will make her worth looking at if she lives to be a hundred."[45]

"I didn't like it at all," said Arthur Laurents. "They jettisoned most of the play. It was an homage to Kate Hepburn who shed more water than there is in Venice. I did write a screenplay. She came in and ran the show. I met with David Lean a lot. I thought he was very upset because of his wife Ann, whom he'd left, and I thought he was mad for Kate. I found him a cold fish. We talked about the screenplay, and I came back to be told by a minion that it was over. I didn't even see him again. Talent is no excuse for bad behaviour. I knew Kate. When it was all over she told me, 'You won't like it. But I'm brilliant.'

"They just did the first act. I liked the photography - it was a beautiful travelogue of Venice. They made love to fireworks. She loses her virginity on the Fourth of July. I call it The Virgin Strikes Back."[46]

"I was told that any time David went to Venice," said Teddy Darvas, "and on to the Piazza San Marco, the bands on both sides immediately struck up the theme of SUMMERTIME."[47]

"It had an enormous effect on tourism," said David. "I remember the head of a hotel chain coming up to me and saying, 'We ought to put a monument up to you.'

"It was a huge thrill making that film. I lived in the Grand Hotel. Chaplin used to come there and I got to know him quite well.

"I remember getting up in the morning, going downstairs and there was a motorboat waiting for me. I'd go off in the motorboat to wherever the location was - really high glamorous stuff. And I just loved it. And I somehow managed to capture a certain essence of Venice. I don't know how, but I did, because it's been remarked upon so many times.

"I thought I might continue with largely exterior pictures. I said to Alex Korda once, 'Why don't you direct another picture?'

"And he said, 'I don't want to go into the studio again. It's like going down the mine.'

"He was quite right. Those huge doors come down and you are in a pitch black mine. I prefer the sun."[48]

CHAPTER TWENTY-FIVE

THE WIND CANNOT READ

Though on the sign it is written
'Don't pluck these blossoms'
It is useless against the wind
Which cannot read

JAPANESE POEM

JUST as he searched in real life for the ideal love affair, David was always looking for the ideal love story. He was attracted to *The Wind Cannot Read*, a novel by Richard Mason. The love story was exceptional and it would take David back to India where he could resume his own love affair.[1] He also saw the project as an opportunity to show the world what the real India was like.

Mason's novel was the story of a young RAF pilot, Michael Quinn, who survives the retreat from Burma. So that he can interrogate Japanese prisoners, he is sent with other RAF men to a language school in Old Delhi. Their instructor, a Japanese academic, announces they are to have a new teacher who turns out to be a beautiful and desperately shy Japanese girl, Suzuki San, the daughter of an exiled democrat. Quinn falls in love with her and calls her Sabby. They have an idyllic affair and she agrees to become his wife. Knowing the authorities would forbid this, they marry in secret. Quinn is then posted back to Burma where he is captured by the Japanese. When he learns that Sabby has become seriously ill, he makes a daring escape and reaches the hospital just before Sabby, who has undergone brain surgery, dies.

David's handwritten notes about the novel, dated 15 March 1954, reveal him to be an avid fan of Richard Mason:

"Page 82. My God you're good. 'It was the first silence we had had without any embarrassment, and you can tell a lot by silences.' *Lovely* scene. Better put that into dialogue. It really is a cracking good scene... Like a Moslem, I go down on my knees to you, dear Richard. Am most touched."

David had given considerable thought to how the film might begin:

"Think we should have an opening with a certain amount of punch. Perhaps not so much punch, as a gripping quality. I wonder what it would be like if we started off in a jungle with a most exotic collection of flowers. After setting a lush atmosphere bring three haggard men out of the jungle into a parched landscape. They are in a kind of delirium. Almost dying of thirst. There is a clap of thunder which they mistake for gunfire. They throw themselves on the ground. They realise it is thunder and look up to see the clouds gathering. The monsoon breaks. Rain begins to fall. They stand with faces upturned to the sky as the drops of water fall on their faces, but a harsh wind blows dust, leaves and earth on their faces. They try to struggle on but collapse in the now quickly forming puddles. They are unable to drink because they are unconscious. They don't realise they have reached the Frontier to India. Figures start running towards them as the wind and rain increases. The camera goes to the blossoms and the notice board. The titles appear. Superimposed under them we see the men lifted on to stretchers. Wrapped in blankets. Put on a train and gradually transformed into an atmosphere of peace. The rain stops. The titles finish. A wonderful view of the Himalayas. Pine forests, and streams of clear water. A balcony of a hotel and our characters stretched out in the sun sipping drinks. We must try and put over an atmosphere of complete peace."

Alexander Korda approved the story and sent David as his representative at the South East Asia Film Festival in Singapore. David would continue to Hong Kong to meet Mason, then to Japan and then to India to work on the script.

David found the trip so exciting that, for the first time in his life, he dictated a twenty-four page letter, via Dictaphone, which he sent to Pamela Mann who distributed copies to his family and colleagues.[2] This was particularly significant, because he found writing such a slow and difficult process. Yet when he did write, more often than not his letters were long. He used the old quote, "Forgive such a long letter, I did not have time to compose a short one."

David described in vivid detail the sea-voyage on the Greek ship, *The Agamemnon*, and the mosquitoes, cockroaches and a huge mouse (mice terrified him) in his hotel at Port Said. He was dismayed by the petty thievery of many Egyptians though the Arab race in general he thought "very fine."

On board ship he had an encounter with an attractive red-head called Mrs Leslie, which conjures up images from Somerset Maugham. She had enlisted David's help in Aden where she wanted to buy a 16mm camera. "Do tell me," she asked, "What are you doing on this ship? People like you don't go on ships." David replied, "But I like ships. My father used to take me on them when I was a small boy." Mrs Leslie did not believe him and was convinced that he was planning a film and was carefully studying the passengers. In her case, she was probably right.

In Bombay he was met by Fred Simmins, Korda's representative. The heat was so oppressive, David had his hair cropped. At the airport he was startled to find a British film crew, headed by cameraman Gordon Dines, who had shot NICHOLAS NICKLEBY, THE BLUE LAMP and THE CRUEL SEA for Ealing.

David's Qantas flight to Singapore stopped in Colombo, Ceylon, which would shortly be his base for THE BRIDGE ON THE RIVER KWAI. "It really does look fantastic coming down over that blue-green sea, with palm trees stretching along a sandy beach as far as one can see. They put us all in a charabanc and drove us to the Mount Lavinia Hotel which is the most glorious hotel on the sea front. I could stay there for days." (He eventually stayed for months.)

In Singapore, David had a dinner jacket made of sharkskin by Chinese tailors in twenty-four hours flat. "I must tell you they are as good as a London cut. Absolutely amazing."

David missed all the films at the festival except a Japanese-Italian version of MADAME BUTTERFLY. The ceaseless parties bored him, until he spotted a Japanese girl who seemed exactly right for the film. His attempts at conversation were greeted by giggles and shyness.

"Imagine my astonishment when a few days later the Best Actress for the whole festival was announced and this girl walked up and got the prize." This made David even more determined to engage her for the film, though she did not speak English and the Japanese delegation was kept rather segregated due to the feelings against them in Singapore as a result of the war.

"That was the most interesting thing as far as I was concerned," wrote David. But this was not true. He later told me about a far more important event.

"At the festival I met a young woman. We knew we'd never meet again and we had the most heavenly three weeks. She was Chinese, tall and very good-looking. We lived together at a place called the Seaview Hotel. I've never forgotten that because she was supposed to be untouchable, as it were. I remember various English film people who were having a great laugh at me, saying, 'You know, we're laughing, but we're terribly envious.' She saw me off with tears streaming down my face. I couldn't stop crying, knowing I'd never meet her again. I don't know whether there was a husband, lover or what. I really can't tell you about it. How does one describe a love affair?"[3]

In Hong Kong, Richard Mason was finishing another novel called *The World of Susie Wong.* Mason suggested that David stay at the same hotel. "I went out there and it was called the Luk Kwok Hotel and it turned out to be near as dammit a brothel. I stayed three weeks. I didn't touch any of the girls. Richard knew all the girls there and he was very occupied with Susie, who was called Susie, although not Wong."

Mason knew the local police who arranged a raid on an opium den for him. David went along as well.

"This absolutely thrilled me to bits because it [was] just like the films. As soon as we got to the first location, a timber yard, a Chinese was arrested. He was a 'watcher.' The opium traders pay these watchers a small salary simply to watch out for the police.

"As soon as this man was arrested, the police started to run through a sort of muddy yard and then climbed over a fence and before I could say 'knife' police were running over roofs of a kind of bungalow town - absolutely poverty-stricken place - and pulling open one of the roofs - they just pulled it off with their hands. At that moment three men carrying opium pipes dashed out of another roof and ran away.

"The police dived through the roof and we gingerly followed. There was a small room and a double decked line of beds. On the beds were lying seven men. All had opium pipes and hadn't been smoking long because they were not all stupefied. The police collected all the pipes. The men were all very calm and smiling, the police started to smile (the Chinese have a great sense of humour) and it was all looked upon as a great joke, and they were arrested. It was a joke until I suddenly saw a policeman bring out a long cord, and instead of handcuffs these seven Chinese were roped together. We went out into the street again where a huge gathering of people had collected.

"All the men were marched into a Black Maria and off we went. The whole thing was exactly like a movie and the police, trained by the English, were behaving in a way that English policemen would behave. There was no rough stuff. It was all done with the most frightfully good manners."

David and Richard Mason left together for Tokyo. "Now," wrote David, "I am no good at packing and since Richard knew all these girls, four or five of them packed my two suitcases. They were all Chinese and all charming. They were absolutely sweet, not the sort of tarts you would imagine from the English point of view. They were gentle, kind and not at all tough. Scrupulously clean and all the rest of it.

"I must say I can understand the Americans going out to these places and marrying these girls and bringing them back to America. It makes absolute sense."[4]

David and Mason took a DC6 to Japan and were greeted at Tokyo airport by a battery of press photographers. David wondered if there was a famous general on board. But the cameramen were for David and Mason and they posed and waved self-consciously on the gangway until two Japanese film stars presented them with bouquets of flowers.

Mason, of course, preferred a traditional rather than a western-style hotel. David was attended by six Japanese maids, kneeling and bowing and discreetly undressing him when he requested a bath. At last he had discovered a country which outshone even Switzerland for spotlessness.

"The Japanese woman," he wrote, "is brought up to look after men. And this is a man's country. I'm like a Pasha. I just lie back and everything is done for me."

Their contact in Tokyo was Nagasama Kawakita, a leading distributor, who showed them the sights and overwhelmed them both by his kindness. He also persuaded them to move to the Imperial Hotel and here David had a shock. The hotel was American (it was designed by Frank Lloyd Wright) and David began to realise the extent to which Japan had been "westernised." He discovered that the Japanese people had a deep inferiority complex:

"They think they are vastly inferior to Europeans," he wrote. "They were astounded by the success of RASHOMON when it came to London and the producer, in fact, didn't want to send it because he was ashamed of it. Then it started to win awards and of course they now accept it for what it is."

David's purpose for visiting Toyko was to find his leading actress for THE WIND CANNOT READ. He asked to see the film which won the Best Actress prize in Singapore. It was called THE REFUGE.

"Before it was over, I was absolutely sold on her. She's a wonderful actress and for a girl of twenty-two - that's all she is - quite, quite remarkable."

Most of Japan agreed with David because she was the biggest box-office draw in the country. In fact, she was so popular that she and two other actresses had formed themselves into the Carrot Club (named after the runaway in Duvivier's POIL DE CAROTTE) and had escaped the big film companies and their onerous contracts.

"I was amused by this, and also very relieved," wrote David, "because I thought it would give me a chance to get her, for having seen her film I was absolutely set on her."

The name of the actress was Kishi Keiko. David and Mason met her at a restaurant and discovered that she spoke only a few words of English. David gave her a Japanese edition of Mason's novel.

A few days later, Kishi Keiko asked to meet David and Mason again. The novel excited her - "that is," wrote David, "as far as a Japanese can become excited. It's bad manners to become too excited. But I could see it in her eyes. She said, 'I love Sabby. I cry.'" David began to realise that she could speak more English than she had let on.

"I am absolutely astounded by this actress," wrote David. "Here she is, a famous Japanese film star, and when one goes out into the street, people stop and stare, and as big crowds collect as collected in Venice with Katharine Hepburn. And yet she is nothing like any film star I have met in my life. She is like a very simple, very shy young girl of twenty-two. She has no side, no airs and graces and does not behave like a sophisticated actress in the least."

Kishi Keiko liked the novel so much she said she would do the film for nothing. David and Mason were invited to meet her parents and to stay the night, an unusual honour. Keiko's mother had made kimonos for them and installed a new sofa and armchairs in case they should tire of sitting on the floor. There was a meal of an infinite number of courses and even knives and forks had been thoughtfully provided.

Kishi Keiko in London to take the lead in THE WIND CANNOT READ.

David and Mason were stupefied by the hospitality. "It was one of the happiest times Richard and I have spent in our whole lives - we were *deeply* touched," wrote David.

Returning to the Imperial Hotel, the two men went straight to a press conference and announced that Kishi Keiko had been chosen to star in THE WIND CANNOT READ. She would be taught English in London by the girl who had taught Mason to speak Japanese.

The film would be made in CinemaScope.[5] Since David had never worked with this widescreen process, he decided to teach himself by making two short documentaries - one on the island of Bali in Indonesia and the second in Bangkok. Mason agreed to go with him.

An Arriflex camera with a CinemaScope lens was shipped over from London. However, David had to do without a CinemaScope viewfinder - when he looked through the Arriflex, the image he saw was "squeezed" into the normal ratio: i.e., people and objects were distorted and made taller and thinner. David edited the film on a standard 35mm Moviola and quickly realised that if a cut looked good squeezed, it looked equally good when projected with a

CinemaScope lens on to a wide screen. He described his work as "touristy". But it served his purpose.

David had insisted to Harold Boxall, who ran British Lion, that Pamela Mann should be sent out First Class on the *Stratheden*. This compensated a little for the fact that she was grossly underpaid and exploited - "I had to live with mum and dad and they thought it was wonderful I was working for David Lean, so they never complained."[6]

Pamela Mann stayed for two weeks with David and Mason in Bombay, where it rained ceaselessly. "It was with some relief that we set off for New Delhi," she wrote in a letter to her parents, "a drive of some thousand miles ahead of us in David Lean's brand new Aston Martin car.[7] We had been warned that the roads were terrible, that we might be held up by floods, bandits operated at night, and that the hotels were anything but luxurious. But the three of us set off in high spirits.

"We drove through hundreds of villages - some of them with mud huts and thatched roofs, others nearer the towns, made of petrol tins and bits of board. A picture of misery and poverty such as I have never seen. And yet amongst all this dreary, muddy brown, one could pick out the bright colours of the women's saris: shocking pink, bright emerald green, scarlet, brilliant yellow, orange... They really look wonderful."[8]

When they reached Indore, David was reunited with Leila. "I remember Richard and I kicking our heels around Indore Lake while David was closeted with Leila," recalled Pamela Mann. "By that time, Leila had had a nervous breakdown and was having shock therapy."[9]

Leila had experienced this before. It was something David hoped their life together might cure, so her sudden return to mental illness was a bitter blow.

They drove on, the rivers were swollen, the roads deteriorated and so did the mood inside the sports car. "David and Richard began bickering because this Aston Martin, a big powerful thing, had only two seats," wrote Pamela Mann. "The back seat was what they called 'an occasional three or four' which meant it had two tiny seats and you had to sit sideways. Most of the time I was in the back but occasionally David would say, 'Richard, I do think you ought to give Pam a turn at the front.' Richard didn't like that. On one occasion, David ran into a flock of parakeets - bright green birds with red beaks - and Richard accused him of doing it on purpose."[10]

They reached Agra, where David showed his companions the Taj Mahal, which would feature in the film, and then set off for Delhi. By now, the Aston Martin was behaving badly. David discovered that from Gwalior the petrol was adulterated with so-called 'power-fuel,' a by-product of molasses. But they limped into India's capital city and separated to stay at three hotels - Pamela

Mann at the Maidens, David at the Swiss and Mason at the Cecil. "Richard was shacked up with a Sikh girl," said Pamela Mann, "He used to leave notes saying, 'I'm playing hide and sikh tonight.'" [11]

They had been in Delhi some weeks when Leila arrived and, for reasons of propriety, she stayed in yet another hotel. Norman Spencer arrived on 2 September 1955.

"When I got to Delhi," said Spencer, "David was droopy and miserable. He would complain a lot about his life, his income tax problems and how broke he was. It was probably the heat. I remember one breakfast when Richard Mason said, 'David, you make me sick. You're a famous film director, you've got all the money you want, and you do nothing but moan, moan, moan from morning to night.' A terrible stand-up row ensued." [12]

Tension between David and Mason had been growing for some time. Mason had told David that he was going to dedicate *The World of Susie Wong* to him but after one of their arguments he said he had changed his mind.

A decision was made to split the group. While Mason and Pamela Mann remained in Delhi to work on the script, David went off with Leila and Spencer to scout locations. This time, Leila and Spencer took turns to sit in the painful rear seat of the Aston Martin.

As sections of the script were completed, they were sent to Korda in London. Korda was currently in dispute with the technicians' union, the ACT, which had objected to the fact that his last production, SMILEY, was filmed entirely in Australia. The union, fearing their members were losing work, announced that Technicolor laboratories or British Lion studios would not do any post-production work on SMILEY until Korda agreed to shoot studio interiors of THE WIND CANNOT READ in England.

Korda sent a cable to David: "MOST AWFULLY SORRY BUT CONVINCED SCRIPT IN PRESENT FORM NOT GOOD ENOUGH FOR STARTING WORK STOP MY CRITICISM FAR TOO BASIC TO BE ABLE TO DISCUSS BY CORRESPONDENCE STOP IMPORTANT YOU COME DIRECT TO PARIS STOP" [13]

Close behind came another cable, assuring David that this was only Korda's private opinion: "PLEASE DISREGARD UNTIL BRITISH LION POINT OF VIEW RECEIVED TOMORROW."

Norman Spencer, who had returned to London, cabled David the next day to explain that Korda felt the script had failed to capture the spirit of the book. Spencer had argued with Korda for hours over this but had to agree that there were some weaknesses.

David and Leila were in Srinagar, Kashmir, when British Lion's opinion came. While they were more enthusiastic than Korda, they wanted changes made to save money. David was urged again to come to Paris.

David was astounded by the reaction to the script and felt that Korda must have read an earlier draft... "WHICH HAS DISTASTEFUL SECOND HALF SOLO RICHARD EFFORT STOP MY FINAL VERSION ONLY POSTED SIXTEENTH AND TAKING NO ACTION UNTIL CONFIRMED."

Spencer cabled back so say that Korda had reached his conclusion after the first seventy pages and was talking of abandoning David's script and starting again. In his reply, David said he was "BLOODY BUT UNBOWED STILL THINK BEST SCRIPT HAVE HAD STOP" He was going to fight the "old bull".[14]

When Korda had read David's open letter with its enthusiastic description of Japan, he said to Norman Spencer, "David is a man with no fundamental erudition but with a great intellectual curiosity. He has discovered Japan and wants the world to know what it's like, totally ignorant of the fact that the world knows already."[15]

Korda felt David had now fallen in love with India and had produced a script that was too sweet and loving of its background. He pronounced it sentimental bosh.

"Also," said Spencer, "it irritated Korda that after weeks and weeks of expenses-paid foreign living, a talented man like David should succumb so naively to the charms of a country to the extent that it overrode his creative vision which Korda felt should have been more astringent, aware of the bland trap into which he was falling.

"In my heart of hearts, I knew it just wasn't good. I thought, still think, and events have borne it out, that Korda was right. He saw in the cold light of London what David, bemused by India, couldn't see."[16]

Korda had decided to withdraw from the project when David was ordered to return from India. He said to Pamela Mann, "I'll be back to make the film." Pamela had been left alone at the Maidens Hotel, somewhat forgotten during all the arguments over the script, and had become nearly suicidal with boredom.

In Paris, David had to face the fact that he would not make the film. "David had a great shock," said Spencer, "It really shook his ego. For a week he couldn't get over it."[17]

David had wanted Kenneth More to play the hero, Quinn, and here he met with a knockout punch from Korda. "Alex said, 'I'll tell you something, David. You're not going to have Kenneth More. I'll tell him not to do it and he won't do it if I tell him not to.' It was all very strange. A few weeks later, Vincent came to me and said, 'You must forgive Alex. He's not well, he can be very unkind, I don't think he means it.'

"I don't know what Vincent knew. I don't know what Alex told him. He *was* terribly ill and he *was* very eccentric at the time. He died within a couple of months."[18]

Pamela Mann was in Delhi when news reached her of Korda's death. She remembered David saying, "The top of the mountain has gone."[19]

On 11 January 1956, Kishi Keiko arrived in London, chaperoned by Mrs Kawakita.

"We found a finishing school in Leicester," said Spencer. "It was run by a genteel, rather snobbish lady who specialised in teaching elocution, good manners and deportment and who lived with her brother in a large house. I visited Kishi Keiko several times. She was the only pupil and learned English quite fast. She stayed for about three weeks but of course it came to nothing and she went back to Japan."[20]

David said he decided against making THE WIND CANNOT READ

The final version starred Dirk Bogarde and Yoko Tani, and was directed by Ralph Thomas for producer Betty Box in 1958. It used the script written by David and Richard Mason and some of the locations chosen for David's film.

because he respected Korda so much and valued his opinion. But the project withered for another reason. The dates tell their own story:

23 January 1956	Korda dies.
1 February 1956	David and Spencer meet Sam Spiegel to discuss THE BRIDGE ON THE RIVER KWAI.
4 February 1956	David receives a letter from George Archibald of Rank, turning down THE WIND CANNOT READ.
7 February 1956	Spiegel urges David to sign contract for KWAI.
23 February 1956	Kishi Keiko leaves London, "bitterly disappointed at the turn of events," according to Spencer.

When Alexander Korda died, the script for THE WIND CANNOT READ, along with many others, was sold to Rank. The producer, Betty Box, acquired it and gave it to her partner, Ralph Thomas, to direct. He was an old friend of David's and had been one of his editing assistants. When he ran the trailer department at Rank, he produced the trailers for the Dickens films.

"David told me he thought it was a great love story," said Thomas. "I told him

I didn't think it was. I thought it was a magazine story. I didn't fiddle with his script - there were no substantial changes. David was working in Ceylon and I spent a week there talking with him about it." [21]

"When the new version was announced," said Pamela Mann, "I wrote to Betty Box and gave her a list of contacts. She wrote to me asking if I would like to do the picture as location secretary, which I did. The girl who played the lead, Yoko Tani, was so coarse-looking compared with Kishi Keiko." [22]

The film, released in June 1958, starred Dirk Bogarde and was made in many of the locations which David had selected. Despite Korda's disdain, it was a commercial success. Although Rank used David's name on their publicity - "Adapted by the author and David Lean" - the screen credit was for Richard Mason only.

"David saw the final film," said Ralph Thomas, "and said he'd like a share of the profits, please. I always felt that David fell in love with THE WIND CANNOT READ because of meeting Leila." [23]

PART TWO

THE POET OF THE FAR HORIZON

"Before he did it, sir, I'd have said it couldn't be done."

MR DRYDEN TO GENERAL ALLENBY IN
LAWRENCE OF ARABIA

CHAPTER TWENTY-SIX

ENTER SAM SPIEGEL

THE BRIDGE ON THE RIVER KWAI I

SAM Spiegel was announced. He entered the room, wreathed in smiles, and threw his arms around Orson Welles and kissed him. I wished I'd brought my camera. But this was the fiftieth anniversary of the British Film Institute, an event held at the Guildhall, and cameras would have been infra dig.

Spiegel, choking with emotion, said, "This is a fantastic moment for me." He must have been as shaken as the rest of us by Welles's size - he was then around twenty-eight stone - but he murmured, "God, Orson, you look wonderful. You never grow old."

"My God," said Welles. "I am Methuselah."

Spiegel dashed out. "Where'd he go to?" asked Welles. I told him I thought he had gone to fetch someone, and indeed he returned with actress Patricia Hodge. As Welles kissed her hand, Spiegel said proudly, "This is the leading lady of the picture I've just finished [BETRAYAL]. You must see it - she's great."

When Spiegel had gone and a suitable pause had elapsed, Welles said, "I have many great Sam stories, but the one I remember best was when he offered me the lead in BRIDGE ON THE RIVER KWAI. I said, 'Fine. I'll do it if I can direct.' He agreed. When I read the script I said, 'I don't think this part is right for me, but I'll still be glad to direct it."

Welles said he was at Cannes, at the Carlton Hotel with Darryl Zanuck, and Spiegel was also there. Welles opened *Variety* and read that Spiegel had given the film to David Lean. He showed the piece to Zanuck, who walked over to Spiegel and poured a jug of iced water over his head.

"Sam wasn't expecting it, of course, so he sat there, like living sculpture, as water poured over him. The upshot of all this was that Sam hasn't spoken to me until tonight. But he called Zanuck round to discuss a deal the following morning."[1]

Magnificent raconteur though he was, Orson Welles was no more to be trusted with a tale like this than Spiegel himself. I have not found a solitary witness to corroborate this event: Cannes was held at the end of April 1956, and *Variety* had announced as early as 8 February that Spiegel had signed David to direct the film in Malaya for Columbia release. During Cannes, *Variety* announced only that Charles Laughton was returning to the screen to star in the picture.[2]

In 1956, David was a leading director in English eyes only; internationally he was a minor player. Under normal circumstances, he would not have been offered such a prestigious subject as KWAI, not when men like John Ford, Howard Hawks or William Wyler were available. But Spiegel had spent a year looking for a director, and he felt that Hawks and Ford[3] had completely misunderstood the novel. Fred Zinnemann turned it down and, much to Spiegel's dismay, so did Alec Guinness. What drew him to David was the fact that he was enthusiastic from the moment he read it. Although when he was asked, years later, why he chose David, Spiegel replied, bluntly, "Absence of anybody else."[4]

One of the films David most admired was Jean Renoir's 1937 classic, LA GRANDE ILLUSION, a study of the relationship between the German commandant of a PoW camp and his French officer-captives during World War One. Whilst KWAI provided little opportunity for the profound humanity of the Renoir film, it was a subject David felt drawn to, despite his lack of military experience.

Pierre Boulle's[5] satirical novel *Le Pont de la Rivière Kwai* was published in Britain in 1954, two years after its original publication in France. Although written by a Frenchman, it had been translated by an Englishman, Xan Fielding,[6] and was a British story, set in a Japanese prisoner-of-war camp deep in the jungle.

Colonel Nicholson, described by Boulle as the perfect example of the military snob, regards any plan of escape as an act of disobedience from the moment the Commander-in-Chief had signed the surrender. He is therefore perfectly willing to help the Japanese build a railway bridge to further their war effort and endures torture to uphold the rule that officers do not work alongside the men. Under Colonel Saito's command, the building of the bridge progresses so badly that he has no alternative but to give in to Nicholson's demands and allow the British to build it themselves. Nicholson does the job with such ruthless skill - enlisting hospital cases and even persuading the officers to work alongside men - that the bridge is completed on schedule. Then commandos are despatched from Allied headquarters to destroy it.

Carl Foreman, who had written HIGH NOON for Fred Zinnemann, had been blacklisted by the Communist witch-hunts and had come to live in England where he read scripts for Alexander Korda's London Films. He optioned Boulle's novel and Zoltan Korda thought he might direct it. Alexander Korda, too busy to read it, was eventually persuaded to do so by his wife. He called a meeting and told Foreman and Zoltan they were insane. Colonel Nicholson was either a lunatic or a traitor, and the portrayal of British PoWs helping their enemies was a thoroughly anti-British idea.[7]

After Foreman formed a partnership with Spiegel, Zoltan Korda left the project. Alexander Korda sold the rights to Spiegel, retaining a ten percent interest. He later sold this percentage for "something like £10,000"[8] and Spiegel and Foreman settled down to write the script.

One of their first dilemmas was whether to blow up the bridge, as all the rules of cinema demanded, or to remain faithful to the novel and leave it standing. Boulle came to London and told them that he had wanted to destroy the bridge but couldn't work out how. "If you can do it, God bless you," he said.[9]

"While I was doing SUMMERTIME," said David, "I got a cable from Sam Spiegel, whom I hardly knew - I think I had met him once - asking if I would direct the film. So I went to Kate Hepburn, who had worked with him on AFRICAN QUEEN, and who had terrible quarrels with him, and I said, 'Look, Kate, what shall I do?'

"And she said, 'Take it. You'll learn a lot from him. And he'll learn a lot from you.' And that proved absolutely true. We both learned a lot from each other.

"Pierre Boulle's book was wonderfully funny but as far as movies are concerned he went too far. Boulle was having a great joke against the British when he wrote it. It was just not believable when Clipton comes up and says to the colonel, 'I suppose you're going to have the thing painted, sir?' 'Don't even think of such a thing, Clipton,' said the Colonel, testily. 'The most we could do would be to give it a coating of lime - and a fine target that would make for the RAF, wouldn't it! You seem to forget there's a war on.'[10]

"I thought that was going too far. I went over to Sam Spiegel and said, 'If I can tone it down, if I can do it like the book but take the excesses out, I'll do it.'"[11]

Sam Spiegel! What an operator! Another "frightful old pirate" and, perhaps, the last authentic movie tycoon.

He was born around 1901 in Galicia, that part of Poland ruled by Austro-Hungary, and he was a Jew who rebelled against his Jewish background. Had he been born a few years earlier, he might have joined the migration west and ended up as a Hollywood mogul, for he looked the part - heavily built, with the face of a bad-tempered boxer. But he went to Palestine after World War One and then travelled widely as a stock promoter and cotton broker, and became something of a linguist. He did not reach America until 1927.

Universal Pictures eventually sent him to Berlin, where he became their general manager at the time of ALL QUIET ON THE WESTERN FRONT. Shortly after this great pacifist film opened in 1930, the Nazis released stink bombs and white mice in the cinema and shouted, "*Judenfilm!*" (Jewish film!) in the hope of having it suppressed.[12]

The disturbances brought about the desired result - a ban, which Spiegel fought, using somewhat unscrupulous means. The ban was eventually lifted in 1931 and Spiegel's proudest moment was when he presented the film at the

League of Nations.

When the Nazis came to power in 1933, Spiegel became one of the many émigré producers struggling to survive in England. He helped finance a disastrous comedy, AN OLD SPANISH CUSTOM, with Buster Keaton, which resulted in a flurry of dud cheques and a short prison sentence before he was deported. In Hollywood, as an illegal alien, calling himself S.P. Eagle, he had such a rough time that it is to his credit that he managed to produce anything at all.

In 1951, he formed Horizon Pictures with John Huston and produced the hugely successful THE AFRICAN QUEEN, filmed on location in the Belgian Congo, with Katharine Hepburn and Humphrey Bogart. He reverted to his real name for ON THE WATERFRONT, which earned him his first Oscar.

Although Spiegel made his films with Hollywood backing, he was based in London. He arranged a meeting with David and Norman Spencer in his flat in Grosvenor Square.

"Spiegel greeted us," said Spencer, "and offered us each a huge cigar which neither of us took, and he said, 'I've got this marvellous script by Carl Foreman - it's out of this world. David, I'd like you to come to New York. Carl is there and you'll want to work on it and go through it.'"[13]

David was dazzled by Spiegel (the name in German means mirror). "Sam was a tremendous charmer," he said. "He was very bright, a huge personality, and very keen on films. I was thoroughly seduced by the man."[14]

David, who had very little money at this time, needed a project and Spiegel seemed to have the right connections. As luck would have it, David had been chosen by the New York critics as best director of the year - for SUMMERTIME - and United Artists gave him an air ticket to go and collect the award in person.[15] He arranged to meet Spiegel and Foreman as soon as he arrived.

"Spiegel was too crafty to give David the script at our first meeting," said Spencer. "He held out this promise of a 'magnificent script' as a carrot to keep him intrigued, meanwhile creating time for any revisions that Foreman might want to make. In matters like ensnaring people and getting his own way, Spiegel never hurried."[16]

When David saw the script, he thought it was appalling. Foreman's original script has been missing for years - David threw his copy away - but a copy has been located by the Canadian researcher, Ron Paquet, who has organised a David Lean archive.

This script, which was never credited to Foreman, but bore the name of Pierre Boulle, opens in the Malayan jungle with a sequence of a train racing towards a tunnel as two commandos, Shears and Warden, try to set their explosives. They destroy the train, but are nearly caught by a Japanese convoy. We next meet them aboard a British submarine, where all the officers are bearded and wear sarongs. The following dialogue ensues:

SKIPPER

This is where you'll bunk. We've got some cots for you. Hope you won't feel too crowded.

SHEARS

(surveying the assorted beards)

No, it's cozy. Don't change a thing. I've only got one question. We lost our razors - what's your excuse?

(the boys laugh, delighted)

WARDEN

Yes, I should think if you chaps shaved now and then, there'd be more room in these submarines.

As the submarine is depth-charged, the script flashes back to the PoW camp. We cut to pile-drivers in action at the construction site, and Clipton, the camp doctor, being given permission by the Japanese to release Nicholson from solitary confinement. Later, Shears attacks the bridge in company with a commando troop and some female Siamese bearers, including a strapping woman referred to as the Amazon, whose broad comedy was at odds with David's idea of the way Oriental women should behave.

The script includes a great deal of the confrontation between Saito and Nicholson, but its arrival so late in the drama astonished David. He had only read the first forty-six pages of the script when he wrote a memo to Spiegel:

"I am attracted by this subject because I like the method the author has used of telling the story. He has somehow contrived to give the whole thing an epic quality. It has real size and style. In a curious way, it reminds me of a Shakespearean drama. One feels almost at once that the stage is set for a tremendous clash of wills, and that the situation can only be resolved by a mighty climax in which some of the leading characters are bound to die. The author presents us with a situation; then brick by brick he develops it. It grows and grows like a sprouting seed, and it is the inevitability of this growth that fascinates me as a film-maker. The script has discarded practically all of this."

David had the impression that Foreman was out of sympathy with the book and merely wanted to use it as a basis for a melodrama.

"Quite frankly I am in a dilemma because if I had read the script only I would have said after the first thirty pages that the subject didn't interest me. I would have felt that it was an Eastern Western and that many Hollywood directors were more qualified for the job than me. However, you, Sam, talked about the whole project in a completely different way. The script is a contradiction to your expressed views. Hence my dilemma."

Colonel Nicholson, David felt, was a magnificent tragi-comic figure well out of the usual run of film characters. As a director, he had to make this extraordinary hero understandable to an audience.

"If they don't understand and admire him in spite of his misguided actions, his stature will diminish - and being the cornerstone of the film, the size of the film will diminish with him.

"Bringing the conflict with Colonel Nicholson and Saito so late into the film was like paying money for a boxing match and coming in at round ten. The characters were cardboard cut-outs: how could you admire the Colonel for standing up to Saito unless Saito was a formidable adversary? He behaves like a stock B-picture villain.

"Look at poor Shears and the embarrassing running gag with the unattractive Amazonian female. Last night I saw Jimmy Durante doing exactly the same on TV. It got howls of laughter. Poor Monsieur Boulle. If he were dead he would be revolving gently. All his fine writing has been vulgarised to a point I would have thought impossible."

David objected strongly to the commandos, who behaved like overgrown schoolboys. He had known quite a few men who had been on dangerous exploits during the war; they did not look upon their work as a patriotic lark.

"War is not fun except in bad films and bad books. I haven't yet met a man who wanted to come face to face with the enemy and 'wouldn't want to miss it.' These ideas are false. Not only will they be laughed at by the thousands of men who know better, but in my opinion these heroics are a positive disservice to youthful audiences who have no idea of war. War is the greatest plague on earth. I don't think this is a time to minimise its horror and film it in false colours. Those are my views as a private individual."

He objected to the almost insulting way the Americans are made to regard the British, and warned that while the British were able to laugh at Errol Flynn winning the war in Burma, this treatment would infuriate them. Perhaps, suggested David acidly, the scriptwriter was irresponsible or perhaps, like the Colonel, he didn't fully realise what he was doing.

"The subject is pretty tricky at the best of times. If it misses it will be a bad miss. To put it over, one has to have a real understanding of the British mentality or it will be offensive. Mr Foreman hasn't got the first glimmer and he is offensive. Monsieur Boulle, on the other hand, knows what he's talking about. We do have an inordinate respect for discipline and the team spirit. We make almost a fetish out of doing a job well. Sir Henry Royce once fired a mechanic whom he overheard saying, 'It's good enough.'

"We love the letter of the law. We are 'superior' and stubborn as mules. Boulle has taken all these characteristics, and with a great deal of warmth, admiration and understanding. He has shown these characteristics of the old school tie carried to tragic lengths.

"The story of the building of a bridge over the River Kwai is the story of a folly. It is a folly to which all of us might subscribe under the pressures, emotions and tempers of war. If we can show this minor incident as a miniature reproduction of the greater folly which is the War itself, we shall have a great film. That is why I want to treat Saito with dignity. I don't want to say that Saito is an uncivilised little Oriental. I want the Colonel to say it. I want the audience to see him as another human being not so unlike the Colonel. Boulle starts off his book with this statement. He shows all the characters as victims of a great joke, with Clipton as the only man with a suspicion of the truth. The script transforms this ironic piece of writing into an adventure story pure and simple. I have only just realised this fact as I write. I have been groping for this basic flaw for days. I have beaten around all the bushes, but have only now stumbled on the truth. I think it's a huge leap forward and I'm very excited. All sorts of things start sliding into position. I, too, had not fully appreciated the book. Now I think I will."[17]

What David could not understand was how Spiegel - a man who claimed to revere ALL QUIET ON THE WESTERN FRONT - could have permitted the script to degenerate so far. Spiegel thought he had made a brilliant partnership with Carl Foreman, and his confidence must have been severely shaken by David's impassioned response.

Norman Spencer was at home in Denham when a call came through from David.
"He said, 'Norman, could you come to New York?'
"I said, 'Yes, but why? How was the script?'
"He said, 'Fucking awful. Fucking terrible.' These were his exact words.
"'Have you told Sam?'
"'Yes.'
"'What did he say?'
"'He went white. I've told him that if he wants me to do the picture, the script must be thrown out of the window. You and I are going to sit down and open the book at page one and start again.'"

Spencer flew to New York on 15 February 1956 and, after a discussion with Spiegel, work began on the new script.

"When we came to the men marching into the camp," said Spencer, "I remember David saying, 'God, I wish we could have them singing. Can't we have "Colonel Bogey" with the soldiers' words "Bol-locks and the same to you?" I know, let's have them whistling it, at least the English audience will know what we're after.'"

Each day, Spiegel would ring Spencer to find out how they were getting on. Spencer said, "All this old-fashioned, heavy producer pressure. He was terrified to talk to David. David scared him. They were scared of each other in a funny way, so I was the intermediary."[18]

According to Carl Foreman, Spiegel told him that David liked the book but hated the script. Unwilling to see anything wrong with his script, he translated David's attitude as "the somewhat in-built antipathy to Americans that you find in some Britons."[19] But David liked Americans; he merely had an antipathy to this one.

As Spencer and David reached the end of the novel, they encountered the dilemma of the bridge. They felt no compunction about blowing it up - you could hardly cheat the audience of that. The question was how.

Said Norman Spencer: "We couldn't decide whether a mortar shot should wound Colonel Nicholson so that he fell on the plunger or whether he should suddenly realise the enormity of what he'd done and blow it up himself, or whether a shot should land on the control box, as if God blew it up. I think this controversy raged up to the day of shooting it."[20]

They finished their treatment on 30 March 1956.

"Spiegel had started to talk about casting," said Spencer. "We all had dinner one evening with Cary Grant. When we came out of the restaurant there was deep snow and I remember David and I playing snowballs after we had said goodnight to Spiegel and Cary Grant."

Cary Grant was considered for the part of Shears - he could have played it as an Englishman or as an American. For Warden, the commando leader, they had Jack Hawkins's agreement to play the part. For Colonel Nicholson, Spiegel had already tried Noël Coward (an idea which startled David), Laurence Olivier and Alec Guinness, who David thought would be wrong. When they had dinner with Katharine Hepburn and Spencer Tracy, David discovered that Spiegel had even offered the part to Tracy!

Norman Spencer's diary records a dinner and then a lunch with Charles Laughton, but Spencer insists Laughton was not a serious contender. "He was talked about for the part, but David said, 'It's ludicrous. Much as I'd like to have him - he's a marvellous actor - you can't have a fat man among all these half-starved people.'"[21] Yet David cherished the hope that Laughton might lose weight for the role.

Carl Foreman had made an American the leading character and Columbia were demanding a major star. But there was no American in Boulle's novel, and whilst the diktat thoroughly annoyed David he complied. He had the idea of placing an American in the camp at the start - as a gravedigger - and then having him escape, to be sent back with the commandos.

The presence of Americans among the prisoners was not entirely a Hollywood expedient. In his research, Foreman had discovered that Americans - usually naval personnel - were indeed among British prisoners of war. With Humphrey Bogart - Spiegel's choice - out of the running, and after David had interviewed Montgomery Clift, the search began for a major American star. And for an actor to play Colonel Nicholson.

In April, David and his agent, Christopher Mann, flew to the tax haven of Bermuda to sign the contract. Spiegel was accompanied by his lawyer, Irwin Margulies, and Sam Rheiner, his New York office accountant and manager. The contract was signed just in time - on 4 April 1956 - one day before the end of the 1955/56 fiscal year.

"It was because of this close call that Chris Mann advised that Bermuda be chosen," said Norman Spencer. "The belt-and-braces safeguard against the Inland Revenue."[22]

The contract stipulated that David was to be paid $150,000 in instalments, less $2,000 for an unusual loan.[23] "I was absolutely broke," said David. "As soon as I signed, I borrowed two thousand dollars from Columbia to get my teeth fixed."[24]

They flew back to New York the next day. David had all his teeth out and returned to England with a set of first-class American teeth, of which he was inordinately proud. He stayed in England for only ten days. He would not return for almost two years.

Spiegel was always playing politics. He now started trying to winkle Norman Spencer away from David by offering him films to produce. Like Korda, he wanted to be David's sole producer. Spiegel also wanted to keep Carl Foreman on the project for despite David's opinion of his script, Foreman was, after all, the writer of HIGH NOON.

"Sam's velvet-covered octopus arms could bend you to his will very easily," said Norman Spencer, quoting a comment by Billy Wilder. "David did not have a very strong will and he found himself, whether he liked it or not, working with Carl Foreman."[25]

Spiegel suggested they next meet at the Hotel George V in Paris, when Foreman would again be with them. They all stayed there two weeks. Leila arrived and on 28 April, Cecil Ford, the production manager, came over from London together with cameraman Jack Hildyard, art director Don Ashton and Columbia's London representative, Bill Graf. It was decided that the film would be shot in CinemaScope, the new widescreen format which David liked very much after his tests with the process for THE WIND CANNOT READ.

Apart from production details, a great deal of time was spent on script conferences at which Spencer could sense Foreman becoming restive. David's dislike of the man was only too apparent, and he would gladly have been shot of him. But Foreman, anxious to become a producer, needed this project. The tension was all part of Spiegel's grand plan.

"The best scripts," he once said, "emerge out of the friction between the people who work on them. No picture is prepared properly without frantic discord between the writer, the producer and director, everyone wrestling with his own doubts."[26]

To add to the tension, both Spiegel and Foreman had an aversion to "Colonel Bogey" which they called a "limey song" and suggested that David's fondness for it showed just how parochial the British were. Spiegel informed David that the song could not be used because the copyright holders were asking a fortune for the rights. As an alternative, David suggested "Bless Em All", which he had already used in THE SOUND BARRIER.

"He was always very persuasive," said David. "I never suspected at the time that they possibly weren't asking a fortune. He'd always say, 'Look, please, baby, think of an alternative. We're not going to be strung up by these crooks.' And could I earnestly, like a good old beaver, go away and think?"

But after much argument, David had his way with "Colonel Bogey". "They went to the copyright people and found that the man who'd written it was a British army officer, Kenneth J. Alford. He had died and one of Sam's representatives went to the widow and asked for permission.

"She said, 'No, because such a lot of rude words have been made up around that song and I don't want my husband made a mockery of.'

"The representative assured her that it was going to be used in the most dignified way and she finally agreed. She was paid, I think, a percentage of the music rights - a very clever move because I'm sure Sam thought they wouldn't make a penny."[27]

In his novel, Pierre Boulle placed the bridge near the Burma frontier, two hundred miles from the actual bridge in Thailand. Since the bridge was the centre of the story, and since it had to be shown under construction, it would be impossible to use a miniature. Spiegel, anxious not to go too far from Europe, started hunting for a site in Yugoslavia, then Sicily, thinking that the jungle could always be matted in, so long as they had the river and the hills. David put a stop to that, insisting that the film should be made in the Far East.

Art director Don Ashton went to Thailand, to the original site, only to find that the area was flat and not in the least wild. Furthermore, a bridge had already been built, thirteen years before. During the war, Ashton had been stationed at Kandy, in Ceylon, with Mountbatten's staff, and in 1945 he married a tea-planter's daughter.

"During my sojourn there, I remembered there were plenty of mountains and jungles and rivers so I went down there to have a look." With construction manager Peter Dukelow, who would become one of David's most valued collaborators, he surveyed a stretch of river sixty miles from Colombo, near the village of Kitulgala. This location seemed ideal. Ashton returned to Paris and told David and Spiegel that the bridge would take at least a year to build, and unless work was started they would have no picture. Spiegel was extremely nervous about allocating huge sums of money before he had signed a single actor. What if the project collapsed? Ashton said that, at worst, he would have a bridge for sale. Spiegel said, "OK, go ahead."[28]

Because he was a tax exile, David had flown direct from New York to Paris. "I remember flying over England to land in Paris. It was most curious, looking down at our island, my home, and realising I couldn't put a foot in it. I felt quite a twinge."[29]

In Paris, he paid a brief courtesy call on Pierre Boulle, then he travelled to Cannes, where the Welles-Spiegel incident allegedly occurred, and then flew to Ceylon, arriving on 28 May. Pamela Mann flew out three weeks later. Spiegel kept Norman Spencer in London.

Carl Foreman sailed for Ceylon, using the time to work on the script, incorporating David's ideas and sending pages ahead at each port the ship visited. David's notes on what he called the "Boat Version" show that he liked the new opening very much.

The film fades in on a hillside overgrown with thick tropical vegetation, a huge red flower swaying in the breeze to reveal a startled cobra, and then a pan to reveal a full shot of the River Kwai, over which the titles appear. As the last title fades, we become aware of an irregular line of men emerging from the jungle - the prisoners, escorted by their Japanese guards.

But even as he noted his satisfaction with the opening, David added, "Always saw prisoners sitting in a train. Lead in to Main Titles poor? Always saw camp coming first, then Nicholson and 'Col Bogey.' Think we can contrast the two opponents, Nic. and Saito, better during walk in. This is the start of Saito's inferiority feeling. Think Saito's speech should give him much more character. I know already he is a rather stupid puppet repeating stuff he has been told. Not a good enough opponent for Nicholson. Think first impression should be of much more impressive individual character."

Foreman had Saito leaping on to a box and addressing the troops with the words, "I hate the British!"

"Surely," wrote David, "he should start calmly and rather frighteningly and then as the unyielding atmosphere develops he should lose his nerve and start shouting - then try to control himself again. This may seem a small point but illustrates what I feel to be a completely wrong approach to Saito. This is anti-Oriental. It's the old tradition of yelling yellow monkeys and I don't think we can do it."

Foreman must have been dismayed by the pages of needle-sharp notes allied to blunt writing. But there was praise, too, for some of Foreman's work.

Inevitably, an agonising period of writing and re-writing followed.

"By this time it was the third or fourth version and it was getting a little wearing because the changes were very minor," said Foreman. "We began to have friendly arguments about whether a character would scratch his face or not. (I had the same problems with Fred Zinnemann.) We never quarrelled but we got on each other's nerves a bit."[30]

When Foreman realised that David wanted to make a full sequence out of the troops marching into the camp whistling "Colonel Bogey" he made his position clear. David recalled Foreman saying, "With all due respect, you are an art-house director. You have only made small British films. You have no experience of the international market. They won't stand for all this. You can't take up three minutes with British troops walking into a camp whistling a tune nobody's ever heard of - you can't expect people to sit in their seats. It won't hold."

David said, "I bet it will hold."[31]

Foreman claimed they never quarrelled, though David remembered an increasing series of disagreements. "In the end I said, 'Well, you can say what you like to me about my inexperience and everything else. I badly want to do this film because I need the money. But if I've got to do this stuff that you've written I won't do it, and that's flat. Either you go, Carl, or I go.' Sam made his decision and Carl left."

Foreman flew to New York from Colombo on 25 June. Spiegel, who had come out from London, followed him a few days later.

"Sam said, 'Do your best, baby,' and left. I sat down at the typewriter and I thought, I've bloody well got to do it myself. I had done it with the Dickens films. So I sat down - desperation stakes - and I wrote that script. I couldn't cope with the American character, that stumped me, so Sam said he would send me out a writer."[32]

A copy of Foreman's final draft, dated June 1956, survives in the Special Collections of UCLA. It includes elements that could only have come from David, such as Joyce's dialogue when he talks about his dreary work as an accountant. However, given the fact that David spoke of "desperation stakes", it is surprising how close to the final version it is. The relationship between Saito and Nicholson is very much as it is in the shooting script. The main difference is that Saito, who is frequently drunk, is still too much of a caricature.

It was David's idea that the American character, Shears, should escape early in the film, and much more is made by Foreman of the terrors awaiting him in the jungle - ants, wild boar, leopard, elephants, and a pursuit by jackals. On the return journey there is an elephant charge against the commando camp. Since none of this is in Foreman's original version, and since it is so reminiscent of the silent picture CHANG, I would guess it was David's suggestion. But Pamela Mann assured me that David disliked it and eventually cut it out. The women who return with Shears are less exaggerated in this version, though Foreman refused to part with his Amazon.

In the prison camp, most of the Japanese are slovenly or incompetent. Saito reveals a pre-war sojourn in London and praises Shakespeare, and says he loathes his prison camp work. While much of the dialogue was changed for the final shooting script, some of it remains the same. Much of the action is the same, too - Nicholson's reverie on the bridge is delivered to Hughes, rather than Saito, but he still strokes the wood with the same pride and affection. That gesture was given him by David, and while it is impossible to know the extent of David's contribution, one can assume that it was fundamental to this version. Nevertheless, the hard work of writing the script was Foreman's and one can understand his dismay when David summarily rejected his contribution.

In New York, Spiegel searched for another writer. Foreman recommended a friend of his, Michael Wilson, another blacklisted writer who lived in Paris. "Sam took Mike's address and number, but didn't use them. Instead he got an American writer called Calder Willingham, who wrote END AS A MAN, which Spiegel made into a movie." [33, 34]

The encounter with Willingham was an experience David would never forget. He wrote to Spiegel, saying how he thought American writers spoke well but wrote badly and were *so* touchy... "And the money they get!"

"On arrival he [Willingham] was scathing about all the work done to date. He spoke a lot of sense on many aspects of the script, and then in a burst of enthusiasm wrote me a scene along the lines he thought Saito and Nicholson should go. I will give you an excerpt:

SAITO:
He's dead, dead, dead!
(Glares furiously)
And you're going to be dead, too! I promise you!

NICHOLSON:
(With a grand calm, and a bored contempt)
Get along with it then, you bounder.

SAITO:
(His eyes bulge at the enormity of this insult)
What did you call me?

NICHOLSON:
You heard me. I called you a bounder, and that's just precisely

what you are, a beastly, uncivilised bounder.

SAITO:
(With a desperate rage slaps Nicholson, and almost beside
himself, screams)
You're an English donkey!
(Slaps Nicholson again, and in a fury.)
Do you hear me, you stupid donkey?

NICHOLSON:
Certainly I hear you.

SAITO:
(Reduced almost to a helpless pulp; panting, running with perspiration, eyes
bulging, trembling with helpless emotion; and now with an almost hysterical,
pitiful fervour)
Well, say something intelligent, then!!

NICHOLSON:
(With a majestic calm, as he stares off into space)
You're a beastly, uncivilised, repulsive bounder.

"That was my first introduction to Calder's writing," David continued. "I must tell you I could hardly believe my eyes, and found it very difficult to know quite what to say to him especially in view of all the high flown talk which had preceded it. That evening ended in Calder sulking off to bed at midnight after telling me that he liked to be praised. Next day he had the grace to apologise and things got on to a better footing. Unfortunately he gave me a copy of his *The Girl in the Dogwood Cabin* as a parting gift on the following night. I did not dare comment on this as I was most anxious to give him every chance, and not to offend him further, but I must tell you it's the biggest lot of trash I have read for many a year, and I became more and more perplexed for the reasons for your faith in him."[35,36]

Willingham left Ceylon at very short notice, leaving David to soldier on alone. But within weeks David received a cable from Spiegel: "I am sending you somebody you will be very pleased with. Do not wish to mention names in a cable. He will be arriving Tuesday week."

Michael Wilson arrived in Colombo with Spiegel on 8 September 1956. A former marine, Wilson had been blacklisted in 1951 and won an Oscar that year for A PLACE IN THE SUN. He later wrote SALT OF THE EARTH, a left-wing film, and FRIENDLY PERSUASION, a story of Quaker folk which William Wyler directed and for which Wilson received an Academy nomination, despite there being no screenplay credit on the film; such were the complexities and absurdities of the blacklist. While he was working on KWAI, Wilson's name was disguised in all communications as "John Michael". He worked on the picture for five months.

David liked Wilson immediately. "He was a very civilised, good chap and he wrote the American part and sort of polished up and tightened up all that I had done. It was really Mike's and my script. I give Mike a huge amount of credit - he never got any credit for it until I lately proclaimed this."

While they were finalising the script, David used to visit the prop room to see all the objects being assembled. This gave him something of the atmosphere, and added to his confidence that the film would be made. He was delighted by the unit Spiegel sent out. Although, much to David's regret, Margaret Shipway's health was not good enough for her to come to such a humid climate, he liked production manager Cecil Ford enormously and felt there wasn't a glimpse of a dud amongst the lot. He wrote to Spiegel:

"You will be thrilled by the prison camp. Don [Ashton] has got several of the huts up and one can see exactly what it is going to look like. I thought of all the people who said, 'Another prisoner of war story?' It may be, but it is something very different from that line of German prison camp movies. Somehow at the back of one's mind has always been the lurking fear that the construction side of this enterprise is too big to undertake in these parts. Yesterday I went up to the bridge site. They have practically finished the road and have done it in record time. It quite staggered me. Very efficient and impressive. The bridge will look terrific."[37]

CHAPTER TWENTY-SEVEN

BLOODY MILLIONAIRE STUFF

THE BRIDGE ON THE RIVER KWAI II

DURING the long months of writing and re-writing the script, David was based at the Mount Lavinia, then an old colonial-style hotel on the beach south of Colombo.

Spiegel was anxious that David should not intrude upon his personal life - he was as keen on women as David was - and Spiegel, in turn, did his best to stay clear of David's. But Spiegel was aware that David had formed a relationship with a Danish catering manageress at the Mount Lavinia, Inger-Grethe Mortensen. This, Spiegel felt, created problems where Leila was concerned and might distract David from the picture.

Trained as a domestic science teacher, Mortensen came to Ceylon to teach at a convent but was tempted away by the hotel's manager who put her in charge of her own restaurant, The Little Hut, where she met David. Their relationship began on a low note - Mortensen declared she had never heard of David, nor had she seen any of his films. But she was impressed by David's kindness, his concern for the staff at the hotel, and his shyness. While she was in Ceylon, she lost both her parents and had to fly back to Denmark. She said David was very considerate over her loss and met her at the airport on her return. "He was a very soft person, David Lean."[1]

The affair seems to have ended when Leila arrived and brought with her a whole set of different problems. She had been taken ill in India while visiting her children, Poupee and Ranju, in Indore. The depth of David's feelings are expressed in a cable he despatched to her, care of his friend, Dr Raam Rishi:

"Tremendous shock. Implore you cable some idea what has happened. Forgive panic. Have you money? Beg you guard yourself. Leave first suspicion of old trouble no matter what. Keep balance by constant touch Rishi stop."[2]

Leila's illness - bacillary dysentery - seems to have been triggered by David demanding that she get a divorce, which was unacceptable in her social circle. David had the latest drug rushed from American to India and asked Dr Rishi to "forgive presumption. Give fondest love and please feed best tinned soups foods available insisting muslin covers against flys [sic]."[3]

As soon as she recovered, David urged Leila to join him in Ceylon. "Unable remain passive here any longer and unless you wire positive reassurances am planning to fly Delhi collect you next Sunday. My devoted love."[4]

"When Leila arrived," said Pamela Mann, "Sam came to me and said, 'We've got to get some channa-dal from Bombay. Leila has been all over the market here - she always washes her hair in these lentils.' Fred Simmins in Bombay bought channa-dal, gave them to a BOAC pilot who flew them to Colombo so Leila could wash her hair. Absolutely ridiculous."[5]

Inger-Grethe Mortensen thought Leila was a very kind woman, but one with many psychological problems. "She was too 'heavy' for David. She talked like a machine all the time and had so many things to explain. He tried to get her up again [help her recover]. But I think it was not meant [David and Leila's relationship]."[6]

David and Leila.

Later that year, Leila left for America, intending to rejoin David in Ceylon in December. It was at this point that Sam Spiegel overstepped the mark. When David discovered what Spiegel had done, he wrote him a devastating letter:

"Dear Sam,

"I returned here after my Kandy trip to find two letters from Leila. The first one told me she had managed to book a seat on the KLM flight arriving here on December 1st. The second letter - written a day later - said that André Morell had taken her to see you. I shall quote you what she says.

"'He took me to Sam Spiegel's at seven. Sam was not there, so we waited. He came in half an hour and was awfully sweet, but he told me I was not to come on the 1st December as you would not be anywhere where I could be. He was very forceful, and said that I could never go into those outlandish places, and there was no meaning in my coming. He was very pleased with your work, and was as warm and sweet as Sam always is. He is going to Paris and will be back on Monday and said he'd call me.

"'I realise you are stuck, and Sam tells me I shouldn't dream of coming out to you because I won't see you. He advises me not to make any plans for two weeks - and then we'll see. When will you be in Colombo or Kandy? I suppose I can't even expect to hear from you often if you are in such remote places. Oh, why after this gruelling experience - should this happen to take away my hopes and my dreams?'

"I sent Leila the following cable yesterday: 'Been trying telephone you explain Sam liar and knows I'm living Mount Lavinia until at least January sixth and all weekends so cease contact with him and try re-book KLM.'

"I find it difficult to continue this letter because you obviously believe that a film contract entitles you to complete ownership of a human being. You are a dictator with no respect for human dignity and individuality. You believe that the end always justifies the means, and if the tragic recent story of your own noble race has not made you question your methods and way of thinking, how can my small voice hope to reach you?

"Leila and I have had an agonising time these last few months. If I were to put our story on a screen it might touch your celluloid heart. But this is real life flesh and blood, and it rattles off you like dice on to a plate. Your bridge must be finished on schedule, and you will lie, charm, and hack your way through to your objective. That is what makes you a good producer - but you have one gaping flaw. You are a *lousy* leader. It springs from the fact that you are incapable of trusting anybody.

"You don't trust me. That is why you are trying to manage my private life backstage. You fear that Leila's presence here may affect the quality of my work on the picture, and so armed with the belief of the end justifying the means, you have lied to her behind my back. And she believed you, Dear Sam…

"Like a blundering bull in a china shop you have crashed into a very delicate situation and taken it into your own hands. You know nothing except what you see on the deceptive surface. You don't know that the specialists have been working towards this reunion with me. It's been a long, dangerous, and hard battle. I am not going into details, but you can take my word that you have barged into a hair-trigger situation, and I don't know that I will ever forgive you for it…

"I can still hardly believe what you've done. You have no right *whatever* to interfere with my private life in this way. I wonder if you can imagine what you would feel if I went to Betty [Spiegel's wife] behind your back? I wonder how you would react if I told her a lie and thereby caused her to cancel her flight from New York to London without a word of consultation with you…

"I only hope you are not contemplating coming out here in the next few weeks. It would be difficult for both of us as I should refuse to have any personal contact with you whatever. I would of course meet you in conference and hear your views and wishes about the film - but there it would end. It would be much better if we corresponded by letter and cable - or better still - via Bill Graf. I will not sit down with you and listen to your explanations over this affair. *I am incensed by what you have done and how you did it.* Your reasons for doing it are beside the point. (That probably makes no sense to you.)

"One day you may realise that I am a professional and I should have thought the last six months might have made an impression on you. If you fail to appreciate the discipline I have inflicted on myself, it is because you have not the requisite antenna to understand the stress I have been under, and the temptations of flying to London - or even giving up the film - which I have resisted. When the film is finished you may perhaps find it in you to apologise to me. It's not good to be so under-estimated. Sincerely, David.

"P.S. I ask you very seriously to have no more communication with Leila. You are on more dangerous ground than you think. Leave what is mine to me."[7]

In October, David - still a youthful forty-eight - received a telegram from his son informing him that he was a grandfather. Nicholas Andrew Tangye Lean had been born on 12 October 1956. David was shaken by the news, partly, one assumes, from the guilt he still felt at his abandoned responsibilities. He sent no answer to the telegram.

Columbia, having read the script, was concerned by the lack of love interest in the picture and Spiegel went along with them. David, against his better judgment, agreed to include such a scene and called Norman Spencer in London about screen tests for possible actresses. Spiegel was advocating Ann Sears, the sister of Heather Sears. Spencer shot the test - after David insisted that Spiegel had no part in it - which David thought was excellent.

"Apparently," said David, "Columbia felt here was a picture of men, English and Japanese. The only women you see are natives. There had to be a love scene between one of the characters and a nurse. So it was written by Mike Wilson. It wasn't his fault. And of course I gave in and shot it. It's bloody awful. What else can one do?"[8]

Spiegel, meanwhile, had still not found Colonel Nicholson or the American, Shears. Due to theatrical commitments, Ralph Richardson was unavailable to play Nicholson. Anthony Quayle was suggested and Spiegel considered Ray Milland and James Mason. He also thought of Douglas Fairbanks Jr and wrote to David, "Please react having first overcome the initial shock." He then returned to a pet idea. "What do you think of approaching Guinness again, or do you feel that he is as wrong as ever?"[9]

David replied that he was under the illusion that Spiegel was lining up Ronald Colman for Nicholson. "I think he is the best so far. As you know, I always thought Richardson was the next best to Charlie (Laughton). Alec Guinness I am still against in that I don't think he will give us the 'size' we need. He could do it of course, but in a different way from what we have visualised."[10]

But Spiegel went ahead and made a last-ditch attempt to sign up Alec Guinness by inviting him to dinner. "He was a very persuasive character," said

Guinness. "I started out maintaining that I wouldn't play the role and by the end of the evening we were discussing what kind of wig I would wear."[11]

"I was at the Galle Face Hotel and David was at the Mount Lavinia," said Pamela Mann. "He was there for private reasons. It was more romantic. David did love women and he couldn't leave them alone and they fell like ninepins. Broken hearts strewn across the world. Anyway, Sam rang me and said, 'I want you to tell David I've got Alec Guinness and I'm very happy about it.'

"I remember getting a taxi out to Mount Lavinia to tell David this and he wasn't very happy. I think the reason he didn't want Alec Guinness was because he knew they wouldn't agree about the part."[12]

Alec Guinness said that when he arrived in Ceylon he was greeted by David saying, "They sent me you and I wanted Charles Laughton." David consistently denied this happened. "He denied it on television," said Guinness, "but I assure you it is true."[13]

The idea of Charles Laughton as a serious contender for the role of Colonel Nicholson is a controversial one. Although one of Laughton's biographers, Charles Higham, states that David offered Laughton the role, Laughton's agent, Paul Gregory, said, "I absolutely know for a fact that Laughton was not offered the part."[14]

Yet David had met Laughton twice in New York, once with Spiegel. Norman Spencer insists that it was all wishful thinking. "The idea of Laughton playing Colonel Nicholson always came a cropper on David's common-sense objection based on the difficulty of audiences suspending their disbelief. 'Fatty' Laughton could never have been acceptable as a British officer starved on prison camp rations."[15]

Guinness undoubtedly wished Laughton *had* taken the part for it did not appeal to him and Guinness was a man who was very careful about the roles he accepted. Since OLIVER TWIST, he had played in a series of comedies for Ealing which had made him one of the best-loved figures on the screen. Now he was being asked to play a man who was neither funny nor lovable, nor even, to Guinness, convincing:

"I couldn't believe in Colonel Nicholson. I thought he was such a humourless ass that it would turn out to be dull, but Spiegel persuaded me otherwise. The book I had read and enjoyed. I thought it rather disturbingly anti-British,[16] but it was interesting, and the final script was a good script."[17]

Over dinner, Guinness asked David to describe Nicholson. "In that no-nonsense manner of his, David said, 'If you and I were having dinner with him tonight, we'd find him an awful bore.'

"I said, 'Oh, I see. You're asking me to play a bore.'

"'Well, you could say that, yes, but it's not true. In the context of the story he is far from being a bore. He's a fascinating character.'

"'No, you said it all right. You told me he was a bore.'

"'I'm not going to argue about it.'

"'No, I don't want to play a bore. I'll pay my own fare home.'

"'Don't be ridiculous. It's a marvellous part.'"[18]

"He didn't go, of course," said David, "but it was difficult from that moment on."[19]

While David wanted Nicholson played absolutely straight, Guinness searched the script for moments where some humour might be introduced.

"I said a line in some way which had a kind of dry amusement behind it. It was about the only place that I could find, and I knew I had done it decently and I could tell from the other actors, and the crew, although of course they don't laugh out loud during a shot. But I caught their amused reaction and I thought, that's exactly what I want. But David was furious because it was not deeply serious. Funny... and yet, God knows I've done six films for him and I admire him enormously. I don't want you to think that I don't. But I think that on KWAI probably he was a bit jealous of a possible success."[20]

David had lived with the character in his mind for months. He had scripted him in minute detail, and Guinness's fresh, tongue-in-cheek portrayal did not correspond to the character in his head.

"I think one has to take into account David's lack of humour," wrote Guinness. "Such humour as he displayed was usually dyspeptic and cynical."[21]

The making of KWAI was a thoroughly wretched experience for David and the harsh memories were not softened by nostalgia.

"I remember James Donald," said David, "who played the doctor,[22] standing on the parade ground and putting a paternal hand on my shoulder. The night before he had told Sam that I was a sadist who had unfortunately picked on him as my whipping boy. He had an expression of smiling and pitying condescension as Sam told him that he was mistaken and he should try and be a friend to me. Armed with this new approach he said, 'You know, David, the only director who's been able to handle my talent is George Cukor. Now, don't misunderstand me, the best thing for *you* to do is just to give me the mood and I'll understand what you want.'

"James had decided that I was making an anti-British film. He told the rest of the cast, including Alec Guinness, who I think went along with it."[23]

Consequently, David took an active dislike to the British actors. During a scene with Guinness on the bridge - the scene in which Guinness reflects on his career against the setting sun - David exploded when Guinness queried why the camera was on his back and not on his face. Guinness had loved the dialogue for this scene and after debating the camera angle with David he took great care to time the speech to the setting of the sun.

Instead of congratulating Guinness, David said, "Now you can all fuck off and go home, you English actors. Thank God that I'm starting work tomorrow with an American actor. It'll be such a pleasure to say goodbye to you guys.'"[24]

The American actor was William Holden, who had been cast as Shears and whose agent had arranged a deal for KWAI which made him, at the time, the highest paid film star in the world - $300,000 plus ten percent of the profits.

"I suppose you could say he was a bit of a college boy," said David, "but he was highly professional. Worked like hell, never late, knew his lines. Had I said, 'We'll start the day with you standing on your head under that tree,' he'd say, 'Oh, I see. Okay.' And he'd do it. If you asked some of the English actors to do much less, they'd start to argue.

"Trouble was, he was the biggest box-office star in the world when he did KWAI. He was so good-looking and so accomplished that people kind of smiled - 'Dear old Bill Holden, yes, very good,' - and dismissed his talent. He had a huge talent and because it was so apparently effortless, Bill never got the credit he deserved. After all, SUNSET BOULEVARD was no easy part."[25]

Cast as the Japanese commandant, Saito, was a great star of silent pictures called Sessue Hayakawa. At first, Hayakawa was not impressed by the script - he skimmed through it and noted at once the lack of love interest, and the fact that the whole thing took place in the jungle. His wife, Tsuru, pleaded with him to read it again; he read it four times and each time, he said, the story got better.

Once he accepted the role, Hayakawa said that he and David enjoyed an excellent rapport: "We never found ourselves in opposition. But he was less than slightly beloved by some of his associates, being broiled by the hot sun and infernal humidity of Ceylon during the stifling months we were isolated there."[26]

To the unit, which, like an army, consisted of predominantly young men, Hayakawa seemed fragile and very old. In fact, he was sixty-eight.

"I remember telling my mother-in-law we'd got Sessue Hayakawa," said camera operator Peter Newbrook. "She was absolutely flabbergasted. He was her childhood idol and she didn't know he was still alive. His command of English was limited so a lot of the stuff he had to speak phonetically."[27]

David's memory of the Japanese actor was not as charitable as Hayakawa's was of him.

"He was a jolly good-looking leading man. He was quite old, and was going a bit ga-ga. The first time he appeared was when the British prisoners come on to the parade ground whistling 'Colonel Bogey.' He gets on to a box and says, 'You British prisoners have been chosen to build a bridge across the River Kwai.' We had a rehearsal and ran through it and I thought, what's wrong? Over in no time."

Hayakawa had taken the script and had learned only the lines which he

Alec Guinness, Inger-Grethe Mortensen, William Holden, David. Photograph by Peter Newbrook

needed to speak before the camera. Those lines of his which would be heard over shots of Guinness he had not bothered with, thinking they could be dubbed in later. When David told him he had to say the whole speech, Hayakwawa said he needed a day to learn the lines.

"And I spent the whole of the next day," said David, "doing close-ups of Alec, close-ups of feet, anything I could do without Sessue. Then he came along and did it."[28]

"His memory wasn't that good," said make-up man Stuart Freeborn. "He had long speeches and he couldn't always get his lines out. He would go so far and suddenly he'd blank out. It was retake after retake.

"I remember a very tense scene with Alec Guinness and Sessue Hayakawa would start fine but as he was almost at the end he would crack up. After about the twenty-fifth take, Alec was still doing his stuff, but he began to do it automatically. David wasn't concentrating on Alec, he had faith in Alec to be the same each time. On the twenty-sixth take, Sessue did it.

"David said, 'Great, print.'

"But Alec said, 'No, no. That was dreadful for me.'

"It was the first time I'd seen Alec and David go at each other. But there was a reason for it."[29]

Teddy Darvas kept a copy of the script, marked up with the slate and take number of each shot. What is apparent, despite all the grim stories, is that most of Hayakawa's work was professional enough to suit anyone - take one... take four... The highest number of takes recorded for Hayakawa on a scene with Alec Guinness is twelve. And even David's favourite, William Holden, sometimes required more than twenty takes.

Yet Hayakawa was curiously naive. When David rehearsed the scene in which Hayakawa follows Guinness off the bridge to where he had discovered the wires laid by the commandos, Hayakawa had no idea he would be killed.

"The real script was one inch thick," said David. "Sessue's was about an eighth of an inch thick. He'd gone through the script and put a cross at the top of

The British prisoners enter the camp.

every page where he had dialogue and he'd taken the script to bits, put all the pages with crosses together and thrown away the rest. So he just had his part. He didn't know he was going to get killed. And he was nominated for Best Supporting Actor!"

The tense atmosphere on the set was exacerbated by a strike. There were two men on the generator crew, and when the driver went sick, his mate took over his duties. All the unions went on strike. Since it was not clear whether responsibility for the driver lay with the Transport and General Workers Union or the Electrical Trades Union - it had to be decided by London - the strike lasted longer than had been intended. All of which made for bad blood.

Once work resumed, the heat grew more and more intense. Since the valley was without benefit of a cooling breeze, David allowed the cast and crew, at the end of every completed shot, to jump into the river and swim for ten minutes.

"How wise that was I don't know," said David, "but it was delightfully cool. I dived in one day and came up opposite this character, Eddie Fowlie. He was our property master. And he said to me, 'Bloody millionaire stuff!'

"I said, 'What do you mean?'

"He said, 'Even a millionaire couldn't do what we're doing now.'

"And of course he was right." [30]

This was the beginning of what was perhaps David's closest and longest-lasting friendship. Eddie Fowlie became property master on all David's subsequent films - and many other big productions as a result.

A tall, powerfully-built, pugnacious-looking character, with a florid face and black hair, Eddie would have been ideally cast as a British redcoat sergeant. He had been in the army - briefly - in the Scots Guards. Injured on manoeuvres, he was in hospital just as the casualties from the North African landings were arriving.

"They were wheeling these poor sods in without arms and legs and I thought, Christ, I can do without that."

He eventually got a job at Teddington Studios, near where he had been born in 1921. He stayed until the fifties when he decided he had had enough of studio pictures. When Spiegel sent him out on KWAI he was in seventh heaven.

"We were doing the bit in the opening of the film, where the prisoners are coming down. There is a train in the foreground; they come off the train and walk down through the forest.

"David was sitting under a big tree and we talked for a while about a butterfly, a big moth on the tree, which was beautiful. After a bit, I said, 'David, there's something wrong, isn't there?'

"He said, 'The scene doesn't feel right. There's something wrong with this location. It's not right.'

"I said, 'It's fuzzy. All the tops of the hills are fuzzy. Perhaps it wants an arsehole cut there. They're coming out of this arsehole in that fuzz.'

"He said, 'Go and do something about it.'

"I went up and spent the whole morning cutting down trees. As a matter of fact I split my head open with the vines of one tree tangled in another. Pulled it down and it hit me on the head, and I had to fill it up with Lifebuoy soap to stop the blood. When I went back, black and all covered in ants, the unit was playing cricket.

"I said, 'Where's the moth?' and then, 'What do you think about it now?'

"He said, 'Get the camera out and let's put it there.'

"When he got the thing set up he said, 'Eddie, get me a branch and offer it in right of frame and give me a pair of scissors.' After taking down all the bloody trees he got his little bit of foreground. He would never shoot without foreground. He had to have foreground - or depth. He would say to me sometimes, 'Go and put some smoke over there, Eddie, about four miles away.'"[31]

Fowlie sorted out misunderstandings, put pressure on recalcitrant members of the crew, did stunts when stunt men proved reluctant, and when David was sunk in gloom he was able, by a sort of sixth sense, to put into words what was bothering him. The words may not have been pretty, but the result often was.

While it was Fowlie's enthusiasm that first caught David's interest, it was his commitment, his almost Teutonic sense of purpose and his rake-hell temperament - with more than a flash of Robert Newton (and perhaps Mrs Egerton?) - that won him a friend for life. That, and his ability to produce exactly what David needed - from a convincing explosion to a frozen lake in high summer.

One sequence involved the commandos floating down the river on a make-shift raft packed with dynamite.

"I'd made about ten of them," said Fowlie. "I thought I'd gather them back each time and be able to keep ahead. But it was terrifying because the way David went on and on, I was running out of rafts. And I had to work all night to be sure I had another dozen ready for the next morning. I didn't expect him to shoot so much and I didn't expect him to do so many takes on it. I was judging him by other directors. While another director would say, 'That's it,' David wanted it right. We soon got to know each other well.

"It wasn't long into the shooting - two or three weeks - when he said to me, 'I want to show my appreciation for the work you've done. I want you to use my apartment in the Mount Lavinia. Use my things, play my gramophone records' - they were mostly Noël Coward - 'use my dressing gown…' He knew I wouldn't live with the unit. I always lived my own way, and I was living in a rest house. It was a bit rough. So that's what happened. It was rather lovely to do that."[32]

Roy Stevens, who worked with David on his three subsequent pictures, explained the friendship between David and Fowlie: "I think David as a man would have preferred to have been Eddie Fowlie than David Lean, because he reckoned Eddie had so much more fun than him. He had great respect for him, loved his outgoing personality, his 'couldn't give tuppence about anything' attitude. David's Quaker background prevented him from getting to that point himself, therefore the nearest he could get was to have a good friend who was like that." 33

"It was a sad picture in certain ways," said David. "I enjoyed some of it, but there was a bad atmosphere among the actors. They thought I was hopeless. A lot of the crew didn't think I was any good at all, either. I had some people who were

really nice to me, among them Eddie Fowlie, the property man. And Jack Hildyard, the camera-man, he was jolly good. He used to go home too early at night, he wouldn't stay and discuss the day's work, and that's really why he didn't get LAWRENCE.

"But it is a miserable experience if you have the cast and crew against you. My assistant director proved to be my biggest enemy - Gus Agosti. It is particularly miserable when your assistant thinks you're hopeless." 34

David checks a set-up for the raft sequence.

"What he had," said Don Ashton, "was a very efficient unit who really hated the jungle. It was most uncomfortable living in this heat and humidity, with snakes and leeches. It was all right for me and my gang - we were used to it. But taking the boys out by plane and just dumping them in the jungle meant an unhappy existence for them. So everybody was a bit on edge. And David's manner didn't help - he used to take hours or days to get a shot, so there wasn't a lot of harmony." 35

"There was a tense scene on the set one day," said Geoffrey Horne, who played Joyce, one of the commandos. "David, like some local preacher scolding the community, started to castigate the entire crew for their inefficiency and lack of interest in the film. He said everybody was guilty, and Fred [Lane], the carpenter, shot back, 'Everybody, boss?' And David said, 'No, not you, Fred.' And not Eddie Fowlie, of course. Eddie could do no wrong. But the rest all hung their heads in shame." 36

While it is tempting to place the blame on David for not being a more inspiring leader, the average British film technician of the fifties was about as easy to inspire as a foot soldier in the Peninsular War. He certainly grumbled as much and was equally bloody-minded. Working on a David Lean project should have been as much of an honour as serving with the Iron Duke, but relatively few of these men had more than a passing interest in the results of the work they were doing.

"Some of the English people were wonderful and I stuck with a whole lot of them," said David. "But, oh boy, when the English become - I don't know how to describe it - something to do with unions but not to do with unions, a sort of maliciousness and a love of this sort of power, of really bitching it up for a director as much as they can, because they're not interested in films at all."[37]

To the young American, Geoffrey Horne, David "was like a stern father but a loving one." It was Geoffrey Horne who saved David from drowning.

"We had a day off, funnily enough, if you can believe it," said David. "We all went swimming in the river and I got swept off by the current. Everyone thought I was joking, until Geoffrey realised I was not and jumped after me and saved my life. He was the youngest and the strongest."[38]

To the casual observer, it appeared that David was so engrossed in thinking about the picture that he was not conscious of anything else. Yet he was deeply concerned about the safety of his crew.

David ordered a trial run for the scene at the end of the picture where Nicholson discovers the bridge has been mined. Stuntman Frankie Howard, playing a Japanese soldier, had to run along the top of the bridge, get shot and fall into the river. The river had been dammed for the scene where the level dropped overnight.

David wanted to be sure that Howard would be able to swim clear. They did a dummy run, and Howard managed it easily. But when they shot it the following day, Howard found the currents too strong. There had been heavy rainfall up country during the night and the volume of water over the dam was so great it sucked Howard down. To everyone's horror, they realised he was drowning. Prop man Tommy Early dashed to the edge with a rope and dived in to help, even though he couldn't swim a stroke.

"So now there are two men, aren't there?" said Fred Lane. "Then there was a Singhalese lad who accidentally fell in. So now there are three men who are literally drowning in front of his eyes.

"David said, 'Gus, for God's sake get on that Tannoy - I want nobody else in the water. Nobody at all.'"

As far as the unit was concerned, the men had drowned. But the mere fact that they had stopped struggling enabled them to survive; they went under, and the current carried them to where Eddie Fowlie's team of Singhalese men could swim in and pull them out.

"Frankie was sent home to England, and he had a bug in his stomach and he died in the Hospital for Tropical Diseases."[39]

Three members of the crew - Stuart Freeborn, Gus Agosti and second assistant John Kerrison were also involved in a terrible car crash. Sixty miles from Colombo, on a jungle road, their car car collided with a lorry.

Freeborn shut his eyes and heard the breaking of glass and the crashing of metal. "Then it all went silent. I opened my eyes and I was flying over the treetops. Then whoompf, a branch hit the back of my neck and nearly broke it. I woke up lying on a huge anthill which saved my life. My spine was broken in two places."[40]

Freeborn somehow managed to prevent the local police from manhandling him into their truck, which would have killed him. He ended up in an English tea-planters' hospital where John Kerrison died.

"When we heard about this thing," said Eddie Fowlie, "David sat for a few minutes, rather sad, and then he said, 'Well, get the camera out... nothing else to do.'"[41]

Freeborn was placed in a plaster cast, surrounded by a screen, and received only a few visits from members of the crew. "I was feeling so desperately depressed, I felt I was going to die. I went into a coma.

"One day I heard a little bit of noise. I was aware of somebody standing behind the screen. I strained my eyes and got a very vague glimpse. It was David Lean. I knew it was him. Absolutely. I thought, my God, David Lean himself has come all this way just to look at me and try to wish something. I felt it, from his mind to mine. It was so strong. How do you explain a thing like that? From that moment, I changed completely. The nurses said, 'You have made a most extraordinary recovery. We thought you were going to die.' I said, 'Yes, there's one person responsible and it was David Lean.' That was the kind of man he was."[42]

The strange thing about this episode is that David's record of attending invalids, even among his own family, is near to zero. But Don Ashton is convinced that David - because of the strange circumstances in which they were all living - actually did go. As Freeborn so earnestly believed, the mysterious visitor might conceivably have been David.

"It was a very long and very arduous production," said camera operator Peter Newbrook. "I went out in September of 1956 and we didn't stop shooting until April 1957. I can tell you by the end of the picture there were probably only four people that David wanted to talk to. The rest of them he'd written off. David didn't miss a day through illness but I think everybody bar five was taken ill, mainly with dysentery or allied tummy troubles, being bitten by leeches or whatever. The ACT people who never took a day off as far as I can remember were the three of us - Jack, David and I. Angela Martelli [the continuity girl] worked right through, and our gaffer Archie Dansie did. Also Eddie Fowlie and my assistant Tommy Nichol. Everybody else was taken ill at one time, or were absent from production for some reason or other.

"We got well behind schedule. Because Bill Holden's contract was going to expire, we had to start a second unit. David really wanted Jack [Hildyard] to be second unit director, but he refused. So David asked me. I directed second unit, paid but not credited. I did all the building of the Japanese bridge, the opening sequence [behind the titles] and part of the end. As cameraman, Jack suggested an old friend of his, Freddy Ford [another Korda veteran], who was great on exteriors. Freddy came out and shot all the second unit with me."[43]

As production neared its end, the Alec Guinness situation was still causing a great deal of tension.

"David and I used to have dinner together," said Teddy Darvas. "One evening we were at the bar having a drink and there was Alec having dinner all by himself. David said to me, 'We're not speaking.'

"I said, 'It seems silly after all these years, here you are in the same hotel and you don't speak.'

"David said, 'You're absolutely right. I'm not having dinner with you.' He took his drink, sat down with Alec and they made it up. That lasted about forty-eight hours..."[44]

In an attempt to reassure Guinness, David invited him to see a rough-cut of some sequences.

"One week, his wife Merula and his son Matthew came to Ceylon and he asked to see it. I had a bedroom in the Mount Lavinia Hotel and opposite was a smaller bedroom which I used as a cutting-room. We had a Moviola, the lens of which could be used to project the picture three feet across the wall. We had painted the wall white. I ran well over an hour's stuff for Alec, Merula and Matthew. There were terrible moments when they sat in solid silence as we threaded up the next thousand-foot reel.

"It ended at a scene Alec had been very sarcastic about, when he walks across the parade ground to Colonel Saito's hut, and people come to the salute. Bloody good shot. He hadn't liked it at all. 'Are you expecting me to walk that distance?' he said. I said, 'Look at it with a stand-in, will you please?'

"He said, 'Well, I think it's an awful, terrible walk, much too long, but all right, David, I'll do it for you - it's just another of your technical tricks.' And he did it in the most murderous bad temper.

"I ended up on that shot. They hadn't said a word all this time. Now they said, 'Thank you very much' and walked out of the room.

"The assistant cutter, Teddy Darvas, put the film away and I said, 'Good-night, Teddy, what did they think of it, any idea?'

"He said, 'I've no idea.'

"I returned to my bedroom when I heard a knock on the door and it was Alec.

"I said, 'Hello, come in.'

"He said, 'No, I won't. Merula, Matthew and I are having a talk after seeing that stuff, and before going to sleep tonight I ought to tell you that all of us thought it was the best thing I've ever done. Goodnight.'

"And he went."[45]

Although the word "epic" has often been attached to KWAI, it was not made on an epic budget. Because Sam Spiegel was unwilling to spend money sending extras to Ceylon, members of the unit were appropriated, and their faces made up. The company also drafted in the local population to work as extras.

"We used a lot of Singhalese with whited faces as prisoners," said David. "We used to have the local bank manager, and we could have him from three to seven on such and such a day, and I had to shoot round him for the rest of the time. We really did skimp, skimp, skimp."

Much of the money went on building the bridge itself. In fact, there were two bridges. Art director Don Ashton discovered that a British engineering company called Husband and Co. was building a dam in Ceylon. Keith Best, aged thirty-two, from Yorkshire and a wartime sapper, was the engineer in charge. Ashton and Best realised that in order to transport equipment to the location a second bridge would have to be built, spanning a small valley. "Which was a godsend," said Ashton, "because we practised building a bridge on that bridge."[46]

David came out to approve the site, and since there was not even the vestige of a bridge Best had to swim across the river with a rope around his waist, clamber up the bank and pull it taut at deck level, to give him some idea.

Two miles down the road was a tea plantation. Production manager Cecil Ford transformed the house into unit headquarters, surrounding it with bungalows equipped with showers, and providing on the ground floor a dining room and kitchen operated by Phil Hobbs, a genius of a caterer who managed to provide English food for everyone who wanted it.

Ashton had designed something like the Forth Railway Bridge which, Keith Best noted, was nothing like the actual bridge on the Burma-Siam railway. He suggested that the bridge be built to withstand no more than foot traffic with an occasional light vehicle. The train could be mocked up using a jeep towing property carriages.

"Then," wrote Best, "out of the blue, a steam locomotive was offered by Ceylon Government Railways. It was a 2ft 6in gauge K-Class loco. It had been made by Hunslet Engineering of Leeds in 1900.

"The ever-cautious Sam Spiegel, having been prevailed upon to build a full-scale bridge, needed a lot more persuasion before believing that it could carry a full-scale steam train. So I had long sessions in his suite at the Galle Face Hotel where he was surrounded by a group of 'Yes, Sam, No Sam, Of course Sam' programmed disciples."[47]

The contractor for the bridge was Equipment and Construction Co., a Danish firm that had built Naragala Bridge. The labour force was local and elephants were hired from haulage contractors to drag logs across the river.

"The elephants were wonderful," said Eddie Fowlie. "They used to knock off every four hours, like trade unionists. They wanted to lie in the water and that was that; you couldn't make them move."[48]

"As the bridge took shape," wrote Best, "there were the customary alarms and excursions. The day after filming a sequence showing the partly-built bridge, there was a storm in the hills and the river rose twenty feet in a few hours, bringing a lot of debris and washing away the six legs of the left bank pier. We then borrowed an anti-submarine net from the Royal Navy at Trincomalee and put it about two hundred yards upstream for protection from floating flotsam. Despite innumerable other setbacks, the bridge was finished almost on schedule in January 1957."[49]

Three months later, this magnificent structure was destroyed. Sam Spiegel came to witness the event, bringing his wife Betty with him. He revealed an understandable nervousness about the bridge, which was not soothed by William Holden and Don Ashton's habit of launching hot air balloons, made from air-mail copies of the *Daily Telegraph* and powered with kerosene, into the wide blue yonder. One of these, landing on the timber bridge, could have ruined ten months' work.

The evening of Spiegel's arrival, carpenter Fred Lane was having dinner in the hotel restaurant when David asked if he could join him. Lane wondered why David was not having dinner with Spiegel. He had seen the two men pacing up and down, but hadn't realised the gravity of it all. David told Lane that he did not so much greet Spiegel as have an altercation with him. Spiegel's message had been blunt: David had gone wildly over budget. He had been back to Columbia twice. There was no more money. David was to blow up the bridge and that was the end of the shooting. The entire crew would then be shipped back to London.

"David said, 'I've still got one or two shots I want to do. As soon as we blow the bridge up, I'll get rid of the main unit and keep the few I need - about eight or ten - and spend a couple more weeks. We'll go out each morning, and if I find what I want we'll shoot it, if I don't we'll start again the next day.'"[50]

On 10 March 1957, the Prime Minister of Ceylon, Solomon Bandaranaike, his wife, and a hundred dignitaries, including ministers and businessmen who had provided facilities for the picture, arrived to see the bridge destroyed. A platform was built downstream, well clear of the bridge, a sort of Ascot enclosure with tables and umbrellas. The explosion was scheduled for eight in the morning and some of the VIPs had been travelling for hours.

"Sam was terrified the bridge wouldn't blow up," said David, "so he got two or three ICI people over, and they placed the charges. They said, 'Look, there's going to be great big hunks of wood travelling at least a hundred miles an hour through the air and you've got to be very careful that the camera crew are out of the way.'"[51]

The cameras were concealed in dugouts and trenches were dug for the camera crew. There were five cameras, one located one hundred and fifty yards downstream at a control point where David, Spiegel and the main crew were stationed.

"I'll always remember Sam standing there with his stick and his hat on, taking tranquillisers," said Don Ashton. "He was terribly nervous."[52]

Ashton had designed a control panel, a wooden board consisting of light bulbs set in a circle, one for each of the five cameras, two for security and one in the centre which indicated that the engine driver had reached the entry point to the bridge, and had jumped from the locomotive. Each camera position was linked to the control by field telephones. It was agreed beforehand that David would not give the order to blow up the bridge until that circle of lights was complete.

"We didn't know what was going to happen," said Peter Newbrook. "When you got the command to switch on, you turned over, made sure the camera was up to speed, and the last thing we did before we left the bunker was to switch the light on."[53]

Don Ashton and Keith Best had the honour of destroying the bridge they had built. Each had a firing button, for there were to be two explosions in rapid succession.

The train run was rehearsed many times. To achieve the effect David wanted, with plenty of smoke, the engine had to gain speed very quickly. It was fitted with a regulator - a lever like an aircraft speed control. The engineer - Ceylon's most experienced - was to open the regulator to full throttle.

"But if he kept that up," said Stuart Freeborn, "the engine would be going too fast for the driver to be able to jump off when it went over the bridge. So they had a white cross on the trees as he went round the corner. When he saw the white cross, he was supposed to take the speed down so that he could jump off without injuring himself. If it was going at top speed, the locomotive would plough through the sand drag and topple over the parapet at the other end."

Now everything was ready. As soon as Gus Agosti saw the train, he gave the signal for the cameras to turn over. In his panic to get out of the way of the explosion the engine driver jumped, forgetting to throttle back. But he reached shelter, suffering only a twisted ankle.

"I don't know how the train stayed on that curve," said Don Ashton. "It went across at thirty miles an hour."

One by one, the lights had come on - all but the last. David had three or four seconds to make up his mind. The fact that one camera was not working was immaterial; far more serious was the thought that the cameraman was not in his trench and might be exposed to the blast. The dignitaries were waiting to see one of the most spectacular and expensive shots in film history. But the risk was too great. David cried, "Don't blow the bridge!" and Ashton and Best stayed their hands.

But the train tore on, across the bridge, into the sand drag, and collided with a generator, almost sending it into the ravine.

Eddie Fowlie and Peter Dukelow rushed to the locomotive. The generator was teetering on the edge like something from a Harold Lloyd movie. Spiegel came up, white-faced and breathless, and asked, "How long to get it ready again?"[54]

"I did not give the order," explained David, "because I thought somebody might be killed. One of the cameramen, Freddy Ford, had forgotten to turn it on, you see. I felt sorry for him. Sam was nearly berserk, and went for him unmercifully."[55]

"If Sam could have had Freddy Ford executed he would have done so," said Peter Newbrook. "But David was marvellous. He was so magnanimous. He asked Freddy to sit with him at his table that evening because he knew the poor man would be terrified beyond measure; he might even be suicidal, knowing that he'd been responsible for this catastrophe."[56]

"I asked Freddy to dinner," said David, "because he'd become the laughing-stock of the unit. Sam was furious: 'You can't take the biggest idiot to dinner to congratulate him for fucking up the scene!'"[57]

Most embarrassing to Spiegel was having to face the disappointed dignitaries, in their smart suits and Ascot hats. He promised them all they would be brought out for the retake - but it proved an empty promise. David felt that it had been bad luck having them there in the first place.

There remained the problem of getting the train back on the tracks. There was only one crane capable of doing the job but when Ashton telephoned the minister responsible, he discovered that as he had not been invited to the explosion, his wife had lost face, and he flatly refused to help. So the unit's railway liaison man decided the only alternative was to jack the train back on its tracks. A lorry arrived with fifteen men and they spent the rest of the day sweating over the engine, moving it inch by inch.

The bridge, ready to receive its first train, with one of the elephants that helped to build it.

By two in the morning, the train was ready again. Ashton told David and Sam, who were still up, they could blow up the bridge in the morning. "I thought I'd better have a couple of hours sleep and went and had a shower when my driver came rushing back - 'Master, master, the bridge is on fire!'

"So with a towel around me, I jumped in my jeep and raced up and sure enough a lorry was blazing away. We had fire extinguishers all down the bridge - Sam had managed to get some sort of insurance on it - and they were all empty. We grabbed handfuls of earth and managed to put the fire out - it had been started by a driver filling up with petrol and a chap holding an oil lamp so he could see. Luckily they didn't blow the tank up."[58]

The next day, 11 March 1957, everything went smoothly. The train came across at the proper speed - with Eddie Fowlie at the controls this time - all the lights came on and David gave the order. Explosions demolished the bridge and the train, its carriage full of dummy Japanese, cascaded with the debris into the boiling water.

It was tremendously effective, but it was not how David had envisaged it.

"I had wanted to blow up the piles on one side of the bridge only so that the whole bridge and the train would fall into the water. When I told the ICI people this, Sam was so frightened he made them put explosives under every pile. So the bridge just sank. It looked good enough but it would have been wonderful to see the whole bloody thing keel over with a moving train on top of it."[59]

Once the scenes around the shattered bridge had been completed, and all the scenes in the Peradinya Gardens in Kandy, Spiegel ordered the main unit home, leaving behind a skeleton crew, together with Jack Hawkins and the bit-part players in the commando troop. Peter Newbrook became director-cameraman with Gerry Fisher as his operator. They shot for three more weeks.

The scene which closes the picture is taken from above, looking down on the shattered bridge and the wrecked train; the tiny figure of the doctor can be seen on one side of the river, and as the camera pulls back the five figures of the commando team are visible on the other. The script called for the camera to be in a helicopter, pulling up into the sky.

"David wanted to replicate the idea of the bird, the hawk which opened the film," said Peter Newbrook. "The idea was that it was the bird looking down at these lunatics - the bird's free and everyone else is either killed or captured.

"We got a very intelligent pilot - he was English, although in the Ceylon Air Force - and I got Eddie Fowlie on the ground setting fire to the remnants of the train, and a walkie-talkie to cue the double for James Donald. I did six takes.

"It was very dangerous, because we had to fly three-quarters sideways, otherwise we had the problem of getting the rotor blades in the picture - this being CinemaScope you could damn near see round the back of the plane."[60]

David himself was not in the helicopter; he was shooting the scene at the waterfall. But the final shot angered him to his dying day.

"Money was so short," he said, "and Sam was whipping actors out as soon as they finished their part. The last scene was James Donald saying, 'Madness, madness.' And he turns away and walks off up the beach. But of course James Donald was on the plane back to London as soon as he got the 's' of madness out of his mouth. We had to use a double. And you can see it. I always say to producers, 'We cannot use a double because even in a long shot nine times out of ten the double will be incapable of thinking the scene right. If you think right, you walk right.' And this man is walking like a marionette. He just sort of lurches across the sand. So the end is simply terrible."[61]

David discovered from Ilya Lopert that Spiegel had worked out a scheme to bring in an American editor to cut the picture. When Lopert told Spiegel that he was getting rid of the best editor in the world, David was allowed to work with Peter Taylor who had been an assembly editor on SUMMERTIME.

"David was incredible," wrote Taylor. "Such a wonderful director and a great editor. It was a great privilege to work with him. After the first film I did for him, he gave me a book for Christmas and in it he wrote these words: 'There's always room at the top.'"[62]

Because David could not return to England, the picture was cut in Paris where Spiegel behaved with the kind of extravagance he would have berated his directors for.

"Every night he threw tremendous parties at the George V for the people working on KWAI," said Malcolm Arnold, who was flown over to compose the music. "Sam's girlfriend, who was a showgirl, came over and the chauffeur's girlfriend, who also had to have a girlfriend." David asked who was paying, knowing perfectly well that all the parties, as well as Sam's gourmet dinners, were being charged to the production.

David was so deeply immersed in the editing that he left Leila to her own devices. Malcolm Arnold befriended her, and they used to go shopping. "She was enchanting," he said, "but the loneliest person I have ever met."[63]

David finished the editing by mid-August 1957. "It's been a hell of a time," he wrote to Peter Newbrook, "and Sam's pressure almost did me in. I have never worked so fast, but I've done a good job and I think you will like the result. We used almost every shot and all the trek stuff you and I did on our own. Think it probably a film and a half. It runs for about two hours forty and doesn't drag. Sam thinks he will bring me a finished print here by the end of September. I doubt it."[64]

"I had to write KWAI in less than three weeks," said Malcolm Arnold, whose arrangement of "Colonel Bogey", complete with whistling, became world-famous.

"The whistlers, incidentally, were a piccolo and seventeen members of the Irish Guards. They weren't handpicked; anybody can whistle. I said, 'Look, gentlemen, we all know both world war versions of "Colonel Bogey". But here, because of censorship, you've got to whistle it.' I had the piccolo to give them the pitch. And I'd already recorded the military band, so I had that over my ear and I conducted them to the picture and that was a nightmare - terribly difficult to fit."

David and Malcolm Arnold were a mutual admiration society. "He adored what I did with the films he made," said Arnold. "He never cut a single quaver, and he observed all my decrescendos. When it came to the scene of the troops marching into the prison camp, David said, 'Look, Malcolm, take "Colonel Bogey" and add the guards outside Buckingham Palace to it. Give it a grandeur, a real swagger.'"[65]

"Malcolm did a marvellous job," said David. "He made 'Colonel Bogey' twice as good as it was. I love those swaggering marches."

Malcolm Arnold did not attend the dubbing because David had reassured him that Win Ryder would be in charge - "he thought he was gold dust, he was so precious to him," said Arnold.

David also chose not to attend the dubbing sessions in England but left long and extremely detailed instructions for Ryder: the sound of insects, the rustling of foliage, the echo of explosions, the sudden screaming of a bird, the use of music... nothing escaped his attention.

Confident that his instructions would be carried out impeccably, he took Leila on a touring holiday through France, Italy and Austria. There had been a significant development in their relationship: David was no longer a married man.

In July 1957, Ann Todd was granted a decree nisi in an undefended suit at the Divorce Court because of desertion since 1954 by David Lean.

"David is not the sort of man that husbands are made from," said Todd in a press interview some years later. "He is too tense, too mercurial. But I shall always admire him and have love for him."[66]

David's father, who had accepted the divorce as inevitable, and who received a charming note from Ann Todd, sent a letter to David:

"I fervently hope that you will not marry again - least of all anyone of different race, colour and religion. It could not last and it can only lead to another tragedy in time to the repeated distress of all concerned and especially

An everyday occurrence in the Japanese prison camp.

those who have your happiness and welfare so much at heart."[67]

David felt that he had been badly treated by Ann Todd, that she "used" him, and that she cared nothing for him as a human being.

"I had to leave my country in order to pay this woman for the harm I was supposed to have done her," he wrote, years later. "Like a fool I resisted pressure to make her the guilty party when I had every opportunity - and I ran. I think I substituted England for her. I remember how I tried to avoid all English people for months. I think that's why I, as it were, embraced the Orient. I was unknown and able to start again with only an occasional whiff of my English shame. Perhaps shame is too strong but it is not far off."

He felt deeply humiliated by Ann Todd, and this contributed to his touchiness about recognition from the British establishment. "Even to the extent of half wanting to tell them all to jump in the lake if they ever went so far as to offer me a knighthood."

David alleged that Ann Todd spread rumours that his friendship with her son was unhealthy.

"I thought that everyone knew and believed. So I was waiting for an attack or a look of disapproval whenever I met an English person. It all seemed real at the time because I had no resistance and very little self-respect. The English lawyers were so dreadful in their cold logical way. It was something to do with being stripped of everything useful like a butcher with an animal - and you are left with the bones."[68]

When Peter Newbrook wrote about an emotional problem he was having, David replied that he understood very well, having had very recent first-hand knowledge.

"Oh dear, oh dear. We English seem to keep our adolescence right up into our middle age, and then one day something happens and we wake up and find we have outgrown our toys. I am one who has gone through it all - this late growing up - and have nearly come out on the other side. I know so well the feelings of guilt, and the helplessness to put right the hurts one has caused. I was lucky indeed because this last disastrous marriage of mine was so hopeless, and the lack of love so apparent, that I have none of these feelings - but it's my good luck and nothing else. To become more and more pontifical, I have so many times in the last three years thought of dear old Shakespeare's 'To thine own self be true, and it will follow as the night the day thou will be false to no man [sic].' No matter what, it's no good attempting to live an emotional lie because the attempt will bring added misery in its wake for all concerned. On top of that, the attempt is certain to break down if there has been a real emotional landslip. One is no longer the gay young hilltop."[69]

Sam Spiegel was as good as his word and had a print of KWAI ready in September.

After the screening for the cast and crew, Alec Guinness wrote to David:

"I think it's TERRIFIC. I was gripped, moved, stimulated and all the right things. It has real authority behind it and eye and ear are constantly alive and fascinated. I do congratulate you. Anyway, I'm vastly proud to be associated with it.

"I was enormously impressed by Jack [Hawkins] - when I read it I thought it rather a map-pointing part such as he has often played - but his reality etc etc are remarkable. Bill [Holden] I liked too - I thought he was fine and made an almost oversardonic character most likeable and intriguing. Liked Geoffrey [Horne] - very appealing. Even liked Guinness - though I thought he was a bit flat here and there (at moments you suggested to him he was and didn't believe) - and only greatly regretted his playing the Pied Piper Hospital scene with a hand in his pocket and not being definite enough at his death. The only thing I didn't care for was the girl on Mount Lavinia beach. Thought the Siamese enchanting. A wonderful film. Thank you for having me. As ever, Alec.

"PS: Clever you've been with silly old J. Donald - he's very effective. So's Sessue."[70]

Some members of the crew, proud of their part in the film, were dismayed to find their names missing from the credits.

Credits on a David Lean film were awarded in an illogical manner. Teddy Darvas, who had been sound editor on HOBSON'S CHOICE, was refused a credit on that film because David told him it was not a big enough job to warrant one. Although he was assembly editor on KWAI, he was buried among the editing assistants. The second unit director was denied a credit and yet, against past precedent, the chief electrician was given one.

"Archie Dansie was quite magnificent," said Darvas, "quite apart from how hard he worked. It was one of the few times a 'sparks' had screen credit, and as far as Archie was concerned that was like getting a knighthood. And I think people miss that feeling of achievement that with non-contractual credits you only got a credit if you'd done something rather good. You get the Jobfit Trainee on the credits now."[71]

The screen credits were the final responsibility of Sam Spiegel, and David found himself in an awkward situation when it came to the screenplay. "I said to Sam, 'If anyone's going to get a credit for the script - and particularly if Carl Foreman's going to get a credit - I want a credit, because I certainly did much more than he did.' And Sam sort of mumbled. When it came on the screen I was absolutely amazed to see 'Screenplay by Pierre Boulle.' Pierre Boulle had written not one line of the script."[72]

"The press show of KWAI was an extraordinary event," said Norman Spencer. "David hated the press. He said, 'These buggers - you spend years devising the beginning of a film and you see these bloody press people coming in late. It's been on the screen ten minutes before they arrive.'

"Sam said, 'We'll stop them this time.' He announced on the press show tickets that the doors would be shut five minutes before the film went on the screen and he stayed in the foyer, and I stayed in the foyer, to see what would happen. They shut the doors and locked them and all sorts of well-known critics came and tapped on the windows, wondering what had gone wrong. They wouldn't let them in. Half the press didn't see the picture at the press show.

"It didn't seem to affect the reaction. I think the critics were a little embarrassed to say they were late. The film was so good, it hit people between the eyes so strongly, that they realised it would have been unfortunate for them personally if they had given it a bad notice while everybody else around was giving it a good one."[73]

This was not the case, though, with one particular critic. Lindsay Anderson - who has been so helpful as far as this book is concerned - was a bugbear for David Lean. At the time of KWAI he was a documentary film-maker and a critic for *Sight and Sound* magazine.

"I sometimes subbed for the film critic on the *New Statesman*, William Whitebait [George Stonier], a friend of mine," said Anderson. "I had to review the Boulting Bros version of LUCKY JIM, which I thought was quite bad, and wrote a whole column analysing it. The next week THE BRIDGE ON THE RIVER KWAI opened. It was hailed as a masterpiece and was mentioned in the same breath as ALL QUIET ON THE WESTERN FRONT. Being, I must admit, lazy, I thought I can't write another long analysis on why I don't think it's good. Everyone else thought it was a masterpiece, so naively I thought, 'no one's going to mind what I write,' and anyway in the *New Statesman* they won't even see it.

"So I had the idea of writing a review of Wajda's A GENERATION, which I'd liked very much and which was not showing in London. Being a Socialist paper, I was sure the *Statesman* would approve of my writing about something which the system was not giving us. When it came to KWAI I wrote three or four lines of rude dismissal. I thought no more about it. But later, Peter Taylor, who edited my film THIS SPORTING LIFE, said to me that the only review he had heard David Lean mention was this one in the *New Statesman*.

"Many years later, my film THE WHALES OF AUGUST was shown at Cannes in the presence of Prince Charles. Afterwards, there was a reception and the room was filled with British film-makers. I remember saying, 'Isn't that David Lean?' Barry Spikings said, 'Yes, I'll go and mention...' I said, 'For God's sake don't,' but it was too late. He came back, grinning all over his face. He'd mentioned my name and David Lean had said, 'That man has trashed every film I've made for the past twenty-five years.' The truth was I had hardly seen any of them."[74]

Anderson dealt with KWAI in a nine-line review: "The week's ration for the public screens may be shortly dealt with. BRIDGE ON THE RIVER KWAI (Plaza) is a huge, expensive chocolate box of a war picture. Inside it is perhaps a better and ironic idea; but it takes more than the word 'madness' repeated three times at the end of the film to justify comparisons with ALL QUIET ON THE WESTERN FRONT. They'll be saying that the new Jayne Mansfield is better than Lubitsch next."[75]

David did not attend the London premiere on 2 October 1957, his accountant having warned him to play safe. Thus he had to experience his first smash-hit through telephone reports and newspaper cuttings. He felt cut off and was grateful for an enthusiastic cable from Mike Frankovich, a Columbia executive in London with whom he had formed a friendship.

"I thought you had a fit and were exaggerating," wrote David from Ceylon. "When I arrived here and read the notices it was I who had the fit. 'Great! Shattering!' What happened to them all? I thought - in a few grandiose dreams - that the New York critics might pull out a few superlatives, but the *London* critics!"[76]

In the run-up to the American launch, he had one unpleasant surprise. As an equal partner with Sam Spiegel, he had not realised Spiegel would give his own name above-the-title prominence. The advance advertisements bore the legend, "A Sam Spiegel Production". David had never had worse billing, even in his early days, and at the moment of his greatest success it made him feel cheated. He fired off a cable to Spiegel:

"THRILLED OUR EVER-WIDENING OVATION VERY EXCITED MEET YOU CELEBRATE OUR JOINT TRIUMPH STOP YES TWO REQUESTS CUM DEMANDS WHICH BEG YOU IMPLEMENT IMMEDIATELY THUS PREVENTING RIFT AND PRESERVING OUR ADMIRABLE RELATIONSHIP STOP FIRSTLY CHANGE SCRIPT CREDIT AS I WILL NOT REMAIN SILENT WITNESS THIS FARCE AND FOREGO POSSIBLE ACADEMY NOMINATION AFTER STARTING SCRIPT FROM SCRATCH AND TEN MONTHS DEVOTION TO IT STOP SECONDLY KEEP FAITH SPIRIT OUR UNDERSTANDING AND PUT ME ABOVE THE LINE ALONGSIDE AMERICAN LAUNCHED SPIEGEL SPUTNIK STOP LOVE FROM BOTH ROCKET."[77]

The New York premiere was held at the RKO Theatre, on Broadway and 47th Street, on 18 December 1957.

"I remember arriving in New York," said David, "and turning on the radio and the first thing I heard was Mitch Miller's jazz version of 'Colonel Bogey.' I turned to another station and there it was, played again. It was a smash hit. Played everywhere. It must have sold millions of copies.

"The widow of the composer, Kenneth J. Alford, unexpectedly made a small fortune. She had been born in South Africa and she had always longed to go back to see it just once more and she could never afford it. So when the film brought in all this money for her, she took a great lump of what it had earned and went to South Africa and then came back to England and died."[78]

The film was received as enthusiastically in New York as it had been in London. "It was obviously a crashing great success," said David. "You could see it immediately with the audience. It was electric. And then we went up to the St Regis roof for the reception. James Donald came up to me and said, 'I don't know what to say to you. Can I shake your hand?' And he put his arms round me and said, 'I'm so, so sorry.'"

On 22 December 1957 Noël Coward saw the film, "A really magnificent picture," he wrote in his diary. "Brilliantly directed by David and acted superbly by Alec, James Donald, Jack Hawkins, Sessue Hayakawa and Bill Holden. Really satisfying. I rather wish now that I had done it."[79]

When David won the Screen Directors, Guild award and the film was nominated for eight Academy Awards, the bogus screenplay credit inevitably caused some controversy and confusion.

"When I arrived," David wrote to Michael Wilson, "Sam was in a fine old state because he was worried your wicked name might get out of the bag and 'ruin our chances, baby.' He told me that you were the one who was most anxious to have it hidden as it would put you out of work. Have no idea if this is true. Consequently I lied like a trooper to all who asked me if you did in fact write it. I made up a long story about Boulle and me in Paris - to overcome the people who said they just didn't believe that a Frenchman who had never written a script in his life could produce such a work. It came to a climax when the Boston critics flew down here for the premiere and Sam had to tell them in my presence that I had done it with Boulle and didn't wish for credit as directors and producers took it as part of their job.

"By now, whether you like it or not, everyone knows you did it. They all know, Mike - I must say I am very glad. You are in fact the top screen writer this minute - but it's acknowledged in whispers! A real farce. Everyone wants to have you on a script and I suppose you are innundated [sic].

"There was an article which I didn't see - in the *Reporter* - apparently saying that Carl said he had done it. This is not believed as I told everyone quite openly that he didn't do more than the first attempt which I threw out..."[80]

Wilson corrected this in a letter to Ring Lardner Jr: "Lean's statement is most unfair to Carl. It is not true that all his work was thrown out, although I did alter it considerably and introduce new elements.

"I received $10,000 for my work on KWAI. Carl had already contracted for twenty-two percent of the profits, which so far have made him a quarter of a million dollars richer. Since he earned twenty-five times the amount I earned on the picture, it is only logical for his lawyer to boast that his contribution was twenty-five times greater than mine."[81]

In a letter to Columbia's Mike Frankovich, David wrote of his frustration over the bogus credit.

"I am entirely responsible for the anti-war angle and the general tone and style. Lines and lines of dialogue are mine. I thought of the big camp scenes such as Nicholson coming out of the oven and being greeted by all the men racing across the parade ground. It's the best thing I've ever done *and Sam didn't even ask me or inform me of what he was doing.* I am quite bewildered by such treatment and I don't think anyone could blame me if I hit out and used the weapons which are in my hands. The script was written by two people - and I was one of them. In the wildness of my distress I could have happily pulled down the whole edifice and exposed its rottenness. But this is American 'show business.' They pay well and I suppose this is the price. This is a little cry from the heart to you - just as a friend who was kind to me about the film."

The Academy Awards were presented on 26 March 1958 at the Pantages Theatre in Hollywood. THE BRIDGE ON THE RIVER KWAI won Best Picture and Alec Guinness won Best Actor, beating - of all people - Charles Laughton in WITNESS FOR THE PROSECUTION. Jack Hildyard won for cinematography, Malcolm Arnold for his music and Peter Taylor won the award for editing. David won the Best Director award.

However surprised he might have been by his film's successes, he was stunned when one of the two screenplay Oscars went to Pierre Boulle.

"I went up later and took my Oscar for best director. In those days it was more or less the same as it is today. You take the Oscar, you walk round the back and you follow a chalk line with crosses. You stop at each cross; the first cross is broadcasting, and they ask you a lot of questions, the second cross is television and it goes on and on and on. At one of them, a man held out a mike to me and said, 'Mr Lean, who wrote the script of THE BRIDGE ON THE RIVER KWAI?'

"I said, 'You're asking the 64,000 dollar question, and as you have not got 64,000 dollars I'm not prepared to tell you.'

"I thought this was very good at the time, because it was just off the cuff, and it was repeated all over America, on all sorts of stations, and Sam went berserk. I remember standing outside the theatre after the Oscar ceremony with Sam holding his Oscar for best picture and shaking it at me in fury. I shouting back at him, brandishing mine. It was a ridiculous scene."[82]

Although Boulle himself did not attend the ceremony, the award irritated the Hollywood film commmunty because they realised the credit was a sham.[83] According to David, it was Carl Foreman who kept the controversy alight.

A spectacular end for the bridge on the River Kwai.

"It kept coming out in newspapers that Carl Foreman had written the script," said David. "He was always giving interviews and saying, 'I wrote it, but I couldn't take credit because I was a witch-hunt writer.' He used to say it was his trademark if he had characters in a script named Grogan and Baker (named for his agents). I didn't trouble to change Grogan and Baker, and he said that was proof that he had written the script.

"On one occasion I met him at a party at Sam's at Grosvenor House. I said, 'Carl, the next time that you claim that you wrote the script, I'll show them what you wrote.' That was a killer. In fact, I hadn't got the script. I hadn't kept it, unfortunately. I was bluffing. That stopped him claiming it, but still the rumour went round that Carl Foreman wrote the script.

"Years later, the credit was rectified and Mike Wilson got his name up on the screen, and quite rightly. I should have been there, too, but I never tried for it because in those days I never took credit for screen writing."[84]

Carl Foreman thought that what had emerged was "a fantastically successful film which waved the flag and to the colourful strains of 'Colonel Bogey' sentimentalised the essential horror of the actual story. I tried to depict the two faces of heroism, the sometimes dangerous concept of military honour and the tremendous human as well as material waste of war."[85]

"The ending of the film was not in the script I left behind," Foreman told Adrian Turner. "I am sure it was written by Mike Wilson at David's request. I didn't like the 'madness, madness' line because it seemed to state the obvious. But David was also very visual and that is part of his genius. We haven't seen each other in years because there is resentment between us over the Oscar thing. I felt he should have behaved more generously.

"I felt very badly about seeing Boulle's name on the credits as author of the screenplay. I thought I was entitled to sole credit and Mike felt he was entitled to joint credit and in the end he probably was. But the decision was made by Spiegel and Columbia to have Boulle's name on the screen. Boulle was amazed, but Spiegel told him it was his book on the screen, that he had just put a few camera angles on it and what do you care? Actually, it was the best thing that ever happened to Boulle because it made him a millionaire."[86]

In Japan, hardly the place where one would expect the film to be popular, KWAI was nominated as the second best film imported during 1957.[87] Perhaps audiences were relieved to see their armies' wartime atrocities presented in so mild a light. For while the film depicted the Japanese behaving brutally towards British prisoners, it was far from the grim reality of life on the Burma railway. But had David shown the extreme brutalities of torture, starvation and suicides, the film would have been unbearable to all but an audience of psychopaths.

Nevertheless, KWAI aroused - and arouses still - passionate protest from those who had suffered from Japanese brutality for not declaring the fact that it was almost entirely fiction. The most articulate of these critics was a former PoW called Ian Watt who gave a talk for BBC Radio on 23 March 1959 and pointed out that the Japanese military engineers had been perfectly capable of planning their own bridges and forcing prisoners to build them.

"Their methods were always rough and ready, and often very confused; but given the need to finish the nearly three hundred miles of railway in less than a year, over a route which a previous survey by Western engineers had pronounced insuperably difficult, and with fantastically inadequate material means, the methods of the Japanese were probably the only ones which could have succeeded.

"It certainly seemed odd that Boulle should base his plot on the illusion that the West still had the monopoly of technological skill, when the Japanese capture of Singapore had made their ability to adapt Western methods to their own purposes so painfully obvious."

Watt was impressed by the visual beauty of the film, but said that except for a few brief flashes, it failed to recreate the peculiar horror of life on the railway. He also explained why the Japanese behaved so brutally.

"To the Japanese, the idea of being taken prisoner of war is deeply shameful, and looking after prisoners shares some of that humiliation. Consequently most of the Japanese staff were men who for one reason or another were thought unfit for combat duty: too old, perhaps, or in disgrace, or just drunks. The engineers usually despised the Japanese troops in charge of running the camps almost as much as they despised the prisoners."[88]

Although Pierre Boulle said he had based his Colonel upon two officers he had known in Indo-China, there had been a Colonel who achieved what Nicholson set out to achieve. Colonel Philip Toosey, a territorial from Cheshire, resolved that as many men as possible should survive. "He first awed the Japanese with an impressive display of military swagger," wrote Ian Watt, "then proceeded to charm them with his ingratiating and apparently unshakeable assumption that no sort of difficulty could arise between honourable soldiers whose only thought was to do the right thing."[89]

Toosey persuaded the Japanese that tasks such as issuing tools or allocating the workload could be better handled by his staff. He won the confidence of the Japanese, with only a slight increase in the level of "collaboration", and saved countless lives.

Toosey himself did not approve of the portrayal of Colonel Nicholson, nor the fact that in the film, unlike the book, the bridge was blown up.[90]

Ian Watt summed up the film's appeal in unexpected terms: "Its story merely developed Boulle's central situation in a recognizable universal fantasy - the schoolboy's perennial dream of defying the adult world. Young Nicholson cheeks the mean old headmaster, called Saito, he gets a terrible beating, but the other boys kick up such a row that Saito just has to give in. Then they carry the victor in triumph back across the playground and in the end, of course, he becomes the best head boy Kwai College ever had."[91]

It would be unfair to give Ian Watt's jest the last word. For many people, THE BRIDGE ON THE RIVER KWAI is a brilliant allegory about collaboration. The British were never faced with it on their own mainland, so the French author, whose homeland was overrun, staged it elsewhere, and showed that the British were just as vulnerable as his own people. As a German put it, "Most of us were against Hitler, but once he came to power, we did our damndest to make it work."

KWAI had cost $2,800,000 (£1,100,000) and by 1980, *Variety* ranked it twenty-third in the top-earning films, its domestic (USA and Canada) gross being $17,195,000, and its worldwide gross well over $22 million. Of this profit, William Holden, it should be remembered, received ten percent.

David's precise financial participation is hard to determine. Whilst he received a regular income from KWAI, Norman Spencer believes that David sold his percentage to Spiegel, at Spiegel's suggestion, for something like £150,000.

From his profits, Sam Spiegel acquired a Park Avenue penthouse where he was able to display his collection of French Impressionist paintings. He also bought a five-hundred-ton yacht, *The Malahne*.

Yet although Spiegel had promised the crew they would be paid for Sunday work, he failed to do so. Carpenter Fred Lane was so indignant he took Spiegel to court. He spent four years trying to get him into the box, but once there he won the day. He was awarded the £120 owing to him.

After the Oscars, David was inundated with offers, including MGM's remake of MUTINY ON THE BOUNTY - a job which was eventually given to Carol Reed who was later fired - and Kirk Douglas's Roman epic SPARTACUS which finally went to Anthony Mann and he, too, was fired. Spiegel suggested another novel by Pierre Boulle called THE OTHER SIDE OF THE COIN which was later optioned by Otto Preminger and never made.

The most unexpected offer came from William Wyler who took David round the MGM art department when he was about to start BEN-HUR. He said, "I'm going to put a proposition to you. Would you undertake to direct the chariot race? Think about it for two or three days. You can have full screen credit - 'Chariot Race directed by David Lean' - I won't interfere at all, you can do exactly as you want and I'd love you to do it."

David thought about it and decided against it. David admired Wyler both as a director and as a human being. He felt that he had the qualities all great directors needed; he was both a dreamer and he was intensely practical. He also liked the fact that he was one of the "no-nonsense brigade" and had a sense of humour about himself.[92]

When David had been editing KWAI in Paris, he gave a great deal of thought to India.

"I love it so much (outside the towns)," he wrote, "and even now I am still a little frightened by this West of ours. Paris is so damned clinical. It's like a bone without any marrow in it. There's such a show of affection and warmth but so very little devotion. The waiters, the servants, and all the rest of them are so brittle, and I long for a sweet Indian bearer with all his faults.

"I shall go back as soon as I can, and one day I may buy that small house in view of Nanga Parbat and grow those crisp Kashmiri apples."[93]

CHAPTER TWENTY-EIGHT

GANDHI

THE idea of a film about Gandhi goes back a surprisingly long way, right back to the silent era.

D.W. Griffith, who had directed THE BIRTH OF A NATION, and who had been encouraged by the British government during the First World War to make a propaganda picture, was approached again in 1923 to make a spectacular film to counter the devastating impact of Gandhi on the British Raj.[1]

But Griffith did not make the film. Nor did Gabriel Pascal, who travelled to Venice in 1953 to meet the impresario Mike Todd, a possible source of finance for his film, which was to be called THE LIFE OF GANDHI. Having spent some time in India attempting to set up the picture, Pascal struck misfortune when the one British actor who might have won him international backing, Alec Guinness, turned down the title role.[2]

There was also another problem: few financiers could be expected to enthuse about a film which lionised a man who stood for everything they did not.

Gandhi's shadow had fallen across David's path long before he was a director, for while the events which shaped Indian history were happening, he had edited the newsreel coverage of Gandhi being greeted by hysterical crowds. This obviously made an impression on him, for among the handful of frames he kept from his newsreel days were two scenes from the Bombay riots that erupted in September 1930.

When David proposed to make a film about Gandhi, Sam Spiegel was only one of the producers competing for his services. David wanted to be able to pick the best possible screenwriter and avoid the misery he experienced on KWAI. He therefore financed the early stages himself, conducting his research in Venice while he waited for the monsoon season to pass in India. And since Alec Guinness and he were now reconciled, he offered him the role.

Guinness said to David, "No, no, no, you must have an Indian. I will never be quite small enough, quite thin enough. You must have an Indian and preferably a Hindu."

"No, no," replied David, "The Indians can't act."[3]

This went on for about two years, when Guinness capitulated. "Of course I'm with you over Gandhi," he wrote to David, "as you really think I can play it. I'm not sure I can, but I feel I'm ready to play something big and it might as well be Gandhi and I could only pull off a really big thing with you I believe - and that's God's truth. So count me in."[4]

David read as many books as he could find on Gandhi (he also began reading about another famous historical character, Lawrence of Arabia.[5]) The principal research source of his Gandhi project was *The Life of Mahatma Gandhi* by Louis Fischer, published by Cape in 1951, which began with Gandhi's death.

For once we have David's carefully typed notes, which indicate his attitude towards his subject:

"Chapter One: find something quite tremendous about this final chapter of Gandhi's life. It immediately poses a basic construction problem. Will an audience remain in their seats for more than a few moments after the assassination - if the scene is shown at the end of the film? I almost automatically recoil at the thought of starting the film with the incident and thereby creating a flashback - but I also feel it would be a wasteful shame to condense and hurry through this great climax.

"I can't imagine why Fischer - as a writer - decided to start a book in this manner, but I presume it was because he felt it gave the whole thing a wonderful 'head.' (Perhaps the same reasoning applies to a film.) It certainly tells a reader or an audience 'we are going to tell you the story of a man who had become, to thousands of his countrymen, a living God. We tell you this before starting his story because he was, at first sight, a very ordinary little man - so don't be misled - watch very carefully.'

"On the other hand - if only one could somehow contrive to keep that restless and impatient audience in its seats - it is the most terrific climax in the grandest of classic forms. By putting it at the beginning one may loose [sic] certain emotional reactions because the character is still unknown, but I can't believe it wouldn't have a tremendous impact. I try to examine myself as to how much my pre-knowledge contributed to my emotional reaction, and if I would have been as moved if I had known nothing about him. I'm not sure. What then are the points that I am loath to miss - apart from the actual shooting which would be in either version?

"1: The almost inescapable yet unspoken conclusion that Gandhi was a modern Christ. He is attended by women in flowing robes. Women show him the greatest devotion, but obviously have no romantic attachment to him. Then the men - as devoted as the women. Nehru - his head buried in Gandhi's bloody clothes. Then the mass devotion."

David listed other extraordinary elements: the funeral cortege - "a million and a half marched and a further million watched"... the guns of Allahabad Fort firing a salute as the ashes are scattered on the water - "The little bones flowed quickly toward the sea"... and Nehru, shaken, shocked and cramped with sorrow, speaking on the radio: "Our beloved leader Bapu, as we called him, the father of

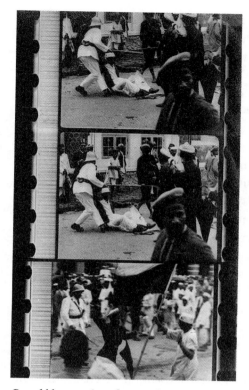

David blew up these frames of the Bombay riots in September 1930 from Movietone Newsreels supplied to Gaumont Sound News.

our nation, is no more."

"At this early stage I cannot believe we can afford to loose [sic] all this. Not only is it the basis for great 'cinema' from a pictorial point of view, it is tremendous in its mass emotional appeal. Mass goodwill and love towards a fellow human being not a King or an Emperor - just a very ordinary-looking little man whose possessions amounted to no more than the clothes he stood in.

"He was loved and respected for himself alone, and for the love he gave all human beings. Who before him ever attracted such demonstrations of spontaneous affection? Has it ever happened before? Have such scenes ever been shown on a cinema screen? Can we afford to underplay it?"

David returned to India in the autumn of 1958 and took with him Michael Powell's erstwhile script-writer, Emeric Pressburger. David admired Pressburger's work and he was a Hungarian Jew, like David's hero, Alexander Korda. It had been Pressburger who had scripted TAJ MAHAL for Korda.

Michael Powell described Pressburger as a conundrum. He was an energetic man - he had been an athlete in his youth - and he had to know what was going on. "He worried for hours when he missed the news."[6]

Anthony Havelock-Allan regarded him as "pure Teuton. One half of him would have made a frightfully good Gauleiter. Despite being a Jew, he was as quintessentially German as you could imagine. He was an enormous eater and a tremendous disciplinarian."[7]

And yet when Pressburger applied for British citizenship, David said, "But Emeric is more English than any of us!"[8]

Pressburger had just experienced the shock of being blamed for a big flop - MIRACLE IN SOHO, which he had scripted and produced. John Davis made it plain that he had no future with Rank, so the offer from David came as manna from heaven.

The subject of the film they had come to research remained confidential, as it was potentially explosive. Their main Indian contact was Hiten Chaudhury, a writer and poet connected with the film industry, who told them at the airport that Filippo Del Giudice had been trying to finance a film on Gandhi. David and Pressburger were astonished by the news and when they revealed that their film was also about Gandhi, Chaudhury was equally surprised. Leila was with them, and David had to struggle with twenty-eight pieces of luggage when he and Emeric were separated in the customs shed.

All this is contained in Emeric Pressburger's diary, which gives a vivid account of their travels, although most of it is the equivalent of David's home movies - descriptive of the scenery but not of the politics. Pressburger is fascinated by the Indian people and by his own state of health. "I feel so rotten I have to go upstairs - David is very sweet and around 7 pm I feel OK."

The most important task facing them is to win government co-operation. They take immense care to go through the right channels. In order to get a meeting with Nehru, Chaudhury suggests they approach his daughter, Indira Gandhi.

David, meanwhile, drives Emeric around India in a purple Rolls-Royce, hardly the most unobtrusive car when trying to pass unnoticed through crowds of beggars. Pressburger records that David is brilliant at remembering the road but tends to forget his car keys.

On 4 November, a telegram arrives from Alec Guinness saying that the *Evening Standard* in London has a story about him, David and Gandhi. Other papers pursue David, track him down and begin telephoning. Photographers and newsmen arrive. The cat is out of the bag and the Indian press emphasise the controversial nature of David's project. He and Emeric get their meeting with the Prime Minister.

"Nehru wears a black coat with a tiny red flower," wrote Pressburger, "looks a little like Rex Harrison." Indira Gandhi asked David to tell her father of his plans for the film. "Too long a silence follows," wrote Pressburger. "I feel David would speak but he doesn't. I meekly intervene saying we never imagined this moment just like this. David collects himself and begins. Mr N listens and when D is stuck, helps. His reactions; a good film on G is welcome. He talks of previous attempts - Pascal. David tells of Pascal's legend with Shaw. Then we start talking of Gandhi. Mr N remembers and draws him with simple, loving care. Gandhi wouldn't preach or scold; when in a third class carriage, somebody spat, he would take a piece of paper and wipe it up, again and again. Indira Gandhi is rather impatient with Gandhi's whim of travelling third class, but keeping the whole carriage; below decks, but upsetting the whole ship."[9]

"I'll tell you something," Nehru told the two men. "It cost us a small fortune to keep Gandhiji in poverty."[10]

Although David was proud enough of his association with Mountbatten on IN

WHICH WE SERVE, he was positively awe-struck by his contact with Nehru.

"He was very kind to me and often asked me round to Parliament House. He was the most attractive man I've ever met in my life. Tremendously gentle, a real gentleman. Terribly good-looking, dreaming eyes, then go down the face, which was bloody good, and you have a kind of sensuality around the mouth.

"I remember having dinner with him and his daughter Indira, who was later Prime Minister and who was assassinated. He said, 'Do you know how to prepare a mango?'

"I said, 'Well, I know the conventional way.'

"He said, 'Come, let me do it for you.' And he prepared me a mango with a very sharp knife with the care of a great surgeon. I was highly impressed, and flattered." [11]

David sometimes dined with Nehru at his house in Allahabad which was decorated with pictures of all the viceroys. After David remarked about the pictures, Nehru told him of a visit from Khrushchev and Bulganin in 1955. Khrushchev had wondered why Nehru liked to have these pictures - these relics of colonialism - on the walls. Nehru replied, "You cannot change history by turning faces to a wall."

"Another day," said David, "Nehru rang up and said, 'Would you like to come round for dinner, tonight? I think you might be amused. There's a Russian delegation here. And Lady Mountbatten will be there.'

"It has since turned out that she was his mistress. I went along and there were all these Russians and Nehru announced, through an interpreter, 'Please forgive me, we're going to be half an hour late for dinner. Lady Mountbatten's plane has been delayed at Agra. But please help yourselves to drinks.'

"For the Russians to have the Indian Prime Minister bearing no malice towards the ex-vicereine, but waiting for her to arrive for dinner, was wonderful, I think. And they were absolutely nonplussed." [12]

When Nehru died in 1964, Hiten Chaudhury wrote to David to say that Indira Gandhi remarked that he had never been so open with any person on first meeting. "I also think that none other than his very close friends have found him so near for such a long period." [13].

The project was going so well that David brought in Sam Spiegel as producer. However, tension was growing between David and Pressburger. It was perhaps encouraged by Leila, who may have wanted to be alone with David; one can only surmise. Pressburger records an argument with Leila - "an unfortunate scrape" - and David takes her side.

"I have decided this morning to go home," Pressburger wrote on 30 November. "D turned up very gloomy at breakfast, after which we had a talk in the sun. I told him of my decision and he recalled some of my crimes of the past six weeks, including telling Hitu that the French brandy was not French and doubting that his green tea was green tea. The whole thing is just idiotic. We agreed that the only thing to do is what I wished to do."

By lunchtime, Leila had arrived wreathed in smiles. "We were both mighty sorry and I promised to talk to D." When he finally does so, David suggests that they cut their trip short, go to Benares without Leila and prepare a short synopsis so that Pressburger could be home by Christmas.

Which is more or less what happened. Pressburger thinks up a title - WRITTEN IN THE STARS - and he gets some solid work done. This is helpful, because Indira Gandhi asks to see something in writing. He creates the character of an American doctor, and David imagines William Holden in the part. Someone recommends he see Yul Brynner in DeMille's THE TEN COMMANDMENTS and he and Pressburger go to the Odeon, but David doesn't like him.

On Pressburger's birthday - about which he breathes not a word - he sees some of the doctor's character destroyed by David. "I don't mind. It was a red balloon. [I think he means a red herring!] I didn't like it either."[14]

Pressburger flew back to London and David returned to Venice. After hearing nothing for three months, David wrote him a letter:

"I'm mad keen to know how you are getting on. Don't let Sam bulldoze you. He's king at it and one has to grow an extra skin or the work suffers or one has a breakdown!"

The treatment of GANDHI was written in the form of a novel. This was standard practice for Pressburger; turning it into a script was a later stage for him. It has a suitably epic, David Lean opening - a parade in Delhi to welcome the Viceroy in 1912, which is shattered by a bomb explosion. Gandhi returns from South Africa, and the treatment intercuts between his activities and those of a sympathetic policeman, John Holdsworth, who eventually marries an Indian girl and as a result finds himself passed over for promotion.

Another prominent character is the American doctor, through whose eyes we experience much of the poverty and disease afflicting India. Although the Amritsar massacre is more restrained than in the 1982 Richard Attenborough film - we arrive after it is all over - the treatment does not flinch from depicting the British in an unflattering light. This would have seemed far more radical in 1958 than when Attenborough released his film.

The treatment did a serviceable job of incorporating the major events of Gandhi's campaign, but while it managed to characterise him, it failed to do as much for the other people. And while it suggested an enormously expensive production, it did not suggest a film with wide appeal: much screen time was devoted to cholera, which would not have appealed to David. There was one authentically epic scene - set in a weaving-shed of a prison - but on the whole, the treatment did not have the stature of a David Lean film.[15]

"Pressburger was a fine writer," said David. "He could turn his hand to anything. I was convinced we had an understanding of how the film should go. He eventually produced a treatment which was simply awful. It was so bad I was able to tell him so. I said, 'Emeric, this simply isn't what we talked about. It isn't what we agreed. It's got nothing to do with the India we saw and it isn't anything I want to make.'" [16, 17]

The relationship with Pressburger dissolved and GANDHI was put on the shelf, though David would take it down every few years. David and Spiegel's attention abruptly turned to the exploits of T.E. Lawrence.

While it was simple enough for the director and producer to switch course in this fashion, what about the actor who had been keeping himself available all this time? Alec Guinness considered that in this matter David acted like a moral coward.

"Over a period of two years," Guinness said, "I never accepted any job of any sort - theatre or film - without writing or phoning David, saying, 'Any sign of the Gandhi film, because I have been asked to do such-and-such?'

"He would write back saying, 'No, you will be perfectly safe to do that. I think it will be at least six months.' And so it went on. After about two years he was back here and he contacted me and said, 'I've got some material for you. I will come for the weekend.'

"He brought me stacks of photographs of Gandhi, articles about Gandhi, Indian press things and gramophone records of Gandhi speaking. But he was curiously silent over the weekend.

"With all this stuff, I was rather expecting his usual enthusiasm. I mean, we'd thumb through it and listen to the records, but he didn't pursue it much. He left at about nine-thirty in the morning, driving himself to London, and it so happens that a little after he had gone there was a telephone call. I had to go to London for a lunch, so I went up by train about an hour after he went.

"Before the lunch I went to a bookshop in Princes' Arcade which I used quite a lot. The chap who ran it said, 'Oh, two friends of yours just came in here.'

"I said, 'Oh, who were they?'

"'Mr David Lean and Mr Sam Spiegel.'

"'Oh, and what were they buying?'

"'Everything they could lay their hands on about Lawrence of Arabia.'

"I said, 'How odd.' And by sheer coincidence, later that afternoon, somewhere in Mayfair, I came face to face with David and his agent walking in the opposite direction. He cut me dead. He was as close to me as I am to you and he walked straight past me. A day or two later it was announced they were doing LAWRENCE OF ARABIA. "Why couldn't he have said, 'Look, the Gandhi thing is not happening,' or 'I've made a bloomer. I'm sorry, perhaps another day' or something? It's so curious." [18]

The GANDHI project kept David away from Europe for so long that when he returned to England, in April 1959, the *Daily Express* ran a story portraying him as a mysterious, hunted man.

"In his luggage Lean brought the bulky script of the film about Gandhi that he wants to make with Sir Alec Guinness. Behind, in a hotel near the hot, bustling bazaars of New Delhi, he has left the lovely Indian girl who has become the central figure of his absence from the film studios.

MR. AND MRS. PETER LEAN WITH TWO-YEAR-OLD NICHOLAS LAST NIGHT

LAST CONTACT: A FAMILY CIRCULAR

DAVID LEAN, leading British film director, has returned secretly to this country after two years in the East. And last night his 29-year-old son Peter telephoned me to ask: "Can you help me to find my take me on holiday sometimes, or else I would see him at the film studios.

"Then four years ago, while I was working at Guildford, I got married. Father did not know about it till the ceremony was over. Then he came haring down to Guildford and gave us

"In India he has lived in secluded style. He has moved from hotel to hotel, making his whereabouts known to only his closest friends. He has avoided almost all contact with film associates and visitors from Britain and America.

"Why has he lived a hunted man? A close Indian friend in New Delhi told me, 'David is like a coil of wire when he is working. His tensions get tighter and tighter as he gets wound up in himself. But the deepest reason for his retreat into being a recluse is that he feared his love for Leila and hers for him would not survive in the social circles he once knew. That feeling is slackening a little now, but he is a terribly sensitive man and they are from very different worlds.'

"He has told friends, 'She is the only woman with whom I find peace and tranquillity.'" [19]

When Peter Lean read that his father had "secretly" returned to England, he telephoned the *Express* and appealed to them for help in locating him, for he wanted David to meet his two-year-old grandson, Nicholas.

The reporter who took Peter's call smelled a story. He arrived at Peter's home that evening with a photographer and carried out an interview. The result, published the following day, bore the headline, 'The grandson that David Lean hasn't heard of...' together with a photograph of Peter, June and two-year old Nicholas. "I gather that David was furious," said Peter. "Buncs was furious. The whole family was up in arms."

The *Express* quoted Peter as saying, "I could never get very close to father. I was at boarding school and then I was doing my National Service. Father would take me on holiday sometimes, or else I would see him at the film studios. Then four years ago, while I was working at Guildford, I got married. Father did not know about it till the ceremony was over [a misquotation]. Then he came haring down to Guildford and gave us his blessing and a four-day honeymoon trip to Paris.

"That was the last time I saw father. After that there were spasmodic letters. The last one came two years ago while he was out East. It had been dictated on a tape recorder and sent to London. Then it was duplicated by a secretary and copies were circulated to members of the family. It was like a travelogue of his activities. Fascinating, but still…

"Since then there has been no word at all. And Nicholas is two-and-a-half years old now, you see. I would just like father to see him. I know father gets terribly caught up in whatever he is doing at any particular moment, but it would be nice to see him."

The *Express* story concluded, "But last night in London there was still no sign of David Lean contacting his family. Said a close friend, 'He's very busy, and I suppose he will get round to things in his own good time.'"[20]

David did not contact Peter after the article. He did not meet his grandson until Nicholas was twenty-nine. A second grandchild, Tracy, was born on 6 March 1960. He did not meet her for thirty years.

CHAPTER TWENTY-NINE

INTO THE FURNACE

LAWRENCE OF ARABIA I

On 4 July 1960, David married Leila Matkar in Paris. The ceremony was attended by twenty-eight guests including Sam Spiegel, Marlon Brando and Jack Hawkins. Barbara Hutton gave the bride away. Leila wore an ivory silk sari, a family heirloom, embroidered in gold.

"When I met them in Paris," said an Indian friend, "Leila would come through the George V like a Persian miniature - barefoot, gold anklets, jingle, jingle, across the lobby. She always dressed like a Moghul princess, the embodiment of the Mumtaz Mahal, for whom the Taj Mahal was built."[1]

It has been said that David Lean married his women when other men would be divorcing them - a twisted tribute perhaps to his Quaker past. The marriage to Leila occurred at a particularly unfortunate moment, because David was about to make her a "celluloid widow" as he embarked on what would prove his greatest film. And because of this film, David would meet a woman he *should* have married.

As a child, David had been taken by his father to several illustrated lectures, and it would have been a satisfying coincidence if he had been taken to the Albert Hall to hear Lowell Thomas speak on *With Allenby in Palestine and Lawrence in Arabia*. Alas, he was not.[2] David and Edward's Christmas treat for 1919 was more likely to have been Maskelyne's Theatre of Mystery near Oxford Circus. Nevertheless, the Lawrence legend enthralled David as it did so many of his generation, and after Captain Maskelyne he became his earliest hero.

Lawrence was the first political or military figure to be transformed into a legend through the power of moving pictures. Lowell Thomas, an American journalist, accompanied by a cameraman, Harry Chase, had been searching the war zones for a colourful hero. At first he thought he had found him in General Allenby, but when he presented his illustrated lecture in New York and London, he found his audiences responding with far more enthusiasm to the lecture entitled *With Lawrence in Arabia*.

Lawrence, who enjoyed publicity and despised himself for doing so, suddenly found out what it was like to be a matinée idol. After revelling in it for a while - meeting the greatest men in the land - he soon retreated to monastic-like seclusion at All Souls College, Oxford. Throughout his life he had longed to produce a work of art; now he began his story - "the most splendid ever given a man for writing." He called it *Seven Pillars of Wisdom*.

Lawrence's father - like David's - deserted his wife and children. Sir Thomas Chapman, seventh Baronet of Westmeath in Ireland, set up a new home with his children's former governess and they lived an outwardly respectable life as Mr and Mrs Lawrence. Since Lady Chapman refused a divorce, Sir Thomas committed a sin even more heinous by the standards of his time; he proceeded to have children. In the Victorian era, this was regarded so seriously that some people committed suicide rather than live with the stigma of illegitimacy.

Thomas Edward Lawrence, who was born in 1888 in North Wales,[3] would not learn of this until he was ten. So shaken was he by the discovery that he set out to prove himself superior to everyone around him. He was, in any case, phenomenally gifted; he claimed he could read and write before he was four. Through scripture readings, he acquired a passion for ancient history, and toured medieval castles with his father.

In 1909, he embarked alone on a walking tour of Syria and Palestine, indulging his passion for Biblical history. He lived among the Arabs, learning their language and dialects and gaining a fascination for the Middle East and its people which would never leave him. His thesis - on the influence of the Crusaders on European military architecture - won him a first class degree in Modern History. Magdalen College, Oxford, granted him funds to visit the site of the ancient city of Carchemish, on the Euphrates, which the British Museum was excavating, and he took the official photographs. Here he met Selim Ahmed - Dahoum - who might have been the mysterious "S.A." to whom he dedicated *Seven Pillars*.

A man with such accomplishments was an ideal candidate for British Intelligence and early in 1914 he reconnoitred the Sinai peninsula. When war broke out he became an Intelligence officer posted to the Army's Information Service in Cairo, where he worked mainly on maps. The enemy was Turkey; the Ottoman Empire ruled almost the whole of the Middle East and was allied with Germany. Turkish brutality led to an Arab revolt, started by Sherif Hussein, which broke out on 10 June 1916. Lawrence, eager to be a part of it, made himself so unpopular at GHQ that he was granted ten days' leave to accompany his friend Ronald Storrs[4] to Jiddah, where they were to meet one of Sherif Hussein's sons, Emir Abdullah.

In Lawrence's opinion, Abdullah was not the leader the Revolt needed but his brother, Feisal, was. Although Lawrence knew that Britain and France planned to carve up Arabia between them,[5] he persevered in his attempts to assist the Arabs in their fight against the Turks. He felt that if the Arabs united and were victorious, the British could hardly overlook their moral claims. He therefore formed an uneasy alliance with Auda abu Tayi, leader of the Howeitat tribe, a medieval tyrant distinguished by both his courage and his brutality. Together they raided Turkish positions, blew up sections of the vital Hejaz Railway and captured Aqaba without firing a shot. Lawrence's commanding officer, General Allenby, whom he deeply admired, realised the value of "Britain's least conventional soldier" and kept him in the desert.

Place any normal, sedentary academic in this situation - travelling a thousand miles a month on a camel - and how long would he last? Not only would he have machine-gun fire and furnace-like heat to contend with, but fleas, camel-flies, dysentery and even bitter cold. This is where those who try to undermine Lawrence's reputation come unstuck; the only way to dispel the legend would be to prove that he was not there, that it was someone else whose exploits he had taken as his own. And that is no more likely than a revelation that David Lean did not direct LAWRENCE OF ARABIA.

In any case, one of the most energetic detractors was Lawrence himself. He felt he was a confidence trickster on a grand scale, and he fully expected - and even hoped - to be killed on the campaign. He set himself feats of endurance, determined to be as physically hard as his fighting men. Anthony Nutting, one of his biographers, believed he achieved spiritual exhilaration through pain. He kept going despite fever and exhaustion, and his achievements impressed the Arabs, who pronounced his name "El Aurens" as though he were already a prince.

Lawrence eventually succeeded in leading the Arab army, under Feisal, into Damascus in October 1918. Yet his name in England was virtually unknown. It was the moving picture - and Lowell Thomas's romantic words - that created his legend.

A film about this dashing desert hero was inevitable, yet it took a surprisingly long time. In 1921, Rudolph Valentino turned the eyes of Hollywood towards the Arabs with THE SHEIK, yet that film - as with the imitators it spawned - avoided any reference to the war in the desert.

In 1923, British Instructional Films released a film about Allenby's campaign called ARMAGEDDON. The film has been lost, but it was apparently strictly factual, using newsreels and maps and only a limited amount of re-enactment. In their review, the *New York Times* said, "An illustration of the great help Colonel E.T. [sic] Lawrence rendered through his marvellous persuasive ability with the Arabs is also shown and one would like to see more of this, together with pictures of this modest and gallant gentleman."[6]

By the time it was released, Lawrence was condensing his vast text, *Seven Pillars of Wisdom*, and planning a limited edition. Although he allowed *Revolt in the Desert*, a shortened version of *Seven Pillars*, to be published in 1927, he did not want to profit from his experiences with the Arabs and the result was that the lavish *Seven Pillars* enterprise cost him far more than he could recoup and he fell deeply into debt.

One way of clearing that debt was to sanction a film. Herbert Wilcox claimed that Lawrence visited him in 1926, though the producer rejected the idea of making a film about Lawrence's exploits as "extremely interesting but not good cinema,"[7] which hardly rings true.

Lawrence had no liking for motion pictures. In 1935 he wrote to Robert Graves, "My rare visits to the cinema always deepen in me a sense of their superficial falsity... The camera seems wholly in place as journalism; but when it tries to recreate, it boobs and sets my teeth on edge. So there won't be a film of me."[8]

The same year as the possibly apochryphal Wilcox visit, Rex Ingram wrote to Lawrence and asked for a copy of *Seven Pillars of Wisdom*. Lawrence replied from the RAF Cadet College at Cranwell, where he was a humble AC/2 hiding under the name of T.E. Shaw, saying that his application had come too late. Ingram and Lawrence began a correspondence. Ingram sent him photographs of his sculpture which Lawrence, an unsuccessful sculptor himself, admired. He said he would try to get him a copy of his book which, he added, was "no good, but it's the best I can do."[9]

Ingram eventually received two copies, by accident, and wrote a letter full of enthusiasm. He offered to send some books in return. Lawrence replied from India where the press had him fomenting rebellion in Afghanistan, though he was merely working in an engine repair depot.

"Karachi is not amusing as a place of exile. I have to stay here till the chatter stirred up by Cape's publication of my little book *Revolt in the Desert* dies out. Three years I believe. India makes me homesick, for it is a shoddy-feeling place. The people seem ashamed of us, and I feel ashamed of myself before them. The Arabs appealed to me because they had complete self-respect and no sense of being inferior to the English. That pleases me, for I'm Irish too, more or less."

Ingram was clearly working towards asking the most difficult question: would Lawrence agree to his making a film about him? But Lawrence forestalled him.

"I do not envy you your film job. It must be a very difficult art, an expression of yourself (and the author of the scenario) at two removes. Indeed I wonder that it is ever so good as it seems to be.

"They babble sometimes to me of making a film of *Revolt in the Desert*. I have no property in it, so that I hope they will not. Hollywood offered £6,000 or something, which the Trustees turned down. Long may they go on turning it down. I'd hate to see myself parodied on the pitiful basis of my record of what the fellows with me did."[10]

At that point, Ingram abandoned hope. But the following year - 1928 - it was announced in the British trade press that *Revolt in the Desert* would be filmed by M.A. Wetherell. The cameraman was to be F.A. Young. It would be more than three decades before Freddie Young would join forces with David Lean in the Jordanian desert to film the epic on a scale which would have delighted David's mentor, Rex Ingram.

In the thirties, the most persistent of those wanting to put the Lawrence legend on film was Alexander Korda. Lawrence vacillated between apparent co-operation and attempts to sabotage the project. At one point, he agreed to a film starring Leslie Howard, written by the author of WINGS, John Monk Saunders, and directed by Lewis Milestone, because it might keep Hollywood travesties at bay.[11] But after lunching with Korda in January 1935, Lawrence wrote to Robert Graves, "He was most decent and understanding and has agreed to put it off till I die or welcome it..."[12]

Five months later, on 19 May 1935, Lawrence died after a motor-cycle accident. He was forty-six.

"Colonel Lawrence was the greatest personality I have ever met," said Korda. "If his relatives or close friends object to the film being made, it will never be made by me and no-one else will be allowed to make it. I could never contemplate such a thing."

The day after this statement appeared in the press, Korda cabled Robert Graves asking if he would write a scenario.

When T.E. Lawrence died, the youngest member of the family, Arnold Walter Lawrence, or "A.W.", became his brother's literary executor. He had been given the same education and T.E. aroused in him the same interest in archaeology and medieval history. Despite an attempt to use him politically as a substitute for T.E., "A.W." remained closeted deep within the academic world.

He permitted the general publication of *Seven Pillars* and when 100,000 copies were sold in England alone T.E. Lawrence's box-office potential soared. Korda cast Walter Hudd[13] in a version to be directed first by Zoltan Korda, then by Brian Desmond Hurst, an Irishman who had fought the Turks himself, and who had known Lawrence in the Middle East. The Korda film collapsed just as Hurst was about to leave for Jerusalem because the British Governor of Palestine had refused to permit any large assembly of Arabs.

The project was revived in 1937 with Leslie Howard starring and American William K. Howard directing. This time, the Turks objected - and since Britain wanted Turkey as an ally in the event of a war with Germany, Korda cancelled it. In 1938, he tried again, promising to show the Turks as "heroic opponents", and considered John Clements, Clifford Evans, Robert Donat and even Laurence Olivier in the lead. Columbia announced a film with Cary Grant, to be made in collaboration with Korda. Burgess Meredith was to star in another in 1949.

Even Alan Ladd wanted to play the role.

In 1952, Harry Cohn of Columbia revived the idea and offered it to Michael Powell and Emeric Pressburger, who reluctantly turned it down.[14] Cohn then approached the director he recalled from OLIVER TWIST. Adrian Turner found this letter in the Columbia files:

1 Ilchester Place
London W8
May 2 1952
Dear Harry Cohn
This is to tell you how excited I am by the Lawrence of Arabia idea... I can't think of a better subject for my first film in America.
Best wishes, David Lean

Around the same time, David was approached by Terence Rattigan with another Lawrence project. Rattigan - whose father had been a diplomat and a friend of Sir Ronald Storrs and who had spent part of his childhood in Cairo - was fascinated by Lawrence, his ambiguous sexuality and the way he buried himself in the RAF. Professor A.W. Lawrence objected to Rattigan's proposal, according to Adrian Turner, because of the hints of homosexuality.[15]

The Professor's dislike of the Columbia project was rooted in his innate distrust of Hollywood, even though the Hollywood company had, in this case, a reputable British director. But David decided to back out when he was presented with a firm contract from Korda to make SUMMERTIME.[16] Columbia eventually pulled out themselves when they realised they would never be able to please the Professor, who demanded script and casting approval.

In 1955, Rattigan revived his Lawrence project and spent three years on a script to be directed by Anthony Asquith and produced for the Rank Organisation by Anatole de Grunwald. Dirk Bogarde was to have played Lawrence. They had no sooner returned from a location hunt in Iraq when revolution broke out, the King was assassinated and the whole project was aborted, leaving the stage clear for Sam Spiegel.

Spiegel's first task was to persuade Professor Lawrence to part with the rights to *Seven Pillars of Wisdom*. To this end he hired Michael Wilson as screenwriter. He also sent David to meet Robert Graves, classical scholar and author, whom T.E. Lawrence had taken under his wing at Oxford.

"He was one of the most interesting people I met," said David. "Graves was sitting in a bed in the public ward of a London hospital, looking eccentric. He had known Lawrence very well, and he used to laugh about him. He told me all sorts of things which were fairly useful, but he was slightly malicious. He obviously admired him very much, but he did think he showed off. That wonderful expression of Lowell Thomas summed it up - 'He had a genius for backing into the limelight.' And that side of Lawrence tickled Graves."[17]

David's enthusiasm clearly impressed Graves for in a postscript to a letter to Professor Lawrence he wrote, "I am very happy to hear you are allowing Spiegel, David Lean and Mike Wilson to make the T.E. film. It will be historical and heroic; the film of the year. The Rank picture would have been a disaster."[18]

The Professor had not yet agreed! Before he would consider selling the rights, he asked to meet David. Spiegel cleverly arranged that the meeting, held on 8 February 1960, would be preceded by a screening of KWAI. Lawrence, who seldom saw films of any sort, was suitably astonished. He then asked to see a treatment by Michael Wilson.

Wilson was an exceptional writer; he had proved it with his work on KWAI, and he proved it again with his work on LAWRENCE, his first contribution being a discussion of Lawrence and his aims, called Elements and Facets of the Theme, dated 20 September 1959:

"In trying to serve two masters, Lawrence betrayed them both. Part of Lawrence's tragedy was his intellectualism. With his inheritance of western culture, he could never really hope to submerge himself in an alien and primitive culture... Did he not serve to introduce into the Arab world the very evils from which he had fled?... He was a man who, fleeing blindly from a deadly disease to a healthy land, himself afflicts it with the plague."

Wilson argued that in the general disillusionment following World War One, the western world needed an authentic hero to shore up the ideals for which the war had allegedly been fought.

"A shining symbol was needed to prove that chivalry and nobility had not vanished, that we had not fought in vain when individual genius could rise out of mass horror. The Lawrence legend was created to fill that need. The prime mover in the creation of the legend was, of course, Lowell Thomas. But willingly and/or unwillingly, Lawrence himself contributed heavily to the myth... The contrast between the legendary figure and the actual man is the meat of drama... *Our picture should unveil a mystery*."

It was precisely this approach, I suspect, that eventually led to Wilson's downfall. For the image of Lawrence he conveys is a sordid one, the story of a cold-hearted opportunist who uses the desert revolt - which the British were already orchestrating - to play his own melody.

Because Spiegel had not yet acquired the rights to *Seven Pillars*, Wilson had to concoct a script based on Lowell Thomas's book, and various biographies - all of which drew lavishly on *Seven Pillars*. When Wilson produced a treatment, Spiegel sent it to Professor Lawrence who was so impressed that the next day he wrote to Spiegel that he would grant him the rights to *Seven Pillars*.

David was in India, and when he was reached, at the Taj Mahal Hotel in Bombay, Wilson wrote to him: "It is perhaps not immodest to assume that my approach to *Seven Pillars* helped to bring the old boy around."[19]

David despatched a cable: "WHAT A MASTERLY JOB YOU ARE DOING STOP YOUR EXTRAORDINARY GRASP AND INVENTIVE APPRECIATION OF COMPLEX SUBJECT FILLS ME WITH ADMIRATION AND EXCITEMENT STOP WARMEST REGARDS YOU AND FELLOW SUFFERERS STOP DAVID"[20]

Wilson must have felt exhilarated; if David was so pleased with the treatment, before the incorporation of *Seven Pillars*, how much more delight would he feel when he read the script?

Professor Lawrence was undoubtedly as relieved as he was impressed by the treatment, for Lawrence's life had been simplified to the two years of the Arab revolt, so all the difficult questions - which Wilson nonetheless planned to address in the final script - were omitted.

David returned to England and was present at the meeting when Spiegel finally acquired the rights. Professor Lawrence was accompanied by G. Wren-Howard, chairman of T.E.'s publishers, Jonathan Cape. The Professor, charming and endearing as he was, and resembling T.E. as he might have looked had he lived to the same age, was not a man of this world. Had he known he was facing the most ruthless negotiator in the film industry he would not have come, but Spiegel had made sure he had so far only encountered David, whose disdain for matters financial was equally spectacular.

Spiegel asked if Lawrence had a figure in mind. He hadn't, so Spiegel suggested £22,500. The Professor, who presumably considered this a suitably vast sum, said "Done" and they shook hands. Spiegel had himself a bargain. If David had filmed the meeting he would have lingered on a close-up reaction shot of the man from Cape, who had urged the Professor to hold out for £100,000.

The contract, signed on 11 February 1960, stipulated that should the Professor refuse to permit the company the use of the title *Seven Pillars of Wisdom* within four weeks of receiving the final script, the sum of £5,000 would become repayable.[21]

On 17 February 1960, Columbia Pictures staged a press reception at Claridge's Hotel to announce the picture. The reporters were not interested in how faithful the film would be to the original work; they wanted to know who was going to play Lawrence. Spiegel announced that Marlon Brando had been chosen. Had he declared "Edith Evans" the reporters could not have been more astonished. One of them mischievously asked if it would be a speaking part (Brando was already famous for mumbling his way through his films).

"In a way, they are very much alike," said Spiegel. "Both have that mystic, tortured quality of doubting their own destiny. In 1917, Lawrence was barely thirty, Brando is the same age." Spiegel added that Alec Guinness would have loved the part, but he was about fifteen years too old...[22]

No one told Professor Lawrence about this crucial decision, but it turned out he had no idea who Brando was anyway.

Spiegel's announcement of Brando was not simply a producer's whim; David had seen Brando as a German officer in THE YOUNG LIONS and thought he looked "an absolute god - would look wonderful in those clothes." In a series of lengthy notes on *Seven Pillars*, written in India, David wrote that Brando would be good as Lawrence because an audience should never feel certain about the man:

"They should sometimes look on him with affection and admiration, and sometimes in horror - not quite understanding. Lawrence is not a stock character, and that's his fascination."[23]

The launch was not a complete waste of time because it produced an exchange of letters between David and Henry Williamson, a close friend of Lawrence (in fact, Lawrence had been killed returning from sending a telegram to him). Somewhat discredited after the war for his sympathy for Hitler, Williamson was nonetheless an exceptional writer, admired not only for his best-known work, *Tarka The Otter*.

Williamson wrote to David: "I wish we were nearer - because I know the key to TE's *behaviourism*. Last night, in little lost Ilfracombe, I saw for the first time James Dean in REBEL WITHOUT A CAUSE, and was moved to praise for the truth of the characters - just a wee bit larger than life but NOT James Dean. There was TEL. But TEL was *terribly* hypersensitive. He was like beaten gold leaf in stale air - quivering to every pressure beyond any air drift or waft. But he had a terrible problem. He was *not* homosexual. He was impotent, in the sense of a wild true animal being impotent with the wrong conditions... You have a tremendous opportunity to make a penetrating, beautiful (because true) and explicit film, that every man will recognise in himself - we are all part fear, part love, part hero, part coward - and as the hypersensitive TEL wrote to me, 'bust themselves trying to be bigger than they are.' TE was noble and cocky-rude; self immolating and Wagner-like in his dreams... He was aloof, but tortured by longing for love and affection or deep friendship, as are all mammals... He is perhaps the brightest star of my life - pure oxygen - but inwardly haunted."[24]

Less than two weeks after the launch, Terence Rattigan signed a contract with Captain Basil Liddell-Hart acknowledging the use of his authorised biography of T.E. Lawrence in the production of a stage play called *Ross*. When Spiegel realised that the aborted Rank film had been adapted for the stage, he was furious and goaded the Professor into trying to block it. Rattigan responded that if he could not put *Ross* on the stage, he would put it on television, where the Lord Chamberlain's archaic rules of censorship and propriety did not apply. Game, set and match.

Rattigan's play opened at the Theatre Royal Haymarket, on 12 May 1960 and starred Alec Guinness. The play received excellent reviews, and by arousing public speculation over Lawrence helped create anticipation for the film.

Yet Spiegel regarded any incursion into what he now regarded as "his" subject as a hostile act. His failure to suppress *Ross* made him determined to buy the rights to any book that contained the basis for a rival version. Spiegel acquired no less than seven literary properties.

He was thus incensed to learn that despite all these expensive precautions the film rights of *Ross* had been bought by Herbert Wilcox, and that he planned a film to start shooting in March 1961 with Laurence Harvey. At this point, David had nothing so positive as a starting date.

Wilcox had given Rattigan a cheque for £100,000, a photograph of which Rattigan wryly included in his memoirs. Spiegel threatened an injunction.

"I would have gone ahead and made *Ross*, defying Spiegel," wrote Wilcox, "and could have shown my film a year ahead of his since David Lean, although a great director, is very slow. However, the City wanted no part of litigation, and so I had to let the whole subject drop since no distributor would finance me with an injunction hanging over my head. Not a penny of the £100,000 did I recover."[25]

Spiegel was a cunning politician. Realising it would need a miracle for a Jewish producer to make a film in Arab locations, he set out to find a miracle worker. He found one in Anthony Nutting.

In his late thirties, Nutting had all the advantages - good looks, an Eton education, and two qualities rare enough among politicians, let alone film producers, a sense of humour and a sense of principle. When he was Under-Secretary at the Foreign Office, he was sent to Cairo by Winston Churchill to help draft an agreement for the British withdrawal from Egypt. He got to know and like Colonel Nasser, and when he found the government had broken the agreement he had signed with him, he was outraged. When the new prime minister, Sir Anthony Eden, sanctioned an invasion of Egypt after Nasser had nationalised the Suez Canal, Nutting resigned as Minister of State for Foreign Affairs, thereby earning the undying respect of the Arab world.

David was alarmed when Spiegel told him he had hired Nutting. "Oh, no, no, no," he said. "I couldn't possibly work with somebody like that. He's Establishment. He's an ex-Minister. He was in the government." David expected him to be dry, pompous and dictatorial.

"After we'd had dinner," said Nutting, "he realised that I didn't have three heads and that I was a reasonable human being who was interested in the project and we settled down and developed a very close and interesting relationship. And the book I wrote of Lawrence - which I wrote because I had nothing else to do -

was largely the result of these discussions, and the conclusions that David and I came to, together with Robert Bolt when he came into the picture as screen-writer. It was because of the way David probed into the character of the man that we evolved this concept of Lawrence as this twisted character. I can honestly say that any success that I had with the book - and it was a bestseller for a considerable time - was largely owing to David. I wouldn't have probed so deeply myself if it had not been for David constantly needling me to do so."[26]

In April 1960, David, production manager John Palmer and interpreter George Littledale went to Jordan. When David returned he tried to reach Michael Wilson in Paris by telephone, and we should be grateful he failed, for he sent him an epic letter:

"I saw both the English and the American Ambassadors, and the King. The King is *the* king-pin. I saw him for only about ten minutes because he was so welcoming there was nothing more to say. He said he was most keen on the film, and for us to make it in Jordan. He asked what we needed and my only request was for an Army jeep and an officer who knew the desert. 'Wouldn't you care for a helicopter?' Being the original cowardly flier I wouldn't. The King had seen KWAI three times and was so impressed that he arranged morning shows for all the soldiers stationed in Amman at nominal prices."

The three men set off, with an officer who turned out to be a distant relation of Auda Abu Tayi, and ten men of the Desert Patrol.

"The overriding first impression is that Lawrence was right all along the line. The real desert people are most impressive. Great manners, hospitality, good humour, and the gentleness of real men. The town Arab is pretty horrible and on a par with the towns themselves.

"The desert is *wonderful*. It gave me a bit of a shock as it wasn't at all what I expected from my boyhood diet of THE SHEIK, THE GARDEN OF ALLAH and BEAU GESTE. Perhaps the reason is that all these entertainments have dealt with North Africa. The *Seven Pillars* country is something quite different. At first I was terribly worried by not finding what I expected. I thought I would find miles and miles of flat sand and rolling sand dunes and they're just not there. Then suddenly I came to and realised that what I was seeing was better than what I'd hoped to see."

The group visited Petra, the ancient city built by the Nabateans and later annexed by the Romans and made famous by Dean Burgon's poem as "A rose-red city, half as old as time".

David was ecstatic about Petra. "The rocks *are* rose red and the whole place is much more impressive than any pictures we have seen in any of the books. I won't try and describe it because I hope I've caught a little of it in my pictures, but the trouble is one needs Todd-AO. I have never seen the Grand Canyon, but can't believe it has anything on Petra."

David's enthusiasm for the desert increased as he saw more and more of it.

"Am I mad? Can I make audiences share my thrill? I know I'm a sort of maniac because the thrill of seeing these places makes up, by a long chalk, for the discomfort of the living conditions. I do realise we've got a tough time ahead, with a British unit who'll expect mashed potatoe [sic] with every meal and won't care a damn for Lawrence, the desert or me...

"The old port of Aqaba is just as it was! We can run camels through the palm groves straight into the deepest blue Jamaican sea. It looks wonderful - or perhaps it was the contrast after all the barrenness. Eilat, the Israeli port across the gulf, can easily be masked by palms, and so can modern port installations.

"Rumm. At first I was a little disappointed that it wasn't quite what I expected from Lawrence's description. Later I found it the most exciting place of all. Again it's vast. The narrowest part, and this is where I was surprised, is

David's photograph of Wadi Rumm, an important location for LAWRENCE OF ARABIA.

about a mile across. It's red rock rising straight out of the plain and going up to God knows what, and some prehistoric giant's had a game and poured a sauce on top of the pudding giving it a grey-white top."

After Rumm, they had their hardest day's driving across the desert to the railway and Mudawara, the fort which Lawrence captured, and the mudflats at El Jafr where David experienced a mirage.

"The mirage on the flats is very strong and it is impossible to tell the nature of distant objects. Jeeps look like elongated ten-ton trucks even when they are quite near. Men look as if they are on stilts and walking in water. You certainly can't tell a camel from a goat or a horse. If a walking man sits down on his haunches he disappears into the 'lake' and you can't see him at all... All the Lawrence blob stuff is true and I found myself thinking of introducing Ali this way. There could be a certain amount of tension about such an appearance because you really don't know what's coming towards you.

"The railway is as was. There are lots of remains of Lawrence's blowing ups, and we've been given permission to blow up anything else we like. The railway goes through any sort of desert or hill country you wish. There are lots of wrecked carriages on the side of the line and Mudawara station is still a wreck with the top of the water tower still lying in the sand. The railway itself is in good condition as I think it was Abdulla who got the line itself put back in order. The King thought we could find engines to blow up also.

"I have taken a few pictures of Jerusalem streets as they might be our best bet for Damascus - and we can use them. There was one terrible sort of yard in the middle of the city which was once a caravanserai. It must have been the sort of Inn where there was no room. (Take a few Italian old masters there.) I wondered if it couldn't be our hospital after an art director had got at it.

"I think we did a good job and I hope Sam is fired by the pictures I have taken. One thing I do know and that is that you've just got to come out and pay this place a visit soon after you've finished this present version. There is a smell in the air which one can't pass on. You will click in on the people, and I think you'll even more understand some of the alternating currents which ran through our hero.

"I can also see how the desert can mean something, little or nothing to various people. I found it a stimulant. George quite liked it, and John was happy to get out of it. It somehow threw me back on myself and made me very concious [sic] of being alive. There you are. Just you and it. You can't sit down and be entertained. Everyone is somehow more on their own out there, and perhaps they just have to come face to face with themselves if they come under its spell. It's probably more dangerous for the town dweller, for as in Lawrence's case, the foundations are in dreams. For me I know it's just a passing fancy, and when the film's finished I'm sure I'll never go back there as I do to the Far East.

The people don't dream much in those parts. I believe they have no word for beauty. You bloody well have to be practical to survive.

"I'm now glad I didn't get you on the phone because this says more than I could have coughed up there and then. I have wondered so much how you are getting on, and have brought you an old Turkish cartridge case. The desert's fairly full of them."[27]

Back in London, Brando had dropped out, preferring to play Fletcher Christian in the remake of MUTINY ON THE BOUNTY. Attention turned to Albert Finney, a twenty-four-year old from Salford, currently appearing in *Billy Liar* at the Cambridge Theatre. His performance in Karel Reisz's SATURDAY NIGHT AND SUNDAY MORNING would create an immense impact in England when it opened a few months later and would strike critics as the first authentic portrait of a working class youth in British film history. But as for playing Lawrence, that soft-spoken "don on a camel", did he have it in him?

In August 1960, David spent four days at the MGM studios in Borehamwood, with cameraman Geoffrey Unsworth, shooting elaborate tests with Finney.[28]

Finney did the tests in Anthony Nutting's Arab robes, which he had been given by King Saud. Unlike David, Nutting thought Finney would have made a superb Lawrence.

"David said, 'I can't work with this beatnik.'

"I said, 'What's wrong with him?'

"'He doesn't even wear a suit.'

"I thought this was funny coming from David, who objected to me on the grounds that I was Establishment. Sam sent him to his tailor and got him to wear a suit and a tie, but obviously Albert Finney was uncomfortable."[29]

"Albert Finney was rather too young for it," recalled David. "But the tests weren't half bad. When we saw them on screen, Sam Spiegel said, 'What do you feel about him? Will you take him on?'

"I said, 'Sam, to tell you the truth, I think I can just about drag him through it, but I can't say more than that.'"[30]

Early in September, Spiegel told David that Finney had turned the part down.

"I went to Albert," said David, "and asked him why he was doing this - why waste four days? He said, 'I think this may make me a star and I don't want to become a star.'

"'Why?'

"'Because I'm frightened of what it will do to me as a person.'

"I said, 'If you become a star, you will be offered the best parts. It's up to you what you do with them."[31]

"What really finished Albert for this whole caper," said Nutting, "was that

Sam's contract bound him to several other pictures after LAWRENCE."[32]

In an interview at the time with the *Evening Standard*, Finney said, "I hate being committed - to a girl, or a film producer, or to being a certain kind of big-screen image."[33]

The Finney tests are preserved at the National Film Archive, and have become their most requested item for viewing. So many people told me what a revelation Finney was, and how remarkable the tests themselves were, that my disappointment - when I finally got to see them - was inevitable. I found Finney startling in that he looked so unlike his normal self; disguised by a wig and clever make-up, he bore a passable likeness to Lawrence. The tests were lavishly mounted and Finney carried himself with authority and skill. He coped with the Oxford accent amazingly well. But he is stiff and self-conscious and lacks the one essential for the role - charisma. As soon as you get used to him quoting from the Wilson script and reciting from *Seven Pillars*, it all becomes a trifle repetitive.

The editor hired to cut the tests was Anne V. Coates, a niece of J. Arthur Rank, who had just finished cutting TUNES OF GLORY for Ronald Neame. She was nervous about editing for the great David Lean, and even more nervous about showing her rough-cut to the assembled unit.

"I never saw a frame go by, I was so frightened. At the end, David got up and to the whole unit he said, 'That's the first time I've ever seen a piece of mine cut exactly as I would have done it.'"[34]

"We had nobody for the leading role," said David, "so I used to spend my days in cinemas in the West End, and one day I went to a film called THE DAY THEY ROBBED THE BANK OF ENGLAND with an Indian friend of mine called Dr Raam Rishi. And there was Peter O'Toole, playing a sort of silly-ass Englishman in a trout fishing scene.

"I said, 'I'm going to use him as Lawrence.'

"Dr Rishi couldn't understand how this silly-ass Englishman could be transformed into Lawrence, but I was convinced. I thought he had a wonderful face and could act."[35]

When David told Spiegel about his discovery, Spiegel said, "I tell you, he's no good. I know it."

Spiegel had good reason to be so dismissive, though it wasn't until David was well into production that he learned why. When Spiegel was making SUDDENLY LAST SUMMER, he discovered that his star, Montgomery Clift, had a drink problem. Spiegel began testing young actors to find one to take over from Clift if he became incapable. He tested O'Toole (not realising his own alcoholic tendencies). During the test, O'Toole, improvising the role of a brain surgeon, turned to the camera and said, "It's all right, Mrs Spiegel, but your son will never play the violin again."

Despite Spiegel's lack of enthusiasm, David insisted on testing O'Toole. "We spent just one day on the same set we'd used for Albert Finney - just a lot of sand - and he looked great. I said to Sam, 'That's it as far as I'm concerned.'

"Sam said, 'A little better than I thought.'

"He suggested one or two Hollywood actors - I've forgotten who they were, but hopeless, hopeless, hopeless. And so finally he had to agree." [36]

No sooner had O'Toole accepted the role than he caused disruptions. It transpired that he was supposed to begin rehearsals at the Shakespeare Memorial Theatre in Stratford and director Peter Hall refused to release him. When Spiegel invited the Royal Shakespeare Company to sue him, Hall decided they could not risk the cost of a drawn-out case. Hall later wrote, "If an actor doesn't want to act for you, there's nothing in the world you can do to make him." [37] Hardly surprisingly, O'Toole was never asked back.

Peter O'Toole was born in Connemara in Ireland in 1932 and moved to Hunslet, Leeds, within a year. Mainly due to illness, he had a poor education. He began working for a newspaper at the age of fourteen and, for two afternoons a week, he took classes in English Literature. After national service in the Royal Navy, he won a scholarship to RADA. He was there at the same time as Albert Finney.

He suffered from his eyes; he had eight operations on his left eye alone. He also suffered from intestinal trouble and relieved the pain by drinking. He adopted the persona of the professional Irishman, and became noted for such eccentricities as never going out with his front door keys. "I just hope some bastard's in," he said. [38]

When Albert Finney took a part in Willis Hall's army play, *The Long and the Short and the Tall*, he went down with appendicitis. O'Toole, who coveted the role, took over, arousing a great deal of favourable comment. Katharine Hepburn, who was in London for SUDDENLY LAST SUMMER, spotted his talent and spread the word.

People in the industry were fascinated to know if Alec Guinness would appear in the cast. He had already played Lawrence in *Ross* - perhaps that was one black mark against him? - and after the KWAI and GANDHI episodes people in the business assumed he and David were at daggers drawn.

A story went the rounds which was so irresistible that it has appeared in print several times. David, so the story goes, had started shooting the film when he discovered that Spiegel had cast Guinness behind his back. He stopped work at once and announced he was leaving the picture.

"According to legend," wrote Andrew Sinclair, "Spiegel fell to the ground, the apparent victim of a heart attack. Rushed away to the hospital, he was put in an oxygen tent. The stricken Lean visited him, offering to give Spiegel anything he wanted, anything, if it would help him recover. Spiegel immediately revived and smiled and said, 'You're so nice. So we cast Alec Guinness.'"[39]

Much of film history is woven from apocryphal stories, and it is a shame to spoil this one. But of course Guinness was due to have played the lead in GANDHI and while David was in Jordan, he invited him to play Prince Feisal.

"As a boy," said Guinness, "I was endlessly throwing a towel over my head and tying a tie around it and pretending to be Lawrence of Arabia." But he was now forty-six whereas Lawrence in 1917-18 was in his late twenties. When he was offered the role of Feisal, he needed no persuasion.

"I should have been much thinner and smaller. But I liked the script. And I wanted to know more about the Arab world. I copied the accent from my first meeting with Omar Sharif."[40]

Casting the technicians was every bit as complicated as casting the actors. But those who worked on LAWRENCE would eventually win the kind of respect accorded the men of Agincourt. The production designer, particularly, became an industry hero.

Born in 1920, John Box had been taken as a child to Ceylon, returning to England at the age of twelve and eventually training as an architect. He was in the army during the war - he took part in the Normandy campaign - and left at twenty-five as acting colonel.

Entering the film industry in the fifties, he worked with Alex Vetchinsky in the art department, where Carmen Dillon was a major influence, and helped transform Wales into China for THE INN OF THE SIXTH HAPPINESS which was photographed by Freddie Young.

With a moustache as clipped as his conversational style, Box still resembled an army officer, albeit a highly unusual one, for he was full of unconventional ideas.

"I was just peeking my nose up into more important films," he said. "I met David at the George V in Paris and he said, 'Go to Jordan. I've seen it. I want you to see it and appraise it.' I went. I hated Jordan - I came to love it later - and I returned to be met by my assistant who said, 'I think you ought to know that John Bryan is on the film.'

Bryan, who had become a producer, had decided to revert to design just for LAWRENCE. Then Bryan fell ill with kidney trouble and was forced to resign. "I never knew why John Bryan had been taken on," said Box. "I asked David several times and he simply said, 'Sam told you, didn't he?' Sam denied any knowledge and perhaps David got cold feet about hiring me and needed help from John. I never knew.

"And John Bryan was the reason I came into films. I'd seen GREAT EXPECTATIONS and OLIVER TWIST - John Bryan was my god. And once I was in films, he plucked me from nowhere and put me on THE MILLION POUND NOTE. Strange, but even when we met for dinner later on I didn't ask him."[41]

Box worked closely with the costume designer, Phyllis Dalton. Trained at Ealing School of Art, she had been a Wren at the secret code-breaking establishment at Bletchley Park and found it "unbelievably boring." In 1946 she leaped with relief at a job in wardrobe at Gainsborough Studios, Islington.

She was hired for LAWRENCE after she had done the Finney tests and went about her work in admirable fashion. "I was terrified by the sheer scale of the picture," she said, "but I'd seen *Ross* and was fascinated by Lawrence. I was a bit of a romantic and I loved the desert. David was interested in costume in that he knew the effect he wanted. If he didn't care for something and you said, 'It's the right period,' he'd say he couldn't care less about the period. And he was right."

Dalton had O'Toole's regulation uniforms made by Hawkes, the firm which made uniforms for Allenby. For the Turkish costumes she travelled to Istanbul and for the Arab costumes she scoured the bazaars of Damascus.

"It was one of those films that started off with people saying, 'Oh, the Arabs, they'll wear their own clothes.' They think it's going to be easy. But each of the tribes had a distinct colour plan. I had ten identical outfits for each of them because the costumes had to be at various stages of breaking down - or 'distressed' - as they crossed the desert. Mind you, it was the wardrobe staff who were distressed, especially when David wanted something altered overnight."[42]

Roy Stevens, in his mid-twenties, had been assistant director on Fred Zinnemann's THE SUNDOWNERS and at Zinnemann's recommendation David took him on as subsidiary first assistant, to be in charge of the second unit and to handle the action of all the big scenes. When the first assistant resigned Stevens said he would handle it all himself.

David decided to give Stevens a crash course in film production and asked him if he took still photographs.

"I said, 'I take snaps.'

"'Do you have an enlarger and a darkroom?'

"'No.'

"He said, 'Right. Organise a darkroom and take photographs and learn to print them and enlarge them. Show me the negatives and then do me six different formats with the enlarger. We've got six months preparation on this and by the time we get out there I want you to have a full knowledge of the whole process.'

"I thought, 'He's sending me up. But anything for the job, I'll do it.' I had to go in on Monday morning with the photographs that I'd taken and he would tell me about framing. And when we actually got out there, he was changing the lenses around and demonstrating the difference. He took a very green lad and taught him the business - editing, everything. I went through all aspects of film-making with him. It was a great education for me."[43]

"I never understand the people who think they can direct films and they haven't learned the rudimentary principles of film-making," said David. "I would say to anybody who wanted to be a director, 'Do you take photographs?' You will tell a hell of a lot from the photographs he takes. If you haven't got an eye for a camera you're in trouble if you want to be a movie director."[44]

For David, photography was a passion; he was always eager to seize the newest ideas. When Mike Frankovich, who now ran Columbia in England, suggested making LAWRENCE in Super Panavision 70 - a 65mm negative producing 70mm prints of astonishingly sharp definition - David agreed at once. Since no British film had been made in this process, why not hire Robert Surtees, the man who shot BEN-HUR in 70mm and won an Oscar? Unfortunately for David (and for Surtees) he was shooting MUTINY ON THE BOUNTY in the South Seas.

David had originally wanted Geoffrey Unsworth. He had done the tests and he was the husband of Maggie Unsworth (née Sibley). But Unsworth was working on a film in the United States. Maggie could not be available either, since she had young children to look after. Barbara Cole would become the continuity girl.

Columbia's Bill Graf recommended Freddie Young. But David, who remembered their clash on MAJOR BARBARA - "Don't teach your grandmother to suck eggs" - resisted the suggestion. He considered Jack Hildyard. David got on well with him, but felt he wasn't really a "dedicated maniac". In any case, he was working on the early stages of CLEOPATRA.

Guy Green, who had become a prominent director, was making a film in Ireland when he had a call from Sam Spiegel: "I'm doing a film with David Lean, and he wants you to photograph it. It's called LAWRENCE OF ARABIA."

"That's marvellous, Mr Spiegel," said Green, "but I'm in the middle of directing a picture."

"That doesn't matter. David wants you," said Spiegel, as though that were the end of the argument.[45]

All the other top cameramen - Ossie Morris, who had operated on OLIVER TWIST, Jack Cardiff, who had shot THE AFRICAN QUEEN - were tied up, either having accepted big pictures, or, as in Cardiff's case, having turned to direction. It was like a full-scale industry conspiracy.

Michael Wilson's first draft screenplay was completed by 4 August 1960. After a brief prologue, it opened with the motor-cycle accident, then Lawrence's death is broadcast to the world and we cut to the memorial service at St Paul's Cathedral, as in the final film, with similar comments: "Putting him up there alongside Nelson and Wellington...that's a bit much." The script then flashed back to Lawrence's army career.

Wilson's decision not to romanticise the story gives his script a strong sense of desolation and anti-climax - the emotions Lawrence himself must have felt. It throws the obscenity of war into strong relief, and depicts Lawrence as anti-hero, sarcasm falling from his lips. Ali distrusts and finally abandons him, and there is a scene of Lawrence, suddenly aware of his loss, striding through the newly captured city at Damascus crying, "Ali!" His love for the Arabs is shown to be as threadbare as his costume.

But the Arabs are depicted as greedy, venal and hopelessly disorganised, and while this is present in *Seven Pillars*, there is little of the nobility and self-respect which is also there and which Lawrence so admired. Another drawback lies in the dialogue, which, on the whole, is merely serviceable. There are many Americanisms. For instance, Lawrence refers to the nomads as "tumbleweeds."

Because David was often in Jordan, Wilson had not worked as closely with him as he had done on KWAI. Perhaps Wilson was trying to avoid a repetition of that experience, for David was beseeched by both Wilson and Spiegel to restrict himself only to the most major criticisms until the completion of the next draft.[46]

There were meetings in Venice, London, Paris and at the Burgenstock Estate, a luxury hotel above Lake Lucerne in Switzerland. But at none of them was David able to delve into the kind of detail he found so necessary. Adrian Turner discovered Wilson's notes of David's comments:

"Prologue is too long and at the moment not related to theme... Lose the Desert Song quality wherever it exists... Do we want to make a western? Must not fall into visual cliché... Too many train raids, which do not contribute to L's character. We lose the theme, the drive to unite the tribes. Many faceted aspects of Lawrence's character not yet in the screenplay. Example: masochism. Other examples: vanity vs shyness, solitude vs gregariousness, glimpses of his pride in the British... Let us not avoid or censor out the homosexual aspect of Lawrence's relationships... The incipient homosexuality of Daud and Farraj must be emphasised."[47]

The masochism was one of Anthony Nutting's discoveries, which would be revealed in his book. In Wilson's notes, David compared the Lawrence-Ali relationship to BRIEF ENCOUNTER - deeply felt, but unconsummated. David was also concerned about the scene at Petra, which would close Part One of the film. Wilson noted, "David feels Petra is the pinnacle - it means 'I am' not 'I can be.'"[48]

Because David had to return to Jordan to finish choosing locations, he was forced to relinquish control of the script to Spiegel whose impatience was obvious. When David left for Amman - on 14 November 1960 - something made him suspicious.

"I said, 'Sam, I have the feeling that you are tricking me into starting shooting with only part of the script written.'

"He said, 'Do you think I'm mad? Baby, how could you suggest such a thing?'

"I said, 'Well, I *am* suggesting it.' We walked for a whole day and he swore on his mother's health and everything else he could cook up. I even went to the extremely unpleasant length of refusing to get on the plane until he gave me his promise."[49]

Wilson completed his next draft and it was sent out to David in Jordan. Wilson flew out in mid-December, to be met by David who told him bluntly that the script wasn't working. He put his thoughts on paper to Spiegel.

"We've got to make big cuts in what we already have, and I'm almost certain that the final result - if the present technique is kept - will appear as the story of Lawrence who made a longish desert trek to Aqaba; returned to Cairo; then made another moderately long trip to Damascus. Now, put that in a box and hold it."

David declared that he was in favour of the kind of flashback technique used in BRIEF ENCOUNTER and IN WHICH WE SERVE, even though Wilson's script already began with Lawrence's death.

"I find it harder and harder to believe that anyone telling the story of Lawrence, and not telling the story of his retirement to the RAF monastery, must be out of his bloody mind. If the story of the monastery is omitted, the story of Lawrence becomes the story..." And there, frustratingly, the letter ends, the remaining pages lost.[50]

Michael Wilson, who had worked for a year, walked off the project in a state of high dudgeon. He had one more draft under his contract, which he delivered on 31 January 1961, and then he was paid the remainder of his $100,000 fee. Wilson pointed out that his resignation should have no effect on his right to a screen credit.

Spiegel had offered Wilson screen credit if he would produce a statement denying any connection with the Communist Party, a statement he could use if he had to. Wilson produced no such statement. Nevertheless, McCarthy was dead and the first of the blacklisted writers (Dalton Trumbo) received screen credit in 1960 thanks to the courage of Kirk Douglas and Otto Preminger.

When the time came, Wilson received no credit at all and the ease with which he was written out of the history of LAWRENCE was as effective as any blacklist. David mentioned Wilson to me as infrequently as he did his wives. It was a sad end to what had been a brilliant partnership. Ironically, it was supplanted by an even more brilliant one.

It was the ubiquitous and ominiscient Baroness Budberg who brought Robert Bolt to the attention of Sam Spiegel. She had seen Bolt's play, *A Man for All*

*Season*s, and suggested that Spiegel went at once to see this outstanding new writer's work.

Spiegel always said that he was very impressed and that he persuaded David to go, saying, "I have discovered a new writer." David is said to have been equally impressed. But there is strong doubt that David ever saw *A Man for All Seasons*, which had opened at the Globe Theatre in July 1960. He was in Jordan for much of the time and, with Wilson hard at work on the script, he had no need to look for another writer.

"The story that David had seen my play never rang true with me," said Bolt. "After all, when would he have seen it? He never mentioned the *Man* script - either play or film - to the day he died."[51]

Robert Bolt was born in 1924, in Sale, near Manchester. His father ran a furniture shop. His family were Methodists and his childhood was even more puritanical than David's - he once referred to the two of them as "wistful Cromwellians". Like David, he had a brother who was more brilliant than he was.

After attending Manchester Grammar School, he worked, like David, in an office for a year - for the Sun Life Assurance Co. In his spare time, he practised writing and studied for the entrance exam to Manchester University.

Drafted into the RAF, he also served three years in the army, becoming an officer and (briefly) a member of the Communist Party. He took a degree and became an English master, first at a village school, then at the progressive but expensive public school, Millfield, near Street in Somerset. The radio plays he wrote for the BBC in his spare time brought him to the attention of the agent Peggy Ramsay. It took five plays before she accepted one - *Flowering Cherry* - which was staged in London in 1958 with Celia Johnson and Ralph Richardson and ran for more than a year, enabling Bolt to give up teaching. It was followed by *A Man for All Seasons*, about Sir Thomas More who was beheaded on the orders of Henry VIII for refusing to betray his principles and religious beliefs.

When the offer came from Spiegel, via Peggy Ramsay, Bolt's reaction was typical of a man of the stage.

"I was a playwright, not a scriptwriter, so I was insulted. What, a film?! I was also intrigued, and Peggy said, 'Go and see what they say.' And I went and saw Sam Spiegel. His office was furnished, apart from the acres of mahogany and leather chairs, with prizes for his last three films, ON THE WATERFRONT, AFRICAN QUEEN and BRIDGE ON THE RIVER KWAI, all of which I had seen and liked. I learned, much later, that Sam had made a lot of money out of those, but nobody else had.

"He talked and talked, and offered me a cigar, and whisky. I glanced at the label. It read, 'Specially bottled in the Highlands of Scotland for Sam Spiegel.' I should have known then that one doesn't win with Sam Spiegel."

Spiegel explained that David Lean was out in the desert of Jordan, all ready to go, but wouldn't shoot because of the low standard of dialogue in the script. Spiegel was asking Bolt to re-write it.

"I was quite outraged. I explained I was a playwright and didn't do things like that. Eventually he said he would pay me I forget how much, say £10,000 for seven weeks' work. I said that was different."

Bolt read the script on the train back to Richmond. He felt the problems lay not only with the dialogue; none of the characters had any substance. On the phone to Spiegel he said, with relief, that he would not, after all, accept the assignment. But Spiegel was persistent and had Bolt agreeing to work for the seven weeks. Bolt asked, "But who's to take over when my seven weeks' work is over?" Spiegel said, "That's up to me. Do it."[52]

David was apprised of none of this. He found himself stranded in Jordan, trying to organise facilities with no support, or even communication, from Spiegel in London. He knew that Spiegel had another writer in London - David Garnett[53] - but had little real knowledge of the true position of the script. After two months, David despatched a stinging rebuke to Spiegel from the Philadelphia Hotel in Amman. David knew so little about the arrangement with Bolt that he spelled his name Boult, as in Sir Adrian Boult.

"My dear Sam,
Do you realise what a dreadfully frustrating situation I am in out here? You left over two weeks ago, Mike has walked off the picture in circumstances partially beyond my comprehension, the script is nowhere near right and I sit here with the physical preparations going ahead with little or no information about what is happening on the re-write. John Box got in last night, with a sheaf of notes about various subjects and a message from you to say that both Boult and David Garnett are doing good work. I hadn't until that moment realised that any writing was being done at all, or that Garnett was contributing except as a critic...

"This horrid situation puts me in a position of writing this letter as a moaner - but what else can I do? I have tryed [sic] very hard to be reasonable for months, in fact I now realise I have gone too far in that direction. I was most upset by Mike going as he did because to others, but not to me, he holds me responsible as being the villain of the piece. I have never been kept so far away from a script, and now it's happening all over again with Boult.

"You know as well as I do that no top-rank director will work in this way. Up till this moment I blame myself because I allowed myself to be eased out for reasons of expediency in getting preparations started on location, but now I realise - at least from Mike's point of view - that he never intended to work with me on the detail work, let alone the overall pattern, for when he saw I had a lot to say he just went.

"As far as Boult is concerned he is taking his briefing from you direct, and you again know as well as I do that the first briefing sets the stage and style more than anything else. Once he starts thinking along those lines it will be very hard to get him off them, and if I don't fall in line I will again be resented by him in turn... I'm saying this to you because I want you to realise that when the above happens it's not my fault and that I'm not going to be eased out again for the sake of keeping things sweet.

"The method of the past God knows how many months has ended us up with a near disaster script. There's barely a scrap of my particular style, bloom, call-it-what-you-will in the three hundred pages, and again work is being started without my having said a word to the men concerned. I not only feel miles away out in the cold, but the whole film is gradually drifting away from me. It's a very dangerous situation as I'm not Mike Curtiz who can take over a script Saturday and start shooting Monday. For both our good I've got to get back into the swim of it and have got to talk to Boult by myself.

"I hope you realise how *very* far off we are. To my mind it's almost as far off as the KWAI script which you and Carl did before I came on the scene. The character of Lawrence which was what fascinated us in the first place hardly peeps through at all - and I don't think it ever can with the present way of telling the story. I've been doing some very hard thinking and see a glint of light in the distance, but oh God do I need help... For the love of God bring Boult out here quick. Let me see his and Garnett's comments. Give me some news! Love from David" [54]

When David heard the following day that Horizon was engaging a crew for a starting date of 28 February 1961, Spiegel received another angry letter:

"Here I sit impotently waiting out a script crisis on the toughest film of my career - a crisis which I'm told is being resolved, but I don't know how! What has happened to you, Sam? Marcel Hellman wouldn't do this to Harold French... I have been on this eighteen months or so. I am the one who will be out in the summer heat while you in your job will be paying only occasional dips into the furnace. But above all this towers the fact that this film has got to be the best my talent can make it, and from the point of view of Columbia's enormous financial outlay, and from my point of view as a craftsman, I will not embark upon it until we have done all possible to ensure as far as we can that the result is the best we can give. It's not going to make any difference to the world if the film comes out in 1962 or 1963, so why play Russian roulette? No one but a madman would start the film without a script." [55]

Spiegel's reply transformed David's mood: "I can't tell you what an impact your longest-ever letter has had on me!" The letter discussed casting, which showed how incredibly far behind schedule they were in choosing the last of the leading players. Cary Grant was still on the cards for Allenby. "Bugger and blast the star system," wrote David. "I tell you [Jack] Hawkins would make a mighty good stab at the Allenby part."

Olivier was suggested for Auda and, before Guinness was offered the role, Prince Feisal. "Let's never forget that he's one of the great actors," wrote David. "In this awful industry he's been relegated to second place by second rate little minds. We need some glitter and bravura in this picture and there isn't anyone who can hold a candle to him... just imagine what Larry would add to the bloodbath scene."[56]

But Anthony Quinn was cast as Auda Abu Tayi, to be transformed with a beak of a nose. As David made notes on the character, he confessed that a sort of automatic pilot took over. "I came on the description of Auda's treachery with a pang of hurt cliché. 'That magnificent looking old Robin Hood doing a *double-cross*!' and immediately finding myself thinking that we can change him into a true-blue lovable pirate and if treachery is needed we can put it into a small part villain-character. In other words, if I'm not very careful I automatically start thinking in terms of traditional film cliché - not even realising it is a cliché."

One of the most difficult and crucial pieces of casting was that of Ali, the Arab who kills Lawrence's guide, Tafas, and yet becomes Lawrence's principal ally and friend. David noted an incident when Lawrence visited the rooms of artist Eric Kennington to inspect the illustrations for *Seven Pillars*. He spent longest in front of the portrait of Sherif Ali Ibn el Hussein "and seemed almost reverential."[57]

David wondered if Ali might have been the mysterious "S.A." to whom Lawrence dedicated *Seven Pillars*.[58,59] Once he decided that Ali would be a major character, a first-rate actor was essential.

David's first choice was Horst Buchholz, a twenty-eight-year old German who had recently had a big hit playing a Mexican in THE MAGNIFICENT SEVEN. Buchholz was promised a life of luxury aboard Spiegel's yacht and a helicopter wafting him to work each morning. But he could not extricate himself from a commitment to a Billy Wilder film.

Alain Delon, who was rising to great heights in France, was offered the part by Spiegel (although David was none too keen) but he was involved in a play.

Spiegel surveyed a gallery of swarthy French actors before selecting Maurice Ronet, who had played in the British war picture CARVE HER NAME WITH PRIDE and who had appeared with Delon in PLEIN SOLEIL. Spiegel signed him in rapid time and despatched him to Jordan.

"I knew from the moment I saw him that he was wrong," said David. "He was blue-eyed and when I put him in Arab dress it looked like me walking around in drag. I did a test and sent a message to Sam saying , 'I can't use him. He can't even walk like an Arab. He doesn't suit the clothes.'"[60]

Ronet added to David's dismay by refusing to wear brown contact lenses because the sand whipped up by the wind caused him agony. He also had a strong

18. *Peter O'Toole as Lawrence of Arabia at his most heroic - on the wreckage of a Turkish train he has just blown up, embodying the spirit of the man of whom John Buchan said "I would have followed Lawrence to the end of the world."*

19. *When Anthony Quayle came out to this location, Wadi Rumm, he said to David, "You're like a bloody general out here. I'm madly impressed." David had command not only of a large film crew but, in effect, of the Bedouin, whose tents are spread across the desert in a careful composition.* 20. *Omar Sharif as Sherif Ali.*

Printed direct from the original 70mm frames, these images from LAWRENCE OF ARABIA capture something of the magnificence of Freddie Young's photography. 21. The famous moment when Lawrence blows out the match. 22. Anthony Quinn as Auda Abu Tayi. 23. Lawrence's fury, just before the massacre of the Turks.

24. THE BRIDGE ON THE RIVER KWAI: Colonel Nicholson (Alec Guinness) leads Colonel Saito (Sessue Hayakawa) to where the mines are concealed. Behind them stands the bridge, itself packed with explosives, which has cost so many lives to construct.

DOCTOR ZHIVAGO: 25 and 26. The visual aspect of the film was carefully thought out. A number of scenes were photographed through frost-encrusted windows. Omar Sharif as Zhivago, with Julie Christie as Lara. 27. The Bolshevik partisans decide Zhivago's future: a scene which might have come from a Russian painting of the revolutionary period.

28. *Cursed by the Irish weather, David ensured that his village was built of stone, capable of withstanding just the sort of storm he depicted in* RYAN'S DAUGHTER. *29. Atmospheric lighting for the wedding night in* RYAN'S DAUGHTER - *Sarah Miles as Rosy, Robert Mitchum as Charles.*

French accent, which would require re-voicing.

Meanwhile, David had asked Spiegel to find him a small stock company of Arabs. "I said, 'Look, I need at least six real Arabs who can speak English. I don't mean that they should be wonderful actors, but they can do the odd line here and there. They should not be totally inexperienced. I'll put them in as I want them in various parts of the film.

"A long time later, Sam told me he'd been to Cairo. He produced about twenty photographs which I went through and I was suddenly stopped short by Omar's face. Sam said he was once quite a big Egyptian film star, but something happened and he had faded from view.[61] 'I like that. He looks good,' I said. I was desperate, can you imagine?"[62]

Omar Sharif remembered Spiegel sending him to Jordan to test for a small part which had still to be scripted. "I thought, 'small part, not yet written' and they need a test? Meticulous people. That's why we don't make good films in Egypt. I didn't think it was worthwhile. I was a star in Egypt. But I went really to meet David Lean."[63]

He flew to Amman and then to the first location at Jebel Tubeiq. "There was no landing strip, nothing except this lone figure standing in the desert. You can imagine how impressive this was to see from the air. The plane taxied over to David Lean. He took my hand and shook it and as he was saying, 'Hello, Omar, so glad you could come out here,' he was looking me over very sharply. Once the inspection was over, he put his arm round me and said, 'Let's go and get a costume.' He took me to the costume tent and sent everyone out, saying he could handle this himself, and he started going through the costumes. He said, 'What do you think of black, Omar?' Then he took me to make-up and started fixing me up. First he tried a beard, and that wasn't right, so next he tried a moustache.

"Without being aware of it, David Lean had just changed me at least in my physical appearance. That wouldn't be the last time. He would have a preponderant influence over my career."[64]

Sharif was introduced to Peter O'Toole. He already knew Maurice Ronet, having met him at the Cannes Film Festival. Sharif did a test as Tafas - which must have worried Zia Mohyeddin, who was playing the part - and then he did a test in the Auda role with Ronet who hoped that Sharif would get the part - whatever it was - because he could help him with his English.

David thought the tests marvellous, and told Spiegel that he was the one to play Ali. Sharif was flown to London where Spiegel made him sign what he termed a "normal contract for a beginner". It was actually a seven-picture deal for $15,000 (£8,000).[65] Meanwhile, Maurice Ronet was told he could go home to Paris because he wasn't needed for a while.

"I had the most unpleasant mission to tell an excellent French actor that he was not wanted," said Spiegel. "I did it with the help of Columbia; they offered him two French pictures in compensation for taking him off this one, so as not to offend his pride."[66] Ronet was also paid his entire $50,000 fee.

Horizon's offices had been set up in the former Indonesian Embassy on Jebel Weibdeh in Amman. John Box and costume designer Phyllis Dalton made their headquarters here. The place was known as Horizon 1.

Horizon 2 was the camp at Aqaba, the only port in Jordan. Captured by Lawrence from the Turks, it had been the British headquarters in 1917, and a dilapidated ex-army barracks formed the nucleus of the unit camp, built by construction head Peter Dukelow. The catering genius Phil Hobbs, who had provided roast beef and two veg to the crew on KWAI, helped to reorganise the place, which soon blossomed into a tent city. A mile away was the Beach Camp, designed for relaxation, with dining hall, canteen and a bar called The Star Tavern Middle East Branch. Every Saturday, they held an open-air 16mm film show.

The preparation period took place in the relative cool of the winter, so the crew became acclimatised to the heat as spring turned to summer. This period was an endurance test for David. With the script, casting and the selection of the crew being largely the job of Horizon Films, he felt pent-up and frustrated. Meanwhile, Spiegel kept on about the starting date.

Despite David's pleas, there was still no sign of Robert Bolt. In his place, Spiegel despatched a young playwright called Beverley Cross who had scripted DANGEROUS SILENCE for Norman Spencer and who would later adapt the stage hit *Boeing Boeing.*

"I met David in Jordan," said Cross. "He was a strange man, a genius in my opinion. I thought he was sunshine and light. Mike Wilson had finished his script and I thought it was very good. But David wanted something different. So while Robert Bolt was writing his, I produced dummy runs for the second unit, almost as an exercise, to keep them occupied. We would script a battle or a skirmish, complete with storyboards, and [second unit director] Andre Smagghe would stage it while David looked at locations. We didn't shoot anything, it was just marking time. It was the phoney war.

"I was never a threat to Robert Bolt. All I witnessed was the stunt man, Johnny Sullivan, teaching Peter O'Toole to ride a camel and I went to wonderful places with David, like Petra. Sullivan and I were appointed guardians of O'Toole when we went to Beirut. It was our job to get him back again. It all reminded me of the army. David was the affable but stern colonel and John Palmer was a very busy adjutant. Eventually, after three or four months, I had to come back for a play."[67]

Once the political and passport problems had been surmounted, Sam Spiegel and his yacht arrived at Aqaba. In April, he held a party to celebrate Leila's birthday. John Box was invited, and recalled Sam becoming uncharacteristically morose.

"Sam said, 'We cannot go on with this film. I have to protect the money. We're in this terrible place with these terrible people, you have fired one scriptwriter, we still have no script and we're getting close to shooting. I, as the producer, am in a most terrible situation. We have to stop.'

"David paused, looked at Sam and said, 'Look here, Sam, when we made KWAI we were equal partners, Columbia and you and me. I'd been broke at the beginning. Afterwards I had a million dollars in the bank and you had three. At the end of LAWRENCE I'm hoping to have three million in the bank and you'll probably have nine, so can we stop this futile conversation and get on and make the film?'" [68]

David rather resented Spiegel's yacht and knew that its expenses and maintenance would be charged to the production, a practice David referred to as "stealing the stuffing from the turkey" and which added to his distrust of producers.

"It had an English captain," wrote David, "a crew of seven or eight and wonderful food. Sam had the enormous master's cabin up forward and other visitors were confined to smaller stuff in the stern. On putting one's head to the pillow, the hum of the generator bored into one's ear like a dentist's drill." [69]

To David's relief, Robert Bolt - his seven-week contract extended - was invited to work on the script aboard the *Malahne*. Not until he reached Jordan did Bolt discover the existence of the other writers. He became angry and was told that Cross and Garnett would be quietly dropped overboard, metaphorically at least. Bolt then became the sole writer on the project and settled into one of the cabins on the yacht.

"David came in about every week from the sand to discuss the scenes I had written," he recalled. "He had some things to say about my writing. He said I underlit certain passages, like the cut from the match burning Lawrence's fingers to the sun coming up over the sand dunes. But on the other hand I didn't say enough about certain other passages. There's a scene where Lawrence has just executed [Gasim]. He's talking to Allenby, saying how guilty he feels, and then mentions that there's 'something else,' apart from the guilt.

"David said, What is something else, Robert?'

"I said, 'Well, he sort of enjoyed it.'

"David's script went up in the air. 'For heaven's sake, why don't you put it in?'" [70]

Robert Bolt had the playwright's snobbery about the cinema, and regarded it as an inferior art - an opinion radically revised when he began to work on it. He was also an intellectual, a fact which alarmed David.

David and Robert Bolt aboard the De Havilland Dove flying to the location.

"He reminded me of my brother, who used to say, 'David, you really just cannot do that sort of thing - but I suppose you can in the movies.' Robert had this sort of attitude, you know, every now and then. He was very superior in those days."[71]

To avoid the mass of conflicting facts in the biographies and histories, Bolt decided to assume that *Seven Pillars* was absolute gospel. To condense it for the script, he said, he had to use an axe rather than scissors. He also chose to alter history for dramatic purposes - for instance, the film maintains that Lawrence knew nothing of the Sykes-Picot agreement - to divide Arab land between Britain and France - when so much of his mental turmoil was caused by the fact that he did. The many British officers who served in the desert were condensed into the single figure of Colonel Brighton (Anthony Quayle) while diplomats and archaeologists like Ronald Storrs became Dryden (Claude Rains).

Bolt regarded Lawrence as a romantic fascist and made him a more flamboyant character in every respect. Lawrence's "moral conscience" became Sherif Ali, as David had suggested. All those who read it agreed that the script was far superior to the majority of film scripts, especially those for epics. It was literate, witty and intelligent.

Anthony Nutting objected strongly to what is undoubtedly the most famous scene in the film - when Sharif emerges out of the mirage and shoots Tafas at the well.

"I said, 'No Arab would do it. He might tell him to get the hell away from his well, but he would never shoot a man. That just wouldn't occur to him. It wouldn't be honourable."

Nutting also objected to the scene in the chaotic council chamber at Damascus where Auda leaps on the table. "First of all, Lawrence's own description of that was an exaggeration and not truthful at all. There was a lot of argument and heated discussions about which tribes should take over which functions in the newly-liberated Syria, but it was never the shambles Lawrence depicted. And Bolt's was an exaggeration of Lawrence's exaggeration. I said I didn't think we ought to do that. Anyway, I was overruled."[72]

The council chamber scene was in the second part of the film, and Bolt had not even finished the first half when it was decided that shooting would have to begin. Spiegel, who had promised David he would not start with an unfinished script, now began to ship actors and technicians out.

"You don't send actors out if you're not proposing to shoot,' said David, "they're expensive commodities. And it sounds mad, but that forces you to shoot because what do you say to them: Go home?"[73]

Perhaps the first moment when David felt that the film would be something exceptional came when Freddie Young arrived. Young had been hired in January 1961 and on reaching Jordan he went up to David, held out his hand and said, "Don't teach your grandmother to suck eggs." From that moment on, their relationship blossomed.

David had known of Young's talent long before 49TH PARALLEL. In one of the few articles he ever wrote he said, "There is one more strenuous job than the director, the cameraman... Freddie Young has the stamina of an ox and a knowledge of the movies which has been more than useful to one or two so-called directors." He might also have mentioned that Young was a first-rate disciplinarian.

David knew he had no need to hover at Young's shoulder. As he wrote to him, years later: "For the most part I will give you a set-up, fiddle around with the props, talk to the actors or go off and have a cup of tea. You are on your own. I know a bit about lenses, consider myself rather bright at composition and, at a pinch, make a suggestion or minor criticism about lighting - but on the whole you're a lonely man left to your own devices."[74]

"I loved working with David," said Young, "because he was one hundred percent behind me whatever I would try to do pictorially. Where another director would say, 'Oh, to hell with that, let's get on with it,' that was something I never heard from David."[75]

After checking the locations in Jordan, Young flew to Hollywood to organise and select the camera equipment. "I met Robert Gottschalk, the inventor of the Panavision camera and the President of the company, and I spent about a week there choosing all this stuff. If you're going into the desert you have to take everything you need. You can't suddenly ring up Samuelson's to send out another lens.

"Just before I left Jordan, David had said, 'Freddie, I'm anxious to get a mirage shot. I don't know how the bloody hell we do it, but give it some thought.'

"So while I was in the camera department I saw this long lens and immediately thought, 'That's the lens to get a close-up of the mirage.' Gottschalk was only too keen to hire it out because it wasn't being used at all. It was just a long barrel of a lens."[76]

King Hussein, Sandhurst-educated and an Anglophile, could not have been more co-operative towards the film. To everyone's surprise, he became engaged to Toni Gardiner, who ran the switchboard at Horizon 1, and married her in the teeth of religious and political opposition. Thereafter, said Anthony Nutting, the Horizon telephones never worked properly.

King Hussein gave the company a remarkable guide called Aloosh, whom David adored, and also his personal pilot, Jock Dalgleish. Jock had retired with high rank from the RAF, and having been based in Jordan he stayed on and taught King Hussein to fly.

"What had happened was that one day he was flying the King in a small plane," said David, "and another Arab country, hostile to Hussein [Syria], sent up a fighter to shoot him down. Jock was a superlative pilot and he out-manoeuvred the fighter and saved Hussein's life. And of course Hussein never forgot it."[77]

Dalgleish piloted an eight-seat De Havilland Dove, emblazoned with "Lawrence of Arabia" in English and Arabic, which took the unit to Beirut for long weekends. It was an essential link, making almost daily trips across the desert and logging more than a hundred and fifty thousand air miles. A Royal Jordanian Air Force Dakota DC3 was chartered to fly in the crew from Horizon 2 to Horizon 3 - the location - to join the "dedicated maniacs" who would live under canvas in the desert.

There was no water. Phil Hobbs, facing the catering challenge of his life, had to use oil tankers, thoroughly washed out, to ship the water from an oasis two hundred and sixty kilometers away. But it wasn't just the water - still tasting slightly of kerosene - everything had to be shipped in. And in a place where the temperatures soared by day and plunged to freezing at night, there had to be a medical team. It was headed by Dr Eustace Shipman, whose daughter had played Oliver Twist as a baby.

"In the desert," said Freddie Young, "we had a generator and a refrigeration truck to keep the film stock and the food cool. We used to have marvellous food which was flown in from Jerusalem or Beirut. We'd even have strawberries and cream, ice cream and roast beef steaks."[78]

"It was made as comfortable as possible," said camera operator Ernie Day. "We had a great crew, people who were dedicated. They were hand-picked. People who didn't like working with David soon dropped by the wayside and were replaced. With him one did have to be dedicated otherwise you couldn't handle the pressure. And there were lots of pressures because of his intensity."[79]

John Bryan had summed up David when they had been location hunting in the desert. "He suddenly looked at me and said, 'I know what you are. You're a bloody boy scout.' In a way, I am. I'm a grown-up boy scout. Because I love going to these mad places."

Perhaps a proper boy scout would have insisted on a tent, but David was accommodated in a motor-caravan from which the wheels were removed and which was hauled on to the back of a Mercedes truck.

"That's where I lived for jolly nearly a year out in the desert, and you don't know what it's like living out in the desert. It's something unbelievable, the loneliness of it, the majesty of it, the wonder of the sky at night, whether it's starlight or moonlight. Just wonderful."[80]

David's encounter with the desert was, for him, the greatest gift of the production. "I used to go out at night," he said. "If there was no moon I'd walk across the flats and see the vague shape of these pyramids - not man-made, but wind-made. And countless stars that one's never realised before. When you're in the desert, you look into infinity. It's no wonder that nearly all the great founders of religion came out of the desert. It makes you feel terribly small, and also in a strange way, quite big."[81]

Eddie Fowlie set up his caravan, twelve miles away, near the spot chosen for the opening scenes. He laid a square of artificial grass, and put a teapot on the table so he could invite David for tea on the lawn the next morning.

"The first night in the desert," he said, "I turned on my little Zenith short-wave radio to try to find some news. And just as an enormous sun came up over the horizon - and it made my hair stand on end - the music from KWAI came on. And I thought, 'Christ, if that's not a good omen...'"[82]

The first official day of shooting was 15 May 1961, the climax of nearly two years' preparation. "David Lean," wrote unit publicist Howard Kent, "was determined that his picture would show scenery unmatched anywhere in the world. In Jebel Tubeiq his dream came true."

Were the history of Jebel Tubeiq to be written it would be a slim volume, for it had known no dwelling since a monastery was abandoned in the seventh century AD. The ruins were still visible. It was a desolate, awe-inspiring place, a wilderness of red sand dunes with black mountains.

The first day of shooting on any picture is of enormous importance. It sets the tone for the rest of the production in terms of the relationship between the director, the crew and the actors. And, in this case, the elements.

The first scene to be shot for Lawrence could not, on the face of it, have been simpler; just two men riding camels across the dunes. But pull back from the riders and you would have seen the monumental nature of the production - two hundred people involved, reported Howard Kent. The Panavision camera and ancillary equipment had to be hauled up an almost perpendicular sand dune, using a five hundred foot "ski-lift" - half a mile of rope with block and tackle. The camels and their riders had to be hauled up too.

"Although the summer has scarcely started at Jebel Tubeiq," wrote John Woolfenden, head of publicity, "the heat radiates like the proverbial blast furnace from the desert floor to a height of a thousand feet. Cast and crew wear goggles, for not only does the dazzling colour hurt the eyes after a prolonged gaze, but also the sand itself, blown by the 'khamsin' or desert wind, stings like birdshot.

"David Lean, burned almost as black as the surrounding volcanic buttes after more than six months of preparatory work in the southeast Jordanian wastelands, waves his hat for the camels to advance. His assistant, Roy Stevens, signals frantically for a moment's delay. He has spotted a white plastic cup, being whipped by the wind right into the camera's line of view.

"The riders touch the neck of their camels with thin wooden guide sticks. But Lean wants a special effect of the wind blowing the sand from the top of the

Filming the journey across the desert of Lawrence and Tafas.

dune. It creates an unearthly golden light as the grains whirl and eddy in fantastic patterns above the red sand carpet."[83]

David spent nearly a month filming Lawrence and Tafas crossing the desert. Tafas was played by the Pakistani actor Zia Mohyeddin, who had played the part of Dr Aziz in the London stage production of *A Passage to India*. LAWRENCE was his first film, and he was dismayed when a simple scene in which he said to O'Toole, "Here, you may drink. One cup," required twenty-five or thirty takes. David was prepared to continue the following day.

"I thought Jesus, a big two-camera scene. The world's greatest director. What did I do wrong? There was no come-back. He wasn't saying, 'Too much' or 'Too little.' None of the direction that one might expect. Weeks later he winked at me and said he didn't want me to think it was going to be easy. It was a kind of sadism."[84]

For the men who had to handle the equipment, the huge and heavy 65mm camera created its own pyramid of problems. Its weight meant that everything connected to it was proportionately heavy, and you could not get away with a lightweight dolly. Instead, they had the Wickham dolly. If this had appeared in the desert war, Lawrence would have blown it up, since it ran on railway tracks - the sand often had to be bulldozed flat - and was driven like a miniature locomotive. "It could hit thirty miles an hour," said Peter Newbrook, "and was quite a sight to see with all the gear on board and a camel caravan tearing alongside."[85]

Fitted with a crane, it could raise the camera to the level of a camel rider. Later, a Chapman crane was imported from America. Its six-wheel drive and large tyres proved ideal for soft sand, and it saved much time. A four-wheel drive camera car, appropriately called the CAM-EL (camera-elevator), designed by second-unit cameraman Skeets Kelly, had a built-in darkroom with a camera lift and even a toilet. Every night, an American mechanic from Panavision had to strip down the cameras, using a compressed air blower to clean them of sand.

"Many things came up in shooting that we could use," wrote Freddie Young. "Light conditions were a constant surprise, and peculiar phenomena such as spirals of sand, called dust devils, would arise from the desert and, whirled by some heat currents of air, travel rapidly at us in long sideways column, taking sunshades and other paraphernalia with them. David cleverly used these moments in the finished film, creating an atmosphere of unreality which complemented the performances.

"The compositions were worked out between us. For example a shot early in the film starts with the camera low down. The backs of the camels' legs go past the camera, and as they pass the camera rises on the crane to disclose an endless vista of the desert beyond. We worked out the set-up together, then it was David who suggested the embellishment of having the camera go up.

"I've heard him say to a carpenter, 'What do you think? How would you do this scene?' More often than not the chippie retreats, terrified, but sometimes he gives an opinion and David will reply, 'Very good, we'll do that,' or 'Thanks, but I don't think that's quite right.' He was the final arbiter.

"David complained that when he knew how to shoot a scene people were full of ideas but when he was stuck and he asked for advice the reply was, invariably, 'Whatever you think, sir.'"[86]

David was delighted with his crew. In a letter to Mike Frankovich of Columbia he said, "Crack technicians down to the last man. I just have to ask for it and they do it. No excuses this time, believe me. The ponderous weight of film technique has been transformed into the ease of lifting a pencil."[87]

After shooting at Jebel Tubeiq was completed, the unit moved to the mudflats at El Jafr. "By comparison with El Jafr," wrote Howard Kent, "Tubeiq was paradise. If there is a divine purpose in Jafr it is that God has placed it on earth as a warning of what hell is like."[88]

It was at El Jafr that David decided to film the mirage and the entrance of Sherif Ali. It was shot on 12 and 13 June 1961, with two cameras.

"You cannot shoot a man coming from a mirage into reality," said John Box. "It just doesn't happen. It ceases to be a mirage. David had to work it out; the cuts were to be long, beginning with long held-shots on the mirage and short reaction shots, then shorter on the mirage to get him out and longer on Lawrence. Then the sound was to be critical. If you listen to that sequence very carefully - swish, swish - strange sound.

"Just before we started, I felt something was wrong. There was something bland about the shot. What are we going to do? You're going to paint the desert with these fingers which point towards where the man is coming from. In other words, concentrate the eye. The painter painted a white line, a camel track coming to the well. Black pebbles were placed on another line."[89]

The script called for Lawrence and his guide to reach a well. While the guide draws water, Lawrence sits on the sand, whistling; he slowly becomes aware of the curious shape on the horizon.

Eddie Fowlie had built a well in the foreground. Omar Sharif and his camel were sent a quarter of a mile from the cameras by a roundabout route to avoid camel tracks being visible to the lens. It was Sharif's first day of shooting; his first appearance in the film.

Two jeeps drove around in circles, stirring up the sand in the background and an aircraft propellor blew more sand so that a kind of screen was created.

"I used the long lens I'd found in Hollywood," said Freddie Young. "We had Omar Sharif go practically out of sight until he was a little pinpoint in the distance and David told him to ride straight towards the camera, and we shot a thousand feet. Nobody had done it before and nobody had done it in colour in 70mm."[90]

"That was actually done in one take," said Peter Newbrook. "The shot ran for eight or ten minutes. It started with nothing in my viewfinder and ended up on a head and shoulders close-up."[91]

At the end, David went up to John Box and said, "You'll never do a better bit of designing in films, ever!"

"The painted path to the well," David wrote later, "and the black tongues of pebble pointing towards the approaching figure was a created pattern, a design, which was part of the drama. Not an affectation. No one noticed it but I'm quite sure it helped contribute to the impact of that sequence. Perhaps it would have been good if we had made it much stronger so that they had noticed it - which a painter like Dali would certainly have done - but we get scared because those damnable 'rules' of reality jump up and censor our imaginations."[92]

When he finally came to cut the sequence together, David felt he had lacked the courage of his convictions. "Originally, I had Omar coming out of the mirage at double the length and it was better. I lost my nerve and cut quite a bit. Wish I hadn't."[93]

The search for Gasim was also filmed at El Jafr. The script demanded that Ali berate Lawrence for turning back and risking the entire enterprise for such a worthless individual.

Omar Sharif told Adrian Turner that he was exceedingly nervous about the scene, for it was his first real show of emotion. Each time it was scheduled, it had to be cancelled because of sandstorms.

"Then one day we came to do it and my camel, a wonderful animal called Alia, was behaving badly and couldn't hit the mark. I was yelling and screaming and the camel was going nuts. That took a lot out of me and I started sobbing and had a sort of nervous breakdown."[94]

It was not perceived as such. "Omar worked himself up to a state of tension for the scene," said continuity girl Barbara Cole. "He sat by himself, tears falling down his face, and David warned everyone to stay away."[95]

Lawrence's return with Gasim is one of the most emotional moments in the picture - it is the moment when Lawrence becomes "Aurens". Yet the filming was close to farce.

"On the day we were supposed to shoot that," said Barbara Cole, "everybody was acting very strangely. David said to me, 'Have you any idea what's wrong?' I talked to one of the boys, 'What's everyone giggling about?' He showed me. He'd got what looked to me like an Oxo cube - it was apparently hashish. How they got it out there in the middle of the desert, heaven knows. I suppose from the Bedouin. We couldn't shoot it that day. All their eyes were closed up. David didn't get very mad about that. He just said, 'Oh, let's call it a day,' and went back to the caravan."[96]

Robert Bolt returned to England, astonished at what he had witnessed. Not being a film person, he could not understand why it was necessary to move mountains to produce the molehills of each individual take. He described it all to the newspapers with a memorable, but wounding phrase. He said life on the location was "a continuous clash of egomaniacal monsters wasting more energy than dinosaurs and pouring rivers of money into the sand."[97]

"Sam was livid when he read this," said Bolt, "and David sort of laughed. Sam Spiegel spent far more than necessary."[98]

Perhaps this press attention triggered Spiegel to a self-defeating act of impatience. He sent David a telegram saying, in effect, "If you don't move faster I shall have to come out with a big new broom."

"I was furious," said David. "That day I got hold of a big broom and I had myself photographed on 70mm. I was sweeping up the desert. I said, 'You come out here, you bugger,' or words to that effect, 'and try having a go in my place. You wouldn't last an hour.'

"And this came up - I knew it would, of course - in the rushes in London. He was mortified, in front of everyone who saw it, and that caused a terrible rumpus. He was frightfully offended. But it was also funny, and so he couldn't do much about it."[99]

When Anthony Nutting visited David on location, his plane landed in the middle of a sandstorm and he was worried that the driver would get lost trying to find the company.

"When I arrived at the camp, the first person I saw was David. Even though he'd been in the caravan when the storm was on, he was caked with dust. It looked as if he'd been with a make-up artist who'd really laid it on thick. So I said, 'Well, what do you think of my desert now?' I thought there was going to be an almighty explosion.

"He said, 'Anthony, everything you said was an understatement.'

"I thought, Oh God, here's another Englishman going potty in this bloody desert."

CHAPTER THIRTY

OLD FASHIONED ROMANCE

LAWRENCE OF ARABIA II

On one of my visits to Narrow Street, I found David sitting in the garden with Sebastian, his gardener. The following conversation was under way:

"I think women are at least, if not more sexually active, more sexual than men," said David. "Men are like goats, in and out, bang, bang, good afternoon. But women really have the lingerers about them."

"But women have that maternal instinct that is alien to man, or a lot of men," said Sebastian.

"What, they don't like being treated as mummy's boy, you mean?"

"No," said Sebastian, "I think women look for a more stable situation, whereas a lot of men, because of their basic sexuality, go out and have casual little affairs."

David said, "You see, casual affairs doesn't mean basic sexuality. I think it means randy little cat. I don't really think that means anything. I mean, most women are much more deeply sexual than men."

"I don't know," said Sebastian, who was gay. "I can't really speak from experience."

"I think pretty well the whole of this creativity is sex. There's no two ways about it. And if you want to go and make a good movie, well, you know, the fact of it is that sex is terribly important. If you want to make a good movie, get yourself a new, wonderful woman and that movie will be fifty if not seventy percent better than it would have been if she hadn't existed. It lights everything up. I mean, I'm too old for that now, but..."

"Doesn't it take up all your energy?" I asked.

"No, it's very energising," said David. "You see, I think lack of energy and tiredness is sexual failure. If you've had a miserable affair with somebody, you're tired out."

I said, "But one hundred percent of your time is devoted to that picture. How can you also have an affair with somebody?"

"I can tell you you can."

"I'll take your word for it," I said.

"You'll have to."

There followed a David Lean pause. "No, you're right up to a point. Of course you are. And you've got to have a very understanding woman, and you've got to have a woman who loves the movie that you're doing."[1]

Barbara Cole was a no-nonsense New Zealander in her early forties. During the war she married an RAF pilot who was shot down over Germany when her son, Peter, was a couple of months old. Money was short, she had a young brother and her mother was suffering from tuberculosis, so she had to earn her living. She went into the film industry as a continuity girl, at first in documentaries and then in "quota quickies". She graduated rapidly into A features, such as THE SQUARE RING, THE MAGGIE and HUNTED.

Married to the head of a television company in the Midlands, she started her own documentary-advertising company. When her husband began an affair with an actress, she left him and went to London. A friend introduced her to Spiegel and she was assigned to LAWRENCE as continuity girl.

Barbara flew out to Jordan with the camera crew. Because it was such a long flight she decided she had to sleep - even though she could never normally sleep on planes - and took a sleeping tablet. All that happened was that she grew more and more exhausted, and woozier and woozier.

Arriving in Amman, it was too early to go to bed. Someone decided she needed a tomato juice.

"I drank this thing, realised it was vodka, and I was soon absolutely drunk. I thought, 'If I can stand up, I'm going to my bedroom to sleep this thing off.' Before I could do that, David Lean walked down the hall towards me and sat down beside me. He said, 'Hello, you must be Barbara.'

"I thought, 'Oh, God, I hope he doesn't find out I'm drunk.' So I sat there and answered his questions and eventually he got up and walked away and I felt very happy. If he'd realised I was drunk I'd have been back on the aeroplane the next morning."

Very soon, Barbara went down to Aqaba where Spiegel's boat was moored in the bay. Her job, initially, was to assist Bolt with the script.

"David came on board and stood behind me. I'm not the greatest typist, and I thought, 'I'm going to get through this page without a mistake.' I managed it and he said, 'Oh, that was very good.' He little knew how nervous I felt.

"Then we went out to camp. David wanted the main crew round his caravan and he wanted my tent in a certain place. A man from the production office said, 'I don't know what's going on between you two,' and I thought, 'Don't be stupid.' In the evenings, David started asking me up to his caravan to take notes and I still didn't realise what was going on. I was attracted to him, obviously, he was a very handsome man. Then one night he tried to kiss me and I said, 'Now look, David, I'm not going to have one of these film romances. In two months we'll be quarrelling and I'll be sent home. I don't want anything like that.'

Barbara Cole relaxing in her tent.

"He said, 'No, no, you don't know me. I'm a very faithful man.' Which, knowing his history, made me laugh to myself."[2]

At the end of one of the three-week stints, Barbara went to Beirut on her own. David had offered her a lift in the company plane, but Barbara decided she wanted to be alone.

"The crew were very cross with me because David decided to stay behind and do a recce. When I got to the hotel the man on the desk said, 'We've been told that anything you want you can charge to your hotel bill.'

"I thought, 'Oh dear, here we go.' I stayed there a day by myself. Next morning they said, 'We've been told to advise you that David Lean is flying in today.'

"I thought, 'That's it. I give in.' So that's when we started having an affair. And from then on we lived quite openly for the next seven years."[3]

Some members of the company found it a useful relationship. Costume designer Phyllis Dalton said she could suggest something to Barbara and if David woke up in the middle of the night worrying about a scene, she knew just what to say. "The only tricky bit," said Dalton, "was when Leila came to stay at Aqaba. Everyone kept quiet."

"David very nicely said that it was thanks to me that he got through LAWRENCE," said Barbara. "He was a very passionate man, making love to me at night and working all day. People say that an artist is a selfish person. Well, all geniuses have to march down this narrow corridor and not be put off by things left or right. Outside of work I think he was a very generous, sharing and caring person. At work, he wanted what he wanted."[4]

Inside the caravan was a large bed, designed by David and Leila, a couple of easy chairs, a work table and a gramophone on which David played records of Stephane Grappelli and Erroll Garner.

People have been quoted as saying that David was up two hours before anyone else and he would leave his caravan to contemplate the desert. Barbara said this was absolute myth for he was a bit slow in the mornings. "He used to arrive an hour after everyone else. He'd generally given the camera crew the set-up the night before, so he gave them time to get ready.

"David didn't believe he should mix much with actors socially while he was filming, because he thought he couldn't go out next morning and give them instructions. When I'd say, 'Why don't we have a few people in for drinks at the weekend?' he'd say, 'No, no. Not while I'm working.' I like having little parties, I do it all the time, but I couldn't persuade him. He was very tolerant about things that didn't directly affect his work. But if it did affect his work, then he was intolerant."[5]

One thing was guaranteed to make David furious: if anyone walked across the freshly swept sand just before the camera turned.

"On one occasion, we arrived on location and David saw a lorry driving across the sand dune. He got out of the jeep and ran after it, screaming and shouting. But he was not angry often, because everyone worked jolly hard and did their best not to make him angry."[6]

Barbara recalled that David sometimes did not know how to stage a scene and would get furious with himself and start yelling at the crew.

"David always knew that a scene could be shot," said Ernie Day. "His problem was finding the most perfect way of shooting it. I'd come on the set and think it all looked wonderful. And then we didn't shoot for another eight hours because they were getting it even better."

David's work was all-absorbing, which gave him an odd sense of time.

"If we were doing a tracking shot," said Barbara, "David would spend a long time peering through the viewfinder. I'd have to go up to him and say, 'Hey, David, you've been doing this for forty-five minutes.' He'd say, 'Oh, my God. Have I? Thanks for telling me.'[7]

"David used to make me laugh a lot. He wasn't a great wit exactly. He had a sarcastic sense of humour, but kindly sarcastic, not this awful digging wit. He'd be very funny about the things that happened during the day, things that hadn't worked."[8]

After shooting at Jebel Tubeiq and El Jafr, the company moved to Wadi Rumm, a valley which lay about twenty miles north-east of Aqaba.

"It was entirely different from the other areas," said John Box, "with its towering red cliffs rising two or three thousand feet from the pink sandy floor of the desert. It was grand, romantic, but more sympathetic to man than Jebel Tubeiq."[9]

T.E. Lawrence loved Wadi Rumm, calling it, "Vast, echoing and God-like." "We wheeled into the avenue of Rumm," he wrote, "still gorgeous in sunset colours; the cliffs as red as the clouds in the west, like them in scale and in the level bar they raised against the sky. Again we felt how Rumm inhibited excitement by its serene beauty."[10]

In front of the camp, there was an airstrip for the DC3s and the Dove, which took the crew to Beirut for R&R every three weeks and flew in actors from England - Alec Guinness, Anthony Quinn and Anthony Quayle among them.

"I remember Anthony Quayle coming out to the location," said David. "I remember him saying, 'You're like a bloody general out here. You've got a huge army under your control. I'm madly impressed.'

"I had never thought of it that way. I suppose it was rather like that. You do have a lot of officers and privates and God knows who else. And you get to know them all very well. That's really why I like working with the same people. Because you can talk to them in a sort of shorthand, just a point here or there and they know what you mean, and you can work quite fast."[11]

David used Wadi Rumm like John Ford used Monument Valley, which it vaguely resembles. In one extraordinary scene, as the Arabs set out for Aqaba, the men begin to sing and the women ululate from the rocks, and David cuts to extreme long shot. The tiny figures, dwarfed by the almost Byzantine architecture of the massive rock formations, lend it a religious atmosphere, as though these are Crusaders parading past a cathedral in the Middle Ages.

"The way we did those big scenes was straightforward," said David. "An assistant director would arrange everything and rehearse it, then he'd stage it for me. I'd watch it and say, 'Look, I think we're wasting this, or I don't like that. I think you ought to make it much more simple.' I'd sort of build it up and then we'd have another go and when it had come together, we'd shoot. It isn't really so difficult because they know what they're meant to do. The extras are meant to run over there, the camera pans and meets that lot of horses coming down the hill. It isn't as wonderful as all that."[12]

The assistant director, Roy Stevens, put a lot of it down to plain good fortune. "I didn't find it difficult, strangely enough. I was a bit cocky, I suppose... I loved him. I said to him more than once after I got to know him, 'I love you like a second father, David, and would do anything for you.' Because he taught me everything. He really did, and made sure I learned. Although he used to make me sweat a bit."[13]

The routine was for the unit to work from around eight o'clock until eleven o'clock. By then the sun was almost directly overhead, the light was too harsh and the heat at its most severe.

"From eleven to three we didn't shoot anything," said Barbara Cole. "We made the motions of setting up. Then we'd start again at three and come home when dusk fell. The worst time in the desert is not the middle of the day, because we had the facilities. You could always get under an umbrella or something. But about four o'clock in the afternoon it is awful: the sun hits you smack on from head to toe and it's really exhausting."[14]

Every morning, Freddie Young would walk the hundred yards from his tent to David's caravan.

"I would go in about eight o'clock to start the day's work. He would be having breakfast - toast and marmalade and coffee. I'd say, 'We'd better get cracking, David, it's going to be a nice day.' And he'd say, 'Sit down and have a cup of coffee.' And he'd sometimes say, 'I don't know what we're going to do today, Freddie. I don't know how to start and frankly I don't feel like it.'

"And he'd put on a tape of Robert Bolt discussing the scene in the script which we were going to do that day. David would listen to the whole tape and then say, 'All right, let's go,' and we'd go out and start shooting."[15]

"Robert was a wonderful reader of his own lines," said David. "I'd often read an exchange of dialogue typed in draft form and I'd say, 'Now, Robert, I don't understand this. What is it?' He'd say, 'Let me read it.' And when he read it, it was just wonderful with the intonations he gave it. After a while, it reached the point where I would ask Robert to read the script as he wrote it. And I would have it recorded. Hardly any of the actors would take advantage of it. Omar would do it, and I think Peter might have listened to some of it. But Alec Guinness wouldn't come near it. I think he somehow felt that his creative ability might be taken away from him. I don't know why that should be the case, as the creation comes from the writer."[16]

Alec Guinness avoided listening to the tapes because he felt it would make his performance more mechanical. "I'd have the feeling that I'd be copying someone, or it would be in the back of one's head. If something's too slow or too fast, or missing the meaning, tell me, but I don't want to get someone else's spirit, because I'm a better actor than that."[17]

To any actor or technician who came to him with a query and who hoped to spend a cosy half-hour sipping coffee and listening to the tapes, David would say, often quite bluntly, that everything an actor needed to know was in the script.

"And it always was," said Ernie Day. "He could pre-empt everybody because he knew what people looked for; they looked for their own angle and would miss out everything else, which he didn't. That's why he spent so much time on scripts, plotting and putting everything in that would be necessary for the scene, and usually that was it. If you missed something, it was because you were busy looking at something else."[18]

Although David was not a believer in improvisation, his imagination was never nailed down by the script. When Lawrence tries on the Arab robes for the first time, he watched O'Toole play the scene as written.

"There's something missing here," he said. "What do you think a young man would do alone in the desert if he'd just been given these beautiful robes? There's your theatre. Do what you like."

O'Toole had the idea that Lawrence would want to see what he looked like and, lacking a mirror, he would pull out his dagger and peer at the blade. "Clever boy," said David. The scene produced one of the best-known still photographs of the film. The image was repeated later in the film, during the blood-bath, when Lawrence stares at himself through the bloodstains on his dagger, once again unable to believe his eyes.

O'Toole disliked prancing around in his Arab robes; he felt foolish and embarrassed.

"Another thing he felt foolish about" said Barbara Cole, "was when he's riding a camel, singing 'The Man Who Broke the Bank at Monte

David directs Peter O'Toole.

Carlo' and making echoes. He said to David, 'I don't understand why I'm doing this. It seems stupid to me.' David had to persuade him."[19]

Bringing the cast and crew in by air every day represented a high risk, especially with the superannuated Dakota. Anthony Quinn, cast as Auda, refused to travel on it. Indeed, he refused to travel on any twin-engine plane, so a four-engine Heron was chartered from the Royal Jordanian Air Force.

"As David and I waited for this plane to arrive," said Roy Stevens, "this Heron approaches and gets lower and lower. I thought, 'He's got to put the wheels down,' but he didn't - he belly-landed. The plane just disappeared in this mammoth cloud of dust. We got in the Austin Gipsies and drove madly out there, just in time for the door to open, and for Anthony Quinn to appear - exceedingly white, except for the false nose, which was dead brown. Quinn said, 'At least it saves the fucking steps.' And with that he walked straight past us all, got into his jeep and drove off."[20]

David was impressed by any display of physical courage.

"We had a scene where Anthony Quinn had to lead a whole column of Arabs down Wadi Rumm and he was mounted on an Arab stallion. Tony was petrified of that horse. I think anybody would have been petrified.

"I said, 'Tony, the light's going and I'm going to try a take. Will you have a go at it?' I turned the camera and said 'Action!' and Tony pulled himself together, put all his fear out of his mind and he managed that stallion as if he'd done nothing but ride it all his life, and we finished that take and did it in one."[21]

Only one man was allowed to apply Quinn's false nose and that was Charlie Parker, the make-up man. "Charlie Parker was a Canadian," said Eddie Fowlie. "In the desert he kept saying, 'My child bride is coming out to see me.' One day, sure enough, she showed up in Wadi Rumm. How she ever got there I can't imagine; she was a small Jewish woman. Anyway, they were always fighting and back in the camp at Aqaba she hit him. He said he fell over a tent peg, but there was a different story to it; she broke his foot that evening.

"The next morning we're all out on the set and Tony Quinn is sitting there waiting to have his nose put on. And Charlie's late. He eventually came with his leg all plastered, being helped along with crutches. David knew what had happened. They put Charlie in a chair and put his foot up beside Tony Quinn. David never even looked at the leg. He pretended it wasn't there. He just said, 'You're late.'

"Charlie said, 'er...er..' and pointed to his leg. David looked at the leg with scorn and said, 'You can hop, can't you?'"[22]

Of all the actors, Peter O'Toole presented the biggest headache for David, for he *was* the film; he would be on the screen throughout its entire length. When he arrived in Jordan with a monumental hangover, Anthony Nutting warned him that he was now in an Arab country and that if he got drunk the Arabs would throw him out, film or no film.

O'Toole contented himself with a bottle of champagne when he finished work. But the lack of hard liquor (though wine and beer were available) affected him almost as badly as a drunken binge, and the suspicion that he might not last the course began to take root. If O'Toole should have a breakdown, or sustain a serious injury,[23] the picture would either have to be abandoned or restarted with another actor, a thought too appalling to envisage.

"Peter O'Toole had a really hard time," said Roy Stevens. "I was hard on him. David was hard on him. He and Omar struck up a huge friendship and I think they helped one another get through it. They were great mates, because they were both inexperienced, so it was a huge burden for them to carry.

"David rather considered that they were paid for it, they were puppets. He was a very generous man in all sorts of ways. But he could not give praise. However good a performance of an actor, it was not in him to say, 'That was really good.' I think that was why the actors felt he despised them and why he had problems with people on long shoots. They might have been sitting there in costume in the heat since six in the morning, and doing that for four or five months. His mind would not stretch to thinking that he might go to the actor and say, 'I'm terribly sorry, but you know what it's like. Next time we'll try and get you in half way through the day.' There was a meanness of spirit in that respect."[24]

If David thought O'Toole was simply doing his job, and saw no reason for praise, O'Toole was in despair. He assumed he was incompetent and considered walking off the picture. Fortunately his wife, the actress Siân Phillips, came out to the location and gradually O'Toole recovered.[25]

Barbara Cole felt that David and O'Toole got on perfectly well. "They never had an open difference as far as I know. He never came home at night and said, 'Oh God, I wish Peter would do so-and-so.' He admired Peter.

"One night, I don't know whether he was drinking or what it was, but Peter put his hand in a rage through the window of a caravan and cut himself. He had one or two of these outbursts before we started shooting; this was probably because he was so tense about it. But I liked him very much and I thought he played his part magnificently. We were never held up because he was drunk or difficult."[26]

And when it was all over, what were O'Toole's feelings? "The most important influence in my life has been David Lean," he said. "I graduated in Lean, took my BA in Lean, working with him virtually day and night for two years. I learned about the camera and the lens and the lights, and now I know more than some directors do."[27]

Years later, when O'Toole had a son, he named him Lorcan, the Gaelic equivalent of Lawrence.[28]

David's relationship with Freddie Young and the crew was unusually good, though not without its stormy moments.

"Freddie and I had awful rows at the beginning," said David, "because he didn't like my idea of lighting. Eventually, we became a terrific combination, Freddie and I, and we sort of changed each other quite a lot with our bitter words, but we worked very well."[29]

Freddie Young has no memory of these quarrels. He is a practical man and, unusually for someone so brilliant, a well-balanced one. He knows what is necessary to produce a big picture, and temperament is no more memorable than the odd hair in the gate. While David threw him more challenges than any other director he had worked with, his chief recollection is of disagreements due to David dragging his heels.

"It falls to the cameraman to try and move things along," said Ernie Day. "But with David, it was no good doing that. He wouldn't be dictated to. I've seen him shoot very quickly - a whole day, and at the end of it he said he was on a high because we'd shot so fast. But everything had to be in its place - the light, the weather. The minute it didn't and there was something niggling him, it wasn't good enough."[30]

"On one particular day," said Peter Newbrook, "John Box and I had gone ahead on one of our leapfrogging jobs and laid out a new set-up. It wasn't a particularly difficult one - it was to be shot at sunset and by the time David and the full crew arrived, all the principal work was completed. It was all propped and dressed, positions all marked out with stand-ins and pre-lit. All David had to do was substitute the principals for the stand-ins, rehearse them and shoot it.

"He looked at me and hummed and hawed - then, as usual, he sat down and went silent. As the light was beginning to go and there was not too much time left, Freddie tried to urge him to shoot it. Freddie, after all his years with MGM, was a very good company man and never one to waste time. After a while, Freddie made one further appeal to David and that did it - he just got up, stormed off the set, got into his jeep and went back to his camp. That night, and for a couple of days, things were decidedly touchy and it took quite a while until normal relations were restored. The silly thing is that when he finally did the shot, it was virtually identical to the one that he had refused to shoot."[31]

Ernie Day explained David's behaviour on these occasions: "So much thought went into it. Compositions would cut on colours and not shapes sometimes. On exteriors in the desert, different shades made all the difference. Freddie would have set-tos about 'You've got to shoot it now,' but David didn't want it now. He wanted the light a little bit lower across the sand dunes and the faces of the rocks, which had different hues at different times of the day. He would take film to its ultimate.

"Over the years, budgets have changed and there is no way now - with a few exceptions perhaps - that you can wait for the light to be right when the whole unit is there and everything is all set. But David wouldn't compromise. It never did matter about time."[32]

Sam Spiegel, though, *was* concerned about time. Hating the desert, he made only two visits to the location in Jordan. On one visit he arrived with a crowd of photographers.

"Sure enough," said David, "they pulled out their cameras and Sam was photographed for a day looking at camels, stroking camels, looking at me, stroking me, and going around with the cast. He took all these photographs back with him and they were put out one a week to the trade press as if he were out there in Jordan continuously."[33]

Classic confrontation: all they need are Stetsons and Colt .45s. David and Sam Spiegel.

David was in a deep sulk when Spiegel was due to make this visit because he was grappling with a problem - how to shoot the scene where Daud (John Dimech) dies in quicksand. When Freddie Young tried to spur him into action, David snapped, 'You shoot it.'

"I said, 'Don't be silly, David.' He repeated that I should shoot it, so I insisted on his being in a chair and watching. He sat down and we shot all day with me directing."[34]

When the unit returned to camp, Spiegel had flown in on his photographic safari. He was alarmed by David's behaviour and told Barbara that he needed to be brought under control.

"I said, 'Sam, I can't do that. I'm not his keeper.' David was very worried because he thought Sam was asking me if I wanted to leave. Next day we went back and David had by then worked out what he wanted to do."[35]

"He had the camera unit open the cans and throw away all the film that I had shot," said Freddie Young, "and we re-shot it."[36]

According to Young, there were no problems with the cameras or the raw stock despite the heat. "We had a wet cloth over the camera and a big sunshade. The only problems we had once or twice was when you got a plague of flies or moths or ants, and we had a big spray gun to cope with that."[37]

By far the biggest problem was making the desert appear as though only Lawrence and his men were in it. The moment the unit arrived it looked like the day after El Alamein. Eddie Fowlie developed equipment to "virginise" the sand, including powder puffs on the end of long canes. Property men used to brush out the footprints, working back to the camera. Fowlie even had camel-shaped hoofmarks fitted to the soles of boots.

"When there was a dust storm," said Freddie Young, "you just had to cover yourself up and wait for the dust to clear. Dust storms in the film we made ourselves with the wind machines. The actual dust storm is just like a thick fog; you can't see anything and everybody is choking and blinded, sometimes for several hours at a stretch."[38]

There were two scares for the camera department. A report from Technicolor said that the film was mottled, and it was thought that perhaps the radar on the plane had affected it. When Technicolor washed the negative again, it proved to be a dirty wash. Then they learned that there were fingerprints in the middle of a roll. Freddie Young insisted that no clapperloader could touch the film in the middle of a scene and although everyone at Technicolor put on cotton gloves, the rushes still had fingerprints. Young suggested that the culprit must be Kodak, so Kodak in Rochester, New York, made everyone wear gloves. But still the fingerprints.

"So they fingerprinted everybody," said Freddie Young, "and traced it to the chap who did the perforating. He worked in pitch blackness and used to touch the film now and again to see if it was going all right and he had sweaty fingers."[39]

David was not able to see any of the footage he had shot until his return to London. "Sam explained that because Jordan was so tight on customs he couldn't send me any rushes, because they wouldn't let the film into the country. I accepted this at the time. He was always very persuasive and maybe I was an ass. I don't know.

"I shot all that desert stuff and I never saw the result, never saw a foot of film. For six weeks I had no news except the laboratory reports and then I was told that Sam was coming out. I was furious by the time he arrived because I thought, and I still think, that it was bloody mean not to let me know. Not a single word, complete silence. And there he was, sitting in London, seeing the stuff as it came in. I remember meeting him out there in the desert. As soon as I got him alone I said, 'Sam, what the hell do you think you've been playing at?'

"'What do you mean, baby?'

"'You haven't let me know what the rushes were like for six weeks.'

"He looked at me - and this is typical Sam - and said, 'Baby, I hadn't the heart. The quantity was so little and the quality so poor, I hadn't the heart to put it in a cable.'

"I was knocked out by this, because it was the last thing I expected. It was very clever; you hit somebody hard below the belt and it gets you off all sorts of hooks. In fact, it was some of the best stuff of the picture, including Omar Sharif coming out of the mirage.

"I told that story to the head of publicity at Columbia, a chap called Bill Blowitz. I said, 'Can you explain that to me?'

"He said, 'Yes, of course. Can't you see it? The producer's got no power at this stage in the picture. The biggest power is the power of withholding and that's what he was doing to you.'"

"In all fairness," said Roy Stevens, "I don't think Spiegel understood what David was doing. I think it was more the sort of situation, 'Come on, baby, let's get on with the story.' He used to beef to me and say, 'We've got to get him out of Jordan. I don't want any more pretty pictures of Jordan.' Spiegel was quite convinced that if he didn't pull the rug from under his feet he would be there till now shooting pretty pictures."[40]

According to Peter Newbrook, David saw one batch of rushes and then decided against seeing any more.

"The idea was that Technicolor would send us rushes in reduction prints from 65mm to 35mm," said Newbrook, "but the quality was so poor, projected on a funny little screen somewhere in the desert. They weren't properly graded, just quick reduction prints to see the action. David said, 'If that's the best we're going to get, I'd rather see nothing.' And he did see nothing."[41]

But David's account of the way Spiegel withheld information is borne out by a letter he wrote to Spiegel at the end of the Jordan location:

"I wonder if you realise that you have never once written me about any of the rushes? You have said a few words on your few visits, and cabled me briefly saying 'Delighted' (three times), 'Absolutely delighted' (once) 'Excellent,' 'Satisfied' or 'Satisfactory' (several times). You have given me no idea of the impact I am certain some of my work must have on the screen and if fifty percent of some of the outside appreciation is true I will feel like... one doesn't write such things. I had a wonderful letter from Mike Frankovich [and] a relayed message from Jules Buck via Peter... Haven't you got the imagination to understand how my tongue has been hanging out for even a little detailed appreciation of the impact on the screen?

"I have longed to know how certain of the unscripted ideas have come off. Did Auda's ride into the well capture the 'explosion' idea which was written unfilmably in the script? Did the beginning of Peter's walk capture the 'mystique' of Lawrence we have so often spoken about? Does Auda's son come off? I could go on and on because after all, you have written nothing. This is not being a partner or a producer; it's being a promoter. Since your boat sailed from Aqaba you are not really in this film any more. I have the feeling that it has become just a terrible worry to you which you can't wait to get done with…"[42]

In London, the rushes arrived from Jordan twice a week and were viewed by Spiegel and Anne Coates.

"As soon as we got them, Sam was on the phone every two minutes wanting to see them immediately. Those days we dreaded. They were nightmare days. The boys were trying to sync stuff up without any clapper boards… Sam used to arrive two hours late. He couldn't be on time. But there wasn't a foot of film that Sam didn't see.

"I didn't really cut anything for ages - apart from the first batch, for which David sent me cutting notes. We just put the rushes into sequence order, which was quite complicated because there was a lot of material, and a lot of desert stuff which could have gone anywhere."[43]

Anne Coates was all set to go to Jordan - she had no fewer than seven injections - though the call never came. David moved further and further into the desert where the thought of editing became purely academic. On his mind were more immediate things like camels spitting and belching during takes, cavalry horses and their attendant plague of horse flies, Arab extras wandering off just when they were needed…

Money, though, was of little concern to him; the film would cost as much and take as long as it needed. KWAI had cost $2.7 million and Spiegel had promised Columbia that LAWRENCE would cost no more than three million. However, the studio executives began to distrust this budget very quickly. Bill Graf warned Columbia's New York head, Leo Jaffe, that LAWRENCE might cost ten million. Jaffe then telexed Mike Frankovich, the overall head of the company: "This info shocking based our recent conversations with Spiegel who advised max figure of three million."[44]

In an attempt to keep the costs down, the production was shut down in Jordan on 28 September 1961. David had been shooting for 117 days.

Spiegel, who was convinced that David had become obsessed with the desert, was anxious to complete the picture in Spain which offered deserts and Moorish architecture, together with plenty of technicians accustomed to working on epics such as Samuel Bronston's KING OF KINGS and EL CID.

Spiegel was also anxious to leave Jordan because, during his visits, he was convinced he was being poisoned and because he was worried about security (during one of his trips, the Minister of State for Foreign Affairs had been blown up by a bomb). Unfortunately, Spiegel did not have the moral courage to explain all this to David.

Then David wrote this extraordinary letter from Wadi Rumm:

"My dear Sam,

"The camp which seems to have been my home for years is being pulled down this very minute, and tonight I shall spend my last night in this caravan. The unit members have said their farewells and they will all be off tomorrow, cameras and all, and you've had your way and got us out of Jordan.

"It's a sad day for me, because I've put all I've got into this venture of ours which started out as a partnership, and I now find myself way out on a limb not having the faintest idea of what you are proposing for the future. Only by a letter from John Box yesterday did I have any news about your cancellations of the Suez sequence (and the fact that you had ordered the cameras out of the country) and even he only hints at some future date. Not a word from you.

"I gather that the equipment is being shipped to Spain; whether for interiors or exteriors I have no idea. I have just finished part of the Raiding Party sequence in which they all ride into some future location. Not a word, not a photograph, not even a sketch giving me a remote idea of what I am supposed to be matching it to. The conspiracy of silence has become a unit joke. It's rather like working on some top-secret nuclear project in which you are the only man holding the key plan!

"I hope there is a plan, because from what I can gather, no proper recce has been made of any other country with the exception of studio space in Spain. The name of the studio and the date is, of course, secret... Jock Dalgleish is a blunt Scot with no ear for undertones. He told me that the Dove is being checked and serviced for flying in Spain. This sounds like extensive location work. I did my best to pump Percival [Hugh Percival, replacement production manager], but he grew more and more like a pipe-smoking owl by the minute. 'Exteriors in Spain? I believe Sam may be considering them, but I couldn't really say. Devilish difficult - the camel situation in Spain - we would need a hundred... but I shouldn't be talking about something I *really* know nothing about, old man...' And off he went.

"You have skillfully [sic], and *very* politely, left me with more egg on my face than a Bob Hope stooge. As Alex Korda once said during his early days in England, 'You say I know fuck nothing! Let me tell you I know fuck all.'

"I can almost hear you say that you were saving me from worry. In one way you probably are, but in another you are driving me slowly into the most ridiculous situation a producer has ever rigged for a director. You yourself are forever complaining about being kept in the dark, but have no compunction about doing that very thing to me...

"After we started shooting I think for the first time you began to realise what an enormous operation this film was. You had done one drive with me through Rumm and back to Akaba. You spent a couple of hours on Jafr mud flat, and I think that was all. You then flew in to Tubeiq after previous conferences in Amman with John Box and Palmer. You came in armed with a plan for cuts and getting out of Jordan come what may as soon as possible. Scenes were transferred, the dust storm was cut from Jordan altogether, (a madness) the hardship scene with the camel dying whittled down and now forgotten, the oasis cut by cable, Sinai - forgotten. The battle scenes postponed with a complete reverse of all your arguments when you wanted to start with them. Jerusalem and the Allenby office which you promised me on the boat - also forgotten. Petra?

"Everything has gone into reverse and as far as my information goes you haven't really much more than a very vague idea as to where everything is going to be done. My guess is that you are hoping to rush me into a start in the studio with as little actual work, from my point of view, on the script as possible. Cut out all desert stuff you possibly can and bring camels to Spain and hope the weather isn't cloudy. Then as a last resort we will pick up what is absolutely impossible to do in Spain and send me with a half-arsed unit back to Jordan with no track facilities and no proper camps...

"I am worried to death by the dreadful state of unpreparedness and inefficiency. I write you like this because of late it has become impossible to talk

to you. You whip out every argument under the sun to suit whatever scheme you have in mind. You even told me that it was good we had no finished script!

"We have worked through the hottest summer they've had for years and now it's an almost perfect Mediterranean climate - and will be until May. Europe and North Africa will be cold and cloudy. The light won't match and you won't touch this place for backgrounds, for after all they are the real backgrounds. Everything is sitting here ready for work and you are wrapping it up out of sheer stubborness [sic] and your own personal feelings about the country. You say that the place is too crooked and too expensive. Any other Arab country will be worse because they are more sophisticated and you won't get a camel and a man for a pound a day which is what we are paying them here. We provide water, but they provide the food. You can't beat Aqaba for Aqaba - with the original old port. You can't beat those fantastic wadis at the back of Aqaba. You won't find another Petra. You won't be able to find the savage faces and I doubt if you will find the same sort of camel to match those we have already shot - if you believe Lawrence.

"We are really 'in' here and have literally trained the Bedu to work very efficiently. Any place will have its difficulties and you are throwing a very valuable investment down the drain and starting anew. As a director I find words fail me to express not only my disappointment, but my feelings of being involved in such a terrible waste. Because you have never been on the technical end of things you underestimate the work of finding new places in new countries. I must visit the places wherever they are going to be, and please don't hope I'm going to act on Box photographs. Spain will probably be ideal for scenes of camels in snow and some of the winter sequences - but I don't know it.

"My biggest worry which I must state in no mean manner is that the second half of this picture has got to better the first. You and Robert continually play down the backgrounds and long to get stuck into the dialogues. I don't disagree with you about the great importance of our real scenes, and if they are not top notch we haven't got a picture. But listen to me, Sam. The thing that's going to make this a very exceptional picture in the world-beater class are the backgrounds, the camels, horses, and *uniqueness* of the strange atmosphere we are putting around our intimate story. Audiences have seen good scenes and good characters before; they haven't seen what we are showing them to date in the first half of this picture. This is our great spectacle which will pull the crowd from university professor to newsboy. For God's sake, I beg of you, don't underestimate it. This can be one of the greats. It's the most wonderful combination of spectacle and intimate character study which ever fell into a film maker's lap. Don't muff it. I don't say this to you because of some so-called creative fad. I know where I'm going and I know my job. I want backing up and encouragement.

"Please do think and think again. I know you have made up your mind and everyone thinks we are finished here, but I think the mistake is creatively almost criminal and something must be done to retrieve the situation and get some sense in to what has become a real mess from your point of view.

"All best wishes, Sam, David."[45]

Spiegel's decision to leave Jordan was supported by John Box. "There was no way we could have built Cairo or Damascus out there. We couldn't shoot in Jerusalem, that would have been impossible. The unit was exhausted, we were losing people, they had to be flown home and medicine and replacements flown out."[46]

And yet Box understood David's desire to stay, because the desert had affected him as well. "I tell you what, I cried. I didn't want to leave the desert. I really did give the family terrible trouble when I came back because I couldn't adjust to anything. The desert was pure. But we had to leave."[47]

The saddest aspect of the move from David's point of view was that among the best locations he had left for the second half was Petra. "Robert had a glamorous idea of Lawrence riding in through the very narrow gorge with a desert gazelle round his neck and throwing it to his Arab bodyguard."[48]

David's dark thoughts about Spiegel's motives for leaving Jordan eventually left him with this theory: "I cannot prove this and I may be quite wrong, but I would guess that there were a lot of complaints about all the Jewish dollars.[49] It sounds funny now, but it was a very serious problem for Sam. He could have been accused of being a kind of traitor. And I have always guessed that he was forced with a gentle velvet glove into the position, and we never returned to Jordan.

"I knew Spain pretty well and I said to Sam, 'You go out and find where I can shoot it.' And he started going off to various places with various people. In the end he failed to find anything and then said, 'We must go to Morocco,' which we did.

"And the last part of the picture - the blood-bath scenes and all that - was all done in Morocco. It's always been a source of regret to me because it could have been better scenically if we had done it in Jordan. I'm not complaining, really, it looks all right."[50]

Among the legends that have grown up around LAWRENCE is that David was so unwilling to leave the desert that he stayed on with his beloved Jordanian guide, Aloosh, living in a tent and enjoying the peace. While it is tempting to see David as a Bedouin manqué, the story eliminates Barbara Cole who was with him until they caught the plane to England, and who says the story - sadly - is simply not true.

When the film was shut down in Jordan, Robert Bolt had still to finish the second half of the script. There was an obvious urgency about this, not helped by the fact that Bolt himself was languishing in jail.

On 17 September 1961, Bolt had taken part in a demonstration organised by the Campaign for Nuclear Disarmament. Ten thousand people blocked Trafalgar Square and Whitehall - the heart of government - and refused to move. Bolt was arrested, along with Vanessa Redgrave, John Osborne and other prominent CND activists. He was hauled into Bow Street Magistrates' Court and given the option of recanting and swearing not to take part in further demonstrations, or going to prison. As the author of the play about Sir Thomas More, Bolt could hardly recant and he was duly sentenced to one month's imprisonment at Drake Hall in Staffordshire.

Bolt counted on being able to continue working on the script in prison, but the authorities forbade this. Anything produced in Her Majesty's Prison would be confiscated or destroyed - unless he signed recognisances of good behaviour, which he refused to do.

Spiegel sent a blitz of cables to Bolt saying that he was delaying the whole project and putting the massive investment at risk; scores of people were going to be unemployed just so that Bolt's conscience might be satisfied. But Bolt would not budge. Finally, Spiegel went to the prison and met with Bolt face to face - and God knows what threats he made. The other imprisoned CND activists understood Bolt's dilemma and urged him to sign. And, with a heavy heart, he did. He was driven away from jail in Spiegel's Rolls-Royce.

"I have never forgiven him for getting me out of jail," said Bolt. "It was the most shameful moment of my life."

Before the unit moved to Spain, there was an entr'acte in London. "When we arrived, Spiegel's people came to meet David and they whisked me off into a separate car before anyone could say a word," said Barbara. "They didn't want us to be seen together. I went home to my flat in Maida Vale and David stayed in Piccadilly at the Athenaeum." [51]

In London, David saw something like ten hours of rushes and cut sequences.

"Due to his remarkable powers of selection," said Anne Coates, "by the time he went to Spain a week later, I was able to start rough-cutting all the material. I had very much hoped to be able to show him these cut sequences when I finished them, but by that time he was too engrossed with the shooting in Spain and consequently I was unable to work on them much further. However, from then on I took rushes down to Spain once a month, so I was at last able to keep more or less up to date with the cutting.

"For me, these trips were extremely interesting as it was the first time I had been able to see any of the film being shot. In the usual way I think it is most important for the editor to spend as much time as possible on the floor since one is able to assimilate a lot of the mood of the film and the director's intention."[52]

"David came to Spain in a very bad mood," said John Box. "He didn't like it at all. I've never forgotten these two rather formidable gentlemen, Lean and Bolt, in the Wellington Hotel in Madrid. I hadn't got all that amount of reputation at the time and David put his piercing eye on me and said, 'John, are you certain we can finish LAWRENCE OF ARABIA in Spain?'

"I said, 'Of course, no doubt about it.'

"I left the room and thought, 'What have you said? You don't know where the hell you're going to do Cairo. All right, you think you're going to get away with Damascus down in Seville, but you don't know where you're going to do Aqaba. It's all ridiculous."[53]

In the end, Seville would provide all the exteriors and interiors for Cairo, Jerusalem and Damascus, although many of the buildings - the headquarters of the British Army in Cairo, and the Officer's Club, were actually anachronisms, having been built for an international exhibition in the thirties.

A drawback to Spain from David's point of view was the fact that he was reunited with Leila. She had visited the camp at Aqaba on one or two occasions, when Barbara and the rest of the crew behaved as discreetly as possible, but this was the first time in nearly a year that she had been with David to any real extent.

"Leila was very nice but she was very floppy," said Barbara Cole. "If we were going on a recce sometimes she'd ask to come and she'd end up by saying, 'I don't want to be a trouble but...' And that meant somebody had to take her to the nearest place where she could lie down in the shade. It got to be her password. 'I don't want to be a trouble, but...'

"I remember one day in Seville she'd asked Phyllis Dalton to take her shopping for materials to make saris. Phyllis was a very busy lady. She turned up at the hotel and Leila said, 'Oh, I can't come. I've just washed my hair and that's enough for one day.' So she wasn't exactly vital."[54]

Shooting resumed in Seville on 18 December 1961. Members of the unit required iron injections. Barbara Cole had the misfortune to be injected by a local doctor with a dirty needle, and she contracted hepatitis. O'Toole was injected by the same man, and developed a boil on his behind which made camel-riding sheer agony.

"Spanish hospitals weren't too good at that time," said Barbara, "so I was sent home. Dr David Sacks [the Columbia doctor] was sent to see me and he said, 'You're going to be in bed for at least a month. You've got to take it quietly.' He rang Sam Spiegel from my bedside and I heard Sam exclaim, 'A month!' Sacks said, 'Perhaps three weeks.' Then Sam rang me and he said, 'Hey, darling, I hear you're going to be sick for a week.'

"The first letters David ever wrote me were when I was ill in London. They were very erotic letters, which unfortunately I destroyed, because I didn't think I should carry them around with me, and I didn't want to leave them at home because they would have shocked my mother. So I'm afraid I burned them all which is a very wicked thing to have done. And mostly because everyone says what a cold man he was, which wasn't true at all. He was a very passionate and erotic man privately."[55]

Assistant director Pedro Vidal had just finished working with Anthony Asquith in Spain when he was asked to work on LAWRENCE.

"Once David was in Spain," he said, "he gave himself completely to the film and forgot he wanted to continue in Jordan. He had a tremendous capacity to bring out your talent, if you had any, because of his sensitivity, the way he pushed you, the way he searched. Maybe through my enthusiasm, he saw I really loved the thing. My ex-wife said once that David needed a touch of madness, and one of the reasons we worked so well together is because I'm quite wild. So is Eddie Fowlie, who is his best friend. We have more than a touch of madness.

"The first day we did the scene with the Turkish Bey. José Ferrer spoke perfect Spanish - he was Puerto Rican. The first take between the Bey and Lawrence was so magnificent, they were both so powerful that when David said 'Cut' the Spanish electricians started applauding, even though they couldn't understand one word. Very few times in my life have I seen the magic of that scene. And that was just the first day."[56]

According to *Seven Pillars of Wisdom*, the encounter with the Bey was one of the most traumatic experiences of Lawrence's life. Historians are divided whether Lawrence was flogged and raped at all, but since Bolt had decided to ignore all contradictory evidence, and take *Seven Pillars* as gospel, he and David had to pay exceptionally close attention to the scene.

"The material of the incident is violence," wrote Bolt in the script. "There is a danger that it will be seen as nothing else, that is, that it will not make its point. That is my reason for advocating a somewhat ritualistic as against a nerve-storming entry to the sequence. If it 'goes over the top' so that the understanding of the audience is simply swamped, we have failed."

Using enormous close-ups, magnified still further on the 70mm screen - in particular the staring eyes of Lawrence and the lascivious mouth of the Bey - David tried to convey the homosexual undertone without showing anything graphic apart from the flogging.

He was not satisfied with the result.

"At the end of the Bey scene," he wrote to Bolt, "we should have had just one more beat to explain that he had been defiled by the Bey - which was missed by ninety percent of our audiences. Our failures within a particular film spring, I think, from not taking enough care and falling back on an attitude of, well, if they don't get it, they don't get it... and bugger them."[57]

Jack Hawkins, playing General Allenby, recalled that David was fascinated by the effect of military boots clattering on the marble of the building standing in for the headquarters in Cairo.

"He insisted that I had steel tips fitted to the heels and toes of my riding boots, and I always had to wear my spurs rather loose. Every time I took a step, it sounded like knights in armour on the rampage."[58]

Hawkins became very friendly with Peter O'Toole. This worried David, and one day he took Hawkins aside and asked him not to be too familiar. David felt that Allenby was a father figure to Lawrence and Hawkins must therefore be rather aloof with O'Toole. David said, "I think you should be careful that your friendship does not intrude into your performance."

For a brilliant film director, thought Hawkins, this was an extraordinary observation. "I ignored his advice, because I couldn't see the point of it. The fact that we used to have some rousing sessions together in no way impinged upon our work; maybe it even improved our performances."[59]

Alec Guinness, who had made another film - HMS DEFIANT - between Jordan and Spain, watched a scene with O'Toole and Hawkins. "The scene I saw was a long, well-written, very intense scene. Jack was marvellous. I could see the

Many have said that David lacked a sense of humour - but it depended on the situation. Here he is with Peter O'Toole, who is collapsing with laughter.

actors slightly tensing up, but nevertheless doing it frightfully well. After about six or eight takes, David said, 'Cut. Fine, that's it' and they all said, 'Thank God.' Jack unbuttoned his uniform, flung it in the air, and did a silly, camp sort of dance.

"David was furious. He couldn't believe it. He said, 'A serious scene and you end it like that!' Jack said, 'Well, I didn't end the scene like that. You said it was OK.' 'Disgraceful behaviour!' said David."[60]

"You don't have fun on a David Lean picture," said Roy Stevens. "You'd have the occasional laugh. He likes the set tense and the rehearsal absolutely quiet. You don't move around. The actors don't like it but that's the way he wants to operate. It's almost a slight to his ability if people are having a joke in the background. There was a feeling of going to church when you went on to his sets."

This atmosphere was essential to enable David to think - hardly the least important of a director's functions.

"In the scene, near the end, where Lawrence is dismissed," said John Box, "we had a desk with a polished top. David came in that morning, sat down and wouldn't move. He said, 'I'm stuck, John.'

"'What's the matter?'

"'I don't know how to start the scene.'

"The unit sensed it and drifted away to have coffee and he sat in his corner like an old gnome, smoking.

"'Is it something I've done,' I asked, 'Props wrong, or something?'

"'No, no. It's here, but I can't get it.'

"I wandered around the room and suddenly he said, 'The camera goes here.'

"I said, 'What is it?'

"He said, 'You moved across the desk. And I saw your reflection. Reflection, no substance, they've taken the Lawrence character apart, he was nobody and he's going to be nobody again.'"

Despite his desire for total control, David had to accept some second unit directors and greeted them with an icy stare.

"In Seville, André Smagghe and a guy called Noel Howard were introduced as second unit directors," said Pedro Vidal. "David said, 'Gentlemen, nothing personal but I *loathe* second unit directors.' I remember the word 'loathe' because I'd never heard it before.

"David said, 'Have you seen BEN-HUR?' They said, 'yes.' He said, 'What did you like the best? 'The chariot race.' And David said, 'That will never happen to me.'"[61]

Another second unit director was André de Toth, a Hungarian of flamboyance and charm. Born in 1900, he grew up with the cinema. He directed a couple of films in Hungary before the war, then went to England where he worked for Korda as second-unit director. In Hollywood, he made B westerns and thrillers. He became famous for his 3-D film HOUSE OF WAX: only Hollywood would have signed a director with one eye who could not see the stereoscopic effect of the finished film.

"I knew Sam Spiegel," De Toth told Adrian Turner, "and was hired by Mike Frankovich. Mike said they had a little problem with LAWRENCE. They were over schedule, over budget and had only forty-five minutes of film. I watched the footage and saw it was absolutely magnificent. I went to Jordan to meet David and he sent me to Spain to look for locations with John Box. It was a way of saving time and David trusted me to find good places to shoot. I flew my own plane and went all over the place. Then I found Almeria."[62]

Almeria is so hot, barren and rugged that it is impossible to believe one is in Europe. The jagged hills and sandy plains make an ideal background for the spaghetti westerns that are still shot there. Although the new location lacked the stunning grandeur of Jordan, David and Box hoped that keeping the camera angles closer to the action - which suited the dramatic intensity of the second half of the film - would leave the audience unaware of the change.

There was one last large vista needed for the taking of Aqaba, which David had originally planned to shoot in Jordan. In Almeria, Box located a dry river bed leading to the sea at Carboneros and designed an extraordinary set, far more impressive than the real Aqaba, just as the battle was far more exciting than the real event.

André De Toth's job was to prepare the charge for Aqaba and the blowing up of the Turkish train, a job which David regretted having to delegate for he considered it to be one of the film's jewels. De Toth's cameraman was Nicolas Roeg, later a famous director himself.

"André was trying to do things for himself that David didn't want," said Roeg. "He was very meticulous about the movie in his mind, and jealous of every shot which wasn't done by him. He was quite right; I can understand that sort of film-maker. André didn't understand that. They were just completely different people."[63]

Roeg found De Toth, this romantic sixty-year-old Hungarian with a black eye-patch, rather endearing. He was full of wild ideas, and Roeg heard him suggest one to David, a scheme for the blood-bath sequence, in which Lawrence is so enraged by the atrocities committed on an Arab village that he lets loose his army on the retreating Turks.

"'We get a whole row of tall mirrors, maybe thirty foot wide, and they would be set at an angle,' De Toth explained to David. 'Behind these mirrors, we hang blood bags and we see the Turkish army coming in these mirrors and when the Arabs charge we will machine-gun the mirrors. The bullets will go into the desert and the blood bursts all over the screen.'

"André was very enthusiastic about his fantastic idea," continued Roeg, "but David said, 'How disgusting.' It was a most crushing blow for this man who had dreamed up this amazing shot. I saw André wandering around on the beach after that. A little later he came up to me and said, 'I'm leaving tomorrow.'"[64]

De Toth, who was not given a credit, held no grudge against David when I contacted him in California, though he sounded regretful about his blood-mirror idea.

"It was a bit too revolutionary," he said. "You look at David; he was a great master of yesterday. You cannot compare Rembrandt to Picasso or even Kokoschka. David was a slow river," he added, enigmatically, "whose undercurrents washed the banks and eventually tumble them in. He was never a mountain stream. But I think he was one of the really great men."[65]

When De Toth left, David told Roeg that he wanted him to direct the second unit. "Oddly enough, we got on rather well,' said Roeg, "because we were distant from each other. I don't think anyone could get very close to David. He was a unique character. If somebody from Mars walked on to his set, they would walk straight up to his chair. There would be no doubt. Nobody else sat in his chair. Nobody went near it. He was absolutely in command.

"He was a very handsome man and he was very acute, but there was a narrowness in his terms of reference. He was focused solely on the film. His attitude was that there is a right way and a wrong way, and that was it. But he did have a giant quality about him."[66]

While the train-wrecking scenes were being shot, the Art Department under John Box and the Construction Crew headed by Peter Dukelow were completing the town of Aqaba. Box had a severe shock when heavy seas washed part of the set away, but little damage was done and it was quickly rebuilt. He gave orders for the three hundred houses to be built a few feet off the ground to give the water less resistance in case it happened again.

"André de Toth said such a charge could never happen at Carboneros," said Box. "He was a horseman, he said, and there were too many stones. What he didn't realise was that we were taking up the stones to build our houses."[67]

Box's set was designed to be photographed from just one angle. "If you walked through it," said David, "the whole place looked ridiculous, but it worked from the camera set-up. The chief point of focus was the gun, pointing out to sea."

David had conceived a bravura way of photographing the charge for Aqaba: as the Arab army sweeps into the town from a high-angle he pans from the charging horses across the town and ends with the gun pointing impotently out to sea. It is one of the most celebrated shots in the picture.

"I was very pleased with myself," said David, "because I took my courage in both hands and the main scene I did in just one big panning shot. I took a great big gulp when I saw it and said 'Cut. That's it.' And that *was* it."[68, 69]

"It was a very bold shot," said John Box. "Several times I said to him, 'Aren't we going over the top? What about a cut?' 'No John,' he said, 'Be bold.' He had the ability to do it. I think that sequence shows what good movie-making is all about. Freddie Young's work, the choreography of the stuntmen, David's direction - masterly. Robert Bolt - just a little bit of dialogue - 'Garlands for the conqueror, tributes for the prince, flowers for the man.' Perfect."[70]

Incredible as it may seem, Spiegel was thoroughly dissatisfied by the rushes of the Aqaba charge.

"There had been a terrible accident in a horse race in England," Anne Coates told Adrian Turner, "when several horses crashed and were killed. A few days later we had the Aqaba rushes and Sam was furious. 'There were more horse falls in the Grand National than in the battle of Aqaba!' he cried. He thought he would be seeing horses and camels falling all over the place. He couldn't see how David was going to cut the sequence."[71]

Despite the work of the second units, Spiegel was becoming exasperated with the slow pace of the production; he had worked on films which had been shot, cut and released in the time it took for David to move from Jordan to Madrid.

On one of his rare visits, Spiegel arrived in Spain with William Wyler. "I was doing that scene with Alec Guinness and Peter O'Toole when the wind starts to creak the inside of a tent and I said, 'Right, do the make-up,' and I turned round and there was Willy standing next to me. It nearly froze me. But in those days I didn't mind. I was so used to him - a benign figure as it were - and I knew he wished me well."[72]

"Sam Spiegel wanted to push the film," said Pedro Vidal, "because everybody said that David was so slow, and he did the same thing again and again. My personal feeling is that Sam tried to impress David, because he was so cunning, in order to say, 'Look out, because I can always have William Wyler.' It was a very subtle thing."[73]

So subtle that the message probably missed David altogether, particularly since Wyler was famous for doing far more takes than anyone else.

As David suspected, Spain was no match for Jordan, and the company eventually ran out of locations. Obliging as the topography had been, it could not disclose a vista of desert bleak enough for the blood-bath sequence. Nor were there enough horsemen, let alone camels, even though a number had been imported for the film. The decision was made to go to Morocco.

Spiegel had assigned Norman Spencer to produce a film called DANGEROUS

Morocco: the start of the massacre of the Turks sequence. The camera crane is strengthened against wind vibration with planks. (Photograph by Ortas)

SILENCE which Robert Parrish was to direct with Jack Lemmon.

"It came to nothing," said Spencer, "because Spiegel didn't want it to come to anything. He just wanted to get me away from David. We spent years trying to get a script done - even Billy Wilder worked on it - and every time we got a script, Spiegel said, 'It's not quite right yet.' Sad. But now, Spiegel revised his tack and said, 'I'd like you to go and work with David. You speak French.' So I was deputed to be in charge of production in Morocco."[74]

Spencer and Sam Spiegel met King Hassan of Morocco and Crown Prince Moulay Abdullah. Spiegel then made a private deal with a Moroccan playboy who became his contact man with the Royal Family.

All the equipment was loaded on to a coastal steamer and shipped across to North Africa. Spiegel sailed his yacht to Casablanca, but never stayed long enough to be of any help.

"I cannot tell you the amount of material the crew had," said Spencer. "You know those British lorries they used to call Queen Marys - a long low-loader on which you could put the fuselage of an aeroplane. We needed thirty Queen Marys to take the material from the docks at Casablanca to Ouarzazate.

"It was really the biggest Cecil B. DeMille rig, and I was in charge of it. I prided myself that no one was going to be held up because the material wasn't there, and so I was supervising it night and day. Absolute nightmare."[75]

In June 1962, David drove Barbara Cole and Freddie Young from Almeria to Gibraltar, and the Rolls was then ferried across to Morocco. After a production meeting with Norman Spencer, David drove the five hours to Marrakesh, where they spent the night. Once they had driven through the pass over the Atlas Mountains, the landscape changed, as if all traces of green had been subjected to an optical wipe and the heat increased to the point where they thanked God for the Silver Cloud's air conditioning. David drove on for four hours until they reached a small village called Ouarzazate - "the asshole of the world," as Anthony Quinn described it.

The romantic in David failed to respond to Ouarzazate, even though he knew his idol, Rex Ingram, had come here in 1931. "A terrible place," said David. "The production office was in a building that was once occupied by the French Foreign Legion. When we were there they were sending the legionnaires there as a punishment. The heat was tremendous and we shared the punishment with the legionnaires."[76]

Norman Spencer has preserved minutes of the meetings with government ministers, governors, army commanders and Caids and Super-Caids which went on for two months before David and the rest of the crew arrived. The water supply was salty... the authorities could only offer three hundred camels and Jeremy Taylor, Master of the Camel, had to mount an expedition to the Sahara and bring in a hundred more... too few troops were offered, and they had to negotiate an increase... It was the equivalent of mounting the Crusades.

The amazing thing is that with all the stress and all the responsibility, David did not collapse. Throughout the entire sixteen months of production, he only fell ill once when he was given some injections during a typhoid scare in Jordan. He asked John Box to take over, and was back the next day "feeling awful, but I did it."

John Palmer, listing the casualties on his daily report sheets, must have felt like a town clerk during a plague: "Peter Carey indisposed with rash on body... John Box in bed with allergic condition... A.G. Scott [chief hairdresser] in bed with enteritis... Ted Brown [electrician] in bed with very bad attack Malaria... George Sanders [sound maintenance man] in bed with complicated condition... Please note Ted Brown and George Sanders were evacuated by Medical Military plane to Casablanca for further diagnosis and treatment in clinic there."[77]

"Everybody went off their heads," said Norman Spencer. "The heat, the conditions, the wind, the living in tents... the army officer we had attached to us as military adviser suddenly started shooting live bullets out of his tent at night. Anything he saw, he shot at. We had to have him taken away."[78]

The crew had to struggle to keep up their enthusiasm against the enervating heat and the unending problems. The Moroccan soldiers, on the other hand, had no such struggles as they had no enthusiasm to start with.

"I can understand their lack of interest," said Ernie Day. "They were dragooned into doing it by officers, which didn't make for good liaison. They didn't like being out in the heat - for what? Talk about mad dogs and Englishmen; they could see us under shades, parasols and things, and they were out there with no shade, except what they could get from their camels or horses."[79]

"The troops got nothing," said David. "We paid the king. The cheques went to a bank account in Paris. So the troops got pretty fed up. At one point they started firing over my head. I had never heard a bullet whistling before. They were a tough lot. They'd do one take and if you asked for another they went over the hill and that was the end of them. I never saw them again for the rest of the day. No one had any sort of command of them at all."[80]

The plan for the blood-bath was to show Lawrence's horror at what the Turks had done to the population of an Arab village, and to have one man, who came from that village, charge the Turks in a solitary display of defiance. As he is shot, Lawrence gives the order to attack the column of retreating Turks. In *Seven Pillars*, Lawrence gives the order by saying, "The best of you brings me the most Turkish dead" and, a page later he says, "By my order we took no prisoners, for the only time in our war." Bolt's script simplified this to the cry, "No prisoners!" and the slaughter begins.

"We aimed to get to the final dramatic point as quickly as possible to show the desolation of the battlefield," said John Box. "Lawrence had indulged in an orgy of killing, and we had to show the effect this had upon him."[81]

The massacre near Tafas was so bloodthirsty it would have been hard to watch if presented realistically. As Lawrence wrote in *Seven Pillars*, "In a madness born of the horror of Tafas we killed and killed, even blowing in the heads of the fallen and of the animals; as though their death and running blood could slake our agony."[82]

David filmed this so that one felt one saw the horrors without their being too graphic (one shudders to think how a present-day director would handle it). He then showed the unforgettable image of Lawrence staring in horror at his reflection in his blood-soaked knife, having given us the sight, rare in the cinema, of a super-hero committing a crime against humanity. David and Bolt confronted this atrocity - which would have had Hollywood film-makers hastily altering history and whitewashing their hero - and in doing so they helped us to understand Lawrence and the obscene nature of warfare a little more.

After the unit had spent nearly four months in Morocco, Spiegel flew in, determined to bring the production to an end. David's output was now down to a daily average of twenty-four seconds (three minutes a day was the average for feature film production in those days) and shooting had taken almost as long as the actual Arab revolt.

"There was a full unit call so that Sam Spiegel could address us all in the patio of the hotel," said Nic Roeg. "He was brilliant. It was so cleverly done. He went up to the rigger and said, 'How are you, Bill, my boy? Hello, Ned!' He knew everybody, like Napoleon. He had learned all their names.

"He said, 'I don't think I will live to see a penny from this film but I just want you to know that you've done a wonderful job and I'm proud of you. But, boys, we've got to go faster!'

"Only David could set the pace, obviously. And only David was absent from the meeting. He had a later meeting with Sam on his own. He wanted to return to Spain to do further shooting there.

"The next morning we were sitting in the desert and Sam's plane circled and buzzed the crew. David looked at it and said, 'Bastard! Bastard! Last night he told me he'd had a heart attack and made me promise we were not going back to Spain. Made me promise. Bastard! I know he's going back to some girlfriend in the South of France. Heart attack! He's a better actor than I've got on the set.'"[83]

Spiegel, though, had wanted to make some kind of gesture of appreciation towards David. He said, "Baby, the production will take the cost of your air conditioning on board."[84]

The main unit returned to England to film Lawrence's fatal motor-cycle accident and the Memorial Service at St Paul's Cathedral. Nic Roeg and a second-unit crew remained in Morocco to do a couple of close-ups of the blood-bath.

One of Lawrence's "tulips" destroys a Turkish locomotive - recreated in Almeria, Southern Spain.

"I was actually the last person with David," said Roeg. "After the final shot, he sat in his caravan and I thought it was time to leave. As I moved away from him I saw that he was on the verge of tears. Understandable. John Huston said movies become a village - the actors go, the editor goes, they've all gone. Your little village has become uninhabited." [85]

When David arrived back in England he had to have an operation and some plastic surgery on an eye. Because he had refused to wear protective goggles in the desert, insisting they interrupted his chain of thought, specialists had discovered sand embedded behind one eyelid, which had begun to droop over the pupil, affecting his sight.

Spiegel now thought of a way of ensuring that the production reached a swift conclusion; he arranged for LAWRENCE to be given a Royal Film Performance in the presence of the Queen on 10 December 1962. This gave David just four months to have the film ready.

"I must say it was a master stroke on Sam's part," said Peter O'Toole, "fixing the premiere date and inviting the Queen before we were even through. He knew we were going on too long - David and I had begun to forget we were making a film. After two years it had become a way of life. So Sam nailed us with a date and that was that." [86]

David was not well pleased; his feelings about Spiegel had by now sunk as low as they could.

"At the end of the picture, I was not on speaking terms with Sam. He knew I liked the old Berkeley very much, when it was in Piccadilly. 'Look, baby,' he said. 'We haven't spoken for four weeks. Let me take you out to dinner at the Berkeley.' After a couple of drinks, I said, 'Sam, answer me this. We could have had a very happy picture with LAWRENCE. Most of the time it was absolutely horrible. Why did you behave so badly to me?'

"He took a great gulp and said, 'Baby, artists work better under pressure.'" [87]

Anne Coates was able to show David two hours of cut material and nine hours of uncut rushes, including the blood-bath, which was covered by several cameras.

Now the editing began in earnest, day and night, seven days a week. Anne Coates had her team based at Warwick Films, in South Audley Street, Mayfair. On the floor above, David was given his own cutting-room which had a small flat attached. There was a television set and David, who had been far from films and television for so long, was startled by what he saw. He was so impressed by one of the early *Z-Cars* he wrote a fan letter to the director - and was quite hurt when he failed to reply. [88]

The editing sessions transformed David from the grim-faced, stubborn and often bloody-minded film director in the desert.

"He was another person," said Anne Coates. "He was so happy in the cutting-rooms. And we used to have lots of laughs, considering we were working those long hours, and were very tired. I remember him telling us stories of his early life, his girlfriends and all sorts of things - I loved it."[89]

"He was very pleasant," said First Assistant Willie Kemplen, "very friendly and very generous. When we were working weekends, he'd take us to the Dorchester for lunch. But he was slightly cold. He was dedicated to making that film. I felt that if I'd fallen over dead in the cutting-room, he'd say, 'Oh, what a shame. Could you get him out of the way? I must just look at this shot.'"[90]

"David worked on a Moviola in his cutting-room upstairs," said Barbara Cole, "a Chinagraph pencil stuck across his mouth, which he regretted because he said that was why he had those deep lines by his mouth."[91]

"David wanted an assistant to work with him." said Coates. "I had the choice of bringing in Norman Savage, who had worked with me before, and who was going to be one of the sound editors, and Malcolm Cook, who had never worked with me, but whom I knew well and who was also on sound. David liked them very much. I had a sort of loyalty towards Norman because he was a friend of mine, but Malcolm had a bit more experience. Spiegel didn't like Norman for some reason and that made me more determined to put Norman with David. And he went on to cut ZHIVAGO and RYAN'S DAUGHTER.

"The decision was made to cut the second part first which had all the big sound sequences in it, the trains and the blood-bath, so the sound department could get on with the sound. When we got that finalised, and sent it off like a complete film, basically we didn't touch it again. We didn't have time. Then we cut the first half.

"David didn't get up too early so we started usually about half past nine or ten. Then we worked to midnight, or later, every night, so much so that the boys who were working with me - I only had three assistants - had to be put up in hotels because it was dangerous for them to drive home at that time of night when they were so tired. We did four months and we never had a single day off. Sunday was no different to any other day."[92]

What Anne Coates learned about the craft of film editing stayed with her for the rest of her career.

"We were having an argument," she said, "about a very simple cut of going through a door. I wanted to cut to the inside, where Lawrence goes into Brighton's office, and walks past Dryden. I wanted to cut inside the office as soon as he got to the door and started to open it because I wanted to see where you were going to. And David said, 'Oh no, you should cut half way through the door. You're wrong because there's only one right frame to cut on.'

"I said, 'David, there may be a right frame for me and a right frame for you.'

"He said, 'Yes, but I'm the director and my frame is more right than yours is.' With that twinkle of his. And of course it's true.

"He said to me things like, 'It's what you take out which makes the movie, not necessarily what you leave in.' He taught me to be brave. If stuff wasn't right, even if it was a great sequence, cut it out. That was something which stood me in very good stead. He also taught me confidence. I am a fast cutter because he taught me to be very definite in what I do. Make your cuts powerful and strong, always cut for a reason, always know why you're cutting. He also taught me to hold on to shots. I don't think I would have held on to those shots in the desert as long as he did. He was brave like that."[93]

But in the late fifties and early sixties, editing styles were undergoing radical changes. Anne Coates was struck by the "jump-cuts" of the French New Wave and suggested that David looked at some of the films produced by it.

"David hadn't really seen any of it. But he went off and saw some Chabrol and that sort of thing and I think he was impressed because he then came up with all sorts of great ideas. They're famous now in LAWRENCE. But if you read the script, it actually says 'dissolve,' it doesn't say 'cut.' The blowing out of the match for instance, is marked as an optical in the script. But David was so brilliant that if you put an idea into his head, he then improved upon what anyone else had done on it at that time."[94]

"One of the cleverest things in LAWRENCE," said David, "I'm not sure whose idea it was - probably John Box's - concerned the Arab robes. Lawrence is given these robes fairly early on, when he's accepted by the Arabs and then the rot starts to set in, and he is seized by a sort of power mania. What the costume people did was gradually to change the texture of the material from which his Arab clothes were made, and they made it thinner and thinner until it was just muslin, and at the end he looked almost ghostlike. Nobody ever spots it."[95]

There has long been controversy over who cut LAWRENCE - did Anne Coates earn her title as editor, or did David dictate every cut? After LAWRENCE, she became one of the industry's most sought-after editors.

"I was lucky to cut as much as I did, because he didn't have time," said Coates. "He was doing cutting on scenes, and I was doing cutting on scenes. I was altering his stuff and he was altering my stuff. I mean, the last word in editing was David's, but then the last word on any film is the director's. He had a more acute feeling for editing because he was a very famous editor, and he had marvellous ideas. But in four months, there's no way one single editor could actually have cut that film. You had to have two people."[96]

One of the most famous cuts in film history was the transition from the close-up of Lawrence blowing out the match to the sun rising over the desert.

"I thought Lawrence should blow out the match," said David, "and I wanted the sound to blow in the desert. What I did was this. He holds up the match and he blows. Now, I laid the first half of the blow over Peter and the last half over the sunrise in the desert, so that the blow noise carried from his close-up over to the long shot. He was still blowing on the long shot. If I'd had him blow out the match and after the sound had faded I cut to the long shot, it wouldn't have had that same effect.

"I was terribly pleased with that. It worked first time. Now the next thing was when to bring the sun up. I thought, 'Blow, desert, one, two, three, four seconds - sun.

"So I would get a bit of blank film and I'd have my foot on the Moviola and I'd go 'blow' and press the pedal and the film would start running. One, two, three, four, put a chalk mark on the film, got it. I then get the real scene and I find the place where the sun appears and I put a cross on the sun appearing and I go back to the beginning and I cut the sunrise where I started to time it, so I have one, two, three, four when I go forward and the sun comes up after a count of four.

"Then I said to Maurice Jarre, the composer, I'd love to have the feeling from the music that something is about to happen. So it's a red screen, ting, ting, ting, ting, sun. Absolutely mechanical, and it works a treat. I think it's the cut I'm most proud of in anything I've done."

As far as David was concerned, there had never been any question over who should compose the music - it had to be Malcolm Arnold, who had done KWAI. Sam Spiegel, obsessed with prestige, acceded to David's demand, then added an even more distinguished name.

"He wanted Sir William Walton to write all the dramatic music," said Malcolm Arnold, "and me to orchestrate and conduct the whole bloody score. I said the only man who can do these Eastern things is my good friend Aram Khatchaturian. You can contact him in Russia. He will do it as he knows it's me."

According to Anne Coates, Arnold and Walton, having imbibed too freely at lunch, arrived in no mood to take the film seriously. They sent it up.

"We saw about two hours of it," said Arnold. "I said, 'William, it's terrible.' He said, 'I know, but I need the money.' I said, 'So do I. But it's so bad.'"[97]

Walton felt it was a travelogue needing hours of music.[98] Arnold had been asked to telephone Spiegel with an immediate decision, but delayed doing so until the evening, when he called Spiegel from Wheeler's Restaurant and turned the film down on behalf of them both. Walton never saw the completed film and he never saw David Lean again.

Having been turned down by two composers, Spiegel then involved three. Maurice Jarre was a thirty-five-year old French composer who had written the music for the documentaries HOTEL DES INVALIDES and TOUTE LA MEMOIRE DU MONDE and features such as Franju's horror film, EYES WITHOUT A FACE. He was a pupil of Arthur Honegger and he collaborated with Pierre Boulez on productions for the Renaud-Barrault theatre company.

Sam Spiegel asked Jarre to come to London to compose the "dramatic" - i.e incidental - music and to co-ordinate the work of two other composers - Khatchaturian, who would handle the Oriental music, and Benjamin Britten, who would write the British Imperial music. Jarre felt very honoured to be among such company.

In his room in Half Moon Street, Jarre began to write. Spiegel telephoned to say that Khatchaturian could not leave Russia and Britten asked for a year to do the work so he was out too. "Bad news," said the delighted Jarre. Then Spiegel went to New York and reported that he had done a fabulous deal with Richard Rodgers, best-known for his musicals, who had also written a memorable theme for the television series, *Victory at Sea*.

In the middle of September, Spiegel summoned Jarre to meet David and to hear a pianist play the Rodgers themes. "He hid David from me because I was his discovery. Then I saw this really handsome man with grey hair, and this is David Lean. I was very impressed. He sat down and Spiegel was there and this British pianist and I was in my corner and the pianist started to play the Arabic theme. 'Now the love scene' - love scene? - I couldn't believe it. 'Now the British theme.' And the pianist turned, without reading the music, and said, 'I know that, it's an old military march.'

"At that point I saw David jump up from his chair. 'Sam, what is all this rubbish? I am supposed to be editing and you take up my time with this nonsense?'

"Sam turned to me and said, 'Maurice, didn't you write anything?'

"I said, 'Yes, I have a little bit of music.' I went to the piano and I start to play what became the LAWRENCE OF ARABIA theme. And I felt a hand on my shoulder. 'This chap has got the theme. He's really got the mood of what I want. I want him to do the music.'

"Sam said, 'Maurice, you are going to do it. In six weeks I want everything recorded.' I barely survived the experience from the physical point of view. I was only sleeping about two or three hours a night."[99]

To Jarre's music, David added 'The Voice of the Guns,' perhaps superstitiously, for it was composed by Kenneth Alford, who had written "Colonel Bogey".

The music was recorded at Shepperton studios by the London Philharmonic Orchestra, whose principal conductor was Sir Adrian Boult.

"Sam was always mad on names," said David. "Sam got Sir Adrian Boult to come down and conduct the opening titles. It wasn't very good. He left the recording studio and Maurice Jarre stepped up to the podium and we re-took it. So Maurice Jarre did it all, but Sam gave Adrian Boult credit on the screen. And this was typical Sam."[100]

As the date for the premiere approached, the pressures on the editing staff were intense. Yet they managed to send the first ten reels of the second half of the film to the labs for negative cutting two days ahead of schedule.

The pressure was equally intense on the sound department. It was so large that there were not enough cutting-rooms at Shepperton and they had to move into caravans. Winston Ryder had booked what he considered sensible dates for post-synching and dubbing the first part, only to find David and Anne Coates still editing, so he could not even work from dupes.

"LAWRENCE was an awful experience," said Ryder, recalling incidents such as the sand, needed for the post-sync sessions, being dumped outside the sound stage in pouring rain; it would have sounded more like Flanders mud than the scorched surface of the desert. And yet he and his department wrought the miracles David expected of them.

"I'm terribly conscious of the sound track," said David, "which is almost as important as the pictures. For instance, when Omar Sharif comes out of the desert, Win Ryder put in the pad, pad, pad of the camel's feet. It wasn't a real sound, but it added immeasurably to the silence of the desert, the size of it all." [101]

And then, right in the middle of editing, David started shooting again, though just for one day. Peter O'Toole explained what happened.

"He wanted another close-up to help build the tension of that amazing entrance of Ali. So having been in the wilderness of Zin, we find ourselves in the relative wilderness of Hammersmith in a tiny little room with an old blue wall and a bit of dry ice…"

O'Toole was shocked when he saw the footage edited into the material.

"He showed me it and it was extraordinary, for I was twenty-seven in the first shot; cut to the figure coming through the mirage; twenty-nine in the second shot and twenty-seven in the third. The difference was astounding. I'd lost the bloom of youth. We're in a strange situation, film actors. We can watch the decomposition of the flesh." [102]

CHAPTER THIRTY-ONE

THE JELLY IN THE SUNLIT POOL

LAWRENCE OF ARABIA III

WHEN David was in Morocco, Professor Lawrence was able to read a copy of the script. "To say that I am extremely disappointed is a gross understatement," he wrote to Spiegel.

The Professor had left himself with only one weapon in his armoury, the witholding of the title of *Seven Pillars of Wisdom*. Since the film had been called LAWRENCE OF ARABIA from the beginning, the old title was only of academic interest. No one imagined, least of all Spiegel, that it would cause a stampede to the box office.

However, Spiegel was not a man to let five thousand pounds slip, and he informed Lawrence's lawyer that he still planned to call the film *Seven Pillars of Wisdom*. As anticipated, Lawrence refused permission and Spiegel got his money back, in accordance with the contract. Since the final cost of the film would be thirteen million dollars, the five thousand pounds was small beer, though Spiegel would happily have paid ten times that amount for an endorsement from the brother of the film's hero.

Spiegel invited the Professor to see a rough-cut, which he saw with his wife, Barbara, at South Audley Street on 5 September 1962. The print was far from complete; there were no opticals, it had no music nor had it been dubbed. Some of it was mute and David had still to shoot the opening scenes in England.

David attended the showing and was shaken by the Professor's reaction. "Lawrence was furious," he recalled. "You felt the seats were heaving about five minutes before the end. He stood up and shouted at Sam, 'I should never have trusted you!' There was a horrendous row and he stormed out of that little theatre with his wife in pursuit, trying to placate him."[1]

Anthony Nutting felt that the Professor was protective to an almost unreasonable degree of the Lawrence myth, mainly because there was a family secret.

"What appeared on the screen was a very muted version of what I put in my book, where I called a spade a spade and said that Lawrence became a physical and emotional masochist. If you like, as Freud says, everything goes back to sex; he got his sexual kicks in that manner. There is considerable evidence that he enjoyed being flogged. That, of course, did not come out in the film, but there is a sort of muted element in the way he reacted to questions about his suffering in the desert and the agonies he went through." [2]

However, the film accuses him more of sadism than masochism - of Gasim's execution, he says, "I enjoyed it" and Lawrence clearly launches the blood-bath with relish.

Although Lawrence wrote in *Seven Pillars*, "In my last five actions, I had been hit; my body dreaded further pain," he did have masochistic tendencies which became public when a Sunday newspaper published an interview with a former Tank Corps private who carried out ritual floggings, at Lawrence's request, from 1925 to 1934.

When Professor Lawrence was interviewed in 1986 by Julia Cave for her BBC documentary *Lawrence and Arabia*, he finally confessed the family secret:

"He hated the thought of sex. He had read any amount of medieval literature about characters - some of them saints, some of them not - who had quelled sexual longings by beatings. And that's what he did. I knew about it immediately after his death, but of course said nothing. It's not a thing people can understand easily."

Perhaps the Professor's anger had been inspired not so much by the picture's hints at sadism or masochism, but by the fact that so deeply personal a matter should have been presented to the public in what he considered so shallow a medium. As his *Times* obituarist put it, "He dissociated himself from the film... not from a desire to conceal the truth but from a concern to see such subjects discussed seriously, not sensationally." [3]

That David was also worried about the sensational aspect was revealed when he wrote to Robert Bolt, referring to the blood-bath scene, "which is interpreted by eighty percent of the audience and ninety percent of the press as meaning that the enigma of Lawrence was that he was a sadist. We could have saved this impression by showing that the coming upon the Turkish column was a devilish twist of fate, a thousand-to-one temptation - a crashing piece of bad luck which most of us are never exposed to." [4]

Would Professor Lawrence have been happier if the film had been made from the Michael Wilson script? It is doubtful, for Wilson's script was very different from his treatment and his Lawrence would have lacked the romanticism and charisma of the Bolt characterisation.

Wilson, curious about how much of his work remained in the new version, managed to obtain a copy of Bolt's script. After examining it, he wrote to Spiegel, saying that while Bolt had done a fine job on the dialogue, the overall structure remained his. "Most of my inventions have been retained - incidents which are not to be found in *Seven Pillars of Wisdom* or any other work about Lawrence." Wilson asked Spiegel for joint screenplay credit but Spiegel, through his solicitors, declared that Wilson had no contractual rights and did not deserve credit anyway. [5]

Wilson also wrote to Robert Bolt:

"I felt I had gone about as far as I could go, that if I lived to be a hundred I could not fully satisfy David Lean. Frankly, I no longer cared about satisfying him, for in the main I had satisfied myself. Not that my work was the definitive 'Lawrence,' but like most writers who have a go at this subject, I developed a certain pride in my interpretation; and I suppose I began to behave more like a playwright than a hired screenwriter and director's right-hand man. At any rate, something had to give. And so I resigned. And thus slipped into the limbo of non-persons the producers of this film chose to forget.

"A few weeks ago, quite by accident, I learned that a solo screenplay credit on LAWRENCE OF ARABIA had been assigned to you. Mr Sam Spiegel had not only failed to inform me of this tentative credit, but had never shown me a copy of the shooting script. As you know, this is a violation of established procedures for the determination of writers' credits. I assume of course that you were unaware of this hankypanky.

"I called Mr Spiegel to register my protest, and belatedly he sent me a copy of the final script. I studied the script with care. It serves no purpose for me to evaluate it here. My sole and selfish concern was to determine whether I deserved recognition; and having found the contribution there I immediately wrote a letter to Mr Spiegel, setting forth the reasons why I felt I deserved joint credit with you on the picture... anyone who takes the trouble to read my stuff chronologically - from the time I wrote my first notes on Lawrence in 1959 until I wrote my third draft screenplay in 1961 - will see where and how the basic ideas and overall conception of this picture germinated. If you were told on taking over the assignment that you were 'starting from scratch' you were misinformed; if you were led to believe there was little to go on except for some technicolor blueprint in David Lean's mind, you were deceived. The blueprint was mine...

"For the past eleven years I have been one of the blacklisted American writers. I have just begun to emerge from that shadowy realm, not through any abandonment of principle on my part, but because at long last I have found an American producer who has the courage to give credit to a writer he engages, and the witch-hunters be damned.

"The men in control of LAWRENCE OF ARABIA lack that courage. If I were 'clean,' my name would already be alongside yours as co-author of this picture. I implore you to believe this is not a paranoid assertion. I am not a man for all seasons; but while martyrdom ill suits me, there are aspects of the blacklist that do fill me with mirth. If I could tell you (and if you're interested someday I shall) the enormous pressures the top brass of this production put on me to 'clear myself' you would see that this is the heart of the matter.

"In view of the producer's violation of current procedure and his refractory position I am impelled to turn the matter over to the British Television and Screen Writers' Guild for examination and probable arbitration.

"I deeply regret that our relationship must begin with a dispute. I hope we shall pass through to friendship for I wish you well. Sincerely yours, Michael Wilson."[6]

Bolt replied: "Your letter came this morning as a bombshell"[7] and insisted to Wilson that all accounts of Lawrence's life followed the same basic story line. Through his agent, Bolt issued a statement asserting that of the dialogue and camera directions, only one percent was Wilson's. Bolt also argued that since Professor Lawrence had approved of Wilson's approach, subsequent events proved that the interpretation was entirely his own.

The Writers' Guild's arbitration committee found in Wilson's favour, and, having presented Bolt with an award for his script, now felt obliged to give Wilson the same award, which they proceeded to do in 1963, a year after the film opened.

Wilson died in 1978. One of the last films on which he shared a credit was PLANET OF THE APES,[8] from the novel *Monkey Planet* by Pierre Boulle, who had written KWAI and who was used by Spiegel to rob Wilson of his credit and his Oscar. Although Wilson eventually won a credit - and a posthumous Oscar - for KWAI, he was not permitted a credit on the restored LAWRENCE, despite considerable lobbying on his behalf.

The Royal premiere of LAWRENCE OF ARABIA was held on Monday 10 December 1962. A screening had been arranged for the crew on the Sunday evening. There was such a demand for tickets that an extra performance was arranged for Sunday morning.

"The night before the Sunday show things were very tight," said Anne Coates. "We only took off two 70mm prints - one was for England and one was to go to New York. And one of the reels got scratched - the British one. So I had to go down to London Airport and get that reel off the American print and take it to the Odeon, Leicester Square for that Sunday morning run. Technicolor had to replace that reel quickly and send it to America. Everything was so last-moment that it was just unbelievable that we ever got there.

"Before that Sunday, none of us - neither David, Sam nor I - had seen the film from beginning to end. Even when we did the grading, we saw the second half first. David didn't even see it that Sunday morning. But I went."[9]

The editing crew had grown accustomed to watching 35mm CinemaScope reductions and black-and-white dubbing dupes. Only a couple of reels of 70mm had been prepared for publicity purposes. Suddenly, on the vast screen of the Odeon appeared images the like of which had never been seen before, images of

As the Queen congratulates Peter O'Toole, Spiegel appears to be casting covetous eyes at David's C.B.E.

breathtaking clarity, so much more beautiful than anyone but Freddie Young had imagined. Anne Coates could hardly believe her eyes.

"David rang me up and said, 'How did it look? How did it stand up, the sound balance and everything?'

"I said, 'Just fantastic. They were swept away.'"

But that audience consisted of the crew and their relatives, most of whom had an immense emotional investment in the success of the picture. The true test would come when it was exposed the next day to the press and public and the invited audience from the industry at the Royal Premiere.

"I'll never forget going to the premiere," said David, "with the Queen and the Duke of Edinburgh. We were all lined up before the show, and the Duke of Edinburgh came up to me, and I bowed, and he said, 'Ah, good evening. Good flick?' And I said, 'I hope so, sir.'

"Now, he had no intention of being insulting, or talking down. But we were 'the flicks.' And that is still the way the English Establishment feels about the movies. Wherever I go now in the world, I am absolutely astounded by the immediate respect I get for being a film director, because if you've done one or two good films you are very much respected, but in England it's still a good old touch of the flicks. And it's a shame." [10]

This attitude was also shared by David's father. "I sent my father tickets and he wrote me a letter saying he was sorry he couldn't come, because it was rather a long journey. He lived in Marlow, on the Thames.

"Two weeks later, I was mortified when he travelled down to Devon to attend the wedding of one of my nephews. He just didn't consider the movies of any importance." [11]

His father's companion, Margaret, and her son, Stephen, did accept David's invitation. "In my mature years," said Stephen, "I realised that David and Buncs did not get on very well. As David became more and more well known, and more and more regarded as outstandingly brilliant, Buncs grew more and more jealous of him." [12]

It was for this reason, he felt, that David visited his father less and less, although he came to see Margaret whenever he could. However, Margaret did not exactly endear herself to David for during the blood-bath scene, Margaret, being a war widow, suddenly said, "I cannot stand this fighting any more" and she and her son walked out.

The reactions after the show and at the party at the Grosvenor House were ecstatic, and David was even able to laugh when Noël Coward said that had Peter O'Toole been any prettier, the film would have to have been called "Florence of Arabia".'

Barbara Cole did not go to the premiere, because David took Leila, but as she emerged on to Leicester Square after a later show she overheard a man saying, "They didn't go to the desert at all. I heard they took sacks of sand into MGM." [13]

"I thought it was magnificent," said Anthony Nutting. "Perhaps this is being a little frivolous, but in a sense it is a picture not so much about Lawrence as about a love affair between a director, a cameraman and a desert." [14]

Sam Spiegel was perhaps more astonished than anybody.

"Any picture is a dream, because there is a white sheet of linen, empty, without anything on it, and a couple of people start thinking how to project their imagination on to it. In most cases one is happy if what emerges in the final cut is half as good as the script that you offered them.

"While you know how lovely an idea is, when you extinguish a match and suddenly the desert opens up for you, when you see it, it exceeds your wildest expectations of what it will look like on the screen." [15]

"I felt in awe of David when I saw LAWRENCE," said Fred Zinnemann. "I went to the opening in New York and I saw the match and the sunrise, and the approach of Omar Sharif through the mirage - I had a feeling of awe because that was beyond my reach." [16]

The reception of the British critics was generally favourable. Alexander Walker, of the *Evening Standard*, wrote, "Here is an epic with intellect behind it.

An unforgettable display of action staged with artistry. A momentous story told with moral force. What on earth has wrought this miracle? The makers.

"Producer Sam Spiegel is a man of culture as well as finance. David Lean is a director who goes out to the wild place to meditate on his films, much as prophets used to contemplate unworldly things. Scriptwriter Robert Bolt is our subtlest playwright of men's emotions. And I think that Allah, in the shape of F.A. Young's Technicolor camerawork, poured down his blessing for the two years of filming. An unbeatable team!"[17]

John Coleman (writing in the *New Statesman*, in which Lindsay Anderson had attacked KWAI) applauded the courage in making the epic, but added, "none of it is good enough. Setting to one side the obligatory, contemptible music, the film never decisively makes up its mind what it's after - a breathing portrait of Lawrence or a series of sandy battles and torments."[18]

But reservations of this kind were swept away by the enthusiasm of reviews such as this one from Dilys Powell in *The Sunday Times*:

"Romantic landscapes, august landscapes - one has seen those often enough on the screen. This is something else. The sun rising on the rim of blood-orange sand; dust storms like the smoke-trails of a djinn; the shapes of infinity, the colours of heat - I think it is the first time for the cinema to communicate ecstasy. LAWRENCE OF ARABIA is full of such beauties, and I can't refrain from singling out the ambush of the train-load of horses and the capture in particular of one proud milk-white creature - a passage which might be out of Homer... LAWRENCE OF ARABIA taken as a whole is a genuine, sometimes even a profound interpretation of character. And that alone, even without the great aesthetic beauties, would make the film unique in the cinema of historical reconstruction."[19]

And yet, thirty years later, the only notice David remembered was by Penelope Gilliatt. "Her subheading was 'Two and a Half Pillars of Wisdom.' You know that's very funny, but not if you're the director."

Penelope Gilliatt's review was headed "Blood, Sand and a Dozen Lawrences" and there was no sub-heading. She considered the film, "a thoughtful picture with an intensely serious central performance, but it doesn't hold together in great excitement."[20]

When it was shown in New York on 16 December 1962, LAWRENCE received a standing ovation. But it had the misfortune to open during a newspaper strike, and one of the few critics to appear in print, Andrew Sarris of *The Village Voice*, called it, "dull, overlong and coldly impersonal... hatefully calculating and condescending."[21] Bosley Crowther of the *New York Times* hated it too. Other, kinder reviewers were syndicated or broadcast their opinions over the radio or on television.

When the show was over, David found himself walking down Fifth Avenue with David O. Selznick. He said to David, "They will do to you what they tried to do to me on GONE WITH THE WIND. They will try to make you cut it. Don't let them. I refused to let them cut GONE WITH THE WIND which they said was going to be hopeless if it wasn't cut because of the length - they could only get two shows a day. It's made more money than any film ever made. Don't let them touch LAWRENCE."[22]

Although Selznick's advice impressed David, he felt, with many others, that the picture *was* too long and was determined to do something about it at the first opportunity. But for the moment, David, Spiegel, Sharif and O'Toole made the rounds of radio and television interviews.

"Sam has just popped in," wrote David to Barbara Cole, "to tell me that the NY box office is jammed with queues bigger than they've ever had... and that a TV personality has just gone on the air saying that anyone who misses LAWRENCE will be depriving himself of one of the greatest experiences of his life... And the Columbia stock has gone up from $14 to $25." [23]

Journalists flocked to David's hotel. What he chose to talk about was significant.

"After a movie is released," he told the *New York Times*, "everyone talks about the wonderful acting, directing and writing. But the crew is a major reason for success with this kind of movie.

"The crew had to withstand temperatures of one hundred and twenty-five degrees... men did not see their families for more than six months... they lived in tents. I was lucky. I lived in a trailer mounted on a truck. Picking the crew was as important as if we were going to explore an unknown jungle or climb Mount Everest. I think they were mad to do it.

"The actors were not in the front line. They could shoot a few hours and get out of the sun. They would have time off when they were not working. The rest of us became very proud. We looked upon the occasional visitor with suspicion, even hostility."

The Los Angeles premiere was held on 21 December 1962. "The Hollywood audience was the best of the lot," wrote David. "They clapped two or three times but had an attentiveness far beyond London and New York. It was a sort of rave show and at the dinner afterwards it was rather wonderful because I knew that everyone present thought we had done something very substantial for the film medium." [24]

On 23 December 1962, from the Beverly Hills Hotel, David typed a long letter to Robert Bolt.

"I don't think I have ever written to you before, so before going any further I must tell you that I can't spell. Having said that I won't apologise any further."

Because it was his first script and because of Michael Wilson's campaign for screen credit, Bolt was worried that his contribution to the film would go unrecognised in America. David allayed his fears:

"When credit *is* deserved it somehow filters through. Most so-called script writers are adaptors and 'added dialogue writers.' The movies don't possess a dramatist. For that reason this film of ours has knocked the top film-makers sideways.

"Among the real ravers are Willy Wyler, Billy Wilder, Fred Zinnermann [sic], Richard Brooks, Joe Mancowich [sic] and the great old-timer King Vidor. They have all been round here to deliver their feelings in person. They are all so bloody generous that every one of them has said words to the effect 'It's out of our class' and really mean it."

The only reservation came from Billy Wilder who "went on and on about the film last evening. Billy says he thinks the film is a tremendous piece of work and 'if my heart had been really touched by Lawrence as a human being I would put it up into the first movie Sistine Chapel stuff. But it wasn't.'

"I think he's right. Came thumping in on me as he said it and I think the rush of the second half is more than half responsible. Funny. Like you I started off against Lawrence and then gradually started to swing round. As an audience I feel like Ali about him now. I have a feeling that given the time to be alone with him a little more we could have gone a stage further and given the audience real compassion."

Wilder, said David, "didn't understand that anything happened to Lawrence [in the Bey scene] apart from the beating and didn't understand why we stayed so long on Omar before he was thrown out into the muck-heap. This, I know, is my fault because with the length panic I didn't allow enough silent footage before the music began after the beating."

David said that "all the papers have had a go about the length. They complain but say they were never bored. It just nags them. No-one has any real suggestion to make and I have talked to Sam a lot about it. My way of thinking is that if we cut out forty minutes - which we can't - I would call it very helpful. But it's no good nibbling at scenes and running the risk of ruining the impact that the film certainly has…"

David had by this time already started to experiment with cuts. "I saw it here in Hollywood with the 'Dine with me in Wadi Rumm!' cutting to the close-up of the little girl in the feast scene. It doesn't come off very well. Quinn declaimed the line in order to lead in to the eyeful long shot - so the cut makes him hammy… It also disrupts the pattern of the picture in some way and we now have one dialogue scene followed at once by another. Don't know quite what to do but somehow that long shot has got to go back.

"My own criticism is that the second half shows the forced pace at which you had to jump from point to point. As it nears the end I get a bit stiffled [sic] with keeping up. Know what I mean? Not your fault of course but a lesson not to be forgotten about starting with an unfinished script."[25]

With LAWRENCE over, Leila must have been longing for the moment when David would resume normal married life. But "normal" for David did not apply to domestic relations; for David, the only sort of normality was his all-consuming passion for work in exotic locations, from which Leila was automatically excluded.

"She said at one moment," wrote David, "that she had settled in her mind for me being a wanderer and that our life would be made up of partings."[26]

Although David had now reached the pinnacle of his career, the difficulties of his personal life did not allow him to drink very deep of his cup of triumph. He missed Barbara profoundly.

"Sometimes it gets almost more than I can take in spite of great efforts at stiff upper lip stuff. This morning I had one of my dreadful crying bouts and had to go to the bathroom and shut myself in. I know 'men' don't do this but I can't help it."[27]

His relationship with Leila lurched from crisis to crisis. "I feel such a shit sometimes and find myself screaming and shouting but can't help it. I don't think I should ever marry and so often hate myself. But I'm better than I was and don't feel so hopeless as I used to. I have told her it's very difficult to run down after the film."[28]

On New Year's Day 1963, David flew to New York to discuss possible cuts with Sam Spiegel. They both thought the film would be better if it could be brought down to three hours, but neither they nor Bolt could think how to lose as much as four reels.

Before David departed on a publicity tour, he left behind detailed notes for Anne Coates which would leave the film twenty minutes shorter. Years later, he would pass responsibility for most of these cuts to Sam Spiegel, claiming he had ruined his masterwork, but at the time he made them in the conviction that they would improve the film. And most people, including critics, agreed with him.

While Leila stayed in New York to see her doctor, David went to Japan, where he was escorted by his old friend Nagamasa Kawakita, and then to Sweden where he managed a reunion with Barbara, but it was hardly straightforward.

"I've come to the conclusion," David wrote her later, "it's no good for either of us to be in those situations where you have, as it were, to retire into the background. It's undignified for you and worrying for me. Much better to be disconnected with social events of that sort. We'll learn by experience."[29]

Barbara wrote to him, "I admire you for behaving in a civilized manner and would be frightened for myself if you had simply thrown up Leila completely to be with me."[30]

The promotional tour circled back to the United States where LAWRENCE OF ARABIA had been nominated for ten Academy Awards. The ceremony was held on 8 April 1963 at the Civic Auditorium at Santa Monica.

"Oscar night is such an ordeal of tension and hysteria," wrote David, "that it's rather like moving around under a drug. It has a very unreal quality and it's done on such a scale. The dinner afterwards, for instance, is in the Beverly Hilton Hotel. A huge room and I suppose something like two thousand people sitting down for dinner at tables for twelve. Huge vases of flowers on all the tables, a large band bashing out brassy jazz, waiters pushing, photographers by the dozen with blinding flashlights and people coming up with congratulations all the time. I really became dazed by the whole effect."[31]

Like KWAI, five years earlier, LAWRENCE won seven Oscars. Sam Spiegel took the award for Best Picture; Best Director went to David; Best Achievement in Cinematography to Freddie Young; Art Direction and Set Decoration went to John Box, John Stoll and Dario Simoni; Best Achievement in Sound to John Cox and Shepperton Sound Department; Musical Score to Maurice Jarre and Best Achievement in Film Editing to Anne Coates. Incredibly, neither Peter O'Toole nor Omar Sharif won and, even more incredibly, nor did Robert Bolt.

Peter O'Toole had forfeited David's sympathy - and perhaps that of Academy members - by his drunken appearances on television shows. But David felt very sorry for the other two.

"The night was almost ruined for me by the fact that Robert and Omar missed out," wrote David. "I felt really quite sick - more directly about Omar as he was sitting just across the aisle from me and everyone thought he would win. It was a real shock - so much so that at the last minute I didn't know what to say and said a few really idiotic words.

"I blame Sam and Columbia almost entirely for Robert's boob because he was entered in the category for scripts from another source - which I think is quite wrong. FREUD was listed as original, and if that's original surely LAWRENCE is too. The Oscars are like any election and there's a lot of local sentiment to go with it. They wanted a local Hollywood film to win some Oscars and I suppose Robert fell under that feeling.[32]

"I spoke to Kate [Hepburn] yesterday and she said, 'No young newcomers ever get an Oscar in the male category. Young girls, yes. The males have, as it were, to win their spurs. The girls do it every time because all the men are suckers. It happened to me, too.' I think she's probably right."[33]

David was delighted to see Hepburn and dined with her and Spencer Tracy. "I find her very refreshing and greatly calmed and more tolerant than the SUMMERTIME days," he wrote to Barbara. "I like and admire her very much. Kate has more energy than anyone I know and we jabber away trying to get a word in edgeways with each other. Two larger than life egotists.

"Kate amazed me by saying she thought that monogamy and marriage as we know it is all wrong. (This is a reaction to all the guilts she used to carry around about her love affair with Spence.) As we agreed, if society suddenly changed and it was alright to have free love we wouldn't all be dancing into any more beds than we do at present. Even less perhaps. She is almost certain that if Spence and she had got married years ago they probably wouldn't be together now. We also (naturally) talked about our own particular ego-nut-cases. She was saying that it's almost impossible to hope that anyone, husband or wife, can understand what it's like when this creative thing takes hold and they find themselves suddenly pushed aside into fourth or fifth place. She also has a theory that if one really loves one doesn't lose that love. Couldn't quite get on to this but as you know I would be hard put to define love. It is a lot to do, surely, with what it brings to ourselves. I do see that one can't possess anyone, and yet I want to possess you to the extent that you won't let anyone else touch you.

"Kate says she finds it damned difficult to live in the same house as a man. Not, I presume, that she doesn't spend a lot of nights up with Spence. I think we are rather like this and our love of separate rooms and bathrooms is part and parcel of the same feeling. She makes me laugh like mad because she's part schoolgirl, part very logical man and part straight as they come woman. We have a very good relationship which I can only describe as brother and sister. No need for green eyes I assure you."[34]

Hepburn drove David to the airport and told him he would have an interesting travelling companion. "She said, 'David, Garbo's on board. You can sit next to her, give me a minute.' And so I waited and sure enough she took my hand and plonked me next to Garbo. She was sweet and I talked to her as we flew across the United States. It took hours in those days - eight or nine hours - and she was very nervous. We held hands when it got a bit bumpy.

"I spoke to her about travel, and she said, 'I don't.'

"I said, 'What do you mean? I know you do because there's a picture of you outside the shoe shop in Venice.'

"'That's the only time I went out.'

"'Go on, what do you mean?'

"'I cannot go anywhere these days without a thousand or two thousand people following me. I cannot be alone.'

"I'm sure this was the origin of the phrase, 'I want to be alone.' This is one of the times when I wish I could remember everything she said. I recall her saying, 'I just don't know how you act outside in the street. I find it frightfully difficult.'

"'Why?'

"'Believe it or not, I am terribly shy. I put up these screens which probably sounds ridiculous to you, because if I see out the corner of my eye two other eyes watching me closely I cannot concentrate on what I am doing, so I put up a screen and pretend I am alone.'"

After the flight was over, Garbo suggested that they meet again. "I was a bloody fool," said David. "I hadn't got the nerve to ring her up. Awful ass."[35]

David's relationship with Leila was a marriage in name alone. A pattern had emerged; after a passionate beginning, David would sooner or later become impotent and he would search for a woman to recharge his batteries. Usually he left the woman with whom he had, to his mind, been a failure, but he remained married to Leila, who was making great efforts to be compatible, even though David was finding life with her less and less bearable.

"L feels very insecure and keeps telling me I make her live in fear and I'm so autocratic.... Last night I felt terrible and drained out like a cabbage. It was very hot. I have no sex at all you know. Really darling Barbara. Last night I got frightened by what I call these cabbage moods. I felt so neuter and get in a panic that I am going to return to the impotent wretch I was before I met you... Our sex together has somehow become a symbol of life to me."[36]

"You probably have no idea,' he wrote in an earlier letter, "of the almost childish fear of sexual failure in a male. There's no midway road like a woman. He's got to 'be a man' to his woman. If he doesn't there's no bluff. He stands there an abject failure. It really is as simple as that."[37]

David was married in all but name to Barbara Cole. They lived first in Madrid, then moved to a hotel in Rome.

It was an unsettling coincidence that David should find himself from time to time in the position of a father to a boy named Peter. Barbara's son had been a unit runner on LAWRENCE, and he often came to stay with them in Rome.

"Peter felt very close to him," said Barbara. "And David was very good with him. I suppose because he didn't have any guilt feelings towards him. That was the trouble with his own son. He had failed him as a father... my Peter wasn't a tie on him."

David and Barbara's life was remarkably self-contained, and they were in each other's company practically all the time.

"David wouldn't even let me go to the hairdresser on my own," said Barbara. "Most of the day he'd read - we read a great deal, books he thought would make films, so many I can't remember any of them except *Hawaii*.[38] Then he'd get on his typewriter and type the relevant pieces out of the book that he thought would make a movie to put them together later for a script. With *Hawaii*, he thought he would make two films.

"We hardly socialised at all. We walked around Rome a lot. He'd point out the carvings or what was over the door. If we went to a new place, he'd work with his camera, and I followed him around with the tripod.

"We visited picture galleries. He took me to the Louvre in Paris and taught me about Degas and the Impressionists. I learned a lot. He always talked about light - 'You see how he's used the light there? You see her face and how the light's reflected from the cloth?' He particularly admired Goya.

"We went to the Valley of the Kings and one of his great dreams was to go on an archaeological dig, not with modern apparatus but with someone who knew. We always packed his 16mm camera, but I don't remember him using it."

When they visited historical sites, David never took a guide. At the Alhambra at Granada, they found themselves with a party of Americans. The guide showed them where Columbus knelt before the Queen and was told to go and discover America.

"David said in a loud voice, 'Bloody fool!' So it was better not to go with a guide. I didn't get uptight with him - when he did things like that, I used to think they were so funny.

"I was an independent woman. When I went with David I stopped being independent. I think if I'd remained as I was I'd have been with him to the end."[39]

Although she had had no real contact with David for many years, Kay Walsh could recognise that his relationship with Sam Spiegel was just as complicated and potentially destructive as any of his marriages.[40]

"David and Sam had fifteen percent participation," said Barbara Cole. "We were over budget, needless to say, and Sam gave away David's percentage in order to get more money to finish the film. Without contacting David. David didn't find out until the film was finished. He was very annoyed. He would have agreed, I'm sure, because the film was the most important thing, but he'd have liked to have been consulted."[41]

In June 1964, David's agent, Christopher Mann, confirmed David's charge that Sam Spiegel had underplayed the film's potential. "Sam said he is reconciled to the probability that the picture will scarcely - or, at the best, meagerly - get into the black during 'the first round' (his expression). It will depend for real profit on reissues in all countries. But he had great faith in the value of these since the picture has a very special revival value. (Certainly, if it matches GONE WITH THE WIND in that respect there is still a fortune ahead.)"[42]

A few months later, Mann succeeded in unravelling the tangle of Spiegel's tax manoeuvres (before the US and Swiss laws were changed) and the way should have been clear for David to receive regular cheques.

As it was, David claimed that for a very long time he got nothing from LAWRENCE whatsoever. "I got my first cheque something like fourteen years after the first showing of the film, because Sam told me it was a flop. He said, 'You'll see it advertised and it will seem to be going very well...'

"It ran for over a year [in London], it ran for a year at the biggest cinema in Madrid, and I pointed this out. 'That's just local interest,' he said. 'Otherwise, it's a complete flop and it's losing money.' And I believed him, you see.

"But I knew somebody who knew Sam very well and he didn't know I was supposed to have a fifty-fifty share with Sam. I said to him one day - this was after about ten years - 'Tell me, how much money has Sam made out of LAWRENCE OF ARABIA?'

'Oh, it's difficult to say. Between seven and eight million.'

"And at that point, apart from my salary, I hadn't made a penny out of the picture. I often think of the proverb, 'A fool and his money are soon parted.' Well, I was certainly the fool.

"I took legal advice, and was told, 'You cannot sue these people because they'll wait till you start another film and then they'll summon you to Cincinnati as a witness and they will bitch your career and they will dog you. Never sue these people. It's not worth it and they will beat you every time.'

"Having taken that advice, which I'm sure is correct, I never did sue. But it's sickening and the biggest crooks are often the people who have done the least in making the films that made them the money."[43]

Film companies know all the tricks to make sure that money reaches nobody but them. But LAWRENCE made so much it would have been impossible to hide it all, and some must have been reaching David. Perhaps he simply didn't realise...

"I remember meeting him one day in the early eighties at the Berkeley Hotel," said his lawyer, Tony Reeves, "and he was asking about LAWRENCE, and complaining about not getting any money and how Spiegel robbed him. I took his unopened mail, as I always did, and as I was skipping through it something caught my eye. I opened it and there was a $40,000 cheque for LAWRENCE royalties. Apparently cheques had been despatched but were never cleared, just put in a bin. They'd been sending them to him for years..."[44]

Buoyed up by the success of LAWRENCE, David began to look for a new project. Whatever it was, he hoped that Robert Bolt would write it. He wrote to Bolt:

"LAWRENCE has been the greatest and most exciting adventure of my movie life. My life, I think. Yes. I know. I have never worked alongside anyone of your calibre before and it's a great reward to know that you are happy about the interpretation. Forgive me, but you know, Robert, we *must* work together again. I think you must understand that I don't say this because I think you are a good writer and working with you will be an easy way to attempt another good film. We might flop like mad. But I think we could spark well together *specially* after having done this...

"I don't know what you plan to do after this present play of yours. You must be deluged like me, but to be selfish I'm just about at the top of my form and looking around me I see how age shrinks the mental and physical capabilities of those in my particular job. This film of ours has so fired me that I'm - for the first time - anxious not to allow too long to go by before making another attempt on something ambitious. People keep telling me - all except Columbia of course - that I ought to do something small and have a comparative rest. But in five or six years I can do something small and do it all from a chair. To hell with it while I have the physique."

David said he realised Robert would not want Sam Spiegel involved in the next project. But now they would be backed to the hilt and could really call the tune.

"Let me plunge on. I think I seemed to dismiss your idea of *Nostromo* without much thought - and *The Reason Why* [45] - but Robert it would be really lazy to do an already written novel."

And then David came up with an idea for another epic.

"Robert. I have an idea. It's been with me for some time. Perhaps I shouldn't call it an idea because in a way it's no idea. It's so frail I don't know how I'm going to convey it you, but at the same time it's enormous if only it could be given a shape. Maybe you'll stare at this page deadpan and think I'm loopy. I can only explain it in a very roundabout way.

"I think one of the great modern-day problems for the average man and woman in the street is a thing I can only describe as a general lack of pride and self-respect. Added to this they have no real faith in anything. Religion. Politics, or what they themselves are. (I continually ask myself, 'What am I? Who am I?') We people are damned lucky. We travel and we are in a continual process of exploration in the imaginative sense. Most people travel up on the same damned train day after day and sit at the same damned desk. They are cogs.

"I remember reading somewhere about the problem of factory workers who spend their days tightening two kinds of bolts on a car chassis or others that bang half completed tennis balls up and down on a bench. None of these people can have any pride in the finished article because they have contributed such a small part to it unlike the old days when a man made a chair and could take pride in the finished result... what, I suppose, I am trying to say it that the average human being of today has no real sense of purpose except in the narrowest sense of trying to earn more money in order to buy a flat, a car or a TV. Their greatest adventure is their two week yearly holiday. Cogs.

"I was walking down Curzon Street from the cutting-rooms one evening. There was the roar of a jet engine and I looked up to see the great silver fish wooshing down towards London Airport. I remember saying 'Bloody marvellous!' It is bloody marvellous! I also remember standing in the starlit garden of the Cecil Hotel in Old Delhi and seeing a bright star which I soon realised was not a star because it was travelling at speed across the heavens. I watched it until it suddenly went out as it entered the shadow of our earth. It was of course a satellite and next day I read in the paper that it had been launched from Cape Canaveral and realised that I had seen it on its first trip around the earth. Bloody bloody marvellous!!

"Now, Robert. Where did all this begin? Where did we begin? If H.G. Wells was right in his 'Outline of History' we began as a microscopic piece of jelly in a sunlit pool. We got out of that pool. We developed lungs, legs and a brain. Then, as Wells says, one tremendous evening one of us looked at a sunset and dimly thought it beautiful.

"Now, having explored our earth we are going outwards once again. My silver fish over Curzon Street is taken as a matter of course because no-one has put a frame round it. The Sputnik is called a Russian achievement, and the fantastic Venus 'probe' an American. They are not. They are us. Us, the jelly in the sunlit pool.

"I have always been rather proud of my grandfather because he was an inventor. I suppose we are all proud of our blood connections with those that have distinguished themselves - but somehow it's all so narrow when viewed from further back. We are a part of the whole human race and I think it's the biggest success story within our knowledge.

"If we could make a movie which said, 'This is the story of you. You sitting there looking up at the screen,' I think it would be a little miracle. I think people would go out with their heads a little higher. Yes, that's just about it. Their heads a little higher. I won't go on about it because if you see at all where I am floundering you will see much further than me. I can only see rather dimly that such a movie - and I think the film medium is the only medium in which it could be done properly - could be an enormous power for peace. It would be anti race-pride, anti suburban mentality - but there I go."[46]

CHAPTER THIRTY-TWO

THE GREATEST STORY EVER TOLD

IN the sixties, David's love affair with the cinema underwent a profound change. He began to visit the cinema less and less. And what he saw began to depress him; this was not a cinema he was familiar with.

Lest he be dismissed as an old codger, I should add that I had much the same reaction towards a certain kind of film - and I was in my twenties. Inspired, presumably, by Jean-Luc Godard and his enthusiastically crude technique, many young film-makers began to feel that in modern cinema, anything went. And to a large extent it did. While the sixties saw a blossoming in terms of themes, it saw a frontal attack on technique. It was this that shook David.

"The films I see don't overwhelm me and more and more I think of some of them as very passing fashions," he wrote.[1]

There were exceptions. In 1963 he saw Fellini's 8½, about a film director suffering from a creative block, which he liked very much. He said he felt exactly the same as the leading character going to work in the morning.[2]

Also in 1963 he saw Frank Perry's DAVID AND LISA, a love story about two psychologically disturbed adolescents, which led to a confession of some significance.

"I liked it," David wrote to Barbara, "but came to the conclusion that I too am a bit off my rocker. Really. I thought I was rather like the boy in the film - not so much so of course - but pretty near the same sort of case! Wonder if you have seen it. I have found some humanity with you but think I'm pretty rum and removed on the whole. Also think that's partly why I can make films so well. I am able to live through a film as I can't in everyday life."[3]

Adapted from the book *Lisa and David* by Theodore Isaac Rubin, MD, the character of David is a tall, good-looking man, always impeccably dressed, who cannot bear to be touched. He turns away efforts at friendship and wanders by himself in the grounds of the institution to which he is sent by his parents. He forms an attachment to a schizophrenic girl, Lisa. Girls find him attractive but it is only Lisa who is able make him relax. He despises any form of amusement and works ceaselessly at geometric problems. Arrogant and pompous, he forms an uneasy relationship with Allan, a psychiatrist. He keeps commenting on the fact that the clock in Allan's office is broken; he seems obsessed by time.

"I plan to construct a masterpiece," he tells Allan, "utterly precise instruments put together in a perfect pattern."

The sixties also saw the rise of some very assured young film-makers, and some of the films David saw, paradoxically, were so well made he felt alarmed by them. He was amazed by the dazzling editorial fireworks of Richard Lester's 1968 film PETULIA and wrote Lester a fan letter which began a friendship between the two directors.

David wrote, "It was my best time at the movies for months and months and months. It's one of those pictures that make me proud of being a director and I came out into the rain-swept street wondering what had gone wrong with the people and the traffic and why it all wasn't moving as it was on your screen. It was a marvellous look at life through a remarkable pair of glasses... I used to think I was a bit of a dab as a cutter but I'm not in your league as an image mixer."[4]

After a while, though, David stopped going to the cinema. Barbara Cole recalled persuading David to see a Japanese film called THE ISLAND which they walked out of.

"I think that's the only film I ever saw with him. I used to say, 'You ought to go - you ought to see the new techniques, you ought to see young actors.' He didn't want to. You'd have thought a man as keen about films as he was would have wanted to see what was being offered."[5]

Still in Hollywood following the Oscar ceremony, David was about to become involved in one of the last and most expensive gasps of the old studio system, the sort of movie which the younger directors were reacting against.

David and Leila planned to return to New York and then sail to Europe aboard the Italian liner *Leonardo da Vinci*. Whilst Leila would leave the ship at Cannes, David would continue to Naples and then travel to Rome to be with Barbara. After two nights in Rome, they would fly to Cairo.

As he was typing the latest travel plans to Barbara, a call came through from Fred Zinnemann who wanted to know if David would consider directing some scenes in THE GREATEST STORY EVER TOLD, George Stevens's film about Christ which had already been shooting for a year in the deserts of Nevada and Utah.

David wrote to Barbara, "George Stevens is under terrible pressure. They have forced him because of being over budget (now something like $15 million) into accepting a second unit on two sequences which are about twenty pages. He rang up Fred in desperation and asked if he had any ideas because it was killing him. Fred said why not ask me? George said he wouldn't dream of presuming. I told Fred my first reaction was yes, but I had to have time to think and that there were two immediate stipulations. 1: I get on the ship on May 7th. 2: That I read the stuff and feel I could do it properly. I think I might do it as I feel very sorry for him and think it would be a good gesture to these director chaps who have always been so big with me. Chance to return it."[6]

The following day, David wrote to Barbara and confirmed that he had accepted the job. It was arranged that David would view some cut sequences and then meet George Stevens. The meeting was held in David's room at the Beverly Hills Hotel.

Stevens's associate, Tony Vellani, remembered that the situation on the film had become so grave, with sandstorms, snowstorms, and casualties among key personnel, that the decision was made to divide the company in two. It was not so much a question of second units, as of finding another director to shoot major sections of the film.

Vellani was present when David and Stevens had their first meeting. "George was a very private person," said Vellani, "very shy. David ordered coffee and there was this moment of hesitation. George was not too ready with conversation. David Lean looked at him, lit a cigarette in a long holder, walked over to the window and looked out and then he turned rather suddenly and said, 'They're fast, aren't they, George?'

"And George said, 'They sure are.'

"David said, 'They're faster than we shall ever be.'

"Neither man mentioned the audience, but that's what they were both talking about."[7]

Stevens suggested that David might like to direct the Nativity sequence. "He says he would like me to shoot in bravura style as far as camera-work is concerned," wrote David to Barbara. "I shall of course take no credit although I am sure there will be a hell of a hoo-haa in the trade press here. For a mad moment I thought I ought to request my own Continuity Girl here! Too risky and rather silly for such a short time."[8]

When David read the script, he realised the Nativity was not for him. He spoke to Lewis Milestone, who agreed to take it over, though, in the end, it was Jean Negulesco who directed this sequence. David talked about other scenes to Stevens, a director he had always admired, and agreed to work on the scenes with King Herod. Since Claude Rains had volunteered to play Herod and José Ferrer was cast in the same scenes, David was reassured to be with old campaigners.

David was unimpressed by the footage he had seen. "Somehow they can't do that sort of thing here," he wrote to Barbara. "I kept thinking of the Arabs in Jordan and comparing them with the clean 'old master' Hollywood versions I was seeing on the screen. Also the American accent just doesn't fit with the Bible. The Swede who plays Christ (Max von Sydow) is rather good though.

"I'm awfully glad to be able to make a gesture to these people out here and of course will work for nothing. By union rules I have to accept minimum rates for a second unit director, but will hand it over to the Screen Directors' Guild Benevolent Fund and they will pay my hotel and car expenses."[9]

David's scenes were to be filmed at Desilu Studios, formerly the Selznick studio whose mock ante-bellum frontage had been the famous Selznick trade-mark. Built for Thomas Ince, the studios had passed to Cecil B. DeMille in the late twenties, and David ate in the ornate "Bounty-style" dining room.

"The Stevens people are very good to me," wrote David. "What a difference from Sam and Co."[10]

On the one hand, David was glad to be working on the film; he could hardly believe he was shooting in Hollywood. On the other, he felt he was quite mad to have taken it on.

"I'm about as lost as I could be with an enormous

José Ferrer and Claude Rains in David's sequence.

bloody set and no ideas yet where to move the actors or put the camera. George is shooting out in the wastes of Nevada somewhere and I sit in his huge office plus madly efficient secretary."[11]

David was also seized by his usual loneliness. Leila had left for medical treatment in New York and David, after the day's activity at the studio, dined alone at the Beverly Hills Hotel, where the three head waiters - French, Czech and Italian - had become his friends. He was given a table overlooking the garden and ate simply because he felt he was putting on far too much weight. And he brooded.

"I was back in the 'who am I?' department," he wrote to Barbara in one of his long and almost daily letters. "Found myself thinking how important sex is. I don't know which group it is, maybe the French existentialists, who say that one lives only through sex. I wondered if it *were* true having said to myself that it was. I'm not interested in living to eat and pass the time. I want to create something even if it's only a still photograph of something which catches my fancy. I get occasional kicks out of something someone has written which twangs a chord where there was previously only a mild vibration. I am lifted up by music of various sorts - more twanging of chords - but most of the time I'm lonely as can be; confined in the cage which surrounds me. We all have our cages and I'm not at all sure that sex isn't the only release. In a certain way it is the only method of communication with another human being.

"Has anyone known you? Has anyone known me? Not much I guess. We have bigger glimpses of each other than anyone else I dare to say. The thing we are always talking about; trust. In the ordinary way of life you know me and I know you because we have the added key of sex, not only as a sort of fifth column behind our facades, but as a giver of confidence to back up certain rather daring reactions with which to cope with the other. By that I mean we are 'on' to each other and dare say so from time to time. I think that's probably why I feel so lonely and want you so much. I'm fed up walking around as me with the shutters up. I could go out with heaps of people, I suppose, but I don't want to. I'd rather be alone than talk and talk polite conversation which doesn't amount to much more than actors speaking dialogue. One can say that sex is enough unto itself. It is the greatest pleasure, but there is more besides the pleasure of physical sensation. I am sure that it's why I always take a pride in your everyday appearance of dignity and, for want of a better word, respectability. Because you show me another side which no one else knows about. I see a you and you see a me - not in the physical sense - which no one else knows about. They can't even guess. I am only just beginning to guess certain deeply hidden secrets which are part of you and part of me. We are not even aware of them ourselves."[12]

David was impressed with the Hollywood crew he had been given, especially the cameraman, Charles Lang Jr, who rather reminded him of Freddie Young and Guy Green.

"The crew is about level with the English," wrote David, "but in the hourly labour vastly superior, and so much more tactful and efficient and educated. All take a real interest in the film and very sensitive to when they should be quiet and so on. I think our electricians would get quite a shock as these chaps are, and behave like, real professionals. Everything moves much faster than in an English studio. Yesterday morning I went in and changed a complete setup which had been lit and rehearsed the previous night. Not one murmur from anyone except that about half a dozen of the workmen came up and said how much better they thought the idea was and hoped I didn't think they took too long making the change! The whole lot want me to come and make a film here.

"The first day I did three minutes and twenty seconds," he wrote to Barbara, "and astounded everyone including myself and you, no doubt!"[13] David did about two weeks work on the picture.

"George Stevens never forgot it," said Tony Vellani. "For years afterwards he always mentioned this act of extraordinary generosity."[14]

David managed to join Leila in New York in time for the sailing of the *Leonardo da Vinci*.

"Because I love the southern route, I took this great Italian liner. I had always thought the only good liners were the English liners. Quite wrong. These Italian ships were sumptuous, and I used to travel on them quite a bit. I've had wonderful times on liners, girls and all. Just lovely."[15]

David was not short of reading material. Columbia had given him a novel called *River of the Sun* by James Ullman. Katharine Hepburn, knowing of David's desire to do another love story, suggested Schnitzler's *Bertha Garlan*. This involved a crippled husband and death by abortion and was hardly David Lean territory. But the idea she was most enthusiastic about was John Buchan's *Prester John*. She knew David was keen on an African project, and she admired the book so much she had once taken an option on it, convinced that the male schoolteacher could be changed to a female so that she could play the part.[16]

Just before he left, David's agent at the William Morris Agency, Phil Kellogg, told him about a Russian novel which nobody seemed to have read but which many considered outstanding; indeed, it had won the Nobel Prize. Kellogg had read it and so had Robert O'Brien, the new president of MGM, who wanted David to direct it. He urged him to read it on the voyage.

"I looked at it with its five hundred and something pages, and I thought, 'Oh God.' We were crossing the South Atlantic and I realised I had to get down to this bloody book. So I propped myself up and I read and read the first night and became more interested. The next night I thought, 'I'll finish it tonight,' and ended up sitting in my bed, with a box of Kleenex, wiping the tears away. I was so touched by it, and I thought that if I can be touched like this, sitting in a liner reading a book, I must be able to make a good, touching film of it. As soon as I landed, I contacted my agent and said, 'Yes, I'll do DOCTOR ZHIVAGO.'"[17]

CHAPTER THIRTY-THREE

STRAIGHTENING COBWEBS

DOCTOR ZHIVAGO I

BORIS Pasternak's novel, *Doctor Zhivago*, had been banned in the Soviet Union, though an Italian company, Giangiacomo Feltrinelli of Milan, had published a translation in 1957 from a smuggled manuscript. When, in 1958, Pasternak was awarded the Nobel Prize for literature, the Soviet Writers' Association expelled him and the Soviet government warned that should he go to Sweden to accept the prize, he would not be allowed to return.

Rather than face exile, Pasternak declined the prize and died two years later, aged seventy. The book, which became a modern classic, translated into many languages, would not be published in the Soviet Union for three decades, until the *glasnost* policy of Gorbachev.

David regarded the novel as the best he had ever read. "Just a man's life," he wrote to Barbara, "but somehow it's all our lives. Don't know if it would spoil in a cut down film version but I'm tempted - particularly so after reading a lot of characterless rubbish."[1]

It is not difficult to find in the novel those elements which excited him. The story is of a doctor who is also an artist, a man who passes from woman to woman, who walks out on his responsibilities, but who is portrayed none the less as an admirable human being, of deep sensibility and romantic nature, who struggles against all the odds to write poems. One of these poems, called "Explanation", ends:

> *"And yet no matter how the night*
> *May chain me within its ring of longing,*
> *The pull of separation is still stronger*
> *And I have a beckoning passion for the clean break."*

The book is immensely visual with brilliant descriptions of nature and searing episodes of violence. It has the breadth and social observations of Dickens, together with Dickensian coincidences - in the second half, Yuri Zhivago meets few people in the vast expanses of Russia that he hasn't encountered in the first.

Pasternak understands what it is to feel guilty; Zhivago starts an affair with Lara even though he worships his wife, Tonya. "At home he felt like a criminal. His family's ignorance of the truth, their unchanged affection, were a mortal torment to him. In the middle of a conversation he would suddenly be numbed by the recollection of his guilt and cease hearing a word of what was being said."[2]

Zhivago is not exactly a pacifist; he identifies more with the Whites, even if he has sympathy with the Reds. Trying to stay clear of both, he is swept into the Civil War when captured by partisans and forced to tend their wounded.

It is a sprawling, episodic saga, with no neat signposts for a self-contained feature film. Its attitude to Communism was as frank as if it was written in the Russia which has thrown off Bolshevism. The peasant, wrote Pasternak, in a typical observation, "had only exchanged the old oppression of the tsarist state for the new, much harsher yoke of the revolutionary super-state."[3]

The screen rights to the novel were owned by the Italian producer, Carlo Ponti, who had ambitions to film it in the Soviet Union and at studios in Rome. A huge budget was needed and Ponti had secured a deal with MGM, then reeling from the disaster of MUTINY ON THE BOUNTY which had cost (and lost) so much money that the studio's President, Joseph Vogel, had been replaced by Robert O'Brien, a no-nonsense Irishman who loved movies and admired David.

"I could and would trust David Lean under all circumstances we would encounter in making a picture," wrote O'Brien. "I regarded him as one of the great jewels of the motion picture industry."[4]

O'Brien proved it when he and the MGM hierarchy flew to Rome to meet David in June 1963 - a unique example of the Hollywood mountain coming to Mohammed. They agreed to pay him the highest salary ever given to a director, along with a generous percentage of the profits.

MGM were not being altruistic; they had to produce a box-office sensation or go out of business. They were also well aware that Columbia were anxious for David to make his next film for them. What they did not know was that David had little desire to return to Columbia for he had made up his mind not to work with Spiegel again. He wanted to be clear of the man, if only to prove he could make a well-produced and financially successful picture without him.

The one stipulation David made to MGM was that Robert Bolt write the script. Bolt, who was in the middle of work on a play when David suggested ZHIVAGO, had the kindness not to remind David of his rejection of *Nostromo* and other novels, nor of his desire to make a film about space exploration. He replied with a letter which matched David's own enthusiasm:

"I am perfectly mesmerised by the idea of ZHIVAGO. I love the book and it would be an honour to work on it with you."

Bolt then launched into an example of the visual style he hoped the film would have: "An ocean of daffodils. A man, tiny, stands in it. What's he doing? (we hold the 'meaningless' shot long enough to raise the question.) Close shot the man; just standing. We move round to see his face; crying perhaps? No, just standing and looking. His POV; the daffodils again, the birch leaves, the white birch branches, we hurl the camera through them, we race, we are drunk, the shafts of black and white drop behind us, below us, we soar, we return, we skim the daffodils and settle at the man's broken-booted feet, ascend slowly to his face. He is as before, but we have been the poet's *mind* for a minute. That kind of thing, David? Risky, but oh worth trying. Would Ponti let us?"[5]

To soak himself in the atmosphere, Bolt renewed his acquaintance with the Russian classics and researched the politics of the period. David teased him about his own brief collaboration with Communism. "No, I'm not Strelnikov, if that's what you take me for," Bolt replied, stiffly, referring to Lara's husband who, from idealistic student, becomes a feared revolutionary commander.

At first, Bolt regarded the proposed film as a political drama and not a love story. David resisted this, saying that the film would be cold and not understood by the mass audience. "The love story being a human basic will touch almost everyone. I'm not saying I think the inner political conflict should be ignored, I am saying that we can't expect the mass audience to follow the refinement of conflict in this area. It must be stated as simply as possible in my opinion. The audience will understand almost every nuance of the love story. If we try to shift the weight on to the other conflict I think they will become impatient."[6]

David thought Bolt should have a taste of the authentic Tsarist Russia and sent him to visit the formidable Baroness Budberg. She told him that whilst she admired Pasternak, she considered him a profoundly self-centred man, caring

The epic shots of the Russian winter had to be taken in Finland, as far too little snow fell in Spain.

only about his art. And Zhivago *was* Pasternak, she declared; otherwise, Pasternak would never have made his hero a poet. She felt Pasternak had an uneasy conscience at taking no part in the Russian revolution and was convinced that the novel was his way of saying, 'Suppose I *had* got involved, what would have happened? This...'

Bolt, now concentrating on the love story, defined what he felt was its central theme. "I suppose it's the old story of the woman falling not for the man but the artist, not realising that only the man and not the artist can return her love."[7]

This summary of Bolt's fascinated David who wondered if it really was an "old story". He said, "Suppose it is, but as you say it's very interesting. I'm not at all sure what an artist is. I've thought about it quite a lot since your letter. I feel rather hot if someone calls me an artist. I am somewhere on the fringe and have a real feeling for things artistic - but an artist...? Pasternak; of course. Chaplin; ditto. Bob Hope? Where does one draw the line? I'm also not at all sure where the man stops and the artist begins. I know they are separate, but at the same time they are not. The artist is surely the human being with the hatches off...

"I won't accept that only the man and not the artist can return a woman's love. Don't tell me that Anne Hathaway didn't experience a full Cape Canaveral count-down - forgive the vulgarity - which she could never have experienced with an uncreative Mr Jones. Shakespeare must be different from Mr Jones in bed. He's just got more life force than Mr Jones. Isn't love-making one of the greatest forms of self expression known to man? (It certainly is to a woman.) Isn't it therefore an art? Doesn't imagination, power, lyricism and the ability to disclose form the basis of both love and art?"

A woman, David wrote, is at the mercy of her man. The man, being a doer, must set a limit on their joint experience according to his ability.

"I have a feeling that women, real women, are fathomless. A man will rise only to his own limitations, but a woman will go right on up the scale alongside the man until he can go no further. The imaginative lover must surely take her further up the scale than Mr Jones... A woman who has been an orchestra with a Beethoven is in a perilous emotional situation if he should leave her... I don't mean that he physically has to leave the woman, but that he may leave her emotionally... She once had the man and the artist - now the artist has gone off to hack away at some marble and is putting all his force into that. May even be another woman. Perhaps sex has left him altogether. I think he will be equally dismayed. One of your prices that has to be paid for the heights.

"That is why I don't really agree with you. It's a damned good way of putting it all on the woman. 'The poor darling was so swept off her feet.' She was damned right to be swept off her feet. She experienced the full bouquet."[8]

David was writing from experience since the last vestiges of his marriage to Leila were falling apart. They were having the worst rows they had ever had. Leila particularly resented David's opinion that she did nothing with her life. "She stung me so much I rose to it. She kept on about how 'superior' I am and how I talk down to her."

Eventually, Leila apologised and delivered a heart-rending plea:

"All I want is to be sure you won't chuck me out and you still love me a little bit at the back of you somewhere. If you will love me a bit I will do anything for you and leave you free to do your work."[9]

But their rows escalated. Leila objected to his snoring, which she attributed to his late-night consumption of brandy. She worried that he no longer took pictures of her. David wondered if she was slightly unbalanced. Her father, he said, had gone clean off his head in the last years of his life. Leila had received shock therapy, and the London specialists had described her as a borderline case.

But there was no lack of mental sharpness when it came to their rows. "If I answer, like a fool, I wish I had never opened my mouth because she will beat me with argument any day of the week."[10]

Leila was very bright, said David. It was her changes of mood which were so disturbing. In a burst of anger, Leila told David that Deborah Kerr had warned her about him and that he had nearly been responsible for putting Kay Walsh in a lunatic asylum.

"She said that I drove women mad because I was - can't remember what it was, rather naturally... Something to do with my moods and my hardness."[11]

David was in a creative haze. Numbed by the misery of his life with Leila, he put off doing anything about ZHIVAGO. He had moved to Venice where loneliness bred nostalgia - "Nearly all my old pals have gone," he wrote, "and not even the motorboat men know me."

He used to leave Leila lying in bed in her darkened room in the Bauer-Grunwald Hotel and walk to the Grand, where he wrote long, uninterrupted letters to Barbara. He knew that his handwriting, neat though it was, was hard to decipher and he preferred to tap away with two fingers on his portable type-writer in his own room.

Bolt visited him in Venice to discuss the project and to start work on a treatment. This visit delighted David, for he was able to give Bolt a tour which he later remembered as "a uniquely vivid and exciting experience. So much so that I almost fear to go back."[12]

When it came to writing, David was a first-class procrastinator, but on this film, Robert Bolt outmatched him. Trouble with his own marriage and work on a play usurped his attention and it took months for the two men to produce even so much as a treatment - the sort of rough outline David and Ronald Neame had once hammered out in three weeks at a seaside hotel.

Robert Bolt at work on DOCTOR ZHIVAGO.

In April 1964, ten months after the deal with MGM had been signed, David and Bolt's treatment - entitled *An Account of the Intended Script* - was sent to MGM. The reactions from the story department were positive, the few criticisms intended to be helpful. Bolt, though, was incensed.

"I bridled to read that 'in general Bolt and Lean are to be commended.' Who in Hell is Russell Thacher?[13] There's something about these letters from MGM, even O'Brien's, which infuriates me really. What possible value can they attach to their own opinions when nine-tenths of what they like turns out to be palpable muck? Let them ask us. We'll tell them whether it's good, bad or indifferent... they are passengers and should not disturb the engineers and drivers with their childish chatter."[14]

David began to grow alarmed by Bolt's slowness and general attitude and, in a letter, insisted they both move to Madrid. Quite apart from his anxieties about the script, David was also desperate to get away from Leila. Bolt resisted the pressure from David and declared he would not come out until 29 June.

David hastily apologised. "I think you must know how very much I dislike pressure tactics and if my letter to you was seemingly ambiguous it was only because I was bending over backwards to avoid them and at the same time be tactful. I use the word ambiguous because right away, in your first paragraph, you say that you think that I think you'll write faster in Madrid than you do at home. I didn't say that but the truth is I do."

David, who was under pressure from Ponti, was growing frantic, because at the present speed Bolt was moving slower even than on LAWRENCE. He referred to him, playfully, as a prima donna, and ended the letter "with real affection - and my usual admiration."[15]

With David en route to Madrid, Bolt did the best thing he could possibly have done; he sent a batch of the script via production manager John Palmer. He received a cable from David: "THINK YOU ARE DOING QUITE A WONDERFUL JOB. PARTICULARLY STRUCK BY YOUR CHARACTER BUILDING."

"The cable gave me a big kick," replied Bolt. "Yes, I am a prima donna, and petulant with it I shouldn't be surprised. You do believe in pressure, David, and I do see why you do. Everybody in film does, has to."[16]

David wrote to Barbara: "There are very great problems in the Lara-Zhivago love story. I have a feeling they are so near Pasternak's own real-life experience that he has veered away from a lot of the more intimate moments which he should have recorded. There may have been a difficult situation with his wife for I swear that the woman in the autobiography[17] who committed suicide must have been his great love.

"I become a little worried because I think a side of Robert will also veer away from such things because they are on his horizon and he may fear their glare. [Bolt was facing separation from his wife, Jo.] The more I read the more I am amazed I took so little in on the first reading - there are difficult patches - but I think most of the confusion comes from the number of characters and the, to us, curious names. Unlike you, I still find it difficult to get such a really clear picture of Tonya. I don't really see why Robert thinks she's such a wonderful character. These common-to-all-of-us situations and characters are so dangerous because we start to read our own situations into them. Maybe Robert is really saying, 'Jo is a wonderful character.'"[18]

If Bolt was a slow writer, David took almost as long to read and re-read the material - "you have to make allowances for me being a slow taker-inner," he wrote to Bolt. He said he was bowled over, lifted up and deeply touched by the whole of the Moscow sequence. "I'd better stop or you'll be *unbearable* when we meet and I won't be able to say all sorts of things I'm writing notes about, dear Higgins."

It turned out that David had not understood some of Bolt's writing - he knew that all sorts of points had gone clean over his head. He hoped that in discussion with Bolt these confusions would be clarified - for his own sake and that of the audience.

Having expressed his admiration, David took Bolt to task for the "rumble of technique" in some of his scenes which he felt were straining for significance.

"This is all a lot of pretentious balls because if we want to do things which are only appreciated by our bright friends we shouldn't be working in a mass media [sic]. You should be writing books for a limited circulation and I should be making films for a top budget of $400,000.

"Being, as it were, quite outside your task I can't help but appear rather clottish and insensitive to you who are in the thick of it. You are entitled to react in the way I react to people who come in with brilliant ideas in the middle of cutting and I'm miles ahead of them most of the time."

This letter to Bolt took David three days to write, for while he thought Bolt's handling of Tonya superb - "better than Pasternak" - he was desperately worried by his treatment of Lara.

"I beg, beg, beg you, Robert, not to be offended. You can hardly help be because in this rum job of ours I'm in the position of having to do something I'd never do in real life. I'm being personal and critical about a woman you're in love with… Like all big talents you go down a wrong track with the same intensity and intention as a right one."

David was so convinced that Bolt had walked into a trap that he suggested he disclose the letter to Bolt's agent and friend, Peggy Ramsay. "I have a feeling she would be just the right person, though I don't know her."[19]

Bolt thought this "a marvellous letter," as indeed it was, an epic example of constructive criticism which had not offended him in the least: "I'm sure what I meant Lara to be like is what you and I both want her to be like… I wake every morning with this story stretching in front of me like a road in a mist; I can see the next stretch in front of me and the last stretch behind me, but for the general trend of it I have only a sort of instinctive compass which sometimes goes mad and I walk in circles for a day or two, ready to throw back my head and howl with rage and helplessness. I've never done anything so *difficult*. That *bugger* Pasternak! It's like trying to straighten cobwebs."

Bolt admitted he was dotty about Lara, and in a prescient description, considering who would eventually play her, he said he saw her as "rather heavy and sweet, like a pot of fermenting honey. I see her even a shade on the sulky side. I agree with every damn thing you say about what Lara ought to be, and thought I had made her that. Jesus, what a mess…"[20]

Behind many of David's comments on Bolt's handling of the Lara character was the conviction that Robert was confusing Lara with his wife, Jo.

"He first presented her as an awful bitch," said Barbara Cole. "Everybody had a different idea of Lara. She was some people's mother figure, some people's glamour figure, and, in Robert's case, a bitchy wife."[21]

Bolt's marriage did eventually end when Jo left with the children in November 1964. Bolt was desolated, and David asked him to come at once to Spain. He was grateful for the invitation, "I nearly went straight to the airport," he said, "but I should be a death's head to you if I came out now. It is all too bloody for words."[22]

Bolt also poured out his despair in a letter to Barbara: "Wherever I turn I seem to see an infinite black void with a howling wind of loneliness in it."[23]

When Bolt eventually joined David in Madrid, we lose those fascinating letters. Face to face, the work became no easier. David was hardly the most articulate of men and it took him a long time to absorb what Bolt had written and even longer to know whether it was right or wrong for his film. And then he found it difficult to put his racing thoughts into words. Confronted by this eloquent, pipe-smoking intellectual, no wonder David issued orders like a slave-driver or retreated into sullen silences.

We can guess what Bolt must have said to him, because there is a significant paragraph in one of the last letters he wrote David before he left:

"I sense that we are in great danger, or that I am. It's not the sort of stuff that can be written 'on approval.' It needs a lot of heat and commitment and confidence; we can't write those scenes as a committee of two; I must write them myself so that they are one thing, one vision - otherwise, however well they may fit a list of specifications, they will not be alive, will have no style or idiosyncrasy; and yet they must be what you want because you have to direct them and they will be as hard to direct as to write; so we must thrash at it until we are sure we understand one another, and then you must leave me alone to do it. I'm scared stiff about this predicament and can find nothing in my mind but doubts." [24]

Pasternak's novel was not only immensely long, it used a technique which might have been designed specifically to defeat a film-maker.

"DOCTOR ZHIVAGO covers a great span of time," wrote Bolt in his introduction to the published screenplay. "And this time is not covered flowingly but in sudden leaps. At the end of Chapter 14 Lara and Yuri have parted, Strelnikov has shot himself; the main story is over. Chapter 15 commences, 'It remains to tell the brief story of the last eight or ten years of Yuri's life...' and finishes with the reported death of Lara. At the start of Chapter 16 another gulf of years has been jumped; we learn of the existence of Yuri and Lara's daughter, now grown-up, and hear from her the story of her childhood, which is at least as poignant as anything in the story of her parents. As if this were not enough, the last section of this chapter begins, 'Five or ten years later...' and reflects upon the possible place of Yuri's poetry in the post-Stalinist thaw.

"Now, the reader of a novel can accept these very vigorously wagging tails to the main story as a pleasurable bonus. But in the film, with its overriding need for continuity, we felt that it would be hard to keep the audience in the cinema when the main story had ended and ended so tragically - and that to interest them in the emergence and the story of an entirely new character (the daughter) so late in the evening would be very difficult indeed. But we felt that it had to be done if we were not to betray the book. The device we employed was the well-tried one of the narrator. Following a hint of Pasternak's, we promoted the shadowy figure of Yevgraf, Yuri's half brother, to this post, and still following Pasternak, we placed him half in and half out of the story." [25]

Beyond any problems of compression and exposition, however, was the way the towering figure of Zhivago was diminished by transferring him to film.

"The way to make a man have stature dramatically is to make him do things that have great stature. And the whole point about this book is that Yuri does nothing that has great stature except write poetry. And how to make this seem to a cinema audience a heroic justification of what looks like a rather useless sort of life was a very considerable problem. We solved it by calculating as carefully as we could towards the climax of his relationship with Lara, where everything is knotted together in this desperate situation at Varykino, where the revolution is closing in on them, where the fearful cold is closing in on them. What they were doing is in practical terms nonsense, if not highly irresponsible. The only justification of it is the intensity of their love for each other. We hope to have shown by this time that they are unusually mature people. So we're hoping that the audience will now believe that this was a kind of *Tristan and Iseult* situation, a great, grand passion. And we have tried to arrange this sequence so that the climax of it shall be the writing of this poetry. In that way we hope to make poetry the crown of the film."[26]

In Madrid, the writing was affected by Bolt being suddenly becalmed by a problem - solved by David simply pointing out that what happens next is the next thing they should write. There were also regular disputes.

"I'll say I had arguments with him," said Bolt. "I remember we met once for three days and neither of us said a word. And I was right. He admitted I was right when the film was finished. I thought Pasha [Strelnikov, played by Tom Courtenay] ought to come back and see the poems that Yuri had written and blow his brains out then. Very good." [27]

And yet David rejected this striking and dramatic idea. The difficulties of writing the script were summed up in an image recalled by a friend: tears of rage and frustration dropping on to the script as Bolt struggled to write it in his hotel room in Madrid.[28]

Bolt was profoundly grateful when the experience was over and equally grateful to have gone though it. Just before he left the Hotel Richmond in Madrid, he sent David a morale-boosting and charming letter:

"Before I pack away this machine (which I do very gladly) I'll write what I couldn't say nor you hear: that my admiration has mounted steadily during these months. Your many-sided talents and dedication are alike amazing to me. I hope I can remember some of what I've learned from you. The trouble is, you don't meet the same problem twice, or do, and don't recognise it; but perhaps I can retain the flavour, vaguely, of your flair and your detestation of the peripheral, the torpid and the hinted at.

"I'm proud of our script - 'ours' not 'mine' - and I think that when you've employed your various other skills upon it, the result may well be exceptional."[29]

CHAPTER THIRTY-FOUR

ARRIVALS

DOCTOR ZHIVAGO II

IN June 1964, the *Evening Standard* published a photograph of Greta Garbo with the news that she might make another film - if David Lean directed her. Although a journalistic fantasy, David had been dreaming of a young Garbo to play Lara. But as the script progressed and he studied the novel more closely, he realised that his vision was totally incorrect; he needed someone far less ethereal. Carlo Ponti had just the actress in mind: his wife, Sophia Loren.

"Ponti invited us for dinner," said Barbara Cole, "and Sophia came along, in a little plain dress with a lace collar, looking very innocent, speaking very good English and being really very nice. When we got home, David said, 'If anyone can convince me she's a virgin, I'll let her play the part.' But it must have been very bitter for her and for Ponti."[1]

David felt so threatened by this idea that he wrote to Robert O'Brien at MGM: "I find it hard to believe he [Ponti] had not got her in mind when he first put hands on this subject. *He has behaved with the utmost correctness* and never once has her name been mentioned to me by him, but at the same time, the atmosphere is such that I would be an insensitive clot if I didn't realise what was in his mind and I find it a great and unspoken embarrassment.

"As the seduction progresses, the audience must witness, understand and therefore sympathise with the overwhelming of this girl by her newly discovered passions. This is why I want a young actress. Innocence cannot be acted except on a superficial level. I would not believe this was Miss Loren's first encounter with sex and if I don't believe it I would think she's a bitch. This is why I want to play young people (as Pasternak wrote them for good reason) in these parts. To explain Zhivago, Lara and Tonya, we have got to see them flower into adult human beings. If we present them in full bloom their behaviour will seem inexcusable and we will have a sordid story nothing to do with the novel except in plot.

"Everyone knows about this problem and at last it is coming into the open. Only yesterday I read in an English paper that a certain respectable body had approved lessons in contraception to the unmarried. A week or so ago a leading Quaker reminded another middle-aged gathering that they perhaps forgot the strength of teenage sexual passions. Our story is so topical and well-timed; don't let's turn it into a routine story about middle-aged promiscuity."[2]

Despite this attempt to influence the casting, David found Ponti's style of producing most refreshing.

"I remember having one talk with Carlo and I never saw him again. He never came near the picture until he arrived at a music session at Culver City. That was the first time he had seen any of it. The film was produced by me, with John Palmer, the production manager, John Box and a few others."[3]

MGM wanted Paul Newman as Zhivago. Oddly enough, Newman had just made a film for MGM called THE PRIZE, in which the leading character, achieving what Pasternak was unable to achieve, goes to Stockholm to receive the Nobel Prize for literature. Perhaps that was why MGM thought of Paul Newman; he played a great novelist in one film, so why not a poet in another?

David went to see Newman in THE PRIZE and wrote to O'Brien: "Oh dear. I do hate to disagree - not about his star name - but his aura as an actor. I can only see him as a very practical young man who would be able to arrive at a decision on most things without any difficulty whatever. I can discover nothing of the dreamer about him. I think he got away with being an author because it wasn't really a film about the Nobel Prize but a whodunit with the prize as the background. Doctor Zhivago is the exact opposite; he is deeply impractical and he finds it, in the best sense, hard to make decisions. He sees too far too deeply and all the big crises of his life are taken out of his hands by fate. I hate going on like this because it makes me sound unappreciative of Newman, which I'm not [and] it makes our Zhivago sound a dreaming bore, which he is not."[4]

When O'Brien arrived in Rome, one of his first questions had been "What stars have you lined up?'"

David could not produce a single name beyond Max von Sydow, who had impressed him in THE GREATEST STORY EVER TOLD. But the MGM people were frightened of Von Sydow and feared that from now on he would be associated with the role of Christ. O'Brien, having seen the actor in some of his films for Ingmar Bergman, was also worried that Von Sydow was cold. David said that Bergman was an icicle and he should not judge Von Sydow just from his Bergman films.

Ponti urged David to consider Burt Lancaster and begged David not to prejudge him until he had seen his performance in Visconti's THE LEOPARD.[5] Bolt, though, had seen Lancaster in THE ROSE TATTOO and thought him "unbearable". When David suggested Jeanne Moreau for Lara, Bolt raised a barricade of paragraphs against her.[6]

For the part of Komarovsky, David originally made a startling choice. "You will be relieved to hear," David wrote to O'Brien, "that Marlon Brando did not answer my letter. I gave him a month and wrote to James Mason. He replied by return and signed it, 'Elatedly, James.'"7

They had arrived at James Mason after much thought. In their casting notes, David wrote, "Komarovsky is a man of the flesh; delighted and uncritical of his body and its desires; food, comfort and sex - so long as it is discreet. He is highly intelligent in his business as a lawyer and respected accordingly. The actor must have enough dexterity and personality to convince an audience that he could not only weather the Revolution (changing sides as he does) but that he could end up Minister of Justice. He must be old enough to make his seduction of the schoolgirl, Lara, shocking, and not attractive enough to be in any logical sense a rival to Zhivago. The danger with Mason is that he has overtones of a dark, dreaming Svengali. I think he's a good enough actor to overcome this."

Omar Sharif was to have played Strelnikov. While this may take some adjustment for those who know the film, David wrote, "Think him almost ideal. First rate as the idealistic student Pasha whose youth and 'cleanliness' so impresses Lara, in contrast to Komarovsky, and believable as Strelnikov, 'The Executioner.'"

With Loren politely sidelined, the possibilities for Lara had been Yvette Mimieux - a suggestion from MGM's Robert Weitman - and Jane Fonda, whom David favoured, although he was concerned about her accent - "Lara with an American accent will bring out the critics with their biggest hatchets." Fonda's agent was asked if the actress would agree to her voice being dubbed if that became necessary.8

During one of the discussions about Lara, David brought up the name of Sarah Miles.

"No, no, no," said Bolt. "She's just a north country slut."

David said, "No, you're wrong. You've just seen her films and believed her publicity."9

David was exasperated by this endless shuffling of actors. But then came a call from MGM. "We got to a total impasse. One evening I was in the Richmond Hotel in Madrid and Bob O'Brien rang up from New York. 'David,' he said, 'I've been hearing about your difficulties of casting. I've had a talk to my people and I want to tell you that you can cast anybody you like and I will accept them.'"10

Freedom can sometimes paralyse one's mind as surely as any lack of it. But Roy Rossotti - casting in London - had suggested that David look at John Schlesinger's BILLY LIAR. David was as attracted as everyone else had been by the shots of a girl walking down the street, swinging her handbag, a scene which became an icon of the sixties. The actress was twenty-four-year-old Julie Christie.

"I have never met her," wrote David in his cast list, "but she has an extraordinary screen presence."

However, he could hardly cast so important a part without checking and

O'Brien was with him when he did so. David put a call through to John Ford.

"When Ford came on the line the spirits of both men obviously had a big rise. They were happy to be in contact. David told John that he had no Lara. As he had been told good things about Julie Christie, he wanted to know what John thought of her work in YOUNG CASSIDY, which John was shooting in Dublin.[11] John was most enthusiastic. 'She's great, the best young actress that has ever come into the business. No one in the past has shown so much talent at such an early age.'"[12]

Julie Christie had a very different impression of herself. She thought "they must be off their nuts" and went to Madrid not so much for the test as for a free holiday.

"I wouldn't even have rated myself as an actress at the time," she said. "My tendency was to put myself in the position of a child, and David was paternalistic. He behaved like an authoritarian but kindly father. He must have had some expectation after what Ford said, but it doesn't seem to me I did very much. After the rape scene, for instance, he wasn't getting what he wanted, and he and Freddie Young had a long talk, they put more sweat on me and then suggested I breathe more deeply and look into the camera.

"He was obviously used to power and authority and he understood his position. I wasn't scheduled to work for weeks and we were based in Soria. This was a wonderfully beautiful part of

Julie Christie as herself.

the countryside. My boyfriend[13] had flown over and I was longing to travel round it with him. I asked permission and was forbidden to go. David wanted us all to be there. I was as furious as a little girl - with a certain amount of justification. I suppose this wasn't a very democratic time in film-making, was it?

"But I did trust him. He was an old-fashioned gentleman. Whatever he asked you to do professionally, you knew it would be okay. I never got to know him very well, but I liked him. He seemed distraught about his personal life a lot of the time. That was one of the reasons I liked him. He was a human being who couldn't quite sort things out. I found this rather touching, considering how hugely powerful he was.

"Like many people who are insecure, he didn't realise how autocratically he acted. And he could easily be hurt by people not realising his vulnerability."[14]

Barbara Cole was convinced that David, as many people suspected, was somewhat smitten by Julie Christie. "I noticed it during the scenes where she's having a mixed-up relationship with Komarovsky. I thought to myself, 'He's really attracted to this woman.' But I was there."[15]

Julie Christie as Lara.

As for the role of Zhivago, David wrote, "If I had to decide at this moment I would go for Peter O'Toole. Zhivago has to be a sensitive but strong young man; no popular idea of a long-haired dreaming poet and not the one-layer deep action hero who knows where he's going and the difference between right and wrong. O'Toole is in fact too much of an extrovert for ideal casting, but I would rather suppress his exhibitionism than attempt to coax strength out of a lily. Unfortunately Zhivagos do not become actors."[16]

Sam Spiegel then came back into David's life by refusing to release O'Toole from existing commitments - THE CHASE, which O'Toole never made, and THE NIGHT OF THE GENERALS, which he did make, with Omar Sharif. But O'Toole let it be known that he wanted to do the part whatever his contractual problems. He was eliminated by a curious and unfortunate incident.

"The script was never sent to O'Toole," said Barbara Cole. "I typed the script. I had a copy, David had a copy and the other copy was sent to Ponti. There were no other copies. So someone photocopied the only script in Rome one night - it's the only answer - and they sent it to Peter. It wasn't the final script, and David didn't want anyone to see it at that point, which was why we didn't make more copies. We heard that Peter had read the script and rejected it, but he hadn't been offered it by David. Maybe he had been by Ponti. People kept coming to David and saying, 'Oh, Peter O'Toole says you've made a mistake this time,' and people were going to Peter and saying, 'David wouldn't have you anyway,' and it was all a lot of lies and people making trouble."[17]

David had run out of ideas - Zhivago was a character on a page, not a flesh-

and-blood actor and the part itself was possibly unplayable. "One of the hardest things to cast is a good man. The more 'good' they are the more dull they appear when they reach the screen."[18]

It was Barbara Cole who came up with the answer.

"David was saying, 'Who the hell do I get? Who's known internationally?'

"I said, 'What about Omar? Not all Russians are blond.'

"David said, 'By Christ, you're right.'"[19]

"So I rang him up and offered him the part," said David. "His agent called to find out how much I was willing to pay. I said, 'I'll pay what Omar asks.' And that's what we did. And I've been friends with Omar ever since. I wish I'd offered him more parts. The trouble with Omar is that he suffers from that awful thing of being too good-looking, and almost too expert, and people smile when they mention his name. It's something to do with jealousy, particularly with men. A kind of scathing put-down. There's a whole class of people like that. It's a shame."[20]

The idea of an Egyptian playing a Russian should have been no more curious in theatrical terms than an Englishman playing an Arab. And Sharif, when he heard the news, had just played an Armenian in THE FALL OF THE ROMAN EMPIRE and was in Yugoslavia playing the Mongol warrior, Genghis Khan. But David found many people astonished at his choice of casting.

"It was sort of a stretch," said David, "but in that part of the world, well, he could have been Manchurian. So we pulled his eyes back with tape, to take the orbs out of it, though Omar still has those large orbs. The critics liked making something of that. And we straightened his hair. Sort of made it look like mine."[21]

Hoping to use Audrey Hepburn, David opposed the idea of Geraldine Chaplin as Tonya, but since the suggestion came from Carlo Ponti he was obliged to give her a test.[22] She arrived, dressed in jeans, and looking about sixteen, and David's heart sank. Tonya starts the film aged nineteen and ends up with two children. She needed maturity, character and charm, and what David described as real womanliness.

"I thought it was pretty hopeless on the age count alone," David wrote to Oona Chaplin, "but there was just something about her and I decided to do the test. I suggested we had a quiet little run-through expecting I'd have to spend quite a time slowing down her movements, changing intonations and explaining this and that facet of mature behaviour. Not at all. Did it like a bird! All the technicians madly impressed and a lot of talk between all of us about her Mum and Dad - and that's why I'm writing this. I hope she does the part - and it's a very good one - and I hope I have your blessings. Please don't trouble to reply. Geraldine does not know I have written this."[23]

Geraldine Chaplin aroused a fever of excitement from the press, not only because she was beautiful and was in her first proper role, but because she was Charles Chaplin's daughter. At a press conference staged to announce the start of shooting, the excited newshounds sped past players like Alec Guinness, Ralph Richardson and Siobhan McKenna - and even Julie Christie - and hovered round Chaplin as though she were the only celebrity.

Alec Guinness did not respond with enthusiasm when David offered him the role of Yevgraf Zhivago. David wrote to Guinness to explain the role more fully and to reassure his old friend:

"Yevgraf is the story-teller. As such he holds a unique position vis-a-vis the rest of the characters. He, as it were, holds the film in his hands, while the others are just playing out their parts in it. It gives him the reins in a way that spoken dialogue could never do. Do try and see this point. The very 'standing back' which you refer to is just what I like. I would understand if Yevgraf were left there with egg on his face while his voice does the work for him, but I don't think you'll find one place where this happens. On the contrary I think it adds another dimension to him, over and above the others.

"Are you sure you're not jibbing at a commentary prejudice? Do try reading it again as a story-teller and not a commentator. I love so-called commentary in films. If it's well done I think it gives a special sort of intimacy. I wonder if you

remember BRIEF ENCOUNTER. It was almost fifty-fifty commentary and dialogue, and the curious thing is that no-one remembers it as such. I think you're off your rocker when you say the audience will feel words to the effect, 'Here's that bore again breaking the mood.' But don't let's argue about you being a bore. I seem to remember we've had that one before. I'm sure you're doubtful whether your talent will reach to speaking commentary, and not at all surprised you'd have preferred to play Alexander.

"You could have had him at the drop of a hat. He's a sweet, cosy old pipe-smoker and although a good part he's not in the *same fucking street as Yevgraf!*"[24]

Guinness replied from Munich: "I have just sent you a telegram saying Yes. I hope this pleases you - well, I know it does. I equally hope you will understand my initial shillyshallying; the script in two halves and separated by a few weeks, embarking on a new film, a discomfort about that commentary etc. Anyway reading it flat out *as a whole* makes a huge difference. I am still unsure about *some* of the commentary - I think it needs to be very clear indeed and not too clever."

With the casting complete, David explained that what he had tried to do was to assemble a cast that would win the full approval, if he were still alive, of Boris Pasternak himself.[25]

CHAPTER THIRTY-FIVE

DEPARTURES

DOCTOR ZHIVAGO III

CARLO Ponti had urged David to make ZHIVAGO in Yugoslavia, which might bring the budget down from seven million to five million dollars. David, Barbara and John Box set out from Rome in the Rolls-Royce.

"They gave us a young man as interpreter," said Barbara, "but the people were so rude. If you pulled in for petrol, there were enormous queues and they were very rude serving you. We stopped at a lovely lakeside hotel where we ordered trout for lunch. It arrived in pieces so I asked the waiter, 'What's wrong with the trout?' He said, 'It's overcooked, what do you think?' and threw it on the plate."[1]

"I don't think we could have worked there," said David. "I remember going into a restaurant with a large group and we asked if we could put three or four tables together. The chap who was looking after us said, 'Now you'll see how Communism works. I will have to ask permission.' He called over all the waiters, explained what we wanted and they had a pow-pow and finally said, 'Yes, you can put the tables together.' And so we sat down and that was it. But I mean, the ridiculous idea of the waiters deciding whether one could put three or four tables together - because they owned the restaurant, as it were. And you can't work like that."[2]

To make absolutely sure, John Box returned to Yugoslavia in the winter. "I took a script and walked up and down in the snow, playing all the parts to myself, and realised that nobody could give a performance in those temperatures."[3]

This also ruled out shooting for extended lengths of time in the Soviet Union. Whilst the authorities in Moscow were keen on the prospect of foreign currency, they were less than keen on the project.

"The go-between with the Russians was Lord Archibald," said David. "He had been the boss of Independent Producers. He was a very efficient man and I liked him very much indeed. He knew a lot about movies, too. And he was a diplomat. He knew the Russians and he said, 'They want you to come over to see what a pack of lies ZHIVAGO is.' For an idiotic statement, that takes the prize, because how can going to Russia today tell you about a book written for another age? He said, 'They'll show you everything, take you anywhere. But if you insist on making the film after you've been there you'll be persona non grata.'

"I said, 'Tell them to make me persona non grata this minute. I'm going to make the film, but I'm not going to be put under that sort of strain.'"[4]

David and John Box took the Rolls[5] up to Scandinavia and Finland. Box was as keen a stills cameraman as David.

"I was not quite as romantic, a bit more gritty. I was taking pictures in a harbour and he said, 'Why are you taking all those pictures of that ship? It's absolutely horrible.'

"I said, 'You take yours, David, and I'll take mine. And when you're too old to direct you can take the photos for the Pan-American calendars.' That stung him.

"The next day he walked into Hasselblad in Stockholm and bought me a camera like his. David loved precision and beautiful machinery appealed to him. I was using an ordinary Pentax. And he said, 'Here we are. It's not a gift. It's simply so we can start even. You go on shooting shit and no more talk about Pan-American calendars, if you please, John.' We went on and had a happy recce."[6]

Spain had not only satisfactorily reproduced the burning sands of Arabia, it had also provided the snow-covered Sierra Nevada mountains for a scene in LAWRENCE. A study of recent weather patterns was what finally convinced the production team to set up their base in Madrid.

David told MGM that while they would be based at CEA studios, one hundred and fifty miles to the north-east was Soria, four thousand feet up, "guaranteed snow from December to March, sometimes waist height." Nearby were large plains with railways, there were pine forests... It was, indeed, Russia.

Thus, on a rubbish dump at Canillejas, outside Madrid, tsarist Moscow began to rise. "I had never been to Moscow," said John Box, "so I took all the references I could find and tried to create the heart of the city."[7]

Construction started on 3 August 1964, to the fascination of the inmates of a nearby prison, who were able to see "Moscow" from their cell windows. The Kremlin was at the end of a street half a mile long with scores of shops, all of which changed with the thirty-year span of the story. Side streets led to factories in the workers' section of the town, and tramcars ran the entire length.

The first problem encountered by the art department concerned the Russian lettering on shops and revolutionary banners. A Russian émigré in London named Eugene Mollo, who had served in both the Red and White armies, was enlisted as technical adviser.

The Spanish signwriters didn't think a technical adviser necessary. They had been evacuated to the Soviet Union when the Fascists won the Civil War, so they spoke Russian. What they did not realise was that after the Revolution there had been a change in Russian orthography and a number of accents and letters had been deleted from the alphabet.

Eugene Mollo was able to point this out and to provide a wealth of information, but he was dismayed that no one seemed prepared to listen. He passed the job on to his son, Andrew, which dismayed me because he happened to be my film-making partner at the time.

We had just finished making a story of the imaginary German occupation of England, IT HAPPENED HERE, the previous year, and had been trying - unsuccessfully - to get a toe-hold in the industry as professional directors. Andrew had worked as an assistant director on films such as SATURDAY NIGHT AND SUNDAY MORNING, but he was, essentially, a military historian. I had been amazed at his knowledge, for he was only sixteen when I first met him, and twenty-four when we finished the film. There was a lot of David Lean about him - terrific enthusiasm, astonishing skill (he was art director as well as co-director on the film) but often remote and abstracted. Nevertheless, he was my closest friend. I was sorry to lose him at so crucial a time in our careers, but realised that whatever the drawbacks, a credit on DOCTOR ZHIVAGO would be of inestimable value to him.

Carlo Ponti had told David that he could have any technician who had worked on LAWRENCE. When he sent out the call, it was like Napoleon's to the Grande Armée. This answer came from Ernie Day: "Dear David. Exquisite relief! I had almost resigned myself to not being there when the first shot of ZHIVAGO is printed. Thank you for your letter, guv'nor, and the extremely nice things you said. Above all, thank you for inviting me to become one of your dedicated maniacs again."

David had far less excuse than Napoleon for not remaining in touch, yet he hardly ever contacted his "dedicated maniacs" between productions. This built up a level of resentment which could easily have been avoided by the occasional tactful phone call. Yet the curious thing was, according to Barbara Cole, that David hardly ever used the telephone.[8]

"At the end of a picture, David had what he wanted from the crew, and that was it," said Roy Stevens. "That was the thing that used to upset me, and everybody else. A nucleus of six or eight were so close to him all the way through - like Ernie or myself. When it was over Ernie wouldn't get a telephone call, I wouldn't. John Box wouldn't, except when he needed him. So it took a long time to get back to the warmth you had felt for him because you felt you had been totally neglected. You had been superfluous to his requirements."[9]

On ZHIVAGO, David's crew suspected him of gross disloyalty. For out of the blue, Nic Roeg, who had been second-unit cameraman on LAWRENCE (and who had been trained by Freddie Young before that), received a telephone call inviting him to become Director of Photography.

"I don't think David even wanted to discuss it," said Roeg. "He just wanted me to do it. It was a very strange thing. I couldn't get my own crew. It was very much, 'You will become the servant of the Lean organisation.'"[10]

Roeg was told that he had been chosen because Freddie Young was working on another film, but he soon realised there was more to it than that, because when he arrived in Spain, he was treated as a kind of traitor by the other LAWRENCE veterans. They somehow gained the impression that Young had not even been asked.

But Freddie Young *had* been asked. David had written to him in July saying, "I hope to God you will be able to photograph it. Do please try as it wouldn't be the same thing at all without you, you have ruined me for everyone else."[11]

Young said he would do it and David wrote to say how delighted he was. "Better start thinking about portable electric blanketing for ourselves, too. God, I hate the cold. Our combined early morning bad tempers should warm up the unit daily. (Trouble is, they laugh at us too.) But we'll have some high-octane reserves up our woolies to surprise them."

But by the time David was ready, Young was booked to photograph Basil Dearden's KHARTOUM, which was ironic, since it was intended to capitalise on the success of LAWRENCE.

Although David considered buying Young out of his contract, he was concerned that if ZHIVAGO collapsed, MGM would have to foot the bill. Whilst a skilled negotiator might have helped Young's agent to find a way out of this muddle, David decided to look for someone else. He had, anyway, been urged on several occasions to give a younger cameraman a chance.[12]

When he first read Pasternak's novel, David came across a quotation from Tolstoy which struck him with such force he wrote it down: "The more a man devotes himself to beauty, the further he moves away from goodness."[13] It was as well no critic located it, or they would have used it to attack David for what they saw as his "chocolate box view of history". And yet nothing could have been farther from David's mind as he embarked on shooting. Prettiness was the one thing he wanted to avoid.

David and Bolt had the idea of making the film in 70mm black and white. David mentioned this to Freddie Young. "Don't jump and say 'Oh no!!' until you've read the book. I will be very interested to hear what you think. I even had a mad day dream the other day about the old coloured bases of our youth. [He was referring to the tinting and toning of silent films.] I remember how wonderful snow looks in lavender, and thought about how spring might look in sepia. I fear colour may pretty it up and make it earthbound. Black and white is already one stage removed from reality and I think it might give it a force which colour might dissipate."[14]

But the idea of black and white was an early casualty of box-office pragmatism. Nonetheless, David determined to handle the colour creatively - the ugliest scenes, like the killing of the Cadets, were to be filmed in beautiful light while love scenes were to be drained of colour and set in the cold.

A further casualty was 70mm. "We did not shoot ZHIVAGO in 70mm," said David, "because of the usual screaming about expense. Everybody said it would cost a fortune, it would break us. They also said, 'Nobody will notice the difference if you shoot on 35mm and blow it up.'"

Amazingly, David gave in.

"When David opted for Spain," said Nic Roeg, "he got all the forecasts. The first shot was supposed to be in winter - the burial of Zhivago's mother. What a day! We had bright blue sky, glorious sun and yellow cornfield. Thank God I was able to get hold of some brutes. I used a blue filter. I had the brutes on as backlight to get the sky white and brutes on their faces. It looked great in the end. Things started to go very well.

"Bob O'Brien came up after the first day's rushes and gave me a box of cigars, saying, 'You only need three great shots in a movie to get an Oscar and you've got them already. Thanks a lot.'"[15]

David had taken a tremendous risk in hiring Roeg, for he belonged to a generation with a very different set of priorities. A mercurial and amusing man, Roeg shared a passion for cinema with David, but little else. He was like a fresh young subaltern reporting to a company commander who had been in the trenches for the entire war.

Roeg felt uneasy from the moment he arrived. The dismay that Young was not on the film was almost tangible. "I felt like a Judas," he said. This must have been apparent to David, for Roeg noticed how close to his crew he was, and how possessive he was of them. He kept their families at one remove. Roeg's wife had accompanied him to Madrid and when David asked him to dinner, he excluded her, rather as an army officer would exclude a civilian.

"I remember we were all on a recce," said Roeg, "and we were at dinner with Roy Stevens, John Box, Roy Rossotti and a few others. David was at one end of the table and I was at the other. And he knew that I knew, and I knew that he knew, that this question was aimed at me. David said to Roy Stevens, 'Have you ever been angry with me, Roy? Tell me, we've been together for a long while.'

"Roy said, 'Oh yes, David, I remember that charge at Aqaba...'

"David said, 'Your bloody camels came in line. I really gave you a hard time, didn't I?'

"Then he asked John Box. And I thought, 'This is coming right down to me.' And it did.

"He said, 'Do you think you'll be angry with me, Nic, at any time?'

"I said, 'If you give me cause David, I'm sure I shall be.'

"He said. 'I bet you would.' It didn't augur well. Now probably no one at that table would even remember, but it's as clear as day to me and it was one of those moments when alarm bells rang in my head."[16]

Roeg found the atmosphere on the set far too tense and reverent. He recalled the occasion when Rod Steiger (who had replaced James Mason as Komarovsky) arrived in Madrid, and called upon David in his caravan.

"I was sitting with David and Barbara Cole. David was musing. Everything was very tense, as usual. Rod opened the door and said, 'What's the matter? Somebody's father just died?' I cracked up."[17]

According to Roy Stevens, David was fond of Nic Roeg but could not understand his sense of humour.

"Nic would send him up absolutely rotten. He took to copying David with his cigarettes. You could see David smoking by the camera, then Nic would light up his Gauloise and hold it in exactly the same way. We were all falling about, and David didn't realise what was going on at all. Yet he would have been really offended if he had twigged."[18]

Some of the time, David was impressed by what Roeg was doing. In the scene where Komarovsky places his hand on Lara's in the troika, and the hand disappears under the fur cover, Roeg gave the impression of passing streetlights.

"I did it with a swivelling pup, so it seemed like a turn of the hand, and the hand's gone. It came back with the light. When he saw the rushes, David said, 'That was brilliant. I'd never have thought of that.'"[19]

Roeg was sometimes too bold. "Zhivago had fallen in with the Bolsheviks," he said, "and they're all in a log cabin plotting. Zhivago was sitting huddled with his cap on, and I lit him so he looked like a skull, so that his eyes were black, with the tiniest pinprick in his black eyes. David hated it. 'You've lost his beautiful eyes,' he said. I realised I was on the wrong planet."

One morning, Roeg and David were sitting on the camera crane, arguing about a shot. "He said something, and I could have clapped my hand over his mouth, because he went to a place it was impossible to come back from. I suppose I was being too pushy. He said, 'You think I'm old-fashioned, don't you?' As he was saying it, I was thinking, 'Don't let that out of your mouth, please, David!'"[20]

The final confrontation came with the demonstration on the big Moscow set. Roeg had done some research and had come to the conclusion that the Muscovites would not have left their lamps on during the disturbances; although the street lamps would have been lit, he felt that the windows of the houses should have been dark.

David said, "No, I think we'll have the lights on because I want people to see the set."

And Roeg said, "Oh, you want it Hollywood, do you?"[21]

Freddie Young and David on DOCTOR ZHIVAGO.

"It was a clash of personalities," said assistant director Pedro Vidal. "On the Saturday we shot, on the Monday he wasn't on the set. Manuel Berenguer [2nd unit cameraman] kept going until Freddie arrived."[22]

"I always used to say that Nic would be a wonderful director," said David. "We did not agree on the way certain things should look. I remember saying to him, 'Nic, the trouble is that what you think is good, I think is bad, and what I think is bad you think is good. We've got to have a break. I promise you I have not got a cameraman in mind, but I think we ought to change. Will you see me out until we get somebody else?' And he did. It was a terrible thing asking him to go. But he behaved impeccably and we're good friends now; we meet and talk and there are no hard feelings that I'm aware of."[23]

"We all got thoroughly drunk in Madrid," said Roy Stevens. "We thought it was really sad for anyone to have to leave the picture. We all thought, 'Christ, that could happen to me. Your career's finished. If David gets rid of you, you might as well go and dig graves.' That was the feeling we had."[24]

Another outsider who found life difficult was technical adviser Andrew Mollo. "I was never formally introduced to David Lean. I would appear early in the morning when they were preparing to film and wander around. Everybody studiously ignored me. David was always busy and surrounded by people, so he was quite unapproachable.

"We had to do the first scene in which we see the partisans. For at least the week before I had tried to find out what these partisans were going to wear. I spoke to props and they hadn't done anything about issuing swords. On the morning, when it was still dark, I remember going out to the location and there were all these extraordinary figures on horseback, all looking like extras from TARAS BULBA, with sheepskins and shaggy fur hats. No swords, no weapons. But apparently, word of my anxiety about these partisans had filtered through to David. He knew intuitively almost everything that was going on. He was obviously very delicately tuned.

"The assistant director said, 'The director wants to see all the partisans.' So they were all assembled and David came out of his caravan. He used to wander around in a rather stooped position, a cigarette always in a holder, with a rather pensive look on his face. But at the same time watching everything out of the corner of his eye. He came up to me and said, 'I don't think you're happy with the way these people are dressed. What's the problem?'

"I explained to him that the partisans at the time were mostly demobbed soldiers and they wore army uniforms without any badges and the only means they had of fighting was on horseback, with swords, and they carried rifles. The extras had some pack horses and I said the Russians never used pack horses, they used carts. So he said, 'I see.'

"He told the wardrobe department to go away and take off all the shaggy furs and dress them up in military uniform and he said, 'We must make sure we get swords.' And off he went.

"It turned out that props were just being awkward. They said David hadn't asked for swords because he didn't want it to look like the charge in LAWRENCE. Eventually we got them correctly dressed and the prop department handed out swords. But that was the David Lean way of handling the situation."[25]

Eddie Fowlie refutes Mollo's story, and yet both men have reliable memories. This is what Eddie told me:

"Can you really believe that my well-stocked and properly researched prop room did not have masses of weapons of every kind? I refute the statement that I, the property master, went to Andrew to ask where I could get swords. I can tell you, if I had made such a mistake, I would not have survived."[26]

One might have thought that costume designer Phyllis Dalton would have been pleased to see the back of Andrew Mollo, especially when he was instrumental in having Tom Courtenay's costume as Strelnikov altered. But Dalton, a true professional, was only too grateful to draw on the Mollos' vast knowledge. "I'm not sure we'd have managed without the photographs they had, the sample uniforms and all sorts of things. One owes a debt."[27]

Mollo thought he would work on the film for two weeks. "I kept on saying, 'Do you want me to stay?' The production manager, John Palmer, would say, 'I don't know. I'll have to check with David.' Several days later, he'd say 'He'd like you to stay on.' 'For how long?' 'At least another two weeks.'" Andrew Mollo stayed with ZHIVAGO for fifteen months.

"The way David directed, he didn't worry, really, about the morale of his crew. It was all done on a level of uncertainty. He had such a reputation, everyone was desperate to do exactly as he wanted. I never once heard him go up to any of the more junior members of the crew and say, 'Well done.' He didn't make an effort to chat with them or joke with them.

"A film crew is no different to any other crew - building an oil rig or fighting a war. People need praise. There was a funny sort of atmosphere. David was cold, very correct, very English, very reserved.

"You felt that not even David Lean himself actually enjoyed it. It was like orchestrating an incredibly complicated piece of music with thousands of musicians. He was so preoccupied with that that you never felt there was any spontaneity or elation at all. There was a rather anxious atmosphere all the time. At the time I thought I was the only person who felt like that, but I spoke to quite a number of people who worked with him before, and it was the dominant atmosphere on his sets."[28]

David prepares to shoot an advancing Russian army at Soria.

It was hardly surprising that the atmosphere was marked with anxiety. David was directly responsible for a massive production which was gradually going further and further over budget, from $7 million to $15 million.

Mollo was as taken aback as everyone else when he encountered David Lean's legendary silences. In the midst of much concentration, he seemed barely aware of the people around him. David explained these silences by saying he was a slow thinker.

"I envy people who receive sudden flashes of genius, because I don't. I try to work out every possible way to do a scene and then choose the way that will surprise audiences. If I seem to be in another world when friends and unit people speak to me, it's because I don't have the scene solved. I'm frequently thought to be rude when I'm really in a mental turmoil."[29]

But for those, unlike Mollo, who belonged to the inner circle, the "dedicated maniacs", the experience was far more significant.

"It was a great education for me," said camera operator Ernie Day, "about photography, about directing, about staging. I was absorbing everything he could tell me as well as presenting what he wanted on the screen.

"Sometimes, I was a go-between. As in all these associations, the director tells you a lot of things that he doesn't want anyone else to know, then the cameraman tells you a lot of things he doesn't want to go any further, so you're a kind of reservoir of thoughts which also affects what you put on the screen. Especially if you're operating for someone like David who had so many esoteric thoughts he wanted the camera to say to the audience. Sometimes this meant not being smooth on this part of the pan, to give some little agitation, so esoteric that you think, 'Wait a minute, it will look like a mistake.' But it didn't. Or, 'Let the actor go a little before you catch up with him.' That sort of thing. When you saw it on the screen, it made sense. But it didn't always at the time."[30]

The hours for the leading members of the unit were punishing - twelve hours a day, six days a week. When shooting finished, many of them still had more work to do - typing up continuity and daily report sheets, canning up rushes, preparing sets and costumes for the following day. And the chosen few had to remain on call, in case David wanted to have dinner with them, to discuss the problems of the next day.

"He expected his crew to be there day and night," said Roy Stevens. "The other fellows would say, 'We're going to this marvellous restaurant.' You couldn't go if David said, 'I thought we were having dinner tonight.' Oh, yes, David, we are having dinner. Absolutely. Sorry, fellows, I can't make it tonight. You were on call, no question about it."[31]

The most essential member of the crew for David was his property master, Eddie Fowlie. Aesthetically, he may have been more dependent on Bolt and Freddie Young, but from the practical point of view he needed Eddie more than anyone. The relationship puzzled many of those around David, including Andrew Mollo. But I understand it, because Andrew fulfilled that role - and more - for me when we made IT HAPPENED HERE.

A film director has to be extremely practical, and the odd thing is that very few are. No matter now many people he hires to make up for that deficiency, they will invariably be deficient in some area or other themselves. Imagine finding someone who has all the skills you lack, has the intuition of a magician and is so compatible he becomes your best friend.

Inevitably, Eddie aroused resentment from other members of the unit. As one said, "David liked him because he was a roughneck and a rebel, as David would like to have been. He was David's slave. He used to wash his Rolls and polish it. No wonder David liked him." ("Nonsense," said Eddie, "I got a prop-man to wash it.")

Yet, although David's friendship with Eddie had grown over the years, and they used to go on holiday together, there was little evidence of it on set or location, apart from Fowlie's sixth sense.

"Off-stage we were friends," said Fowlie. "As soon as we were on-stage it was work, and I never ever attempted to take any advantage of that situation and he never presumed that I would.

"I could say things to him that perhaps other people couldn't - but always in a diplomatic way. Other people would say things to David almost as criticism. You couldn't do that. David wouldn't take criticism from anybody. I would sow a seed and stand back because if it was any good at all it would grow. If we were filming and he was looking for a set-up, I would go and just stand where I thought a good set-up would be. Not a word would pass between us, we wouldn't even look at one another. Presently, as I walked away, David would stand there and look. And more often than not, he would choose it. That was the subtle part of it. It was no good shouting to David, 'Look, it's good over here.' Then it was not his idea.

"The same thing if I wanted to criticise a scene. He would permit it, but I wouldn't say it to him. I might make a little note of a suggestion on a piece of paper, or even on a tape recorder." [32]

If ever Eddie Fowlie proved his value, it was high up on the plains at Soria, where they would shoot the snow scenes. Inspired by an engraving on an old Russian stamp, John Box had built an amazing set of Varykino, the Zhivago's country house. Then everyone waited for it to snow.

"We waited till the end of November," said David. "No snow. December, January and February and there it was, sitting out in this huge plain with yellow stubble all around it. In the first week of March we got a telephone call; it's snowing!"

"We'd be shooting in Madrid with the Spanish army," said Phyllis Dalton,

David and John Box before Varykino.

"and just as we got them dressed and ready the command would go out: 'Drop everything and go to Soria!' You'd scramble into cars and go up there by which time the snow would have melted. Nightmare."[33]

On one occasion, there was just enough snow to shoot the establishing shot of the house. But the snow wasn't nearly deep enough. The furrows in the fields were still visible. Eddie Fowlie had located a marble factory and had bought tons of white marble dust which he scattered around the location, augmenting it with lengths of white plastic sheet, placed over hedgerows in the distance. Bushes and trees were sprayed with whitewash.

"Just before the snow came," said David, "I was told that Mr O'Brien was coming and would I show him some of the rushes? He saw them in Madrid and I was told he was going to come the following day to see me at Soria. 'How are you, David?' 'All right, thank you.'

"We carried on talking pleasantries until I couldn't stand it any more, and I said, 'Bob, I know that I am three million dollars over budget, it's because of the snow. I just don't know what to say to you.' I thought he was going to say, 'Cut the next twenty pages of script' or something. He said, 'I know about that, David. I've seen what you've been shooting. You carry on as you're doing and let me look after the money.'

"I was his slave from then on." [34]

As they were filming the scene when Zhivago and Lara part at Varykino, David asked Fowlie if he could make the snow glisten.

Fowlie said, "I can but it won't look real."

"I don't want it to," said David.

Fowlie spread cellophane over the snow laden trees and bushes.

"I wanted it all to look not real," said David. "I wanted their memory of the scene, all glistening in the moonlight with wolves howling in the distance." [35]

Fowlie and John Box performed another miracle for the scene when the Red Army has to charge across a frozen lake. The scene had to be filmed in the oppressive heat of a Spanish summer.

"There wasn't a lake there at all," said Fowlie. "It was just a great big field. I spread it all with cement and in certain places I put down sheet iron. I used an awful amount of crushed white marble on top, thousands of tons of it, which we ironed out with steamrollers, so the horses were able to slide on that in a more natural way." [36]

The illusion of a lake was completed by a rowing boat, apparently moored on the shore.

The interior of Varykino, or "The Ice Palace", was a studio set, and David and Robert Bolt wanted it to have a strange and other-wordly look. John Box designed it to resemble an Arctic Miss Havisham's.

"I had seen a still of Captain Scott's hut in the Antarctic," said Box, "and it showed how, through a little hole, ice and snow had got through. I thought that was the clue for us.

"Mind you, we didn't know how the hell to do it. Eddie Fowlie and I worked it out between us. He went round with a bucket of hot candlewax and he threw it at the set and I walked behind him with a bucket of freezing water and a pressurised Hudson spray. We added mica after that." [37]

But not even Eddie Fowlie could spread enough marble dust for the long shots of Russia in the grip of winter, nor for the frozen battlefront, nor for lingering tracking shots from trains, so in March 1965 a reduced unit was sent to Finland. This costly trip was authorised by O'Brien himself.

They stayed at the lumber town of Joensuu, four hundred miles north of Helsinki and within seventy-five miles of the Russian border. Finnish Railways provided thirty-two railway carriages and two wood-burning locomotives, altered to resemble Russian engines. The main shooting was on the frozen Lake Pyhaselka and Lapland gipsies were recruited as refugees. The railway line that

David celebrates his 57th birthday in Finland with a cake decorated with a diesel locomotive.

was needed for the sequences had actually been laid during the Russian invasion of Finland in 1940.

The trip to Finland consumed the best part of two weeks and was hampered by poor visibility and equipment seizing up in the sub-zero temperatures. David and Omar Sharif were given honorary citizenship by President Urho Kekkonen and, for his fifty-seventh birthday, David was given a vast cake emblazoned with "Happy Birthday" in Finnish. David left Finland on 28 March 1965, leaving behind veteran cameraman Desmond Dickinson and second-unit director Roy Rossotti who shot more train footage.

Train scenes were also shot in Spain and provided a disproportionate degree of frustration. David had an almost aristocratic level of disdain when he was displeased.

"The shot was a train coming across the screen from right to left and Mr Lean stood there with his jacket off and his ever-present cigarette holder," said Rod Steiger. "The train came all the way from Madrid and it took an hour and a half to get there to do this shot.

"'What are we doing here?' he said to his first assistant.

"'We're trying to do the shot of the train.'

"'Yes, we are. Will you tell me which way the sun is shining?'

"And the sun was shining from the wrong direction, the train was coming from the wrong direction and they had to send it back to Madrid and turn it around in the big yard and send it the other way.

"'That's all the shooting for today. Thank you.' And Mr Lean walked away."[38]

Another train scene gave David one of the worst moments of his career. A woman with a child (a dummy) was supposed to run alongside the train and grab Zhivago's hand and be hauled aboard. But a miscalculation was made and instead of the woman holding Omar Sharif's hand, he was instructed to hold hers.

"She started panicking," said Ernie Day, who was watching it all through the camera, "but he didn't understand her. She was trying to make him let go, and when she did finally wrench her hand away she stumbled and disappeared out of the viewfinder."[39]

It appeared that the woman had fallen beneath the train. Horrified, David ordered the train to stop, and hardly dared look, expecting to see mangled flesh.

"What a terrible feeling it was," said Pedro Vidal, assistant director. "Yet nothing happened to her. She had a lot of contusions but nothing great. David was very worried so we took her to the hospital. And David was wondering, 'Do we stop shooting or not?'" He was asking himself, he was not asking Pedro.

"I didn't answer because I knew David very well. He said, 'I think we'd better continue, Pedro, for the morale'"[40]

It turned out that the actress, Lili Murati, a Hungarian survivor of the Holocaust, had bunched up as she had fallen so the wheels had not severed her limbs. She was also wearing thick clothes, which protected her further. Her stumble can be clearly seen in the finished film.

"We carried on shooting with other scenes," said Barbara Cole. "Three weeks later, we re-shot it and the same actress came back and did it again. An amazing feat; I don't know how she had the courage."

The Spanish winter was so mild that the actors sweated in their heavy costumes and thousands of daffodil bulbs, imported from Holland in December, started sprouting and they had to be dug up, put in pots and kept under cover until it was considered safe to plant them again.

"We had a scene, much laughed at and scorned," said David, "the coming of spring when Omar looked at the crystals on the window and they melted and the colour came up with an absolute rush. I did it with daffodils, because I love daffodils. In the scene before we had Zhivago and Lara sitting around in freezing weather in the cottage at Varykino. We went in there and sprayed everything grey - took out all the colours. Freddie Young was practically crying when he said, 'Leave me that little pink thing on the table.'

"'No, Freddie.'

"'It'll look just bloody awful photography.'

"I said, 'It won't when it's run on the screen and the daffodils come up and people will gasp because the sudden advent of colour after three minutes of greyness will catch them by the throat.'

"And it did. For everybody except the critics. But it worked and I'd do it again tomorrow."[41]

In Franco's Spain, the Communist Party had been outlawed. "We were doing the demonstration scene," said Andrew Mollo. "David said, 'The Chief of Police is worried about playing revolutionary songs over the loudspeakers as playback for the extras.' Could I come up with a well-known Russian revolutionary song which wouldn't mean anything to the Spaniards?

"I listened to some of the old Russian songs and there was one very haunting refrain which I thought would be good. I rang my father in London, and he had never heard it used abroad, and didn't think anybody would know it. So I went back to David with this record and he played it on the gramophone in his caravan and said, 'Yes, that's fine.'

"We had two thousand extras, Cossacks, God knows what, assembled and the Chief of Police came round to watch. When they started playing the song, almost spontaneously the extras started singing it in Spanish: 'A las barricadas.'"[42]

Komarovsky (Rod Steiger) and Lara (Julie Christie). Barbara Cole left, with David centre, Freddie Young behind.

"I think I never suffer so much," said Pedro Vidal. "I thought the police were going to come and get me and it's the end of everything. But when we did the scene, nothing. The police know it was a film about Russia. But really, the extras, especially everybody that was close to the Communist Party, they were so enthusiastic. And also the 'Internationale,' forbidden for so many years, now they could sing it as loud as they wanted and nobody was going to stop them, so it was cheered."[43]

The scene where the revolutionaries are charged by dragoons was intercut with a fashionable restaurant where Komarovsky is entertaining Lara.

"In the script," said Andrew Mollo, "it was written that the officers in the restaurant were dressed in white uniforms, and I had to point out to David that there was only one regiment in the Russian army that wore white uniforms, but they wore them on duty. When they were in the restaurant in the evening they would wear a different uniform, which wasn't white.

"David said, 'Yes, I understand that. The problem is that it must look very obvious to the audience that these are White Russian officers - tsarist - and therefore it is important for dramatic purposes that they are in white.' I accepted that as being a reasonable argument."[44]

Film historians have often compared the charge of the dragoons with the famous Odessa Steps sequence in Eisenstein's silent classic, BATTLESHIP POTEMKIN. David, though, had never seen Eisenstein's film and thought such montages of violence had been overdone. As he told Robert Stewart, who interviewed him during production:

"I'm fed up in these battle scenes of people pulling out swords in close-up and 'crash' a man gets his head bashed in in another close-up and that sort of thing. I decided that as they clash, as the dragoons hit the crowd, I cut to Zhivago and just stay on his face for about a minute, just with the sound on it. And then, at the end of it, cut, and there are bodies in the street and the dragoons are gone. Now I've taken myself out on a limb because I haven't shot anything beyond the actual charging down the street, so if it doesn't work on his close-up, I'm cooked."[45]

Omar Sharif revealed that David's direction for this all-important close-up was somewhat unconventional:

"David told me to think of being in bed with a woman and making love to her," he said. Instead of staring transfixed at the horror, he should imagine he was at the moment "just before the orgasm."[46]

Because he saw hardly anything of the work of men like Eisenstein in the twenties, David was never as inspired by the Russian classics as he was by American silent films of his youth.

"King Vidor was a wonderful film crib - I copied him absolutely direct in

Tonya (Geraldine Chaplin) and Zhivago (Omar Sharif).

DOCTOR ZHIVAGO. In THE BIG PARADE, John Gilbert falls in love with Renée Adorée and the day comes when they're told to move forward up to the front and the trucks all leave and she runs along with a truck and hangs on to it. What a nerve! You wouldn't dare do it now. She lets go and he gets farther and farther away. She comes to a stand-still and there she is with the trucks going past her. It was just wonderful. I copied it with Julie Christie. It was a slight twist around but it was a straight copy."[47]

Now that David had his old cameraman back, he urged him to be daring in his lighting. When David wanted Zhivago's face plunged into black with pin-pricks of light in his eyes (perhaps a memory of the Nic Roeg attempt?), Freddie Young said, "I was brought up at MGM and the first rule was, 'You've got to see the money.'"[48]

But once David made him realise the extent of his freedom, Freddie Young's genius blossomed. After Lara's mother attempts suicide and her stomach is pumped out, Zhivago wanders into the dimly lit machine room, looks through an inside window into Lara's room and all he sees is her hand, picked out by a spot as she sits in the dark. Young suggested lighting the scene in that striking way and David supported him. "An almost black screen and a lighted hand," wrote David, "it was your idea completely. Very daring. Not realistic. Magic. Sensual delight."[49]

David felt the best thing they achieved together was when Zhivago, having tramped for days through the snow, reaches Lara's house, looks in a mirror, and an exhausted, haggard face gazes back.

"You had that bright idea of using a white gauze with a hole in it and gradually flooding it with light so that everything went white but Omar's face - then we cut to Tonya running away across a white snowfield; 'Tonya! Tonya!!' - straight cut back to Omar surrounded by white. Dim out the light, and there he is in bed looking up at Lara, not Tonya. It was done so simply and so expertly that I'll bet no one realized how much those three images had told - or even that they were very way-out images. In a few seconds they covered a four-week illness, told the audience that he was guilty about Tonya but loved Lara and at the same time gave an impression of almost peeping into his most intimate thoughts.

"Note also, my old Fred, that there was no question of bad photography - completely the opposite."[50]

Production lasted two hundred and thirty-two days, from 28 December 1964 to 7 October 1965. When shooting finally ended, Omar Sharif said that the cast wept. David said, "I don't want it to end."

The film was not shot in continuity: winter scenes were often staged in the severe summer heat which meant that the cast, dressed in thick furs and heavy uniforms, and denied drinks, were in a dangerous state of dehydration. "As soon as you sip water," said Geraldine Chaplin, "you sweat."[51]

The report sheets listed a myriad of delays and minor disasters; too much sun when snow was wanted, too little sun when sun was wanted; trouble with mist machines; rain washing the artificial snow from the sets; Omar Sharif pulling the muscles of his legs; an extra being knocked cold in the demonstration scene; the Chapman crane getting stuck in the mud; actors proving "absolutely useless" and having to be replaced.

The fact that such a monumental production could be produced against such odds was proof beyond doubt that David did not need a Sam Spiegel. His ideal producer was Robert O'Brien, a man with faith as deep as his resources. Carlo Ponti might have qualified, but there was something of the absentee landlord about him. The line producers, of course, were men like John Palmer, John Box, Roy Stevens, Pedro Vidal, Eddie Fowlie, and David Lean himself.

He might have quoted, along with the comment by Tolstoy, a line from Pasternak, "The fabulous is never anything but the commonplace touched by the hand of genius."[52]

CHAPTER THIRTY-SIX

SEIZE THE DAY!

DOCTOR ZHIVAGO IV

With his editor Norman Savage, David had tried cutting the film in Spain at weekends, while he was shooting.

"The results were awful," he said. When he looked at his work a few months later, he tore it apart and started again.

"Bob O'Brien begged me to get it out in time for the Academy Awards, because Metro was in a bad way at the time. I said, 'I'll do it, but it won't be absolutely perfect. Will you promise me when we see it with the public that I can recut it and redo the music where necessary?' He said, 'You can have what you like.' He really trusted me."[1]

Leaving his precious new Silver Cloud in a garage in Madrid, David moved to the MGM studios in Culver City, California.

"I had a wonderful place at the studio," said David. "It used to be the schoolroom for Mickey Rooney and Judy Garland when they were young kids and had to be educated while they were shooting films. They turned this bungalow into a place for me. There was a sitting room, and a kitchen and they gave me a black maid to look after me. They also gave me a suite at the Bel Air Hotel."

"We actually slept in a cottage in the grounds of the Bel Air," said Barbara Cole. "But we worked nights so often and there was nothing open except takeaway chicken, which no one wanted. So I used to cook the midnight meal at the bungalow. We would come home at two in the morning and be back at the studio at eleven.

"We had very nice American assistants who were keen on working these hours. They all had some kind of scheme. One wanted to build a swimming pool and he had a picture of it in outline and every night he pencilled in a new piece."[2]

"Norman Savage was very correct and very English," said Tony Lawson, who worked for him as an assistant. "He came from a working class background, and had pulled himself up, as the expression goes. He used to love wearing suits and ties, with a handkerchief in his top pocket; he was always very correct in the way he dressed and in his behaviour. And he liked the good things of life. He was wonderful to work for; a really nice man, very generous.

"He was very much in awe of David. He loved him as a person and David nurtured him. He became one of David's protégés. He certainly never expressed anything other than a love of the man and a deep respect for his work. Also, I suppose, David represented a sort of acceptance into another society."[3]

"He had a great sense of humour," said Roy Stevens, "and wasn't at all put out by David playing with the film and in the end they trusted one another implicitly. I worked with David on three films and the best relationship he had was with Norman Savage."[4]

"David and Norman worked as a matter of course until two and three in the morning," said Ralph Sheldon, an editor and friend of Savage. "The schedule was so gruelling that they had to keep going on vitamin injections."[5]

Three months is a reasonable editing schedule for an ordinary film, although I have spent a year editing a ten-reeler. DOCTOR ZHIVAGO was an immensely complicated twenty-reeler and the challenge of completing it so quickly must have appealed to David. He may not have been a swift director, but he could be astonishingly fast as an editor.

Although he had to accept a team assigned by MGM, David insisted that his indispensable sound editor, Win Ryder, be brought out from England to supervise the sound-editing, pre-mixing and dubbing. Ryder was horrified by what he found. Sound editors seemed to be regarded by the all-powerful sound mixer, a giant by the name of William Steinkamp, as "one above the lavatory cleaner". He would roar at Ryder, "Take this fucking crap and bring it back so I can mix it!" Fresh sound editors kept being assigned to the picture and pre-mixes were done with no reference to David's requirements. Win Ryder felt he would have a nervous breakdown unless the log jam was broken.

It was the first time a British production had been brought to Culver City. "They thought we Limeys were bloody idiots," recalled Win Ryder. "When David finally understood the problem, his anger was roused. He got Merle Chamberlain, the executive in charge of completion, out of bed at three in the morning and said, 'You'd better ring New York, because I'm not going to make the date.'"[6]

David caused enough panic for Steinkamp to be fired, after which the log jam cleared and the sound side proceeded more smoothly.[7]

One department at the studio filled David with pride - Metrocolor, the MGM laboratory.

"They were fabulous. I'd never known anything like it. I remember talking to a timer [grader] and I said, 'Look, I'd like to talk to you about this scene. You see, what happens is that the girl has done this...'

"And he said, 'Yes, I know.'

"'Well, how do you know?'

"'I've read the script.'

"Now, for a timer to have read the script - I'd never imagined such a thing and I'd never met it in England. His name was Dick Martin."[8]

David was also delighted when the technicians at Metrocolor told him that they particularly liked his pictures because sitting there, seeing his rushes silent, they always knew what was happening.

David had not been in contact with Maurice Jarre since LAWRENCE. Jarre was in Los Angeles and suddenly received a summons to the set in Madrid. Although MGM's music director wondered if Jarre was the right person for ZHIVAGO - "Mr Lean, if I may say so, Jarre is very good for

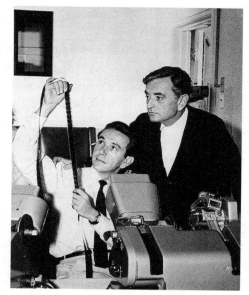

David with Norman Savage in their cutting-room at MGM.

open spaces and sand. We have better composers here in Hollywood for Russia and snow"[9] - Jarre flew over to watch some of the filming and to gain an idea of the Russian atmosphere.

"I take a lot of trouble over music," said David, "and I like to write where we're going to have music into the script. On several films, I've actually selected a piece of music, put it on tape and played it on the set when they're acting the scene. This is a hangover from the silent days when the star of the picture was asked what he or she wanted played during an emotional scene. It helps a lot, it relieves the tension, and I did the same with ZHIVAGO. I listened to a lot of Russian music, and I got every balalaika sound track I could put my hands on and I found a tune which I considered just lovely. I said to Maurice Jarre, 'Look, I know how hurtful it must be for you, but I want to use this as the theme tune.'"

To Jarre's relief, MGM could not trace the copyright to the tune and were worried about using it. "At any moment somebody could pop up and say 'I wrote it' and they could be sued," said David. "So we had to give up that piece of music. I then said to Maurice, 'It's over to you.'

"He had four or five goes at it and on the last one I said, 'Yes, that's it' and that's the one that went out and made such a lot of money for him. Mind you, I think he had to pay half the Lara theme to one of his wives in a divorce settlement. These ladies are quite clever, you know."[10]

Discussions about music, and the recording itself, cut swathes through David's editing schedule. According to David, they only just made it - with the last reel flying to the Capitol Theatre, New York, on the day of the premiere, 22 December 1965.[11]

After the premiere showing, O'Brien and the MGM top brass held a dinner for David on the roof of the Americana Hotel.

"Around midnight a terrible hush descended on this dinner," said David. "I said to somebody, 'What's happened?' And they said, 'The newspapers have just come in.' Everybody was reading the reviews, which were terrible. One notice was worse than the next. They were the worst I'd ever had in my life. As they left the room, lots of people said, 'Well, David, I liked it. I thought it was a good movie. I don't understand them.'

"I felt absolutely sick at heart and ashamed. I thought the picture was rather good. I thought it worked. I couldn't believe it was as bad as they said it was. The notices were so awful I didn't want to go out to a restaurant because I thought people would be staring at me and saying 'There's the chap that made that terrible film.' It's a wretched feeling.

"Next day I saw Bob O'Brien, because we were going off to Los Angeles for the premiere there. And he said, 'David, I think it's a good movie. I'm going to put another million dollars into it. I'm going to hold it in that theatre and I'm going to try and get some solid publicity.'

"For the first week that theatre was empty and MGM was paying to keep the film on. The second week it picked up a bit, the third week it picked up more and by the fourth week you couldn't get a seat. He relied on word of mouth. That was all due to Bob O'Brien. It was an enormous gamble on his part. And I wasn't cheated - that was because of Bob O'Brien again, I'm sure. ZHIVAGO made more money for me than all my other films put together."[12]

Despite David's memory of the bad reviews, the six daily film critics in New York were evenly divided and opinions ranged from the Kate Cameron in the *Daily News* ("One of the finest of our time") to Judith Crist in the *Herald-Tribune* ("ultimately tedious epic-type soap opera").

Crist, who had praised KWAI as "a flawless film," now wrote of "cardboard characters shuffled through a ridiculous plot." Most maddening to David would have been this comment: "David Lean is one of those rare directors who has proved himself not once but twice master of the spectacular, with THE BRIDGE ON THE RIVER KWAI and LAWRENCE OF ARABIA (both, it is worth noting, with Sam Spiegel as producer; Carlo Ponti, a spectacular-maker of a rather different batting average, let alone stripe, took over ZHIVAGO production chores)."[13]

When *Time* magazine came out, on 31 December, it went some way to rescuing the situation.

"The star of DOCTOR ZHIVAGO is director Lean himself, who has effectively captured on film the essence of Pasternak's belief that men are priceless as individuals, not as cogs in a superstate. Lean speaks for humanity in a language of unspeakably beautiful images. His sentimental ZHIVAGO is perhaps warm and rewarding entertainment rather than great art; yet it reaches that level of taste, perception and emotional fullness where a movie becomes a motion picture event."[14]

Then appeared the all-important *Life* magazine with a rave review from Richard Schickel: "It succeeds, in the last analysis, because of the perfection of visualisation by Lean [who] with careful, conscious artistry, has created the visual equivalent of Boris Pasternak's novel. He has received surprisingly harsh criticism from some reviewers, who apparently had hoped he would trump up some high adventure sequences like those that enlivened his two Academy Award winners. But Lean simply refuses to inflate his material for idle effect."[15]

MGM telephoned Robert Bolt in London and read him Schickel's review.

"How can *that* and Miss Crist's be both about the same article?" Bolt wrote to David. "The critics are simply bewildering. The same article can't be at one and the same time despicable and a near masterpiece. And it's not as though it were a difficult film, open to misunderstanding. It is as you say (and as we both said two years ago) the highbrows are more concerned to preserve the book as their own recondite property than honestly to appraise what we put on the screen. We'll get the same here, you know, and more so. Unless by then it's been learned here that the film's a smash with intelligent audiences there."[16]

As soon as Christmas and the New Year holidays were over, David and Norman Savage returned to Culver City and began re-editing some of the scenes.

"As we finished a reel," said David, "they'd ship it to New York and take out what was playing there. After five or six weeks, we got the orchestra back and the film was improved more than somewhat by my cutting and the new music."[17]

David also flew up to San Francisco, a city he had never visited before and which he liked more than any he had seen in America.

"The Premiere went off alright but the two notices not all that good - as usual! Then last Sunday out came an interview with Sam Spiegel about THE CHASE which opens today, with a lot about me. What a *sod* that man has turned out. He had met the critics a couple of weeks before and done a sort of benevolent uncle act about me. Words to the effect that I am great at detail but fail therefore in taking proper perspective of the whole. Then all about how he didn't send the rushes on KWAI and LAWRENCE but stayed in London 'studying' them. Obviously he's been doing this all over the place and it naturally has its effect in a subtle sort of way. But doesn't matter as business is booming all over and we are ahead of BEN-HUR with MGM delighted."[18]

Leila joined him in San Francisco and David was grateful to MGM, whose kid-glove treatment gave her "an enormous lift and feeling of importance." Conveniently, her friend Barbara Hutton, the Woolworth heiress, was living in the hotel next door.

On 23 April 1966, David flew to London to attend the British premiere. He then went to Paris to do foreign versions of ZHIVAGO and to meet Barbara again. Leila wanted to stay with a friend near Paris, but David vetoed that for fear she would come to his hotel.

"I was tempted for a moment but it would be too much of a cat and mouse. The fact is that now she feels confident of being Mrs D.L. she is doing her best to leave me free and unquestioned. Think I probably owe a lot of that to Kate [Hepburn] as she said she'd been very frank with her - and if she says frank she means frank."[19]

The London premiere, wrote David to Barbara, went exceptionally well. "Best audience yet - with (Anthony) Armstrong-Jones [now Lord Snowdon] coming into the theatre after the interval, leaving his wife [Princess Margaret] standing and rushing over to me in my seat saying, 'Must tell you we think it bloody marvellous.' Very nice.

"The notices were bloody awful except, of all things, *The Times* (John Russell Taylor) and the *Evening News* (Felix Barker). The *Standard* (Alexander Walker) started, 'When a director dies he becomes a photographer.' You can't get much crueler [sic] than that can you? Perhaps you can. Tynan ends his piece today with, 'An orchestra without a conductor.'"[20]

Behind the reference to Kenneth Tynan, the most celebrated critic of his generation, lay an incident in which David threw down a challenge to this much-feared intellectual.

"I remember going down to Wembley studios for an interview with Kenneth Tynan. He was very pleasant, and then suddenly turned. I said, 'Now, look, just stop it. I know what you're at. You're building up your name as one of these acid interviewers, and you're not doing it on me. Shall we stop now or go on?' And we went on.

"Tynan did a series of profiles, so-called, in the *Evening Standard*. He did Vivien Leigh, and that was pretty bad, and he did Laurence Olivier, which was really awful. It would be interesting to dig it out.

"He then asked to do a profile of me. I refused, citing the Olivier piece. His reply was 'I shall do it all the same and it will be much worse if you really do refuse to see me.' The piece was not written.

"When Larry started at the National Theatre he said, 'You know I think it would be better to have him inside pissing out than outside pissing in. Let's have him as literary adviser.'

"He was an exceptionally good journalist, no two ways about it, and wonderfully entertaining to read, but not when one was bringing out a new film or play. He did terrible things to a lot of people, and was completely ruthless about coming in late for a movie."

When Tynan arrived at the ZHIVAGO press show thirty-five minutes late, David broadcast this fact on ITV, adding, "He is no doubt now sitting down to pen a caustic review of the proceedings."

"Somebody reported this to him and he rang me up in a frenzy. I said, 'Look, Mr Tynan, do you blame me?' He said, 'You've misunderstood me completely. I was going first thing in the morning to see it from start to finish.'

"I said, 'I'm sorry, but I don't believe you.' When the fate of a film and the careers of actors and technicians depended on what a critic wrote, the least he could do was turn up on time. I was told that he did go - only because of me, obviously. It can be very frightening when these erudite people attack one. He was much cleverer than me. I doubt if he could have directed a movie, though."[21]

The reactions of those who had worked on the film were as divided as those of the critics.

"I thought visually it was lovely," said Andrew Mollo. "I'm a great admirer of John Box as a film designer. He's an amazingly talented man. Visually, I couldn't find fault with it. But there were the same problems that arise with all period films. You do have to make concessions to modernity, I feel sometimes that these detract. I don't think it was as dramatically tight as KWAI. Sheer romanticism isn't enough for me in a film. I know many people find it the great romantic experience of their lives. I'm proud to have worked on the film, but I don't think it's his best."

Mollo was bitterly disappointed to discover that he did not receive a screen credit. "And I felt I deserved one. I made quite a contribution to that film. In my opinion, it's a matter of leadership again. If you're not interested in your crew and you take their co-operation for granted, you don't think of things like that. You get a credit not because you've been particularly helpful, but because it's in your contract."[22]

Alec Guinness said: "It was romantically wonderful to look at and all that, but mind you I could never read the book, so I can't really discuss it. I tried to read the book but I was so bored by it. The script was kind of OK, but writing poems with frozen ink in fairy-tale palaces in the middle of God knows where I find pretty peculiar."[23]

"It is a *tremendously* good film," wrote Robert Bolt. "Anyone who doesn't like it condemns himself. It's moving, powerful, beautiful, serious, and continuously held my rapt attention. Peggy [Ramsay] and I sat like a pair of housemaids and ended with sodden handkerchiefs. What's more, although it is always simply told and therefore intelligible, it is not in any way vulgar. It is simpler than the novel, of course, but it isn't a trivialisation of the novel. I can't tell you how proud I am to be your lieutenant in the enterprise. I don't care what happens to the film (an easy claim since I'm sure it's going to make money). It's a fine piece of work and one which I'm going to draw comfort from for the rest of my life."[24]

After ZHIVAGO had opened in London, David went to Lydd where he put his car on an aircraft for the Continent.

"There was an AA man at the desk and he said, 'Oh, Mr Lean, how nice to meet you. I've always admired your films.' Then there was a dreadful pause and he said, 'Sir - what went wrong?'"[25]

The Oscars were presented on 18 April 1966 at the Civic Auditorium in Santa Monica. Although ZHIVAGO was nominated for ten awards, and won five, William Wyler telephoned David to warn him that he wasn't going to win this time, saying, "They never give it to you three times in a row."[26] Wyler was proved right; Robert Wise won the Best Director award for THE SOUND OF MUSIC.

"The worst moment," David wrote to Barbara, "was that immediately after me not getting the director's award (which everyone thought I would), I had to go up and receive Robert's [Bolt].[27] I think I did quite well as everyone - including strangers - came up afterwards and congratulated me on being such a wonderful loser etc! I don't quite know what I said but it must have been all right.

"I sent cables to the winners and one to Norman [Savage] saying I was sorry we had both muffed it but we'd try again. Today there's been a big swing of indignation from the movie people saying that no matter how good a piece of light entertainment SOUND OF MUSIC is, that it makes the Academy vote non-serious. I really don't mind at all and keep thinking of the sea in front of your house and how I said it put all this sort of thing into perspective."

Julie Christie won an Oscar as Best Actress, not for ZHIVAGO, for which she was not nominated, but for John Schlesinger's DARLING. David wrote, "Julie Christie's Oscar was very popular with a great roar of applause. Julie accepted for herself and was also practically bowled over by emotion."[28]

DOCTOR ZHIVAGO was to make a personal fortune for David. As a gesture of gratitude, he gave substantial sums to some of the technicians as soon as the film began to make money. Sandy Lean estimated he gave away a million dollars.[29] The film eventually grossed over $200 million worldwide and is still earning money from television and video sales.

"I must tell you," said David, "I think ZHIVAGO takes a bit of beating as a love story, and I could do it better now than I did then, but I'd have to have Julie and she's too old now, of course."[30]

CHAPTER THIRTY-SEVEN

INDIA AND THE PROCESSION OF LIFE

WITH ZHIVAGO completed and on release, Robert Bolt wrote to David in America to say that he was more and more attracted to the idea of making GANDHI.

"I see it, tentatively, in black and white (again), but that's a detail: but I think you could put something universal and visually terrible, beautiful and reassuring by turns onto the screen with it." [1]

Once again, David decided to abandon the project. His usual explanation for this - and the one he gave to me - was that he did not think that the script Bolt eventually produced did Gandhi justice. He always felt it was like making a picture about Christ (and by this time he may have been deterred by the disastrous failure of THE GREATEST STORY EVER TOLD).

On top of this, David's relationship with Bolt had been put under strain when Bolt blamed David for the break-up of his marriage, claiming he had been kept away from home for too long. Bolt had then forged another relationship, with Fred Zinnemann, which would soon result in A MAN FOR ALL SEASONS, winning Oscars for both of them. GANDHI was about to pass into new hands.

"Fred Zinnemann wants to do GANDHI with Robert Bolt but feels guilty and wants to know my reaction," wrote David to Barbara Cole. "They seem to have overlooked the film of the same subject which Richard Attenborough[2] is doing according to an interview I heard on the BBC." [3]

David told Zinnemann to go ahead, though nothing came of that project, either. However, India would shortly feature again in David's life and in a most dramatic way.

At Katharine Hepburn's instigation, George Cukor invited Leila to help him on a film he planned to make in India, NINE-TIGER MAN.[4] In order to make the contacts, Leila left for India in April 1966, and David decided to go with her, to make up for what she called her "ZHIVAGO widowhood".

On the plane, David read a review in *Time* of a book by Alan Moorehead, *The Fatal Impact*, about the baleful influence of naval explorers and missionaries in the South Seas. He bought a copy and was enthusiastic about what he read. He contacted his agent, Phil Kellogg, and asked him to let Moorehead know of his interest. Despite the rift, he also sent a copy to Bolt, who was equally fascinated by the material.

Suddenly, they dropped the idea. "We think it's asking for trouble in being too near another beautiful eyeful," David told Barbara.[5] But David would not forget Moorehead's book and a long and tumultuous sojourn in the South Pacific would ensue a decade later.

Albert Broccoli, who co-produced the James Bond films, gave David a book of South African history, an epic about the Boers called *Rags of Glory* by Stuart Cloete, which he considered for a time. "It might be a good moment to show such a thing - what these people did to get what they now want to hold. Just show it with no actual comments." wrote David to Barbara from New Delhi. "I have decided to take no notice of what the highbrows say and go ahead and do just what I want to do, even if they do say I can't do anything but epics. At any rate I'll make the best epics."[6]

David later changed his mind about Cloete's book. "Very good in an awful sort of way. Horrible revelations, to me, of white slave traffic and how they used to batter wretched girls into tartdom. Very shocking and I see exactly how Cubby Broccoli will make an enormous money-spinner out of it - but not with me."[7]

After three months in India, David left Leila and joined Barbara at the Richmond Hotel in Madrid. He had acquired land at Carboneros, near the "Aqaba" location of LAWRENCE. This was to be David and Barbara's new home. Eddie Fowlie built a house there and, later, opened a hotel next door. While Barbara coped with the building and the furnishing of the house, David flew to New York to meet Robert O'Brien, with whom he was now on very close terms. O'Brien disclosed the astonishing news that DOCTOR ZHIVAGO was expected to gross $52 million.[8] "He thinks I will make more money than Willy Wyler did on BEN-HUR - which was a sort of director's record."[9]

While in New York, David was surprised to find himself the centre of attention. Nobody seemed to remember the bad reviews for ZHIVAGO; they seemed aware only of its phenomenal success.

"I have a terrible embarrassment because all these American people think I'm in a special class of my own - and say so," David wrote to Barbara. "I get awfully hot around the collar and try to cope with their compliments - which they give me in a sort of factual way which I find even worse. I feel such an awful dud - as you well know - and I find it all very difficult. I even get it in the street. Walking up 5th Avenue yesterday a chap passes me and says, 'Thanks!' I thought I had heard wrong and turned back to see who said it only to be met with a great big friendly grin from a young chap passing in the opposite direction.

"The trouble is - and I don't know why I should find it a trouble - that I'm an interpreter. I wish I could be treated as such. I'm not an author and am not really creative. I'm like a horrible kind of journalist waiting for someone else to write the 'story.' I suppose that's why I feel a sort of fake - and I'm not really because I can, as it were, translate."[10]

In September 1966, David flew to the Far East for the start of a holiday-cum-promotional tour for ZHIVAGO.

"The flight from Hong Kong good," he wrote, "and to my great surprise we flew right over South Vietnam. No sign of war. A much bigger country than I realised, with huge tropical forests in which a million Americans could be swallowed up without notice. They can never win that war without making it a full-scale horror."[11]

From Hong Kong he went to Singapore and then to India, where O'Brien had asked him to talk to the Foreign Affairs people since the Russians, who had great influence in India at the time, were trying to have the film banned.[12]

Because the Indians did not wish to disturb their good relations with the Soviet Union, they decided to censor ZHIVAGO. David had always thought the Indian Censor Board the most backward in the world; had they not banned SUMMERTIME in its entirety?

O'Brien had given David authorisation to withdraw the film if he considered the cuts damaged the picture, and this he threatened to do. The cuts, he said, were politically motivated stupidities, "and making the twenty-three they wanted was like cutting out twenty-three pages from a novel." He argued them out of all but seven brief eliminations which added up to less than a minute.

At the same hotel in India as David was Alexander Trauner, the legendary art director who had designed the films of Marcel Carné and who had also worked on HOBSON'S CHOICE. Trauner was in India to scout locations for Cukor's NINE-TIGER MAN, the film on which Leila was also working.

David thought him very intelligent, though his love of precision made him a strain to be with, "like looking too long at a complicated crossword. But he's very kind and I like him in not too big doses."[13]

David decided to take Trauner on a tour of Old Delhi and called in at his favourite hotel, the Cecil. David's association with the Cecil came to an end when they forbade him to stay there with Leila before they were married.[14] He had become friendly with the elderly Mrs White, the younger sister of Miss Florence Hotz, the manageress. When David arrived with Trauner he learned that Mrs White, a lady of the Raj, had recently retired. He was also saddened to discover that the hotel was now used as a Catholic school and had gone somewhat to seed.

They moved down to Agra and Laurie's Hotel which, to David's relief, was unchanged; there were even some of the old bearers from the Cecil. A tall blonde girl of about twenty took David to his room. He asked after Mrs White.

"She's retired to South Africa," said the girl. "She's not at all well. She's nearly blind and her memory's gone. I'm sorry."

David felt a profound sense of loss. "It was as if a huge lump had fallen away from my life in a landslide. Poor old 'Mummy,' as I used to call her, her eyesight half gone - and her mind too."

The girl remarked that David's room was the one he had had when he was last at Laurie's; she had looked it up. David noted that the girl had a rather lovely classical face with fair hair and green eyes. He asked how long she had been doing the job.

"Three days."

"Did you know Mrs White?"

"She's my great-aunt - I'm what they call the Last of the Hotzes."

When David asked if she was going to take over the business, she said no, she was very unpopular because she preferred to go to an American or English university to attain a professorship.

"Seems silly to have taken two pages to tell you all that," David wrote to Barbara, "and I don't quite know why it affects me so much."

Going away and coming back had given the changes a more dramatic shape. Besides which, he was now able to see the last part of his life in the same dramatic way.

"I see the awful fool I have been, so that here I sit, alone in this room, thankful for the aloneness and knowing that tomorrow night I drive back to Delhi and the strain of this peculiar marriage of mine which I should never have entered into." [14]

The relationship with Leila was reaching the point where David felt it would be kinder to make a complete break. He began to have nightmares about her in which her softness had become venomous and she became a snake coiled about his neck.

The one thing Leila prided herself on was her musical talent, particularly her singing voice. As she sadly confided to a friend, "The psychiatrist says, 'You lose what you value most.' So I've lost my voice." This was something David could understand, and he was sorry for her. In a long letter to Barbara, David untangled his relationship with Leila.

"She has nothing to fall back on within herself. That's the real trouble. The loss of the singing voice is a minor tragedy. A real one with which I have sympathy - because the singing was all there was in life minus me - but the circus around it gets out of all proportion.

"She can't stand it here - and I understand her up to a point. She says she is now part of the west and only wants to come here for short visits to see the children. Also cannot understand why she can't be with me 'even in the same town.' Has no idea whatever about you or anyone else for that matter.

"We were with her doctor friend the other day and were having a conversation about this country. She suddenly started crying. Got in a terrible state. I have had tears in two restaurants which I can't help squirming at because everyone stares. Afterwards the doctor said he didn't understand and that it must be a pathological case. The next day she said how sorry she was and couldn't understand why she had cried. Then added, 'Perhaps there is something wrong with me somewhere.' Awfully sad, because that is the truth and she dimly sees it from time to time. She says she knows I don't love her but she can't help loving me. I want so much to be kind and the other day told her I thought perhaps I was being cruel in not making a break. She says, 'Then I have nothing to live for.' On other occasions she is more than maddening and I go almost up the wall with a sort of frustrated impatience.

"She can barely do this job [NINE-TIGER MAN], which God knows is pretty simple and consists of contacts with people she knows. I've spent nearly all my time in Delhi backing her up and visiting people with her.

"I am feeling very good because I have somehow developed an enormous selfishness which is hard to describe. I am no longer got down by it all - except at very odd nervous moments. Can't quite describe it but suppose I had to adopt some sort of attitude to save myself from an involvement which would have drowned me, too. I suppose I react badly because tears are a pointing finger to one's own guilt, so when they appear in public it makes it a public accusation of guilt. But I have thought to myself, 'I can't help these lack of feelings on my part. I haven't wilfully adopted them in any kind of spite. Therefore accept them as unfortunate and be as kind as you can - but protect yourself.'

"In some ways I surprise myself with my own terribly selfish nature. In the end as many ladies have said, I always save myself in a quite ruthless manner. Do you know, darling, I have got to a point where I am very nearly untouched (in any deep sense) by L's unhappiness? I don't know if this is very bad or if it's plain common sense - and I don't even worry about the answer. Enough."[15]

This new attitude had quite the wrong effect. Leila reverted to the state she had been in before the shock therapy, which David described as "complete disintegration, self-hate and hopelessness. Spending most of the day in bed with the blinds drawn, unable to sleep at night, pills by the dozen, doctor with various injections and a seeming desire to collapse completely. I know this is all to do with me going away again and that it's a subconscious blackmail."[16]

On 18 November 1966, David wrote what must have been the most difficult letter of his life. It had been a month since he had last written to Barbara. Now he had to explain what was happening to Leila, and to himself:

"I think I must have come pretty close to breaking point. It was like flying in dense cloud for days at a time. As she got worse and worse I didn't know much more where life was leading or what I was doing in it. I couldn't do anything but sit and read *Time* or order endless teas with L in the next room trying to sleep in her darkened room, tottering on the verge of a breakdown. I didn't even want to go out and didn't have any strength or perhaps I should say self-respect. I kept thinking of how I never really helped you with the house except in odd spurts which I never followed through; of the way I always wanted to drive the car because, looking back, I felt that was the one thing I could do."

David's account intercut between Leila's mental illness, and the pre-production on the Cukor picture. Trauner decided he had to see the erotic temples at Khajuraho, a place which David adored. Since he had lost interest in doing anything, David tried to slide out of the arrangement, but Trauner said the trip would do him good. Even Leila agreed with him. They hired a car and tried to make the whole trip from Delhi in one day. But fate acted like the script-writer in a melodrama; as they reached Agra the car's air conditioning broke down and the driver suggested they stayed at Laurie's while he arranged for a replacement vehicle to be sent from Delhi.

David and Trauner retraced their steps to the Taj Mahal and David telephoned Sandra - Sandy - Hotz, the girl at the hotel. They had lunch and then spent the evening together, "all of us talking and talking," wrote David. "I found her like a bright light shining through the mist of my lifelessness. Optimistic and quick-minded in a way which made me spark back in a way I'd almost despaired of ever being again. I wasn't carrying on a flirtation, I think you know me to that extent. It was just a sudden return of life - and I didn't even feel the danger ahead."[17]

David and Trauner reached Khajuraho the next day and then returned to the Imperial Hotel, New Delhi, where David was met by Leila's sister, Maya, and her husband, who told him that Leila was in a very bad way and threatening suicide.

"It was like a ghastly psychological game being played in order to hang on to me - because the date for my return was near. I don't remember much about that week because as you know I black out these terrible things in an effort to escape the effects of their memory."[18]

The decision was made to take Leila to Bombay. Her depression worsened and a French friend took her to Paris for a new "sleeping cure". David decided he would do everything to avoid joining her in Paris; instead he sent a cheque to cover her medical and other expenses. Rather than stay in Delhi or leave for Europe, David decided to return to Laurie's Hotel.

"This is when it all started," said David, saying everything and nothing.

When David had previously written to Barbara about Sandy, he was going to add that she was just the sort of girl he would love to have had as a daughter.

"I didn't because I thought it would sound rather ridiculous and sentimental. But it was true. Not quite twenty-one. Born in India with dual nationality of Swiss and English. An English accent with traces of American from an American missionary school up in the hills where she had her education. Trau and I asked her how she knew so much about modern trends in painting, music and the young people of the rest of the world. She said she had read and read, listened to the radio and gramophone records and had more or less taught herself in this direction."[19]

By now he had to face breaking the news to Barbara. In one of the most recent letters, he had closed by saying, "You have been simply wonderful to me over these last months. I know how difficult it must have been for you. I don't really understand your selflessness - being a very selfish person myself - but don't think I don't appreciate your sweet human understanding. You often make me feel very humble. I'm so glad we came together after the hashes I have made. I might not love and appreciate you as I do."[20]

He came to the conclusion that the only thing he could do was to tell Barbara the truth.

"I have fallen in love with a young girl. In my bloody arrogance, I used to say I could never understand such a thing, that I was immune, above the common crowd. I feel almost as if I don't understand anything any more. It's a sort of final fall from my too arrogant pride...

"I don't know, dearest, if this is the best or the cruelest [sic] letter I could write to you. I have spent several days over it... You're the best friend I've ever had in my life. You've taken me as I am and never given me a single hurt. There must be a better way to treat you than this letter - but I don't know one. I keep thinking of Pasternak because for the first time I've come up against what almost amounts to a game carefully laid out by some sort of fate... so it seems to me. I took Leila away on this trip, not wanting it at all. I wasn't looking for anything. I only wanted to get back to you. I came here to Agra almost as an escape - thinking I'd never come back again. I almost fought not to come back again, but did so as a favour to Trau and only stayed here because a car breaks down. Almost as if this whole trip was planned, to lead me back here into this situation. Perhaps I'm making an effort to make fate and not me responsible for this hurt to you. I suppose I am trying to tell you I have schemed nothing. I cannot even find guilt within me, for my only guilt is in the hurt to you...

"To use Pasternak again, I am not at war with you and I pray to God you won't be at war with me... Forgive, if you can, this terrible mess."[21]

Barbara replied with a letter which, according to Sandy, was astonishingly magnanimous, saying in effect that it was a fantastic situation, "which it was," said Sandy "and although she was desperately sorry, she wished us both well."[22]

"If it hadn't been for the coincidence of meeting me," Sandy added, "Barbara would have been the best wife in the world for him. She loved him, she supported him. And because they were in the business together, she understood. She accepted that the film work always came first."[23]

"I think the reason David had so many women," said Barbara, "was that he had passionate likings for things and then wanted a new thing to inspire him. And I know that one of the things that went wrong with David and his women was that after a time they failed to attract him sexually. I know that happened with me. What happens is that he meets someone else who does excite him sexually, and he needed this sexual excitement to work. As soon as he started a new affair he used to go off with his camera and take pictures. I think he was generous and caring so long as people interested him. When they ceased to interest him, well then, of course, he dropped them.

"I met David again in Madrid, and I managed not to cry, and we had a drink together. I asked him if he was happy with Sandy, and he said 'Yes, but you've got no right to ask me that question.' I said. 'I think I have every right.' I didn't see him again.

"But I was not embittered. There were stories - one that I went off with the Rolls-Royce and he had to chase me across Europe to get it back. I was a most surprised person to hear that. I count myself a fortunate woman. Very few women have such a fantastic experience with such a lovely man. I love David to this day and I think I am the one who loved him most."[24]

At her house in Carboneros, Barbara showed me a silver ring which David had given her. Inside were the initials D and B together with the words "Tubeiq, Jafr, Rumm", a souvenir of the most romantic assignment any continuity girl could ever have had.

David remained at Agra for five more months. His stay at Laurie's was marked by increasing tension since his relationship was becoming a source of general gossip and Sandy's parents, not unexpectedly, were shocked by the liaison between their daughter and a married man more than twice her age.

In March 1967, David and Sandy left India and flew to Switzerland, so that David could have business meetings with his bank. The cool air of Switzerland was a delicious contrast to the emotional and physical heat of India.

Early in April they flew to Madrid, where David had stored his beloved Silver Cloud.

"He wanted to show me the locations of DOCTOR ZHIVAGO," Sandy recalled. "David longed to be back in Spain, but the idea of running into Barbara put him in a funk, so instead of moving back to the hotel where he'd lived during the making of ZHIVAGO we holed up in this odd little furnished apartment. And whenever we went out to a restaurant he hid behind his menu."[25]

Four months later they began a long meandering trip through the south of France to Italy. They arrived in Rome in July.

Thus began David's relationship with Sandra Hotz.

"I was born in Gujrat, Pakistan, in 1946," said Sandy. "I was twenty years old

Sandy Hotz photographed by David Lean.

when I met David and he was fifty-seven. I knew almost nothing about him. He'd made a film called THE BRIDGE ON THE RIVER KWAI, I knew that. But by coincidence I'd just seen LAWRENCE OF ARABIA in the cinema in Agra. And I'd been overwhelmed by it. You know how you walk out onto the street into the daylight, and it's all less real than the screen? That was the first time it happened to me. Those astonishing images, they stayed with me for days.

"Beyond that, David was simply this extraordinarily charming man who came to the hotel with Alexander Trauner and had to stay the night because their car broke down.

"A week later he came back with his suitcase and his camera, and he stayed for five months. My parents were very upset, in fact they stopped speaking to me. In the end, we waited till my twenty-first birthday in February, and four days later we left. That was how it began, the next twenty years of my life.

"He was still married to Leila for twelve of those years because he was in terror of her threats of suicide and her general helplessness, and he was still fond of her and terribly guilt-ridden. You know, I think most of David's involvements with women were held together by guilt. Just when another man would have divorced them, he married them.

"Actually, to have taken Leila on in the first place was a sort of madness. Because even when he met her, she was in the midst of a breakdown. When she went to Ceylon on KWAI, she was seriously depressive. I remember him talking about the horror of having her there on the set, sitting slumped in a chair with her hands hanging between her knees and her head down, not looking at anyone. She'd already been in and out of mental hospitals, and she'd had electro-shock therapy, before they'd even met.

"But he told me that he met her on the rebound. I wonder, by the way, if it wasn't true of most of his relationships. Ann Todd had been this cold, tight, pulled-together film star, very tough, very contentious. After her, Leila seemed wonderfully Oriental, so soft and fragile and exotic. He told me she used to sit at his feet and light his cigarettes for him, that kind of thing. Then he takes her on this trip around the world, a way of making up to her for his lack of attention during ZHIVAGO. And it's a disaster. She ends up lying in a hotel bedroom in Delhi with the curtains drawn all day, and he goes out and wanders about on his own. And then he meets me and I'm a rebound from Leila.

"David had very few friends. He had this great loneliness. I think it stemmed from his reluctance to trust people. The people he trusted were Brian Goodberry, for instance, the hall porter at the Berkeley Hotel, or Maggie Unsworth and Eddie Fowlie, who were truly devoted to him. But finally, I think, it was a comfort to David to feel that they were in *his* camp. Because he very much had the feeling that you were either for him or against him. With David, there was no middle ground."[26]

CHAPTER THIRTY-EIGHT

A LITTLE GEM

RYAN'S DAUGHTER I

"WE were in Naples," said Sandy Lean, "because David wanted to show me Capri. We'd only been there a couple of days when this script arrived from Robert Bolt, and it was *Madame Bovary*.

"In his covering note, Robert said, 'Even if you don't want to do it, please write and tell me what you think.' David sat down and read it with a terrible concentration, taking copious notes, and when he was finished he wrote Robert a ten-page letter explaining why he couldn't possibly make the film.

"When he got to the end of the letter, he tore it up and began another, much longer letter, saying that given changes - major changes - he would be willing, in fact excited, to work on it.

"I remember sitting in that gloomy mausoleum of a suite at the Excelsior, with its high ceilings and chandeliers, for almost a month while David slaved over his portable typewriter, never going out, eating in the hotel dining room night after night. In the end, I found a bookstore but the selection of English books was very small. I remember reading *Gargantua and Pantagruel* over a weekend, not something I would willingly do again. So I never got to Capri. But that was the beginning of RYAN'S DAUGHTER."[1]

David proposed not merely changes to *Madame Bovary*; he wanted to devise an entirely original story, using Gustave Flaubert's classic novel as the source. Once his letter had been dispatched to England, David and Sandy returned to the Hotel Parco dei Principi in Rome.

Although Bolt mourned the loss of his beloved *Bovary*, he was impressed by David's analysis. "Here was an amazing thing," he said. "You would give him something like *Bovary* to read and he would deliver so fine and far-reaching a critique of it and he didn't think anything of his ability to do that."[2]

Bolt had written the script for Sarah Miles, to whom he was now married. David's wedding gift to them had been a Lamborghini sports car. Bolt had already suggested the idea of casting Sarah Miles to David when he was in Agra. This raised David's eyebrows - he did not think a writer should impose an actress on a director. "I can imagine what rehearsals would be like," he complained to Barbara Cole, "with Miss M knowing more about Robert's intentions than anyone else, including me."[3]

David wryly recalled Bolt's dismissal of Sarah Miles when they were casting ZHIVAGO, and was at a loss to know how to tackle the matter, and since he never did, she took the lead somewhat by default.

Once they began working together, however, at the Hotel Parco dei Principi in Rome, David's respect increased. "I thought, 'Well, why not?' I like Sarah, she's a damn good actress and I think she was jolly good in the film."[4]

Because the emotions of Flaubert's novel were universal, they were anxious to remove the story from its French background. After considering Sicily, the Shetlands and Sardinia, they decided on two alternatives, India and Ireland. While David thought it would have been fun to do an Indian version, in which the glamorous hero would have been a young Maharajah, his recent problems inclined him towards Ireland, which he had never visited.

"We chose Ireland," he said, "because we had to have an outside conflict, something over the hill to come in and affect the characters. The 1916 Irish situation suited us rather well, and in fact the Troubles come into the village and go out again."[5]

As David described the story to Freddie Young: "A girl marries her teacher who, because he taught her about great men and their music and their romantic imaginings, she believes he has similar heroic greatness. He has none at all; he is just a simple, good man and no match for her romantic youthful imaginings. Their bed does not set off a Brock's Benefit in the way she supposed it would.

"In this situation comes a real life hero from the Western Front; a shell-shocked VC, a strange, withdrawn man who thinks that life is over. Explosion of Brock's Benefit. Running parallel is an IRA sub plot of gun-running of German arms. Gun-running partly thwarted by storm and totally arrested by VC. But what no one knows is that in the aftermath of the storm floats a box of dynamite at the feet of the cuckold husband who knows about his wife's infidelity... The VC is blown up and there is a happy ending which should be really touching."[6]

While working on the epics, David affected to despise "those beastly little British films," complaining that the "wretched" BRIEF ENCOUNTER kept being revived and spoken about. In his new project he saw an ideal opportunity to show those critics who said he couldn't do anything on a reasonable scale that he still had the talent that had once produced BRIEF ENCOUNTER.

A colleague was dining with Norman Savage when David joined them and described his next project as "a little gem" which he intended to shoot in ten weeks. "Seeing the total disbelief in our eyes, he told us very firmly that he'd done it in the past and was going to show everyone that he could do it again."[7]

He repeated this to director Richard Lester when he visited Sandy and David at the Parco dei Principi. "He had a lot of the top floor. And the hotel is right next to the zoo. You'd wake up in the night and hear these bloodcurdling sounds and I thought to myself, is this his life? A couple of these green-and-white tiled

The energy of David Lean - at 76, one of the oldest directors ever to have made a feature film - astonished those who worked with him on A PASSAGE TO INDIA. 30. They expected a quieter, more contemplative character, as portrayed above, in Kashmir. 31. David with Peggy Ashcroft and Judy Davis. Photographs by Frank Connor.

32. *Lean succeeded in making* A PASSAGE TO INDIA *look more expensive than it was: the arrival at the Marabar Caves. Photograph by Ken Bray.*

David's fascination with photography, which began when he was given a box camera as a child, never left him. He took carefully composed pictures wherever he went. The only time he left his camera behind was when he was directing. 33. Tahiti. 34. India.

THE LAWBREAKERS. *After an interlude with Maurice Fowler, Tony Pratt took over the art department, and his designs capture the spectacular qualities David wanted the film to have.* 35. *In the breadfruit garden, under the gaze of the fertility god, the Bounty sailors - after months at sea - surrender to the lures of Tahiti. David wanted to suggest a parallel between their behaviour and that of the generation watching the film, many of whom would have surrendered to the spell of drugs. Tony Pratt designed this for the VistaVision ratio, which was then under serious consideration.* 36. *In an early draft, Christian and Bligh survey the East Coast collier Bethia, stripped down to the bare hull after purchase by the Admiralty at Deptford. She will emerge, at a cost to the taxpayer of £64,000, as The Bounty.*

37. *THE LAWBREAKERS. Bligh steps aboard his new command, The Bounty, at Deptford. 38. The Bounty vainly tries to batter her way around the Horn, but is forced to "go about" and retrace her steps on the longer route to Tahiti via the Cape of Good Hope.*

39 and 40. Reminiscent of the Dickens films are these designs by John Box for the discovery of Hirsch in the Custom House in NOSTROMO. *The complicated background has been simplified in the second version, and the monochrome effect makes the splash of colour all the more startling.*

rooms on the top floor of the hotel, after all he's achieved? There was the Zenith Intercontinental radio on the shelf, people arriving bringing Walls Pork Sausages, which I assume he got the kitchen staff to cook for him, and these terrible roaring lions at three in the morning. I thought, dear God, what an awful way to live."[8]

Fate obligingly placed some crucial people in Rome that summer. John Mills was there with his wife, Mary Hayley Bell, to make a film.

"We went over to the hotel that they were working in," said Mills. "We opened the door and we literally couldn't see either David or Robert Bolt, it was so thick with cigarette smoke. David said, 'We've got another scene to write, get a breath of air with Mary and come back.' I went back in and said, 'That's a nice pool outside.' 'What pool?' said David. The pool was a few yards from the window and they'd been there for months.

"Anyway, we had dinner and Mary said, 'You know, you made four pictures with Johnny and they were all smashers. Why haven't you offered him any more?'

"He said, 'Well, there's been nothing for him.'

"Mary said, 'What about RYAN'S DAUGHTER?'

"'No, nothing in that, unfortunately. Pity.'

"He went rather quiet and towards the end of the dinner he suddenly said, 'Well, I've got an idea, Nob. Do you think you could play a village idiot?'

"I said, 'Well, it's type casting, isn't it?'"[9]

When MGM questioned the casting of Mills as Michael, the village idiot, David organised a test with Charlie Parker, the make-up man. "Look," said David, "You've heard of The Hunchback of Notre Dame, haven't you? Make him look like that, make him look ridiculous. Bloody great nose, one eye, head five times the size." He showed the test to MGM executives who thought it was perfect.

"I think a part of his brilliance was the fact that once he decided I was going to do it, he very much left me alone," said Mills. "So I said to Charlie, 'I want the smallest make-up you can manage that looks great.' After a week we came up with what you finally saw. Sixteen minutes in the chair in the morning - that's all it took. I stuck on the end of a nose, he made some teeth to stick on mine with a twisted mouth with a bit of plastic. Shaved the eyebrows. I had this ghastly haircut with strands hanging down over a bald pate and that was it. The marvellous thing was I didn't feel made up."[10]

Also in Rome was another old friend, Anthony Havelock-Allan, who was producing Franco Zeffirelli's ROMEO AND JULIET with John Brabourne. David showed him the script so far. At that stage the project was called MICHAEL'S DAY (so Mills had the title role), later to be called COMING OF AGE; it was Havelock-

Allan who suggested RYAN'S DAUGHTER. David asked him if he would be the producer.

"It was sweet of him to ask me," said Havelock-Allan. "I was really a passenger. I knew our budget was nine million, which was very big in those days. If you're going to spend that kind of money, you can't do it without big names. I don't think Metro would have gone for it. They would let David do almost anything, but without a big name they could hang above the canopy, I don't think it would ever have got off the ground."[11]

David and Bolt created a character called Charles O'Shaughnessy, the village teacher, who was based on Flaubert's Charles Bovary. In the novel, this character was a doctor; in the film, a schoolmaster. Bolt had been a teacher and there are traces of David's teacher, Scott Goddard, in the new character. After Paul Scofield turned it down, Bolt was convinced that either George C. Scott or Robert Mitchum would be at least as good.

"Particularly Mitchum. Warmer and gentler than Scott, and I know he can do an Irish voice. Was speaking to someone who'd seen him with his wife on telly, doing an interview, and was amazed by the dignity and mildness of the actor as against his swaggering tough-guy image. And if he's half what Roy Stevens says he is to work with [Stevens had been with him on Zinnemann's THE SUNDOWNERS] he'd be easy to have about the place, whereas Scott is, so they say, a bit neurotic and given to sudden violent tempers."[12]

David considered this the most interesting piece of casting. "He's a jolly good, dull character. Now, if you get a jolly good, dull actor and play him in that part, the audience will be yawning their heads off in five minutes flat. So we decided to cast against type. I remember thinking of all the times that Hitchcock cast against type - the most amiable people playing absolutely horrible villains. We went through what we thought were really good actors and ended up with Mitchum. The only trouble was that he didn't like me. So we had a bit of a fracas every now and again, but I still think he was damn good.

"He was a sort of gifted tearaway. I remember seeing him years ago in a film called BUILD MY GALLOWS HIGH. A wonderful performance, I thought, in those days. On top of which he was without doubt a star."[13]

"I thought Mitchum absolutely wrong for the part," said Havelock-Allan. "I said that I didn't think any audience in the world would believe that Mitchum would stand by for one second and allow somebody else to pinch his girl from under his nose without making a protest. He's not that kind of man. You're playing him as a weak man and he quite patently isn't. He's a tough guy, a reactor, and a violent one at that. And I don't believe in him in his nightdress looking out of the window and watching his wife go to meet a man whom he'd half kill in real life.

"I wanted to play Gregory Peck who is Irish and, curiously enough, a cousin

Some of the character of Scott Goddard went into the schoolmaster played by Robert Mitchum. (Photograph by Ken Bray)

of a man who was the civil engineer for the little town in Ireland where we shot the film.[14]   But he walked away from it the moment he heard negotiations had started with Mitchum.

"David never hit it off with Mitchum, almost from the word go. We had to stop shooting twice because David got so upset he couldn't go on.

"The clash with Mitchum came over the fact that Mitchum has a cynical disregard for films. It's a job, that's all [Mitchum was paid $870,000]. For David it's an art, and indeed it is. It happened right away at the beginning, when David wanted to see how he was going to dress.

"He said, 'Hey, what is this? I've never done a dress parade in my life before. Give me the clothes and I'll put them on. I'm not gonna march up and down like a tailor's dummy.'

"Later on, people came to see him and he used to bring them in to rushes without asking David or me. There were times when we had three weeks with no work at all, and then he'd give parties in his house and never ask David or myself. Mitchum's whole attitude was, 'I'll do what I have to do,' while David's was, 'We're making something marvellous, something very important.'"[15]

Mitchum did his best not to make the film. He wanted to retire and had no intention of playing a part in which he had to work every day. Bolt called him and said they had found several gaps in the schedule that would allow him a ten-day holiday. Mitchum then found another reason to decline the part, telling Bolt that he planned to commit suicide. Bolt was startled, and said, "Well, if you would just do this wretched little film of ours and then do yourself in, I'd be happy to stand the expenses of your burial."[16]   Mitchum laughed and said he would do the part.

"The day they shot the scenes of Mitchum wandering along the beach in his nightshirt," said Tony Lawson, assistant editor, "after he's found out about the affair, they didn't start shooting until well into the afternoon, by which time the rumour on the set was that he was on to his second bottle of vodka. In the rushes you could tell he was absolutely paralytic. I remember when we were cutting we had to look for the bits where he looked like he wasn't about to topple over."[17]

David was no stranger to actors working through a haze of alcohol, but Mitchum lacked the warmth of Robert Newton. He complained ceaselessly - with some justification, because he never got his holiday. If he was not in his caravan, Mitchum was generally to be found leading the revelry in Ashe's pub.

"Theirs was the funniest relationship," said Sarah Miles. "Our three caravans were all in a row. I was pig in the middle, and also the go-between, because the mountain would not go to Mohammed, nor would Mohammed go to the mountain. So there was me trailing notes between these two great men.

"'Tell Robert he's got to wear his shirt out of his trousers.'

"'Tell David I'm fucking not going to wear my shirt out.'

"'Tell him he's got to!'

"So I'm running back and forth, holding the collar of a shirt!"[18]

Mitchum frequently got a rise out of David by laughing and joking with the crew until "Action" was called, and then doing it perfectly first time. "Lean would be almost tearful," said Mitchum, "and he'd say, 'Bob, that was spot on! I can't tell you how lovely it was, that was simply marvellous.' And instead of saying 'Thank you,' I'd ask, 'You don't think it was a little too Jewish?' It would just drive him crazy the way I kept putting him on."[19]

Cameraman Bob Huke said that because Mitchum was so laid back, David was convinced he gave not a damn about his work.

"Yet Mitchum - a fine actor - *was* involved, despite all the signs to the contrary. David felt that he wasn't getting the performance out of him that he wanted - he had to come over as an introverted failure. And then we shot a scene in the cottage where Sarah Miles was knitting and Mitchum was putting leaves in a book. I remember at rushes, Mitchum was extraordinarily good. You suddenly realised that this man was out of his depth with this woman. After rushes, David said quietly to Roy Stevens, 'That's what I wanted. Now we have it - that is the character I want from Bob. We're going to retake everything so far.'

"Roy said, 'But we've been shooting for weeks!'

"David said, 'I want to retake it because I know now how to get it and I know exactly what he's going to give me.'

"Roy said, 'What am I going to tell MGM?'

"And David said, 'Tell them I didn't like his hat.'"[20]

Mitchum, who had as little understanding of David's attitude as David had of his, came up with a memorable wisecrack:

"Working for David Lean is like being made to build the Taj Mahal out of toothpicks."[21]

However much Mitchum sent up the experience, in hindsight a part of him appreciated the experience that David subjected him to.

"I knew that he was an eccentric," he told radio journalist Erwin Frankel, "but I didn't know in which direction that manifested itself. The rewarding part of it was that I finally met somebody who considered the medium as important as I did. Only he suffered it. I rather insulate myself against suffering. But David suffers and I suffered along with him. And I think he's rather shy in the revelation of his own feelings."[22]

David offered the part of Father Collins to Alec Guinness, explaining that it had been written for him. "You must balance it against your other offers in the normal way," David wrote. "I assure you that I won't take umbrage. I say this because I've still got a guilty feeling about Yevgraf and have a nasty feeling you would never have done it but for our rather special relationship."

Whatever he thought of the part, David asked Guinness for his views on the project. "It's a different kind of film for me," wrote David, "I think it's exciting. Very ugly, some of it. Much more intimate and private than the last two films. It's an original story so I'm more lost than usual on how good or bad it is - but it's a movie alright."[23]

Guinness was not impressed by the few pages he was sent of the script. A convert to Catholicism, Guinness objected to the technical inaccuracies concerning the priest who wore the soutane, the long black robe, whereas one of the grievances of the Irish at the time was that their priests were not allowed to wear it; they had to wear ordinary suits. Guinness also took exception to the scenes in which the priest and the village idiot go out fishing for lobsters in heavy weather.

"You don't go out in twelve-foot waves in a coracle," he said. "But David hated reality as such - this is where we fell apart so often. He wanted it romanticised all the time."[24]

Guinness listed all the points he feared were wrong. David said "Thank you for being so frank" and gave the part to Trevor Howard.

"I remember at the beginning, poor old dear, he went for me. He said, 'You passed me up for all sorts of wonderful parts since we worked together.' What was he thinking of? I suppose it was KWAI and various other things, and he said, 'I just don't know how you could forget old friends like that.'

"Well, I couldn't say, 'I didn't think you were very good.'

"Then we started the film. On the first day, before we'd shot a foot, he came up to me and said, 'You know I'm only doing this because of you.'

"I said, 'Oh, come on, why? It's a bloody good part.'

"'It's a terrible part.'

"'I said, 'Look Trevor, you and I had better take a walk.' We took a walk, and I explained what Robert and I had been aiming at with Father Collins. He was a man with tunnel vision. He knows the difference between right and wrong - no two ways about it - and he began to see. In fact, he caught on very fast to the fact that it was really a wonderful part and he'd somehow missed out on one side of it. Actors often do this; they just miss out on something.

"After all those years, he had developed a kind of screen weight. Robert and I used to judge the results of an actor playing a part by marks out of a hundred. A hundred was what in our wildest dreams we thought of as the best performance that could be given at the time we finished it. We used to think ourselves jolly lucky if an actor gave you seventy. At the end of RYAN'S DAUGHTER we both agreed that out of a hundred we'd give Trevor five more - a hundred and five - because it was better than we imagined it."[25]

David had asked Marlon Brando to play the role of the British officer, Randolph Doryan, and he had accepted. The character, written specifically for Brando, was a war hero who had won the Victoria Cross and had lost an arm. In case Brando dropped out, Bolt recommended Richard Burton, then Richard Harris and finally, Peter O'Toole.

"The trouble is that Peter is such a victim always, these days," Bolt wrote to David. "There ought to be something about Randolph which makes us admire him but also makes us secretly relieved that Rosy and he are parted. He ought to have some quite forbidding darkness in him. Brando and Burton could both do that. Peter might appear sullen or posturing."[26]

Brando used to call David about his attempts to make the loss of an arm look real. "He said, a bit self-consciously, 'I've got it so I look absolutely fine from the front and absolutely fine from the back, but I can't turn from the front to the back and make it look convincing. Can you think of anything else?'"

David and Bolt decided to drop the missing arm and gave Doryan a bad leg instead. Then Brando dropped out - the film he was making in Colombia, QUEIMADA, had run into problems. David had to look for someone else to play Doryan.

"John Box was making his first film as a producer. He always longed to be a producer, I don't really know why, but he did. He was making THE LOOKING GLASS WAR by John le Carré and he wanted me to see one of the actors."[27]

"I wanted him to see Anthony Hopkins," said Box, "because I thought he should play the school teacher. But David ignored Hopkins and fixed on Christopher Jones."[28]

Sarah Miles, who was present at the screening, recalled that Christopher

Jones spoke with a convincing Polish accent. "We all agreed that he had a lot of presence and a great Polish accent. David didn't really go into it any further. He said, 'Hire the bugger!' It turned out that he was American. Another actor had post-synchronised his voice."[29]

"Nobody seemed to think anything of him," said David, "but he had this extraordinary quality of screen personality which I always find terribly difficult to describe or even to understand. I went for him, out of the blue."[30]

David knew nothing of the background of the young man he had taken on. Christopher Jones came from Tennessee. He was separated from his parents when he was three and placed in a boys' home in Memphis. His mother died of TB and he only occasionally saw his father. He ran away when he was sixteen and joined the army, which he loathed. He went AWOL, determined to get to New York, and wound up in jail. But at least the jail was on Governor's Island - he was so close to New York he felt he could reach through the bars and grab it.

From the moment he had seen James Dean on the screen in REBEL WITHOUT A CAUSE he knew he wanted to be an actor and he had quick success in the New York theatre, being cast with James Farantino in *The Night of the Iguana*. It was during the run of this play that he met Susan, the daughter of Lee Strasberg, of Actors' Studio fame, and they embarked on a fiery 1960s-style romance, replete with drug-taking. They were married for only six months before divorce proceedings began, but they produced a daughter who had a hole in her heart. This caused despair for Christopher, who felt drugs might have played a part.

He had been accepted as an observer at the Actors' Studio, where Paula Strasberg thought he had the same animal magnetism as James Dean or Brando. He was given the lead in a television series and starred in such pictures as WILD IN THE STREETS and A BRIEF SEASON.

As a bonus for A BRIEF SEASON, producer Dino de Laurentiis gave him a Ferrari; it was, however, made a condition that he would not bring it to Ireland. "One night," said Anthony Havelock-Allan, "we came out of the hotel and there it was. And that very night he turned it over on the edge of a cliff with himself inside it, unhurt. Thereafter he would spend long periods in his hotel room. He was a very tortured young man. He had absolutely no idea what an English cavalry regiment was. So he was in a fog and didn't get gentle treatment."[31]

Christopher Jones had been trained along totally different lines to those of David Lean. "I don't know why he cast me," said Jones. "He tried to change me totally. He wanted certain things which I didn't think right, but he was David Lean so I went along with it. I didn't have any input hardly. He just wanted it a certain way and I did it that way. I resisted him once - in the bar scene. He just kept shooting it over and over again and getting madder and madder at me. I didn't know what he was looking for. Then about four days later, when the rushes came back, he came over and said 'I'm sorry. I couldn't see it from where I was.' I was doing it for the camera. I mean, I wasn't doing a performance for the crew there. I guess I was working small, you know what I'm saying?"[32]

"David thought he did a superb job on that scene where he collapses in the pub," said Roy Stevens. "He said 'You really did that well.' Certain parts of it, Lean was very pleased with him."

In order to help Jones with his accent, Havelock-Allan arranged for a tape-recording to be made of the voice of the son of a friend, Lord Dunraven, who lived nearby. Jones was given the tape six weeks before shooting but, in Havelock-Allan's opinion, it was not so much his voice with which he had such difficulty, it was his acting.

"It wasn't that he was a bad actor; he was an actor who needed to be told exactly how to do it. He needed a director who loved actors, had infinite patience and could see where the boy was going wrong. David didn't like to have to struggle to do that, so it was rather unfortunate. When he knew David was getting impatient with him, the boy got scared and his nerve went."[33]

Freddie Young didn't think Jones could act at all. "In the scene where Gerald Sim is leaving and going to France, and Christopher Jones is taking his place, Sim is saying, 'You've seen the war, you're a hero.' Implying how scared he was to be going to France the following day. Jones sat there with no expression on his face at all. He didn't say anything, he didn't do anything.

"David said, 'Cut. For Christ's sake, Christopher, what's the matter with you?'

"Jones said, 'I'm not an actor.' There was a very stony silence. David took me to one side and said, 'For God's sake, throw his face in shadow.' So I left him with just a little light in his eyes, and David worked it out so that Gerald Sim did all the acting.

"We did the same thing when he was waiting for the bus. I threw him into backlight and I had a brute with a tiny slit shining into his eyes. It made him interesting, whereas the chap couldn't act at all."[34]

"We did our best," said David, "and I think he came through rather well. I don't know how responsive he was to my direction. I don't know how much he understood what I was talking about, quite honestly. Strange young man, but quite a character on screen. He looked jolly good. He was certainly watched, you know. I think that's one of the great requirements of a screen actor. Some people can walk across the screen and you'd hardly think a shadow had gone across."[35]

When the script was finished in Rome, Bolt could look dispassionately at his work. He likened it to a big jet, which took off and kept climbing right up to the point where Charles wears his nightshirt on the beach. "I would claim that at that point we have - taking the audience with us - high tragedy," he wrote. "I believe in the sufferings of all three characters... can see them as credible human beings caught in a vice, can see no happy outcome - in short, tragedy."

At this point the jet levelled off and maintained its altitude for a further fifteen pages, when Rosy came back and found her husband missing. On page 178 the landing flaps come cranking down and the plane drops, juddering. Charles's discovery of the affair, and Rosy's response, caused Bolt to lose interest, and he no longer cared whether they stayed together or not. "Randolph's death does not shock Rosy or Charles into any kind of nobility; they leave the village behaving well, no more.

"At the eleventh hour, Father Collins suggests a happy marriage may yet lie before them. I'm not terribly interested. Only Randolph remained true to his promise and met the disastrous end which I feel was really in store for all three if they really were what they pretended to be in the first three-quarters of the film. In short I feel that this happy ending is horribly sad."

David and Bolt had argued many times over the ending and Bolt had lost. "When you tell me that Rosy is not Joan of Arc, that Sarah is not Greta Garbo and I am not writing *Tristan and Yseult* I am not only silenced, I am undermined within... I feel I am about to make an ass of myself and of Sarah and that I am asking you to risk your enormous reputation on some highly personal spree of my own. But that is mere weakness of character; more important is the fact that working as we do, so closely, it is literally impossible for me to write at all unless we are agreed as to general direction. It becomes pure strain and unhappiness for us both. Certainly, it would be out of the question for me to write an end with both men dead and the girl tarred and feathered in the teeth of your conviction that it ought not to be so. And probably out of the question for you to direct it even if I could under those circumstances write it... I am in fear that we are going to disappoint the audience by failing to deliver in the last quarter what we promised in the first three. And I do not believe that a catastrophic ending such as I want would disappoint them." Alas, Bolt decided against letting David see this letter.[36]

Despite Bolt's serious reservations about the final sections of the script, MGM was delighted with it and expected a smash hit. Russell Thacher, MGM's executive story editor, wrote to say they were all immensely enthusiastic, "Impressed with the beauty of the writing and the strength and power of its themes." But privately, Robert O'Brien and Thacher felt that Randolph's suicide was a let-down.

Thacher suggested that the IRA man, Tim O'Leary, come upon Randolph just before his suicide and instead of taking his life because he was a "burnt out case" he might sacrifice it to thwart O'Leary's escape. "In short, still commit suicide, but with more of a purpose."[37]

Bolt wrote a thoughtful letter back, arguing that the arbitrary death was what he and David wanted.

"The First World War was not (we wish to say) an act of mass murder, but something worse: a world-wide suicide pact. The best soldiers were destroyed by it, either literally or internally. It is a fact that men on leave from the Western Front, though they longed for leave when they were in the trenches, longed for the trenches when they were on leave because 'Home' had no reality for them. They had been rendered unfit for ordinary life, and the black reality of the Front pulled at them - not because they enjoyed the Front, of course, but because it was an ultimate sort of experience, so vivid and intense that their homes by comparison seemed papery and ghostlike.

"Randolph is meant to be a paradigm of this condition. He hates and fears the Front but is sexually and emotionally incapacitated away from it. His affair with Rosy is a last blaze of natural life, which he and she and, we hope, the audience understand to be foredoomed."[38]

"Robert and I were in a mess on RYAN'S DAUGHTER," said David. "We had the basic triangle situation. As Robert explained, 'We're in trouble, because as soon as the glamorous young man appears you know she's going to fall in love with him, and he with her. We've got to think of an idea to get them together quickly because otherwise the audience will be ahead of us and that would be fatal. How do we do it?'

"We thought they could bump into each other in the street, they could see each other in the pub. All as flat and predictable as ABCD.

"You go to bed absolutely obsessed with these things and that's why it's impossible to be married to a film director. I woke up at four in the morning. When you're half awake, your mind's freer for fantasy. I thought of Johnny Mills in the pub. I thought if he started kicking his leg against the bar, let the shell-shocked war hero be sitting there and become fascinated by this banging, and you see it having a nasty effect on him. And then I thought to myself, this could easily end in him having the shakes. The use of sound effects turns into a bombardment on sound only and the noise gets louder and louder and the officer stands up, looking most peculiar and wild. Johnny bolts from the bar, slamming the door behind him, and the officer turns round.

"Then I thought we'll cut from a close-up of him to a shell going off in the sky - it seemed terribly daring - and then the music starting and in the end he dives under a table, puts his hand over his ears and Sarah, seeing him in distress, finds herself kneeling beside him, cradling his head in her arms... Just the fact that someone else is holding him brings him out of his shell-shocked state. He looks up, they look into each other's eyes and kiss, and we're home. I leaped out of bed, grabbing hold of an envelope and a pencil, terrified of it evaporating like a dream."

The next morning Sandy told David that she thought this idea was too outrageous. However, Bolt liked it and it went into the script. "And it worked a treat. It's one of the sequences I'm most pleased with because it gets straight to the point, it's miles ahead of the audience, it's very dramatic and I can only say it works. I think it's one of the best scenes I've done."[39]

David and Bolt were convinced that 70mm was essential for RYAN'S DAUGHTER. Although the blow-up from 35mm to 70mm on ZHIVAGO had been adequate, neither felt it could compare with the real thing. And after the muddle on ZHIVAGO, David did not want to risk losing Freddie Young again. From Rome he sent him a long letter praising his work, and trying to express what he wanted this new film to achieve. As he used to say on location, "Freddie, I want you to make this absolutely marvellous. I don't know how to explain, but I think it's just got to wring the emotions of the people. Just make it marvellous, Freddie!"

David felt that one of the reasons the critics had attacked ZHIVAGO was the very perfection of its style. Movie photography, David believed, had reached a plateau of perfection and had gone stale. No one was doing anything to push it up the next hill, because they didn't think there was one. The critics were saying, "We are bored by your facile expertise. We have seen it all before."

David said that he worked much more closely with the writers and the actors than he did with Freddie, and this had to change. He itemised the ideas Freddie had contributed to the other films, and how bold and effective they had been. In each case they were daring and not realistic. He would now be more dependent on him than ever.

"I have a horrid feeling, which I only half admit to myself, that I'm coasting along on my past experience. I think we've got just about the finest collection of technicians in the business and it makes me hopping mad to sit back and watch a bunch of untrained, semi-talented whiz-kids stealing all the thunder with a half-arsed ill-lit amateur night at the Classic."

David acknowledged a flaw in both of them; they were roaring romantics, who were in love with beauty. "Nothing wrong with that, but we tend to beautify everything we touch - even the ugly - and that amounts to what my dictionary calls 'a picturesque falsehood'. I hope this Irish picture is going to give us both a chance to show our hand. It contains hard down-to-earth squalor and the full glamorous romantic. The beauty of working with you is that you have such great technical skill that you can do any style that is called for. Some of it should have the voluptuous quality of an erotic thought."

David was already aware of the danger posed by the erratic Irish weather. "Most of the beach stuff should look extremely beautiful in contrast to the almost sordid village and its mostly second-rate inhabitants. Small rooms and

David has a lonely lunch on the beach location. (Photograph by Ken Danvers)

claustrophobia set against great stretches of wild coastline which, on the screen, could perhaps have the grandeur of Wadi Rumm. The terrible worry is sun with scudding cloud shadows on white sand. I've had mad moments when I've wondered if we could do some of the sun stuff in some place like the Channel Islands or Portugal. A lot can be shot in dull weather of course but not knowing Ireland I can see the rain coming down for days on end."[40]

"When David called me," said Eddie Fowlie, "I was in Spain. He said, 'I'm going to make a little gem, so don't do anything else.' A little later he called me and said, 'I don't think it's going to be a little gem, it might be a bit bigger. Come to Rome.'"

Fowlie was sent to scout locations. Because of worries about the Irish weather, he tried Spain and Wales and then took the ferry to Ireland with the Rolls-Royce which David had given him. On a map of Ireland he had marked Dingle in County Kerry.

"When I'm setting off on a recce, I read the script and I always think, 'What is it that only God can do? The rest we can do.' I figured that the most difficult thing to find would be this long, beautiful beach with a cliff that falls to the sand and a place on top with heather where they can have their picnic and a cave underneath. You don't often find cliffs that fall to sand: they fall to water. So I went up and down the coast - and I came back to Dingle, looked at the map again, walked across two or three farms and I came to this place. It made my hair stand on end. I'm on top of where they have their picnic, with a cave below and it's a great beach - it's actually where the IRA landed their weapons during the Troubles."[41]

Because John Box was involved with THE LOOKING GLASS WAR, David had to find another production designer. He finally chose Irish-born Stephen Grimes, who had been art director on LAWRENCE. Grimes was a bluff, redbearded giant, who spoke in a whisper, which led to many misunderstandings.

The decision was made to build a complete village, rather than use an existing one. "In nearly every country in the world," said David, "if you put up a movie camera you will have crowds of people. Working on a specially built street, although everyone laughs, is miles cheaper and if you have a place which is entirely under your control you're in clover and you can work very fast."[42]

The site chosen was near Dunquin, at the end of the Dingle Peninsula. Starting in November 1968, two hundred Irish workers constructed forty full-scale structures, built of traditional material - slate, thatch and granite - hauled from several quarries. They worked in appalling conditions through the winter months - gale force winds, rain and sleet and bitter cold. Many of the buildings were equipped with electricity and plumbing and properly fitted interiors. The set, completed by March 1969, was called Kirrary and, while it stood, it was the westernmost village in Europe.

County Kerry was one of the poorest parts of Europe. When the film company arrived - and stayed for a year - local people found out what it was like to live in a goldmining town. They rented their cottages and moved into caravans and retired on the proceeds. One bed and breakfast landlady, who renamed her house Kirrary in honour of the film, said "They were great days in Dingle when there were beautiful film stars walking up and down the street when I went to put out my bins."

It is estimated that MGM spent a million pounds in Kerry. "To a great extent," wrote Micheal de Mordha, "the money was used to the benefit of Dingle and its environs at a period when times were poor."[43]

"The film accelerated emigration," said *The Observer*. "Local boys put on the payroll at what seemed like fabulous wages wouldn't return to farming. The film's release roughly coincided with the collapse of herring fishing and forced local people to move from a closed community to a tourist economy catering for visitors who wanted to see where the film had been made. Outsiders came to stay. By the end of the Eighties, sixty percent of Dingle's population came from elsewhere."[44]

One of the first scenes to be shot, in March 1969, was at Coumeenoole Cove, known for its dangerous currents. The camera was set up for a long shot of John Mills and Trevor Howard rowing out to sea in a curragh. Two experienced rowers doubling for them returned to say it was too dangerous.

"To my horror," said crew member Fred Lane, "David said, 'Right, let's have a try with the actors.'"[45]

Trevor Howard was late, so John Mills did some dummy runs on his own. At last Howard arrived.

"All right," said David, angrily, "get in the bloody boat. We'll just make it."[46]

The actors were on safety ropes, but there was still as much danger as discomfort. "The wind blew up and I don't think we should have done the shot," said John Mills. "It was very dangerous, and they had frogmen in with ropes, in case anything happened. And it did happen. I was coasting on a wave and the boat turned upside down and hit me on the back of the head. The funny thing was that I had taken the teeth out. I had a feeling that something might happen. I thought, 'I don't want to swallow the bloody things and choke to death.' So I took them out and put them in my pocket.

"Now, Charlie Parker used to watch the filming through a telescope. He saw the boat spill over, and I was knocked out and drifting out to sea when I was grabbed by two frogmen and carried unconscious up the beach. Somebody rushed over to Charlie, who was sitting on a rock, and said, 'Charlie, have you seen what's happened to Johnny?'

"Charlie said, 'Never mind about Johnny. Where are my fucking teeth?'"[47]

"We ran some terrible risks on that film," said David, "because those Atlantic rollers have immense force in them. Johnny did get a horrible great mouthful of water and got bashed on the head on top of it, but he was very game, a real professional."[48]

Mills, who was rushed to hospital in case he had suffered concussion, was found to be in excellent shape and was on the set the next day.

Although Dingle was near wild and remote country, there were forty-nine bars to choose from. Nevertheless, the thought of being marooned there for six months was anathema to many of the actors and technicians. Little did they realise that the six-month schedule would be doubled.

"It's a terrible trap, Ireland," said Anthony Havelock-Allan. "It can be the dullest place in the world and there is nothing to do but drink. All the actors had long periods of not working but they couldn't go away because if the sun shone they were needed.[49]

"Some of the locations were down twenty-five miles of narrow Irish roads. We were like Barnum and Bailey's circus.[50] We never got anywhere much before half past nine, even if we started at eight. And time and time again we'd start shooting sunshine scenes and by midday it would cloud over. By one it was raining - or conversely, we'd go out to shoot rain scenes, having been told there would be rain, and the rain would clear and the skies would be blue. Day after day would go by. To get a minute and a half of screen time was simply miraculous. We never went into a studio. The whole thing was done on location - every scene."[51]

David hated this circus and frequently wished there was a simpler way to make the film. It was a monstrous technical jigsaw coping with the weather and the logistics. But the main problem remained one of morale. If you isolate a group of actors and technicians in a small location, you soon have material enough for a dozen novels. When two of David's players embarked on an affair he was outraged.

"We spent a year in Ireland and poor David had such miserable luck," said Sarah Miles. "Once we did half a scene and I remember waiting in my caravan for three solid weeks before there was enough sun to finish the other half of the scene.

"For one year we were either waiting for the sun or the rain or whatever it was we needed, and when the right weather would finally hit we'd do as many as thirty scenes [set-ups] in one day to make up lost time. Then another two weeks of shooting went down the drain because the laboratories ripped the film in half. The technical problems were endless. I thought I'd go bonkers before it was over." 52

During the ceaseless bad weather - when there was nothing on the exposure meter except the maker's name - the unit was able to use the practical interiors of the village as cover sets. But they had so many weeks of rain that they were running out of interiors and still hadn't got the exteriors they needed. And summer - or what passed for it - was almost over.

The unit was regularly visited by journalists on trips organised by MGM's publicity department. When Alexander Walker of the *Evening Standard* requested an interview with David in Ireland, he was turned down. Walker had written a devastating dismissal of DOCTOR ZHIVAGO - "When a director dies he becomes a photographer" - and received the reply, "Since the director is supposed to be deceased he will not be able to see you."

But *American Cinematographer* editor Herb Lightman was able to visit Dingle and observe some of the filming.

"I get a graphic demonstration of the horrendous matching problems when they are shooting inside the pub. This set had large windows opening onto the village street. When they start the sequence there is a pea-soup mist outside that blocks out all detail. Then the weather clears suddenly and there is blazing sunlight outside... In another hour, the skies go leaden, the wind begins to howl and rain beats down on the roof. While Freddie copes with the exterior balance, the soundman supervises covering the roof with felt and rubber mats to deaden the pounding of the rain."

Lightman noticed that Lean and Young appeared to jog everywhere - "up and down vast stretches of beach, selecting camera angles. Their vitality is absolutely incredible, very much like that which teenagers are supposed to have. Freddie, in his red hat and socks, seems to be in eight places at once, personally checking out every detail relating to the camera.

"The rapport between director and cinematographer is a lovely thing to behold - two highly individualized cinema craftsmen functioning as a single creative entity. One can finally begin to understand how LAWRENCE and ZHIVAGO came into being." [53]

David submitted to implacable pressure. In order to use Robert Mitchum and Sarah Miles, who had other commitments, it had been necessary to rush into production - to cast hastily, and even to forego an essential support for David's confidence, the shooting script, which contained a wealth of detail about camera angles, sound effects and lighting.

"We had the script that he supervised with Robert, but we didn't have a shooting script," said Anthony Havelock-Allan. "Before we started I said, 'We are forty minutes too long.' David cut out thirty minutes from the script - and it all went back in again."

The inevitable result was that the twenty-six-week schedule which had been presented to MGM soon proved inadequate and, as the picture soared over its nine million-dollar budget, certain executives at MGM began to lose their faith in David Lean.

Admittedly, MGM was in serious difficulties. In October 1968, an attempt to dislodge Robert O'Brien as President had begun. In January 1969, the company announced a loss of $2.5 million. O'Brien was ill and in his absence Louis F. "Bo" Polk Jr, a thirty-eight-year-old executive from the cereal industry with no film experience whatever, was elected President. By July, MGM's losses were running at $14 million.

A Las Vegas hotel operator and corporate raider called Kirk Kerkorian had set his sights on the vulnerable MGM and set about buying up all the shares. By August 1969, after spending an estimated $100 million, Kerkorian owned a controlling interest. In October, he placed James T. Aubrey - known as "The Smiling Cobra" - in charge as the new President and Chief Executive Officer.

At once, a ruthless economy drive began with the wholesale firing of studio personnel, and the sale of Freddie Young's old workplace, the MGM studio at Borehamwood, and ended with the public auction of MGM's props and costumes. Aubrey's ruthlessness resulted a year later in a net profit of one million dollars.

The spirit of the day seemed resolutely opposed to the kind of film David was making. EASY RIDER, a film made on a budget of $400,000 and aimed at the youth market, appeared in 1969 and was a stupendous hit, earning $16 million for Columbia. Aubrey calculated ruefully that he could make twenty of these little pictures for what he was paying for RYAN'S DAUGHTER.

One of the rumours that persist in the industry is that Fred Zinnemann's film of André Malraux's *Man's Fate* was cancelled by MGM at the last minute because David's film had gone so heavily over budget.

"There were so many contributory causes," said Zinnemann. "I'm quite certain that RYAN'S DAUGHTER didn't help because it was over budget, very much so, and was probably one of the reasons why MGM was getting into great problems. Which resulted in O'Brien having to resign and that's when our friend Kerkorian came in. But to say RYAN was the cause is an oversimplification. It was one cause, probably a minor one. Even without it, we would have ended up that way because the management felt [MAN'S FATE] was too pink a subject politically and would never make its money back. They were in bad shape, and they had to get rid of some of the pictures which were not promising commercially and we were one of them. I would not like to say that David had very much to do with that disaster." [54]

Aubrey placed a limit of two million dollars on all future projects. "Clearly, at those numbers," wrote Peter Bart in his chronicle of MGM's demise, "the days of the DOCTOR ZHIVAGOs were over." [55]

To try to ensure those days *were* over, Aubrey flew to Ireland to meet David. Fortunately, David's agent from William Morris, Philip Kellogg, was in Dublin at the same time. Aubrey issued an order: "No agents" and David responded, "No meeting." Aubrey lost round one, and Kellogg attended. Aubrey explained the studio's financial situation and asked David to slash his budget.

"Even as Aubrey shook hands to leave," wrote Peter Bart, "he sensed his mission had failed." So much for round two. Aubrey lost round three, a few months later, when he dispatched Herbert Solow, a considerably more amiable character, with a coterie of minions, to ask David to economise.

"We were going well over schedule, well over budget," said associate producer Roy Stevens, "so all the MGM top brass jumped on their private 707 and flew over to Ireland. A whole planeload came over to rap David's knuckles. They certainly cleaned me out; how could I allow this to go so over budget, so over schedule?

"I said, 'Don't talk to me, the director's on the set. He's the man, because if the seagulls and the weather and the clouds aren't right he doesn't shoot. You can bawl the skin off me and fire me if you like, but it isn't going to make any difference.'

"I'd primed David on the radio that they were coming, so he was ready. He said, 'Okay, cut. Everybody go for tea.' And he sat in a chair. And they all sat, so polite and so fawning it made me almost sick listening to them. He just sat there, and finally one of them said, 'David, look, shouldn't you be getting on?'

'David said, 'No, I'll sit and answer all the questions you like. If it is important enough for you to fly all the way from America to see me, I'll abandon shooting until such time as you're completely happy.' They were gone the next morning. But they came with the idea of getting the stick out and seeing the film finished in a few weeks."[56]

Eddie Fowlie, searching for a bluebell wood for one of the film's love scenes, was directed to the Kenmare Estate which was owned by an allegedly flint-hearted Englishwoman. He won her permission, he insists, largely by accepting a Scotch at nine in the morning.

David had succeeded in capturing several spectacular establishing shots of the wood, carpeted with bluebells, and of the lovers riding their horses through them. Six horses were shown to David and he chose two. Phyllis Crocker, in charge of continuity, objected to them and was overruled.

"We filmed three scenes," said stills photographer Ken Bray, "and were ready to do a close shot when the continuity lady protested once more. 'You cannot have a close-up,' she said, 'because Sarah Miles's horse is a stallion.' Panic broke out, because in an earlier scene Ryan [Rosy's father, played by Leo McKern] had given his daughter a mare. David called on Charlie Parker, the make-up artist, and he went to work on the horse with camera tape and grease paint and performed a sex-change in thirty minutes."[57]

This scene was shot on a Sunday which upset the local population, so a priest said mass before work began. But after that Sunday, the weather turned slate grey and David was unable to continue the sequence until September. He then got as far as the start of the love scene, when Rosy and Randolph dismount and Randolph begins to undo the buttons of her dress. The general reaction was one of relief and delight at the beauty of the rushes. Freddie Young had used his lights so skilfully that no audience would notice the change in the seasons.

Robert Bolt, though, was not as impressed with the woodland scenes as everyone else. "They are beautiful certainly but, perhaps because they are artificially lit, they are beautiful in a distinctly theatrical manner and look to my eye more like an unusually good Stratford production of *Midsummer Night's Dream* than the rest of the film, where the quality of light is so natural, the sense of wind and cloud and weather so true as to be almost palpable. Moreover, though I am not a naturalist, the woods in those rushes have a distinctly Autumnal flavour to them, something dark and opulent and damp, rich and fruity rather than lyrical and budding. And we are in the last week of September now."[58]

Bolt thought David had four options: to stick to the script and hope for good weather; to come back the following Spring; to take Sarah and Christopher Jones to woods in Italy or even New Zealand; or to rewrite the love scene in a location less dependent on the weather.

Bolt proceeded to stress the last alternative, writing a sequence in which the lovers meet at an old tower, which is spooky, ruined and ominous, a strange place for love-making. Rosy enters the dark place and Randolph follows her.

The roof has gone, disclosing blue sky framed in nodding white convolvulus, the stonework warmed in the bright sunshine. A curtain of honeysuckle cascades above them, red and golden bracken makes a bed for them...

Bolt thought this was an improvement on the woodland sequence because it told the audience something about Rosy. A decision was needed at once, and although Bolt recalls David liking the new version, he clearly preferred the original.

Suddenly it was December. The leaves had fallen and the ceaseless rain had turned the wood into a sea of mud. The prospect of waiting another four or five months to complete the sequence alarmed David. He turned to Eddie Fowlie.

"David asked, 'How are we going to finish this sequence, Eddie?'

"'The only place I know is in New Zealand.'

"'Oh well, we'll just have to go to New Zealand.'

"'I'll build it here, David.'

"'Don't be silly.'

"Anyway," said Fowlie, "I rented a dance hall in another village [Murreigh] and prepared the floor. I put down soil and I put down thick hair felt and tarted it all out with watercress and grass seed and put some heat and humidity in it and started to grow it. And I dug up all roots and things out of the forest and sent them over to Waterford into a cold store for a couple of weeks and then into a hot house and they started to grow. I had a lovely forest in there - I got butterflies from a farm at Romsey, and I had a net curtain over the door."[59]

One night, Eddie drove David a different way home, stopped in front of the dance hall, drew aside the net curtain and switched on the light. David was so astounded and grateful that he instructed Anthony Havelock-Allan to make out a substantial cheque to Eddie.

"Stephen Grimes put in a cyclorama right the way round," said Freddie Young, "and it was warm in there, with a lot of brutes lighting it, the foliage was growing luxuriantly, the trees kept perfectly well. And we had birds in there, twittering in the trees. We shot in there probably for a week. As a final symbolic touch, Eddie had kept some dandelion heads and at the climactic moment, the seeds were gently wafted by a blow dryer across the pool."[60]

The symbolism was not a substitute for the love scene itself. Bolt had written it so that the lovers were naked, and while David intended to shoot them discreetly, to include only their heads and shoulders, there would be no doubt what was happening. Then Bolt insisted on a brief flash of Rosy's breasts.

This gave David some soul-searching; his love stories were famous for their restraint and he did not approve of the new permissiveness that was affecting the cinema.

"Robert told me he saw a play in which the leading actress suddenly bared a breast. The whole audience gasped and he said you could have dragged a dead camel across the stage and no one would have seen it. If you are telling a story you've got to be careful of shocking an audience because if it's pure shock they are going to forget the character - they are going to become self-conscious and the story will go down the drain. You won't be able to tell anything for the next ten minutes."[61]

The love scene had to convey eroticism to audiences who were growing accustomed to nudity. Sarah Miles had no inhibitions as far as the nude scene was concerned. What no one had foreseen was that Christopher Jones would suddenly be seized by an attack of histrionic impotence.

"This made it difficult," said Sarah Miles, "because Rosy's first real climax was meant to be the most important moment of her life."[62]

The actor was well aware that Sarah Miles couldn't stand him, he knew he was a grave disappointment to David, and he refused to do the love scene.

"Now come on," said David. "You've signed for it. Don't embarrass me or Sarah any longer."[63]

"So Chris said, with Sarah there, 'David, she doesn't do anything to me'" said John Mills. "He was getting his own back. He'd had a really rough ride."[64]

"Looking back on it,"said David, "it was hysterically funny. Christopher Jones had to touch Sarah Miles's breast. Well, he didn't like her and he didn't like her breast and so she got cross, he got cross. I had to behave like some awful schoolmaster, saying, 'Now, look, you two. You've both got to pull yourselves together. It doesn't matter what you think of each other...'

"Christopher said, 'I don't want to touch her.'

"I said, 'Well, now, look, stop being stupid. That's just what you're going to do and you're going to enjoy it.' Terribly funny."[65]

Sarah Miles thought she had explained Jones's attitude when, in her book *Serves Me Right*, she revealed that he was in a state of shock over the Sharon Tate murder. Jones admitted that he had been upset by this - he knew Sharon Tate from England - but that was not the reason.

"Like David said, Sarah and I didn't get on too well. Also, I was going with Olivia Hussey [who had played Juliet in Zeffirelli's ROMEO AND JULIET]. We were going to get married and we didn't get married, and hell hath no fury like a woman scorned. And my ex-wife Susie was coming over. And we were in Ireland for a year, right, and he would not let us leave. I suppose he was trying to get us in the mood, like on LAWRENCE OF ARABIA in the desert or something. But London was only, what, an hour and a half away? Have you ever spent a year in Ireland? And I'd just come from Rome - boy!

"But you know, I loved Lean, and he liked me and we got along great most of the time. Just a few times it was head-to-head. But I totally respected him. A brilliant director. The best there was."[66]

CHAPTER THIRTY-NINE

THE SEVENTH WAVE

RYAN'S DAUGHTER STORM SEQUENCE

ROBERT Bolt had written a storm sequence into the story of RYAN'S DAUGHTER. And not just a storm; this was to be a meteorological convulsion on a Biblical scale. As Father Collins says, gazing at the fuming clouds above, "You'd think they were announcing the coming of Christ."

Cameraman Bob Huke had come out in January 1969, three months before the main unit, to try to capture a storm. He and David shot in a number of storms, but none of them reached the ferocity necessary for the story.

When Freddie Young arrived in March, a storm sequence was staged on a beach near Dingle, where the rough seas were augmented by fire hoses and wind machines aimed directly at the shivering actors. When he saw the rushes, David felt the footage was still too tame; he wanted the kind of storm Robert Flaherty had captured in MAN OF ARAN. David even went to Aran and found more weather than even Dingle endured.

Eddie Fowlie was sent in search of storm country. He found it at the Bridges of Ross, near Ennis in County Clare. It wasn't too far from Dingle, so they could carry on shooting and await an encouraging forecast.

"I should think the storm sequence took four or five months to do," said Freddie Young. "Because when you got a storm warning, it was about two hours from Dingle and you'd get there early in the morning, set up the camera and by the time you're ready to shoot the storm would fade away and you'd go back and get on with something else." [1]

"It was very hard working in those conditions," said David. "The storms came in sort of gusts. You would see a huge black cloud approaching a few miles away. It was rather like a cold version of the desert with those dust storms that used to come at us. As they approached, you put your head down, covered your face and you could hear the sand rattling against your headgear. In Ireland, as the blackness comes it turns to rain and within seconds the rain turns to hail. We used to look at each other with the blood running down our cheeks.

"I remember one scene and you can see it in the film, but you don't realise what it is - it's a river pouring over a cliff and being blown back by the force of the wind. Fantastic. I like that sort of thing. That's why I call myself a boy scout, and it's all to do with Major Charles Gilson from the *Boys' Own Paper*." [2]

"We were all in wet suits," said Freddie Young, who grew a beard to protect his face from the driving rain. "The camera was chained to a rock and it was as much as you could do to hold on to the tripod and crouch against the wind."[3]

How do you prevent the rain and hail driving straight at the lens, obscuring all the action? A lens hood would be useless, as the wind often drives the rain horizontally, and umbrellas would be swept away, like Rosy's in the opening sequence. This is one reason why storms in films are nearly always artificially created. David's passion to shoot a real storm might have been defeated were it not for a brilliant idea. And here I have come upon an embarrassing conflict of memory. This is what David told me:

"When I was on IN WHICH WE SERVE I was amazed by the windscreen - in a car, you call it a windscreen, in a ship I'm not sure what you call it. It's a round piece of glass which revolves, driven by an electric motor. And I thought, 'My God, we could adapt this for a camera.' And we got Panavision to build it. We used to put it up in front of the camera lens, turn on the switch and gradually this piece of glass would turn faster and faster. On the first exciting occasion, we turned the camera on and I took a bucket of water and threw it at the lens, which was covered with this revolving glass. And within a second it was clear. I should think you could chuck a bucket of milk and you would only see a white flash. It would clear immediately. And now Panavision have taken it over and you can go out and hire this piece of apparatus."[4]

Leo McKern took great punishment on RYAN'S DAUGHTER.

Freddie Young hotly disputed David's claim. "I did that with the camera mechanic, Nobby Godden. We got a ship's Clear Screen and adapted it to the camera and put a plastic bag around it and Gottschalk [of Panavision] produced one after we'd done ours. It had never been done before. This was the first time a Clear Screen had ever been used. It was a very simple idea. It's just having the thought, like the long-focus lens for the mirage."[5]

Roy Stevens still has one of the two Clear Screens, or Rain Deflectors. "It was totally Freddie's idea," he said, "and the camera mechanic set it up. The glass revolves at 2,000 rpm and they'd set up the camera so the lens was close to the centre. Freddie said, 'No, you have to set it right at the bottom, or the top or the side - it has to be on the outer edge, that's where you're going to get the speed.' And it worked perfectly. Because it was something quite personal to me, I bought them at the end of the picture. One was destroyed at a fire at Twickenham, and other one is at home. Not that it's any use to anyone, it's just a souvenir."[6]

David was not usually one to claim credit for the ideas of others, but towards the end of his life, as he gave more and more interviews, so he simplified his stories; the number of characters grew smaller and smaller until he predominated, apparently responsible for every aspect of his pictures.

The confusion over the Clear Screen was indicative of a greater confusion over the whole sequence. For it was obvious to everyone that the storm would have to be shot by a second unit. It was a sequence requiring endless days of waiting, endless hours of mercilessly hard work, and endless rolls of film. It was against all sensible practice of commercial film-making for the director to involve himself in such a sequence. A storm, like a chariot race, could take longer to shoot than an entire feature film.

David's dislike of second units appeared to have diminished somewhat, for he had agreed to his old colleague Charles Frend, who had directed THE CRUEL SEA, coming to Dingle.

"I liked Charles Frend very much," said David. "He had hit a bad patch in his career and I said, 'Come and help me with some second unit.' He did a lot of the raft shots, but was not involved in the storm."[7]

It is true that Charles Frend was not involved in the storm, but why was David so anxious to make the point? Frend was not in the best of health, and according to Roy Stevens he was also "exceedingly old". (He was a year younger than David.) But this had nothing to do with it and David's fear of second units was, in fact, as strong as ever. It would be a tragedy, he felt, if the second unit produced inferior material. It would be an equal tragedy if their work was better than anything he managed to obtain.

Roy Stevens was worried about David's obsession with the storm. "It was apparent when we tried to get the first few storms that David just couldn't operate under such conditions. In fact, it used to exhaust him so much that I can remember having to lift him back into the Land Rover because the sheer cold and rain completely froze him."[8]

Anyone who imagines this kind of film-making is exhilarating should stay on the location for longer than ten minutes. No amount of clothing can resist a biting wind hurtling across the Atlantic at the speed of the Royal Scot. And yet David *did* find it exhilarating.

"I remember working all day in the pouring rain and getting in to my car. As I put my hands on the wheel, I felt a rush of water going down my sleeves. I had to drive for an hour, absolutely soaked and feeling very cold. It had grown dark, but as I drove along the cliff road you saw these sheets of water and you realised they were waves bursting against the cliff. You sometimes had to drive through a torrent of sea water which swamped you and you had to pull up and think, 'God, what's all that salt water going to do underneath me here?'

"But great fun, you know. Terrific."

After David had managed to achieve the essential long shots for the sequence, working in three storms, there was a sickening lull. No storms. No sun. Constant drizzle.

After a week of this, Stevens told David that the money they were spending doing nothing could take them anywhere in the world. He should consider moving to where there was guaranteed sunshine so they could at least complete the other sequences.

Anthony Havelock-Allan telephoned a South African friend who was familiar with Kerry. He recommended the beaches on either side of Table Mountain in Cape Town.

"When are you going to South Africa?" David asked Eddie Fowlie, who immediately started peeling off his wet suit. He said, "Well, now." David said, "I don't mean *now*. Tomorrow morning."

"We flew straight to Cape Town," said Fowlie. "I went with Doug Twiddy, the production manager with one eye knocked out when he was a commando, marvellous fellow. I didn't go to a hotel. I got an aeroplane and flew all around the beaches."

The next morning, Fowlie chartered a helicopter and flew to the location he had chosen, took photographs, packed some sand in a cellophane bag and flew back to Ireland.

"David had a little office in this hotel in Dingle. He never usually uses an office but he happened to be in it and I went to see him.

"He said, 'I thought you were going to South Africa.'

"'I've been to Africa.'

"He said, 'Don't be silly.' I showed him the sand and he said, 'Look, pack it

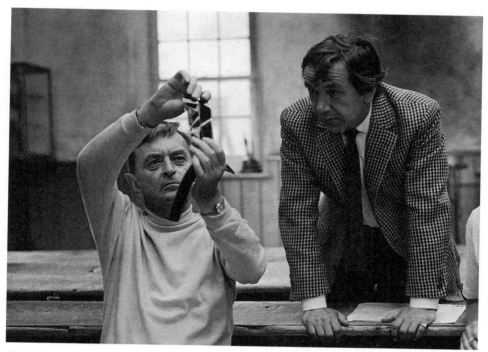

David examines a trim with a worried-looking Norman Savage. (Photograph by Ken Danvers)

up here, put it all on an aeroplane and we'll go down and finish it in South Africa.'

"David said, 'You know, you are the only one, including the great John Box, who ever says to me "we'll do it this way" or "we'll do it that way." Everyone else says, "I think it will be all right" and leaves me to fall in the shit.'"9

As soon as the Christmas holidays were over, the company chartered a plane, loaded their equipment - tracks, dollies, lights - and flew to South Africa.

"The Cape Town beaches looked just like the Irish beaches," said David. "We just had to spray the white rocks black. And I'll tell you, if you showed me the film now, I'd have to think hard which beach was Ireland and which was South Africa."10

Before leaving for Cape Town, David realised he had no alternative but to surrender the storm to a second unit. He did not, though, suggest a single name to direct that second unit.

Roy Stevens found himself talking to Fred Zinnemann and asked him if he would direct the storm sequence for David, though probably without credit. Zinnemann said he would do anything for David. Then Stevens, thrilled that he had solved the problem so quickly, told David the news over dinner.

"I thought he would say, 'Wonderful! How marvellous!' He went through the roof.

"'How dare you! How dare you do that! Get on the phone!'

"'But David, you told me we were looking for somebody...'

"'How dare you!'"

Fred Zinnemann was told that a mistake had been made, and everyone waited for another name to be suggested. Roy Stevens was both relieved and amused when the buck appeared to stop at the camera operator, Ernie Day.

"I remember giggling to myself and thinking, You're in the hot seat there, Ernie. You're on a hiding to nothing. If you do it well, you're in for a bollocking. If you do it badly, you're in for another bollocking."

Then David turned to Roy, and asked him to work on the sequence.

"No, absolutely not, David. It's hard enough as associate producer."

"Look," said David, "Ernie will do it, but he needs a bit of help organising the crowds and all that stuff on the rocks. You and Ernie stay to do it."

"That was how it was left," said Stevens. "We broke for Christmas for two weeks and I had a call from Anthony Havelock-Allan on Boxing Morning, saying 'I've spoken to David in South Africa. He really can't survive without his 'eyes' - Ernie Day - so I've fixed you up with another cameraman.' I was lumbered. I was well and truly trapped."[11]

Stevens had spent every Sunday for four months at the storm location, studying the pattern of the waves. He took photographs and created a file devoted to the storm. He looked at the storm sequence in MAN OF ARAN and flew by helicopter to Aran, where he realised how clever Flaherty had been in selecting small cliffs and rocks that made an angry sea look positively tumultuous. He then located similarly low cliffs near Ennis - but the sea was still dangerous.

"We were doing stuff with wind machines and tip tanks where the raft is in the water, and the stuntmen are pulling it out. I was on the edge with a viewfinder, trying to get a set-up, and there was a sound like an express train. I looked behind, and my cameraman Denys Coop and the operator were backed up against the rock, and it caught me - the green water threw me down and I was concussed. Anthony Havelock-Allan was there, and they whisked me into this medical van, wet suit and all, and took me to the hospital.

"We were lucky not to lose people on it, actually. The only person who got injured was me. The storms were so violent that you couldn't put the artists into the sea, you could only use it as a background."

To give the illusion that the actors were in the sea, the second unit was equipped with five-hundred gallon tanks which were filled with water and emptied on the actors from above.

"You time it," said Stevens, "with the waves in the background. You dump it on people. It's not like a wave which would knock them off their feet. But it looks like a wave."[12]

Leo McKern endured the most rigorous experience of anyone on the film (except perhaps his stunt double, Peter Baldwin) because he was so prominent in the storm sequence. In interviews, McKern said he came close to drowning and that the experience had encouraged him to give up film-making for good - luckily he didn't.

"We probably did only about four set-ups a day," said Stevens. "The most we got was six, because the storm went on all day. We used to get them to drill plugs into the granite everywhere there could be feasible positions for a camera. The wind was so violent that you couldn't even talk to each other, so on a plan you'd got them all numbered. You'd look at the plan and say, 'We'll go to number six.' Everyone knew where that was and the camera could hook on to that place. The waves used to come and knock them off their feet, but everyone had a safety harness so they couldn't be swept out.

"Then we had to get the camera off that position and on to the next one. And that was a race because you would do it bit by bit. As the wave would recede, you'd run down like crazy and get that bit secured. Then you'd run back before the next wave came in and you'd run like crazy with the batteries, and then you'd run back and connect them - hopefully they worked and you could start getting people in position.

"We had to have lights, of course. The risers were covered in all sorts of protective stuff. We must have gone through miles of plastic. We lost one arc - swept out to sea - and that was anchored down.

"Out of the eight weeks, we only had five days of storm. I used to send Polaroids out to David of an absolutely dead flat sea, a beautiful blue sky and the crew in swimming trunks with sunglasses."[13]

David returned from South Africa and settled into the Great Southern Hotel, Killarney, where he had installed a complete editing suite and all facilities. A few weeks later, Stevens arrived with all the storm footage.

"I knew I had some good stuff," said Stevens, "even though it was overlong. Eventually, we had lunch and David said, 'Let's go and have a look at your material.'

"I said, 'No, David, I'm not coming in there with you.'

"He said, 'Why? Come on. I hear you've got some good stuff. Come and see it with me.'

"I said, 'No, you will be saying all the way through, 'Why didn't you put the camera three inches to the left or nine inches to the right?' I'd rather you saw it by yourself."

David finally agreed and viewed the footage with the editor, Norman Savage. At one point Savage came out of the screening room and said to Stevens, "Oh boy, are you in the shit! Up to here, I can tell you."

When the screening was over, Stevens went in to see David.

"He was sitting in the corner, looking depressed. The lines of his mouth were way down. He said, 'I don't know how the fuck you did that. All I know is I wish I'd done it. Now fuck off.'

"From then on, he hardly talked to me. We went right through the post-production, where to talk to me he would have to talk to Doug Twiddy, who would relay it to me.

"Two years later, when I was in Rome setting up a picture with Kirk Douglas, he found out I was staying at the Hotel Parco dei Principi, which he used as his mailing address. He said, 'You can't stay here. You're going to stay with us.'

"I didn't think it was a good idea, because I hadn't talked to him for two years, but he was insistent and he was extremely friendly with my wife, Jackie.

"On the third night, David - who couldn't handle his drink, by the way - had two whiskies which loosened his tongue to the point where he actually apologised. He said, 'I really have been evil to you. I do apologise.'

"It had been the most miserable time, because the atmosphere was horrible. I hated it. That gave me the feeling that I didn't really want to work with him again because he really had put me down so badly. One does one's best for his sake, and then one really got kicked in the teeth. He wouldn't have wanted me after that, anyway, because with David, once something had happened with somebody, it was difficult to get back in. Not that we had a row: he just didn't talk to me. So that was the end of our association.

"But I loved him dearly. I'd defend him like crazy. He was the most brilliant man you could ever meet, the most wonderful film-maker. But his personality was not of the same quality as his ability as a film-maker."[14]

Photography on RYAN'S DAUGHTER was completed on 24 February 1970. The "little gem" which David had talked of, the film which would remind everyone of BRIEF ENCOUNTER, had taken fifty-two weeks to shoot.

CHAPTER FORTY

LOSING THE LIGHT

"WHEN a picture is absolutely finished," said Carol Reed "and there is nothing more you can do about it, it is like falling out of love. Making a picture is all work and worry and fear and panic. But not making a picture is worse. There is no happiness in this business."[1]

When RYAN'S DAUGHTER was released, David faced a level of hostility which, for a man who couldn't bear criticism even in its mildest form, was a cauterising experience. His film was subjected to a critical reaction so venomous one might have thought he had released a couple of hours of undisguised pornography - although had he done so, he might have been given a warmer reception.

"Nobody felt it would be anything but a success," said assistant editor Tony Lawson. "We thought we were working on class product - class with a capital C. David was a Lord already in most people's eyes - he was untouchable. People wouldn't dare.

"Now I can analyse my own reactions - then I was a bit green, but I remember feeling the cringe factor quite high as far as one or two of the performances were concerned.

"It was a time in the British film industry when we were in one of our depressions. I remember meeting a director who was absolutely incensed that David had been given X million dollars. He said he could make three films for that budget. He was incensed that he had essentially stolen it from other film-makers. That was the general feeling at the time. People were very critical of the apparent waste."[2]

Freddie Young considered that all this was mostly jealousy. "Things were bad in the film industry," he said, "and there we were in Ireland over a year and everyone was terribly jealous about David spending all this money on one film when a dozen could have been made for the same amount of money. People were out of work and the critics gave it a slating, but it's a bloody good film."[3]

David thought that in one area at least, he had made a mistake which, had he thought about it, might have deflected the critics.

"The photography of RYAN'S DAUGHTER was dead straight until the appearance of the Major, and she falls in love with him. Suddenly, the world changes. Everything centres around that man and girl. I decided that when they fell in love, we'd change the photography into a mood of wild romance. I went at it full tilt. We had exotic lilies growing in the garden of the schoolhouse, bluebells in the woods. I told Freddie to make it as lush as he could and 'think of the times when you first fell in love.'

"The critics, of course, all laughed at it. They wouldn't have laughed if Father Collins had said to the girl, 'Rosy, you're seeing everything through rose-coloured spectacles,' and you had a good cut to something wildly romantic. If I'd told them what I was up to, it would have worked."[4]

But this would hardly have reduced the outcry, which was all the more strident because so much was expected of a David Lean picture. There were some good reviews - and the MGM publicity department managed to extract enough strong comments for a striking advertisement - but the overwhelming impression conveyed by the critics was one of distaste. They thought he had wasted millions and produced not an epic, but an inflated B-picture.

"I haven't seen it for such a long time," said David. "I'm sure if I saw it, I would want to tickle it around a bit, and could probably succeed in doing so. I think I'm right in saying that it's a much better picture than the terrible notices it got suggested. I think there were some good performances. I think it had a good atmosphere. Lots of people now come to me and say how much they've enjoyed it, they've seen it on television or something, and I tell them the story of the notices. They can't believe it. And you know, the press, the critics, in some mysterious way can become a pack, so when you've reached a certain stage in your career, they can literally hound you. There is a kind of invisible contact between them all.

"When forty people burst into print and tell you that your film is a load of rubbish, you tend to believe them. At least I do. Because when you finish a film, you are at your most vulnerable. Almost anybody could come to me at the end of a film and say 'Why did you do that?' And they can go on and on and the more they talk the more you believe they must be right.

"Producers know all about that. So when you've completed your final cut, a producer can come in and say, 'Look, that just doesn't hold up.' You find yourself agreeing with them, because you are at your most insecure."[5]

"The critics are intellectuals," he told *Time*. "I'm always frightened of intellectuals. I think one tends to take the critics too seriously. Because you can't, as it were, meet the general public, and if your mother or aunt tells you the movie is great, you say, 'Yes, very sweet of you, but you would.' The only people who really don't give a damn, who are out there giving their opinions, are the critics. They are the only people, as it were, you can believe. You read it there in black and white and think it must be true."[6]

"David got some tough reviews on LAWRENCE," said Sandy Lean, "and he got some terrible reviews on ZHIVAGO, but both films were huge popular successes.

RYAN'S DAUGHTER wasn't. The public deserted him and he was left alone with the critics. And the critics were ferocious.

"And then there was an extraordinary evening at the Algonquin Hotel. David had been invited to an evening with the National Society of Film Critics[7] and he'd made it a point to go because it seemed such an honour.

"We were shepherded there by Nat Weiss, the publicity man for MGM, and his wife. David had assumed we'd been invited for dinner, but when we got to the hotel nobody had arrived. So we sat in the lobby and waited.

"When the critics arrived, it was all in a group. I remember them filing in and thinking what a strange physical assortment they were. There were no introductions. They escorted David across the lobby into this private room. I remember glimpsing this huge bare table. Then the doors closed. And for the next couple of hours we sat there, Nat and his wife and I, with our coats in our laps, picking at the cashew nuts and wondering what was going on inside."[8]

The chairman of the meeting was Richard Schickel.

"The National Society of Film Critics was founded in the late sixties," he wrote, "as a counterweight to the conservative middlebrow New York Film Critics, which at that time confined its membership exclusively to the newspaper reviewers, who were not a very distinguished lot. We thought we were slightly finer stuff and in those days tended almost automatically to give our prizes to Ingmar Bergman and a few other Europeans of his ilk.

"At some point we conceived the idea of inviting directors to meet with us for informal, off-the-record, give-and-take dialogues. This was a good idea in theory, a bad one in practice. The gentlemanly exchange of ideas that some of us envisioned, a means by which creators and critics could see each other's human faces, rarely happened. Instead, the critics tended to attack and the directors tended to be shocked by their vehemence. They were used to being interviewed by the rather tame movie press and were entirely unprepared for the passions vented by people who professed to care greatly for the 'art' of the film.

"In the sixties and early seventies, when literary New York made the wonderful discovery that film was an 'art,' we, the critics, were for a time lionized, became demi-celebrities, and this had an unfortunate effect on a lot of egos. Of the directors who appeared before Lean, I can only remember John Frankenheimer, who was a feisty guy and gave as good as he got. Lean was much too gentlemanly for that sort of roughhousing. He arrived directly from the airplane and was visibly jet-lagged.

"I was chairman of the Society that year, and, frankly, was expecting trouble. The screening of RYAN'S DAUGHTER at the Ziegfeld the Sunday before had not gone well. Moreover, at that time the standard American critical line on Lean was that his small films were superior to his spectacles. I don't hold with that view; I liked them all. Still, I didn't like RYAN'S DAUGHTER any more than anyone else did.

"In welcoming Lean, I listed his past triumphs, paid tribute to his distinguished career. There followed an interval of polite sparring. Then Pauline Kael launched a brutal critique, and this opened the floodgates. And it was an angry torrent. I pretty much lost control of the meeting, caught between a director I revered and colleagues for whom I had more respect than I do now. Lean did not counterattack; instead he went into a shell. I seem to recall plaintive bleats from him, to the effect that he was unprepared for a dialogue of this intensity and for the lack of respect being shown. This was a legitimate complaint and I tried once or twice to divert the discussion to calmer areas. But to no avail. Lean grew less and less responsive. At some point he said, 'I don't understand all this; why are you doing this to me?'"[9]

"After an hour or so," said Sandy Lean, "the door opened and Pauline Kael burst out. She rushed over to us and said, 'Let's get some dames in here. We've gotta break up the tension.' And she grabbed me by the hand and said, 'C'mon, c'mon.' I was so surprised, I just sat there. So she went back in and then there was nothing until David came out on his own and then the whole lot came out and filed off.

"Afterwards, though he talked very little about it, it was clear that he'd been devastated. It was shocking to find himself confronting a roomful of strangers who bore him so much malice. He was such a lonely man, you see, he didn't have any framework of friends. There was the great public out there and then there were the critics, but the only voice he really heard was that of the critics."[10]

"The meeting was one of the most horrible experiences I have ever had," said David. "It was very CITIZEN KANE - this huge dining room. They had a big table in the middle. The lights were not strong enough to illuminate the whole room, so it was very sinister and very heavy. I remember Pauline Kael meeting me at the door and leading me by the hand to the table where there were ten or twelve critics and they sat me at the head of the table and within seconds they started grilling me in the most unfriendly fashion. One of the most leading questions was, 'Can you please explain how the man who directed BRIEF ENCOUNTER can have directed this load of shit you call RYAN'S DAUGHTER?' It really cut me to the heart, and that was Richard Schickel. I think he's a jolly good writer, by the way. And it got worse and worse. Pauline Kael said to me, 'Are you trying to tell us Robert Mitchum is a lousy lay?' I was a fool to stay there, of course. I remember saying to Pauline Kael at the end, 'You won't be content until you've reduced me to making a film in black and white on 16mm.' And she said, 'We'll give you colour.'

"In their defence, I think they were pretty tight."[11]

Richard Schickel considered that Pauline Kael was the leader of the attack on David and has long resented David's misquotation of his remark. In Stephen Silverman's book, the line is quoted as he greeted David. According to Schickel, it occurred well into the meeting.

41. RYAN'S DAUGHTER. *David on Coumeenole Beach, near Dunmore Head, Dunquin, Co. Kerry.* This was the unit's 1969 Christmas card. *Photograph by Ken Danvers.*

42. (Overleaf) *David and camera crew brace themselves against hurricane-force winds to film the storm. The camera is equipped with a plexiglass windscreen rotating at high speed.* Photograph by Ken Bray.

43. *David demonstrates how he wants a scene played.* 44. *Robert Mitchum as the diffident schoolmaster tries to make contact with his wife, Rosy (Sarah Miles).* 45. *Robert Mitchum in receptive mood.* 46. *David faced problems getting the performance he wanted from Christopher Jones (Major Doryan).* *Photographs by Ken Bray.*

47. *(Overleaf) Robert Mitchum in the schoolhouse at Dunquin - Freddie Young left, with beard and glasses; boom operator, Bill Cook. The schoolhouse still stands. Photograph by Ken Bray.*

48 and 49. Trevor Howard and John Mills set out in angry seas at Coumeenole and promptly capsize. Rescuers race to their aid. Photographs by Ken Danvers.

"What I was doing was all-too-bluntly summarising the subtext of the questions that were being put forward. I think the way I put it was this: 'What they're trying to say, Mr Lean, is that they don't understand how someone who made BRIEF ENCOUNTER could make a piece of bullshit like RYAN'S DAUGHTER.' There is, I hold, a substantial difference between a 'greeting' and a summary offered well along in a difficult discussion when tempers had grown short. There is also a nuanced difference between shit and bullshit in American colloquial usage.

"In other words, mine was a perfectly accurate summary of the meeting's tenor. But, of course, it was not felicitously or kindly put, and I regret that. On the other hand, I confess a certain amount of impatience with Lean's demeanour at this point - his evasions and his silences. I was an impatient younger man - thirty-seven at the time - and a believer in the value of free, open exchange of opinion, the more outrageous the better. I am now no longer so sure of the value of such exchanges. I have also learned what I should have known then, that directors are peculiarly vulnerable in the weeks before their films go into release.

"In the years since, as Lean repeated this story, I became increasingly dismayed, and then angered, by his behaviour. First of all, I did not set the tone of this meeting; Pauline and her pals, and Lean himself, did that. I resent being made the symbol and scapegoat for what was an almost universal response to the film."[12]

When I asked Pauline Kael for her comments, she said she was still bound by her agreement with the National Society of Film Critics and would not reveal what was said at that meeting.

"Even if I weren't bound, I wouldn't trust myself to report what various people said at a talkative gathering twenty-one years ago. I always felt bad about that evening because everything that was said about the film seemed to go wrong, and Lean was so offended. He seemed determined to misunderstand the remarks made and to take even jocular comments and attempts to be soothing as affronts."[13]

Kael's review of RYAN'S DAUGHTER, published in *The New Yorker*, summed up the critical reaction:

"As a director, he is a super-technician, and probably he doesn't really have anything he wants to do in movies except to command the technology. He probably enjoys working his characteristic gentleman-technician's tastefully-colossal style. But tasteful and colossal are - in movies at least - basically antipathetic. Lean makes respectable epics, and that's a contradiction and self-defeating. Humorlessly meticulous, his pieces have no driving emotional energy, no passionate vision to conceal the heavy labor...

"The only reasons for placing this story in 1916 were to legitimize the fact that every idea in it is shopworn, and to build sets. For years, during the making of a Lean film, publicity people send out photographs of the handsome director standing in the cities he has built, and then the movies arrive and he never seems to have figured out what to do in those sets. They have a gleaming pictorial look, a prepared look - everything is posing for a photograph...

"[Bolt and Lean] don't have it in them to create Irish characters; there isn't a joke in all the three hours (three and a half, including intermission), except maybe the idea that an Irish girl needs a half-dead Englishman to arouse her. There's no point in asking 'What's it all for?' We know what it's for; it's to try to repeat the financial success of DOCTOR ZHIVAGO. The question is, 'Can they get by with it?' Will the public buy twinkling orgasms and cosmetic craftsmanship? The emptiness of RYAN'S DAUGHTER shows in every frame, and yet the publicity machine has turned it into an artistic event, and the American public is a sucker for the corrupt tastefulness of well-bred English epics." [14]

Nic Roeg renewed acquaintance with David at this period. "He had never had reviews like he got on RYAN'S DAUGHTER. He was in shock and fury and startled and dismayed and he didn't know what to make of his feelings at all. He had had some poor reviews, but he had never been smashed. Maybe he'd been lucky. I've had a real kick in the arse. [15] It gets you going, it gets you angry. But he was in a state of catatonic shock from it. He couldn't believe it." [16]

David felt the shock waves for quite a while. "After RYAN'S DAUGHTER, I didn't like going out to a restaurant because I thought I'd be pointed out as the chap who made that disastrous, terrible, horrible film. I felt very ashamed. [17]

"I used to go to a well-known tailor in Los Angeles, and the owner always came up and greeted me. Some time after the film came out I walked into the shop and suddenly saw a face looking at me from between the suits at the other end of the corridor. It dived straight though the suits and into a door and never came out again. I suppose one has to have a certain amount of sympathy because if you have just read the most horrendous review - 'This is a real turkey, take it away' - there's not much to say, is there, except a sort of funeral parlour approach? [18]

"I thought, 'What the hell am I doing if my work is as bad as all this?' I didn't want to do another film. I thought. 'I'll do something else.' I went travelling round the world and I didn't make a film for fourteen years. I thought, 'What's the point?'" [19]

CHAPTER FORTY-ONE

WILDERNESS YEARS

IN a sympathetic article for *Sight and Sound*, published after David's death, Hugh Hudson wrote:

"The result of this devastating attack was a self-imposed exile from film-making for a period of fifteen years, during which time Lean travelled the world, visiting among other countries Kenya, India and Tahiti, where he spent a good deal of time. While living in Tahiti he became familiar with the language, discovering the word *Pwew* - an expression the Tahitians use when they are particularly upset about something and spiritually 'disappear' until things get better. David Lean went *Pwew* for fifteen years."[1]

After his experiences with the critics, David liked to convey the impression that he gave up the idea of making films. There is only an element of truth in this. Throughout 1971, he was trying to set up GANDHI and when this became subject to more and more delays, he began to relax into a leisurely life with Sandy.

During the making of RYAN'S DAUGHTER, they bought a house in Rome. Because David was unable to leave Ireland, Sandy surveyed the house and took photographs, which was enough to convince David of its beauty. It was called La Metella, just off the Appia Antica at 53 Via dei Metelli, and had been named after the nearby tomb of Cecilia Metella, a Roman noblewoman. David employed Stephen Grimes to redesign it and in March 1972 they moved in, surrounded by workmen who were still completing the swimming pool and the garden. David installed a 16mm cutting-room, together with projection facilities and a sound-mixing panel.

"We had the house in Italy," said Sandy Lean, "that we enjoyed. We did a lot of travelling, but he was always looking round for something, make no mistake; it was just that he couldn't find anything.

"Certainly, he'd been devastated by the critics, but I think that if he'd found the subject, he would have been after it like a terrier after a rat. It was paralysing; you know this happens with so many directors. Their very success paralyses them and they've always got to top the one before. It was some record he was trailing, some trail of tin cans, as he would have said."[2]

When I first met him, David said that he had a wonderful time during his so-called "wilderness years". "Funny, if I'd worked, at the end of it I'd have a pile of twenty cans. Perhaps I'd rather have had the other."

He laughed. I did not believe him.

As it happened, David had no need to work again for he had touched not a penny of his capital.[3] He was paid a million dollars for each of his last two pictures, quite apart from the percentages. While most of his money came from ZHIVAGO, there was a substantial income from KWAI and LAWRENCE. David was able to afford the best hotels and the best suite on the QE2 when he and Sandy crossed the Atlantic.

"I have no greed for money whatever," he wrote to a friend, "and it doesn't mean anything to me except being free of the worry of being without it - which I know very well. I give quite a bit away one way or another - and it's one of the great pleasures of my life."[4]

However generous he was - and he was extremely generous - he still resented the punitive taxation that awaited him at home.

"Thank goodness I had to leave England," he wrote to his friend André Morell. "With the envy tax as it is I would still be broke. I hate these socialists and their 'what you have got that I haven't got I'll take from you although I can't have it.' I think it too awful that people like you and I who have worked hard and honourably all their lives have to worry about our old age and the well-being of our loved ones. I have known so many of these chaps; as soon as they get money they change completely and very often leave the country themselves."[5]

"Whenever David was in England," said Judy Scott-Fox, "I think he felt rather abandoned. It's funny, but this man who was so famous and so brilliant

David at the Kia-Ora Hotel, Rangiroa, photographed by Sandy.

had rather few friends. I think like a lot of famous men, people were afraid of him, or felt they didn't want to impose themselves on him because he was this great man. As a result of that, he was incredibly lonely. He was very fond of Fred Zinnemann and also of Richard Lester. And of course there was the solid friendship of Maggie Unsworth and Eddie Fowlie. But he wasn't an easy man."[6]

In January 1973, one of David's close friends, Norman Savage, died of leukemia. He had died whilst he was editing Robert Bolt's directorial debut, LADY CAROLINE LAMB, for which he had installed a cutting-room in the hospital. Bolt, whose friendship was even closer, wrote about him to David with a touching poignancy.

"What was it that Norman had? I think he had innocence. Which doesn't connote either ignorance or foolishness or indeed a lack of anything whatever. I mean he wasn't seriously tempted to be anything but truthful - truthful to himself. It didn't seem to cost him much effort. And that's why the memory of his little foibles (the hair and the natty suiting and the grumbling over food) is so painfully charming. His foibles about which he made such to-do emphasized the goodness of which he was almost totally unaware. I miss him amazingly. But he serves to remind me that goodness is both possible and effective."[7]

On 9 December 1973, David's father died. He was ninety-five. To add to David's guilt was the realisation that he had seldom visited him at the Thamesbank Nursing Home, Goring, where he ended his life and where Peter Lean's daughter-in-law, Anne, was a nurse.

In his last years, Frank had deteriorated to the point where he was extremely difficult to deal with. David's brother, Edward, visited him fairly regularly and felt that the old man's horizons had shrunk to a few feet around his chair.

In his will was a request that he be cremated, and his ashes interred at the grave of Helena, who had died in 1962, at Falmouth in Cornwall. Sara Lean discovered letters between David and Edward discussing this strange request. The cremation was duly organised, but between them, the brothers decided to do nothing else. They considered the idea of a man who had spent most of his life with his mistress wanting to return to his wife in this way outrageous.

It wasn't as if David had faded from people's thoughts. He was still considered an important director and he was still sent scripts. In 1973, Fred Zinnemann was given J.G. Farrell's book *The Siege of Krishnapur*, which later won the Booker Prize. Zinnemann knew that David had always wanted to make a picture in India and he sent it to him. David liked it well enough to plan to take up the option, but then he wrote to Zinnemann saying he had decided not to proceed.[8]

"I think he turned against *The Siege of Krishnapur*," said Judy Scott-Fox "because it was so depressing. He said, 'I can't face the idea of those dead bodies all over the place.'"9 David also toyed with a project about the Nile.

Sara Lean, Edward and Doreen's daughter, who was a painter, spent many of the "wilderness years" with David and Sandy. I asked her if it was true that the critical reaction to RYAN'S DAUGHTER put him off making films.

"I think it's sort of true. He was very hurt by it. But it has to be said that in those years he became a human being, a family man, which he'd never been before in his life. He became very close to my father, for the first time. He said that was due to Sandy. He and Sandy were terribly close and did everything together. If Sandy came round here for an hour, David would ring up - 'Are you all right? When are you coming back?'

"In the first of those years, he spent a lot of time with my parents. There had been this rift between them. He and my father were terribly jealous. No one talks of my father being jealous of David, but I think my father could have done with some of the worldly splendours.

"David was always in awe of my father, and right up to the end he insisted that my father had been offered a knighthood and had turned it down, which would have been the right and proper thing to do, and he later said how terrible it was that he had accepted the knighthood. 'Can you imagine?' he used to say, 'Mr Picasso, meet Sir David Lean!'

"David admired my father so much and thought that he looked down upon him as a rather stupid gadabout. They were actually terribly compatible and during the first part of those years they spent a lot of time together. My father would go and stay with him in Rome and he and Sandy would come and have endless dinners with my parents in London."10

"I adored Edward," said Sandy. "He was so wild and funny and so *literate*. He didn't just speak in sentences, he spoke in paragraphs. He was the antithesis of David. Where David was smooth, Edward was rumpled. David was always in his neat white polo neck and his dark blue cardigan and Edward would slouch with his wild long hair and his sandals and an old shirt with the tails hanging out. He was crazily eccentric, David was conventional." 11

"My father wasn't vain in the same way as David was," said Sara. "David was extremely vain. At the same time very beautiful. My father was always taking the piss out of him. I remember vividly in Rome my father, who was quite podgy, parading around David's immaculate swimming pool and saying 'Do you like my bathing dress?' and giggling like mad. David would never have done that. In all our trips to Tahiti, he never took his clothes off. He didn't like the idea that his body was old. He surrounded himself with young people - Sandy, me and my then husband, Christopher Coy, who was my age and starting out as a film editor.

"I remember going up Kilimanjaro with David and my husband and David taking great pleasure in saying, 'Now, come on, come on.' We're out of breath and this man in his sixties was striding out. He was very competitive and at the same time very good with young people. He took a lot of time with a lot of my friends.

"I think he was quite a young boy himself. He never grew up. He never had a lot of wisdom - he had a sort of acquired wisdom. You'd ask him an important question and he didn't like to say anything that was wrong. He would consider a long time before answering so he didn't make some terrible faux-pas. We spent many evenings getting slightly tiddly all around the world and then he would consider for hours before he pontificated - and then he'd giggle. He was quite capable of giggling.

"I think he was always more vulnerable than my father. My father was happy to laugh at himself and laugh at anything in a very kind way, whereas David was slightly more malicious.

"David had this style of making you feel that when you were with him you were the only one who really mattered. He did that with everybody. It was his charming way. So it was quite hard to tell who he really liked and with whom he was just happy to spend an evening.

"The whole of the time he wasn't working, he was, in fact, working. You'd be in a foreign country and he'd be soaking up ideas. Wherever you were, there was something going on. I don't know if someone like that ever does stop working.

"There we were in Egypt. He'd get tombs opened up and we'd go in. It was a film in itself - a mammoth organisation. We went in with lights. He used to pretend he wasn't going to take a picture and was just playing around, but I knew he was trying to get me to relax so he could shoot. He never took photos or shot film on an off-chance."[12]

Judy Scott-Fox - who worked at the William Morris Agency - was one of the few to see these films.

"It was marvellous stuff," she said. "Because he wasn't doing anything else, he became completely obsessed by these films. He and Sandy would go and stay at Mount Kenya Safari Club[13] and he would film a lot round there - and then they'd go off with a couple of guides with tents for weeks on end. A lot of the film was scenic shots, and there were a lot of shots of animals. Amazing."[14]

"I took round a very good 16mm camera," said David, "an Eclair, a crack French camera - and I loved photographing with it. It gave me a really great pleasure to hold a camera. I have hundreds of feet taken in the South Pacific which I had developed at the MGM lab. And they said, 'David, come and see it. Do you know we could blow this up to 35mm and people wouldn't know, the quality is so good.'

"I've always had movie cameras - 8mm, 16mm, all the rest of it, and I've always had still cameras. I had a Hasselblad that I loved dearly and whenever I touch it I think of that Hasselblad left behind on the moon. It must be in pristine condition up there. The trouble with the Hasselblad is that it's bloody heavy and when you make an exposure and press the shutter it goes off like a cannon and every bird in the district takes flight, so you can't creep up on things.

"Through my brother, I graduated to Leicas and I've got a beautiful Leica now. I've taken slides on that - I alternate between slides and negative film - and I've blown them up to six feet across and they're pin sharp from side to side. I cannot recommend a better camera than the Leica. I've got thousands of photographs scattered all over the place."[15]

Sara regarded David as a modern visionary, a William Blake character. "He would see the world in a grain of sand. He was very shy, very humble, very lacking in confidence. And yet very positive about what he thought. The combination often fools people. They think, 'Here's a man who knows exactly where he's at.' I don't think that was the case at all.

"I think people were unaware of the fact that his perfectionism carried over into his private life. He was like that not just about his films but about everything, right down to sausages and eggs for supper. They'd got to be exactly right. If he wanted to enjoy something it had to be perfect in his own eyes. He would have endless dinners with me of sausages and eggs because he was living at the Berkeley and he couldn't stand all their fussy food, so Sandy and he would go

David's photograph of his new home in Rome.

to Harrods and buy the sausages and bring them round for me to cook. He loved it. It wasn't a perfectionism based on things being expensive - it was a way of looking at the world. And it's a tremendous quality to be able to get as much pleasure out of an old sausage as you do out of the best smoked salmon. And the sausages weren't always bought at Harrods; sometimes they were bought round the corner."[16]

"Our daily life was very static," said Sandy Lean, "in spite of the fact that we never stopped travelling. We'd have breakfast in the hotel room, lie in the sun, lunch in a cafeteria, go for a little drive, buy a couple of books. In the evening we'd dress for dinner and eat in the hotel restaurant. We had no roots, either of us. So this was our domesticity.

"Another thing was that when David wasn't working or filming he was passive, almost like a machine with the switch flipped off. No, that's not quite true, if you listened you could hear the motor humming. He was always observing, his eye was like a view-finder, composing what he saw. And of course he wanted you to see it *his* way, on the screen and off.

"I was passive, too. But my passiveness was about hanging back in his shadow. I did it for a long, long time. I was the perfect wife, the secretary you long to marry because she always remembers how much sugar you take in your coffee. I carried the suitcases, booked the airline tickets, set up the tripod, took the light reading, sat on the coral reef just to the left of frame to give the picture some scale.

"Film directors can become curiously helpless creatures. David wasn't unique. As a director you're in this amazing position, buoyed up by an assemblage of people who are there to fulfil your every whim. They can do anything for you, they can create castles out of thin air. They can also fix the plug in your bathroom, and put gas in your car. After a while it becomes a necessity, having someone to sort out the practical details of life. You forget how to do it yourself."[17]

In October 1973, the Directors Guild of America presented David with the D. W. Griffith Award,[18] an event which filled him with pride. The award was presented by George Stevens, whom David had helped out by filming scenes for THE GREATEST STORY EVER TOLD.

"Awfully nice, he was," said David. "Gave me a wonderful dinner in the poshest restaurant there and a private little orchestra and a whole lot of interesting people."[19]

At the reception, David said how touched he was. "From early on, I've owed a great deal to American generosity."

After the ceremony, David and Sandy flew from Los Angeles to Tahiti. With fond memories of WHITE SHADOWS IN THE SOUTH SEAS, he had long wanted to make a film in the Pacific. David's agent, Phil Kellogg, joined them for a tour of Tahiti and its neighbouring islands - Moorea, Bora Bora, Huahine, Rangiroa.

David felt he was at the end of the world: the sense of space, the vast beaches, the reflection of the sky in the ocean, the colours that changed every few moments, soothed and exhilarated him. With just the lap of water and the breeze in the palms, David felt completely at ease. Perhaps for the first time, he could contemplate retirement. He was, after all, sixty-five, the age at which the majority of men are expected to step aside.

"Bora Bora is just about the most beautiful island you will ever clap eyes on," he wrote to his old friend André Morell, who had often spoken to him of Moorea. "You fly from Papeete in a Fokker Friendship, very old but with two Rolls-Royce turbo props. The flying time is forty-five minutes. The landing strip was built on the reef by the Americans in the last war. You are met by boat and taken across the lagoon to the Hotel Bora Bora. Wonderful colours. Only one pass in the reef. The mountain in the middle of the island over two thousand feet. We would put you up in overwater bungalows which are out over the lagoon some fifty yards from shore. You go down steps from the veranda straight into deep blue water, warm as toast."[20]

"We used to live in an overwater bungalow at the Bora Bora Hotel for weeks on end," said Sandy. "Dino de Laurentiis used to stay there, too. Being Dino, his wheels were always spinning. He couldn't understand how David could sit day after day on his balcony, watching the sky. 'But what does he *do*?' he would ask plaintively."[21]

David acquired a boat, a Boston Whaler which Sandy piloted.[22] It was seventeen feet long and had an eighty-five horse power engine. They had a private anchorage at the hotel and another in the middle of town. Their other form of transport was a Mini.

While David was in these remote parts, friends in America and Britain clipped items from newspapers and sent them to him. One small paragraph must have caused him astonishment: Carlo Ponti was producing a remake of BRIEF ENCOUNTER as an NBC television special, and the stars were Richard Burton and... Sophia Loren! Anyone less like Noël Coward's middle-class housewife would be hard to imagine, yet the *Hollywood Reporter* considered her performance "fine."[23] The following month the *Reporter* announced a musical version of GREAT EXPECTATIONS to be photographed by Freddie Young for Lew Grade's ATV in association with NBC.

David and Sandy were in England for one important event.

"I remember it so vividly," said Sandy Lean. "We were in the Berkeley restaurant, sitting at our usual table. The wine waiter had just brought us dry martinis. The telephone rang at the head-waiter's desk by the door, and the call was for David. He went to the phone. It was just a few yards away and I heard him say hello. The wine waiter was still standing at the table. He was talking and talking and I remember nodding and smiling and watching David and knowing something was wrong. He was just so still standing there.

"He came back to the table and sat down. 'That was Sara,' he said, 'Edward's died.'

"It was as though everything in the room stopped moving. 'What shall we do?' he said. 'We go over there, right now,' I said.

David's brother, Edward Tangye Lean, CBE, Assistant Director of External Broadcasting at the BBC, at his home in Albert Street, Camden Town, London, with his daughter Sara, 1958.

"We got a car and drove over to Albert Street, and stayed with them through the night and came back to the hotel at dawn the next morning."[24] It was 28 October 1974. Edward was sixty-three.

David refused to go to the funeral - if he hated anything to do with illness it was because of his fear of death. But he organised the party afterwards and laid on lavish supplies of food and champagne.

"He was terribly good about it all," said a family friend. "He was very good to Mrs Lean, who was extremely distraught. We were all very miserable. Tangye Lean was a most wonderful man, immensely charming and kind and pleasant and erudite and fun. He had a much closer circle of friends, I feel, than David did."[25]

The *Times* obituary called Edward, "a man of quite exceptionally strong and distinctive personality; highly intelligent, passionately enthusiastic, magnanimous, kind and gifted with a sense of the absurd which could blow away pretentiousness and meanness in hoots of laughter. Not an easy man, but a most lovable and entertaining one."[26]

After the funeral, David and Sandy went to Rome and returned to England to spend Christmas with the family. Sara had just left Oxford, and as the New Year began, David decided she needed cheering up. He sent Edward's widow,

Sara Lean with Sandy in California, photographed by David.

Doreen, on a trip to America with a friend, then he and Sandy took Sara on a world tour.

It is entirely characteristic that David should have treated his niece, Sara, as a daughter, while he continued to ignore his son. Although Peter and June received regular birthday greetings and Christmas presents from Edward, they saw little of the family and only learned about his death by seeing an obituary notice in a newspaper. They did not attend the funeral. David remembered Peter and June at Christmas, too, though they never met him during this period.

"David took over completely as the father figure," said Sara. " My father had taken me to Italy and shown me all the classical sites. David showed me all the visual, beautiful sites - Tahiti, Venice, Africa, America.

"He took me to Bora Bora. There was no talk of making a film there; he was fed up with films at that point. We'd go to these places, supposedly on holiday, and we'd have to carry the tripod, wear the right colours - every single day was a shoot. But at the same time it was very relaxed. It was a side of David few people know about. He really enjoyed life. He'd love to go off for the day in a little boat, off to a coral island and just mess about all day. He'd get quite drunk quite regularly. He never got legless, but he'd get very, very tiddly. He'd take my arm and roll around. You always knew when David was relaxed because he'd start drinking wine instead of whisky.

"He taught me an awful lot about photographs. I got myself a camera and he taught me about composing pictures and getting the right light and then I brought home all my films and took them to the local chemist and David rang up and said, 'Well, what are they like?' I would say, 'They're disastrous. That's it. I'm giving up. I'm going back to my painting. It's far more reliable.'

"And he said, 'This is nonsense. Give them to me.' I gave him my negatives and he took them to his place in Switzerland and it turned out they hadn't been graded properly and he cropped them and presented me with some wonderful photographs which encouraged me to go on."[27]

Back at La Metella in Rome, David and Sandy were asleep when burglars broke into the house. They stole two Oscars and a Golden Globe - "I suppose they thought they were gold," said Sandy - and they consumed half a bottle as they rummaged through the contents of the house and ransacked cupboards just outside the bedroom door.

"We heard nothing," said Sandy. "The *carabinieri* said they must have pumped gas under the door. It sounded absolutely fantastic but the police insisted it was a common thing. David was very upset. It was a bad time in Rome, with a great deal of street violence and kidnapping."[28]

In 1973, Paul Getty III, the sixteen-year old grandson of J. Paul Getty, had been kidnapped in Rome. Getty refused to pay the ransom and the boy's ear was delivered to his father by mail. A million dollars was eventually paid and the boy was released. A spate of kidnappings followed and David, fearing for Sandy's safety, reluctantly abandoned La Metella in 1976, leaving two servants and their teenage daughter in charge of the house and its two-acre garden.[29]

David's accountant had long since given him word that he could return to England. Having decided to leave Rome, David and Sandy seriously considered moving to London, and Judy Scott-Fox helped them track down prints of those of his films he hadn't been able to get.[30]

But instead of moving to England, they went back to Bora Bora. David could not know what lay ahead - four years of intense and wasted effort, shattered relationships and tragedy for Robert Bolt. David was about to set in motion the grandest project of his entire career.

CHAPTER FORTY-TWO

SUNSHINE LOYALTIES

PANDORA'S BOX 1

DAVID had three ideas for films to be made in the South Pacific. He considered Alan Moorehead's book, *The Fatal Impact*, and also spent a great deal of time on the story of Captain Cook, the farm labourer's son, educated by Quakers, who discovered Australia. And Eddie Fowlie had given him a copy of Richard Hough's 1972 book, *Captain Bligh and Mr Christian*, which was a fresh account of the famous Naval mutiny of 1789. David was so impressed by Hough's book that he abandoned his other ideas.

Fowlie, who had written his own treatment of Hough's book, had accepted a job on THE GREEK TYCOON when a call came through from David. "What the hell are you doing in Greece? We're going to do your thing."

"And out of that," said Fowlie, "came all those lovely years down in the Pacific, paid for by Warner Bros. David once told me that the happiest days of his life were the four of us in the South Pacific."[1]

When David first arrived in the South Pacific in 1973, he had contacted Robert Bolt with only a vague idea of making a film there. Bolt was enthusiastic but had committed himself to a play, *The State of Revolution*. By this time, Bolt had made his directorial debut with LADY CAROLINE LAMB, an eighteenth-century melodrama starring Sarah Miles which was widely perceived as a flop. Bolt and Miles separated shortly afterwards. After Bolt's screenplay for GANDHI had been rejected by David, it seemed as if this brilliant partnership was collapsing.

Now, in May 1977, David again contacted Bolt and for once the timing was propitious. Bolt had just turned down a project called *Shogun* for James Clavell and was working on a play about Augustus John[2] for his own pleasure. Bolt loved the idea of the Bounty and said he would join David in the South Pacific in July.

"Now don't get silly and impatient," he wrote to David. "You only found this project a week ago yourself. I haven't even read it. And here I am committing myself to it and you, which as you know is a thing I don't do lightly. If you go and get another writer now you'll just waste time and money and then call me in anyway. No, I don't think I'm the best writer in the world, I do think I'm a good writer for this particular film. The background, the themes, the characters are right up my alley. Perhaps even too obviously so. We mustn't do merely what we've done before. There really is in this one the opportunity for what we've always wanted - a strong narrative plus a bit of free-wheeling magic."

Ten days later, Bolt sent another letter. "I'm so excited by our project. We mustn't argue too much about this one or it will get too cut-and-dried and conscious. I want to dream it under your direction."[3]

David's knowledge of the mutiny aboard the *Bounty* was founded, like most people's, on the MGM film of 1935 with Charles Laughton as Captain Bligh and Clark Gable as Mr Christian. It was a film he liked very much and was based on a series of novels by Nordhoff and Hall.[4] When he read Richard Hough's account he was amazed at the difference between the facts and the fiction.

"The difficulty is you don't quite know why they mutinied, because, in fact, Bligh was quite a benign captain. He flogged much less than Captain Cook, and was a wonderful seaman, as was demonstrated when they put him off in a small boat and he went across the Pacific.

"You've got to have some reason for the mutiny, and Nordhoff and Hall met the difficulty by saying that Bligh was a flogging brute, which he wasn't. I think he was a terrific chap, though he had no sense of humour. Christian was a young man who just got swept away by the South Seas. Robert and I worked on this script and I think we nearly got it. It was a story of the seduction of men who come in from the sea and who land in paradise, where the women are only too easy to sleep with. And then, when the men had to go home, they couldn't bring themselves to return to England."[5]

In 1776, William Bligh had been sailing master to Captain Cook on the *Resolution* and charted the coastline of Hawaii. He was a superb navigator and even an artist. He was also a diarist, botanist, astronomer, geographer and anthropologist. And to attract David even more, he was Cornish.

"David loved authority figures," said Sandy Lean. "I don't mean figures within the establishment, but men with personal authority. He fell in love with Bligh and wanted to rescue him from his Hollywood image as a flogger and a bully."[6]

When Bligh set out on his ill-fated voyage he was thirty-four. His mission was to procure breadfruit plants in Tahiti and transport them to Jamaica where they would be used as cheap food for the slaves. Bligh selected his crew himself and was especially friendly with Fletcher Christian, whom he promoted over the heads of other officers and with whom he dined every other night. Hough suggests that there might have been a homosexual relationship (not unlikely in those days of "rum, sodomy and the lash") and David was inclined to agree with him. Bligh was considerate towards his crew, doubling their rest periods, ensuring they had proper exercise, and supervising their diet to prevent outbreaks of scurvy.

After a prolonged attempt to round the stormy and treacherous Cape Horn, which was the shortest route to Tahiti, Bligh took the *Bounty* across the Indian Ocean and past Australia, arriving in Tahiti several months later than scheduled. In a crisis Bligh was a great leader, but when calm returned he seemed to lose his authority. After so long at sea, discipline lapsed as the crew abandoned themselves to the arms of the Polynesian women. When Bligh saw Christian settle down to a life of indolence with a Tahitian girl, he grew angry and vindictive. When he found his officers had neglected their duties, and discovered sails mildewed and an anchor rotten, he was beside himself, and blamed Christian.

As the *Bounty* sailed for Jamaica, after six months in Tahiti, she was, to quote Robert Bolt, a floating barrel of gunpowder awaiting its spark. The crew had become soft and lazy, loathing the prospect of a hard voyage across to Jamaica. Bligh tried to restore discipline without much success. For Fletcher Christian, a sensitive and intelligent man of twenty-four, much loved by the crew because he was reliable, thoughtful, and made them laugh, the change in his friend's attitude was impossible to endure.

The mutiny, which occurred a few months before the French Revolution, began, like so many dire events, in accident and farce. Bligh decided that someone had been stealing coconuts and once again blamed Christian. While Christian had been planning to slip off the boat on a raft, he was encouraged by Ned Young to take the ship by force.

On the morning of 28 April 1789, as the ship lay off the Tongan island of Tofua, Christian seized the ship at gunpoint. Christian gave Bligh his sextant and supplies sufficient for a few days and cast him and his supporters adrift in the longboat. Bligh promptly became a great leader again and, after sailing for forty-one days across 3,618 miles of ocean, they made landfall at the Dutch settlement of Coupang, on the island of Timor in the East Indies. It is now recognised as the longest journey ever made in an open boat, and one of the greatest feats of navigation in history.

Christian took the *Bounty* back to Tahiti to pick up women and extra men and to leave behind those members of the crew, loyal to Bligh, who could not be squeezed into the longboat. Christian's plan was to start a colony on a remote island, though his first attempt - at Tubai - proved disastrous, due to the hostility of the natives. Christian returned once more to Tahiti, gathered provisions and then went in search of an uninhabited island. Nine months after the mutiny he and his little group of mutineers and Polynesian men and women reached Pitcairn Island, a tiny, uninhabited dot far from the main sea routes.

Bligh returned to England and a hero's welcome. He was received by George III and entertained at a series of celebratory dinners and banquets. And at the Royalty Theatre, a "fact told in action" spectacular entitled *The Pirates!* drew enthusiastic crowds.

The Admiralty demanded retribution and sent a heavily-armed ship called the *Pandora* to apprehend the mutineers. She was commanded by Captain Edward Edwards, a truly ferocious martinet who behaved exactly like Charles Laughton's Bligh. When the *Pandora* reached Tahiti, the men who had had no part of the mutiny swam or canoed out to the ship with much delight, only to be clapped in irons and incarcerated in a wooden cage known as "Pandora's Box". The mutineers who had chosen to remain on Tahiti were quickly rounded up and were put in the box along with the innocent.

After searching in vain for Christian and the other mutineers, Edwards turned the *Pandora* homewards. Lacking Bligh's skills, he wrecked the ship on the Great Barrier Reef and four innocent prisoners were drowned, trapped in the box. The survivors clambered into the longboats and after an arduous voyage they, too, staggered ashore at Coupang.

When the ten surviving prisoners were brought back to England, Bligh was on another voyage, determined to discharge his original commission, of carrying breadfruit from Tahiti to the West Indies. When he returned to England, he found public opinion had turned against him. The real story of the mutiny had reflected badly upon him and Christian had become a popular hero. Nevertheless, three men were hanged. Bligh subsequently became a vice-admiral and governor of New South Wales. On tiny Pitcairn, quarrels over women and land rights developed into full-scale warfare as the Tahitians rose in revolt. The killings went on and on until only one mutineer, Jack Adams, was left alive. Shaken by the horror of their brief history, Adams and the Polynesian survivors turned to religion. The God-fearing little community was not discovered until 1808. When the Admiralty finally learned the fate of the *Bounty*, Adams was allowed to live out the rest of his days in peace. The island's only settlement is named in his honour.

The *Bounty* saga had everything - elements of Moorehead's *The Fatal Impact* and the explorational aspects of Captain Cook's story - and it was undeniably dramatic. It was, as David might have said, the entire story of colonialism and exploitation neatly packed into a box, a Pandora's Box. As far as the film business was concerned, it would live up to its title.

"The stature of the film," wrote Bolt in one of his thoughtful letters to David, "depends utterly on the fact that they were both right, but from irreconcilable points of view. Bligh believed that without order, duty, self-abnegation, factual precision and foresight, life is impossible. Christian believed (though less consciously) that without spontaneity, freedom, self-expression and emotional gratification life is not worth living. Every human being is lumbered with this tension and everyone will recognise it and it is this which, with luck, will raise our film to the level of tragedy. Tragedy is not pessimism, it is the opposite of pessimism because it shows that even at its worst and most unjust life is worth living." [7]

Attached to the film was Stephen Walters, an Englishman who was one of the world's foremost authorities on maritime history and the *Bounty* affair.

According to Walters, "David was Captain Bligh in the sense that he recognised his own frailties and blamed himself when he made mistakes. In blaming himself, he forced a reaction on others. It was said to me when I was learning the sales side of a business, 'You only have yourself to blame if the person you choose doesn't make the grade, because you chose him. You either chose the wrong person and you should know better or you chose the right person but you don't give him the tools to get on with it.' In the David Lean-William Bligh mould, you become intolerable. David couldn't see the damage he was causing because it was secondary. The primary thing was getting the film made." [8]

Director John Boorman, perceptive as always, pointed out that the two protagonists - the authoritarian Bligh and the sensualist Christian - represented the two extremes of David's personality, and he must have felt sympathy for both of them. [9] The fact that the action took place in the South Pacific - David's favourite place in the world - rendered the project irresistible.

David was well aware that remakes tended to do poorly at the box office, no matter how good they were, and initially he was wary of making a third film about the mutiny. [10] But the freshness of the approach gave him confidence.

"I gather you want me exclusively for a solid year," wrote Bolt. "I hope that proves excessive. If we're still working on the script after a year, we'll be in trouble." [11]

Philip Kellogg, David's personal representative at the William Morris Agency and co-head of their Motion Picture Department, was told he had to retire when he reached sixty-five in 1977. David, who was four years older, considered this the height of ingratitude. He was devoted to Kellogg and, as a gesture, he dismissed William Morris as his agents and made Kellogg his producer.

Kellogg was known in Hollywood as "Gentleman Phil". An ex-navy officer, he habitually wore dark blue suits, white shirts and blue ties. He had the reputation of being immensely decent, which was both a strength and a weakness; like most agents, he wanted to convey only good news. But Kellogg, who represented David in almost all of the difficult negotiations over the Bounty project, would have to face being the harbinger of bad news. The result was often confusion.

Kellogg first brought Marvin Meyer into the project as his attorney. Then he moved to organise the acquisition of the rights to Richard Hough's book and to negotiate contracts for Bolt and John Box.

Even before David had found this subject, Kellogg had advised him that

Warner Bros., with the management team of Ted Ashley, Frank Wells and John Calley, was the right home for his next picture. Now he was able to bring them a complete package.[12]

John Calley, who was President of Warner Bros., said, "I'd always been an enormous fan of David's. From the time I got the Warner's job I kept after Phil Kellogg. Every three or four months I'd call him and say, 'Listen, if David Lean ever goes to work again, I'd like him to do it for us.' It almost got to be a habit, so I was shocked when one day Phil called and said, 'You've been ardent for so long, and I've told David that, and he'd like to come to you with a project.'

"So in April 1977 the three of us - Ashley, Wells and myself - flew to New York and met David at the Hotel Pierre. Phil introduced us and David told us that Eddie Fowlie had brought him a book about the *Bounty* and that he was completely enthralled by it.

"David wanted to tell the story of the events immediately preceding the mutiny, and the dismissal of Bligh and his crew in the small boat, with some kind of remarkable dramatic compression. The actual film was to be the story of this remarkable feat of navigation in which Bligh, with no serious navigational gear, charts or anything, manages to find Coupang. I'm kind of a nautical feat freak myself and it seemed like Shackleton what Bligh had done with those people. David hadn't thought of the framing story. The film's main narrative was to be this incident. He intended to describe what happened to all the participants in a crawl [a moving title] at the end. It was never to be dramatised.

"We had such reverence for David, we embraced the idea completely. He and Phil said they could do the picture for seventeen million dollars. We were a little bit nervous about that, but we said, 'Let's hope so.'

"I had another concern. It was going to be awful tough dramatising that number of people in one small boat. For me, it rang a bell - Hitchcock's LIFEBOAT, where you've got all these guys sitting around with their nicknames and their idiosyncrasies - and I was afraid it might be a little boring. But I knew that was one thing you couldn't accuse David of. I assumed that if it had caught his fancy, he had visualised something we would all want to see."

Warner Bros. announced the project publicly on 22 June 1977. By this time, though, David had a rather grander scheme in mind.

"In the process of developing the screenplay" said Calley, "David felt that, yes, this navigational incident was breathtaking, but that in the drama of the overall story it was a fragment. He wanted to begin with the story of Bligh getting the commission to deliver the breadfruit and the story should be expanded.

"I was troubled by the budget but was comforted by the idea that what we were getting for our money now wasn't just four men in a boat, it was a real David Lean movie. The other guys were a little anxious, but I really wanted this one and was selling it to them all the time: 'Yeah, it's going to cost us twenty but for twenty you get sunsets and islands and happy natives and human sacrifice. We're not talking about dysentery anymore.' You'd have paid ten million for no dysentery anyhow."

Calley suggested that a German company, Abeking and Rasmussen, could build a working replica of the *Bounty*.

"They're the best yacht boatyard in the world," he said, "and they're imbued with a sense of tradition. I've owned four or five of their boats myself and they're quite wonderful.

"David liked the idea. However, I knew that building a boat would cost a lot of money. So I started to do some personal research and discovered that existing Scandinavian trading vessels, the so-called Baltic traders, were almost exactly the same size as the *Bounty*. We could have bought one for about forty thousand dollars and spent another four hundred thousand on it and had the *Bounty* ready to go."[13]

In September 1977, Calley, Kellogg, John Box and Paul Hitchcock, Warner's English production representative, flew to Copenhagen and toured the Ring Andersen Shipyard where they found four or five possible boats.

"Some time later," said Calley, "Phil called me and said, 'We've talked to David, and John Box has shown him photographs and sketches, and David doesn't want to do it. He wants to build a full-scale *Bounty* from scratch.'

"I said, 'Well, it's going to cost a lot more money.' I felt that building the *Bounty* was emblematic of the kind of extravagance David had got a name for on ZHIVAGO. Put aside the fact that ZHIVAGO was a hit, there had been escalating financial panic during the production. I'm sure every MGM staff meeting was infected with rumours: 'there's no snow today, so what they're going to do is move everybody and the sets to Tierra del Fuego... there's no snow there, so now they're going to Finland....' A kind of migration of film people wandering around the world trying to find the right sunset.

"And Phil, of course, giving everybody what they wanted to hear, said 'No, no, David wants to dispel all that. As it happens, it was Bob O'Brien's idea to take ZHIVAGO to Finland, but David has been saddled with that rap, and it's unfair. He's just as concerned as you are about the budget, believe me.' I suspect Phil then went to David and said, 'You're absolutely right about building the boat. The guys at Warners will come round, they're a little bit soggy about it, but it's going to work out, believe me.'

"Now, after all, I had raised the spectre in the first place when I said, 'Build the boat and get it right.' And if they'd decided to build it at Abeking and Rasmussen I probably would have endorsed it. But then this momentum began to develop to build it at some Mickey Mouse yard in New Zealand and that scared the shit out of me. I felt that when the deal was signed, they would do what they wanted to do and it would be too late to do anything about it from our point of view.

"The crusher came when Phil flew from Tahiti to see me. He said, 'David and Robert have considered this carefully, so it's not a capricious idea, but they feel that the canvas is so immense that it can't be covered in a single film. It should be two films. And so what we want now is to have you commit to making two films and let us shoot them simultaneously.'

"The first film was to be the mutiny and the second was Pitcairn Island and the court-martial. Not a bad idea, by the way. But remember that we started at seventeen million with a bunch of guys in a small boat. Suddenly, we had two movies and a slice of English maritime history.

"I knew I had a real probem. I said, 'Have you any idea what it can be done for?' By this time everybody was just sort of winging numbers. Phil thought thirty-four or thirty-five million for the two films. I said, 'Let me talk to the guys.' And I did and everybody said, 'Well, Jesus, it's scary.'

"Their plan was to shoot the whole thing, then cut the first film and release it, and then cut the second, which would come out the following year. Then there would be the ultimate re-release, when you could see the whole thing. Which was all great, except that we didn't want to do it.

"We said, 'Let's spend twenty-five million and make the first movie. We have the option to make the second movie but if we make a loss and it doesn't work - if it just sort of lays there like the Brando picture - we don't want to be locked into a second one.

"So that you understand the problem in its context, if I'd gotten a call from Phil Kellogg saying, 'David's got his next project. He and Bolt are working on a really extraordinary, two-part action adventure about the mutiny on the *Bounty*, the whole thing is going to cost thirty-seven million,' I think we might have said yes.

"But it was the *slide* that got to me. I couldn't keep saying to my colleagues, 'Hey, you're not going to believe this. The guys have another great idea. Now they want to tie it into the space programme. You end with the court-martial and you cut to John Glenn on the launching pad, a kind of history of the world starting with the *Bounty*.'[14] I just couldn't get my guys to go with it.

"We were on the hook. We were committed to making the movie and building the boat. They had us. What *was* a deal-breaker was that we would not do a two-part movie. We wouldn't shoot them both at the same time. We would only commit to a one-part mutiny and if that didn't work we weren't going to do a second half.

"We expected Phil to go back to David and say, 'They won't do a two-parter,' and David to say, 'Right, I understand. Let's scale it down and we'll do it in three hours and fifteen minutes, it will be a one-parter with intermission.'

"What happened astonished me. I still don't understand. Phil came back to us and said, 'We don't want to do a one-parter, we want to do a two-parter and we want to be out of the deal.'

"We said, 'Give us our money back, and let us off the hook?' And he said, 'Absolutely.'

"I thought, 'Jesus, this guy is nuts.'"[15]

John Calley did not realise that David and Kellogg had found a new partner. However, apart from his own disquiet at the way the project was inflating, Calley learned that all was not well within David's camp and this was partly why Warner Bros. were keen to get off the hook.

Three months earlier, when the finance from Warner Bros. seemed assured and with Bolt starting work on the script, all was serene in Bora Bora. There was no reason why another great David Lean production should not have been underway. Yet disaster - the first of many - soon struck. David was standing with John Box, gazing out to sea, when a disturbing conversation took place.

"Isn't it beautiful?" said David. "And yet you seem to hate the place."

"I don't hate it," said Box, who was about to leave for England. "I hate it only from the point of view of having to do the film here. I don't know how to do it. I haven't got the facilities. How do we create snow and ice? How do we show the ship going round the Horn? I can't even get a box of matches. And everything is so expensive."[16]

"We have lost John Box," wrote David to Phil Kellogg. "I feel quite sick in the stomach because I have lost a good working friend... it's a failure on my part as far as the film is concerned.

"John had become more and more remote and depressed and I had a strong instinct that he had it in mind not to return. Last evening there was one of those silly all-too-frequent muddles based on umbrage where John and Bob Laing [his art director] failed to show up for drinks at seven and we finally ended up by having the final dinner separately. I woke up early this morning and decided I just had to have it all out with John.

"We went into the bar and I put my worries to him quite straight. I said I had a fear that he had made up his mind not to return and would he please tell me if it were true or nonsense. He asked me why I asked him this question. I said he gave me the impression of being some sort of disinterested friend out here on a visit and if I were a fly on the wall I would never dream he was on the payroll. He then said he had indeed intended to go back to England and discuss the whole subject with Doris [his wife] and did I require an answer now, 'before we get up from this table?' I said I did. 'In that case,' he said, 'there can only be one answer. As you force me into the situation, I must leave the picture.'

"I asked him to be quite sure in his own mind that he wasn't playing some sort of game with me. He then launched into a rather highly-charged series of statements about how he was dangerously near the point of idolizing me - and that his friends laughed at him about it. That I had changed a lot since we last worked together and had become very dictatorial. (I said that idolatry was a double-edged and dangerous emotion and that I had become dictatorial with him to fill the vacuum of his constant wooflings.) He told me he had worked with other directors besides me and 'because I am hitting sixty I cannot afford to spend two years of unhappiness on any film.'

"In fairness to him he made a great effort to make me postpone a decision there and then, but I am not at all sure it wasn't because he wanted me to carry the responsibility of his leaving.

"At the moment he has no idea at *all* what this picture is going to look like and as a result he feels very inadequate and has to remind himself and everyone else of his great creative ability. As soon as John sees the first page of *written script* he will be a changed man. John's vision has always been better than mine once the scene has been written and explained to him. He's quite brilliant and he is *always* like a beached whale at the start of things."[17]

"Up to that point," John Box told me, "our relationship couldn't have been better. People said we looked and behaved like brothers. But brothers who got on very well. Robert tried to make me stay but I was determined to go. I wish now I hadn't.

"David had got a bit grandiose, to be honest. I'm talking about somebody I'm immensely fond of. If you can't be God, be a film director. I think they all get a touch of that from time to time. And that's why he didn't do a film for years. But if we'd kept on the rails correctly, it would have been a very good film, there's no question about it."

Box flew home via Los Angeles, where he opened his heart to an old friend, Bob Shapiro, who had been his agent and was now in charge of production at Warner Bros.

As a result of Box's meeting with Shapiro, rumours spread like smog in Hollywood. The idea that David was acting like a megalomaniac in Tahiti soon became common currency. Such rumours, distributed far more conscientiously than any film, spread to Europe, and anyone who might have considered financing the project had serious doubts. David and his group blamed Box for everything.

"I thought what I had to say wouldn't have affected David's position at all," said Box. "I felt awful."[18]

"What a dreadful month it has been," wrote David to Kellogg. "I still feel very upset about John's departure; more in a personal than a professional way. If, after a night's sleep, he had come back here and confessed to a mistake things would have been different. The very fact that he boarded that plane to Los

Angeles shows the depth of his inner convictions." [19]

David would not speak to John Box for nearly five years.

Why did Phil Kellogg decide to pull out of what seemed an excellent deal at Warners? One evening, he was summoned to meet Frank Wells and Bob Shapiro. "I was told that Warner Bros. did not intend to continue to fund the development of the project - let alone the two projects - unless we presented a complete screenplay which they could budget at $19 million or less. Furthermore, they would not pay for the building of the *Bounty*, which was essential to meet our production plans."

Since Bolt had so far written only part of a first draft screenplay, Wells's ultimatum meant postponing the construction of the ship and that was estimated to take a year.

"I told Wells this was not our deal," wrote Kellogg. "He said that rather than going ahead with the picture, he would pay full cash commitments to David, Bolt, Box, Fowlie and me. I told him we did not want to be paid for not working; we wanted to make the pictures. Frank pointed out that Warner Bros. was in trouble with the first SUPERMAN picture which was vastly over budget. Our two big projects, having no limit on their costs, would present a corporate suicide pact. If he agreed to proceed with our request, he should be fired, he said. He left me no option but to go to David and give him his position." [20]

Wells gave Kellogg a memo from Warner's English production representative, Paul Hitchcock, who had returned from Tahiti and predicted a cost of $27 million for just one film.

When David heard the news from Kellogg he prepared a letter to Wells saying how shocked he was by Warner Bros.' lack of confidence in him.

"I wish you could have written me a few personal lines," wrote David. "As it is, I am faced by your somewhat embarrassed emissary, a photostat of an inter-office memo and the discomforting realisation that I have misjudged your confidence in me. I really have done my best to demonstrate my concern for cost by deferring my own salary - a point which would escape readers of your memo. You have stung me in photostat, a very public thing, and all of you who read this reply please remember that."

David wrote that he felt conned by Paul Hitchcock's presence in Tahiti - he had shown him the sights without realising he was drawing up a budget. He thought he had scared Hitchcock because "he is not an outdoor type" and that Hitchcock had distorted the cost of the ship by adding items such as livestock and a studio-built deck on rockers, for which he had added one million dollars. "May I suggest if director develops paranoia during shooting add $2 million?" [21]

David asked Kellogg to take the letter back to Frank Wells. As luck - or fate - would have it, the Italian producer, Dino de Laurentiis, was in Bora Bora. He offered Kellogg a ride to Los Angeles in his private jet.

"En route," wrote Kellogg, "he asked me about the progress of the picture, since he had always wanted to work with David. I told him David wanted to do two films and I was going to discuss some problems with Warner Bros. He told me he would gladly do two films with David and would get Paramount to distribute them. I told him if I had trouble with Warner Bros. I would come to him."[22]

That evening, De Laurentiis offered Kellogg an agreement which he signed. It was understood that it would be subject to both David's and Warner Bros.' approval. Kellogg flew back to Bora Bora; his trip was so rapid that David had not realised he had even left.

"I showed him the conditional agreement for the two pictures," wrote Kellogg. "He did not understand it and asked Robert to read it. Robert was elated and told David I had turned a disaster into a triumph. I went back to Frank Wells and asked for our release, which he granted. Wells never saw David's letter."[23]

If the executives at Warner Bros. were startled when Phil Kellogg withdrew, Dino de Laurentiis was stunned.

"At first," wrote Kellogg to David, "he didn't comprehend that we were clear from WB. He had been too elated that you were willing to make a deal

DINO DE LAURENTIIS has acquired the rights to new material about the best known and least understood event in Naval History. He announces two separate but related films which together tell the full story of His Majesty's armed vessel Bounty.

"THE LAWBREAKERS"

and

"THE LONG ARM"

Both screenplays are by ROBERT BOLT. They will be directed by DAVID LEAN. Produced by PHIL KELLOGG and photographed in Polynesia.

Photograph by David of John Box, used as advertisement: The Hollywood Reporter, December 1977.

with him for two pictures. Then he became even more elated as he realised the deed was done. He rushed around his desk and shook hands and almost danced."[24]

With his long experience of big pictures, De Laurentiis must have seemed the ideal backer for the *Bounty*. He took some time to read what script there was available, for his English was not too good. He often had scripts translated into Italian and this may have been the case with the *Bounty*. Eventually, he cabled

David to thank him deeply for the joy he had given him.

"It is the best material I have ever read, the construction is excellent. It has rhythm, it is always interesting, with suspense and beautiful dialogue and all the characters from Bligh to the very last sailors are superbly built. Bolt is without doubt unique. Together, you have done a truly excellent job and I am sure it will be the best script ever written."[25]

The agreement drawn up by De Laurentiis was for two pictures budgeted for no more than $40 million, the first picture costing $25 million. De Laurentiis gave David joint business and total creative control, including the final cut. David would receive one million dollars upon execution of the transfer from Warner Bros. and ten percent of the distributor's gross up to break-even point, when half a million dollars would be paid, plus twenty-seven-and-a-half percent of the gross. De Laurentiis declared these to be the most generous terms for a director that had ever been given.

In early 1977, after the contracts were signed, De Laurentiis took out full-page colour advertisements in all the trade papers to announce the project. Printed on a photograph of a man standing in the shallows of the ocean, lit by the moon, were the words:

DINO DE LAURENTIIS has acquired the rights to new material about the best known and least understood event in Naval History. He announces two separate but related films which together tell the full story of His Majesty's armed vessel *Bounty*.

THE LAWBREAKERS
and
THE LONG ARM

Both screenplays are by ROBERT BOLT
They will be directed by DAVID LEAN
Produced by PHIL KELLOGG and photographed in Polynesia.

"David and Dino," said Judy Scott-Fox, "was a marriage made in hell."[26]

De Laurentiis authorised the construction of the *Bounty* at Whangerei Engineering and North Island Construction Ltd, New Zealand. Against everyone's advice, Kellogg had recommended this shipyard, though it proved to be a good decision. The masts and sails were to be supplied by a British firm, Spencer Thetis Wharf, at Cowes, on the Isle of Wight. The construction was to be supervised by "Mac" McGuire, a senior marine officer for Lloyd's of London, who was appointed captain of the *Bounty*.

Julie Laird, who had recently worked for the Victoria and Albert Museum, and who had some acting and playwriting experience, was invited by Bolt to travel to Bora Bora to join the unit, bringing his and Sarah Miles's thirteen-year-old son, Tom.

"I remember my first meeting with David," said Julie Laird. "He looked at me and said, 'You're very white.' Apparently, as I learned afterwards, he didn't want anyone to come at all. He kept saying to Robert, 'Who is this person you're bringing down? I want us just to work. I don't want any distractions.'

"Robert said, 'She comes from the Victoria and Albert Museum.' And I gather David had gone around saying, 'A museum? We don't want anybody from a *museum*!'"

However, Julie Laird was so un-stuffy, so attractive and so intelligent, that David was quickly won over.

"When you saw how fastidiously David lived," said Julie, "he might as well have been living at the Berkeley. The fact that he was living in Bora Bora didn't alter how he approached life. There would be a 'royal command' which said, 'My boat is leaving and you will come' and so Robert and I used to go. We wore clean gym shoes but we had to dust the sand off frightfully carefully before we actually stepped on the boat.

"When we got to these spotless islands, Eddie would put down something across the sand and there would be a tree and this chair would be placed beneath and David would sit on it, immaculate, without a crease in his linen trousers. That's how he enjoyed it. The scenery, which I know he passionately loved, looked as though David had produced it. We'd all caper about a bit, then we'd have to clean ourselves up before we'd be allowed back on the boat.

"What David loved about it all, the rest of us began to hate. The mournful crash of the sea on the reef, a sound you couldn't escape from, the splat of coconuts falling from the trees on to the concrete paths between the bungalows - how we escaped being hit we never knew - the lazy, enervating heat, the remorseless breakfasts in the open dining room full of the latest batches of three-day American and Japanese trippers, and frangipani on the scrambled eggs.

"Robert and I kept asking ourselves, 'Why can't we be back in Earl's Court on a wet Saturday night, going to the movies?'

"Robert hired a battered old jeep - which again didn't please David, because everything he had was immaculate - and went to the other end of the island where Dino de Laurentiis was making HURRICANE. But David never did anything with anybody - his was the most extreme isolation. And Sandy obeyed it.

"He couldn't understand if you wanted a rest while you were working for him. He actually said to me, 'There aren't any weekends.' Mind you, I feel it too a bit, so it wasn't too difficult to go along with that enthusiasm.

"But I tell you why I worshipped him. Quite often at night there is this phenomenon called a green flash - scientifically I can't explain it, but there is no twilight, and as the light goes you can sometimes see this extraordinary green flash just above the water on the horizon.

"David suddenly said, 'Come on, Julie, come and have a look at this.' So I went to the window and I could see this phenomenon. I said, 'Gosh, isn't that amazing?' or something equally original, and he said, 'No, no, look at it like this,' and he put his arms over my shoulders, and made a square of his hands, as directors do, and said, 'Just shift your head a little to the right. Now look.' I don't know what he'd done, but it was totally different. It was breathtaking. It made you gasp with beauty and astonishment. I remember turning round to him and saying, 'Oh dear, oh dear. Now I know why I'm here.' I went round seeing things in a different way. You would die for a man like that.

"The fact that he wanted to show me what he was seeing, I think must be what he wanted in his films to show everybody. And I think that's how the battles over the script came about. Robert was concerned about what the character was thinking and the motivation; David couldn't have cared less about that. He knew what the ship was going to look like as it crested the waves and that was what he was going for. So there were bound to be clashes. But I think that what came out of it was awfully good."

Julie Laird eventually left Bora Bora because Tom had to be taken back to a more formal education in England. When David learned of this, he immediately suggested she should take over the research in London.

"I shall never forget the tremendous kindness of David. When I was leaving he came down to the little jetty and said, 'Are you all right for money? I'm giving you some because you deserve it anyway.' He'd worked it out that I would be a bit short of cash when I got back to England. He was terribly good like that." 27

With Julie Laird gone, Robert Bolt felt bereft. He wrote to her in London: "David, guessing doubtless at my lowered spirits, says that he thinks this is the best script he's ever had to direct. And even if he isn't right about that he's right in thinking it would lift my spirits to be told so. He is strangely compounded and sometimes puts me to shame. His egoism is so extreme and takes such finnicking forms that I get into a locked posture of rejection; and then he takes me off guard with some little act of thoughtfulness and generosity like that....

"My script is fairly good; everyone thinks it's a masterpiece which it damn well isn't. Oh, why has everything got to be larger than life? It's so exhausting and it always leads to tears."28

Despite Bolt's modesty, the script of the first film - THE LAWBREAKERS - reads most impressively. Whilst relatively little is made of the new facts included in the Richard Hough book - Bligh is still a martinet, albeit highly skilled - the intercutting between the mutiny, the court martial and even the play of *The*

Pirates! is dazzling. Characters are introduced in original ways - the dreadful Quintal, for example, is revealed in the act of murdering an elderly man in a Docklands alley - and the imagery leaps from the page. No one reading it could doubt that it would make a remarkably exciting film.

David decided to leave remote Bora Bora and base himself and his team on the island of Tahiti itself. While Bolt and the Fowlies found apartments, David and Sandy installed themselves in a suite at the Beachcomber Hotel, near the airport of Tahiti's capital, Papeete. It was here that a curious diversion took place.

In August 1773, Captain Cook had nearly lost one of his ships in Tahiti and had been forced to cut a main anchor adrift. This was well-known in the islands, and there had been many attempts to find it. While examining the log books, Eddie Fowlie became convinced that the anchor lay off Tautira on the north-east coast of Tahiti. A dive team was assembled and, after an encounter with a shark they spotted a vague shape fifty yards away at a depth of one hundred and twenty metres.

"They went towards it," said David, "and sure enough it was Cook's anchor, encrusted with coral. Eddie was right and everyone else was wrong."[29]

David was as excited by this discovery as any marine archaeologist, and he decided to finance the recovery of the anchor himself at a cost of ten thousand dollars. He thought that the raising of the anchor was important enough to be filmed, and although he had his own 16mm camera, he wanted it done by a professional documentary company. He wrote to a director he knew in New Zealand, Wayne Tourell, asking him if he could organise a crew.

When Tourell received the request, the name of David Lean struck a match to the flashpowder of his ambitions. Why not build the film up from four or five minutes of salvage footage to include the earlier *Bounty* films, the fabulous Tahitian locations, the historic appeal of Captain Cook..? David liked the idea and ten days later Tourell and producer George Andrews, of South Pacific Television, arrived in Tahiti with a crew including New Zealand diver and marine historian Kelly Tarlton. Tarlton quickly reassured David that the anchor, buried in coral, was almost certainly one of the three anchors lost by Cook in 1773. The two smaller ones might also be nearby.

David agreed to help finance the documentary but he also told Tourell and Andrews that he was too preoccupied with the Bounty project to become closely involved in making it.

"However, he would like to mention two things," wrote Andrews. "The first was that the moment when the anchor stirred from the ocean floor for the first time in two hundred years was 'tremendously exciting' and that we should make sure we filmed it properly. The second was who did we think would narrate the film? This, too, would be very important. By then I had known him just long enough to make the suggestion I think he was after. 'Why not do it yourself?' 'I'd be delighted,' was his reply."[30]

Andrews dispatched a script to David and a crew of seven followed. The weather in Tahiti was superb and technical trials were conducted on an expensive magnetometer which David had ordered from England to help find the other two anchors. But shooting was slower even than on a David Lean film. Because of the depth at which the anchor lay, cameramen faced danger from the "bends" - Tarlton had lost three friends that way - and no dive could last more than eight minutes. There had to be a wait of eight hours before the next descent.

A Saturday lunch was organised for David to meet the crew. "After lunch, the bombshell," wrote Andrews. "David told us that he had been thinking about some shots for the opening of the film and would it be all right if he took Ken [Dorman, cameraman] away the next day to do some shooting? Wayne and I were dumbfounded. What scenes for the opening? How would they fit in with the opening we had already written in the script, which we had sent David weeks earlier? And what about the filming we had in mind for Ken the next day, and the schedule we were trying so hard to keep to? Who was the director on this picture anyway?"

The delicate matter was resolved by submitting to David's wishes, and using the underwater cameraman [Lynton Diggle] for the scheduled shooting.

"We should have realised what was happening," wrote Andrews. "To David, who hadn't, after all, made a picture since RYAN'S DAUGHTER, the temptation to get involved once again in filming was proving irresistible.

"David's first filming day was a great success. He had Ken frame him some marvellous shots of the Tahiti coastline. He composed his shots superbly, with an energy and vigour that shamed those thirty years his junior. But how was it all going to integrate with the script that Wayne was already shooting? We got our answer that night. David and Robert Bolt, we were told, were now working on a new script for our film which they were sure we would like."[31]

Although David was paying for the actual raising of the anchor, South Pacific Television were paying for the costs of filming and those costs were escalating. Andrews was later shown David and Bolt's script at a restaurant outside Papeete. Whilst the original script was written as a documentary - a film in which events would be covered as they happened - David and Bolt's re-write was to be shot like a regular, fictional feature film.

"It was, of course, an impossible situation - hardest of all on our director, Wayne," said Andrews. "It was quite clear that if we wanted to involve David Lean in the film there was only one way it was going to be done: his way. Once we accepted that decision, life changed enormously. We soon reached the stage where we were not only shooting to a David Lean script, we had David Lean as director as well."

To George Andrews, a documentary purist, it was sheer heresy when David suggested that the raising of the anchor could be reconstructed. David persuaded Tarlton to haul the anchor from its coral grave and re-bury it in shallower water where there was no danger from the "bends" and where filming could be achieved swiftly and in more favourable light. Tarlton didn't argue.

David ordered a full-size mock-up of the anchor and, on dry land, he rehearsed precisely what the divers were to do and what the cameraman would cover. David even asked Bolt to write the dialogue which Tarlton was to deliver as he apparently "discovered" the anchor. Tarlton duly recorded this, and when he went underwater to do the scene, it was fed through the underwater communications system. Tarlton mimed to his own commentary, matching every movement to his words, while the underwater cameraman filmed to David's instructions.

"As a lesson in how to control an awkward filming set-up it could hardly be bettered," wrote Andrews. "As an example of the difference between the approaches of an old pro of the cinema and a young television documentary team, it was equally unforgettable."

A further shock was in store for the New Zealand crew when they viewed the first week's rushes. David said they were the worst he had ever seen.

"What he saw was a full four hundred feet magazine [10 minutes] of underwater stuff being shot every time our divers went down," wrote Tourell. "It was a long way down and when the visibility was good you shot the whole mag in case you never got down again. The cameraman always got a bit light-headed - a bit drunk, if you like - so the last few minutes was usually a lot of visual nonsense as the divers blew water rings at each other during the various decompression stages of the ascension to the surface. I'm afraid that was just too much for him.

"There were a lot of silent, depressed faces as we left that first showing. We all felt a little sick. How could we carry on when the greatest film-maker in the world and our co-producer hated it?

"I got a hint of things to come when he came over to me outside - probably after seeing my despair - put his arm around me and said, 'I will teach you how to make real films.'

"As my teacher he was very avuncular... as my boss he was a tyrant. As first assistant, I was constantly abused and reprimanded for everything from the weather and sea conditions to plonking the camera in the wrong place for the day's first set-up. I was not unfamiliar with drama. I had already won two New Zealand Television awards. I could see the potential and I grabbed the opportunity with both hands. It wasn't demotion but promotion. How many directors in the world would have given their right arms to be taught personally by the master! And teach me he did, although he kept saying I'd never make a good director because I was too nice."[32]

Before travelling to New Zealand for the editing and dubbing sessions, David sent a letter to Andrews and Tourell, giving his instructions. The "space signal" - a sound effect which was written into the Bounty script - was also to feature in the "documentary".

"Get the sound department on to cooking up a good electronic 'peep... bleep...peep...bleep' to go over the underwater stuff. It doesn't matter a damn if it makes such a noise or not. I can see you, George, twisting in your seat but in my book sound effects are orchestrations like musical accompaniments and are the more interesting for being only suggestive of reality..."

David suggested that they find a recording of "Rule Britannia" - "played by a rather eighteenth century-sounding orchestra, not a marine band with jingoistic overtones" - and play it over the shots of the anchor rising through the water, slowly drowning out the noise of the lifting crane. David also suggested that Nathaniel Dance's famous portrait of Captain Cook should be intercut with the shots of the anchor.

David added a PS: "The 'Rule Britannia' may - of course - not work. The worst thing about reading about it is the actual title which had different con-notations. It would certainly be a failure but for the crane noise which we hope might take the curse off it because of its grinding and harshness. I'm trying to defend ourselves but in my experience some of the really best ideas sound quite mad when told in cold blood."[33]

When David reached Auckland he was careful not to behave like a dictator. When Tourell took a week off for another project, David rang him every day and, when Tourell returned, he went over his cuts in detail. He told his team, "You know, I get just as excited about this film as I do on any of my big ones. Every morning I wake up at five o'clock thinking of a cut. It's marvellous making movies, wonderful. It's magic, really, isn't it?"[34]

Once the anchor was raised and cleaned, David presented it to the Musée de Tahiti et des Isles, where it stands at the entrance, with a report from a Tahiti newspaper detailing the rescue with a photograph of David and Phil Kellogg.

The film, called LOST AND FOUND: THE STORY OF AN ANCHOR, was an enjoyable diversion for David though he admitted that it "wasn't terribly good."[35] But then, he never regarded documentaries with the same respect he accorded feature films. *Variety* reviewed it when it was shown on Auckland TV-2 in May 1979, saying it "lacks magic and shows no sign that it is the work of a major cinematic talent."[36] However, it played to top ratings and very good reviews in the New Zealand papers. Bolt, who considered the whole episode a maddening and unwanted distraction, regarded the film as "beneath contempt."

I remember seeing it at the London Film Festival in 1980 and being somewhat disappointed since the name of David Lean had set up such expectations. Seeing

David directing LOST AND FOUND, *with Ken Dorman at camera and Wayne Tourell.*

it again for this book, I found it rather charming. The re-enacted scenes with David, Robert Bolt, Eddie Fowlie and the shipwreck expert, Kelly Tarlton, are hilarious because the performances are so amateurish - all except David, who proves once again that he was a natural actor. He also reads the narrative very compellingly. The film is lovely to look at and its underwater material justifies all the liberties taken. When the anchor breaks surface and Tahitian girls swim out to lay garlands on it, David's unashamed use of "Rule Britannia" works well. This isn't exactly the equivalent of the raising of Henry VIII's ship, the *Mary Rose*, but it is exciting.

We are also given a glimpse into the kind of research that David was undertaking for the Bounty films. In one scene of LOST AND FOUND he shows us a ship's biscuit, with its Admiralty markings, and taps it against the side of his Boston whaler. That sound, he explains, was heard all over ships of the period - it was the sound of men knocking out the weevils. The film ends with David and Bolt at Papeete airport, saying farewell to their crew and looking a little lost. Then David puts his arm around Bolt and says, "Come on, we've got a film to make."

"Now that Bligh and Christian are on the home straight," wrote Bolt to David, "let's break off from THE LAWBREAKERS and tackle LONG ARM. The point is that as you say there are no more decisions of content to be made in LAWBREAKERS; it's a question of style and emphasis, and these will be dictated by LONG ARM, particularly its commencement."

The letter ended on an unexpected and, in the light of what happened next, a somewhat sinister note:

"A contractual point which I hate to bother you with, but you ought to know: my contract is, strictly, with Dino only. The Director isn't mentioned. Phil assures me that Dino knows that I'm working with you, regardless of dates, and that he wishes me to go on doing so. But as we go I'm going to be in breach of contract unless Dino OK's this (to you, Phil or me) in writing. I've asked Phil to get this OK for me (on May 1st as I remember) and I expect he will. Just thought you ought to know. Affectionately, Robert."[37]

In August 1978, Leila finally granted David a divorce. "After years of living - half-living - with my Indian wife," David wrote to a friend, "I married her knowing it was a mistake because of her 'intolerable position' back in India. After something like twelve years of asking for a divorce, interspersed with breakdowns and threats of suicide, I finally got it for a final settlement of a million dollars."[38]

Leila seldom admitted the divorce to her friends and acquaintances. She continued to call herself Mrs David Lean and lived quietly with her daughter in Bangalore. A statement of hers was picked up by the press:

"David and his work are more important to him than I am. He really only lives when he works. Life has only one meaning for David - his film-making. He is obsessed. He will do the impossible for a film. He will go to the moon. The film is his father and mother and brother and son. His concentration is total. I never talk to him unless he talks to me. Even if he is just shaving or tying his tie. If I speak to him, it startles him.

"His greatest love apart from making motion pictures is taking still ones. He has the most marvellous eyes. He can see a spot on the horizon that no one else can see."[39]

Ten years after the divorce, on 7 July 1988, David was told that Leila had died a tragic and bizarre death. In London for a cosmetic operation, she had choked on a croissant at the Grosvenor House Hotel. The coroner recorded a verdict of misadventure.

David told me, "She was a dear woman. Wonderfully glamorous, terrifically good-looking, I mean, a real show-stopper, and very nice, very intelligent and very funny. It's a pity that it didn't last. I think it's entirely my fault."[40]

CHAPTER FORTY-THREE

FATAL IMPACT

PANDORA'S BOX II

WHEN the 1935 version with Charles Laughton was made, people spoke of a BOUNTY jinx. The production was marred by accident - a man was killed - and incompatibility. But at least the film made money and won the Oscar for Best Picture. When the Brando version of 1962 went down with all hands, it was assumed that no one in their right minds would ever tackle the subject again.[1]

David's Bounty sailed into a series of whirlpools. At the centre of the first vortex was Dino de Laurentiis.

A veteran of the Mussolini era - he was born in 1919, three years before the March on Rome - De Laurentiis produced his first film by the time he was twenty. He was behind that notorious sex-and-neo-realism sensation BITTER RICE and married its seductive star, Silvana Mangano. In collaboration with Carlo Ponti, he produced Fellini's LA STRADA and King Vidor's WAR AND PEACE. After this film, made with backing from Paramount, he parted company with Ponti and produced a series of historical spectacles for Hollywood studios, notably BARABBAS and THE BIBLE. In the Soviet Union, he produced Sergei Bondarchuk's massive WATERLOO, and in 1976 was responsible for the lavish remake of KING KONG, which was a famous box-office flop.

Phil Kellogg's lightning deal had been signed while De Laurentiis's company was trying to produce HURRICANE, a remake of a venerable John Ford film, an epic which was to go $10 million over budget. The producer was De Laurentiis's daughter, Rafaella, and the stars were Mia Farrow, Jason Robards, Max von Sydow and David's old chum, Trevor Howard, playing a grizzled Catholic priest not unlike his part in RYAN'S DAUGHTER.

To facilitate the production, De Laurentiis had built a luxurious hotel on Bora Bora, the Marara, to be used by the cast and crew. This $3 million investment,[2] together with the budget for HURRICANE and other lavish productions, as well as a chain of restaurants and delicatessens - called the DDL Foodshow - left him without sufficient assets for David's epics. It began to look as though he might be trying to wriggle out of his commitment.

The first indication was the argument over his fee. One factor that had persuaded David to accept the deal was that, as an independent, De Laurentiis would have no justification to demand the vast fifteen percent overhead of a major studio like Warner Bros. When De Laurentiis claimed that such an overhead was a standard feature of his deals, Kellogg guessed that Paramount were squeezing him; he could not sell the idea of the two pictures at forty million and had to have an overhead factor "or some way he could hold off Paramount's distribution terms so that they would make a deal and he could live with it."[3]

De Laurentiis's lawyer, Norman Flicker, drew up a detailed contract which outraged David's lawyer, Marvin Meyer. The overhead was written in and creative control was taken away. "It had everything in it that you might have expected under the Columbia-Spiegel days - or worse," wrote Kellogg.

Knowing that De Laurentiis was in financial straits, Kellogg also knew they could not possibly turn to another company. Dino simply had to make the Paramount deal, even if David had to make concessions - such as the overhead; otherwise they might be killing the goose that lays the golden eggs. Kellogg wrote to David, "I know that you and I do not need the difference in profits that amount represents if it costs us the making of the pictures."[4]

In addition to the overhead, De Laurentiis also insisted on a fee of $500,000 - and defended it in a most original fashion: "Not only do I know that this is what Warner's got, but Paramount knows it also. How am I to make a deal with Paramount that is straightforward and honest, when I am asked to deny what is a fact? In view of these facts, the overhead charge cannot be discussed."[5]

With the sole exception of Robert Bolt, De Laurentiis terminated all the contracted salaries (he had already stopped paying Kellogg) and tried to take over as producer, even though the agreement limited his role to that of financier. He also brought in Bernard Williams, a young associate producer who had worked with Stanley Kubrick and who, therefore, knew all about perfectionists. Williams told David that the age of the big movie was over, explaining that Paramount had just spent $6 million on a film called SATURDAY NIGHT FEVER which looked like earning $100 million.

Williams was instructed to prepare a budget. Kellogg believes the idea was to show the project to be irresponsibly expensive in order to justify De Laurentiis's withdrawal. Because De Laurentiis had several projects on the boil at the same time, he was able to prevaricate, leaving David dangling in Tahiti. As David made no secret of his impatience, De Laurentiis decided it was politic to send him a letter:

"Rumors have reached me that you are unhappy because you are convinced that, after a year of hard work on the script, I have lost all interest in this project and no longer intend to produce it. Believe me, if this was the truth I would have immediately told you because I consider myself a very straight person.

"If this is what you feel, then I must tell you that you are wrong, at least for the following reasons:

1 - It has always been my wish - and still is very much so - to produce a

David Lean picture, and you can therefore imagine what two pictures means to me, as in this particular case;

2 - I have not changed my opinion on the script, which I consider beautiful, and I still feel very strongly about it;

3 - I was born a winner, and thus I never give up; if I ever had to withdraw from the project because of any circumstances, I would be a loser."[6]

Whatever other charges might be levelled at De Laurentiis, one could not deny his almost poetic sense of irony. For by this point - August 1978 - it must have been blindingly obvious to him that he was going to have to ditch both the Bounty projects.

Ever since he was a boy David had been fascinated by wireless, and he had recently bought a short-wave radio - a Sony ICF7600 - which enabled him to tune to the BBC World Service, which he called his "umbilical cord", and into such unexpected transmitters as airliners. It provided much harmless entertainment until David discovered that he could pick up De Laurentiis's radio messages from Bora Bora to Papeete. Fortunately, Sandy was able to translate from the Italian.[7] But it was rather like the British breaking the German code; David could not act upon the information without giving away his source.

In mid-September 1978, De Laurentiis summoned David and Phil Kellogg to an urgent meeting in Los Angeles. David never publicly revealed what happened, and when I asked him, he claimed he had blocked it out of his memory. Fortunately, he put it all in a letter to Julie Laird:

"Dino personally presented us with his budget [for the first picture] which came to a figure of $34 million. Dino assured us that this was without any contingencies for going over budget or even inflation. In fact, with such contingencies it would almost certainly reach something like $50 million. With the script in his hand he also informed me he could tell by the sheer weight of it that it would run for four hours.

"'I cannot afford it, David. We must talk tomorrow - just Phil and your lawyer.'

"The talk tomorrow consisted of Dino reiterating the cost which he couldn't afford and saying he could not continue because I had not 'used my best endeavours' (quoting from the contract) to bring it in at a reasonable cost - round about $25 million.[8] This, he said, put me in breach of contract and he was therefore no longer liable to me. When my lawyer replied to this statement, Dino answered with, 'I cannot talk to you. You must talk to my lawyer.' That was it.

"He sent a lawyer to New Zealand to see the boat builders and asked them to slow up the work and give him a year to pay. The only person he kept on in unaltered circumstances was our friend Robert. It took a little time for the truth of the situation to dawn on me.

Sandy Hotz photographed in the South Seas by David.

"Because of Robert's tax problems, Dino had already paid out three quarters of his money. With the outlay of another quarter he would own two scripts. Now, he knew very well how close I was to those scripts and how much I wanted to do them. The normal thing to do in these circumstances is to give what is known as a 'turnaround'[9] with a sixty-day limit. Dino then produced his trump card. (He owed me one and three quarter million dollars if I made the film or not; called 'Pay or Play.') He said he would give me the turnaround if I signed a paper saying I relinquished all the payments he owed to me and that I would promise not to say a word against Dino or mention the method of getting my release.

"We got Eddie out to LA and soon found out that the budget had been padded out and that the real and probable cost was in fact in the region of $25 million. But there I was. Dino was the undisputed owner of both scripts. If I didn't agree to his conditions he could make both scripts himself, cut both scripts into one script by using another writer and have it directed by anyone he could get."[10]

"The best thing David or his representatives could have done," said John Calley, "from the point of view of self interest, would have been to say to Dino de Laurentiis, 'I'm sorry, Dino, no turnaround. We're going to make the movie. You don't want to make it with David? Good luck. You owe David X million, you owe X million for the boat, you owe John Box, Phil Kellogg, Robert Bolt.... Dino would have had to have written a cheque for six or seven million dollars to walk away from this thing. Because of the combination of either bad agenting, producing or legal advice, they accepted these onerous turnaround terms, and David assumed the burden for the production expenses to date, except for the boat. As it was, it was catastrophic."[11]

David described his lawyer, Marvin Meyer, as "a bloodhound on a leash. He said he had a cast iron case contractually, but he couldn't do anything if I insisted on getting hold of the scripts again because the only condition for doing so was to sign away the money owing to me."

Seeing David so determined, Meyer and Kellogg advised him to accept Dino's arrangement because he was in a "very dangerous mood" and fighting him in the Californian courts could take years. In order to keep the film alive and have the chance of finding another backer, David accepted, although he refused to sign two clauses which Meyer described as "obscene". The first stated that De Laurentiis was forced to give up the film because of David's extravagance, and the second stated that David would never disclose the contents of the agreement to anyone.

With those two exceptions, David signed the agreement on the night he left Los Angeles for Tahiti to continue work with Bolt on the script. However, Meyer warned David not to tamper with the script until De Laurentiis had been paid in full.[12]

"So for $1,750,000 I got the right to find a new producer-financier for the two films within sixty days," said David. "Even then Dino wouldn't sign until the last minute! It's my worst experience in the whole of my career."

Now that David had accepted full financial responsibility, and given up every penny due to him, he received an account, forwarded post-haste from Marvin Meyer, for $31,000.[13]

David and Kellogg had two dozen copies made of the first script and these were distributed to the major studios. "Without exception they said it was the best script they had read for years," wrote David. "Some said it was the best script they had ever read."[14] However, they were all frightened of two films with the second not even written.

But one man, Joseph E. Levine, appeared to have no fear. He offered $50 million, perhaps $55 million, for the two pictures. Without knowing of Levine's offer, John Calley telephoned Meyer offering an original scheme for a deal: Calley had spoken to his partners, Frank Wells and Ted Ashley, and suggested that the Motion Picture Association of America, consisting of all the major companies, should join together to finance the pictures and draw lots for the rights of distribution at cost.[15]

It was the kind of brave gesture towards film history that Hollywood producers had never been imaginative or unselfish enough to implement before.

Nor did they implement it on this occasion. In any case, David refused to enter into any discussions on this basis since he felt a loyalty to Levine who then looked like being the saviour of the project.

Although David was deeply touched by Calley's enthusiasm, he wanted to behave correctly with Joe Levine because he thought he had the blood for it. He had been appalled that a producer like De Laurentiis could take away a script: "It's the kind of situation I would have thought well-nigh impossible to be clobbered with," he wrote to Kellogg. "In your terms it's as if someone had separated you from your wife and was bargaining for her return.

"For my part I can only tell you that never before in my career have I felt the certainty I now have about those two films. I have had the same feeling about certain parts of some of my other films; the prisoners marching into the camp whistling at the start of RIVER KWAI, Omar Sharif coming out of the mirage in LAWRENCE, the train journey across Russia in ZHIVAGO. But there have always been areas of doubt as to whether certain scenes would work or if the subject matter in certain parts would really appeal to big audiences. I don't have these sort of doubts with these pictures. I know I will have to come up with a bit of magic here and there, tickle quite a few talents and pull out some stops - but it's all there in the air waiting for me to catch it. It also has a certain power of its own; something to do with the power of certain legends and characters. It's magnetic.

"Films have been my life. These are the last two big pictures I'll ever make and I'm determined to make them. The quality which scares people with me is my so-called perfectionism."[16]

David offered to defer every penny of his salary until Levine had recovered it from the box office. If he went over the agreed budget, he would sacrifice his salary, dollar for dollar - if it went two million over, he would have worked for nothing and if that offer was refused, he would invest another two million from his own capital. There was only one definite "no". He was not going to be put in a situation where he made two films which made a fortune for everyone except himself - because he went over budget.

"If the two pictures cost $57 million instead of $55 million I would not be prepared to see Joe sit back with a profit of nearly $10 million and I only get $2 million because I had forfeited nearly all my percentage points. In those sort of circumstances it would be very advantageous to everyone else if I did go over budget - and my pride won't take it."[17]

It is certain that Levine could never have been presented with "so eloquent a commitment" as Kellogg put it. Alas, Levine was not up to such a challenge and withdrew. David had to find support elsewhere.

A letter survives which hints at the discomfiture Bolt felt about his position. He sent David fifty-nine pages of THE LONG ARM and wrote, "I fully take your point that at this moment I am working only for Dino and that you have neither the desire or authority to influence my writing on this second script. That is very proper and correct. Meanwhile, however, you remain my friend I trust, and I want your comments on what I've done so far, as I would on any other script I was working on. I hope you will be willing to do that for me, simply as a friend. I think it would be pedantically scrupulous for you to refuse."[18]

David replied in a way which suggests his suppressed anger: "By the time you read this, we will already have spoken together and you will therefore have some idea of my reaction. We have had many such post-reading encounters - and I have hated and been embarrassed by them all. This promises to top them all. I generally take you on five to ten pages at a time. This one, including your accompanying letter-cum-thesis, is sixty-three. I have scarcely known you more enthusiastic and am therefore the more put out.

"To add to my difficulties the script and letter are written as if from two different people. The letter is a highly intelligent appreciation concerning the aims and pitfalls of writing this second script as a dramatic scenario. An appreciation which the writer of the script has failed to read. Unfortunately, you are one and the same person and I am going to have to go into battle against the intellectual who will defend the script with some pretty good verbal acrobatics."

David then broke the script down into sections, criticising the method of story-telling for having nothing to do with the first film.

"The first film I would call athletic, unpredictable and dramatic. It is also told in a series of time slips. The second film is told in the style of a slightly dramatised documentary."

He thought the script far too slow and nearly all the major dramatic points were blurred by too much detail.

"When the *Pandora* arrives at Tahiti the main point is surely the race of the non-mutineers to be first on board - only to be clapped into irons. This is completely blunted by the crowds of Tahitians running forward with fruit, pigs and flowers."

The greatest character distortion was the *Pandora*'s captain, Edwards. Bolt described him as an interesting and recognisable psychological study, not just an inexplicable monster. David thought the script portrayed him differently: "I find him not only way over the top but an inexplicable and disgusting pervert which reminds me of your description of Ken Russell's VALENTINO."[19]

When David returned to Tahiti, Bolt, who was considerably overweight and who had been smoking and drinking too much, disclosed to David that he had experienced slight discomfort at Los Angeles airport, returning from a holiday in France. He was told it had been a heart attack. David made arrangements for him to catch the next plane to Los Angeles, to have this confirmed by experts.

Bolt was kept in St John's Hospital for over a week, then discharged with a long list of regulations. He had to give up smoking and drinking and he was ordered to take regular exercise, such as swimming.

Bolt returned to Tahiti in November, when he and David continued their discussions on THE LONG ARM. He would have much preferred to have flown home to England, for he had become desperately homesick and complications with his family were causing him anguish. What he referred to as "the bloody endlessness of it all" maddened him.

He found himself alienated from David, yet living only for the work: "Demanding and forceful he is: fertile and fortifying he isn't. He has that blinkered quality which characterises all great achievers - apart from the very greatest. Perhaps even they? Alexander used to enjoy mocking himself, but I expect that was really a matter of style. On the whole I don't think I like the breed. But I don't like ineffectuals either. Oh, I am hard to please."[20]

He felt that, in every area, 1978 had been "a sort of catastrophe, like a silent film of a street accident in slow motion."[21]

Bolt was so desperate to get the script done that he suggested to David that they ignore Christmas Day and work as usual. David, who looked a trifle startled, agreed, and then phoned later to say that Sandy was dismayed and would he mind if they took the day off?

"I fell in with this readily, feeling, however, that a valuable point has been made in the most, indeed the only, effective manner. He simply can't believe in the reality of any experience not his own. That people might want time off from his project of the moment for decent not deplorable reasons is a thing he has always felt to be highly dubious, smacking of hypocrisy."[22]

Bolt's frustration grew worse. David was constantly picking at pages which he felt had been finalised.

"David, for Christ's sake be careful," he wrote. "I know you when you get like this. What we've got is pretty damn good. Don't let's pick it to pieces for fun. What is familiar never seems as good as a new idea. You can go on for ever like that and end with a mess."[23]

"The bugger of writing for a brilliant film director," wrote Bolt to Julie Laird, "is that while you are certainly writing for a superior skill you may be writing for an inferior mind. You can't ponder the nature of Black Holes with a man who has never heard of gravity and feels insulted if you attempt to tell him of it. I try to slip in my little contributions as I drive my pitons into the cliff face and work us along from one directorial 'opportunity' (shipwreck, sacrilege, rape or sunset) to the next, but that's the most I can really do. David thinks that left to myself I am highbrow and moralizing; and for all I know he's right. I think that he left to himself is inconsistent and jejune. Trouble is that like all Great Directors he really regards the writer as a troublesome sort of fountain-pen with a perverse will of its own. At a pinch all of them without exception think in all sincerity that if they put their minds to it they could write, act, design and photograph the film better than their actual colleagues. They really do. That their colleagues may know something which they don't themselves simply doesn't occur to them and would seem almost blasphemous if it did."[24]

David found Robert equally maddening. He had even less business sense than David, and had caused David embarrassment when his agent, Peggy Ramsay, demanded payment for the second part before he had even finished the first.[25]

David must have taken legal advice, yet he relinquished none of his possessiveness towards the scripts. As soon as he had recovered from the De Laurentiis débâcle, he set to with his customary dedication.

"I see us rather like workers in a diamond mine, armed with pick axes and hacking away at a wall of rubble," he wrote to Bolt. "This morning I've been reading five possible versions of how Christian ended his days on Pitcairn. But we are not miners; we are diamond cutters and it's very intricate work, far removed from the wall of rubble. It's such hard physical work - this hacking one's way through the theories and facts - that if we can produce an interesting narrative line we tend to think that the job is done."

David was ready with some theories designed to provoke the socialist in Bolt. "There's the whole racial theme. It's not unlike Africa. The whites came in and turned the bush into fertile farming country. The men from the *Bounty* came to Pitcairn with their western implements and building 'know-how' and turned the place into a small colony. The Tahitian man is not a worker and he's not a thinker. The Demi and the Chinese and the French have now taken over Tahiti and the Tahitians - particularly the men - are resentful. All they've got to do is pull their finger out - but it's no good - there's nothing behind the finger. Rage, fury and frustration. Violence the only outlet. It's all very modern and I wouldn't half mind showing a few home truths. (I can see you recoiling as if I'd let loose a rattlesnake.)"[26]

David also took Bolt's literacy to task. In a bizarre letter, he quoted a line from the script - "Tonight I want as much hot mush as every man can eat" - and asked Bolt why "he can't just say, 'as much hot food as every man can eat?' When I hear 'mush' I think, 'What's mush? Must be an old-fashioned word for food.' And by the time I've had that thought I'm no longer touched because it's been an interruption."

To rub it in, David referred back to an exchange of dialogue in LAWRENCE - "Themistocles, sir, a Greek god." "I know you're educated, Lawrence, it says so in your dossier." (Bolt must have noticed that David had misquoted the line, for Themistocles was not a Greek god, merely a writer and philosopher!)

"I would like to blow cocaine up everyone's nostrils," David continued. "Yours, the designers and the actors. If we could create a kind of Gauguin-like atmosphere, exotic and heavily perfumed, I think we could put the film up into another class." [27]

In New Zealand, the *Bounty* had been faithfully reconstructed from plans supplied by the National Maritime Museum at Greenwich. She was made of steel - which was not apparent to the eye - and below decks were two powerful engines. The ship, which was registered at Lloyd's as a yacht, was estimated to cost two million dollars.

"She was beautiful," said David, "an exact replica on the exterior. Down below we had the generators and all the rest of it. It was much smaller than the ones built for the Brando or Clark Gable films. They thought the original would look too small on the screen, but the whole point was that you couldn't walk below decks without bending over, and it was so cramped you were stooping the whole time." [28]

The ship was launched at Whangerei on 16 December 1978. Sadly, David could not attend this momentous event - he was represented by Eddie Fowlie - since Kellogg had summoned him to Los Angeles to meet a representative of Lew Grade. But it turned out that Grade's man, like everyone else, was interested only in one long film.

David was so desperate by now, and so bereft of options, that he agreed to consider it. As he searched for a backer, David and the Bounty had become known to Hollywood insiders as "The Old Man and the Sea".

Then David remembered United Artists. He had already met the two young men who now ran the company - Steven Bach and David Field - and had liked

The launch of the Bounty *in New Zealand.*

them. They were enthusiastic and friendly and their detailed questions about the script proved they had read it carefully. Bach and Field examined the De Laurentiis budget and thought it exaggerated. David told them the whole sorry story.

"Lean startled us both," wrote Steven Bach, "by announcing in his silvery voice that he could not imagine the two pictures together costing twenty million. 'I should imagine more in the area of nineteen,' he offered, all sincerity and crisp British inflexions. My first thought was either he was trying to outhustle De Laurentiis or he was seriously out of touch with the inflation that had taken place over the decade since RYAN'S DAUGHTER."[29]

Since the first picture was budgeted at more than twenty million, I found these figures difficult to accept, and wrote to Steven Bach, who has since become a film historian and biographer.

"The whole Lean-Bounty thing was mysterious then and remains so," he replied. "I remember the incident vividly just because of the surprising figures Lean cited, which was why we paid a great deal of money to send Lee Katz to Fiji and New Zealand to come up with some sort of budget arena. Lean was working with somebody called Eddie Something (you will know) whom he trusted and Katz thought a charlatan so far as budgets were concerned. My real connection with Lean was through Phil Kellogg. 'Gentleman Phil' (as he was known) was far too circumspect and, it must be said, inexperienced at production to contradict Lean about the budget or even make a guess of his own.

"Lean was so sure that Dino was robbing him blind that he may have arrived at the figure by simply subtracting what he assumed Dino had paid for the hotel, for the boat, for his own lavish life-style, expenses and fees, etc, etc. Then there was whatever overhead Dino was charging him (we charged none, which was of great interest to Lean). I suggest in the book, and still think it possible, that Lean was not above his own brand of 'pitchmanship' in selling the project. His desire to get it made was palpable. And to an extent it worked. Lean was far too sophisticated at the business of show not to know that and be able to exercise it in his elegant way.

"In any case, what I say he said in the book is truly what he said, and I've checked my notes to confirm it. Obviously at the time he said it, he didn't know we were going to call him on it by sending Lee Katz to chase down the figures."[30]

As far as the script was concerned, David and Bolt were at loggerheads over the start of THE LONG ARM. David had set a fresh course, which Bolt disagreed with. He felt that the first dozen pages, which had been sent to UA, were too leisurely, and while he was amused and charmed he was not gripped until the *Pandora* set sail to catch the mutineers. He wrote a long letter detailing his worries to David.

"Sorry," he concluded. "All of this is so destructive; I hope very much that I'm barking up the wrong tree and that you'll talk me out of it; but I'm feeling it strongly at the moment. Everything tells me that we've struck the wrong rhythm altogether. It wouldn't be right not to say so. I mean - I'm all for grace notes and finishing touches, I really am. I love all that. But these pages seem to be made up of grace notes; there's no melody."[31]

Another letter from Bolt, almost as long as the script itself, followed a few days later. David poured gallons of cold water over it and pointed out that they faced a crisis. UA had been delighted by the first fourteen pages of the new script, which had pretty well "sold" them on the film.

"Now at this critical moment you come along and say that those first pages are so much rubbish and we should begin again at page one... I am shocked by it' because after what you said about the first pages sent to UA I expected something so interesting and so good that I would be happy to part with those pages."

He attacked Robert's work, saying that his new construction had done considerable damage to the film. And for the first time, as though suspecting that something dreadful was about to happen - legal action perhaps - Sandy added some notes to David's letter. She considered some of the circumstances "rather odd", that Robert was behaving strangely and David was finding the material he submitted "way below standard."[32]

By the end of January 1979, Bolt had written eighty pages of the second script. It opened with black and white freeze-frames to remind the audience of the events of the first film, and the colour faded in as Bligh walked up the ramp at Coupang to be greeted by a bizarre sound - a burst of applause. This provided a cut to the Royal Society for the Advancement of Knowledge, whose President has just bestowed on Bligh its Gold Medal.

This second script, no more of a straight narrative than the first, cuts excitingly from the mutineers burning the *Bounty* on Pitcairn to the *Pandora* and her vicious captain, Edwards, setting out to capture them. We see Bligh back in Tahiti, and his public humiliation in London at a performance of *The Pirates!* The script also includes an intriguing observation from the American whaling skipper who landed at Pitcairn in 1808. Meeting Bligh, years later, he comments that Jack Adams had never heard of Nelson or Trafalgar, Wellington or Waterloo. "He'd never heard of Napoleon Bonaparte!"

With Lee Katz, David flew to Fiji and then on to see the ship and studios in New Zealand where government representatives had once promised every assistance. Now they offered no such thing. Katz estimated the two films at $42 million - not much more than De Laurentiis's original budget, but twice David's.

"And a week later," wrote David, "we had a call from Phil Kellogg saying, 'You can open the champagne.' We did. Then silence."[33]

Not until several precious months had passed did they hear the rumours about HEAVEN'S GATE, Michael Cimino's folly, and how its budget was assuming the proportion of a war debt. UA were not anxious to take on another big exterior film.[34]

As the work on THE LONG ARM drifted into drudgery, David and Bolt's relationship deteriorated. While David had been away with Katz, Bolt had turned the script in yet another direction David did not approve of. There was a confrontation and then Bolt fell ill with fever.

"It became very bitter and very painful," said Sandy Lean. "They had been working interminably, sometimes with a great deal of rancour. Robert hated rewrites and over this David was implacable. They fought over every scene."[35]

"There were genuine points of aesthetic morality and taste at issue, but also, I fear, a good deal of fairly pointless macho," wrote Bolt to Julie Laird. "The result, predictably, was a dead heat, with both contenders carried out of the ring. However, I had the ignoble satisfaction of seeing him exhausted and near to tears before we both decided to call it quits and now he is being hilariously polite and considerate and I hilariously eager to see merit in his ideas and justice in his criticisms of my own. It hasn't been a complete waste of time. We couldn't have gone on as we were. He to my mind had become a little too high-handed, even for a Great Director. I, to his mind, was no doubt wilfully intractable. Anyway, the happy upshot is that the second script is under way again and proceeds apace."[36]

On 7 March 1979, David left for Los Angeles to take over responsibility from Phil Kellogg and to see if he could put the deal together himself. Bolt felt sure he would not succeed and, worse, that the films would not be made. He told Julie Laird that the money men disliked being confronted by detailed, finished scripts. They preferred a vague "project".

"Another damaging factor (I think) may be David himself; he does not and will not understand or even consider as a possibility the fact that in his old age his admirable self reliance has hypertrophied to the verges of megalomania. It shows itself in a myriad tiny ways but it does show itself; and megalomaniac directors have a terrifying reputation for squandering backers' money. We have had several brief scuffles and (a week ago) one stand-up battle on this subject and it's no good going on about it. David is deeply convinced he is the most unassuming and self-effacing of men, almost culpably moderate in his demands. It is all a great shame and I'm exhausted by the effort of writing and trying to perfect something which in all likelihood will not be seen."[37]

David knew that the extension of the turnaround - to ninety days - was about to expire. In extremis he decided that the only man capable of saving the film was Sam Spiegel, and he flew on to New York to see him.

What a moment of triumph for Spiegel! His career had been in the doldrums since he and David had last worked together in 1962. He had tried to top David's success on ZHIVAGO with an epic about the last Tsar, NICHOLAS AND

ALEXANDRA, which was photographed by Freddie Young, designed by John Box - and directed by Franklin Schaffner. It had been a financial failure. Even more spectacular was the failure of Elia Kazan's THE LAST TYCOON, based on F. Scott Fitzgerald's unfinished novel about Hollywood.

David's arrival on his doorstep was a sign to Spiegel that he still had power and prestige and he proved it by extending again the De Laurentiis turnaround. But he made David suffer by informing him that under no circumstances would he agree to two films. It would have to be one or nothing.

"I must say I never had much excitement for the subject," Spiegel told Adrian Turner, "as it had been done several times before, but David's passion was contagious. I just felt compelled to make it happen."[38]

Spiegel put Kellogg through an interrogation for two days. With his role now ended, Kellogg told David that he would resume his producing deal with Warner Bros., which Frank Wells had requested after the Bounty deal had been concluded. If the Bounty went into production, Kellogg would be happy to return, as long as David wanted him.

At this crucial juncture, Robert Bolt flew to Los Angeles because of renewed heart trouble. Awaiting his appointment at the hospital, he stayed at the Beverly Hills home of Michael Caine and his wife, Shakira. At dinner one evening, the Caines noticed that Bolt was seriously ill and they rushed him to hospital. He was given a triple bypass on 9 April 1979 and two days later he suffered a massive stroke which paralysed him and left him for a while unable to read, write or even speak.

Despite David's hatred of sickness, he went to the hospital only to learn that Bolt did not want to see him. His son Ben (now a film director himself) rushed to Los Angeles when he heard the news. He had the difficult job of explaining the situation to David.

"Robert felt very muddled and confused," said Ben Bolt's wife, Jo. "He'd get frantic when Ben said, 'David is here to see you.' His reluctance was partly due to the fact that he couldn't speak."[39]

Perhaps because of this, a rumour circulated that Ben Bolt, distraught at seeing his father in such a desperate plight, had accused David of being responsible for it by driving Robert so hard.

"It's not remotely true," said Ben Bolt, indignantly. "Who told you? A lot of people wanted to see him and he didn't want to see them because of the state he was in."[40]

"David was actually incredibly generous and sweet," said Jo Bolt. "There was some muddle over the medical insurance and David paid for the operation."[41]

Nevertheless, David was upset and hurt and felt in some way responsible. He wrote to Spiegel about the build-up to the crisis.

"By the behaviour of Robert's son, Ben, and very vague hints from Julie Laird when I was in London, I gathered that Robert had been giving a very different picture from the truth in his letters home - and in some way I was the villain of the piece. This feeling was so pressing that it put me in a difficulty when I was about to leave Robert after his stroke in the hospital. By asking him questions and receiving his answers via nods and the pressing of his left hand I gathered he was having great worry over his medical bills... I said to Sandy, 'If I pay his bills his friends and family will think I am doing so because of my guilt.' Because of the seriousness of his situation and my very genuine compassion for him I paid all the medical accounts to date. They amounted to $25,600."[42]

David later changed his mind about the medical bill. Not wanting to have this accusation hanging over his head, he asked for a refund from Bolt's agent, Peggy Ramsay. To his surprise, she told him the money had been sent long before to Los Angeles.[43]

After sixteen weeks in hospital, Ben and Jo took Bolt back to England and looked after him for the first few months, "for which," Bolt said, "I feel a debt of infinite gratitude."[44]

David stayed miserably in Los Angeles until Spiegel arrived to set up meetings with some of the major studios. Warners returned centre stage and offered $100,000 for David to find a new writer. David flew to London to talk to George Macdonald Fraser, author of the *Flashman* novels, but he was tied up on another project. David also read a script about Nijinsky which had been written by Melvyn Bragg, though he didn't think Bragg was right for the Bounty. But when David flew to New York, Spiegel flew Bragg over for an interview. David found him very agreeable and hired him to write the script. Since Bragg was adamant he would only work in London, David and Sandy booked into the Berkeley Hotel in June 1979.

Within days of David and Sandy's arrival in London, the *Evening Standard* ran a story about the film in its Londoner's Diary column: 'Bragg sets sail for the $40 million Bounty?' The reporter found Bragg a little cautious, but his worries about upsetting Robert Bolt were dismissed by Peggy Ramsay.

"He doesn't give a damn who takes over from him," she declared. "I feel sorry for Melvyn, he won't know what hits him. Believe me, whatever money he gets, you can double it in blood."[45]

When Ramsay wrote to David a few weeks later, asking for copies of the script, she received a frigid response: "You must appreciate that your malicious contribution to the *Evening Standard* precludes anything but an impersonal reply to your letters."[46]

"I'm sorry you thought the *Evening Standard* column malicious," replied Ramsay. "When a newspaper rings up, one must expect something absurd to result from it. There was certainly no malice. I am only concerned with Bob, and the fact that if one goes out for the really big killing you should be sure that your constitution and temperament can stand it - very few can. Though Bob is improving, I don't suppose he will be able to write for the cinema again, but nobody knows."[47]

Melvyn Bragg, the well-known novelist, had taken a sabbatical from his job at London Weekend Television, where he was editor and presenter of the *South Bank Show*.

"I thought David was wonderful to work with," he said. "And I wished I'd met him at the beginning of my career because he'd have taught me to write screenplays. But during a fine summer, I felt incarcerated even though it was a lovely suite at the Berkeley. I'd turn up at ten in the morning and we'd spend the day until about six-thirty working through two or three lines here, two or three lines there. Occasionally I'd be let off to go and do some writing.

"David led an extraordinarily enclosed life. By telling him what was happening in the outside world, it was as though you were bringing news from Mars. You had to keep feeding him this stuff; you were his newspaper, his link, and I found this very difficult.

"There was a great confusion about Robert because David had been accused in no uncertain terms of bringing about Robert's collapse, which he thought was a great affront. It hurt him, or it rang true with him, I don't know which. He was oppressed by that. He wouldn't talk about Robert and he wouldn't go and see him, which puzzled me.

"I went to see him. We had one memorable dinner together when he had the greatest possible difficulty in speaking, and Robert's summary of David was, 'Always remember he began as a cutter. And that's what he does. He cuts.' He meant he did so emotionally. Now I found David not only charming but helpful and generous in every way, but I saw the truth in what Robert said.

"The idea was to make a single film, which David was reluctant to consider, but that's what he had to do. That was the only option. David would much rather condense everything into a single film from material he and Robert had already arrived at, but that proved to be impossible; it was much too long, the way they had conceived it."

For Bragg, who had read the log of the *Bounty* as part of his preparation, the story became fascinating when he came to the conclusion that Fletcher Christian was far from the hero of popular myth.

"In my view, Christian was a shit. He left Bligh and the men on the boat with so few provisions that no one in their right mind would have thought they'd do anything but starve to death. He took people away from Tahiti by force and landed at Pitcairn where there was soon a racial war. Bligh was a victim of black propaganda run by the Christian family so that should Christian ever be captured, which they thought very likely, then he might have a chance of getting off this heinous crime of mutiny because the man Bligh was such a shit. These things excited me a lot."[48]

As David and Bragg got down to work, another set-back occurred in New Zealand. Dino de Laurentiis had been unable to keep up the payments on the ship and in August 1979 the *Bounty* was seized by order of the supreme court of New Zealand and a writ was nailed to its mast. It was four months before the writ was removed.[49]

After a few weeks' work, David, with his years of working with Robert Bolt, found it hard to deal with his new collaborator.

"He'd got this second writer on his hands," said Bragg, "who wasn't being the tame little chappie and clearing up after Robert Bolt. He'd got a whole set of ideas which were intriguing but got in the way. And I think that got him down. The working relationship was strenuous to a degree. It was very, very difficult. He could be back in Tahiti. He could take a whole day to tell me about the views, the blue of the water, the smell of frangipani - I got a lot of that - and he would show me the photographs. We were never less than polite, we never lost our tempers with each other. But it was such a strain."[50]

In the basement of David's home in Narrow Street I found a bundle of hand-written sheets and some type-written pages from Bragg's script. The title page reads:

PANDORA'S BOX
based on
THE LAWBREAKERS and THE LONG ARM
by
ROBERT BOLT
First Draft Screenplay
by
MELVYN BRAGG

The opening was entirely fresh: "The screen is filled with a vast shot of the Pacific Ocean. This is taken from such a distance that we can see the curve of the earth. The camera moves closer through dissolves to frigate birds hovering in the sky. We follow them as they make for their objective - a black tip of land, where they loudly and excitedly beat their wings.

"CUT underwater. Suddenly silence in this rich, tropical sea embroidered with so many glittering colours and shapes. Here too, though, is a sense of panic as the thousands of fish speed and flick towards the camera as if fleeing something.

"CUT to a woman's face under the water. It is the face of a smiling, slant eyed nymph. The painted face of the figurehead of the PANDORA. Tiny, brilliant fishes dart about her. A pair of chained hands come across her mouth and grab her shoulder.

"CUT to a wider shot. We see the full figurehead - the woman holding a box (which has been smashed) and the name PANDORA on what we recognise as the bow of a sunken ship. The man's feet are chained together as are his hands. He is young, we can see, and almost naked. He is covered in cuts and we see that his head has been badly hurt, which is why he is moving desperately slowly trying to get some leverage to push himself to the surface. He finds a foothold on the box; it gives way as he pushes himself to the surface."

"I'd worked with Sam Spiegel before," said Bragg. "I admired him a lot. But it became a tug of war between Sam and David. They had completely fallen out. David thought he'd been well and truly cheated by Sam over the royalties [for LAWRENCE]. And he felt Sam had taken far too much credit. David both envied and despised Sam's worldliness, his friends, his yacht, his social life."[51]

David was suspicious of the friendship between Spiegel and Bragg. "When, Melvyn, you and I started working together," he wrote, "I thought we were aiming to turn the idea of making two films into a one-film idea. I also thought that Robert and I had done an exciting job on the LAWBREAKERS script and that we were aiming to keep as much as possible in the new framework of one film."

David was under the impression that all three of them liked the actual method of telling the story. It was fast and full of surprises. "Because of this we set ourselves a new beginning in order to provide a new end. The wreck of the *Pandora* gave a smashing introduction to the new title and enabled us to make a lot of short cuts at the end of the film."

David was also becoming alarmed by the introduction of sex scenes. "I beg you both to remember that the discovery of Tahiti as it then was started a concept which swept through the whole of the civilised world. The concept of the Noble Savage. Tahiti was and still is a magic name. Just think of the people who have been drawn there - and it was very difficult to reach. Gauguin, Melville, Robert Louis Stevenson, Somerset Maugham, Rupert Brooke. Even Noël Coward said that Bora Bora was the most beautiful place he'd ever seen. We must not lose this magic."[52]

But David thought they were in danger of doing just that. "Spiegel and Bragg joined forces against me," he wrote. "Spiegel wanted to inject a lot of bare-breast sex into the Tahiti scenes. I thought they were ruining the script and I finally suggested that they write their script and I write mine. I chose Switzerland because Spiegel begged me to go 'somewhere where the telephone works' and I had to admit it doesn't work in Rome. Weeks later, the Bragg script was delivered, discarded and paid for with the Warner money."[53]

David continued work on the script alone, delivering it to Spiegel in December 1979. Copies were sent out - to Filmways, to Warner Bros. - and Rona Barrett talked about the project on American network television, which led to an enquiry from the President of MGM. But no one took it any further.

Spiegel decided that what was needed was a major star to lure the studios. In March 1980, he announced that he wanted Robert Redford to play Captain Bligh. In the early days of the project, David had thought of Oliver Reed and then Anthony Hopkins for the part. His first idea for Fletcher Christian had been Christopher Reeve who had been recommended by Katharine Hepburn. But David thought Redford was completely wrong for the part. "Meeting him would be an embarrassment," he wrote.

Spiegel now dropped a bombshell: Dino de Laurentiis wanted to come back on the film and would require not only a percentage of the profits, but reimbursal for all the money he had spent on scripts and expenses. He would sell the ship, still in dry dock at Whangerei, to the film at cost, provided it was returned to him after shooting. David would have none of this: "After LAWRENCE and KWAI I expected Spiegel to cheat me, but with the two of them together...!"[54]

Although the ship was once again the property of De Laurentiis, David refused to work with him in any capacity. Spiegel then became more and more off-hand about the project. David suspected something was going on which he couldn't explain. Something certainly was. Spiegel had learned that Paramount had just loaned De Laurentiis $32 million free of interest to help pay for the script and the ship.

David and Spiegel finally parted because Spiegel insisted on an equal division of artistic control. "I dared not accept this," wrote David, "because it would give him the power to negate all my ideas including casting and script - a clause no major director would accept."[55]

There were a couple of last desperate efforts to save the rapidly sinking ship. John Heyman, who had helped Spiegel finance THE LAST TYCOON, had attended a couple of meetings shortly after the De Laurentiis fiasco. He recalled, "Spiegel would scream at David, 'It's too late to bring me in on this - you always bring me in as an afterthought.' Then he did all in his power to make it work, at no expense to himself. It was one of the few totally thought-out scripts I've ever come across. Both commercially and artistically it would have been an absolute beauty."[56]

David was then introduced to a millionaire Israeli, Arnon Milchan, who diverted the Bounty back towards United Artists just as the HEAVEN'S GATE débâcle reached its climax, and UA pulled out again. Milchan then started a fruitless search for tax shelter money. Before David finally relinquished the project, he and his historical adviser, Stephen Walters, attempted to adapt the two screenplays into a thirteen-part series for television, hoping that Time-Life might finance it. But television was not in David's blood.

David had two other ideas which he had been thinking about for some time. The first was a film about the early days of the movies. He gave this up in August 1975, indulging instead in a luxurious cruise and turning his attentions to his 16mm camera. He returned to his idea in 1981, writing reams of his experiences for the benefit of a new scriptwriter, Dennis Potter.

Potter recalled that a meeting over lunch began compellingly enough, and then steadily became more uncomfortable. "Mr Lean began more and more to rail first against 'the critics' and then, in particular, about the acting abilities of one of his most recent (British) stars.

"But I was intrigued by the half-idea and thought I might perhaps be able to come up with something to flesh it out. I was working on something else at the time, and took a few weeks over the book-readings. And then he wrote a sharp little note to Judy Daish, my agent - 'The silence emanating from you and Dennis Potter is truly explicit.' He asked for the return of his notes."

Potter replied to David, "It seems very clear that you have been badly offended by a silence you take to be the equivalent of unresponsiveness. I am extremely sorry. It did not for one moment occur to me that you would take such umbrage."

Potter went on to explain that he had been having problems with the drug he had to take for his skin trouble and that he did not realise there was any hurry. But he needed time "to prowl around a subject" although he was very swift once he started writing.

"The very degree of your reaction means, alas, that a shadow has fallen upon any possible working relationship and so I, in turn, find it sad, but necessary, not to seek to pursue what could have been such an exciting venture."[57]

Potter later recalled, "I thought, God! I'm better out of that! I duly sent all his books back. End of non-story. A pity, really..."[58]

David's other idea was to make a film from Karen Blixen's novel OUT OF AFRICA, which had first been suggested by Barbara Cole. No sooner had he unpacked at the Mount Kenya Safari Club than Arnon Milchan telephoned to say there was immense interest in the Bounty from Universal, and in the other ideas from other companies. How soon could he return to London? David, though, insisted on first visiting the Karen Blixen farm outside Nairobi.

While 20th Century-Fox expressed interest in the early movie idea, a deal with Universal on the Bounty fell through because Paramount revealed they were the owners of the Bolt scripts and put up a series of impossible conditions.

"It is now clear," wrote David, "that Paramount under Barry Diller were determined to stop the film being made. The reason is that they have just about finished a film called REDS which is being directed by the actor Warren Beatty, a close friend of Diller's. They are far over budget and it is said the cost is something over $50 million. It will cost Diller his job if it fails. Paramount dare not make another big budget film until REDS has come out. If they allow Universal to buy over the rights and the film turns out to be a success the shareholders will ask why they made REDS and turned down the Bounty. So the film is finally off." 59,60

David gave Eddie Fowlie and his wife Kathleen his Mercedes diesel as a gesture of appreciation. David had previously given Eddie his Rolls-Royce.

"Did you know I found out what David wanted and sent him a cheque which came back with, 'I always wanted to give you a Rolls-Royce. I think you'd look rather good in one', written across it. Later, he gave the Mercedes in Tahiti to my wife Kathleen and shipped it to Europe. Later again, Sandy gave to Kathleen the Mercedes she had in India. They were both very kind and generous people. Not just with us but to a hell of a lot of others. They helped so many, at times at quite big cost." 61

Sandy and David packed up their suite in Tahiti and flew to Los Angeles to see Paul Kohner, the veteran agent who controlled the rights to OUT OF AFRICA. They picked up their current Rolls-Royces and, with Eddie and Kathleen, spent a month driving across the States via Charleston and the Deep South, before sailing from New York on the QE2 with both cars. They arrived in London on 29 June 1981, staying at the Berkeley, as usual, where they were met by Stephen Walters.

"David put his arm around me and was crying. He said, 'I'm afraid it's finished because Universal just won't play.' He thought Universal was his last chance - they were used to sea pictures, they understood the problems of boats, waiting for the clouds to come up behind the mast, with the wind in the right direction.

"In a sense, he had been reliving elements of his past. David relished the enjoyment of pre-production. But he hadn't got the thing off the ground and was being kicked up the arse financially to make it happen. He funded much of that time out there himself. He did have money from Warner's, but in the end he was hoping Universal would fund it."

An idea that came out of the Bounty was inspired by Stalin's daughter who "hopped across the border as though on a pogo stick," as Walters put it. David wanted to parallel this modern story with the story of Omai, a Tahitian whom Captain Cook brought to London and who became a favourite at court. Omai was eventually returned to Tahiti where he aroused such envy that he was killed.

Although David came up with some remarkable ideas and imagery, the idea came to nothing.

One producer David had not yet approached was the white hope of the British industry, the man behind CHARIOTS OF FIRE and THE KILLING FIELDS, David Puttnam. Would he be interested in producing OUT OF AFRICA? Even though David was well aware that Puttnam did not work with veteran directors - he preferred directors he could initiate - the two men had a meeting at the Berkeley.

"We had a long talk," said Puttnam, "I had re-read the book. He was concerned only with the magnificent scenery and the animals. I pointed out that the book was about the impact on a woman of syphilis. I had done research on what would happen to her, and the 'cure' in those days was quite horrendous - it involved ripping out her genitalia. David was absolutely horrified. This was not a field of interest to him.

"I didn't see how he could leave the syphilis question out to make a film about Africa and animals. He thought he could. I have to say that history proved him right - the Sydney Pollack film [which won several Oscars] was hardly a film about syphilis."

Puttnam was deterred from working with David for another reason. "One evening, we were having dinner, and in some detail he slagged off all producers - starting with Sam Spiegel. He did it in an interesting way. He said the reason why he wanted to work with me was because I was different. The others were all thieves or incompetent. It was a nonstop tirade. But I realised that I'd be next. He basically resented the notion of a producer. They were an ugly and unfortunate necessity."[62]

Puttnam suggested that David might give a series of lectures to students at the National Film School. When David turned the offer down, Puttnam felt he had evaded his responsibility as a film-maker. But David declined because he thought the students would laugh at him. He knew, from other film-makers who had visited the school, that the students had no compunction about informing their guest speakers exactly what they thought of their work.

While David was still thinking about OUT OF AFRICA, producers continued to send him novels and scripts. David Niven Jr wanted him to direct a picture called SANTA CLAUS. "The combination of David Lean and Santa Claus sounds like and would be magic," he wrote, hopefully.[63]

Judy Scott-Fox wanted him to make *Howard's End* and sent him the novel. But by that time David had made up his mind to direct another story by the same author, and the film which would prove to be his last, E.M. Forster's *A Passage to India*.

CHAPTER FORTY-FOUR

REGAINING THE LIGHT

A PASSAGE TO INDIA I

Just before LAWRENCE, David had married Leila. Just before A PASSAGE TO INDIA he married Sandy. David and Sandy both maintained that Lord Brabourne was the first to suggest they regularise their relationship. "The film was going to get a lot of exposure in India," said Sandy, "and there could have been shots taken of us in the press."[1]

Lord Brabourne denies this vehemently. "The idea never entered my mind. If it had, I wouldn't have interfered."[2]

If anyone was responsible for the marriage, it was David's lawyer, Tony Reeves, bringing a hint of his primitive Methodist background to bear. "I suppose you disapprove?" David asked one day of his relationship. "I can't see why you haven't married the girl after all this time," replied Reeves.[3]

"So John Brabourne proposed," said Sandy, "and Tony Reeves seconded. In the end we rather liked the idea ourselves. Why not, we thought? Seventeen years, that's an awfully long engagement."

The wedding took place on 28 October 1981 in Thalwil, Sandy's family's town of origin in Switzerland, shortly before they left for India. To everyone's surprise and dismay, the marriage proved, technically at least, to be David's shortest.

The story of E.M. Forster's novel *A Passage to India* concerns the friendship between a Moslem doctor, Aziz, and an English schoolmaster, Fielding (based on Forster himself), who has little time for the British. A young lady from Hampstead called Miss Adela Quested sails out to India with Mrs Moore, the mother of the young man, Ronnie, she intends to marry. Miss Quested wants to see "the real India" and at a tea party at Fielding's she meets Aziz. On the spur of the moment, Aziz invites them on an elaborate picnic expedition to the Marabar Caves. Something happens in the Caves: perhaps Miss Quested was touched by a guide, perhaps she was so disoriented by the echoes and the pitch blackness that she gave way to hysteria. She accuses Aziz of what the British community takes to be rape and he is put on trial. Fielding is ostracised by the British after he gives Aziz his support. When Miss Quested withdraws her complaint, Aziz is found not guilty, to the apoplectic fury of the English. Fielding returns to

England. Aziz hears he has married Adela and is deeply upset, but he's made a mistake for Fielding has married Mrs Moore's daughter. When Fielding returns to India he tries to resume the friendship, but succeeds only briefly. The ending depicts Aziz and Fielding on horseback: "We shall drive every blasted Englishman into the sea," says Aziz, "and then you and I shall be friends." "Why can't we be friends now?" asks Fielding. "It's what I want. It's what you want." The men ride off in opposite directions.

Edward Morgan Forster, who was born in 1879, came from a wealthier position in society than David, but as an artist he, too, reacted against his suburban background. Forster first conceived the novel during a stay in India in 1913, but put off completing it. He returned as a private secretary to a Maharajah in 1921. He loathed most of the English he met there, comparing them unfavourably to the intellectuals he knew at Cambridge. The novel was published in 1924, five years after the British army's massacre of civilians at Amritsar.

Even though Forster avoided topical references, the novel was regarded as political for it gave a remarkably unsympathetic view of life under the Raj. It sold well, aided by controversy, and was quickly accepted as a classic, the mystery of the 'rape' in the Marabar Caves obsessing literary critics.

Curiously enough, Forster was a frequent visitor to T.E. Lawrence's cottage, Cloud's Hill, in Dorset. He recalled how delightfully casual the atmosphere was, how they drank only water or tea - no alcohol - and ate out of tins. "We weren't to worry about the world and the standard the world imposes." Forster had been deeply impressed by *Seven Pillars* and had written the last two chapters of *A Passage to India* under its influence.[4] These two literary geniuses had one thing in common; a profound dislike and distrust of the cinema.

Convinced that any film of his novel would be a travesty, Forster rejected every offer to buy the film rights. He did, though, allow the Indian authoress Santha Rama Rau to adapt for the stage the courtroom scene, and this became the basis for the Oxford Playhouse production of *A Passage to India*, directed by Frank Hauser, with Zia Mohyeddin as Aziz, Norman Wooland as Fielding, and Enid Lorimer as Mrs Moore.

It was one of the few plays David saw - probably at the invitation of Norman Wooland - at the Comedy Theatre, Panton Street, London in 1960. He was so impressed he made enquiries about the rights.

He struck the usual brick wall. However, he discovered that an old friend of Santha Rama Rau's family was Anthony Havelock-Allan, who did his best on David's behalf. But Forster still said "no". Moura Budberg intervened - she was also turned down. And when Santha Rama Rau suggested writing a script for the great Indian director, Satyajit Ray, Forster still rejected the idea.

"I think that Forster was simply terrified of the cinema," said David.[5]

Forster had approved of the play and this made it difficult for him to reject a television version, to be directed by Waris Hussein, a talented Indian working for the BBC. Hussein's sister, Shama Habibullah, subsequently became the production manager on David's film.

"Waris knew Forster," she said, "because he had been at Cambridge. He pleaded with him to allow him to do a little bit of filming because he didn't want to do it as just a courtroom drama. So Waris was allowed to do some second unit in India."[6]

Hussein cast Zia Moyheddin as Aziz and Sybil Thorndike as Mrs Moore, and his television play proved very effective. But having given this limited permission, Forster then cracked down again on anyone trying to make the film.

"I had also seen the play in 1960," said Fred Zinnemann, "and I, too, wanted to make it into a film. I couldn't reach Forster, but two very good friends of mine, Peggy Ashcroft and George Rylands [who controlled the rights on Forster's behalf at King's College, Cambridge], tried to persuade him to let me have it, but Forster didn't give in. Then he died. David didn't know of my interest - it was just another curious coincidence."[7]

After Forster's death in 1970, his literary executors at King's, and Donald A. Parry, chief executor, turned down all approaches, including those of Joseph Losey, Ismail Merchant and James Ivory, and Waris Hussein, who now wanted to make a feature film version.

When Professor Bernard Williams, the husband of the politician Shirley Williams and a film enthusiast himself, became Provost of King's in 1980, the situation changed. Forster's literary executors decided to sell and, since the rights had been bequeathed to both King's and Santha Rama Rau, the consent of Miss Rau was essential.[8]

Lord Brabourne, whose father had been Viceroy of India, and who was married to the daughter of Lord Mountbatten, the last Viceroy, had been after the rights for twenty years.

"I went to see Forster about it and I pestered him so much he eventually agreed. But when he died, he had forgotten to tell his literary executors."[9]

Brabourne asked Professor Williams to look into the matter, and having tried for so long, he learned that he was, at least, top of the list. In March 1981, Santha Rama Rau and King's College transferred the film rights to Mersham Productions - later G.W. Productions - run by Brabourne and his partner Richard Goodwin. The contract stipulated that Santha Rama Rau would write the screenplay and it reserved the right to approve the director. The screenplay appeared, with commendable speed, in April. A list of six directors was submitted, with David's name at the top.

When John Brabourne telephoned David at the Berkeley, and asked to come and see him, David asked what it was about. Brabourne was non-committal.

"What happened in the caves?" said David.

"And he nearly dropped the phone. I'd heard a rumour that he'd bought *A Passage to India*. He came to see me and said, 'I'd very much like you to do it.'" [10]

"You can imagine what I felt," said Brabourne. "David Lean was my idea of the great British director. The scale of the films is what I like so much. The way he saw everything in such a huge way. Think what he did with THE BRIDGE ON THE RIVER KWAI, think of LAWRENCE. I mean, think of it. I adore ZHIVAGO. And I loved the Irish one." [11]

By September 1981, David had been approved as director, and Santha Rama Rau had completed a second draft of her screenplay. Those who have followed our story this far will immediately recognise an anomaly. How can a writer, no matter how distinguished, complete a script independent of David for a David Lean picture? Particularly when David had already done preparatory work with Stephen Walters on Forster's manuscript notes.

David moved to the Dolder Grand Hotel, Zurich, planning to return to London in November, when Santha Rama Rau would fly in from New York. But first he wrote her one of his epic letters.

It is a remarkable letter - Santha Rama Rau described it as "magnificent" - but it has one curious aspect. It goes into great detail about the problems of adapting a difficult book, and the pitfalls that lie ahead, but except for two minor references it studiously ignores Santha Rama Rau's script. The underlying message was that the entire work had still to be done. Another danger signal was the mailing of David's final version of the Bounty script - PANDORA'S BOX - presumably intended as an example of how a film script should be written:

"Dear Santha Rama Rau,

"Firstly this is to tell you how delighted I am at the prospect of working with you. I was introduced to *A Passage to India* through your play at the Comedy and it was the reason I said yes to this film without even re-reading the book. When I re-read it I had something like a week of blind panic - the ambiguities, hints and half-defined characters. The feeling that ghosts are hovering over some of the pages. I nearly sat down to write you a letter saying, 'Please tell me the story of our film on half a sheet of paper.' (I rather like that old idea of writing plots or scenes on postage stamps. It keeps one to the point and we're certainly going to have to keep on the point - just from the point of view of length.) However, that phase has passed and I'm now quietly excited, making notes and coming up with some ideas.

"I face you with a certain amount of trepidation. You knew Mr Forster personally, the book is a revered classic and you've been intimately connected with it for over twenty years. You are going to have to put up with an awful lot of swearing in church and you're going to have to be patient because I'm a slow study.

"Before we come to any conclusions I think we must face 'the notorious unsolved riddle of the caves.' We have to face it head on and without evasions because the conclusion will affect the whole film, the character of Miss Quested in particular.

"As you know, he first wrote the scene in the cave as an assault by Aziz: 'She struck out and he got hold of her other hand and forced her against the wall, he got both her hands in one of his, and then felt at her breasts...'

"I have a feeling that Forster found himself out of his depth in this scene and changed it, rather carelessly, into a sort of mystery. (Perhaps he was even making a joke at his own expense when he has Fielding say, 'A mystery is only a high-sounding term for a muddle.') He left in the broken binoculars - which I can't but see as rather bad Agatha Christie. (Old or not a leather strap doesn't break that easily.) Then there's that guide. I cringe at him being our suspect rapist; he's just a bad red herring. To tell the truth, the cave begins to strain my credibility from the moment Aziz takes offence at Miss Quested's query as to how many wives he has. He bolts off into one cave to allow her to go off into another. (I really admire the way you handled this whole incident in the play. What a teaser it must have been with the limitations of the stage!)

"I think we have to agree between ourselves exactly what did happen. At the moment I can only see it as an honest to goodness hallucination. Difficult, but interesting. Apart from withholding it until the trial I believe we should play fair with our audience and have no truck with red herrings, it's not that sort of film.

"Another problem of the incident is the revolution in social and sexual attitudes since the book was written. Our audience is tough and emancipated. Unless we play our cards true and right they'll be only too ready to laugh at Miss Quested having a self-imposed fit of the sexual horrors in a dark cave. We're on very thin ice; the place and the period will help us to a certain extent - but they're going to have to know an awful lot more about Miss Quested than is told in the book. More about her later.

"By way of introduction, a few more notions. In making a film I'm always very conscious of the audience. A lot of the time I almost feel they're sitting with me behind the camera. It's very much a two-way medium and I try very hard to be clear and interesting in telling them the story. I like them to know where they are in terms of geography whether it be a house or a town. When someone has seen our film I would be pleased if they could describe Chandrapore in the same way they could describe the place where they spent last summer holiday. They're an impatient lot, very quick, easily bored, and run almost entirely on emotion. But they sit in the dark. It's all very intimate, almost confidential, and I begin to see this film as a sort of eavesdrop - particularly on Miss Quested. I think it can be fascinating. But back to earth:

"Our audience are not going to know much about present day India and almost nothing whatever about the Raj. We have somehow got to give them this background information. (I think I've nearly cracked this nut - but will reserve it for the paper.) Now, you started with the train journey. I'm very tempted to go back further and start in England. Cold and grey. It was such a long way in those days and if we're clever and economical we can tell a great deal very quickly. By the time we arrive in Chandrapore we should know Mrs Moore and Miss Quested quite well. I'd like to know the reason for their trip and meet one or two people - Turton and wife coming back from leave? - whom we'll meet again in Chandrapore. It's got a good sweep to it. And it's moving pictures.

"The other big nut to crack - and as yet I haven't done it - is how we make the time lapse of two or three years and bring Fielding back with the unseen Stella - and keep the audience in their seats while we do it.

"India. We are back in the twenties with the interplay between the Indians and the English - so beautifully described in the book with the Bridge Party[12] - but it takes nine pages. We can't afford that time to describe the social scene. We have to find some sort of shorthand. I often think of a film as a train journey. The permanent way, the rails, are the story line. Very soon after the titles the train gathers speed and reaches its narrative cruising speed. Tickity-tat. Tickity-tat. Tickity-tat. Woe betide us with that impatient audience if we slow down to examine an interesting detail of the passing landscape. They'll open the popcorn, kiss their girl and light up a cigarette. We'll have to show them those details while we're still travelling or it'll take an earthquake or an elephant charge to regain their attention. I mention the bridge party as an example. Perhaps there is a way of showing it while we're travelling. Apart from the Indian-English incomprehension we badly need the humour.

"We have an enormous lot to tell. I think our first stop is at the Marabar Hills. That's where we're going - and I think we must resist temptations to dilly-dally on the way. The caves provide the catalyst for the real drama of the story. The journey to them - and it's very attractive and important - is only a preparation for the real drama to come. The caves suddenly put all the characters under stress and it's that stress which opens them up and makes them so fascinating. We have got to leave ourselves time. If we take time here and there we might have to skimp some of the most important aspects of Forster's extraordinary piece of work. Back to the characters:

"Aziz. Late 20s - early 30s. Forster describes him as, 'An athletic little man, daintily put together, but really very strong.' Aziz is one of our biggest characters. He has to carry much of the Indian side of the race theme. I have no wish to glamorise him or turn him into into an Indian Sidney Poitier in GUESS WHO'S COMING TO DINNER? I don't mind if at first the audience find him very 'foreign.' But after a while I would want them to like him very much. I understand Mr Forster saying he's a little man, daintily put together but in the run of the book one forgets this rather denigrating description as his character takes over - but on the screen his physical presence is there to remind us all the time.

"Fielding. About 45. 'Outwardly the large and shaggy type.' He has both culture and intelligence - which makes the people in the Club distrust him. 'The men tolerated him for the sake of his good heart and strong body; it was their wives who decided he was not a sahib. They disliked him.' Can't do better than that.

"Miss Quested. I find her translation to the screen our biggest character problem of all. In the book I find her a pale shadow beside the events she puts in motion. For the first 150 pages I don't know her and can only guess at explanations for her behaviour. At the trial I find that she has intelligence and real courage. I think I could grow to like and admire her very much - but she must be at least partially explained. I have a strong feeling that Forster didn't care for her and was only interested in using her as a somewhat tiresome tool in the plot.

"As far as we are concerned she is a young woman who has a hallucination that Aziz has raped, attempted to rape, or molest her. The illusion is so vivid that she bolts out of the cave, plunges down a gully filled with cactus bushes and collapses into the arms of Miss Derek, a very level-headed person, who is completely convinced of her veracity. Miss Quested is certainly aware of the disastrous results of her experience but they in no way shake her belief in the experience.

"The hallucination is pretty lurid stuff for this respectable young woman. It took place in her mind only - and was therefore invented by her. This sexual explosion is presented right out of the blue. I don't really think it works in the book and am as certain as I can be it won't work in a film. We're not given the slightest clue to this side of her character. I think everyone will presume her to be a virgin who has not even been to bed with Ronnie.

"They're so controlled and repressed that we are confirmed in our belief in her pale chastity. We are wrong, and I think it can be very exciting. She leaves England in the rain, pale and pure. Then the sun comes out. Suez, the desert, the heat of the Red Sea. India. I've often wondered why Europeans first arriving in the East either like it or hate it. Lids tend to come off. Some become deeply disturbed. I knew one man who went straight back to the airport and took the next plane out. Another who left me flat and spent the whole of his first night in a brothel. It may be that India somehow reflects echoes out of our distant past where our inhabitants weren't so strong. In a sense we do walk down our aircraft steps into the past.

"I have a few ideas of how to walk Miss Quested into some of this past. She's very attracted by it, almost impelled from the outset towards her appointment at Marabar. This is the eavesdrop. Only we will know about it. (With perhaps the exception of Mrs Moore?) When the explosion comes it will have the same effect on the other characters but I believe it will be much more exciting and credible.

"My instinct is to show as little as possible and rely on our powers of suggestion. When we do show Miss Quested immediately after her experience I think it should be sudden, shocking and what's known as very 'real.' (I like your idea of her topi bumping down the gully.) All this boils down to the fact that the actress who plays Miss Q must be given a part that is playable. I'm willing to place two small bets right now. 1: That the part will make some unknown a star. 2: That it will turn out to be the best part in the picture. I only wish we could think of something which could keep her going to somewhat nearer the end.

"Mrs Moore. In some ways I find her the most unique character of all. We're going to have an interesting time with her. She's going to have a much more prominent part in the film than in the book because a great deal of film acting is re-acting. She's going to have a lot of close-ups watching people, tilting a scene this way or that with a look, or just being dead pan. I feel she needs a little more explanation - particularly round about her reaction to the cave incident and her very quick departure. Regarding her appearance, I'm not mad about her having a red face. First of all I thought of Peggy Ashcroft. Then Celia Johnson. Ashcroft could give her a more remote elegance. Celia more down to earth, more emotional, kinder. Goodness me she's a wonderful actress.

"Ronnie. Almost a complete non-part. Stock dull. We'll have to come up with a good idea or he will do damage to Miss Quested by association. He's surely one of those very presentable young men whose barely discernible faults were brought out and encouraged by colonial life in Chandrapore. I thought it might be good if she didn't immediately recognise him at the station. It would give us a chance to see the relationship gradually slide down the hill instead of presenting Ronny as a fully developed bore. I even wish we could build him up so it were possible to feel for him at the end.

"Godbole. Another type of bore. Sententious and obscure. I know that's the point of him - and I've met them all over the place - but as a film character I still think he's lacking in entertainment value. I don't know how the idea will appeal to you but I would love to introduce some snatches of Hindu philosophy. Every visitor to India is plied with it. I think it might be intriguing, amusing and highly relevant.

'I don't know if you've ever heard of Gabriel Pascal. A lovable old rogue to whom Shaw gave the film rights of *Pygmalion*. He died broke in the New York Athletic Club just before *My Fair Lady* opened. He had a good percentage in it. He believed in reincarnation and in answer to my doubts said, 'For the sake of simplicity just accept that we are given three visits to this world.' I'd love to see Godbole having an earnest conversation with Miss Quested along these lines.

Certain visual effects appear and reappear in David Lean's work. 50. Pip (Anthony Wager) at his mother's grave in GREAT EXPECTATIONS. *51. Oliver Twist (John Howard Davies) is ordered to sleep among the coffins at Sowerberry's undertaking establishment.*

52. *OLIVER TWIST: The Artful Dodger (Anthony Newley) spying on Oliver and Fagin (John Howard Davies and Alec Guinness) on John Bryan's set of London's East End. 53. Trevor Howard and Celia Johnson on L. P. Williams's studio-built station set for BRIEF ENCOUNTER. 54. Katharine Hepburn and Rossano Brazzi in Venice for SUMMER MADNESS.*

55. *LAWRENCE OF ARABIA* Turkish troops flee the advancing Arabs just before the massacre. A scene shot in Morocco. Photograph by Ken Danvers.

56. *Extras playing Russian partisans in* DOCTOR ZHIVAGO *prepare for a scene - smoke is laid to accentuate the shafts of light.* 57. *David's own photographs show the same eye at work. A desert policeman poses at Petra from his* LAWRENCE *location trip - Sam Spiegel forced him to leave Jordan before filming here.*

58. *David waited patiently for the light to fall on the statue (left) at Karnak in Egypt.*

Probably going too far. The other day I even thought of Alec Guinness playing the part but fear it'd upset all the balances. Very funny though!

"That's about it. I hope I haven't introduced myself as a bore - and I also hope you didn't mind me asking Richard to forward you the Bligh script without even a note. All best wishes, David Lean."[13]

Far from dismaying her, David's letter encouraged Santha Rama Rau. "I can't tell you," she wrote, "how pleased I am that you will be directing A PASSAGE TO INDIA. It has been such a long-standing dream of mine, and at last it is coming true."[14]

In November, the two met at the Berkeley for ten days of discussions. "We talked all day and every day about the plot," said Santha Rama Rau, "the characters, the dialogue and the themes. Lean had never met Forster. Naturally I poured out all I knew."[15]

They parted on cordial terms with the understanding that they would work together on the final shooting script. On 9 December 1981, Goodwin dropped her a note from India saying that the authorities there had genuine enthusiasm for the project. "David seems to be in fine form but I suspect hasn't done a lot since you left."[16] David himself wrote to Santha Rama Rau from the Maurya Sheraton, New Delhi:

"I feel more and more guilty about you as each day goes by. I haven't written you a word for weeks." He described his own efforts with the script. Fielding's tea party and the bridge party had been "real buggers. Nonstop, more or less static talk. Death to any movie." He thought he had come up with a few good ideas which he wouldn't reveal until she read the result. "I'd rather reserve you as a completely new eye."[17] He looked forward to seeing her when she arrived in Delhi. But the invitation to her was never confirmed and she heard nothing more for the best part of a year.

I discovered David's copy of Santha Rama Rau's script in the basement of Narrow Street, together with a letter David had typed which introduces the bicycle ride to the temple with the erotic carvings and a flashback to it while Miss Quested is in bed that night. The letter is unfinished, and Santha Rama Rau never saw it. It is possible that David made up his mind then and there to write the script himself, which is why he did not go over it with her.

For her script is the work of a playwright. Long scene-setting instructions are followed by lengthy dialogue scenes with no sense of the camera. But the atmosphere and the dialogue are so strong, so close to the spirit of Forster, that it would have taken little to turn it into a first-rate film adaptation.

John Brabourne, however, thought the script "disastrous", and David considered it "amateur".

"It was too wordy and literary," said Brabourne. "It just wasn't a script. We had a talk and David said, 'Well, we've got to do another script.'

"We had money for that. EMI were financing us. I said to David, 'Well, why don't you do it?' He said, 'I've been thinking the same thing. I wrote the others with Robert Bolt. I never got any credit for it. Why shouldn't I get credit on this one?'

"He went off to India and wrote it. Richard and I used to go out occasionally. He loved writing the script and we used to have a lot of discussions about casting. That was really a very pleasant relationship."[18]

David's determination to capture credits - and thus possible Oscars - would damage relationships on this film and would cause resentment out of all proportion to their value. The most serious breach was with Santha Rama Rau.

David was optimistic at the beginning that he could persuade her to alter her work fairly radically. But since he felt he was capable of adapting a novel, as he had done with Dickens, he began a few experiments with Forster. And the deeper he got into it, I suspect, the more proprietorial he felt. He had always envied writers, and now he was one himself. He probably had no intention of discarding Santha Rama Rau at the beginning. By the end of his travails, he had absorbed her work into his own and, consciously at any rate, almost forgotten her.

While he was studying the book he wrote, "The more I read the more I respect Forster as an artist. He has a deceptive simplicity, a wonderfully touching feeling for human beings and *honesty*. There are several very emotional moments about the basic loneliness of human beings which, if we can transfer them to the screen, will make our picture very special."[19]

David's scriptwriting technique began with the purchase of a copy of the book in which he underlined, as he had with Dickens, everything he felt would work in a film.

"I wrote the script for PASSAGE in a room at the Maurya Sheraton Hotel in New Delhi," said David. "I couldn't stay in New Delhi for more than six months or I'd be caught with Indian income tax, which is hefty. So I moved out just before six months. I went to the Dolder Grand Hotel in Zurich and spent about three months there, finishing it. I wrote the whole script in my own handwriting and then typed it out. I only type with two fingers, which is a huge advantage because it slows you up and you get to know every word and examine everything more carefully than if you just rattle it off. Then Sandy typed it properly. She went to the American missionary school in the Himalayas and learned typing as part of her course, which no English school would ever do, of course - far too practical."[20]

David doubted that the friendship of Aziz and Fielding was the theme of the book. As he wrote to Brabourne and Goodwin, "Even Santha says, under pressure, that left to themselves Fielding and Aziz wouldn't have all that much to say to each other after a couple of hours. Their relationship is an attempt at a friendship. It's about the enormous difficulties of human contact. I know nothing about Forster's friend, Syed Ross Masood, but whatever Masood felt, Forster was able to fill in the blanks with sex - albeit unrequited. Because of the same sexual difficulties he misses out on Miss Quested. She's fine until the Caves, and then blacks out until she confesses to the hallucination during the trial. It's Forster who blacks out, and I say that with the greatest respect. I just don't believe one can write about something of which one has absolutely no experience and I don't believe a homosexual relationship can stand in for a heterosexual relationship simply by changing the name of Masood to Adela."[21]

David at Srinagar, Kashmir.

David largely abandoned Forster's plain, intelligent and well-meaning girl. "I added the scene of Adela bicycling through the fields and finding the ancient Indian erotic statues in the ruins of a temple. I used that scene to show her as-yet-untapped sexuality. I always imagined to myself - although nobody ever said so, Forster certainly didn't - that she was brought up in some vicarage somewhere and both parents died. She was a very repressed girl. I wanted to say she was opening out. One of my favorite places in India is a place called Khajuraho. A couple of Englishmen were hunting tigers there and found themselves in the forest with a lot of undergrowth. They saw stone figures amidst the vines and soon discovered that they were erotic figures. In fact, there were more than sixteen temples covered with this erotic statuary. I've always been fascinated by that, and it gave me the idea of showing Adela in a new light. Also, I enjoyed doing that scene - I think it's a piece of cinema."[22]

David would raise a few eyebrows about the way he had softened Forster's view of the British Raj. To one interviewer he said, "Forster was a bit anti-English, anti-Raj and so on. I suppose it's a tricky thing to say but I'm not so much." David didn't believe the British colonials were a lot of idiots. "Forster rather made them so. He came down hard against them. I've cut out that bit at the trial where they try to take over the court. Richard wanted me to leave it in. But I said no, it wasn't right. They wouldn't have done that."[23]

To another interviewer he said, "It's all very well to criticise the English but just take a look at New Delhi, look at the railway system, look at the postal system - which works. We've left them all sorts of bad things, I suppose, but they also got some very good things."[24]

David felt that the story could be made into a very good, moderately inexpensive picture.

"What I believe we're all hoping for is a movie which is true to the book but which will also appeal to the man in the street. We are blessed with a fine movie title, A PASSAGE TO INDIA. But it has a built-in danger; it holds out such promise. The very mention of India conjures up high expectation. It has sweep and size and is very romantic. If we don't fulfil those expectations I fear we will lose a great part of our mass audience. That is why I was immodestly rather pleased with those first few pages of script: it's the opening of a big picture... I am not suggesting we turn the whole thing into an Indian 'Spectacular.' I'm talking about the backgrounds... I can't for the life of me think why we should present a kind of poor man's India when, for the same cost, we could show such visual riches."[25]

Late in 1982, David sent his script to a few close friends. Fred Zinnemann thought it was very good indeed, and was particularly struck by the scene in the temple with the monkeys.

Alec Guinness thought he had done a marvellous job, "telling a difficult story with a complicated background truly, clearly and excitingly." However, he had a few minor points about the characters, particularly Godbole. Guinness foresaw that David's idea of having Godbole singing his song after the guests have left rather than embarrassing them while they are trying to leave, as in Forster, would leave the sequence vulnerable. "I know that if the film is running too long it is a lump that would be cut out, and that would sadden me - partly because it would rob Godbole of much of his mystery... If the film gets made I'd love to play Godbole - it excites and intrigues me - no other part in ages has so attracted me - but I might be embarrassing and just plain awful in it."[26]

Santha Rama Rau was sent a copy of the script and was startled to see that only David's name appeared as screenwriter. But her letter to David - as tactful as she could make it - spoke of her admiration. "I think it extraordinary, marvellous, gripping. And with some of the most economical and ingenious exposition of very complex situations that I ever expect to see. In particular, the whole of the beginning and the scene in the mosque seem to me absolutely brilliant. So I hope you will forgive me, if in this letter, I concentrate on the points that worry me, some of them very trivial, some of them less so."[27]

She then listed instances where she felt David had disregarded Forster's intention. Comparing David's screenplay with her own, she found close similarities as well as wide discrepancies. She was dismayed to see several scenes she had written herself which had not appeared in the novel. But she was most distressed by the new scenes - Miss Quested's encounter with the erotic carvings, houseboats in Kashmir - none of which had anything to do with Forster.

In hindsight, she thought it was just as well that David hadn't confided in her. "I think I would have had a fit if I had known in advance that the film was going to contain the sequence of a lonely 'brave' Memsahib cycling about the Indian countryside and coming upon erotic sculptures in the jungle only to be scared into flight by a pack of shrieking monkeys. This sort of vulgarity was so remote from Forster's oblique, equivocal approach to Adela's sexual malaise that I'm sure I would have argued furiously against it if I'd been given the opportunity.

"David used to call me 'the Keeper of the Flame' (not as a compliment) because when he went off on one of his frequent flights of irrelevant fancy, I kept referring him back to Forster's very dramatic, visually arresting novel which, in my opinion, didn't need the extra heavy-handed emphases that David felt the audience would have to have in order to get the point of this or that scene."[28]

She also sent her list of her objections, which ran to seven pages, to King's College and to Brabourne and Goodwin. When he received her letter David telexed John Brabourne:

"OVERALL SHE HAS BEEN VERY GENEROUS ABOUT MY SCRIPT UNDER DIFFICULT CIRCUMSTANCES. YOU CANNOT EXPECT ME TO AGREE WITH MOST OF HER SUGGESTIONS BECAUSE WE ARE APPROACHING THE SUBJECT WITH DIFFERENT OBJECTIVES, SHE AS KEEPER OF THE FLAME AND ME AS A FILM DRAMATIST. APART FROM THIS SHE IS A COMPLETE AMATEUR AS FAR AS WRITING FOR THE SCREEN IS CONCERNED WITNESS HER THREE ATTEMPTS TO DATE.

"I DON'T WANT TO HURT HER SO WILL HAVE TO SPEND THE NEXT TWO DAYS SPELLING OUT SOME BASICS OF DRAMATIC CONSTRUCTION IN A LETTER. WHAT ALARMS ME IS THAT YOU HAVE OBVIOUSLY LED HER TO BELIEVE THAT SHE IS COMING TO LONDON TO WORK ON THE SCRIPT WITH ME FACE TO FACE. THIS IS EXACTLY WHAT I BEGGED YOU TO AVOID. I THINK THIS IS AN IMPOSITION FROM WHICH YOU AS PRODUCERS SHOULD HAVE SAVED ME. YOU ARE MERELY DUMPING HER IN MY LAP AND LEAVING THE ROOM. I'M NOT HAVING IT.

"IF YOU SERIOUSLY BELIEVE THAT SANTHA HAS FURTHER CONTRIBUTIONS TO MAKE I CAN ONLY REPEAT, LET HER PUT THEM ON PAPER AND SEND THEM BY POST."[29]

"The fact is," said Sandy Lean, "David accepted A PASSAGE TO INDIA out of sheer bravura. It was such a good joke to be able to say to John Brabourne, 'Yes, what happened in the caves?' It happened so fast, he'd agreed to make the film before he'd even finished reading the book. Then one day the honeymoon was over and he woke up and found himself in bed with Forster and of course it was a shock.

"David adored the classics, but he had no reverence when it came to adapting them into his own medium. What he had instead was a kind of fearless innocence. He'd say, 'Look here, this bit about the British, he's simply got it wrong.' After all, what made Forster an expert? And then, being David, he tried to fix it. Well, you don't fix Forster any more than you fix the Taj Mahal. You love him or leave him, but you don't fix him." [30]

The script had already been sent to King's College when John Brabourne and Richard Goodwin took David to lunch there on 3 December 1982.

"Lovely looking place," said David. "We had lunch in the dining-room and the dons were all friendly, old-looking gentlemen. Old gentlemen? Younger than me, I think, who turned out to be some of the greatest experts on English literature you could find anywhere in the world. I'm glad I didn't quite realise it at the time. We sat down and had about two spoonfuls of soup and one of them turned to me and asked why I had done a certain thing with the script - I don't remember now exactly what - and I said, 'I wish you'd left that for the sweet.'"

"We told him we were surprised at the ending and didn't like it," said Dr Donald Parry, the chief executor. "David Lean put down his knife and fork and made a wonderful speech. He said, 'We are talking of one of the greatest novels in English literature, which will live forever. As for my film, in five or ten years, it will have been forgotten and you can make another film if you want to.' But while he was making the film, it was his film and that was that. He stuck his Adam's apple out in an ostrich kind of way and carried on with the meal." [31]

What David did not know as he lunched at King's was that Goodwin and Brabourne were facing the collapse of the project. The development money of one million dollars from EMI had run out.

Goodwin and Brabourne had been to Hollywood in October 1982 and were consistently turned down. Goodwin became so frustrated that he kicked one of the swans in the ornamental lake at the Bel Air Hotel.

"Brabourne believes very much in the presence, in being in the right place," said Goodwin. "We never intended to stay so long - we stayed a month. We had terrible trouble with the major studios. One man, confusing Forster with Forester, said 'I thought he only wrote Captain Hornblower.'" [32]

"Another studio said they'd do it if we put in an explicit rape," said David, "thereby ruining the story, of course. And a producer wrote a fascinating memo to me: 'Our audiences are young people. Young people are bored by old people. Cut out the old dame.'" [33]

"They couldn't understand what it was we were trying to make," said Goodwin. "They were terrified of losing their money and terrified of Lean." [34]

"It doesn't make any difference my films have made millions of dollars,"

David told Denise Worrell. "I hadn't made a film in fourteen years. The studios thought, 'Maybe he's lost his touch. Maybe he's forgotten how to do it. Is he strong enough?' They all kept on saying, 'What's the bottom line?' In the end I had to initial every page of my own script to promise that I wouldn't invent a herd of elephants or something which would cost more. It's humiliating; the money people have you over a barrel. They're just frightened people. It's one of the things about movies today. Instead of old boys like Goldwyn, Mayer, Selznick, Cohn, who, though some were absolutely illiterate, loved movies, the new people at the top don't care about movies. I hardly meet a person now who loves films. They love money. They're all obsessed by money. Anyway, I thought, to hell with this. They'll find the money somehow or other."[35]

It was John Heyman, who had tried to help David with the Bounty films, who saved the day. "John Heyman did an amazing job of getting it all together," said Richard Goodwin. "Columbia put up one-and-a-half million, HBO put up eight-and-a-half and the balance of the sixteen-and-a-half million came from Thorn-EMI."[36] The Completion Bond Co - headed by Lee Katz, who had represented UA during David's negotiations with the Bounty - provided the guarantee.

"There was a lot of squawking from Verity Lambert at EMI on this film," said David. "She hated me because I had an argument with her about the script. She started telling me how to do the script and I said, 'Look, Miss Lambert, you're just moving that cup from here to there. If you have a suggestion that we shouldn't have the trays on the table or we shouldn't have the table, I'll listen to it and respect you. But you cannot just move things here and there.'

"She said that with the cost of A PASSAGE TO INDIA she could make five films. I'm sure she could. But I think the quality article is terribly important. And producers are no longer keen on doing a quality article. It used to be our English forte. We used to do wonderful things.

"Rolls-Royce did not make an enormous profit on some of their early cars, but they still put on their twelve coats of paint. People couldn't see it, but they were there. That attitude has gone out of business now.

"I asked Spielberg, 'Why did you do INDIANA JONES here?' He said 'Because you've got a better finish to sets than we have.' Wonderful."[37]

CHAPTER FORTY-FIVE

MOVING MOUNTAINS

A PASSAGE TO INDIA I I

IN 1981, before setting off for India, David made a visit to the National Film Archive in Aston Clinton. In July of that year, a parliamentary Green Paper had stated, "the case for comprehensive national archives of sound and visual recordings has yet to be made."

"That's the English attitude in a nutshell," wrote David. "In this country the government is all too ready to give its support to the performing arts. We are in awe of the theatre, ballet and opera, but when it comes to the flicks we aren't interested. We don't take them seriously.

"The same is true of the industry itself. Go to the Archive and see the brilliant film directors and artists we have produced - and just look what has happened to them. It's not talent we lack, but people who are prepared to take a financial gamble on that talent. It's a question of confidence, and an understanding of what film can do." [1]

Two years later the British Film Institute, of which the Archive is part, decided to award David, along with his heroes Orson Welles and Marcel Carné, one of its first Fellowships. It was made a condition of acceptance that the winner travel to London to attend the Guildhall banquet marking the fiftieth anniversary of the BFI, and even Orson Welles agreed. David was in India, but since he could hardly be left out, the BFI reluctantly agreed to present it to him in absentia.

David telexed the BFI's chairman, Sir Richard Attenborough:

DEAR RICHARD, I DID NOT REALISE YOU WOULD AWARD A FELLOWSHIP TO AN ABSENTEE, BUT THANK YOU VERY MUCH FOR SPEAKING FOR ME. PLEASE READ THE ROLL-CALL OF CHARACTERS WITH A TOUCH OF THE LARRYS. 'YOUR ROYAL HIGHNESS, LADIES AND GENTLEMEN. I AM VERY SAD NOT TO BE WITH YOU TONIGHT BUT I HAVE JUST STARTED DIRECTING A FILM IN INDIA. HOWEVER, IT IS MOST FITTING THAT THIS HONOUR SHOULD BE ACCEPTED ON MY BEHALF BY SOME VERY OLD FRIENDS. MAY I CALL UPON MR HERBERT POCKET, FAGIN, COLONEL NICHOLSON, PRINCE FEISAL, GENERAL YEVGRAF ZHIVAGO AND PROFESSOR GODBOLE OF A PASSAGE TO INDIA.' [2]

Sir Alec Guinness received David's award from the Prince of Wales, Patron of the BFI. It proved to be the first of many awards and honours that David would receive in the years ahead.

Since December 1982, David had been using his own money to scout locations in India with Sandy, and Eddie Fowlie and his wife, Kathleen.

They did not have an easy time of it. No sooner had they arrived at Delhi airport than Kathleen, being an Irish citizen, was refused entry. David's only document of authority was a letter to Lord Brabourne from the Indian Ministry of External Affairs, which the immigration officials immediately spotted was a photocopy and a year out of date. Fortunately, a friendly travel agent talked them in on a twenty-four hour visa. They were then blocked by customs officials. When they finally cleared the airport, their taxi promptly ran out of petrol.[3]

David had been warned he might be arrested if he took pictures of bridges or railway stations - areas of strategic importance - but he knew he had no alternative. He had to find railway stations, tracks and bridges, and he was very worried that his cameras or film might be confiscated. He felt in despair at his lack of official authorisation.

The location trip was hair-raising - the bus drivers seemed bent on suicide and some roads were appalling. David thanked heaven for his new white Mercedes station wagon which had been purchased and shipped to India by Stephen Walters. (When David took delivery of the Mercedes he sent a telegram to Walters which said, "THANKS FOR CAR. CAN I HAVE SOME MUSTARD?" David loved mustard and was tired of the tubes available in India. Walters sent him tins of Colman's mustard powder.)

They set off in the Mercedes. Again and again, David found just what he was looking for: ancient Swiss steam locomotives in perfect condition rolling over ravines and bridges, and spectacular scenery.

He found the perfect location for Fielding's house - in the garden of the West End Hotel in Bangalore. "The main feature is a lovely group of ten very old trees with wonderfully shaped trunks and branches reaching up to a leafy covering some forty feet above. It would require only a few clever touches to give the place the air of an ancient Moghul garden - and very beautiful too. And in the hotel grounds if you please!"[4]

As he walked around the site, David found himself longing for the talent of John Box...

For the main studio "backlot", they found an ideal site in the vast grounds of a maharajah's derelict palace which was just seven minutes away from the hotel where the cast and crew would be based. It was here that David would build the city of Chandrapore.

"This is the first chance I have had of seeing the settings for our film outside my imagination," he wrote. "I have not, as a director, been so excited since I was at the same stage on LAWRENCE OF ARABIA. Forster has given us some wonderful characters and words. I now know that the visuals, the action and the atmosphere are going to match them."[5]

David at the "Marabar Caves" at Savandurga. (Photograph by Ken Bray)

The key location, however, was the Marabar Caves. While the interiors of the caves were to be shot on sets back in England, David needed to find exteriors which provided all the elements called for by the script. Although Forster had actually described, in exact detail, the caves near Patma, his location was not big enough for what David had in mind.[6]

"The government said there could be no filming there because of bandits," said David. "Goodwin took pictures and made a tape of the echo. I was rather disappointed. The echo was all right, but the caves Forster wrote about were at the bottom of rocks only thirty feet high. I'd always seen on the screen in my mind caves at the bottom of a cliff face.

"Eddie went out on a fast reconnaissance trip near Bangalore. He found some rocks and cliffs. We went to look. The trouble is, if you have a cliff, you generally have boulders at the bottom of it, and we couldn't find a place without the boulders, and they were too heavy to move. Then Eddie found a place for Mrs Moore's cave, that first cave they go to. And I said, 'I don't think that's any good is it?' And he said, 'Just think a minute.' There was a great big bowl in the rock, covered with scrub about ten feet high, and he said, 'Imagine that all cleared out.' And he was dead right. I'm very grateful to him. We cleared the whole thing and we made it just bare. There were wonderful water marks running down the rocks."[7]

The place was called Savandurga.

"One of the problems," said production manager Shama Habibullah, "was that there were no caves there. He knew he was going to shoot the interior in the studio, but he had to have at least the entrance. What happened next caused some controversy in India. The reports in the papers that said the rock was blasted to make caves were not quite true. I admit the rocks were cut, to exactly the shape David wanted them. In order to see that no real damage was done, we got people who were carvers - temple carvers of statues - which is a highly skilled job. They cut those entrances. No dynamite, beyond the little charge you use to loosen where you drill. We could never have dynamited a hole. That would have been impossible, apart from being extremely dangerous and wasteful.

"It was a hard, meticulous and slow operation. Where you see Miss Quested run down the hill, above that, high on the hill, was the most enormous black wasps' nest. It was a gruelling job for the people working there - mostly Indian craftsmen and two supervisors from the English art department.

"Half way through this process, someone came back with the message that the priest on the temple at the back of the hill was upset because it was a holy hill. In India any outcrop of rock of a certain shape can become a shrine. So Richard Goodwin had to go there and do a Puja ceremony - to offer his apologies and blessings to the rock. Because of the controversy, we invited a lot of townspeople so that everyone knew we were being blessed as well for working there.

"Shortly after this, the wasps attacked. One of the English people, running down the mountain, broke his arm. The Indians had very little protection. They retreated to where they'd cut the rock and covered themselves in plastic sheeting. Some were quite badly hurt. We had to take them to hospital. It was quite nasty. But in some way, people could see this as some kind of retribution for using the mountain."[8]

David's use of the cliff face continued to cause controversy when he started shooting. Patrick Cadell, assistant director, said, "One or two journalists came out from Europe and they were told they couldn't go to the location. If somebody travels all that way, especially if he is a journalist, it's a bit silly not to allow him to come on the set. But Lean wouldn't allow it. We had a man from *The Sunday Times* who wasn't allowed on the set, but who managed to root out that something was going on at the caves."

The result was a devastating article in *The Sunday Times* by Ian Jack which was subtitled, "What if an Indian director decided he would like to rearrange Stonehenge?"

"Long before the birth of all that is thought of as 'eternal' in India - the Himalayas, the Ganges - these rocks existed," wrote Jack. He described the arrival of David Lean, in white Mercedes with Swiss numberplates, who looks about him and is enthralled. The Conservator of Forests refuses his permission, so Lean appeals to higher authorities in Bangalore and Delhi and permission is granted.

"Lean blasts several holes in the ancient and previously untroubled granite and scars and pits the smooth rock-face with scaffolding." Jack described how Dr Singh, a "noble-looking young Sikh with a long black beard, feels almost as insulted in real life as Dr Aziz in fiction. For he is the Director of Mines and Geology for the state of Karnataka."[9]

Several members of the unit considered this merely a journalist's attempt to get his own back, and that it was unfair and unjust. Even Peggy Ashcroft thought the talk of blowing out the caves was total nonsense.

"You could say, I suppose, that I desecrated the cliff face," said David, "but it was a newspaper story that blew it up into the Englishman who desecrated this wonderful Indian landscape. In fact, only a mile down the road, the Japanese were cutting rock by the ton and shipping it off to Japan because it's wonderful granite."[10]

In addition to finding locations in the south of India, around Bangalore, David and his team also went to the northern state of Kashmir where, high in the Himalayas, he decided to shoot the final sequence of the film.

Shama Habibullah said, "The book doesn't actually have anything to do with Kashmir. Godbole goes away to his own state. It should be somewhere in central India. But David chose Kashmir because he wanted a complete contrast to the burning part of the plains - he wanted the snow.

"I arranged for them to stay on houseboats. It was so much nicer than hotels. He didn't want to do that. So Richard Goodwin and I took over the houseboat and David and Sandy came to visit and David was very cross that he hadn't actually done it.

"The man who ran the houseboats was named Mohammed Wagnoo and I think a lot of Mohammed came into Aziz. Mohammed was driving us around, looking for locations, and at one point he had a tremendous argument with a man operating a toll gate; he displayed such passion - his vocal cords were standing out - and he was gesticulating. David was fascinated. He kept on talking to Mohammed after that and watching him."[11]

Despite his exhilaration at finding excellent locations, David felt he had been left to get on with it, and for someone accustomed to working with a smoothly-oiled team, this irked him. He wrote to his producers:

"In my whole career I have never been so completely alone in these first vital stages of a production. You have left me to pay everything out of my own pocket while you, thousands of miles away, sit behind your own particular brand of plate glass. From time to time great waves of resentment sweep over me. Columbia, E.M.I., Home Box Office and Mersham. Silence. (But thank you for your Christmas-New Year telex, Richard.) I somehow believe we are going to make this film and I dislike those waves of resentment and believe the best way of clearing them is to come straight out with it. I do hope you understand."[12]

In the end, however, he came to rely on his producers and if Richard Goodwin went away for more than a couple of days, he became anxious. David thought they had done a marvellous job of putting the project together against all the odds.

During the long reconnaissance trip, David fell ill. "He had something wrong with his neck," said Eddie Fowlie, "and it was terribly painful for him. Maybe it was the beginning of all his problems. He was complaining quite a lot about it before, but when we got to Srinagar it was so agonisingly painful he couldn't move and I got a doctor. I don't think he did any good; he just sort of massaged him. And then we were marooned there, we couldn't get out because of avalanches and snowfalls. Finally there was a plane and we managed to get David and Sandy on it. Kathleen and I stayed up there with the car, trapped for a couple of months."[13]

David avoided seeing films on similar subjects which he felt might influence him. He refused to see Waris Hussein's BBC version of *A Passage to India* as well as the TV series *The Jewel in the Crown*, in which Peggy Ashcroft played a character not dissimilar to Mrs Moore. For a long time he avoided seeing Attenborough's GANDHI, no doubt because of the heartbreak it would have caused him.

"I have not seen his version," David told *Encounter*, "but I think all these films on India are a good trailer for this one. You know, I do not think that anybody has made a good Indian film. Perhaps Jean Renoir did in THE RIVER, but all the others, like BHOWANI JUNCTION and the rest, are terrible. I do not think anybody has caught the Raj yet - in the cinema at least."[14]

Film people were startled that he failed to mention the great Indian director Satyajit Ray. Was it because he hadn't seen any of his films? Perhaps he had seen one or two and found them wanting. In any case, it showed how out of touch David had become.

John Box had been contacted by Brabourne and Goodwin and put on standby for "a film about India" - no title, no director. When they revealed who the director was, Box explained that his row with David precluded him from working on the film.

But when Box was told that David felt that bygones should be bygones, he gave up the film he was working on in Australia and came back to England, from where he wrote to David:

"I ask as humbly as I can that when the appropriate time comes you will give me some consideration to being part of your team. Much more important than all that - I ask you for your forgiveness for my wretched behaviour in Bora Bora and after. It has given me untold shame and considerable misery - I should have written to you before - I was pressed by several people to do so, particularly Omar, but I found it difficult."[15]

When Box was told that David had changed his mind, he swore a lot, then wrote another letter, saying how sad he was and adding, "I am sure you are going to make a very special film. My best wishes go with you and I shall be thinking of you."[16]

But David changed his mind yet again, and both men swallowed their pride.

"John Box is a very good art director," said David. "He nearly ruined my career on the Bounty - he pretty well did, actually - and because I think he's very good, on PASSAGE TO INDIA I said, 'Well, we'd better have him again.' And people said, 'You're absolutely mad. He betrayed you.' I said, 'I don't mind as long as he does a good job on the film.'"[17]

David did not demand absolute authenticity in the design of the film, perhaps because he felt the period of the mid-twenties - which coincided with his own boyhood - was not a particularly attractive one. This resulted in a crop of anachronisms which led to complaints when the film was released. One of these, showing Fielding

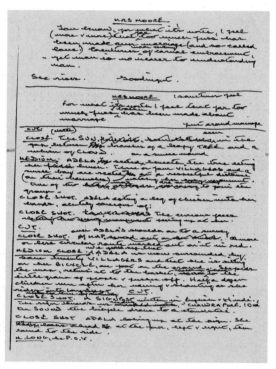

A page of David's script.

using a shower - an unlikely refinement in the India at the time - contrasted with the Waris Hussein version, where Fielding was shown washing himself in a bucket. However, the design of the film was generally considered to be amongst John Box's finest achievements.

"My greatest joy on that film was to encounter John Box and to have access to the art department," said Shama Habibullah. "To look at what they were doing was a privilege. The company had taken over most of the West End Hotel and had built the art department in one of the old bungalows there. It was something I don't suppose I'll ever see again in my life. It was so incredibly organised. I've seen art departments - I've seen the one on GANDHI - but this was absolutely extraordinary. I think it was because John Box suddenly had everything he ever wanted around him. He had one wall which was just photographs of the colours of India. People would feel themselves into the areas they were in. There was a sketch artist with his own section working out things even like the make-up for Aziz. You could see how Aziz would change and what would happen.

"John would sometimes say to me, 'Come up when David's here. I want you to tell us - it's better coming from you - how would Aziz sit, or how would he use his hands.' All this went into the sketches. They were done by a man named Bill Stallion.

"The most intricate model was for the matte shot at the beginning where you get the Gateway of India. That was a triple matte shot. The sea had to be matted at the back, because that's now a dry dock area, then the Gateway itself and then the square in front of it where you see the British troops. That is not an open space, but a garden with a statue and parked cars. That part of the matte, with the troops, was shot in Delhi, the Viceroy coming through it in Bombay. I just thought it was amazing."[18]

As with the village in RYAN'S DAUGHTER, the exteriors of the town of Chandrapore were specially constructed. In his *Sunday Times* article, Ian Jack had criticised David's unbridled extravagance in building his "India-within-India".[19]

But, as with the earlier film, David had sound reasons for building sets. "In India, they're film mad," he said. "It's their great entertainment. As soon as you set up a camera you've got three thousand people round you and you can't work. I think you can work much better on sets, because you can make it a concentrated bazaar, which is more of a bazaar than a real bazaar. It's the difference between a painting and a photograph. You can make the painting much better."[20]

Freddie Young was not asked to do A PASSAGE TO INDIA, presumably because he was even older than David. As David had promoted Ronald Neame's operator, Guy Green, so now he promoted Freddie Young's operator, Ernie Day.

Ernie Day was born in 1927, the year David entered the industry, and he, too, was a film-struck child. He grew up near the Warner Bros. studio at Teddington, where his elder brother worked, and which he himself joined during the war.[21]

Day had worked with Geoffrey Unsworth, who got him a job with Technicolor. In the early fifties he worked as assistant cameraman on MONSOON, which took him to India, and on John Ford's THE QUIET MAN. He became the first British camera operator to work in 65mm, on Otto Preminger's EXODUS. It was then that he was hired for LAWRENCE OF ARABIA.

After RYAN'S DAUGHTER he became a director of photography, then a second unit director, and he finally got his chance to direct a film, GREEN ICE, when he took over from a director who did not get on with the actors.

When David invited him to light A PASSAGE TO INDIA, it may have seemed as though he was being asked to drop a rung on the ladder but, according to Ernie Day, it was an accolade he could not turn down. It was not long, however, before he wished he had.

"Ernie was the most brilliant man, and a sweet person," said Patrick Cadell, "but he had an immensely difficult job because he was, in effect, filling Freddie Young's place, and Freddie Young had done so much and so well for David. Ernie had operated for Freddie for so long, of course, and David expected Ernie to do what Freddie had done. I don't think you can expect any operator to do exactly the same. They have their own styles.

"The relationship between David and the camera crew wasn't very good. They were perfectly professional. But it is so important for David to be surrounded by people who really had a passion and were prepared to throw everything in, and also had sensitivity. These professionals were not quite right and I think that was why there were difficult moments."[22]

"David worshipped Ernie," said Sandy Lean. "Ernie was a brilliant camera operator, the absolute best. And David felt that he and Ernie had this amazing synchronism of taste. I remember him telling me about this game they used to play: David would zoom into a composition, then deliberately change it and pass the camera to Ernie. And Ernie always ended up framing precisely the same composition.

"I think he thought that because he knew Ernie so well, and trusted him implicitly, taking him on as cameraman would turn out all right. It was the purest wishful thinking.

"It wasn't long before he was hating the rushes. The exterior shots were all right, but the close-ups and interiors, he felt, were really marginal. David was no good at sitting down and talking through a situation: he just got angrier and angrier and more and more upset. And in the end he just froze Ernie out. He stopped talking to him, stopped having anything to do with him. The rancour on the set was awful, and it spread a kind of poison through the film."[23]

"I think David, after fourteen years of not doing anything," said Ernie Day, "was probably, I hate to say it, out of his depth. Things were different, pressures were different. I suppose it's understandable.

"Soon after shooting began, David asked me to operate the camera as well as photograph the film. He never forgave my refusal.

"The camera crew had never worked with a director who insisted on shooting strictly in continuity, with the resulting delays in completing the day's work. Someone had to be blamed - inevitably it was the camera department. The atmosphere on the set was disappointment in working for a fallen idol.

"David committed the crime of getting old. Because of the way the film business had changed in the intervening years, he didn't understand it as well. I

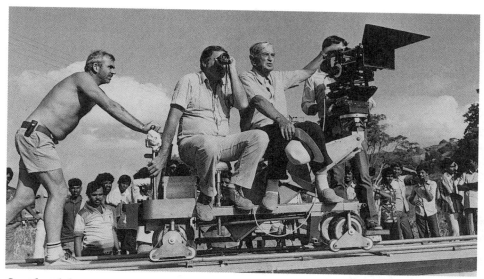

David with his camera crew on A PASSAGE TO INDIA. *(Photograph by Frank Connor)*

don't want to sound as if I'm maligning him. It's just that being close on a film, you do notice things. He started off so well, and then the story was that all the information about the progress of the film was being fed into a computer in America. The scenes planned for today were x, y, and z. They were not completed because David wasn't happy. Suddenly the computer was claiming that nothing was being completed on time, so what's happening out there? Those sorts of pressures got to him because, frankly, he wasn't used to that. 'What do you want,' he'd say, 'a film or a computer read-out?'

"It was all a question of budget, but it made him very edgy, which was such a shame because directors of his stature do worry. They may not give that impression but they do. All those pressures built up over the months.

"The cameraman has to keep things going, but it's no good if it comes to a stop with a director who doesn't want all that nonsense. He wants to make the film he wants to make. So you get a certain animosity. It's tough shooting a film, it's a tough way of making a living."[24]

"On PASSAGE TO INDIA," said Sandy Lean, "David was working for the first time in his life on a film where money was really tight and where there were restrictive conditions on him personally. He actually had to forfeit salary if he went over budget or over schedule. It was one of the conditions of the completion guarantee, but he never stopped resenting it.

"And there were so many other pressures, he felt besieged. The camera crew was in revolt, the actors were in various states of dudgeon. In the end he just lowered his head like a bull and charged the lot of them. Richard Goodwin took a lot of heat for David. So did Maggie Unsworth. She was so calm and wonderful, Maggie, half Mother Teresa and half mother hen."[25]

There are many things to account for David's irascibility. In addition to the budget pressures, he had been forced to abandon his beloved widescreen format and shoot the picture in the television ratio. And he had just given up smoking, which often leads to tetchiness. A heavy smoker since his teens, David had a chest X-ray before leaving for India which, his doctor said, revealed slight emphysema.[26]

"I'm sure it was a mental thing, due to the pressure," said Ernie Day. "We had laughs on all the other films, he had a sense of humour. He had no sense of humour on PASSAGE, none at all. Such a shame. It may have been better to quit at the top and do a lecture tour. It got so intense, you'd go to rushes and it was like a cathedral. You'd walk in and you'd sit there and no one would say a word. He'd just sit there. 'Are we ready?' No reaction. He would only react to say something derogatory - 'You are about to see one of the worst performances in the history of the cinema.'

"I think he was looking for agreement and yes men. Not everyone likes to be cast in that mould. If my opinion is asked, I like to be able to give it in all honesty. But he seemed to have gone off all that, and didn't accept it any more. We didn't end up friends at all. I've had such good times with David. I can't say enough about him. I keep saying it; he was a completely different person."[27]

David remained remarkably ungenerous about the experience.

"Oh God," he said, "what a mistake. Deathly mistake. Ernie Day ought to be down on his knees to me. I mean, he's not speaking to me. I thought Ernie would do a wonderful job and it's an absolute disaster. I've never worked so hard in a lab as I did with that. Three weeks. And the final result didn't look bad."[28]

Ernie Day's work was highly praised and it was nominated for an Academy Award. As any film-maker knows, altering the colour balance in the laboratory would not by itself convert the photography from the category of a disaster into that of an Oscar nominee.

Every director has found himself working with an incompatible camera-man, and it is an appalling experience. David, super-sensitive about the cinema-tography, was probably aware of deficiencies the rest of us might not notice. Having worked with Ernie for so long, he expected him to produce work duplicating that of Freddie Young. But if cinematography is an art, as well as a craft, no two cameramen will produce the same result.

He had often said, "I can make any cameraman look good." So the anger directed at Ernie Day must have been only a fraction of the anger he felt at himself.

CHAPTER FORTY-SIX

VICTIMS OF VISION

A PASSAGE TO INDIA III

"SHOOTING A PASSAGE TO INDIA, I didn't feel I was getting old," David told Denise Worrell. "I didn't feel more tired than I was used to. It's a curious thing, you know. I feel I've got much more experience, but I feel as I did when I was twenty-five. I have never been ill in my life. You get very trim doing these big location pictures. When I'm out on my feet all day long, climbing rocks, doing God knows what, I stay fit. I didn't feel this movie would be my last."[1]

Shama Habibullah's mother, the writer Attia Hosain, had known David when he first went to India for TAJ MAHAL. She had found him then to be "a stimulating, sympathetic and intelligent human being". The David she met this time had changed to a "watchful person", not wholly in tune with the India for which he had once expressed such enthusiasm.

David takes part in a traditional ceremony in the grounds of the Maharajah of Mysore's palace before the start of shooting on A PASSAGE TO INDIA. (Photograph by Ken Bray)

David watches Victor Banerjee doing his Douglas Fairbanks act. (Photograph by Frank Connor)

Before the start of a film in India, a traditional Mahurat, a religious ceremony, is held to bless the production and the people working on it. Even the camera is garlanded with flowers. In the Bombay film industry this ceremony can be accomplished in a few minutes, but working on this film was a Brahmin of the highest caste, who went on for an hour and a half with everyone wilting in the heat in front of the Bangalore Palace.[2]

David considered he was very rusty when he started. "I was like an engine that needed running in again. But my producers were very good to me. They let me kick off with some simple shots."[3]

"The first scenes were with Peggy Ashcroft, Judy Davis and Nigel Havers," said John Mitchell, sound mixer. "David arrived around eight thirty and said, 'I think we'll rehearse the scene.' He sat them round the table. As you know, he really didn't like actors all that much, but he loved props and he spent an age - he was wonderful to watch - moving a vase slightly, adjusting an ornament.

"'Well,' he said. 'I think when Ernie has lit the scene, we'll shoot.'

"Ernie said, 'I'm ready.' We had one rehearsal, and he sat in his chair under the camera for the first time for fifteen years, and he said, 'Action.' And they played the scene. About three quarters of the way through, he got up in front of the camera, looked around and said, 'Cut. I don't think we can do better than that. Print it.'

"From then on, everybody was on their toes. They thought they could bumble along and he'd probably print take twenty-three."[4]

Gag shot of Richard Goodwin - for once David relied on a producer.

David's work with his actors was a series of confrontations. In the case of Victor Banerjee, who was playing Aziz, and who had been recommended by Satyajit Ray, the shadow of Peter Sellers fell over their discussions. David wanted him closer to the character of another comedian.

"As for Aziz, there's a hell of a lot of India in him. They're marvellous people, but maddening, sometimes, you know. He's the young Charlie Chaplin, and what I mean by that is that you laugh at him, but you cry with him too. That's it - he's a goose. But he's warm and you like him awfully. I don't mean that in a derogatory way - things just happen to him. He can't help it."[5]

Banerjee agreed that there was a Chaplin element at the beginning, because an audience has to be made to love him - "his obsequiousness, his excess of hospitality, his midsummer madness of falling in love - in order to accept his final arrogance. But once he is in the dock, all trace of Chaplin disappears. Nor will you find any Chaplin in Forster. I think that is one major change between the book and the film; the other is that Forster's Aziz, a most complex character, is a Muslim and there is no mention of that on screen."[6]

Over another matter Victor Banerjee crossed swords with David and stood his ground. "Victor thought I was making an anti-Indian film," said David. "I wanted him to do it with a chi-chi accent, you know, the Welsh-sounding Indian accent. He thought I was making fun of Indians. I wasn't, but I think he missed a huge trick there, probably lost him the Academy Award. I wanted to start him off as this rather naive creature who gradually grows up into this quite considerable person, Aziz. And he wouldn't do it. I think he ruined the part.

"Banerjee buggered himself up. If only he'd listened to me. Right at the end he started to trust me. I don't know why they mistrust me. I don't know what they think I'm up to."[7]

During one row, Banerjee told David to his face he was being "obnoxious" and that he wasn't the greatest director in the world. He had worked with Satyajit Ray, who, if there were any justice, would have been making this film.

"Playing one Englishman's idea of another Englishman's idea of an Indian isn't my scene," said Banerjee.[8]

Banerjee was obstinate, refused to adopt the "chi-chi" accent, and when he got his way, after four days of prevarication, he offered Lean his hand. "What the hell for?" said David.

"He shook hands the next [day], however," reported Jay Cocks for *Time*, "and on the last day of principal photography, when Banerjee brought off an especially tricky scene in one take, Lean came from behind the camera and embraced him."[9]

Eventually, Banerjee, who was interested in learning about directing, spent most of the nine months' shooting on the set whether he was in the scene or not.

For the role of Fielding, David always had Peter O'Toole in mind. "The part itself could be played with success by several good character actors," he wrote, "but it's got to shine. Peter has that star quality. He can be very sensitive to distress. He also has another asset: a strange sexual ambiguity which I played up

David (centre) with Victor Banerjee, Alec Guinness and Judy Davis at the pool in the grounds of the West End Hotel at Bangalore. Patrick Cadell, assistant director, right.

in LAWRENCE but would play down with Fielding."[10]

In the event, James Fox was cast. The brother of Edward Fox, he had been a child actor for Ealing Studios under his real name, William Fox. Changing his name to James, he starred in Joseph Losey's THE SERVANT in 1963 and six years later - after starring with Mick Jagger in Nic Roeg's controversial directorial debut PERFORMANCE - he abandoned acting for religion.

David treated him somewhat roughly but, as a practising Christian, Fox was so forgiving that he was too soft a target. He tended to find David's scorn amusing.

Far more of an opponent was Judy Davis, an Australian actress who had first come to international attention in MY BRILLIANT CAREER. David had selected her after talking to her for a couple of hours in Thorn-EMI's office in London.

"At the time it looked as if the finance was not going to come through," said David. "I had a couple of rooms filled with the packing cases that contained our work on the film. At the end of those two hours I said, 'If we ever make PASSAGE you will be Adela.' She wanted the part and she waited for it."[11]

Alas, Judy Davis and David Lean came from different planets. "Miss Quested is written as a rather dowdy spinster, who is lost in India, and Judy Davis geared herself to play it like that," said Peggy Ashcroft. "But David wanted her this elegant, pristine creature, beautifully dressed."[12]

"I thought that I had to find a way that fills her out a little more," said David, "to let you see that she is beginning to awaken sexually... because India can do this, you know. There are two lots of people that go to India. Some get off the plane and want to get the next plane out; others want to stay for six months. She is one who wanted to stay for six months, and I wanted to catch a bit of that."[13]

While David thought her an excellent actress, he was aware that she was highly suspicious of him and didn't like him at all.

"She thought I was a commercial hack and was terribly rude. I remember her saying, 'I've only seen one film you've made and that was a prisoner of war story. I don't think you can do women, can you?'

"I said, 'Well, every now and again, I suppose.'

When Davis was told about BRIEF ENCOUNTER she went to Richard Goodwin and asked him to get her a copy. "I want to see what his work is like with women."

"I mean, real cheek, you know," said David. "Richard must have fudged it, because the film never appeared."[14]

"I think I was frightened of him right up to the end," said Judy Davis. "He made me feel inadequate initially and, I thought, unfairly. He was very nervous about making that film, he hadn't made one for so long. He did it to all of the actors in turn, made them feel bad, and then kind of forgot about it and passed on to something else. Everybody reacted in different ways. James Fox used to try

David with Alec Guinness as Professor Godbole. (Photograph by Frank Connor)

and laugh through it. While Lean was exploding, James would laugh, 'Oh, ho, ho, unbelievable, isn't it?' Victor got highly nervous and tried desperately to make him happy, Peggy Ashcroft floated above it all magnificently and I got bullish."[15]

"She was terrible to him," said Alec Guinness. "In front of the whole unit, 'You can't fucking well direct. You haven't directed for fifteen years, you don't know what's fucking well happening. You don't know what the process is at all.' And a whole lot of Australian stuff. She went too far. David was amazed, but he sort of laughed. He couldn't get over it for days."[16]

"Judy Davis thought I was a kind of goof," said David "She would start every day by saying, 'You know what I think of the script. It's not nearly as good as the book.'

"I'd say, 'I know you feel that, but we've got to do it.'

"Oh God, you can still see it in the film - a scene at a polo match, you see her leaning over the rails, her nails filthy dirty. And she said, 'Well, it's natural, isn't it?'

"After a while, I got really fed up with her. Yet she's a wonderful actress. Absolutely fantastic."[17]

Richard Goodwin was anxious to keep the conflict in proportion. "It was minor compared to a director like John Guillermin. Nothing to write home about. David was too civilised for that. But I got them together and said, 'Either you make up your differences or we stop.' I stuck them in my room, and they sat on the terrace and screamed at each other, and then they became the best of friends, so we were all right."[18]

"There was never any talking at all with Lean, really," said Judy Davis. "It was difficult finding a common language with him because he had restrictions on the way he would talk. He would explain the shot: 'Dear. You come in here and the monkeys are here. You look up and see the statue.' Never any discussion about the internal workings; he was uncomfortable with that kind of dialogue. That was fine. I had seen the character slightly differently, so I needed to talk it through with him, but he blocked that.

"He was a very emotional man and I don't think he was confident of his intellect, so he'd get nervous. If the conversation got too intellectual, you could see him getting nervous, gripping the seat for support. He'd then swing back to sweeping statements and big emotional strokes - that made sense. You had to go into his language and then you'd get somewhere. He would say things like, 'Dear. You're lying in bed. Moonlight coming through the window. And you can smell the frangipani. And you remember the monkeys and the statues.' He'd paint the picture for you. Actually, I liked that scene. I thought it was lovely. And I love the idea of the smell of frangipani."[19]

"I don't know what happened," said David, "but towards the end of the film when we came back and did the trial scene her attitude towards me completely changed, and for the first time I had a kind of rapport. I made suggestions, and she accepted them, and we got on very well together.

"She thought I despised her because she was a colonial. I found that out on the grapevine. I can't prove that I'm not anti-colonial. I don't know what one does about that sort of thing, and we had a miserable relationship until the very end when she gave me a very nice little figure wrapped in newspaper, shoved it into my hands and said, 'I've learned more from you than I thought I'd ever learn from anybody.' And ran. That was her goodbye to me. It's awfully difficult to cope with these personal hates. I'm not very good at it."[20]

"Judy Davis in the end came to a very happy conclusion," said Kees T'Hooft, an assistant film editor. "For his birthday she bought him a present and he was completely bowled over. There were several occasions when they had clashes during the filming and yet in the cutting-room he called us over. 'Look at this,' he'd say, showing a scene of hers. 'This is what's in the script, this is what she says. It's beautiful. Just how I wanted it.'"[21]

"I was suddenly the golden girl for a while," said Judy Davis. "After we shot the court scene, Lean liked the way I'd done it. He came up to me one day (impersonates Lean's conspiratorial hiss), 'Dear. Come with me.' And he strode off. We went through one sound stage and across the courtyard, then through another sound stage, then the final sound stage. There was a set being constructed. What's this? He said, 'This way.' We walked up these temporary wooden steps and it was the set of a room with a window and desk. 'Dear. The last scene of the film. You're at the window. Fuck Alec Guinness.'"[22]

At the casting stage, Alec Guinness was having dinner with David and Sandy, and he suggested Peggy Ashcroft for Mrs Moore. Guinness asked what David's other casting ideas were and wondered who was going to play Godbole.

"Well," said David, "I was rather hoping... you."

"David knew he was wrong about Alec Guinness," said Richard Goodwin, "and he couldn't get out of it. We begged him not to do it. He said, 'I need my old friends around me. I've got to have Alec. I can't direct an Indian.' He just couldn't face trying to explain to an Indian what he wanted. But it was a big mistake. A very unhappy sequence."[23]

In Forster's novel, Professor Godbole was a Deccani Brahmin. Since David wanted to finish the film in the Himalayas, this had to change. "We've now made him a Kashmiri Hindu," said David.

"Well," said Guinness, "it's a Muslim country so Hindus are a bit rarer there. I went first to Delhi to pick up the atmosphere, and sought out anything to do with grand Hindus, and indeed met a man from Kashmir, a grave man dressed in white robes. A very intelligent professor. I met him in a rather grand house and talked to him quite a bit and thought, That's got his accent fairly well, that's a help. I arrived and set off doing that. David said, 'Do you want to stay in all this white stuff?'

"It's up to you, but it seems to me all right and the man I met in Delhi was in white."

David had meanwhile discovered that no man with the name of Godbole would come from Kashmir. The solution was to have the character originate from somewhere in the west and to wear a red and gold turban.

"I can't tell you," said Guinness. "I think I had five different sets of things to wear. The wardrobe people must have gone mad. One didn't know where one was."[24]

Even at the time, Guinness told Victor Davis of the *Daily Express* that he thought the casting was "absolute madness."[25]

David was depending on the character of Godbole to provide the mysticism in the film, and gave him a more important role than he had in the book.

"Godbole is everything," he told Harlan Kennedy. "He's a sort of first cousin to Mrs Moore, he's got a sort of extrasensory perception - at least, I gave him that; he's part mumbo-jumbo, part highly intelligent, part cynical, part funny. It's a real bag of tricks to contain in one character."[26]

"I did a day's work," said Guinness, "one little scene with James Fox. David said, 'Absolutely spot on. It looks marvellous. Don't alter it a fraction.'

"I was a bit astonished and thought, well, that's a relief."

A few days later a report came from London which said that Guinness's make-up was too pale and that they should start again with a darker tone. Guinness's argument that Forster had described Godbole as having a European complexion was rejected.

"At that point, I said to Richard Goodwin, 'Look, I think a mistake has been made. I certainly won't ask for a penny of salary as long as you pay my fare back.'

"He said, 'Oh, nonsense, nonsense...'

"I mean, that was Goodwin, really. He was so nice about the situation. Later I said again that I was perfectly happy to go home because I felt the whole thing was not going to function. And a thousand other details."[27]

"I thought Alec Guinness would be wonderful as Godbole," said David. "Why shouldn't he be able to play an Indian? There are not many very good Indian actors, there really aren't, because they come from a different school. They find it difficult to stand still, hold a look, they tend to exaggerate everything.

"Alec was terrified I was trying to make him be a copy of Peter Sellers. It never entered my head, actually. He should have played it dead straight, I think it would have been bloody good, but he didn't. I am not quite sure what he did with it. But if he'd played that part straight it would have been very good. I think he kind of changed the whole colour of the film - in fact, I know he did. I had to cut out the last sequence because he wouldn't do it simply.

"It was a sort of dance, but it wasn't really a dance. Alec met somebody in Delhi and he learned all these eye movements. I didn't want eye movements and that caused a bit of trouble. It was an unhappy experience. And then he burst into print in several papers saying various things I made him do, or didn't make him do. I always find it rather hard to read what one's colleagues have said about you. It's all right in later years, I suppose, but hot on the heels of an event it's a sort of shock, and Alec is pretty free with his criticisms. He really rattled me on PASSAGE TO INDIA."[28]

Guinness gave an account to Richard Findlater of the difficulties he had had with his part, and it appeared in *The Observer*:

"There won't be any Godbole dancing in the film. I don't know whether there's any singing. First I was given a Hindi psalm to learn, which was infinitely difficult however one tackled it. I'm not musical, and I don't sing. Then I was given another psalm in Sanskrit. *That* was tricky enough to learn: I gave it an hour every day for two weeks, enormously assisted by John Dalby, who was responsible for it. Then I used to go - if I wasn't working directly on a scene - to a very nice Hindu, with an enchanting wife, who taught me the Hindu dance. I'm a bit better at that than I am at singing, but it wasn't easy stuff.

"After a couple of weeks of this David said to me one day, 'Oh, I hope you're using the right kind of cymbals.' I hadn't been using *any* kind of cymbals; nobody had told me to do so. I then had to go back and learn a new dance, with some special cymbals bought in northern India by the film company. The Hindu teacher laughed when he saw them. 'Those are *Tibetan* cymbals,' he said. 'They have nothing to do with Hinduism at all.' So I learned *another* dance, a fairly simple one. I had to dance along the perimeter of a giant wheel, along the spokes and into the centre. But David never saw me do the dance, and it dawned on me that he didn't really want me to dance. He said suddenly one evening, 'I just want you to stand in the middle of the wheel and twiddle around.' I couldn't refuse, but I did lose my temper.

"If he'd come to me - preferably earlier, but even on that evening - and said, 'Look, you've got to forgive me, but after all your hard work we shan't be able to use your dance,' I shouldn't have been pleased but I would have accepted it. As it was, it made me feel an absolute fool."[29]

When I asked Guinness what put David off the sequence so much that he cut it out, Guinness said, "Me, I should think. It got altered in the script before I arrived. He brought in a crowd of children and so on where it should have been a lonely Indian thing purely facing up to the weather, the rain and the monsoon. So you became a victim of his... vision."[30]

"Alec Guinness practically ruined the film because of the dance," said David. "We had a very big set, which was supposed to be in Kashmir, with a wheel of life with Alec on it, which tied up the whole business about life as a wheel with many spokes, which he talks about. It was there at the end, at the end titles really, and he's on this wheel and he just couldn't do it simply. All I wanted him to do was to have cymbals, and people joining in and music coming up and the titles over it.

"Pictorially it was wonderful. I thought of the idea of doing it all in reflections in the pool in front of Fielding's house, and I put the camera upside down and photographed the whole thing in reflections so that they were all reflections, the right way up. There was just slight movement - it gave them an unreal quality - lovely. And Alec just couldn't do it. It was so bloody awful I had to cut it out.

"Now he writes in the newspaper that I ruined his part by cutting out some of the dance and he writes me a private letter[31] thanking me for doing it. Saving him from the shame of its being seen."

"And yet with it all," said Guinness, "the last two times we met, we both fell over backwards to be affectionate, and I mean affectionate. I do have an affection for him. He was a very strong personality. God knows, if it hadn't been for him, I wouldn't have been involved in making two or three successful films, or won an Oscar. But I have to trust my instincts, and sometimes my instincts went contrary to David's."[32]

During a party given by David and Sandy for a Hindu holy day, Peggy Ashcroft slipped and twisted her ankle.

"She couldn't help it," said Ernie Day, "but it was almost looked upon as a plot against him, preventing him from forging ahead. Here was another thorn in his side. He hated suffering and couldn't go near it. He recoiled from cripples in India. He was Aries, and I am an Aries too, so I can understand why he recoiled from people who were ill. I can't remember him ever consoling anyone personally. He would always be very sorry if anyone was suffering, but he would never contribute by his presence." [33]

Alec Guinness found it strange that even though Peggy Ashcroft was in the same hotel, David didn't go and see her, whatever the degree of exasperation. [34] But Peggy Ashcroft was as much of a trouper as David, and as soon as she could, she returned to work - albeit on crutches.

It was curious that these two great figures had never worked together before. Peggy Ashcroft, who was born in Tirlemount Road, just a few hundred yards from David's birthplace in Blenheim Crescent, Croydon, had made her first film, fifty years before, with Maurice Elvey. She had risen to become perhaps the finest actress of her generation - on the stage. Her occasional forays into the cinema had never aroused in her more than a vague interest.

Perhaps sensing this, David veered in a very different direction. He had originally decided to have Katharine Hepburn and to let her play Mrs Moore as the New Englander she was. Hepburn turned it down. [35]

Peggy Ashcroft had also seen the Santha Rama Rau play of *A Passage to India*, in the company of one of her oldest friends, Dr George Rylands, Master of King's College, Cambridge, and one of Forster's literary executors.

"I went to the last performance," said Peggy Ashcroft, "and I remember meeting Forster afterwards and him saying to me, 'I hope one day you'll play Mrs Moore.'

"I thought to myself, what me, play an old girl like that?

"When I was approached about PASSAGE, I had lunch with David at the Berkeley. I said, 'You see, Mr Lean, I am seventy-five and I think I'm beyond doing another work in India.'

"And he said, 'I'm seventy-five too.'

"As a result of that conversation, I agreed to do it. He was enormously enthusiastic about the book. And he had done the script himself. I fell madly for him. He was the most charming man I had ever met." [36]

When it came to working on the film, however, she admitted her attitude changed. "I thought him absolutely inspiring because of his visual feeling, and his perfectionism. I don't think very much of him as a director of actors. I don't think he likes actors very much. I never had any problems with him myself, except once.

"He asked me to look at Aziz 'and blush like a young girl.' Well, I was stunned. It was lucky we were doing this at the end or I'd have had a great deal of difficulty playing Mrs Moore. I was staggered - he had an attitude which was totally different to the book, totally different to Forster. It was David Lean's vision, not Forster's. I said I couldn't possibly do it like that and he said, 'Oh well, if you can't, you can't.'

"My unhappiness was due to his lack of sensitivity where the young actors were concerned, Victor Banerjee and Judy. A director shouldn't really treat actors like that. There was a lack of respect for their attitudes to the part. He was an autocrat. I heard him say that he casts people he knows are absolutely right for the part. It isn't a case of being absolutely right, is it? It's how to play it. And then you've got to allow that they have their attitude to the part. Judy had a completely different conception of her role and she was bulldozed. I loved Judy Davis and admired her enormously. He did not. That was a bone of contention."[37]

David with his indispensable Maggie Unsworth. David Nicholls behind.

There was another occasion when Peggy Ashcroft's ideas clashed with David's. "I was foolish enough at the beginning of the picture," said David, "to try to explain the part to Peggy Ashcroft and she kept on throwing it in my face. I said, 'Mrs Moore and Godbole are very closely allied. You're both about four or five inches off the ground.'

'Off the ground? What do you mean?'

"I said, 'Peggy, I don't know how to put it, but not quite real. A touch of the ghost about you. And two ghosts understand each other. And yet you're not ghosts.'

"And she looked at me absolutely blankly. That proved to be one of the great bones of contention throughout the film, and it's one of the things which she missed in the film - this slight second sense. It could have been wonderful but she missed it. She's got no poetry in her."[38]

This is a comment which those who have seen Peggy Ashcroft's stage work might quarrel with. The problem was that she felt a profound loyalty to the Forster original. "I found it difficult to accept that David said, perfectly frankly, 'This is my version of A PASSAGE TO INDIA', whereas I thought it should be E.M. Forster's."[39]

David invited her to look at scenes through the viewfinder of the camera, hoping to intrigue her with the magic of cinema, but she found this neither exhilarating nor challenging, just another example of David's passion for having everything set in concrete.[40]

"She was wonderful in the film," said Sandy, "but she didn't understand cutting at all. Camera lefts and rights were a mystery to her. And she was baffled that she could step down out of frame in Ooty and land on the platform in Bangalore and it was still the same scene.

"At the same time, David felt Peggy was missing a lot of the character, that Mrs Moore was a more sensitive, more intuitive person than Peggy was making her, that there was much more tragedy there. Funny, because she turned out to be the best thing in the film."[41]

"The great strength and comforter of the film was darling Maggie Unsworth," said Peggy Ashcroft, "who kept David level at difficult moments and was a great comfort to me. She and I shared a flat in the same bit of the hotel. David and Sandy were upstairs. I love her."[42]

In the end, though, after all the sweat and tears, David joined in the general admiration for Peggy, which culminated in an Academy Award for her performance.

"I think Peggy Ashcroft is wonderful. Did you see the Olivier memorial service on television? Her authority, her dignity, her mastery of the language is tremendously impressive. It was not an entirely satisfactory relationship again. I don't know why not: I think it was probably my fault. Alec Guinness and I have a funny relationship, and they used to spend a lot of time together. He's an old friend of Peggy's and I used to imagine, probably quite wrongly, that she was catching Alec's suspicions of me, which are pretty considerable. So I began to look on Peggy as a sort of joint enemy with Alec, and I think I was wrong because she's obviously got a mind of her own."[43]

"What I never, never understood was David Lean's chucking the end of the book, which is one of the most amazing situations," said Peggy Ashcroft. "He said it wasn't cinematic. I would have thought it was the most cinematic thing you could have. Instead of that very sentimental end which he invented the book ends with Aziz and Fielding having recriminations and they ride out on their horses to the edge of a precipice. Their conversation ends and they part - one going one way, the other the other. Agreeing that they have to agree to disagree. In a sense, I think it sums up the book. The inability of East meeting West. But dealing with the efforts to do so. He cut out Mrs Moore's degeneration because she remains gracious to the end. He didn't want to complicate the tale.

"David went to India in his youth and he had put that impression on the screen, which isn't really the book. The little town was a rather small and dingy bit of the British Raj, not grandiose like we had it, with almost an embassy and hundreds of well-off Indians. It was a small town, small community, small

David during the shooting of the departure of Mrs Moore. (Photograph by Frank Connor)

people. But there it was. It came out as quite a successful film, didn't it?"[44]

David's ending showed the two men parting warmly, their friendship intact. He dismissed charges that this countered everything Forster was trying to say.

"Look, this novel was written hot on the movement for Indian independence. I think the end is a lot of hogwash so far as a movie is concerned. It's highly symbolic. They both like each other very much, those two men. It's finished, that. India's free. It may have been relevant at the time, but I can't expect an audience to pick that up now."[45]

Despite her reservations, Peggy Ashcroft eventually sent David a letter congratulating him on the final result. "I must say I'm in good company," said David. "It used to be the same with Willie Wyler. They always used to say about Willie, 'I'll never work with him again.' Until they saw the film."[46]

Even as shooting progressed in the seclusion of the maharajah's estate and in the garden of the West End Hotel, the "real India" was not entirely excluded and its unceasing drama would reveal another aspect of David's character.

During production, a multi-storey building in Bangalore collapsed and a number of people were killed. David was one of the first to make a generous contribution.

"We had a security guard who was killed as he went off-duty," said Shama Habibullah. "His young wife and child came to the office a day later and immediately he gave a donation to her. There was a whip-round among the unit as well. And in this way, he was very responsive. It was an odd thing; the humbler you were, the better he would be with you."[47]

"He was very, very generous," said Alec Guinness. "I know an actor with whom he became friendly and who was in financial trouble - he owed money to someone - and David wrote a cheque for forty thousand pounds without a tremor.

"There was a kid of about fourteen with a crippled leg. He was beautifully clean, always had a sparkling T shirt, but he lived on a board with wheels and got around on his hands. The unit befriended him and invented jobs for him to do and gave him little bits of money. He was a charming child and people were worried about what was going to happen to him when we left and so a subscription was got up and people put in what they thought was suitable. A sum of money was collected and it was decided to set him up with a soft drinks and cake store - the kind of thing they have all over the place. I heard this from Maggie Unsworth. David was brought into it and had the imaginative and expensive idea of saying, 'Fine, but we could really give him one-upmanship if I gave him a fridge. Then he can serve ice-cold drinks.' With those sorts of things he was very good."[48]

CHAPTER FORTY-SEVEN

CREDIT TAKEN, CREDIT LOST

A PASSAGE TO INDIA IV

"It was on PASSAGE TO INDIA," said Sandy Lean, "that I began to exist as a person distinct from David. It came as a surprise; I saw that people on the unit weren't reacting to me simply as David's wife. When I accepted it, I started coming out of my shell. I discovered that I loved the atmosphere of the film set, being on location, hanging out with the crew - it was like being given a whole new sandlot of children to play with every day.

"I began to have this new sense of confidence and started to become aware of other people in quite a new way. My emotional life had always been intensely inward. Suddenly that was changing and it was happening so fast I could hardly keep up with myself.

"I don't know how much David was aware of. There's always gossip on a film set. Someone told me, much later, that David thought I was having an affair with Nigel Havers. In any case, he said nothing to me. Perhaps he felt that by discussing nothing there would be nothing to discuss."[1]

The way it affected David was to make him more stubborn than usual. And this came to a head in Kashmir.

The set of Aziz's clinic had been built by the river with the wooden houses of the Old City of Srinagar in the background. All the television aerials had been taken down, but because the sun was in the wrong place David decided to do the shot later.

"So that meant," said Shama Habibullah, "that for ten days, two weeks, people had to do without their television sets. Every day I'd expect a riot in the Old City. What you do in such a case is to find the strong-arm man of the area and ask him to go and do it. You don't do it yourself because it's far too large an area. But every day he'd come back to me and say, 'I can't hold this much longer.' At one time, I gave them all two-band radios and said, 'Distribute these to the people making a fuss.' Suddenly, one had visions of giving the whole of the city radios or I'm shot! And it was all because the light wasn't right."[2]

The mountain David wanted to photograph was covered with less snow than usual; he wanted it right down to the middle of frame. So David decided to wait for the snow.

Eventually, Richard Goodwin lost patience. "I said, 'If you don't shoot this afternoon, we're going home and that's it.' It was the end of the schedule. It was very depressing to have to say that to him. He knew perfectly well that he had to pack it in, but he was sort of mesmerised by this and depressed by his wife. And then he made the fatal mistake of putting her in the picture."[3]

"They needed someone to play Stella, Fielding's wife at the end of the film," said Sandy. "It didn't turn out to be easy. You see, she appears for such a short time, and she has to convey a presence that's completely fresh and at the same time weightless. Every actress they came up with, David turned down. This had gone on for months, and time was running short.

"One day Richard and Priscilla John, the casting director, came to David and said they thought they'd found the perfect person for the part.

"'Who's that?'

"'Your wife.'

"He was rather tickled by the idea, but I was in a panic. I said to him 'You know I can't act.' And he said, 'I can make dogs and children act, don't worry. Besides, there's no dialogue, all you have to do is *think*.'

"It became my private nightmare. I was fitted with a costume, and each time I went for a fitting they had to take it in because I'd lost weight. Then, two weeks before we moved to Kashmir, Priscilla and Richard came to me and said, 'You know, you don't have to do this if you don't want to.' And I thought, 'What do they know that I don't know?'

"In the end, of course, it wasn't so bad. In fact, in my relief, I almost enjoyed it. But would I ever do it again? No, thank you. I'm not an actress."[4]

Only after she returned to England did Sandy realise how unhappy she was.

"When we got back to England," Sandy recalled, "all the balances changed. The film crew, which had been such a tightly-knit group, was unravelling. Instead of being out on location, the unit was in the studio. And I was forlorn: after being on the set every day in Bangalore, driving David out to the location and back again, suddenly I was back at the Berkeley, watching television and going shopping. My life was slipping back into its old groove.

"And now, when I'd ask David, 'Can I come on the set today?' he'd usually say, 'No, I don't think that's a very good idea.' Later, during the editing, he said, 'No, you'd just be a distraction. There are too many of us in the cutting-room as it is.'

"So for the next four or five months I saw him very early in the morning, and very late in the evening, when he came back exhausted from editing."[5]

One of the reasons David preferred editing to directing was the sense of peace after the turmoil of production.

"I love editing - to sit back in the cutting-room, the circus has disappeared, just wonderful. I know the shots I've taken, and before I cut I sit there and think of the flow of shots - I see it in my mind's eye as I sit there at the Moviola before running a foot of film. And then I try to copy in reality what I see in my imagination.'[6]

A young Dutchman, Kees T'Hooft, was second assistant. He had been at the London International Film School, and had initially been hired by Win Ryder to help sync the rushes.

"David Lean managed to build up a fairly awesome reputation, but he was determined to make the cutting of the film a pleasure for everyone involved. He wanted to cut the film himself. The editor, Eunice Mountjoy, was not briefed about this at all, so she was disappointed when it transpired, after a few weeks of work, what method of editing he envisaged. The atmosphere in the cutting-room was fairly tense."[7]

Eunice Mountjoy[8] was living in Capri when she was telephoned by Lord Brabourne and asked to work on the film. She flew to England, and after signing a three-month contract as editor, she contacted, as first and second assistants, Ann Sopel and Kees T'Hooft. Three months' worth of rushes were piled up, and had to be numbered, logged and broken down.

In the cutting-rooms Kees T'Hooft was accustomed to making Nescafé, but when David was due he decided he should have something better, and brought in his own cafetière and made proper coffee. After a while, Sandy insisted that David be given decaffeinated coffee. David soon caught on to this, and sought Kees out to ask him for the real thing. "I need a charge," he would say.

Sometimes David would go to the studio doctor for a Vitamin E injection to give him greater energy. It was this technique that he felt had got him through the hectic editing schedule on DOCTOR ZHIVAGO. But the doctor refused at one point, saying it was an unhealthy practice.

"David was very keen on his health," said Kees. "Both his parents lived into their nineties, so he expected to outlive them if he was careful."[9]

Although David got on perfectly well with Eunice Mountjoy, he did not feel she was a fellow spirit.

"I was always explaining to her why I was doing this and why that, and why I really fuss over cuts. One or two frames can make a terrific difference. I was explaining things to her and she didn't really understand. I said, 'Look, aren't people interested in smooth cuts nowadays?' She said, 'The old ones.' I said, 'What about the new ones?' She said, 'Oh, they can't be bothered.' I found that a fascinating remark, 'Can't be bothered.'"[10]

"He would sit behind the Moviola," said Kees, "and be handed all the different takes in order, and he would make with a chinagraph pencil a mark where he wanted it cut. Eunice at the editing bench would make the physical cuts and he would look at it again and make his changes.

"Eunice was very professional. She was at first surprised, but then fairly reconciled to her position. What really got her was that she hoped for an editor's credit. I think Lean assumed it was made clear to her when she was hired.' [11]

"Because I'm very proud of being an editor," said David, "I decided to take the credit, 'Directed and Edited by.' I said to John Brabourne, 'Look, I'm going to take editing credit on this.' That was a terrible thing because he'd promised her that she should have editing credit while I was in India. And as he hadn't got the courage to tell her, he left me to do it. I said, 'Look, Eunice, I'm going to take credit for this.'

"And she said, '*What?* But you've never taken credit before.'

An argument followed, during which David insisted she had not made a single cut herself. He offered her a credit as Associate Editor, saying, "I think that's bloody generous and you know it is." Eunice told him that she had wasted six months of her life. [12]

That, anyway, was David's story. Eunice Mountjoy told it rather differently.

"He didn't do it to my face. I had a telephone call from Lord Brabourne. 'I've got some very bad news for you,' he said. 'David wants the editing credit.'

"I said, 'Well, he can't have it, John. You employed me as the editor. I've got it in black and white.'

"He said, 'I know, but we're in terrible trouble and he says he wants it.'

"I was very angry. So I said, 'This really isn't on. You've employed me as an editor. There is no way I would even have considered taking the film on for an assistant editor's credit.

"So he said, 'Will you think about it?'

"The next morning, I had David in my cutting-room for about two hours. He said, 'Eunice, you're young. Your life is ahead of you. This is my last film. I've wanted to have the editing credit on all my pictures. And I'm doing it on this one.'

"I said, 'There is no way, David, I would have come back from Italy to work for you as assistant editor. I admire you. You're a great man. But I can't understand why you're doing this.'

"He said, 'Well, I want to, and that's that. Anyway, I'll give you a jolly nice credit...'

"He gave me Associate Editor. The producers didn't want to know. All they wanted was for the film to get finished. They'd had enough. They could see it going on for months and months. Unfortunately, I didn't have an agent. I didn't have a leg to stand on. Also, the union didn't want to know about it.

"David took a dislike to one of my sound editors because he was short and overweight, and smoked and drank. David had his downs on people, and when it came to the credit titles, he just crossed him off because he didn't like the man. Unbeknown to David, we had the titles remade. He was a wicked man. But you couldn't help liking him.

"When I got married, he filled my car up with Harrods boxes full of the most beautiful willow pattern china. It must have cost him a fortune and I was totally taken aback. And every time I look at these cups and saucers, I think of David, don't I? At the time, after what he did, I wouldn't even open them. They went in a cupboard and I didn't even use them, I was so angry with him. I've got over that now, of course. It's a lovely memory from David. They're on the dresser."[13]

"It was extraordinary," said John Brabourne, "that at the end of his career he should be worrying about what sort of credit he was going to get. Perhaps all the time he had resented not getting all the credit. The jealousy really destroyed him. It ate into him. I thought it was sad."[14]

Meanwhile, Santha Rama Rau was also expecting to see her name on the screen. She had neither seen nor heard from David after his letter from New Delhi in which he spoke of writing the script himself. Two years had passed and the picture was nearing completion. However, a rough-cut screening was arranged for her at the studio and since a hostile reaction was anticipated, David stayed away.

"When I realised," she said, "how far the film strayed in action, tone and spirit from Mr Forster's novel - even totally contradicting his original ending - I was pleased not to have my name in the credits except as the author of the play on which the film was based... The sad truth is that David wanted to make *his* film about India, behind the shield of a famous novel. Yet because he so basically disagreed with Forster on just about all matters - social, political, the Raj, Indians, British officialdom - he couldn't make *Forster's* film about India."[15]

In 1984, David was startled to be invited to lunch with Mrs Thatcher at Chequers, the prime minister's official country home in Buckinghamshire. He was equally startled to see that another guest was Rex Harrison, with whom he had had no contact since BLITHE SPIRIT, forty years earlier. Also present was Sir Richard Attenborough.

When the *Daily Mail* reported the names of the lunch guests, Peter Lean's daughter-in-law, Anne, decided she would use the opportunity to meet her elusive grandfather. She managed to locate the telephone number of Chequers, said her name was Anne Lean and would David please phone her back?

"Literally, two minutes later they phoned back," said Peter Lean. "A woman RAF officer, presumably to check out that it wasn't someone she shouldn't be... She explained she was married to David's grandson, who would very much like to meet him as he was in the country. We later learned that this woman RAF officer gave him a note with Anne's name and phone number as he was leaving. Maggie Thatcher came with him to the gate. David opened the note and was very embarrassed because he thought Maggie would know what was in it."

"The next thing I knew," said Maggie Unsworth, "I was sitting in the garden and the Rolls pulled up with David and Sandy. He said, 'The most *awful* thing has happened.' And he told me the story: 'Oh, I was so embarrassed - in front of Maggie Thatcher.' He thought she was wonderful. He admired her no end. But he was very embarrassed by that."[16]

Maggie Unsworth decided to bring the family together at long last. First she asked Peter and June to tea at a restaurant in Sonning, then she arranged for them to come to tea at her house.

"It wasn't until we got there that she sprang the bombshell," said Peter. "She said, 'Your father will be here in half an hour's time.'"

Maggie had mentioned it to David at Pinewood one lunch hour.

"Long silence," she said. "I heard nothing from him for the rest of the meal. Right at the end, as I was getting up to go, he said, 'Oh Maggie, by the way, what time on Sunday?' Nobody forced him. He made his own mind up."

The encounter was initially very awkward. David had no idea what to say and began talking to Maggie about music. When Maggie produced a batch of stills from David's earliest days at Gaumont, collected for London Weekend Television's *South Bank Show*, the ice was broken.

"When they sat down together," said Maggie, "looking at those stills, you'd have thought there was nothing in the world that was wrong."

The reconciliation was an emotional one - too emotional for Peter, who had always imagined he wasn't wanted. "We'd been close enough at Pinewood. Then, that's enough, thank you very much. Out of my life. I've always thought that."

It was the first occasion he had met Sandy and he thought she was charming. He was convinced she had a lot to do with what happened next.

The next meeting took place at the Savoy Hotel. Peter and June were invited, together with Nicholas and Anne. It was the first time David had met his grandson, since Peter's first attempt in 1959, via the *Daily Express*, which had so badly misfired.

"During most of the meal, David was on whisky or brandy and he got a little tight," said Peter. "By the end he was very jolly. Our daughter Tracy was in America, nannying. She had been out there for a year and June and I thought it would be a nice break to go out at Christmas to see her. We found that air fares to America had literally doubled two or three weeks before Christmas. When we found this out we had to phone Tracy up and say 'we're sorry, we can't make it.' I don't know how he found out. I reckon Maggie must have said something because over the meal at the Savoy he suddenly produced tickets for June and I to go on Concorde. Not only did he provide the tickets, but a Hertz car and a whole bundle of travellers' cheques.

"Then we had an invitation to go to Pinewood to see the first print of PASSAGE TO INDIA - Nick and Anne were invited to that as well. Then I wrote to him and Sandy and said would they come down to see us one Sunday? I gave them two dates to choose and Sandy phoned June and down they came and had lunch and tea. Nick and Anne were there and I thought there was a chance we'd see each other on a regular basis - not weekly or monthly, obviously, but once or twice a year. But that wasn't to be."[17]

The invitation from Margaret Thatcher was the harbinger of one of Britain's highest honours. On 16 June 1984, it was officially announced that David would be awarded a knighthood.

Among the many letters of congratulation, David received a few lines from Emeric Pressburger. Their disagreement over GANDHI had not prevented Pressburger staying in touch.

"Dearest Emeric," replied David. "What a sweet card you sent me. It was the warmest and best received of all the many good wishes. I'm very touched and hope we might have dinner together when I've finished cutting the film I've just done in India! Much love David."[18,19]

David formally received his knighthood on 30 October 1984. He said little about it in the cutting-room, but Kees T'Hooft was in Win Ryder's cutting-room when David dropped in, as was his habit, before going home. He said that everyone at the Palace had been surprisingly friendly, and that he and the other knights-to-be had received a briefing on how to behave in front of the Queen. There was an orchestra to entertain the guests, and when his turn came, it played themes from his films.

A PASSAGE TO INDIA had its world premiere in Los Angeles on 13 December 1984. David refused to attend the New York premiere the next day because of his bitter memories of the New York critics after the opening of RYAN'S DAUGHTER.

But as the film approached its American premiere, Richard Schickel, now a film critic for *Time* magazine, joined forces with another David Lean devotee, Jay Cocks, to campaign for a cover story on David.

Schickel had chaired that unhappy dinner at the Algonquin Hotel. "This was in no sense an act of atonement," wrote Schickel, "as I did not know, at the time, that I had anything to atone for. We meant this to be a tribute to a great figure on what we imagined might be his last film. Management was not all that fond of the idea, but ultimately acceded to our passion, and off we went to London to see the movie and for Jay, who was to write the profile of Lean himself, to interview him. I was to write a critical consideration of the film.

"A couple of days before the screening, I got a call at the Savoy from the Warner Bros. publicist in Los Angeles, informing me that Lean had barred me from the screening, citing the Algonquin incident as the cause. I was astonished, and also placed in a highly embarrassing position. After my campaign for this story - and after having spent the company's money on this venture - how could I explain what seemed about to happen?

"Eventually, I got in touch with Richard Goodwin, the film's producer, who told me to forget Lean's animus and come along to the screening. I'll never forget Goodwin's comments: 'Don't worry, after what we've been through on the picture, this is nothing.'

"Eventually Lean got his *Time* cover. My story was a nightmare to write, for knowing what I now knew, I found myself almost totally blocked when I sat down to write it. Now that it had been pointed out to me, I did feel compelled to

atone for my youthful indiscretion. At the same time, I had to fulfil the usual journalistic obligations to judiciousness and objectivity. I suppose you could say that as I hunted and pecked my way through this assignment, agonizing over every word, David Lean finally got his revenge on me."[20]

And this is part of what Schickel wrote:

"In Lean's cinema, there is no such thing as an idle shot, something that survives to the final cut merely because it is striking in its beauty or novel in its impact... Like Forster, Lean uses India not just as a colorful and exotic setting but as a decisive force in shaping the story he is telling, almost as a character."

Schickel acknowledged the wasted years. "He passed some of the ensuing years in bitterness, wounded by reviewers who so often tend to listen to movies more intently than they look at them, thus missing much of his special grace and subtlety... For a man like him, austere and passionate, to attempt a comeback after these misadventures, and at his age, was an act of extraordinary creative nerve. To do so with an adaptation of a book that, however beguiling its surfaces, has been a conundrum for readers ever since its publication sixty years ago, was flirting dangerously with calamity... That Lean has brought this essentially schizoid work to the screen with such sureness, elegance and hypnotic force is akin to a miracle."[21]

Another critic at the Algonquin meeting, Pauline Kael, was also full of praise for David: "He knows how to do pomp and the moral hideousness of empire better than practically anybody else around. He enlarges the scale of Forster's irony, and the characters live in more sumptuous settings than we might have expected. But they do live. Lean knows how to give the smallest inflections an overpowering psychological weight..."[22]

Vincent Canby, in the *New York Times*, felt it was "by far his best work since THE BRIDGE ON THE RIVER KWAI and LAWRENCE OF ARABIA and perhaps his most humane and moving film since BRIEF ENCOUNTER. Though vast in scale and set against a tumultuous Indian background, it is also intimate, funny and moving in the manner of a film-maker completely in control of his material. Lean shares with Forster an appreciation for the difficulties involved in coping with the universe."[23]

David told CBS News that he felt a bit of redemption about A PASSAGE TO INDIA: "It must seem strange to you, but if you're a - I suppose, an actor or director - the press means a lot. Because they're the only people who you think tell you the truth. Your friends will all be nice and say, 'I loved it, etc., etc.' But the press, there they are. And another thing - the power of print. There it is in black and white, it's absolutely horrible."[24]

The New York Critics gave the film their award as the best foreign film.

"The American reaction to PASSAGE was very good,' said David. "We got fourteen [actually, eleven] Academy nominations. I got three. I was very pleased, because I hadn't done anything for so long.

"And then AMADEUS won the lot - all except one, Best Supporting Actress, which went to Peggy Ashcroft."[25,26]

When I asked if this had upset him, David nodded silently. As he had admitted in his interview with Jay Cocks, "I've just begun to dare to think I perhaps am a bit of an artist."[27]

"I certainly ended up admiring him enormously," said John Brabourne. "It's a tragedy he's gone, because with all that I'd loved to have made another film with him."[28]

And David's own summing up of the experience?

"I enjoyed doing this last picture, but I didn't have any fun."[29]

CHAPTER FORTY-EIGHT

A NAME TO CONJURE WITH

AFTER years of living abroad in hotels, David had begun to think of living permanently in England and of buying a home. Many exiles, when they reach a certain age, feel compelled to return to their native roots. David's homecoming, and homemaking, would prove to be dramatic.

The English countryside did not appeal to him. David asked Alec Guinness where he would choose to live in London. "I would want either to live very high up in Hampstead or somewhere on the river where I could see what's going on on the Thames," said Guinness.

"I've often wondered about the river," said David.

Guinness told David and Sandy of an architect acquaintance who had a flat in a converted warehouse. He also mentioned an estate agent, next to the Connaught Hotel, who was advertising warehouses for conversion. David and Sandy went round immediately.

"David loved the idea of being in the city and yet not being in the city," said Sandy, "of being able to look out across the sweep of the river. 'I don't want to look at house-fronts,' he said, 'I want to stretch my eyes.' And with his passion for Dickens, and Chinatown, and the Limehouse Blues, just the thought of living in the docks was romantic."[1]

The original idea was a penthouse apartment in Narrow Street, on a wide loop of the Thames. Next door was an abandoned warehouse. "We wandered in," said Sandy, "and the view was breathtaking. We decided to buy it."

Stephen Walters, who was David's historical adviser on the Bounty project and had become a trusted associate-cum-assistant, explained that David had other reasons for liking the riverside setting.

"He liked the fact that he had a spectacular view both up and down the river. Bligh had lived just round the corner. The *Bounty* had been altered by the Admiralty just down the river and the theatre which had staged *The Pirates!* was in Wapping."

Next door was a smaller building, and beyond that a huge warehouse, a gaunt shell gutted by fire. In rapid succession, they bought all three.

At first David considered demolishing the entire site and building an apartment block, where he would live rent-free and lease other units. An architect produced plans, but David and Sandy disliked them. Walters urged

David to retain as much of the original buildings as possible since they were historic, if only because of their age.

The decision was then made to convert the site into a large home, free of the problems which might be caused by neighbours. The two smaller buildings were combined into a single house with terraces on the upper floors. The third was converted into an elaborate garden, its high north wall and ruined arches enclosing a series of grassy roofless rooms that opened on to the river.

"What's the use of having money in the bank?" said David. "We had it built beautifully. The first thing people say when they come into the house is, 'We didn't know the English could do such wonderful carpentry and such wonderful brickwork.' And it's all over the house; it's like good sets. I'm terribly keen on quality. Everybody says you go back to your roots and I guess that's true. I mean, I just love it here. It's my home."[2]

"The house cost six to seven million pounds to build," said Tony Reeves. "David came into it one day and they were putting in an extra light switch. He asked the builders how much it cost. It was something like thirty-eight pounds. He went up the wall. 'It can't possibly be thirty-eight pounds for this! I can't afford it. You mustn't do it.' I find that's quite common with very rich people. They can't deal with a million, but they can focus on the cost of a cup of coffee as real money.

"The Quaker upbringing had an effect. Frugal is the wrong word; he never regarded himself, nor did I, as profligate. But yes, he travelled First Class and, yes, if he wanted something he had it."[3]

"I went once when it was being built," said Alec Guinness, "David and I

The derelict warehouses at Narrow Street, photographed by Sandy.

walked in the garden and he said, 'This is the best thing I've ever done in my life. It's more important to me than any of my films.' I think that was just a momentary thought - it *couldn't* have been more important than his films - but he was proud of it."[4]

For Sandy, still in her thirties, the life which David chose to lead was suffocatingly restrictive. Although they remained at the Berkeley, awaiting the completion of Narrow Street, they might have been in a suburban backwater - Croydon, perhaps - with David repeating the possessiveness which had so maddened him about his mother.

"We had lived together twenty-four hours a day for all those years, but David didn't see it that way," said Sandy. "So when I wanted to spend the day with Sara, say, or simply go off on my own to a bookstore or a movie, he saw it as a betrayal. He couldn't understand how there could be something I wanted to do that he didn't. Or that I could want to be on my own."[5]

David and Sandy had a routine. Every evening they would dress for dinner and sit formally and silently in the Berkeley restaurant. One evening after dinner, David startled Sandy by announcing he was going out for a walk.

"Now this is not a man who ever walked for pleasure. But I just thought, 'Well, poor man, I'm making him so miserable, it's no wonder he wants to get away.'

"The next night he went out again, and the night after that. At first he would leave at nine o'clock and come back at eleven or midnight. And then it got to be two or three o'clock. And then one morning I woke up and his bed hadn't been slept in. And still I suspected nothing. It seems impossible to me now, but if you'd asked me then what I thought he was doing night after night, I couldn't have written you a plausible scenario.

"One day I went to have lunch with Sara. She knew how wretched and guilt-ridden I was. In the middle of lunch she suddenly said, 'Tell me something. Would it make a difference if you knew David was having an affair?'

"I said, 'Of course it would, it would make all the difference in the world.'

"She said, 'Well, he is.'

"I was sitting at the table with a glass of wine in my hand, and I started to laugh and she said, 'You'd better put that glass down before you spill it.' I was shivering so hard I couldn't hold the glass.

"But when it finally came to the break-up, it took place over an absurdity. What happened was this: David used to snore. And when he snored particularly horribly I used to grab the pillow and the blanket off my twin bed and go and sleep on the sofa in the sitting-room.

"One morning he came out of the bedroom in a rage. 'You're behaving in a most inappropriate way,' he said, 'No proper wife would behave like this. It's only because you're spoilt, living in this extraordinary suite in a luxury hotel, that you can afford to behave like this.'

"Now, I'd never confronted David before, but this was so absurd that I heard myself answering back. 'Look,' I said, 'whatever is making you angry at this moment has nothing to do with me getting up and sleeping on the sitting-room sofa.'

"He said, 'You're right, you're right. I'm very unhappy.'

"I said, 'I know. It's my fault. We're drifting apart, and I'm terribly sorry.'

"He said, 'What do you want to do about it? Do you want to leave me?'

"I couldn't believe it. I said, 'Yes.'

"'Very well,' he said, 'I'll get Tony Reeves to call you tomorrow.' And he left the room and got dressed and went out.

"The next morning Tony called me. He had a draft agreement of the settlement of assets ready. I signed it three days later. And six weeks after that we were divorced. And in all that time David and I hardly exchanged six words. It was as though there was nothing to discuss. This took place after I had found out that he was having an affair. Curiously enough, if I hadn't found out I don't think I would ever have had the moral courage to go off and leave him. His affair let my conscience off the hook."[6]

"First time it had ever happened in my life," said David. "Gave me a hell of a shock. And she was smashing. I shall always be fond of Sandy. Smashing person. We had a great time together. She liked travelling. She was very adventurous, we were jolly good companions. Just a great big shame, but there you are."[7]

On 12 November 1985, Sandy went back alone to Thalwil, the small town outside Zurich where she had married David three years before. After a short court appearance, in the company of Peter Hafter, David's Swiss lawyer, she was divorced.

"One of the things that kept me with David for so long," said Sandy, "was the sense that, if not me, who would he have to look after him? He was so helpless in practical life. The other was a sense of indebtedness. I owed him, I still owe him, so much. I don't know what or where I would be if it weren't for David. Kate Hepburn, bless her, said to me, 'You've paid your dues, you were a wife to him for twenty years, more than any other woman was.'

"But it didn't help. To this day I feel guilty."[8]

"He was desperately unhappy when Sandy left," said Tony Reeves. "And he was very concerned about her welfare. He used to make me look him in the eye and confirm she was all right, that she had enough money. He had made a good settlement on her, he gave her the house in Rome and would constantly ask me, 'Have you spoken to her?' A few years after they separated she found she hadn't any need for the Rome house and she gave it back to him. She kept in contact with Maggie in relation to David and he assumed a sort of caring obligation relative to her that was genuine and continued right to his death."[9]

When Sandy left David, someone was waiting for her. She had first encountered John Calley in 1977 when, at the start of the Bounty project, he had flown with Frank Wells and Ted Ashley from California to meet David at the Pierre Hotel in New York.

"I'd been out shopping and came back and there were these three guys sitting in a row on the sofa," said Sandy. I said, 'Hello' and went and shut myself up in the bedroom, waiting for them to go away. That was how I first saw John, the guy in the middle with the beard and the glasses."

David's friendship with Calley survived the bitter fall-out from the Bounty project and Sandy was impressed by the fact that Calley never failed to contact them whenever they were in the same city.

"John was the funniest man I'd ever met," said Sandy. "He was witty and spontaneous and unpredictable. He lit up your life. We both adored him. I thought he was David's greatest fan. Much later I told him that and he said, 'Didn't you ever realise?' And then, when things finally started to fall apart between David and myself, there on the doorstep was John."[10]

Produced to coincide with the British release of A PASSAGE TO INDIA, the *South Bank Show* Special, *David Lean - A Life in Film*, was shown on Sunday 17 February 1985. Besides being more than twice as long as most *South Bank Shows*, it contained an exceptionally good interview with David, together with interviews with his friends and co-workers and remarkable footage, specially shot in India, of the making of the film. Directed by Nigel Wattis and produced by Nick Evans, it was presented by Melvyn Bragg.[11]

One of those most impressed by the programme was Sandra Cooke, who was a David Lean aficionado. Then in her mid-forties, Sandra Cooke was an art dealer working for a gallery in St James's. To look at her casually, you might have mistaken her for an Egyptian; in fact, she was English with Russian antecedents. Her black hair fell in a fringe across her eyes, which she accentuated with make-up, like an actress of the twenties. She looked younger than her age, and was very slim.

Gazing with fascination at David on her television screen, she thought how intelligent and different he looked.

"I didn't think he looked English, and I wondered what other side he had to him. I didn't know he was Cornish."[12]

This was to set in motion a bizarre sequence of events. Sandra and a friend, Tessa Lefroy, an Irish woman who was staying in her basement to work on a book, went to a Greek Orthodox clairvoyant who told Sandra she was going to have "a wonderful few years" with somebody whose name began with "Da". Sandra then went to Harrods, which was not far from her house in Alexandra Place, and in the Food Hall she came face to face with David Lean.

She asked the assistant, whom she'd known for years, if it really was David and he confirmed it. "He always comes in here because he loves muscatel grapes."

But when she turned round again, David had vanished.

"That was that. I walked through Harrods and on my way out I found myself abreast with David. I thought, what the hell, I'm going to go up and say how much I love his films. So I approached him and said, 'I'm so sorry to invade your privacy. It must get awfully boring because people must do this all the time. I just wanted to congratulate you on your work which I've always found wonderful. What do we have next?'

"He started to talk, about the weather and his movies, and then he said, 'Have you ever been to Tahiti?'

"I said, 'No, I love the Bahamas.'

"He said, 'You can throw the Bahamas in the ocean. Wait till you go to Tahiti.'

"He was quite chatty and we went on talking for about quarter of an hour, at which point I thought I'd better say goodbye. No names. No address. No phone number. He didn't ask."

Sandra went home and dropped in on her writer friend whose cousin, Diccon Swan, happened to be visiting. They spoke about the clairvoyant, and then Sandra told Swan that she had met David.

Swan was astonished. It turned out that he had visited the same clairvoyant the day before - with David's wife, whose name was also Sandra. "And what's more," he said, "I'm dining with them both tonight."

Of all the coincidences in David's life, the involvement of Diccon Swan is perhaps the most remarkable. Swan, from an Anglo-Irish background, had been a close friend of Sara Lean when they were both at the Ruskin School of Drawing at Oxford. Thanks to Sara, he met David in 1970, although he was closer to Edward, whom he came to regard as a second father. For a time, he lived in the basement of the Lean home in Albert Street, Camden Town. As David and Edward forged a new relationship, Swan saw David more frequently.

"David was immensely kind to me," said Swan. "When I was setting up as an artist I wasn't certain whether I could afford to do so or whether I was going to have to go back to teaching. David said, 'It's ridiculous to go back to teaching. You've got the talent. So get on with it.' He gave me - certainly with Sandy's help as well - a cheque for £10,000 just so that I could survive for a while. I was immensely touched and grateful and it kept me going for two years while I did enough work for exhibitions."[13]

Later, Swan heard about a clairvoyant in Upper Norwood and mentioned him to Sandy. She decided she had to consult him, and persuaded Swan to take her. He sat reading magazines until Sandy emerged looking vaguely dissatisfied. Swan was then given a consultation himself and was told a string of facts which had no connection with him at all - about his mother, an uncle who had died young and a house he was building by a river…

On the way back in the car, he repeated these facts to Sandy who said, "Wait. This is extraordinary. He's talking about *me*, not you." Sandy made up her mind to return.

Sandy then had to persuade David to let her go on another expedition. He was difficult about it and kept saying, "Well, what am I supposed to do?" Sandy suggested he went shopping in Harrods.

In his newly acquired house in Brixton, Swan showed Sandy a copy of *House and Garden* with a photographic feature on a house in South Kensington belonging to someone called Sandra Cooke. He thought it a fantastic place, and wanted his own house to look like it. At that precise moment, David was meeting Sandra Cooke in Harrods.

After the second session with the clairvoyant, Sandy was unusually silent. Swan did not hear for some time what the clairvoyant had said. "He predicted precisely what was going to happen later that year. He said she was going to be able to leave David with a clear conscience. He told her exactly what she wanted to hear except that she couldn't possibly believe it."

A few days later, Swan heard that his cousin, Tessa Lefroy, was in town, and he went to see her in the basement at Alexandra Place. He was introduced to Sandra and shown over the house, which he recognised at once from the pictures in *House and Garden*.

The next morning, Swan told Sandra of his dinner with David and Sandy. David had mentioned the woman he met at Harrods - he described her as a "fascinating Oriental" - and was surprised when Swan said he knew her. David asked Swan to arrange a dinner.

"It was a very successful evening," said Swan. "It was quite obvious that David and Sandra got on very well. There must have been some furtive glances we didn't actually take in. David was very nice to me and very amused by Tessa's husband, Geoffrey, who'd been in the army."[14]

After the dinner party, Sandra received a brief note from David:

"Please meet me in Harrods bookshop at twelve o'clock."

Sandra kept the assignment, and thus began their relationship.

"He came around to my place every evening until I had to say, 'You've got to go, David. Your wife is in the Berkeley. What does she think you're doing, sitting on a park bench? I was saying to myself, I'm going to get hurt. I swore that I wouldn't get involved with a married man because it hurts. I didn't want to break up a marriage and on the other hand I didn't think it would ever have been broken up.

"I was getting near to saying, 'David, this can't go on,' because my life was being taken away from me. I was just waiting for David. He demanded that I was here at half-past-five for his phone call. He would have dinner with Sandy at eight, and he would be around here at a quarter to nine every day and he wouldn't leave here until four in the morning. And that was a man of seventy-eight.

"So finally I was going to deliver this speech. It wasn't easy because I found myself actually falling in love with David, and I had to wrench myself away from the relationship, because I thought, it's never going to be. I didn't think it fair to her, and it certainly wasn't fair to me, and it wasn't really fair to David. So all in all, it had to end."

But Sandra never had to make her speech.

"He called me at nine o'clock the following morning and appeared on the doorstep ten minutes later. He came up and sat down, rather depressed. I sat on the floor. There was a long David Lean pause, which by that time I'd got used to.

"I said, 'David, is there anything wrong?'

"He said, 'Yes, she's left me.'"[15]

While Sandy remained at the Berkeley for the next two weeks, David moved in with Sandra at Alexandra Place.[16] Subsequently he learned that Sandy planned to live with John Calley, the one studio executive in Hollywood whom he trusted.

David refused to speak about his split with Sandy, and Sandra did not press the point.

"Sandy obviously knew about me," said Sandra. "I don't know who from, but she knew. Nothing was talked about, nothing was said. He seemed happy. There must have been some remorse, and some ghastly ache going on within

Sandra and David, just before their wedding in 1990.

him, I'm sure, but he never talked about it. And I didn't see any anguish going on inside him, quite honestly, so maybe David was the sort of person for whom when it was over, it was over. He had an enormously retentive memory. The only thing he'd forget was what he wanted to forget. He blocked it out. And went on to the next one. It was history repeating itself, really, only this time I thought it would be worse because *she* had left *him*. It was a shock because she was the sort of girl that he thought silently read books and stayed beside him.

"He was an insecure man. And I think a lot of women suffered because of that. I suffered a lot of the time, because if he was under stress, he would take out all that stress by digging, very quietly, with a little needle, until you rose. And if you rose to it, God help you. But you have to, if you're a person with any opinions of your own. And I was nearly fifty years old then, and I think probably I was the only person that did that, so there were slightly more arguments with us than maybe with Sandy, who didn't rise to it.

"But if a woman interfered with David's work, that was it. David, as we all know, has tunnel vision and any woman that comes between David and movies - out. He would twist it into it being her fault. David could be very ruthless when he wanted something.

"Yet he was, I think, the most sensitive man I've ever met in my life. He needed affection, he needed love. And he denied it to himself."[17]

Sandra and David departed on an ambitious trip. Sandra planned the itinerary and felt obliged to cut off all her activities as an art dealer.

"We booked to go to Singapore, Australia, Tahiti, Hong Kong. What actually happened with David, who is a complete nomad, we started off on the schedule, but when we got to Tahiti, we just didn't leave. I simply adored it, so we were there two months. And there I got to know David very well. He was a man who could sit for hours looking at the sky, at different cloud formations. From time to time he would say, 'Get me my camera, get me the light meter, get me the fifty.' I'd take the lens cap off, I'd fit the lens to the camera, I'd put the camera in his hand. He taught me the lenses, and how to use a light meter."

In Bora Bora, David handed Sandra a copy of *Empire of the Sun*, J.G. Ballard's novel about the Second World War in China. Sandra, who read the book in a day and a half, told David what she thought of it.

"It's the war seen through the eyes of a little boy," she said. "It doesn't seem to be your sort of movie. It hasn't got a story and I always remember you on Melvyn Bragg saying, 'Character, story.' It's got no dramatic arch, it's a diary of events. I suppose you could change it, but I don't know how much."

David's main problem, Sandra recalled, was that there was no satisfactory ending. He talked about changing the ending, but each time he came up with an idea he said, 'No, it's not going to work.'"

When they eventually moved from Bora Bora, they travelled to Hong Kong and then to Shanghai, to scout possible locations.

"We took a car and found it all. The European houses were as they had been fifty years before, except that they were inhabited by Chinese, with washing hanging out. I even found the prison camp. Sure enough, there was a railway line beside it, and I crossed the railway, leaving David sitting in the car. He shouted at me to come back, because I could be shot. I climbed up on the wall - he was petrified - and sure enough, over the wall were still the bunkers, the huts, and everything that had been described in the book.

"Anyway, that was Shanghai. We stayed in a hotel with no bath plugs and the things that happened were terribly funny. David refused to work there. 'It's like bloody Yugoslavia when I was with John, trying to find locations for ZHIVAGO. Fucking Communist country. I'm not going to stay here. How could anyone shoot a film here?'"[18]

Nevertheless, David made his usual copious notes on the novel and the problems of adaptation. Steven Spielberg had agreed to produce it.

"I worked on it for about a year," he said, "and in the end I gave it up because I thought, 'This is like a diary. It's bloody well written and very interesting, but I don't think it's a movie for me because it hasn't got a dramatic shape. I may be talking nonsense; I'm not sure if I am or not. Anyhow, I gave it up and Steven said, 'Do you mind if I have it?' I said, 'Of course I don't.' And he did it and I must say a bit of what I felt, I felt about his film, too."[19]

On their return to London, David and Sandra moved into the newly completed Narrow Street. David also fell ill with double-pneumonia and Sandra realised she could not cope without help.

She knew a capable girl, Sarah Foster, who had worked as a cook for the Queen Mother and was now working as a PA for a floral decorator in Motcomb Street. She, too, had avidly watched the *South Bank Show*. So when Sandra offered her a job she accepted with alacrity.

On 26 May 1989 - five days after the restored LAWRENCE opened in London[20] - Sarah Foster began working as personal assistant to Sir David Lean.

David had just returned from hospital and Sandra was taking care of him. He had purchased a house in the South of France, at Mouans-Sartoux, not far from Nice and the Victorine Studios.[21]

"I thought he was going to be extremely gregarious and very easy to talk to," said Sarah. "But he wasn't. To begin with, I was so petrified of him, Sandra used to have to push me into the study some mornings. I said, 'He's going to snap my head off.'

"Sandra said, 'Take no notice. He doesn't mean it.'

"He told the most wonderful stories. He had so many Sam Spiegel jokes, he would have me almost on the floor, with tears streaming down my cheeks and in stitches, and the more he saw you laugh, the funnier he would become. He could also be very crude, and he would do it on purpose because I laughed at his vulgarity.

"David wasn't very good at talking about anything but films. If he wasn't the centre of attention, he would switch off and not be interested at all, or he would tell Sandra and I to change the conversation totally.

"We would sit in France at the dinner table, just the three of us, having dinner every night of the week. If he wasn't interested in what Sandra and I were talking about, he would push his chair away from the table and say, 'I'm going to sit by the fire.' Not, 'Would you excuse me?' He was so stubborn in that way. If it wasn't done to please him, forget it.

"Whenever we went out with David, none of us would see the price list, so we didn't know how much it was costing. He was very generous and he loved to give people a good time. But I remember once we went to a restaurant in the South of France and I ordered a chocolate mousse. It was huge, with a chocolate butterfly on top. I took one mouthful and it was so rich I thought, 'If I finish this, I'm going to be ill.'

When David realised that Sarah had hardly touched it, he flew into a rage.

"How dare you order something and not finish it? It is one of the most expensive things on the menu."

"He made me feel so small. In fact, his doctor, Peter Wheeler, was with us and he ate it. But David made a real thing of it and Sandra said, 'That's from his Quaker upbringing.' He was brought up to believe that if you ordered something, you finished it, whether you were going to be sick or not."[22]

Sixty years after he had left Leighton Park, David was invited to return. The school was producing a video and he had agreed to supervise the event. As soon as he approached the grounds, he said, "Why have you moved the entrance?"

The opening scene for the video was a recreation of the first day in the school's history. A small carriage had been hired, and the pupils and the headmaster played in the scene. David sat alongside the camera and gave advice.

"He was fascinated," said John Allinson, "by the fact that there were now girls at the school. He enjoyed the visit. It was a warm, sunny day and the school looked much as it had when he left it.

"He talked about the pond where they had art classes. He said, 'It was very beautiful, and I used to sit and dream.' The day was reassuring to us. I thought he might be rather dismissive of his schooldays."[23]

David had bulrushes planted at his last home, in the South of France, to remind him of Leighton Park.

CHAPTER FORTY-NINE

RESTORATION DRAMA

FROM Hollywood came news that meant more to David than all the Fellowships and Honorary Degrees,[1] perhaps even his knighthood. He was told that LAWRENCE OF ARABIA was to be restored and re-released.

To those who live normal lives and have not experienced the lunatic world of the cinema, it may seem a trifle odd that a film as recent as LAWRENCE would need restoration, a word usually applied to medieval paintings or Roman remains. After all, what greater responsibility did a giant company like Columbia have than to preserve its wealth in the form of its films?

It sounds simple enough, but almost all the studios have behaved with a criminal lack of care towards their old films. Several volumes could be filled with horror stories of the deliberate destruction of celluloid to clear vaults, and the accidental destruction through negligence. More than half the films produced in America before 1950 have been lost. Those in charge of a film like LAWRENCE simply assumed it was properly preserved and never bothered to check. After all, to do so might have taken time and, worse still, cost money.

When it came to launching the restoration, Columbia didn't know whether to castigate itself or pat itself on the back, so their publicity hand-out did both:

"Twenty five years of records indicated that the original negative had never been touched and that full and complete black-and-white 65mm protection materials were available. Columbia (then under David Puttnam) gave the go ahead."

Later, the handout states, "No print of the premiere version was found to have survived. Columbia had no written continuity, no record of any kind of what the 222-minute version even contained."

Film restoration became glamorous in the eighties. Despite the fact that unsung heroes in archives had been restoring films for decades, it was perhaps the success of my restoration of Abel Gance's NAPOLEON, achieved with the National Film Archive, which triggered the quest for lost films and the restoration of cut ones.

To be strictly accurate, it wasn't the restoration which had the glamour - NAPOLEON had been restored for nearly a decade. It was not until it was presented with a live orchestra playing Carl Davis's score at the Empire Theatre, London, in November 1980 that people took notice.[2] David missed this initial performance and saw it when it was repeated at the Queen Elizabeth Hall. He was as amazed by Gance's cinematic wizardry as everyone else. The film was launched at New York's Radio City Music Hall in January 1981, with a score by Francis Coppola's father, Carmine, and this, too, was hugely successful.

Behind the American launch was Tom Luddy, who worked for Francis Coppola's Zoetrope Company, and Robert Harris, who ran a distribution outfit called Images Film Archive. Harris, who had been instrumental in locating some of the missing footage for NAPOLEON, was now the driving force behind the restoration of LAWRENCE.

Unlike NAPOLEON, which had literally been dismantled and dispersed, LAWRENCE had lost thirty-five minutes of its original 222-minute running time. The question was, who ordered the cuts?

"No one really knows for certain who decided to cut the film or for certain why it was cut," Robert Harris told the BBC. "The consensus that has come down is that it was a combination of studio and producer who, under pressure from theatre owners, wanted to make the film shorter."[3]

David told me, as he told everyone else, that it was the awful Sam Spiegel who, having persuaded him to take a few minutes out after the premiere, sneaked the negative back and sliced out further chunks.

"I didn't know that Sam had been nibbling at it," said David. "I'd no idea that stuff was cut, they didn't tell me. I helped on cutting six minutes out of the beginning, that I was responsible for, but I didn't realise they'd cut another twenty minutes or more out of the body of the picture, and without telling me."[4]

Either David's memory betrayed him, or the mystery appealed to his sense of showmanship; anyway, he went along with Harris's theory for the sake of the restoration. But all the evidence suggests that the cuts were made with David's knowledge and, to the extent that he left detailed notes, participation. He felt the picture was too long on its initial showings, and while he was less anxious to reduce it again in 1970 for its television showings, he did so, albeit at Spiegel's urging.

Adrian Turner has the theory that David, wanting money for NOSTROMO, seized on the restoration of LAWRENCE as the opportunity to create a legend of himself as hero, Spiegel as villain and the film as a sullied masterpiece. And it didn't hurt to have the film placed in the same category as NAPOLEON.

It would therefore have made no sense for David to have said, "I took these scenes out in 1963 because I thought it would help the film. Now I'm putting them back because I think it will help the film."

David tailored his account to the occasion - sometimes claiming he cut as much as twelve minutes, always making Spiegel the villain - which bewildered people like Anne Coates who saw nothing shameful about the original course of events.

Harris and his partner Jim Painten knew that LAWRENCE had been released at 222 minutes. In 1963, it had been shortened by twenty minutes and in 1970 by another fifteen, reducing the running time to 187 minutes. All they had to do was locate the missing footage.

The project began in the summer of 1986 at the suggestion of Dennis Doph, head of Columbia Classics, though it took several months for Harris to receive clearance to examine the materials at Columbia's vaults in Long Island City. By this time, Columbia Pictures had been bought by Coca-Cola who hired David Puttnam as the studio's President and Chief Executive Officer. Puttnam was enthused by the project and asked if LAWRENCE could be ready for Cannes, in five months' time. Columbia was the soul of co-operation and assured Harris that while the prints may have been cut, the negative itself had not been tampered with. They said there would be "no problem" - that most ominous of modern expressions.

At the first examination, Harris and Painten realised that the camera negative had indeed been cut - twice. The cutting continuity (or post-production script) of the original version had been junked, and there were no guidelines.

"I wanted to get in touch with David Lean," said Harris, "and the studio said, 'No, we're going to handle this our way,' and David Puttnam apparently sent him a letter. The other person I was trying to find who I felt could have helped - who I was told not to get in touch with - was Anne Coates. I started calling around without success."[5]

Harris even called me, hoping that, as a former film editor, I might be able to help. Alas, I had no idea of her whereabouts. It was only when he was talking on the phone to producer Jon Davison at Laird Studios (the old Selznick Studios) that he discovered Anne Coates was right next door cutting a picture.

Anne Coates asked Harris, "Have you found the goggles?"

"Goggles?"

"Yes. The first shot in the film that you'll be missing is Lawrence's goggles hanging from a branch."

In mid-January 1987, a truck pulled up at Harris's office in Mamaroneck, NY, near where D.W. Griffith once had his studio, and unloaded three or four thousand pounds of miscellaneous 65mm and 70mm film. These were mostly negative cuts and trims. Harris and his co-workers began examining and cross referencing it.

"I went back to my place with my partner Jim Painten," said Harris. "It was eleven at night and we were sitting there, and I said, 'Wait a minute. If there are black-and-white trims with sound tracks on them - slash dupes, made of the original colour workprint - these could be the trims from the [original] version.' So in the middle of freezing February we got in my car, drove back down to

Mamaroneck, put a few of these black-and-white pieces up on the flat bed, and what did we find? The goggles!

"Eventually we found about half of the twenty minutes of deleted scenes. We could have used this for restoration if we'd had to, but it was dirty and black-and-white - the one thing you wouldn't want to use. But at least we had it."[6]

Since Bob Harris was not permitted to contact David, Anne Coates did it for him. The following day she called back and said, "David wants a word with you."

"I could feel myself breaking into a cold sweat," recalled Harris. "What had I done? How would he react?" Harris regarded Lean as "akin to God."

After plucking up the courage he called David in Los Angeles and was reassured by the friendly voice at the other end.

"I'm coming back through New York on Tuesday," he said, "Stopping by to see Kate." The voice didn't sound seventy-nine years old, thought Harris.[7]

Nor did the man who arrived at his office look his age - "tall, slim, ramrod straight, his white hair blowing in the breeze, he looked more fifty-five than nearly eighty."

That first day, Harris showed David his work print.

"It was filled with black slugs [spacing] where footage should probably go, and dupe where we found some missing shots. He sat, viewed... and remembered. Not just basic information, but specific shots, sound to look for, possible alternatives and so on."[8]

"Let's suppose you can find the missing bits of picture," said David. "But what if you can't find the tracks?" David suggested that if the sound was missing for any sections, he would contact Omar Sharif, Peter O'Toole or whoever was necessary to re-record the dialogue.

On that first visit, said Harris, the emphasis on the reconstruction had changed from "you" to "we." He began to share David's confidence and enthusiasm.

"Bob Harris was very nice and he let me begin cutting immediately," said David.[9]

Harris must have lost a stone when David told him he wanted to cut something he was trying so earnestly to restore. Restoration usually means putting things back, not cutting things out. But David saw the chance of correcting longueurs that had irritated him for twenty-five years. He recalled a remark of Hitchcock's about British films - "Every scene seems to start a minute before it should start and ends a minute after it should end."[10] He made sure that charge wouldn't be levelled at LAWRENCE and made his trims. He was also able to make more sense of the blood-bath sequence by showing Lawrence surveying the slaughtered Arab women and children.

"There was one scene which we just couldn't put together," said David. "It's the scene where Allenby points out to Lawrence that he's got blood on his back. And he says, 'Come outside... Your name will be a household word when nobody will remember mine.' And we had to cut one of Robert's favourite lines - 'I'm a gardening sort of general' - because the track had been thrown away, all the continuity sheets had been thrown away. We didn't know what they were saying. We tried to sync it with Charles Gray, who used to do Hawkins's voice when he got throat cancer. And we just could not fit his voice to the scene. We gave up and made a huge cut - about three minutes went because we couldn't find the material. Columbia were completely ruthless. They didn't save anything."[11]

Those who run film companies cannot bear to see outsiders earning money from their property. They would rather burn it than have someone else exploit it. When, in March 1987, they realised what was happening with the restoration, Columbia threw a spanner in the works, altered the deal with Bob Harris and brought everything to a grinding halt in time-honoured fashion. Arthur Goldblatt, of the studio's pay-cable division, was concerned by the project and legal letters to Harris and Painten accused them of "tampering with Columbia property."[12]

Harris had to start shipping the material back to the studio vaults, where so much of it had already perished and where the negative was gradually fading. Puttnam was approached and he agreed to try and get the project moving again. Then Puttnam was replaced. The new president was Dawn Steel, an admirer of David Lean, and she permitted the restoration to be resumed. Martin Scorsese and Steven Spielberg became involved as figureheads. Harris moved to Los Angeles to complete the work, with Anne Coates as supervising editor.[13]

Eight minutes of the rediscovered material had no sound whatever, and effects had to be recreated using sound from other parts of the film. Since there was no script available, Harris brought in lip-readers to work out what the actors were saying. Arthur Kennedy and Anthony Quinn re-recorded their dialogue in America and in London the post-synchronising sessions with Peter O'Toole and Alec Guinness were supervised by David. Much technical wizardry was needed to conceal the fact that the pitch of their voices had changed in the course of twenty-five years.

An Indian fortune-teller had informed David that he would die when he was sixty-four. For his eightieth birthday, on 25 March 1988, Barbara Cole sent him a card saying, simply, "The Indian soothsayer was wrong, wasn't he?" which David thought very amusing.[14]

Sandra organised a surprise party worthy of the event, and I was delighted to receive an invitation to Narrow Street. The taxis and limousines made the street live up to its name.

David greeted everyone warmly in the living room, where a fire roared in the grate. Eddie Fowlie gave a conducted tour of the house which was lit by candles. I spotted many of David's leading players - John Mills, Bernard Miles, James Fox - together with Freddie Young, who was himself eighty-five.

James Fox was particularly fascinating. He said that in working with David "one is on railway lines." Unlike John Milius, with whom he had just made FAREWELL TO THE KING in Borneo and who "practically made the film from his bed, he was so bored with it," he thought David cared passionately about the film. He wasn't great at directing actors, but he surrounded them with such visual style, brought them up to the camera and set them off so superbly, that their appearances were often unforgettable.

The buffet was exotic and at the height of the party the house was crammed with guests. In the kitchen was a cake, decorated with eight candles and the words: GREAT EXPECTATIONS. David walked in and announced, "Come this way. There's something happening. But not in the kitchen!"

We followed the cake as it was ceremoniously carried out, and took our positions around it. But before David had a chance to cut it, he was led to the balcony and suddenly the night sky was torn by the most vivid flashes and deafening explosions that he could have witnessed since the Blitz on the docks in 1940.

After the firework display had faded, an obviously emotional David cut the cake, stood back and said "I'd no idea about any of this. Thank you all so much for coming." This got a giggle because it sounded as though he was bidding us goodbye.

Later, David spoke to me about Ingram's THE FOUR HORSEMEN OF THE APOCALYPSE and how he had seen it again in the seventies with a forty-piece orchestra at the Los Angeles Filmex Festival. He urged David Gill and me to stage it in London - something we were able to do in 1992. We dedicated the event to him.

At the Cannes Film Festival in May 1988, BAFTA held a gala birthday tribute to David, who took the opportunity to berate Dino de Laurentiis for his behaviour over the Bounty project. Whilst he said little short of the bare facts, they were alarming to an audience accustomed, on these occasions, to polished platitudes. And after he had dispensed with De Laurentiis, David launched an attack on Sam Spiegel.

"I think it's time that all of us moviemakers band together to get rid of these crooks, every producer who has his hands in our pockets."[15]

David singled out Stephen Frears' hit MY BEAUTIFUL LAUNDRETTE as not having the weight of big pictures to carry an industry, "as good as it is." He ended with a plea to his fellow film-makers not to lose the passion for making big movies.[16]

David threw hand grenades of controversy in all directions - sometimes unwittingly. Praising Columbia president Dawn Steel for her support for the

LAWRENCE restoration, David upset David Puttnam, who told people afterwards that the person most responsible for putting the project back together, Dennis Doph, had been fired when Steel's regime succeeded his.

The final stage of the LAWRENCE restoration was fraught with drama. Almost at the start of the project, Metrocolor Laboratories had started test-printing the negative and had carefully re-humidified it to make it more pliable. But Columbia transferred it to New York, where it had dried out again. When, in February 1988, Harris went to examine the negative in Los Angeles, he was shocked to find that it was unusable; the splices fell apart and the negative was ripped. Even though this problem continued throughout the restoration, Metrocolor heroically overcame all these disasters and David was full of praise for the final print, which was of extraordinarily high quality, with few signs of the neglect and carelessness it had endured at the hands of its owners.

"When we reissued it everybody told me, 'David, be prepared for the American audience, they are not what you remember. They chatter, they shout at their friends three rows in front, they make a noise. You may get a hostile reception.'

"We went on with the film in New York, Washington and Los Angeles. I have never had a reception like that film received when we put it out in its full length. Three hours and thirty five minutes. You could have heard a pin drop. It was almost as if they were mesmerised. I don't know if it was the size of the screen - they installed new sixty-foot screens for it - and the MGM Lab did a wonderful print. The lab is now gone, terrible shame. And the Goldwyn Studio which has a wonderful sound department took the old soundtrack [for the deleted sections] - just an old married print with a mono sound track, the original had been thrown away - and they put this through their digital system, took enormous trouble with it and the sound is now miles better than it was originally.

"It received absolutely staggering notices and at places like the Ziegfeld, you couldn't get a seat. It went around like nobody's business.

"I looked at some of those scenes, I mean twenty-seven years old or whatever it is, and thought, 'That's bloody good, you know.' Because I know I was there, but it doesn't feel as if it has anything much to do with me. And that gave me great pleasure. It's so long ago. I could almost anticipate the dialogue, but I feel tremendously removed from it. At the time, your nose is right up against it, and it's very much to do with you, when you put it on the screen. But when, after thirty years, it seems very remote, and you can sit back and say, 'Well, that comes off,' or 'I wish I'd done that a bit quicker.'"[17]

In the opinion of many of those who saw the restored LAWRENCE OF ARABIA, it was, quite simply, the most impressive film they had seen in their lives.[18]

CHAPTER FIFTY

THE TREACHERY OF SUNKEN ROCKS

NOSTROMO

IN 1985, David was invited to give a talk to the Cambridge Film Society. A questionnaire distributed to the students asked what novel they would suggest he adapt for his next film. A surprisingly high percentage voted for *Nostromo* by Joseph Conrad.[1]

Maggie Unsworth read the book and rang John Box who felt that Conrad transferred poorly to the screen. He thought Carol Reed had made a mess of AN OUTCAST OF THE ISLANDS, and that Richard Brooks's film of LORD JIM, despite brilliant 70mm photography by Freddie Young and an outstanding performance by Peter O'Toole in the title role, had been a failure. Nevertheless, Box decided to read the novel.

"At first I was appalled, because he had a very strange way of writing. It was not straight narrative. Then it clicked; it started to make sense. Maggie and I persuaded David to read it. He rang up and said, 'What are you and Maggie doing to me? It's really boring.'

"I said, 'Read another twenty or thirty pages.' The scale got to him, the Englishman in a strange country, the silver mine and the extraordinary characters."[2]

David always made detailed notes when he read a book he was considering filming. For NOSTROMO, he made two sets of notes. Having read it the first time, he wrote that he was sunk in depression. It had taken one hundred and sixty-seven pages before he was able to write, "At last a paragraph or two which holds my attention." A few pages later he had become more optimistic: "A brilliant paragraph, 'one of those profound pauses that fall upon the rhythm of passion.'"[3]

His enthusiasm increases at pages 226-7: "Wonderful scene between N and the dying woman. 'Did you think you could put a collar and chain on me?'" And page 230: "Fantastic description of N and Decoud making their escape on the lighter." Although David ran aground on Conrad's more cerebral passages, especially at the end, he made up his mind to make the film. By the second reading his approach is largely practical, although there was one intriguing comment:

"If only I could free myself from present-day screen conventions I could put this in a flow of pictures... I know this could be really good and in a very short time could put over the whole background to these poor people and show the size of this vast country."

Having decided to make NOSTROMO, David called Steven Spielberg who agreed to produce it for Warner Bros. To begin with, it was as simple as that.

Although David had written his last screenplay more or less on his own, he knew he would need the equivalent of Robert Bolt to tackle the complexities of this one. Since he and Bolt were still estranged, Maggie Unsworth recommended Christopher Hampton.[4]

David and Hampton had already met each other. They had discussed the project on Stanley and Livingstone which David was toying with when Bolt was otherwise engaged. This was around 1973, when Hampton was still in his twenties, although his plays *Total Eclipse*, *The Philanthropist* and *Savages* had already won him praise and awards.

"I met him again in early 1986 to talk about NOSTROMO," said Hampton. "He wasn't in contact with Robert Bolt. I think David felt, rightly or wrongly, that he was to some extent held responsible for Robert falling ill. And I think he felt very strongly that it wasn't his fault. You know how touchy he was. He would pull away from people rather abruptly if there was any question of bad feeling."[5]

Hampton was subjected to an interrogation on the first day.

"The first question was, 'Have you seen many of my films?'

"I said, 'Yes, I think I have. I've seen most of them, probably.'

"He said, 'Well, which one do you like best?' And I said, 'GREAT EXPECTATIONS' and he said, 'Quite right.' He was surprisingly self-critical. I don't know why I had this idea he was somehow pleased with all his films; not a bit of it. He was very, very hard on them, I thought.

"He was dependent on writers. He told me stories about Robert Bolt sending him tapes of the dialogue. And he talked a great deal about all the writers that he'd worked with - H.E. Bates, Terence Rattigan, Noël Coward - and always sympathetically.[6]

"The one thing that made him nervous about me was that I came from the theatre. Somewhere in the past, he'd felt very patronised by theatre people and he'd been made to feel that the cinema was inferior, so he was rather defensive about everything that he regarded as being fancy intellectual talk.

"One thing which touched me a good deal was that he actually went to the theatre, to see *Liaisons*.[7] He complained bitterly, quite rightly, about the leg room in the Ambassadors - it is appalling. But I think he liked the play. I think he felt it went on a bit and there were one or two of the performances he wasn't crazy about. But yes, he did like it."[8]

On their first morning together, David asked Hampton how the picture might begin. Hampton said, "Shall we start with an image of the body of Decoud sitting at the bottom of the sea with silver coming out of his pockets?"

David said, "Umm, that sounds good. Umm."[9]

Hampton remembers being "quite careful not to get into any theoretical discussion about what I thought the book was about, which suited him fine. He didn't want to talk about what Conrad might or might not have had in mind.

"My perspective on the story was that it was about these three completely different men: Gould, the capitalist, who becomes obsessed with the silver, who finishes up never going home, but sitting in the mine, actually sitting on the money; Nostromo, who's corrupted by the silver in quite a different way, and Decoud, the intellectual who can see the problems but is in a sense even less competent to deal with them than Nostromo or Gould and kills himself. One of the things we never saw eye to eye about was the characterization of Decoud. David once said he was a sort of Kenneth Tynan figure.

"I said, 'What do you mean?'

"David said, 'Well, you know, one of those smart-arse intellectuals who have no grasp of reality.' I thought differently. I thought Decoud was somebody who did understand but, like Hamlet, couldn't cope with it at all. Here was a dilettante who in the end couldn't engage with what was going on because he couldn't help but see it as basically idiotic."[10]

Despite their different perspectives on the novel, Hampton was enjoying the work and thought David was, too. "Of course, a lot of it was agonising. He would put you on the spot and say, 'Well, this isn't quite good enough.' And then you'd be expected to come up with something better. But if you did come up with something better, he was very chuffed about it.

"What he wanted was for you to be there. I suppose I spent about six weeks or so writing the first draft. He phoned up a lot and got very restive, saying, 'How is it going?' And then, as soon as he had the script, I would get a cab every morning to Narrow Street. I would arrive at ten and work till six-thirty."[11]

In January 1987, to avoid the British winter, David and Sandra went to the Marbella Club in Spain for three months. "I would go out Tuesdays to Friday and work with him and then come back for the weekend," said Hampton. "That was the time when the work was at its best; we'd got it to a shape that we were both very pleased with.[12]

"He liked it in Spain. We would have a meeting from ten in the morning until two in the afternoon. Then I would go across to my room - they had a bungalow and I had a nice little room with a balcony - and write five or six pages. I would often be writing until dinner time. And then we would have dinner and I would show him the pages after dinner. He liked that very much, he liked the immediacy of it. There was one day when we started work at ten-thirty in the morning, and then some sandwiches came in at some point and I remember Sandra putting her head round the door and saying, 'The restaurant's closing in a minute.' We'd been working ten hours straight without stopping.[13]

"He was very stimulating to work with because so much energy went into the work. And then, in the calmer moments, there were all those reminiscences which were very interesting to listen to.

"The reason I found it an educational experience was precisely because he would attack a scene quite ferociously in terms of insisting that it didn't simply carry information, that it somehow moved the story forward. And the thing that was most instructive was the attention paid to how to move from one scene to another, the editor's eye. He was very good at saying, 'No, this isn't the right way to go from this part of the story to that part.' It really made me think about all that in a way I hadn't before."[14]

David was determined to shoot the picture in 65mm and was willing to forego his salary to pay for it.[15] He had the idea of trying to emulate the look of Preston Sturges's 1941 classic SULLIVAN'S TRAVELS which had been shot (though neither David nor I remembered) by John F. Seitz, formerly cameraman for Rex Ingram. David thought the Sturges picture was "wonderfully photographed in this real tough lighting." The flashbacks were to be toned blue, as in silent pictures.

He met with cameraman John Alcott who was famous for his work with Stanley Kubrick. "We had a day-long meeting with John, who was going to light it,"[16] said Hampton. "David said, 'The problem is that this is a scene that is supposed to take place in pitch darkness. It's the principal action scene of the film, so how are we going to light it?' David had this idea of artificially lighting the whole scene by using the silver, which is a fantastic idea.

"Phosphorescence was my idea, because I'd found some nineteenth-century travel book about South America which described how extraordinary in certain seas around South America the phosphorescence was and how the rain would create more phosphorescence as it struck the water. So it was all going to appear to be lit by the stars and the silver."[17]

David would be very excited by specific sequences in the book and these gave Hampton his greatest problems.

"In the book there is the moment when Montero and his men, having marched over the mountain, come into the town. Decoud is on the island and Nostromo has passed out on the beach, having swum ashore, and Gould is in his house with the doctor. The idea was that there would be a sort of montage: the bells would ring in the church and everyone hearing those bells would know that they meant the army had arrived. And you would sum up the position that each character had got into by cutting from one to another. Thinking what order these seven or eight images should go in was incredibly intricate. It ended with a sequence which I thought was more or less a perfect way of doing it, which was that the first person to hear the bells was Gould, sitting at his table with his wife and Monygham. He looks up, hears the bells and in a perfectly logical order you went from one listener to another - Decoud on the island and Nostromo waking up on the beach. And you come back to the room at the end of the sequence to find Gould getting up to close the window to shut out the sound.

"To do that sort of work was very exhilarating. What was dispiriting was that three months later he would say, 'I don't think I like this sequence,' and chuck it out. That was difficult to cope with. He was very radical about making changes and continued to be so. I grew to dread the words, 'Well, let's go back and have another look at scene one.'[18]

"Another sequence that he loved was bringing the silver from the mountain to the harbour. He spent an enormous amount of time on the details of all that - where the actors would be in frame, whether it would be a cut or a dissolve. He once had a storyboard made, three postcard size drawings, one of which was the last image of one scene, another the first image of the next scene, and another the dissolve, to see whether he preferred the cut or the dissolve.

"David wasn't like Fred Zinnemann, whom I also worked for - and liked very much indeed - on a project called THE LAST SECRET about the forced repatriation of the Russians after the war, which was never made. He was a worshipper of the juggernaut of narrative and there could be nothing quirky. But David loved out-of-the-way details or bizarre moments.

"We got tremendously excited about the use of a lighthouse - there was a love scene when Nostromo first sleeps with the other sister. We had this idea of the light coming round every few seconds and they would be at some different stage of love-making. He loved that sort of thing.

"And he always wanted you to see it. He couldn't understand how you could write it if you didn't see it. He would say, 'Describe the room.' I would say, 'I'm not interested in the room. I'm trying to write dialogue.' He didn't like it if you didn't see everything. It gradually made me think in a different way about writing films."[19]

As they worked on the script, David and Hampton would also have constant discussions about casting.

"I remember him once saying that Alec Guinness was always being awkward. I said, 'What do you mean?'

"He said, 'Well, there would be a scene where I'd imagined him sitting down and he'd want to stand up.'

"You'd think if Alec Guinness had said, 'I might stand up here,' any other director would give it a go. But the idea that an actor might have something to bring to a project was very foreign to him, although there were actors that he absolutely adored - Katharine Hepburn, Charles Laughton, Claude Rains. And often, when we were trying to cast the film, I would say, 'Who from the past would you ideally have in this situation?' It would help him. So he would say, 'Well, Ingrid Bergman for Mrs Gould,' which is no doubt why he eventually offered the part to Isabella Rossellini.[20] We used to say things like, 'Basil Rathbone for Sotillo.' For Nostromo, he wanted the young Brando - from VIVA ZAPATA. Montero was to be played by Brando himself.

"The casting was all revised, because he talked about casting a lot. The only survivor was Paul Scofield. We'd talked about him right at the beginning and I'd written Monygham with him in his mind, with his voice very much in my ear."[21]

George Correface was a young Greek, born in France, who worked with Peter Brook's Paris theatre company, and played in *The Mahabharata*. Correface was given a full-scale test at Shepperton with costumes, sets and supporting cast, but David was unhappy about the lighting, so the entire thing was done again.

"He was very interesting," said David, "in the sense that he looked like a working man, but there was a sort of strange sensitivity or melancholy about his eyes that registered very strongly on the screen."[22]

Correface recalled how impressed he was by David's demeanour. "I could see he was in his element. He was where he most liked to be, behind the camera. He was extraordinarily happy and alive, in a contained way. He was also very inspiring. His presence, the tone of his voice; I could feel his involvement, I could feel how much he wanted the test to be a success."[23]

"I remember David saying that he hadn't been so excited by a young actor since Omar Sharif," said Hampton. "He was terribly good, I thought, and absolutely right for the part.

"He tested Alan Rickman as Decoud on my recommendation because he was then in *Liaisons*. He said, 'He's got a tremendous amount of screen presence,' which has proved to be the case.[24]

"I thought Conrad was a very good match for David's temperament," continued Hampton, "because he was very positive about individuals, but very pessimistic about the human race in general. Conrad was profoundly pessimistic about people in general and found consolation or hope in individuals; all his work was about valuable individuals being crushed by malign forces of people's inertia or greed.[25]

"I was basically very fond of David. I thought he saw the world in such black and white terms that it seemed a difficult way to live, to have to condemn everyone outright, or put them on the side of the angels. There wasn't much room for fine shading in his life. But he was amusing and incredibly sharp all the time I was working with him. I don't know how his health in the last couple of years might have affected him, but he could certainly work me under the table.

"I formed the impression towards the end of my time with him there was a sort of contrary pull in him that didn't want to make the film. There was a period when he went out to Mexico[26] and took a lot of photographs of locations. At that point, which was six months into our work, you could see that the whole thing was absolutely concrete. Then somehow it began to become less so...[27]

"I remember him saying, 'I shall probably be eighty before I start making this film.'

"And I said, 'That's all right. What's worrying me is that *I* shall probably be eighty before we start making it.'"

The first draft of NOSTROMO was sent to Spielberg and David was invited over to discuss it.

"The trip to America was a disaster in all kinds of ways," said Hampton. "When he arrived, it turned out that Spielberg had 'flu and he asked if the meeting could take place at his house rather than at his office. Steven had done only a few pages of notes, which he proceeded to go through. And this incensed David."[28]

The notes survive in the form of a memo from Spielberg on Amblin Entertainment paper dated 13 February 1987. It begins: "Let me first of all congratulate Christopher Hampton and yourself for taking Joseph Conrad's best and most complex novel and organizing it into something that a layman of literature, like myself, can follow, understand, and admire. Only in your hands do I believe this will make a riveting motion picture."

Spielberg asked for more character time for Gould, the mine owner, because "he is the man responsible for opening Pandora's box... You promise so much in his marvelous set-up at the mines, and then he sorts of drifts out of the picture, only reemerging with strength on page 78, in a brilliantly written scene between he, Montero and Gamacho."

He said that Decoud was his least favourite character and didn't know what motivated him. He knew so little about him, he didn't care that he committed suicide. "I was also confused as to what Sotillo wants in the story. Now that I know Sotillo wants the silver as well, shouldn't we make this clear much earlier?"

Spielberg said he was confused trying to keep track of everything; he couldn't work out where the coups were happening. "Dare I suggest a map in someone's office that could give us some suggestion as to where all the game players, all the armies, all the antagonists and protagonists are located?"

Spielberg was amusingly self-deprecating: "Here's an incredibly stupid idea; when Gould refuses Hirsch's dynamite, and for that matter Hirsch's company, could Hirsch have sold dynamite to the dissidents and the leaders of the mob knowing there was going to be a riot? As much as I like Hirsch, we need to know more about him...

"NOSTROMO is written so well it is somewhat embarrassing for me to make any suggestions about how to improve it. Except for Decoud, I loved every character, and would only like to see more of a continuity of corruption as seen through Gould's experiences. He would then be a story-teller, and there would be somewhat of a linear thread from beginning to end that would not, in my opinion, disrupt the unorthodox approach you've consciously taken with this material."

However, Spielberg missed a Herculean confrontation between Montero and his promises to take back the silver mine: "I miss Gould's defending his mine against Montero's army." Spielberg hoped for a race to the rescue, Nostromo bringing Barrios's armies just as Gould is about to lose the mine to Montero: "Just a little bit of a 'movie' in a great film," he wrote.

"I hope these notes do not frustrate you beyond Exedrin," he concluded.[29]

Unfortunately, the criticisms had entirely the wrong effect on David, who was absolutely furious with Spielberg.

"When he came back he was in a rage about the whole thing," said Hampton. "He decided he didn't want Warners to have it any more and that he'd been insulted. And I remember him waving these notes and saying, 'Who does he think he is?'

"I said, 'He thinks he's the producer, and he is.'

"You see, they had met on Concorde and Steven had told David that he was his idol, and he said, 'If there is any time I can do anything to help you on any project that you make, I will.' I think David took that to mean, 'I will give you carte blanche, I will facilitate the whole thing for you.' And when he realised that wasn't the case he was very upset in a completely irrational way.

"Right at the beginning, I had a meeting with Spielberg. He confessed to having some trouble reading the book and said, 'Let's talk in very basic terms. Who's the hero of this book?' I thought this might be a trick question. I said, 'Nostromo.' And he said, 'Yes, I can see that. In that case, who is the villain?' I said, 'The villain is money.' There was a longish pause and he changed the subject. But those were the only questions he asked me about it before I started writing.

"He withdrew from the whole thing because he could see there would be some sort of fight between him and David and he wanted to avoid that. Once the Warner Bros. thing began to collapse, it started to feel as if the whole project was on self-destruct."[30]

At an *Evening Standard* Awards dinner, Hampton found himself seated next to Robert Bolt. Bolt asked how NOSTROMO was going and said it was a great sadness to him that he'd lost touch with David.

Hampton said it was absurd, and that he would try to get David to ring him. But when he suggested it, David refused.

"Would you mind if he rang you?" asked Hampton.

"No, I suppose not," said David.

Robert Bolt renewed contact with David when he and Sarah Miles were invited to Narrow Street. Hampton's kind deed ended his own association with David Lean.

"I think that was inevitable anyway," said Hampton. "I gave in my notice, as it were, in order to go and do LIAISONS [the film version]. I said, 'When I've got it done, I'll come back again,' which I intended to do. David, quite clearly, was unhappy about the fact that I was going. And I was feeling that I'd done everything I could. I'd worked exactly a year, August 1986 to August 1987.

"I had begun to feel that the film would never be made and that somehow we were doing draft after draft to no particular purpose by that stage. It had been very exhilarating for about nine months, because I'd gone on with the feeling that it had kept getting better. Then that gave way to a feeling that it was just being changed, rather than getting better, if you take the distinction.[31]

"I gave him a month's notice. I know he got grumpier and grumpier as the end approached and I was working until ten in the evening of the Saturday of the last week."

Hampton kept in touch with David until one morning he sounded constrained.

"Is this a bad time to talk to you?" asked Hampton.

"I'm here with Robert," said David, and the conversation ended.

"When you were working with him," said Hampton, "you were family, and so he just replaced one family with another."[32]

"The terrible thing is," said David, "that Christopher got fed up with me, which in a way I don't blame him for at all. He said in some magazine that he just dreaded the moment we'd get to a certain point and I'd say, 'Well, now, we'd better go back to page one,' which I would do at the drop of a hat because I always think I can get it better. As a matter of fact, I find this is one of my biggest assets. I just plod and plod and plod away. And by the time you've gone through it I don't know how many times, all sorts of cats fall out of bags. It's part of my make-up in some curious way that I go on and on.[33]

"And then one day I met Robert and I'd not met him since he'd been really ill, and he said, 'How's the script?' 'Well,' I said, 'I think it's coming all right; bloody difficult.' He said, 'Yes, I know it is. Can I read it?' And I said, like a rock dropping into mud, 'YES!' And of course he started to spark right away, and because we know each other so well we could talk to each other in shorthand. Robert and I can carry on a conversation which is probably unintelligible to a lot of people but it means a lot to us. It's wonderful because I think that working together again has improved his disability. It's done something for his confidence, I think. In fact, I'm sure he'd agree if he was sitting here."[34]

"I received an invitation to his eightieth birthday," said Robert Bolt. "I went to it. He, I suppose, wanted to make sure that he could understand what I was saying. No conversation about NOSTROMO took place at it. Shortly after, I received a further lunch-time invitation. Alone this time. He mentioned NOSTROMO and the fact that I had recommended it to him as far back as LAWRENCE.[35] I said I was agog to see what he and Christopher had done with it. In other words, I said that

I would be willing to have a go at it, if that was in his mind. He, of course, did not say so, neither did I. It was understood. I read it at my home. Responded with a few criticisms and praise in a letter."[36]

Bolt wrote in this letter that it was remarkable how close Hampton and David had kept to the original story-line. "Nevertheless, I would take a much freer line with it, make it more about Nostromo and less about the blessing (and curse) of the Gould silver." Bolt sketched a new outline and ended up by saying, "Forgive all this, if this is a confounded cheek."[37]

And so this remarkable partnership which had begun twenty-seven years earlier was reforged. Although Bolt still found it hard to speak, the working relationship prospered.

"They had a shorthand together which was quite amazing to watch," said Sandra. "Robert was very bright first thing, but he would become a little dyslexic as the day went on. And over lunch, they continued talking and Sarah [Foster] and I had to shut up. Very often, David went through a whole lunch silent because it was all ticking over in his head. I'd always thought I'd done something wrong, but I hadn't.

"Robert would come up with a word, 'MMMo…' and I would go 'Monygham?' 'Yes.' A sentence would come out of his mouth back to front and David would say, 'Robert, are you trying to say…?' 'Yes.' They understood each other so well; one sparked the other, you could see it, it was like fire."[38]

"The relationship was better than before," said Bolt with a laugh. "I have this stroke, so every now and then I could say, 'David, I'm going to bed…'"[39]

According to Julie Laird, Bolt wrote a letter to David saying, "I will never forget what you have done since I was ill."[40]

"I must say that he went out on a limb for me," said Bolt. "He has been so patient, listening to me burble on with my speech defect! Because I was much less articulate when I took it on - awful. But he stuck with me, and he has turned out trumps."[41]

Melvyn Bragg presented another programme for the *South Bank Show* about their relationship.[42] Bragg and his team were very anxious about the way Bolt would cope with it, but he was delighted that it was being filmed, and it did wonders for his self-confidence, particularly when relatively few of his comments had to be subtitled.

In January 1989, David had an attack of shingles. Although it was caught early, and eventually cleared up, it was the beginning of a series of illnesses.

By the summer, he had difficulty breathing and was admitted to the Wellington Hospital where they diagnosed fibrosing alveolitis, an inflammation of the lung. He was put on high doses of steroids which improved his breathing, but as they reduced the dose, David found it more and more difficult to move. This was put down to a steroid-induced myopathy, a rare condition where the taking of high doses of steroids makes one paradoxically weaker. A specialist had been brought in, and he had agreed with the diagnosis. In desperation, Sandra called Peter Wheeler, who was also the doctor of Fred Zinnemann and John Box.

"Sandra phoned me in November to say David had been unwell for about six months and she was very worried about him," said Peter Wheeler. "He couldn't walk, he was swollen up, and she thought he was dying. That evening, I went over and saw him and he *was* dying. He'd got extreme oedematous - swelling in his legs, arms, back. He couldn't move, he couldn't even scratch his nose. He could speak perfectly well, he had all his faculties, but he couldn't do anything else. He was lying there, an inanimate swollen object."[43]

Dr Wheeler carried out blood tests, which suggested that David was suffering from Polymiacitis, an inflammation of the muscles, which had been masked by the steroids, together with a few other ailments such as abnormal liver function. He decided to put David back on steroids - Cortisone - which alarmed Sandra, who had meanwhile tried every other treatment she could think of, including homeopathy. Since nothing had worked, she was eventually persuaded to accept the new treatment and by Christmas, 1989, David was much better.[44]

That Christmas, David wrote to Robert Bolt:

"I have been thinking quite a lot about death lately. The other evening a great flight of geese passed by my window in the half dark. I did not even see them. It was the swoosh of their wings, beautiful but doom-laden, which arrested me.

"I would like to try bringing in the sound of the 'goose' theme over the shots of Mrs Gould seeing the devastation of the forest for the first time. Show her looking up and seeing the birds fleeing from destruction.

"At the end of the film I would like to try bringing in the sound of the goose wings just before Nostromo dies in the Paio. Even show Mrs Gould and Nostromo looking upwards listening to their passing.

"At the Lighthouse Linda steps out into the darkness, calls: 'Gian Battista - Gian Battista.' The sound of the geese passes overhead and disappears. Nostromo's body is carried into the Cathedral. A triumph in death which he never experienced in life.

"I do hope you like it because I think it adds a whole new dimension to the character of Nostromo and to the picture."[45]

After Spielberg had withdrawn from NOSTROMO, David formed a partnership with Serge Silberman, whom he had met at a dinner organised by Adrian Turner of the National Film Theatre for Akira Kurosawa, whose film RAN Silberman had helped to produce. Born in Poland in 1917, Silberman had produced many of

Luis Buñuel's films and offered to take on NOSTROMO. So expertly did he ingratiate himself into David's good books that the two men seemed ideally suited.[46]

"I also tried to get NOSTROMO financed," said Judy Scott-Fox, who was now Christopher Hampton's agent. "At one point, I had John Heyman ready. John had helped raise the money for PASSAGE TO INDIA. He was going to Japan, and I said, 'They've just spent $30 million for a Van Gogh painting. Why don't they pay $36 million for a David Lean film?' He went to Japan and found someone to put up the money, but by that time, David had got himself involved with Serge. And he said, 'Oh no, my lawyer says I can't get out of it.'

"I think he could have got out of it, but he was strange. Although he was ruthless in some ways, in others he was not ruthless enough. I'm sure it was his Quaker background; he wouldn't get rid of Serge because he felt they had a handshake deal."[47]

By the time I started working on this book, in February 1990, David had been profoundly disillusioned. He and Silberman had exchanged acrimonious letters and Silberman had faxed to say he had lost all desire to make the film.[48] Tony Reeves brought the two sides together again, but the meeting had been a disaster. David told me about it just after it had happened.

"You know, Kevin, I suppose while we're doing this, all sorts of curious things will pop up and probably not be used. But while I'm in the white heat of fury, I'll tell you of meeting a producer, i.e. Serge Silberman. For weeks he's been trying to get me alone, and I've always avoided that because I'm no good at business and he wanted Tony Reeves out of the way. And finally he succeeded. I felt the walls closing in around me as he started to talk."

At first, they argued about casting. Because Paul Scofield had decided to do a play, David had offered his part to Eric Porter, and when Scofield's play ended its run, David felt unable to re-offer Scofield the part because of his commitment to Porter. But Silberman, making a commercial judgment, wanted Scofield.

"And he started pressuring me; it became pretty nasty. In fact, nobody's talked to me like that, I don't think, ever. He said, 'I'm going to tell you something that'll probably shock you. Warner Bros. dislike you, don't want you and don't want to have anything to do with a film that you've got anything to do with.' You know, rough stuff.

"I tried to talk about other things and the trouble with Serge is he cannot listen. He's always got to butt in and push his own ideas forward. And he got more and more nasty and it all revolved around a situation in which they wanted me to sign a letter saying that if I keeled over and died, or could not direct the film, that they could still call it 'A David Lean film.' I said, 'I'm not going to do that. I'd have queues of people willing to pay me quite a lot of money to say they could have my name on a film although I'd had nothing to do with it.'

"And he said, 'I am taking a gamble. If I take a gamble, you should take a gamble.' I said, 'Look, there's no gamble for you. The gamble is for me.' And it got worse and worse. A most unpleasant scene. In the end, he reminded me of how much money he'd spent, how much I'd let him down by becoming ill and he walked out of the room. My heart was going bang, bang, bang. I had to call him back. I said 'Look, you've left your briefcase.'

"There is a terrible thing that happens to people's faces when they get like this. You see a face that you've never seen before, sort of twisted and mean. He came back, got the briefcase and walked out of the room.

"I said, 'Come back, you've forgotten your stick.' So he came back and collected his stick. Then I said, 'You've forgotten your book.' And he collected that, and swept out. It left me absolutely shattered."[49]

David turned to other topics, but he kept coming back to Silberman.

"I think he's putting two million of his own money, maybe even more. So he's in the tweezers all right. But it wasn't really that; it was the awful thing of seeing the fangs. Rather frightening. Because he's very polite in the usual way and comes along with champagne and flowers. He's always telling me, 'I love you' on the phone. So when you really meet the fangs at the end, I mean, it's terribly upsetting. I suppose I'm going to have to meet him again. But I don't want to meet him again. I've been doing a sort of stupid sulk."[50]

David had to resume the partnership - he dare not risk a producer sinking NOSTROMO as one had sunk the Bounty.

"They're not interested in

After consultation with David, John Box did roughs for the story-board which Michael White executed. This is the scene where Nostromo and Decoud are mown down by a steamer.

movies as movies," said David of modern producers in general. "Practically every day I thank God I'm doing what I'm doing, and I bet you that none of those people thank God they're doing what they're doing."[51]

"I'd always encouraged him not to make the film" said Peter Wheeler. "I think physically it would have been very difficult for him. I said to him, 'Why on earth do you need to do this film? You're wealthy enough. You don't need to do it. Suppose it goes wrong and you're shot to pieces again?'

"He said, 'I have to do it. It's in my blood.'"[52]

David's age and the possibility of him dying during production was having an effect on the budget of NOSTROMO, adding to Silberman's problems. "They are terrified of me dying," said David. "There are no two ways about it. So I'm insured for this enormous amount - the premium is more than I'm paid - and it goes on the budget. This is a new way of getting money. Nobody over seventy-five, I think it is, can make a picture now unless they get massive insurance.

"I have to put up the name of a man - preferably three - who, if I die halfway through the picture, would be capable of finishing it. He's got to be agreeable to the completion guarantor and to the insurers and to the banks and to other people who are putting up the money. Well, modesty prevents me saying a lot, but that is the situation. Because they have no tact about this at all, I've been bombarded with lists of people they think would agree to finishing the picture. On a whole lot of the names I said, 'He's too highbrow... he's too literary...'"[53]

David favoured Robert Altman as his stand-in. "I met him at the Cannes Film Festival. I was most impressed with him. Not as I thought he would be at all. Very nice. Real gent. And he thinks very highly of me."[54] Among others who were considered were John Boorman, Peter Yates, Arthur Penn and Guy Hamilton, who was the final choice.[55]

In November 1989, Steven Spielberg had called to say that David, by unanimous consent, had been made the beneficiary of the American Film Institute's Life Achievement Award. The ceremony was to be held in Los Angeles on 8 March 1990.

Since previous recipients had included John Ford, William Wyler, Billy Wilder and Orson Welles, David was deeply moved and determined that he would overcome his illness. From that moment on, the American trip was his goal. Physiotherapists were brought in and he had a personal trainer.

But a month before the ceremony, David declared that he could not possibly go; he was not nearly well enough. Despite the improvement in his health, he was still not walking. Sarah reminded him that since the whole event depended on his presence and he had agreed to go, there was no alternative. David asked Peter Wheeler to go with him.

Sarah Foster contacted the AFI and discovered they were only prepared to pay for David's flight. "I told them that David had to have his doctor with him, I'll be coming and his girlfriend will be coming. He also had his night nurse with him, so there were five. David ended up paying for all of us.

"Sandra and I arranged special VIP treatment with TWA, which took a lot of organising. But Sandra had been in the art world and still had her old chums in the airlines. So we were whisked through - it was absolutely fantastic - straight into a white stretch-limo, off to the Beverly Wilshire. It was a long flight, but David loves aeroplanes, so he was quite happy."[56]

Wheeler was impressed by the fact that as they drove down the boulevards, people driving alongside would open their windows, lean out and say 'Hey, aren't you David Lean?' Even in his wheelchair, in the street, people would come up and tell him how much they liked his films.

"I thought that was remarkable."

Fred Zinnemann was in Los Angeles at the same time, and Wheeler took David to lunch with him at the Beverly Hills Hotel.

"They were very sweet with each other. They reminisced about the thirties and the forties and spoke with a lot of affection for each other and each other's work. Fred said David's films were all about gallantry and the feats of mankind and David said Fred's were all about the little man fighting back. They were quite emotional with each other, hugging and kissing - and there were tears in David's eyes. It was lovely to be there; I was in a privileged position to listen to them."

At the dress rehearsal, the organisers asked David if he could walk from the door to his table, a distance of about forty yards. David said he didn't know, but thought he could.

"We had tried to see if he could walk along the corridor in the hotel," said Wheeler, "but he got anxious and nervous, and I don't suppose he did thirty feet before he started panicking. He had to be carried on and off the aeroplane and he couldn't walk any length of the corridors at the airport. Even at the hotel there was a major problem; could he walk up three or four ordinary steps? With everyone by his side, of course, he could do it. His legs were very floppy and weak and so he had a stick to lean on. David was basically a rather lazy person. If he didn't have to walk, he wouldn't walk. And since he didn't know whether he could walk it was all rather frightening.

"I remember James Fox was there and he said, 'I don't think he can walk that far. He can hardly stand.' That afternoon, David was in a terrible state. I walked the distance with Sarah; we thought that with the adrenalin he probably could do it if we didn't tire him too much before."[57]

On top of all this were his other concerns. David was only too aware that NOSTROMO was still not fully financed.

"While we were in Los Angeles, problems with NOSTROMO came up," said Sarah Foster, "and he had a huge row with Serge Silberman. David said to Sandra and myself, 'If I don't get the go-ahead for this film by tonight, I'm going to stand up there and tell them that the movie's off.'

"So Sandra and I immediately panicked and I ran into my bedroom and I was on the phone for over an hour trying to find Tony Reeves. He was fishing in Scotland. We needed to get him to ring David and say, 'Everything's okay. You've got the green light.' Just so he could stand up and deliver his speech.

"He hadn't written his speech and he wouldn't write it. A few hours before the event he said, 'Right, everybody out. I'm going to write my speech.' He must have sat there for three or four hours, and he didn't do anything. Then it was time for us to get ready. It was an absolute nightmare as far as the organising was concerned, and keeping David under control. He was worried about this walk. He was bloated and feeling very sorry for himself, and there was nothing anybody could say to make him feel better."[58]

"That evening," said Peter Wheeler, "he was rather embarrassed by all the people milling around outside the hotel waiting for the film stars. He didn't want to be seen in a wheelchair. The nurse brought him up in his chair to a hotel room that was put aside for him. When the time came, they'd worked out a route round the outside of the hotel, along the corridors, through the kitchen, and then four husky blokes carried him up a staircase to the make-up area at the back of the hall. We went and sat in our places, and then David had to make his entrance.

"He psyched himself up and behold, he came in with his cane and walked the forty yards to where we sat. Sandra kept feeling she should hold him up and he kept pushing her away because he wanted to look his best. He was a bit bloated in the face, but he did look good."[59]

"We thought he was going to keel over, but he didn't," said Sarah. "It was a most incredible feeling, being with somebody who is so famous and so much loved, with all these stars, and there's me sitting at the top table with my boss and his girlfriend and Johnny Mills and Billy Wilder. It was a wonderful evening. It was so highly charged with emotion I don't remember much about it, nor does Sandra. But now, having seen it about thirty times on tape, I just hadn't realised how special it was. Sandra and I spent most of the evening in tears, because it was so magnificent."[60,61]

During the ceremony, Steven Spielberg said, "David brought me here and in fact, you could say bought me my ticket. Because it was two of his films, THE BRIDGE ON THE RIVER KWAI and LAWRENCE OF ARABIA, that most made me want to be a film-maker. I was inspired the first time I saw LAWRENCE. It made me feel puny. It still makes me feel puny. And that's one measure of its greatness.... David Lean makes movies that are the equivalent of great novels. With one difference. When you read, it's your imagination that sparks the imagery. But in films you trust the director's imagination. And if he's a good director, you don't betray the trust. But if you're a great director like David, you can even go past it. He puts pictures on the screen that not even imaginations can anticipate. Gregory Peck quoted someone as having said that David Lean is 'the poet of the far horizon.'[62] And for me, Sir David Lean brings that horizon closer for all of us. And then he sails right across it. And his movies are truly the voyage of a lifetime. And I'm here to say, for everyone, thank you for taking all of us with you."

Martin Scorsese said that David was a great picture maker. "His images stay with me forever. But what makes them memorable isn't necessarily their beauty. That's just good photography. It's the emotion behind those images that's meant the most to me over the years. It's the way David Lean can put feeling on film. The way he shows a whole landscape of the spirit. For me, that's the real geography of David Lean country. And that's why, in a David Lean movie, there's no such thing as an empty landscape. Thank you, David."

Billy Wilder ended his tribute with two little questions for the AFI: "Who else and what took you so long?"

David extemporised his speech, and it proved controversial. Here it is without the cuts that had to be imposed on it for the television programme:

"The trouble with me is that I got so nervous over this, I tried to write a speech over the last week and completely failed. And so I have got no speech at all. But I'll try to meander for a moment. I must say, I'm very surprised at some of the shots I saw this evening. They're better than I thought they were.

(Light applause)

"Another great thing struck me, and I do hope you'll forgive me if I seem presumptuous in this great honour you've given me. I promise you that everything I'm going to say comes from my heart; it's completely sincere and it's because I love movies. (Applause) You know, Noël Coward once said to me in our early days, 'My dear, always come out of another hole.' Now, he said a lot of other things, but I found myself thinking that nearly everything he told me and everything I learned in those early days, seems to be contradicted today. We don't come out of any more new holes. We try to go back and we come out of the old holes. Parts one, two, three and four. And I think it's terribly, terribly sad.

"Looking at this list here [previous winners of the AFI Award], in this wonderful programme, nearly everybody there is an innovator, a pathfinder, they found new things to do in the movies. And all of us live on new things. Okay, do old things parts one, two and three, but don't make them a staple diet. We'll sink if we do.

(Applause)

"Oh thank you so much. I'm awfully relieved about that because I was worried and it seemed a sort of cheek. But I really believe this. I think we're running into deep waters. I mean, the rubbish that happened today to me. Two hours before I came here I get the okay after months that we were going ahead with NOSTROMO.

(Applause)

"It's a sort of asinine game that we people who create the movies should be strung along to within two hours of a great event like this. I really resent it. I really do.

(Applause)

"This business lives on creative pathfinders and there are a whole lot of you here. I terribly miss, we all miss I think, somebody like Irving Thalberg. He had a foot in both camps. He understood us people and he understood the money people. We're in terrible danger. I think there are some wonderful new film-makers coming up now. I don't mind if that sort of thing happens to old birds like me. I really don't. It hurts, but that's it. But I think we've got to protect the young ones. And there are a lot of you coming up now. They are going to be our future. Please, you chaps in the money department, remember what they are. It's a very, very nervous job making a film. They need help and if I could only find a piece of paper which I have, I would like to read you something. It came from my old friend Fred Zinnemann, who I had lunch with the day before yesterday. He found something that was said by Irving Thalberg: 'The studio has made a lot of money and they could afford to lose some.'[63] I think the time has come where the money people can afford to lose a little money taking risks with these new film-makers.

(Applause)

"I think if they give them a break, give them encouragement, we're going to come up and up and up. If we don't, we're going to go down and television's going to take over. Anyhow, wish them luck. I do. Thank you so much."

(Applause/ovation)[64]

"Afterwards," said Peter Wheeler, "they put him in a thing like a birdcage to sit in, for all these people to come and pay homage. He couldn't bear it. There was some chap from a film magazine who asked him some nasty questions and he said, 'Get me out of here.' I got Telly Savalas to come and help us back with the chair and we went off out of it, out of the hall."[65]

Some Hollywood financial people were as outraged by the speech as they were no doubt intended to be. Judy Scott-Fox met one head of production who took it as a personal insult, partly because his company was responsible for more sequels than any other, and partly because he was stung by David's remarks about the way he had been treated by the money men. His reaction was one of retrospective petulance.

"I was going to put the money up for NOSTROMO, but now I'm not going to."[66]

On his return to England, David resumed work with Bolt on the NOSTROMO script. Sadly, their partnership, recently re-forged, was coming to an end. David took exception to many of Bolt's ideas and decided to complete the script on his own.

"I sat in on the rewrite with Maggie," said Sarah Foster, "and they must have been the foullest two weeks I ever spent with him. He was a nightmare because he couldn't get it right, and because he still wasn't very well.

"He'd be in his study at ten, a quick break for lunch, and then back again. Maggie would have to leave to get home and he would say, 'Do you mind working late?'

"I'd say, 'Not at all.' We'd sit there and about eight o'clock he'd say, 'I'm afraid I'll have to stop. I'm so tired, I can't concentrate. But I know what'll happen - tomorrow morning I'll wake up and it'll come to me like that.'

"And sure enough, it did. The next morning he'd have written it before I got in. He loved doing the script, but it was laborious to him; it was the processing of it that he disliked so much. And he hated being forced to a time limit. He wanted to do it in his own time without being pushed. He'd sit for hours, not saying a word. When Sandra was there, she and I would say, 'Have we done something wrong?' He'd say, 'I'm thinking about the script. Shh, I need silence.' There would be lunches of silence and dinners of silence, because he was thinking about what he wanted to put down. When he thought he'd given an idea to Robert, and that Robert was going to get it perfectly, he didn't. That used to upset him.

"I think the Cortisone accounted for eight-five per cent of his mood, which was such a shame. When he was on sixty milligrams a day, he was frightful. When I reminded him of his bad moods he said, 'Was I really that bad? How awful.'

"But he was such a sweet man, for all that. All the goodness overcame the bad. He was such a dear. He was very caring, in a funny sort of way. He always wanted to know what was going on. He wasn't interested in anybody's past life, and he wasn't interested if you had a family life. But he was lovely. He was very much like a grandfather to me."[67]

David, Sandra and Sarah spent the entire summer of 1990 in the south of France. In September, Peter Wheeler went to France at the request of Columbia Pictures, who had come into the project as American distributors and had insisted on a medical examination before shooting on NOSTROMO began in January. "In order to have a cardiogram, it was necessary for him to climb a long flight of stairs. He had to struggle hard, but he managed to do it."[68]

Peter Lean tried to keep in touch with his father and he telephoned Sandra to ask if he could go over. Sandra said she'd have to ask. The message came back - yes, you can go. Then Peter asked if he might bring Tracy, David's thirty-year-old granddaughter whom he had never met.

"I got the message back - okay," said Peter. "We went in October 1990. The evening we arrived we were all taken out to a restaurant in the village, the Moulin de Mougins. My daughter is not only a vegetarian, she's a vegan. The head waiter was summoned and told what she couldn't eat. We had a very nice meal, but halfway through dad started retelling a story from KWAI. It was supposed to be a funny tale, but it was interspersed with four-letter words. He looked across the table at Tracy. 'Why aren't you laughing?'

"She said, 'I don't think swear words in jokes are anything to laugh at.'

"The conversation went stony silent and that topic was changed altogether. Tracy says what she thinks. He says what he thinks. The two collided a bit."[69]

"Sandra had gone to London for a couple of weeks," said Sarah Foster, "and David and I sat down to dinner one night and he said, 'Dear, I think I'm going to ask Sandra to marry me. What do you think?'

"I burst into tears. I said, 'David, that's just wonderful.'

"He said, 'We could get married in France, couldn't we?'

"I said, 'I'm sure Sandra would love that.'

"So for the next two weeks that's all we talked about. I had assumed that when Sandra came back, he would whisk her off for a quiet romantic dinner and propose to her and that would be it. One night he said, 'Dear, get Sandra on the phone will you?' And he just popped the question to her over the phone.

"They decided to get married on 15 December. Sandra came back and we started organising. So we had this huge job, hauling people over from America and England, Kenya, Switzerland and Spain - all their chums - finding accommodation for them and picking them up from the airport. Forty people were invited on the Friday for the civil ceremony in the village and back for drinks afterwards to the house. And in the evening, we had them to a sit-down dinner at the Moulin de Mougins. The following day we had about two hundred in the main house for a big party. It was just fantastic. David was on top form."

The preparations so disturbed David, as he struggled to complete the script, that he decided to move to the Hotel Negresco in Nice.

"It absolutely flummoxed him" said Sarah, "because Sandra didn't oppose the idea. He was expecting her to burst into tears. She just said, 'Okay, darling, if that's what you want, you go.' That totally threw him, so off he went like a little lost schoolboy to a prep school and he came back, five days later, just two hours before the wedding.

"Sandra and I got his Rolls-Royce over from London so he could be chauffeured down to the village in his Rolls, his best friend. We took him out to see the car and he couldn't believe it.

"Then I took him their wedding present from the studio, a Great Dane puppy. David had wanted one but he had no idea he was being bought one, so his face was a picture. We'd gone all over France to find this particular puppy and got hold of it at huge expense.

"What I hadn't been able to tell David was that at the town hall, there were thirty steps he had to climb. I kept it quiet and David was on such good form that day that I don't think anything would have mattered to him. I said, 'David, there's one thing I must tell you before we go. You've got to climb thirty steps.' And he didn't bat an eyelid. We got there and he flew up those stairs without even a breather, as if nothing had ever been wrong with him.

"The party was fantastic. We had Dawn Steel, Mike Medavoy of Columbia TriStar, Maurice Jarre, who had composed a special orchestral piece for the occasion, and we had all the villagers as well. David stayed up till four o'clock, chattering away, absolutely thrilled he'd finally made Sandra his wife.

"And that's when his illness began. He started to choke. He couldn't swallow. On the day of the wedding, we didn't think anything about it, we thought it was just nerves.

"His appetite had been lessening for a while. We thought he was nervous about the script. He'll eat when he wants to eat. The day after the wedding he hardly ate at all. We were sitting at dinner and I'd actually have to get up from the table because he was choking so badly I just couldn't bear it. I felt so sorry for him. Sandra brought in his dentist from London, putting the problem with his throat down to a set of new dentures."[70]

But it was far more complicated. The drawback to heavy doses of steroids is that they reduce the body's immunity to other diseases.

"He didn't sound right on the phone," said Peter Wheeler. "He almost sounded drunk. It was obvious he had something horrid going on in his mouth. But I didn't expect a tumour, I must say. When he came back in January, they went straight to Sandra's house in Alexandra Place - he could get up the stairs and walk around. It was a great shock for him to go downhill almost as soon as he had reached the pinnacle of his well-being. He went and saw Ian Hannam at the Westminster, and he found this tumour involving much of the back part of his tongue.

"When I went to tell him the bad news, his attitude initially was, 'That's it. Let's all go round the world. Sod it. We'll forget the film and we'll go and enjoy life and wait till I die.'

"That was his normal approach to things until he'd given it a bit of thought. He then decided, 'I don't want to die; maybe I can still do the film if I get better.'

Everyone was very optimistic, but there really wasn't a lot of hope because it was such a big tumour. It seemed to respond quite well to radiotherapy, but he felt rotten and had more and more difficulty swallowing. He was very brave. He went on, did five or six weeks at it, and had radiotherapy burns to his neck by the time he had finished, which is normal, but it goes to show how much tissue damage was being done."

During the radiation treatment, I visited David at Alexandra Place, which Sandra had decorated, like the house in France, in Florentine and Romanesque style. David was in bed and the problem with his throat made him sound almost mentally deficient. How ironic, I thought, that both Bolt and David had been almost silenced by illness. He spoke a little about his childhood, at long last, and remembered an episode from IN WHICH WE SERVE involving the RAF using enemy planes. He seemed encouraged that he had been able to remember such a significant incident, despite his illness.

He came downstairs for lunch. He had seen DANCES WITH WOLVES in France and he, Sandra and Sarah had been impressed by it. He had tried to hire its cameraman, Dean Semler, whilst its star and director, Kevin Costner, was under consideration as a standby director for NOSTROMO. He took little part in the lunch, since he found eating so difficult, and the constant interruptions maddened him. I withdrew as soon as I could, walking back to the Tube through the snow, feeling very sad about the plight of this extraordinary man.

The following day, he received a visit from his friend John Boorman, the director, who described it vividly in his book *Projections*.

"He told me in detail the history of his cancer and described his radiation treatment. He said the tumour is regressing, responding well, and he had hopeful signals from the doctor. He told me of a dream he had had. 'It was more than a dream,' he said. 'It was so real, so sharply focused, almost a vision.' He dreamt that he woke up with the feeling that there was someone in the house. He went downstairs and there he sensed that this dread thing was in the basement. He walked down the dark stairs and opened the door. There was a burglar. He stood there with an insolent grin on his face and David said, 'I know who you are.' 'Who am I?' the man asked. 'You are cancer,' said David, 'and I'm going to beat you.'"[71]

When I next saw him, a week or so later, he had been transferred to Narrow Street. He sat in a vast bed, looking like a depressed old dog. He had a few more treatments to go and was very weak. His memory seemed to be fading and he could not remember the name of the street where he had been born. I produced a map of Croydon, but it didn't help. I turned to the subject of the Second World War, which he had always avoided.

To try to bring back memories, I ran a video-cassette of Humphrey Jennings's wartime documentary LISTEN TO BRITAIN. In the middle of it he said, "Kevin, what do you think of this chap?" I hate people talking during a film, and I was shocked that he, of all people, would break the atmosphere. I was also surprised that his television set was so poorly adjusted. We reached the end and he said, "Jolly good" (not his highest compliment!) and he spoke not of the war, but of how the "superior" documentary people of that era disapproved of him. I could not, however, get him to talk about them. The flood of memories of the war I had hoped for was not forthcoming, either.

"I feel so detached from that time," he said apologetically, adding, "The women didn't look very attractive, did they?"

I made another attempt to bring him back to his childhood, producing the same model of 9.5mm hand-cranked camera that he had purchased in the twenties. This astonished him. He gazed at the tiny box, examining the mechanism and feeling its unexpected weight. He kept saying, "Good lord!" and "Look what we've come from!"

Look what he's come from, I thought.

Just before I left, he turned to me suddenly and said, "Blenheim Crescent! Number thirty-eight!" He had been trying to recall that distant fact all the time I was there.

I said farewell, and he said, "Awfully good luck to you," as though he doubted we would ever meet again.

David asked Eddie Fowlie to come from Spain, and he sat with him every day for weeks.

"After one of our long quiet spells I asked him what he was thinking about when he was lying there. He thought for a few seconds and said, 'Women'."

Eddie returned to Spain and was asked to come back as a matter of urgency since David's condition had worsened. Dr Wheeler was moving him to the King Edward VII Hospital in Marylebone.

"That was the news that David didn't want," said Fowlie. "He wanted to resist, especially when he was to go in an ambulance. No way would he be carried on a stretcher. As he left the bedroom he said to me, 'I want my flowers.' These were rather wilted sunflowers in a vase by his bed. I said we'd get fresh ones. 'No,' he said firmly. 'I want those.' And so they went with him. David loved sunflowers."[72]

"He was miserably unhappy there," said Peter Wheeler. "He was effing and blinding at all the nurses - they had never heard such language. It was typical of him, really. He didn't really mean it. It was just one way of expressing himself. I think he was upset that people felt there was anything wrong with it. But he didn't really care in the end."

I knew when I'd found the hospital, because outside a woman was unloading a huge armful of daffodils from the boot of her car. I was directed to his room on the second floor. David was lying down, looking more depressed than ever. He stared blankly at me, and I realised he had no idea who I was. I told him my name and he said "Kevin!" and tried to sit up.

If the interviewing was slow-going when he was in reasonable health, it was impossible when he was ill. All the surgery had been in the region of his throat, which made speaking hard. He answered as helpfully as he could, but he spoke in monosyllables. There was a knock on the door and an explosion of daffodils lit up the room like the scene in DOCTOR ZHIVAGO.

I was impressed to see how carefully Sandra looked after him. She was there when I arrived and there when I left. Whenever he needed to be moved, Sandra always helped the nurses. Gradually David found it more and more difficult to speak and his answers became shorter and shorter. Eventually, David Lean silences turned into real silences; he had apparently switched off.

"He spent his eighty-third birthday in King Edward's," said Peter Wheeler. "By that weekend, he had developed severe inhalational pneumonia, and we treated that and then he went home to Narrow Street. He seemed to have recovered, but we made a decision that if he got another pneumonia we'd treat it urgently, but really it might be kinder to let him go, because the whole thing had become horrendous for him"[73]

"I went to see him at Narrow Street," said John Box. "He had had an awful night. He said, 'I woke up and it wasn't dark. It must have been dawn. There was a strange noise of wind - a great flapping sound - these Canada geese went past. I thought I must be dead.' I joked with him, 'I suppose you thought they were angels.' But in the script, as Nostromo dies, there is an extraordinary sound and strange birds fly overhead. I wouldn't have used Canada geese; if the film is ever made I'll make sure they're white birds. But you see the coincidence."

Script Extract:
NOSTROMO is trying to say something. Mrs GOULD bends closer.

NOSTROMO
(very quietly)
I want to tell you where I hid it...

She gently places a hand over his mouth.
MRS GOULD
No. No Capataz. Let it be lost forever.

A smile spreads across his face. MRS. GOULD turns and beckons to GISELLE.

NOSTROMO reaches up for GISELLE's hand then looks up: A FLIGHT OF GEESE are passing overhead. He looks after them. The mournful sound of their wings fades away. NOSTROMO's head slumps to one side. He is dead.

Sandy Lean had heard that David was ill, but the news of his final decline came as a shock.

"John and I were at a health spa in the Berkshires, I remember," said Sandy, "sitting in the dining room with Mike Nichols and his wife Diane Sawyer, when there was a long-distance call for me. I picked up the phone and it was Sara.

"She said, 'I've something to tell you. I'm sure nobody else has, and I know you'd never forgive me if I didn't. David is dying. If you want to see him again - and I think you probably do - you'd better do something now because there isn't much time.'

"So first I called Maggie, and then I called Tony Reeves. I said, 'Tony, I can't just turn up there. Will you ask him if he'll see me?'

"Tony said, 'As it happens, I'm going down to see him tomorrow. I'll ask him if I have the chance, but it's difficult. His concentration comes and goes and he's looking terrible. He's hooked up to a tube, and he's very wasted. You'd hardly recognise him.'

"I said, 'All right, but please get back to me.' We drove back to Connecticut that evening. I stayed in the house, waiting for the phone. And a day went by, and another day.

"Then Tony called and he said, 'I've talked to David. He wants to see you, but first he wants to get a little better. You have to understand, he doesn't want you to see him looking like this.'

"I said, 'Do you think he has any idea how ill he is?' And then I asked him, 'Would it be all right if I sent him some flowers?'

"Tony said, 'I think he'd probably like that.' So I called up Pulbrook and Gould, and asked them to send round a huge bunch of spring flowers. David loved spring flowers - oh, hell, to make sense of this I have to tell you that he always used to call me his spring flower - and the girl said, 'What shall I put on the card?' And I said, 'Just put, 'Thinking of you. With all my love, Sandy.'"[74]

"Everything had improved," said Sandra. "His doctors had checked his throat and they pronounced the tumour completely gone. He was having difficulty eating, but he had worked out a way. He was longing to go back to France.

"Then I heard that Sandy wanted to fly over. I am a grown-up woman. I'm not jealous of David's past. David did not want to see her. He had had pneumonia in the hospital and was very weak anyway. He couldn't cope with it."

When Sandra heard that 'Lady Lean' was sending flowers she was at first confused and then realised that they were from Sandy.

"Sarah said we should chuck them in the river. No, I said, I'm an honest woman and they should be delivered. I'll take them in. Well, that did it. The card said, 'Thinking of you. All my love, my darling David.' She hadn't got in touch on his eightieth birthday, nor at Christmas, she had built this house and dumped him in it, as he himself said. Suddenly her guilt was getting the better of her. Anyway, I said absolutely no to her flying over.

"David was terribly depressed by the flowers. He said, 'I'm in the middle.' And David always used words at their face value. If she said, 'All my love,' she still loved him. The emotion was too much for him. 'That's it,' he said, 'The battle's over.' I kept him away from emotion as much as I could. We talked of France and the garden and animals.

"Then suddenly this terrible depression. He wouldn't talk to me. I asked him what the matter was and he wouldn't tell me. I was robbed of the last week with him."[75]

"Tony called me," said Sandy, "to tell me David had got the flowers. I asked him what David had said, and he said, 'Nothing. He just started to cry.'

"The next morning I was woken by a telephone call from Austria. It was our friend, Vita Hohenlohe. She said, 'Do you realise what a terrible thing you have done? I've just had Sandra on the phone and she's in a frightful state. David won't eat, he won't talk, he's gone into a deep depression. It was selfish and thoughtless of you to interfere. You have nothing to do with him any more, you're no longer part of his life, don't you understand that?'

"And I remember holding on to the phone and saying, almost shouting, 'I understand, Vita, I understand.'"[76]

"He'd developed a pneumonia again and was really quite frightened," said Peter Wheeler. "He had a high fever and was hallucinating. He seemed to know that people were around him. Sandra, some friends of hers, Sarah and the male nurse all left the room. I think he knew he was dying at that stage. He said, 'Goodbye, old chap,' as if he knew he was going. I left at midday and I thought, that will be the last time I'll see him alive. Almost as soon as I got back I was told he'd died. He died very quickly, within an hour or so. I went back and certified him dead. I felt he was still there. I was very upset about him dying. I'd grown to like him a lot. He was a nice man to me. I think he was pretty horrid to some other people, but he was always very nice to me."[77]

David died on 16 April 1991. On that day, more than a century before, Charlie Chaplin had been born.

When news of his death reached Dingle, the flag over the Phoenix Cinema was lowered to half mast.

The next time Tony Reeves called Sandy, it was to tell her that David was dead.

"After that, well, it was made quite clear that I wouldn't be welcome at the funeral," said Sandy. "And so I didn't go. I comforted myself with the thought that David hated funerals. In the end I didn't go to the memorial service either. It sounded like such a huge production and there would have been enough wives there without me.

"I knew at the time it was the right thing to do and I'm so glad, because we'd had no contact at all, and it was good for him just to know that I still cared about him and was thinking about him. I don't regret it and I don't think it was the wrong thing to do, I really don't."[78]

The funeral was held at Putney Vale Crematorium on a sunny but cold day, 22 April 1991. Two policemen were on duty. I spotted Alec Guinness, John Mills, even John Justin from THE SOUND BARRIER.

As we were ushered inside the chapel, a gentle flow of people quickly became a flood and many had to stand. After an opening hymn, the simple service was given astonishing impact when a tall, iron-grey man strode stiffly forward. He had a military bearing and the lined face of a man who had experienced much. It was Group Captain Lord Cheshire, VC, OM, DSO, DFC.

I thought, what on earth could this man - the most admired RAF bomber pilot of the war, observer of the Nagasaki Raid, and organiser of homes for the terminally ill - possibly have in common with David Lean?[79]

"Just a few moments ago," he said, "I was asked to say something about David. I shall have to speak as the spirit moves. He was one of the greatest men of this century and he was great in all sorts of ways, not just in the making of films. When I was having problems in India thirty-five years ago, he helped me out and he became perhaps my greatest friend."

How was it that I could have listened so long to David Lean and never heard him so much as mention the name of Leonard Cheshire?

At a gathering in Narrow Street, after the funeral, I looked for Cheshire but saw no sign of him. Most of his other friends and collaborators were present, including John Box who told me that he had to break the news to David that his sets for NOSTROMO were being torn down at Rex Ingram's old studios, La Victorine. Box said there was then a long silence. I would imagine that from that moment, David Lean gave up. For films were his life, and while he had given up on projects, this was the first time a project had given up on him. He had beaten the cancer only to succumb to pneumonia. This must have been a final blow.

A short, grey man in his seventies whom I had never seen before marched up to me and said, "The sets were built, everything was ready!" and marched off again. Enquiries revealed it to be Serge Silberman. His accusing tone suggested that David had somehow insulted him by fading out so inconsiderately.

By this time, the Canary Wharf tower was finished. Director Hugh Hudson, who had been best man at David's wedding less than four months earlier, pointed through the window and said, just as David would have done, "Wonderful shot." The tower stood out from a threatening cloud bank with the sun streaming upon it and converting it from a brash example of modern architecture into an incandescent mirage to which only Turner could have done justice. Turner, or David Lean with Freddie Young...

Leonard Cheshire's portrait dominated the entrance hall when I arrived at the headquarters of the Cheshire Homes in Westminster. I was ushered upstairs to his cramped office, where I was introduced to "GC" as everyone called him - short for Group Captain. He was casually dressed, in an open necked shirt, and was slightly shy. He apologised for the state of the place; they were moving next door and the racket of building work filled the air.

He was easy to talk to, a bit like David in his rather boyish attitude to cerebral matters. He gave no impression of lofty eminence, as one might have inferred from his chilly dignity at the funeral. He smiled a lot, and was full of charm. Most of his references and comparisons were with the war, and I noticed that whenever an aircraft passed overhead, his eyes flicked up to the window.

"I think David was almost my best friend," he said. "I don't have a social life,

Leonard Cheshire visits David during DOCTOR ZHIVAGO, *1965.*

because once you have a social life, where do you stop? But once or twice a year, I went out and spent an evening with David, or went and saw him on the set. I can't tell you how much I miss him. I keep thinking, 'I must talk to David about that,' and then realise I can't."

Leonard Cheshire first met David in 1958, when he was living in Dehra Dun, north of Delhi. He had already established his Cheshire Homes for incurables in England. Leila's son was at the Dun School, the Indian equivalent of Eton, and David, while he was up there, met an architect who told him of Cheshire's transportation problems. David asked to see him.

"We walked across the dry river to this thirty-acre jungle site - no water, no electricity - and I told him I had plans for a little place for leprosy patients, the mentally retarded and others. He looked round and said, 'Hmm... I just wouldn't have the faintest idea how to begin.'

"I said, 'But David, I wouldn't have the faintest idea how to begin a film.'

"He drove me down to Delhi in his Rolls-Royce and he transported the tents and the tentpoles back to Dehra Dun. That started our friendship.

"He invited me out to LAWRENCE and I visited him on DOCTOR ZHIVAGO in Madrid a couple of times. One thing which struck me about David. I'd never seen him anywhere but in a hotel with two suitcases. When he invited my wife [Sue Ryder] and myself to Rome - she's never forgotten it, it was a complete rest for her, as she's always working - I saw him in a house. He was incredibly keen on gardening. He showed me around and as he was very busy, I said could I help him with it? He said no, he just wanted to be alone in the garden. He didn't want me around him. That struck me as a side of David I'd never seen.

"He also gave me a first-class ticket for my wife and myself - she couldn't come - to Fiji when he was working on the Bounty. I've got the original [script], copy number three, which he sent me.[80] We went driving round the island looking at the sights together. Then he invited me to Auckland, because we've got a big Ryder-Cheshire set-up there, but I spent the first two days with him.

"I think he had real affection for me. I liked his penetrating mind. He was so interested in everything. Whenever I saw him he'd either been to the National Portrait Gallery or he got biographies of great people... he had a very enquiring mind. I found him very easy to talk to. Some people you don't; you wonder what to talk about.

"I think he had been a pacifist in the war. But he wasn't a pacifist when I knew him. I talked to him about the atomic bomb and the deterrents - the fact that you have men of violence and therefore you must have a police force within the country and your security forces between nations to contain violence. The absence of war is not peace, it's an immense blessing, but without security forces you can't be sure that you won't be attacked. I think he agreed with that. I wrote a book on the fortieth anniversary of the dropping of the atomic bomb -

The Light of Many Suns - and I know he read that two or three times.

"I went through a period when I was making amateur films, because every time I tried to get a documentary made, the film-makers had their own ideas of what they wanted and I never got what I wanted. So I embarked on some films and he helped me financially with them. Then I did a series of video interviews and he very kindly came to watch them going on at the studio, and directed three of them.[81]

"I'll never forget the arguments he had with the video boys because they wanted to do the cuts as we were going along. He said, 'Nothing doing, you can't get a proper cut that way. Record it, then we'll go back through it and decide what we want to edit and how we'll do it.' They didn't like that, but in the end they agreed he was right. This was after RYAN'S DAUGHTER, where they had him up at the Algonquin and gave him a real going for, and that drove him into retirement in a way. After he had done the third film, he turned to me and said, 'Thank you, Leonard, for bringing me back to the sweet smell of the studio.'

"I noticed on the set that he was a very strict disciplinarian. Everything had to be right. We used to discuss this, because I said that in the war if there was a man who wasn't doing his job properly, I had no hesitation about removing him because nothing mattered except winning the war. I didn't care who it was. And he said, 'Same with me on a film. I've got a plumb line and the good of the film is the plumb line. And if people don't fit, they go.'

"There was a little incident when he was producing one of the video films. An assistant cameraman dropped something while the camera was rolling and David turned to him and said, 'That was a very poor show.' The man was really upset. He'd never been spoken to like that before; he belonged to a Methodist communications centre, they made religious films. It showed me that for David, once he was on the job, everything had to be right. But in his private life he'd find that very difficult to do.

"He was extremely generous. When he directed those three films, he said, 'How much has this cost, Leonard?' I said, 'In the region of six thousand pounds.' Immediately he paid for it.

"And when I needed some money for a film on a leprosy boy that I was making, I wrote to him. Was there any possibility of his signing a letter for me to a funding agency? He rang up my secretary and said it would be much easier for him just to give her the money. I couldn't believe it. I mean, it was three or four thousand pounds in the early sixties and for me that was huge money.

"I'd never meet him without a discussion on religion. I think he reacted against his Quaker upbringing. He quite often used to tell me how protected he was and how strict they were as regards the facts of life. All that went out of the window.

"But he had a clear starting point. 'If anybody tries to tell me that a Rolls-Royce has not been made by anybody, it's just come about by chance, I'd think he's mad. But what is it that's made it,' - using it as an analogy to the creation - 'Who knows? Perhaps an electrical force or something.'

"I said, 'David, an electrical force hasn't got a brain. For the creation to be brought into being presupposes an unbelievable mind and power.'

"And then he shifted from that. 'Yes, I think God must have created everything but now he's abandoned it. Like an artist who makes a beautiful painting and then just leaves it.'

"I said, 'David, that won't stand because the survival of that painting presupposes an environment to keep it in and the proper temperature and climate and people to look after it. Just thrown out into space it wouldn't survive.'

"That's about as far as we got before he died. You never got away with anything with David. If there was anything false, anything put on, he'd immediately detect it and show you that he knew it. I liked that.

"I genuinely think he was a searcher for truth. The disappointment I shall never get over was that I didn't see him more often in that last period in hospital. I thought he was in France. And when I did go he was very pleased."

When David was with Cheshire, he had to overcome his horror of illness and never forgot a visit to one of the Cheshire Homes when he saw the rapport between his friend and an ailing woman.[82] And when David was dying, he recalled that visit again.

"He said, 'Leonard, will you do me a favour? When we were together in that home, you put your hand on that lady's forehead. Would you mind putting your hand on mine?' So I put my hand on his forehead but I didn't know quite how long to keep it there. So I left it until he said, 'Thank you.'"[83]

Leonard Cheshire did not live much longer than David. Shortly before he died, I received a note from him:

"What I forgot to say was that he was continually wanting to give me gifts of one kind or another. Whenever possible I stopped him, but he still used to give me a lot."[84]

The Memorial Service was held on 3 October 1991, at St Paul's Cathedral, where David had filmed Lawrence's own Memorial Service. The event was stage-managed by Sandra and Sarah, and David would have been proud of them. The Royal Philharmonic Orchestra was assembled in strength and virtually all the surviving figures of David's life and career attended. Even Alec Guinness, who had said he would not attend, slipped inside incognito.

In his address, the Dean of St Paul's referred to the scene in LAWRENCE, set in the crypt below: "Anthony Quayle says, 'He was the most extraordinary man I ever knew.' Then an actor, bearing a striking resemblance to my late predecessor

Dean Inge, says, 'But did he deserve a place, in here?' It could be David Lean writing about himself."

John Mills read the opening of GREAT EXPECTATIONS, John Box delivered a moving tribute and Maurice Jarre conducted the orchestra in themes from David's films. Robert Bolt, assisted to the microphone by Sarah Miles, succeeded in making a short speech, and Sarah Miles herself spoke the ward-room address from IN WHICH WE SERVE. Tom Courtenay read a passage from Pasternak's *Doctor Zhivago* and Omar Sharif read a passage from *Seven Pillars of Wisdom*. Peter O'Toole read John Donne's sonnet, "Death Be Not Proud".

A surprising moment came when a dark, bearded young man strode to the lectern and introduced himself as George Correface. He read the opening and closing sections of the script for NOSTROMO.

Melvyn Bragg delivered an address which embraced David's entire career, not omitting the friction that sometimes occurred on the set. Bragg said that David's favourite word was "Cut" and characterised him as a Victorian explorer: "In the jungle of the set the shooting would begin. No prisoners taken... He was meticulously inflexible... No one knew as much about the film as he did and you deviated at your peril. 'Actors,' he said almost cheerfully, 'hate me.' All the actors here would contradict that but several, I suspect, and many others from the crew, would permit themselves a quiet little nod. They know what he meant."

I could not help musing on the fact that this man who had started life against the stark background of a Quaker Meeting House - *sans* music, colour and ornamentation - had ended it in St Paul's Cathedral with two thousand people, a massive orchestra and the architecture of Sir Christopher Wren. He would have been very surprised and, as the Dean said, not a little amused.

How would he have directed it, if he were putting his life on film? I imagine he would have started in extreme long shot and craned slowly over the crowd towards the frail figure of Isabel. She was the only one there who had known him when the idea of such an event was too preposterous to imagine. David would have laid her voice over the scene, like Celia Johnson in BRIEF ENCOUNTER. She would have been just as reticent and perhaps just as moving, for she loved David and was deeply hurt by his departure. And he probably felt a greater sense of guilt about her and their son than about anyone else.

A final *coup de cinéma* was the band of the Blues and Royals, playing "Colonel Bogey". The St Paul's authorities, only too aware of the unofficial lyrics, would not permit it to be played inside, so Sandra had the brainwave of stationing them on the steps. When I saw them in their glistening helmets, looking for all the world like David's "Buckingham Palace swagger" come to life, it brought tears to my eyes.

It was a terrible shame he had to miss it...

David told me one day at Narrow Street, "The fascinating thing about my job is the tremendous power my early experiences have had on me. Everything that I've been talking about to you has affected my work. It has a lot to do with secrets. Secrets are what you confide to people in the dark. I think one of the things we've lost in the cinema is intimacy. Now you see appalling things happening and high excitement, but you rarely get right into people. The old films we used to go to had a tremendous intimacy about them, the good ones. You were really given a peep into private things."

As I packed up my tape recorder, he came out with one of those disarmingly modest remarks that made me so fond of him.

"You will say if this turns out to be absolute balls?"[85]

In the fifties, David copied out from Louis Fischer's book on Gandhi the Mahatma's comment on death:

"This is such a sweet sleep that the body has not to awake again, and the dead load of memory is thrown overboard. So far as I know, happily there is no meeting in the beyond as we have it today. When the isolated drops melt, they share the majesty of the ocean to which they belong. In isolation they die but to meet the ocean again."[86]

CUT

DAVID LEAN *A Biography*

SOURCES FOR PHOTOGRAPHS AND DESIGNS

Front cover: David Lean Collection
Back cover: Sandy Lean
Frontispiece: Cornel Lucas
End papers: David Lean Collection

Plate Section

Academy of Motion Picture Arts & Sciences 26
British Film Institute Stills, Posters and Designs 1, 2, 6,
     7, 9, 11, 12, 13, 14, 15, 16, 17, 50, 51, 53, 54
John Box 8
Joel Finler 4, 45
Ron Grant Archive 24
David Lean Collection 10, 13, 28, 33, 34, 35, 36, 37,
     38, 39, 40, 41, 43, 44, 46, 47, 52, 55, 57, 58
Kobal Collection 25, 27, 29, 30, 31, 32, 42, 56
Roy Stevens 5, 48, 49
Adrian Turner 18, 19, 20, 21, 22, 23
Tim Unsworth 3

Text Illustrations

Barbara Beale 441, 495, 514, 522, 529, 531, 738
Ken Bray 557
British Film Institute Stills, Posters and Designs 55, 76,
     80, 83, 92, 95, 102, 104, 120, 124, 139, 142, 148,
     163, 166, 174, 176, 179, 184, 186, 189, 197, 204,
     232, 233, 242, 246, 255, 260, 261, 268, 274, 283,
     286, 291, 299, 303, 319, 322, 340, 434, 445, 446,
     460, 468, 479, 511, 512, 630, 653, 660, 672, 674,
     680
Vera Campbell 137
John and Catrine Clay 97

Croydon Public Libraries 22, 27
William K. Everson 524
Joel Finler 246, 271
Ron Grant Archive 306
Guy Green 236
David Lean Collection 127, 170, 207, 218, 224, 229,
     234, 237, 265, 273, 278, 293, 361, 368, 379, 382,
     389, 413, 430, 449, 465, 533, 551, 590, 594, 598,
     611, 619, 624, 664, 667, 669, 670, 671, 682, 691,
     723, 751
Doreen Lean 74, 597, 598
Isabel Lean 68, 72
Peter Lean 37, 39, 56, 60, 61, 193, 194, 371, 395, 566,
     579
Sandra Lean 700
Sara Lean 5, 11, 14, 34, 35, 37, 46, 58
Peter Miller 159
National Maritime Museum 7
Peter Newbrook 367
Photofest 238
Photoplay 42
Michael Santoro 117
Norman Spencer 210, 336
Roy Stevens 454, 500, 503, 527, 576
Sheila and Hilary Tangye 400
David Tree 128
Kay Walsh 107

DAVID LEAN *A Biography*

FILMOGRAPHY

DAVID LEAN
A CONDENSED FILMOGRAPHY

Films Edited by David Lean:
(some without credit)

1930
THE NIGHT PORTER
Director Sewell Collins
Cast: Donald Calthrop, Trilby Clark

1931
THESE CHARMING PEOPLE
Director Louis Mercanton
Cast: Cyril Maude, Godfrey Tearle, Ann Todd

1932
INSULT
Director Harry Lachman
Cast: John Gielgud, Hugh Williams

1933
MONEY FOR SPEED
Director Bernard Vorhaus
Cast: John Loder, Ida Lupino

MATINEE IDOL
Director George King
Cast: Camilla Horn, Miles Mander

THE GHOST CAMERA
Director Bernard Vorhaus
Cast: Henry Kendall, Ida Lupino

TIGER BAY
Director J. Elder Wills
Co-editor: Ian Thomson
Cast: Anna May Wong, Henry Victor

SONG OF THE PLOUGH
Director John Baxter
Cast: Stewart Rome, Rosalinde Fuller

1934
DANGEROUS GROUND
Director Norman Walker

Cast: Malcolm Keen, Joyce Kennedy
SECRET OF THE LOCH
Director Milton Rosmer
Cast: Seymour Hicks, Nancy O'Neill

JAVA HEAD
Director J. Walter Ruben
Cast: John Loder, Anna May Wong

1935
ESCAPE ME NEVER
Director Paul Czinner
Cast: Elisabeth Bergner, Hugh Sinclair

TURN OF THE TIDE
Director Norman Walker
Cast: Niall McGinnis, Geraldine Fitzgerald

1936
BALL AT THE SAVOY
Director Victor Hanbury
Cast: Conrad Nagel, Marta Labarr

AS YOU LIKE IT
Director Paul Czinner
Cast: Elisabeth Bergner, Laurence Olivier

1937
DREAMING LIPS
Director Paul Czinner
Cast: Elisabeth Bergner, Raymond Massey

THE LAST ADVENTURERS
Director Roy Kellino
Cast: Niall McGinnis, Kay Walsh

1938
PYGMALION
Director Anthony Asquith
Cast: Wendy Hiller, Leslie Howard

1939
SPIES IN THE AIR
Director David MacDonald
Cast: Barry K. Barnes, Joan Marion

FRENCH WITHOUT TEARS
Director Anthony Asquith
Cast: Ray Milland, Ellen Drew

1940
SPY FOR A DAY
Director Mario Zampi
Cast: Duggie Wakefield, Paddy Browne

1941
MAJOR BARBARA
Director Gabriel Pascal
Cast: Rex Harrison, Wendy Hiller

49TH PARALLEL
Director Michael Powell
Cast: Leslie Howard, Eric Portman, Laurence Olivier

1942
ONE OF OUR AIRCRAFT IS MISSING
Director Michael Powell
Cast: Eric Portman, Hugh Williams

Films Directed by David Lean

1942
IN WHICH WE SERVE
Two Cities. Directors Noël Coward and David Lean.
Associate Producer Anthony Havelock-Allan; Story Noël
Coward; Photography Ronald Neame; Editors Thelma
Myers and Jack Harris; Art Director David Rawnsley.
Cast: Noël Coward, Bernard Miles, John Mills, Celia
Johnson, Kay Walsh, Richard Attenborough.

1944
THIS HAPPY BREED
Two Cities. Producer Noël Coward; In charge of
production Anthony Havelock-Allan; Screenplay Noël
Coward, based on his own play; Adaptation David Lean,
Anthony Havelock-Allan, Ronald Neame; Photography
(Technicolor) Ronald Neame; Editor Jack Harris; Art
Director CP Norman. Cast: Robert Newton, Celia
Johnson, John Mills, Kay Walsh, Stanley Holloway.

1945
BLITHE SPIRIT
Cineguild-Two Cities. Producer Anthony Havelock-
Allan; Screenplay Noël Coward, based on his play;
Adaptation David Lean, Ronald Neame, Anthony
Havelock-Allan; Photography (Technicolor) Ronald
Neame; Editor Jack Harris; Art Director CP Norman;
Costumes Rahvia; Music Richard Addinsell. Cast: Rex
Harrison, Constance Cummings, Kay Hammond,
Margaret Rutherford, Joyce Carey.

1945
BRIEF ENCOUNTER
Rank-Cineguild. Producer Anthony Havelock-Allan;

Screenplay David Lean, Anthony Havelock-Allan, Ronald
Neame, based on the play 'Still Life' by Noël Coward;
Photography Robert Krasker; Editor Jack Harris; Art
Director LP Williams; Music Sergei Rachmaninov. Cast:
Celia Johnson, Trevor Howard, Cyril Raymond, Stanley
Holloway, Joyce Carey.

1946
GREAT EXPECTATIONS
Rank-Cineguild. Producer Ronald Neame. Screenplay
David Lean, Ronald Neame, Anthony Havelock-Allan,
Kay Walsh, Cecil McGivern, based on the novel by
Charles Dickens; Photography Guy Green; Editor Jack
Harris; Production Designer John Bryan; Costumes
Sophie Harris and Margaret Furse; Music Walter Goehr.
Cast: John Mills, Valerie Hobson, Bernard Miles, Francis
L Sullivan, Finlay Currie, Martita Hunt, Alec Guinness.

1948
OLIVER TWIST
Rank-Cineguild. Producer Ronald Neame. Screenplay
David Lean, Stanley Haynes, based on the novel by Charles
Dickens; Photography Guy Green; Editor Jack Harris; Sets
John Bryan; Costumes Margaret Furse. Music Sir Arnold
Bax. Cast: Robert Newton, Alec Guinness, Kay Walsh,
Francis L Sullivan, John Howard Davies.

1949
THE PASSIONATE FRIENDS
(US: One Woman's Story)
Rank-Cineguild. Producer Ronald Neame. Screenplay
Eric Ambler, based on the novel by H.G. Wells;
Photography Guy Green; Editors Jack Harris, Geoffrey
Foot; Production Designer John Bryan; Costumes
Margaret Furse; Music Richard Addinsell. Cast: Ann
Todd, Claude Rains, Trevor Howard, Isabel Dean, Betty
Ann Davies.

1950
MADELEINE
Rank-Cineguild. Producer Stanley Haynes. Screenplay
Stanley Haynes, Nicholas Phipps. Photography Guy
Green; Editor Geoffrey Foot; Sets John Bryan;
Costumes Margaret Furse; Music William Alwyn. Cast:
Ann Todd, Ivan Desny, Norman Wooland, Leslie Banks.

1952
THE SOUND BARRIER
(US: BREAKING THROUGH THE SOUND BARRIER)
London Films. Producer David Lean. Screenplay
Terence Rattigan; Photography Jack Hildyard; Editor
Geoffrey Foot; Set Design Vincent Korda; Music Malcolm
Arnold. Cast: Ralph Richardson, Ann Todd, Nigel
Patrick, John Justin, Dinah Sheridan.

1954
HOBSON'S CHOICE
London Films. Producer David Lean. Screenplay David

Lean, Norman Spencer, Wynyard Browne, based on the play by Harold Brighouse; Photography Jack Hildyard; Editor Peter Taylor; Art Director Wilfred Shingleton; Costumes John Armstrong; Music Malcolm Arnold. Cast: Charles Laughton, John Mills, Brenda de Banzie, Daphne Anderson, Joseph Tomelty.

1955
SUMMERTIME
(GB: Summer Madness) London Films in association with Ilya Lopert. Producer Ilya Lopert. Screenplay H.E. Bates, David Lean, based on the play *'The Time of the Cuckoo'* by Arthur Laurents; Photography (Technicolor) Jack Hildyard; Production Designer Vincent Korda; Editor Peter Taylor; Music Alessandro Cicognini. Cast: Katharine Hepburn, Rossano Brazzi, Isa Miranda, Darren McGavin.

1957
THE BRIDGE ON THE RIVER KWAI
Columbia-Horizon. Producer Sam Spiegel. Screenplay (credited to Pierre Boulle) Michael Wilson, Carl Foreman, based on the novel by Pierre Boulle; Photography (CinemaScope, Technicolor) Jack Hildyard; Editor Peter Taylor; Art Director Donald M. Ashton; Music Malcolm Arnold. Cast: William Holden, Jack Hawkins, Alec Guinness, Sessue Hayakawa, James Donald.

1962
LAWRENCE OF ARABIA
Columbia-Horizon. Producer Sam Spiegel. Screenplay Robert Bolt; Photography (Super Panavision 70, Technicolor) FA Young; Editor Anne V. Coates; Production Designer John Box; Costumes Phyllis Dalton;

Music Maurice Jarre. Cast: Peter O'Toole, Alec Guinness, Anthony Quinn, Omar Sharif, Jack Hawkins, Claude Rains, Arthur Kennedy, Anthony Quayle.

1965
DOCTOR ZHIVAGO
MGM. Producer Carlo Ponti. Screenplay Robert Bolt, based on the novel by Boris Pasternak; Photography (Panavision, Metrocolor) Freddie Young; Editor Norman Savage; Production Designer John Box; Costumes Phyllis Dalton; Music Maurice Jarre. Cast: Omar Sharif, Julie Christie, Geraldine Chaplin, Tom Courtenay, Rod Steiger, Alec Guinness, Ralph Richardson, Rita Tushingham.

1970
RYAN'S DAUGHTER
MGM - Faraway. Producer Anthony Havelock-Allan. Screenplay Robert Bolt. Photography (Super Panavision, Metrocolor) Freddie Young; Editor Norman Savage; Production Designer Stephen Grimes; Costumes Jocelyn Rickards; Music Maurice Jarre. Cast: Sarah Miles, Robert Mitchum, Trevor Howard, John Mills Christopher Jones, Leo McKern.

1984
A PASSAGE TO INDIA
Thorn EMI-Columbia-HBO.
Producers John Brabourne, Richard Goodwin. Screenplay David Lean, based on the novel by E.M. Forster; Photography (Technicolor) Ernest Day; Editor David Lean; Production Designer John Box; Costumes Judy Moorcroft; Music Maurice Jarre. Cast: Judy Davis, Peggy Ashcroft, Victor Banerjee, Alec Guinness, James Fox, Nigel Havers.

BIBLIOGRAPHY

Aldgate, Tony, and Richards, Jeffrey. *Britain Can Take It* (Blackwell, Oxford, 1986).

Allen, Louis. *Burma: The Longest War* (J.M. Dent and Sons, London, 1984).

Ambler, Eric. *Here Lies Eric Ambler* (Weidenfeld and Nicolson, London, 1985).

American Film Institute, The Eighteenth Annual AFI Life Achievement Awards, 8 March 1990 (Tribute Book published by American Film magazine, John Johns and Associates).

AMPAS, *The White Book.*

Anderegg, Michael A. *David Lean* (Boston: Twayne, 1984).

Arroy, Jean. *En Tournant Napoleon avec Abel Gance* (Editions la Renaissance du Livre, Paris, 1927).

Attenborough, Richard. *In Search of Gandhi* (Bodley Head, London, 1982).

Bach, Steven. *Final Cut* (Faber and Faber, London, 1985).

Barrow, Kenneth. *Mr Chips: The Life of Robert Donat* (Methuen, London, 1945).

Bart, Peter. *Fade Out* (Simon and Schuster, New York, 1990).

Bates, H.E. *The Sleepless Moon* (Michael Joseph, London, 1956).

— *The Cruise of the Breadwinner* (Michael Joseph, London, 1946).

— *Fair Stood the Wind for France* (Book Society and Michael Joseph, London, 1944).

Bergman, Ingrid, with Burgess, Allan. *My Story* (Michael Joseph, London, 1980).

Berwick Sayers, WC (ed). *Croydon - The Official Guide* (Abbey Publicity Service, Croydon, 1930).

Best, Keith. *Best Endeavours* (Keith Best, 1992).

Billington, Michael. *Peggy Ashcroft* (John Murray, London, 1988).

Bishop, James. *Social History of the First World War* (Angus & Robertson, London, 1982).

Bogarde, Dirk. *Snakes and Ladders* (Chatto and Windus, London, 1978).

Bolt, Robert. *Doctor Zhivago: The Screenplay* (Collins and Harvill Press, 1965).

Boorman, John, and Donohue, Walter (eds). *Projections 1* (Faber and Faber, 1992).

Blakeston, Oswell (ed). *Working for the Films* (Focal Press, London, 1947).

Boulle, Pierre, *The Source of the River Kwai* (Secker and Warburg, London, 1967).

Boulton, David. *Objection Over-ruled* (MacGibbon and Kee, London, 1967).

Brunel, Adrian. *Nice Work* (Forbes-Robertson, London, 1949).

Budd, Mike (ed). *The Cabinet of Dr. Caligari* (Rutgers University Press, New Brunswick, 1990).

Calder, Robert. *The Life of Somerset Maugham* (Mandarin, London, 1990).

Callan, Michael Feeney. *Julie Christie* (W.H. Allen, London, 1984).

Callow, Simon. *Charles Laughton - A Difficult Actor* (Methuen, London, 1987).

Castelli, Louis P. and Cleeland, Caryn Lynn. *David Lean, A Guide to References and Resources* (G.K. Hall and Co, Boston, 1980).

Christian Discipline of the Society of Friends, Vol 1: Doctrine and Practice; Vol 2: Church Government (Headley Brothers, London, 1906).

Close Up (1927-1932).

Cole, Hugo. *Malcolm Arnold, An Introduction to His Music* (Faber Music, London, 1989).

Conrad, Joseph. *Nostromo* (Penguin, reprinted 1990).

Coward, Noël, *This Happy Breed, A Play in Three Acts* (Samuel French, London, 1945).

Croydon Advertiser

Croydon Directory 1915-1934, Croydon Corporation.

Croydon Times

Curran, James and Porter, Vincent (eds). *British Cinema History* (Weidenfeld and Nicolson, London, 1983).

Darlow, Michael and Hodson, Gillian. *Terence Rattigan* (Quartet Books, London, 1979).

Dawes, Edwin A. *The Great Illusionists* (Chartwell Books Inc, New York, 1979).

Deans, Marjorie. *Meeting at the Sphinx* (McDonald, London, 1945).

Dickens, Charles. *The Adventures of Oliver Twist* (Chapman and Hall, London, 1850).

— *Great Expectations.*

Douglas, Kirk. *The Ragman's Son* (Simon and Schuster, New York, 1988).

Eells, George. *Robert Mitchum* (Robson Books, London, 1984).

Eisenschitz, Bernard. *Nicholas Ray - An American Journey* (Faber and Faber, London, 1993).

Eliade, Mircea (ed). *The Encyclopedia of Religion*, Vol. 12, (Macmillan, New York, 1987).

Encyclopedia Britannica (15th edition, 1989).

Epstein, Jerry. *Remembering Charlie* (Bloomsbury, London, 1988).

Eyles, Allen. *Rex Harrison* (W.H. Allen, London, 1985).

Eyles, Allen and Skone, Keith. *The Cinemas of Croydon* (Keystone Publication Co, Sutton, 1989)

— *London's West End Cinemas* (Keystone Publications Co, Sutton, 1989).

Falk, Quentin. *Anthony Hopkins: Too Good to Waste* (Columbus Books, London, 1989).

Fine, Marshall. *Bloody Sam: The Life and Films of Sam Peckinpah* (Donald Fine, New York, 1991).

Flaubert, Gustave. *Madame Bovary* (Penguin, London, 1979).

Fleming, Kate. *Celia Johnson* (Weidenfeld and Nicolson, London, 1991).

Foot, Sir Hugh. *A Start in Freedom* (Hodder and Stoughton, London, 1964).

Francis, Anne. *Julian Wintle, A Memoir* (Dukewood, London, 1986).

Freedland, Michael. *Peter O'Toole* (W.H. Allen, London, 1983).

Gent, John B. *Edwardian Croydon Illustrated* (Croydon Natural History and Scientific Society, Southern Publishing Co, 1981).

Gent, John B. *Croydon Between the Wars* (Croydon Natural History and Scientific Society, 1987).

Graham, John W. *Conscription and Conscience* (Allen and Unwin, London, 1922).

Grantley, Lord (Richard Norton) and Wood, Mary and Alan (eds). *Silver Spoon* (Hutchinson, London, 1954).

Graves, Robert. *Goodbye to All That* (Jonathan Cape, London, 1929).

Guinness, Alec. *Blessings in Disguise* (Hamish Hamilton, London, 1985).

Hall, Peter. *Making an Exhibition of Myself* (Sinclair-Stevenson, London, 1993).

Harrison, Rex. *Rex, An Autobiography* (Macmillan, London, 1974).

Hawkins, Jack. *Anything for a Quiet Life* (Elm Tree Books, London, 1973).

Hepburn, Katharine. *Stories of My Life* (Viking, New York, 1959).

Higham, Charles. *Charles Laughton* (W.H. Allen, London, 1976).

Hirschhorn, Clive. *The Films of James Mason* (LSP Books, London, 1975).

Holroyd, Michael. *Bernard Shaw, Vol. III 1918-1950 The Lure of Fantasy* (Chatto and Windus, London, 1991).

Hough, Richard. *Captain Bligh and Mr Christian* (Hutchinson, London, 1972).

Howard, Leslie Ruth. *A Quite Remarkable Father* (Longman's, London, 1960).

Huntley, John. *Railways on the Screen* (Ian Allan, Shepperton, 1993).

— *British Film Music* (Skelton Robinson, 1947).

Huntley, John and Manvell, Roger. *Technique of Film Music* (Focal Press, 1957).

Huston, John. *An Open Book* (Alfred A. Knopf, New York, 1980).

Hyde, H. Montgomery. *Solitary in the Ranks* (Constable, London, 1977).

Irwin, Margaret. *The Gay Galliard* (Chatto and Windus, London, 1943).

Jacobson, Artie, and Atkins, Irene Kahn. *Artie Jacobson* (Directors Guild of America and Scarecrow Press, New Jersey, 1991).

Kent, Howard. *Single Bed for Three* (Hutchinson, London, 1963).

Knight, Vivienne. *Trevor Howard* (Beaufort Books, New York, 1986).

Knightley, Philip and Simpson, Colin. *The Secret Lives of Lawrence of Arabia* (Nelson and Sons, London, 1969).

Korda, Michael. *Charmed Lives* (Random House, New York, 1979).

Kulik, Karol. *Alexander Korda, The Man Who Could Work Miracles* (W.H. Allen, London, 1975).

Lawrence, A.W. (ed). *T.E. Lawrence and His Friends* (Jonathan Cape, London, 1937).

Lawrence, T.E. *Seven Pillars of Wisdom* (Jonathan Cape, London, 1940 edition).

Lean, Tangye. *Voices in the Darkness* (Martin Secker and Warburg, London, 1943).

Lesley, Cole, Payn, Graham and Morley, Sheridan. *Noël Coward and His Friends* (Weidenfeld and Nicolson, London, 1979).

Loder, John. *Hollywood Hussar* (Howard Baker, London, 1977).

Low, Rachael. *The History of British Film 1918-1929* (George Allen and Unwin, London, 1971).

— *Film Making in 1930s Britain* (George Allen and Unwin, 1985).

Macdonald, Kevin. *Emeric Pressburger* (Faber, London, 1994).

Madsen, Axel. *William Wyler* (Thomas Crowell Co, New York, 1973).

Manvell, Roger and Neilson-Baxter, R.K. *The Cinema* (Pelican, 1952).

Marshall Cavendish Encyclopedia of the First World War I, Vol 2, 1914-15 (Marshall Cavendish, New York, 1984).

Maugham, W. Somerset. *The Summing Up* (Heinemann, 1938/Penguin 1973).

Mayer, J.P. *Sociology of Film* (Faber and Faber, London, 1946).

McFarlane, Brian (ed). *Sixty Voices* (BFI Publishing, London, 1992).

McGilligan, Patrick. *George Cukor - A Double Life* (St Martin's Press, New York, 1991).

Mills, John. *Up in the Clouds, Gentlemen, Please* (Ticknor and Fields, 1981).

Minney, R.J. *Puffin Asquith* (Leslie Frewin, London, 1973).

Moore, Alderman H. Keatley. *Croydon and the Great War* (Corporation of Croydon, 1920).

Moorehead, Alan. *The Fatal Impact* (Hamish Hamilton, London, 1966).

Moorehead, Caroline. *Sidney Bernstein, A Biography* (Jonathan Cape, London, 1984).

Mordha, Micheal de. *An Rialtas Ab Fhearr!* (Coisceim, Dublin, 1993) (Ryan's Daughter, Irish edition).

More, Kenneth. *More or Less* (Hodder and Stoughton, London, 1978).

Morley, Robert, and Stokes, Sewell. *Responsible Gentleman* (Heinemann, London, 1966).

Morley, Sheridan. *A Talent to Amuse* (Heinemann, London, 1986).

— *Robert, My Father* (Weidenfeld and Nicolson, London, 1993).

Morley, Sheridan and Payn, Graham (eds). *The Noël Coward Diaries* (London, 1982).

Morris, L. Robert and Raskin, Lawrence. *Lawrence of Arabia: The 30th Anniversary Pictorial History* (Doubleday, New York, 1992).

Nutting, Anthony. *Lawrence of Arabia: The Man and the Motive* (Hollis and Carter, London, 1961).

O'Toole, Peter. *Loitering with Intent* (Macmillan, London, 1992).

Parker, J. Francis. *Some Notes on the Tangye Family* (The Journal Press of Evesham, c1958).

Parrish, Robert. *Hollywood Doesn't Live Here Anymore* (Little, Brown and Co, New York, 1988).

Pascal, Valerie. *The Disciple and His Devil* (Michael Joseph, London, 1970).

Pasternak, Boris. *Doctor Zhivago* (Collins and Harvill Press, London, 1958).

Patch, Blanche. *Thirty Years with G.B.S.* (Victor Gollancz, London, 1951).

Perry, George. *The Great British Picture Show* (Little, Brown, Boston, 1985).

— *Movies from the Mansion* (Elm Tree Books, London, 1983).

Pickard, Roy. *The Award Movies - An A-Z Guide* (Frederick Muller, London, 1980).

Poolman, Kenneth. *Zeppelins Over England* (White Lion Publishers, London and New York, 1960).

Powell, Michael. Vol I: *A Life in the Movies* (Heinemann, London, 1986).

— Vol II: *Million Dollar Movie* (Heinemann, London, 1992).

Pratley, Gerald. *The Cinema of David Lean* (A.S. Barnes, New York, 1974).

Punshon, John. *Portrait in Grey, A Short History of the Quakers* (Quaker House Service, London, 1984).

Quinlan, David. *British Sound Films* (B.T. Batsford, 1984).

Ramsey, Winston (ed). *The Blitz - Then and Now* (After the Battle, 1988).

Rangoonwalla, Firoze. *A Pictorial History of Indian Cinema* (Hamlyn, London, 1979).

Reisz, Karel and Millar, Gavin. *The Technique of Film Editing* (Focal Press, London, 1953/1968).

Roberts, Jerry. *Robert Mitchum - A Bio-Bibliography* (Greenwood Press, 1992).

Sharif, Omar with Guinchard, Marie-Thérèse. *The Eternal Male* (Doubleday, New York, 1977).

Shaw, Bernard. *Major Barbara* (Constable, London, 1907).

Sieff, Marcus, *Don't Ask the Price* (Weidenfeld and Nicolson, London, 1986).

Silver, Alain and Ursini, James. *David Lean and His Films* (Leslie Frewin, London, 1974).

— *David Lean and His Films* (rev. ed. Silman James Press, Hollywood, 1991).

Silverman, Stephen. *David Lean* (Andre Deutsch, 1989)

Simmons, Dawn Langley. *Margaret Rutherford, A Blithe Spirit* (Arthur Barker, London, 1983).

Sinclair, Andrew. *Spiegel: The Man Behind the Pictures* (Weidenfeld and Nicholson, London, 1987).

Singer, Kurt. *The Charles Laughton Story* (Robert Hale, London, 1954).

Spoto, Donald. *The Life of Alfred Hitchcock* (Collins, London, 1983).

Stevenson, John. *British Society 1914-1945* (Pelican, London, 1984).

Stewart, John. *To the River Kwai* (Bloomsbury, London, 1988).

Strasberg, Susan. *Bitter Sweet* (Academic Press, Toronto, 1980).

Tangye, Nigel. *Facing the Sea* (William Kimber, London, 1974).

— (ed). *The Air is Our Concern: A Critical Study of England's Future in Aviation* (Methuen and Co., London, 1935).

Thomas, Lowell. *With Lawrence in Arabia* (Hutchinson and Co, London, 1925).

Thorpe, Frances, Pronay, Nicholas and Coultass, Clive. *British Official Films in the Second World War* (Clio Press, 1980).

Todd, Ann. *The Eighth Veil* (Putnam's Sons, New York, 1981).

Tracey, Michael. *A Variety of Lives, a Biography of Hugh Greene* (Bodley Head, London, 1983).

Tree, David. *Pig in the Middle* (Michael Joseph, London, 1966).

Turner, Adrian. *The Making of David Lean's Lawrence of Arabia* (Dragon's World, London, 1994).

Tynan, Kathleen (ed). *The Letters of Kenneth Tynan* (Weidenfeld, London, 1994).

Villa, Brian Loring. *Unauthorized Action; Mountbatten and the Dieppe Raid* (OUP, Toronto, 1989).

Walker, Alexander. *It's Only a Movie, Ingrid* (Headline, London, 1988).

— *Rex Harrison* (Weidenfeld and Nicolson, 1992).

Wallis, Isaac Henry. *Frederick Andrews of Ackworth* (Longmans, Green and Co, London, 1924).

Walmsley, Leo. *So Many Loves* (The Reprint Society, London 1945).

Walton, Susanna. *William Walton Behind the Facade* (OUP, Oxford, 1988).

Wapshott, Nicholas. *Carol Reed* (Chatto and Windus, London, 1987).

—— *Peter O'Toole* (New English Library, 1983).

Wells, H.G. *The Passionate Friends* (Macmillan, London, 1913).

West, Anthony. *Aspects of a Life* (Hutchinson, London, 1984).

Wood, Alan. *Mr Rank* (Hodder and Stoughton, London 1952).

Wood, Linda. *British Films, 1927-39* (BFI Library Services, London 1986).

—— *The Commercial Imperative in the British Film Industry: Maurice Elvey, a Case Study* (British Film Institute, 1987).

Worrell, Denise. *Icons - Intimate Portraits* (Atlantic Monthly Press, New York, 1989).

Wright, Basil. *The Long View* (Secker and Warburg, London, 1974).

Wyand, Paul. *Useless If Delayed* (George Harrap, London, 1959).

Yeager, Chuck and Janos, Leo. *Yeager* (Century Hutchinson, London, 1986).

Young, Freddie. *Autobiography* (unpublished manuscript).

Ziegler, Philip. *Mountbatten* (Collins, London, 1985).

SOURCE NOTES

Where a source note refers to an interview conducted by the author, the interviewee's name is followed by the page number from the transcript of that interview. If the reference comes from a book then the title of the book is given, sometimes in abbreviated form (full references can be found in the Bibliography). In later chapters, references to some letters are followed by the initials "UoR". This stands for the University of Reading, to which Barbara Cole donated her correspondence with David Lean. The initials "TR" stand for Tony Reeves, David Lean's lawyer, who provided many letters I would not otherwise have seen.

1: A Child of Light

1   Philip Ziegler, *Mountbatten*, p.25.
2   Institute of Chartered Accountants records.
3   The visitors' book and its contents were described in an article on David Lean in the magazine of Leighton Park School.
4   *The Friend*, 3 April 1908, p.224.
5   For a full account of the launching see Parker, p.14
6   Denise Worrell, *Icons - Intimate Portraits* p.159.
7   *The Friend*, 15 October 1920, p.660.
8   Ann Todd to author / Nigel Tangye to Gerald McKnight.
9   One relative who was kind to the family was Harry, Reginald's first cousin. When Sheila qualified and lived in Birmingham during the war, he invited her to dinner every week. A young man called Christopher Tangye was often present - he was the man who designed the hydraulic machinery for P.L.U.T.O (Pipe Line Under The Ocean), the fuel system used for D-Day. Christopher married into the Cadbury family, the influential Quaker family which owned the *News Chronicle* where Edward had worked.
10 *Encyclopedia of Religion*, p.130.
11 John Punshon, *Portrait in Grey* p.51.
12 Ibid, pp.1,131.
13 DL to Denise Worrell, op. cit., p.162.
14 Bernard Ellis, *The Friend*, 21 May 1915, p.393.
15 Bernard Ellis, *The Friend*, 21 November 1915, p.873a.
16 *The Friend*, 3 December 1915, p.903a.
17 16,000 conscientious objectors went before military tribunals and 10,000 went to prison. Men 'forcibly enlisted' were taken in irons to France where field punishment for refusal to obey orders included crucifixion to a gun wheel.
18 Barbara Cole, p.9.

2: The Break

1   66 Park Lane.
2   Kay Walsh, p.20.
3   Norman Spencer, p.112.
4   Private source.
5   David Lean, p.1.
6   Ibid.
7   David Lean, *Notes For A Film*, p.7.(Unpublished)
8   David Lean, p.5.
9   Ibid, p.4. John Nevil Maskelyne occupied the Egyptian Hall in Piccadilly, where some of England's first moving pictures were shown. But in 1906 he had moved to St George's Hall where the Maskelynes remained until the building was sold to the BBC in 1935. (Edwin A Dawes, *The Great Illusionists* p.165.) David remembered the name Maskelyne and Devant, so it is possible that he was taken when he was very young, before the partnership split up in 1915.Maskelyne died in 1917 and the act was run by his son, Nevil and Edwin Archibald, together with three of Nevil's sons, Clive, Noel and Jasper. David particularly remembered Clive and Nevil.
10 David Lean, p.4. / *Notes For A Film*, p.3.
11 Until 1920, the headmaster was the Major's brother, George Atkinson. The Major died in 1933. The

Limes was evacuated in the Second World War and never returned to Croydon. The buildings now form part of Croham Hurst School for Girls.

12 David Lean, p.112.
13 Maurice Cooke, phone interview, 18 December 1991.
14 David Lean, p.453.
15 Ibid., pp.8,10.
16 Kingston Monthly Meeting Minutes, Society of Friends Library.
17 David Lean, p.453.
18 Ibid., p.458.
19 Ibid., pp.358,361./David Lean to Denise Worrell, op. cit., p.162.

3: The Laws of Lip

1 David Lean, *Notes for a Film*, p.6.
2 David Lean, pp.21,42.
3 *Film Comment*, Jan-Feb 1985, p.32.
4 Stephen Silverman, *David Lean* p.22.
5 David Lean, p.128.
6 *The Croydon Times*, 28 September 1921, p.7.
7 David Lean, p.128.
8 Many Friends had avoided the major public schools, feeling they created too many social ambitions and too little principle, and that they led boys away from their religious background. (*The History of Leighton Park*, p.13.)
9 Letter from Harold G Atkinson to Charles Evans, 19 December 1921, courtesy Tim Unsworth.
10 Letter from Charles Evans to Francis Lean, 21 December 1921, Leighton Park School Archives.
11 Stephen Silverman, op. cit., p.19.
12 F.L.Woolley phone interview, 20 December 1991.
13 David Lean, p.456.
14 Maurice Blundell phone interviews 21 February 1991, 7 July 1991.
15 David Lean, p.13.
16 *The Leightonian*, Autumn 1956, p.233.
17 David Lean, p.466.
18 David Lean to Denise Worrell, op. cit. p.160.
19 *The History of Leighton Park*, p.130.
20 Ibid., p.135.
21 Norman Spencer phone interview, 17 December 1991.
22 David Lean to Sarah Miles.
23 David Lean, p.522.
24 Ibid., p.425.
25 Ibid., p.442.
26 David Lean, p.423. Scott Goddard was at Leighton Park from 1921-26. The schoolteacher, played by Robert Mitchum, in RYAN'S DAUGHTER, who has a great passion for music and has a gramophone in his living room, clearly owes a great deal to Scott Goddard.
27 *The Leightonian*, Autumn 1956, pp.232-33.
28 David Lean, p.298.
29 Sheila Tangye, p.1.
30 David Lean, p.476.
31 Ibid., pp.475,479.

4: City Lights

1 David Lean, p.682.
2 Ibid., p.316.
3 John Box phone interview, 14 October 1992.
4 David Lean, *Notes for a Film*, pp.5-6.
5 David Lean, p.317/Denise Worrell, op. cit., p.164.
6 Stephen Silverman, cut section of manuscript.
7 Sandy Lean, p.25/phone interview, 31 May 1993.
8 David Lean, p.358.
9 Ibid., p.460. There were many accidents at the old aerodrome, partly because pilots had to climb uphill before taking off. In 1926, construction started on a new airport which opened two years later on the newly-built Purley bypass.
10 David Lean, p.302. David gave these words to Lt Joyce, a Canadian officer being interviewed by Colonel Green:
GREEN
You were an accountant in Montreal?
JOYCE
Yes, sir. Not really an accountant, sir. That is, I didn't have my charter.
GREEN
Exactly what did you do then?
JOYCE
Well, I just checked columns and columns of figures which three or four people had checked before me. Then there were two other people who checked them after I had checked them.
GREEN
Sounds an awful bore.
JOYCE
Sir, it was a frightful bore.
11 David Lean, p.7.
12 Ibid., p.404.
13 Ibid., p.613.
14 Freddie Young, unpublished ms. p.3.
15 Linda Wood, *Maurice Elvey*, pp.1,39.
16 David Lean, *Notes for a Film*, p.2.
17 Ibid.
18 The number of British films released in 1926 was a mere 27, compared to 103 in 1919. Whilst Gaumont's schedule for 1927 was nine features, the major studios in Hollywood depended on releasing 52 features a year.
19 Linda Wood, *British Films, 1927-39*, p.1. The percentage was a modest five percent in 1928, rising to seventeen-and-a-half by 1934. A revision to the law reduced the percentage in 1938.
20 The book was originally published in 1914; David's copy was a 1923 reprint.
21 David Lean, pp.307,310.
22 Murnau's SUNRISE (1927) is now acknowledged as

one of the most innovative and important films
ever made.

23 *Close Up*, March 1929, pp.8,86.
24 *Close Up*, August 1928, p.34.
25 *Close Up*, August 1927, p.20.

5: The End of the Rainbow

1 David Lean letter to Dennis Potter, 1 January 1981.
TR.
2 David Lean, p.308.
3 Ibid., p.354.
4 Ibid., pp.164-65/Notes for radio interview of
1943.
5 David Lean, p.312.
6 Barbara Cole, p9/David Lean, *Notes for a Film*,
p.25.
7 Maurice Elvey to author, 1960.
8 Alan Lawson phone interview, January 1991.
9 The first British Acoustic film was completed on 11
February 1926 at the Weissensee Studios in Berlin,
eighteen months before THE JAZZ SINGER which
used disc apparatus rather than optical film.
10 The most famous example of this editing technique is
to be seen in Eisenstein's BATTLESHIP POTEMKIN
(1925) which was first shown in London in 1928.
David never saw it.
11 Ibid., p.308.
12 David Lean, pp.313-14.
13 *Stills* magazine, March 1985, p.32. David
reproduced Milestone's tracking shots of trench
warfare in both DOCTOR ZHIVAGO and RYAN'S
DAUGHTER.
14 The Avenue Pavilion was the Curzon of its day.
Bombed during the war, the cinema was rebuilt and
named the Columbia and then, appropriately, the
Curzon West End.

6: Commitment

1 Isabel Lean, p.2.
2 Ibid., p.10.
3 842 marks out of 1000. The course ended in
December 1929.
4 David revealed his attitude to pregnancy many years
later in a letter to Robert Bolt, concerning the
pregnancy of a character in DOCTOR ZHIVAGO:
"Let me start off by saying I'm almost certainly one
of the worst judges of this particular item of married
bliss. The curse being a couple of weeks late has
always filled me with forboding [sic]; a woman who
announces 'I'm pregnant!' is telling me, with pride
mark you, that the bill has arrived from the
entertainment tax people. And the congratulations
heaped on a young man for performing the greatest
of pleasures with a desirable girl is quite beyond
me." (20 August 1964, UoR.)
5 David Lean letter to Isabel Lean, 2 February 1930.

6 John Stevenson, *British Society 1914-45*, p.119.
7 Kay Walsh, p.138.
8 David Lean, p.299.
9 Isabel Lean, pp.12,13.
10 Roy Drew letter to *South Bank Show*, 7 August 1984.
11 Fox, which owned Movietone, had a stake in
Gaumont Sound News and they often exchanged
footage.
12 In fact, David did not join the union until 1938,
though this was still considered early.
13 Isabel Lean, p.11.
14 David Lean, pp.552,613.
15 Kay Walsh, p.137.

7: Flight

1 Isabel Lean, p.3.
2 Sid Cole, p.1.
3 Although Isabel believes the test was made at B&D,
my guess is that it was made at Gaumont, probably
by Oswell Blakeston. The test was filmed with a full
aperture silent camera, which suggests Gaumont
rather than B&D where Academy ratio apertures
would have been used, even if the test was without
sound.
4 Isabel Lean, p.7.
5 David Lean, p.557.
6 Isabel Lean, pp.9-10.
7 David Lean, p.301.
8 Kay Walsh, p.19.
9 Julie Laird, p.1.

8: Top Flight

1 David Lean, p.49x.
2 Merrill White had worked on Paramount's WINGS
(1927) and then edited the studio's first talkie,
INTERFERENCE. A tall, red-headed man with a
fiery temper, White pioneered music and film, when
dubbing was considered an impossibility, and worked
on Lubitsch's THE LOVE PARADE (1929) and
Mamoulian's LOVE ME TONIGHT (1932). He
came - reluctantly - to England to cut a film for
Herbert Wilcox which was cancelled. But White
stayed in England.
3 David Lean, p.61.
4 *Films in Review*, November 1957.
5 David Lean to Robert Stewart, p.12.
6 Peggy Hennessey phone interview, 23 November
1992.
7 David Lean to Denise Worrell, op. cit., p.163.
8 *Moviemen* interview, p.2, nd.
9 L.P.Williams, pp.1-2.
10 Vera Campbell, p.1.
11 Ibid., p.6.
12 John Mitchell, p.3.
13 Dickinson always referred to David with warmth and
respect. Lutz Becker, who worked with Dickinson in

his old age at the Slade School, said that he chose
LAWRENCE OF ARABIA as the film to celebrate
his retirement from teaching. "He took a great deal
of pleasure from David Lean's success." (Lutz
Becker, 5 March 1993.)

14 Rachael Low, *Film Making in 1930s Britain*, p.160.
15 David Lean, p.363.
16 *British Film Reporter*, 2 June 1934.
17 Gordon Hales, p.5.
18 Mary Clinton-Thomas phone interview, 20 February 1992.
19 Rank, whose move into films would have a major effect on David's career, had formed British National Films with Lady Yule, who had inherited millions from her late husband, John Corfield.
20 They stayed at the Ritz until their marriage was announced - when the Ritz ejected them because they weren't married.
21 Allgeier had been the cameraman on Leni Riefenstahl's famous documentary on the 1934 Nuremberg Rally, TRIUMPH OF THE WILL. "He was anti-semitic and didn't like Paul or Elisabeth," said Dallas Bower, "which was a problem. His assistant, Gutzi Lantchner, was just as bad."
22 Patricia Danes phone interview, 13 July 1991.
23 Philip Hudsmith letter to author, 24 July 1991.
24 Dallas Bower, p.1.
25 *Esquire*, 23 May 1965.
26 A famous example of breaking the eye-line rule can be seen in John Ford's STAGECOACH (1939) where the Indians and the fleeing stagecoach can be seen racing in different directions. Yet the sequence is never confusing and is one of the greatest action scenes ever filmed.
27 Susanna Walton, *William Walton*, p.87.
28 The daughter of Mrs Freda Dudley Ward who was the mistress of the Prince of Wales. "She was a darling, I loved her," said David. "I thought she would marry David Tree but she married Carol Reed." (David Lean, p.604.)
29 David Lean, p.59.
30 Ibid., p.58.
31 Catrine Clay, p.1.
32 Ibid.
33 Ibid.
34 Colonel P.J.D Toosey (later Sir Philip), commanding officer of the Hertfordshire Yeomanry.

9: Love Cutting

1 Hugh Stewart, who worked on a musical at Beaconsfield called IN TOWN TONIGHT, could still remember the song she sang: "My name is Lu-Anne Meredith / I wouldn't do without it / It doesn't rhyme with anything / But you can't make gags about it." (Hugh Stewart phone interview, January 1991.)
2 Isabel Lean, p.9. The date of the divorce hearing was

17 February 1936.
3 Isabel Lean, p.10.
4 Kay Walsh, pp.124-25.
5 David Lean, p.553.
6 Michael Holroyd, *Shaw*, Vol III, p.382.
7 Dallas Bower, p.1.
8 David Lean, p.556. £60 a week was the salary of a top lighting cameraman and even that was exceptional. For an editor, it was unprecedented.
9 Dick Best letter to author, 14 June 1991.
10 David Lean, pp.60-62.
11 Dallas Bower, p.2.
12 Vera Campbell, p.5.David recaptured this experience in his 1949 film, THE PASSIONATE FRIENDS.

10: Dreaming Lips

1 SECRET OF STAMBOUL (1936), directed by Andrew Marton.
2 At that time, many people called their daughters Gemma, after Gemma Jones, the character Bergner played in this film.
3 In NOW, VOYAGER (1942).
4 Kay Walsh, p.89.
5 Ibid. p.119.
6 Tickets at the Curzon were two shillings and sixpence, against one shilling and sixpence at the Academy.
7 Inevitably, this idyllic spot has been demolished.
8 Kay Walsh, p.124.
9 With his lack of interest in politics, David was probably unaware that by 1936 Lang was in Hollywood, a refugee from Nazism, whilst Lang's wife had remained in Germany, a committed National-Socialist.
10 The Blue Train to Rome
11 Kay Walsh, p.117.
12 Quisisana means, 'Here We Heal You.'
13 Kay Walsh, p.38.

11: Climbing Back

1 Eric Cross, p.7.
2 Kay Walsh, p.105.
3 Ronald Neame, p.48.
4 The prospect of Kay making a third film with Formby came to nothing when Formby turned her down, saying he did not want to create a team like Astaire and Rogers.
5 *Isis*, 2 November 1938, pp.10-11. In a letter of 6 January 1972, Edward reminded David of this incident, "when he sent you away with a handful of cigarettes."
6 David Lean, p.76 et seq. Shaw's biographer, Michael Holroyd, wrote that men saw in Pascal only a colossal imposter whose surname should have begun with an R. Shaw would probably have agreed;

he warmed to the man because he reminded him of another charlatan, the Irish writer, Frank Harris. According to his secretary, Blanche Patch, "GBS never met a human being who entertained him more." (Holroyd,op. cit., p.386/Blanche Patch, *Thirty Years with GBS* p.118.)

7   David Lean letter to Edwin A Davis, 12 November 1964, UoR.

8   Leslie Howard, *A Quite Remarkable Father*, p.229.

9   David Lean letter to Edwin A. Davis, 12 November 1964, UoR.

10 Wendy Hiller had made just one film - a "quota quickie" called LANCASHIRE LUCK (1937) which was produced by Anthony Havelock- Allan. She confessed that she "looked down her nose at the cinema."

11 Michael Holroyd, op. cit., p.390.

12 David Lean, pp.78,351.

13 Michael Holroyd, op. cit., p.392.

14 David Lean, p.83.

15 Also on the crew were others who would work with David. John Bryan was art director; the camera operator was Jack Hildyard and the second assistant director was Michael Anderson who would work on IN WHICH WE SERVE and later became a famous Hollywood director. Also on PYGMALION, as clapper-loader, was Freddie Francis, later a celebrated cameraman. The film also marked the screen debut of Anthony Quayle.

16 Bob Huke, p.1.

17 Vera Campbell, p.9.

18 David Lean, p.603. Howard later directed PIMPERNEL SMITH and THE FIRST OF THE FEW.

19 David Lean, pp.29,620.

20 R.J. Minney, *Puffin Asquith* p.97.

21 For PYGMALION, David moved into the Pinewood Club and lived at the studio for much of the production.

22 Michael Holroyd, op. cit., p.392.

23 Kay Walsh, p.5.

24 *Film Weekly*, 17 September 1938, p.31.

25 *Picturegoer Weekly*, 29 July 1939.

26 Kay Walsh phone interview, 7 March 1992.

27 The Max Fleischer cartoon of 1940.

28 Kay Walsh, p.110.

29 Ronald Neame, *South Bank Show* transcript, p.9.

30 Kay Walsh, p.111.

31 Vera Campbell, p.6.

32 Kay Walsh, pp.68-69.

33 David Lean, pp.361-62.

34 Rushed into production at the outbreak of hostilities, it was on the screen only six weeks later.

35 David Lean, p.496.

12: Major Barbara

1   David Lean, p.621.

2   Kay Walsh, p.107.

3   Michael Holroyd, op. cit., p.436.

4   Elstree Studios were requisitioned and eventually turned out parts for the Mulberry Harbour. Pinewood - previously managed by Norton - was closed, eventually to become a food storage depot and an out station of the Royal Mint - the first time, so the joke went, that Pinewood ever made money. The only films made there were those of the Crown Film Unit. (George Perry, *Movies from the Mansion*, p.53 / Alan Wood, *Mr Rank*, p.104.))

5   Deborah Kerr letter to author, 27 February 1992.

6   Valerie Pascal, p.97.

7   Robert Morley phone interview, 14 December 1991.

8   Allen Eyles, *Rex Harrison,* p.46.

9   Ibid., p.72.

10 Ronald Neame, pp.62-64.

11 Wendy Hiller, p.1.

12 Ronald Neame fax to author, 21 July 1992.

13 Ronald Neame, pp.56-58. Tragedy struck Harold French during the production. His wife was killed when a German air-raid destroyed their London home.

14 Ronald Neame, pp.50-51.

15 Kay Walsh, p.97.

16 Harold French, pp.4-6. French is credited as Dialogue Supervisor and Assistant in Direction. And his name still came before David's!

17 Vera Campbell, p.8.

18 Ibid., p.6.

19 Kay Walsh phone interview, 13 July 1992.

20 Wendy Hiller phone interview, July 1991.

13: 49th Parallel

1   Bergner's excuses were quoted in the press: "The part was not suitable. She wanted her husband to direct her. Her ears were so bad she could not stand flying back to England to finish the film, so she'd gone to Hollywood." (*Picture Post*, 4 October 1941.)

2   Michael Powell, Vol I, *A Life in the Movies* p.373.

3   Ibid.

4   Hugh Stewart phone interview, 11 February 1992.

5   Michael Powell, Vol I, p.379.

6   Sid Cole, p.2.

7   He is quoted in Powell's book as saying he saw eight hours. But every other time David has referred to this he gives the length of five-and-a-half hours.

8   David Lean, p.621.

9   David Lean, p.634.

10 Michael Powell, op. cit., p.380.

11 Sid Cole, p.2.

12 It was retitled THE INVADERS in America and was later nominated for three Academy Awards, including Best Picture. Another propaganda film, MRS MINIVER, directed by William Wyler, won the main award though Pressburger won for writing

the original story but not for his screenplay.

13 David Lean, p.606.

14 Rank turned it down - to Powell's regret - and the film was made with British National.

15 David Lean, p.433.

16 Betty Curtis, p.2.

17 Another cameraman, responsible for the models and miniature explosions, was Freddy Ford who would play a role in blowing up the Kwai bridge.

18 Guy Green, p.18.

19 Ibid., pp.16-17.

20 Michael Powell, Vol I, p.397.

21 Ibid., p.399.

22 Ibid., p.315.

14: In Which We Serve

1 Stephen Silverman, op. cit., p.48.

2 David Lean, p.245.

3 The LSO film was made in 1943 as BATTLE FOR MUSIC, directed by Donald Taylor.

4 David Lean, p.442.

5 When I interviewed Mountbatten in 1976 for the *Hollywood* TV series, he said his efforts to get films screened aboard naval ships went back to 1923.

6 Noël Coward, *Future Indefinite*, p.208.

7 Stephen Silverman, op. cit., p.35.

8 Ronald Neame, p15.

9 David Lean, p.435. David first saw CITIZEN KANE with Kay Walsh and Leslie Howard at a private screening at Denham. It became his favourite sound film. He had been so impressed, he told me, that he had written an article in praise of it. After many months and a great deal of help I tracked down the article which had the by-line Tangye Lean - David's brother, Edward. David offered a great deal of advice and perhaps he regarded himself as co-author because of all he put into it. His memory may have been coloured by the fact that years later Orson Welles embraced him and told him how much the article had meant to him at a time when the film had encountered hostile or uncomprehending reviews... David did write occasional articles himself and in one of these he referred favourably to CITIZEN KANE, so perhaps that is where the confusion first arose.

10 Coward faced fines for breaking currency regulations in America, while working on government business and using his own money. He was devastated and convinced that someone in authority was out to get him.

11 Kay Walsh, p.52.

12 Philip Ziegler, op. cit., p.171.

13 A book, *Unauthorized Action*, by the Canadian academic Brian Loring Villa, accuses Mountbatten of spending too much time on the fine details of 'a movie glorifying himself and the men of the *Kelly*' (p.200) and not enough on the planning of the Dieppe raid which ended in disaster and a sixty percent casualty rate. Villa claims that Mountbatten was an "immature" man, "dazzled" by Hollywood. In his book there is a photograph taken on the set of IN WHICH WE SERVE at the time of the visit by the King and Queen. A dark figure identified by Villa as Mountbatten is actually David Lean.

14 Norman Spencer, p.118.

15 David Lean, p.437.

16 Betty Curtis letter to author, 23 November 1991.

17 Kate Fleming, *Celia Johnson*, p.90.

18 Ibid., p.15.

19 Kate Fleming to author.

20 Kay Walsh, p.94. Noël Coward's small godson, Daniel Massey, son of Raymond Massey, took the part of Captain Kinross's son, Bobby, with Ann Stephens as his daughter, Lavinia. (Massey would later play Noël Coward in Robert Wise's film, STAR!) Coward also liked to have members of the crew play brief roles (although he never got David in front of the camera). Assistant director Norman Spencer played a part, with false beard, as a naval officer. John Brabourne, Mountbatten's future son-in-law and co-producer of David's last film, A PASSAGE TO INDIA, was an extra in the Dunkirk sequence.

21 David Lean, pp.589-90.

22 *Noël Coward Diaries*, p.13.

23 Ibid., p.14.

24 Ronald Neame fax to author, 27 April 1991.

25 Noël Coward, *Future Indefinite*, p.213.

26 Norman Spencer, p.5. William Hartnell later played in two films for Carol Reed - THE WAY AHEAD and ODD MAN OUT. He was also the first Dr Who on television.

27 John Mills, *Up in the Clouds*, p.177.

28 Michael Anderson was credited as Unit Manager. "He was ridiculously young." said David (he was twenty), "He was the best assistant director in the country. And later Mickey directed a lot of films including AROUND THE WORLD IN 80 DAYS." (David Lean, p.440.)

29 *Noël Coward Diaries*, p.15.

30 Kay Walsh, p.95.

31 Richard Attenborough, *The Golden Gong*, BBC-TV, 21 August 1987.

32 John Mills, p.9.

33 Ibid., p.4.

34 Maggie Unsworth, p.2.

35 David Lean, pp.82,141,438.

36 Norman Spencer, p.112.

37 Kay Walsh, p.47.

38 Guy Green, p.21.

39 David Lean, p.605.

40 James Hill to author, 14 August 1992.

41 David Lean, p.605.

42 The Enemy Flying Circus was officially known as 1426 Enemy Aircraft Flight and had in its charge a

Heinkel, a Junkers 88 and a Messerschmitt BF109E, the first aircraft to be captured in the war. (*Aircraft Illustrated*, February 1970.)

43 Kay Walsh, p.48.

44 Ibid., p.129.

45 Ronald Neame, p.89.

46 Norman Spencer, p.7.

47 Allen Eyles, letter to author, 8 January 1992.

48 Anthony Havelock-Allan, p.17. *The Express* was written into the final draft of the script.

49 Sir Vincent Massey, High Commissioner for Canada, was Raymond Massey's brother.

50 David Lean, p.128.

51 Noël Coward, *Future Indefinite*, p.231. There was a showing of the film at Buckingham Palace on 12 October 1942 (Villa, p.187.)

52 Mistake or not, names missing from credit titles would be a recurrent source of resentment on David's productions.

53 *Daily Mail*, 25 September 1942.

54 *Daily Express*, 24 September 1942.

55 *The Observer*, 27 September 1942.

56 *The Sunday Times*, 27 September 1942.

57 *The News of the World*, 27 September 1942.

58 Ronald Neame to author, 11 February 1993.

15: This Happy Breed

1 In the silent days, in America, there was an attempt to do for film what the Theatre Guild had done for the theatre. It was called The Film Guild.

2 David Lean, p.246.

3 Kay's sister.

4 Peter Tanner letter to author, 28 April 1992/phone interview 19 May 1992.

5 Peter Tanner went on to edit some of the classics of the post-war British cinema, including KIND HEARTS AND CORONETS, THE BLUE LAMP, THE CRUEL SEA and THE MAGGIE.

6 Anthony Havelock-Allan phone interview, 9 February 1992.

7 David Lean, p.134.

8 David Lean, p.581. "I didn't like the style he chose. I didn't think it worked to go from extreme stylisation into a realistic charge as they had. I thought some scenes were wonderful but as a complete film I wasn't mad about it."

9 Ronald Neame fax to author, 27 April 1992.

10 Anthony Havelock-Allan, p.73.

11 David Lean, p.130.

12 Graham Greene, then a drama critic, complained of Coward's ear for 'common speech,' saying, "Mr Coward was separated from ordinary life by his theatrical success and one suspects that when he does overhear the common speech he finds himself overwhelmed by the pathos of its very cheapness and inadequacy. But it is the sense of inadequacy that he fails to convey, and with it he loses the pathos."

(Sheridan Morley, *A Talent to Amuse*, p.259.)

13 David Lean, p.132. Before Robert Newton was offered the part, Robert Donat had turned it down. (Kenneth Barrow, *Mr Chips*, p.85.)

14 Kate Fleming, op. cit, p.118.

15 Kate Fleming interview, 14 February 1992.

16 Kate Fleming, op. cit, p.120.

17 Ronald Neame, pp.24-25.

18 Noël Coward, op. cit., pp.238-39.

19 Eileen Erskine phone interview, 24 April 1992.

20 Ronald Neame, pp.24,27.

21 Norman Spencer, p.118.

22 Kate Fleming, op. cit., p.121. The horses were needed for Olivier's HENRY V.

23 Gerald Pratley, *The Cinema of David Lean*, p.46.

24 Guy Green, p.6.

25 Kay Walsh, p.101. Noël Coward passionately opposed appeasement and detested Chamberlain. (Tony Aldgate, *Britain Can Take It*. p.188.)

26 David Lean, p.128.

27 Stephen Silverman, op. cit., p.47.

28 *The Observer*, 28 May 1944.

29 *The Sunday Times*, 28 May 1944.

30 Stephen Silverman, op. cit., p.52.

31 Kay Walsh, p.148.

32 Doreen Lean to Gerald McKnight, p.9.

16: Blithe Spirit

1 Anthony Havelock-Allan phone interview, 8 February 1992.

2 Sheridan Morley to author.

3 Qu. CA Lejeune, *The Observer*, 27 February 1944.

4 Ibid.

5 Anthony Havelock-Allan phone interview, February 1992/also pp.32-33.

6 Michael Powell, op. cit., p417.

7 Ronald Neame fax to author, 21 April 1992.

8 Rex Harrison, *Rex*, p.81.

9 Anthony Havelock-Allan, p.72.

10 Thames TV, 2 December 1987, interview by Patrick Garland.

11 David Lean, pp.346-347.

12 Constance Cummings, pp1-2. Cummings had a strong influence on the lives of David and Kay. Politically, Kay was left-wing enough for Noël to refer to her occasionally as "Red Emma". Cummings' husband, Benn Levy, was hoping to become a Labour MP. There were many political discussions and Cummings made a number of public appearances for the Labour Party which David and Kay attended. David, apolitical as always, was under unusually strong pressure and according to Kay Walsh, voted Labour in the historic 1945 General Election which swept Churchill from office. "We did it with a heavy heart," said Kay, "because we thought we were betraying Churchill." (Kay Walsh phone interview, 25 May 1992.)

13 David Lean, p.146. Bernard Vorhaus had been the first to cast Margaret Rutherford in a film - DUSTY ERMINE (1936). But it was BLITHE SPIRIT which would launch her career as the perhaps the pre-eminent British character actress.

14 David Lean, p.39. The American version of BLITHE SPIRIT was aired on 15 January 1957.

15 Thames TV, 2 December 1987, interview by Patrick Garland.

16 Kay Walsh, p.41.

17 *New Statesman*, 7 April 1945.

18 *Daily Mail*, 16 April 1945.

19 *The Observer*, 8 April 1945.

20 *The Sunday Times*, 8 April 1945.

21 Perhaps the kindest dismissal came from Coward himself: "I will draw a light, spangled veil over BLITHE SPIRIT." he wrote, "It wasn't entirely bad, but it was a great deal less good than it should have been." (Noel Coward, Future Indefinite, pp.211-22.)

22 Kay Walsh, p.118.

23 Sheridan Morley, op. cit., p.253.

17: Brief Encounter

1 *Penguin Film Review* No.4, p.33.

2 *Still Life* was part of a cycle of twelve plays called *Tonight at 8.30*. In the original production, Noël Coward played the doctor and Gertrude Lawrence was Laura. The plays were bought by MGM, then sold to British producer Sydney Box who sold them to Rank. When Cineguild wanted the rights to *Still Life*, Rank charged them for the entire cycle of twelve plays - £60,000. (Anthony Havelock-Allan/Vivienne Knight, Trevor Howard p.56.)

3 Ronald Neame, p.82.

4 David Lean, p.445.

5 "Lineshoot", in wartime slang, meant any kind of showing-off.

6 Vivienne Knight, op. cit., p.56.

7 Ibid.

8 Kate Fleming, op. cit., p.137.

9 Stephen Silverman, op. cit., p.64.

10 David Lean letter to Peter Lean, 1 February 1945.

11 Professor Alan Earnshaw letter to author, 28 March 1995.

12 When production manager E.J. Holding went to organise accommodation for the cast and crew, he found the hotels packed with refugees from southern England. He had to book hotels in five different districts - Carnforth, Ambleside, Lancaster, Morecambe and Bolton-les-Sands. (Cineguild Production Story, BFI.) Now stripped of much of its original fittings, Carnforth is still used as a railway station and the main buildings are still there. There are organised tours for BRIEF ENCOUNTER fans and there are plans to convert the derelict buffet into a 'Brief Encounter Restaurant,' even though the buffet in the film was a set at Denham studios.

13 "This being 1945, with the blackout officially in force, the glare from the film lights, covering one end of the station to the other, might have panicked drivers - from a distance, Carnforth appearing to be an inferno. So official notice had to be given: drivers were instructed not to slow down but to pass through the station at high speed." (John Huntley, *Railways on the Screen*, p.15.)

14 Kate Fleming, op. cit., p.140.

15 Robert Krasker had succeeded Ronald Neame as cameraman. Born in Perth, Australia, in 1913, his parents came from France and Austria. Krasker had been camera operator to the great Georges Perinal on Korda's REMBRANDT, THE FOUR FEATHERS and THE THIEF OF BAGDAD.

16 L.P. Williams, p.1.

17 David Lean, p.399.

18 Billy Wilder found the character of Stephen so interesting that he used the situation of a man lending his flat for the sexual indulgences of others in his 1960 film, THE APARTMENT.

19 Anthony Havelock-Allan phone interview, 14 April 1992. Mount Royal was also the home of art director L.P. Williams's first wife.

20 David Lean, p.386.

21 Gerald Pratley, op. cit. p.55.

22 David Lean letter to Freddie Young, 16 July 1968. David repeated the effect in THE SOUND BARRIER (as Ridgefield listens to the pilot on the radio) and even more dramatically in RYAN'S DAUGHTER when Rosy and Doryan meet in the pub.

23 David Lean, p.285. This scene is much abbreviated in the film as there is a dissolve to the entrance of the flats.

24 Kate Fleming, op. cit., p.144.

25 Kay Walsh phone interview, 16 April 1992.

26 Susanna Walton, op. cit., p.92.

27 Charles Saunders phone interview, 5 June 1992.

28 John Huntley phone interview, 14 October 1992.

29 *Films and Filming*, January 1963, p.15.

30 David Lean, p.79. On the Terry Wogan show in April 1988 David told this story and gave a hilarious imitation of the woman's laugh.

31 *The Listener*, 29 November 1945.

32 FLAMES OF PASSION was the title of a 1922 film produced by Herbert Wilcox, directed by Graham Cutts and starring Mae Marsh. The title stuck in Coward's mind because it was playing at a cinema next door to the theatre in Manchester where the local watch committee had refused to allow the title "Easy Virtue" because it was too risqué. (Sheridan Morley, op. cit., p.104.)

33 This was curious, because there was a strong anti-British feeling in French film criticism - later the film was strongly attacked by *Positif*. It was seen as a film against 'l'amour fou' - a film about surrendering to bourgeois conventions. (Bernard Eisenschitz.)

French critics also thought the scene in the flat implied that Stephen was a homosexual who was infatuated with Alec.

34 *Penguin Film Review*, No.4, p.32. The film cost £174,370 and eventually made a profit, according to Havelock-Allan, of £168,000. In America, it was released as a supporting feature to SONG OF SCHEHERAZADE, about Rimsky-Korsakov (at least it wasn't about Rachmaninov!)

35 David did not win, but he could hardly have objected to the winner - William Wyler for THE BEST YEARS OF OUR LIVES. Celia Johnson was nominated for Best Actress, having earlier won the Best Actress Award from the New York Critics Circle. In 1946, David received the Grand Prix for the best British film shown at the Cannes Film Festival, and the four hundred press men and film critics voted it the best film of the year, against such competition as Billy Wilder's THE LOST WEEKEND.

36 David Lean, p.386.

37 *Noël Coward, Diaries*, p.135.

38 Kay Walsh, p.148.

18: Great Expectations

1 Steven Spielberg, *The South Bank Show*.

2 Kay Walsh, pp.7-8.

3 Stephen Silverman, op. cit., p.170.

4 Ronald Neame, p.32.

5 Clemence Dane had named herself after Wren's church in the Strand; her real name was Winifred Ashton. She was a novelist, painter and sculptress as well as a dramatist, a close friend of Noël Coward and had won an Oscar for Best Original Story for Korda's PERFECT STRANGERS.

6 Ronald Neame, p.49.

7 Norman Spencer, p.114.

8 Bryan had been art director on PYGMALION and MAJOR BARBARA.

9 David Lean, p.224.

10 Roger Manvell, R.K.Neilson-Baxter (eds), *The Cinema*, p.20.

11 David had forgotten that Sullivan had played Jaggers in Stuart Walker's 1934 version for Universal.

12 Alec Guinness, p.1.

13 Norman Spencer, p.18.

14 Ronald Neame, p.83.

15 Peter Lean to Gerald McKnight, p.9.

16 Peter Lean, p.1.

17 Ronald Neame, p.87.

18 Guy Green, p.12.

19 Bob Huke, p.2.

20 David Lean, p.607.

21 Ronald Neame, p.83.

22 Norman Spencer, p.117.

23 Ibid., p.32.

24 Kay Walsh, p.142/phone interview, 11 September 1992.

25 Kay Walsh, p.143.

26 Colette described a very young man who was so attractive that he could make women tremble simply by turning his eyes on them. He has a long affair with a woman 25 years older than he - but walks out on her as he walks out on his marriage. He returns when he feels like it, and the woman forces him back to his wife.

27 *New York Times*, 15 June 1947.

28 Alec Guinness, p.7.

29 Valerie Hobson, pp4,6,8. Valerie Hobson had played in the 1934 version of the film, though her scenes were deleted. In David's film she played both Estella and her mother.

30 *The Technique of Film Editing*, p.240. It is actually 31 frames!

31 *Pinewood Merry-Go-Round*, October 1946.

32 *Kine Weekly*, 1 August 1946. David had been dismayed by an Ealing film in which everyone spoke with "ridiculous accents. I felt ashamed. No one talked like that except in films. I wondered what on earth the Americans would make of us." (David Lean to author.)

33 John Huntley phone interview, 14 October 1992.

34 Win Ryder, p.9.

35 Geoffrey Foot letter to author, 27 November 1991.

36 *Film Book 1*, pp.51-52 (The original quote combined two visits to the censor, for GREAT EXPECTATIONS and MADELEINE. I have separated them.) Also David Lean p.593.

37 Yet the salaciously advertised Howard Hughes film, THE OUTLAW, with Jane Russell, was given a U certificate.

38 *Pinewood Merry-Go-Round*, February 1947.

39 *News Chronicle*, 11 December 1946.

40 *Daily Express*, 15 December 1946. Stephen Watts later married Maggie Furse.

41 The film was showing at the Gaumont, (later the Odeon) in Haymarket, and also at the Marble Arch Pavilion.

42 David Lean, p.110.

43 American Film Institute tribute, p.12.

44 Anne Coates, p.4.

19: Oliver Twist

1 David Lean, p.450.

2 Kay Walsh, p.9.

3 Gerald Pratley, op. cit., p.77. Although set in the Victorian era, OLIVER TWIST's story of social evils such as crime, slum housing and child poverty, must have struck a chord in a country emerging from a war, with a Labour government intent on establishing a welfare state and a more equal society.

4 Mary Benson, p.1.

5 Kay Walsh, p.99. Haynes completed CARNIVAL, which was photographed by Guy Green.

6 Mary Benson, p.2.

7   Kay Walsh, pp.3-4.
8   Norman Spencer, p.28.
9   Ibid.
10 William K Everson to author, 4 May 1991.
11 Tree's son was Carol Reed who in 1968 directed the musical version of OLIVER! with a much less sinister Fagin, played by Ron Moody. Reed's nephew, Oliver, played Sikes.
12 David Lean, p.239.
13 Alec Guinness, p.12.
14 Stuart Freeborn, pp.1-3.
15 *Films in Review*, May 1951, p.3.
16 Stuart Freeborn, p.4.
17 John Howard Davies, p.2. Davies later became one of British television's most prolific and successful producers of situation comedy. When the film was made, David thought Davies was as angelic as he looked. "I should think television has knocked some of the angel out of him."
18 Dorothy Davies letter to author, 10 August 1992.
19 John Howard Davies, p.4.
20 Dorothy Davies letter to author, 10 August 1992.
21 Mary Benson, p.2.
22 *International Journal of Psycho-Analysis*, No 50, 1969, p.261.
23 Kay Walsh, p.97.
24 Guy Green, p.27.
25 Oswald Morris, p.3.
26 David Lean, p.108.
27 Guy Green, p.4.
28 David Lean, p.230-31.
29 Norman Spencer, p.118.
30 John Howard Davies, p.4. Davies said that amongst the extras in the mob were Peter Sellers, Spike Milligan and Harry Secombe, all just out of the army and finding small parts and work as extras.
31 Peter Newbrook, p.3.
32 Clive Donner, p.4.
33 John Huntley, *British Film Music*, p.1.
34 Huntley and Manvell, *Technique of Film Music*, p.94.
35 Eric Ambler, *Here Lies Eric Ambler*, p.3.
36 Stuart Freeborn, p.7.
37 *The Cinema Studio*, 7 July 1948, p.16.
38 Alec Guinness, p.12.
39 When Ben Hecht, the Hollywood scenario writer, who had given money to the terrorists, publically rejoiced in the killing of British soldiers, American films in which Hecht had been involved were boycotted by many theatres in Britain.
40 *Films in Review*, May 1951.
41 Ronald Neame, p.93.
42 David Lean, p.214.
43 *Life*, 7 March 1949, p.38.
44 *The Times*, 22 February 1949.
45 *Life*, 7 March 1949.
46 Norman Spencer letter to author, 21 September 1992.
47 David Lean, p 214-15
48 Ibid., p.214.
49 Norman Spencer, p.33.

20: The Passionate Friends

1   David planned to follow OLIVER TWIST with Paul Gallico's THE SNOW GOOSE. Gallico was a friend of Tony Havelock-Allan; his wife turned out to be the former Mrs Gabriel Pascal. The film was to be produced by Pascal for Rank but after the fiasco of Pascal's CAESAR AND CLEOPATRA, Britain's most expensive film - £1,200,000 - Rank decided to write it off, even though it cost them £30,000 to do so.
2   Ronald Neame fax to author, 26 June 1992.
3   David Lean, pp.256,266.
4   Ronald Neame, pp 36-9.
5   Eric Ambler, pp.1-5/phone interview, 8 June 1992.
6   Ibid., Ambler abandoned his position as producer and resigned from the board of Cineguild, although his contract still entitled him to a share of the profits. He later teamed up with director Ronald Neame (and John Bryan) and wrote the screenplay for THE CARD which starred Alec Guinness and was a great success.
7   Norman Spencer, pp.40,114.
8   Marius Goring phone interview, 25 August 1995.
9   Geoffrey Foot, p.1.
10 Oswald Morris, p.2.
11 Ann Todd, p.20.
12 Ibid., p.43.
13 Norman Spencer, p.114.
14 Oswald Morris, p.2.
15 David Lean, pp.257-8,266./Geoffrey Foot, p.2. An illustrated breakdown of this scene can be found in Karel Reisz's *The Technique of Film Editing*, pp.90-99.
16 Peter Lean, pp.2-3.
17 Norman Spencer, p.116.
18 Ann Todd, p.16.
19 Norman Spencer, pp.42,115.
20 Geoffrey Foot, pp.1-2.
21 David Lean, p.255.
22 *Evening Standard*, 27 January 1949.
23 Gordon Hales, pp.4-5.
24 Kay Walsh, p.143.
25 In those days it was necessary to prove misconduct and it often had to be staged at a hotel for the benefit of a private detective, as Ann Todd said it was in this case.
26 In his autobiography, Nigel Tangye found himself "paralysed in a vacuum" and went to Paris where, feeling utterly helpless, he contemplated suicide. (Nigel Tangye, *Facing the Sea*, p.154.)
27 *The Times*, 12 May 1949, p.3.
28 This was Ann Todd's third marriage. She first married Victor Malcolm in 1933, by whom she had a son, David. She married Nigel Tangye in October 1939.
29 David Malcolm phone interviews, 7 May 1993/29 June 1994.

30   Ethel Tuke had been financial comptroller to the Marquis of Anglesey. David thought she looked like Queen Mary. "She was very grand and very deaf," said Sandy Lean, "and had four silk dresses, all cut on the same model, in different colours, that she wore on a rotating basis." Ethel Tuke eventually became David's secretary and stayed with him for sixteen years.

31   Norman Spencer letter to author 12 July 1991.

32   Norman Spencer p.43.

21: Madeleine

1   LETTY LYNTON, a famous MGM film of 1932 directed by Clarence Brown and starring Joan Crawford, had been adapted from a novel which had been suggested by a 'famous Scottish murder trial.' The film was involved in a trial of its own when the playwrights of *Dishonored Lady*, which opened in 1928, sued for plagiarism. The script carried an unusual tribute; "The authors salute with gratitude Miss Madeleine Smith of Glasgow whose conduct in 1857 suggested to them this play. Accordingly, they make a friendly and admiring bow to her across the years." A film of *Dishonored Lady* was delayed because of objections raised by the Hays Office but was later made in 1947 with Hedy Lamarr and directed by Robert Stevenson.

2   Ann Todd, p.41.

3   Norman Spencer, p.43.

4   David Lean, p.588.

5   Ivan Desny letter to author, 2 January 1992.

6   Mary Benson, p.3.

7   Ann Todd, *The Eighth Veil*, p.97.

8   Low, a left-wing New Zealander, had created the cartoon character of Colonel Blimp, which was the inspiration for Powell and Pressburger's film. Low was a keen filmgoer whose daughter, Rachael, would write the definitive history of the British cinema from its origins to the end of the Second World War.

9   Ivan Desny letter to author, 2 January 1992.

10   *Cine-Technician* No 85, Jul-Aug 1950, p.104.

11   "At the height of the Rossellini-Ingrid Bergman scandal," wrote David, "Bergman wanted to come to London to meet her husband and get some rest. Being a friend of Rossellini's, I put her up for a few weeks. Everything was arranged with great precautions. The papers were shouting 'Bergman Disappears etc.' They all thought she was hiding in Italy. The scheme was a great success and we all congratulated ourselves. Imagine our astonishment when, at the end of the first week, she said, 'I want to hold a press conference.' She did, too." (David Lean letter to Dennis Potter, January 1981.) See also Ingrid Bergman: *My Story*, pp.279-280.

12   Geoffrey Foot, p.12.

13   Actually in Camden Town, later renamed the Parkway and closed in 1994. The cinema was specifically chosen for previews because it was one of only two theatres which could run "double-head" - i.e. sound and picture on separate reels. The other cinema was the Granada, Slough. (Jim Pople.)

14   Geoffrey Foot, p.3.

15   Clive Donner, p.13.

16   David Lean, p.252/ *Notes for a Film*, p.24.

17   The film has now been donated to The National Film Archive by David Malcolm.

18   Ann Todd, p.39.

19   Alan Wood, *Mr Rank*, p.245.

20   David Lean, p.450.

21   Peter Lean, p.3. He went to L'Ecole Hotelière in Lausanne and stayed ten months, celebrating his twenty-first birthday there.

22   Diana Cooke phone interview, 31 July 1993.

23   Peter Lean, p.4.

24   Norman Spencer, p.56. Clive Donner remembers seeing THE ASCENT OF EVEREST (1953) and David saying afterwards, *"That's* the kind of film I want to make." (Clive Donner phone interview, 4 July 1993.)

25   *Picturegoer*, 21 July 1951.

22: The Sound Barrier

1   David Lean, pp.401,626/AFI Seminar transcript.

2   Stephen Silverman, op. cit., p.91.

3   146 Piccadilly had been the home of the Duke of York before he became King George VI.

4   David Lean, pp.401,405,409. It was closer to thirty years before he got his knighthood.

5   David Lean, p.452. Stanley Haynes was forty-eight when he died. He had been working on a CinemaScope version of Dickens' A TALE OF TWO CITIES which had been postponed because of casting problems. Haynes himself had been fired.

6   Sidney Gilliat letter to author, 6 January 1992.

7   In the film, Nigel Patrick buys a newspaper - with the headline, 'JET PLANE EXPLODES: Geoffrey de Havilland killed FASTER THAN SOUND?' - and it was probably this image which remained in David's head and convinced him that De Havilland's death was a recent event. The newspaper used in the film was an original copy of the *Evening Standard* dated 24 September 1946.

8   Gerald Pratley, op. cit., pp.102-3.

9   De Havilland had three sons: Geoffrey, Peter and John. Geoffrey was killed in 1946 and the youngest, John, was killed in 1943 in a mid-air collision between two Mosquito aircraft during test flights.

10   Norman Spencer, p.52.

11   Ralph Richardson had directed a film himself, HOME AT SEVEN (1951), repeating a performance he had done on the stage. Richardson rehearsed the film for three weeks and shot it in less than two. To help him with this nerve-racking task, Korda visited the set

every day with two of Carol Reed's key men and David's cameraman, Jack Hildyard. David himself came and these top talents held discussions at the beginning of each new scene, leading to a studio joke, "We've shot ten minutes of credits so far and three minutes of story." (*Daily Express*, 21 November 1951.)

12 David Lean, p.391.
13 Gerald Pratley, op. cit., pp.100-103.
14 Norman Spencer, p.53.
15 Anthony Squire, p.1.
16 John Derry had been born in Cairo in 1921 and joined the RAF directly from school. He was commissioned in 1942 and trained in Canada as a pilot in 1943. He flew Hawker Typhoons over the Low Countries during the Liberation and was awarded the DFC. He joined De Havilland in 1947 and on 6 September 1948 he became the first British pilot to break the sound barrier. (*The Times*, obituary, 8 September 1952.)
17 Anthony Squire, p.2.
18 Ibid., p.16. The shot is recognisable because of increased grain and a scratch on the negative.
19 Ann Todd phone interview, 18 August 1992.
20 Vincent Korda designed the film but left the technical material to Hawkesworth.
21 Anthony Squire, p.2.
22 Ann Todd, pp.5,41/phone interview, 28 July 1992.
23 Teddy Darvas, p.2.
24 Ibid., p.8.
25 Geoffrey Foot, p.3.
26 Malcolm Arnold, p.1.
27 Geoffrey Foot phone interview, 27 November 1991.
28 *Today's Cinema*, 14 October 1952.
29 Norman Spencer, p.55.
30 *Today's Cinema*, 14 October 1952.
31 Two decades later, David would return here to complete the beach and cliff scenes for RYAN'S DAUGHTER.
32 David Lean, p.564.
33 Stephen Silverman, cut section of manuscript, p.177. John Derry and his observer, Anthony Richards, and twenty-five spectators were killed.
34 David took another flight to Rome in the Comet in 1954. The same plane exploded a few days later.
35 Chuck Yeager, *Yeager* pp.220-21.
36 At this time, the Festival Mondial du Film et des Beaux Arts in Brussels asked film-makers for their lists of the Ten Best Films ever made. David's list was surprising for he completely forgot Rex Ingram. His list was: INTOLERANCE; VARIETY; THE CROWD; CITY LIGHTS; WHITE SHADOWS OF THE SOUTH SEAS; A NOUS LA LIBERTE; LA GRANDE ILLUSION; LES ENFANTS DU PARADIS; LE JOUR SE LEVE; CITIZEN KANE. Noël Coward included BRIEF ENCOUNTER amongst his choices (as did Robert Bresson) and the film tied for last place with THE THREEPENNY OPERA, INTOLERANCE and MAN OF

ARAN.*Sight and Sound*, Jul-Sep 1952) *Sight and Sound* subsequently conducted a poll amongst international film critics in which BRIEF ENCOUNTER tied for last place with Clair's LE MILLION and Renoir's LA REGLE DE JEU. (*Sight and Sound*, Oct-Dec 1952) In every decade since, *Sight and Sound* has conducted similar polls - CITIZEN KANE winning every poll and LA REGLE DU JEU ranked third in 1962 and second ever since None of David's films have since made the top ten or been listed in the runners-up.

37 Arthur C. Clarke phone interview, 31 July 1992.
38 Norman Spencer, p.80.

23: Hobson's Choice

1 Originally written as a contemporary piece, its period was transposed to the late 1880s before the first production.
2 There had also been a 1920 film, directed by Percy Nash.
3 Sidney Gilliat letter to author, 6 January 1992.
4 Norman Spencer, p.57.
5 Ibid., p.58.
6 David Lean, p.30.
7 Simon Callow, *Charles Laughton*, p.130.
8 David Lean, pp.218,369.
9 Teddy Darvas, p.10.
10 Ibid., p.11.
11 Robert Donat was only too aware of his age. Harold Brighouse, as it happened, was an old friend, and he wrote him a letter saying he was too old to play Willie Mossop. "Nevertheless, I'm all set to do it. Any hint and tips and prods in the right direction will be gratefully accepted. I hope we can make a smash hit and that we'll be proud of it." (Kenneth Barrow, op. cit., p.183.)
12 Ibid., p.183.
13 Ibid., In 1954, Donat faced the same insurance doctor to play in a film about a parson with only a year to live. On this occasion, Donat passed his medical - LEASE OF LIFE co-starred Kay Walsh and was directed by Charles Frend. Donat died in 1958 after completing his last film, THE INN OF THE SIXTH HAPPINESS, with the aid of oxygen tanks.
14 Paul Gregory, p.1.
15 Peter Newbrook, p.10.
16 John Mills, *Clouds*, op. cit., p.224.
17 Prunella Scales letter to author, 17 July 1992.
18 Norman Spencer, pp.60,116.
19 Preliminary design work had been done by Alexander Trauner, the great French art director who had worked on LES ENFANTS DU PARADIS.
20 Joe Marks letter to author, 14 July 1991.
21 Norman Spencer, p.60. A decade later, A TASTE OF HONEY and other films of the British New Wave were shot in Salford.
22 Teddy Darvas, p.10.
23 Billy Russell was born Adam George Brown in

Birmingham on 16 July 1893. His father was a scenic
artist at the Theatre Royal in Birmingham. He started
acting at the age of twelve and during the First
World War he played in concert party as Bruce
Bairnsfather's cartoon character 'Old Bill.' This
formed the basis of Russell's post-war navvy act, 'On
Behalf of the Working Classes.' In 1969, he was cast
by Lindsay Anderson in the Royal Court production
of *In Celebration*. He played in Stanley Kubrick's A
CLOCKWORK ORANGE but was cut out. He died in a
London TV studio in 1971. (Roy Busby, *Music Hall*,
p.156.)

24   Norman Spencer, p.61.
25   Teddy Darvas, p.10.
26   Ibid.
27   Norman Spencer, p.64.
28   Peter Newbrook, p.47.
29   Hugo Cole, *Malcolm Arnold*, p.61.
30   Malcolm Arnold, pp.2,4.
31   *The Sunday Times*, 28 February 1954.
32   *New Statesman*, 6 March 1954.
33   *The Observer*, 28 February 1954.
34   Korda had already announced the film as the first to
      be made in 3-D outside America and that it would be
      made in both Hindi and English with an Indian and
      European cast. A few months later, CinemaScope
      was introduced and 3-D faded out.
35   David Lean, pp.481-2.
36   Barbara Cole, pp.1,2.
37   Attia Hosain, p.14.
38   David Lean to Barbara Cole, 15 September 1966,
      UoR.
39   David Lean to Santha Rama Rau, 7 October 1981.
40   Ann Todd, pp.40-42.
41   Daily Express, 21 May 1954.

24: Summertime

1   Private source.
2   Notes for Japanese fan magazine.
3   Korda had formed a new partnership with Ilya
      Lopert who was connected to Robert Dowling's
      City Investment Corporation of New York which
      owned such properties as the Empire State Building
      and the Carlyle Hotel. Dowling invested $500,000
      in Korda's London Films (Karol Kulik, *Alexander
      Korda*, p.324). According to Michael Korda,
      Dowling was a tough businessman with an interest in
      art - his private lift boasted a Van Gogh. A powerful
      man in every respect, he had once swum around the
      island of Manhattan and hoped one day to swim the
      Hellespont, like Byron (Michael Korda, *Charmed
      Lives*, p.316).
4   Norman Spencer, p.66-67.
5   Katharine Hepburn, p.3.
6   Norman Spencer, p.67.
7   Pamela Mann, p.7/phone interview 16 November
      1992.

8   Ibid.,p.7. Brazzi had started acting in Italian
      films in 1939 and had recently played in two
      American films made in Italy -THREE COINS IN
      THE FOUNTAIN and THE BAREFOOT CONTESSA.
9   Norman Spencer, p.68.
10   Ibid., p.72.
11   David Lean, p.506.
12   Ibid., pp.377,508.
13   Pamela Mann, p.3.
14   Norman Spencer, p.70.
15   Peter Newbrook, p.8.
16   David Lean letter to Dennis Potter, January 1981,
      TR.
17   Katharine Hepburn, p.2.
18   Peter Newbrook, p.16.
19   David Lean, p.623. In fact, the trip occurs when
      Hepburn has been stared at by Brazzi in the antique
      shop. She is so flustered that she trips as she crosses a
      bridge. David liked the effect so much that he asked
      Peter O'Toole to repeat it in LAWRENCE OF ARABIA as
      Omar Sharif emerges out of the mirage.
20   Leonard Mosley, who interviewed David in Venice,
      claimed that Hepburn did it six times (*Daily Express*,
      26 August 1954.)
21   Peter Newbrook, p.16/letter to author 10
      September 1992.
22   Stephen Silverman, op. cit., p.108.
23   Norman Spencer, p.70. Miranda received the best
      actress award at Cannes for AU-DELA DES GRILLES.
24   David Lean, p.377.
25   Maggie Unsworth, p.1.
26   Norman Spencer, p.71.
27   Katharine Hepburn, p.4.
28   Norman Spencer, pp.72-74.
29   Ibid.
30   Pamela Mann, p.3.
31   David Lean letter to Dennis Potter, January 1981,
      TR.
32   Katharine Hepburn, p.9.
33   Ann Todd to Godfrey Winn, *Daily Sketch*, 26 July
      1956.
34   Norman Spencer, p.81. The film was given an 'A'
      certificate in Britain, meaning that no child could see
      it unless accompanied by an adult. India adopted a
      stricter attitude. "In my experience," wrote David,
      "the Indian censor board is the most backward in the
      world. They banned SUMMERTIME in its entirety,
      presumably because it showed a brief encounter
      between an American spinster and a married Italian,
      in spite of the fact that he was separated. I have
      several good friends in the Indian film world and
      their efforts to raise their home product up out of
      the hackneyed song-and-dance rut of the average
      Indian film are being badly hampered by those no
      doubt worthy Victorian moralists at the top." (Qu.
      Film Book I, p.51.)
35   Norman Spencer, p.79.
36   Peter Lean notes 15 May 1992.

37 Pamela Mann diary, 5 February 1955.
38 Peter Lean to Gerald McKnight, 10 October 1983.
39 David Lean letter to Tony Reeves, 14 July 1981. David went to Paris on 2 April 1955. According to Norman Spencer, "I remember him telling me that if he went abroad for a year (before the start of the fiscal year on 5 April) and had no domicile in the UK during that year, he would pay no UK tax for that year. He said he was told he could spent a maximum of sixty days in England but to make it really safe he should stay away and not return to the UK until the second year. I remember Forsyth saying that three years was the maximum time this tax-avoidance ploy could be utilised." (Norman Spencer letter to author, 21 September 1992.)
40 Jacqueline Thiédot letter to author, 11 August 1992.
41 David Lean circular letter, 8 July 1955 (Pamela Mann.)
42 David Lean letter to Peter Newbrook, 27 April 1955.
43 *Daily Herald*, 30 September 1955. At the premiere in Venice, local people laughed at the way the film's editing played havoc with the geography of their city.
44 *The Observer*, 2 October 1955.
45 *The Sunday Times*, 2 October 1955.
46 Phone interview with Arthur Laurents, 11 March 1992. Richard Rodgers' 1964 musical *Do I Hear A Waltz?* was based on the play and the film.
47 Teddy Darvas, p.6.
48 David Lean, p.509.

25: The Wind Cannot Read

1 David travelled in the summer of 1955, shortly after Otto Preminger arrived in Bombay to make a film about Gandhi to be called THE WHEEL. The project would collapse, leaving the way clear for David's own project.
2 David Lean letter dictated to Pamela Mann, 8 July 1955. All quotes from David in this chapter are from this letter unless otherwise stated.
3 David Lean, p.560.
4 Ibid.
5 CinemaScope was a development of a wide-angle lens designed for the periscopes of tanks used by the French army. Professor Henri Chrétien thought he could use the device to bring panoramic pictures to the screen without the need for two additional projectors, which was the technique used by Abel Gance for NAPOLEON. Only one film was made using Chrétien's invention - Claude Autant-Lara's CONSTRUIRE UN FEU (1929). Not until 1953 did 20th Century-Fox buy the rights from Chrétien and rename the process CinemaScope. That same year, Chrétien won an Oscar. The first film released in CinemaScope was THE ROBE (1953).
6 Pamela Mann, p.2.
7 The Aston Martin was shipped out with Pamela Mann on the *Stratheden*.
8 Pamela Mann letter to parents, 18 August 1955.
9 Pamela Mann, p.8.
10 Pamela Mann letter to parents, 18 August 1955.
11 Pamela Mann, p.8.
12 Norman Spencer, p.48.
13 Cable from Alexander Korda to David Lean, 17 November 1955, TR.
14 David Lean cable to Norman Spencer, 19 November 1955.
15 Norman Spencer letter to author, 13 September 1993.
16 Ibid.
17 Norman Spencer, p.49.
18 David Lean, p.562. In his autobiography, Kenneth More claims that both David and Korda were keen for him to play the part and that he thought the script was "flawless." But he decided not to play this "Rupert Brooke of the RAF" and regarded it as his greatest professional mistake. (Kenneth More, *More Or Less*, pp.227-8.)
19 Pamela Mann, p.8.
20 Norman Spencer, p.50. In 1956, Kishi Keiko married a French director, Yves Ciampi, and appeared in two of his pictures. They had a daughter, Delphine, but the marriage ended in divorce and Keiko returned to Japan. (Jacqueline Thiédot letter to author, 11 August 1992.)
21 Ralph Thomas phone interview, 9 June 1992.
22 Pamela Mann, p.5.
23 Ralph Thomas, phone interview, 9 June 1992.

26: Enter Sam Spiegel: The Bridge on the River Kwai I

1 Orson Welles, Notes, p.4.
2 *Variety*, New York Sound Track column, 25 April 1956, p.4.
3 John Ford told Spiegel, 'You'll have to get a director who understands the Colonel - I don't.' After he saw the film, Ford said he understood. (Stephen Watts in *Films in Review*, April 1959, p.245.) Nicholas Ray was also approached along with Humphrey Bogart! (Eisenschitz, *Nicholas Ray* p.192.)
4 Melvyn Bragg interview, *South Bank Show* transcript, p.2.
5 Born in 1912, the son of an Avignon lawyer, Pierre Boulle went to Malaya in 1936 to work on the British rubber plantations. When the war broke out he enlisted in the French army in Indo-China and then, when the Vichy regime was established, he joined the Free French forces in Singapore. After training as a spy, he sailed a bamboo raft back into Indo-China and was soon captured and sentenced to forced labour. He managed to escape in 1944 to Calcutta.He returned to France in 1948 and embarked on a successful career as a writer. He

died, aged 81, in 1994.

6 Major Xan Fielding lived as a youth in the South of France and was a friend of Michael Powell and Rex Ingram. He was twice infiltrated into wartime Crete where he organised an intelligence network, later dramatised by Powell in the 1955 film ILL MET BY MOONLIGHT. Fielding was later parachuted into Northern France and in 1954 published his autobiography, *Hide and Seek*.

7 Carl Foreman to Adrian Turner, 1 November 1982/Kulik, *Alexander Korda*, p.211.

8 Ibid.

9 Carl Foreman to Adrian Turner, op. cit.

10 Pierre Boulle, *Bridge on the River Kwai*, p.120.

11 David Lean, pp.380, 502, 575.

12 It was undeniably Jewish, being produced by Carl Laemmle Jr., and directed by Lewis Milestone. Among its extras was an even more talented Jew, Fred Zinnemann.

13 Norman Spencer, p.83.

14 David Lean, p.622.

15 At the Critics Awards on 21 January he met Errol Flynn. "I liked Errol Flynn, because he was a great mover, like Doug Fairbanks. I found his Robin Hood very impressive. He came up to me at Sardi's and said, 'Look, if you ever get the chance, do give me a part. I really can act a bit, you know. But for the last twenty years they've put my sword in one hand and my prick in the other and I've been told to go to it.' He was a slightly nutty character, and sad, I should think." (David Lean, p.364.)

16 Norman Spencer letter to author, 22 February 1992.

17 David Lean memo to Sam Spiegel, 31 January 1956, TR.

18 Norman Spencer, pp.82-84.

19 Carl Foreman to Adrian Turner, 1 November 1982.

20 Norman Spencer, pp.90-91.

21 Ibid., pp.84-85.

22 Norman Spencer letter to author, 21 September 1992, p.3.

23 Kwai contract 4 April 1956, TR.

24 David Lean, p.502.

25 Norman Spencer phone interview, 10 June 1993.

26 Sam Spiegel to Ludovic Kennedy, *The Producer and the Film*, BFI Compilation Unit, 1962.

27 David Lean, pp.524-5.

28 Don Ashton, p.1.

29 David Lean, p.264.

30 Carl Foreman to Adrian Turner, 1 November 1982.

31 David Lean, p.533.

32 Ibid.

33 Carl Forman to Adrian Turner, 1 November 1982.

34 END AS A MAN (1957) - THE STRANGE ONE in US - was a film directed by Jack Garfein about brutality in a Southern military institution.

35 David Lean letter to Sam Spiegel, 10 August 1956,TR.

36 Shortly after KWAI, Willingham would be one of three writers credited for Stanley Kubrick's World

War One masterpiece, PATHS OF GLORY. Willingham later co-wrote the screenplay for THE GRADUATE, based on his own novel.

37 David Lean letter to Sam Spiegel, 10 August 1956, TR.

27: Bloody Millionaire Stuff: The Bridge on the River Kwai II

1 Inger-Grethe Mortensen, p1. Mortensen played briefly in a scene, filmed at the hotel, which had been made into a hospital, though she could never find herself in the final cut.

2 Rough of David Lean cable 21 June 1956, TR.

3 Rough of David Lean cable 2 July 1956, TR.

4 Rough of David Lean cable 16 July 1956, TR.

5 Pamela Mann, p.5.

6 Inger-Grethe Mortensen, p.1.

7 David Lean letter to Sam Spiegel, 22 November 1956, TR.

8 David Lean, p.94. The love scene, played on a beach, is between Ann Sears and William Holden, who has escaped from the camp and has arrived at British GHQ. The scene lasts for little over a minute.

9 Sam Spiegel letter to David Lean, 6 August 1956, TR.

10 David Lean letter to Sam Spiegel, 10 August 1956, TR.

11 Guinness quoted in *Focus on Film*, Autumn 1972, p.20.

12 Pamela Mann, p.1.

13 Alec Guinness, p.18.

14 Charles Higham, *Charles Laughton*, p.200. Higham claimed Laughton turned down the role "because it involved several harrowing months in the tropics of Ceylon, and because of the somewhat warlike, militant nature of the story."/Paul Gregory phone interview.

15 Norman Spencer letter to author, 30 July 1991. "Incidentally, Ronald Searle published a book of serious and moving drawings he had made when he was a PoW in one of those camps, and the illustrations played a big part in our general thinking."

16 "Anti-British sentiment?" wrote Pierre Boulle. "Who has dreamed that one up? I am very indignant about this. The truth is that all my books contain a sarcastic nuance towards my fellow men (most often towards the French). May I mention here my first novel, *William Conrad* [1950] which was a vibrant *hommage* to England at war." (Pierre Boulle letter to author, September 1992.)

17 Alec Guinness, p.18.

18 Ibid.

19 David Lean, p.341.

20 Alec Guinness, pp.18-19.

21 Alec Guinness letter to author, 8 September 1992.

22 James Donald had also played the doctor in IN WHICH

WE SERVE.

23 David Lean, p.339.

24 Ibid.

25 David Lean, p.376. The director of SUNSET BOULEVARD, Billy Wilder, was much admired by David, and the character which Holden played for David had much in common with the character Holden played in Wilder's prison camp comedy STALAG 17 (1953) for which he won an Oscar.

26 *Films and Filming*, February 1962, p.21 seq., extract from Sessue Hayakawa, *Zen Showed Me the Way*. David remembered Hayakawa from his inferior British films rather than his American masterpieces, such as THE CHEAT (1915) which David never saw. Hayakawa had already played a Japanese prison camp commandant in THREE CAME HOME (1950) produced by Nunnally Johnson and directed by Jean Negulesco.

27 Peter Newbrook, p.26.

28 David Lean, p.103.

29 Stuart Freeborn, p.18.

30 David Lean, pp.337-338.

31 Eddie Fowlie, pp.27.

32 Ibid., pp.5-6.

33 Roy Stevens, pp.11-12.

34 David Lean, p.339. David sadly forgot Fred Lane, Peter Newbrook, Teddy Darvas, Stuart Freeborn and others who supported him with total loyalty and commitment.

35 Don Ashton, p.1.

36 Geoffrey Horne, quoted in Stephen Silverman, op. cit. p.123.

37 David Lean, p.343.

38 Stephen Silverman, cut section of ms, p.228.

39 Fred Lane, p.2.

40 Stuart Freeborn, p.17.

41 Eddie Fowlie, p.11.

42 Stuart Freeborn, p.17.

43 Peter Newbrook, pp.29,31.

44 Teddy Darvas, p.4.

45 David Lean, pp.339-340.

46 Don Ashton, p.3.

47 Keith Best, *Best Endeavours*, p.34.

48 Eddie Fowlie, p.22.

49 Keith Best, op. cit., p.36.

50 Fred Lane, p.2.

51 David Lean, p.116.

52 Don Ashton, p.4.

53 Peter Newbrook, p.31.

54 Don Ashton, p.4. and Eddie Fowlie letter to author, 14 August 1995

55 David Lean, p.116.

56 Peter Newbrook, p.32.

57 David Lean, p.116.

58 Don Ashton, p.4.

59 David Lean, p.116.

60 Peter Newbrook, p.30.

61 David Lean, pp.286, 625.

62 Peter Taylor letter to author, 19 June 1993.

63 Malcolm Arnold, p.5.

64 David Lean letter to Peter Newbrook, 13 August 1957.

65 Malcolm Arnold, p.3.

66 *Films in Review*, May 1974, p.279.

67 F.W. le Blount Lean letter to David Lean, 6 June 1957, TR.

68 David Lean letter to Barbara Cole, 14 April 1963, UoR.

69 David Lean letter to Peter Newbrook, 13 August 1957.

70 Alec Guinness letter to David Lean, 9 September 1957, TR.

71 Teddy Darvas, p.3.

72 David Lean, p.535.

73 Norman Spencer, p.90.

74 Lindsay Anderson, pp.1-2.

75 *New Statesman and Nation*, 2 October 1957.

76 DL letter to Mike Frankovich, 16 October 1957, Brigham Young University.

77 David Lean, draft for cable, December 1957. David's earlier draft made the point somewhat better: "secondly put me above the line alongside newly launched Spiegel sputnik which has left behind its Rocket."

78 David Lean, p.525.

79 *Noël Coward Diaries*, p.370.

80 David Lean letter to Mike Wilson, 30 January 1958, Adrian Turner collection.

81 Michael Wilson letter to Ring Lardner Jr, 19 September 1961, Adrian Turner Collection.

82 David Lean, p.535.

83 Boulle explained to me how his name appeared on the credits: "Since many writers (two or three) had worked on the screenplay, Spiegel decided to give me the credit, the novel being his basis. I accepted without knowing that the real reason was the famous Black List. I found this out when it was too late. But I have never claimed to have written the script. In fact, I did not care a damn about the script!!" Boulle was critical of the ending of the film. Otherwise, he enjoyed the film. Pierre Boulle, letter to author, September 1992.

84 David Lean, p.537. Carl Foreman was also given full screenplay credit, alongside Michael Wilson, for the video and laser-disc versions issued in 1992.

85 Allen Eyles, ed., booklet for John Player Lecture, National Film Theatre, London, 5 January 1969.

86 Carl Foreman interview with Adrian Turner, 1 November 1982.

87 *Evening Standard*, 12 February 1958.

88 Transcription for *The Listener*, 6 August 1959, p.216 seq.

89 *Observer Magazine*, 1 September 1968.

90 Louis Allen, *Burma: The Longest War*, p.629.

91 *Observer Magazine*, 1 September 1968.

92 David Lean, p.270.

93 David Lean letter to Peter Newbrook, 13 August
    1957.

28: Gandhi

1   "The British Empire wants peace in India," said
    Photoplay. "The effective answer to Gandhi, and the
    effective appeal to the potential colonists of the white
    world can, these British leaders feel, be more
    forcefully phrased in the motion picture than in any
    of the other media of modern propaganda."
    Photoplay, August 1923, p.27.
2   "I may be very wrong, but I think Pascal was flying a
    kite when he asked me to do Gandhi. I never saw a
    script and the project didn't last long." (Alec
    Guinness, letter to author, 8 September 1992).
3   Alec Guinness, p.19.
4   Alec Guinness letter to David Lean, 15 August 1958.
5   David Lean to Tony Reeves, 14 July 1981.
6   Michael Powell, Vol II, *Million Dollar Movie* p.121.
7   Anthony Havelock-Allan, p.72.
8   Michael Powell, op. cit., p.523.
9   Pressburger Diary, 11 November 1958 (courtesy
    Kevin Macdonald).
10 David Lean, p.459.
11 Ibid., p.487.
12 Ibid., p.457.
13 Hiten Chaudhury to David Lean, UoR.
14 Pressburger Diary, 5 December 1958.
15 Emeric Pressburger, *Written in the Stars.* (courtesy
    Kevin Macdonald).
16 David Lean, p.617.
17 According to Stephen Silverman, David's next
    choice after Emeric Pressburger was French writer
    Romain Gary, who was the son of silent star Ivan
    Mosjoukine. After Gary turned it down, Spiegel
    approached Albert Camus, the existentialist writer;
    he died in a car crash. The contacts with both writers
    were made by Sam Spiegel. (Stephen Silverman, op.
    cit. p.127).
18 Alec Guinness, p.20.
19 *Daily Express*, 29 April 1959.
20 *Daily Express*, 30 April 1959.

29: Into the Furnace: Lawrence of Arabia I

1   Private source.
2   David Lean, p.468.
3   Lawrence was born on 16 August,
    Napoleon's birthday.
4   Oriental Secretary to the British Residency in Cairo.
5   This plan was known as The Sykes-Picot Treaty,
    drafted in January 1916.
6   *The New York Times*, 13 January 1924.
7   Herbert Wilcox, p.204.
8   Malcolm Brown (ed.), *The Letters of TE Lawrence*,
    p.520.
9   T.E. Lawrence to Rex Ingram, 5 October 1926,

author's collection.
10 T.E. Lawrence to Rex Ingram, 21 July 1927.
11 Morris, L. Robert & Raskin, Lawrence, *Lawrence of
    Arabia*, p.14.
12 Malcolm Brown (ed.),op. cit., p.520.
13 Hudd had been approved by Lawrence himself who
    had seen him in Shaw's *Too True To Be Good* in
    which he played Private Meek, a thinly-disguised
    Lawrence.
14 Michael Powell, op. cit., p.202.
15 Adrian Turner phone interview, 14 August 1991.
16 Adrian Turner, *The Making of David Lean's
    Lawrence of Arabia*, p.33.
17 David Lean, p.669.
18 Morris & Raskin, op. cit, p.32/Robert Graves
    letter to Prof Lawrence, 16 November 1959.
19 Adrian Turner, op. cit., p.65.
20 David Lean cable to Michael Wilson, 3 February
    1960/Ibid.
21 Adrian Turner, op. cit., p.38.
22 Morris & Raskin, op. cit., p.33. Spiegel was
    slightly mistaken about Brando's age - the actor was
    six years older than he thought.
23 David Lean memo, October 1959.
24 Henry Williamson letter to David Lean, 12 May
    1960, TR.
25 Wilcox, p.205. Wilcox later declared for
    bankruptcy.
26 Anthony Nutting, pp.1-2.
27 David Lean letter to Michael Wilson, 24 April 1960,
    Adrian Turner collection.
28 Several sources state the tests cost £100,000 - surely
    a wild overestimate since the cost of all 72 sets for
    CLEOPATRA at three British studios was only £50,000.
29 Anthony Nutting, p.13.
30 David Lean, p.85.
31 Ibid., p.363. According to Barbara Cole,
    Finney had been advised by Tony Richardson to turn
    the part down. Richardson was the producer of
    SATURDAY NIGHT AND SUNDAY MORNING, which made
    Finney a star in Britain, and the director of TOM
    JONES, which would make Finney an international
    star.
32 Anthony Nutting, p.13.
33 *Evening Standard*, 3 February 1961.
34 Anne Coates, pp.1, 2.
35 David Lean, p.384. If David had read *The Times* on
    23 May 1960 he would have seen a photograph of a
    train wrecked by Lawrence - "taken on location in
    Jordan for the forthcoming production of the film
    LAWRENCE OF ARABIA" - and beneath it, a review of
    THE DAY THEY ROBBED THE BANK OF ENGLAND which
    described O'Toole's performance as "most
    unexpected and accomplished." He would have
    made an effort to see the paper because the
    photograph was one he had taken.
36 David Lean, pp.57, 384.
37 Peter Hall, *Making an Exhibition of Myself*, p.164.

38 Nicholas Wapshott, *Peter O'Toole*, p.23.

39 Andrew Sinclair, *Spiegel*, p.99.

40 Alec Guinness, p.22. By a strange coincidence, Albert Finney was Richard Attenborough's first choice for his own version of GANDHI.

41 John Box phone interview, 15 August 1993.

42 Phyllis Dalton, p.1.

43 Roy Stevens, p.2.

44 David Lean, p.417.

45 Guy Green, p.7.

46 David Lean letter to Sam Spiegel, 6 January 1961, TR.

47 Undated Michael Wilson notes. Adrian Turner, op. cit., pp.71,73.

48 Ibid.

49 David Lean, p96/David Lean letter to Sam Spiegel, 6 January 1961, TR.

50 David Lean letter to Sam Spiegel, 7 January 1961, TR.

51 Robert Bolt didn't think Sam Spiegel had seen the play either. (Robert Bolt fax to author, 12 July 1993.) Stephen Walters said David told him he had never seen the play.

52 Robert Bolt, p.3/*Evening Standard*, 11 May 1989, pp.27-29.

53 Garnett was the seventy-year old son of Edward Garnett, who had worked with Lawrence at Jonathan Cape. David Garnett had published *Letters of T.E. Lawrence* (1938) and *The Essential T.E. Lawrence* (1951). Garnett was to have done an editing and rewrite job and perhaps he was retained to do the same for Bolt. As far as David was concerned, it was all a typical Spiegel muddle.

54 David Lean letter to Sam Spiegel, 6 January 1961, TR.

55 David Lean letter to Sam Spiegel, 7 January 1961, TR.

56 David Lean letter to Sam Spiegel, 25 February 1961, TR.

57 *Lawrence by His Friends*, p.221.

58 David Lean memo, October 1959, TR.

59 Robert Graves said on BBC radio that S.A. was a woman Lawrence had met behind the Turkish lines. (*Lawrence of Cloud's Hill*, 3 December 1958.) David undertook a great deal of research into this mystery himself. Most biographers of Lawrence select Sheik Ahmed, as S.A.; he was also known as Dahoum. Lawrence met him during an archaeological dig in Syria before the war and brought him back to Oxford on a visit. The film's Ali is an amalgam of several characters; in the film he is called Sherif Ali el Kharishi.

60 David Lean, pp.86-7.

61 This was not the case. Omar Sharif had made THE BLAZING SUN which represented Egypt at the Cannes Film Festival. Sharif's name was Michael Shalhoub, changed to Omar after General Omar Bradley rather than Omar Khayyam. (Omar Sharif,

The Eternal Male, p.15.) He was born a Catholic in 1932, in Alexandria, and was converted to Islam for his first marriage to a leading Egyptian film star.

62 David Lean, p.89.

63 Adrian Turner, op. cit., p.117.

64 Omar Sharif op. cit., p.13/Adrian Turner, op. cit., p.117/Morris-Raskin, op. cit, p.69.

65 When Spiegel released Sharif for DOCTOR ZHIVAGO he asked $150,000. (Lee Steiner to David Lean, 4 October 1964, UoR.)

66 Sam Spiegel, *South Bank Show*, p.17.

67 Beverley Cross phone interview, 28 March 1994.

68 John Box, p.15.

69 David Lean letter to Dennis Potter, January 1981, TR.

70 *Evening Standard*, 11 May 1989, pp.28-29.

71 David Lean to Adrian Turner, *Lawrence*, p.82.

72 Anthony Nutting, p.12.

73 David Lean, p.96.

74 David Lean letter to Freddie Young, 16 July 1968.

75 Stephen Silvermann, op. cit., p.164.

76 Freddie Young, pp.11-12. *The American Cinematographer* (April 1989, p.95) published an article about the inventors of the lens, which gives the impression it was ordered by Freddie Young and designed especially for the mirage. Young says no one at Panavision knew anything about the mirage and he was bewildered by the article. I have written to author Ron Magid but received no reply. In his article, Magid quoted the inventors of the lens as saying it was "about 482mm" but a photograph taken on the location clearly shows the lens marked as being 450mm.

77 David Lean, p.96.

78 Freddie Young, p.16.

79 Ernie Day, pp.5-6.

80 David Lean, pp.224,265.

81 Morris & Raskin, op. cit., p.80/Denise Worrell, op. cit., p.149.

82 Morris & Raskin, op. cit., p.80.

83 *New York Times*, 15 May 1961.

84 Adrian Turner, op. cit., p.115.

85 Peter Newbrook letter to author, 9 October 1991.

86 Freddie Young manuscript, pp.8-9.

87 David Lean letter to Mike Frankovich, 29 December 1961, Brigham Young University.

88 Howard Kent, p.160.

89 John Box, pp.21-22.

90 Freddie Young, p.12.

91 Peter Newbrook, p.41. Oddly, the continuity sheets reveal several takes, the longest being 260 ft.

92 David Lean letter to Freddie Young, 16 July 1968.

93 David Lean, *South Bank Show* transcript, p.25.

94 Adrian Turner, op. cit., p.121-2.

95 Barbara Cole, p.20.

96 Ibid.

97 Nicholas Wapshott, op. cit., p.82.

98 Robert Bolt fax to author, 9 January 1993.

99 David Lean, p.530.

30: Old Fashioned Romance: Lawrence of Arabia II

1   David Lean, p.221.
2   Barbara Cole, p.4.
3   Ibid/Last line is from Barbara Cole's explanatory note to David Lean letters, UoR.
4   Ibid., p.5.
5   Ibid., p.8.
6   Ibid., p.11.
7   Ibid., p.15.
8   Ibid., p.2.
9   Morris & Raskin, op. cit., p.7.
10 T.E. Lawrence, *Seven Pillars*, pp.423,384.
11 David Lean, p.338.
12 Ibid., pp.336-7.
13 Roy Stevens, pp.6,15.
14 Barbara Cole, p.6.
15 Freddie Young, pp.47-48.
16 David Lean, p.530.
17 Alec Guinness, p.42.
18 Ernie Day, p.11.
19 Barbara Cole, p.11.
20 Roy Stevens, p.42. Another Heron crashed on 20 September 1961 and one reel of rushes was destroyed. That same day the brakes failed on one of the two DC3s and it crashed. (Peter Newbrook letter to author, 10 December 1992, p.2.)
21 David Lean, p.378.
22 Eddie Fowlie, p.13.
23 And the worst nearly happened. On 13 September 1961, O'Toole was sitting on a camel ready for the charge at Aqaba, when an effects gun went off accidentally, in his right eye. The camel bolted and O'Toole, temporarily blinded, was thrown into the path of five hundred charging horses. The camel stood over its master, as it had been trained to do, protecting him and probably saving his life. Luckily, O'Toole wasn't hurt - after all the operations on his left eye, any damage to his right would have been catastrophic - and he was back in front of the cameras the following day. (Howard Kent, p139.)
24 Roy Stevens, p.6.
25 Nicholas Wapshott, op. cit., p.82.
26 Barbara Cole, pp.9, 11.
27 Nicholas Wapshott, op. cit., p.86.
28 *The Observer*, 18 October 1992, p.23.
29 David Lean, p.345
30 Ernie Day, p.8.
31 Peter Newbrook letter to author, 9 October 1991.
32 Ernie Day, p.7.
33 David Lean, p.250.
34 Freddie Young, p.19.
35 Barbara Cole, p.5.
36 Freddie Young, p.19.

37 Ibid., p.17.
38 Ibid.
39 Ibid.
40 Roy Stevens, p.13.
41 Peter Newbrook, p.38.
42 David Lean to Sam Spiegel, 29 September 1961.
43 Anne Coates, p.9.
44 Adrian Turner, op. cit., p.129.
45 David Lean letter to Sam Spiegel, 29 September 1961.
46 John Box, p.17.
47 John Box, p.19.
48 David Lean, p.96.
49 Adrian Turner, who has examined Columbia's legal files, confirms that the company was reluctant to pour any more money into an Arab country.
50 David Lean, p.96.
51 Barbara Cole, p.17.
52 Anne Coates, *SFTS Journal*, Winter 1962-63, p.22.
53 John Box, p.18.
54 Barbara Cole, p.1.
55 Ibid., pp.2,10,22. While Barbara was ill, they shot the scene of the Damascus council chamber with Margaret Prado as continuity girl.
56 Pedro Vidal, pp.4,15.
57 David Lean letter to Robert Bolt, 15 June 1964, UoR.
58 Jack Hawkins, *Anything for a Quiet Life*, p.126.
59 Ibid.
60 Alec Guinness, p.21.
61 Pedro Vidal, p.24. Both men had worked in Jordan.
62 Adrian Turner, *Lawrence*, p.141. Actually, Louis Roberts, Columbia's man in Spain, had recommended Almeria (Eddie Fowlie fax to author, 27 August 1993) but De Toth's aerial survey may have confirmed the company's hopes.
63 Nic Roeg, p.2.
64 Ibid.
65 André de Toth phone interview, 15 January 1993.
66 Nic Roeg, p.8.
67 John Box, phone interview, 15 August 1993.
68 David Lean, p.95.
69 Nic Roeg and the second unit covered closer shots and detail to build up the sequence before the track.
70 John Box, BAFTA lecture, p.1/George Perry tribute to David Lean, BBC Radio 4, April 1991.
71 Adrian Turner, op. cit., p.151.
72 David Lean, p.271.
73 Pedro Vidal, p.23.
74 Norman Spencer, p.96/Robert Parrish, *Hollywood Doesn't Live Here Any More*, pp.9-10.
75 Norman Spencer, p.99.
76 *Films and Filming*, January 1963, p.13/SFTS Journal, Winter 1962-63, p.24.
77 Day 284 of location, 21 July 1962.
78 Norman Spencer, p.102.
79 Ernie Day, p.13.
80 David Lean, p.103.

81 John Box, *SFTS Journal*, Winter 1962-63, p.18.
82 T.E. Lawrence, op. cit., p.654.
83 Nic Roeg, p.9.
84 David Lean, p.103.
85 Nic Roeg, p.3.
86 Nicholas Wapshott, op. cit., p.90.
87 David Lean, p.100.
88 Barbara Cole, p.6.
89 Anne Coates, p.16.
90 Willie Kemplen phone interview, 13 April 1993.
91 Barbara Cole, p.6.
92 Anne Coates, pp.7,11. Coates's assistants were (First) Willie Kemplen, (Second) Ray Lovejoy, (Third) Roy York.
93 Anne Coates, pp.13,14.
94 Anne Coates, p.12. David had seen the early films of the New Wave, such as Chabrol's LES COUSINS, because he refers to them in his long memos on *Seven Pillars* - he said they had the audacity to blow the gaff on the sentimental nature of the average picture and the old movie cliché. As an editor in this period myself, I remember reacting against dissolves; I was heartily sick of them. They had often been beautifully used, especially during the silent period when they were done in the camera, but they had become maddeningly clichéd when optical printers made them the easiest way out of an awkward transition. David himself certainly over-used them in films like THE LAST ADVENTURERS. However, a fresh examination of LAWRENCE reveals that there are just as many dissolves as there would have been had David made this film in the old days - there are literally dozens. But their presence ensures that when there is a strong direct cut, one notices it all the more.
95 David Lean, p.395.
96 Morris & Raskin, op. cit., p.141.
97 Malcolm Arnold, p.2.
98 Susanna Walton, op. cit., p.22.
99 Maurice Jarre, pp.2-3,*RPO/Sound Track* (Belgium), December 1984, p.6.
100 David Lean, p.532.
101 *Stills*, March 1985, p.35.
102 *Film Comment*, March-April 1981, p.51.

31: The Jelly in the Sunlit Pool: Lawrence of Arabia III

1 David Lean, p.609.
2 Anthony Nutting, p.2.
3 *The Times*, 6 April 1991.
4 David Lean letter to Robert Bolt, 15 June 1964, UoR.
5 Adrian Turner, op. cit., p.89.
6 Michael Wilson letter to Robert Bolt, 29 November 1962, Harry Ransom Humanities Research Center, Austin, Texas.
7 Adrian Turner, op. cit., p.93.
8 PLANET OF THE APES contains several sequences in which the marooned astronaut played by Charlton Heston is interrogated by a tribunal of monkeys. Is this possibly an allegory of the McCarthy hearings written by one of the victims of the blacklist?
9 Anne Coates, p.10.
10 David Lean, pp.3,494.
11 David is confusing events - his nephew Anthony married in 1962, but not in Devon. His nephew John, who lives in Devon, was not married until 1967 (although Frank did attend). On the ticket for the film that David sent to his father he had written, "This party will probably be too late for you - starts after the film which will finish at about midnight - I'm afraid the film is 3 hrs & 40 mins. Have been in hectic work - will ring and arrange a hotel for the night. Love David."
12 Private source.
13 Barbara Cole, p.22.
14 Anthony Nutting, p.18.
15 *South Bank Show* transcript, p.23.
16 Fred Zinnemann, p.3.
17 *Evening Standard*, 13 December 1962.
18 *New Statesman*, 14 December 1962.
19 *Sunday Times*, 16 December 1962.
20 *The Observer*, 16 December 1962.
21 *The Village Voice*, 20 December 1962.
22 David Lean, p.167.
23 David Lean letter to Barbara Cole, 17 December 1962, UoR.
24 David Lean letter to Robert Bolt, 23 December 1962, UoR.
25 Ibid.
26 David Lean letter to Barbara Cole, 17 December 1962, UoR.
27 David Lean letter to Barbara Cole, 20 December 1962, UoR.
28 David Lean letter to Barbara Cole, 30 December 1962, UoR.
29 David Lean letter to Barbara Cole, 4 April 1963, UoR.
30 Barbara Cole letter to David Lean, 2 July 1963, UoR.
31 David Lean letter to Barbara Cole, 15 April 1963, UoR.
32 The award for best screenplay (based on material from another medium) went to TO KILL A MOCKINGBIRD, for which Gregory Peck was named as Best Actor. It is possible that one of the reasons why Bolt went unrewarded was the dispute over screen credit - BEN-HUR, which won a record eleven Oscars, did not win the screenplay award for that same reason.
33 David Lean letter to Barbara Cole, 11 April 1963, UoR.
34 David Lean letter to Barbara Cole, 15 April 1963, UoR.
35 David Lean, p.267.

36 David Lean letter to Barbara Cole, 1 July 1963, UoR.

37 David Lean letter to Barbara Cole, 17 February 1963, UoR.

38 Fred Zinnemann worked on the the James Michener novel for a year but it was was eventually filmed in 1966 by George Roy Hill, with Max von Sydow and Julie Andrews.

39 Barbara Cole, pp.9,15,18.

40 Kay Walsh phone interview, 16 September 1991.

41 Barbara Cole, p.16.

42 Christopher Mann letter to David Lean, 8 June 1964, UoR.

43 David Lean, pp.371, 373.

44 Tony Reeves phone interview, 4 January, 1993. When Adrian Turner examined the LAWRENCE files at Columbia Pictures he found a statement which proved that David had received $1,135,985 by 1985. This was probably much less than Spiegel had received, though it does show how David rather exaggerated Spiegel's chicanery.

45 Cecil Woodham-Smith's book about the Crimean War and the Charge of the Light Brigade.

46 David Lean letter to Robert Bolt, 30 June 1963, UoR.

32: The Greatest Story Ever Told

1 David Lean letter to Barbara Cole, 15 September 1966, UoR.

2 Barbara Cole, p.19.

3 David Lean letter to Barbara Cole, 4 April 1963, UoR.

4 David Lean letter to Richard Lester, 26 October 1968. PETULIA was edited by Anthony Gibbs, photographed by Nic Roeg and starred Julie Christie and George C. Scott whom David was considering for RYAN'S DAUGHTER.

5 Barbara Cole, p.7.

6 David Lean to Barbara Cole, 12 April 1963, UoR.

7 Transcript, AFI Seminar, 12 December 1984.

8 David Lean letter to Barbara Cole, 12 April 1963, UoR.

9 Ibid.

10 David Lean to John Box, qu. Stephen Silverman, p.152.

11 Ibid.

12 David Lean letter to Barbara Cole, 27 April 1963, UoR.

13 Ibid.

14 Transcript, AFI Seminar, 12 December 1984.

15 David Lean, p.539.

16 David Lean letter to Barbara Cole, 11 April 1963, UoR.

17 David Lean, p.539.

33: Straightening Cobwebs: Doctor Zhivago I

1 David Lean to Barbara Cole, 15 April 1963, UoR.

2 Boris Pasternak, *Doctor Zhivago*, p.274.

3 Ibid., p.202.

4 Robert O'Brien letters to author, 26 September 1991/15 October 1991.

5 Robert Bolt letter to David Lean, 25 May 1963.

6 David Lean letter to Barbara Cole, 30 June 1963, UoR.

7 Robert Bolt letter to David Lean, 27 June 1963, UoR.

8 David Lean letter to Robert Bolt, 30 June 1963, UoR.

9 David Lean letter to Barbara Cole, 14 August 1963, UoR.

10 Ibid.

11 Ibid.

12 Robert Bolt letter to David Lean, 5 June 1973, TR

13 Thacher was MGM's executive story editor, based in New York.

14 Qu. David Lean letter to Barbara Cole, 10 April 1964, UoR.

15 David Lean letter to Robert Bolt, 18 May 1964, UoR.

16 Robert Bolt letter to David Lean, 21 May 1964, UoR.

17 David had read Pasternak's *An Essay In Autobiography*.

18 David Lean letter to Barbara Cole, 12 August 1963, UoR.

19 David Lean letter to Robert Bolt, 15 June 1964, UoR.

20 Robert Bolt letter to David Lean, 20 June 1964, UoR.

21 Barbara Cole, p.13.

22 Robert Bolt letter to David Lean, 12 November 1964, UoR.

23 Robert Bolt letter to Barbara Cole, 17 November 1964, UoR.

24 Robert Bolt letter to David Lean, 23 June 1964, UoR.

25 Robert Bolt, DOCTOR ZHIVAGO screenplay, p.12.

26 Robert Bolt to Robert Stewart, pp.3-4.

27 Robert Bolt, p.2.

28 John Coldstream, *Daily Telegraph*, 22 September 1984, p.14.

29 Robert Bolt to David Lean, nd, probably February 1965.

34: Arrivals: Doctor Zhivago II

1 Barbara Cole, p.12.

2 David Lean letter to Robert O'Brien, 4 June 1964, UoR.

3 David Lean, p.411.

4 David Lean to Robert O'Brien, 4 June 1964, UoR.

5 David Lean letter to Robert Bolt, 30 June 1963, UoR.

6 Later, Jeanne Moreau was asked to play Lara's mother and replied, with icy dignity, that perhaps

she was a trifle young for the role.

7   David Lean letter to Robert O'Brien, 4 June 1964. It is hardly likely that MGM would have warmed to this idea, anyway, following their experience with Brando on MUTINY ON THE BOUNTY.

8   David Lean letter to Lee Steiner, 1 November 1964, UoR.

9   Stephen Silverman, op. cit.,p.169. Bolt would later marry Sarah Miles.

10 David Lean, p.382.

11 When Ford became ill, he was replaced by Jack Cardiff.

12 Robert O'Brien letter to author, 26 September 1991.

13 Don Bessant, a 24-year-old art teacher from Kent.

14 Julie Christie phone interview, 14 January 1993.

15 Barbara Cole, p.9b.

16 Casting outline, 18 March 1964, UoR.

17 Barbara Cole, p.3.

18 David Lean, p.381.

19 Barbara Cole, p.14.

20 David Lean, pp.381-2. When they were making LAWRENCE in Spain, David involved himself in Omar Sharif's future career. "One month before we finished shooting David told me I was going to be a very big star but I would be in great danger because they would always ask me to play an Arab on a camel. David said I must refuse them [and] said he would lend me some money so that I would feel obliged to him and could afford to turn the offers down. He gave me $15,000." (Adrian Turner, op. cit., p.139.)

21 Stephen Silverman, op. cit., p.165.

22 Part of the test, photographed by Manuel Berenguer on 29 October 1964, can be seen in Scott Benson's *Dr Zhivago - The Making of an Epic* in the MGM/UA videocassette of DOCTOR ZHIVAGO.

23 Oona Chaplin replied, "What luck to be considered for such an important part with you as director. We do hope it works out, but in any case she must be proud of your opinion of her talent." Oona Chaplin letter to David Lean, 11 November 1964, UoR.

24 David Lean letter to Alec Guinness, 11 November 1964. The part of Alexander went to Ralph Richardson.

25 *ABC Film Review*, 11 November 1964, p.10.

35: Departures: Doctor Zhivago III

1   Barbara Cole, p.13.

2   David Lean, p.583.

3   John Box, p.29.

4   David Lean, p.545. The film was not shown in Russia until May 1994.

5   After the recce David took delivery of a new Rolls-Royce Silver Cloud III straight from the Paris Motor Show. It was a left-hand drive model which led one of the crew to joke that David's knighthood would

be delayed for another few years.

6   John Box, p.29.

7   Ibid., p.30.

8   Barbara Cole, p.16.

9   Roy Stevens, p.23.

10 Nic Roeg, p.3.

11 David Lean letter to Freddie Young, 5 July 1963.

12 Joan Young phone interview, 13 April 1993.

13 David Lean letter to Barbara Cole, 30 April 1963, UoR/Pasternak, p.47.

14 David Lean letter to Freddie Young, 18 July 1963.

15 Nic Roeg, p.5. The boy in the scene was Omar Sharif's seven-year-old son, Tarek, and David asked Omar to direct him. (Omar Sharif, *Eternal Male*, p.87.) The funeral and the scene of the boy staring out of the window, with the twigs tapping the glass during a storm, are reminiscent of GREAT EXPECTATIONS.

16 Nic Roeg, p.4.

17 Nic Roeg, p.12.

18 Roy Stevens, p.22.

19 Nic Roeg, p.11.

20 Ibid.

21 Adrian Turner in Pedro Vidal, p.21, confirmed by Nic Roeg.

22 Pedro Vidal, p.21.

23 David Lean, pp.349-350. Nic Roeg drove home with his family pondering the implications of his dismissal. But the incident did not impede his career. He was hired as Director of Photography for John Schlesinger on FAR FROM THE MADDING CROWD starring Julie Christie (David hated it). He made his directorial debut with PERFORMANCE. As David had shown the summer magnificence of Venice, so Roeg showed its wintry, sinister aspect in DON'T LOOK NOW, starring Julie Christie. He soon won a reputation for experimental films noted for their cinematography, but as far from the David Lean style as a space ship from a Spitfire. He was awarded a C.B.E. in 1995.

24 Roy Stevens, p.20.

25 Andrew Mollo, p.2.

26 Eddie Fowle letter to author, 14 August 1995.

27 Phyllis Dalton, p.4.

28 Andrew Mollo, p.3.

29 Gerald Pratley, op. cit., p.17.

30 Ernie Day, pp.23-24.

31 Roy Stevens, p.22.

32 Eddie Fowlie, p.8.

33 Phyllis Dalton p.4.

34 David Lean, p.105.

35 *Esquire*, 23 May 1965.

36 Eddie Fowlie, *South Bank Show*. Eisenstein had shot the Battle on the Ice for ALEXANDER NEVSKY in high summer, too.

37 John Box phone interview, 15 August 1993.

38 Rod Steiger on *Meridien*, BBC World Service, 23 April 1991.

39 Ernie Day, p.20.
40 Pedro Vidal, p.16. Geraldine Chaplin remembered David saying "Dress the double.".
41 David Lean, pp.131-2. David may have been exaggerating here, because Freddie Young was in absolute agreement with the idea of extracting the colour. The pane of glass, which appears to be frozen, was painted by Eddie Fowlie who used a feather to etch the design. In the scene with Lara and Pasha, viewed from outside the window, David wanted the effect of the warmth of the candle melting a circle of ice on the glass. A hair-dryer, operated by Eddie Fowlie, substituted for the warmth of the candle flame and it gradually created a hole in the frozen window pane through which the audience could see the two characters.
42 Andrew Mollo, p.5.
43 Pedro Vidal, p.14.
44 Andrew Mollo, p.3.
45 David Lean to Robert Stewart, p.14.
46 Stephen Silverman, op. cit.,p.165.
47 David Lean, p.624. It is the scene when Lara and Zhivago meet as they walk through crowds of troops deserting the front line.
48 David Lean, p.349/Freddie Young, p.12.
49 David Lean letter to Freddie Young, 16 July 1968, p.9.
50 David Lean letter to Freddie Young, 16 July 1968. Freddie Young used a technique familiar from the silent days. A gauze on a wooden frame was placed in the matte box, and a hole burned with a cigarette in the centre, just large enough to accommodate Sharif's face. Then the gauze was flooded with light, which was shielded from the lens, so that everything burned out but Omar's face. (Freddie Young manuscript, p.139.)
51 Geraldine Chaplin to author, 7 September 1994.
52 Boris Pasternak, op. cit., p.259.

36: Seize the Day! Doctor Zhivago IV

1 David Lean, pp.381,387.
2 Barbara Cole, p.19.
3 Tony Lawson, p.1.
4 Roy Stevens, p.31.
5 Ralph Sheldon to author, 2 February 1993.
6 Win Ryder, p.22.
7 Steinkamp was still given credit, however, and the entire MGM sound department was nominated for an Academy Award.
8 AFI transcript, p.57. On the other hand, David loathed Technicolor because they would provide a good answer print but he felt that their work then deteriorated. He used to drop into theatres and saw prints which should have been discarded.
9 Maurice Jarre, p.4.
10 David Lean, pp.541-2.
11 David Lean letter to Tony Reeves, 14 July 1981. Complete prints would have been needed, however, for the press previews in New York and Los Angeles the previous day.
12 David Lean, pp.107, 411-4. When David told me this, it accorded with my own experience. I happened to be in New York when the picture opened and saw it in a practically empty Capitol Theatre. However, *Variety* reported that the picture opened strongly - $70,224 for the first ten days and between $43,000 and $51,000 for subsequent weeks. After the tenth week at the Capitol, *Variety* reported an MGM executive as saying, "ZHIVAGO has had only one non-capacity showing so far (a strikebound Wednesday matinee) and while L.A run has not been as good it is doing better in fifth and sixth weeks."
13 Judith Crist, *The Private Eye, the Cowboy and the Very Naked Girl*, p.156.
14 *Time*, 31 December 1965.
15 *Life*, 24 January 1966, p.62A.
16 Robert Bolt letter to David Lean, 21 January 1966, UoR.
17 David Lean, p.413.
18 David Lean letter to Barbara Cole, 17 February 1966, UoR.
19 David Lean letter to Barbara Cole, 19 April 1966, UoR.
20 David Lean letter to Barbara Cole, 1 May 1966, UoR.
21 David Lean, pp.137-9. Tynan wrote to say the reason he was late was that his plane had been delayed - he complained of this professionally damaging treatment. David replied that it was the sort of treatment he, as a critic, was used to handing out. (*Letters of Kenneth Tynan*, p.346.)
22 Andrew Mollo, pp.4-5. Said Barbara Cole, "As a rule, the producer- director and the departments put together the credits. I don't know anyone who was left off for reasons of dislike. They probably just plain forgot." (Barbara Cole, p.9.)
23 Alec Guinness, p.33.
24 Qu.David Lean letter to Barbara Cole, 26 February 1966, UoR.
25 David Lean, *Meridien*, BBC World Service, 23 April 1991.
26 Stephen Silverman, op. cit., p.167.
27 Robert Bolt was unable to attend either the American premiere or the Academy Awards ceremony because he was refused an American visa on account of his criminal record (the prison sentence in 1961) and a recent official visit to China.
28 David Lean letter to Barbara Cole, 19 April 1966, UoR.
29 Sandy Lean, p.58.
30 David Lean, p.591.

37: India and The Procession of Life

1 Robert Bolt letter to David Lean, 21 January 1966, UoR.

2   Richard Attenborough, who has chronicled the two decades he spent getting the film made, was rewarded with staggering success which must have shaken David, who did not see the film until a hotel manager in India persuaded him to watch it on video. Because it was incomplete and of poor quality,he always declared that he hadn't seen the film.

3   David Lean letter to Barbara Cole, 22 August 1966, UoR.

4   *Nine-Tiger Man* was a novel by Lesley Blanch, author of *The Wilder Shores of Love* and the ex-wife of Romain Gary, the celebrated French author. Set during the Indian Mutiny, this epic romance included tiger hunting, riots, house parties and inter-racial sex. Terence Rattigan wrote the script. (McGilligan, p.293.) It was never filmed.

5   David Lean letter to Barbara Cole, April 1966, UoR.

6   David Lean letter to Barbara Cole, 27 September 1966, UoR.

7   David Lean letter to Barbara Cole, 12 December 1966, UoR.

8   This was actually an underestimate, it eventually grossed more than $200 million worldwide.

9   David Lean letter to Barbara Cole, 18 August 1966, UoR.

10 David Lean letter to Barbara Cole, 19 August 1966, UoR.

11 David Lean letter to Barbara Cole, 13 September 1966, UoR.

12 David Lean letter to Tony Reeves, 14 July 1981.

13 David Lean letter to Barbara Cole, 15 September 1966, UoR.

14 Ibid.

15 David Lean letter to Barbara Cole, 9 October 1966, UoR.

16 David Lean letter to Barbara Cole, 21 October 1966, UoR.

17 David Lean letter to Barbara Cole, 18 November 1966, UoR.

18 Ibid.

19 Ibid.

20 David Lean letter to Barbara Cole, 18 August 1966, UoR.

21 David Lean letter to Barbara Cole, 18 November 1966, UoR.

22 Sandy Lean, p.2.

23 Sandy Lean fax to author, 23 August 1995.

24 Barbara Cole, pp.10,14,20.

25 Sandy Lean fax to author, 23 August 1995.

26 Ibid.

38: A Little Gem: Ryan's Daughter I

1   Sandy Lean, p.16/phone interview, 31 May 1993/fax to author 23 August 1995.

2   Robert Bolt, p.1.

3   David Lean letter to Barbara Cole, 15 September 1966, UoR.

4   David Lean, p.202.

5   David Lean to Michael Billington, *The Times*, 5 December 1970. "But I think it could happen anywhere." Gerald Pratley, op. cit., p.202.

6   David Lean letter to Freddie Young, 16 July 1968.

7   Peter Miller to author, 15 June 1991.

8   Richard Lester, p.1. At a dinner a few months earlier, Lester's wife had suggested *A Passage to India* as a project for David.

9   John Mills, p.16.

10 Ibid., p.17.

11 Anthony Havelock-Allan, pp.42-44.

12 Robert Bolt letter to David Lean, 22 October 1968, TR.

13 David Lean, p.202.

14 Peck is a third cousin of the Irish patriot Thomas Ashe, who was born near Dingle and who fought in the Easter Rising. His grandmother was Catherine Ashe from Dingle. (Gregory Peck to Howard Prouty, 5 February 1996)

15 Anthony Havelock-Allan, pp.42-43.

16 Jerry Roberts, *Robert Mitchum - A Bio-Bibliography*, p.201/George Eells, *Robert Mitchum*, p.245/Robert Bolt fax to author, 23 November 1993.

17 Tony Lawson, p.5.

18 Sarah Miles, p.3.

19 George Eells, op. cit.,p.248.

20 Bob Huke, p.4.

21 Robert Mitchum to Nigel Andrews, *International Express*, 24 April 1991, p.46.

22 *Sound on Film*, November 1970.

23 David Lean letter to Alec Guinness, 13 September 1968.

24 Alec Guinness phone interview, 4 July 1994.

25 David Lean, pp.159, 160, 201.

26 Robert Bolt letter to David Lean, 22 October 1968, TR.

27 David Lean, pp.196-7.

28 John Box, p.23.

29 Sarah Miles, p.1. The actor who dubbed Jones was Tony Walbrook. (*Film Comment*, July-August 1992, p.35.)

30 David Lean, p.194.

31 Anthony Havelock-Allan, p.52.

32 Christopher Jones, phone interview, 14 December 1995.

33 Anthony Havelock-Allan, p.52.

34 Freddie Young, p40/manuscript, p168.

35 David Lean, p.196.

36 Robert Bolt letter to David Lean, 11 October 1968, TR/ Robert Bolt fax to author, 31 May 1993.

37 Russell Thacher to Robert Bolt and David Lean, 21 October 1968.

38 Robert Bolt letter to Russell Thacher, 24 October 1968.

39 David Lean, p.50.

40 Freddie Young to Gary Crowdus, June 1994/David Lean letter to Freddie Young, 16 July 1968.

41 Eddie Fowlie, pp.36-7. The place Eddie found was Banner Beach, near Tralee.

42 David Lean, p.183. David offered to leave the set standing as a tourist attraction but the Dingle council turned the idea down. Only the schoolhouse was left standing. It is now vandalised and no longer the tourist attraction it once was. However, every local I spoke to agreed that RYAN'S DAUGHTER had led to an explosion of tourism. "They could have had the whole bloody village," said David.

43 Micheal de Mordha, *Ryan's Daughter*, synopsis for book, p.2.

44 *Observer Magazine* 7 June 1992. In 1992 director Ron Howard shot the opening of FAR AND AWAY, with Tom Cruise, on the old David Lean location near Dunquin. By coincidence, it was the first film to be shot on 65mm since RYAN'S DAUGHTER and its title suggests a reference to David's production company, Faraway.

45 Fred Lane letter to author, 19 August 1992.

46 John Mills, op. cit., p.262.

47 John Mills, p.18.

48 David Lean, p.548.

49 Vivienne Knight, op. cit., p.192.

50 With actors' caravans, prop trucks and generators, there were sometimes twenty to thirty vehicles in the convoy. There had been sixty minor accidents since the unit arrived. (*Woman's Own*, 25 April 1970, p.34.)

51 Anthony Havelock-Allan, p.45.

52 *LA Times* Calendar Section, 15 November 1970, p.28.

53 *American Cinematographer*, August 1969, p.788.

54 Fred Zinnemann, p.4. James Aubrey cancelled MAN'S FATE on 21 November 1969, just three days before it was due to start shooting. Although it was a Carlo Ponti production, MGM made Zinnemann personally responsible for the $3.5 million spent on the film so far. Zinnemann filed a lawsuit. MAN'S FATE, RYAN'S DAUGHTER and, another epic, TAI-PAN, would have cost MGM $60 million if they had gone forward as planned, but with the studio fending off creditors such an outlay was out of the question. (Peter Bart, *Fade Out*, p.35.) Another MGM film cancelled at the same time, though possibly for different reasons, was Stanley Kubrick's NAPOLEON.

55 Peter Bart, op. cit., p.40.

56 Roy Stevens, p.8.

57 Ken Bray , p.2.

58 Robert Bolt letter to David Lean, 20 September 1969, TR.

59 Eddie Fowlie, p.39.

60 Freddie Young, p.44/manuscript, p.174.

61 David Lean, *Movie Men*, Granada TV, 1970.

62 Stephen Silverman, op. cit.,p.176.

63 Ibid.

64 John Mills, pp.33-34.

65 David Lean, pp.195-9.

66 Christopher Jones, phone interview, 14 December 1995

39: The Seventh Wave: Ryan's Daughter II

1 Freddie Young, p.31.

2 David Lean, p.188,548.

3 Freddie Young, p.30.

4 David Lean, p.188.

5 Freddie Young, pp.28-29.

6 Roy Stevens, p.28.

7 David Lean, p.610.

8 Roy Stevens, p.27.

9 Eddie Fowlie, p.40.

10 David Lean, p.187.

11 Roy Stevens, pp.27-28.

12 Roy Stevens pp.29-30/phone interview 11 August 1995.

13 Roy Stevens, pp.29-30.

14 Ibid., pp.9,11. In fairness to David, I should point out that he gave credit to Roy Stevens when he was recounting the storm incidents to me, saying, "He did it bloody well." Stevens also received special credit on the film itself as a second unit director: "Roy Stevens (Storm)."

40: Losing the Light

1 Alan Wood, *Mr Rank*, p.137.

2 Tony Lawson, p.4.

3 Freddie Young, p.52.

4 David Lean, p.206.

5 Ibid., p.500.

6 Denise Worrell, op. cit., p.151.

7 The New York premiere was in aid of the Museum of Modern Art Film Department, and the Museum gave David a retrospective in October 1970.

8 Sandy Lean fax to author, 23 August 1995.

9 Richard Schickel letter to author, 22 March 1993.

10 Sandy Lean, pp.19-20/fax to author, 23 August 1995.

11 David Lean, pp.550, 610. Three years later, the Canadian critic, Gerald Pratley, planned a book about David's films but David, still smarting from the Algonquin meeting, refused to co-operate. Fortunately, Pratley had already interviewed David, on the set of DOCTOR ZHIVAGO and at the New York premiere, so he was able to include some direct quotes and anecdotes. Pratley's book, *The Cinema of David Lean*, was published in 1974 and presented David in a most flattering light. The same year another book on David's films, by Alain Silver and James Ursini, was published and this, too, was sympathetic. But David wanted to discourage books about him because he was convinced - wrongly in these cases - that they would be written by "intellectuals" hostile to his work.

12   Richard Schickel letter to author, 22 March 1993.

13   Pauline Kael letter to author, 5 September 1991.

14   Pauline Kael, *The New Yorker*, 21 November 1970. The picture took a long time to go into profit but it did so.

15   Richard Schickel described Roeg's directorial debut, PERFORMANCE, as "The most disgusting, the most completely worthless film I have ever seen since I began reviewing."

16   Nic Roeg, p.1.

17   David Lean, p.500.

18   Ibid., pp.428-9

19   Ibid., p.413.

41: Wilderness Years

1   *Sight and Sound*, September 1991, p.20. Following a hostile editorial obituary, Hugh Hudson's article was the first on David Lean ever published by *Sight and Sound*. "Pwew" is pronounced "few".

2   Sandy Lean, p.19.

3   David Lean letter to Pvt source, 21 February 1979, TR.

4   Ibid.

5   David Lean letter to André Morell, 11 January 1978, p.4, TR.

6   Judy Scott-Fox, p.1.

7   Robert Bolt letter to David Lean, 28 August 1973, TR.

8   Lavinia Greacen fax to author, 22 February 1993.

9   Judy Scott-Fox, p.1.

10   Sara Lean, p.1.

11   Sandy Lean fax to author, 23 August 1995.

12   Sara Lean, pp.2-5.

13   The Mount Kenya Safari Club, an expensive and formal hotel on the slopes of Mount Kenya, had been founded by David's friend William Holden as part of Holden's private game reserve.

14   Judy Scott-Fox, p.2.

15   David Lean, p.551.

16   Sara Lean, p.2.

17   Sandy Lean fax to author 23 August 1995.

18   In March 1974 he was presented with a Life Fellowship of the British Film Academy - then called the Society of Film and Television Arts and soon to be BAFTA - by Princess Anne at the Albert Hall in London. David had arranged for a massive donation to be given to the Society from the profits of DOCTOR ZHIVAGO, becoming their principal benefactor. (*Cinema & TV Today*, March 1974, pp.3,9.)

19   David Lean, p.150.

20   David Lean letter to André Morell, 11 January 1978, TR. When David first arrived in Bora Bora, the overwater bungalows cost a hefty $150 a day. They now cost $700.

21   Sandy Lean fax to author, 23 August 1995.

22   David acquired a second Boston Whaler which was based at Rangiroa. He eventually gave it away to Serge Arnoux, a round-the-world sailor who ran the island's Kia Ora Hotel with a Polynesian girl called Martine, whose name was borrowed for the boat. The boat is still there.

23   *Hollywood Reporter*, 14 November 1974, p.6.

24   Sandy Lean fax to author, 23 August 1995. Edward and Doreen lived in Albert Street, Camden Town, London. David later bought a house for Sara in the same street.

25   Diccon Swan, p.5.

26   *The Times*, 30 October 1974, p.17.

27   Sara Lean, pp.4-5.

28   Sandy Lean phone interview, 31 May 1993.

29   *The Times*, July-November 1973/David Lean letter to Pvt source, 21 February 1979, TR.

30   Judy Scott-Fox, p.1.

42: Sunshine Loyalties: Pandora's Box I

1   Eddie Fowlie, p.32/letter to author, 14 August 1995. "The four of us" included Eddie's Irish wife, Kathleen, whom he met on RYAN'S DAUGHTER.

2   Augustus John had been the artist responsible for some of the most famous portraits of Lawrence of Arabia.

3   Robert Bolt letters to David Lean, 14 May 1977/24 May 1977, TR.

4   Charles Nordhoff and James Norman Hall published a sequence of three novels about the *Bounty* - *Mutiny!* (1933), *Men Against The Sea* (1934) and *Pitcairn's Island* (1935). Hall's son is the Hollywood cameraman Conrad Hall, who was born in Tahiti in 1926.

5   David Lean, pp.368, 414.

6   Sandy Lean fax to author, 23 August 1995. David claimed he never saw the 1962 version with Marlon Brando and Trevor Howard.

7   Robert Bolt letter to David Lean, 15 September 1977, TR.

8   Stephen Walters interview, 15 September 1995.

9   John Boorman, *Projections I*, p.23.

10   A fifth if you count an Australian silent of 1916, THE MUTINY OF THE BOUNTY (filmed in Rotorua, New Zealand, and on Norfolk Island, and directed by Raymond Longford) and the Australian dramatic documentary IN THE WAKE OF THE BOUNTY (1933) which introduced Errol Flynn as Fletcher Christian. MGM bought this film in 1935 and recut it into two short travelogues, used to promote the Clark Gable film.

11   Robert Bolt letter to David Lean, 29 July 1977, TR.

12   Phil Kellogg letter to author, 22 May 1994.

13   John Calley, p.42/fax to author, 5 September 1995. David sent Kellogg and Box to Florida to inspect the ship built by MGM for the 1962 film. David vetoed this since the ship was much larger than the original *Bounty*.

14 This was not Calley's joke. The first script, entitled THE LAWBREAKERS, begins with a space launching to demonstrate that the maritime explorers - the eighteenth-century Argonauts - were the equivalent of astronauts, and a space theme is referred to at several points for the music. Behind the credit titles were to be explorers such as Scott, Lindbergh and Livingstone.

15 John Calley, p.42/fax to author, 5 September 1995.

16 French Polynesia, a department of France, was (and remains) one of the most expensive regions in the world. The currency, the French Pacific Franc, is held at an artificially high exchange rate and high taxes are levied on all imported goods and tourist facilities. The Tahitians themselves pay no taxes on their income.

17 David Lean letter to Phil Kellogg, 22 October 1977, TR.

18 John Box phone interview, 4 April 1993. Maurice Fowler worked on the film for a while. But when De Laurentiis took over, Danilo Dorati, Fellini's designer, was set to do the film. He was delayed on HURRICANE, and to help advance the film, Eddie Fowlie recommended Tony Pratt. "He has no wife," David told Phil Kellogg, "works like a beaver and can really draw. One of my friends was a Pratt. Very bright and they are all related to Boris Karloff who changed his name not to embarrass his family playing in horror films! His brother was a judge if I'm not mistaken - and this sort of background sometimes helps although unfashionable nowadays." (David Lean letter to Phil Kellogg, 26 October 1977, TR.) Tony Pratt proved an excellent choice, and David was impressed by the designs he produced. When De Laurentiis departed, Pratt was left high and dry and David kept him on, paying both salaries and expenses.

19 David Lean letter to Phil Kellogg, 26 October 1977, TR.

20 Phil Kellogg letter to author, 22 May 1994.

21 David Lean letter to Frank Wells, 31 October 1977, TR.

22 Phil Kellogg letter to author, 22 May 1994.

23 Ibid.

24 Phil Kellogg letter to David Lean 7 November 1977, TR.

25 Dino de Laurentiis letter to David Lean, 16 February 1978, TR.

26 Judy Scott-Fox, p.3.

27 Julie Laird, pp.1-6.

28 Robert Bolt letter to Julie Laird, 16 April 1978.

29 David Lean, p.414.

30 George Andrews, *American Cinematographer*, March 1979, p.295seq.

31 Ibid.

32 Wayne Tourell letter to author, 11 July 1993.

33 David Lean letter to George Andrews and Wayne Tourell, 5 June 1978.

34 *American Cinematographer*, March 1979, p.308.

35 David Lean, p.414.

36 *Variety*, 9 May 1979.

37 Robert Bolt letter to David Lean, 31 May 1978, TR.

38 David Lean letter, private source.

39 *Time*, 31 December 1984, p.51./Denise Worrell, op. cit., pp.169-170.

40 David Lean, p.567.

43: Fatal Impact: Pandora's Box II

1 The Laughton version was filmed mainly on the island of Catalina, just off the coast of Los Angeles; only a second unit was sent to Tahiti. The Brando version was shot in authentic Tahitian locations and was delayed by ceaseless rain as well as Brando's erratic behaviour. The production was halted and brought back to Hollywood where director Carol Reed was replaced by Lewis Milestone.

2 In the draft agreement between De Laurentiis and David, the cost of the hotel and its potential profit was to be shared between them. This was crossed out, presumably at David's instigation.

3 Phil Kellogg letter to David Lean, 11 June 1978, TR.

4 Ibid.

5 Dino de Laurentiis letter to Phil Kellogg, 15 June 1978, TR.

6 Dino de Laurentiis letter to David Lean, 18 August 1978, TR.

7 Sandy Lean, p.27.

8 David had in fact sent Eddie Fowlie to recce other possible locations in Polynesia where it was much cheaper. Fowlie reported that there were splendid locations in Fiji.

9 Turnaround is Hollywood parlance for a set period in which a film can be offered to another studio. Should the project by taken up, existing production expenses are re-imbursed to the previous producers. According to film industy expert Peter Bart, turnaround "constitutes a death knell." Peter Bart, op. cit., p.93.

10 David Lean letter to Julie Laird, 24 October 1978.

11 John Calley, p.52.

12 Marvin Meyer letter to David Lean, 12 October 1978, TR.

13 David Lean letter to Tony Reeves, 14 July 1981.

14 David Lean letter to Julie Laird, 24 October 1978.

15 Phil Kellogg to David Lean, 20 October 1978, TR.

16 David Lean letter to Phil Kellogg and Marvin Meyer, 24 October 1978, TR.

17 Ibid.

18 Robert Bolt letter to David Lean, 16 October 1978, TR.

19 David Lean letter to Robert Bolt, 22 October 1978, TR.

20 Robert Bolt letter to Julie Laird, 1 October 1978.

21 Robert Bolt letter to Julie Laird, 24 December 1978.

22 Ibid.

23 Robert Bolt letter to David Lean, 2 December 1978, TR.

24 Robert Bolt letter to Julie Laird, 2 December 1978, TR.

25 Peggy Ramsay to Phil Kellogg, 20 October 1977, TR.

26 David Lean letter to Robert Bolt, 29 October 1978, TR.

27 David Lean letter to Robert Bolt, n.d., probably November 1978, TR.

28 David Lean, pp.414, 516.

29 Steven Bach, *Final Cut*, p.157.

30 Steven Bach fax to author, 22 July 1993.

31 Robert Bolt letter to David Lean, 26 December 1978, TR.

32 David Lean letter to Robert Bolt, 11 January 1979.

33 David Lean letter to Tony Reeves, 14 July 1981.

34 HEAVEN'S GATE cost $36 million and became one of Hollywood's most famous flops. The failure of the film led to the sale of UA to MGM. Steven Bach chronicled the film's production in his book, *Final Cut*.

35 Sandy Lean phone interview, 31 May 1993.

36 Robert Bolt letter to Julie Laird, 7 January 1979.

37 Robert Bolt letter to Julie Laird, 8 March 1979.

38 Adrian Turner, *The Bounty* manuscript, p.11.

39 Jo Bolt phone interview, 14 June 1993.

40 Ben Bolt phone interview, 14 June 1993.

41 Jo Bolt phone interview, 14 June 1993.

42 David Lean letter to Sam Spiegel, 9 June 1979.

43 Ibid.

44 Robert Bolt fax to author, 31 May 1993. Bolt's friend, Ann Queensberry, whom he later married, also took care of him at this time.

45 *Evening Standard*, 22 June 1979, p.20.

46 David Lean letter to Peggy Ramsay, 23 July 1979, TR.

47 Peggy Ramsay letter to David Lean, 24 July 1979, TR.

48 Melvyn Bragg, pp.1-2.

49 *A Fated Ship*, New Zealand TV documentary, directed by Wayne Tourell.

50 Melvyn Bragg, pp.23.

51 Ibid.

52 David Lean memo to Bragg and Spiegel, 1 October 1979, TR.

53 David Lean letter to Tony Reeves, 14 July 1981.

54 Ibid.

55 Ibid.

56 John Heyman phone interview, 11 March 1994.

57 Dennis Potter letter to David Lean, 12 March 1981, TR.

58 Dennis Potter letter to author, 16 September 1993.

59 David Lean letter to Tony Reeves, 14 July 1981.

60 In 1984, Dino de Laurentiis released THE BOUNTY. The picture - an abridgement of Bolt's original script of THE LAWBREAKERS - starred Anthony Hopkins as Bligh and Mel Gibson as Christian. It was produced by Bernard Williams and directed by Roger Donaldson, a New Zealander whom David had met briefly when he was conducting casting research in Auckland. Supporting roles were played by Daniel Day-Lewis and Liam Neeson. The film cost around $20 million and was a box-office flop. De Laurentiis later sold the ship to a travel company who offered Bounty cruises in the Pacific. The ship also appeared in a TV mini-series about Captain Cook and is currently a floating restaurant in Sydney Harbour.

61 Eddie Fowlie letter to author, 14 August 1995.

62 David Puttnam phone interview, 11 March 1993. Puttnam produced a film for television about T.E. Lawrence and the Peace Conference called A DANGEROUS MAN (1992) which starred Ralph Fiennes as Lawrence.

63 David Niven Jr letter to David Lean, 8 November 1981, TR.

44: Regaining the Light: A Passage to India I

1 Sandy Lean phone interview, 31 May 1993.

2 Lord Brabourne, p.3.

3 Tony Reeves, p.16.

4 As Lawrence dedicated his book to 'S.A.,' so Forster dedicated his to the young Moslem on whom he partly based Aziz.

5 David Lean quoted in *The Times*, 9 December 1981.

6 Shama Habibullah, p.5.

7 Fred Zinnemann, p.2. Satyajit Ray also wanted to direct it.

8 Naomi Gurian letter to Walter Jeffrey, 12 April 1984, SRR.

9 Lord Brabourne, p.2.

10 David Lean to Denise Worrell, p.153.

11 Lord Brabourne, p.2.

12 A 'Bridge Party' in this sense was not a card-game but a social gathering designed to 'bridge' the gulf between the English and the Indians.

13 David Lean letter to Santha Rama Rau, 7 October 1981.

14 Santha Rama Rau letter to David Lean, 2 November 1981.

15 Santha Rama Rau quoted in *The Sunday Times*, 24 March 1985, p.15.

16 Richard Goodwin letter to Santha Rama Rau, 9 December 1981.

17 David Lean letter to Santha Rama Rau, 18 February 1982.

18 Lord Brabourne, p.2.

19 David Lean letter to Richard Goodwin and John Brabourne, 6 February 1983, TR.

20 David Lean to Denise Worrell, op. cit., p.153.

21 David Lean letter to Richard Goodwin and John Brabourne, 31 December 1981, TR.

22 David Lean to Denise Worrell, p.153.

23 David Lean to Derek Malcolm, *The Guardian*, 23 January 1983.

24 David Lean to Harlan Kennedy, *Film Comment*, Jan-Feb 1985, p.32.
25 David Lean letter to Richard Goodwin and John Brabourne, 31 December 1981, TR.
26 Alec Guinness letter to David Lean, 20 September 1982, TR.
27 Santha Rama Rau letter to David Lean, 27 September 1982, TR.
28 Santha Rama Rau letter to author, 18 August 1993.
29 David Lean telex to John Brabourne, October 1982, TR.
30 Sandy Lean fax to author, 4 September 1995.
31 Donald Parry phone interview, 7 January 1992.
32 Richard Goodwin, p.18.
33 David Lean, p.663.
34 Richard Goodwin quoted in *Stills* magazine, April-May 1984, p.35.
35 David Lean to Denise Worrell, p.155.
36 Richard Goodwin, p.9. The total budget was $17,514,568 (Budget summary, 30 June 1983, TR.)
37 David Lean, p.42.

45: Moving Mountains: A Passage to India II

1 BFI News, November 1981.
2 David Lean cable to Richard Attenborough, 4 October 1983, TR. By coincidence, another absentee at the BFI banquet was India's most famous director, Satyajit Ray.
3 David Lean letter to Dennis van Thal, 12 December 1982, TR.
4 David Lean to Brabourne and Goodwin, 6 February 1983, TR.
5 Ibid.
6 Richard Goodwin, p.3.
7 David Lean to Denise Worrell, p.158.
8 Shama Habibullah, p.4.
9 *The Sunday Times Magazine*, 8 April 1984, p.33 seq.
10 David Lean, p.625.
11 Shama Habibullah, p.2.
12 David Lean to Brabourne and Goodwin, 12 January 1983, TR.
13 Eddie Fowlie, p.44.
14 *Encounter*, 23 June 1984, p.89.
15 John Box to David Lean, 8 January 1982, TR.
16 John Box to David Lean, 14 June 1982, TR.
17 David Lean, pp.46-7. David always maintained - incorrectly - that Box's report had caused Warner Bros. to withdraw from the Bounty project.
18 Shama Habibullah, p.4.
19 *The Sunday Times Magazine*, 8 April 1984, p.33 seq.
20 David Lean, p.633.
21 His first photographic assignment, in 1944, was to film a flying-bomb for Doc Solomon who ran the studio and was killed shortly afterwards when a V-1 bomb half-demolished the studio. Ernie's brother is

Robert Day, who became a director.
22 Patrick Cadell, p.7.
23 Sandy Lean fax to author, 23 August 1995.
24 Ernie Day, p.17.
25 Sandy Lean fax to author, 23 August 1995.
26 "I don't think I had emphysema because I don't think you recover from it. I know my lungs are clear as anything now. So I think it was probably a kindness. I shall never know." David Lean, p.550.
27 Ernie Day, pp.32,34,37.
28 David Lean, p.173.

46: Victims of Vision: A Passage to India III

1 David Lean to Denise Worrell, p.158.
2 Shama Habibullah, p.4.
3 *Daily Express*, 2 April 1984, p.9.
4 John Mitchell, p.13.
5 David Lean to Derek Malcolm, *The Guardian*, 23 January 1984.
6 Victor Banerjee to John Higgins, *The Times*, 4 March 1985, p.15.
7 David Lean, p.397.
8 *The Sunday Times Magazine*, 8 April 1984, p.33seq.
9 *Time*, 31 December 1984, p.52.
10 David Lean letter to Brabourne and Goodwin, 31 December 1981, TR.
11 David Lean to John Higgins, *The Times*, 4 March 1985, p.15.
12 Peggy Ashcroft to author, 17 December 1990.
13 David Lean to Harlan Kennedy, *Film Comment*, Jan-Feb 1985, p.30.
14 David Lean, p.396.
15 Judy Davis to Gavin Smith, *Film Comment*, Nov-Dec 1992, p.47.
16 Alec Guinness, p.38.
17 David Lean, p.109x.
18 Richard Goodwin, p.5.
19 Judy Davis to Gavin Smith, *Film Comment*, Nov-Dec 1992, p.47.
20 David Lean, p.396.
21 Kees T'Hooft, p.3.
22 Judy Davis to Gavin Smith, *Film Comment*, Nov-Dec 1992, p.49.
23 Richard Goodwin, p.5.
24 Alec Guinness, p.39.
25 *Daily Express*, 17 March 1984, p.20.
26 David Lean to Harlan Kennedy, Film Comment, Jan-Feb 1985, p.32.
27 Alec Guinness, p.28.
28 David Lean, p.398.
29 *The Observer*, 9 December 1984, pp.17-18.
30 Alec Guinness, p.30.
31 "I think the film is marvellously good," Guinness wrote, "and do congratulate you most heartily. It is expansive, handsome, gripping and yet somehow intimate. And the story - which we all know is somewhat complicated - comes over with simplicity.

It didn't seem a minute too long. Also I think it is beautifully acted - with one excruciating exception. Peggy, for my money, gives a truly superb performance and should get a whopping big Oscar. And I thought Victor pulled it off charmingly and splendidly. As did the others. For my own part I thought I was sickeningly awful. I thought it was poor at the time we were doing it but I hadn't realised how wide off the mark I was. I don't in the least blame you, as you were helpful, but I do wish - when I asked Richard, very calmly and unfussily, in the first week, if you'd all like to get rid of me - he had taken me up on it. John Brabourne was right in his original objection. Well, there it is and some of the press have rightly pointed it out. One thing I am <u>now</u> grateful for is the disappearance of the song and dance - at least the agony isn't protracted. Anyway, that's all fairly minor stuff. The film itself is outstanding and I think it combines, happily, your best work from the Dickens films to Lawrence of Arabia. Clearly, it is going to be a huge success." (Alec Guinness letter to David Lean, 16 December 1984. TR.)

32   Alec Guinness, p.40.
33   Ernie Day, p.30.
34   Alec Guinness, p.40.
35   David Lean cable to Richard Goodwin, 20 May 1982.
36   Peggy Ashcroft to author, 17 December 1990.
37   Ibid.
38   David Lean, p.19x.
39   Peggy Ashcroft to author, 17 December 1990.
40   Michael Billington, Peggy Ashcroft, p276.
41   Sandy Lean, p.9.
42   Peggy Ashcroft to author, 17 December 1990.
43   David Lean, p.398.
44   Peggy Ashcroft to author, 17 December 1990.
45   *The Guardian* obituary, 17 April 1991, p.37.
46   David Lean, p.109x.
47   Shama Habibullah, p.11.
48   Alec Guinness, pp.26-27.

47: Credit Taken, Credit Lost: A Passage to India IV

1   Sandy Lean fax to author, 4 September 1995, p.5.
2   Shama Habibullah, p.12.
3   Richard Goowin, p.6.
4   Sandy Lean fax to author, 23 August 1995.
5   Ibid.
6   David Lean, p.286.
7   Kees T'Hooft, pp.1-2.
8   Eunice Mountjoy had worked regularly for John Huston as assistant editor since THE NIGHT OF THE IGUANA (1964). She started her career in the fifties, had cut commercials for ITV and had also been a sound assistant on Lawrence of Arabia. She had been trained by Ralph Kemplen, a veteran who had edited Huston's THE AFRICAN QUEEN (1952) and Zinnemann's A MAN FOR ALL SEASONS (1966).
9   Kees T'Hooft, p.1.
10   David Lean, pp.14x,15x.
11   Kees T'Hooft, p.2.
12   David Lean, pp.13x-14x.
13   Eunice Mountjoy, p.13.
14   John Brabourne, p.2.
15   Santha Rama Rau letters to author, 17 April 1993/18 August 1993.
16   Maggie Unsworth-Peter Lean interview, p.5.
17   Peter Lean, pp.5-6.
18   David Lean letter to Emeric Pressburger, 24 June 1984 from the Berkeley Hotel. (Courtesy Kevin Macdonald.)
19   Pressburger had long wanted to write a script of the Forster novel himself. According to his grandson, David's film of A PASSAGE TO INDIA was the last film he saw "and he truly loved it." (Kevin Macdonald, phone interview, 16 October 1991.)
20   Richard Schickel letter to author, March 1993.
21   *Time*, 31 December 1984, p.44 seq.
22   *The New Yorker*, 14 January 1985.
23   *The New York Times*, 14 December 1984, p.10.
24   Morris & Raskin, op. cit., p.200.
25   Another Oscar went to Maurice Jarre for his music score.
26   While Columbia was lobbying for the film, promoting Judy Davis as Best Actress, the Hollywood Reporter announced that the Academy had voted posthumous Oscars to Carl Foreman and Michael Wilson for THE BRIDGE ON THE RIVER KWAI. The widows of the writers, Eve Foreman and Zelma Wilson, received the awards on 16 March 1985 at the Samuel Goldwyn Theatre, followed by a screening of KWAI. (*The Hollywood Reporter*, 7 March 1985, p.8.)
27   *Time*, 31 December 1984, p.52.
28   John Brabourne, p.4.
29   David Lean, p.36.

48: A Name to Conjure With

1   Sandy Lean fax to author, 23 August 1995.
2   David Lean, pp.47,266.
3   Tony Reeves, p.8.
4   Alec Guinness, p.40.
5   Sandy Lean fax to author, 23 August 1995.
6   ibid.
7   David Lean, p.568.
8   Sandy Lean fax to author, 23 August 1995.
9   Tony Reeves, p.11.
10   Sandy Lean fax to author, 23 August 1995.
11   The researchers of the programme were Caroline Baum, Tony Knox and Steve Jenkins. Maggie Unsworth's son, Tim, was responsible for researching the early years of David's life.
12   Sandra Lean, p.4.

13 Diccon Swan, p.2. Edward Lean had been equally generous in his own way. When Swan was robbed of all the money he had saved up for a holiday, Edward quietly replaced it.

14 Diccon Swan, p.4.

15 Sandra Lean, pp.13-14.

16 Sandy Lean fax to author, 31 August 1995.

17 Sandra Lean, pp.10,18,36.

18 Ibid., pp.34-35.

19 David Lean, p.321. A script for EMPIRE OF THE SUN, dated 11 July 1986,written by Tom Stoppard and Mennio Meyjes, was amongst David's effects. The Spielberg film, released in 1987, was scripted by Stoppard.

20 Such was David's influence, that he persuaded Columbia to replace the giant curved screen at the Odeon Marble Arch with a conventional screen at a cost of £50,000.

21 David had also bought a house in Tuscany, which he planned to renovate for his "retirement".

22 Sarah Foster, pp.9,12,15,16.

23 John Allinson letter to author, June 1991. Both of Edward's sons went to Leighton Park. Maggie Unsworth sent her sons there as well. Another Old Leightonian was Karel Reisz, director of SATURDAY NIGHT AND SUNDAY MORNING.

49: Restoration Drama

1 In May 1986 David had been made an Honorary Doctor of Letters at Leeds University, an honour which must have given him some quiet amusement.

2 My partner, David Gill, was responsible for staging this event.

3 *A Tickling Of Talents*, BBC documentary on Lawrence restoration, produced by Colin Burrows and David Castell, tx 28 May 1989.

4 David Lean, p.108.

5 *Films in Review*, April 1989, p.206.

6 Ibid.

7 AFI Award programme, p.14.

8 Ibid.

9 David Lean, p.610.

10 AFI Award programme, p.14.

11 David Lean, pp.167-68.

12 Jim Painten, letter to author, 8 June 1993.

13 *Films in Review*, May 1989, p.288.

14 Barbara Cole, p.14.

15 Stephen Silverman, op. cit., p.194.

16 *The Hollywood Reporter*, 23 May 1988, p.25.

17 David Lean, p.372.

18 Columbia has still to create protection masters for their most precious film.

50: The Treachery of Sunken Rocks: Nostromo

1 Conrad originally published *Nostromo, A Tale of the Seaboard*, in serial form. The novel was first published as one volume on 14 October 1904 and it was filmed in 1926 as THE SILVER TREASURE. Nostromo - "Our man" - is the name given to an Italian sailor, a reliable man who is thought capable of anything. The expansive, athletic character - literature's equivalent of Douglas Fairbanks, as Harlan Kennedy called him (*American Film*,March 1990, p30) - becomes involved in a plot to smuggle a consignment of silver out of a South American country called Costaguana when the rebels seize power. The precious metal corrupts and enslaves everyone - including Nostromo who informs the owner of the mine, Charles Gould, that it has been lost at sea when, in fact, he has buried it on an offshore island. Nostromo plans to get rich slowly...

2 John Box, pp.30-31. There was to have been an earlier NOSTROMO, produced by Anatole de Grunwald and scripted by John Mortimer, which was planned for 1958.

3 David was reading the Penguin edition and if one reads the rest of the paragraph it conveys itself visually as a silent film montage.

4 Christopher Hampton's sole connection with Robert Bolt was that he had acted in an amateur production of *A Man For All Seasons* (*American Film*, March 1990, p.55). But Maggie knew that Hampton had prepared a version of *Nostromo* for Jonathan Powell when he was in charge of BBC serials. Stuart Burge was to have directed it but the project collapsed when the BBC costed it at £1 million per episode. But in 1995, the BBC made a four-part dramatisation of *Nostromo*, directed by Alistair Reid from a script by John Hale and filmed in Colombia.

5 Christopher Hampton, p.2.

6 Ibid., p.10.

7 Hampton's play, *Les Liaisons Dangereuses*, transferred to the Ambassadors Theatre in 1986. It was later filmed for Warner Bros. by Stephen Frears as DANGEROUS LIAISONS.

8 Christopher Hampton, p.15.

9 David was startled to discover that Rex Ingram's MARE NOSTRUM began in a similar way. And if the title of Nostromo reminded him of Mare Nostrum, it excited one potential financier to express the hope that it would be "just like Rambo". (Silverman, p.193).

10 Christopher Hampton, p.8.

11 Ibid., p.3.

12 Ibid., p.11.

13 Ibid., p.13-14.

14 Ibid., p.5.

15 David Lean, p.300. David also considered using the Showscan Process, a high-speed 70mm system which, like IMAX, could only be seen at specially equipped theatres. The president of Showscan at the time was Peter Beale, the son of Barbara Cole.

16 John Alcott died shortly afterwards at Cannes.

Earlier tests for NOSTROMO were photographed
by David Watkin who won an Oscar for OUT OF
AFRICA, though his system of lighting was not
compatible with David's style. (David Watkin phone
interview, 22 January 1992).

17 Christopher Hampton, p.1.

18 Ibid., p.6.

19 Ibid., pp.5-6.

20 Daughter of Ingrid Bergman and Roberto Rossellini.

21 Christopher Hampton, p.9.

22 *American Film*, March 1990, p.30.

23 George Correface, p.1.

24 Christopher Hampton, p.9.

25 Ibid., p.17.

26 In fact, David went to Cuba, not Mexico, because he
was told that Cuba had all the locations he was
looking for. Besides which, Sandra wanted to go.
"Oh, it gave me the creeps," said David. "We had
some awfully nice people with us but I had the
distinct feeling there were microphones and that
every call we made was listened to. I think quite a
hefty attempt was made to stop us leaving. Sandra
actually got us on the plane and how she did it I
don't know, but she did and I'm jolly glad because I
wouldn't have liked to stay there any longer. You
know, they took all the rich houses, commandeered
them - I don't know what happened to the owners -
and they were used as houses for visitors. Various
staff members appeared and looked after one, and
also one felt they were watching one and I didn't like
it at all. I may be wrong, I don't know. But it was
the same feeling in Yugoslavia when Ponti wanted to
do DOCTOR ZHIVAGO there." (David Lean, p.583.)
John Box and Eddie Fowlie, however, did go
to Mexico and found little of use until they reached
the Baja Peninsula. There they found the mountains
and the offshore islands just as Conrad had described
them. Box took photographs and had one of them
retouched with snow and had it made up as a
birthday card, sending it to David with the message,
"I haven't found gold but I have found silver." (John
Box phone interview, 15 August 1993.) After David
went to Mexico and approved the locations,
Silberman urged them to use Spain which took David
back to the exact locations he had used for
Lawrence. "He sat down on the sand and enjoyed the
sunshine and his private thoughts," said Eddie
Fowlie. "I left him there for quite a long time and he
seemed so contented." (Eddie Fowlie letter to
author, 14 August 1995.)

27 Christopher Hampton, p.18.

28 Ibid., p.13.

29 Steven Spielberg memo to David Lean, 13 February
1987, TR.

30 Christopher Hampton, p.13.

31 Ibid., pp.2-3.

32 Ibid., p.13.

33 David Lean, pp.180, 329.

34 Ibid., p.329.

35 David refers to Bolt's recommendation in a letter to
Bolt, dated 23 December 1962, p13. UoR.

36 Robert Bolt fax to author, 10 May 1993.

37 Robert Bolt to David Lean, 4 June 1988, TR.

38 Sandra Lean, p.27.

39 Robert Bolt, p.5.

40 Julie Laird, p.4.

41 Robert Bolt to Harlan Kennedy, *American Film*,
March 1990, p.55.

42 LWT, tx21 January 1990.

43 Peter Wheeler, p.1.

44 "He was actually under the care of Sir Anthony
Dawson in terms of the strategic management of this
very difficult condition although I looked after him
on a day to day basis." (Peter Wheeler letter to
author, 14 May 1993.)

45 David Lean to Robert Bolt, 18 December 1989, TR.

46 Silber means silver in German.

47 Judy Scott-Fox, pp.1, 3.

48 Serge Silberman fax to David Lean, 23 January 1990,
TR.

49 David Lean, pp.36-39.

50 Ibid., p.41.

51 Ibid., p.381.

52 Peter Wheeler, p.6.

53 David Lean, pp.178,229-30,251.

54 Ibid., p.181.

55 Guy Hamilton, who at sixty-eight was no spring
chicken himself, had been an assistant director for
Carol Reed. He is best known for directing
GOLDFINGER and other James Bond films. By an
odd coincidence, Hamilton did some preparatory
work on THE BRIDGE ON THE RIVER KWAI before
Spiegel hired David to direct.

56 Sarah Foster, pp.2-3.

57 Peter Wheeler, p.2.

58 Sarah Foster, pp.3-4.

59 Peter Wheeler, p.3.

60 Sarah Foster, p.4. The producer was George
Stevens, jr.

61 The TV programme of the ceremony was quickly
shown all around the world, except in Britain, a fact
which upset David. What he did not realise was that
the programme was regarded by the BBC as a ready-
made obituary. They transmitted it on 20 April
1991.

62 Denise Worrell of *Time* magazine. See her *Icons -
Intimate Portraits*.

63 Thalberg's actual quote, in connection with King
Vidor's THE CROWD, was: "I can certainly afford a
few experimental projects. It will do something for
the studio, it will do something for the whole
industry."

64 David's speech had nothing to do with what he had
intended to say. Peter Wheeler kept his notes which
reveal that he planned to speak about his first years in
a silent movie studio with its glass roof and three-

piece orchestra accompanying the actors. "Find myself alongside such a group of film-makers - ALL INNOVATORS. One thing in common to all - love of the medium." This was then to lead into a discussion of the Hollywood moguls -"Louis B Mayer, Goldmann [sic]. Their concern was quality. The love of making a film of quality far exceeded the desire to make a lot of money." David was going to pay tribute to Rex Ingram and had written across his paper, "FOUR HORSEMEN. A guiding hand telling me a story." He was going to mention Vidor and THE BIG PARADE and his admiration of his use of crowd movement against static figures. "The language of the cinema which is nothing to do with literature. A sort of symphonic (?) flow of pictures nearer to music than anything else." And the last note was, "Suddenly found myself seeing that a lot what I had learnt was now being used in reverse - 'Always come out of the same hole' with slight variation." And this led David to the theme that ruffled so many feathers.

65   Peter Wheeler, p.3.
66   Judy Scott-Fox, p.4.
67   Sarah Foster, p.8.
68   Peter Wheeler, p.3.
69   Peter Lean, p.7.
70   Sarah Foster, pp.22-23.
71   John Boorman, *Projections 1*, p.22.
72   Eddie Fowlie letter to author, 14 August 1995.
73   Peter Wheeler, p.5.
74   Sandy Lean fax to author, 23 August 1995.
75   Sandra Lean, p.35.
76   Sandy Lean, p.34.
77   Peter Wheeler, p.5.
78   Sandy Lean, p.35.
79   In May 1948, Cheshire came upon an old man dying of cancer whom no one wanted and who was about to be discharged from hospital. After trying very hard to find somewhere else for him to go, without success, Cheshire took him into his own house and nursed him until he died. He discovered others in the same situation and turned his house into a home for the incurably sick and permanently disabled. His mission expanded all over the world. (Cheshire Foundation Leaflet, 1971, p.2). Cheshire's second wife, Sue Ryder, has her own charitable foundation. His first wife was the American silent film actress, Constance Binney.
80   "I think the script is quite superb," he wrote to David. "It is in the running for the best film ever made - if there can be such a thing as an absolute in an evolving art form." (Leonard Cheshire to David Lean, March 1981, TR.)
81   The videos include *Chance Encounter* and *A Hidden World*. Alas, they are on a video format which is now obsolete.
82   "He was always shocked," said Sandy Lean. "But he was never there for long. He was amazed and fascinated by Leonard and his goodness - that he could touch these people. He and Leonard were crazy about each other - it was hero-worship on both sides, I think." (Sandy Lean phone interview, 31 May 1993.)
83   All quotes from Leonard Cheshire interview with author, 21 August 1991.
84   Leonard Cheshire letter to author, 29 August 1991.
85   David Lean, p.35.
86   Louis Fischer, *Gandhi*, p.367.

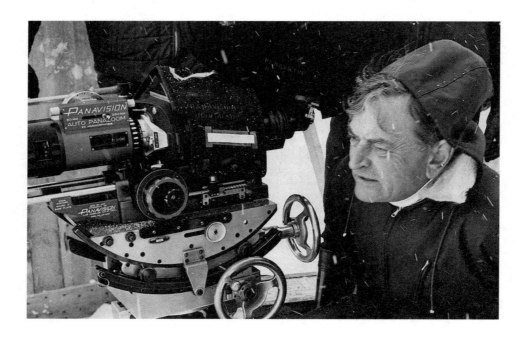

D A V I D   L E A N   *A Biography*

INDEX

"I think we're only at the beginning of making movies"

DAVID LEAN